Book of Biala Podlaska
(Biała Podlaska, Poland)

Translation of
Sefer Biala Podlaska

Original Book Edited by: M. J. Feigenbaum

Originally published in Tel Aviv 1961

A Publication of JewishGen, Inc.
Edmond J. Safra Plaza, 36 Battery Place, New York, NY 10280
646.494.5972 | info@JewishGen.org | www.jewishgen.org

Book of Biala Podlaska (Biała Podlaska, Poland)
Translation of *Sefer Biala Podlaska*

Editor of Original Yizkor Book: M. J. Feigenbaum
Project Coordinators: Max Wald
Cover Design: Irv Osterer
Layout: Jonathan Wind
Name Indexing: Stefanie Holzman

Printed in the United States of America by Lightning Source, Inc.

Library of Congress Control Number (LCCN): 2022952301

ISBN: 978-1-954176-66-9 (hard cover: 730 pages, alk. paper)

About JewishGen.org

JewishGen, an affiliate of the Museum of Jewish Heritage - A Living Memorial to the Holocaust, serves as the global home for Jewish genealogy.

Featuring unparalleled access to 30+ million records, it offers unique search tools, along with opportunities for researchers to connect with others who share similar interests. Award winning resources such as the Family Finder, Discussion Groups, and ViewMate, are relied upon by thousands each day.

In addition, JewishGen's extensive informational, educational and historical offerings, such as the Jewish Communities Database, Yizkor Book translations, InfoFiles, Family Tree of the Jewish People, and KehilaLinks, provide critical insights, first-hand accounts, and context about Jewish communal and familial life throughout the world.

Offered as a free resource, JewishGen.org has facilitated thousands of family connections and success stories, and is currently engaged in an intensive expansion effort that will bring many more records, tools, and resources to its collections.

Please visit https://www.jewishgen.org/ to learn more.

Executive Director: Avraham Groll

About the JewishGen Yizkor Book Project

Yizkor Books (Memorial Books) were traditionally written to memorialize the names of departed family and martyrs during holiday services in the synagogue (a practice that still exists in many synagogues today).

Over the centuries, as a result of countless persecutions and horrific atrocities committed against the Jews, Yizkor Books (Sefer Zikaron in Hebrew) were expanded to include more historical information, such as biographical sketches of famous personalities and descriptions of daily town life.

Following the Holocaust, the idea of remembrance and learning took on an urgent and crucial importance. Survivors of the Holocaust sought out other surviving residents of their former towns to memorialize and document the names and way of life of those who were ruthlessly murdered by the Nazis. These remembrances were documented in Yizkor Books, hundreds of which were published in the first decades after the Holocaust.

Most of these books were published privately, or through landsmanshaftn (social organizations comprised of members originating from the same European town or region) that still existed, and were often distributed free of charge. Sadly, the languages used to document these crucial histories and links to our past, Yiddish and Hebrew, are no longer commonly understood by a significant percentage of Jews today. As a result, JewishGen has undertaken the sacred responsibility of translating these books into English so that the culture and way of life of these communities will be preserved and transmitted to future generations.

In 1986, a group of farsighted JewishGenners started a project to pool their efforts together in groups based upon their ancestors from each town and donate money to get the Yizkor books of their ancestral towns translated into English. As the translated material became available, it was made accessible for free at www.JewishGen.org/Yizkor. Hardcover copies can be purchased by visiting https://www.jewishgen.org/Yizkor/ybip.html (see below).

It is our hope that the translation of these books into English (and other languages) will assist the countless Jewish family researchers who are so desperately seeking to forge a connection with their heritage.

Director of JewishGen Yizkor Book Project: Lance Ackerfeld

About JewishGen Press

JewishGen Press (formerly the Yizkor Books-in-Print Project) is the publishing division of JewishGen.org, and provides a venue for the publication of non-fiction books pertaining to Jewish genealogy, history, culture, and heritage.

In addition to the Yizkor Book category, publications in the Other Non-Fiction category include Shoah memoirs and research, genealogical research, collections of genealogical and historical materials, biographies, diaries and letters, studies of Jewish experience and cultural life in the past, academic theses, and other books of interest to the Jewish community.

Please visit https://www.jewishgen.org/Yizkor/ybip.html to learn more.

Director of JewishGen Press: Joel Alpert
Managing Editor - Jessica Feinstein
Publications Manager - Susan Rosin

Notes to the Reader

The images in the original book were reproduced from photographs from the time of the first edition. These reproductions were already of poor quality, being pre-war and at least 30 or more years old. As a result, the images in the book are the best achievable.

A reader can view the original scans of the book on the websites listed below.

The original book can be seen online at the Yiddish Book Center website:

https://www.yiddishbookcenter.org/collections/yizkor-books/yzk-nybc313693/sefer-byalah-podlaskah

OR

at the New York Public Library Digital Collections website:

https://digitalcollections.nypl.org/items/9bceda00-502c-0133-f858-00505686a51c

To obtain a list of Shoah victims from Biala Podlaska (Biała Podlaska, Poland), the reader should access the Yad Vashem web site listed below; one can also search for specific family names using family name option. These lists are continually updated by Yad Vashem, so it is worthwhile to search these lists periodically.

There is more valuable information (including the Pages of Testimony, etc.) available on this website: https://yvng.yadvashem.org/

A list of all books available from JewishGen Press along with prices is available at: https://www.jewishgen.org/Yizkor/ybip.html

Photo Credits

Front Cover:

Photo of Dramatic Group who participated in the Sholom Aleichem Evening with the participation of Noach Prilutzky from Warsaw. [Page 226]

Background: Town Plan (without Volia quarter). [Page 90]

Back Cover:

Photo of Flower Sale on behalf of the Jewish National Fund (detail), [Page 204]
Photo of Biala Weekly newspapers. [Page 242]
Photo of Biala Podlaska Community Memorial Tablet, unveiled in the Shoah Crypt on Mount Zion in Jerusalem, October 23rd, 1960. [Page 469]

Biala Zionist Administration Seal used on a document issued to Moshe Braverman on his Aliyah to Eretz Israel. Full document is on page 228. [Page 189]

Cover designed by Irv Osterer.

Project Coordinator Dedication

This Sefer of Biala Podlaska is dedicated to the lost history of a once thriving Jewish Community like most others in Poland that were obliterated during the Shoah. After almost 1000 years of presence and contributing to the cultural and social life of Poland. The only history and stories of life in these shtetls, apart from the many cemeteries, are contained in many of these Yizkor books

I dedicate this book in the memory of my late father Laibl Wald Z"L, who for many years was a member of the Biala Podlaska Landsmanshaft here in Melbourne and who was responsible for distributing the original 'Sefer' in the early 1960's in Australia.

I would also like to acknowledge the contributors, who, over the years have answered my call for funds.

Financial Contributors		Translators
Alan Droz	Marcy Yavor	Molly KARP
Aleksandra Zinkovskaya	Martin Broder	Yocheved KLAUSNER
Alexander Gelman	Michael Statman	Libby RAICHMAN
Bev Sackville	Mikhail Matoussov	Gloria BERKENSTAT FREUND
Daniel Wald	Robert Wald	Phillip A. APPLEBAUM
David Zyngier	Rochelle Silver, USA	Pamela RUSS
Henryk Fridman, Germany	Ros Gold	Marc ZELL - Donated translation
Joel Wald	Vivienne Musat	Ofra ANSON - Donated translation
Leon Piterman	Yael Liber	Max WALD - Donated translation
Marcia Ruben	Zelda Schule, USA	Pamela Russ
Ilana Wald	Steven Casper	Ida Selavan Schwarcz
Beverley Sackville	Max Wald	
Melma Hamersfeld	Pebby Wald	

Max Wald, OAM

Melbourne Australia

Project Coordinator Sefer Biala Podlaska

Geopolitical Information

Biała Podlaska, Poland is located at 52°02' N 23°08' E and 92 miles E of Warszawa

	Town	District	Province	Country
Before WWI (c. 1900):	Biała Podlaska	Biała	Siedlce	Russian Empire
Between the wars (c. 1930):	Biała Podlaska	Biała Podlaska	Lublin	Poland
After WWII (c. 1950):	Biała Podlaska			Poland
Today:	Biała Podlaska			Poland

Alternate Names for the Town:

Biała Podlaska [Pol], Podlyashe [Yid], Litvish Biale [Yid], Biala Gadol [Heb], Biala, Biala D'Lita

Nearby Jewish Communities:

Łomazy 9 miles S
Piszczac 12 miles ESE
Janów Podlaski 12 miles NNE
Rossosz 13 miles S
Konstantynów 13 miles N
Międzyrzec Podlaski 15 miles WSW
Wisznice 17 miles SSE
Komarówka Podlaska 18 miles SSW
Niemirów 18 miles N
Terespol 19 miles E
Volchin, Belarus 19 miles NNE
Mielnik 21 miles N

Łosice 22 miles NW
Kodeń 22 miles ESE
Sarnaki 22 miles NNW
Brest, Belarus 25 miles E
Wohyń 25 miles SW
Vysokaye, Belarus 25 miles NNE
Sławatycze 26 miles SE
Damachava, Belarus 28 miles SE
Radzyń Podlaski 28 miles SW
Chernavchitsy, Belarus 28 miles ENE
Mordy 29 miles WNW
Parczew 29 miles SSW
Zbuczyn 30 miles W

Jewish Population in Biala Podlaska: 6,549 (in 1897), 6,923 (in 1931)

Map of Poland showing the location of **Biała Podlaska**

Table of Contents

Preface	Marc Zell	2
Foreword	The editors	4
The Jews in Biala: Tracing their History to the Middle of Nineteenth Century	Dr. M. Handel	5
Jewish Biala During the Last Generation	M. Y. Fiegenboim	34
Total Destruction	M. Y. Fiegenboim	56
The Zionist Organization	M. Bruhel	99
The book	M. Y. Feigenbaum	110
Biala	M.Y. Feignbaum	112
Jews in Biale	Dr M. Hendl	121
Jewish Biale in Recent Generations	M.Y. Feigenbaum	152

The Economic Life

A. Trade until World War 1	M. R.	180
B. Forerunner Of The Banks		181
Jewish Income	M. Y. Feigenbaum	182
Trade	Gedalyahu Braverman	189
A. Factories	M. Y. Feigenboim	191
B. Printing		194
The Biale Estate	Alter Vineberg	195
The Professional [Workers] Movement	Yisroel Hochman	201
The Artisans Union	B. Winograd	203
The Retailers Union	Shmuel Kahan	204
Credit Cooperation	A. Wajs	206
a. Until the First World War		206
b. In Liberated Poland	M. Y. Feigenbaum	207
Workers Consumer Cooperative Einikeit	W. Szuster	213
Cooperative Mechanical Bakery	M. Y. F–M	214
The Interest-Free Loan Fund at the Small Businessmen's Union		214

Parties

The Zionist Organization	M. Bruchl	217
Hashomer Hatza'ir		231
The Revisionist Organization	Jacob Bernstein	240
The Mizrachi	M. Bravermann, A. Brandweinman, Y. Beitl	242
Poalei Zion Left	Avraham Lavi	245
The National Funds		247
The "Bund"	Gedaliahu Braverman	250
a. From the start to 1918		250

b. Between Both World Wars	V. Schuster	258
The Rise of "Agudat Yisrael"	Moshe Braverman	264
The Communist Movement	Gottl Biederman	265
An Anarchistic Group in Biale	Gedalyahu Braverman	268

The Cultural Life

General Overview	M. Y. Feigenboim	271
The "Yavne" School	M. Raboun	279
Nachman Schiwak's Private Elementary School		283
Evening Courses to learn Polish	Gedalyahu Braverman	285
An Attempt at Culture	M. Rabon	285
The "Tarbut" Library	M.Y. Feigenboim	286
The Bundist Library	Gedalyahu Braverman	288
The Library of the Left Leaning Po'alei Tzion	A. Labi	289
Maccabi	Nachman Vineberg	290
The Press	Chaim Rozmarin	296
Dramatic Circles	Gedalyahu Braverman	299
The Dramatic Circle of "Bet–Am"	M. Y. Feigenboim	302
Purim Plays at the end of the 19th Century	Gedalyahu Braverman	304

The Religious Life

General Overview	M. Y. Feigenbaum	307
The Talmud Torah		313
Houses of Prayer	M. Y. Feignbaum	314
The synagogue, The Beith Hamidrash, The Additional Beith Hamidrash, The Beith Hamidrash Of Volia	M. Y. Feignbaum	314
Prayer Houses of Chassidim and the opponents of Chassidism	Fyvl Gold	320
Cantors	Feivel Gold	325
The Rebbe's Court	Asher Hoffer	328
Rabbis and Rebbes in Biala	Meir Edelbaum	330
A Portrait of Rabbi Shmuel Aryeh Leib, a Holy Person of Blessed Memory, the Rabbi of Biale	Shmuel T. Halevi Rubinshtein	340
The Rav R'Zvi Hirschhorn		349
Rebbe Berish Landau		351
Rebbe Ahron Landau		353
Our master and Teacher Rabbi Yitzchak Ya'acov Rabinowicz		354
The Khevra Kadishe		356
The Cemeteries		357

Hassidic Biala in Literature

Between Two Mountains	Y. L. Peretz	359
The Silent Man From Wurk	Y. Opatoshu	366
Poland	Y. Y. Trunk	369

Biala's "Yard"   A. Litwin   374

Social Institutions

The Hospital   M. Y. F – M   377

In the Health Service for the Welfare of the Population   Alter Wajnberg and Asher Hoper   383

"Achiezer"   Moshe Braverman   384

The Children's Home   387

TOZ   Baruch Vinograd   390

The Moyshev–Skeynim   M. Y. F – M   395

Women's Aid Committee   397

Other Voluntary Institutions in the City   M. Y. F – M   399

Personalities, Figures and Types

Political activists   403

Apollinaire Heartglass   Yitzhak Grinboim   403

Apollinaire Heartglass, Moshe Rubinstein, Joshua Fisher   M. Y. Feigenboim   405

Moshe Smolyor   Jacob Aaron Rosenboim   411

Baruch Weinberg   412

Yeshayahu Weinberg   412

Elie Shimsheles (Elijahu Yustman), David Kruses (Goldfarb) Gdaliahu Braverman   413

Elie Bobkes (Elijahu Hoffman), Tankhum Freind   P. Gold   415

Hirsh Richter (Lazar the Carpenter)   417

Rabbi David Pizich   Elijahu Mazor   417

Religious Persons and Figures

Rabbi Dovid'l Karliner   Dr. Shmuel Elyashiv   420

Bialer Yichus (pedigree, O.A.), "The Hoseh" (The Prophet), Rabbi
Noah (The Giant of Biala), Rabbi Moshe Cohen, Rabbi Moshe
Moses (The Great), Rabbi Moshe Shahor (the Little), Rabbi
Shimele Kreidshtein (the "Skoreyi")   Pavel Gold   422

Rabbi Velvel Moses   425

The Rabbi Shmuel Tanhum Levi Rubinstein   425

Rabbi Shmuel Jacob Rubinstein   Shmuel Tanhum HaLevi   427
                                                          Rubinstein

Portraits   428

Yakov Steinman, Menachem Mendel Gelenberg, Moshe Kave, Idel
Schwartz, Alter Zukerman, Hershel Zak, Haim Mustovitch (The
Kobryner), Benjamin Konolstein, Yakov Virnik, Hershel
Nuchovitz, Dr. David Cohen, Dr. Butche Finkelstein, Dr. Nathan
Tsigelnick, Shimon Goldsmith   M. Y. Feigenbaum   428

Social Workers, Writers and Personalities

Ya'akov Kahan   Yosef Zide   443

Aharon Beckerman   Y. Papiernikov   444

Yossel Birshtein, Yitzhak Perlov	Melech Ravitch	445
Ya'akov Cohen		447
Ya'akov Falatitzky		448
Yosef Zide	Yakov Kahan	449
Advocate Avraham Yitzchak Gottlieb	Zalman Gottlieb	450
Fyvel Friedman	F. Gold	450
Bernard Lieberman	Arthur Lederman	451
Dr. Yehuda Leib Davidson	Yosef Babitsh Prozshani	451
Fritz Kornberg	Moshe Ravon	453

Women Characters

Tille Berlin	Yitzchak Shein	456
Rivkah Akivaches, Pesl the "Deaf", Esther the "Lizard"	B. Wineberg	457
Godya Shteinman	Dina Arbitman	460
Chavale Rodzinek	M. Y. Feigenboim	461

Types

Moshe Tuvia the carpenter	B. Vineberg	464
Shmerele Becker (Hochman)	Gedalyahu Braverman	464
Leibe Mednik (Reb Yehuda Leib Bornshtein)	Ya'akov ben Yechezkel	465
Abik Ogrodnik (Abush Rozenblum), Mordche'le Weintraub	Berel Fakman	467
Boruch Sholem the Teacher (Krideshtein), Motl Domatshever, Shualke Cohen, Yossel Vetshik (Gotfried), Pesach Skos, Moshe Bass, Alter Nemirover, Yitzchak Urtsheles, Meir Tallitmacher [lit. prayer shawls maker], Idl Tzinnes (Kanalshtein), Chaim Chaveles, Moshe Bukkes (Puterman), Yos Drozshkarzsh (Gerrman)	F. Gold	469

Folklore

Words, Aphorisms, and Jokes by Biale's Sharp Minds and Fun Lovers; Surnames according to towns of origin, Grandmothers and Grandfathers and occupations; Mocking Surnames and Nicknames; Customs and Charms; Clothes and Fashions of 80 years ago	M. Y.Feigenboim	476

Tales and Legends

"Stoyontse" The "Upright" Burial		483
Without Success		483
The Dead Man	M.Y. Feigenboim	484
The Muddy Neighbourhood	F. Gold	485
Stories	M.Y. Feigenboim	486
In the town they used to narrate the following legends	F. Gold & G. Braverman	488
The "Hero" from Biale	A. Litvin	489
A Blood Libel	M.Y. Feigenboim	491

Destruction and Annihilation   M.Y. Fajgenbaum   492

Survivors Tales

The Beginning of the End   Berish Asenhaltz   557
  A. In the Miedzyrzec Ghetto;   R. Bachrach   558
  B. In a Bunker in the Center of Miedzyrzec   563
Leaving Home   A Bialer   570
Some Memories   Leon Fokman   571
In Liberated Biala   M. Y. Fiegenboim   576

Bialers in the World

In Israel   M.Y. Feigenboim   585
In North America
  A. New York   587
  B. Los Angeles   David Gordon   593
In Argentina   Yakov Aranovitch   594
In France   597
In Canada   Noakh Bresker   598
In Australia   Hershel Orlanski   599
Our Compatriot, Yakov Wirnik a Witness at the Eichmann Trial in
Jerusalem   601

Index of names and places   602

Name Index of this English Translation   693

Book of Biala Podlaska
(Biała Podlaska, Poland)

50°02' / 23°08'

Translation of
Sefer Biala Podlaska

Edited by: M. J. Feigenbaum

Published in Tel Aviv, 1961

In memory of
Benjamin Sivak

Acknowledgments

Project Coordinator:

Max Wald

This is a translation from: *Sefer Biala Podlaska,* Book of Biala Podlaska,
ed. M. J. Feigenbaum, Tel Aviv: Kupat Gmilut Hesed of the Community of Biala Podlaska, 1961 (Pages 501 H,Y)

Note: The original book can be seen online at the NY Public Library site: Biala Podlaska (1961)

Preface

By Marc Zell

Sefer Biala Podlaska, the Yizkor Memorial Book for the town of Biala Podlaska and vicinity, was the result of the combined efforts of many individual Bialans and others following World War II, culminating in the publication of the volume in 1961. But this extraordinary tome would never have been created without the singular contribution of its editor, Moshe Yosef Feigenbaum (1908 - 1986). Before the War, M.Y. Feigenbaum was a bookkeeper in Biala. When the Nazis invaded Poland on September 1, 1939, he was a conscript in the Polish cavalry which was no match for the Teutonic horde. He returned to his native Biala after Poland was decimated. He survived the Holocaust in Biala and nearby Mezritch, after losing his wife and two-year-old daughter, and most of his family, to the Nazi murderers.

From his hiding places in Biala he chronicled the fate of his family and his birthplace on scraps of toilet paper. After the War he published his personal history in two volumes, one of which has been translated into English and appears on this Portal: "Podlasie in Umkum" ("The Extermination of Podlasie -- 1942 - 1944") [Munich, 1948] and "Podlasie in Nazi Klem" (Podlasie in Nazi Chains -- 1939 -1941 (Buenos Aires, 1953). This two-volume memoir served as the foundation for Sefer Biala Podlaska now presented here in English translation.

After the liberation, Feigenbaum, along with a handful of Jewish survivors, collected documentation and other evidence which was used by the Soviet Army to prosecute and punish Nazi war criminals responsible for the destruction of Jewish Podlasie. Leaving Poland for the West, Feigenbaum was one of the members of a small but distinguished group located in Munich that worked to collect materials to document the Shoah. Their efforts formed the basis of the archives that are now housed at Yad Vashem in Jerusalem. We owe an enormous debt to Moshe Yosef Feigenbaum for his prodigious work in perpetuating the history of Biala Podlaska and its surrounding towns and villages, and in creating the basis for documenting the Holocaust for generations to come. May his work and memory be a blessing forever.

as a result of Napoleon's victory over Austria. Western Galicia (including Biala) was taken from Austria and added to the "Principality of Warsaw" created by Napoleon for the King of Saxony (in 1807). For fourteen years the Jews of Biala were Galicians. In 1815 the Principality of Warsaw became a part of Congress Poland connected to Russia –according to the decision of the Congress of Vienna. This transitional period created changes in the constitution and the juridical and economic situation. We should add that this entire period was full of battles, and clearly this fact impacted on the general situation of the town and the community. There was another change as well. In 1813 the Prince Dominik Radziwill died after participating in the Battle of Leipzig, and Biala passed into the hands of his son–in–law, the Russian Prince Wittgenstein. Biala became the subdistrict capital and the academy became a royal gymnazie. In the ledger of the "Chevra Kadisha" [Burial Society] we find a list which hints at the change from 1809. Until then the fees were paid with Austrian money but from then on would be paid with the new monetary units "because of the changing times." In the days of the Warsaw Principality, Biala continued serving as a subdistrict capital. In the chronicle of those years there were three important events: In 1812 there was the Sejm on the subject of joining the Napoleonic trek to Moscow. During that same year there was a Russian–Saxon battle in the Biala area, and it cost the town large sums (payment of tribute). In the fall of 1815 the Russian Tsar Alexander the First passed through Biala on his way to the Congress of Vienna, which was convened to end the rule of Napoleon. At the time of his visit he received a delegation from the Polish Senate.

As for the Jews, during Austrian domination they were required to pay two new taxes: "Kosher tax" which increased the price of meat greatly, and candle tax which had to be paid by every family. Thus the Austrian ruler became the guardian of the Jewish way of life as related to the lighting of Sabbath candles, memorial candles, etc. There was also an increase in the old Polish poll tax (now called Toleranz Steuer, that is, a tax for the right to live and work). There was also a payment for conducting weddings. Life did not therefore become easier. On the other hand, there was an improvement in general conditions because of the new impact upon commerce and industry in providing for the army. In general, Austrian policies toward the Jews included additional burdens: requirements for army service, school attendance, and taking a family name, edicts to outlaw the traditional Jewish dress, and selling liquor in the villages. We do not know how these laws were applied in Biala.

[Page 21]

In the time of the Austrian rule there was a change in the relationship between the Jewish community and the town administration. In 1800 the two sides reached a mutual understanding, and a charter was drawn up which, if it had been observed, would have fundamentally improved the lot of the Jews. According to the charter, the Jews would participate in electing the administration; two Jewish citizens would participate in overseeing the town treasury; Jews would enjoy all the rights of citizenship as long as not prohibited by the laws of the state; the town was obliged to concern itself with the welfare of the Jews as it did for the Christian population; representatives of the community would participate in army draft boards. In return for all of these benefits the Jewish community was obligated to pay an annual sum of 100 Austrian gulden. But it was not certain that Jewish hopes for a change would be fulfilled. Indeed, in the constitution of the Warsaw Principality of 1807 it was stated "that all citizens are equal in the eyes of the law", but it was not clear whether Jews were even considered citizens. The interpretation given to this passage in 1808 did not calm the Jews. It clearly stated that all matters relating to the problem of Jewish citizenship and rights were postponed for ten years. A new series of Jewish taxes and limitations was instituted, i.e. "Kosher tax" and candle tax on the one hand and poll tax (now called "family tax") on the other. A new burden was added, army tax ("Rekrut Steuer"), which the Jews of the Warsaw Principality had to pay in return for freedom from the army draft. Wealthy Jews with European educations were able to acquire special privileges, but the great mass of Jews from the cities and towns, among them the Jews of Biala, were not rich or cultured in terms of the European enlightenment.

When it received the rule over the Siedlce District, the government promised to nullify the "family tax", if the debts of the period of the Jewish autonomy in Poland were defrayed. But this was very complicated and it could not be hoped that it would be done quickly. Meanwhile, they had to pay, and to pay according to the highest exchange rate, even though the real monetary value had depreciated. Meanwhile their usual obligations existed and had to be paid: Maintenance of the congregation, royal taxes, municipal taxes. In 1810, a number of communities got together with Biala (Mezeritch, Siedlce, Vlodavi, Levertov) and presented a petition asking for relief to the Ministry of Interior, in which they claimed: "The war has impoverished us, the amendment about the defrayal of taxes in the high exchange rate cannot be met, the family tax is not applied equitably, the rich pay less and the poor are pressured beyond their means, the subject of old debts from the days of Poland is a complicated problem and should be settled with the old Austrian administration which collected a large sum for them." The request also included a patriotic note: "This heavy burden of taxes lessens our joy in our return to the Fatherland and our hopes for a better future." There is no documentation of a reply, but it was doubtless not positive.

Meanwhile the year was 1812 and Napoleon was defeated, the Principality of Warsaw was abolished, and Congress Poland was created under Russian rule. In the annals of the Jews of Poland, including the Jews of Biala, a new page was opened.

H. The Municipal Budget in the First Years of Congress Poland

With the founding of Congress Poland in 1815, a new period opened in the history of the city and the [Jewish] community. It was the beginning of great changes in the world: the consolidation of the urban bourgeoisie and the industrial proletariat, new ideas inspired by the French revolution, Napoleon's wars, and the industrial revolution in England –the sovereignty of the people, social and economic liberalism, ideas of changing values about social justice, the beginnings of formulating new ways of life especially in the matter of personal and societal hygiene, in the matter of transportation and daily needs, etc. The world seemed to advance somewhat in relation to Jews, with the introduction of the idea of equal rights and emancipation. In some countries there were attempts from 1791 to grant Jews certain rights of citizenship and to make their obligations equal. This was true of the western countries which had experienced the changes of the French –Napoleonic conquests. However, in Russia the old situation continued. In the course of time the period of industrialization began in Congress Poland with the rise of the urban bourgeoisie. But in the beginning there was very little change. As to the Jews, they had to continue to struggle as in the previous period, to try to survive, for the right to settle, to work, etc.

With the beginning of the new Poland the wheels of history seemed to turn backward in regard to the Jews to the events of the Middle Ages. In 1816 there was a wave of blood libels. The blood libel also affected the community in Biala, not only because these libels suddenly appeared in nearby towns, Mezeritch, Vladavi and Sielce, but also because of tragic events in the prison in Biala castle. Here the prisoners from Mezeritch were tortured before being transferred to the prison in Chentshin, in order to remove them from closely populated Jewish environments. Also the prisoners from Vladavi were held there until they were freed in 1821. From an official document of 1817 one can infer that there were conspiracies about Jewish use of Christian blood.

In the following two chapters we shall deal with some of the important features of the fortunes of the Jews of Biala. But first we must present a picture of the town in the 1820s as seen in the municipal budget, which reflects the situation of the community. The items deal with expenses and income. They are a reliable picture of the town and the perceptions of the government inspectors who prepared the budget. And here are the numbers:

Municipal Budget for 1819/20

Income	Zh'
Municipal tax for maintenance of rota for cleaning chimneys	1000
Tax on Christian population	934
Income from various municipal fees	920
Community participation in maintenance of municipality administration	374
Toll tax on bridges	176
Income from municipal pasture lands	160
Income from abattoir	100
Tax on publicans	42
Total	**3706**

[**Translator's note**: The abbreviation for monetary units is Zh' which may stand for zehuvim, gold, the literal translation of zloty or for zlotych the old Polish plural of zloty]

[Page 22]

Expenditures	Zh'
Salary of Mayor/Head of financial administration	1200

Salary of chimney cleaners	1000
Salary of municipal employees	400
Salary of two night watchmen	200
Contribution to salary of municipality affairs of Wojewodztwo [Province]	144
Rent for Magistrate's dwelling	100
Office and lighting expenses	150
Subscriptions to official publications	21
Refurbishing municipal stalls in market	50
Special expenses	141
Total	**3706**

The amounts and kinds of expenses speak for themselves. One of the important persons in the municipal administration was the chimney sweep. His salary constituted 27% of the total budget. And no wonder: A poor town, which did not have enough money to pave the streets, to buy new fire- fighting equipment and for other needs, had to have at least good services for cleaning chimneys in the wooden houses prone to fires. And the town paid various taxes to the Court: there is no mention in the budget of these expenses but they existed and were a burden until the 1860s. In Mezeritch, for example, the bridge and market payments belonged to the Court; and even though the Prince waived this payment and was obligated to provide wood to heat the magistrate's dwelling, he could require many different fees from the municipality which the budget did not mention. This municipal budget presents a depressing picture, especially compared to the budget of 70 years before, which reached 1000 zlotys at a time when the real value of money was greater. The government was budgeted 165 zlotys (144+ 22) but in reality one has to add the item called "special expenses". In the document approving the budget it is clearly listed as "for the Ministry." Hence it is obvious that there was no independent municipal rule, even in petty matters, where the business of the town was dependent not only on the Wojewodztwo but directly on the Ministry. Thus, for example, in approving the budget, the administration of municipal affairs changed some items to release the sum of 27 zlotys for the Mayor for the surety he pledged at the time he received his position.

As to expenses, the taxation system was still primitive, and there was a need for certain special taxes, e.g. maintenance of fire-fighting equipment. In the course of time two important sources of income were created: Consumption tax on publicans and "industrial tax" on merchants and artisans. In 1863 these two sources provided 3300 zlotys. In analyzing these sources one can see this table:

Direct taxes	2350 zlotys	63.4 %
Indirect taxes (bridge and market tolls)	1096 zlotys	29.5 %
Income from municipal property	260 zlotys	7.1 %
Total	**3706 zlotys**	**100 %**

Of particular interest is the income from the collective payment of the community (374 zlotys). According to the agreement of 1800 the Jews as an entity were required to contribute 100 Austrian Gulden. In exchange they were promised certain rights, but the agreement remained on paper only, and the contribution was never imposed. In the planning of the parliamentary budget of 1819/20 the question of the 100 Gulden was raised and the Christians argued that since the number of Jews had increased and 31 households had been added, the number of Jews was 2020 while there were only 1475 Christians, therefore the Jews should pay proportionately to their number, and generally more than was imposed on them in 1800. The Wojewod also concurred and in presenting the municipal budget for the confirmation of the Ministry it suggested imposing a tax of 1308 zlotys on the entire city, with the understanding that an agreement would be reached between the Christians and the Jews on how to divide the amount between them. Meanwhile the city asked for only 374 zlotys from the Jews. It seems that the number of residents as noted was incorrect. The Jews did not let this pass in silence. They presented a memo to the Ministry in which they noted that the conditions of the 1800 agreement had not been fulfilled, therefore the debt owed by the Jews should be cancelled. They also stressed that their number was not 2020 as argued by the Christians and that during the Napoleonic War they had carried most of the burden of contributions and housing the soldiers. Their claim was that the community was a kind of municipality in itself, and maintaining it cost the Jews a great deal of money as well as the burden of the payments to the Court and the government taxes, especially the specific Jewish taxes, Kosher tax and army recruitment tax. The Ministry did not respond to the Jewish appeal and in the approval of the budgets for the following years (1821-1826) it insisted that the Jews and the Christians had to make an internal agreement. The municipality began to change its tactics and demanded that the Jews pay half the total sum, that is, 654 zlotys. The Jewish appeal to the Ministry now received a clear response: that since all trade was concentrated in the hands of the Jews, and they were more in number than the Christians, it was only right that they should pay half of the overall sum, that is the 654 zlotys requested by the municipality. And this is how the situation remained for many years. The Jews who had not agreed to pay 374 zlotys were forced to pay almost twice that. The Jews benefitted from one point in the municipal budget. They were lessees of the indirect taxes.

In conclusion, we can state that Biala was a small city, in which the Christian population worked as small farmers, and the Jews in trade, as artisans, tax lessees and publicans. For the sake of comparison we bring other numbers. In 1826 the municipal budget of Biala was 3899 zlotys, that of Mezeritch was 4810 zlotys, and that of Radzin was 1256 zlotys.

[Translator's note: The writer does not seem to differentiate between zlotys, Gulden, and z'h i.e. zehuvim, gold.]

---

1. I collected this information at the Polish Archives between 1933 and 1935. At the time this article was edited, it became necessary not infrequently to examine the original material afresh, but this was no longer possible. Who knows whether this material still exists; a portion of the material consisted of isolated pages that were thrown about the attic of the Biala municipality. Due to a lack of suitable material in the libraries of Israel and due to a lack of primary sources, I was forced regrettably to give up on writing the interesting chapter about the participation of the Biala Jews in the Polish wars for liberation in 1794, 1831 and 1863. Also I did not spend much time on the chapter about Hasidism in Biala.
2. *Regyesti i Hadpisi, II*, pp. 142 – 143 (materials on the history of the Jews in Russia, published by the Jewish Society for History and Ethnography).
3. In his book on the history of the Jews of Krakow (in Polish 1912), Professor Balaban mentions a Jew from Biala by the name of Jesko Szlomowicz in 1533 (p. 268). It turns out that this was a mistake. In a Russian document from 1533 on which Balaban relies it speaks about a *Zhid byelski* and according to a Latin source from 1542 it would seem that the reference here is to the town of Bielsk and not Biala.
4. Raphael Mahler, "A Fragment from the Jewish Commerce Between Lithuania and Poland in the Sixteenth Century," *Historishe Shriften fun YIVO*, Vol. 1, pages 130 – 204.
5. A. Yaari, "Emissaries from the Land of Israel," pp. 80 and 248 (and perhaps this R. Uri is not from Biala in Podlasie?).
6.
7.
8. To my chagrin I was not able to obtain a town plan from this period, but Bialans will definitely be able to identify the foregoing street names with those of the recent time.
9. The concept "juridical" – "Jurdyczna" means houses belonging to the Court of the Prince, the inhabitants of which were not subject to the jurisdiction of the municipality, but were directly subject to the Court.
10. Plabania, Plabanski, Plabanszczyzna, Fara – are names that symbolize the Christian Church and the houses associated with it.
11. The Synagogue is given the name here "Szkola" [a school]; the Jewish cemetery is "pole" [a field].
12. It is worth noting that among the providers we also find women: storekeepers, a glazer and a silversmith.
13. Wax is an important commodity for making candles. Lighting the palace required many wax candles.
14. Karawka was an indirect tax primarily on meat.
15. Plett – a slip of paper that designates to which home–owner the charitable recipient had to apply for his allowance (room, board etc).
16. The Parnasim would rotate from month to month.
17. This impoverishment had begun after the terrible events of 1648. Sources of livelihood dwindled and the tax burdens increased.

[Page 23]

The Jews in Biala (cont'd)

Section translated by Rabbi Molly Karp

I. The Struggle of the Jews Over the Right of Residence in the city; The Idea of the Establishment of the Jewish Ghetto

For generations upon generations the struggle between the Jews and the Christians continued in the cities of Poland that yearned to distance or at least to minimize the danger of competition from the Jews. One episode on that front is the fight for the rights of residency in the city. The Christian population sought, in legal and illegal ways, to drive the Jews out of the center of the city and the streets that surrounded it. There were even cities that obtained writs of rights, according to which it was forbidden to Jews to dwell within them. This kind of writ of rights, which was known by the name "Privilegium de non tolerandis Judaeis", "The Privilege of Excluding the Jews", was among others also in the hands of the cities of Warsaw and Vilna, and a protracted war about it was carried out in many cities, among them Krakow and Lublin. Also in the 19th century this struggle was continued, and it even grew more serious on the occasion of the new invention of "Moral" reasoners: it was the lot of the Jews to suffer because they are "decadent" – because they lack European culture, because they are not productive in their activities, only in trade and inn–keeping, because they are set apart from the general population in their dress, in their customs, and in their language. The claim of this ideology is that before the Jews are offered an expansion of their rights, they must undergo a process of moral correction in these areas (dress, language, customs, and productivity). That is to say, they must become different people, and to assimilate; this claim came to justify the existing discrimination, and therefore there was conducted in Congressional Poland a protracted and well–thought–out struggle against the Jews, a struggle whose sting was deliberately economic, and whose cover was in a moral explanation. The government nullified the communities and established in their place an institution called "Dazur Bozhnitzi District", whose powers were only religious and fiscal; a school for rabbis was founded in Warsaw, whose intention was clearly assimilationist.

In 1822 two special decrees within this plan were published: one with the intention of reducing the number of Jews in the city, which announced that the Jews would be concentrated in specific neighborhoods, and one simply determining that in the cities where the right of the Christians existed, and with the limitation of the Jews of the type of the privilege mentioned above, it was forbidden in the future for the Jews to settle, unless they obtained the right to a tavern through legal means. If not, they were obligated to leave the aforementioned city within three years. These two decrees contained danger for the Jews of Biala. From within "the desire for good and evil", it was possible to interpret that according to the arrangements in 1621 the Jews could keep only thirty houses in the city: it was possible to interpret further that thirty houses really meant thirty families, and since there were then in Biala 389 Jewish families, that 359 of these families were illegal, and they could expect either expulsion from the city, or concentration in a specific ghetto. And indeed the Starosta [local government officer in the Polish administration] together with the leaders of the city began to make fundamental clarifications in the matter of the arrangement of the Jews in the future. According to the decree of the year 1822 and according to the above interpretation of the writ from 1621, they planned to set up a ghetto; they did not even consider the expulsion of the Jews. The Jews in Biala immediately stood against the danger and on their own initiative – it would seem – the representatives of the communities in Podliasha spoke and sent a message to the Governor, in whose hands was the final authority. On the memorandum were the signatures of Abraham David Cohen of Shedlitz and Aaron Zak from Biala. The memorandum requested only to delay the first decree, that determined that from January 1 1823 only one family would be permitted to live in each Jewish house (the law for any above that number was that they were to leave the house), and requesting to delay the implementation of this decree for six years. Since only a few weeks remained until the specified day, and it would not be possible in that short time to erect such a great number of new houses, when the Wojesodstwa began to implement this law, the Jews delivered an additional request – this time to the Minister of the Interior – to refrain from additional steps for the time being. On the problem of the ghetto the Jews did not yet see a need to speak, for the matter seemed far enough off in the future. At the beginning of December 1822 the answer came from the Minister that the decree would not be nullified, that the date of January 1 was firm and abiding, but the letter promised that those who would carry out the decree would be compassionate, and would consider the difficult situation of those before them. This question however was omitted for the time being from the agenda; regarding officials who would not reveal explicit understanding of the words "to act with lovingkindness" it would be possible to encourage individual persuasion – the giving of a bribe. But in the meantime, the problem of the ghetto entered into the agenda in all its gravity. The Wojesodstwa willingly accepted the idea and the plan that was delivered by the Starasta and the administration of the city and forwarded the matter for the permission of the Ministry. According to this plan, the following arrangements were set:

1. It was forbidden for the Jews to live and own stores in the center of the city (rynek) [marketplace] and in Warsaw, Lublin, Mezeritz, Yanov, Brisk, and Reformatska streets, and also in the alleys between these streets. The Jews who lived on

these streets and in the corner houses between the permitted streets and the forbidden streets were required to leave their houses, until the end of the year 1825. Otherwise heavy financial penalties would be imposed upon them.

2.   The Jews would live only on Prosta Street (above Brisk Street) and Grabonov Street, and beyond that in the streets that would be established in the future: Jerusalem Street (between Brisk and Grabanov Streets), a new street, Rinkawa Street, Dzilna and Rechoka (Dalika) [streets].

3.   On these streets it would be forbidden to build wooden houses; only masonry houses would be permitted.

4.   As a special kindness, two Jewish families would be permitted to live in the streets of the Christians, and these are the terms that are required of them: that they will be important merchants, that they should have in their possession at least 24 gold pieces, that they should be able to speak Polish, French, or German that they send their children to government schools, that they not be distinguished from the general population by any external signs (dress, forelocks, customs, and the like).

5.   Artisans, scholars, manufacturers who employ Jewish workers, wholesalers, Jews who build large houses on empty lots if they meet the cultural requirements of the preceding paragraph.

6.   It is further emphasized that in keeping with the decrees of 1822 it is forbidden for more than one family to dwell in a room of a Jewish house (whether in the permitted streets or the forbidden streets).

It is necessary to explain that paragraphs 1, 2, and 3 are local matters: the rest of the paragraphs are according to the general assimilatory line that the Polish authorities took at that time; they were not invented in Biala, and not in the Wojesodsto in Shedlitz, they came into expression in the mind of the Polish community (in the newspapers, pamphlets, and books) and also in governments plans regarding other cities, with the city of Warsaw at the head.

[Page 24]

The financial details are interesting: the government surpassed the methods that were used in western Europe already in the second half of the eighteenth century, which was to give preference to the wealthy Jew, and compel him to invest his capital in factories that would have a result in the land – in commerce, manufacturing, construction. The directive in the matter of the employ of Jewish workers is reminiscent of the intention of the productivization among the Jewish masses by means of Jewish capital. In short, there is in the plan danger of the complete destruction of the masses of Biala, that the hub of the city (except for two houses), the streets of Mezerich, Yanov and Brisk, would be the important places for concentrations of the Jews. To the joy of the Jews of Biala (and the Jews of other cities), other winds began to blow in the Ministry. The answer that was received to the suggestion of a ghetto is characteristic: which is, since Biala is a central city and the number of Jews is greater than the number of Christians, it is undesirable to concentrate the Jews in it in a special district, and further, the Squire would have to agree to it. In this way this dangerous matter was deferred for one year. In 1824 the authorities in Shedlitz again raised the question, this time from the announcement that the local authority was relying on the decree of 1621, and was not permitting other Jews to settle in the city, but in vain, for what was there to do? From within this position it was clear that also in Shedlitz they abandoned the idea of the ghetto and considered that maybe they could save face by means of raising the question on a new plan: not a ghetto but a restriction on the entry of new Jews. A vague answer was given by the Ministry, which said that the directive from 1822 remains in effect in the matter of cities that have the right of the "The Privilege [of Excluding the Jews]" mentioned above. There was therefore cause to worry that the number of Jews would not increase. It is known from this exchange of letters that the local and central authorities in Poland were in confusion, and life went on in the usual way. The clerks carried on extensive correspondence – reduction of the number of Jews or concentrating them in a ghetto, and the Jews continued to multiply. In the 1860s there were already in Biala 3456 Jews (compared to 2083 Christians). The plan for a ghetto and the plan for maintaining the number of Jews with limited cover passed to the archive; the stringencies of the interpretation of the writ of 1621 no longer had authority, and since the Ministry was convinced of the idea that implementation of the plans of districts was unrealistic, a decision came in 1833 to nullify it completely. Over the course of thirty years (1862), the Jews came to possess, at least according to law, the complete right to free settlement in the cities of Congress Poland.

J. In the Battle Ranks of Jewish Labor in Biala

The second front, in which Jews and Christians in Poland struggled over the course of hundreds of years, was work, or, more correctly, the problem of whether the Jews had the right to engage freely and legally in labor. The determining cause in this field was the professional union of the tradesmen– the Tzach. The tzachim ruled in all aspects of the regulation of the market, preventing competition, maintaining oversight of the quality of the products, purchase of raw materials, work relationships between the employer and his employees, relations between the manufacturer and consumer, and the like. As a social office which was concerned for its members, they established a kind of insurance fund for those without means, for orphans and widows. In the religious life of the local community every Tzach had a restricted area – a special corner in the church, sanctified and set apart for him alone, and in the same way the Tzachim knew to fortify for themselves a suitable place in the autonomous administration of the city. The essence of their power was expressed in the fact that their authority in the field of labor was exclusive, that belonging to the Tzach was a kind of obligation on all of the tradesmen in the profession; a tradesman who did not want to join the Tzach would be compelled in the end to submit, if only in the form of a tax, as compensation to the Tzach for his standing outside of it. Further, control of the Tzach was not only explicitly over labor, but also over the products of the craftsmen, and by means of this they acquired for themselves considerable influence in the field of trade. The Tzach had a religious nature, and in general encompassed members of only one faith. In Poland there also lived members of the Protestant faith, Greek Catholic, Pravoslavie [the eastern Orthodox church]; these were compelled to fight for their right to work within the general (Catholic) Tzach, or outside of it, as a union within itself, and paid for this stance amounts that were not small. The most positive outcome of this was that the Jews joined together amongst themselves and established Tzachim societies of their own. Indeed, in the sixteenth to eighteenth centuries there arose many Tzachim societies that made great strides in the battlefield of the existence of the Jewish worker. Since the question was not merely religious but also and mainly economic, it was clear that the Christian and Jewish Tzach could not live in peace, and the history of Jewish labor in Poland was one long line of conflicts and disagreements accompanied by more than one incident of robbery and bloodshed. On one side stood the general Tzach, which was supported by the city authority, and on the other side, the "Chevrah" – the Jewish "Society", which was supported apparently by the community, and, as agents and arbitrators, the state authority and the king at their head, courts of the legal authority from the lowest to the most supreme authority, and in the private cities, the private landowners who controlled them. The disputes were mostly concluded with compromises, but these were not carried out, as both sides wanted to obtain the most favorable terms, so the struggle continued and did not come to an end. In Biala the struggle was about three professions: shoemaking, hat–making and tailoring.

The Christian shoemakers in Biala in 1693 received from the landowner a writ of permission, according to which all merchants and tradesmen coming to the markets in Biala had to pay, for the benefit of its Tzach, one groschen for every pair of shoes produced. This obligation also fell on Jewish merchants selling shoes in their shops. The first decree was a kind of protectionist tax for the good of the local worker, to shield his production from outside production. The second decree had a fiscal nature to it; its purpose was to weaken the Jewish manufacturer, and it imposed a tax on the Jewish shopkeeper. The words of the privilege were unclear, and the two sides were permitted to interpret them for their own convenience. The question was whether the payment on the sale of shoes was only on market days, or every day, and whether it was levied on all the merchandise in the store or only on shoes, or maybe only on shoes that the shopkeeper bought for his store on market days. The revenue from this tax was budgeted in accordance with the privilege of the religious needs of the Tzach, for candles for the church, purchase of flags, etc. As if that wasn't enough, two years afterwards (in 1695), the Tzach obtained an additional writ of rights, which broadened the previous one, so that from now on the payment was due not only on footwear, but on every piece of leather. In the Magistrate of Biala there were two privileges: this last one was approved anew in the year 1778, hence the Tzach viewed it alone as obligating.

[Page 25]

It was immediately revealed that it was difficult to collect the payment and difficult to oversee the implementation of the whole matter. The Tzach agreed therefore to compromise with the Jews on a sum of 10 pounds of wax[a] a year from each Jewish shopkeeper, for the needs of the church, in addition to the previous payments. It seemed that the Jews did not meet their obligations, and due to the many disputes the matter was transferred to the court of the landowner (1740). He took a position for the good of the church and ruled that the Jews are obligated annually to pay 15 (not 10) pounds of wax from every shopkeeper, and in order for there to be the possibility of overseeing the fulfillment of the first decree, all sales of footwear and leather should be centralized in the marketplace; the ruling further stated that if the Jews did not obey then they would be obligated to pay a fine, half of which would be for the Tzach and half for the judge of the royal court. The judge found that the Tzach had not been entirely in order, therefore he set the collection methods and kept for himself the right to supervise the method of collection of the monies. When the Tzach saw that its standing was strengthened it demanded for itself additional rights, and actually an additional right was given it in 1751, according to which every new Jewish shopkeeper was obligated to pay it a sum of 6 gold pieces, for the same purpose.

It seems that now matters entered a normal course, and the two sides came to a mutual understanding. In the Warsaw archive of "old documents" we find a document from 1754 in which four shopkeepers from Biala request pardon that they did not pay off the wax fine, that they are obligated to pay it before a certain date, and if not they would pay double. From the year 1774 there is in the documents a decree regarding seven shopkeepers who opened new stores and had not yet paid the proceeds from them. In the days of the Napoleonic Wars the arrangements were disrupted and the Jews stopped paying; when the Tzach demanded its due, the Jews responded that they did not recognize the rulings of 1740 and 1751, and that they were ready to conform only to the Privilege of 1695. Thus began a series of claims and counter–claims, and at the end they again reached, in 1815, a compromise: the Jewish shopkeepers would from that point on pay one and a half gold pieces a year, and they would pay off the proceeds from the years 1815–1816 up front. In this way the Jews were obligated to cover the expenses of the judgement: 8 gold pieces. The payments of the workers and the shopkeepers that came to the market remained in force, with this easement, that the sales need not take place in the market, and only for sales in the market itself would they be required to pay the old payment of one grosch for a pair of shoes. Apparently all had been settled, but not that.

In effect there now was opened a new series of struggles due to the new royal decree of 1815. This law was intended to pave a path to the freer development of private initiative for the sake of the movement in the field of labor and manufacturing. These are the important decrees of the stated law:

- The Tzachim would continue to exist, but the power to regulate economic life would be removed from them;
- The method of training the craftsman would be such that it would be his responsibility to undergo the steps of an apprentice and worker and to be tested by the preparation of a sample product;
- Registration with the Tzach would cost 30 – 60 gold pieces;
- The authority of the law would hold over all workers, whether Jews or Christians;
- The Jews would be permitted to be included in the Tzachim, but since they did not hold the rights of citizens, they would not be able to be elected to administer the Tzachim.

When the law was published, the shoemakers rose against it because of the fact that the entire matter was unpleasant; and since over the course of time the Jewish shoemakers had increased, this was for them a double question: the relationship with the Jewish shopkeepers on the one hand, and on the other hand the arrangement of the affiliation of the shoemakers to the Tzach and their acceptance in it was because of official recognition of new competition. It was likewise clear that the Jewish shoemaker who was in the Tzach would reveal anew the problem of the payments and their usage. And further, this: paragraph 145 of the law declared that all the old laws were nullified. It was possible to see from the start that the stated payments were "old laws" and it seems that the Jews apparently stopped paying the amounts to which they had become obligated in 1815. The managers of the Tzach therefore seized upon the rule of the removal of the 60 gold pieces in the rules of Tzach registration fees. The Jews refused to pay, and the matter was brought to the court of the Starosta. He delved into the details of it, and ruled (1824) that according to the law a Jewish tradesman must prove that he underwent the required training steps; if afterwards he fulfilled the ruling, it was within the law that he should be accepted to the Tzach with a registration payment of 30 – 60 gold pieces. If he did not fulfill these requirements afterwards, he did not have the right to consider himself an independent tradesman. In the matter of the payments from the merchants, the shopkeepers, and the tradesmen who were bringing merchandise from outside, for the time being there was no opinion, and they should turn to the supervisors about it. On the surface all appeared clear, but only on the surface, since the Jewish shoemakers claimed that they were experienced tradesmen, as they had been involved in their trades already for a long time, and they should not be seen as new members upon whom the registration payment of 60 gold pieces should be imposed. For its part, the Tzach claimed that it was not so, that the Jews were not in the Tzach, and there was no doubt that they should be treated as new members. Regarding the payments for the marketplaces, Biala turned to Shedlitz, Shedlitz asked the Ministry, and here the matter become stuck; since the officials were not familiar with the entire matter, nor with a similar matter in Garwolin[b], they delayed their response. The matter remained suspended until 1840 when the file was closed and went dormant without a solution. In effect, the Jews won. The matter will be further clarified for us when we examine the list of craftspeople in Biala in 1841; from this list we learn that in Biala there were in all a total of 11 shoemakers and that most of them were Jews – 7 Jews and 4 Christians. The number of Christians grew smaller and smaller from year to year; for the sake of enlarging their prestige they first demanded of the Jews payment for registration as mentioned above, but with no choice left, in the face of lack of desire of the Jews to pay, they gave up. In this way they themselves nullified the marketplace payments. From a number of documents in the city archive (from 1845), it is possible to conclude that only two Tzachim were active, one for builders and one for potters. We can say of the shoemakers that in effect they had no Tzach, since "the Christians were few, and the Jews were impoverished". It appears that in 1853 a Tzach for the shoemakers was re–established. Details about the number of Jews in the Tzach and the arrangements for registration payments are lacking, but one thing is clear: there were only two Christian shoemakers, and, in keeping with the law, these two were made the administrators of the Tzach.

Until now only the leather department was discussed. Now we will turn to the needle department. With the publishing of the law in 1816, there began in Biala preparation for the reorganization of the Tzachim, and there was reawakened – as we have seen above – the problem of Jewish membership in the Tzach. For the Jews it was important to transform the Chevreh [Society] into an official Tzach. According to law, 10 artisans were required for the formation of a Tzach, and 2/3 of them must be Christians, in order that it be possible to elect from among them 2 administrators. It was a serious question: what would be the outcome if there were enough members of this profession or other Jewish artisans in the city, but there were lacking enough Christians to be administrators? The financial authorities of the Tzachim were in upheaval, for it became clear that in many cities there were a great number of Jewish craftsman but the required Christians were lacking.

[Page 26]

After much consideration, in most cases the following two outcomes occurred: either the Jews joined the Tzach for their profession in another city, or they joined a Tzach for a different profession in their own city. This was how it worked, for example, in Sokolow[c]: there were 50 Jewish tailors, and they were included by the authorities in the official Tzach for tailors in Biala. In Sokolow there was not even one Christian tailor, and because of this the official Tzach for tailors was established in Biala. After negotiations that continued for five years (1830–1835), the Jewish tailors of Sokolow obtained an agreement that since membership in Biala was not comfortable for them, they would be affiliated with the official local Tzach of the furriers until such time as they achieved the settlement of two Christian tailors.

How did things fall into place in Biala? We have in our hands a list from 1841 of the religious and professional distribution of the craftsmen of the city, and these are the details: there was one artisan in each of these crafts: chimney cleaner, miller, soap maker, welder, wagoner, weaver – the soap maker and the weaver were Jews, and all the rest were Christians. There were two artisans [in the following professions]: hat–making, book–binding, cotton–wool cleaner, watchmaking; all, except for one watchmaker, were Jews. Three artisans [in the following professions]: tinsmiths, tanners, roofers (all of them Jewish). Four artisans [in the following professions]: painters (three Jews), blacksmiths (one Jew). Five artisans [in the following professions]: floorers (all Jews), leather workers (one Jew). Six artisans [in the following professions]: carpenters (all Jews). Eleven artisans [in the following professions]: meat preparers (7 butchers, 4 pig slaughterers), shoemakers (of them, 7 Jews), potters (all Christians), and in addition 13 bakers, (among them only one Christian), thirteen tailors (all Jews)[43], 17 builders (among them 2 Jews). All together 127 craftspeople, among them 76 Jews and 51 Christians. From the numbers mentioned above it can be deduced that only five types of professionals were on hand to establish a Tzach (excluding the meat preparers), and they are the shoemakers, the potters, the bakers, the tailors and the builders, and actually only the shoemakers, the potters and the builders, since among the bakers and the tailors there was not even one Christian craftsperson. We have already spoken above about the shoemakers; there remain therefore only the potters and the builders, who indeed established organized Tzachim. And then suddenly in 1849 there arose "the Jewish Problem" regarding professional organization, which did not quite contain every job among the craftspeople of Biala – meaning the hat makers. The initiative came from the authorities. The Tzach had to include the hat makers from Biala, Kėdainiai, Piszczac, Lomazy, and Rossosz. Responsibility for the arrangement of the matter was placed on the Magistrate of Biala; however, this was not an easy job, since all of these hat makers were Jews. The Starosta pressured and urged – they needed to search high and low for the two Christians. They searched and searched, but did not find them. The matter was postponed again and again[44], and finally in November of 1850 the Magistrate assembled all the hat makers and established the Tzach; two Jewish hat makers from Biala were chosen as members of the administration, Ephraim Tzinomon and Shimon Leizer Cohen[45]. The head of the city knew that something was out of order, but the Starosta applied pressure, and he had no choice. The Starosta was not familiar with the question, maybe he played dumb, and demanded immediately to establish the Tzach fund. However, in the authority of the gubernia[46] there sat an official who had the most experience with these issues, and he ordered that the Tzach be dissolved. However, four months after the above–mentioned elections, the head of the city assembled the hat makers again, in order to inform them of the sad announcement that the election of Jews to the administration of the Tzach was illegal, and that, lacking Christian hat makers, they had to nullify the Tzach. The Gubernia tried further to remedy the situation, and ordered that all the furriers be included in the Tzach, but also among the furriers there were no Christians. Finally, in the summer of 1851, a solution was found: the furriers and the hat makers from Biala were joined with Losice, Yanov, Konstanynow, and Sarnaki, since among them would surely be found the two redeeming Christians, and a shared Tzach could be formed. In this way the "Painful Jewish Problem" of the hat makers in Biala was solved.

And now to the matter of the tailors. The establishment of a Jewish Society for tailors was already mentioned above in connection to the communal budget in the eighteenth century. From the period following that no material remains, but there is no doubt that the society continued to exist. The issue of the transfer of the society to a new form of an official Tzach is not clear. It is only known to us that in 1825, a new idea of the creation of a shared Tzach for the tailors of Biala and Sokolov suddenly appeared; in Sokolov there were at that time no Christian tailors. Is it possible to suppose that there were any Christian tailors among those in Biala in that same year? At any rate, the tailors from Sokolov did not agree to the joining, and the matter was removed from the agenda. I lean towards the assumption that the tailors in Biala continued to maintain their old association, and vis–à–vis the authorities they appeared as a new division of the Tzach of the hat makers. On the special right of the tailors within the burial society we will dwell in the next chapter.

K. Societies in Biala

The Society within the Jews of Poland was quite developed, and in every community different forms of associations were cultivated – for the sake of learning, social aid, and professional unification. The number of associations was dependent on the vigor and alertness of the men of the community, but at a minimum one Society was found in every community. This was the Society of the gravediggers, whose concern was the care of the cemetery and in burial. In certain communities this society was also responsible for visiting the sick and the Home for the Aged (religious trust). The name that was given to this society was generally "The Holy Society". Actually the names of all the societies were "The Holy Society" (The Holy Society of…) however since the burial society was the most prevalent, the name that included all the societies became attached to it. Regarding the period that we are discussing (from the end of the sixteenth century to the middle of the nineteenth century), we have received no information on any kind of society in Biala at all, not regarding matters of learning, and not for the needs of social aid (except for the tailors' association). Nevertheless, there is no doubt that these societies existed. If as regards the city that was adjacent to Biala, Mezerich, we have knowledge of seven associations (Shas [Six Books of the Mishnah], students of the Gemara, the Candlestick for the Light[d], Midrash [Homiletics], Tehillim [Psalms] and the Morning

Watch, The Charitable Hostel and Aid to the Poor, The Eternal Light)[47], it is impossible to suppose that the societies were entirely lacking in Biala. Rather, what? Their ledgers were not found, or they were not concerned with finding them. Regarding the professional societies, it was known that there was a society of tailors, but we do not have much information about it, since its ledgers and papers were lost. The only society on which we are able to dwell in detail is the burial society, whose name in Biala was "The Holy Society For Acts of True Lovingkindness" ([Abbreviation:] H"K GUCHSHA).

This society had been established some time ago; above we alluded to its part in covering the deficit of the community for the budget year 1749/50. In a ledger that was in my hands I found material regarding only the years 1800 – 1905, accounts for the years 1806–1838, and also decrees from the year 1813 with additions from later years.

[Page 27]

Every Jew was accepted into the society, but only by the general agreement of all the members, "only one could prevent" [meaning that all had to agree]. There existed, therefore, a right of veto, and this was surely for the society an influence on the number of members, and the exclusive nature of the society. The high membership fees certainly also functioned as a fence to the growth of membership. There were two customary levels of membership fees: one who held the erudite rank of "Member" paid 72 gold pieces, and one who acquired the higher title, the title "Our Teacher" – paid only 54 gold pieces. Thus the nominal value and the real value of the amounts mentioned above were both quite high. In the first three years the only new member was by obtaining a position (młodość – that is to say, a youth). His responsibilities were greater; he was required to visit every sick person according to the instructions of the administration, and his rights were fewer, since he had no active or passive rights of choice. All disobedience brought in its wake an extension of the positions for an additional year. Elections for the administration were held every year after Passover, and at the latest before the beginning of the month of Iyar [the month following Passover]. The elections were not direct, and it may be more accurate to call them "appointments" and not elections; they placed the names of all the members in the ballot box, and took out five pieces of paper. These five, who were called "arbitrators", were given the responsibility of choosing the administration. In the administration we find 20 members: four general managers, who took turns from month to month; four "expenders and conveyors" – the conductors of the daily affairs of the society; four account overseers, who oversaw the fund; four regulation supervisors, who oversaw all regulations and authorizations for the initiation of receipt of new regulations; and four handlers, who were expert in matters of burial and the cemetery in general. The arbitrators had the right and the responsibility to review their operations before they appointed the administration of the old and new cemeteries, and to repair any damage or disarray that occurred in the previous year. If they failed to fulfill this responsibility according to Jewish law, they were dismissed, and new arbitrators would take their place. A general manager could be chosen only from those who had served as an "expender and conveyor"; therefore, a general manager would only be appointed for two consecutive years. The "expender and conveyor" could only make expenditures by means of a note from the general managers, and for every expenditure he had to file a report with the account overseer. One of the arbitrators could be appointed to be general manager or expender and conveyor, but only on condition that the three other arbitrators agreed. In the passage of time, two important changes were made to the rules: the manager could not, on his own initiative, expend more than 12 gold pieces in his month of duty; if the need arose to exceed that, it was incumbent upon him to obtain the agreement of the rabbi or two members of the society who were appointed for that purpose by two of the arbitrators (1846). Secondly, new members would no longer be accepted into the Society by general agreement of the membership but rather by the general managers and members of the group of "expenders and conveyors" in conjunction with ten members of the Society (1879).

The regulations don't tell us much about the functions and operations of the Society, in total 4 out of 18 branches (18 regulations). When a Jew from Biala died, the general manager immediately sent – by ballot – six members of the Society to the task. If anyone of these failed to comply, or to send a substitute, he had to pay a fine. During the funeral, the general manager would walk around with the donation box, and afterwards he would give to the expender and conveyor the money that he had collected. The minimum fee for the erection of the gravestone would be 2 gold pieces. One who did not have that sum on hand would give an item for collateral, and if he did not have the funds to redeem it, it could be brought for sale with the knowledge of the general manager, after two warnings to the owner of the collateral. When a member of the Society died, a minyan [quorum of ten, traditionally men, for prayer] was arranged at the home of the deceased for the period of thirty days following the death, and men from the Society were appointed to attend the minyan by ballot. At the end of each month the general manager had to turn over the ledger to the manager for the next month, and if he failed to do that he would be expelled from the Society.

It is surprising that the regulations deal so much with the organizational aspect of the Society, and so little with other matters. It is also surprising that the members did not pay a membership fee. It is possible that there were additional regulations from earlier years, that were not copied into the ledger that we have from 1813. For the sake of comparison, we will bring here regulations from two other cities, from nearby Radzin, and from Pruzhany[48] [in Belarus] which was farther away; perhaps we will find similarities between them.

	Biala 1813 (18 Regulations)	Pruzhany 1715 (18 regulations)	Radzin 1816 (9 regulations)
General Character of the Regulations	Essentially organizational regulations	11 regulations on the obligations of members	2 clauses on the functions of the Society; 7 organizational clauses
Acceptance of Members	Extremely restricted	Also restricted, but without veto power	According to the opinion of a majority of the membership
Enrollment Fees	Very high	Not mentioned	According to the decision of the general managers
Membership fee	Did not exist	One grosch a week	Not recorded
Authority of the General Manager	Quite great	Reduced; could not expend more than two gold pieces without permission of the account overseer	He was permitted to expend only six gold pieces on his own authority
Relationship with the community and the rabbi	The rabbi possessed recognized authority	The Society objected to involvement of the community in its affairs	The regulations were made by the rabbi

We will bring several facts about the budgetary basis of the Society, which will clarify its nature for us. In the years 1810–1812 there were two instances of the imposition of a fine. In the first incident, a butcher (Joseph Butcher son of David Doctor) was caught in an act not proper with a man's wife.

[Page 28]

He was removed from the community for six years, and after it was revealed that he was not repentant, he was expelled from the Society "forever". Thus it was decided that upon his death only the official from the Society would attend him. The second incident touches on a member who "opened his mouth without limit"; he certainly held a critical stance about the administration of the Society, and was removed for three years. It appears that after that he mended his ways, and his transgression was forgiven.

The information about the tailors is important. In 1884 15 tailors were accepted into the Society, and it was recorded in the ledger "the financial managers of the tailors stand in place of the command of the tailors (of the Society)." From this it is possible to learn that the tailors held a special position within the Society, and that they constituted a special unit in itself under the supervision of special managers. Perhaps this was a means of providing legality to the society of the tailors, which existed illegally.

From the budget of the Society it is possible to see that it did not limit itself to matters of the cemetery alone, but rather operated in broader social activity. Here are several details about expenditures: for a woman who married a doctor, for a feldsher[e] for one woman, for guests, "wheat money" [charitable funds for Passover necessities][f], bridal expenses, for the rabbi, for the preacher, wood for the Study House, learning fees for one boy, shrouds for people who died in the poorhouse, for a sick person lacking funds, for a blind man from Kaminetz, wages for the schoolteacher, wages for the custodian of the Study House, shroud for the poor, firewood for the poorhouse, for the cellar, for a cart [or, a calf] for a poor man from Mezerich, three times donations for poor people are listed for converts; a male convert, a female convert, and one hosting a convert. One item is anonymous: "for the one [person or object] that is known". Thus, the Society fulfilled general charitable functions and contributed to the maintenance of the community. From this matter, for example, the budget for one month from 1811: in this month the Society spent 65 gold pieces, of them 16 gold pieces for guests. "Guests" surely refers to poor people who wandered from community to community.

L. A Portrait of the City in the Beginning of the 1860s

In 1860 a ruling was published in the matter of eliminating the debts of private cities to the Polish landowners. It is interesting, therefore, to see what the face of the city was from the legal and socio–economic aspects prior to the elimination of debts mentioned above, and until it gradually acquired the character of a modern city.

There are 344 houses in the city. Only 66 of them are of masonry. 145 houses belong to the Jews, 160 belong to the Christians, to the government, 10, to the city, 1, to the Polish landowner, 16, and 12 to the church. The population of the city stands at 5539 souls, of them 3456 Jews, 2032 Poles, others (Russians, Germans, French), 51 souls; by percentages, Jews: 64.4%, Poles: 36.7%, others: .9%. The number of families is 1753 – 1036 Jewish, 717 Christian (by percentages, 40.9 Christian, 59.1 Jewish). A Jewish family consists of 3.3 people, and a Christian family 2.9. 383 families live in houses of their own; the rest (1370 families) are tenants (kamarnikim). The physical condition, therefore, is not bright. According to the religious make–up, we get the following table:

Jewish tenants	886 families	64.7%
Christian tenants	484 families	35.3%
Total:	1370 families	100%

Jews who don't have their own houses constitute 64.7% of those who are tenants, at a time when in the general population the Jews comprise only 59.1%. Jewish poverty is therefore greater than that of the Christians. The matter is understood also on the basis of another analysis.

In the Jewish Population

3456 souls, which are 1036 families. Among them, 886 tenant families. The percentage of kamarnikim in families in total is 86.5%. Among families in general, kamarnikim are 25.7%.

In the Christian Population

2083 souls, which are 717 families. Among them are 484 tenant families. The percentage of kamarnikim in families in total is 67.5%. Among families in general, kamarnikim are 23.2%.

What Were the Occupations of the 1753 Families in Biala?

120 families were engaged in agricultural work, and they also owned their house and land
62 families were engaged in agricultural work and also labor, and they too owned their house and land
201 Home owners whose occupations were not indicated
1370 Tenants who were engaged in commerce and labor
1753 in total

And now to the matter of the obligations of the town and its inhabitants to the landowner. We have already dwelt on this in the discussion of the communal budget in the eighteenth century. There, before our eyes, were only Jews. In our addressing the elimination of the feudal tax of the city vis–à–vis the princely palace, we will give our knowledge of the general population. A payment for the land preceded every paid–up bill of every homeowner and every landowner, since from a legal perspective, the land belonged to the nobleman. This is the income of the nobleman from this source: 274 rubles from the Christians, 140 rubles from the Jews; in addition to these there was the payment known as the "tithe", in total 284 rubles. The village as an administrative collective unit paid an additional total of 150 rubles as a payment for work in paving in Biala, and therefore there was an argument about the work of the residents of Biala – one day a week. Besides that which was mentioned above there were in the hands of the nobleman other monopolistic rights that brought in for him substantial income: the propensity which included 14 inns owned by residents of the town/the sale of wine and brandy

– 2500 rubles a year, 57 kopecks for each barrel of beer and 13 kopecks for each pot of mead made and sold by residents of the town. He received 15 kopecks from each barrel of salted fish, for milling at home and not at the landowner's mill – 15 kopecks, from the sale of tar and oil he received 5 rubles, for fishing rights he received 50 rubles, for each pig slaughtered he received 7 ½ kopecks. From the sale of imported pig meat he received 7 ½ kopecks. In comparison to the concessions, the nobleman had the following obligations: he paid 30 rubles a year as his share in supporting a system for extinguishing fires, 180 rubles to repair roads and roadblocks.

Aside from that there existed for the Christian population as individuals the following rights: the use of the nobleman's mills at a low price, free grazing in the nobleman's forests, and also a wagon of wood for heating each week. All of these services of the nobleman are valued at an amount of 2250 rubles per year. As stated, only the Christians benefited from these individual rights. For the sake of the city, Jewish and Christian residents paid, for the right of maintaining inns, 135 rubles. Taxes for the right of commerce and labor – 360 rubles; for cleaning the marketplace, 42 rubles; for maintaining a system for extinguishing fires, 210 rubles.

To the national fund were paid the following taxes: house tax, 2019 rubles; land tax, 149 rubles; for the removal of drafted and conscripted soldiers, 64 rubles; personal tax, 1971 rubles; for the billeting of soldiers, 2882 rubles; for the support of the school, 292 rubles. In the detailed monthly budget, there is a value to the amounts included above which is not insignificant; regarding the Jews one must also take into account the additional expenses of supporting the community and its institutions.

M. Summary

We have tried to describe the history of the Jews of Biala over the course of an approximately 300–year period, to the extent that the source material supplied the necessary information. We accompanied them in their struggle for decent lives and we saw that they withstood this challenge with dignity, with maximal unity and aid to the needy; the shadow points that we raised aren't able to darken the general picture. However, all existence was built on sand; the last decades of the existence of the Russian government and the period between the two world wars under the Polish government didn't change much. Then, suddenly, everything collapsed and disappeared from the map of life: the Jews, their houses, their businesses, their books and all the documents that were in them that might have testified to their previous lives.

Translator's footnotes:

    a.   See footnote here: http://www.jewishgen.org/Yizkor/Biala_Podlaska/bia003.html#f9–13
    b.   http://www.jewishgen.org/yizkor/garwolin/garwolin.html
    c.   http://kehilalinks.jewishgen.org/kolbuszowa/sokolow/Sokolow1.html
    d.   In the Wilderness Tabernacle (Exodus 25:31); also the name of a book by Rabbi I. Abohav in the 14th century.
    e.   a medical or surgical practitioner without full professional qualifications or status in some east European countries and especially Russia http://www.merriam–webster.com/dictionary/feldsher
    f.   http://www.chabad.org/holidays/passover/pesach_cdo/aid/1170218/jewish/Maot–Chitim–Wheat–Money.htm

Author's Notes:
    [for translations of notes 1–5, see translation p. 22 http://www.jewishgen.org/Yizkor/Biala_Podlaska/bia003.html#f9–16]

    6.   The title "master" vis–à–vis a Jew is rare; the accepted title is *niewierny*, (the unbeliever).
    7.   The value of red gold in the eighteenth century is 18 gold pieces.
    8.   It is worthwhile to note that among the supporters we find women as well – shopkeepers, a glazier, and a smith.
    9.   Wax is an important commodity for the manufacture of candles.
    10.   Karavka was an indirect tax, mainly on meat.
    11.   The festival of Saint Julian fell on January 25th.
    12.   Plett – a slip of paper that designates to which home–owner the charitable recipient had to apply for his allowance (ASH) "L – abbreviation for food, drink, and lodging).
    13.   The Parnasim would rotate on a monthly basis.
    14.   The impoverishment began after the decrees of 1648: [http://www.yivoencyclopedia.org/article.aspx/Gzeyres_Takh_Vetat]; sources of income dwindled, and the tax burden increased.
    15.   A. Yaari, "Journeys in the Land of Israel," p. 329
    16.   M. Banayhu, "The Holy Society of Reb Judah the Pious", Panels 3–4, p. 175
    17.   "The Ari", (The Divine Rabbi Yitzchak) [Rabbi Isaac Luria] established practical mysticism in the land of Israel in the sixteenth century; see "An Epistle on the Ascent of Rabbi Rovigo", Yaari, Epistles of the Land of Israel, p. 241
    18.   SHD"R – Rabbinic Emissary; the emissary who go out from the land of Israel for the purpose of collecting funds for the poor of the Jewish settlement. In May 1960 the coffin of Hayyim Yoseph David Azulai was brought up to the land of Israel from Livorno and buried in Jerusalem.

19. "The Book of the Good Journey; The Diaries of Rabbi Hayyim Yosef David Azulai" p. 27 [[[[https://searchworks.stanford.edu/view/4409099]. Also see M. Banayhu, "Rabbi Hayyim Yosef David Azulai", p. 146.

20. Y. Halpren, "The Ledger of the Council of the Four Lands" 186 [http://www.chabad.org/library/article_cdo/aid/112038/jewish/Rabbi–Jacob–Emden.htm]

21. Y. Halpren, "The Ledger of the Council of the Four Lands" pp. 362, 364 [http://www.jewishencyclopedia.com/articles/4705–council–of–four–lands]

22. Y. Halpren, "Additions and Supplements to the Ledger of the State of Lithuania" pp. 66–67 [http://www.worldcat.org/title/tosafot–u–miluim–le–pinkas–medinat–lita/oclc/38718090]

23. Y. Halpren, "The Ledger of the Council of the Four Lands" pp. 392–393

24. ibid. p. 374 note 4

25. ibid. pp. 376–377 – pasht – postal fee

26. ibid. p. 378

27. ibid. p. 399

28. ibid. p. 402

29. A Jewish–Muslim sect, the last remnants of which continue to exist in our time.

30. Y. Halpren, "The Ledger of the Council of the Four Lands" pp. 188–189

31. Y. Halpren, "The Ledger of the Council of the Four Lands" p. 401

32. M. Balaban, "Towards a History of the Frankist Movement p. 190 [http://www.yivoencyclopedia.org/article.aspx/Ba%C5%82aban_Majer]

33. *Suplika* – a request. The *Nunciatora* is the envoy of the Pope to foreign countries.

34. Halpren, op.cit., pp. 423–424

35. M. Balaban, op. cit., p. 190 note 3

36. H. Gratz, "Frank und die Frankinsten", p. 33

37. The Pope expressed his opinion in the year 1753 that there was not enough basis for proof that the Jews were indeed using Christian blood, and that in every individual case the details and the evidence should be thoroughly checked.

38. S. Bronfeld, "Book of Tears", Volume 3, pp. 125–126

39. ibid. pp. 138–139

40. According to the memories of Rabbi Dov of Bolichow, pp. 50–51 his grandfather was among the refugees of Mezerich after the Decrees of 1848. [http://www.jewishgen.org/Yizkor/bolekhov/bolekhov.html]

41. Rabbi Zvi Yehezkel Michelzen in the introduction to a publication of the homilies of Rabbi Zvi Hirsch Halberstater, Biala, by the name of "The Crown of Zvi".

42. Rabbi Yehudah Leib Fishman (Maimon), "Princes of Israel", Volume I, p. 11

43. In the previous years there were apparently also Christian tailors in Biala (at least two).

44. One time the representatives from Fishchach and Lomza were late in arriving; another time matters were postponed because the meeting had been scheduled for Yom Kippur.

45. From among the 10 hatmakers that were present, eight signed with a circle, indicating that they did not know how to write.

46. From the year 1837 the *województwa* was called the Gubernia. Until 1844 Biala was included in the Shedlitz gubernia. Until the year 1866 – in the Lublin gubernia, and after that, again in Shedlitz.

47. The material of the regulations of the societies of Mezerich is in my possession in manuscript form. See also about the societies in Sokolow in my article "Towards an Investigation of the Societies of Craftsmen in early Poland", Records, New Series, Volume 5, pp. 131–146.

48. The regulations of the Burial Society in Pruzhany are quoted in "The Ledger of the State of Pruzhany" pp. 100–118. The ledger of the Burial Society of Radzin I saw in the possession of a Jew from Radzin in my visit to the city in 1934.

[Page 30]

Jewish Biala During the Last Generation
(General Review)

by M. Y. Fiegenboim / Ramat Gan

Translated by Ofra Anson

1. Up to the First World War

In this chapter, we will review Jewish life in Biala from the end of the first Polish rebellion against Russia in 1863, up to World War II in 1939. Based on interviews and our memories, we will discuss three sub–periods, divided according to political processes, which affected Jewish life. The holocaust will not be discussed here, as it will be described later in the book, in a separate chapter.

In 1863, Biala's Jews happily welcomed, with bread and salt, the rebels led by Roginski. The Rabbi made a special, festive, prayer and read the message of the people's government.

In 1866, there were about 3,456 Jews in Biala, 64.9% of the population. The town was governed by Russia and, although the Jews were the majority of the population, they did not have any political power and the municipality was controlled by the Christians.

Until the end of the 19th century, Jews chose to live in a ghetto–like neighborhood. Jewish life was centered around the rabbi's courtyard, prayer houses, and houses of study. They hardly had anything to do with the outside world.

The following was written by the lawyer, A. M. Heartglass, in 1927:

"40 years ago, all Biala's Jews were Hasidim. There were two or three Lithuanians, and the rest, almost 100%, were a socially backwards Hasidic mob, ignorant of any modern concepts, without any cultural needs and far removed from any general modern and European cultures. Their narrow world was composed of the rabbi's yard and the landowners around the town, with whom they traded. There was no self–respect in their relationships with Christians. At the same time, in Brisk located only 40 Km away, there was a healthy, culturally developed, nationalist Jewish community.

The Jews in Biala were not interested in general education. Biala did have a state high school, which I attended, but at the time, I was the only Jewish student. Jews did not read Polish newspapers or journals. The only Jewish magazine was "*Hatzfira*", but reading it was forbidden, mainly among the Hasidim.

(Source: "Podalsier Leibn" [Life in Podalska, O.A.] volume 6/2, February 11, 1927, "Tzeiten Beitn Zich" [Times are Changing]).

This Hasidic mob fought against even the smallest deviation from the accepted traditions and managed to freeze Jewish life. Every time they sensed the possibility of a small change, they would scream "Fire on you, Israel!" meaning we must "save" Israel. For "saving", they would not stop at the ghetto's boundaries, but recruited the Czar's administration for help…

"Fire on you, Israel!" – This alarm call was heard when they saw a Yeshiva scholar with shining shoes, or with a tie and collar; or someone carrying something on Saturday when the "Shabbat Boundary" was broken. Not to mention when they found something "unclean" like a secular book such as "The Love of Zion" by Ahad Ha'am.

An article in the Hebrew newspaper "*Hamelitz*" from 1884 (volume 5), describe this period as following:

"H. Abraham Kushzutz, from Biala (Siedlce region), reports that a few youngsters got together to read a general knowledge book. When the Hasidim found out, they allowed some of their members to beat them up. Indeed, the education seekers were beaten so hard, that one of them needed medical attention. The town's administration learned about it, the beaters were forced to ensure medical care for the ill youngster and were made to pay a hundred Rubles fine."

During that period, there were rebels and deviants. Yet, they were very few. We know, for example, that Israel the Builder father of Alther, Baruch, and Joshua Weinberg [members of my father's family, O.A.] loudly expressed his anger because the rabbi forced the people to wait for him for a long time during the high–holidays service. Any person familiar with the authority enjoyed by the rabbi of Biala knows that almost no one dared to behave like that.

Orthodox persons, scholars, and the respected rich men ran the community. They used to meet at the rabbi's and decide important matters (in those days' terms).

[Page 31]

They chose the community leaders who were then approved by the Russian regime.

The memorable leaders from 1890 to WWI (1914) were: Moshe Bergstein, Yeshayahu David (nicknamed "Floken"), Moshe Wyznicher (probably immigrated from Wyznica), Moshe Cohen, David Shachor, Haim Yoske Kashtenbaum, Haim Levi Rubinstein [my maternal grandfather, O.A.], Kalman Sheinberg, Zelman Zak, advocate Kalman Heartglass, and Moshe Lebeberg. Naturally, all the leaders were rich.

The poor did not dare to criticize the leaders. They could not afford to pay community tax and did not have a say in any matter. The rich were not happy with the leaders, because they did have to pay a community tax.

The leaders made a list of the people who should pay tax, and the sum each of them had to pay. They gave the list to the local authority, who collected it together with the municipality taxes.

The leaders used the community tax to renovate the synagogue, the learning place, the Mikveh, supported promising young scholars and set aside some financial aid for the poor. They also covered hospital expenses for Biala Jews who were hospitalized out of town. Later, a special hospital tax was imposed.

The leaders never reported to the community how they spent the money, only to the town's authorities.

Until WWI, the Jewish community did not have an office. All affairs were settled on the street or in the leaders' houses. They never kept notes or references. When the Jewish community was formally established in free Poland, no archive was found.

The community leaders issued their own internal money which was used by the Jews. It was a piece of parchment named "Pruta" (a Hebrew name for a small coin, pl. prutot), with the letters PBg [Pruta of great Biala, O.A.] written on it. Three prutot made one groshen. The pruta was what people gave to beggars. When a beggar from out of town came, he would buy a few prutot in case he needed to give change and changed what he had collected upon leaving town.

There were households who could not even give a beggar a pruta. In this case they would give a sugar cube, which cost less than a pruta.

A few years before WWI the pruta has been replaced by a brass coin.

Several social institutions of those days are worth mentioning: Hevra Kadisha [for burial, O.A.], "Beith Lehem" [feeding the poor, O.A.], "Bikur Holim" [visiting the sick, O.A.], and "Linat Tzedek" [staying all night watching over a sick person, O.A.]. A few years before WWI, "Achi'ezer" was founded, for medical help. (Some of these institutions will be described later in the book).

Jews were merchants, artisans, and brokers. The standard of living was low, as will be demonstrated in the following examples.

Most of the population lived on bread and potatoes. In most households, meat, fish, and *Halla* were seen only on Saturdays and holidays. When someone fell ill, his family went to a rich house with a small pot to ask for some soup. When the price of bread rose by half a Groshen, people went to the synagogue to read psalms. Clothes were of poor quality. Most men's clothes were made of hard, thin material; women wore dresses made of simple material. Shoes were made of thick leather, seeking strength, not appearance. Patched clothes and shoes were common.

Housing was also poor. Most often families lived in one windowless room, sharing the kitchen with other families. The kitchens were equipped with a brick oven and a hob. Hobs were considered a luxury and were hardly used. Instead, an iron tripod was placed on the hob, the pot on it using wood for cooking.

The room was furnished with two wooden beds, a table, two stools, and a box on wheels holding clothes and important goods. The box was frequently used as a bed too.

A wooden cradle hung from a hook in the ceiling for babies.

Saving was a common phenomenon. Even those who earned very little tried to save. The first purpose of saving was a dowry for daughters; yet buying a property, even a part of a house, was the real dream. Many of the artisans had part of a house, although they were quite poor. There were also artisans who were considered to be poor, but actually lent money as mortgages for others to buy property.

Taxes were not heavy on the population. Shop owners bought an annual business license, and paid their taxes at the same time. Evidence of how low the taxes were can be seen in the way pressure was applied. If someone did not pay his taxes, Mr. Kashimovski would come to his house on Friday night or on a holiday eve and confiscate the *Talith* or the brass candle sticks.

The only interaction with non–Jews was through trade and handicrafts. They lived in peace: Christians felt they controlled the villages, Jews felt they ruled the town. On Saturdays and holidays all shops were closed, and the Christians knew there was no point in coming into town for shopping. Jews were rarely harassed, and if they were, it was by Christians from different regions who came for military training in the autumn. The Jews knew that riots could be expected after Succoth, when the new recruits arrived.

[Page 32]

In later years, when the "Bund" started to be active in Biala, it organized a defense, and the rioting soldiers were beaten up.

Jews did not take part in cultural activities organized by Christians until the time of Polish independence.

Most Jews had very little to do with the town's administration except for the courts. The well to do, who had to pay taxes, had to deal with the administration. Most of the clerks could be bribed, and there were Jews that specialized in settling matters, such as freeing a Jewish boy from the army, using bribery.

The residents of Biala, Jews and Christians alike, did not take part in politics. Elections to the Russian parliament took place occasionally, but they had no effect on life in the town.

The elections were very different from those in democratic countries. Biala sent delegates to the region's capital. Only property owners, who paid taxes, had the right to vote for delegates. Once the Jews put forward three candidates, Bernard Raaba, Idel Schwartz, and advocate Kalman Heartglass. That time the Jews were more involved in the election.

As mentioned, the self–imposed ghetto lasted until the end of the 19th century, when Jewish life started to change. A struggle between some of the youngsters and the orthodox began. General education in the state high school. Zionism, and the Bund generated the beginning of change.

The Jews of Biala did not take up the opportunity to send their children to the state high school: but Russian Jews, who could not send their children to Russian schools because of the numerus clausus, sent their children to Biala instead of the local school.

These Russian students met with their local Jewish peers, and under their influence, some of the locals started secretly to acquire a general education. They started to read Russian literature, which impressed them remarkably.

The young Jews who dared to open their minds to general knowledge suffered harassment, in public and in their own families. Yet their forward looking attitude started a trend. Parents started to give their children secular education.

The Zionist movement reached Biala relatively late. Still, in 1894 it encouraged the adoption of the enlightenment movement by Biala's youth. Naturally, the orthodox despised the Zionist movement, and its followers were persecuted. The weak Zionist movement attracted young men who studied in the *Shtibels*, but did not reach the public. The young Zionists had to be careful not to be found out by the community leaders, who would have stopped their studies, sentencing them to social isolation, had they found out. Their activity was thus limited to the cultural sphere.

It was the Bund, the workers' movement, which turned to the public and to the young blue–collar workers in particular. These youngsters welcomed the Bund, especially once they heard of the number of Russians who struggled for the same ideas. The struggle between the traditional Hasidim and the Bund was weaker than their struggle again Zionism, because the Bund organized the workers, not the Torah students. Aside from its political activity, the Bund promoted cultural activity and the reading of serious books. The Bund had the courage to go against the Jewish leadership. It also fought against Jewish criminals that frightened the Jewish population. Needless to say, all this activity was illegal.

After the suppression of the 1905 revolution, the Czar's regime organized riots against the Jews. Siedlce suffered such a pogrom; Biala was probably included in the plan but was saved.

Every year, an Atonement ceremony took place on St. Anthony's day. Thousands of Christians from the surrounding villages came into town. The Czar's regime probably meant to organize a pogrom on that day.

The head of the Russian police, Koryanov, used to visit several Jewish homes. On one of those visits, he mentioned the pogrom planned for St. Anthony's day. Joshua Fisher heard about it and decided to prevent the pogrom.

Joshua Fisher was a member of the Polish Socialist Party and did almost nothing without its approval. He cooperated with the underground of that party and brought news from Biala to the leaders of the party. He used his position in the party to explain to them that it was in their own interest to prevent the pogrom planned by the Czar.

The party leaders agreed with his arguments and decided to actively resist any possible harm to the Jews.

On Atonement day, the party placed members to guard all the roads leading into the town. Each wagon was searched, and possible weapons were taken to be returned when its owner returned home. They also warned the Christian travelers to avoid doing any harm to the Jews, if they did not want their homes to burned.

[Page 33]

The day went by peacefully, and no one was hurt. At the same time, the Jews tried to stay out of sight.

As much as Jewish life in Biala was dull and uneventful until WWI, every now and then a scandal shook the people. The different Hasidic groups had many disputes. There were, for instance, the Radzyn Hasidim, who had light–blue Zizith strands. When the Radzyn Rabbi, Rabbi Gershon Hanoch, came to visit Biala, he had to leave town in a rush because his rivals intended to inform on him.

I would like to describe some of the more memorable events taking place before WWI.

In 1892, a cholera epidemic broke out in Poland. In the absence of a Jewish hospital in Biala, the sick were taken to the Talmud Torah. The treatments were:

1.   rubbing the hands and the feet with alcohol;
2.   putting soaking paper on the belly, leaving a hole for the bellybutton;
3.   wetting that paper with alcohol and spreading paper on it.

Jewish volunteers took care of those who fell ill with cholera; among them were Mendel Shtritz, Yosl Gotfried (nicknamed Votchik), and Avigdor Richter (from Lomazy). The materials were stored in the women's section, managed by Itche Meir Zishas (Cohen), who was extremely devoted to the patients. The Christians were also affected and the municipality ordered the sewage to be whitewashed. The rabbi ordered his Hasidim not to come to his yard during the high holidays.

The cholera lasted for some two months, and many lives were lost. The Jews believed that the epidemic was sent as punishment for their sins. They made sure not to get close to the sewage, where the devils live … As in other towns, a "black Hupa" was set up in the cemetery, and they chose a bride and a groom to marry. The bride was "cold Dosha" the "town's crazy woman".

Closing the old marketplace, located in today's Wlnoshchi Square, generated a lot of objections from the Jewish population. The following story has been told about the struggle:

Esther Perale was a smart woman, with a sharp tongue. Indeed, for many years, any woman who talked back was called "Esther Perale.

In 1902/3, Czar Nicholai the Second passed Biala on his way to Loshno Vyanovo [not sure about the spelling, could not find any reference, O.A.]. When the Czar's wagon entered the market square, Esther Perale jumped out of the crowd, and stood in its way. She spread her arms and forced the driver to stop the horses. She gave the Czar a sheet of paper and returned to the crowd. It all occurred so fast, that the police did not have the time to react. The sheet of paper Esther Perale gave the Czar was a plea to order not to destroy the huts and the stands of the old market. The Czar accepted her plea and gave the order on his way back.

There was a story regarding the Jewish hospital. The wife of a rich man passed away in 1904. Her funeral was delayed by a day, until her husband donated 6,000 Rubles for the hospital (note that according to the Jewish law, the burial should not be delayed overnight. O.A.).

In 1905/6, robbers attacked some Jewish merchants on their way to the market in Lomazy. The robbers ambushed the convoy in the forest near Lomazy and started shooting at it. The convoy stopped, and the robbers went from one wagon to the other and took all the money. They shot and killed two Jewish horse dealers from Mordy, near Siedlce.

The event shook the town. Different versions were told concerning the identity of the robbers, who were disguised.

The funeral was held the next day, in the afternoon. All shops were closed, and everybody went to pay their respects. The bodies were carried in a simple wagon, and had not been ritually cleansed, and were buried as they were found at the site of the murder. The funeral stopped in the yard before the cemetery. Rabbi Shmuel Leib Zak arrived, declared the excommunication of the murderers, and blew a shofar next to the bodies.

Simultaneously, a rumor started to spread in the crowd, that one of the murderers, a Jew by the name of Siroky, a well–known thief, was a "guest" in the brothel run by Krawotzov (a Russian Jew) located in the new market at the end of Grawanover St.

When Aaron Landau heard the rumor, he cited Rashi's interpretation of the weekly Torah portion "Kedoshim". He said, it is time to "eradicate the evil within us", we may yet finish with the house which is a disgrace to our town (referring to Krawotzov house). Let us go there to look for the murderer and destroy this evil and shameful house.

The crowd went to Krawotzov's house, while developing a riotous mood. Aaron Landau was the first one to break the windows and shake the doors. The doors opened forcefully, and people started to empty goods from the house. Suddenly there was a scream – Siroky had been found under a bed. Badly beaten, he was carried to the cemetery. Half dead he admitted he took part in the murder.

Yet, Landau did not want to leave Krawotzov's house. Enthusiastically he called:

[Page 34]

"Do not leave until the house is completely destroyed!" Furniture, pianos, bedding, and looking glasses were thrown out of the windows. An order came that nothing should be taken and everything should be destroyed on the spot. A few minutes later, the yard was full of feathers, ripped clothes, and broken furniture.

Guards led by Koryanov arrived. They shot in the air, but Landau refused to move until everything had been destroyed. Moshe Edelstein and Yeshayahu Agers helped him. Aron Landau was arrested for rioting and resisting the authorities. The next day Rabbi Shmuel Fijytz bailed him out.

There was a major criminal trial, with Aron as the main defendant. Krawotzov hoped to retrieve some compensation for his loss. There was a long investigation before the three–day trial began in the district court, then located in Urmacher's place on Miedzyrzec St.

Four lawyers, led by the well–known Warsaw lawyer Henrik Atinger, represented the defendants. The young Apilinary Heartglass, who had just started his professional training in the office of advocate Zorderland from Siedlce, was also one of the defenders.

Heartglass took a unique approach for the defense. While the other lawyers focused on the legal aspect of the prosecution, Heartglass described Jewish education from early childhood. He emphasized the loathing a Jewish person acquires towards murder and prostitution from a very young age.

All defendants were found not guilty.

One summer night in 1907 or 1908, three Russian policemen were shot next to the house of Springer (nickname). One of them was killed.

It was said that this event, which took place in the Jewish quarter, almost caused a pogrom. Only the Russian captain of the troop placed in the town, who was on duty that night, prevented it.

The suspects were the men of the Charni family (nicknamed Stopes) and they were arrested. There was a rumor that anonymous information had led to the arrest.

After several trials which lasted for years, Ortche Motel, Shlomo and his son Jacob, were sentenced for life with hard labor in Siberia. Hershl and Benjamin were found not guilty.

Ortche Motel died in Siberia. Shlomo and Jacob returned to Biala after the Bolshevik revolution.

One shot police officer in Vollia cost the life of a young Jewish man. He was an orphan who worked for a shoemaker in Vollia. He was arrested, with a few others, as a suspect.

They brought the suspects to the nuns' hospital, to be identified by the dying police officer. The Jewish orphan was the first to be shown, as he lived in Vollia. The police officer nodded when asked if he knew the boy, and that was enough. He was sentenced to 10 years in prison and died shortly after that.

Only two Jews served in the Russian army for the full 25 years during the past 70–80 years. They were the husband of Hadassah, the daughter of Hanna, and Siskind. Siskind worked as a porter in the train station, which was a privileged work.

Advocate Apilinary Heartglass has written about the Jewish porter in his forthcoming book:

"The porters in the train station were all Jewish. I still remember one of them, old Aron, who had a long, white, beard and his formal shirt and hat, with a brass number on his chest. The Jewish porters worked for the Polish regime for about 30 years. They were mercilessly fired by the Russians and replaced by Russian workers.

Four cases of religious conversion occurred during the period described here. Especially of women.

The most dramatic was the case of Reisele, an exceptionally pretty young woman. A Russian colonel fell in love with her, surrounded her house on Janover St. with his soldiers, and took her with him.

Her parents could not bear the shame and immigrated to America. I heard that she joined them with her children later on.

Another special event was the day when the Jewish hospital was opened in 1911. Building such a wonderful hospital, at a high standard for those days, was a very difficult task for such a community. The regional governor and his entourage came to the opening from Siedlce.

Before we finish reviewing the events that took place in Biala before WWI, I would like to mention the case of a blood libel in Jewish Biala, though it happened far away, and was not even heard of in Biala.

The story went like this: in 1881, the Jewish oil merchant Haim Cohen from Brisk was told by his clerk, who was located in Vienna, that the anti–Semitic Austrian newspaper, "Fatherland", published an article by Pinhas Meir. In the article, Pinhas Meir wrote that he saw, with his own eyes, how Rabbi Ashkenazi from Biala, a town close to Brisk, slaughtered a Christian boy after Purim of 1881 in order to use his blood for Matzoth.

The news reached the Jewish community in Warsaw, and Y. L. Perez, who worked in the community administration, was sent to Brisk to investigate the event.

Various Jewish leaders took an interest in the event, and after the investigation, they learned the following:

[Page 35]

Pinhas Meir was from Terespol, probably from the family of Rabbi Shmuel Leib Zak. He studied in Biala for a while, but he did not do well. He was not expelled because he was from the Rabbi's family. One Saturday he tried to hang himself on the Beith Hamidrash chandelier. The Janitor took him down immediately, he was expelled from studies and left Biala.

They also found out that between March 10 and September 10 Pinhas Meir was in Jail in Brisk the time he said he was in Biala. They managed to get a formal document stating this fact.

They sent this document to Dr. Bloch, the editor of the journal "Austrian Weekly". Pinhas Meir was sued and sentenced to 6 years in jail (source: "Blood Libel" by B. Z. Neimark, "Brisk of Lithuania" – the diaspora encyclopedia).

Emigration from Biala was very rare before 1905. A few people emigrated following the riots of 1881 in southern Russia ("The Negev Storm"). After the pogroms, Russian Jews started to emigrate, and a few families from Biala joined them. There were also a few cases of young people who left to avoid army service.

The large emigration to America started only after the defeat of the 1905 revolution. A few went to England. The emigration was not economically motivated. Rather, people left because the revolution, which had raised a lot of hope among the workers, failed. They were disappointed, depressed, and the Czar's secret police was after active revolutionists. The 400 people who left then were mainly laborers.

The Jewish population of Biala, 6,382 already in 1897 (little over 55% of the total population), ignored the emigration. Migrants' families were ashamed to admit they had a member in America. The common wisdom was that in America people worked on Saturdays and they stopped living a Jewish life. No family wanted a non–Jew among their members. The migrants thus usually left secretly, without saying goodbye. There was a saying "He went out to close the shutters and ran off to America".

Immigration stopped when WWI broke out.

The First World War

Although in the beginning, in 1914, the front lines were far away from Biala, the atmosphere in the town was one of war. Many Jewish men were recruited to the army, and many families lost their only provider. Army troops constantly went through the town and although they provided more business, they also increased anxiety and worries about the future.

After a year of war, the Russian army intended to leave Biala. Some Jews decided to join them and escape to Russia. They thus sent their belongings to Russia, and when the German army got closer, they left for Russia.

Some of the Jews that left for Russia had traded with the Russian army and expected to continue their activity. Yet, it is difficult to understand why the others decided to leave. Especially, considering that the Jews despised the Russian regime because of the persecutions. It seems that they followed the Russian army to get away from the front.

The Russians imposed many restrictions and persecutions on the Jews in Poland. Biala, however, was largely spared. There were just a few incidences of robbery recorded when the Russian army left at the end of the summer of 1915.

The Germans entered Biala after a night of shelling which did not do any damage. The Germans walked around the town with confidence, took everything they needed, as if they were in their own place. The Jews had no problem communicating with them in Yiddish.

The German occupation brought about a complete revolution in Jewish life in Biala. The region had been declared a war–zone and was isolated from all the surrounding areas. All economic connections with other parts of Poland were disconnected. The negative consequences of the war and German occupation were now obvious.

The German regime confiscated all the goods in the town, and within a short time there was a shortage of basic ingredients. A strict food distribution program was set up, but clothing was not part of it. The roads around were guarded by the Germans, so that no food supplies would be smuggled in from the villages around. Farmers had to provide the Germans with a quota of their production; failure to fill the quota resulted in severe punishment, and some were even expelled from their land. The German regime made a full list of each farmer's property and production. They exercised many control mechanisms, such as numbered earrings on the pigs' ears, setting the number of eggs per chicken, etc.

Food was distributed by ration cards from the local municipality. Portions were very small, and Jews looked for ways to increase the amount. They stopped reporting deaths, and for each birth, they reported that twins were born.

The main food was rye bread and potatoes. Yet, even these were in short supply, and many families could not afford it.

[Page 36]

Bread was baked at home, and to get a large loaf from the small amount of flour, mashed potatoes were added to the dough.

Trade stopped, and merchants became idle. The better off became poorer and poorer, and started to sell goods from their homes to support their families. The artisans also had a hard time. Tailors and shoemakers made their living by mending old clothes and shoes. Builders went to work for the Germans for ridiculous pay.

There was hunger in the town, but farmers still had products to sell. Despite the road control, some food was smuggled from the villages into town. When the Germans caught smugglers, they punished them heavily.

In many places Jewish workers worked shoulder to shoulder with Russian prisoners. In many cases, the Russian prisoners stole food from the German storehouses, and sold it to the Jews. Later, when the Jews became better acquainted with German soldiers, the latter would come to Jewish houses to sell them food.

Malnutrition brought about a typhoid epidemic.

When the Germans heard about a case of typhoid, they immediately took the patient to the infectious disease hospital on Warsaw Road (later the camping location of troop 34); the Jewish hospital was taken over by the German army. They disinfected the home of the patient, and the family was not allowed to visit him/her. Some said that the Germans poisoned the patients in the hospital. This, of course, was not true, but it seems plausible that patients did not receive the best treatment. Because of these rumors, people took great care not to inform the authorities about cases of typhoid, and hospitalization of a family member was a tragedy.

The Germans neglected the needs of the population, but they were very good in supplying it with forced, hard, labor. They attracted people to work for them, promising them various rewards. The economic hardship drove many people to accept the jobs offered by the Germans. They were sent to various places for hard work and paid almost nothing. Many returned from this forced labor broken and sick.

In order to control the men and to make sure they all worked, all men had to come to the Gere "Shtible" every Sunday morning, for identity card control.

Life was very tight. People felt as if they were suffocating and the curfew added to that feeling. In the summer, the curfew started before sunset. Everybody had to carry a collection of certificates: work card, identity card, and so on, in case a German soldier stopped them.

The houses were constantly inspected. They always searched for forbidden merchandise, and in the conquerors' opinion – everything was forbidden. Two soldiers in particular excelled in searching: "the small beard" (named after his pointed short beard), and the "white underpants" (named after his white trousers). When "the small beard" appeared on the street, the Jewish population was frightened. Yet, with time, they learned how to hide anything that he might like.

The Germans emptied the town of every piece of brass and copper. Even door handles were confiscated, and several brass chandeliers were taken out. A poll tax was added to the regular taxes.

Nevertheless, though life was limited, the economy destroyed, and the Jews extremely poor – cultural, political, and social life flourished.

We know that the same happened in other towns, too. However, given the power held by the religious leaders in Biala, this development seems like a miracle.

The wish for public activity, that existed among young persons with no outlet, broke out. This became the most fruitful cultural period in Biala.

Where were the religious leaders? Why did they not continue to forcefully the new mood? Where were the screams, "Help!", "Fire in town!"?

A few of the religious fanatics, known for their strong objection to the new trends, emigrated to Russia. The others became poor, and their fighting spirit declined. The bases for socio–cultural activity has been set before the war by the Zionists and the Bund. All this changed the rest of the religious fanatics from being offensive to defensive.

Refugees, mainly from Brisk–Lithuania, made an important contribution to the cultural development.

An extraordinary activity was initiated by the Zionists, led by their energetic chair Moshe Rubinstein (my uncle, O.A.), the most outstanding personality in town in those days. Overnight the Zionists became a large association with effective administration. They established institutions that left their mark on a large proportion of the youngsters for the rest of their lives.

The highlight of all institutions was "Yavneh", the Hebrew school, founded by the Zionists.

[Page 37]

Nowadays, Hebrew schools exist everywhere in the world. But in those days they were rare, and whoever remembers Biala before WWI, can appreciate the courage it took to set up the school.

The people who established the school faced several problems: recruiting teachers, devising a study program while they were isolated from the outside world, and raising money. Yet their main problem was recruiting students. Would Biala's parents stop sending their sons to the Heder and send them to school? The very word "school" has a non–Jewish aroma. When we get to the chapter on the children–house, we will describe the means that were necessary to bring the children to school.

The school brought a lot of festivity to the hard life of Biala's Jews. What a wonderful youth it educated! Even the opponents of the Zionist movement admitted that Yavneh School was a milestone in the activity of the Zionist movement in town.

"Beith Ha'am" [people's house, O.A.] was very popular in town. At the beginning, it was used for non–political get-togethers and discussions. It had a library, and the theater club and the choir of the Zionist federation performed their etudes there. It was used for lectures, and "Maccabi" used it for gymnastic exercises. Later, the wind instruments orchestra also practiced there (my father played the trumpet, O.A.).

"Maccabi" was a completely new phenomenon in Biala. It was the first time that Jewish men of the town fostered the strength of their bodies. Christians and Jews alike were surprised to see that. At the end of the war "Maccabi" managed to buy wind instruments from the German army and establish the first civilian orchestra in Biala.

It is worth mentioning that several Jews, members of the Zionist movement, served in the German army. They offered their knowledge as well as practical help to the emerging Zionist movement in Biala.

Religious Zionists, who could not accept the free spirit in "Beith Ha'am established "Hamizrachi". The bund was behind the library, and organized the theater club, and public discussions.

The Bund stopped its political activity. Before the war, this activity had been directed towards the Russian regime's oppression. Now this activity was redundant, as was organizing the workers against their employers. The only employer in town now was the German army.

Two important social institutions were established during WWI: the children's house and the public kitchen.

The children's house played an important role during the war. Established by the Zionist movement, it was one of the best social institutions in Biala.

The public kitchen was located on Brisk Street, next to the Catholic Church. Hot lunch was served to the Jewish poor. The German authorities supported the Kitchen, mainly because of the involvement of the army Rabbi, Dr. Teantzer. All political parties sent representatives who ran the kitchen.

The kitchen was not only a place where hundreds of people had hot lunch daily, but also a place of cultural activity for young people. It hosted lectures, discussions, theater club. The latter donated the income from its performances to the kitchen. Before the holidays, there was a flower sale to help finance the kitchen.

After three years, the German occupation started to crumble. The enormous German war machine started to collapse, and it was clear that its days were numbered. Who would be the next rulers – nobody knew yet. Nevertheless, people felt that a new era was coming; liberal, freedom for each citizen regardless of religion or nationality. The first sign that the Germans were about to leave was the sale of the content of the storehouses to the population.

Public kitchen in front Jewish army chaplain, Dr. Taentzer

[Page 38]

The transition from the German occupation and the new regime lasted for a few months. A few criminal Jews took the opportunity to rob other Jews. Wearing German uniforms, they came at night to Jewish homes and stole money and jewelry.

The Jewish population organized a militia which, armed with German pistols, patrolled the Jewish quarter at nights. One night they spotted two of the bandits and started chasing them. After a short distance they shot them on the butchers' street.

In November 1918, the last German soldier left Biala.

Under the Polish Regime

In the first days of the Polish government, Jewish blood was shed. Polish soldiers entered Moshe Richter's home in Vollia in search of armaments. During the search they beat Richter so badly, that a few days later he died. Often they would kidnap Jews for hard labor, where they suffered abuse. Yet, slowly order was restored. The proper administration was established in town, and the population, including the Jews, started to rebuild what had been destroyed during the war.

The population was extremely poor. The American Joint Distribution Committee came to help and sent large quantities of food and clothes to Biala. A local committee, composed of all Jewish political parties, distributed the goods. A special kitchen provided children with hot meals, and another kitchen sent food to the very poor.

The freedom to have active Jewish political parties in Biala gave each party the opportunity to develop their activities and to reach the different population groups. Elections were coming up, and all parties had a chance to show their activity and organizational ability. A new party joined the existing parties – Zionist, Bund, and Palei Zion: Agudat Israel, the party of the orthodox Jews, started to operate, recruiting most of the older generation.

The main political struggle was between the Zionists and the Bund. The Bund, known for its turbulent nature, attracted mainly workers. Often, they would interrupt the Zionists meetings in order to stop them, which sometimes led to scuffles.

In 1918, the Zionists in Biala sent delegates to the organizing committee of the National Council.

The election to the Sejm [the Polish parliament, O.A.] created a lot of excitement, as well–known party leaders came to Biala to participate in the public campaign meetings. The Zionists won the election in Biala, and Apilinary Maximilian Heartglass became a member of the Sejm.

The first election to the municipality, in which Biala Jews took part, was in 1919. The Bund did very well in this election, and 6 out of the 15 Jewish delegates were Bund members.

Life just started to get back to normal, when the Poland Bolshevik–Russia war broke out. As long as the front was in Russia, or far away from Biala, it had no effect in town. Yet, with the collapse of the Polish army, and its withdrawal, war came to Biala. Troops went through town and behaved brutally. The soldiers of General Haller and those who came from Poznan region showed their courage by beating Jews, cutting beards, and robbing stores. The Jewish community lived in constant fear, and there was no source of help. All Jews were considered by the Polish as Bolsheviks, and as such – could be hustled.

In the summer of 1920, the front line reached Biala. The Polish defense lines were broken through one by one. A few months before the Polish left town, they started to kidnap Jews and send them to the east to dig defense trenches. Christians did not take part in this hard labor at all.

Before leaving town, the important leaders of the Bund were arrested, and sent to the concentration camp in Dąbie.

In the beginning of August 1920, the Red Army conquered Biala. Yet, it left before it managed to set up administration, because of the defeat by the Vistula. The Polish army was quick to chase it.

The Jews panicked to see the Russian leave. Not because they liked the new regime, which lasted only eight days, but because they feared the returning Polish army. Jews and Christians alike cooperated with the Red Army. While the Christians got the better position and Jews only secondary ones, the Polish defined Jews as cooperators against Poland. Christians, of course, were doing it to save their homeland.

Fearing Polish revenge, a few Jewish men tried to run east with the Red Army. Yet because the Red Army left suddenly, those who tried to join it were interrupting the withdrawal, and they were left behind. Most of Biala's refugees returned after a few weeks, broken physically and mentally. Very few succeeded in entering Russia (one of them was Sheima Sheinberg, who became an important commander in the army).

[Page 39]

As much as the Polish army treated the Jews cruelly when it withdrew, its returning was even worse. The Polish army killed and hit Jews claiming that they were Bolsheviks. Robbery was frequent and villagers came daily into town to fill their bags with Jewish property with the help of the Polish soldiers.

Our delegate to the Sejm, Heartglass, presented a question to the Sejm, presenting the situation in Biala in 1920:

"Even before the Russian invasion, Jews and Christians were taken to work. The latter, however, were released immediately. The Jews were hit with the rifles' butts, and their money stolen. This was done mainly by the Poznans. People were allowed on the streets until 10 at night, before the working day was over. Jews had to pay 100–500 Marks each for someone to accompany them home. Complaints to the authorities were disregarded, as the army officer in charge of work was not interested. The Poznans bullied and robbed Jews; on the last day they shot Jews on the streets, wounded a woman, and broke into houses. Before the Polish army left town, they sentenced to death four spies; one was Jewish. A few days before the Bolsheviks entered town there was a battle near Grabanow (a village near Biala, the author). During that battle, Biala Jews provided food for the fighting soldiers and helped the wounded. The headquarters praised the Jewish help.

When the Bolsheviks entered town, the Polish head of the local militia welcomed them warmly (he fled with them when they left), while the Jewish population stood apart. They warmed up to the Bolsheviks after the public meeting in the market square. The Bolsheviks were fair. There was only one case of robbery, in the house of Mrs. Heartglass, where they searched for equipment belonging to her son who was a soldier in the Polish army. The Christian Communists also behaved properly. Jewish Communists, on the other hand, informed anti– Bolshevik community members. As 75% of Biala's population was Jewish, the participation of Jewish youth in the action organized by the Bolsheviks was crucial.

The Revolutionary Committee included a Russian soldier by the name of Juljov, and two local citizens – one Polish and one Jewish. The heads of the different departments were local. A local Polish man ran the agriculture department, a Jew ran the health department; the education and the provision departments were run by communist Christians, both fled with the Bolsheviks when they left. The militia, headed by a non–communist, recruited unemployed persons, most of whom were Jewish. Christians, who were not necessarily communists, held most positions; Jews served as police officers or clerks. Most of them were not communists but left with the Bolsheviks, fearing the returning Polish regime.

Rubinstein, the Zionist, refused to get a position, though the Bolsheviks threatened him twice. Not even as the head of the education department.

When the Polish soldiers returned to town, they immediately shot to death two Jews in Vollia, and robbed them. Then they arrested, with no reason, the Zionist Fisher, the Jewish municipality member Levenberg, and someone by the name of Librant (who was first asked if he was Jewish). They put them against the wall and got ready to shoot them. Fortunately, some local Christians interfered and freed them.

Some Polish residents were not happy with Akiva Kamion the fisherman. He followed the orders given to him by the town's administration and did not let them fish in the ponds of Count Wolopolski. He was informed on to the soldiers, who were about to shoot him before others from the Christian population stopped them. They killed another six Jews they met behind the town. The Bolsheviks took Eliezer Wassermann to work with his horse and wagon. He returned with a Polish document, but the soldiers stopped him between Jonava and Biala. They took his horse and his clothes and forced him into a hole in the ground with the intention of shooting him. One soldier had mercy on him and they left him alone. Six kilometers before Biala, another group of soldiers met him, forced him into the river and ordered him to lie on the riverbed. Luckily, an officer went by and stopped them.

Now, robbery is constantly going on, though with no pogroms. The Jews closed their stores. The robbery involves vandalism. For example: the books and other things that were taken from Rosenstein were piled outside and burnt. Some of the Christians in Biala and its neighborhood encourage the soldiers to keep robbing. They come with bags to take Jewish property. A few young Jews deserted the army and fled with the Bolsheviks to Russia. The municipality, however, recognized that serving the Bolsheviks was necessary to prevent the Bolsheviks from establishing full control in town. Until now, no persecutions against cooperators, most of them Polish, were reported. Still, the Christians in town decided that Jews' salaries should not be paid, and the administration follows this decision. Jews are also not getting their share of the flour the Bolsheviks left behind, though other office holders do get their share.

Only Jews, of all ages, are kidnaped for work. Soldiers assault Jews on the streets. Soldiers go into houses, inquire whether the residents are Jewish, and if they are, their property is confiscated. Jaborski's volunteer horsemen are the worst.

The current administration started to work only on August 26. Its head, Officer Zaloeski, seems to be of good will, and opposes any assaults against Jews.

[Page 40]

I went to see him with one of the victims, and he took care of the matter efficiently and sympathetically.

He set up guards. He spoke to the head of the police, demanding that the municipality provide him with the workers needed, and that the kidnaping of Jews stop. The equestrians' officer Stokolski and others thought that the closed stores were partly to be blamed for the pogroms. I explained to them that the shops had been closed because of the soldiers' behavior."

A few months after the Polish victory by the Vistula, Prime Minister Jozef Pilsudski passed through town. His train stopped in Biala to allow delegates with different interests to talk to him. He asked the Jewish delegation about the size of its community during the war. Yet, when they gently tried to complain about the troubles the soldiers caused them, he stopped them sharply, saying they were probably referring to the Bolsheviks' behavior. Surely, they could not continue…

The Jewish population experienced one bitter Saturday after the invasion, though order had already been restored. A Jew from Constantin, Zalmanke, had been charged with spying for the Bolsheviks. The military trial took place in the house of Mowus, and many Jews paced up and down the street waiting for the verdict. In the afternoon, the defendant was led in the direction of the jail, which was also the direction of the cemetery. Nobody knew the verdict, and people started following him. When they passed the jail, everybody understood that he had been sentenced to death. Indeed, he was led to the cemetery and shot.

This war too was over, and the damage slowly mended. The economy started going again, factories started to work, and the stores to fill with merchandise. Intensive building industry provided work for builders and other artisans.

Many Jews from Biala joined the massive emigration from Poland to America. The news about the good conditions and opportunities in America, in contrast to their poor situation in Poland, increased the emigration stream. Anyone who had any chance to migrate – did. Yet, the majority of migrants were workers and women and children who joined their parents who left Poland before the war.

Emigration to America was no longer considered shameful, and nobody had to apologize for dollars sent to him by family members. On the contrary, such support elevated the social status.

Warsaw, the capital, also attracted the young people. Emigration, within and out of Poland, took many capable people out of Biala. It thus had a negative effect on many aspects of public life. Yavneh School and the children's house were particularly affected. The standard of education in the school declined, and the children's house closed its gates.

Even after the peace treaty between Russia and Poland was signed, in Riga, the Jews were still thought of as Bolsheviks, and the provocations continued. Inciteful literature against the Jews was distributed daily by an organization by the name of Rosvoi, which continued to call for an economic boycott against the Jews. The organization was active in Biala too, headed by a man by the name of Piatchiski. He used to organize public gatherings and speak out against the Jews. Later, the teacher Novotarski replaced him. The tension between Jews and Christians grew, but the Jews did not react and gave the Christians no reason to harm them.

Despite the caution, there was one episode that could have ended with terrible consequences.

Photo at an unknown celebration

[Page 41]

On lag Ba'Omer 1922, Hashomer Hatza'ir went, as usual, to the forest in Vollia. The Maccabi orchestra led the procession. When it got to the high school "Krashowski" the students threw inkwells through the windows onto the heads of the marching youngsters. Upon returning, in the afternoon, young Christians from Vollia attacked the Jewish youngsters. Fortunately, some strong Jewish men accompanied the procession and beat up the attackers.

When Piatchiski, the leader of Rosvoi, learned about the event, he decided to take revenge on the Jews. There were rumors that a pogrom was planned for one of the coming Sundays, connected to a public gathering of Rosvoi.

A Jewish delegation went to the head of the region, told him about the rumors, and asked him to prevent the pogrom. The head of the region did not give a straightforward answer. A day later, he sent a letter saying that he could not interfere because of the aggression of the Jewish youth in Vollia. The Zionists reported the event to the Sejm in Warsaw. A few days later, the head of the region asked for his letter and the Jewish community returned it to him.

One Sunday Rosvoi did indeed organize a public gathering, and Piatchiski made an anti–Semitic speech. The public then proceeded to the regional headquarters but dispersed in peace.

Yet, the incitement continued, and Jews were attacked. The local authority and the police were totally passive. The police refused to interfere even when it witnessed the attacks, as in the case of Mathithiahu Edelstein. Jewish delegates to the Sejm put forward questions regarding these episodes.

At the same time, the relationships between the Jewish and the Christian population were good, unless they were incited by their leaders. There were, however, cases in which Christian youngsters fell upon Jews and hit them. Such cases became more frequent before WWII.

In comparison with the period before WWI, the relationships between the Jewish and the Polish population did change. However, Jews did start to take part in cultural activities organized by Christians, such as theater, dance parties, lectures, etc. Similarly, some non–Jews came to Jewish cultural activities. These closer relationships were facilitated by the enrolment of Jewish students in governmental schools, which brought about mutual home visits.

Both Jews and Christians volunteered in the local fire–brigade, working together in harmony. "*Podlasyer Leiben*" [Life in Podalska, O.A.] issue 77/1 from January 5, 1934, reported that the following Jewish fire–fighters were decorated for long years of service: Officer Jacob Hershberg, for 35 years of service; Abraham Orlanski and Anshel Beckman, each for 15 years of service; Abraham Browarok, Jacob Goldreich, Josef Rosenberg, and Berl Hershberg, each for 10 years. We see, then, that Jews were an important part of the brigade, which would not have been possible if the relationships between the two populations were tense.

The league for air defense also had a Jewish department, led by Michash Hopper. Michash Hopper himself had been decorated with the "Cross of Excellence".

Even without pogroms, Jewish life in Biala was not calm. The economic boycott had catastrophic consequences. The Jews in Biala were never affluent; there were very few rich Jews, most were middle–class and workers. Furthermore, additional economic hardships occurred when the Jews started to break out of their self–imposed residential segregation.

After WWI, the Jewish life–style changed dramatically. Although there was a considerable number of religious fanatics in town, their influence declined. An example of the decline in their power was the boycott declared by Biala's Rabbi on the Zionists. A Hasid showed the rabbi an issue of "*El Al*", published by Hashomer Hatza'ir, which included a poem by David Shimoni that he interpreted as irreverent (*Apicorus*). The Rabbi sent Joel, the janitor, to call all Jews to the Beith Hamidrash. When the people gathered, candles were lit and in a short speech, the rabbi declared the boycott and Joel blew the Shofar.

Anybody who knows Biala can imagine the impression such a ceremony would have had if Rabbi S. L. Zak had performed it before WWI. Now, it hardly had any effect at all.

The Jewish political parties were legal, and each motivated its followers in its own way. Each party established a library, and the number of readers increased constantly. There were theater clubs, which every now and then had quite nice productions. The younger generation participated in politics and acquired education and knowledge.

The standard of living increased and the great majority of the families had an apartment. It was necessary to prepare a furnished dwelling, not to mention a handsome dowry, in order to marry a son or a daughter. The simple clothes, made of rough material, and boots disappeared completely and were replaced by good–looking suits. Nutrition improved and in most houses white bread and meat were consumed daily. There was no need to turn to the rich for a bowl of soup for the sick. Workers and artisans did not need to work from sunrise to sunset anymore.

The Polish policy of economic dispossession against the Jews, which forced a decline in the standard of living, caused a lot of sorrow. The enforcement of the policy tightened, and Gravski started to empty Jewish houses of their property.

[Page 42]

As already mentioned, many persons from Biala, most of them young, emigrated. Now, however, the USA had closed its gates and the new emigrants went to South America, France, Belgium, and Canada. A high percent emigrated to Israel.

There was also internal migration, from Biala to Warsaw and other large cities that offered better job opportunities. The most active members of all parties left Biala, heavily harming the cultural and social life of the town.

After the Pilsudski revolution, in May 1926, the economic conditions of the Jews eased off a little bit. Yet the relief was a short one. The world economic crisis of 1930 affected Poland, including Biala. Some of the big timber dealers went bankrupt, and with them fell many other families and the two credit institutions.

The boycott policy of the *Sanacja* [a political regime set up by Pilsudski, O.A.] against the Jews ensured that the Jews would not recover from the economic crisis. Like all other Polish Jews, Biala's Jews experienced deep economic hardships, which almost paralyzed Jewish public life. The general mood was of despair and apathy.

Jewish shopkeepers lost their Christian customers, Christians did not hire Jewish workers, and the Jewish internal market was too small to provide them with a living. Poverty was hastened by the heavy business taxes and businesses collapsed one after the other.

In those days people remembered, nostalgically, the times of the Czar's regime. Taxes were low, the value of a *Talith* or the brass candle sticks that the clerk Kashimovski would confiscate in case one did not pay. The Czar's taxes now looked ridiculous. Nowadays, all the property of the house was not enough to cover the debt.

Jewish youth had no future. The working youth could not find jobs, and when they did, they were paid very little. Those who studied were not accepted into universities. Consequently, there was a group of unemployed youth, named "Street Rebels".

Given the poor economic conditions, the Jewish population could not support any social institutions. There were only a few charity organizations that offered limited help.

The Jewish hospital, the pride of the community, was closed more days than it was open, for lack of resources. When American community members sent a few hundred dollars, the hospital reopened until the money ran out.

Many families became "customers" of "*Beith Halechem*" [the "house of bread", O.A.], where they could get a Hala every Friday. The Haloth were donated by community members. The "Taz" association, an organization for the welfare of children, helped Jewish children.

Some of the Jewish youngsters turned to Communism out of despair.

In a report on the Biala region, the writer (the deputy head of the Biala Region) states that Jews comprised 39.34% of the communists in the region. He does not try to understand their motives, his purpose being to present the Jewish community as a hotbed of communists. We have no evidence to contradict the numbers he cited, but we do argue that the policy of economic dispossession and antisemitism of the Polish regime were the main factors pushing Jews to Communism.

The communists' propaganda claimed that Russia was a paradise for Jews, who enjoyed equal rights and freedom and experienced no limitations, as did all Russian citizens.

We now bring a few facts to demonstrate how Biala's municipality treated the Jews. 40% of Biala's population was Jewish. The municipality was sure that they had to fill the town coffers without any claim on the town's budget.

The share of the Jews in the municipality's income was much higher that the share of the Christians. On top, the Jews, who were the majority of shopkeepers and artisans in town, had to pay a tax to the government to buy business permits. Yet, only after a struggle by the Jewish delegates in the municipality, did they hire two Jewish clerks (one of them was later fired) and two–three tax collectors.

The budget of 1933/4 was 270,000 Zlotys. Only 10,550, or 3.91%, were allocated to the Jewish community (6,500 to the old age home; 100 to the "Tarbuth" library; 100 to the cultural league library; 300 for "Taz"; 50 to YIVO [Institute for Jewish Research, O.A.]; and 3000 to the Jewish hospital). Even this allocation was rarely transferred.

The names of the Jewish delegates to the town's council were as follows. In the first elected council served: Moshe Rubinstein and Moshe Kaveh (Zionists); Gdalyahu Braverman, Moshe Rodsinek, Nahum Worak, M. Hochman, Haim Brodach, and Geltman ("Bund"); Israel Bialer, Mishe Haim Weisenfeld, Sosha Rosen, and Moshe Melech Silberman ("Aguda"); Moshe Levenberg (not a party member).

[Page 43]

Although Jews were the majority in the municipal council, they did not manage to elect a deputy mayor, and they had to make do with two members on the board. In part, this happened because the "Bund" refused to cooperate with the other Jewish delegates; nevertheless, it is very possible that the central government would not have agreed to a Jewish deputy mayor.

In the election for second municipality council, in 1923, 13 Jewish members elected: Jacob Aaron Rosenboim, Joel Silber, and Israel Cohen (Zionists); Baruch Vinodrag and Menashe Cheshinski (the artisan association); Eliezer Tzelniker and Moshe Kramatzsh (the tenants association); Eizik Sheinberg, Israel Bialer, Sosha Cohen, David Wiseman, Haim Levy Rubinstein (my grandfather, O.A.), and Yitzhak Levi (Aguda).

In the second council, Jews were again the majority, but, again, no Jewish deputy mayor was elected, and all they achieved was one board member position for Israel Cohen. Today, it is difficult to know whether or not they even tried to get a deputy mayor position, knowing that the government would not approve it. Again, all the Jewish delegation achieved was some minute financial support for a few Jewish institutions.

In the third election, 1927, only seven Jews were elected. The new regulations, issued by the government, ensured no Jewish majority in local councils. The disintegration of the Jewish community was also a factor.

The delegates elected were: Israel Goldstein (Zionists); Baruch Vinodrag and Abraham Stricher (the artisan association); David Wiseman and Wolf Weitzman (small merchant organization); Haim Levy Rubinstein [my grandfather, O.A] (Aguda); Yitzhak Pisshitz (merchant association).

There was another Jew in this municipal council, a delegate of the communist party. Needless to say, he did not deal with Jewish issues, and had little to do with the other Jewish council members. After a while he emigrated and was replaced by a Christian.

The Christian majority, again, "donated" a seat on the board to the Jewish community. Emil Weinberg (of Galician origin) got the position.

In the fourth election of 1934, the Jewish representation declined further. One reason was the new regulations, which enlarged the boundaries to include villages and allowed permanent army soldiers to vote.

Thus, only five Jewish members were elected: Baruch Vinodrag and Abraham Stricher (the artisan association); Yitzhak Levi and David Wiseman (small merchant organization); Haim Levy Rubinstein [my grandfather, O.A] (Gere Hasidim).

It is worth noting, that the political parties which took part in the election failed to gain a seat on the council. Almost all those elected represented economic interests. For the Jewish community, then, the priority was protecting its economic interests.

The last election was in 1938, before WWII. The Jewish community had no interest in it whatsoever. The artisan association and the small merchant organization ran in one list; only three were elected: Abraham Stricher, Moshe Rodsinek, and advocate L. Goldfarb.

From the first to the last election, Jewish representation declined by 80%. The decline in Jewish population was only 16%. We see what an effort the Polish authorities took to exclude Jews from decision making, although even when Jews were the majority on the council they did not have any achievements.

The Community

The first elected community institutions (the council and the board) in Biala were founded in 1924. The Jewish population had chosen their delegates from the community in a public election,. All political parties and economic associations in town took part in the election. Yet, the workers' parties excluded themselves.

Unfortunately, we have no archives that can be of help in picturing this period in the life of the community. We shall thus rely on memories, explanations provided by Baruch Vinodrag, who was the secretary of the community (he died in Israel), and on newspaper reports of that time.

The Polish community law demanded minorities to limit their activities to religion only. Yet, by cooperation between its different interest groups, a community could operate in many other aspects of life.

In Biala's Jewish community, religious and the other leaders enjoyed equal power. The religious leaders made sure that their needs were met early in the budget year. The community law was with them, and there was no need to struggle. They did not demand a lot of support, because they did not want to upset their voters by increasing taxes. The income from slaughtering and some tax was sufficient.

The community's main sources of income were a levy on kosher slaughtering and taxes. Yet this was never enough to meet the community's needs. There were leaders that, when it came to planning the budget and thus the taxes, protected the interests they represented and tried to prevent their acquaintances and voters from paying high taxes. Indeed, the rich paid very little tax and even that never on time.

A list of tax payers was published in "*Bialer Wochenblat*" ["The Biala Weekly," O.A.], issue number 29, July 23, 1937.

According to this list, not all the persons who were supposed to pay the community tax actually paid.

[Page 44]

It is unlikely that in a population of more than 7,000 persons there were no more than 584, or 8.3%, taxpayers. Assuming that the average household size was five people, then there were about 1,400 Jewish families in Biala. No more than 60% of these paid taxes. Note that the Jewish community never had a valid registration of its population.

Number of taxpayers	Annual tax in Zlotys
159	5
130	10
41	15
62	20
28	25
30	30
2	35
20	40
28	50
12	60

25	75
13	100
10	125
11	150
1	175
1	200
1	225
3	250
4	300
2	350
1	600
Total 584	**Total** 18465

The table shows that only a few paid 100 Zlotys or more, although, according to the economic situation in the town, there were still many more who could pay. These data show that the rich contributed very little money to the benefit of the community.

The chairs of the community board, Benjamin Kliger and Pinchas Nortman, wanted to charge taxpayers enough to have a realistic budget, which would enable them to meet more than the religious needs. Yet, they were never able to recruit enough support for their ideas.

The Zionists and the artisans' association struggled for a long time in order to transfer the income from slaughtering to the community. The slaughterers, naturally, did not want to share such a good business, and they were supported by "Aguda". When finally it was done, the slaughterers kept sabotaging.

In the local papers we read as follows:

The slaughterers slaughtered without notes from the community, because their demands for a better salary were denied. The rabbi agrees with the board's decision to suspend the work of the slaughterer Y. for two months with no pay. The slaughterers held a strike in protest, and after a day, by the rabbi's orders, returned to work.

"Podlasier Leibn" [Poldalsier life, O.A.], issue 6, December 31, 1926)

Slaughterer P. has been fined with 100 Zlotys for slaughtering fowls without notes from the community [that is, he charged the customers and put the money in his own pocket, O.A.].

"Podlasier Leibn" [Poldalsier life, O.A.], issue 29/145, July 27, 1934)

Yet all these punishments were in vain, because the slaughterers thought that slaughtering was their own private business and nobody should interfere with it.

In 1932, the community paid each slaughterer 75 Zlotys a week. On top of the pay, he would get meat for free. If we compare it with the 30 Zlotys a week earned, on average, by a professional worker, we see that the slaughterers were quite well off.

The financial affairs of the community were carelessly handled, and the community was constantly in debt. In "Poddlasier Lebn", issue 19/51, September 23, 1932, we read that the community property has been put on auction for 70 Zlotys, to cover a 1200 Zlotys debt to the national administrators' insurance.

We shall bring some data regarding the community's budget, as published by the local papers.

In 1927, the Rabbi got 600 Zlotys a month, plus 500 Zlotys a year for rent ("Poddlasier Lebn", issue 23, September 16, 1927).

The early budget for 1933 was 75,000 Zlotys. The expected income was from the following sources: Tax to be collected for 1932 – 8,500 Zlotys; from the cemetery – 3,500 Zlotys; from the community houses – 7,000 Zlotys; tax to be collected for 1933 – 16,000 Zlotys; from slaughtering – 40,000 Zlotys.

The following expenses were expected: for the hospital – 10,000 Zlotys; for charity – 600 Zlotys; for the "taz" – 500 Zlotys; for the libraries" "Tarbut" and "the cultural league" 200 Zlotys; for "Talmud Tora" – 5,500 Zlotys; for the Jewish National Fund and the Foundation Fund – 200 Zlotys ("Poddlasier Lebn", issue 5/70, February 3, 1933).

The above expenses mount up to 17,000 Zlotys. What were the other 58,000 Zlotys for? Most of it went to support the Yeshiva students, and a small part of it was allocated to the salaries of the office team. The later included: Baruch Vinodrag – secretary, Shlomo Hochberg and Yechiel Heibloom – clerks.

We learn that the major part of the early budget, 84.66%, had been assigned to support Yeshiva students and the "Talmud Tora", where the standard of learning was very low. Cultural activity's share was 0.27%, and charity – 14% from the budget.

[Page 45]

It should be noted that the money allocated for the Yeshiva students and the "Talmud Tora" was spent immediately, while the other institutions rarely got their share. The Jewish hospital, for example, was closed more than it was open, because it never received the sum allocated to it.

The numbers cited for the community budget of 1933 show the activity in the community. No wonder it had no influence in town, not even on affairs that were under its authority. Thus, in 1927 all the butchers together raised the price of kosher meat: 3 Zlotys for one kilogram of veal, and 3.50 for beef. Only the Polish government managed to cut the price to 1.80 and 2.40 respectively ("Poddlasier Lebn", issue 10, March 11, 1927).

A few years before WWII, the community experienced a bitter struggle regarding the choosing of a Rabbi to replace the deceased Rabbi, Shmuel Leib Zak. The decision had been delayed for years, and the position was temporarily filled by Rabbi Moshe Utshen. After a time, "Agudad**Error! Bookmark not defined.**" did not like him anymore, and started to demand that a permanent Rabbi be chosen. The Zionist leaders kept delaying the decision, but the religious sector started to push hard. Several candidates came to town, and Rabbi Tzvi Hirschhorn from Jaworzno was nominated.

There were also some positive actions taken by the community board.

There were public buildings in town that were registered as private property. Similarly, there were buildings whose income should have been public, but were also registered to private people. The community never had any control over this money, which was collected and distributed by private persons.

Changing the registration of this property to the community was not easy at all. It was a difficult, expensive, legal procedure demanding constant watch and monitoring.

In the end, the following property was transferred to the community:

The Jewish Hospital, the "Beith Hamidrash" (the one in Vollia too), the synagogue, "Talmud Tora", the inn, the Mikveh, Tile's house in the market square (where the stock bank used to be), the house named "Paradise" on 6, Brisk Street (the place of the community office), three stores in the market, three stores of 3, Brisk Street, and one store on the butchers' street.

The income from the cemetery was taken from "Hevra Kadisha". Naturally, it was not easily done, as the cemetery had been considered to be the property of "Hevra Kadisha" from early days.

The Jewish hospital was supported by the community. The board chair, Benjamin Kriger, and the secretary, Baruch Vinodrag, managed to make it an institution of the community. The hospital's budget was also included in the community budget, and the community board did everything possible to keep it working.

The community had the synagogue and the Beith Hamidrash thoroughly renovated. Local and other painters were invited to decorate it.

A lot of effort was invested in the guest–synagogue and the synagogue's yard. The guest–synagogue had been "conquered" by poor persons from out of town, and local sick poor who had no roof over their head. The sanitary conditions in that place were terrible. The community invested many resources in its rehabilitation, making it into a decent inn. The synagogue yard was dirty and neglected. The community invested in cleaning and maintaining it.

All these consumed considerable time from the community authorities. Each change involved long negotiations with people who did not want it whatsoever.

After "Achiezer" was closed, its medical instruments were kept in the community's office. Until the last days of the Jewish community in Biala, people could borrow these instruments when needed.

Poor pregnant women could deliver in the Jewish hospital free of charge with a note from the community administration. Similarly, documents and letter-writing services were offered to the poor for free.

From "Poddlasier Lebn" we learn that in the years 1926–1933 the chairs of the community board were: Jacob Aaron Rosenboim, Benjamin Kliger, Pinchas Nortman, Arke (Aaron) Weisman, Yitzhak Levy, Moshe Kaveh, Shamai Kalichstein.

We also find the names of the following leaders:

Motel Idelsberg, Sosha Rosen, Israel Cohen, Eliezer Tzelniker, Moshe Kramatzsh, Abraham Stricher, Fibel Sinter, Tzvi Halperin, Velvel Eisenstaedt, Moshe Melech Silberberg, Eitzik Sheinberg, Hanina Kashemacher, Yitzhak Petersburg, Mordechai Piekarski, Haim Levy Rubinstein, Mordechai Josef Goldstein, Joel Shtrumvaser, Saul Batchko, Alther Soknov, Yidel Eidelstein, Avogdor Fireman, Eliezer Applebaum, Itzhak Cohen, Shimon Lichtenstein, and Joshua Eidelstein.

Towards the end of this chapter, I would like to write about a tragic event, that shook the Jewish population for a long time: The burning of the wooden house in the yard of Rabbi Aaron Landau.

"On September 4 1927, one hour after midnight, a fire broke on 25, Natrovitz Street, in the yard of Rabbi Aaron Landau. Five persons lost their lives:

[Page 46]

1. Yitzhak Rubinstein (holy–books writer, aged 60); 2. His wife Esther (aged 58); 3. Their son Israel (21 years old); 4. Their granddaughter Yocheved (aged 3); and 5. Yitzhak Rubinstein (aged 46) from Lubartow, a proofreader, who stayed the night over at the writer's house, and left at his own home a wife and three children. Three Torah books also burnt. The funeral took place the next day, the Rabbi ordered people to close all shops, and declared a fast. Hundreds of people went to Beith Hamidrash after the funeral to read psalms. Some thought that the house had been set on fire after the people inside were robbed and murdered. At the same time, it is possible that they suffocated from the smoke in their sleep (Source: "Podalsier Leibn", volume 22, September 9, 1927).

There was a rumor, that a year later, on his deathbed in the Christian hospital, a Jewish water carrier admitted that he took part in robbing the writer's house and setting it on fire.

A few numbers regarding the size of the Jewish population in Biala, from the 19th century to 1939.

Year	Number of Jews	% of the total population
1827	1,091	54.8
1841	2,220	61.8
1857	2,564	66.1
1897	6,382	55.2
1921	6,874	52.9
1931	6,923	39.5
1939	7,493	36.9

From 1857 to 1897, the Jewish population grew by 148.9%. It is very possible that the earlier figure was not valid, while in 1897, the Czar's regime conducted a large–scale census, which included the great majority of the population. The imprecision of the earlier censuses is apparent from the size of the Christian population, which seems to have grown by 400% during the same 40 years. Consider, also, that in 1927 not all Jews registered, out of fear.

From 1921 to 1931, the natural growth of the Jewish population replaced the deficit caused by emigration. From 1931 to 1939, after emigration ceased, the Jewish population increased by 570 people.

Up to 1921, Jews were the majority of residents in town. The increase of the Christian population was the result of industrialization in the town, which increased the demands for workers, and only Christians were employed. For example, many workers were recruited to the airplane factory from all over Poland. Moreover, as mentioned above, before the elections, rural areas, settled by Christians, were administratively annexed to Biala.

Biala's Jews entered the crucial year of 1939 under these conditions. The economic dispossession continued during the war.

The Jews lived 21 years under the free Polish regime, established after 150 years of subordination. All Polish Jews dreamt of a free Poland and expected equal rights in accordance with the post WWI spirit. Yet disappointment was soon to come. Those who had recently been oppressed quickly became today's oppressors. The Jewish struggle for equality became, in the years to come, a struggle for survival.

WWII found Biala's Jewry depressed, apathetic, and hopeless. They were located close to the new German–Russian border, but only a handful crossed into Russia. Most stayed where they were until the German murderers came. In every corner one could hear the argument: why run away? What is Hitler going to do to us? Can our conditions get worse?...

Sources:

1. "Podalsier Leibn", an independent social weekly, Biala, issues from 1926/7–1932/4.
2. Memories told by: Alther Weinberg, Ashe Hofer, Moshe Ravon (Rubinstein) – Tel Aviv; Gdalyahu Braverman – Petah Tikva; Baruch Winograd – Ramat Gan, Jacob Aronowitz – Buenos Aires; Rabbi Shmuel Jacob Rubinstein – Paris.
3. Janusz Urbach: "The participation of Jews in the fight for Poland's independence." 1938 in Polish.
4. B. Gorny: "Review of Bialski Region". (In Polish).
5. Bohdan Wasiutynski. Jewish population in Poland in the XIX and the XX centuries." Warsaw 1930. Chapter: Jews in the cities.
6. National Jewish club of Sejm delegates adjunct to the temporary Jewish leadership: "Jews and the Bolshevik invasion." A collection of documents and notebooks I. Warsaw, 1921 (in Polosh).

[Page 47]

Total Destruction

by M. Y. Fiegenboim

Translated by Ofra Anson

On the first day of the German–Polish war, September 1, 1939, Biala experienced fire and blood. Vollia was bombed early Friday morning, in an effort to destroy the airplane factory. Bombs fell on civilian houses, including a Jewish house where all members of the carpenter Abraham Itlbaum's family lost their lives.

It was clear that Poland was not prepared for the war. The airplane factory had not been protected, and no Polish airplanes tried to intercept the German attack. Yet, there was hope that, after that day, which took Poland by surprise, things would change.

There were no signs of any of the government promises, "we are united, strong, and prepared". Chaos and embarrassment increased all the time. German bombers flew freely in Biala's skies, wreaking havoc and destruction. People lay on the ground in the fields all day long, and started to move at night, after the German bombers had stopped their work. The first thing they did was to bury the day's victims.

The airplane factory was already in ruins, almost all the Polish army had left Biala, but the Germans kept bombing. Among the destroyed houses were: the beautiful house of Heartglass, the elementary school in Grabanover Street (the house of Motl Mowiness), Shimom Lichtenstein's house on Brisker Street, Papinski's house on Janaver Street, and others.

German tanks entered the town, shooting, on New Year Eve, turned to Brisker Street, and drove to the Brisk Road. A Polish officer, with his small company, opened fire on the tanks by the new market. As a result, most of the huts in the new market caught fire.

Within two weeks, it was clear that Poland had lost the war. Naturally, the future under the German occupation frightened the Jewish population. They found some hope in the information that the Russian army was marching west and that, according to the German–Russian agreement, the border would be at the Wisla, which meant that Biala would be in Russian hands.

Indeed, the Russian army occupied Biala on September 26, 1939, and kept moving west.

Succoth was celebrated heavy-heartedly. They were pleased they did not fall into German hands, but feared the future.

The Russians did not bother to make order in town. They left it to the local population. Several committees were established, all by Christians. Remembering their bitter experience of 1920, Jews avoided cooperation with the new regime.

Shops were often closed, and soon there was a shortage of basic ingredients. People started exchanging goods; in front of each open store was a long line, and people bought anything they saw.

Succoth was not a happy holiday. At the end of September, the radio reported that the border would not be by the Wisla River but by the river Bug. The information soon spread among the Jews, and the fear was enormous.

Although the Russian soldiers denied the truth of this information, there were signs that they were going to withdraw to the east. They started to load valuables on trucks. Even from the Jewish hospital, expensive medical instruments were confiscated.

Some thought to leave the town and move to the other side of the Bug River. It was a real possibility, because the Russians did not restrict population movements to the east. Yet, as mentioned, the Jews of Biala had had bad experiences in WWI and in 1920. Then, those who stayed in the town had a fearful time, while the refugees really suffered. Nobody, of course, could imagine the horrible end. They suspected that the times would be difficult; but when had Jewish life in Poland not been difficult?

They knew that life under the Russian regime would not be easy, and everybody lived in hope that Germany would quickly lose the war, and that a free, open, world would lie ahead. On the other hand, moving to Russia would put the refugees in a camp that was vulnerable to a variety of difficulties and hazards.

The greatest fear was that it would be impossible to leave Russia after the war. Those who decided to leave town had one answer to all questions:

[Page 48]

"We do not want to live with the Germans, and even less with Hitler's Germans!" About 500–600 Jews probably left town, most of them men who left their families behind, assuming that the Germans would be after men rather than the women and children.

Those who left for Russia came from all social strata. Most of them never had any connections to Communism. Those who were known to support the Communist regime stayed in Biala.

One cannot blame Biala's Jews for staying in their hometown. If the leaders of the Jewish Federation did not know about Hitler's extermination program, how could the Jews in this small town know about it?

The End of 1939

On October 10, 1939, the Russian army left, and the German army entered town. The Jews were so frightened, that many, who had not decided to leave town before, left now.

A few hours after the Germans entered the town, they started taking Jews as hostages (the head of the town's administration provided the list). Christians wearing white bands were seen on the streets, and their first duty was to capture Jews for forced labor. The Germans were never short of work, and the Poles were happy to provide them with Jewish labor, even with more than they asked for.

The German regime ordered everyone to open the shops, and tried to get the town functioning. For a few days, they did, indeed, succeed. There was a curfew the whole time the Germans ruled the town and for Jews the curfew lasted longer hours than it did for Christians.

The local government was, for the moment, in the hands of the army. It seems that at this point they did not have any orders concerning the Jews. Indeed, Jews received traveling permission to go to Warsaw and Lodz to bring merchandise. Trade started to flourish, and, free from the heavy Polish taxes, the Jews felt some relief, forgetting the threatening reality. Yet, the relief lasted a short time. In November 1939 the Gestapo arrived and started the Via Dolorosa which led to the total destruction of the Jews.

The Gestapo settled in the palace of the factory of Raabe in Vollia. Its first contact with the Jews was a demand for a contribution of several tens of thousands of Zlotys. In order to expedite the contribution, they arrested a number of Jews and tortured them. They were released when the full sum had been paid.

The Gestapo on the street aroused panic among the Jews, who abandoned the streets. Abraham Lubeltzik, the printing house owner, died from a heart attack when he heard that the Gestapo were on their way to him.

In Beith Hamidrash the Gestapo found the janitor, Joel Greenglass, standing alone in his Talith and Tephilin. They forced him to climb on a ladder they had brought, and made other Jews carry the ladder on their shoulders in the streets around the town.

When the Gestapo entered town, an additional several dozen Jews left the town. Leaving town was more difficult now, as the borders were guarded. Among those who ran away was Biala's Rabbi, Tzvi Hirshhorn.

Any Jew that accidentally met the brown murderers was brutally beaten. They robbed Jewish stores, and took money out of drawers. The economic life of the Jews stopped. The Germans started to eliminate Jewish businesses. The big Jewish stores were confiscated, their merchandise taken on trucks, their owners put in jail until a large ransom had been paid. Workshops and working tools of Jewish artisans were confiscated.

```
Abschrift

                    Biala-Podlaska, den 24.11.1939.

             Anordnung.

             Alle in Biala Podlaska wohnhaften oder
aufhaltigen Juden vom 6.Lebensjahre ab haben als
ausserliches Kennzeichen ab Sofort einen gelben
Davidstern in der Grosse von 15 cm.Durchmesser
von Spitze zu Spitze auf der Vorderseite ihrer
Bekleidung sichtbar zu tragen.Das Zeichen ist auf
der linken Brustseite in Hohe der linken Brust-
warze anzubringen.
             Wer nach dem 1.Dezember 1939 als Jude
ohne dieses Kennzeichen in Biala Podlaska betrof-
fen wird,hat strengste Massnahmen zu gewärtigen.

                    Der Führer der Sicherheitspolizei
                    für den Kreis Biala Podlaska
                         Hildemann
               SS-Obersturmführer und Krim.-Kommisar


             Za zgodność odpisu



                    Przewodniczący
               Miejskiej Rady Narodowej
                  w Bialej-Podlaskiej
```

Order to wear yellow Magen David patches

[Page 49]

In an effort to save their property, some Jewish merchants gave their businesses to Christian acquaintances, ensuring their ownership in legal contracts. Only a minority of these Christians kept the contract; most of them did all they could to get rid of the Jewish owners. There was nothing the Jews, who were already helpless and without civil rights, could have done.

In November 1939, the Gestapo's commissar, Hildeman[a], ordered that each Jew above the age of 6 had to wear a 15cm yellow Magen David patch on the left side of his/her chest. This was later replaced by a white band, with a blue Magen David, on the right arm. Leaving town with no permission from the Germans was forbidden.

One day, the members of the last community committee were called to the Gestapo. They were ordered to organize a "Jewish Council" immediately. The council, which included more members than the original committee, was based in the community hall on Brisk Street.

The Germans now had an agent to which they could turn with their demands. There was a constant stream of demands to the "Jewish Council", which took a lot of resources from the Jewish population. Beside money, they also had to supply hundreds of workers. The workers were never paid for their work, and were often beaten during work. The "Jewish Council" had to organize the workers and to pay them for their work, knowing that otherwise they would have no source of income to support themselves and their families.

The occupation activated all the local governing institutions, and the Polish administration largely cooperated. The latter took revenge on the Jews for Poland's defeat. They took every opportunity to make the Jews be aware of them.

The tax office resumed work, and started to collect the debts of the Jews. The clerks Gerach and Kunitzki were particularly active collectors. A Jew that did not pay his debts immediately was arrested and tortured.

The head of the apartments office, Bieletzki, used to walk around the streets and confiscate Jewish apartments for Christians, who suddenly found out that their current apartments were too small for their needs. They happily helped the Germans to load the Jews' furniture onto trucks; Tchibulski, the jail keeper, was particularly enthusiastic.

Germans and Poles alike asked delegates from the "Jewish Council" for presents every time they came to the town's office on some errand. The worst were the head–of–civilians, Antony Wallawski, his deputy Stephen Shzapan and the head of the apartments' office, Bieletzki.

In addition, these people encouraged the movement of Jews into the ghetto, the smallest and the narrowest possible.

At the end of 1939, Jews from Suwalki and Serock were brought to Biala. These Jews were taken from the market places in their home towns and were taken to other cities in the Lublin Region. They were not allowed to take anything before they were pushed into trains. The refugees told the locals about the inhuman tortures they had already suffered during the few months of German occupation.

About 2,000 refugees came to Biala. The local Jews took in most of them to their own apartments, the rest settled in Beith Hmidrash and the Hassidic prayer houses. Some refugees went to Warsaw and other cities.

1940

At the beginning of 1940, Jewish war prisoners from the former Polish army were brought to Biala from Lublin. They originally came from the far east of Poland.

The road they were taken through was full of their blood and the graves of their fellow Jewish soldiers. They were brought from Germany to Lublin, and from Lublin to Biala they walked by foot. On their way, the Germans shot many of them with their automatic guns. They were locked in Pizitz camp on Brisk Road.

The Germans built Pizitz camp, using the Jewish workers supplied daily by the "Jewish Council". When they started building it, the head–of–civilians, Wallawski, told the Jewish workers that the camp would host Jews, who would arrive at the beginning of April. The workers felt desperate.

The jail was full of Jews who suffered real abuse. Jews were in jail for not paying the contribution or tax; others because they supposedly hid their merchandise; artisans for supposedly hiding the things they had made. For hiding merchandise, the merchants Josef Gitlman, Fishl Wulos, and Moshe Itzhak Biderman sat in Lublin jail.

Jews started to work a little, and got 2 Zlotys for a day's work. This was not enough for living.

Some turned to illegal trade, and were able to make a living. Although Jews were forbidden to travel by train, some risked their lives and went to Warsaw, dressed as Christians, to bring in some goods.

During the day, until sunset, some shops were open.

[Page 50]

Most people could not get anything there, as trade was very limited. A trusted client, however, could get almost everything.

New decrees were constantly imposed on the Jews. Their last economic positions were destroyed by the Germans. Even their small stores were closed and their goods confiscated. Only a handful of shops remained on Grabanover Street, and the Germans often changed the owners. Even the smallest store was marked by a large Magen David which had to be bought from the local regime for a large sum of money.

Two large placards, hung at the entrance to Grabanover Street from the market side, declared: "Epidemic – danger! Aryans are not allowed in". Jews were not allowed in the Market Square, which made access to the post office difficult. Jews tried to avoid the post in any case, because standing in line exposed them to all sorts of hassles. The "Jewish Council" managed to establish a branch of the post office, which also had a telephone. Every day two members of the council went to the German post office and dealt with the needs of the Jewish population.

On the eve of the high holidays, the Jews of Vollia were ordered to move to town, and Vollia became free of Jews.

The use of balconies was forbidden. If the balcony was made of metal, it had to be dismantled. Jews had to give the Germans all the metal they had, while the Poles had to hand in only 3Kg.

The refugees that settled in the synagogue and Beith Hamidrash lived in terrible conditions. The cold winter afflicted them bitterly. All the wood from the Jewish quarter had been used, trying to keep warm; the wood from the floor and the windows of the synagogue and Beith Hamidrash, the wooden fences, and even the trees from the cemetery.

They were pleased when the short winter day passed and the long night came. People locked themselves in, told each other the news, and waited for Germany's defeat.

Although the German-Russian border was well guarded, some succeeded in crossing into Russia. They reported home that many of those who left for Russia desperately want to return to Biala. They were tired of being refugees, and they thought that on the German side of the border the Jews' economic situation was not too bad.

In May 1940, a train from Russia carried refugees who returned to Poland. Among them were many Jews from Biala. They were amazed how well the Germans treated them.

During the war in West Europe, the Germans repeatedly told the Jews that Germany was winning.

One morning, the Gestapo called the "Jewish Council" in. They stood in line while Gestapo Kot read to them a report from a German newspaper, saying that Weitzman troop has been recruited in Israel to fight Germany. For that purpose, a Jewish state, headed by the King of England, had been established. When he had done reading, Gestapo soldiers came into the room to beat the members of the "Jewish Council" with their sticks.

In March 1940, all the Jews were ordered to register for forced labor. Many got a note from a doctor that they were not able to work, and brought the notes to the "Jewish Council".

The sad, forced labor episode started in June 1940. Jews from Miedzyrzec, and later from other cities, were brought to Biala. Pizitz camp filled with Jews, who worked in construction. Most of Biala's Jews managed to arrange easier work that was still considered as forced labor and at the end of the day they returned to their homes. Only a few of them worked in construction, mainly in the town itself.

The German engineer Greenfield managed the construction. The supervisors were SS police and their helpers, ethnic–Germans (I am not sure what the writer means. He may be referring to the fact that the SS first recruited the unemployed and bandits, O.A.).

Jews were looking for ways to avoid forced labor. It was not too difficult, because every German had already found a Jew who dealt with freeing Jews, and the slave trade of Jews began. Naturally, not everybody could afford to pay the large ransom. Indeed, the poor stayed in the camps until the middle of the autumn.

While on one hand the SS freed Jews from the camps and the work for a handsome payment, on the other, trying to disguise these illegal actions worsened the conditions of work and in the camps. One day, the SS Shwach came to the worksite, and, with no reason, shot Jewish workers from Miedzyrzec.

One early morning in July 1940, there was a surprise search for Jewish men. They were taken to the camp on Artillery Street. One might have thought that all Jewish men would be taken from town. The women had a hard time: they could not even go out of their homes, because the curfew was still in effect.

When all the men were gathered by the big ditch next to the 9th battalion, the Germans inspected their work cards. Most of the men were sent back home, others were taken by train to an unknown place.

Similar searches took place in other cities in the Lublin region the same night. They soon learned that the men on the train were taken to forced labor in Belzec.

The "Jewish Council" worked hard to free Biala's men from Belzec. Yet it took time.

[Page 51]

Young Mordechai (Motl) Hofer was one of the victims in Belzec.

The "Jewish Council" established the employment office in the autumn of 1940. The Jews who worked there were: Emil Weinberg, Adek Slobovski (from Warsaw), Tuchshneider, Dova Kreiselman Levi (son of Yitzhak Levi), Chamilevski, Tzimeman (Sulwalki), and a young woman from Serock. Although the "Jewish Council" hired and paid the workers in the employment office, it had very little influence on them. Slobovski, for example, used his position to blackmail his Jewish customers.

The employment office served only Jews, but the German Lehman, a former worker of the airplane factory, managed it. The Jews used to say that he is not a bad 'Goy'. He used to take money from Jews, but did not inform on them to the Gestapo or to the "Special Nazi Court" for misbehavior, and punished them himself. Sometimes he beat Jews bitterly, but they were thankful he did not hand them over to the Gestapo. Sometimes Lehman beat Jews for no reason, but the Jews said that he was nervous and needed to show that the employment office had a real Nazi orientation.

There was a case of young Jewish men who were taken to the Gestapo for not coming to work on time. The "Special Nazi Court" sent them to jail for years. Young Sigelman from Garnzcarska Street was one of them.

After a while, the employment office did not have to make an effort to recruit Jews for work. On the contrary, Jews were begging for work; they needed the few Zlotys they could earn. They also did not want to be identified by the Germans as unemployed; the work was hard, but it was more convenient than staying in the camps. At least they could come home after a day of hard labor and being beaten.

Those days, Jews were still paid 3–4 Zlotys a day. In the carpentry factory, a worker could get up to 10 Zlotys a day. The Christians who worked there could not make that kind of money. On top of this, Jews returned home with bags full of wood they could sell. By comparison, the price of bread was still quite reasonable, 0.75–1.00 Zloty for one kilogram.

Jews were employed mainly by the army or by German firms. Among them were: "Benz", "Mayer", "Seeger–Werner", "Stuag", and "Zid".

"Mayer" and "Seeger–Werner" operated in the airport. Pay was low, beating was frequent. "Benz" was the worst from this respect. Lehman, the manager of the employment office, used to send those who deserved punishment to "Benz".

"Zid" employed Jews to build sheds for the Sicherheitspolizei (SIPO) on Jonava Road. Here, too, Jews worked for low pay and high suffering.

"Stuag" fixed roads. Work was hard and dangerous. They worked with boiled tar that gave off a gas that burnt their faces. They did not have any safety equipment and workers were often brought to the hospital in a serious condition.

Jews also worked in large firms owned by Polish and Ethnic–Germans such as Zawudski's sawmill and the carpentry originally owned by Herzl Tcharni in Raabe's factory and in Housheid carpentry, located in Pizitz's sawmill.

Jews tried to build factories and hand them over to German civilians that came to Biala to confiscate Jewish property. Thus, a brush factory was built on Garnczaska Street, managed by the expert Munia Suchartzik from Miedzyrzec. At the beginning, the "Jewish Council" managed the factory, but it was soon taken over by the German Wanzura, the brother in law of Fritz, the deputy Head of the region.

Wanzura also got the soap factory of Sara Gele Goldfarb in Vollia, and made it into a big factory. The professional managers were the Jewish refugees Bibrovski and Wolf Weitzman. He did not settle for these two, and took the Jewish printing houses of Lubeltzik and Hochman, and made one big printing house on Pilsudski Street.

Biala's Jews had "equal rights" in the working sphere, and even got governmental positions. They worked also in the regional administration and other German positions as couriers, drivers, and mechanics as well as working for the army. For the army, Jewish work was crucial.

Although the employment office supplied all the demand for working men, the kidnaping of Jews continued. There were Germans who simply enjoyed walking the streets and chasing Jews. The kidnapers did not need Jewish work, they just wanted to abuse them.

1941

At the beginning of 1941, the German made an expulsion attempt. One winter morning, the gendarmerie and the police went out on the streets, kidnaped several Jewish women and elderly persons, and took them to Opole, near Rossosz. A few days later all of them returned to town. It was difficult to understand what the Germans were trying to do.

The war epidemic, typhoid, started to spread in the Jewish quarter. Houses were crowded, and sanitary conditions were poor. The yards were also filthy, because they were not suitable for so many residents. The sanitary department of the "Jewish Council" could not keep up with the needs.

[Page 52]

The "Jewish Council" was responsible for the Jewish hospital, which was always crowded. At the beginning of the German occupation, there were no Jewish physicians in town, and the Christian doctors were not allowed to treat Jewish patients. In the summer of 1940, three Jewish doctors came: Dr. Bergman (from Kattowitz), Dr. Hochman (a German refugee who arrived via Warsaw), and Dr. Rubinstein (from Warsaw). The surgeon Dr. Gelfish came in 1941. There were two medics: Haiim Musawutz (Kobriner) and Berish Weisman (from Lomazy).

Attached to the "Jewish Council" was the "Social Jewish Self Help" committee, supported by the regional help committee located in Lublin. Moshe Rodsienek was the chair. They tried to help the poor by providing hot meals and free medical help. Yet, the resources they had could not meet the needs. The committee sat in Jacob Kornbloom's home, on Grabanover Street. Its kitchen used the house where Yitzhak Fogel's bakery used to be, on Proste Street.

In the spring of 1941, the Germans started to build army buildings quickly, mainly air force bases, in Biala and around it. Jews were employed, and the working conditions were better than a year earlier in the working camps. It was clear that the Germans were planning an offensive to the east.

New regulations were imposed on the Jews such as: Jews were not allowed to leave their residence. The Christians were ordered to avoid any contact with Jews, because Jews are dirty, full of lice, and spread typhoid.

Jews could not ride carriages or wagons pulled by horses.

Jewish dwellings were confiscated, and they had to pay rent to an office specially established for that purpose. Rent was collected punctually, and the Jews had to renovate their homes and clean the yards and the streets.

An die

BEVÖLKERUNG

des Kreises Biala Podlaska.

Seit einigen Wochen nimmt die Fleck-typhusgefahr im Kreise überhand. Überall fordert die Seuche ihre Opfer. Die Bevölke-rung wird daher aufgefordert von sich aus alle Massnahmen zutreffen, die geeignet sind, den Flecktyphus niederzukampfen.

Wie macht sich der Flecktyphus bemerkbar?

Do

LUDNOŚCI

powiatu białskiego.

Od kilku tygodni szerzy się na terenie powiatu TYFUS PLAMISTY. Coraz więcej ludzi pada ofiara zarazy. Wzywa się ludność, aby samorzutnie prowadziła walkę z tyfusem.

Jak się rozpoznaje tyfus plamisty?

Announcing the Petechial–Typhoid epidemic. Jews as infectious carriers

The synagogue and the Beith Hamidrash were confiscated too. As refugees and other homeless Jews occupied these buildings, the "Jewish Council" had to pay the rent. When the "Jewish Council" deducted the costs of toilet cleaning from the 53 Rent, a German controller that came especially from Lublin slapped Jacob Aron Rosenboim, the chair, in the face. Still, the "Jewish Council" kept deducting the costs from the rent.

[Page 53]

One of the new rules dictated that Jewish workers would get 20% less for their work than Christians. At the same time, the cost of food increased, and one kilogram of bread was now 6 to 8 Zlotys.

After Passover, the town filled with German soldiers going east. It was clear that they were getting ready for more bloodshed; the German–Russian war was about to start. The Jews hoped that this war would bring Hitler's end closer, but they feared the new struggle. Meanwhile, the cost of living increase;, bread was now 12 Zlotys a kilogram.

On Saturday night, 21 June 1941, the German army crossed the border to Russia. Hopes died soon, and the Jews feared the future.

During the first few weeks of the German Russian war, Russian war prisoners were transported to Biala. When they went through the street, they asked for a piece of bread or for matches. After Moshe Gonski and Akiva Urberg were sent to Auschwitz (and died there) for giving some bread to war prisoners, nobody dared to help them. For the same 'sin' the Nazis arrested the Polish woman Byernatzka, but she was saved.

The Russian war prisoners suffered terribly in the German prison, but the Jewish war prisoners suffered even more. The Germans made every effort to identify the Jewish prisoners and kill them.

One working day, repairing the Brisk Road, a van full of Russian war prisoners passed the Jewish workers. One of them started shouting in Yiddish: "Friends! They are going to shoot us!" The Jewish workers recognized the son of Goldberg the shoemaker from Janaver Street.

By the order of the regional government, the "Jewish Council" set up a Jewish police, which the Germans called "The Jewish Police Service". They were "decorated" with hats similar to those used in the Warsaw Ghetto. The police were responsible for order in the Jewish quarter; to keep people away from the main street of the quarter, Grabanover Street; to bring the Jews who did not want to work to the employment office and to maintain an appropriate level of sanitation in the quarter. Later, after the "Jewish Council" built a jail for tax refusers, the Jewish police were responsible for arrest and preventing prisoners from running away.

The following persons served in the Jewish police: Jacob Goldstein (commander), Heinech Bialer, Asher Rosenzweig, Motl Finkelstein, Moshe Preter, Haim Freidman, Fishl Lebenberg, Jacob Tokarski, Hana Leibson (a saddler from Vollia), M. Hartzman (secretary, the former accountant in Raabe's factory). Tzimeman, a refugee from Sulvalki, became the commander after Jacob Goldstein was shot.

In the autumn, the "Jewish Council" moved from Brisk to Grabanove Street, to the house of Jacob Kornbloom. The purpose of the authorities was to restrict Jews to a given area of the town.

One November morning, the German Police went out to the Miedzyrzec–Biala Warsaw road, and shot each Jew they happened to see. Among the murdered was Berl Jelaza, a flour merchant from Biala. The shooting may have been connected to the order that restricted Jews to the Jewish quarter.

Many could not keep that law and see their families go hungry. They tried to go out to make some living, risking their life. Indeed, some never returned, leaving their family in tears and sorrow.

On Christmas Eve, the "Jewish Council" was ordered to collect all the furs from the Jewish population. The office of the "Jewish Council" became a fur warehouse. Not all Jews hurried to give their furs to the Germans. A few chose to burn them or to destroy them in other ways, although, if caught, they could have been sentenced to death.

A few days later, the German police searched Jewish houses for more furs. This operation had one victim: a short fur was found under the coat of one man, probably mentally ill, and he was shot.

News came that in the occupied territories in east Poland, Jews were being tortured and murdered. Among the victims were Jews from Biala who left in 1939, and who were considered as survivors. Sara Cohen (from the Preter family), who returned from Slonim, brought the news about the terrible slaughter the German did to the Jews. This was the fate of Moshe Orlanski, his wife and their children, the husband of Sara Cohen, and others.

The town was full of German offices, and each one of them dealt with Jews. The fate of a Jew that these offices were interested in was bad.

On Pilsudski Street, there was a station of the SD (the security services). Its commanders were two SS German soldiers, and Glat. On top of the "presents" they demanded from the Jews, they ordered the "Jewish Council" to report what Jews were thinking and talking about. The "Jewish Council" tried to avoid reporting. When the pressure on the "Jewish Council" forced them to give a report, they said that the Jewish population worries about the coming winter, how to get survival supplies such as potatoes, fire wood, and so on. When the SD people heard the report they started shouting: We know: the Russians have reconquered Minsk, Vilnius, and Riga, this is what the Jews are talking about. They sent the "Jewish Council" back after beating them.

[Page 54]

In the German gendarmerie was a man by the name of Apple. He probably was a carter before the war, employed by a Jew. He spoke good Yiddish, with juicy curses. The Jews called him "Yankl Face". He used to pick on Jews, and every day he caught one to beat up. If he found a piece of meat in a Jewish house, he would make a real pogrom there. He would break everything he could lay his hands on, and beat up all family members. When the Jewish shoemaker Baruch Freiner, who was friendly with him, asked him: "Apple, what do you want from us?" He used to answer: "I do not understand. You are beaten and killed and you are still here?!"

In the gendarmerie was a Polish police corporal by the name of Derwantzki, who enjoyed a special status because he spoke German. He had ways of blackmailing Jewish traders. He used to visit Jewish homes, but his demands could not be satisfied. And after he took everything, he handed the Jew to the gendarmes.

The defense police, located on Grabanover Street, used to scream in the middle of the Jewish quarter. Two were particularly cruel: Peterson, whom the Jews called "the yellow murderer", and a stupid person whom the Jews called "Pesil". The defense police had a smithy in the new market, and if they took a Jew to work there, they would treat him in such a terrible way that he would not forget it for weeks. When these two were on the street, the streets emptied immediately.

The defense policemen would break in at night, rape women, and rob the house.

Next to the regional administration was a special police, named "special services". For a while, Gzimek was their commander. They gave the Jews a lot of trouble. They used to come to hunt people for work, and while doing that hit and harmed many.

The agents of the criminal police were also after Jews. They knew who was involved in trade, and blackmailed them; agents Constantin Baldiga, Wolanski, and Golencyovski in particular. In 1941 /2 Baldiga shot to death Weisberg the carpenter (son of Hanan the carpenter) and a young Jewish refugee from the former east Poland.

The Polish police also bothered the Jews nonstop. Jews had to bribe them to keep away from them; for the Germans, Jews were always guilty, and, after all the confiscations, they had next to nothing. Yet the Polish police officers knew exactly where to search.

The clerks from the regional administration constantly asked the "Jewish Council" for expensive presents. They always promised that no new decrees would be issued, but they themselves planned the new ones. The "Jewish Council" members knew their promises were worth nothing.

The Gestapo caused the least of the problems for Jews. They did not kidnap Jews for work, and did not come to beat up Jews. The Gestapo did contact the "Jewish Council" to take its last coins. Thus, the "Jewish Council" was always in deficit. Some Jewish artisans got a lot of work from the Gestapo. The Gestapo set up a tailoring workshop, where the brothers Nahman and Joel Subman, Meyer Rietz, and Aron Wolkowitzki worked regularly. The Gestapo regularly employed the shoemakers Baruch Freiner and Nehemia Dorfman. The Gestapo supplied the materials.

Once in a while, these employees got some information from the Germans. They used to share it in secret with people close to them. They knew who had been put in jail in Raabe's factory, or who had been shot to death in the forest.

One of the first Gestapo prisoners was Michash Hofer, the pharmacist. It seems that the Gestapo itself did not know the reason for this arrest, but did not want to set him free. Hofer used to spend the days in town, but at night had to return to jail. After the Gestapo took all his most expensive belongings, and after many months, he was released.

1942

By the beginning of 1942, the Jews of Biala were depressed, desperate, and without hope. It was their last year in their hometown. Their life became harder before the final deportation.

One winter, in late afternoon, the "Jewish Council" was informed that the defense police had put two young men who worked there in the cellar. In other words, they were sentenced to death. One of the men was the son of Hanan Reich. The police officer who put them in the cellar claimed that he saw them sawing a piece of wood to take home. The "Jewish Council" tried to save them. The police demanded 10,000 Zlotys, a fortune. Still, the money was collected and handed over, but only one young man was set free. Reich had already been shot and died.

[Page 55]

Every day, Christians reported dead Jews lying behind the town. Germans who happened to meet them had shot them. The worst was the gendarme Leon Bush, an ethnic–German from the Posen area.

Next to the church of Vollia, Gendarme Bush killed the boy who worked for Liptche Adelstein, the butcher. A few weeks later, on Shidorska Street, he shot to death the wife of Pinie, the bagel baker, from Miedzyrzec Street.

On the first week after Passover, ten Jews were arrested. All had been punished in the past for breaking Nazis rules. They spent the night in the Polish police station, and the next morning were taken to the Jewish cemetery on Janeva Street, where they were shot. Among the murdered were: the butchers Yurberg and Adelstein, the Sulvalki refugee Bernstein (the brother of Osip Bernstein the photographer), and others.

Similarly, on a June evening, the Polish police arrested Jews and the Gestapo shot them in the morning in the Vulka forest. Among the murdered were: Haim Freidman (nicknamed Beznosek [nose–less, O.A.], Nahum Tenenbojm's son in law, and Jacob Goldstein, the commander of the Jewish police who had been arrested a day earlier by the gendarmes.

Young Moshe Lichtenbojm (the grandson of Leib Mednick) was among those arrested in the Polish police station. He was arrested because he answered back to a Christian woman who insulted him. His parents, who saw the evening arrests, understood that an execution was planned. They did everything they could to free their son, but to no avail. One can imagine their anxiety when they had to return home when the curfew started, without their son. Early next morning they went out to the street, and heard that indeed, all prisoners had been shot, but their son stayed in the Polish police station. Overjoyed, his mother became hysterical. The redheaded police officer, Peterson, had arrested him; the Jewish policeman Moshe Preter knew him. Preter begged Peterson to free Moshe Lichtenbojm, but he refused. It seems that he just wanted Lichtenbojm to suffer, because he asked the Polish policemen to put him in a separate room when the Gestapo come for the others. Thus, with the others he agonized through the night not knowing that he would be saved. Indeed, he said they knew they were going to die, and spent the night confessing.

Meanwhile, Jews from Janeva were killed in Wulka Forest, among then Leibl Rodsinek from Biala, who tried to save Janeva Jews. A Christian woman, Konopka, was supposed to help him, but actually betrayed him.

Shooting became more frequent. All the Jewish prisoners in Lublin were shot. The Germans did not even cancel the discussion of their cases in court. The case of Noah Weinstein (from Prosheki village in the Biala region) is an example of German cynicism. He was arrested for leaving his residence, and transferred from Biala jail to Lublin. His two daughters did all they could to save their father. They hired the famous lawyer Hofmakel–Ostrovski, who had connections with the German law system, for an unimaginable sum of money. Noah himself was not present in court; he was found not guilty, but never came home. The lawyer informed his daughters that he had been sent east.

In the middle of all this, the regional government sent the "Jewish Council" an order to provide a list of candidates to emigrate to Israel and to America. The "Jewish Council" did not advertise it, but the few who knew about it hesitated to register. The "Jewish Council" did not believe that the Germans would deal with Jewish emigration in the middle of the war. In general, Jews avoided putting their names on German lists. Since the regional administration did not repeat the order, the "Jewish Council" ignored it.

Most of the Jewish population worked, and a few artisans still had their workshops. On the other hand, only a few merchants kept their business. In the Jewish quarter there were still 20–25 small shops, most of them on Grabanover Street.

Under these conditions, it was only natural that smuggling flourished. The artisans who worked for the Germans or for the Christians brought in basic products as part of their pay; the workers brought different things from their workplace.

The most commonly smuggled commodity was flour. Flour was smuggled together with the regular supply of flour with the food stamps. With these supplies, they also smuggled groats. The secret service knew about it, and because they were handsomely bribed, they made sure it continued. The bribery increased the costs of the smuggled flour and groats.

The "Jewish Council" got potatoes, a most important basic product, from the Polish "rolnik". Yet, although the potatoes were supplied by government order, presents were still needed.

The butchers smuggled meat. This was dangerous, and the secret services did not support them. On the contrary, they were looking for them. Often, the butchers' fate was horrible. Meat was thus extremely expensive, and only a few could afford it.

The life of the educated Jews was very difficult. Except for the physicians, they had lost their economic basis. The transition to a lower social class was hard, especially as it was accompanied by beatings from the Germans. They sold everything that they had accumulated during years of work. The educated refugees had it even harder in the strange environment.

[Page 56]

They did not know anybody in the employment office, and could not get appropriate working positions.

A rabbi from Philipova came to Biala with the Sulvalkian refugees. After the death of Rabbi Moshe Utshen (who died of typhoid in the winter of 1940/1) people turned to him with their Halachic questions. He had a reputation as a great scholar and person of the world. Yet, his influence was limited, because there was no synagogue or Beth Midrash in the Jewish quarter.

In the high holidays, there were places where several large Minyanim prayed. On other days, small Minyanim prayed three times a day in private homes.

There was no cultural activity in the Jewish quarter. Each person was completely absorbed in his own troubles.

The big "Tarbuth" library moved from Wolnosci Street to Brisker Street. Jacob Aron Rosenbojm, the chair of the Zionist Organization, devotedly guarded this treasure. The "Bund" library moved first to the home of Elijahu Hofman (Bobkes). He cared for it as best he could, but had to move it from his small home to the cowshed as the number of residents in his apartment kept increasing. Mrs. Liuba Tuchshneider ran a kindergarten on Grabanover Street. It supposedly had a permit from the supervisor of the Polish school system.

Many teenagers studied at home, aiming at taking their final exams after the war.

Despite the prohibition on reading newspapers, Polish and German papers were smuggled into the quarter. The Germans used loudspeakers to repeat the news broadcast by the German radio. Children brought the news into the Jewish quarter.

Illegal publications came into the quarter sporadically. A person got a brochure from a Christian acquaintance and brought it in.

News Kidnappers

The cold, short winter days, quickly passed. People would sit at home at night, counting Hitler's failures. The Germans built a loudspeaker in the municipal park, broadcasting political news several times a day. The loudspeaker attracted the public, but the Jews avoided the risk of being found listening to the news.

Since there was a lot of interest in information regarding Hitler's failure, they sent the children to the loudspeaker, and they brought in some news.

Children stood in the bitter cold, their eyes and noses dripping, but their brains ready to absorb as much information as possible. At the end of the broadcast, when the children returned to the Jewish quarter, the adults were waiting for them with questions. The children, however, refused to answer. Each of them had his own audience, and only they would get the information.

I would like to write about one such audience circle. One 11–12-year-old boy, Neta Osenholtz, specialized in collecting news from the loudspeaker in the municipal park. Before the war, he had attended both the *Heder* and the Polish elementary school. He was very thin, literally skin and bones, with burning eyes and a sharp brain.

He used to sneak out to the loudspeaker a few times a day. Dressed lightly, he listened, jumping from leg to leg to keep warm, and taking in the information. In the evening, he would repeat what he had heard and take part in the adults' political discussions. People were amazed at his ability. Being weak with malnutrition, his voice trembled, but he remembered in detail all the headlines, including those from the Far East, and presented news of places no one had heard of. His political knowledge and understanding were outstanding.

People that knew nothing about politics used to come to hear Neta. They came to see how such a weak boy "maneuvers" battle ships, airplanes, and other armaments.

When he was called home, he could not leave the political debates. His mother used to complain, "Well, Neta, I am busy breaking my head trying to find how to get some wood, or something else for the home, and you are doing politics?…"

When Neta went out of the room, people would say each other, "Well, go find such a boy among the Christians! No Christian boy knows so much about current politics."

There were two other "news kidnappers" and talented politicians in Neta's information circle.

One of them was Haim Silberberg, the young son of Joel Silberberg the dentist. He was about 20 years old, unhealthy since birth, and a frequent a visitor to physicians. Just before the war, he graduated from high school, where he was one of the best students. He was exempt from forced labor because of his health condition. Yet he worked hard. He examined the German newspapers thoroughly, searched them for hints and analyzed the information. His room was full of maps to follow the war. Occasionally his mother raised hell, fearing that if the police found the maps in a search, they would be punished.

The second was Moshe Lichtenbojm, grandson of Leib Mednick, about 18 years old. He studied in a *Heder*, and undertook general studies privately. Before the war, he had entered the family business, but was interested in politics. He, too, was well informed on the war fronts. His duty was to get the German newspapers in different ways, and to share them with young Silberberg.

Moshe had a problematic leg since childhood, and he too was exempt from forced labor. Despite the exemption, he went to work in the carpentry of the ethnic–German Krakovski.

[Page 57]

He had to pay a few hundred Zlotys to get the job, but he did it on purpose: Krakovski had a radio, and Moshe was eager to listen to news from abroad. He got friendly with the ethnic–German who had been a communist, and spent considerable time in his home. There he could listen to news from London.

He was also in touch with Jewish young men who served in the houses of Nazi officers, who fully trusted them and gave them their house keys when they went on vacation to Germany. He used to spend the night in these houses, as they were the safest place to hear foreign radio broadcasts. Moshe was indeed full of foreign information. When he started sharing this information people did not let him go for hours.

Moshe did not want to rely on the information brought by Neta, and he did not have the patience to wait for Neta to return. He used to go to the loudspeaker in the park by himself. He succeeded at first, but later was beaten up a few times for his curiosity. After the restrictions on the Jews got tighter, you could find him at the gate of Israel Shaulkes trying to hear something from the park. When the time for broadcasting came, Moshe used to sneak out of the workshop to listen.

Translations by Mira Eckhaus

The first expulsion

On Saturday, 21 Sivan, 5702, (6.6.1942), a rumor was spread in the city that all the Jews in Biala must leave the city. It was later learned that the "Jewish Council" had received an order from the district government, that all the Jews who were not employed by the Labor Bureau must be present at the train station on Wednesday, June 10, for transfer. The order applied to all the Jews in the district. All the country towns would be emptied of Jews and all the working Jews from the whole district would be concentrated in Biala.

The representative of the "Jewish Council", Yaakov Aharon Rosenbaum, dared to ask the messenger Lipkov: Where will the people be sent? He replied: To the West. The representative of the Jewish Council asked again: We know that the Jews from the West are sent to the East, so why are the Jews of Biala so favored that they are sent to the West? Lipkov was embarrassed for a moment, but immediately came to his senses and said: "Don't you see the situation of the people in the synagogue and the other houses of prayer?" Rosenbaum replied: "Indeed, we would not object at all to the improvement of the situation of these people, but we know that the government is not interested in that, therefore, why do you care if these people die here?"

The messenger did not expect such an argument at all. And as he did not have any better answer, he muttered: "You, Rosenbaum, see everything in black colors; in this way, there can't be any cooperation with you".

The "Jewish Council" began a vigorous action to repeal the decree and began to appeal to anyone they could. The Gestapo wondered that such "work" was not handed to them.

The "Jewish Council" learned that the decree was originated in Lublin, but they did not set a quota for the deportees. The district government was interested that the "Aktz'ya" (the roundup of the Jews before sending them to the camps) would be as large as possible.

After all the efforts of the "Jewish Council", it became clear who would be allowed to stay and who would be deported. The right to stay was given to all those who had work cards as well as merchants and artisans, that were approved by the district government, along with their wives and children up to age 14. These women and children had to receive tickets imprinted with the seals of the Labor Bureau and the district government to prove their right to remain in place. Each deportee was allowed to take with him a package weighing only 10 kilograms. Anyone who disobeyed the order was subject to a death penalty.

The government instructed the "Jewish Council" that the entire "Aktz'ya" be run by it and by the "Jewish Order Service". If they did not take control of the situation, the government would be forced to intervene, which would lead to undesirable results.

On the third day, the "Jewish Council" informed the Jewish population about it through street ads, and set the collection point in the synagogue courtyard.

Already on Saturday, when it was realized that it would be possible to be saved from the expulsion with the possession of a work card, many of the Jews invested many efforts in order to obtain such cards. And indeed quite a few succeeded, for large payments, to get these "cards of life".

Single men who had been dating girls for several years and did not want to marry during the war, hurried to get married in order to save their brides from expulsion as married women. Fictitious weddings were also held to save the daughters of Israel.

There were those who did not find a way to be legally rescued and decided not to show up and hide during the "Aktz'ya". Many escaped ahead of time to the villages, to Christian acquaintances and to nearby Mezerich. Those who decided to wander, began to prepare for the journey and packed their packages.

In the country towns of the district, the Jews fled to the forests. They did not even intend to be present for the transfer.

On Tuesday afternoon, the Ministry of Taxation showed its aggressiveness. Almost all of its officials, accompanied by policemen, raided the Jewish Quarter to collect old tax debts and even those not yet imposed by assessment for 1942. They demanded huge sums that had to be paid immediately, and in case of refusal they threatened imprisonment followed by a transfer to the transfer lots on the next day.

That day, Yaakov Malina went to the district government to settle some matter. At dusk, it was learned that Malina was taken out of the city by car and shot by the detective Baldiga.

These were tragic hours for the families. Neither the parents knew what to advise the sons nor the sons their parents. No one had the courage to say to another: Stay home, do not go to the lot, because behind every command the word Death cried out!

On Wednesday, June 10, at 5 A.M., about 700 people had already gathered in the synagogue courtyard, wearing their best clothes and carrying packages. People flocked there from all over. The "Jewish Order Service", which was enlarged specially for this purpose to 50 people, went from house to house and mentioned the obligation to be present at the synagogue courtyard. Those who belonged to the happy ones who remained in the city walked freely in the Jewish Quarter, where no inspection was carried out.

[Page 58]

Representatives of the government came to the synagogue courtyard and watched what was happening. They released from the courtyard handicapped people, the sick and women with children, and announced that patients who were unable to be transferred would remain in their homes. Such a gesture, of course, reinforced the impression that the people were only being transferred to another city. The gesture convinced some of those who decided not to show up, to take their package and go to the synagogue courtyard.

At 2 P.M., when the synagogue courtyard was already filled with Jews, the crowd was led by the "Jewish Order Service", accompanied by several gendarmes, to the train station, where they were handed over to the "special service" of the district government. Some weak Jews were brought to the train in cars.

It is difficult to mention all the people of Biala who marched to the train. Some of them are engraved in memory: desperate and very exhausted marched the well-known and beloved Moshe Cava. The good-hearted teacher Hillel Meir Heiblum marched by him. In the rows also marched the merchant Yosef Gittleman and his family, Fintche Eidelman with his wife and child, Herzl Charni and his wife.

The Jews were forced to wait near the train until the next day, since, apparently, the "Aktz'ya" was carried out before the wagons had been prepared for the deportees. The "Jewish Council" brought them bread and coffee several times.

On the morning of the fifth day, a freight train arrived and at 11 the people were already locked in the wagons. The train moved from its place accompanied by an S.S. man and several Ukrainian guardsmen in the direction of Lukow.

The "Jewish Council" wanted to know where the Jews had been sent. The "Jewish Council" in Lokuw learned that the train had turned in the direction of Lublin. From the "Jewish Council" in Lublin it was learned that the Jews were sent in the direction of Chelm, while in Chelm they announced that the train passed through the city on Friday evening in the direction of Wlodawa. The last news was received from Wlodawa. From Wlodawa it was announced that they knew nothing and they asked not to be asked such questions again in the future.

Therefore, the information route was blocked in Wlodawa. And since such an answer was obtained from there, it was easy to suppose that the people in Wlodawa knew for sure what happened to these people.

The news of these continuous rumors became known to the district government. So, they tried to find out what the "Jewish Council" knew, but the "Jewish Council" replied: We asked the people to be present for the expulsion but we don't know where they were sent, you should be the ones who know about it and not us.

In fact, the "Jewish Council" finally learned where the people were exiled. It turned out that the last stop of their travels was Sobibor, 37 kilometers from Chelm, in the direction of Wlodawa. Sobibor was known before the war as a tiny station in the forest around Wlodawa, from which trees were transported.

Later on, they heard that many Jews had been brought to Sobibor and were kept there in locked wagons, on side railway tracks in the forest, for a few days without food and without water during the summer's hottest days. Later on, the bodies of the dead were removed from the wagons and were burned there.

Weeks passed and the thought of the displaced victims did not stop. It was obvious that the German government became the heir to the little property that the victims left in their apartments. The abandoned apartments were emptied completely.

The month of July passed relatively quietly, and then came the month of August that was full with bloody events.

On Monday, August 3, in the afternoon, Aaron Brodach was arrested by the district government. At the same time, the "special service" began searching for Menachem Finkelstein. When it could not find him, it imprisoned the chairman of the "Jewish Council", Yitzhak Pizich as a hostage, threatening to shoot him if Finkelstein was not found. After a while, Menachem Finkelstein appeared at the district government office, and Yitzhak Pizich was released. The news about the imprisonment of these two Jews made a strong impression in the city, because it was known that both of them had influence in the district government, and they had strong support in the form of the two reporters, the engineers Davos and Neulinger. Indeed, relatives and friends always warned them of the consequences of contact with the Nazis, from whom they had obtained, from time to time, some kind of a favor for a Jew.

Immediately after the arrest of Aharon Brodach, the "special service" searched his apartment. During the search, his sister and wife Haya of the Feigenbaum family and her two sisters were arrested.

All that day, the families of the detainees made efforts to find out something about them, but without success. No one knew what to say, but everyone tried to calm down the others. They thought that this is nothing but a misunderstanding that would soon become clear. Thus, the day passed when nothing happened, and the time of the curfew for the Jews at 7 o'clock in the evening arrived. The families of the detainees were forced to return to their homes with mixed feelings of anxiety and anticipation.

The end was tragic. On the same day, all the detainees, women and men, were shot. People in the city whispered that in doing so, the Germans wanted to erase the traces of contact they had with these Jews, and that Neulinger, the reporter from Passau (Germany), had a big part in this murder.

At the midnight before Tuesday morning, suddenly the footsteps of soldiers were heard rushing through the streets of the Jewish quarter. As soon as dawn arrived, the wild roar was heard: "Mener Reus!" (Men get out). The entire Jewish Quarter was surrounded by gendarmerie, defense police, Polish police, Gestapo and Goring soldiers - pilots, all armed with machine guns and hand grenades. Gravanover Street was filled with men who were chased to the end of the street (towards the new market). Those who lingered on the way received blows from rifle butts. After a while, the Germans began to check the work cards. The check lasted several hours and all the men were released afterwards.

However, this almost "innocent" check claimed 19 Jewish victims, among them: Zalman Levrant, Yukel Listgarten, Friedman (from Poland's country towns, a former prisoner of war) and others. Many of those who came back alive from the check, were beaten there till bleeding.

[Page 59]

This "Aktz'ya" was conducted by the Gestapo soldier Peisker[b] and by the German gendarme Leon Bosch, who especially excelled in this bloody work.

The events in the city began to happen very quickly.

On Friday, August 7, the "Council of Jews" announced that by an order of the government, all Jews must leave their apartments and move to the small quarter, as previously planned.

The Jewish quarter that was formerly located between the streets: Gravanover and the alleys of the synagogue (except for a few houses facing the new market), Yanaver (only its right side), Froste (from the courts onwards) and Tzmentarna, would now be limited, as in a square box, between the streets: Gravanover, without the alleys of the synagogues (from Volnoshchi square to Froste), Froste (only the left side, from Gravanover to Pashkodenia), Yanaver (only its right side) and Pashkodenia, only its right side (from Yanaver street to Froste street).

In this narrow cage, there was a real suffocation, and people housed in barns and pens, because what choice did they have in such a horrible situation.

The "Jewish Council" tried to persuade the representative of the SD Glat, and he promised to work to repeal the decree, and indeed, it was canceled shortly afterwards.

In a conversation between the SD representative and the representative of the "Jewish Council" A. Rosenbaum, the SD representative said that this decree would surely be repealed, since other measures were being planned against the Jews. He didn't say what the nature of these measures was. However, as time passed, this mystery was solved.

On Monday, August 10, a rumor spread in the city that there were wagons near the train station, that would carry about 400 people from Biala to Lublin. The rumor was confirmed when people from the train station called all the German offices and asked to know when the Jews were taking off. Everywhere they received the same answer, that they knew nothing about it.

On Wednesday morning, August 12, a search was made for Jewish men by a foreign protective policeman, with the help of a Ukrainian militia. The detainees were brought to a collection lot in Volya. Among the detainees were many workers in government and German workplaces, and efforts were made to free them. The "Jewish Council" announced this search to the SD Vida, and he went to the collection lot in Volya and released all the detained Jews.

Only a few hours passed and panic arose in the city again, as the search for men was renewed. At the same time, an order was received from the district government, that the "Jewish Council," the "Aid Committee" and the "Disinfection Battalion", should stand in the district government courtyard.

The reporter Lipkov went to those who gathered at this place. He ordered the women of the "Aid Committee" and the "Disinfection Battalion" to return to their homes and he immediately disappeared. A truck with a foreign police officer and several Ukrainians stopped there. The Jews were loaded on the truck and were taken to the train station.

There was despair in the city, as it was clear that with the exile of the "Jewish council", the city was abandoned and the end of the tragedy was close and certain. They were sure there would be an immediate manhunt for the men, as there were still many missing for the number of people abducted in the morning search. And indeed, the search resumed shortly.

The abduction of 400 Jews was not easy because most of the Jewish workers were already in their workplaces. Therefore, the search continued all day, and when evening arrived after nightmare day, a dead Jew with a shattered head was lying in the gutter on Narotovich Street, and in the room was lying dead Bracha Adlerstein (the bride of Moshe'le, the bartender), who did not let a Ukrainian, one of the participants in the "Aktz'ya", rape her.

It was later known, that in the morning, the SD member Vida managed to free the Jews because the one who was in charge of the "Aktz'ya" was not in place but when he returned to the collection lot and saw that they were released, he ordered them to be detained again immediately. He went to the German offices and presented to them, apparently, his power of attorney to carry out the search, and again he encountered no disturbances. On the contrary, they assisted him.

At 9 P.M., the freight train left for Lublin, carrying about 400 Jews inside the locked wagons, including most of the members of the "Jewish Council" and the "Aid Committee".

Here, apparently, the "other measures against the Jews" that were mentioned earlier by the SD member Glat began to be in force. First, they got rid of the "Jewish Council", which, although it usually brought them gifts, at the same time this "Jewish Council" was too active and demanded too often to have various decrees repealed. They also dragged the members of the "Aid Committee" and other institutions, thus helping the foreign protective policeman to fill the quota of abducted Jews, who had to be brought somewhere.

In August, the member of Hashomer Hatzair in Biala, Godya Steinman (the youngest daughter of the well-known Hebrew teacher Yaakov Steinman), was arrested. It was said that this talented girl was engaged in illegal activity and that messengers from the movement met in her apartment. The Gestapo arrested her following the imprisonment of a Polish railway worker, who was arrested on a train after illegal literature was found in his possession, and it is believed that he gave Godya's name and address. She spent a short time in the cellars of the Gestapo prison. The experienced killers seem to have realized that they would not be able to extract any information from this weak-bodied girl, despite the tortures she was going through. The Jewish tailors who worked there heard about the torture she suffered there, and it was even learned from them that they had taken Godya Steinman out by a car to an unknown direction and there she was shot.

[Page 60]

At the same time, Galika Lichtenbaum (the daughter of Leiba Madenick) was arrested and shot by detective Baldiga. It is rumored that this was caused by a popular German from which Galika demanded a repayment of a debt.

There was panic in the quarter every evening because of rumors that at night there would be a search for men. Each went to sleep in his own workplace, leaving his wife and children to their fate.

The German extermination machine was already in full intensity at the time, and in the early stages of the extermination of the Jews, it made an effort to concentrate the Jews, in order to facilitate its work.

The military government informed the Jewish workers that anyone who wanted to work for it must stay in barracks under German supervision. The military government also began to provide food for its Jewish workers. The Jews did not want to lose their jobs and therefore had to agree to it. Every day in the evening one could see such a spectacle: the workers came to their homes from work only for a few moments, and immediately gathered again in the courtyard of the synagogue, where they were held in a military order and marched to the barracks. Anyone who wanted to spend the night at home, was hit the day after about forty blows with a stick.

Only on Sunday would the workers be released from the camp to see their families.

In the meantime, one of the 400 exiles in the direction of Lublin, the former prisoner, Grossman, returned to the city. A new picture of the tragedy unfolded from his words.

It was learned that the 400 people had been brought to the Majdanek camp, a few kilometers from Lublin. There they received camp clothes to put on, but immediately afterwards, an order to return their clothes was received. Officials from the train management came and selected from among them about 350 people for the construction work of a new train line in Golomb, between Demblin and Pulaw, in the Lublin district. In the Majdanek camp remained about 50 people. Most of them were old people, among them: A. Rosenbaum, Yitzhak Pizich, Moshe Rodzinak, Moshe Chaim Wiesenfeld, Israel Bialer, Shmuel Kreiselman, Yaakov Shlomo Zeidman, Yaakov Wolwell Herschberg, Berl Goldberg (pharmacist), Hanan Weisberg and others.

The work at Golomb was done in unbearably difficult conditions. Hard work, poor and little nutrition. For every slight negligence they would have been shot dead. Among others who perished there: Fishel Kantor, Eliezer Lerner and Blumenkrantz (the son-in-law of Yukel Listgarten).

Near Rosh Hashanah, almost all the Jews returned from Golomb.

The wives of the expelled members of the "Jewish Council" began to beg for the return of their husbands. The German officers promised them to fulfill their request, but the promises were not fulfilled. In the meantime, Eliezer Tselniker was appointed as the new chairman of the "Jewish Council", and he, along with several remaining members of the "Jewish Council", tried to carry out some action.

An order was issued that on Saturday, September 19, the "Jewish Council" of Biala, Yanaba and Konstantin, would appear before the SD representatives.

By Saturday afternoon, they already knew the results of this "visit": The "Jewish Council" in Biala was required to collect from the Jewish population a few kilograms of gold. The reason was: thanks to this gold, the SD would be able to protect the Jews of Biala from the government. The "Jewish Councils" of Yanaba and Konstantin were informed that by Friday, September 25, all Jews in these towns must move to Biala.

On Tuesday, September 2, the SD member Glat invited the wives of the two members of the Jewish Council, Pizich and Rosenbaum, who were constantly urging him to return their husbands from Majdanek.

When these two women entered SD member Glat's office, they found there the new chairman of the "Jewish Council", Eliezer Tselniker. In his presence, he asked the women how much it was worth to them to pay for the release of their husbands because there was a possibility of their release. The women replied that their husbands were worth a great deal but unfortunately, they did not have large sums of money that they could pay for their release. The women tried to convince him to bring back all the Jews of Biala, but Glat did not want to hear such an offer at first. Finally, after prolonged pleas from the women, he agreed to try to help with the release of all the Jews. In return for this help, the women undertook to pay him a sum of 45,000 gold coins. He emphasized that the money should be transferred to him as early as possible, as he would probably have to travel to Lublin on Saturday or Sunday to transfer the gold collected by the "Jewish Council", and meanwhile he could start talking there about the release of the people. In doing so, he remarked that everything should remain a serious secret; that if not, the women would be responsible with their lives.

On Wednesday, the first groups of Yanaba and Konstantin Jews were seen. Wagons loaded with Jewish families flocked to Biala. In Yanaba a small group of Jews who worked in "Vigoda" remained.

Some of the 3,000 displaced Jews lived with relatives and acquaintances, and some remained for the time being with their packages in the street, in the open air.

On Thursday evening, Glat visited in the quarter. He promised to provide apartments for the displaced, and for the time being ordered the baker Yitzhak Pratar to distribute bread to the refugees and promised him that on Monday he would return him the flour.

Glat saw there the women Boltsha Pizich and Chaya Rosenbaum, who had been waiting for him all day to hand him the money. He told them to come to his office at 7 PM.

The "Jewish Council" had already supplied the gold it had collected. It was impossible to know whether this quantity of approximately 2 kilos would be considered as satisfying in the opinion of the SD people.

At 7 PM the women were already in the SD office and handed over the sum of 45,000 gold coins. Glat reiterated his promise to the women that he would be in Lublin on Saturday and he hoped to be able to release the men. Meanwhile the curfew began and he gave them permission to walk down the street during the curfew.

[Page 61]

It was clear to everyone that the expulsion was imminent. In the Lublin district, the expulsion encompassed all the Jewish settlements. However, the Jews of Biala did not assume that total destruction was about to happen.

The county government had spread rumors that the expulsion did not apply to the Jews of Biala and that only the refugee Jews from the small towns were intended to be displaced. The Jews of Biala believed these rumors, although they knew that the expulsion of the refugees would include also quite a few of the Jews of Biala. But they had a solution for that as well. They had learned a lesson from the previous expulsion of the Jews of Biala as well as from the great expulsion in Mezrich: they needed to hide. Therefore, the construction of the hiding places was in full force. They did not spare money for this purpose, and a hiding place was created in every house.

Those Jewish refugees from the towns, who were qualified for work, lined up at the Labor Bureau and demanded that they be given jobs. It was known that in the previous expulsion of the Jews of Biala, this was a matter of salvation. Hence, they did not spare money to get a work card.

On Friday, the eve of Sukkot, there was nervous and crowded traffic in the district. The closeness of the danger was felt everywhere. The panic intensified following the news that various officials had come to receive works they had ordered and had not yet been completed from Jewish artisans.

Throughout the day, the "Jewish councils" of Yanaba and Konstantin collected gold from their townspeople, and in the evening handed it over to the SD.

At noon, the workers of many workplaces came to pick up their clothes because they had been gathered in camps. There were talks of 7 camps that would be set up in the city: 1. At the firm "Stoag"; 2. At the firm "Tzaid"; 3. At "Ostaban"; 4. At the "supervision of the water farm" (the only camp where there would also be women); 5. At the airport; 6. In the military bakery; 7. Under military rule. The last camp would be the largest. In this camp, all the workers of the private firms who had a permit to employ Jews would also eat and sleep.

The Jews were divided into three types: one type –campers; the second type - those who prepared hiding places, among them were a few that were about to hide with Christians. Among those who were preparing to hide were also campers who did not want to part from their relative.; The third type were Jews who had no hiding place, or did not want to hide at all and were ready for anything.

The second and the final expulsion

On Saturday, the first day of Sukkot (September 26, 1942), at 5 AM., gunshots were heard in the Jewish Quarter, and it was clear that the bloody events had begun.

A. In the collection lot and on the streets

As it was later learned, the expulsion "Aktz'ya" began before 5 AM. When the gunshots were heard, there were already quite a lot of Jewish victims.

The "Aktz'ya" was attended by the Gestapo, the Defense Police, the Gendarmerie, the Polish police and Air Force soldiers, who surrounded the quarter at 10 o'clock at night.

At dawn, they started the expulsion of the Jews from their homes and walked them to the "pig market". There they were ordered to sit on the ground.

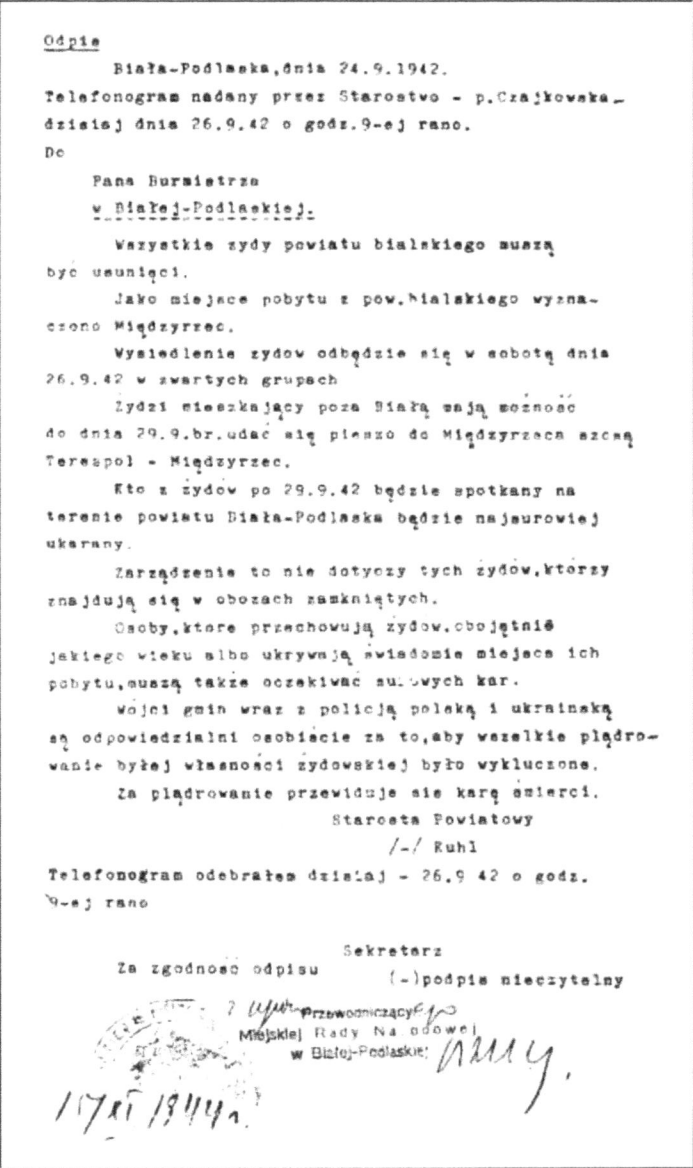

Order for Jews to leave Biala

They broke into houses in which the people were not in a hurry to open the doors. Like raging animals, the Germans entered the houses and brutally beat the people, and even used their guns and shot down casualties. Patients who lay in their beds and could not go to the collection point were shot in their beds. The SD member Glat ordered the man from the "Jewish order service", Heinech Bialer, to enter a Jewish apartment in Haim Gotel's yard, on Froste Street, and check if there were any Jews there. Bialer entered the apartment and found Jews there and told them to hurry. He informed the SD man that he did not find any Jews there. However, Glat did not believe him and entered the apartment and found several Jews there, who had not yet been able to hide. He immediately went outside and shot Bialer right on the spot.

[Page 62]

The Jews on the street who went to the collection point were severely beaten; some of them were even shot.

The three Grodner sisters came to the street with their little brother and hurried to the pick-up point, and here the protective policeman, Patterson, appeared in front of them, and when he saw the younger sister, an incredibly beautiful girl, he said: "It's a shame to take a girl like that to Mezrich, it is better that she stays here". A shot was heard and the girl staggered and fell to the stone floor with a shattered head. The two sisters with the little brother were hurried to the collection point.

In the collection lot, the Jews sat depressed and terrified. At every moment, the Germans chose a Jew, led him aside and shot him dead. A long mass grave was created near the house of the Christian Shidlovsky.

Jewish blood flowed through the houses, on the streets and in the collection lot. There were dead bodies of Jews everywhere.

The protective policeman Patterson, the gendarme Bosch, and the Polish Police Chief Kukzewski raged with extremely cruelty.

Many hiding places were immediately exposed by the executioners. Those who were hiding were led to the collection lot while being beaten aggressively, which caused some of them to fall.

When there were already enough Jews in the collection lot, they began to select people who were capable to work for the camp in the airport, and for Malashowicz (the former Polish airport, near Terespol).

Terrible spectacles took place on the lot: the people were beaten to death constantly and women and children were shot for no reason.

Here they brought the young man from Sarotsek, Zusha Goldberg (a friend of the above-mentioned Godya Steinman), who worked all the time for the protective police, and there they were very pleased with him. Only a few protective cops, that were led by Patterson, resented him for not letting them steal from the warehouses. It is impossible to describe the path of torment that this young man went through until he died. He was beaten and wounded with poles, then his eyes were punctured and again he was beaten aggressively, tortured and abused.

The young man withstood all these tortures with heroism, did not ask for mercy, only hurled harsh words at his tormentors: "You are heroes only against defenseless Jews, but the world and Jews within it will still show you our heroism when you will be defeated in this war!" This infuriated the torturers even more and they intensified the torture until he died.

The people at the collection point were made to hand over their money and jewelry, or else they would face a death penalty. Since they assumed that they were being sent to the extermination camp in Treblinka, they did not take anything with them. Later on, they regretted it, because the Jews were loaded on wagons and were driven to Mezrich.

However, only the elderly and children were seated in wagons; the young people were ordered to line up and walk to Mezrich, and only when many empty wagons were left, the young people were loaded on them as well.

And so, wagons full of oppressed and frightened Jews left, without them knowing where they were being led. At the end of the Biala district, in the Voronezh forests, many Jews were removed from the wagons. They were led to the forest and were shot there.

The victims of the streets of Biala, and the bodies of the dead from the houses, who were thrown out of the windows, were taken by the Christian municipal workers to the cemetery. After lying there for a few days, they were buried by the Christian workers.

At the Jewish hospital, where about 15 patients were hospitalized and two compassionate nurses treated them and did not want to leave them - the Gestapo broke in and ordered the nurses to give the patients good food...

The Christians took advantage of the darkness of the night and took over the houses of the Jews. and took everything they saw. They also stripped off the clothes of the dead bodies that were rolling in the streets.

Jewish cemetery at the time of the Expulsion

[Page 63]

```
Abschrift


Stadtverwaltung                    Biala Podlaska, den 7.Oktober 1942.
in Biala Podlaska


                     Bekanntmachung

                     Es wurde festgestellt, dass nach
               der Aussiedlung der Juden aus dem bis-
               herigen Judenviertel mehrere Fälle von
               Plünderungen durch die Ortseinwohner
               vorgekommen sind. Im Einvernehmen mit der
               Sicherheitspolizei fordere ich die Täter
               zur sofortigen Herausgabe der entwendeten
               Gegenstände auf, wobei ihnen volle Straf-
               freiheit zugesichert wird. Im anderen Falle
               haben sie mit strengster Bestrafung zu
               rechnen. Die Gegenstände sind bis zum
               12.Oktober 1942 einschließlich im Grenz-
               polizeikommissariat Biala Podlaska, Drescher-
               str. 17 abzuliefern.


                            Der Bürgermeister
                            (-)Ing.A.Walawski


                     Za zgodność odpisu
```

Christian population ordered to hand over to the Gestapo goods plundered in the Jews' quarter

On the second day of Sukkot, all the Germans civilians were invited to the Jewish Quarter, and they came in masses dressed in holiday clothes. They wandered around the quarter looking for Jews who were hiding. On their way, they looted the best things they found in the Jewish houses.

The Germans, however, noticed that many Jews did not show up at the collection lot. So, they brought in trained dogs to sniff and discover the Jews who were hiding. The horror visions of the first day returned. Jewish victims were rolling everywhere and streams of blood were spilled.

The district government took Jewish workers from the camps to transfer the Jewish property from the abandoned houses to the synagogue and the Beit Midrash.

Immediately upon the entrance of the Jewish workers in every house, they shouted: "Men, get up and go out!" The men who heard their call came out of their hiding places, joined the working group and in the evening went with them to the camps. Wherever possible, the Jewish workers announced that Biala was "clean" of Jews and that it was necessary to slip away and go to Mezrich at night.

The Gestapo broke into the Jewish hospital again, went from one bed to another and killed all the patients. The fate of the two nurses was the same as the fate of the patients.

They discovered a hiding place at the hospital, too, and all the Jews who were hiding there were killed immediately. Among the dead was the chairman of the "Jewish Council", Eliezer Tselniker.

The Jews who were gathered on the second day for expulsion at the collection lot were also sent to Mezrich.

The roads leading to Mezrich were full with Jewish bodies. Everyone who wanted, stopped the wandering Jews and hand them over to the Germans. This is how the Grozman sisters were arrested by Stiziniach and the "special service" shot them to death on the spot.

From Tuesday, the fourth day of the expulsion, they stopped shooting Jews. The Gestapo took over the management of the Jewish Quarter. Ads were pasted on the streets stating that Jews were allowed to move to Mezrich on their own until October 1, 1942. Any Jew found in the Biala district after that date would be shot to death.

And indeed, in these days no Jews had been killed. Those who showed up on their own and those who went out of their hiding places and were caught – all of them were transferred to Mezrich.

From among the people who volunteered for expulsion, the Gestapo selected a group of 50 people to clean the houses in the Jewish Quarter. Among them were: two women: Mattel Zucker (the wife of Froiem Zucker) and Masha Gelbord (the daughter of Yosele Voiner). The men: Yitzhak Eckstein (the barber), Yitzhak Cohen and his son Gedalia, Hanina Kashamacher, Noah Rudzinak, Anshel Beckerman, the Beckerman brothers (the sons of Yosef Sanies, who now lives in Eretz Israel), Shmuel Lieberman (a locksmith from Siedlce), Yitzhak Grobman, Baruch Feigenbaum, Polosetsky (a carpenter from Lumaz), Davidl Geltman, Shlomo Zucker (the son of Mattel Zucker), Shimshon Yustman, Shlomo Steingart (the son of Motel Aryeh) and others.

The workers were housed in barracks that were on the lot of Shabtai Finkelstein (the barracks were built there in early 1942 and until the expulsion, Jews, who were occasionally removed from the streets outside the closed Jewish quarter, lived there). At night the workers would be put in the barracks, the doors and windows would be closed with planks and the municipal firefighters would guard them until early in the morning, when they would get to work.

The first duty of these workers was to lock all the houses of the Jews. Then they had to go from house to house and empty all their contents. The objects were taken to special warehouses for this purpose, from which valuable items were later taken out and transported to Germany.

An important part of their work in the first weeks was digging graves in the same lot.

As soon as Thursday passed, they started shooting at every Jew they met. This time it was done only by the Gestapo, which turned the lot in the Jewish Quarter into a cemetery.

In fact, again there was no difference between the cemetery on the lot which was in the Jewish Quarter and the official cemetery. The Teutonic barbarism also applied there, when they smashed and crushed all the tombstones and structures on top of the tombs and used them for various purposes.

Section of the Ghetto (garden of Shabtai) where massacres took place at the time of expulsion. In centre,

the house of Hanina Kashemacher where Jewish workers of the Gestapo were housed.

[Page 64]

The fifty workers at the Gestapo service witnessed atrocities. Every day Jews were brought to the barracks, and the workers were forced to prepare a mass grave for them. In the evening, the victims would be brought in pairs, with only their underwear, placing them in front of the pit and shooting them. The rest of the victims would hear the thunder of the shots and see through the slits of the barracks what they could expect soon.

When the shootings ended, the Jewish workers hurried to cover the mass grave with the shovels in their hands.

They brought to the lot the member of the "Jewish Council" David Kantor with his daughter Sarah. He begged the Gestapo man, who had received gifts from him at the time, to let them live because they were still young and fit for work. But two shots were heard and both of them fell dead to the ground.

Sheindel Kornblum, who was brought here with her husband, Yaakov, offered the Gestapo all their property for saving their lives, but the Gestapo man giggled cynically and activated his automatic machine gun.

Atel Richter asked a Jewish worker not to talk about her bitter fate to her son, who was in one of Biala's camps. That evening she was taken out of the barracks with only her cotton on her skin and shot.

Some of the workers saw in the lot how their wives, children and relatives, who had been taken out of hiding places, were shot. They stood in their place motionless and silent, and the victims themselves were silent too, as any slight hint that the victims were relatives of the workers could have brought death on the workers as well.

This is how the worker Hanina Kashemacher saw how his wife Pearl was shot. The worker Shmuel Lieberman put sand over his son's fluttering body. Noah Rodzinak saw with his own eyes the murder of his brother Abraham.

Here is the story of Idel Zimbalist, an official of the "Jewish Council", who was shot along with his pregnant wife Nechama (the daughter of Moshe the bartender). After prolonged efforts by the workers, they managed to persuade the Gestapo man to take Zimbalist to work, but while working, another Gestapo man noticed him, returned him to the barracks of those destined to be shot. When the workers tried to ask the Gestapo man to take Zimbalist to work, he said he could not help because he was brought here with his wife. If they took him to work, what would they do with his wife? They could not and were not allowed in such a case to separate the husband from his wife ... and indeed they did not separate them, but threw them both into the grave.

There were also cases in which Jewish girls were ordered to dance naked on the sides of the prepared grave, next to which they were later shot.

The entire lot with all the yards adjoining it turned into a Jewish cemetery.

B. The hiding places and other means of rescue

The hiding places were made in various places after thinking about it for long nights. Inside basements, walls were built that were divided into two parts. One part remained as it was, and they would enter the other part through a plank board on the floor of the house. They also set up narrow cells near the walls of the apartments, covered them with planed planks and made an opening hidden under the bed or in the closet. Various dens were built in the attics, in the barns, in the pens and in the dairy barn.

Almost all the hiding places were overcrowded, as at the last minute people who had not been taken into account before had to be taken in. In the dens in the attics, the people lay completely naked because of the great heat. The biggest trouble was the children, who did not stop crying and could easily have led to the discovery of the hiding place. There were even cases where such children were strangled by those who were hiding in the hiding place.

The Jewish workers, who worked for the Gestapo in the quarter, later found dead children in the attics, basements, barns and apartments. There was one woman (Rivka, the daughter of the carpenter Shefsel Barazovski) who was giving birth in a hiding place, and because of her cries, her fate was similar to the fate of the children mentioned earlier: those who were hiding strangled her (at the home of Haim the baker, on Froste Street).

Food and water were prepared in the hiding places for a certain amount of time, but for how long could they stay in the hiding places like that? Especially, when the firefighters joined the Germans and engaged diligently in discovering the Jewish hiding places. Some houses, which they suspected were hiding places, were demolished completely.

[Page 65]

In many hiding places people lay down for long days without knowing what was happening in the streets, and if someone took the risk and came out of the hiding place to see what was going on, he never returned to the hiding place because he was arrested and shot dead.

There were hiding places in which people lay for months. In the hiding place in the attic of Haim the baker, the people lay until mid-January 1943 - more than three and a half months. When the Jewish workers of the quarter noticed them, they were already in a terrible situation. It was a good hiding place, arranged with beds, protected from the great cold and even the food was enough for them for the entire period. They benefited greatly from an oven that was in this house and which was full of cholent, which was put into it on the eve of Sukkot. But they did not have water. Once they looked out of their hiding place and saw the Jewish workers of the quarter carrying water, they started calling them to give them water. That evening the workers gave them water and food, and when the workers asked them why they were not going to Mezrich, they replied that they wanted to wait here until after the new year; perhaps a change in the situation of the Jews would finally come.

But from inability to wait any longer until the change came, many came out after many weeks from their hiding places. Everyone made their way alone to Mezrich, but only one person reached Mezrich - the young man Ackerman (the son-in-law of Sheime the tailor). The rest probably died on their way to Merzich.

In another hiding place (in the attic of Moshe Yitzhak Biderman, Yanaver Street) they found a number of dead Jews in March 1943. It was difficult to determine the cause of their death.

The Jews who hid with Christians could not stay there for long periods either. The Christians were afraid to keep them, because they were facing the death penalty for this sin. The Jews flocked one by one, for weeks, to Mezrich. Most of the Jews who were hiding in the villages were arrested and shot.

A minor percentage of Biala's Jews tried to save themselves by obtaining Christian passports that were called "Identification cards", but even then, they encountered great difficulties. They had to pay enormous sums for these cards, and the holders of the cards were subjected to extortion by the Christians, who extorted the last pennies from them, and eventually they returned to the ghetto.

After the war, the ones who obtained the identification cards and survived as they were considered Aryans were: Gotsha Goldfeld, Mikhash Hoffer, his wife and daughter, Mania Warm and her brother Leibel, Emil Weinberger, Berl Sandlerz, his wife and daughter Hala, Krusa Rosenstein and her daughters Ida and Chana, Chaim Friedman, attorney Leon Goldfarb, Brunia Fux and others.

Young women tried to be sent to work in Germany as Christians, but were unsuccessful. Women traveled by train to be taken to work in Germany but they missed their target. Having no documents to prove their origin, they found their deaths instead of their desire. According to the rumor, Doba Altbir (the daughter of Neta Altbir) was among these victims.

A few people, such as the butcher family Applebaum from Yanaver Street, fled to the forests, hoping to join the Russian prisoners there, who had escaped from the German prisoner-of-war camps. But even here the end was tragic. These prisoners, who did no partisan action against the Germans, robbed everything from the Jews, left them with no property and expelled them.

Individuals set up for themselves hiding places in the forests. Every night they would go out to a nearby peasant house and buy something to eat. But also in the forests death lurked. The Jews were murdered either by the Christians or by the Germans. Such an act took place in Hulye Forest that served as a shelter. In the summer of 1943, the Schneiderman brothers (the sons of Rachel Leah from 14 Brisker Street), Hanan Tenenbaum (the son of David the baker), Heinech Cohen (the son of Yitzhak Cohen) and a young man from Mezrich were shot by the Gendarmerie. A Christian from the village of Saltz handed over their shelter to the Gendarmerie.

After the liberation of Biala by the Russian army, in July 1944, the ones who returned from their hiding places were: Barish Urbach, Rivka Bakrach, Favel Buchalter, Shmuel Gwiazda and his wife, Rozke Dejantshul, Sarah Wiesenfeld, Esther Weinstein, Avraham Nochowitz and his sister Rivka, Nehemiah Puchtaruk, Moshe Yosef Feigenbaum, Chaya Feldman with her two sons Yitzhak and Shmuel, Yitzhak Friedman, Noah Rodzinak, Gedaliahu Ridlevitch, Moshe Steinberg with his sister Elka, and Elka Shlitterman.

C. In the camps

We have already mentioned above that according to the rumor that spread in the city, they were going to set up seven camps. At the time of the expulsion, this rumor was confirmed. Most of the men who belonged to the camps, or to the private firms that were recognized by the government, lived in the camps at the beginning of the expulsion, and were not affected by the displacement's "Aktz'ya". In the first days of the expulsion, some Jews infiltrated the camps, some of them managed to stay there, and others were handed over to the Gestapo and shot.

Most of the Jews were concentrated in a camp near the "Wehrmacht" (the armed forces) on the Warsaw Road, near the barracks of the former 34th battalion[c]. The camp was managed by the paymaster of the headquarters (stabsalmeister) Zeman, and the main paymaster Schultz. The Jew Sokolowski was appointed as the "chief Jew".

In this camp there were workshops of carpentry, welding, shoemaking and tailoring, in which a number of Jewish workers were employed.

Every morning a military guard led workers from this camp to the "Vineta" camp in Volya, which was a division of the camp by the 34th battalion. The Jews worked there at various heavy labor, and they received food for their work. Jewish workers who had previously worked for private firms that were recognized by the government were brought there every morning and in the evening were returned by the "Jewish order service" in the camp. They were brought lunch to their working places.

German soldiers would come every morning and take groups Jews to work in military units. The Jews who remained in the camp worked at various hard labor.

As early as Sunday, the second day of the expulsion, there was a Jewish funeral in the camp. The young Haim Hoffer hung himself when he heard that his wife and his children were exiled.

[Page 66]

During the expulsion days, when the Jews of Biala were allowed to go freely to Mezrich for several days, small Jewish children would spend the day around the Wehrmacht camp on the Warsaw Road. At night they would climb and cross the barbed wire fences surrounding the camp, sneak up to the fathers and spend the night there, and leave early in the morning.

In the camp at the airport, where the German firms Maior, Bentz, and Zager Warner were located, the Jews worked in construction and sewage. A large number of workers were employed in loading wooden poles into wagons for the coal mines. At first, the regime there was tolerable, but later the place became dangerous for the Jews. Every day weakened Jews would be bound with barbed wire, put on a cart and handed over to the Gestapo in the ghetto, where they were shot.

In this camp, the leather worker Yitzhak Winderboim cut his neck with a razor and died in agony over several hours, until a German bullet ended his life.

In the "water farm" camp, the men were busy with improvement work, and the women and children with field and garden work. The camp was managed by the German engineer Grinenfeld, who took every valuable object from the Jews. The regime there was not unbearably harsh. The camp was located on the bank of the river.

The Jews worked in various jobs in the German bakery. The camp was managed by the German Hanak. He also robbed quite a bit of Jewish property from his Jewish workers. The few Jewish workers lived quite well there, relatively speaking. The camp was near the mechanical bakery in Volya.

In the "Stoag" firm camp, located in the Hulye forest, the Jews worked in road work. They were managed by German and Polish civilians. The treatment there was not too bad.

In the camp of the German firm "Tzaid", which worked for the Protection Police and under its supervision on the Yanaver road, the Jews worked in the construction of barracks for the Protection Police and sewage works. Life there was unbearable. The German craftsman Bittner excelled in his savagery in the camp.

Next to the train was the "Ostaban" camp, where the Jews worked in loading and unloading wagons, as well as cleaning the railway lines. The regime there was comfortable.

In almost all the camps they tried to employ the craftsmen in their professions, in order to derive the greatest benefit from the holding the Jews in the camps.

The work was not particularly difficult for the Jews in all the camps. However, the inhumane treatment, the humiliations and the hardening, affected people much more than the most difficult physical work. The food was meager. People bought additional food, which was smuggled into the camps in different ways. The sanitation and hygiene conditions were poor. All wages for the Jewish workers were canceled as soon as they crossed the threshold of the camp.

In the first days of the expulsion, many Jews went from the camps to Mezrich, where their families were. They even tried to go to the Jewish quarter accompanied by a soldier, which they achieved in different ways and for a fee. The purpose of the trip to the Jewish Quarter was first and foremost to get the men out of hiding and take them to the camps. In addition, they would take money and clothes out of their houses. Afterwards, walking to the Jewish Quarter became impossible. The soldiers were ordered not to go to the Jewish Quarter, and the Jews of the camps were warned, and threatened with a death penalty, not to leave the camps. Despite all this, Jews risked intrusion into their homes at night, in the Jewish Quarter, which was constantly guarded by Polish firefighters, who murdered quite a lot of Jews, such as Isaac Orlansky (Abraham's son), the son of Moshe Leibzon and grandson of Sarah Chirel the baker (Sushchik).

Shimon Lichtenstein and his grandson, who left the camp at the airport and tried to infiltrate the group of Jewish workers in Vigoda which is in Yanaba, were arrested and shot on the road to Yanaba.

Immediately in the first week of the expulsion, they tried to persuade the paymaster of the headquarters (stabsalmeister) to arrange a place where the Jews could wash themselves and carry out disinfection. They also tried to persuade him to transfer the medicines of the Jewish hospital and the Jewish Aid Committees. It was promised that everything would be arranged. However, at the weekend they felt that there was a different spirit and it would carry away all the promises. They understood that the Jews were being held here as slaves, and the situation would only get worse.

On Wednesday, September 30, the women and children were taken out of the camp near the "water farm" and led to Mezrich. The women resisted and wanted to get out of the cars. This resulted in gunfire, in which Yitzhak Levy's sister-in-law (from Yanaba) was killed and Rivka Novominsky (M.Y. Biederman's daughter) was injured.

The first week passed and Sunday arrived, the day in which they were free from work in the camp next to the 34th battalion. The people stood in groups and talked. In one group they discussed politics, and the "politicians" promised that the end of Germany was near. In another circle, they listed the victims of last week one by one, and in the process included the live people as well.

Most of the workers would reflect on the situation. What was important to them was the behavior of the camp government in the last few days. The question that arose was whether they would continue to detain the Jews here. One commented that they had brought a large quantity of potatoes which was evidence that the Jews would stay there.

Jews with a developed sense of what was happening felt that this silence was like a silence before the storm, and that a great evil would come soon.

On Tuesday, October 6th (25th of Tishrei 5703), at 2:30 in the afternoon, Abba Weissman (the son of Berish the medic) entered the carpentry workshop and said that something changed. His father had just come from the "Vineta" camp and said that a meeting of all the workers was called for 1 o'clock. Also: all the men of the water farm were led to the train. Gestapo men had probably come from Lublin and were meeting with the local Gestapo. Abba Weismann had just left the workshop and the worker Hanan Zuckerman entered and began pounding his fists on his head and shouting: "Already now we are lost! The Gestapo is coming to take us!".

And immediately after him came a man from the "Jewish Order Service", Leybzon, and called the professionals to the camp. The camp was already surrounded by a guard of Gestapo armed with machine guns. The carpenters had already started to leave the workshop, but during that time, the paymaster of the headquarters arrived and ordered them to return. When everyone had returned to the workshop, the director of the workshops, the Polish Karpinski, closed the door and put a lock on it.

[Page 67]

Not much time passed and the Jews were taken out of the camp. Where and why - no one knew.

In the evening, the paymaster of the headquarters came in, ordered them to stop work and declared: You are the last 17 Jews left in Biala. Until when - I don't know, in any case try to work diligently and not go outside the camp.

Is it true that of the thousands of Jews who were in the camps, only 17 remained in the city?

When 17 professionals returned to camp after they finished their work, they found it closed. By order of the government, they settled in the small barracks, which stood outside the camp. As they stood engrossed in contemplation of sadness, they noticed a small group of workers come. It turned out that they also left a group of 16 workers who worked in the Hulye Forest. They said that all of Stoag's workers had also been taken.

Twilight time arrived. The 33 workers sat in the barracks in the dark and there was sad silence around them. Suddenly there was a scream: "All the Jews, come out!" Yes, the Jews thought, they did not forget us either, they had already come to pick us up. The Jews went outside and saw an officer and a soldier in front of them. They ordered them to line up in two lines. They counted the Jews, who were sure that soon they would hear the order "March"! However, they only ordered a few of them to go and get bread, jam and oil for the flashlight. After bringing the bread, jam and oil, the soldier ordered that there be a fair distribution and that a list of the people be made. David Gelassen was elected as the head of the team.

Early in the morning, when the workers in the barracks began to get dressed, the young man Pinchas Grodner, who was led here yesterday with all the other workers, entered into the barracks. The following information was obtained from him: The Jews of the camp next to the 34th battalion were taken to the train, where the workers of the camps "Vineta" and of the water farm were already gathered. They were ordered to sit in the garden next to the train station and not to talk to each other. Later on, they brought the workers of "Stoag", the German bakery and from all the other places where the people of the camp near the 34th battalion worked. They did not bring the Jews from the firm "Tzaid", from the airport and from the ghetto.

In front of the gathered Jews, the Gestapo commissar, Shtilhamer, spoke and said: "You are being transferred to another temporary workplace. For you, men who are capable of working, there is no danger hovering over you, do not be afraid, no evil will befall you". He ended his speech with these words, and called for "order and discipline".

Many accepted his words without question. Those who didn't believe him couldn't help themselves either. One worker, Wolwish Weizmann, who wanted to save himself and ran away, was shot during his run by the Gestapo man Shymanski[d].

The Jews sat in the garden until twilight time. A cargo train arrived and they started loading them into wagons. Only then did they grasp where they were being led. Although there were quite a few wagons, only a few of them were open. The crowd was pushed into the wagons while being vigorously beaten with rubber batons. It was clear to everyone that the people were not being sent to work, but there was some new trick of the sadists here. They started shouting from the wagons: It is better that you shoot us than let us suffocate in this crowd! "A death by a gunshot is too easy for you" - was the answer of the Gestapo man Shymanski. The train started moving in the direction of Mezrich.

In Biala they had already heard a lot about the jumping from the train during the first deportation of the people from Mezrich. And here the people of Biala also started to do the same. Wherever it was possible, they broke down a door and jumped. Where it was impossible to break the door, they jumped through the small window of the galloping train.

However, the jumpers were very few. Knowing that there was no shelter and refuge, many reached the point of giving up their will to live and letting the murderers lead them to the massacre. As soon as the wagons' doors were closed, the dentist Yoel Zilberberg and his son Haim poisoned themselves.

Pinchas Grodner didn't know where the people were being taken, because as soon as the train started moving, he jumped from it and was slightly injured.

At noon, the paymaster of the headquarters came, opened the camp and ordered everyone to take their clothes. At the same time, he announced that each worker was only allowed to take with him two pairs of underwear and one suit. Professionals were allowed to take two pairs of pants. Disobeying this order was subject to severe punishment. The Jews were required to immediately hand over all their documents, photographs, money, watches and jewelry, knowing that whoever was later found to have any of these would be handed over to the Gestapo.

In the next days, all the belongings of the expelled workers were removed from the barracks to the ghetto at the disposal of the Gestapo.

In the following days, all those who jumped from the train in territories that are far from here began to be seen in the camp next to the 34th battalion. Among them the lawyer Leon Goldfarb, Aizasha Rubinstein, the tailor Yaakov Friedman, Shepsel Leibzon, Moshe Sheinberg and Zilberzon. It was learned from them that the train was delayed in Mezrich and Jews from Mezrich were pushed into the empty wagons. It turned out, therefore, that the people were sent to Treblinka.

Only now has it been clarified what were the intentions in the concentration of men, who are capable of working, in the camps. The "heroes" of the Gestapo did not want there to be in the "collection lot" several thousand men capable of working and with physical strength who would see with their own eyes the horrible acts that they were perpetrating on their loved ones. Who knows, maybe at the sight of such a vision, one of them would burst out and the others would follow him to react to their bloody horrible acts, and then, Nazis would be killed as well. But now, when the men with physical strength are imprisoned behind barbed wire fences, they can do with their defenseless wives and children everything they desire...

Some of the people who jumped from the wagons decided to sneak into Biala at night and to check whether there were still any Jews left in the camps. Others turned to the forests, to their bitter end.

The directors of the camps next to the 34th battalion and Vineta tolerated the arrival of new Jews to the camps. Because why should they care if these Jews worked as slaves. It can be assumed that the Gestapo of Biala also

[Page 68]

knew about the addition of Jews in the camps and did not respond. It was more convenient for them that their victims were again concentrated in the camps. In this manner, it would be easier for them to exterminate them when the time came.

At the end of October 1942, the number of Jews in the camp next the 34th battalion was 106 people and in "Vineta" - 47 people. Among the latter were three disguised women: Golda Shapira (the daughter of Avraham Orlansky), Mania Kowarsky (the daughter of Label Goldberg) and Sarahle Glicksberg (the young daughter of Nachman Glicksberg).

The professionals who remained in the camp next to the 34th battalion received one barracks at their disposal. The food was not the worst, but it was too little. Ten kilograms of bread could not satisfy the hunger. However, everyone found a way to do it. They still had their gold, and the Christians who worked in the camp would bring the Jews enough bread with the money they received from them, despite the prohibition of the director of the workshops, the evil Karpinski. And if it was hard to get enough bread, then a kind of spread, such as jam, substitutes for honey and cheese they managed to get quite successfully. Lunch, which was potato soup with a dash of fat, wouldn't be so bad, if the Christian cooks didn't take so much trouble to prepare it in such a way that it would be impossible to eat it. Although after the meal was distributed there would still be enough stew left in the pot and the hungry workers would ask for a small addition, it was convenient for the Christian cooks to pour the rest into the garbage can. Twice a day, in the morning and in the evening, they would get coffee, which should have been sweetened, but instead of reaching the boiler, the sugar was "stuck" at the cooks. Several times they asked if the Jews themselves could run the kitchen, but with no success.

A tragic case happened in the "Vineta camp". One worker named Shmelke Schwartz went with a German to the city, dug in his pen, on Sadova Street, and took out a small package of valuables. A Christian woman (the prison guard's wife) saw it and informed the Gestapo. Some Gestapo men came to the camp and called Schwartz. Schwartz immediately felt the evil that is coming and shoved the package into the hand of a young man. Later on, Pinchas Grodner took the package from that young man. The Gestapo beat Schwartz and he confessed. When the Gestapo arrested the young man and began to beat him, he pointed to Grodner, and said he took the package from him. Schwartz was taken to the prison on Froste Street and Grodner was taken by the Gestapo to their headquarters in Raaba's sawmill.

When Grodner arrived at the yard, he jumped off the carriage and disappeared. A warrant was issued for his arrest and they found him hiding among the wooden planks. When he was taken to the Gestapo prison, he started to run away again. He reached the fence and began to climb over it, but several bullets hit him and knocked him dead from the fence, and he was buried there.

They heard about Shmelke Schwartz, that one night at the end of November, they brought him in a car, along with other victims, to the ghetto lot, and he was shot next to the "Shtibel" of the Radzins Hassidim.

Sad news from other camps would be received at the camp next to the 34th battalion. While in this camp there were punishments with a few strokes of the cane for a serious sin, in the "Tzaid" camp they would shoot for every offense.

Even sick people, who in this camp were tolerated and stayed alive, would be shot in "Tzaid" camp. This is how the worker Yonah Morgenstein (Moshe's son) was actually shot there because he was sick.

The situation was extremely bad in the camps near the airport and in Malashevich (near Terespol), where many Jews from Biala were. In the camps, the superiors made a partnership with the Gestapo: every day they would provide it with a quota of Jews, both healthy and sick, to be shot.

Days and weeks passed in this manner. The workers of the 34th battalion did not behave badly. But no one can forget his suffering. Everyone was depressed and sadness pinched their hearts. From time to time a "singing ball" of Jewish folk songs was held there. However, these songs did not make people happy, but on the contrary, made them even sadder.

The religious among the workers would pray every day Mincha and Ma'ariv in public. They had a very good prayer leader, Avraham Greenglass (the son of Yoel Hashamash), who returned during the war from Lodz to Biala.

At the end of October, a group of young people, led by Zilia Gutenberg, left the camp to the forest. The group managed to get some weapons, ammunition and clothes out of the camp's warehouses. According to the rumor, this group is the one that shot the district general of Biala, Kiehl, on the road to Mezrich.

In the summer of 1943, Zilia Gutenberg lay wounded at the house of a Christian in the village. What happened in the end is unknown. That summer, according to the rumor, young Lustigman, who also belonged to the group that left the camp, was walking in the forests of Mezrich.

At the beginning of November 1942, the Jews from the camps of the firm "Tzaid" and Ostaban" were transferred to the camp next to the 34th battalion. Together with the 47 Jews from "Vineta", the number of Jews now totaled 400. The transfer of the Jews was justified by the fact that from November 1 onwards, no Jews were taken in except in camps controlled by the "Wehrmacht", behind wire fences. And since the above-mentioned two camps had no affiliation to the "Wehrmacht", they transferred the Jews to the "Wehrmacht" camp on the Warsaw Road.

Among the people who had just come to the camp, the most neglected workers were of the "Tzaid" firm, dressed in tatters and starving. Among them were also typhus patients. The leader of their group, who was a prisoner of war from the eastern provincial towns, was somewhat to blame for this situation, according to the people.

In the camp next to the 34th battalion, friendly relations prevailed among the people, the head of the group did not do anything on his own and would consult with the group of professionals about everything. He did not enjoy any privileges. From this camp people would often escape and go to Mezrich to see their families. These people had to be deleted from the list of workers, so that they would not be given food, or else - it could have led to a disaster. Anyone who went would be deleted from the list, if he did not return in the evening from work. However, after a few days the man would return from Mezrich and they would register him under a different name, so that he would not be handed over to the Gestapo in his absence. There were cases where people held such "parades" several times and they were always registered in different names.

[Page 69]

But in no case did they demand any compensation for such an act. Therefore, it was very strange what the Jews from the "Tzaid" camp said about the manager of their groups, who ordered them to give him any good clothes or objects he saw with them. He would even perform tricks in the kitchen, which would worsen their nutritional status.

Because of the arrival of the new people, the previous camp was opened again. Meanwhile, another barbed wire fence was added around the camp, and rolls of barbed wire were placed between the fences. The camp gate was locked at 7 in the evening and opened at 5:30 in the morning. The German guards would patrol the area outside the camp all night and would check the barbed wire fences every time to make sure they were not damaged. In the camp itself, two Jewish guards had to walk along the barbed wire fences, and their role was to make sure that no one would run away from the camp.

Once again, every morning several hundred Jews would go to work in the "Vineta" camp and in the evening they would return. The professionals worked in the workshops, the rest of the Jews were employed in the camp at various kinds of hard labor, and there were also Jews who worked in the warehouses.

Until the new people came, the problem of morbidity did not exist in the camp. Now many sick people were lying in the two barracks, where the "Tzaid" men were housed. There was no doctor in the camp, and they were afraid to ask for a doctor. The experience in other camps showed what the results of a doctor's visit were. If the doctor found that there was a typhus patient in the camp, the patient would be shot and a quarantine would be placed on the camp for a certain time. What did they do? They bought various medicines and several "local" doctors, such as Haim Rosemarin (dental technician) and Label Levenberg (an electrician) used to take care of the sick.

Before the government, they always claimed that these were flu patients, since the flu was also spreading in the city now; the sick people would recover in a few days and go to work.

In the meantime, several deaths also occurred. The dead were brought to the Jewish cemetery for burial. Among the dead were found the people of Biala: Moshe Korenblum (the son of Yaakov) and Spivak (the son of furrier from 21 Gravanover Street).

The typhus epidemic began to infiltrate the other barracks and did not miss the "Vineta" camp. They began to think about isolating the sick in a special barracks. But they were afraid to do so lest this isolation open the eyes of the Germans and they would hand the patients over to the Gestapo. But when the number of the sick reached more than sixty, the healthy began to demand that they be isolated, or else they would all get sick.

On Sunday, December 13, 1942, all the patients were isolated, willingly or unwillingly, in a special barracks. Matityahu Jelazny, Eliyahu Singer and Grubman, who had already recovered from typhus, treated the patients.

At the beginning of December 1942, the paymaster of the headquarters, the director of the camp next to the 34th battalion, ordered the group leader to inform the workers that he had received a permit to continue holding the Jews. He said that as long as he was there, nothing bad would happen to the Jews. He would try to improve the food, and they should know that there was no point in escaping from the camp, since all the previous fugitives had been caught and shot.

When the group leader passed this on to the Jews in the camp, many immediately responded and said: There will surely be news, because always when the German murderers start to reassure and calm us down, the opposite happens; while others tended to believe the things they were told by the camp director.

On Saturday, December 12, the paymaster of the headquarters went on vacation and his place was filled by the main paymaster of the headquarters, Shilf.

On Sunday night, when the gate of the camp was already locked, the Jewish guards inside the camp announced that the main paymaster Shilf and the paymaster Behme had entered the camp.

Both of them started checking the barracks. The main paymaster Shilf was very drunk. He probably came to train his dog on the flesh of the Jews. He placed his whip on every Jew he met in the barracks, and immediately his dog jumped up and climbed on top of the Jew, tore off the rest of his clothes plus a piece of flesh. After his wild behavior with the dog and seeing some Jewish blood, the drunkard left the camp. This case caused a lot of depression, because so far, they had not seen such visions in the camp.

On Tuesday, December 15, the head of the group was called to the "Vineta" camp to be asked about some matter there. When he arrived at "Vineta", the workers asked him if he knew where the forty workers equipped with shovels had been taken. They were also given bread because they would have to work there at night as well. The head of the group replied that he had no knowledge of this.

While the head of the group was sitting there with some Jewish acquaintances and eating lunch, Dehatm Koze asked the director of the groups about the 40 workers. But he also said that he knew nothing. In the meantime, the director of the "Vineta" camp entered, a military official named Balman from Hamburg, who acted in a duplicitous manner towards the Jews. He took the most expensive gifts from them, promised them salvation, but during the "Aktz'ya" of the displacement from the camps, on October 6, he handed the Jews over to the Gestapo himself, so that they would not hide. The tailor Yosef Tischel sewed many diamonds into his suits and the shoemaker Baruch Freiner placed gold Rubles in the heels of his boots, so that he could take all this home when he went there for a vacation. Balman started a conversation with a sick young man who was apparently very friendly with him, and whose father was in the camp next to the 34th battalion. The conversation lasted for a long hour, and in the meantime a rumor spread in the "Vineta" camp, that the forty workers had been shot. The leaders of the group realized that Balman's conversation with the young man related to the case of the forty workers, since he saw that the young man got up from his bed and got dressed. However, the young man promised that he knew nothing about this case.

In the evening, when the workers returned from the "Vineta" camp, it was learned that indeed 38 of the forty workers had been shot. Two of them, Herschel Weissman (the son of David and Rosenberg (the son-in-law of Nachuma'le Sanders), managed to escape.

The fugitives were so embarrassed that it was difficult to get anything out of their mouths. But one thing was more or less understandable: army guards led them from the camp. On the way, a Gestapo man on a bicycle approached them and showed them where to lead the people. These two aforementioned young men immediately realized that the appearance of this Gestapo man was a bad sign, and near the forest of Grabarka they began to run towards the forest. The Germans shot after them but they managed to hide in the thick of the forest. Then they heard the sound of gunshots and screams in the distance.

[Page 70]

A new mourning fell on the camp. Fathers mourned the death of their sons and sons mourned the death of their fathers. Before the gate of the camp was locked, the head of the group went to the main paymaster and informed him that the 40 workers had not returned from their work in "Vineta", and that they were not even in "Vineta". He asked him how this could be explained. The main paymaster and his staff pretended to be surprised. He asked the leader of the group if he did not know where the people were. He replied that he had no knowledge of them. The main paymaster pondered for a few moments and said: They are probably in the camp next to the airport. I will call there tomorrow morning. This answer confirmed the terrible truth.

Wednesday was a normal work day; everyone in the camp was busy with their work. The workers who were working in the "Vineta" camp were also led early in the morning by German soldiers to the camp in Volya.

In the afternoon, the paymaster Behme came to the camp. He walked across the camp accompanied by the head of the group, who gave him a report on everything. The paymaster was satisfied that the number of patients was decreasing. The head of the group casually asked him about the 40 workers. The paymaster was not confused and answered that they were working in the camp next to the airport and would surely return next week.

In the evening, the workers of the "Vineta" camp returned and said that the Jewish group managers were not there. They seemed to have gone to the Christian Shemietanko, who lived next to the camp. Among those who left the camp was also the same young man with whom Balman talked for a long time yesterday, and whose father was in the camp next to the 34th battalion. Is there a son who doesn't want to save his father? Wouldn't the son advise his father to run away from the camp? But his father continued to stay in the camp just as he did until now...

True, it was very difficult for everyone to leave the camp, especially when there were many sick people in the camp, and there was nowhere to go, except for the ghetto in Mezrich - nevertheless, if the people of the camp had known, just as the young man did, about the danger that awaited them, they would all escape on time from the camp in the long winter night. However, all the assumptions revolved around the attitude of that worker in "Vineta" to his father, and they were deeply disappointed. In those terrible days, the family ties also loosened, and everyone tried, first of all, to save his own life, without thinking of the dearest and most loved ones.

And indeed, that worker of "Vineta" got up at night and went to Mezrich while leaving his father in the camp next to the 34th battalion.

After the news of the escape of the Jewish leaders of the groups in "Vineta", the mood in the camp on the Warsaw Road became very tense. Groups that were preparing to escape were organized. Many did not want to hear about an escape, since they already felt "organized" in the place - and where would they turn now in the winter?

On Thursday, December 17, 1942 (9 of Tevet 5703), at 4:30 in the night, the Jewish guards in the camp announced that the camp was surrounded. They saw that outside, in front of the camp gate, two trucks were parking and lighting with their spotlights the entire camp area. By the barbed wire fences patrolled army guards with full ammunition.

Yes, the tragic end is here - thought the Jews of the camp.

In the barracks the workers stood angry and helpless. It was clear to them that their fate would be similar to the fate of those 38 workers from the "Vineta" camp. They said among themselves that in the last hours one should behave with self-worth, since these hundreds of workers cannot be exceptions to the entire Jewish people. Although it was clear to everyone that soon the march to their death would begin, there were still some workers who started to prepare packages to take with them, which caused sarcastic laughter from others.

An opinion was expressed that the murderers should be attacked. Others tried to prove that such an action cannot be organized in advance. Especially when the barracks are separate and isolated; such an action should come naturally, spontaneously.

The Gestapo Commissar Steilhamer entered the barracks with two Gestapo officers, Peisker and Darm. The commissar called one worker to approach and ordered him to line up every 5 people in a row and translate for them what he, Steilhamer, would say. The commissar began by saying: Since there are cases of escape in this camp, it is a sign that the regime here is too easy, therefore, the people will be transferred to another camp. Nothing will happen to the workers, but order must be maintained during the march. Anyone who tries to escape will be shot, and twenty others will be shot with him. He also pointed to the wolf dog, which was by his side, and stated that the dog too would watch the people and not let them escape.

In the barracks they heard cars coming to the camp and leaving again. It was clear that the sick people were being taken out of the camp. It was later found out that in the trucks that awaited in front of the camp gate were the Jewish workers from the "Vineta" camp.

The darkness of the night still prevailed around. Those condemned to death stood in the barracks and waited to be led to the gallows. The silence of the night was disturbed by several shots. As it was later known, some workers who approached the barbed wire fences were shot. In one barracks they found the worker Moshe Leibzon (the son of Yechiel Frondik breaking through the floor to hide under it, and took him out to the yard of the camp and shot him. They also shot a worker who tried to hide in the pit of the toilet.

The last morning of those condemned to death began to infiltrate the barracks. The doors were opened and the order was given to the Jews to leave the barracks and to go to the camp's yard. There they were arranged in rows of 7 people and they were again warned lest they escape. The paymaster Behme worked with all his might to prove that he was not lagging behind in the "holy work" of exterminating Jews. He brought the worker Pinchas Charni (the son of Shlomo Stop who was hiding in a trash can, and handed him over to the Gestapo commissar. The commissar led the worker to the barracks and ordered him to lie down on the ground. Pinchas Tcharni refused to fill the order. Then the commissar pushed him forward, aimed his pistol at the back of his neck and shot him. The Jew fell dead to the ground.

You see - exclaimed the commissar - I keep my promises. - He ordered them to collect 20 people and shoot them, but in the middle of the collection, he announced: exceptionally, I now waive you the penalty of killing 20 people.

[Page 71]

They counted the rows and found that 231 people were ready for the massacre. They were ordered to cross their arms, look only forward and don't talk to each other.

The people condemned to death started marching towards the place of the massacre with their heads down, accompanied by 5 Gestapo officers and 10 soldiers. When they left the camp gates, they saw a dead body lying to the left of the warehouses. Near the homes of the Germans, they saw two Christians with two carts full of shovels. It was clear what they were for.

The people went out onto the Warsaw Road and started marching in the direction of Mezrich. Although it was the second half of December, it was not very cold, but the air was soaked with moisture. They diverted the marchers from the road to the narrow Slavachinska alley, which was full of slush and mud that made the march difficult. Suddenly an order was given "to sing"! The sad melody of a Polish cavalry song was heard and the parade continued to march through the mud. When they were ordered to stop singing, the marchers heard the last sounds of the machine guns. It turned out that these shots killed the people who were taken out of the trucks. Among the dead there were these Biala people: Yaakov Weissman (the son of Arka Weissman), Mania Kovarski (the daughter of Leibel Goldberg), the coachman Butchkela (a nickname), the tailor Yaakov Friedman and his little son, Sarahle Glicksberg, Eliyahu Singer, Matit'yahu Zilazni, Grobman and others.

The death parade stopped, and the Jews saw their grave. A long, deep pit in the ground, known as "Kolikava". On both sides of the pit was piled up the dirt that was removed from it and that would later be used to cover the grave.

As soon as the marchers stopped, the worker Israel Rudzinak broke out of the line and started running to the right. They immediately started shooting at him from all directions, but he kept on running. The dog did not obey his master and did not move from his place.

This whole spectacle only lasted a moment until the worker Senior, a former prisoner of war, shouted the order "Run!" and the crowd began to run away, while shouting wild "Hora". The machine guns and guns began to fire continuously and aggressively at the escapees.

Almost all those who escaped from the killing field headed to the ghetto in Mezrich. Among them was also the hero, the first one to run, Israel Rodzinek. Among the people of Biala who came to the ghetto in Mezrich were the wounded: Yehoshua Weissman, Yerachmiel Lichtenbaum and Asher Feigenbaum (a carpenter).

Later it became known that some of those who escaped from the killing field turned in other directions, and that many of them perished on the way. Among them: Isaac Koifman (a grain merchant, Yanaver Street), Alter Flatt (a tailor), Yaakov Rosenker (a painter), Haim Shimon Rosenblat (a watchmaker), Avraham Gringlas (the son of Yoel the Shamash), Blumenkranz (the son of Yeshayahu Blumenkranz) and others.

Order of Gestapo chief following expulsion to intercept and hand over Jews to the Gestapo

[Page 72]

After the camp workers next to the 34th battalion and "Vineta" were shot, the Jewish workers next to the Gestapo knew that they were also expected to end their lives in this way, so the group managers Yitzhak Eckstein, Shlomo Steingart, Shimshon Yustman and the Schneiderman brothers fled from there.

Yitzhak Eckstein immediately came to Mezrich. Someone apparently told the Gestapo in Biala about Eckstein's arrival at Mezrich and it demanded that he be returned to the Gestapo in Biala. The "Jewish Order Service" arrested him and handed him over to the Polish police, from where he was transferred to the Gestapo in Biala.

One morning they gathered all the ghetto workers in the Gestapo yard, in Raaba's factory. Eckstein was taken out to them, beaten and wounded and the Gestapo commissar demanded that the Jewish workers kill Eckstein. The Jewish workers stood still. - If you fear the God of the Jews - said the commissar Steilhamer, we will kill him. Some Gestapo officers crushed their victims with rods. Eckstein was buried near the fence of Raaba's factory.

In the camp next to the airport, the Jewish workers worked until November 1943, then, as the Christians told, they were shot. Among them was also found a group of Jews from Yanaba, who worked in the "Vigoda" of Yanaba, and were later transferred to the camp at the airport in Biala.

In collecting testimony of the Katowice Department of the Central Jewish Historical Committee in Poland (No. 290), a man named Yazi Rosenbaum from Warsaw, who was in the Poniatow camp (near Lublin), told that in October 1943, 10,000 (ten thousand) people were transferred from this camp to the airport in Biala Podlaska.

Christians from Biala would talk about Jews from Hungary who were brought to the airport. It is assumed that this is related to the shipment of people from the Poniatow camp, but the number 10,000 is certainly exaggerated.

It seems that the information given by the Christians about the killing of the Jews at the airport in November 1943 is true. On November 3, 1943, an "Aktz'ya" was held in the vicinity of Lublin, which was called "special treatment", in which many Jews were shot in the camps, and the rest were taken to Majdanek.

The last surviving remnant of the Jews of Biala was a group of Jewish workers near the Gestapo, who, after cleaning up the former Jewish quarter, were employed in eliminating every trace of Judaism in Biala. This group destroyed the synagogue and the midrash houses.

In May 1943, 17 more Jews from the ghetto in Mezrich were added to this group. This group existed in the city until April 1944. With the approach of the Russian army, they moved the last handful of Jews from Biala to Lublin. Only a small part of this group survived.

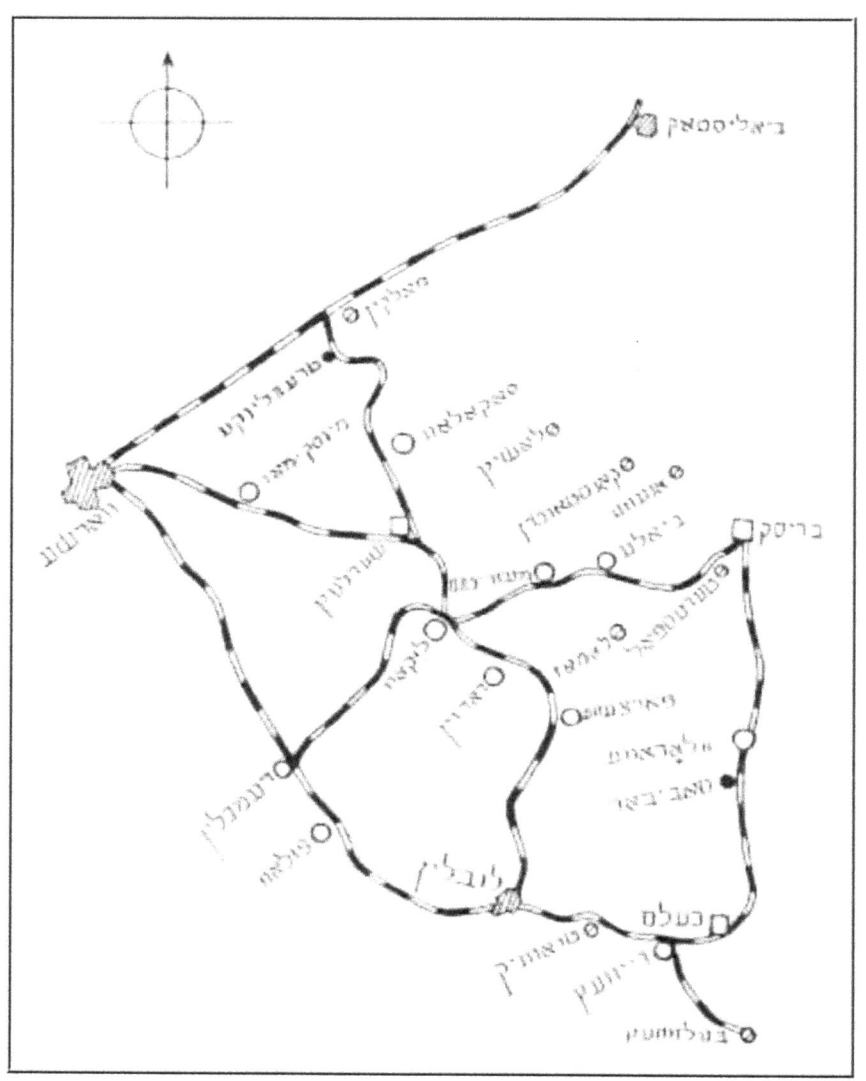

Map of the roads leading to the death camps
"The Jewish Council"

It has already been mentioned above, that on one day in November 1939, the Gestapo in Biala invited the previous community leaders and commanded them to organize as a "Jewish council".

Several of the community leaders joined the "Jewish Council" that was being established, and people from all strata of the Jewish population were added to them. The composition of this "Council" was as follows: Yaakov Aharon Rosenbaum, Yitzhak Pizich, David Kantor, Avraham Streicher, Yitzhak Levy, Moshe Haim Wiesenfeld, Israel Bialer, David Weissman, Shmuel Kreiselman, Menachem Finkelstein, Yehoshua Goldreich, Hanina Kashemacher, Yehoshua Eidelstein, Yehoshua Rubinstein, Berl Goldberg and others.

The "Jewish Council" enjoyed the full support of the Jewish population and no indignation arose in the city against it. Even the refugees who were brought by the Nazis to Biala, had no claim on the "Jewish Council". The extent of the tolerance of the "Jewish Council" by the refugees can be evidenced by the fact that among its office employees was a considerable percentage of refugees, headed by Secretary Rubinstein from Subalak. Many refugees were sent by the "Jewish Council" to important positions in the Labor Office and other German workplaces.

[Page 73]

Everyone in the city knew that the members of the "Jewish Council" did not want their jobs, but were required to do them by the Gestapo, and it was clear to everyone that under these difficult conditions and circumstances, the "Council" had to conduct its work, and how dangerous it was to negotiate with the superiors of the Nazis. When one of the wealthy Jews would complain about the high taxes that were demanded of him, the "Jewish Council" would inform him that it agreed to add him as a member of the "Council". It goes without saying that the complainer would have immediately apologized and justified himself, as no one in the city wanted to be a member of the "Jewish Council".

In the winter of 1941, the "Jewish Council" annexed several members, among them Haim Rosemarin. Since the latter did not at all desire to be considered by the government as a member of the "Jewish Council", he released himself from being a member by providing frequent large sums of money to the "Council". The dentist Yoel Zilberberg also paid large sums of money to release himself from being a member of the "Jewish Council".

There were cases when Jews (among them Avraham Yamnik, the son-in-law of Yehoshua Glicksberg) brought to the "Jewish Council" expensive jewels to be used to perhaps alleviate the situation of the Jewish population. The "Jewish Council" refused to accept the jewels and said: - If it becomes necessary, we will appeal to the population.

The brave and dedicated activity of the "Jewish Council" in Biala should be especially noted. They literally sacrificed themselves for the benefit of the Jewish population. Its members were the first to bear all suffering and hardship, which was something that the Jewish population sometimes had no idea about.

The "Jewish Council" was constantly on guard to cancel the decrees that were imposed on the Jews, sometimes with success.

The courageous stance of the "Jewish Council" towards the government occupiers can be learned by the conversation of the head of the "Jewish Council", Yaakov Aharon Rosenbaum, with the reporter Lipkov, which is presented in the chapter "the first expulsion".

During the first expulsion from Biala to the Sobibor death camp, the members of the "Jewish Council" gave clear hints to the Jewish people not to hurry to go to the collection lot, even though they might be killed for it. Thanks to these hints, the first expulsion from Biala (at that time they still didn't know about the death camps and were sure they were being transferred to other cities) did not uproot many Jews who, according to the decree, were obliged to leave Biala.

The Jewish Council knew well how to take advantage of the contradictions and disagreements of the German rulers among themselves. The Gestapo more than once canceled a decree issued by the district government. This is how the "Jewish Council" embarrassed the Gestapo, which had no idea about the first expulsion decree. The Gestapo was then very hurt by the fact that the news of the first expulsion reached it from the "Jewish Council". Perhaps this is the reason for the passive attitude of the Gestapo on the day of the expulsion and why it passed without bloodshed.

The proud and active stance of the "Jewish Council" must have been the reason that its members were the first victims in the city. A month before Biala became clean of Jews, members of the "Jewish Council" were taken from the city and tortured to death in Majdanek.

The people of Biala in Mezrich ghetto

The Jews of Biala, who were brought during the second and last expulsion (from September 26 to October 1, 1942) to the ghetto in Mezrich, did not find any place for them there. In the narrow ghetto, the people from Mezrich found themselves a place with difficulty, and here they brought thousands of Jews from Biala and the Biala district. In such cases it was clear to the residents of the ghetto, that Jews were being brought there and that a new expulsion was coming. And since in every ghetto they fostered the illusion that they did not mean to harm the local Jews, but only the immigrants, they did not want to interfere with the new residents.

However, the "Jewish Council" of Mezrich had no choice and allocated several houses for the Jews of Biala. Here too, in the ghetto in Mezrich, the Jews of Biala made efforts to obtain work, in order to prolong their life, or perhaps others advised them that in this way they would be saved from death. Some of the people from Biala managed, with the help of various protections, to get work places.

The exiles of Biala had not yet had time to get to know the maze of alleys of the ghetto in Mezrich, and the decree about the second expulsion of Biala's Jews had already reached Mezrich. On the same day, October 6, 1942, when the men were displaced from the camps in Biala, they stopped the train in which they were transported at the Mezrich train station and filled the empty wagons with Jews. The first victims were the Jews of Biala and its district. The people of Mezrich had already managed to prepare good hiding places and workplaces for themselves, and therefore, their part in this expulsion was small.

Before the expulsion, the SD member of Biala, Glat, came to Mezrich and asked where the women Boltsha Pizich and Chaya Rosenbaum were, from whom he fraudulently took 45,000 gold coins, in return for the promise to return the Jews of Biala from Majdanek. Later it was said that during the expulsion, all the women who worked in the field at Pototsky's estate, "Halas", among them the women Pizich and Rosenbaum, were taken from the field during their work day, and led to the wagons at the train station in Mezrich. This assured the SD member Glat that he had got rid of these two women.

During this expulsion, David Weissman (who came to Biala from Warsaw), who was a refugee from Biala in the Mezrich ghetto and the brother of the medic Berish Weissman, refused to leave the house and in no way wanted to obey the Nazi order to go outside. He was shot at home. It was typical that the Jews of Biala would say: I will not be taken to Treblinka. This place is enough for me to die in, why should I trouble myself all the way to Treblinka to die there?

After this expulsion, the number of Jews originating from Biala in the Mezrich ghetto decreased greatly. With each displacement from the Mezrich ghetto, people from Biala were taken away and their number dwindled. The women Hama Kalichstein and Lidzbarski (Moshe Lidzbarski's wife) died in hiding places during the expulsions.

[Page 74]

From expulsion to expulsion, the life of the Jews of Biala was similar to the life of the Jews of Mezrich; a life of fear, overcrowding and filth (typhus ruled in the narrow and dirty houses and a number of Biala people died of this disease), a life of constant struggle with death, a life full of sorrow, grief and longing for the loved ones who perished - and hope for the downfall of Hitler.

The Jews of Biala would risk going to Biala, in order to get something valuable out of the hiding places there. Some of them did not return from such a walk to Mezrich. This is how Moshe Yitzhak Biderman, his grandson (the son of Rivka Novominsky), Yehoshua Englander, Polya Rybak, Eija Rubinstein and others, went to Biala and were never seen again in the ghetto.

After the fourth expulsion from the Mezrich ghetto, in November 1942, only a few of the people of Biala remained. Some of the people of Biala engaged in trade in the ghetto, others would go to work outside the ghetto and would try to smuggle things in order to make a living. There were a few people from Biala who still had money that they took with them when they were deported from Biala. There were also Jews who needed the help of the social department of the Jewish Council in Mezrich.

The people of Biala would meet in the narrow ghetto, and like the people of Mezrich, they were not engaged in any public affairs. Everyone lived their own life.

In the long list of the Jewish victims in the ghetto in Mezrich, who died between one expulsion to the other, or during the expulsions themselves, the part of the people of Biala was very material. We will list here the names that were engraved in our memory:

For leaving the ghetto, in order to make a living, the following were shot: Itke Platt, Miriam Listgarten and her daughter, Leah Kenizshnik, Asha Friedman (her husband was a tailor on Gravanover Street – he was from Lumaz).

In the bloodshed that was caused by the Gestapo in the Mezrich ghetto on the New Year's Eve of 1942/3, most of the victims were women and children from Biala. On this night, the following were shot with Dum Dum bullets: Zissel Rosemarin (from Sircus family), Slava Cohen, Asha Sheinberg (from Wiernitki family), Asha Rosen (from Rosenbaum family) and the two children of the painter Haim Yosef Kenizshnik.

During the search for the fugitive from the police, Israel Lazer Yazshimovski, the former commander of the "Jewish Order Service" in Mezrich, Avraham Ezra Handelman and Bluma Preter were shot.

During the expulsions from the Mezrich ghetto in May 1943, victims from Biala died inside the ghetto, mainly those who were in hiding places that were discovered.

In one hiding place, into which the gendarme Franz Bauer threw a grenade, among the rest were killed: Monia Lustigman (the son of Iser), his wife (from the Yurberg family), her sister, the brother of his wife and two sisters of Monia.

From a hiding place in the butcher Lempert's house, the people were taken out into the street, placed against a wall and shot. Among them were the following people of Biala: Moshe Feigenbaum (the son of Zilia the carpenter) with his wife Bluma (from the Gershkop family), their little son and the wife's sister; Toyvale Lustigman (from the Rubinstein family) and her little son. Elsewhere in the ghetto, Meir Orlansky with his wife and the baker Yitzhak Fogel were shot.

In the Mezrich forests, Yosef Elboim (the son-in-law of Yaakov the Slaughterer) was murdered by the Poles. His little daughter managed to return to the Mezrich ghetto with a bullet-holed hand.

Young people from Biala also tried to escape from the Mezrich ghetto into the forest, to escape the Nazis, but the attempts did not succeed.

In one group that went to the forest were found the following people of Biala: Fayvel Buchhalter, Moshe Steinberg and his sister Elka, Shefsel Leibzon, Nachka Gershkop and David Rosenberg. This group managed to purchase several pistols. At a meeting in the forest with Russian prisoners of war, who had escaped from German camps, the Russians, being armed, surrounded the Jewish group, unloaded their weapons and robbed them. The Jews returned to the ghetto.

In a second group that went to the forest, were the girls Sarah Wiesenfeld and Bass (from the butchers) from Biala. During a large search by the Germans in the Mezrich forests, the group managed to escape from the forest and returned to the ghetto.

In July 1943, the Mezrich ghetto was completely liquidated and together with the handful of the Mezrich Jews, the few remnants of Biala Jews disappeared from there.

After the liberation of Mezrich by the Russian army, it was discovered that a group of young people from Biala was the only one that had a hiding place in the center of Mezrich, and it managed to stay alive. In this group were the sister and brother of the Steinberg family, Buchhalter and the girls Wiesenfeld and Bachrach.

* * *

At the end of these bloody lists of happenings, we will mention two stories from the Nazi camp, which relate to Biala, as well as two lists of Jewish real estate in Biala.

In the official government newspaper of the "General Government" "Krakuer Zeitung", dated October 17, 1942, it is said that according to an agreement between the district authorities of Biala and Radzin, all the Jews of Biala were transferred to Mezrich and that after the expulsion of all the Jews in the city, all the prices were cut to half. The craftsmen who had previously been pushed aside by the Jewish craftsmen now performed their work more diligently.

What was the form of transfer of the Jews - nothing is said about this, of course.

In fact, it was impossible to get anything in the city. The Christians themselves would say that the Jews must have taken everything with them... Every Christian was afraid to trade with another, since a large part of the trade was illegal. When the Jews left the city, the trade stopped completely.

To what extent the Christian craft flourished can be demonstrated by the fact that when the rulers of Biala needed good work they would come to Mezrich to the few Jewish craftsmen who still remained there. The Christian craftsmen in Biala sat without work as they also lacked the materials for work, which had been provided to them earlier by the Jews.

[Page 75]

As it is known, after the war, 21 of the greatest Nazis were tried by the International Military Tribunal in Nuremberg (Germany), and Goring was the most senior of them.

In the stenographic report of the trial, the testimony of Dr. Pritscha, who was the chief editor of the German News Agency (D.N.B. - Deutsche Nachrichte Beyuro) and the head of the news departments of the German Radio, is given. In his testimony, among other things, the district of Biala is mentioned (volume 17, page 177), in connection with the following matter:

Dr. Fritz, the defense attorney of Dr. Pritscha, presented questions to him during his investigation about the fate of the displaced German Jews. When asked by his defense attorney, if he, Pritscha, was interested in the conduct with the German Jews, who were sent to the Jewish pens in Eastern Europe, came Dr. Pritscha's answer: Of course. For example, I learned various things from my former assistant, who was sent to the General Government, and was appointed to an administrative position there in the Biala-Podlaska district. He told me that the area that was under his supervision had become a Jewish area. He would often describe to me the appearance of the displaced Jews and their housing. He also told me about the difficulties in employing the Jews as workers and their work in the plantations. His whole description testified to his humane attitude. He told me that at his workplace, the Jews are treated better there than by the Third Reich.

To the defense attorney's question, what was the name of this man, Dr. Pritscha answered: Chief Government Adviser Hubert Kiehl.

In connection with this statement, it is worth noting this:

There were not found at all any Jews who were displaced from Germany in the Biala district. The aforementioned Hobert Kiehl was the district general who was shot on the Mezrich Road (probably by the group of Jews who went from the camp next to the 34th battalion under the command of Zilia Gutenberg).

Already in the announcement of the district general of Biala dated January 15, 1941, the expropriation of Jewish real estate was spoken about.

From the certificates we received from the Jewish Historical Institute in Warsaw, it is proven that back in September 1943, when the German front in Russia had already been breached, Rommel's African Division was crumbling and the Allied armies had already invaded Italy - the Germans were still engaged in making lists of Jewish houses, whose owners were killed by them.

These certificates are of interest to us first of all, to get an idea of the real estate of the Jews that were remained in Biala.

From the letter dated September 22, 1943, whose photograph we include in our review in Yiddish, we can see that there are about 317 real estate properties in Biala as of August 1943. It is difficult to say that this number includes all the Jewish houses and lots in Biala. From the list we publish in our review above, as edited by the Germans, we see that it includes only 194 units and is missing a whole row of streets. Some of the names are neutered and distorted. On Gravanover Street, the houses of Ahrale Slavatitshor and the Rudzinek family are missing. In Volnoshchi square, the houses containing the shops of Hanna Rachel Reich, Sarah Gele Goldfeder, Winograd, Sapir, Yontel Lipiats, Mendel Tokarsky and Sarah Leah Tornheim are missing. Apart from these, the houses of Avraham Orlansky, Shmuel Fishman and Tila Berlin are missing from Volnoshchi square.

There were rumors about Shmuel Fishman's house during the Nazi era, that the Germans sold it to the German firm Golinker from Bremen.

Due to the discovery of the German list of Jewish real estate and in order to complete it, we provide in our review in Yiddish a list of Jewish real estate, that was edited according to memory and that is not included in the German list. The list contains 98 units and also this list is not complete.

* * *

After the liberation of Biala by the Russian army, on July 26, 1944, about 26 Jews who emerged from hiding places and from the forests returned to Biala. Among these were also people who were not from Biala, but rather were in Biala during the Nazi occupation. The Christian population viewed the return of this handful of Jews with an evil eye. In the first days of their arrival, they refused to sell them anything, and the Jews were forced to ask for bread from the soldiers of the Russian army.

Exhumation of the "Kedoshim" who were shot during the Nazi regime in Biala and buried in various places. After the war, they were interred in a Communal Grave in the destroyed Jewish cemetery.

[Page 76]

With the return of the Polish citizens from Russia, dozens of former Jewish residents returned to Biala. They took out the bones of the Jews shot in Shabtai Finkelstein's lot and brought them to be buried in a mass grave in the Jewish cemetery. With the help of the Jews of Biala that now live in North America, a memorial pillar was placed on this mass grave. However, this pillar stood there only for a short time and was blown up by an explosive. Even this tragic sign of the Jewish destruction has disappeared.

The handful of Biala Jews realized that it was no longer welcome in its hometown, and it left Biala.

* * *

In our descriptions of "the Jewish Biala in the last generations" and "destruction and devastation", we reviewed the life of the Jews in Biala from the end of the nineteenth century until the tragic end.

We saw a voluntary confined life in the ghetto, and the struggle to get out of this ghetto. We accompanied the volatile social life that grew precisely during the years of the First World War. We followed the hopes and expectations for a better tomorrow, which were nurtured and dreamed of at the end of the First World War, but faded away quickly and their place was taken by the struggle for daily existence, a struggle that continued until it reached us, "the people of the philosophers and the poets". And again, we saw the Jews of Biala shut up and confined within a ghetto, but this time not in a voluntary ghetto, but in a ghetto that was forced upon them by brutal force, and from this ghetto, the road led to the terrible destruction.

We broke out into the light of the culture of the West, we longed for its education and science, and now, a part of this West came and brought upon us extermination.

Translated from Yiddish: A. L. P.

Sources:

1. M. Y. Feigenbaum: "Fadlyashe in natsi kalam", Buenos Aires, 1953.
2. M. Y. Feigenbaum: "Fadlyashe in umkum", Munich 1948.
3. "Krakuer Zeitung", October 17, 1942.
4. "Dokumenty i Materialy", Tom I Obozy. Opracowal Mgr. N. Blumental. Wydawnictwa Centralnej zydowskiej Komisji Historycznej przy C. K. zydow Polskich. Lodz 1946.
5. "Trial of the Major War Criminals before the International Military Tribunal Nuremberg".

Original footnotes::

a. He was tried in Biala after the war. The trial lasted for three days in the firefighters' hall. In a six-hour speech he asked for mercy and forgiveness, so he could return to his only daughter in Germany. He argued that he only fulfilled orders he got from Lublin. He also hinted that, since only one party currently ruled Poland, those who execute its policy might have to stand trial in the future. He was sentenced to death by hanging. He was hanged in the yard of the Biala jail (reported by Joshua Weissman, now in Israel).

b. He was tried after the war in Biala and sentenced to 15 years in prison. Among the prosecution witnesses were also Jews from Biala, such as Yitzhak Friedman, Yehoshua Weissman, Israel Beckerman and others.
On the part of the prosecution, the shoemaker W. Ivanitsky, who was the deputy of the head of the citizens of Biala, appeared as a witness against him. After giving his testimony, Paisker rose to his feet and claimed: I was prepared that the Jews would stand against me. I can also understand the appearance of Poles as witnesses against me, but why Ivanitsky is here? It was Ivanitsky, who was a Gestapo agent, who reported about dozens of Poles to the Gestapo and caused their deaths - how dare he appear in a trial against me?!
Ivanitsky was arrested on the spot. The court sentenced him to 10 years in prison and to the loss of his civil rights for 15 years, as well as to the confiscation of his property to the Royal Treasury (the information was delivered by Joshua Weissman, now in Israel).

c. This camp has been described in detail because the author was there from the second day of the expulsion till the end.

d. Shymanski was shot by unknown people in the summer of 1943.

[Page 77]

The Zionist Organization

by M. Bruhel, Tel Aviv

Translated by Ofra Anson

Edited by Rafael Manory

We do not really know if the Hibat Zion (Love of Zion) movement was active in Biala before the establishment of the Zionist Organization, but it most probably was not. However, news of the first Zionist Congress in 1897 did reach Biala–even though there was no organization waving the "Jewish Kingdom" flag–via a few individuals who were in touch with activists of the new movement in neighboring towns. There were even some Hassidic families who received the famous hectograph–printed circulars written by Dr. Cohen-Bernstein from Kishinev and published in Krakow, and the weekly (or monthly) magazine "Der Yid" (The Jew). These families were also the first to get hold of the first small stamp, a little David's Shield with the word "Zion" in its center. These families, however, left the Zionist movement after their religious leaders denounced Zionism. A few preferred to leave their Hassidic milieu, and one of these was Herzl Halberstat, Moshe Cohen's son in law, whose brother–in–law, Dr. D. Cohen, became a famous surgeon in Warsaw.

The first Zionist group was organized in Biala in 1901, by Apolinari Hartglas, a young student at Warsaw University. In his yet–to–be–published memoirs, which he wrote towards the end of his life in Israel, advocate A. Hartglass wrote:

"… during the break between my first and second years at university, I had taken enthusiastically to the spread of Zionism in Biala. I managed to influence a few young Hassidic men. Using my own funds, I ordered many publications in Yiddish and Polish from the "Ahiasaf" publisher in Warsaw. I organized the first group, and we used to get together, hold discussions, and sing songs of Zion. This is how Biala, a town that used to rebel against the light of progress and be part of Hassidic backwardness, became a fortress of Zionism amongst the Polish country towns."

Hartglass described the difficulties he encountered in organizing the first Zionist group in Biala in an article titled "*Tzeiten baiten zich*" (Times change) in the "*Poldasi'er Leibn*" (Life in Poldasy) issue 62, on 11.2.1927. Because of his lack of knowledge of Yiddish, the Hebrew teacher, Shalom Ratstein, offered his help. This was the cornerstone for the Zionist movement, which developed gradually, though in leaps, to become the fortress envisioned by Hartglass. And this is what Asher Hoper, one of the first Zionists in Biala, says about those early days:

"I cannot remember in which year we, a group of youngsters from Biala, became activists for the Zionist idea. At some point Eliezer Beinish Goldfarb came from Mizrich to talk about Zionism at the *Beith Hamidrash* (the religious school). The hall was full of people from all walks of life: *Hassidim* and *Mitnagdim* (opponents to Hassidut), merchants and craftsmen. Even Reb Itche Meyer Cohen and Reb Haim Levy Rubinstein (my grandfather, O.A.), two of the greatest Gur Hassidim, came to hear his speech."

Goldfarb's speech at the *Beith Hamidrash* made a big impression, and we, the group of young Zionists, tried to use this event to enlarge our group. Unfortunately, we failed to recruit new members as the *Admorim* (Hassidic religious leaders) forbade their followers to join us, and they started to persecute the Zionists. Nevertheless, the Zionist Organization was established in Biala by: Kamona Meshedlitz, an agent for Singer sewing machines, Haim Tvarkovsky, a military tailor, and Shalom Ratshein, a Hebrew teacher from Sluzk who was married to a woman from Biala. They conducted their activities from a hall rented from Shimon Kreidstein. Craftsmen and young men from Hassidic *shtibel*s (orthodox schools) used to sneak in, like thieves, so that they wouldn't be seen by the pursuers of Zionists.

Abram Uhrmacher provided some more details regarding this period in his article published on 18.2.1927 in "*Podlasier Leiben*" issue no. 7:

"One Passover between 1903 and 1906, A. Uhrmacher held a meeting of the Zionists for a drink in his house. The participants were: A. Hartglass; Rabbi Gabriel Hasofer; Rabbi David, the son of Moshe Yosel; Moshe Yavor; Shalom Ratshein; Asher Hoper; Benjamin Kliger; Abraham Lubeltzik; Hanoch (Hinch) Cohen; Abraham Gelblum, the *melamed* (young children's teacher) from Borka, some students from the Biala gymnasium who were attracted to Zionism, and about 50 young men who studied in '*Hevrath–Bahurim*' (a religious study group)."

"Abraham Pudlishevsky came from Warsaw to promote the Jewish National Fund. His speech was held in the presence of very few people, in the private dwelling of Haim Tvarkovsky the tailor from Bialsk."

[Page 78]

"Between 1903–1906 the Zionists founded a *Beth Midrash* (religious school) of their own in Shimon Kreidstein's house. Prayers were held on Saturdays and holidays, whereas in the evenings members would get together for lectures."

Joshua Fisher, one of the veterans of Zionism in Biala, a hot–tempered militant man who led the Zionist activity up to WWI, describes it thus:

"In about 1903 I applied to the Odessa–Palestine committee and asked them to nominate me as their agent in Biala. My interest in Zionism started earlier, but my father's objection hindered involvement in any activity. As his opposition declined over time, I started Zionist activity. The committee accepted my nomination and I recruited some members who paid annual membership fees of 3, 6, 10, 15, and 25 Rubles.

We had some 30 members. The most active were Asher Hoper, Moshe Kave, Jacob Steinman, Benjamin Kriger, Moshe Rubinstein (my uncle, OA), and Moshe Braverman. We used to meet at my place and discuss Zionist matters. I did my best to attract the young men who studied at the *shtibel*. The Odessa committee used to send us Zionist publications and materials for fundraising. We would organize the collection on Yom Kippur eve at the synagogue, *shtibels*, Batei Midrash, and in the cemetery. We put a bowl and listed the names of those who donated more than 20 kopecks. In the first year we collected 6 rubles, in 1913 we already collected 100 rubles. However, the fundraising was not eventless; it was disturbed particularly by the hostile Hassidim. One Yom Kippur, Motl Mintz dropped the bowl placed in the Gur synagogue off the table. After I met him and warned him not to repeat this behavior, or I would have to take actions that would spoil his reputation, he refrained from disturbing us any further.

Every now and then, we used to invite a speaker from Warsaw, donating the income to the Odessa–Palestine committee.

Some time after I started my Zionist activity I learned that a Zionist group had previously been established in Biala, by Asher Hoper, Moshe Kave, and Benjamin Kruger. This group ceased its activity because it was prohibited by the Czar's regime."

In 1910/11 a few young people joined the group and worked enthusiastically. New connections were established between the Biala Zionist group and other Zionist centers, and they subscribed to the Zionist magazines: "*Hatzfira*" (in Hebrew), "*Razviast*" (in Russian), " *Die Welt*" (German) and the library of the Zionist Association in Odessa.

Apart from the annual fundraising on behalf of the Odessa–Palestine committee each Yom–Kippur eve, under the leadership of Joshua Fisher, the group also focused on distributing the "Shekel" and raising funds for the Jewish National Fund. All these were performed secretly, as they were forbidden by the Czar. They sent the money by mail to Cologne in Germany, the headquarters of the Jewish National Fund in those days. They also held a lottery for a share in the Anglo–Palestine Bank (today's Bank Leumi). It was a 1–pound sterling share, worth 10 Rubles. Participation cost was 15 kopeks. Some 60–65 people took part in the lottery. Pinie Ribak from the Rogijnize village won the lottery (he later became the son in law of Reb Shloima'le Goldberg, who was appointed by the government to be a Rabbi).

Initially, the group met in private houses, such as those of Joshua Fisher, Israel Finkelstein (Ritkar), and Asher Hoper. The discussions included practical and organizational matters, but also Zionist matters, how to realize their cherished dream. However, as the group grew and became more confident, they began to feel that meeting in private homes was not enough. They wanted a place of their own, where they could meet and spend time together. They also needed a place to prepare their activities and express their enthusiasm for action, which grew stronger with every meeting. They could not set up such a place openly during the Czar's regime, under the watchful eyes of the Russian police. So they decided to establish a charity institution named "*Achiezer*" (Brotherhood assistance) to provide medical help for the poor and to lend out medical instruments. Such a charity was already operating in Shedlitz, and Biala followed this example and emulated its rules of operation.

This charity deserves a chapter of its own. In this article I focus on the Zionist activity that was secretly conducted under its cover. As mentioned, the real motivation in establishing "Achiezer" was to promote Zionist activities. The group contacted well to do, respected, men and invited them to cooperate with the initiative. The head of the charity was Idel Schwartz, and the directors were Moshe Kave and others. All the charity work, the administration and the lending of medical equipment, was done by the young people. It was a place where the Zionists could meet every evening, play chess, talk, have a good time, and mainly be together. "*Achiezer*" became the club for young people and the leaders of the charity not only knew this, they welcomed it wholeheartedly, as they felt that only the youth could carry out its important activities and make its existence possible.

The first location was in a brewery; then it moved to a bigger hall in David Pasels' house. Here the Zionists used to meet on Friday nights, secretly, without the management's permission, read Zionist literature and invited *Shlichim* (emissaries) from other cities.

For several years, Zionist work continued in this manner. A connection with the Zionist center in Warsaw was established, though indirectly.

[Page 79]

We found its address via Berlin and Petersburg. As recommended by the center in Warsaw, Biala sent one representative to the 11th Zionist congress, Dr. Monosovitch. He was supposed to report to Biala's Zionists after the congress, but unfortunately, this never happened. By now the group was able to operate in the open. Public lectures were organized in Haim Yoske Kashtenbaum's hall: one was given by Rabi Isaak Nisenbaum from Warsaw, the other by Dr. Shmuel Eisenstadt from the Hebrew University of Jerusalem.

The first movie from Israel was shown in 1912 or 1913. It showed the "Herzlia" gymnasium and the first houses in Herzl Street in Tel Aviv. If I am not mistaken, we also saw the Passover Festival, celebrated annually in Rehovot in those days. The contacts with the Zionist movement of Warsaw were maintained via the Press, too. The newspaper "Hatzfira" had a special section for provincial cities, where it also published reports from Biala. One of these reported Rabbi Isaak Nisenbaum's visit to Biala.

"A public lecture about Eretz–Israel and its settlement was held in Biala, located in Schedlitz region. It attracted a large audience, including members of Hassidic *shtibels*, as they are very interested in matters related to their fatherland, and they are eager to learn what is happening there. There are several different Hassidic group in Biala, yet all sat together without any incidents. Nevertheless, there was a commotion in the *shtibel* of the Partshev Hassidim when they learned that some of their members went to this "agnostic" lecture; almost as if they had recreated the golden calf… on the first Saturday after the lecture, when the Holy Scroll was brought out, an announcer came forward calling the people who took part in the Zionist event to refrain from coming to the synagogue in the future. There was a venerable teacher among the Partshev Hassidim of Biala, a renowned Kabbalist who was thoroughly versed in the *Sefer Hayetzira* (The Book of Creation) and was busy trying to create a living creature from the earth… and when he heard about this great affliction which had spread within the walls of his *shtibel*, he was sorely troubled, lest the devil's emissary be running loose within these holy walls. He quickly summonsed the 'sinners' to appear before him and explained to them the gravity of their crime to think that The Land of Israel could really become the State of Israel… heaven forbid we should think such unthinkable things, these are the thoughts of *apikoiresim*, the *zionisten*. And really, 'as the true believers know, The Land of Israel is to be found wherever our people live… And if such an abominable thought did cross your mind', added the teacher, 'you should fast until your heart breaks, and the good Lord will forgive you'". (*Mimahazot Hahaim* (from the Theatre of Life)–*Hatzfira*, issue no. 174, 15.8.1913).

At this point it became impossible to hide the Zionist work done by the *Achiezer* charity. The managers and board members of the charity were both excited and angry. In particular, they were upset to learn that such activity had taken place without their knowledge … the charity, which had been developing so well, was in danger. Even Moshe Kaveh, who resented the Hassidic perspective, stood by Idel Schwartz, the head of the charity, who felt betrayed. Some feared that Dr. G. Zito (my father's cousin, O.A.), an assimilated Jew, would leave *Achiezer*. Yet the youth were determined to keep the charity going, even if the well–to–do left. The crisis was over without any turbulence.

World War I started on the Jewish date of 9 Av (the fast over the Temple) in summer 1914. A dark cloud spread over Jewish life. In Biala, refugee camps were set up for Jews from cities in Galicia and in Poland as the front moved towards Russia. All Jewish movements and organizations stopped their activities and concentrated on helping the Petersburg Committee for refugees. The Zionist activity in Biala stopped, too. That summer, as the German army moved eastward, part of the Jewish population of Biala left. People were worried that the battle around the Brisk castle would be a long one, and the cities close to Brisk would have a hard time. Many left for Russia, believing that the war would not reach there. Some of the young men whose families stayed in Biala went to Schedlitz to avoid being drafted into the Russian army.

In the summer of 1915 Germany occupied Biala. The Zionists who stayed in Biala resumed their activities, hoping for greater success under a European regime than under the Czar's government. The initial Zionism–related consultations were between Moshe Rubinstein and Joshua Fisher. They looked for an activity that would attract as many young people as possible. From one idea to the next, they eventually decided to organize Hebrew lessons for adults, and they called upon the help of the Hebrew teacher, Jacob Steinman. Finally, they decided to set up a Hebrew school and a children's home, for families whose heads were drafted to the Russian Army or went to America.

Intensive preparation and publicity work started in mid–winter of 1915/6 with the aim of starting the "*Yavneh*" school on Passover 1916. The school is described later on in this book. Here we would like to point out that this was the starting point for Zionist activity under the German occupation. From the start, it was clear that the impact of the school went far beyond its main function. After school, the 12–13–year-old pupils came home looking encouraged and joyful, after learning Hebrew songs and stories about Jewish history, fairy tales and anecdotes that aroused their imagination. Their older siblings were envious, sorry that they were too old for the school, and asked the younger ones to repeat what they learned.

The school, which was located in the wooden house of Reb Haim Levy Rubinstein on Kashiva Street, was like a burning flame, attracting all light–seekers. During classes, young people would stand close to the windows trying to hear what the teacher was saying.

[Page 80]

The Hebrew songs learned in school could be heard everywhere shortly after they were taught.

Lag Ba'Omer (the 33rd day of the Omer period, a traditional bonfire night), arrived just few weeks after the school opened, and the pupils went for a field–trip in the forest. They marched through the town in festive clothes, singing songs in Hebrew. Naturally, this first public parade of the school attracted other youngsters, celebrating Lag Ba'Omer, a holiday that had never been celebrated in the town before.

All this created a Zionist atmosphere in Biala, and motivated the Zionist leaders to build on this resounding success and to expand the movement. The Zionist circle expanded steadily as the refugees started to settle down in Biala, among them active Zionists. By that time, Haim Barlass, who came with his family from Brisk had joined in as well.

In the summer of 1916, further efforts were made to bring Zionist ideas to the youth. Every Saturday afternoon there was a lecture in the big hall at the school. Many came to these lectures, including individuals and groups who opposed the Zionist movement, such as active Bundists, who were friendly with some Zionists at the personal level. Fulia (Rafael) Lederman lectured there about the Bundist ideology, and even Wasskin, a refugee from Brisk who represented assimilationist ideas, was allowed to take part in the discussions.

The Zionist group grew and expanded. Many came to the lectures, and after a while, an important Zionist group developed. On the one hand, one weekly meeting was not enough anymore (the school's hall could not be used during working days), but on the other hand, people were tired of the endless arguments with opponents and the incessant repetition of proofs and counter–proofs. So it was decided to establish a Zionist "*Beit Am*" (People's House) as a meeting place for the Zionist youth and their supporters. Beit Ha'Am was to be managed by an elected committee and chaired by the chair of the Zionist committee.

The house was initially located in the house of Meir Korman, on Grabanover Street, at the corner of a narrow alley. It included two rooms and a corridor.

Beit Ha'Am opened in the winter of 1916/17, with a big festive ceremony. The festive atmosphere was evident not only in the high spirits, but also in the formal, elegant dress of the participants. Moshe Rubinstein, the chair of the Zionist committee, also chaired the Beit Ha'Am committee. Other elected members were: Haim Barlass, Mendel Kaveh, Jonah Steinman, and others.

A period of intensive organizational work started. Committees were elected for each topic, thus involving a large number of people in the movement. Each committee was autonomous in its field of responsibility, and reported to the managing committee and participated in its meetings. The cultural activity included frequent lectures, some on literature and some on current political issues. There was a dramatic club, directed by Mordechai Piekarsky, and a choir conducted by Shimon Blankeider ("the skinny"). Later, a branch of "Maccabi" was established, and it had a brass orchestra.

The different committees used one of the two rooms, a different committee each evening, except for the evenings of general assemblies or balls, when both rooms were needed.

Every Saturday afternoon the Hebrew group met to read Hebrew journals or classic Hebrew literature.

Two Jews who served in the German army stationed in Biala joined the activity of the Zionist group: Fritz Kornberg (an architect) and Dr. Schwabe, the chair of the sailing club (Rudder Club) of the Jewish students' union "*Ivria*" in Berlin, who worked in the Police Administration. Their activity was limited, according to what could be accommodated beside their army duties, but it was very important, nonetheless.

On the corridors of Beit Ha'Am, the Weinstein sisters (daughters of David, the tile–layer) ran a food stand. Their younger sister, Shayne Weinstein [who today lives in New York], became a student at the *Yavneh* school, and thus they were also coming to Zionist activities.

The work developed well. Young people came from all walks of life, even from groups that were far from Zionism. Many were influenced by their younger siblings who studied at the school, and also Beit Ha'Am was the only venue that was open to all, and allowed the youth to spend some leisure time together. The freedom on which Beit Ha'am was based had eventually led to conflicts with older and religious Zionists, some of whom left and established *Hamizrahi*.

The first general assembly of Beit Ha'Am took place in the summer of 1917. It was supposed to be a meeting of a strong, cohesive, group of people who had been working hard for quite a while. The two rooms, which were not that large, were full to overflowing. After hearing the report of the chairperson on the achievements since the opening of Beit Ha'Am, the participants started arguing. There was a strong opposition, not to the way Beit Ha'Am was being run, but to the principle that the same person held both positions–the head of both the Zionist committee and Beit Ha'Am.

The opposition came from within the Zionist committee, from Haim Barlass and Mendel Kaveh. Almost all the assembly joined the opposition. Only Dr. Shwaba, a prominent, very experienced, organizer, stood by M. Rubinstein. They both argued that a joint function was necessary to maintain the Zionist orientation of Beit Ha'Am and avoid repeating the experience of the Saturday meetings in the school, which became a place of arguments and dispute.

The general assembly lasted three days. At the end it was decided that the Zionist committee and the Beit Ha'Am committee should remain unchanged. From then on, Beit Ha'Am formally became a Zionist institution, both as a club for members and as a home for all Zionist activity.

In 1917, as the Zionist Organization grew, the Zionist center in Warsaw decided to hold a Zionist opinion poll in all cities and towns of Poland, combined with a fundraising campaign on behalf of the Jewish settlers in Tel Aviv and Jaffa, who had been deported by the Turkish government. The main purpose, however, was the opinion poll, which was supposed to be a pro–Eretz–Israel [called Palestine at the time–RM] demonstration at a time when people believed that the war would bring about freedom for all oppressed people. Polish Zionists were asked to sign the following declaration, with their name and address:

[Page 81]

"We recognize the extreme importance of the help provided to our pioneering brothers in *Eretz Israel*. The Jews of Poland express their wish that they will not lose heart. The great world revolution which will bring freedom and liberty to all oppressed peoples and nations, will also fulfil the historical ideal of the Jews and create for them a legally assured homeland in *Eretz Israel*, their historical native land."

The newspaper of the Orthodox Association, "*Das Yudishe Vort*" (the Jewish Word), declared war on the poll, and warned the Orthodox Jews against signing it. But the Zionist Organization in Biala participated enthusiastically in the poll. A couple of its members visited each Jewish household, told the families about Eretz–Israel and the hopes for an appropriate solution to our aspirations when the nations reached a peace agreement after the war. They collected dozens of pages, which included hundreds of signatures, and Biala contributed substantially to the 250,000 signatures collected in 200 towns of Poland.

Zionist activities developed quickly and demanded more time and space. The hall, that until then had been big enough to release the energy of the Zionists, could not contain it anymore. Appetite grows with eating, and each group (the theater group, the choir, the band and Maccabi) demanded more time, more rooms, and a larger hall.

They started looking for a larger place and in the winter of 1917/8 Beit Ha'Am moved to the house of Moshe Levenberg, on Briskai Street, for a short time. This was also the time of the first clash between the Rabbi of Biala and the local Zionist Organization, which happened as described below.

In the winter of 1918, Biala learned of the death of the Zionist leader, Dr. Yehiel Chelinov. The committee decided to hold a public memorial at the Central Synagogue. Zionist activity, such as assemblies and parties, which took place at the *Yavneh* school or at Beit Ha'Am, had been criticized before, but this time the whole Jewish population was invited to pay respects to a Zionist leader. On the day of the ceremony, the rabbi called Godel Binies, the *Gabbai* [keeper of the finances of the congregation who also is in charge of day–to–day running of the synagogue–RM] of the synagogue, and ordered him to lock the synagogue and give him the keys.

That afternoon the city was in tumult. Some went to the Rabbi in an effort to prevent a clash, asking him to allow the memorial to take place in the synagogue, but to no avail.

In the evening, at the appointed hour, people arrived at the synagogue, but it was locked. For half an hour the synagogue yard was full of people. The response to the Zionists' invitation was a success.

The Rabbi's stubbornness upset the Zionist youth, and Maccabi members, originally assigned to keep order during the memorial, got ready to force the synagogue open, which was not that easy: it had double doors and heavy locks. It was a difficult decision, but there seemed to be no chance that the Rabbi would reconsider. Moreover, they did not want to appear to show disrespect or desecrate the synagogue by breaking the doors.

However, when it was clear that the Rabbi was not going to change his mind, they decided to open the synagogue from inside, and to avoid any damage. Three Maccabi members, led by Asher Feigenbaum (son of Moshe the glassmaker), climbed up to the ladies' section on the third floor, managed to take out one of the bars of a window, and through this opening, Feigenbaum managed to jump into the synagogue. Half an hour later the doors opened from inside. The synagogue filled up immediately, and hundreds of people remained outside for lack of room. Members of the Zionist Organization eulogized the deceased, and the prayer for the dead (*El Male Rahamim*, God is full of mercy), was sung by one of the members, Pintze Libman, as the cantor was absent at the rabbi's command.

Through this incident, the first in a string of battles with the anti–Zionists and, in particular, the Rabbi, the Zionists felt stronger and capable of gaining social acceptance. This was the "pioneering incident" of a series of public social clashes that were to occur in the near future.

A while later Beit Ha'Am moved to the house of Kalman Sheinberg, on Sadova Street. This was where the real Beit Ha'Am, *Tel Talpiot*, for the youth, was located. It consisted of five rooms, two of which were combined by knocking down the wall separating them, to create one big hall for assemblies, and an exercise room for Maccabi.

Once again, activities were divided between the different committees; each was given time and space according to the new possibilities. The council, which included all the committees, met every fortnight. There were frequent lectures on literature, and current affairs, law, etc. In short, there was a tremendous upsurge in Zionist activities. Youth movements began to appear, first the "Zion Youth" and later, under the Polish regime, *Hashomer Ha'za'ir*. All were hosted in Beit Ha'Am.

This was happening already in 1918, near the end of the war. People had already begun to feel some freedom. The borders of the German–occupied territory, formerly tightly controlled by the army, which were fenced and blocked off, with no connection to the outside world, were gradually breached, and news from outside penetrated the blockade. As the Germans advanced in 1917, the Jewish soldiers who had taken part in the Zionist activities and had allowed for some indirect connection with the Zionist committee in Berlin had left Biala.

There was almost no connection with Warsaw. It was impossible to attend the 3rd national Zionist meeting as the German military administration did not issue travel permits. Yet, step by step, it became easier to have external connections and to receive news from different parts of Europe. Those who had fled to Russia when the front came close to Biala were sending books, newspapers, and memoranda published by Zionist centers and the "*Tarbut*" (Culture) organization, which gave some idea about the extent of the Zionist activities in Russia. The above–mentioned Fritz Kornberg, who was now in Krakow, would send news about himself and also material published by the "*Tse'irei Zion*" (Youth of Zion) movement in Ukraine, where he was active at the time.

[Page 82]

Later on it became easier to contact Warsaw. Letters could be sent and received, and exit permits were more easily obtainable. It was then that we learned about the Balfour Declaration, although the Germans preferred that the Jewish population would not know about it. In short, we came out of the straits and onto the wide way. We began to feel that important political and social events were about to take place, and also the German military effort started to die down and its end was near.

At the end of the summer of 1918, the first returnees began to arrive from Russia. Among them, there were two very different groups: some who had become extremists on the left, who brought to Biala the ideas of the Bolshevik Revolution and its ideals; at the other extreme came the Hassidic middle class, for whom the *shtibel* was the center of the world before the war. Some of these people later established *Agudat Israel* [To this day a political religious party in Israel– RM].

All these political groups started to demand their place in society. The Zionists, who until now had the hegemony, had to adjust to interactions with other parties (for instance, in the American assistance committee, chaired by Moshe Rubinstein, where all the parties were represented), and sometimes had fights with the opposing parties.

In the fall of 1918 the Zionist movement in Poland was strengthened by the return of the powerful leader, Itzchak Grinboim, from Russia. His first step towards organizing Jewish life in Poland was his plan to call for a general Jewish congress during which a national committee was supposed to be elected, a committee that would lead Polish Jewry and manage its affairs. This initiative encountered strong opposition from "Aguda, the "Bund", the "Polkists", and even from the Zionist–Socialist party. The central Zionist committee decided to call for a pre–congress conference in December 1918, in which both the Zionists and unaffiliated people took part.

In Biala, these elections were the first time that the Zionists had encountered other parties in a political contest. Their main opponents were the members of Agudat Israel. Public meetings took the place of Tora studies. The Aguda was fighting against the idea of a general Jewish national committee that was not based on the Tora and on keeping all commandments. In one of the meetings, Iche Meyer Cohen represented Aguda; before the war he had never dealt with secular matters, but when he returned from Russia he felt that he could speak to the public. His ultimate argument was that the secular Jews did not wear *Tzitzit* [a Jewish garb with four fringes that is worn by Jewish orthodox men under the shirt–RM].

The elections for the pre–congress committee took place on a winter day, and Moshe Rubinstein and Haim Barlas were elected. The conference enabled Biala to meet personally for the first time with the Zionist leadership in Poland, and from then on to occupy a central place in the Polish Zionist movement.

The first elections for the post–war Polish parliament (Sejm) took place in 1919. For the Jews, the "renewed" Poland began with pogroms in Lvov and Kielce (Keltz), attacks from the "Halerchiks" (General Haler's soldiers), and the Poznanchiks (Polish soldiers from the Poznan region), who were very active in cutting off beards of Jewish men, throwing Jews from fast moving trains, and other such "heroic" acts, in Biala as elsewhere.

At that time the Zionist leaders in Biala started to get ready for the election campaign. Four regions had to vote in Biala: Biala, Radzin, Vladova, and Janeva. Before the election, a meeting was called for all the towns and cities in these regions. The convention took place in Biala's Beit Ha'Am. It is worth mentioning, as a memorable episode, that a non–Jewish candidate from Mezrich also came to the convention, claiming that he was a liberal Pole who objected to anti–Semitic incitement and needed support to be elected as the candidate of the Jews in the Sejm… Haim Barlas and Moshe Rubinstein reported to the participants, who accepted the Zionist election platform and established a regional election office in Biala to manage all the election affairs.

The Zionist youth became actively, and enthusiastically, involved in the elections. The work was organized locally, and there were frequent contacts with the towns and cities of the four regions, via circulars, letters, and visits. No financial aid from Warsaw was necessary. Soon after the list of candidates was published (which included the lawyer Apolinary Hartglass, the lawyer Alexander Hertz Olshwanger, and the engineer Moshe Kerner) the list received the number 5, and a fundraising campaign to cover expenses was organized overnight in all four regions, selling pins marked with the number 5. During the two months of the election campaign, Beit Ha'Am was a busy administrative center.

As the elections grew closer, meetings of the different parties took place. The campaign heated up. Biala was liberated late from the Germans, and thus was the last to conduct the elections. All the parties could send their best speakers and instructors. The elections were held on a Sunday. The weekend before, Biala hosted several young Zionist speakers from Warsaw: Dr. Esther Mangel, Yitzhak Aitkin, Mordechai Yoffe, and Jacob Pyontnitzki, who talked at the different meetings. On Saturday night Noah Prilotzki spoke in a Polkists' assembly. From the Zionist side, Dr. Esther Mangel answered, presenting counter–arguments.

After this meeting, which was attended by many people, the nationalists decided to call for another meeting the next day at the same place (the movie theater of Yoske Kashtenbaum), at which Yitzhak Grinboim would speak.

Grinboim came to Biala on Saturday night. The hall was full of people impatiently waiting for the speaker to start. There was a lot of tension; opposition parties recruited many of their members in order to disturb the meeting. The Bund in particular was determined to break up the assembly and not to let Grinboim speak. Grinboim stood on the stage surrounded by a group of strong people, but he could not speak.

Bundists stood at the foot of the stage shouting and screaming things unrelated to the elections. Finally, Grinboim succeeded in overcoming the noise. His speech, too, was not related to the elections that were to take place the next day, but was a thorough analysis of the Bolshevik revolution and the Jews. The audience listened with much concentration.

[Page 83]

This made the Bundists even more furious. They screamed and shouted that in a certain town the Zionists had informed on members of the Bund. Grinboim promised to look into the matter. One Bundist called Grinboim a "provocateur", and Grinboim slapped his face, saying: "One should pay with blood for such an accusation". A fight started and the meeting could not go on. It was also felt that there was no need to continue. After the party in honor of Grinboim, he was escorted to the train.

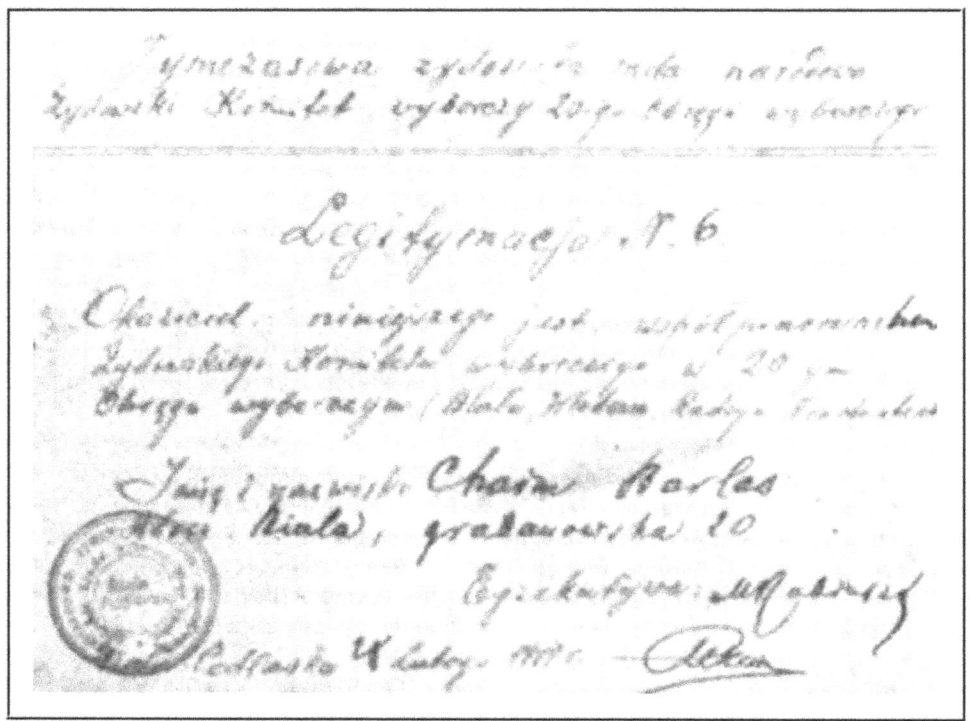

Certificate issued by the Zionist organization in Biala during the elections to the Constitution Sejm (Parliament)

On Sunday morning, they were all at their work stations, and performed their tasks diligently. Now came the long wait for the results of the hard and stressful preparations. On the one hand, this was a time of relief from the tension and stress of the campaign; on the other, a period of anxious expectation for the results. Members of the Zionist organization who roamed about impatiently in the corridors of the regional court, where the votes were being counted, learned ten hours before the results were formally announced that their efforts were not in vain: their candidate, the lawyer Hartglass, was going to strengthen the group of Jewish nationalists in the Polish Sejm.

The general elections were the first political action taken in post–war Poland. At the same time, the local government and regional councils (Starostawa) were established, and this Council started to control political parties and social organizations, and immediately banned the activities of the Zionist organization.

Yet, the resourceful Zionists found a way around this. From the first contact with the new authorities, it was clear that asking for a permit would be a long and unreliable process; they thus took a shortcut: they used a Royal order (Note: Poland was a kingdom until 1919 – RM) that automatically validated all associations that existed legally during the German occupation. The truth was that even this way was not strictly "kosher", but it was quicker. This struggle with the new Polish regime was described in the Zionist daily newspaper "Das Yidishe Folk" ("The Jewish People") that was published in Warsaw.

In August 1919, the fourth national Zionist convention took place and Biala sent two delegates: Moshe Rubinstein and Jacob Aharon Rosenboim. It was during this convention that the Youth of Zion was established as an independent organization. The Zionist

Organization started to split up into democrats and the right wing, which later became the democratic *Al Hamishmar* ("On Guard"), and the right wing *Et Livnot* ("Time to Build"). Biala joined the democrats.

In the same year, 1919, there were also elections for the Biala municipality. All Jewish parties presented candidates. From the Zionists, Moshe Rubinstein and Moshe Kaveh were elected.

In the municipality itself, all Jewish members, except the Bundists, joined together and voted as one party. Sometimes, when a Jewish matter was discussed, and it was clear that an anti–Jewish vote was unavoidable, the Jewish parties would stop the meeting by walking out and thus breaking the quorum. There were frequent fights between the Bundists and the Jewish Party.

A meeting of all Jewish representatives in the municipalities of Poland took place between December 30th 1919 and January 1st 1920. The purpose of the meeting was to unify the activity of all Jewish representatives.

During 1920, Biala's participation in Zionist work in Poland increased. Yet, the local activities declined, as the main activists went to work at the headquarters of the organization in Warsaw. After Purim 1920 the Zionist organizations around Seidlitz held a convention there. There were speakers from Warsaw, a delegate from Seidlitz, and one from Biala, who talked about social work. In post–war Poland most Jewish social work was done by self–help organizations, funded by the Joint Distribution Committee (JDC). In most parts of Poland this work was undertaken by assimilated Jews or by the orthodox. In Biala, however, a large committee was established, and all the parties–left and right–participated in it constructively under Zionist leadership. It was a rare and interesting phenomenon, and for that reason the delegate from Biala was invited to speak on the topic. They wanted to know how this was achieved.

In 1920 there was a crisis in the Poland–Russia war. The front was approaching Biala closer and closer. Life became increasingly difficult, people were afraid to step out of the houses, not to be kidnapped for forced labor. The civilian regime left the town, leaving just a military government.

[Page 84]

During these days of tension, a civil Polish– Jewish militia was organized by our members to keep an eye on Jewish affairs. The militia members were allowed to move freely in the city, even during the hours that movement of civilians was forbidden. However, this militia was brought to an end with the Red Army occupation.

The military regime under the Red Army immediately organized the "Revcom" (the revolutionary committee), and slowly rebuilt the administration by trying to replicate the previous government departments. At first, they did not look for communists, and appointed any person that offered to work. Later they searched for any person able to take on administrative work and demanded his/her cooperation.

Members of the Zionist group debated whether or not to cooperate with the new regime. It was impossible to hold a meeting and to reach an agreement in the matter, because had an open debate ended up with a negative decision and the authorities found out about it, it could bring about the capital penalty in a revolutionary court under accusation of sabotage. Thus, the discussion was carried on in secret, by exchange of ideas by hints, but no decision was taken. Each person decided for himself and did not try to influence those who did not do the same.

Nevertheless, one meeting was held to discuss the matter. It was held on a Saturday, six days after the Russian occupation. That morning one of the Jewish leaders was invited to the department of culture and education that was located in the high–school building. He was informed that he had to take on the responsibility of supervisor of the Jewish schools in Biala and Yaneva. He tried to refuse by saying that he was a Zionist and he could only establish schools based on teaching Hebrew and Bible. He was promised that the authorities would not interfere with the school program. His appointment was issued the same day, and he was told to come the next day to look for an appropriate apartment that would be confiscated for his office. That Saturday afternoon a small group of Zionists got together for a meeting, disguised as a visit to the bedside of a sick female friend. It was the first time that the question had been clearly raised. Most participants thought that the appointment should be accepted, because it would leave the school in the hands of the Zionists. Some, and the appointed person among them, suggested that they should wait for the outcome of the battle over Warsaw. If Russia conquered Warsaw, it would be possible to consult with the central Zionist committee.

The next day, Sunday, the person did not go to confiscate an apartment. In the evening the Russian authorities put out announcements on the streets that within 24 hours he would be charged with sabotage and judged by the revolutionary court. It was decided that he would present himself for the office the next day. Yet, by Monday the military situation had changed and that evening the Russian army left Biala.

The sudden retreat of the Russian army forced those who had worked for the Russian administration to leave the town in fear of revenge by the Polish regime. They ran East. Some stayed for a while in places where they were complete strangers and were not recognized and later returned to Biala; others left for Russia.

The reorganization of Zionist work after the Bolshevik invasion was slow. Some of the active members were absent, the relationships between the Jews and the Poles were tense, making public work difficult.

Soon after the Balfour Declaration was approved by the League of Nations, the Jews of Poland started to immigrate to Israel. The policy of the Zionist Organization was to prefer people who had a profession. A training course for woodworking was set up in Biala, in Freidman's yard (nick–named "Paradise") on Natrovitz Street. Several people took the course in preparation for *Alia*. The person in charge was Asher Feigenbaum (son of Moshe the glazier).

In 1920 some individuals got ready to make Alia [immigration to *Eretz Israel*]. The first woman to leave Biala and go on *Hachshara* [training in agriculture for the purpose of Alia] at the pioneering farm in Grochov near Warsaw was Feige Ita Uhrmacher, who indeed became one of the first to immigrate to Israel. Zelig Rosenfeld and Pearl Wiesenfeld, from the youth, also made *Alia*. From the older people, Solomon Weissberg (the hatmaker), Yesha'ayahu Agres, Alter Weinberg, Shalom Rogalski, Noah Mann and others made Alia.

At the end of the summer of 1922 the first term of the Polish Sejm ended. Preparation for the election of the new Sejm began, and the Jews also started to prepare themselves for this.

A regional convention of delegates from all four regions was organized in Biala, and the delegates Yitzhak Grinboim, Joshua Heshel Farbstein, and Apolinary Hartglass reported on their activity in the first Sejm. This meeting took place on a Sunday, in the hall of Haim Yoske Kashtenboim. In the morning there was a public talk, and then the delegates received delegations from the different institutions and associations. In the afternoon, there was another meeting in the Beith Midrash. The streets leading to it were overflowing. Biala had never seen such a crowd in the Beith Midrash. In the evening, the delegates of the four regions got together in the hall of Kiakovsky to make a list of candidates for the Biala constituency to the second Sejm. Learning from Biala's experience, similar conventions were then held in other parts of Poland.

In 1923 the Zionist movement in Poland experienced a sharp dispute, which divided it into two groups: *Al Hamishmar* and *Et Livnot*. The *Al Hamishmar* group was a minority in Biala, and only members of *Et Livnot* were sent to the sixth Zionist congress. The prominent members of *Al Hamishmar*, who had represented Biala in past congresses, were elected to represent other localities.

[Page 85]

The reactionary forces, namely the town Rabbi and his followers, could not digest the Zionists' enthusiasm and called upon their old weapon–excommunication. The reason for excommunication was a poem written by David Shim'onovitz (Shim'oni), which was published on the front page of a *Hashomer Hatza'ir* newsletter, and was titled El Al (upwards toward heaven). It was handed to the Rabbi by one of the Radzin Hassidim, and was "spiced" by "appropriate" interpretations… The boycott of the Zionists was called by the Rabbi himself, with all the ceremony of lighted candles, Shofar blowing, curses and excommunications, all of which made a strong impression on the superstitious public.

A quick and strong counter action was necessary to stop the irrational fear. The next day the Zionists declared that they accepted the challenge, and that they were going to fight the Rabbi and his helpers without fear or hesitation. One result of this struggle was the first newspaper in Biala, called the "Bialer Echo" (The Echo of Biala). The newspaper mocked the excommunication; the ceremony was presented as a comedy. People read it and rolled with laughter, which was exactly what was needed.

The Zionist Organization in the town got ready for the elections. Several fundraising events were organized. One of them was a concert with the famous Chazan Gershon Sirota and his daughter. After all was ready and ads were posted around the town, Sirota sent a telegram apologizing for canceling the concert, following the Rabbi's request. The Zionists did everything in their power to convince him to change his mind, and succeeded.

On Purim of 1924 there was a big party in an open hall. A special satirical piece was written for this occasion about the excommunication, beginning with: "Ich bin fun reb zu dir geshikt" ("I was sent by the Rabbi to you", a parody on H. N. Bialik's Yiddish poem "Dos letzte vort" (The last word)). The performance was announced in the program, which upset the Rabbi's followers. They tried different ways to avoid the reading of the satire, but the Zionists did not give in, and read it during the ball.

With this courageous fight the Zionists prevented the revival of the Middle Ages.

After the excommunication, the anti–Zionists exerted a lot of pressure on Kalman Sheinberg to clear Beit Ha'am from his house, and unfortunately succeeded. The Zionist organization was forced to leave the big spacious hall and move to Mendel Goldfarb's home on Mizrich St. This house also included a library, which was already quite rich by then, and lectures were held there.

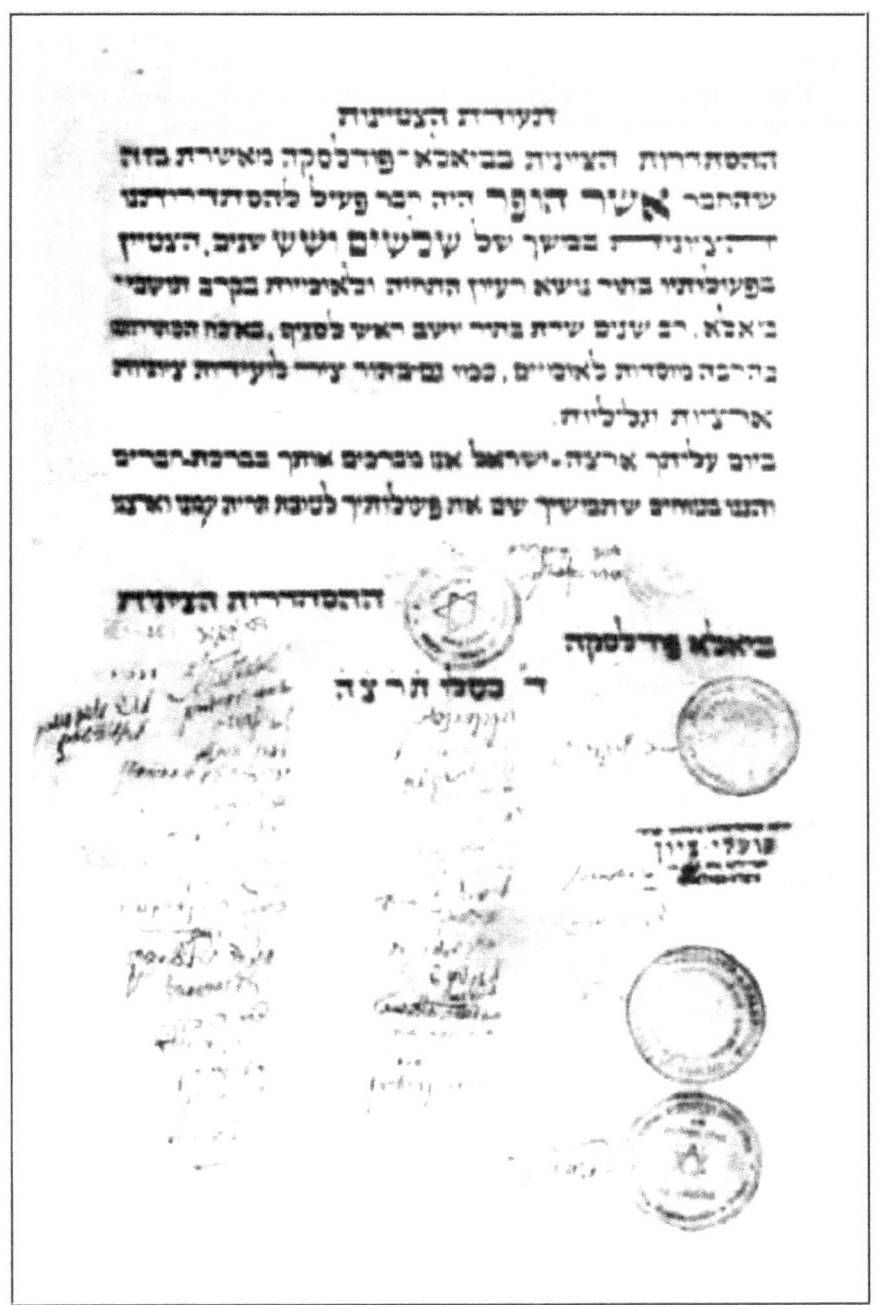

Certificate issued in connection with the aliya of Asher Hoffer signed by all Zionist groups in Biala, 1935

Addition to the article by M. Bruhel

by M.Y. Feigenboim

Translated from Yiddish by A. L. P.

Translated from Hebrew by Ofra Anson

Edited by Rafael Manory

After Moshe Rubinstein moved to Warsaw, and from there to Israel, general Zionist activity in Biala weakened. The reduced activity was also reflected in the events and the splits in the World Zionist Federation. Until the 1920s, the Zionist Organization in Biala was a united body, which attracted all the Jews with Zionist sentiments. *Mizrahi* was a separate autonomous organization, but, except for its cultural activities, it cooperated with the Zionist Organization in all other aspects. *Hashomer Haza'ir* was just a group of scouts at the disposal of the Zionist Organization for all its political activities. After 1920, other Zionist groups developed in Biala, as in other towns, and these groups were subject directly to their respective centers in Warsaw. They did not cooperate with the Zionist Organization, and sometimes acted in opposition to it. Not surprisingly, the new groups attracted members of the Zionist Organization and practically arrested the recruitment of young people to the Zionist Federation itself.

At that time, *Hashomer Haza'ir* stopped being a scout association and became an independent youth federation, with its own ideology. The revisionist party came into being and bitterly fought the old Zionist movement. The *Hehalutz* movement started to operate, and actively recruited the working youth. *Hehalutz* sent its members on *hachshara* (agricultural training for aliya–RM) encouraging them to make *aliya*. During the 1930s a branch of the right–wing *Poalei Zion* (workers of Zion) began operating. The League of the Workers in *Eretz Israel* also operated in Biala.

Naturally, this differentiation among the various Zionists had a strong effect on the previously united Zionist Organization, and it became a branch of the general Zionist Organization of Warsaw, which was also split into Aleph and Beth divisions. Only the old generation still belonged to it, with no youngsters. Economic hardships also contributed to the decline in enthusiasm and activity.

After Moshe Rubinstein left, the leadership of the Organization was taken over by Israel Goldstein, M. Mishkin, Benjamin Kliger, Asher Hoffer, Jacob Aaron Rosenboim and a few others. Haim Myudak served as a secretary for many years, doing a great job. During the later years the home of Moshe Goldstein, the butcher, on Chasna Alley, housed the hall of the Organization. It should be noted, however, that despite the differences between the Zionists in Biala before WWII, all were united in the activities for the Jewish National Fund.

In the elections for the 18th Zionist congress, on July 23rd 1933, 968 votes were cast of the total 1027 eligible members. List no. 1 (*Al Hamishmar*) got 59 votes; List no. 2 (*Et Livnot*)–5 votes; List no. 3 (*Mizrahi*)–132 votes; List no. 4–0 votes; List no. 5 (The block of "Working *Eretz Israel*")–574 votes; the Revisionists–251 votes; List no. 7–7 votes (from *Podliasier Lebn* (Life in Podlaska), volume 19/9, 28.7.1933).

———————

[Page 87]

The Book

Translated by Libby Raichman

In the year 1933 we, a group of Biala residents, started making enquiries about publishing a book of records that would portray a comprehensive picture of the Biala Jewish settlement since its inception. We wanted to provide insights into the past, compare it to the present and extract inferences for the future. The difficulties of our daily lives that each one of us endured and the lack of financial resources, brought our plans for this project to nought.

And what an irony of fate: Far from our birth town, the book about which we dreamt in 1933, is now published. But the present is no longer here to compare to the past and there is no one for whom to extract inferences for the future. The bloody flood that descended upon Polish Jewry reached our town too. The German horde destroyed the Jewish Biala and annihilated the Jewish population. Instead of this being a book about, and for, a living community, the book has turned into a gravestone in memory of the slaughtered Jewish community, whose unknown graves are scattered over almost the whole of Europe. Instead of being a stimulus to an active and spiritually rich Jewish life, this book is the conclusion to a chapter of Biala Jewish life, that existed for hundreds of years and that ended in such a gruesome and tragic way; a memorial to all those who perished so bitterly at the hands of the German murderers.

Our Biala, like other Jewish settlements in Poland, forged a ring in the chain of Jewish life and creativity on Polish soil. Our town contributed her modest portion to all political and social aspects that enriched, beautified and stimulated Jewish life in Poland.

We were substantially represented by the Chassidic movement, that in its time brought a revival of Jewish life. Biala scholars were famous throughout Poland and we regarded them very highly.

The idea of a return to Zion had many loyal followers in Biala who, because of their beliefs, endured much persecution. Among the builders of the Land of Israel and the Chalutz movement our participation is evident.

On the altar of the revolutionary movement, Jewish Biala sacrificed more than one victim. Under Czarist rule in Poland one could find Biala Jewish revolutionaries as exiles in white Siberia. In Poland from before the 2nd World War, many Biala youth were tormented in the prisons for their revolutionary convictions.

In the history of Polish Jewry, in the period between the two wars, Jewish Biala wrote many articles through a fellow citizen, Advocate Apolinari Hartglas, who was known as a proud Jew and one of the most important representatives of Polish Jewry. He distinguished himself with his uncompromising courageous struggle for equal rights for Jews in Poland.

[Page 88]

In the struggle with German tyranny in the 2nd World War, there was no lack of participation on the part of Jewish Biala. In the resistance movement in Biala, around Biala and far from Biala, the people of Biala were active. Most of them perished in the struggle with the German monster.

It was not easy for us to set up this book. The necessary material was not easily available and not accessible to us. We succeeded only with our research into archival material from the earlier periods of Biala Jewish settlement. Material from Jewish life in recent generations was reconstructed from testimonies and from memory.

Our intention was to present a review of Jewish life in Biala. It is understandable that the book does not pretend to be perfect. We are, however, convinced that for the most part, what has been told about our birth town is presented in an objective way in this memoir.

In the book there is material taken from the Biala weekly news. Certain corrections were made, in order to adapt the material to the general framework of the book. Certain works extend beyond the prescribed framework but we could not shorten them as they contain many details of former Jewish life in Biala.

We must mention here fellow townsmen Alter Weinberg and Asher Hoffer (may his memory be blessed), who despite their advanced age and weak state of health, did not tire of sitting with the writer of these lines for long hours. They shared important details about Jewish Biala with love and devotion. Thanks to the outstanding memories of these two fellow townsmen, we were successful in reconstructing pieces of history that would have, without doubt, remained in oblivion.

We owe thanks to:

The historian Dr Michael Hendel (Tel Aviv), who in his time was director of the Gimnazye (High School) in Mezrich, gathered valuable historical material about the Jews of Biala and here, in Israel, revised it and gave it to us.

The researcher and author Mayer Edelbaum (New York), a descendant of neighbouring Mezrich, for his interesting chapter "Rabbis and Teachers in Biala".

All those who responded to our call and contributed essays for the book; Mr MosheTsinovicz (Tel Aviv) for referring us to specific sources and the members of the committee who helped to prepare the book for publication.

Our birthplace Biala was destroyed, every memory in the town obliterated where once a vibrant Jewish life existed. Our nearest were annihilated in a gruesome manner and we have not remained with a grave to their memory at which we could have stood, petrified in our eternal sorrow and dampening the earth of the grave with a tear. Destroyed is our Biala on earth. Let us create a Biala in the world above and impart her beauty and her innocence from generation to generation.

Y. Feignbaum,
Ramat Gan
Adar 5721 (March 1961)

———————————

[Page 89]

Biala

by M.Y. Feignbaum, Ramat Gan

Translated by Libby Raichman

On the Warsaw–Moscow highway, 40 km west of Brisk-D'Lita [Brest] lies the town of Biala Podlaska that can be confidently regarded as one of the most beautiful towns in Poland. The town is beautifully built in urban style and is noted for its cleanliness. The River Kazhna flows through the town. Its source is at Lukov–Podlaski [Lukow] and in the vicinity of Brisk it flows into the River Bug. The Kazhne River divides the town into two sections: on the left is the town and the right – the suburb called Volye [Volia]. The train station is located in Volye [Volia] and from there the trains travel in the direction of Warsaw and Brisk.

In a few short lines we will trace the general history of the town.

The founder of the town was Piatr Yanovicz Biali and the town actually bears his name. Piatr Yanovicz Biali was the Governor of Trok, founding land–owner of Great Lithuania, the first Chief Commander of the Cossacks. He died in 1498. It is therefore reasonable to assume that the town was founded at the end of the 15th century. In the 16th century Biala was the property of the Lithuanian magnate Ilinicz and in 1568 Prince Radzhivil Sherotka bought the colony and from then on the town acquired additional names like: Radzhivilishe Biala, "Alba Dukalis" (in Latin: a Prince's Biale).

This very ancient colony was, it appears, a defence stronghold which is evident from the high rampart and deep ditches that encircle the castle. The high, strong tower of the castle still stands to this day. The beautiful castle was built by Radzhivil Sherotka. During the Swedish–Polish war a division of Swedish soldiers, at the command of the Swedish King Karl the 12th, destroyed the town and the castle in 1706. The castle was restored quite quickly and regained its former splendour. During the reign of the Polish King August the 2nd, wealthy noblemen of Biala lived in the castle and the courtyard was used for entertaining guests, for recreation and for presentations. The last of the Radzhivils who spent time in the castle were: Karol, the Governor of Vilna who was called "Panye Kichanko" (he died in the castle on 22nd November 1790) and Dominic.

In the year 1650 Biala received from Prince Michael Kazhimi–erzh Radzhivil, together with other freedoms, the town's coat–of–arms that represents the image of the holy Michael, who fought with the snake. The same coat–of–arms was used in the official seal of the town council.

Already in 1628, the Biala Gimnazye (High School) is mentioned which at that time was called Academy and was a branch of the Krakow Academy.

Amongst the oldest buildings in the town were the three churches. The church near the Gimnaziye was built in 1520, the church in Reformatzye Street in 1671 and the church in Brisk Street was built at the end of the 17th century. In the course of these hundreds of years they were constantly renovated and their appearance was certainly altered.

Biala belonged to the former Lithuanian state and lay close to the Polish border. With the closing of the "Lubliner Unye" (Union of Lublin) in 1569 that united Poland and Lithuania, Lithuania became part of the Polish State and Biala fell under Polish rule. At the time of the last partition of Poland in 1795 (between Russia, Austria and Germany) the town was allocated to Austria and the Austrian government ruled until 1809 when it was transferred to the Warsaw Duchy. From 1815 Biala belonged to Poland that was then under Russian rule.

[Page 90]

During the former Polish rule, the town belonged to the district and circle of Brisk-D'Lita. Under Austrian rule Biala was converted to a circle–town. During the Russian governance of Poland, Biala again remained a circle–town and from the beginning belonged to the Shedletz [Siedlice] Province and later to the Province of Chelm. The annexation of Biala to the Province of Chelm happened for religious reasons. In the outer region of Chelm there was a greater number of Christians, called "Unitten", so attaching the Biala region to the Province of Chelm gave the Russian Church the upper hand over the Roman Catholic Church in Chelm and the Biala region (the persecution of the Roman Catholic Church at that time, in the areas mentioned, is described in the collection: "Martyrologia Podlasia" and in the book "Z.Ziemi Chelmskiej" by the famous Polish writer ST Raimont).

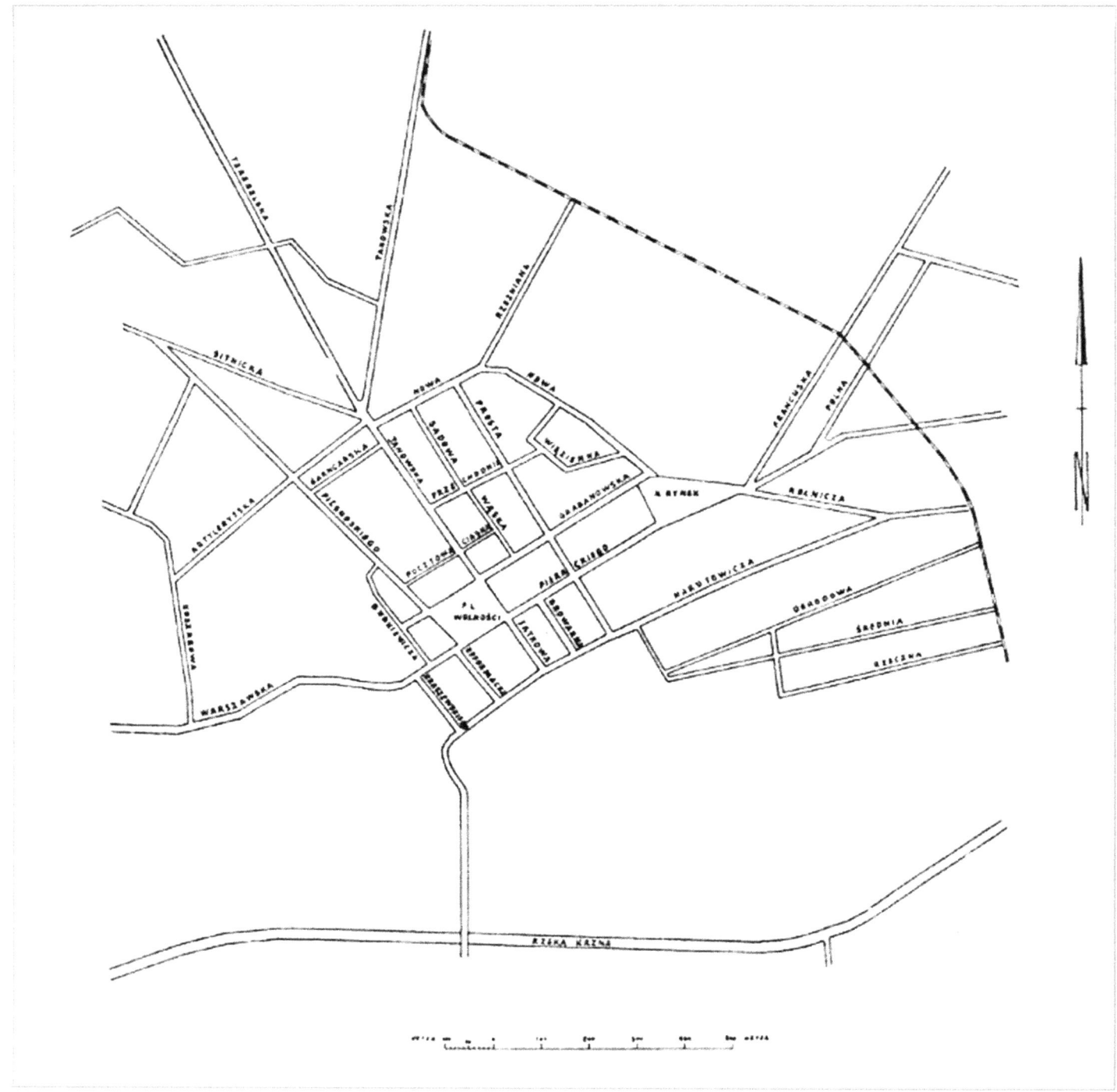

Town Plan
(excluding the suburb of "Volye" [Volia])

The name of the town was changed by the Russians to "Bi–ela". The Gymnaziye was transformed into a Russian training institution and the Russian Government tried with all its might to Russianize the social life in the town.

[Page 91]

The Railway Station

The people of Biala took an active part in the uprising against the Russian Government. In the town during Russian rule the following offices could be found: The District office, the District Court, the Peace Court of the 3rd circle for the people of Biala and Terespol, the Circle Court, the Tax Management of the 4th circle and the Finance office.

The District offices responsible to the Governor of the province in Polish times could be found in the market place in the building that later belonged to Shmuel Pizshitz. Later it moved into the Mevius building. The District Court called in Russian "Siyezd" was at first located in the High Court and later in the premises of: Fradel Shmad, Bergshtein, Avrom Urmacher [Ormacher] and finally in the Mevius building. The Peace–Court was at first located in the house of Kotshemoyenik, later where the Polish Police Station stood on Brisk Street and finally in the Mevius building.

The Mevius building (on Brisker Street) in which the Government offices and courts were housed

The Circle–Court, called in Russian "Akruzshnayi Sud", was located in the High Court, later in the premises of Urmacher [Ormacher] and finally also in the Mevius building. The finance office was located on Mezrich Street where later the Polish "Uzshond Skarbovi" was located.

The municipality was located in the same building in the market place as it is now. Even the oldest residents did not remember when the building was erected. They only remembered the big renovation that was carried out there.

The council was led in Russian times by a nominated Mayor and there was no elected administrative body. Council taxes were only paid by the wealthier people and the money was used to light the streets and clean the chimneys and another tax that was called "kanefatsedre".

In 1915, during the 1st World War, the town was occupied by the German army. The transition of the town from Russian to German rule did not create any disturbance to daily life. Both the town and its inhabitants hardly suffered at all.

Then the town was incorporated by the Germans into the territory of the "Bug Army" who made the entry into the town and the exit from it difficult. Economic life was almost paralysed. The agriculturalists had to surrender their produce to the government who operated a strict regime of food distribution for the population.

The Civil Administration was led by the German Civilian organisation and also the German town Police at the head of which stood Mayor Punk. This mayor Punk already then had a reputation for his bestial attitude and draconian decrees. If the snow was not immediately cleared from the streets, he punished the merchants by ordering them to keep their shops closed for a few days. For not greeting him, although he did not respond to those who did, he sent them to the Police Station where they would receive a due portion of lashes. Throughout the time of the German occupation, the inhabitants were obliged to observe a strict curfew.

During the entire period of German occupation, for the first time the council began to function as an administrative body, dealing with matters of the town. These duties were carried out by local citizens. V. Klimetzki, a Pole, was nominated as Mayor and from the Jewish population the advocate Kalman Hartglas and Chaim Levi Rubinshtein were nominated as aldermen.

[Page 92]

A Peace–Court dealing with civil disputes functioned in the town. The judge was a German officer, Dr Hauser. Kalman Hartglas and Sholem Vinograd would appear as advocates. The assistant–secretary in court was Chaim Barlas. Grinshtein the Jew (Yechiel Hersh's grandson), was appointed bailiff.

The monument in the market place that was erected by the Russian Government to eternalise the transit of the last Russian Czar through the town was removed by the Germans and the metal was transported to Germany.

German occupation lasted until the end of 1918, and after they left the government took over the newly elected Polish State.

The repossession of the town by the Polish Government occurred without incident. When the German army left in the direction of Brisk and a Polish military division entered the town, it was welcomed with music by the Biala Maccabi Orchestra. The German army retreated slowly from the Brisk Circle and because of the rapid advance of the Polish military division there were clashes between the Polish and German military units in a few places. One such incident occurred at Zalessiye [Silesia] where tens of Polish soldiers fell.

Biala again remained a circle–town and was attached to the Lublin military. The following offices existed in the town: the office of the Governor of the province, Circle and Peace– Courts, Finance office, Tax–office, the office of the Polish Government etc.

The Bolshevik invasion in 1920 did not avoid our town which was one of the main arteries through which the Russian army streamed into Warsaw. In the month of August, the town was occupied by the retreating Red Army because of the failure of the Russian offensive in Warsaw; and Biala, after one week of rule by the Red Army, again came under the rule of the Polish Army.

Hitler's world–conflagration that flared up on the 1st September 1939, seized our Biala amongst the first Polish towns because of the local aeroplane factory. Biala was one of the few centres in Poland that was bombed by the German air force immediately after the outbreak of the War.

In the beginning Biala was settled by the Soviet Army but after two weeks' rule, she withdrew and delivered the town into the hands of the Germans. The German occupation of the town lasted until the end of July 1944.

[Page 93]

In every war that cut its way through our town, the Jewish and Polish inhabitants had to endure suffering and pain. This time however, during the murderous rule of the Nazis, the Jewish population was entirely annihilated.

At the end of the 19th century and the beginning of the 20th century, fires and floods in Biala were a fairly frequent phenomenon. We will describe a few of them here:

Approximately in Elul 1883 at noon, a fire broke out that actually destroyed all the houses in the town. The houses at that time were mostly wooden houses. A fire started in Kshiver Street in Mayer Kroch's house next to Ky–yovske's [Kaiyovski's] brick house and ended at Brisk Street at Pizshitz's house.

The fire devoured the house of Ky–yovske [Kaiyovski] up to the church on Reformatzke Street, that means on both sides of Kshive Street; the more distant houses on the left side of Kshive Street (coming from the Volye) up to the Jewish bath house. All that remained was the wooden house on Reformatzke Street where the wash house was later located. The houses on Gimnazye Street, except for the Gimnazye building itself, the houses on Reformatzke Street, except for Klimetzki's house on Yatke Street and in the small streets of the bath house up to the winery, were all destroyed in the fire.

They did not manage to establish the cause of the fire. The Jewish inhabitants lived for a long time in the synagogue and the Chassidic prayer houses. They proceeded to build new wooden houses.

In approximately 1890, one Elul night a fire broke out at the "Deftik" (the name was taken from the fact that at that place a blind horse would constantly walk on a wheel that belonged to the mill), later known as the place of Shimmele (Shimon), the son of Chaye Raize. During the fire, the houses on Shmoller street burned down, and Grabanove Street and Proste Street, except for the Talmud Torah.

At the place where the jail stands today, they quickly made "zemliankes" (earthen huts) and those who were burned settled there for a while. They again proceeded to rebuild the town but this time the government forbade the building of wooden houses and they were only permitted to build houses of stone.

In approximately 1904 on the night of Tishah B'Av, a fire broke out on Proste Street. Amongst others, the houses of Chaim Becker, Shlayme Stop, Yosef Itshe Ash and the winery burnt down.

In 1885 or 1886, Purim time, there was a huge flood in the town. The ice on the river melted and the floating ice–blocks on the river smashed all the bridges on the Volye river. The river overflowed its banks and flooded large areas. Communication between the town and the Volye was severed. The waves carried away a house. There were no human fatalities.

In addition to the frequent fires, in 1892 a plague of Cholera engulfed Poland at that time and brought devastation, sorrow and shock to the town.

The frequent fires and the growth of the population changed the appearance of the town.

Already in 1910 the booths and stalls on the market place (today called Volnoshtshi [Wolnosci] Place) were transferred to the new market. The market place was enlarged so that the centre of the town acquired a more beautiful appearance.

The inhabitants, however, could not grow accustomed to the idea that the market was situated "so far" behind the town, so a large number of the stalls transferred to the yard of Chaim Levi Rubinshtein. This is where a section of the market was situated until 1919 when, according to a decree, the market trade moved over to the new market place.

The town developed rapidly. Already during the German occupation in the 1st World War, when Biala was the seat of the headquarters of the Bug Army, there was an extension to the town, particularly in the suburb of Volye. The Germans brought in a small train that isolated Biala from the surrounding small towns of Yaneve [Janow Podlaski] and Konstantin. They built an electricity station in the winery and Biala saw electric light for the first time. The inhabitants began to enjoy electric light only under Polish rule. The Germans also introduced numbers on the houses.

The "corner" of Volnotshti [Wolnosci] Place (Liberty Square) – the place of the porters of Biala

Intensive building development began in the town only after the end of the Polish–Bolshevik War, mainly after the establishment of the aeroplane factory alongside the Volye, in whose vicinity a new neighbourhood was built.

In 1934 Biala occupied an area of 3200 hectares, of which 350 hectares was used for construction. The rest was agricultural land. In 1878 the number of houses reached 350 and in 1934 there were 1100 houses. In the years between 1926 and 1930, a strong building movement developed. In these years 193 wooden houses were built and 36 stone houses, and together they contained 915 rooms. Thanks to this, Biala did not experience a shortage of housing. The largest number of houses was built on the Volye and only a very small percentage by Jews.

The beginning of the Biala local self–administration dates from the year 1919 when the first elected town council was constitutionalised. The following were the Mayors between 1919 and 1939: Barkovski, Kuchayevski. Klimetski, Zakshevski and Valovski.

Before the 2nd World War the town possessed two electricity stations that were managed by Kavalevski the engineer, in an exemplary way. Biala was preparing to supply electric current to Mezrich and Lukov. On the Brisk highway they built a modern local slaughterhouse with a cool room and a factory producing large blocks of ice.

There were two hospitals in the town – one, the so called hospital of the nuns, and the second – the Jewish one.

In Biala there were 5 cinemas, 4 in the town and one at the Volye. (Before the 1st World War there was one cinema, in the house of Chaim Yoske. Of the most important monuments in the town, it is worthwhile to note:

1.   The monument on the market place that the Poles built from stones to remember the establishment of the government in 1918 (in the place where the Russian monument once stood).
2.   The Krashevski monument (of red granite) on the site of the Gimnazye on the Warsaw highway.
3.   The monument at the barracks of the 34th regiment (of concrete) on the Warsaw highway, in memory of the regiment of soldiers who fell during the war with Russia in 1920.

[Page 94]

Grabanover Street —seen from Proste Street (Winter 1944/5)

The Christian population lived on the periphery of the town and until 1918 were mainly engaged in agriculture. Some worked as clerks and workers in various factories. The Jewish population were engaged in commerce and worked as tradesmen. After the Polish State came into existence in 1918, large parts of the Christian population were employed as clerks in government and local offices, in factories and other enterprises. Some began entering into commerce and learning trades.

The numbers of the population showed no growth between 1827 and 1857. It started to grow recently, as the table below illustrates:

1827	3818 inhabitants
1841	3588 inhabitants
1850	3456 inhabitants
1857	3881 inhabitants
1878	7112 inhabitants
1897	11556 inhabitants
1921	13005 inhabitants
1931	17620 inhabitants
1939	20307 inhabitants

The flood of blood and fire that lasted six years (1939 – 1945) was over. The town of Biala at that time emerged intact and was even beautified during the war. From a few Jewish shops they built one large business with beautiful display windows, but the builders of the town, the Jews, were no longer there, and even the smallest sign that they were once there did not exist. The synagogue and the houses of prayer and study were removed right down to their foundations. The grave stones in the cemetery were taken and the earth was ploughed and sown. The sign with the name of the family on every Jewish house was removed. And in case they would have wanted to erect a memorial on the site of the Jewish cemetery after the war, in memory of the holy ones who perished in that gruesome period, our former Polish neighbours could not bear it; and even the stones, the only trace that Jews once lived here, were destroyed.

We always used to hear this saying from the Christians: "The streets are ours and the houses, yours". Jewish ownership of property would not let them rest. We acquired those properties over generations with so much toil and drudgery. Now they can paraphrase this saying: "The streets are ours and the houses are ours".

Bibliography:

1.   "History of Polish kings" Warsaw 1880
2.   Bogdan Wasiutynsky: "Jewish People in Poland in the 19th and 20th centuries", Warsaw 1930
3.   "Podlassiyer Leben" Independent Social Newspaper of Biala, examples from the years 1926/7 and 1932/4.
4.   Testimonies from: Alter Weinberg, Asher Hoffer, Moshe Reuven, Gedalyahu Braverman and Ya'kov Aronovicz.

[Page 95]

Jews in Biale[*]

by Dr M. Hendl, Tel Aviv

Translated by Libby Raichman

(Their history from the end of the 16th century to the middle of the 19th century)

A. The town of Biale

Old Poland consisted of two parts: Crown–Poland and Lithuania. Biale belonged to Lithuania, lying close to the border between Lithuania and Crown–Poland. In Poland there were two kinds of towns: state towns, whose inhabitants determined the level of development amongst the people, and private towns that were founded by the Polish nobility on their land. Biale was a private town. It was connected to the great princely family of the Radzshivils, who – thanks to their enormous estates, their strong military power and the high positions that they occupied in the running of the state – developed a significant force, that for the most part, had little to do with the government, its laws and decrees. The main centre of the Radzshivil "kingdom" could be found in Ni–esvi–ezsh, but there were times when Biale[1] also occupied a most prominent position.

Among the Radzshivils there were princes who were noted for their outlandish characteristics, and their wild whims were famous throughout the whole of Poland. It is understandable that their reign was a huge scourge for their subjects – Jews and Christians. One summer, one of the Radzshivils had a desire to drive a sledge so he ordered that the path be strewn with salt. Another Radzshivil prince who lacked birds to shoot, sat a Jew in a tree, told him to imitate a bird, and then shot him.

A story is told about one of the Radzshivils (in the 18th century), who had a kind of fantasy of love for Judaism. He chose Jewish advisors; he learned Yiddish and Hebrew and on the Sabbath he used to wear a prayer shawl together with his military awards. His family wanted to restrain him and placed him under strict control – first in the Biale castle and then in Slutsk. But he did not sever his contact with the Jews. The Jews of Slutsk suffered a lot because this. The Rabbi of Slutsk was even imprisoned in the Biale jail. The story only ended with the death of the Judaising sympathiser in 1781.

Historians also mention good rulers, who cared for their subjects and ruled with kindness. The historian Bartoshevicz, who is himself from Biale, writes for example, about the princess Anna. Under her rule Biale was a happy town and a city of refuge for the poor.

The local inhabitants of Biale – Jews and Christians – benefited from the princely court–trade, the work it provided and the economy. On the other hand, the court oppressed the town by placing upon it various burdens and taxes.

Among the institutions that existed in Biale, the Biale Academy must be mentioned separately. It was an educational institution that filled the place between a middle–school and a high–school. The town Jews and Christians were obligated to contribute to the budget of the Academy; but they also profited from it, through trade and contracting. Students were ordered not to contact any of the inhabitants of the town or those passing through, not to offend them by word or deed and not to carry arms without the knowledge of the rector. The fact alone that such a warning was included in the oath of every newly–enrolled student, shows that the relationships were not ideal, and that there were probably some clashes. We know from other towns that the school–youth were in many cases, the cause of anti–Jewish excesses.

The Polish writer Krashevski, who took a great interest in Biale (he studied in the Biale Gimnazye) wrote that the town did not have a rich history: "She lived in herself and for herself". Yet it is worthwhile mentioning that Biale endured a few historical experiences besides the political events in the stormy life of the Polish government and Polish party–conflicts, in which the Radzshivils played a substantial part.

[Page 96]

We will enumerate a few events here:

In 1665, a sitting of the Lithuanian Senate was held in Biale. Three years later the Polish king Jan Kazshimierzsh visited the town. During the North–War (at the beginning of the 18th century) in which Poland sided with Russia against Sweden, the town was run by the Swedish army. In 1789 the German Kaiser Josef the 2nd travelled through the town on his return from a visit to Petersburg. The events mentioned (except for the Swedish occupation) made little impact on the population. However one section of these historical events had a major effect on the town: these were the frequent fires, from which the town suffered in the course of centuries. One has to remember that the town consisted mostly of wooden houses. As the Polish historian Bartoshevicz said: "Biale burned constantly, always burning and always rebuilt anew". After one of these fires that happened at a time of a raging plague (1711) – it was said that in Biale and the surrounding villages a total of 559 Christians souls suffered and according to the declaration of the leaders of the community, Koppel ben Yitzchak and Shmuel ben Meir, the "inhabitants and civilians" – numbered 37 (Jewish) souls.

B. The Biale Community

The Biale Community, with regard to Jewish self–administration, belonged to Brisk (the holy community of Brisk), that together with the communities of Vilna [Vilnius], Pinsk, Grodne [Hrodna] and Slutsk developed the Jewish Autonomous Central–organisation for Lithuania (the committee for the State of Lithuania). In 1705 when the representatives of the communities that belonged to Brisk gathered to divide the state taxes that Jews were compelled to pay in the form of a head–tax, the Biale community had to pay the sum of 510 zlottes[2], the third–largest sum after Brisk [Brest] (1384 zlottes), and Visokke [Vysokaye] (700 zlottes). Those communities who had to contribute less were: Pruzshanne [Pruzhany] (485 zlottes), Vlodavve [Wlodawa] (400 zlottes) and Shedletz [Siedlce] (230 zlottes). From this we have an approximate idea about the place that Biale then occupied among the towns and villages of the Brisk [Brest] Circle.

We do not know exactly when Jews settled in Biale. We are also missing the exact date of the founding of the Biale community[3]. We have the lists of payments between Crown–Poland and Lithuania, in Bielsk and in Lukov from the year 1580[4]. In those lists Jews from the following towns are mentioned: Tiktin [Tykocin], Bielsk, Vengrov [Węgrów] and Kotzk [Kock] and Christians from: Tshechanovtze [Ciechanowiec], Loshitz [Loštice], Bielsk, Kobrin, [Kobryn], Mezrich [Międzyrzec], Brisk [Brest] and Pinsk. They travelled through carrying merchandise from Crown–Poland to Lithuania or vice–versa. However we do not find here even one mention of Biale Jews or Christians. Is this merely a coincidence? We have to accept that specifically in this connection, with the border–trade between both parts of the Polish state, the Jewish settlement in Biale is to be thanked for the existence of this border–trade.

The first known information about Biale Jews, we found out by chance and the incident has a connection to the Land of Israel. A Biale Jew, Reb Uri bar Shimon, emigrated to the Land of Israel at the end of the 16th century and settled in Tsfat [Safed] which at that time was experiencing a period of economic and spiritual prosperity. From there he was sent to Europe to organise the collection of money for the material needs of the Jewish population in the Land of Israel. In 1575 we find Reb Uri in Italy where, for propaganda purposes, he printed a list of the holy graves in the Land of Israel[5].

We do not know who this man Reb Uri was, and when he left Biale. It appears that he was a Jew who was skilled in worldly–matters, and was therefore chosen to be an emissary for the community in Tsfat. No matter what the situation was – thanks to this Reb Uri we can establish that around 1575 a Jewish community already existed in Biale. Here it is worthwhile noting that in regard to missions from the Land of Israel to Jews in the diaspora, Biale occupied an important place: the greatest and most important emissary, Reb Chaim Yosef Dovid Azoulai who lived in the 18th century, was the grandson of a Biale resident; we will talk about this in further chapters.

We have actual knowledge about Biale Jews for the first time in 1621. This shows that in this year Jewish settlement in Biale was already well established. As in other Polish towns, also here, conflict between the Christian and Jewish populations increased, with regard to dwelling rights, trade, employment and taxation.

The nobleman, Prince Radzshivil, was forced to regulate in an official document, laws that would alleviate the conflict. From this very document we learn about a series of important details regarding the situation of the Biale community.

[Page 97]

The Biale Jews had earlier privileges from the court even before 1621, according to which they were freed from various payments to the nobleman's court; they were obligated to pay 6 groshen annually for local needs. Their main employment was in trade. As the most important trading place was the central point of the town, i.e. the "Rynek", [market place] it is understandable that they lived mainly in the houses that stood there. From now however, i.e. from 1621, they were forbidden to continue to settle on the "Rynek" and in the whole town they were not allowed to possess more than 30 houses in total and specifically, small houses (that means: single–family houses that occupy not more than one plot for each house). It was explicitly stressed that here in these 30 houses, free trade could be conducted and only the occupants of the 30 houses could enjoy the privilege of being free from the payments to the court and from the right to pay the local treasury not more than 6 groshen per year. And now comes an important point, that shows that the number of Jews that lived in Biale was much larger; the clause reads like this: "If however it would turn out that Jews in Biale own more than 30 houses, then the Jews of these houses would bear all the taxes (landowners and local) equal to the Christian population.".

The picture it seems, is quite clear: a community of more than 30 families, whose members live in their own houses, mainly in the "Rynek" and are engaged in trade. It must be assumed that this was the general situation during the 17th century: with the passing of time however, the number of Jews and their houses grew considerably, as we will see in further chapters.

How did Biale Jews live and maintain their relationships with the town and with the landowner? What was their economic situation? We will learn the exact details from later events. Here we will end with the legal position of the community.

It appears that the autonomy of the community was severely restricted and the court intervened in all the details of community life: the budget had to be presented to the court and even in regard to appointing a Rabbi, they meddled; they even took upon themselves the right to depose a Rabbi, if they did not like him and to nominate a new one in whom they had more trust. This was at least the situation in the 18th century. One can assume that it was most probable that the situation was better in earlier times. In the course of time the number of Jews increased and the conflicts with the Christian population became more acute. Anti–Semitism became stronger and more aggressive in aggravated economic situations, and also in the climate of growing religious fanaticism. The economic position of the entire Polish Jewry was strongly undermined in the second half of the 17th century. So it is therefore no wonder that the social and legal situation of the Jews also became worse, and as a result Jewish autonomy was restricted. Here we will compare two contracts that the Biale court made with Jews, that took into consideration the income that the lessees earned from managing the Biale noblemen's estates; one in 1645 and one in 1736. The first contract concerned a Jew, Pinchas ben Shmuel, from Brisk who received the right to judge with full legal power the peasant population of the Biale estates ("the gentleman lessee[6]himself or his official"); but in the case of a punishment that could lead to the death penalty, the landowner secured the right to provide a judge from his side. Even in situations where free landowners were being judged, Reb Pinchas had the right to propose a judge from his side (a nobleman landowner). In contrast, in the contract with the "General–Treasurer" named Shmuel ben Yitzchak (a Biale resident) of 1736 it means explicitly: "in the case of a severe punishment, the agent Reb Shmuel, may not judge or sentence the subject and no Jewish hand may touch a Christian". The difference, it seems, is clear and does not need further explanation.

Now let us see how restrictions on Jewish autonomy in the 18th century impacted on their lives. Legal acts demonstrate to us four important examples regarding this matter: two from 1736 and two from 1763 to 1765. In 1736 Princess Anna began to "make arrangements" in the Biale community and ordered the above–mentioned General–Treasurer Shmuel ben Yitzchak to look into all community matters, and "prepare the budget of income and expenditure". Under threat of serious punishment she ordered the community to present to Shmuel all the lists and all other acts and papers, follow all his orders and "not to do a single thing without his knowledge". Reb Shmuel received the right to depose the elected community committee and nominate another in the event of the community not obeying his orders. The princess announced these decrees in the synagogue so that from then on everyone would know what she expected regarding the community management committee. It must be added that the decrees contained one item that showed that the highly regarded, just princess had good intentions in championing the cause of the poorer classes of the Biale community.

[Page 98]

She specifically stressed in the decree that the budget must be constructed in such a way that the rich should not be privileged at the expense of the poor and that one must not suffer for the good of the other. We have here a clear indication of the social contrast of the reign of the wealthy in the Jewish communities in the 18th century at the expense of the poorer classes. According to the historians, this situation contributed a lot to the downfall and ruin of the Jewish autonomy. Whether our Reb Shmuel maintained the social detail of the princess's decree cannot be ascertained but we do have a certain indication. In 1748/9 Reb Shmuel allegedly paid not more than 15 zlottes in tax (in fact he paid not more than 9 zlottes) and in the year 1749/50 he paid even less, not more than 7 zlottes. Reb Shmuel was certainly a rich Jew; his position as General–Treasurer of the court must have without doubt given him a substantial income, and if so – and if he still had his former legal power in the years 1748 – 1750 – then one might ask, why does he pay so little when others are paying sums of more than 250 zlottes?

Let us now see how the aforementioned decree of the princess worked. It appears that there was an uproar in the community as they did not want to give in to Shmuel, the princess's lessee and General–Treasurer, and as one can imagine, they decided to excommunicate him. The princess, however, was resolute in her dealings. For her it was not a question of Jewish autonomy or not Jewish autonomy. For her that was not the fundamental issue. She was more interested in her income. A community that dares to rebel against her is, from a fiscal point of view, not a loyal subject and must therefore be severely punished. Three days after announcing the aforementioned decree (9th September 1736) about the legal power of Reb Shmuel, the princess deposed the Rabbi and imposed upon him a considerable fine of 100 red gulden[7]. Reb Shmuel was given the legal authority to appoint a new Rabbi and bring order to the community. As an introduction to this very ruling, the princess specifically said that the reason is a fiscal one; that the transfer of the lease to the General–Treasurer (by this she meant also the supervision of the community's economy) was done with the purpose of assuring her, the princess, of an income from the Jews. She also said that the community, as well as the Rabbi, wanted to reduce her income. We see therefore that the community was in her eyes, merely an object, as were all her other possessions. How long Reb Shmuel ben Yitzchak's reign lasted is unknown. From a chance article in a German newspaper, we learn that in 1751 he had already passed away.

In 1763 we are faced with new information about the aristocratic rule over the community. The prince informed them that "from various places people spoke to him in praise of the scholarship and humility of the Jew Reb Yosef ben Ya'akov and he therefore nominated him as Rabbi of the Biale community." He transferred to his hands the authority to judge and carry out sentencing and reserved the right to be an appellate judge. The appointment was for six years (that means until 1769). The new Rabbi (unfortunately we know nothing about him) wanted to be secure in his new position, for which he was surely well paid and – after prolonged negotiations – he received, in 1765, an official confirmation of his position from the highest state official, from the very Interior Minister himself.

C. Biale Jews and their economic situation in the middle of the 18th century

The number of Jews in Biale amounted to approximately 200 families in the mid–18th century. 110 families lived in their own homes and approximately 90 families as "komornikkes" (tenants) who lived with strangers. Assuming that each family averaged 5 souls – man, woman and children – we reach the sum of approximately 1000 souls. One must remember that the statistical figures for those times were not clear and therefore not accurate. In one list, the number of residents in Volye (a suburb of Biale) were counted together with the Biale residents and in another list – not. In one list the Jews of Biale, Dokudov (the village of Dokudovve) and in the surrounding villages are calculated together and in another – only Biale. In one list the whole Jewish population is counted plus all the children and in another, only the children over 10 years of age were included. One list speaks about houses and another – about families or house-owners. The fires and plagues, on the other hand, often altered the numbers. The assertion that in the mid–18th century, Biale had 1000 souls is only an assumption that approaches the truth but it is not an accurate one. In each case it appears that Biale was considered not as a small town in regard to the Jewish population. We know, for example, that in 1764 the community of Lublin (the town only, not counting the surrounding villages) numbered 1383 souls; the Lukov community – 543, Radzin [Radzyń]– 537, Shedletz [Siedlce] – 332, Krashnik [Kraśnik] – 921, not counting children under one year of age. Compared to these towns Biale can be considered a large community.

We have a list from 1742 of Biale residents, also according to the streets, and though this list is not a precise one, yet it gives us a picture of the Biale population.

[Page 99]

The Biale population according to the streets

Name of street	Houses		Families	
	Christian	Jewish	Christian	Jewish
Rynek (Street of Market)	14	17	14	18
Briske (a)[a]	20	22	24	34
Reformatn	15		22	
From Blonye to the market	23	2	27	3
From Reformatn to Volve	6		9	
From Reformatn to Yurizditshne[b]	6	–	8	–
Lublin	7	–	8	–
Lublin Yureditshne (b)	15	–	18	–
Piebonsk behind the Farre	15	–	17	–
From Church, at the back	6	–	6	–
In the town from Piebanshtshizne	7	4	9	6
Mezritsh	31	7	35	10
Garntsarske	17	–	18	–
Loshitze	16	22	17	28
Yanover	25	1	29	1
Zashkolne from Yanover (c)[c]	–	24	–	45
Total	242	112	281	166

What do we learn from this list? Let us draw a few conclusions:

a. 447 families lived in Biale in 1742, of which the Jews were about 37%. We know that in the 19th century the number of Jews grew significantly and outnumbered the Christians.

b. In Biale there were 354 houses (excluding Volye), of which the Jews occupied 32%.

c. In every Jewish house lived 1.36 families; in every Christian house – 1.16 families.

d. The Jews lived in almost every street, but they were concentrated mainly at the "Rynek" (market place), on Briske Street, on Loshitze Street and in the vicinity of the synagogue. In the streets where no Jews lived, the houses were occupied mainly by public servants; that means that in those houses families of the court–servants lived, or they were also inhabited to some extent by Christians (with one exception, of Garntsarske Street where only Christians lived).

e. Generally Christians lived together with Jews but in a certain circle around the synagogue, there was not one Christian house.

Let us now see how Jewish people made a living, what their occupations were. The list from 1742 does not give us an entirely precise picture, yet the indications are quite clear. Not less than 53 income earners of the 166 Jewish families were tradesmen (approximately one third). Tailors and cap–makers as amongst all Polish Jewry at that time, occupied first place – 22 tailors and cap–makers amongst 53 tradesmen (approximately 42%). Amongst the other tradesmen there were: lace makers, goldsmiths, boiler makers, bookbinders, turners, metal workers, glaziers and understandably, also butchers. Before 1748 the following were also listed: wagon drivers, bakers, stone cutters and free occupations such as: musicians and medical assistants. Of the non–working population, the Rabbi occupied himself with trade and inn–keeping[8]. The rich conducted greater farming trade with the town and with the court, and also acquired an income by leasing land owned by the nobility of the surrounding estates.

Footnotes:

(a) The Jewish hospital is located here
(b) The Christian hospital is located here
(c) The synagogue is located here

[Page 100]

Jews bought agricultural products from the court and added various products for its maintenance. We find in the various accounts in the statutes that the court was not always punctual in paying their debts. Here we have a list of the debts (from 1791) that the court owed merchants and tradesmen: 4716 zlottes for supplies of milk, wax, coffee and meat; debts for other provisions – a sum of 8000 zlottes; debts for work completed – a sum of 2836 zlottes (that included tailors and cap makers 869 zlottes, the turner – 1384 zlottes), and in addition a whole list of other smaller and larger debts.

An interesting example of how the court did not pay its debts can be seen in the accounts for the year 1780. That year the court owed the community 3756 zlottes for additional wax[9]. The community received 400 zlottes in cash and to the value of 900 zlottes, it received 40,000 bricks. The Prince undertook to pay the remaining 2456 zlottes by the end of the year, but in fact we still find that debt in 1795 amongst the other 5000 zlottes of debt that accrued in the course of the years. In order to reduce the debt, the prince declared that he was prepared to deduct 500 zlottes annually from the sum that Jews pay him for the meat tax[10].

The differentiation in community–membership from the point of view of their material possessions we can see with the support of a tax list from the mid–18th century. One must however remember that also here the preciseness is not entirely certain. We know that also today the tax burden is not an altogether exact reflection of the true situation of the taxpayer. In a certain sense, however, we do have from the list an approximate picture of the situation. We have here before us a list of 214 taxpayers that takes into consideration almost all the taxes for 1749/50.

Taxpayers

Those who paid nothing	27
Those who paid up to 1 zlotte	3
Those who paid 2 – 5 zlottes	26
Those who paid 6 – 10 zlottes	46
Those who paid 11 – 15 zlottes	25
Those who paid 16 – 20 zlottes	25
Those who paid 21 – 30 zlottes	20
Those who paid 31 – 40 zlottes	12
Those who paid 41 – 50 zlottes	9
Those who paid 51 to 60 zlottes	8
Those who paid 61 – 70 zlottes	3
Those who paid 71 – 80 zlottes	2
Those who paid 81 – 90 zlottes	1
Those who paid 91 – 100 zlottes	1
Those who paid 101 – 150 zlottes	3
Those who paid 151 – 200 zlottes	1
Those who paid 201 – 250 zlottes	1
Those who paid more than 250 zlottes	1
A total of	214

Considering the payment of up to 5 zlottes for the poor, up to 40 zlottes – for middle–income earners, up to 100 zlottes – for the rich, more than 100 zlottes – for the very rich – we have here the following income levels in Biale:

Poor	56	26.2%
Middle income	128	59.8%
Rich	24	11.2%
Very rich	6	2.8%
	214	100%

It is worthwhile mentioning amongst those belonging to the middle income group, we find many tradesmen.

D. The community budget in the mid–18th century

From these details we can understand the general situation of the community and its members. We will have an exact picture of the functioning community machine, its competency and relationship with those in power: the court, the state and the town, by analysing the budget of the community – its income and expenditure. As the budget of a private person is known, so too, in greater measure, is the budget of a public–societal corporate body, one of the most reliable indications of its situation, its needs, its aspirations and wishes. We will pause here at a budget for the year 1748/49 ("of the holy year 1748 until the holy year 1749"[11]), and analyse its particular position and compare information of other years. It does not have to depend on the fact that the budget bears a Christian date and not a Jewish date (from Tishrei to Tishrei or from Nissan to Nissan). It is a clear indication that the economy of the community is not purely a Jewish venture but a "partnership" with the master, the landowner, who is the underlying influence on the community. Firstly let us see the figures and then we will stop to look at their significance from a fiscal and economic point of view.

[Page 101]

The Biale community budget for 1748/9

Income

	zlotte
Direct taxes (possession and head–tax)	3133
House tax	661
Director's tax from the leases in the villages and estates that belong to Biale	604
Income tax from small trade	900
Meat tax (Korobke)	3225
A separate tax to cover the loss of money from the noblemen's promissory notes	231
Income from the Mikveh (ritual pool) and the bath house	150
Fines	15
Payments from free places	30
Loans	1079
Total	10028

Expenditure

State taxes	1035
Payments to the court	2609
Payments to the Catholic Clergy	2534
Separate gifts for the court and for the Catholic Clergy	365
Payments to the town council	112
For our own Jewish needs	1467
Various expenses	529
Debts and interest	2075
Repairs	342
Total	11,068

Before we begin to explain the meaning of every entry, we must say a few words about the procedure for the community house–keeping. Outwardly the community was conducted as a single body, and the community was the official representative and mediator between every individual and every external government organisation. On tax issues, that means, every burden, every obligation and responsibility did not lie with the individual, but with the community. The community had three ways of collecting the necessary money:

    a.   by imposing direct taxes – according to the assets of the individual committee members.
    b.   by imposing indirect taxes on unused articles as, for example, meat.
    c.   when both sources did not suffice, the community had to go into debt, borrowing money from Christians or from Jews – at high rates of interest, incurring debt in this way for future years, that might perhaps be better. The Biale community operated in these three ways as did other Polish communities.

In order to impose direct taxes, they used to elect an assessing committee (assessors) and they would, according to specific procedures, impose the tax. Unfortunately the community book of records does not exist so we do not know how the assessment committee functioned in Biale. In any case, one must remember that the direct tax also served as a key to political and social rights, and only the highly taxed had the privilege to vote or to be voted on to various organisations of community management and administration. The executive committee that collected taxes were the trustees and the beadles; and it appears that they also received help from the court personnel.

The indirect taxes were leased by the community and the lease–holder had his income from them. Sometimes the lease–holders were in trouble, when the court imposed too high an assessment of the lease–money, or it expected assurance of the punctual delivery of meat for daily use. In this way, for example, the community paid a one–off sum of 60 zlottes to bribe the landowner's supervisor, so that he should not in these cases, punish the lease–holder.

And now we will see what each item means, firstly – the expenses.

Jews paid the government two kinds of taxes: a house tax that amounted to 8 zlottes, approximately, from each house (paid in two instalments): A. in the budget year that we are speaking about here, 70 houses were taxed (the sum of the tax amounted to around 537 zlottes). B. a head tax, that according to its value, the Biale community had to negotiate with the Brisk community, and through its mediation, the state –treasury was paid. In 1748/49 the head–tax came to 498 zlottes. This method continued until 1764. In this year Jewish Central autonomy was abolished, and the head–tax was imposed personally on each individual for the amount of two zlottes annually for each soul, except for children under one year of age.

The community paid the court various amounts that were of a threefold nature. One kind of payment was actually disbursements by the court for members of the community, as for example, interest on the plots of the Jewish houses. The other kind – those were various gifts for various occasions. The third kind – those were payments, that according to the feudal system that ruled Poland then, and also almost the whole of Europe – all its subjects, first and foremost the farmers, were forced to make payments in favour of the nobility.

[Page 102]

Of the 2609 zlottes paid to the court, actually only 609 zlottes were evident as a fee for actual payments in favour of the Jewish taxpayer. The rest, as much as 2000 zlottes (and perhaps more than that) were payments of the second and third kind. Let us list a few situations: spanning a horse to a wagon "for various court needs (twice to Warsaw)"; horse and cart for various field work; repairing the fences and field gates; light for the main guard and other guards of the court; to approve once again Jewish rights; gifts for Christmas and Easter; money for good wishes for a birthday and other similar occasions of this kind. To this list also belongs the not small charge of 808 zlottes that the community had to pay the court to compensate for the devaluation of the Polish currency. Various rates of exchange circulated in Poland and there was no stable mutual rate of exchange. The people of the Biale court garrison received their salaries at a good rate of exchange and the Jews were obligated to pay the difference between a good and bad rate. There were still a few situations that were difficult to decide – whether they belonged to the first kind of payment or to the second and third. Therefore the reader should decide where he wants to insert the expenses that are written in the following columns:

"For bringing order when many Jews, simple folk, did not want to pay any taxes and payments according to the existing custom".

"For lawsuits with small dealers, male and female, who did not want to pay what belonged according to old customs and agreements".

"For bringing order when the community did not want to buy corn and oats, that the court obligated them to buy".

"Bribing an officer to treat fairly one of the representatives of the community that was in prison".

"To support other Jewish prisoners who are serving prison sentences in the castle–prison".

We see that the court made the Jews pay harshly for the favour of allowing them to live in Biale. The court knew well how to secure its income, without considering other financial obligations with which the Biale Jews were burdened. We hear, for example, that in 1849/50, Biale Jews approached the Brisk community to arrange to pay only 340 zlottes head–tax (instead of 498 zlottes). As the Biale Jews would not, or could not, pay the general head–tax that was imposed on the entire Polish Jewry, other communities had to pay the sum as the court would not forego its income from the Jewish population and demanded payment to the last cent.

A small portion of the payments to the Catholic clergy was interest on loans taken, but they were mainly for gifts for various priests and churches, for nuns and monks; for the Academy, its rector, its professors and its students; for the Home for the Aged that was located in one of the Biale churches (a full 336 zlottes), for light and milk in the churches. All these payments, that exceed by more than 1000 zlottes the funds required for the needs of the community, are clear evidence of the Feudal system in which the Christian clergy enjoyed the same privileged position as the nobility. The leadership of the clergy also belonged to the noble classes, possessing large tracts of land.

With regard to the town, the community was quite independent of it. The town and the community were two units that were under the court, but each on its own. Yet the town was more privileged, as the community had also to give gifts to the town leadership and assist in maintaining the town administration; the mayor, the chimney–sweep and others.

The needs of the Jewish community (1467 zlottes) amounted to not more than 13.25% of the whole budget. That says a lot and needs no further explanation. If we should include in our calculations part of the expenses that figure in the budget as "various expenses", the picture would change very little.

Among the Jewish expenses, the salaries of the religious ministrants take the highest place. The Rabbi receives 360 zlottes, besides his house; the trustee 224 zlottes; the town–preacher 156 zlottes. Then there are beadles, the treasurer that is concerned with social assistance and distributes "allowances"[12] to the poor, the slaughterer, the cantor and singers, community officials and finally – the community night–watchman. The community employees receive, besides salaries, also payments in kind, like meat for the festivals, and some receive boots.

It is worthwhile mentioning that the community was not punctual or consistent in its payments of their employees because their finances did not allow it. So the Rabbi, for example, received (in the year that we are discussing) only 166 zlottes (in the next year only 93 zlottes); the preacher only 57 zlottes etc. The community was prompt in covering expenses of other kinds because the authorities did not keep quiet.

[Page 103]

The salaries paid amounted to 969 zlottes i.e. approximately 2/3 of the expenses for purely Jewish needs. Another important aspect concerns social help: donations and support for travelling Jews passing through and particularly preachers. All these preachers who passed through Biale were given support by the community and besides that, a wagon, to go further. In our budget–year, Biale was visited by no less than 26 preachers (from: Horchov [Horokhiv], Kurov [Kurów], Lemberg [Lviv], Pintshev [Pińczów], Ostre [Ostroh], Pshemishl [Przemyśl], Yavorov [Yaroriv], Slutsk, Radzin, and Tiktin [Tykocin]). Biale receives Yeshiva–students from other towns, it assists poor widows with making a wedding, it receives emissaries from the Land of Israel, or a cantor, a messenger from the Brisk community who comes to collect the head–tax or a poor Jew who arrives in town, either from Poland or from a foreign country (in our budget–year, two emissaries come to collect donations from as far as Prague) – each one turns to the community representative[13] for a donation and the community does not refuse.

In 1748 a sum of 234 zlottes was collected for small donations. The community did not give this willingly, particularly as the preliminary budget that the nobleman put together, did not foresee this kind of expense. The community sent a special delegation to Brisk [Brest] to find a solution and requested that they not send so many preachers and random poor people through Biale. This helped a little (in 1749 only 66 zlottes were spent for this purpose). In later years, however, the number of people seeking hand–outs grew larger, because the need was great and Jews were impoverished[14].

A third aspect of the expenses were of a representative nature. The community had to present well and it was a custom that if an important visitor came to town, a rabbi, a cantor or just a communal worker, then the community representative would honour him and entertain him with liquor. Of these individual aspects one can imagine that at most, the community representative could send two bottles of mead (at 19 groshen a bottle). Jews would often come from other Radzshivil towns to take care of various matters at the court and this also cost the community a significant expense –in 1748, 24 zlottes and a year later 34 zlottes. It was also customary for the community to send liquor on the occasion of a wedding in the family of one of the leaders of the community. In 1748, eight weddings cost the community 14 zlottes.

A fourth aspect was administrative–expenses like: liquor for the assessors that arrange the taxes, for the selectors that carry out the community elections, contract money when leasing the meat–tax, renovations to the ritual bath–house, religious items, community butcheries etc.

Finally there were also the expenses of covering debts and paying interest. This issue plays an important part in the history of Polish Jewry in the 18th century. With the growth in poverty (the large number of wandering preachers serves as certain proof of this) and the rising taxes, the amount of debt also increased. In this way, for example, it reveals when the central Jewish autonomy was abolished (in 1764) that the debt of the Polish Jewish representation reached an amount of 2½ million zlottes. We do not know exactly what the situation was regarding the Biale community. On the grounds of the little evidence that is available to us, it can be assumed that Biale was not largely in the wrong and that the court kept a firm hand on the community and did·not allow it to create new debts. If it was apparent that a loan was absolutely necessary, then the court expected an exact account. This is what occurred in 1745, when the community wanted to borrow a sum of 3000 zlottes from the priest of Vohin.

And another explanation about the sum of 342 zlottes that appears at the end: "renovation" (deficit). This was the amount submitted as the income from taxes that had to flow in according to the "lists" that the assessors drew up; in actual fact a number of payers remained owing, others died or left Biale and the community had to write off that income. It did that by its own initiative or according to a draft from the court. All these write–offs (62 of them) were recorded as expenditure. In 1748 the deficit amounted to 342 zlottes from an original 5529 zlottes (from direct taxes and additional taxes to cover the debt arising from the rates of exchange of the court funds), therefore hardly 6.2%. We will still add that amongst the 62 cases of write–offs there were: 8 cases from Jews who left Biale, 6 cases where the debtor died, 5 cases where the court itself decided to write off the debt, 2 cases where the write–off occurred in connection with honoured members of the community, that were according to a community law or according to an order from the court freed from the tax; and finally 2 more cases in which the money apparently flowed in, in the form of registered work on the part of the payers in favour of the court – we will then come to the conclusion that the tax system worked well and it was difficult to free oneself from it. This is how it must have been, because the government–supervisor, the nobleman, involved himself in every detail and saw to it that everything was in order. So, for example, we see a fact from 1742, when a contract was sealed with the lessee of the meat tax and the court immediately put out an account of how the money was to be spent. Just as this or the other expense amounted to 55 zlottes more than the income from the lease of the meat–tax, the court ordered that this amount should be regarded by the lessee as a tax. Evidently the lessee had to deposit the whole sum of the preliminary expenses into the hands of the nobleman.

[Page 104]

Going over to the income, we immediately see that the direct taxes are foremost. When we divide the income into four sections we have this picture:

	Zlottes	**%**
Direct taxes	5529	55.1
Indirect taxes	3225	32.1
Loans	1079	10.8
Other small income	195	2.0
Total	10028	100

According to modern conceptions of the politics of a budget of a public corporate body, it can be assumed that the Biale community–budget was a progressive one, from the fact that it attempted to lessen the income from indirect taxes. It is only a question whether the burden of the direct taxes was correctly divided, so that the rich paid more and the poor – less.

Now we come to the balance. We see that the budget left a deficit of 1040 zlottes. The situation will become clearer if we look at the relationship of the situation in 1748/9 and also consider the economy of the community for the year 1749/50. For these two years we find in the legal acts a court document that looks like a preliminary one, that was put together by the court commission. The preliminary estimation for both years can be seen here:

Zlottes	
Income Not specified	Total: 18434
Expenditure	
For the clergy	5045
Government taxes	2712
Horse and cart, materials for the court – for covering the deficit of the rate of exchange for the court	1074
Light for the main guard of the court	86
Payment for houses and places	83
For the executioner	74
For the chimney–sweeper	156
Gifts for the Christian holidays	600
Salary for the Rabbi	720
Salary for the beadle	312
Salary for the trustee	312
Salary for the cantor	416
Gifts for the above for the Jewish festivals	200
Total	12582
Therefore there remains a surplus of	5852

In fact the situation was quite different. Here the court is granted a sum of 2409 zlottes for the two years (dividing the amount for the Christian holidays in two parts, half for the court and half for the clergy), but from the previous analysis, we know, that in the year 1748/9 alone, the court received a sum of 2609 zlottes and a half from the separate gifts, 182 zlottes, therefore together 2791 zlottes. The preliminary estimate is therefore not realistic, because the court kept secret a fine sum of money as it was sure that it would receive it anyway. As opposed to that the court ignored the actual Jewish expenditure. In 1748/9 alone, the community spent 1467 zlottes on Jewish needs. In two years the expenses should therefore amount to 2934 zlottes and not 1960 zlottes, as is stated in the preliminaries (Rabbi, beadle, trustee, cantor and gifts for them).

The actual account is presented in reality here:

	Income zlottes	Expenditure zlottes
1748/9	10028	11068
1749/50	10214	8940
Total	20242	20008

It is evident that the surplus for both years is only 234 zlottes and not 5852 zlottes. Also this surplus is only on paper. The loan of 1079 zlottes of the year 1748/9 is not covered; the debts from the salaries of the community employees were not paid; and in the year 1749 the community took new loans: from the priests 350 zlottes, from Shmuel the shopkeeper 105 zlottes, from Yosye the tailor 321 zlottes – altogether 776 zlottes. And another interesting fact: in 1749/50 the community found itself forced to burden the budget of the synagogue, of the Burial Society (Chevra Kadishah) and also the tailors' society with a combined sum of 245 zlottes. How can one speak of a surplus? And where is the money to cover the debts from the years before 1748/9? Something is therefore not right here. The court knows this full well but it ignores it and does not want to forego its income. The Jews know this well. They moan, they bargain, they rebel, they go to jail, make various combinations and money transactions, but the court is in possession – and Jews pay, pay more than they can. A hole in the year is covered with a patch and the hole in the patch is covered with a new patch.

[Page 105]

One must add that the above budget expenditure does not include all the Jewish expenditure. Jews also paid membership taxation to the Burial Society and to the Tailors' Society to maintain the hospital and the Society for Visiting the Sick (Bikkur Cholim); the Jews who live in the "Rynek" make separate individual payments to the court and the town; for inn–keeping – a separate individual payment to the court and the government; Jews that sell footwear and leather pay a separate tax to the Shoemaker's guild. If we add to this expenses after a fire, expenses after a plague, expenses from separate events in the life of the state, the court, the community and general happenings that affected the whole of Polish Jewry – we have a picture of how difficult and bitter their situation was. The struggle to exist was hard and tough but Jews endured the struggle with honour.

E. Events in Jewish life

The internal life of the Biale community did not differ from the lives of other Jewish communities: trading and peddling, the pains of raising children, learning Hebrew and Yiddish, rabbinical college, synagogue, small and large community disputes, Rabbis and others holding religious positions, disputes with the town council and with the court of the nobleman, suffering from living in the diaspora and hope for the coming of the Messiah – this was the arena in which daily Jewish life functioned. But apart from this the Biale community had to record three events of general Jewish significance, in which Biale Jews played a specific role, and in the last two, a major role. All three events were linked with the furore that ruled the whole of Jewry in general, and Polish Jewry in particular, in the 18th century.

In 1666 Shabtai Tzvi took on the Islamic faith and it was hoped that with this, his mission had come to an end. In truth however, it was different. His followers did not retract, they saw in his conversion a means of concealing the redemption that would come soon. In the following decades, there appear in various countries, and to a great extent in Poland, miracle–workers and prophets that urged the end, who called for repentance and faith in the coming redemption. And as the general situation of the people was an oppressed one, it is no wonder that they found many followers. The belief in Shabtai Tzvi and in his mission as a Messiah was reawakened and a violent struggle ensued in Jewish life.

One of the leaders of the anticipation of the coming of the Messiah was a Jew from Shedletz [Siedlce], Reb Yehuda Chossid, who together with another Polish Jew, Chaim Malach, organised a large emigration to the Land of Israel. Among the emigrants were ardent followers of Shabtai Tzvi as well as ordinary believers, who wanted by the ethical way in which they conducted their lives, by repentance and torment, by attaching their path in life to the land of Israel, to pave the way for deliverance. When they left Poland the group numbered 120 souls, then it grew to 1500 souls, of which about 500 died on route. After a long period of wandering over Austria, Hungary, Germany and Italy that lasted a whole year, the remaining Jews arrived in Jerusalem on Rosh Chodesh Cheshvan 5461 (October1700). But luck was not in their favour. Five days after arriving in Jerusalem, Reb Yehuda Chossid died. The material situation of the emigrants was a very difficult one. Many of them fell into despair, and the result was, that part of them converted (those were the ardent followers of Shabtai Tzvi) and part of them returned to Europe. But those for whom the emigration to the Land of Israel was a religious and nationalistic life choice, remained, hoping for better times. Among those who remained was Reb Yosef Bialer.

It is quite natural that the movement that left Shedletz [Siedlce] had an impact on Biale. We do not know how many Biale Jews were amongst the emigres, but we know two of them by name: one, Reb Zalman Bialer, died immediately after his arrival in Jerusalem and he was buried on the same day as Reb Yehuda Chossid[15], and the second, the above mentioned Reb Yosef Bialer, for whom the emigration to the Land of Israel was a true beginning of a new life of holiness and purity.

In 1712 a group of immigrants from Italy arrived in Jerusalem under the leadership of the kabbalist Reb Avrom Raviga from the city of Modena. In the group we find Shabtai Tzvi followers on the one hand, and on the other, Jews who were believers, who wanted to find in the land of Israel a way of improving their personal, general religious lives and nationalistic aspirations. In the intermediate weekdays of the festival of Passover 5462 (April 1702) Reb Avrom established a yeshivah and among the ten elected members who were to educate the minds and hearts of the yeshivah students, we find our Reb Yosef (besides him, we find amongst them another five Polish Jews from the Reb Yehuda Chossid group: a Jew from Kalish [Kalush], from Opotshne [Opoczno], from Semiatitsh [Siemiatycze], from Lukov [Lukow] and also the son–in–law of Reb Yehuda Chossid). The ten selected members had to sit " – – nights and days, – – and in their prayers, they called out and cried and confessed with their broken and depressed hearts until they pierced the heavens – – and immediately after their prayers, in holiness and purity, with the tallit and tefillin on their heads, they chose to study the book of the Zohar, and after that the writings of (Haari)[16] the kabbalist Rabbi Yitzchak Luria until the time of the afternoon prayers"[17]. In this way through the personality of Reb Yosef who had a large following, there was a large emigration.

[Page 106]

We know nothing of his later life, but there is an opinion that he was a familiar personality in the Land of Israel and that he proved to be one of the respected Sephardic leaders. Reb Azoulai formed a relationship with him by taking his daughter as a daughter–in–law. This marriage produced a son Chaim–Yosef–David, and the Biale grandson Reb Chaim Yosef David, born in 1724 in Jerusalem, died in Livorno, Italy, in 1806 and is famous to this day as one of the most important emissaries[18], as a great scholar and bibliographer. He wrote more than a hundred books, amongst them a bibliographical lexicon called "The Great Names" and a book of memories, "A Good Circle", about his journeys in Europe and North Africa as an emissary for the Land of Israel.

His first mission took place between 1753 and 1758 when he wandered through Italy, Germany, Holland, England and France. His second mission took place between the years 1772 and 1778. That time he visited Tunisia, Italy, France, Belgium and Holland. To all those places he brought living greetings from the Land of Israel and aroused an interest in the land and encouraged a preparedness to help the settlement there. He searched and found hand–written books and printed books. What a pity that he did not visit Poland; it is possible that he would have given us some information about his mother–town, Biale. It is evident that he had a keen eye and a talented quill to describe everything that he saw, and he presented it with full richness in his book of travels "A Good Circle". In Kislev 5515 (1756) while staying in the west German town of Cleve, he found an aunt there " – – a sister of his mother, she is Mrs Gitli the daughter of Meilech my master, the elder, the Rabbi, the pious Kabbalist, man of God, holy, our teacher, Rabbi Yosef Biali, may his memory be blessed – –"[19].

In 1756, however, our Reb Yosef had already died. Unfortunately we cannot dwell any longer on the interesting personality of Reb Yosef Bialer. We do not know about his life before his emigration, about his life in Jerusalem and his ties to his father's home–town, while staying in Jerusalem.

The second great event to affect Jewish life in general, and in which Biale Jews played a large part, almost the main part, was their connection to the renewed turmoil surrounding Shabtai Tzvi.

In the middle of the 18th century the entire Jewish world was stirred up because of the suspicion that fell on the Rabbi of Hamburg, Reb Yonatan Aybeshitz, one of the greatest rabbinic authorities of that time, that he had leanings towards the views of Shabtai Tzvi. The Jewish rabbinical and social world fell into two camps: one that sided with Rabbi Yonatan Aybeshitz and cleared him of every harm and suspicion, and the second, that denounced him on the grounds that he distributed amulets to children and the sick, claiming that he did this with signs and wonders. They tried to prove that Reb Yonatan was lost to heresy, and if so, he must be persecuted, excommunicated and deposed as a Rabbi.

The leader of those opposed to Reb Yonatan was Reb Yaakov Emdin, the son of the wise man Tzvi Ashkenazi, the former Rabbi of Hamburg. Reb Yaakov ben Tzvi Emdin lived in Altona (one of the parts of the Hamburg community) and there he stirred up a stormy life and death battle against Reb Yonatan. He set himself the objective, just like his deceased father, to root out all the bad elements of Shabtai Tzvi'ism. For both parties it was outwardly important to win the sympathy and support of the autonomous organisations of Polish Jewry, whose authority was recognised not only in Poland but also in the entire Jewish world. With Yaakov ben Tzvi Emdin, were two Jews, one might say his main agents in Poland, who were both from Biale. One was the Biale Rabbi Reb Yitzchak bar Meir (who was at the same time, the Rabbi in Slavatitsh, where it seems, that it became a custom that both communities should share a Rabbi). He was the son of the famous Rabbi Reb Meir MRH"M from his name – our teacher the Rabbi Reb Meir Izenshtat, the brother–in–law of Yaakov ben Tzvi Emdin. The second was a Jew who came from Volin [Volhynia] and settled in Biale, Reb Boruch ben David, who was known by the name Reb Boruch from the land of Greece. This Reb Boruch was a wealthy Jew who conducted financial business with the Polish–Saxon minister, Bril, and with the Polish finance–minister Shedlnitzki. He could therefore help with religious matters through government intervention. He later proposed a marriage between Nechama, the daughter of Yaakov ben Tzvi Emdin, and his son Eliezer.

This is how Reb Yaakov ben Tzvi characterised the activities of Reb Baruch in his memoirs ("The scroll of the Book"): " – – he was a man who fought the wars of God, for my sake — — even though he could have taken bribes for his own benefit, if he sided with those who were against me, but he would not take bribes and he did according to God's will and fought against those mentioned above. He gave of the little that he had to glorify and bless the name of God and because of his passion for the Torah — —".[20] And the battle was not an easy one. The Rabbi of Lublin, Reb Yaakov bar Avrom bar Chaim, and his father, Reb Avrom bar Chaim, had great ideas of becoming one of the elected heads of the Synod of the Four Lands [Greater Poland, Little Poland, Belorussia and Lithuania] and were followers of Aybeshitz and in 1751 they excommunicated Reb Yaakov ben Tzvi Emdin. But Reb Boruch did not take fright.

[Page 107]

This is what he wrote after the excommunication to the Rabbi of Amsterdam who was one of the important fighters for Reb Yaakov ben Tzvi Emdin: " – – every day, at every time and at every hour, I drew the attention of the honoured Rabbis, loyal heads of the community when I said: why are you silent — — I was persistent and I guarded the doors of the faithful Rabbinic leaders — —". When he saw that from the Jewish side he could not hope to get help, he turned to his supporter, the Polish finance–minister Shedlnitzki, who put Reb Avrom in prison. From Avrom's side they wanted " – – to pay me a few hundred as a bribe to silence me, but matters like these did not deter me and I would just respond by giving them the cold shoulder but even this I spread around from the little that God gave me and he was gracious unto me — —". In short this is what Reb Boruch wrote to Amsterdam: and in all this I am thankful to God that I stood my ground, I was an antagonist against them all – – ".[21]

All this however did not help. The Aybeshitz party was stronger both in the Lithuanian committee and in the Polish committee so they spoke out in his favour. In Kislev 5512 (1751), the Lithuanian committee of the state decided: " – – we will ban and ostracise and curse and damn, whoever will dare to verbally denigrate — — against our teacher, our Rabbi the genius – – Yonatan – – ".[22] In Cheshvan 5514 (1753) the Polish Synod of the Four Lands [Greater Poland, Little Poland, Belarussia, Lithuania] spoke out in favour of Reb Yonatan as a Jew " – – in whom the spirit of God rests and he is worthy of being Divinely inspired — — he is absolved of wrongdoing and he sent his explanation that was sufficiently rooted in holiness, the amulets of the genii of the time — — and whoever suspects him, it is as if he suspects the Divine Presence".[23]

And the committee decreed that all the writings that had been published against him had to be burned — those were the writings of Reb Yaakov ben Tzvi Emdin and his followers.

In the course of this entire time, 1751 – 1753, Reb Boruch and Reb Yitzchak stood guard and were present at every important meeting and session. They tried to influence whomever they could. For them this was a holy–war but according to the official directive of Polish Jewry, their view about Aybeshitz was not the right one. For Reb Boruch it was easier to carry out his activities as he had the necessary means to do so and his influence was greater. In contrast, for Reb Yitzchak it was more difficult. More than once he complained that the fight was dragging him into great expense: I am compelled to travel to a gathering of the Four Lands, to the holy congregation of Kostantin [Konstantynów] and God will compensate me for my great expense".[24] " — — I was in conflict with the writings in my possession and I gave an amount of 12½ gulden in coins — — ".[25] I was there (in Brod) [Brid] for a month in order to guard the path of Torah, — — and to remember for good deeds the name of the master of the Torah, my Rabbi, our teacher, the scholar and our master Reb Boruch from the land of Greece, who supported me strongly and whole–heartedly — — and the wise Rabbis decided to send two Rabbis to the holy community of Hamburg, of whom I was one — — the main thing that is missing from the story is, who would pay for the expenses — — who would have to give a few hundred gold coins for one hour".[26] Reb Yitzchak kept on believing that he would manage to do something and renew the battle against Aybeshitz: "and I am still active in the committee whose gathering will take place on the 12th Tammuz 1755, an event that is approaching for our good in the holy community of Kostantin".[27] "— — for how long can we be under threat and turn the other cheek, for in every place where the desecration of God's name occurs, the Rabbi is shown disrespect — — ".[28]

Reb Yitzchak and Reb Boruch were prepared to fight further but in the meantime something else occurred in Poland that was worse than the amulets of Reb Yonatan Aybeshitz. This is the third act of the general Polish–Jewish history, in which Biale Jews – this time again Reb Yitzchak and Reb Boruch – played a large part.

At the end of 1755 the Podolye [Podolia] Jew, Yaakov Frank, returned to Poland. He spent a lengthy time in Turkey and there he was in close contact with the Shabtai Tzvi sect of the "Denmayer"[29] [a Jewish/Islamic sect]. In Poland, all the followers of Shabtai Tzvi gathered around him, and if until now Frank was inclined towards Islam, from now on he began to turn his gaze towards Christianity. Frank and his followers lived a licentious way of life, one of vice and heresy, in defiance. The idea of taking on the Christian faith was ripe. They came as far as making an accusation that the Talmud commands the use of Christian blood on Passover.

One sees clearly the difference between the opinions of Yaakov ben Tzvi Emdin – Aybeshitz and the Frank problem. One was a purely Jewish matter and the other, a great danger that threatened Polish Jewry. In those dark times, blood–libel was the order of the day and the testifying of Jews could bring about a great tragedy.

The Jewish leadership immediately went out in protest against the terrible situation and a fiery battle broke out. In Sivan 5516 (1756) the committee in the region of Lemberg [Lviv] excommunicated the followers of Frank and this excommunication was substantiated by the Synod of the Four Lands in Konstantin (September 1756). On the side of the Frankites was the Kamienietzer Catholic Bishop and he decreed an open public dispute between the Jews and the Frankites. The dispute ended according to a verdict by the Bishop with the defeat of the Jews and with the decree to burn the Talmud (June 1757). Frank took his agitation further and as a candidate for Christianity he won the support of the king. He appealed to the Lemberg [Lviv] archbishop, saying that one more dispute should take place between his followers and the Jews, in order to prove that the right observance of Judaism and messianic belief leads of necessity to the acknowledgement of Christianity. The Jews consented with honour to the dispute from Lemberg (July – August 1759) but the Christian authorities declared that the Jews were defeated.

[Page 108]

However, in one aspect the Jews had a partial victory but the details were the most dangerous: the Canon that led the dispute left open the question of blood–libel, as he was awaiting an answer from the Pope, to whom the Jews turned for help.

The Frankites now openly took on Christianity. Frank himself, however, came into conflict with the church and was sentenced to life imprisonment in the Tshenstochover [Częstochowa] fortress. During the first division of Poland (1772), the Russians freed Frank and he and his followers settled first in Berne (Austria) and later in the area of Frankfurt on Maine, where he died in 1791 at the age of 91.

We are interested here in the entire history, in the role of the Biale Jews in the battle against the Frankites. Rabbi Yaakov ben Tzvi Emdin writes in his memoirs "The scroll of the Book": also my in–law, the wealthy, the honourable Reb Boruch, mentioned above, will be remembered for good things in this matter, because here too, he played his part and stood like a pillar of steel before the king of Poland and his ministers — — to change their opinions and nullify their bad thoughts about Jews, so he volunteered to pursue them with all his soul and all his might so that they get what they deserve.[30]

At the forefront of the conflict in the first years stood our Reb Yitzchak. In a letter from Reb Boruch to Yaakov ben Tzvi Emdin he writes about the Konstantin committee: "And also he, (Reb Yitzchak) was here for some time and he attended the meeting of the Great Synod — — and he was strengthened in his faith and he appointed himself as head of the language and he did not involve himself in any activities other than the observance of the commandments — —".[31] Reb Boruch, on his part, did extensive work so that the issue should not be considered a Jewish one but also a matter that concerns the Christian church: "And also we will gather our strength before them, we will stand before the rulers and the Bishops to judge these cursed ones in fire because to their law, he who creates a new faith will be judged in fire — — ".[32] His view was correct. Using this tactic, one could hope that the battle would be easier and more successful.

After the Kamienietzer decree, Boruch turned to minister Bril and described to him the developments of the events: "I opened my lips with a cry and a plea for mercy so that he would request of our master the king to deal harshly with the sect of Shabtai Tzvi may his name and his memory be erased". Bril advised him to write a memorandum to the king (August III, 1734 – 1763), requesting that he take further action with the help of the Pope. Reb Boruch immediately composed the memorandum and sent it to the king. But he did even more, as he relates this anecdote: "And I did more than this by taking people with me — —, and I made a request for judgement to the diplomatic representative of the Pope[33] — — and I, as if I had the hand of God upon me, I gave an amount of one hundred red gulden for the necessity of dismissing this judgement — —".[34]It is also worth mentioning, that in his activities he treats Reb Boruch not as an influential person who takes matters into his own hands but he consults with him and gives an account to the official leadership. Reb Boruch is hopeful that matters with the Frankites will now come to an end. He writes: "When our eyes saw the burning of the Torah, it was as if one was seeing one's own daughter burnt in a fire"[35] and at the same time he asks Reb Yaakov ben Tzvi Emdin to approach the Amsterdam community to turn to the Pope through the community in Rome.

We saw above how the issues developed further. Reb Boruch became involved in the course of events once more. When Frank sat in the Tshenstochover [Częstochowa] fortress, he made contact with Moscow and Petersburg expressing the view that he would be prepared to take up the Slavic faith. Here Reb Boruch threw himself into the battle again ("he truly relinquished all his activities and occupied himself entirely with the work of God") and he managed to reveal the true face of Frank and his followers: "and these evil ones were led astray in disappointment".[36]

In summing up the whole matter, we have evidence that the two Biale Jews represented the viewpoint of Jewry with great honour; it is not their fault that they did not manage to do a lot.[37] Here too, we must comment that it is a great pity that we do not know more about Reb Boruch and Reb Yitzchak besides what we have related above. It would have been very interesting to know what such important leaders as these two men did within the Biale community itself.

F. The Community and the outside world

In the rich history of suffering, persecution and evil decrees that Polish Jewry experienced, the Biale Jews also had a significant part. We do not have any direct information about the decrees that the Biale community endured thanks to Chmielnitzki, but according to indirect intimations, it can be assumed that Biale was also involved in the tragic events. The main chronicler of the decrees, the scholar Reb Natan Hanover, who himself experienced this tragic chapter, pauses little on the fate of the Lithuanian communities. He satisfies himself with a general quote that: "and the people of the holy community of Slutsk, and the holy community of Pinsk and the holy community of Brisk-D'lita [Brest] fled, a few to greater Poland, a few to Dansk [Gdansk] on the water on the River Visel. Of the poor people as well as the remnants of the holy community of Brisk and the holy community of Pinsk, a few hundred were murdered for the sanctification of God's name". "Many Jews gathered in the holy community of Vlodava [Wlodowa] and there about ten thousand souls were murdered in different ways. And in the rest of the large communities in Lithuania, Jews were killed in their tens of thousands".[38]

[Page 109]

In the introduction to the Penitential Prayers that were composed by the great Talmudist Reb Shabtai Cohen, the author of the famous commentary of the Shulchan–Aruch "The Lips of Cohen", who was himself a victim of the decrees that were inflicted on Lithuanian Jewry and regarding the painful after-effects of the decrees, we read: " – — in the holy community of Vladvi there was a great slaughter — — also in the holy community of Brisk [Brest] and in the holy community of Minsk and in all the surrounding regions, there was no place where there were no killings. Whole families were destroyed there".[39] In another chronicle ("Place of Suffering" by Reb Shmuel Fyvish bar Natan Fytl) the decrees of various communities are listed "in the state that is called Podlashia".

In the list of the communities, Mezritsh [Miedzyrzec] is mentioned three times – (Great Mezritsh, Small Mezritsh and Great Mezritsh) and there is no doubt that one of the three towns is Mezritsh near Biale. About Mezritsh we have incidentally, quite direct information: In the 18th century we find the well–known writer of memoirs, Reb Ber Bolechover [Bolekhiv] in the Galician town of Bolechov. From his text we can accept that his great–grandfather, Reb Yehuda Leib, is a descendant of the fugitives of "the Great Mezritsh close to Brisk D'lita".[40] Biale itself is not mentioned anywhere, but it is certain that its fate was the same as the fate of the entire Brisk vicinity.

From the beginning of the 18th century we note two personal tragedies amongst the Biale residents. In 1710 a Biale Jew was sentenced to death in connection with a case of blood–libel. A few years later something happened in Biale that has not been historically proved, but it is definitely based on fact. The event concerned the famous son of the Rabbi of Lemberg [Lviv], Reb Tzvi Hirsh ben Reb Naftali Hirtz, whom the Biale Jews were honoured to have as a Rabbi and head of their Yeshivah. In the sources he is called Reb Tzvi Hirshli Halbershtater (in honour of his position as Rabbi that he accepted in Germany after he left Biale), but, it appears that he took the name Biale as his surname.

Reb Tzvi Hirsh had a beautiful daughter and the nobleman wanted to take her for himself. The Rabbi and his wife wanted to rescue their daughter and quickly arranged a marriage with the Rabbi's student, Reb Moshe of Brisk During the marriage ceremony the nobleman suddenly appeared and wanted to take the bride by force. Fear spread amongst the guests but the young groom was not afraid and with a mighty blow threw the nobleman to the ground and ran away with the bride. The nobleman was burning with rage and to avenge the great shame that was brought upon him, he imprisoned the rabbi and his family. The prisoners were threatened with the death–sentence, but here the powerful Jewish mediator and financier, Reb Yissachar bar Lehman, intervened. He had great influence in government circles and Reb Tzvi Hirsh together with his family were allowed to go free. Reb Tzvi Hirsh could no longer remain in Biale. Also the tragic news that his daughter died three days after her wedding placed a heavy burden on the whole family. Reb Tzvi hirsh therefore accepted the proposal of Reb Issachar Bern and arrived as a Rabbi in Halbershtat, taking with him Reb Moshe who then became a Rabbi in Pressburg.

The following is told about his rabbinical tenure in Biale: when he was in the town of Biali, all the people of the town loved him and honoured him greatly. They knew and understood that their Rabbi was one of the great scholars of his generation, unique and extraordinary in the diaspora community. The people honoured him from the depths of their hearts, for his great modesty, the charity that he distributed to the poor and the respect that he showed everyone in his community, each according to his worth and his honour. No man wanted to distract him from Torah learning to which he devoted himself day and night and he spent all his time, in the intellectual pursuit of Halachah.[41]

In Halbershtat Reb Tzvi led a great yeshiva and he himself excelled in great scholarship – his nickname was "Kharif" (sharp–witted). He was involved in many activities as spiritual leader of his community. He died in 1748. Two of his rabbinic writings were published: "Ateret Tzvi" (the Crown of Tzvi) and "Kos Yeshuot" (The cup of Salvation). Rabbi Yehuda Leib HaCohen Fishman praises him in his book "Sarei Ha–meah" (masters of the century) as: "— — a master of Torah, and a holy and pure genius — — a wonderful and endearing personality, winning hearts, a person of influence and generous spirit; there is none like him".[42]

In the middle of the 18th century, we came across by chance, news from a German newspaper of 1751, about the former general–treasurer and lessee of the court in Biale, Shmuel ben Yitzchak, who was mentioned earlier. While conducting business of the court, he entered into a dispute with the economic government organisation of the Prussian king and with his main contractor, Ephraim. It appears that the dispute had serious repercussions for the finances of the court and, as a Jew was involved in the dispute, the nobleman took revenge on the Jews of Slutsk and Biale and imprisoned 92 of them. After various negotiations, the dispute was crushed in 1751. Trade between Prussia and Biale–Radzhivil resumed and the nobleman freed the 92 Jews from prison. He gave gifts to the Jews that he freed, and in particular, he demonstrated his generosity to the family of Reb Shmuel (who died in the interim) providing "lavishly for them, for life". This information originates from correspondence from Danzig. We can assume from this that the dispute broke out regarding the trade of products from the Radzhivil estates at the Danzig sea–market.

[Page 110]

There is one more piece of information from the 1760s, that came to us by chance. It is in connection with a great Rabbi. In 1744, the great Rabbi, Reb Meir ben Yitzchak, died in Isenshtat (Hungary). He was known by the name "maharam", the first letters of his title (our teacher Rabbi Meir Isenshtat). We find his son Reb Yitzchak bar Meir as a Rabbi in Biale in the 1740s and we have already conveyed information about him in the previous chapter. In 1766, Reb Yehuda, a brother of this Reb Yitzchak, also a Biale Rabbi, published his father's book "The Hidden Light" in Fiorda (Germany) – new comments on tractate writings and the laws regarding "libation wine" (wine touched by heathen hands that is forbidden to Jews). In the introduction he tells us the following: " — — when our great and holy community was in turmoil — — in the time of the kingdom of Poland — — in the year 5524 (1764), — — I was given forbidden wine, and in the same year — — on the 1st and 2nd days of Tammuz, the enemy came to our community with a thundering noise and told all the others to do as they wish with the Jews, whatever their hearts desire, that is called in the German language, plundering. They gave permission to the slaughterers and for three hours they stole and tortured from time to time, Heaven Forbid. No one can appreciate the magnitude of the horror, particularly what the enemies did in the Great synagogue and in the community's House of Study. They plundered and stole all my possessions, they undressed my wife and me and our children and left us without clothes, naked. Despite this I gave thanks to God, for with his help, the God of mercy, they did not damage our souls. God should remember with mercy the holy community of Brisk D'Lita for their good deeds and protect them, for the rulers (the leaders and benefactors) of the holy community mentioned above, warned of the coming disaster. Our enemies and thieves left our community and went to the community mentioned above. It was decreed that whoever buys from the spoils taken from our community is obligated return them. They were to be redeemed without profit and this was of great help and comfort to our community. We lost many of the holy writings of my father, the Rabbi, the teacher, may his memory be blessed, and nothing remained except the book about the Torah, The Coat of Light, and new discoveries about the laws of libation wine and the tractate of Ketuvot".

From the introduction, we learn something else: in 1764 at the time of the turmoil that broke out in Poland in connection with the election of the last Polish king, Stanislav August Paniatovski, the Biale community experienced a small pogrom, that by some miracle ended without any loss of life. Our Reb Yehuda, it appears, suffered greatly and was most upset about his great father's writings that were lost during the pogrom.

Two years after the pogrom he undertook a journey to towns in Poland, Austria and Germany, to collect money to publish the remaining writings of his father. He gave the manuscript of the book "Coat of Light" to the son of his sister who lived in Biale, who was a Rabbi in Zabludove, and he actually printed it. He published the book "The Hidden Light" himself. We know, by the way, from his stories, how well they were treated by the Brisk community and how they helped Biale Jews to return to a normal way of life.

G. Transition–period from Old Poland to the new Congress–Poland (1795 – 1815)

In 1795 Poland ceased to exist; the third division of the remaining Polish territory was enforced (after the first and second divisions of 1772, 1793) and the three great countries: Russia, Austria and Prussia enriched themselves again with new Polish provinces. The entire Lublin and Shedletz area, and with them also Biale, fell to Austria, creating the province of "West–Galicia". Fourteen years later (1809) came a new change: as a result of Napoleon's victory over Austria, West–Galicia (and Biale in its midst) were cut off from Austria and attached to the Warsaw principality that Napoleon created in 1807 with the Saxon king at its head. For 14 years therefore, the Biale Jews had the "privilege" of being "Galicians" and then they returned again to Poland. The long period of transition dragged with it changes in legislation and in the legal–economic situation. It must still be added that this period was a time of wars. Napoleon did not let the world rest. Austria and the Warsaw principality were in a state of war all the time and it was clear that this fact must have had its consequences. The Jews of Biale had to experience yet a third change; in 1813 Prince Dominic Radzhivil died in Germany after he had participated in the great Napoleonic slaughter of Leipzig. Biale fell under the rule of his son–in–law, the Russian Prince Vitgenshtein.

During the Austrian occupation Biale became a circle–town, and the academy was converted to a Kaiser type of High School [Gimnazye]. In the record book of the "Chevra Kadisha" (Burial Society) we found a note that informs us about the changes in 1809. The note mentions that until today, Austrian money was in circulation but from today membership fees for new members must be paid in the currency of the new state "because of the changing times". In the time of the Warsaw principality Biale remained a circle–town and her chronicles of this particular time record three greater events.

[Page 111]

In 1812 there was a government decision to refrain from joining the great movement of Napoleon towards Moscow. In this year a Russian–Saxon battle played out in Biale and it cost Biale a huge sum of money. In Autumn 1815 the Russian Czar Alexander 1st passed through Biale on his way to the Vienna Congress where they wanted to overthrow Napoleonic rule. During his stay in Biale, he held an audience with a delegation from the Polish senate.

Regarding the Jews, the Austrian government brought in two new, special taxes: the "Kosher tax", which meant increasing the price of meat for the meat–eating consumer and the "light–tax" that every Jew had to pay. In this way the government made itself the guardian of Judaism with regard to the lighting of Sabbath candles. And when we also add that the old Polish head–tax was significantly raised (it is now called "tolerance –tax" meaning a tax for the privilege of living, dwelling and working in Austria) and that they also implemented a high payment for making a wedding – it will become clear that life did not become easier. The state of war on the one hand, with new opportunities for trade and work, alleviated the struggle to exist, but on the other hand, it was a heavy blow to the Jews because in Austria, Kaiser Joseph II implemented general compulsory military service for Jews.

In general, Austrian Jewish politics displayed specific liberal tendencies, but the intention was to lead Jews to assimilation or even to conversion; and only when they experienced internal revolution would they be privileged to have equal rights. In the meantime Jews only saw and felt negative aspects to government politics: a decree about synagogue visits, a decree to take on Christian names, a decree to overthrow traditional Jewish dress, a decree for Jews to give up inn–keeping in the villages etc.

In Biale however, we find also positive signs of a liberal trend under Austrian rule: in 1800 a situation arose paving the way for a reconciliation between the town council and the community that could have had important outcomes. The terms of the reconciliation contained many important statements: Jews will participate in the election of the town council; two Jewish representatives will participate in the revision of the town finances; Jews will enjoy all rights of citizenship as long as they are not contrary to government laws and decrees; the town council is obligated to cater for Jewish interests in equal measure as for local interests; the Jewish community will take part in the recruitment of Jewish soldiers; as a counter offer the community undertakes to pay 100 Austrian gulden annually.

If the terms of the agreement had been honoured, it would certainly have had a great impact on the general situation of the Biale community. However, as we will see further, it did not happen.

In the constitution of the Warsaw principality of 1807, it was decreed that "all citizens are equal regarding this law", but as far as Jews were concerned, it was not clear whether they were actually citizens. And they did not have to wait long for an explanation. A year later (Autumn 1808), a decree was issued that the question of political rights for Jews was being postponed for 10 years. So concerns about Jewish taxes and dwelling rights etc. began again. The "kosher–tax" and the "light–tax" on the one hand and the "head–tax" on the other (now it was called "class–tax or family–tax") put great pressure on the impoverished Jewish towns, and in addition there was also the "recruitment–tax" where Jews in the Warsaw principality were compelled to pay the outrageous sum of 700 thousand zlottes annually as compensation for being released from military service. Rich and Europeanised Jews wove various concessions for themselves, but the greater mass of Jews in towns and villages, amongst them Biale, were not rich and not Europeanised.

When the government took over the rule of the Shedletz [Siedlce] area in 1809, they promised to abolish the "family–tax" as soon as the Jewish debt of the old autonomy organisation of Polish Jewry was adjusted and repaid. But for that one would have to wait a very long time. In the meantime they had to pay, and pay according to a good rate of currency exchange, without taking into consideration, perhaps intentionally, that the old money had lost its value. And besides the heavy government taxes, Jews still had a whole row of other financial commitments: to maintain the community, added taxes for the town budget and various repayments to the court. In 1810 a few communities, together with Biale (also Mezritsh [Miedzyrzec], Shedletz [Siedlce], Vlodave [Wlodowa] and Lubartov) made a request to the Minister of Interior asking for mercy: "the war impoverished us, the decree that we pay a good rate of currency is an edict that we cannot sustain and the "family–tax" is not fairly distributed – the rich and the well–to–do pay little and the poor are oppressed.

[Page 112]

The debt of the old Polish period is a complex matter and should be regulated with the former Austrian government that demanded a substantial amount of money for this account". The petition attempts to play on the patriotic strings: "the heavy charges and the great needs of the people diminish the joy of returning to the homeland, and the hope of a better future". The answer to the petition was not found amongst the acts, but it is clear that it was not a positive one.

In the meantime the new war of 1812 crept up and as a consequence of it, the Warsaw principality was abolished. The Polish kingdom was established under Russian rule (Congress–Poland), and the history of Polish Jewry and also Biale Jews opens a new page.

H. The Town Budget in the first years of Congress–Poland

In the middle of 1815, with the establishment of Congress–Poland under Russian sovereignty, a new chapter begins in the history of the town generally and in the Jewish community in particular. We find ourselves at a time of the beginning of a new era; a time of the rise of a new social power: the town bourgeoisie and the factory–proletariat; of new ideas that draw their benefits from the French revolution, from the Napoleonic wars and from the English Industrial Revolution – the sovereignty of the people, social and economic freedom, ideas of reconstructing a more just society, the beginning of new living standards and new life–concepts with regard to social and personal hygiene, and in regard to communication of daily needs.

The world also took a small step forward in its attitude to Jews. The question of equal rights and emancipation surfaced in the past years. In some countries attempts were made to give Jews rights as citizens and, with regard to debts, to give them the same treatment as all other citizens. This is the way it was in Western and Middle Europe. It was the same in all the lands that experienced the French–Napoleonic occupation but in Russia everything retained its old ways. In the course of time, a new period of industrialisation began in Congress–Poland with stronger emphasis on the power of the town's bourgeoisie but in the beginning the changes were hardly felt.

Concerning the Jews – again they had to fight as in earlier Polish times – the old battle for existence, the battle for dwelling rights, for the right to free employment etc.

Right at the beginning, in the first years of Congress–Poland it seemed as if the wheels of history were turning backwards, and Polish Jews began to experience a return to the middle–ages. In 1816 a wave of blood–accusations went through Poland, and cases of blood–libel came close to the Biale community: not only because the blood–lie came to the fore simultaneously in nearby towns such as Mezritsh [Miedzyrzec], Shedletz [Siedlice] and Vlodave [Wlodowa], but also due to the tragic fact that the Biale prison played a sad role; here the accused Mezritsh Jews sat for some time before being transferred to Chentshin [Chęciny] in order to isolate them from the purely Jewish vicinity. The accused from Vlodave were also imprisoned in the Biale prison and were tormented for a long time, until they were freed in 1821. According to the official document of 1817 it can be assumed that in Biale itself there was talk of a blood–lie, but further information is missing.

In the next two chapters we will look at details of the fate of the Biale community. First we will present a picture of the town in 1820s, in the light of the town budget, that mirrors, in a certain sense, the situation of the Jewish community. The individual entries, those of the expenses and those of the income, give a true testimony of what the town was like, and what the goals of the government supervisor who put the budget together were. But first, let the numbers speak for themselves.

The Town's Preliminary Budget For the year 1819/20

Income

zl.

Town taxes to maintain the chimney sweepers	1000
Taxes from the Christian population for the town administration	934
Income from various market repayments	920
Contribution from the Jewish community for the town administration	374
Bridge repayments	176
Income from local pastures	160
Income from the local meat market	100
Contribution from the taverns	42
Total	3706

[Page 113]

Salary of the Mayor who is also the treasurer	1200
Salary of an Alderman who is also the secretary	300
For the chimney sweepers	1000
Two town servants	400
Two night watchmen	200
Contribution to the salary for the representatives of local matters in the military	144
Payment for the premises of the magistrate	100
Writing materials and lighting	150
Publication of official journals	21
Representatives of local butchers	50
Extraordinary expenses	141
Total	3706

The high level of the amounts detailed in the expenditure speak for themselves. One of the most important expenses of the local budget was the chimney sweep and his assistants. Their salaries amount to 27% of all the expenses. It is no wonder: a poor little town, that complains that it does not have money to pave the streets, to buy new tools to extinguish fires and other needs, must at least, have good service for the chimneys. One must remember that the town consists of almost all wooden houses and experience has taught that firstly, something must be done to avoid a fire.

To the above listed expenses one must also add the expenses that the town pays the court. This is not reflected in the budget but they did exist and were only abolished in the 1860s. In Mezritsh [Miedzyrzec], for example, the bridge repayments and the market repayments belonged to the Mezritsh court. If in Biale the court waived these payments, then on the other hand, they took upon themselves the obligation to provide wood to heat the house of the magistrate. In this way they found a means of covering the deficit in the form of other incomes of the town, about which the town's budget tells us nothing.

The local budget makes a notable impression, particularly when compared to the community budget of 70 years earlier, that amounted to approximately 10.000 zlottes, at a time when the actual value of money was greater.

In the budget the government predicted a sum of 165 zlottes (for the representative of local matters and for publishing official journals), that make up 4.5% of the budget but in truth they also have at their disposal funds under the title that reads "extraordinary expenses". In the certified budget the entry received another name, where it was called "at the disposal of the ministry". So we see that in reality, we can speak very little about an autonomy and an independent management committee, when in such minor matters, the state economy is dependent not only on military power but also directives from the ministry. By the way, it should also be noted that the legal custodians made a small change in the list of items of expenditure, in order to free up a sum of 27 zlottes as provision for the security of the Mayor when taking up his position.

And now about the income. The tax system was still primitive in those days; one sees that clearly from individual entries. Over time, two important sources of income were implemented: a concession tax for inn–keepers and a kind of industrial tax for the traders and artisans. In 1863 these two taxes brought in 3300 zlottes.

When analysing the income, we have this picture:

	zl.	%
Direct taxes	2350	63.4%
Indirect taxes (market and bridge repayments)	1096	29.5%
Income from local estates	260	7.1%
Total	3706	100%

Speaking about the direct taxes we will look at the amount of 374 zlottes that burdens the Jewish community. According to the agreement of 1800, Jews had to contribute the amount of 100 Austrian Gulden to the local budget, and for that they were to receive a list of citizen rights. The agreement, however, remained only on paper. They never actually collected this tax. When the preliminary budget for 1819/20 was being reviewed, the question of reconstructing the income of 1800 arose. Among the Christian population opinions emerged that since 1800 the number of Jews had grown significantly, that 31 more Jewish houses had been added and that the number of Jews had reached 2020 souls as opposed to 1457 Christians. If that is so, then the Jews would have to pay tax in the same proportion as the Christian population. So the magistrate presenting the budget for certification to the ministry alerted them to the fact, and the ministry certified the budget and put in a common entry of 1308 zlottes, as a citizen tax to cover the expenses of the town's administration, with a note that Jews and Christians must work out between themselves how to divide the sum.

[Page 114]

In the meantime the magistrate imposed only the 374 zlottes mentioned above. Jews, however, did not keep quiet. The Biale community requested a meeting with the ministry and showed that as the magistrate did not fulfil the terms of the agreement of 1800, the Jewish obligation to contribute to the town's budget was void. The community also demonstrated that the number of Jews was, in fact, less than the number of Christians and that during the Napoleonic wars Jews carried on their shoulders the entire burden of contributing to military quarters etc. Now, the petition says further, the Biale community has become impoverished and cannot bear the burden of 374 zlottes (that the magistrate imposed, on the grounds of certifying the budget).

The ministry did not report the petition to a higher authority and stressed the view that Jews and Christians must arrange the equal division of taxes amongst themselves in this budget and in later years (1821 – 1826). Now that the magistrate saw that he had the ministry on his side, he actually began to demand that Jews pay half of the whole sum, that means, 654 zlottes. The Jews again appealed to Warsaw. This time the ministry gave a clear answer, that as the Jews have the entire trade in their hands and overtake even the number of the Christian population, it is fair that they should pay the same as the Christians. And so it remained for a long time.

Regarding the indirect taxes, it is worth noting that the task of collecting repayments was placed in Jewish hands.

Resuming the details up till now, we come to the conclusion that Biale was a small town with a Christian population whose main employment was working the land and small farming businesses; and with a Jewish population that was employed in trade, labour, leasing and inn–keeping. Two more numbers for comparison: in 1826 the Biale town budget reached 2899 zlottes, in Mezritsh 4810 zlottes, and in Radzin 1256 zlottes.

I. The Jewish struggle for dwelling rights

The battle between Jews and Christians in Polish towns lasted for generations. The Christians attempted to sideline what was, for them, fierce Jewish competition. One chapter of the struggle was the question of dwelling rights.

The Christian population tried by legal and illegal means to see that Jews were banned from the Rynek and the nearby streets, and certain towns even earned the right to demand that Jews could not live in them at all. Amongst them were also Warsaw and Vilna and a long–lasting battle about this question also took place in Lublin. This was called "non–tolerance of Jews".

This battle continued in the 19th century and in certain instances was even intensified. They also added to the restrictions of "moral" reasons: Jews must suffer because they are corrupt; because they do not have a European education; because they are not productive, employed only in trade and inn–keeping; because they separate themselves from residents in the vicinity by their dress, customs, language etc. Before they will allow Jews to have elementary rights of freedom of movement and freedom to practise their professions, they expect them to "improve morally"; they should change their ways. For many years in Congress–Poland there was a well thought out and wide–branched battle about economic purposes and "moral" excuses. Jewish communities were dismissed and in their place the "Dozur Buzshnitski" came into existence whose competence was limited only to religious and fiscal matters. A school was established for Rabbis in Warsaw with an outspoken assimilatory character, and at the same time in 1822, two important anti–Jewish decrees were published. One presents various measures that will restrict the number of the Jews in the towns and simultaneously it says that in various towns separate areas will be organised for Jews. The second decree states that Jews may no longer live in the towns that had previously the right of "non– tolerance of Jews" unless, in the interim, they legally acquired a concession for an inn. If not, they must leave the town within three years.

Both decrees were terrible for the Biale Jews. With good–bad will, one could interpret the decree of 1621 to mean that Jews were allowed to own no more than 30 houses. One could go still further and claim that 30 houses means 30 families. And as there were 389 Jewish families in Biale at that time, it means that 359 of them are not legal and they are compelled to drive them out of the town, or in the best case, to be concentrated in a separate Jewish ghetto. In fact the circle–commissioner and the town administration began to occupy themselves intensively with the issue and, supported by the decree of 1822 and the indicated interpretation of the decrees of 1621, worked out specific plans to create a Jewish ghetto; there was no talk of exile.

[Page 115]

The Jews of Biale immediately assessed the danger and, it appears, of their own initiative, the Jews of Podlashe [Podlasie] decided to communicate with a written request to the Head of State who had the highest power in Congress–Poland. In the request (signed by Avrom David Cohen from Shedletz [Siedlice] and Aharon, from a line of saints, from Biale), Podlashe Jews ask that the time given to put the edict of the first decree into effect, that says that from the 1st January 1823, only one family may live in each Jewish house and all others must move out, should be prolonged for six years because it would be impossible to erect so many houses in such a short time (barely a few weeks remained until the 1st January 1823).

As the local government began to carry out the above–mentioned task, an appeal was also sent to the Minister of Interior requesting that in the meantime, no further steps should be taken.

On the 9th December the reply arrived from the ministry, that the decree could not be altered. They were only assured that those organising the execution of this procedure would treat the matter with favour, considering the difficult situation of the Jews concerned.

Regarding this matter therefore, the Jews of Biale were safe for a certain time. Now a new danger drew near. The plan for a ghetto in Biale, as mentioned above, found favour with the local government and in 1823 it was sent to the ministry for confirmation. The plan states that:

1.   Jews are forbidden to live and have shops in the market and in the following streets: Varsheve, Lubline, Reformatzke, Mezritshe, Yaneve and Briske and also in the small streets between those mentioned. Jews that live in these streets and also in the corner houses (between the permitted streets and those not permitted) must move out by the end of 1825. If not – they will be punished with large money fines.

2.   Jews will be allocated Grabanovve and Proste streets (from Brisk Street upwards) and besides that, a row of new project streets as for example: Yeruzalimske (between Briske and Grabanovve), Nye Street, Rinkovve, Vytte, Dzshelne.

3.   Only stone houses may be erected in these streets and not wooden houses.

4.   As a favour, two Jewish families will be allowed to live in Christian streets. They must, however, observe the following conditions: they must conduct substantial trade, must possess 24,000 zlottes, know Polish, French or German , send their children to government schools, not make themselves different from their surrounds with outward signs (Jewish clothes, customs etc.). In addition to them, the following will also receive permission to live in Christian streets: artists, educated people, manufacturers who employ Jewish workers, big wholesalers, Jews who undertake to erect multi–storied houses on empty plots; they must, however, observe all the aforementioned cultural stipulations.

5.   In addition it was stressed that, in accordance with the agreements of 1822, only one Jewish family may live in each house (both in the streets permitted and in the forbidden streets).

[Insert town plan]

Points 1, 2 and 3 are purely local Biale matters. The others are general and show without clarity, the trends of assimilation and repression that existed in leading Polish social circles. Neither the Biale locals nor the Shedletz [Siedlice] local government created them. They are the result of general public opinion, as was printed in the press, brochures, in books and also in government plans for other towns, mainly for Warsaw.

[Page 116]

The economic matters are also interesting. Polish society and the government followed the path that was marked in Western and in Middle Europe already in the second half of the 18th century, i.e. to favour the rich Jew and force him to be of greater use to the country by his investment of capital in substantial trade, industry and housing construction.

The issue that compels Jewish manufacturers to employ Jewish workers, if they themselves want to live in Christian streets, is characteristic. In truth, did they seriously mean the question of professional upheaval?

Or did Biale Jews know about the new decree that threatened the existence of so many Jews? The whole of the market, except for two houses, the whole of Mezritsh, Yaneve and Briske streets were occupied by Jews. Unfortunately we have no information at all about this.

Fortunately the ministry ruled differently regarding this matter. They realised that the threat to Jewish existence also threatened the income of the government. The ministry issued an opinion that as Biale was a district town that contains a Jewish settlement, whose number exceeds the Christian population (1457 Christians and 2020 Jews), the establishment of a Jewish precinct was not worthwhile. More than that, it would then be necessary to acquire the approval of the Head of the Town. With this in place, the matter was put to rest for a whole year. Only in summer of 1824 did the local government in Shedletz [Siedlice] turn again to this matter. They asserted that according to the edict of 1621, only 30 Jewish families could live in the town. Afterwards the decree from Warsaw stated that in those towns where they had the authority previously to restrict Jewish dwelling rights, the restrictions were valid, then and in the future, so the circle–commissioner tried not to allow new Jewish families to come into the town. However, he did not manage to enforce this and the number of Jewish families continued to grow. It was therefore up to the ministry to express its intention regarding the future.

We see from this that in Shedletz [Siedlice] too they changed their views and thoughts of a Jewish ghetto were abandoned. It is possible that this happened because of Jewish influence. The answer of the ministry to this, was that the lower organisations of government should abide by the above–mentioned regulations of 1822, and see to it that the number of Jews should not increase. The answer was intentionally clouded because in the ministry, as we have seen above, there was no definite line of thinking regarding the introduction of Jewish precincts. As a result the Circle–Commissioner did not know what else he had to do.

And life went on its way. The government organisations continued to exchange a comprehensive correspondence and the plan to reduce the Jewish population or to create a Jewish ghetto precinct was postponed from year to year. Jews continued to live freely in Biale and their numbers increased. In the 1860s there were 3456 Jews in Biale and 2083 Christians. The plan to create a Jewish quarter and regulations regarding the number of families in the individual houses remained on the statutes. The difficulties with the badly interpreted act of 1621, until now, as well as in the future, meant that the act could not be enforced. As they convinced themselves in the ministry, that the whole plan for a Jewish precinct could not be carried out (in Sokolov for example, Jews returned to their dwellings at night, and in the morning they were removed again), it was decided in 1833 to annul this decree entirely. Thirty years later (in 1862), Jews received full dwelling rights in the whole of Congress–Poland, at least, on paper.

J. The struggle for work for Jewish people

The second battle field on which Jews and Christians wrestled in Poland over an entire century, was about work or more precisely – the right of Jews to legally engage in various professions. The authoritative opinion in the domain of work was the professional organisation of tradesmen – the guild. The guilds regulated the links between production and consumption. They judged in all matters regarding the market, eliminating competition, supervising good work–practice in handling products, purchasing of raw–material etc. They had welfare–boxes for the poor, the sick, orphans and widows. They had their own areas in the churches and each guild was assigned a separate part along the town– walls that they were obligated to defend in case of a war. In many towns they also had an important say in the town council. Their power was increased due to two factors:

> a.   belonging to a guild was obligatory and the tradesman who tried to free himself from the guild and its regulations experienced many problems, and finally he had to bear all the payments that the guild imposed on him without benefiting from his rights as a member.
> b.   The guilds regulated and dominated, not only production, but to a certain extent also trade; every guild according to the products of its trade.

[Page 117]

As the guilds bore a distinct religious character, it is clear that only followers of a particular faith could belong. The Polish guilds were of an overwhelming majority Roman–Catholic and the other tradesmen were: Protestant, Greek–Catholic and Greek–Orthodox who had to withstand a difficult battle for their existence in the guild, or from without the guild. Understandably, it was not possible for Jews to belong to the guild. Jewish tradesman established their own guild–societies, mostly tailoring. And as the matter was not only a religious one, but to a much greater extent, an economic one, it is clear that the Christian guilds (who saw themselves as the solely official and entitled) and the Jewish societies of tradesman could not live together in peace. This is also the story of all Polish towns, filled with battles between Christian and Jewish tradesmen, battles that lasted decades and centuries. On the one side, stand the Christian guilds and the town council that protects them, and on the other side – the Jewish societies and the community. The mediators and arbitrators were: the government, all the way to the king, the courts – from the highest to the lowest, and in the private towns, also the landowners. Sometimes it ended up with bloodshed. A contract would be sealed, and both sides agreed with the full intention of not honouring it. The issues would be referred to the courts and again new contracts would be sealed, sometimes in favour of one side and sometimes in favour of the other side and the battle never ended. And life went its way – legally and illegally the numbers of Jewish tradesmen and their societies increased and somehow they organised themselves. In Biale the battle concerned shoemaking, hat–making and tailoring.

The Biale Christian shoemakers organised themselves and in 1693 they elicited a document from the nobleman, according to which they were given the right to establish a guild organisation. In this document, the rights and duties of the members were formulated and the entire internal organisation of the guild was determined. In order to increase the income of the guild, they imposed a tax on all merchants and tradesmen that came into the town to the fairs with footwear for sale. They had to pay one groshen to the guild for each pair of footwear that was brought in. The Jews who had shoe shops also had to pay one groshen for every pair of boots. The first regulation concerns a kind of protection–tax. It aims to protect the local tradesman against external competition. The second regulation, in addition, was of a fiscal nature, that aimed to weaken Jewish competition and also imposed a random tax on Jewish shop owners. The regulation is very vague: it is not clear if the tax applies only to the fairs or to everyday trade; is the tax only imposed on the items sold or on the entire merchandise in the shop. One could also interpret that the payment is valid for those shopkeepers whose merchandise was purchased during the fair. The text of the regulation infers that evidently this applies only to the pairs of boots sold at the fair. But as the rule is not a clear one, it created distress and caused uncertainty in the Jewish shoe–trade. The income from the taxes was earmarked for church purposes by the guild (lighting and a guild flag etc.). The shoemakers were not satisfied with this: two years later for instance, in 1695, they again approached the town–authority and without mentioning the regulations of the previous two years, requested that they confirm a new rule that differs from the previous one, in one particular aspect – the one that imposed on the Jews a duty to pay, not only for every pair of footwear, but also for every piece of leather. The nobleman confirmed the document and from then on the guild used the last rule only as a basis for its needs regarding the Jewish shop–owners and merchants. The Biale magistrate kept a copy of both regulations. On the second, that contains the additional clause, there is confirmation from 1778. Apparently it was only this rule that the guild presented for confirmation. It chose rather not to mention the first.

Already in recent years it became known that the taxes were difficult to collect and that it is simply difficult to control the whole issue. So the guild compromised with the Jews, that instead they should give 10 pounds of wax annually to the church and in exchange they would receive the right to free trade.

The Jews, however, did not keep the agreement. Disputes increased and the matter was finally handed over to the High–Court. In 1740 a judgement was delivered stating that Jews had to give a total of 15 pounds of wax annually. In addition, in order to enable the guild to control the shoe–trade with foreign shopkeepers and tradesmen, Jews were forbidden to buy, or to sell, other than in the market place, under threat of a severe monetary fine, half of which went to the guild and half to the Chief Justice. The judge, however, realised that the guild's expectations were unfair, and determined exactly the manner in which the payment was to be collected. He also secured for himself the right to have control over the utilisation of the money.

[Page 118]

The guild, seeing that he was in control, after 11 years (1751), elicited an additional right, that every new Jewish shopkeeper pays the guild six zlottes for the same purpose. Now it appears the ratio is more or less controlled: Jews paid and the guild was satisfied. In the Warsaw "archive of old acts" we find a contract from 1754, in which four Biale shopkeepers ask to be pardoned for not giving the wax. They commit themselves to giving it over a certain period, and if not, they will pay double. In 1774 there was another decree for seven shopkeepers who opened new shops and did not pay the tax to the guild.

In the time of the Napoleonic wars, the Jewish shopkeepers again stopped paying and when the guild demanded payment, the Jews argued that they did not acknowledge the regulations of 1740 and 1751 but they were prepared to fulfil the agreements according to the regulations of 1695. The mutual negotiations finally brought them to the point where in 1815, they compromised on the following points: the Biale shopkeepers must pay ½ zlottes annually and in addition they must pay this amount for the years 1815 and 1816 in advance. The shopkeepers must also cover the cost of the lawsuit in the amount of eight zlottes. The payment by the foreign shopkeepers and tradesmen, remains as before but with one important change, that the trade does not necessarily have to take place in the market place and only for the price that that it would be in the market, is the old groshen tax paid.

In 1816 a new decree regarding the guild was brought in. The decree aimed to pave the way for a freer development of private initiative, in order to enable an upswing in work and industry. The form of the guild remained but the guild was no longer the regulator of economic life. In the decree, amongst other issues, the development –path of the tradesman is described: he must first go through the steps as a student journeyman, and after participating in an appropriate "master's course" and demonstrating that he has learned his trade well, he is then registered as a master, and pays 30 to 60 zlottes. The decree applies to all tradesmen.

As already stated, this decree of 1816 applies to all tradesmen, both Christian and Jewish. The Jews were now permitted to be taken into the guilds with the restriction that as they do not have equal right of citizenship, they cannot be elected to various guild offices.

When the above decree came out and people began to think about it, Biale Christian shoemakers realised that for them the whole matter was an uncomfortable one. And as in the course of time, Jews also turned to shoemaking, the matter for the Christian shoemakers was twofold: the proportion of Jewish shopkeepers that trade in footwear, and secondly – the issue of Jewish shoemakers. Taking the Jews into the guild meant that with their own hands, they would create right–minded competitors. It could also have been a suspicion that the Jewish shoemakers might open the question of payments and also perhaps about the distribution of the money. And another thing: paragraph 145 of the decree of 1816 confirms that all old guild customs are abolished. It was easy to imagine that the tax that is discussed here had to be thought of as an "old guild custom". And it seems really that on these grounds, after 1816, they again stopped paying the tax, to which they themselves were agreeable in 1815. The guild therefore had to consider what to do, and it found a solution. It took this same decree and interpreted it in this way – that all Jewish shoemakers, as new guild members, must pay a registration fee of 60 zlottes. The guild hoped in this way to collect a substantial sum of money. The Jews, however, did not keep quiet. The shoemakers and the shopkeepers went to the circle–commissioner and accused the guild and in 1824 he formally ruled that every new tradesman must substantiate how he fulfilled the regulations about a course of education with a qualified master. Those who could not bring evidence of this were not allowed to work as independent tradesmen. Those who have attained the prescribed qualifications must pay 30 – 60 zlottes as determined by the guild leaders. And concerning the tax to be paid by the Biale shopkeepers and foreign merchants and tradesmen at the market and the fairs, the Circle–Commissioner stated that he would turn to the higher powers regarding this matter. The first question has again remained unclear. Most Jewish shoemakers were considered professional tradesmen from before, although they did not belong to the guild. The guild, on the other hand, considered them as newly qualified and demanded the tax. Therefore the disputes between the guild and the Jewish shoemakers increased. In the second matter the Circle–Commissioner turned to the town administration in Shedletz [Siedlice] and from there they asked the ministry if, according to the decree of 1816, the taxes could remain. The ministry postponed the decision for some time. A lecturer even added that he had to give an opinion on a similar matter in Garvollin,

[Garwolin] but no decision was taken. The decree was not mentioned in Biale or in Shedletz. In 1840 the matter was shelved in the acts of the ministry.

[Page 119]

The reason for the silence will be clarified afterwards when we look through the list of the Biale tradesmen of 1841. Evidently in this year there were 11 shoemakers in Biale and amongst them only 4 Christians. Now everything becomes clear. With each year the number of Christian shoemakers fell. They wanted then to save their prestige, expecting up to 60 zlottes from every shoemaker but afterwards, it appears, they resigned from this. Of its own accord, the taxes for the footwear and leather shopkeepers surely must have ceased to exist. In the local archive of 1845, we discover that only two guilds functioned in the town: bricklayers and pot makers. Regarding the shoemaker guild, it means apparently that it simply did not exist "because there were very few Christian master tradesmen and the Jews were very poor".

The shoemaker's guild, it seems, reorganised itself after eight years (1853). We do not know how the question of the Jewish taxes and the rights of the Jewish shoemakers was organised in the new guild but we can accept with certainty that the tax of the Jewish shopkeepers was abolished entirely. We do not know how many Jewish members there were in the reorganised guild of 1853. One thing is clear – There were no more than two Christian shoemakers and they were actually in agreement with the regulations of 1816, elected as the guild leaders.

Until now we have spoken about the "leather–line of business". Now we will look at the matter of the Jewish hat–makers and tailors.

When the decree of 1816 came out, the guilds in Biale also began to reorganise themselves. As in many other towns, the question of Jewish membership of the guilds and their right to vote presented itself here as well. The decree could be interpreted in different ways, particularly in cases where there was not a full complement of ten master tradesmen who were legally necessary in order to form a guild or inversely, when there was a large number of Jewish master tradesmen but the two Christians who were needed in order to form a guild committee were non–existent. It was important for Jews to belong to the guild, firstly because it protected them from non–professional competition. The Christians, again, did not want to allow the Jews to have the privileges that the guild offered. For this reason, long disputes and negotiations took place in which the government, in a purely formal manner, referred to the decree that Jews had no passive voting rights in the guild. In this way it emerged, for example, that 50 Jewish tailors from Sokolov [Sokolow] were attached to the Biale tailors' guild because in Sokolov they were short of the two Christians to stand at the head of the guild. Only after protracted efforts (1830 – 1835) did they manage to extract an agreement from the ministry that they would be added to the local cap–makers guild until a few Christian tailors settled in Sokolov.

And what was the status quo regarding this matter, in Biale? We have a list from 1841 of the membership of the professional tradesmen, that states:

attached to each master tradesman in the town there is: a chimney sweep, a miller, a soap–maker, a locksmith, a wheelwright, a lace maker; all except the lace–maker and soap–maker were Christians. To every two master tradesmen there were: hat–makers, carpenters, bookbinders, makers of wadding, watchmakers. All except one watchmaker were Jewish. To every three master tradesmen there were: metal–workers, tanners, roofers (only Jews). To every four master tradesmen there were: carpenters (one Jew amongst them), painters (three Jews amongst them) blacksmiths (one Jew amongst them). To every five master tradesmen there were: pavers (only one Jew), harness–makers (of them only one Jew). To every six master tradesmen there were: joiners (only Jews). To 11 master tradesmen there were: butchers (of them 7 Jewish, and 4 pig slaughterers), shoemakers (7 of them Jews), and pot–makers (only Christians). Besides them, 13 bakers (amongst them only one Christian), 13 tailors (only Jews), and 17 masons (amongst them two Jews). A total of 127 tradesmen, of whom 76 were Jews and 51 Christians.

From the numbers above we can see that there were only five kinds of tradesmen that could organise a guild (not counting the butchers and pig slaughterers because these are in fact, two different trades), those are; the shoemakers, pot–makers, bakers, tailors and masons. From this number we remove the tailors and bakers as they do not have the required two Christians to form a guild committee. We have written previously about the fate of the shoemakers' guild and about the position of the Jews in it. The masons and the pot–makers were therefore the only tradesmen in Biale who had a legal guild.

In 1849, suddenly the Jewish question arose in the organisation of a profession that did not feature in Biale – the hat–makers. When there was an initiative to establish a hat–makers' guild, the government withdrew. This guild was to accommodate the hat–makers from Biale, Kodniye [Kodnya], Pistshatz [Piszczac], Lomaz [Lomazy] and Rososh [Rossosz]. The Biale magistrate was supposed to be involved in its organisation. It was immediately evident that there were 4 hat–makers, in Kodniye also 4, and in Lomaz and Pistshatz, one each, and in Rososh there were no hat–makers. All these hat–makers were Jews and the Circle–Commissioner, it appears, was not very involved in

[Page 120]

the matter. When this became clear to him in 1850, he began to urge them to find the Christian tradesmen. They searched and searched but did not find any. After another two postponements,[43] the Biale magistrate gathered all the hat–makers and in November 1850 the guild was established. As elders, Ephraim Tsinamon and Shimon Lazer Cohen were elected, both from Biale[44]. The magistrate knew that something was not right here but the Circle–Commissioner demanded it, so there was no other solution. As was mentioned in the beginning, the Circle–Commissioner again did not want to be involved in the situation. As soon as the elections took place, he ordered the magistrate to organise a cashbox for the new hat–makers' guild. A couple of months later, however, he received instructions from the provinces[45] that the elections were illegal and had to be annulled. The magistrate did so and four months after the founding–gathering the hat–makers got together again, in order to receive the sad news. As the Jews could not be elected and as there were no Christian hat–makers, they had to dissolve. For the provincial administrators the whole issue was embarrassing so they still tried to maintain the guild in Biale and in order to make it acceptable, ordered that the hat–makers' guild include all the cap–makers. However, it again became known that also among the cap–makers there were no Christians.

Similarly in the summer of 1851, after an investigation by the district chief, it was established that a cap–makers' guild was being formed that would comprise all the cap–makers and hat–makers of Biale, Loshitz [Łosice] , Yanneve [Janowo], Konstantin [Konstantynów] and Sarnak [Sarnaki]. The centre of the guild would be in Loshitz. It is probable that amongst such a large number of tradesmen they finally found the two necessary Christians.

This is how "the painful Jewish–issue" was solved in the Biale hat–makers' guild.

Unfortunately we know very little about the tailors. We have already mentioned the existence of a tailors' society in the chapter about the community budget in the middle of the 18th century. No material has remained from the later years, but there is no doubt that the society continued to exist and it certainly had a similar story to all the other tailors' societies in Poland from the standpoint of organisational and professional–societal activity. A history of converting the society into an official guild is not clear. We only know that after 1825 there was a plan to create a partnership with the tailor guilds of Biale and Sokolov [Sokolow]. The plan was in the framework of the guild regulations of 1816: if a town did not have two Christian master tradesmen to form a committee then a guild could be formed to which tradesmen from a few towns could belong.

In Sokolov [Sokolow] there were no Christian tailors. Should we assume that in Biale there were Christian tailors? Whatever the situation was, it immediately emerged that Sokolov did not agree to the plan to merge and it was removed from the agenda. I am inclined to the supposition that the Biale Jewish tailors re–established their old society according to the Jewish formula and that from a government point of view they appeared as a division of the hat–makers' guild. In the next chapter we will talk about the individual right of the tailors in the Chevra–Kaddisha.

K. Societies in Biale

The social life of the Jews of Poland (and not only in Poland) was very well developed. In every community, large or small, we find societies of various kinds and with various goals: study groups (studying the Talmud, the society for Ayn Ya'akov [the Talmudic collection of legends and homilies of Rabbi Ya'akov, the son of Shlomo Ibn Haviv], and a group studying the Psalms), groups for social assistance (dressing the poor, visiting the sick, marrying off a bride etc.), professional organisations that were of similar character to the guilds (the tailors' society, the charity society and others). Some communities had more and some fewer societies, according to the social activity of its members but there is one society that could be found in every community, that is, the burial society whose realm of activity centred around the cemetery. In some communities the work of the burial society included visiting the sick and maintaining the home for the aged (the holy). The name by which the society is generally known is "Chevra Kaddisha". In fact all the societies bore the name "Chevra Kaddisha" (the holy society), like: "Chevra Kaddisha for charity, "Chevra Kaddisha for tailors etc. But as the burial society was the most extensive and the most popular, the name of all the other societies was transferred to it.

Prior to the time that we are dealing with here (end of the 16th century to the middle of the 19th century), we do not know about any study groups or societies for social help in Biale. There is, however, no doubt that groups such as these did exist. If in the neighbouring town of Mezritsh [Miedzyrzec] we find seven societies, why would such societies not have existed in Biale? What does this mean? Either that their record books were not found or the "people" did not take the trouble to find out. Regarding the professional societies, it is certain that Biale had a Tailors' society (to which other tradesmen also belonged) but also about this society, we know little, because it appears that its record book was lost. The only one on which we could rely more precisely is the burial society, whose exact name in Biale was "The holy society, bestowal of loving kindness and truth".

[Page 121]

The Chevra Kaddisha had been in existence for a long time; we have indicated above the role it played in covering the deficit of the community in 1749/50. In the record book that was accessible to me, however, I only found entries from 1800 – 1905, accounts from 1806 – 1838 and statutes from 1813, with addendums from various later years. It appears that this record book was opened in 1813 and part of the material from earlier years was transferred to it. Every Jew could belong to this society, but to be accepted into the society one had to have the general approval of all the members, "even if one person voted against, the applicant would not be admitted to the society". There was therefore a veto–right, and this had without doubt an influence on the number of members of the society and its exclusive character. Also the high membership fee could have been an obstacle. There were two kinds of fees, according to the level of scholarship: a Jew who had the study–title of "associate" paid 72 zlottes; when, thanks to his scholarship he attained the higher title of "our teacher", he paid only 54 zlottes. Both payments, according to their nominal and their real worth, were quite substantial. In the first three years of membership, the member was only a candidate (nominated — it means of course, a young man); he has greater obligations (he must visit every sick person according to the orders of the committee) yet he has no rights, not active and not passive voting rights. For not following orders, he is threatened with an extension of his period of candidacy for another year. The voting for the committee took place every year after Passover and at most, until the first days of the month of Iyar. The voting was indirect, and it would be more correct to speak about nominations and not about voting. All the names of the members were placed in a ballot–box and five names were drawn out. The five members whose names appeared on the notes that were drawn out were called "arbitrators" and they nominated: the committee, that consisted of four "trustees" (they held office in rotation, each one for one month), four "executives" (these are the actual administrators of the society), "four auditors" (treasurers and managers of the cash), four "keepers of the statutes" (their duty was to keep the laws, and see that everything was conducted according to the regulations. In their year of office they could also bring in new laws), four burial attendants (those were the experts in all matters concerning burial and the cemetery). Aside from this honour and duty of nominating, the arbitrators still had one more responsibility: before they could carry out a nomination, they had to go to the old and the new cemetery and repair the damage and disorder that occurred during the year. If they failed to fulfil this duty, they would be declared unfit to hold office and would be replaced by other arbitrators. Only a person who had already served as an executor could be appointed as a trustee. Also, a trustee could not be nominated for two consecutive years. The executor could not incur any expenses without a note from the trustee and when he had incurred the expense, he had to give an account to the auditor. One of the arbitrators could also be nominated as a trustee or as an executor, on condition that another three arbitrators agreed.

In the course of time, two important changes were made to the regulations:

a.   The trustee may not take it upon himself to spend more than a sum of 12 zlottes a month. If he needs to spend more, he needs to have the approval of the Rabbi and another two members of the society who have been appointed by the arbitrators (1846);

b.   New members are not accepted by the vote of all the members with a veto–right from each one, but by the trustees and the executors together with another ten members (1879).

The statutes of the society tell us little about the activities of the society (not more than four paragraphs of the 18 – 18 regulations). If one member dies, the trustee of the month immediately selects six members whose names are drawn from a ballot–box and sets them to work. If the member does not obey the rules and does not send a representative, he pays a fine. During the funeral the trustee goes around with an alms–box and the money that he collects is handed over to the executor. For putting up a gravestone, one pays not less than two zlottes. Whoever does not make a payment immediately, must make a pledge. When the time comes to redeem the pledge and the debtor does not have the money to pay, then the executor, "with the knowledge of the trustee" can sell the pledge after he has warned the debtor twice of his commitment.

In the field of social activity of the society, we have one regulation that states, that if one of the members dies, a "memorial service" must be held for him in the course of 30 days and the names of the members who are expected to attend are drawn from a ballot-box.

The last regulation that can be cited, is the one that states that the trustee of the month is obligated at the end of his term of office, to hand over the records of the society to the new trustee of the month and if, after three warnings, this is not done, he is excluded from the society.

It is notable that the statutes are concerned mainly with organisational matters and very little with other issues. It is also surprising that in the society a record of the duty to remit weekly payments through each member does not exist. It is probable that there were other rules from earlier times, that were not transferred to the new record book of 1813. To compare we will present the statutes of Pruzshanne [Pruzhany] and Radzin [Radzyn][46] with whom Biale was surely in contact.

[Page 122]

Biale (18 statutes) 1813	Pruzshanne (18 statutes) 1715	Radzin 9 statutes 1816
Mainly organisational paragraphs	11 paragraphs of the duties of the members; 7– organisational	2 paragraphs of the duties of the members; 7 organisational
Very restricted	Also very restricted but without veto–rights	Much less; without the accountant's approval he may only spend 2 zlottes
Very high, Non–existent High enough	Not mentioned. A groshen a week. Much less; without the accountant's approval he may only spend 2 zlottes	At his own responsibility he may only spend 6 zlottes
The Rabbi is the acknowledged authority	The society secures itself from the interference of the community in societal matters	The Rabbi has a very high position here; the statutes are made with his approval

From the history of the Biale Chevra–Kaddisha and its budgets, we will highlight a few facts, that will clarify its essence. In the years 1810 – 1812 there were two cases of members being disciplined. The first case was in connection with a butcher (Yosef ben – Dovid Roffe), who was caught in an unpleasant incident of having a relationship with a married woman. He was barred from the society for six years and after it was apparent that he was not repentant, his name was deleted altogether from the members' list, "forever". As a punishment it was decided that when he died, the servant of the society would see to his burial. The second case concerned one who "spoke illegally". He must have certainly taken a critical view of the management of the society and they therefore kept him away from the society for three years. It appears that he improved afterwards and they forgave him the sin.

The knowledge about the society of tailors is important for us. In one year the society accepted 15 tailors and it was noted: "the tailors are under the supervision of the appointed trustees and financiers" (of the society). This shows clearly that the tailors had distinct rights in the society, and that they formed a separate group with their own trustees. It can be assumed that in this manner, an appropriate way was found to incorporate the tailor's society (that was illegal) into the Chevrah–Kaddisha.

From the budgets of the society one can see quite clearly that it was not limited to matters relating to burial and the cemetery, but that it also conducted broad social activities. And here a few entries will bear witness to the expenditure: For a woman who travelled to a doctor, to a surgeon for attending to a woman, wood for the house of study, study fees for a boy, shrouds for people who died in the poor–house, to a sick assistant–teacher, to a blind person from Kemnitz, for hiring a teacher, for hiring a beadle for the synagogue, shrouds for the poor, wood for the hostel for the poor, for the cellar, a wagon for a poor person from Mezritsh [Miedzyrzec]. Three times we find donations for strangers (a righteous male convert, a female convert, a visiting stranger). One entry is anonymous "for the sake of identification". The society therefore fulfilled the duties of a general charity–character, and also contributed to the community budget. What is interesting for example, is the budget for one month in 1811; in this month the society spent 65 zlottes, of which 16 zlottes were for visitors, and visitors means none other than poor people that wander from one community to another.

L. A view of the town at the beginning of the 1860s

In 1866 a decree was issued about doing away with the town taxes with regard to the administration of the private towns. It was very important to see what the town looked like from a judicial and social–economic point of view before such a decree could be imposed, and until it slowly assumed the character of a town in a modern sense.

[Page 123]

In the town there were 244 houses: 278 wooden and 66 stone houses. Of the 344 houses, 145 belonged to Jews, 160 to Christians, 10 to the government, 1 to the town, 16 to the nobleman and 12 to the church. The town consists of 5539 residents, of them 3456 Jews, 2032 Poles and 51 others (Russians, Germans and French). (Percentage wise: Jews – 62.4%, Poles – 36.7%, others 0.9%). The 5539 residents form 1753 families: 1036 – Jewish, 717–Christian (percentage wise: 59.1% – Jewish and 40.9% Christians). 383 families live in their own houses and the remaining 1370 families live in houses that are not their own, as "tenants". The financial situation is therefore not a bright one, but it is worthwhile comparing the situation of Christians and Jewish families.

	Families	Percentage
Jewish tenants	886	64.7
Christian tenants	484	35.3
Total	1370	100%

The Jewish families who did not own their own homes, therefore make up 64.7% of the general number of tenants while they are only 59.1% of all the families. The poverty amongst Jews is on average, greater than the Christians. This is also evident in another analysis:

In the Jewish population:
3456 people – 1036 families – of which 886 are tenants which comes to 85.5% of the general number of families and 25.6% of the general number of people.

In the Christian population:
2083 people – 717 families – of which 484 are tenants, i.e. 67.5% of the general number of families and 23.2% of the general number of people.

From what does the Biale population make a living? The 1753 families are engaged in:

	Families
Agriculture; they possess houses and land	120
Agriculture and trade, they also possess houses and land	62
Home–owners whose professions are not given	201
Tenants who are engaged in trade and labour	1370
Total	1753

What commitments did the town and the residents have to the nobleman? We have already dwelt on this a little, when dealing with the community budget in the middle of the 18th century. There we only had the Jews in mind, now, standing before the abolition of the local taxes in favour of the nobleman, we will deal with all the residents. Firstly every house and ground–owner pays a tax for bathing, but from a judicial point of view, the bath–house is the property of the authorities. From this tax the nobleman has the following income: 274 rouble from the Christians for bathing and 140 rouble from the Jewish shop–owners. Those who own plots of ground pay a tax called "a tithe" (284 rouble). The town as one unit still pays the nobleman 150 rouble as a ransom for their work (people and horses) at the rake at the Volye and it consists of a dispute about work (one day in the week) by the residents of the Volye. Besides this the nobleman has a few monopolies that bring him a substantial income:

The proceeds (14 inns that sell wine and brandy) bring him 2½ thousand rouble annually. From beer and mead production, that every citizen is permitted to sell, the nobleman receives a payment of 57 kopecks from every barrel of beer, and 15 kopecks for every pot of mead. For every barrel of herring sold, the nobleman receives 15 kopecks. For using home–made millstones to avoid the nobleman's mills – 15 kopecks. For dealing with tar, oil and wheel–grease, 5 rouble. For the right to catch fish, 50 rouble. For every slaughtered pig – 7½ kopecks. For trading with imported bacon – 7½ kopecks.

As opposed to this the nobleman had a few obligations to the town: he paid 30 rouble annually as his share in maintaining the fire–brigade and another 180 rouble for repairing the tarred roads, the field gates etc. Besides this every Christian resident had the following benefits from the court: the use of the court mills in exchange for a small fee, free pasture in the court forests, and the right to a wagon–full of firewood every week. These payments from the court were rated at 2250 roubles annually. As already mentioned, only the Christians had the right to enjoy the benefits; for the Jews no benefits existed.

Biale citizens, Jews and Christians, paid the following taxes to the town: for inn concessions (135 rouble), a head tax (360 rouble), for cleaning the market–place (42 rouble), for maintaining the fire–brigade (210 rouble).

The following taxes were paid to the state treasury: house–tax 1219 rouble, ground tax 149 rouble, for transporting recruits and vagabonds 64 rouble, for a fire–tax 1971 rouble, for supporting the school for children 292 rouble, a lodging tax 2882 rouble.

In the private monthly budget of every citizen, all these obligations had real meaning. As regards Jews, one still has to add the expenses to cover the needs of the community.

[Page 124]

M. Conclusion

We have tried to portray the history of the Biale Jews in the course of approximately three hundred years, as much as the available material allowed. We accompanied them in their struggles in life, and we saw that they endured their battle with honour, attempting to help and support all those in need. Their whole existence was built on sand, and suddenly everything was destroyed.

Original footnotes:

    a.   Unfortunately I did not manage to find a plan of the town from that time, but Biale people will certainly easily be able to identify the above mentioned names of the streets in their time.

    b.   By Yuredich houses are those that belong to the court, and their residents are not subject to local rule.

    c.   Zoshkalne – means the street of the synagogue; towards the field – towards the cemetery.

Coordinator's footnote:

    * The translator has used the Yiddish names of towns. Current names have been entered in square brackets for research purposes. I have retained the Yiddish name "Biale" now known as "Biala" as it appears many times in the document.

Translator's Footnotes:

    1.   I gathered this material in the Polish Archive between the years 1933 and 1935. When writing this document in 1953, the necessity arose more than once to look again into the acts, but unfortunately this was not possible. Because of the lack of specific historical literature in the Israeli libraries, unfortunately I had to forgo the interesting chapter about Biale Jews in the Polish national struggles in the years 1794, 1831 and 1863. I also did not pause at the chapter about Biale Chassidism.

    2.   11 (1910) pages 142– 143. (material concerning the history of the Jews in Russia published by the Jewish historical–ethnographical society).

    3.   In his history of the Jews of Krokke (written in Polish 1912), Professor Ballaban mentions a Jew from Biale named Jesko Szlomowicz (Hershke? Ben Shlomo) already in the year 1533 (page 268). It appears that this is an error. In the Russian act of 1533, that Professor Ballaban uses to support his theory, it speaks of Belski. What the word Belski means is clearly evident from a Latin act of 1542, in which is written, Jesko Szlomowicz de Bielsko.

Russian Jewish Archive I, no. 152, no. 340. The reference is therefore to Bielsk and not to Biale.

    4.   R. Mahler: "a fragment about Jewish trade between Lithuania and Poland in the 16th century". Historical writings from "YIVO" volume 1, pages 130 – 204.

    5.   A. Ya'ari : "Emissaries of the land of Israel" (5711 – 1951) page 80, 248 (and perhaps this Reb Uri is not from Biale–Podlaska?).

    6.   The title "Mr" is seldom found preceding a Jewish name; the usual title is "non–believer" one who does not believe (in the Christian faith).

    7.   In the 18th century, a red gulden was worth 18 zlottes. A zlotte comprised 10 groshen.

    8.   It is worth mentioning that amongst the income earners, we also find women: shopkeepers, glassmakers and goldsmiths.

    9.   Wax was an important commodity and it served to provide light. The illumination of a large courtyard required a lot of wax.

    10.   "Korobke" – an indirect tax, mainly for meat.

    11.   The holy year falls on the 25th June.

    12.   Accommodation tickets – given to a poor person passing through the town, assigning him to a home where he would receive lodging and food.

    13.   A leader for a month – the leaders (representatives of the community) rotated their leadership role each month.

    14.   Poverty set in after the decrees of 1648; the internal and external conflicts and the taxes that kept rising.

    15.   "Pray for the peace of Jerusalem" by Reb Gedaliah Mesimiatitz; see A. Ya'ari "Journeys in the land of Israel", page 329.

16. Ha'ari (title of the Kabbalist Rabbi Yitzchak Luria, the founder of the practical Kabbalah, in the land of Israel in the 16th century.

17. "Notes on the emigration of Rabbi Avraham Raviga" in A. Ya'ari's "Notes about the Land of Israel", page 241.

18. The emissaries of the Rabbis, the emissaries who went to collect money for the settlements in the Land of Israel. The bones of Chaim Yosef David Azoulai were brought from Livorno (Italy) to Israel and were buried in Jerusalem on the 20th Iyar 5720 (17.5.1960).

19. Rabbi Chaim David Azoulai: "The complete book of the good circle" page 27.

20. Ya'akov Emden ben Tzvi "The scroll of the Book", 5657 (1897), page 186.

21. Y. Heilprin: "The Book of Records of the Synod of the Four Lands", pages 362 – 364.

22. Y. Heilprin: "Additions and Supplements to the Book of Records of the State of Lithuania", pages 66 – 67.

23. Y. Heilprin: "The Book of Records of the Synod of the Four Lands", pages 392 – 393.

24. Y. Heilprin: "The Book of Records of the Synod of the Four Lands", page 375 (note 4).

25. Y. Heilprin: "The Book of Records of the Synod of the Four Lands", pages 376 – 377.

26. Y.Heilprin: "The Book of Records of the Synod of the Four Lands", page 378.

27. Y.Heilprin: "The Book of Records of the Synod of the Four Lands", page 399.

28. Y. Heilprin: "The Book of Records the Synod of the Four Lands", page 402.

29. A Jewish Islamic sect that still exists in small numbers, to this day.

30. Ya'akov Emden ben Tzvi "The scroll of the Book", pages 188 – 189.

31. Y. Heilprin: "The Book of Records of the Synod of the Four Lands", page 408.

32. Professor M. Balaban: "The History of the Frankite Movement", page 190.

33. A request

34. Y. Heilprin: "The Book of Records of the Synod of the Four Lands", pages 423 – 424.

35. Professor M.Balaban: "The History of the Frankite Movement", page 190 (note 3).

36. H. Gratz: "Frank and Frankites" 33 ff.

37. The Pope who was supposed to judge regarding the various cases of blood–libel in Poland at that time, stated in 1753 that there was not sufficient evidence to charge the Jews with using Christian blood, and in every case the concrete evidence must be precisely and accurately investigated (see: R. Mahler "The History of the Jews in Poland", pages 344 – 345).

38. Sh. Bernfeld "The Book of Tears" 111 (5686 – 1920) page, 125 – 126.

39. There, pages 135 – 136.

40. "Memories of Reb Dov Mabulichov", the edition of Dr. M. Vishnitzer, pages 50 – 51.

41. Reb Tzvi Yechezkel Michelzon in the introduction to the publication of Reb Tzvi Hirsh Halbershtatter (Biale): "The Homilies of the Crown of Tzvi".

42. Rabbi Yehuda Leib Ha Cohen Fishman (Maimon): "The Ministers of the Century" volume 1, page 11.

43. Once Fishman and Lomaz came too late; the second time, the matter was again postponed because the magistrate designated that voting take place at the end of Yom Kippur.

44. Of the 10 hat makers indicated, eight signed with rings, that means that only two were able to write.

45. From 1837 the magisterial districts became known as provinces. Until 1844 Biale belonged to the province of Shedletz, from 1844 to 1866 – to the province of Lublin and then again to the province of Shedletz.

46. The regulations of the Chevrah–Kaddisha of Pruzshan were printed in the "Book of Records of the Town Of Pruzshan" (1930), pages 100 – 118. I saw the hand written Book of Records of Radzin, from a Jew from Radzin.

[Page 125]

Jewish Biale in Recent Generations
(general overview)

by M.Y. Feigenbaum

Translated by Libby Raichman

1. Until the First World War

We will reconstruct a picture here of a specific period of time, based on witness testimonies and personal memories. It begins after the last Polish revolt against the Russian regime in 1863 and ends in 1939 with the outbreak of the Second World War. We will divide this period into three time–sectors, that are connected to the changes that took place in the general political situation, and had an effect on Jewish life in particular. We will deal with the life and destruction of the Jewish population under Nazi rule in a separate chapter.

During the Polish rebellion against the Russian regime in 1863, the Biale Jewish population happily received with honour the rebel division of Raginski (leader of the division). The Rabbi, under instructions from Raginski and his officers, delivered a fiery prayer in the synagogue and read the manifesto of the national government.

In 1866, approximately 3456 Jews lived in Biale. This constituted 64.9% of the general population. The town found itself under Russian rule, and although the Jews were in the majority in the town, they had no influence on the administration of the town, which was in Christian hands.

Almost until the end of the 19th century the Jews lived as if in a closed–off ghetto, of their own free will. Jewish life was centred around the Rabbi's courtyard, in the small prayer houses of the Chassidim and in other prayer houses. They never came into contact with the outside world.

In 1927 our fellow–citizen, Advocate A. M. Hartglas, writes about this period:

"Forty years ago Biale was a town purely of Chassidim, two to three Litvaks [Lithuanians] and the rest, that means, almost the whole 100% – a backward Chassidic mass, without any modern concepts, or any cultural needs; far, not only from modern culture but also from European culture in general. Their whole world was locked into the Rabbi's courtyard and trading–businesses with the surrounding landowners. They had no feelings of their own personal self–worth in their relationships with the "non–Jews". And this was the time, when only 40 verst [Russian measure of distance – each verst equal to 2/3 of an English mile] from Biale there was a town with a healthy national, and cultured Jewish community – Brisk D'lita.

The Jewish population of Biale had no interest at all in any general education. There was a government high school – but I was the only local Jew among the students. Jews did not read Polish newspapers – the only Jewish newspaper at the time, the Hebrew "Ha'tsefirah" ["The Dawn"] was forbidden particularly amongst the Chassidim" ("Podlassia Life", number 6/2 of 11.2.1927, "Times are changing").

The rigid observance of this Chassidic mass impacted on Jewish life. They fought against the slightest deviation of accepted traditions. When noticing the smallest divergence from the customs of that time, one immediately heard the cry "help! it's burning!"; this was a means of informing people that someone must be "rescued". And in order to "rescue" them, they did not stop at the borders of the "ghetto", they also harnessed the help of the Tsarist regime–

You could hear the "help! it's burning" when a young man was seen with a pair of polished boots; a young man with a cravat; someone carrying something on the Sabbath when the Eruv was in disrepair.

And also someone talking about a parcel that was packed that was "not fit, and flawed" like, for example, Avraham Mapu's book "Love of Zion".

Resonating from that period, we find correspondence in the Hebrew newspaper "Ha'melitz" "The Advocate" [first Hebrew newspaper in Russia, founded 1860], number 5 of 1884, where we are told:

[Page 126]

"From Biale (district of Shedletz [Siedlce] Mr Avraham Kushtsitz notified that a few of the young men of the town got together and formed a group – to read books of enlightenment. When the Chasidim heard about this, they gave permission to a few of the masses to attack the enlightened youth. They came to the synagogue and beat the young men heavy blows with their fists and one of them fell ill. When the matter came to the attention of the commissioner of the town, he ordered that the attackers be punished, to heal the sick youth and pay a fine of 100 rouble".

One cannot say that in those days there were no rebels, although one could count them on your fingers. It is a known fact that on the High Holy days, Israel Mulyer (the father of the brothers Alter, Baruch and Isaiah Vineberg) publicly expressed his disapproval, that the Rabbi allows the people praying in the synagogue, to wait so long for him to arrive. Whoever was familiar with the authority of the Biale Rabbi, Rabbi Shmuel Leib, of holy descent, would agree that this was a very daring act.

The matters of the community were dealt with by religious personalities, scholars and respected home and business owners of the town. They would gather at the home of the Rabbi and make decisions on every important matter (according to the beliefs of that time). They also elected the wardens, who were later confirmed by the Russian regime.

The wardens that are remembered from approximately 1890 until the First World War were:

Moshe Bergshtein, Isaiah David (called: a pole), Moshe Vishnitzer (apparently from Vishnitz), Moshe Cohen, David Shachor (called David Reb Isaacs), Chaim Yoshke Kashtnbaum, Chaim Levi Rubinshtein, Kalman Sheinberg, Zalman of holy descent, Advocate Kalman Hartglas and Moshe Lebenberg. Naturally, all these wardens came from the wealthy classes.

The poorer classes in general were afraid to say a bad word about the wardens. And as they did not pay any community taxes, they also had no say. The rich people were also unhappy with the wardens, because they had to pay community taxes and this alone was already grounds for dissatisfaction with the trustees of the town.

The wardens would make a list of the tax payers with the amounts due, and hand over the information to the magistrate who would collect the community taxes in the same way as the municipal taxes.

From the community money that was collected, the wardens would renovate the synagogue, the house of study, the ritual bathhouse, pay support to the clergy and allocate certain assistance to those suffering and in need. The community taxes also covered the expenses of Biale Jews in hospital, away from home, on the basis of them having a note from the wardens. Later the community also paid the so–called hospital tax, according to the list of the wardens.

The masses never received accounts from the wardens about their activities, and only the government used to receive activity reports.

Until the First World War the community did not even have an office. The wardens dealt with all the matters on the street, or in their own homes. Typical of the activities of the community leaders, is that no records remained of their activities, no document has ever been seen. Even regarding the founding of the community and the liberation of Poland, not the least sign of archival material was found and there was nothing to transfer from the wardens.

Until the First World War the community even had an internal coin, the so–called "prutah". This small coin was cut out of parchment and on it was stamped "P B G" that stood for: "Prutah Biala G'dola", "coin of the great Biala". This coin was distributed by the wardens and three coins were equal in value to one groshen. The prutah served the paupers who used to wander from house to house. The day of the paupers was Tuesday or Thursday. If a pauper from another place came into town, he would buy a certain number of prutot in order to be able to give change from a groshen or from a larger coin. When they left town they would exchange the prutot that remained with them.

There were houses where even a prutah was too large a coin; there they would give such a pauper a piece of sugar, that amounted to a very small part of a groshen.

A few years before the First World War, the parchment prutot disappeared and prutot made of thin brass plate took their place.

Of the societies that existed in those times, the following must be mentioned – the Chevrah Kaddisha, the Food Kitchen, Visiting the Sick, Hostel for the poor. A few years before the outbreak of the First World War, the "Achiezer" was established whose members were active in distributing medicinal necessities to the community.

The Jewish community occupied themselves in direct trade, labour and as middlemen in trade. The standard of living was low and we will illustrate this with a few examples.

Most of the community sustained themselves with bread and potatoes. In most Jewish houses, fish, meat and challot would only be seen on the Sabbath and festivals. If someone took ill then they would arrive at the home of a wealthy man in the town with a little pot and ask for a little gravy. Once, when the price of a loaf of bread rose by half a groshen, the people were called to the synagogue to say psalms.

[Page 127]

Clothes were of very cheap quality. The men wore clothes made mostly of fabric that was as stiff as sheet metal. The women wore calico clothes. The shoes they wore were made of thick cartilage, and more attention was paid to the strength of the shoe than to its beauty. It was a normal sight to see patched clothing and shoes.

The living conditions in those times were also not ideal. You only heard of people living in an alcove, that means, in a small room that often did not have a window; they had a shared kitchen, that all the occupants of the alcoves used. The kitchen was a small room, where there was a built–in oven made of brick and added to it was the kitchen for cooking. However, seldom did one use such a kitchen, which in those days was actually regarded as a luxury. In such a kitchen a metal tripod was set up and under it – a few pieces of wood. A pot was placed on the tripod and this is how they cooked. The alcove furnishings consisted of two wooden beds, a small table, two stools and a trunk on wheels, in which their whole wardrobe and the valuables belonging to the family could be found. Very often at night this trunk served as a sleeping place.

A so–called "koyke" was affixed to a hook in the ceiling. The "koyke" (an open flat basket in the shape of wide circle, plaited with tree branches) served as a child's crib.

Therefore in those times, the idea of saving was widespread in the community. No one suggested the idea but it was almost self–understood. Even those who earned a little, also managed to save. They saved to have a dowry for a daughter, but mainly in the hope that they would be able to acquire a little piece of land, like buying a quarter of a house. This explains how many tradesmen in the town who, although they led a poor life, were owners of houses, or parts of houses. One might also encounter tradesmen who passed as poor in the town, whose names appeared on mortgage documents of houses, as money–lenders.

The community was not heavily taxed by the town council or the government. The shop and workshop owners would buy up a patent every new–year, from which the authorities would cash in almost all the taxes. That the taxes were minimal is demonstrated by the fact that when a Jew did not pay his taxes, the sequestrator Kshimovski would appear purposely on a Friday or on the eve of a Jewish festival, and remove the person's prayer shawl or the brass candlesticks.

Contact between the Jewish and Christian communities took place only in matters of trade or labour. Their mutual regard was cordial and as the Christian saw himself as the leader, in charge of out–of–town areas and the villages, so the Jew saw himself as the leader in the town. On the Sabbath and on Jewish festivals, the stores were all closed and the Christians already knew that there was no point in coming into town, because there would be nothing for them to buy. When peace in the town was disturbed on occasion, and Jews were being beaten, the Christian perpetrators, who were strangers to the town, would arrive in autumn as recruits to the local regiment. Jews already knew that after the festival of Sukkot they needed to prepare themselves for recruit–unrest and be able to stand up to the hooligans. In later years, when the "Bund" was active in the town, the resistance was organised and the recruits were given a good beating.

Attending events that were organised by Christians, like various artistic evenings, happened later in liberated Poland. Of that there was no question at all.

The Jewish community hardly came into contact with the local officials, unless in court. Mostly, the leaders of the community dealt with them and they were obligated to pay taxes in favour of the magistrate. These officials were mostly open to bribery and already had their Jews, that helped them in their work. These Jewish intermediaries used to manage to appeal to the officials to repeal a minor decree or buy back a Jewish child from Christian hands, during conscription.

Jews and Christians alike took no part in political life. On a few occasions there were elections to the Russian parliament, but the elections in the town occurred without any disturbance for the Jewish community.

These were not elections in the modern sense, but delegates were sent from Biale to the Russian provinces. Those who had the right to vote for delegates were owners of substantial immovable property, who paid taxes etc. Once, the following candidates from the Jewish community were presented for election as delegates to the provinces, Bernard Raabe, Idl Shvartz and Advocate Kalman Hartglas. It also happened once, that at the time of these elections to the Russian parliament, a small skirmish took place on a Jewish street.

[Page 128]

As said earlier, the voluntary ghetto lasted almost until the end of the 19th century, when changes in Jewish life began to be noticeable. A dispute between a sector of the youth and the religious circle began, caused by various factors like the Jewish High School students, the "Bund" and Zionism.

As the Biale Jewish community did not take advantage of the possibility of sending their children to the local government High School, so Russian Jews took advantage of this opportunity. They were unable to send their children to their own High Schools because of restricted intake percentages, so Jewish children came from Russia, in order to study in the Biale High School.

This High School made contact with the local youth, and under its influence, part of the youth began to secretly study worldly subjects. Gradually they were drawn into a circle actively involved in the study of Russian literature, and the effect that the Russian literature had on the young minds is not difficult to imagine.

The youth who were bold enough to savour worldly knowledge had to suffer much hardship. They had to endure persecutions, as well as clashes that took place within their families, but this pioneering trend was not lost. With time parents themselves began to give their children worldly education, naturally, according to the ideas of that era.

The Zionist movement, whose dates reflect a belated appearance on Biale soil, only in 1894, also assisted greatly in an attempt to see that the enlightenment–movement should become a natural part of the lives of the younger generation. It is understandable, that in Chassidic circles Zionism was forbidden, and those that sympathised with this cause were severely persecuted. The weak Zionist movement in Biale attracted mostly young boys that studied in the small Chassidic study–houses, but they did not reach the masses. These young people had to be very careful about their activities, because at the slightest suspicion they could be thrown out of the Chassidic study–house, that in those days meant actual isolation from the social life of that time. Their activities were concentrated mainly in the field of culture.

Enormous credit must go to the "Bund" for organising, activating and revolutionising wide circles of the Jewish community, and mainly the workers' foundation in Biale. They came to the Jewish masses and mainly to the youth with slogans that captured their ideals. Particularly, as all around them they saw so many fellow fighters that inhabited Russian territory — people who shared the same views. The battle of the Chassidic circles against "Bund" sympathisers was weaker than their battle against the Zionists, because here they were not involved with any of the students of the Chassidic study–houses. Besides their political activities, the "Bund" was also involved in cultural matters and influenced their friends to take it upon themselves to study worldly subjects and primarily, to begin reading serious work. The "Bund" had the courage to speak out against those who took upon themselves the right to rule the masses. The "Bund" also fought against the underworld, that terrorised the Jewish community mercilessly. Understandably, all the activities of the "Bund" were illegal.

After the suppression of the revolution in 1905, the Tsarist government organised pogroms against Jews. Such a pogrom took place in 1906 in neighbouring Shedletz [Siedlce]. It appears that Biale was also part of the pogrom plan but by chance Biale Jews were saved from a slaughter.

Every year in summer a great event would take place in Biale called "Shvienti Antoni" [a Christian religious festival called "Antoni"]. From all directions thousands of Christians would come into the town. On this day, it appears, the Tsarist government wanted to use the opportunity to settle scores with the Biale Jews.

In Biale at that time, the chief of police was a Russian, named Koreniov, who would enjoy spending time in certain Jewish homes. This Koreniov let a word slip out in a Jewish shop about the impending actions during the event of "Shvienti Antoni". News reached Yehoshua Fisher who decided to undertake to employ whatever means possible in order to avoid a pogrom against Jews.

Yehoshua was very close to the circle of the PP"S (Polish Socialist Party) who hardly did anything without his support. He worked together in the conspiracies of PP"S and he was their reporter to the higher courts of judgement. Using his status in this party, Yehoshua Fisher gathered together the leaders of the PP"S and notified them of the news of the impending pogrom. He informed the Poles, that this deals with a provocation that will be implemented by the Tsarist government using the Polish population. He explained that it was in the interest of the party not to allow the Tsarist government to use the help of the Polish population to carry out their political plans.

[Page 129]

The party leaders agreed with Y. Fisher and decided that they would actively resist any anti–Jewish public offensive.

On the day of the event the PP"S deployed its people to all roads leading into the town. Every wagon was searched and anything that could be used as a beating instrument was confiscated, with a promise to return these on their way home. They also warned the travelling Christians that they should guard against any public action against Jews, because, in retaliation, revenge would be taken and they would burn their cottages and leave them in ruins.

It appears that this worked and the authorities did not manage to provoke the incoming Christian mass to a public offensive against the Jews. The day passed without incident. On that day, however, the Jewish community were not too visible.

No matter how peacefully and monotonously the lives of the Jews in Biale flowed until the First World War, from time to time their lives were overturned by some kind of occurrence that shook up the community. There was no shortage of disputes amongst the Chassidism in particular. In Biale, there was a known battle against the Chassidim from Radzin for wearing a blue cord in the tassels of their prayer shawls. The Rabbi of Radzin, Rabbi Reb Gershon Hinech, the discoverer of the purple dye while on a visit to Biale, had to leave the town in a hurry because of a denouncement from the opposing Chassidim.

We will mention here a few events that occurred before the First World War that became ingrained in the memories of the Jewish inhabitants.

In 1892 Cholera raged in Congress–Poland and did not bypass Biale. The Jews who were affected by this shocking illness, were taken to the Jewish school (a Jewish hospital did not yet exist). Medicinal assistance consisted of: 1. rubbing alcohol into the hands and feet; 2. placing a piece of blotting paper on the stomach, with a hole cut out for the navel, that remained exposed; 3. The paper was soaked in alcohol and thrown on to the person.

Those who worked with the sick were volunteers from the Jewish community (amongst the rubbers – who used to rub alcohol into the bodies of the sick – were: Mendl Shtritz (nickname), Yossl Gottfried (nickname – Vetshik) and Avigdor Richter from Lomaz). The alcohol and the paper were stored in the women's prayer house under the supervision of Itshe Meir Zishes (Cohen) who truly sacrificed his own life for the sick. The epidemic did not spare the Christian population (children were not affected by the illness). The government arranged to lime–wash the gutters. In the Biale Rabbi's courtyard they forbade all the Chassidim who were from other locations to come to the Rabbi for the High Holy Days.

The Cholera, that began on the eve of the festivals, lasted for two months in the town, and destroyed many lives.

In the Jewish community, there was the belief that the Cholera was a punishment for Jewish sin. People were afraid to walk in the gutters, because the demons were there– As in many other towns during the epidemic, the community arranged for a couple to marry at the cemetery. The bride was the town's mad woman the "cold Dashe".

In the chapter "Biale" we told of the liquidation of the market place in what is now called Volnoshtshi Place and transferring it to the new market. The liquidation of the market place in the centre of the town did not happen so smoothly, and not without a battle on the part of the Jewish community. With regard to this battle the following would be told:

In the town there was a woman, Esther Perele, well–known for her glib tongue. Even in recent years a woman with a sharp tongue was called "Esther Perele".

In approximately 1902/3, Tsar Nikolai passed through Biale on his way to Leshne and Yaneve. When the coach with the tsarist couple appeared in the market place, Esther Perele tore away from the crowd, stepped down on to the pavement, planted herself in the path of the approaching coach and signalling with her hands, she forced the coach–driver to stop the coach. Esther Perele quickly approached the coach and handed a sheet of paper to the Tsar and returned to stand amongst the crowd. This all happened in the blink of an eye so that the police did not even manage to react. The sheet of paper that Esther Perele handed to the Tsar was a request to him that he should issue a command that the stalls and booths should not be removed from the market place. On his return journey, the Tsar actually stopped the decree.

In the town they used to tell about the funeral of a rich local woman that took place in approximately 1904. They demanded a large sum of money from her husband and children in order to build a Jewish hospital in Biale. The funeral only took place on the second day after the sum of 6000 rouble was paid.

[Page 130]

In the year 5666 (1905/6) there was a sudden attack on Jewish traders who were on their way to a fair in Lomaz. A group of robbers held up the caravan of wagons, when they passed by the Lomaz forest and began to shoot, forcing the travellers to stop. The robbers went from wagon to wagon and robbed the traders of their money. During the shooting two Jewish horse–traders from Mord [Mordy] (a village in the direction of Shedletz [Siedlce]) were killed.

The incident shook the whole town. Various versions circulated about the robber–murderers who were masked during the attack.

The next afternoon the funerals of the two murdered Jews took place. All the stores in the town were closed and the whole community took part in the funeral. The victims were taken in a normal wagon (because according to the law they had not been purified, but were to be buried as they were found after the murder). In the space in front of the cemetery the funeral procession stopped and the Rabbi Reb Shmuel Leib of holy descent, announced a ban on the murderers and then the Shofar [ram's horn] was blown beside the bodies of the victims.

At the same time a rumour spread amongst the crowd that one of the murderers was a Jew by the name of Siroki, a well–known thief, who came to Biale "to take a star role as an actor" and was happily lodging in the house of Kravtsov (a Russian Jew) that was situated at the new market place, at the end of Grabanovve street.

When the news reached Reb Aharon Landau, he called out: — Jews! "in every place that you find a guard against immorality, you find holiness" (Rashi section on holiness). As we are now standing before the holy victims, now is the time to fulfil the precept "and you will remove the evil from your midst", to "guard against immorality" and perhaps the merits of these holy ones will stand by in the demolition of the house that is a stigma for our town. Let us all go there to find the murderer and destroy the nest of all this evil.

The crowd ran to Kravtsov's house. As they approached the house, a mood of a pogrom arose immediately. Reb Aharon Landau was actually the first one to knock out the window panes and begin to storm the doors. All the entrances and exits were guarded. They began to carry out various valuable possessions. Suddenly there were screams that this Siroki was found under the bedlinen. When he was already half dead from the beatings he received, they took him to the cemetery. After the murderous blows that were inflicted, he confessed to taking part in the murder.

Reb Aharon Landau, however, did not want to give in and withdraw from the house, so with holy fervour he shouted: "Jews, do not leave until this house is utterly destroyed!". From every window in the house various pieces of furniture began to fly, pianos, mirrors and bed–linen. They were ordered, for the sake of God, not to take anything, and that everything should be destroyed on the spot. In a matter of a few minutes, the place was filled with feathers and torn bed–linen, with pieces of broken furniture and with torn clothes.

A patrol of soldiers approached led by Koreniov, the chief of police. At the time extraordinary conditions ruled in the land. The patrol released a volley of rifle shots into the air, but Reb Aharon Landau did not move from his place until he finished his work of destruction. Assisting him fervently were: Moshe Adlershtein and Yeshayahu Agress. Reb Aharon was arrested for inciting a pogrom and for resisting the authorities. The next morning, after Reb Shmuel Pizshitz paid the authorities the appropriate bail, Reb Aharon was released.

A charge of criminal action of a very serious nature was brought against Reb Aharon Landau and a few others who were complicit in the attack on the house. Reb Aharon Landau was exposed as the main culprit. In this way Kravtsov hoped to receive money for the damage that he suffered. After a long investigation, the proceedings took place over three days in the circle–court, which at that time was housed in the home of Urmacher, on Mezritsh street.

The defence consisted of four advocates, under the leadership of the well–known advocate Henrik Ettinger from Warsaw. Among the other advocates was the young advocate, a fellow–citizen, Apolinari Hartglas, who at that time began his advocate practice in Shedletz [Sieldce] with Advocate Zunderland.

The form of Advocate Hartglas's defence was characteristic. At the time when the other advocates were occupied with the legal side of the accusations, Hartglas described a Jewish upbringing that began with elementary school. He brought out the aversion that every Jewish child absorbs from his earliest childhood against murder and prostitution, presenting to the three Russian judges a picture of the prevailing Jewish world.

The result was that all the accused were released.

On a summer evening in 1907 or 1908, three Russian policemen were shot near "Shpringer's" (a nickname) house. One of them died on the spot.

At that time people said that this occurrence almost caused a pogrom against the Jewish community, because the shooting took place in a purely Jewish area. They were protected from a pogrom by the captain of the Kaluzshesk regiment who was on duty at the time.

[Page 131]

The men of the Tsharni family (nickname "Stoppes") were arrested as suspects in carrying out the attempted assassination of the policemen. According to a rumour that circulated in the town, the "Stoppes" were arrested on the grounds of anonymous information that was passed on to the authorities.

After a series of trials that stretched over years, Urtshe Motl and Shlayme and his son Ya'akov were given life sentences of hard labour in Siberia, where they were in fact sent. Hershl and Binyomin were allowed to go free.

Urtshe Motl died while in exile in Siberia. Shlayme and his son Ya'akov returned to Biale after the Bolshevik Revolution.

On a second occasion when a policeman was shot on the Volye, again a young Jewish boy paid with his life.

The boy, an orphan, worked for a shoemaker on the Volye. At the time of the arrest, after the shooting of the policeman, the boy fell into the hands of the Gendarmerie.

They began to parade those who were arrested before the dying policeman who was lying in the hospital run by the nuns. As the orphan was from the Volye, he was the first to be brought before the dying policeman who was asked if he recognised him. The policeman nodded and with that it ended.

On these grounds, the boy was sentenced to ten years in jail. After a short period of languishing in the Warsaw Citadel, the innocent boy exhaled his last breath there.

In Biale, in the last 70 – 80 years, only two Biale Jews were known to have served in the Tsarist army for the entire 25 years. They were: Hodessl Chantshe's husband and Ziskind. The latter worked at the trains as a porter; he received this work as a privilege.

This is what Advocate Apolinari Hartglas writes about the Jewish porters at the trains in his unpublished memoirs:

"The porters at the trains were, without exception, all Jews. Still today I remember one of them, the old Aharon, with the long white beard, dressed in uniform with his blue shirt and official hat, with the big brass number on his chest. The Jewish porters who worked for the Polish administration for approximately 20 years, were removed without mercy. In their place came a band of porters from Russia".

During this period, that we mention here, there were about four cases of conversion, and those mainly by women.

Particularly dramatic was the case of one called Raizele who was very pretty and who fell in love with a Russian Colonel. The officer and his group of soldiers besieged the house on Yaneve Street where Raizele lived, and Raizele left with him.

Raizele's parents left for America in shame. According to what was later heard, Raizele and her children returned to her mother, in America.

In the monotonous life of the Biale Jewish community, the day of celebration in 1911 when the Jewish hospital was opened must be mentioned in particular. It was no minor effort for such a community to build such a hospital that was splendid for those times. For the opening the governor and his retinue came down specially from Shedletz [Siedlce].

In ending this article about perceptions of events in the period before the First World War, it is worth mentioning a case of blood–libel against the Jews of Biale, that took place far from Biale and about which the Biale Jews never had any idea.

In 1881, a Brisk resident Reb Chaim Cohen received information from his employee in his petroleum store in Vienna that in the Austrian anti–semitic newspaper "Faterland" ["Fatherland"], a man called Pinchas Meir published a notice, in which he tells that after Purim and before Passover in 1881, he witnessed a Biale Ashkenazi Jew, a Rabbi in Biale, near Brisk, kill a Christian boy and use his blood for making matzah.

This information also reached the Warsaw community which then delegated Y.L. Peretz to go to Brisk and find out details about this matter.

A few Brisk communal workers became interested in the matter and after certain investigations they succeeded in discovering this information:

The writer of the notice originated from Terespol and was a nephew of the Biale rabbi (apparently they meant Rabbi Reb Shmuel Leib of holy descent – M.Y. Feigenbaum). This Pinchas Meir studied in the Biale house of study for some time and did not conduct himself appropriately.

[Page 132]

Being a relative of the Rabbi, they did not remove him from the house of study. One Sabbath night he hanged himself on a light fitting in the house of study and the beadle noticed it and rescued him from the hanging. After this incident he was driven away from the house of study and he left Biale.

The communal workers learned that from 10th March to 10th September 1881, Pinchas Meir was arrested and jailed in the Brisk jail. They succeeded in extracting an official confirmation of his arrest in this period, relating to his false accusation.

The confirmation was sent to Dr. Bloch, the editor of the "Estreichisher Vochenshrift" [Austrian Weekly"] who took action against the slanderer. The tribunal sentenced Pinchas Meir to six years in a fortress. ("Blood–libel by Ben Tzion Nymark, "Brisk D'Lita" – Encyclopaedia of the Diasporas).

Until 1905 emigration had hardly been heard of in Biale. There were a few cases of emigration in Biale after the pogroms in Russia in 1881, when the emigration of Russian Jews dragged a few Biale residents with them. There were also a few cases of emigration due to military service.

It was only after 1905, after the strangling of the revolution by the Tsarist government, that there was a large emigration from Biale to America and a small percentage to England. The emigration was not for economic reasons. People left the old home due to the failure of the revolution, on which the workers placed great hope, and the failure brought with it a state of depression. The atmosphere became stifling for these people and some of them, who were active revolutionaries, had to escape in any case, from the Tsarist guard. This was an emigration almost entirely of workers and reached a number as high as 400 people.

In 1897 the Jewish population of Biale, that already in reached 6382 souls, little more than 55% of the general population, thought little of emigration. Those that emigrated did not bring their families great honour, and the last ones did not even confess that they had family in America. It was assumed that in America people worked on the Sabbath and became like non–Jews, and who wants a non–Jew in the family? – Many of the emigrants left mostly in secret and did not say goodbye to anyone. An expression went around the town: "went out to close the shutters and left for America".

But the outbreak of the First World War interrupted this small emigration stream.

2. The First World War

Although the front lines were far from Biale at the time of the outbreak of war in 1914, the mood of war was strongly felt in the town. Firstly the Jews were mobilised into the army and in some families the only bread–winner was enlisted. The constant military transports, that passed through the town, cast a fear over the population and a concern for tomorrow. Despite this there was an upturn in the economic situation due to the greater presence of a military garrison in the town.

Six months after the war began, it became clear to the Biale population that the Russians would evacuate the town. Some Biale residents considered leaving the town and going to Russia. With this aim in mind they sent part of their household possessions to Russia and with the approach of the German army to Biale, these Jews left for Russia.

Amongst the Biale Jews that evacuated to Russia were some who had business connections with the Russian army and they went to Russia to continue their trading. It is, however, difficult to understand what motivated simple Jews to leave the town and to migrate. The Russian regime was hated by the Jews because of its persecutions, so why would they want to go there? Did they then, at that time, have grounds to fear the approaching German army? Perhaps their fleeing was connected to the thought of being as far as possible, away from the front–line.

The oppression that the Jews of Congress–Poland endured at the hands of the Russians during the war and when they were evacuating from the territory was known. Fortunately Biale Jewry did not know about these problems. When the Russian army left at the end of summer 1915, there were only a few incidents of robbery that could be attributed to it.

There was a short round of night–time, artillery–fire on the town by the German army, that did not cause any damage. In the morning we could already see the town in German hands. They moved around with such confidence and wherever they went it seemed as if they had already been in charge for a long time.

[Page 133]

The Jews did not find it difficult to understand them because of the similarity of German to the Yiddish language.

The German occupation brought complete upheaval to the way of life of the Biale Jewish population.

The Biale district was declared a war–zone and was hermetically sealed from the surrounding areas. All economic matters in which Biale was involved were interrupted. People began to feel what war meant and how German occupation could affect them.

The German regime conducted requisitions of all merchandise, and after a short time the town was emptied of all its stock–reserves. People began to experience the shortage of new articles. A strict rationing of food items was introduced. The German regime did not care at all about the allocation of clothes and footwear. Guard posts were erected on the highways to guard that no food items be brought from the villages into the town. Contingent deliveries were imposed on all agricultural products. For not delivering the assigned contingent at the proper time, the agricultural suppliers were severely punished and often even chased off their land. The German regime used to conduct precise inventories of everything that the agriculturalists owned and produced. They implemented systems of control, like putting numbered rings on the ears of pigs, receiving information about how many eggs a hen lays etc.

The products that the people received were rationed and they were issued with ration cards by the magistrate. And as they wanted to receive as many cards as possible, the Jews found a solution: they registered a single birth as a twin, and did not inform the authorities in cases of death– .

The main foods were black bread and potatoes but even these were restricted. In many houses they did not even possess the amount required to buy the most meagre ration. In every house people baked their own bread with flour that they received, and in order to increase the amount of bread to be baked, they would knead grated potato into the dough.

And when trade diminished, the merchants had nothing to do. The once important merchants and a large portion of the middle class became impoverished, even selling everything in their homes to maintain their existence. The Jewish tradesmen were also hard hit. The work of the tailors and shoemakers consisted of renovating old clothes and patching footwear. The building tradesmen and labourers went to work for the German authorities for a pittance.

In such an abnormal situation, people in the town were suffering from hunger yet in the nearby village there was the possibility of buying food, that was impossible to bring into the town. As a result there developed a smuggling of food products from the village to the town. Although the Germans guarded the streets the smugglers still managed, by various means, to smuggle in some products. More than once the smugglers fell into the hands of the Germans and paid dearly for the risks they took to avoid complying with the decree of the occupiers.

In many work places, Jewish workers worked together with Russian prisoners of war, who would steal various articles from the warehouses and sell them to the Jews. Later, when the Jews developed closer associations with the German soldiers, the latter would also bring a variety of items to sell in Jewish houses.

As a result of the malnutrition in the Jewish community, the typhus epidemic was a frequent guest in Jewish homes.

As soon as the German authorities became aware of a case of typhus, they would take the affected person to the hospital for infectious diseases, on the Warsaw Highway (later – the place of the 34th regiment). The German army took possession of the Jewish hospital. The house of the infected person was thoroughly disinfected and no member of the family was allowed to come close to the invalid. Word went around the town that patients in the hospital were poisoned. Understandably, this did not occur in reality; it can be assumed, however, that proper care was not taken of the sick. Because of these rumours people were reluctant to report cases of typhus to the authorities, and taking an invalid to the hospital was truly a tragedy for the family.

The German authorities were not much concerned about supplying food and clothing for the people. However, they had in mind to employ the population in forced labour. Using various strategies they deceived the people about work, promising a variety of opportunities. Finding themselves in difficult economic circumstances, many Jews allowed themselves to be taken in by these promises and put themselves in the hands of the German authorities. These people were sent to different places where they were employed in very hard labour without reward. The Jews returned from this forced labour, broken and sick.

[Page 134]

In order to have control over the male population, to determine whether every man was actually employed, there would be a compulsory gathering for all the men in the courtyard of the Gerrer Chassidim house of study every Sunday and there they checked each person's documents and certificates.

Entire lives were governed by iron constraints, that did not really allow the people to breathe freely. In the same way, throughout the period of German occupation they were bound by a curfew. During the summer they would hear the trumpet–call of the Commander some time before sunset, that announced that they needed to lock themselves in their homes. They always had to carry with them a parcel of documents, so–called certificates like: "permit certificate", "discharge papers", "work papers", "personal documents" etc. in order to be able to legitimise themselves with all these papers.

The houses were inspected endlessly. They searched constantly for illegal goods. And what was indeed legal in the eye of the occupier? Two German military figures were particularly zealous in these searches: the "little beard" (so–called by the Jews because of the pointed little beard that he sported) and the "white breeches" also a nickname given by the Jews because of the white trousers that he always wore). The appearance of the "little beard" in the street cast a fear over the Jewish community. With time, however, the Jews found a solution to the searches by organising good hiding places and concealing everything that might appeal to the "little beard".

The German authorities emptied the town of almost every bit of copper and brass. Anything that had any connection to these metals had to be handed in to the authorities. Even brass latches were removed from the doors. They also dragged out heavy brass chandeliers from the synagogue and house of study.

Besides the taxes that the community had to pay the magistrate, the ruling powers added a separate tax, the so–called "head tax".

It is remarkable that the community was not in a state of depression. The economy was in ruins and the Jewish masses were impoverished, yet, despite this, in these same years there was an upturn in the town in cultural, political and social aspects.

We know of similar cases in this period in other towns too, but when the specific conditions in Biale are taken into account, where the religious forces ruled with an iron hand, the phenomenon was indeed a wonder.

The collective social energy that poured out from the youth and the adults did not waver throughout this time and was now released with great impetus and scope. One can boldly say, that in the realm of cultural–achievement, this was the most beautiful period in the lives of Biale Jews.

How did it happen that all the disturbances by the powerful members of the community [Chassidim] suddenly disappeared? How did the alarm "help! it's burning!" disappear?

A number of religious Jews who were most prominent in their battle with those who sought freedom, migrated to Russia. Those who remained in the town became economically impoverished and therefore lost their enthusiasm for the battle. The ground for the social and cultural work mentioned previously had already been stimulated earlier by the activities of the Zionists and Bundists. All this forced the remaining religious fighters to stay on the defensive.

A few refugees, mainly from Brisk-D'Lita who turned up in Biale during the war, made a significant contribution to invigorating cultural life.

Under the energetic leadership of their chairman Moshe Rubinshtein who was the most popular personality in the town, the Zionists displayed outstanding zeal. Overnight the Zionists grew into an organisation with a large membership, and with a well–functioning operation. They established institutions that were the pride of the town and influenced large sections of the youth for their entire lives.

The crown of all the institutions in the town, was without doubt, the Hebrew "Yavneh"–school that was founded by the Zionists.

It is difficult to describe today, the revolutionary steps that were taken in those times, to establish a Hebrew school that in our times would be a normal occurrence. Whoever remembers Jewish life in Biale before the First World War, would understand the daring of such an act.

In founding a school of this nature, one did not have to solve the problems of staffing and curriculum only, but at a time when they were cut off from the world, they still had to worry about a budget. The main concern, however, was where would they find students. Would the Biale parents suddenly discontinue sending their children to the Cheder [religious elementary school] and send them to a school? The word "school" itself smells of non–Jewishness. And when we read the chapter about the Children's –Home, we see what kind of measures we had to take then to solve the problem of students for the school.

[Page 135]

How much festivity the school brought into difficult Jewish lives! What a superb youth the school raised! Even opponents of the Zionist party had to admit that the establishment of the "Yavneh"–School was a beautiful page in the activity of this party, in the town.

"Bet–Am" was a popular venue in the town that was initially used for gatherings where political meetings and discussion–evenings took place and was later changed to the seat of the local Zionist party. The building housed a library and held rehearsals of the dramatic circle and the choir, and presented performances of the Zionist organisation. Readings and debates took place there. In the same place Maccabi held gymnastic events and later the wind–orchestra practised there.

An entirely new phenomenon on the Jewish street was Maccabi, that was established by the Zionist organisation. For the first time Biale residents witnessed Jewish youth devoting themselves to cultivating their physical strength and this was also something new for the Christian population. At the end of the war Maccabi managed to purchase a complete set of wind–instruments from the Germans and the Maccabi orchestra came into existence. In those times, it was the only civilian orchestra in the town.

It must be mentioned that a few Jewish military personnel, that were followers of the Zionist organisation in Germany, came to assist Biale Zionists with advice and practical aid.

From this Zionist organisation, the "Mizrachi" came about in Biale, established by a few religious Zionists who could not tolerate the free atmosphere that prevailed in "Bet–Am".

The "Bund" concentrated on cultural activities like: organising a library, a dramatic circle, and various social and discussion evenings that were held in their premises.

The political activism of the "Bund" was established before the war to counter Russian oppression. Understandably, in the course of time their activities were minimised as there was no actual struggle against Russian oppression. The "Bund's" activity in the realm of organising the workers' union in its battle with employers was limited because there were almost no private employers; there was one employer – the German.

In the area of social activity, two very important institutions were established: the Children's Home and the Folk–Kitchen.

The Children's Home that was established by the Zionist organisation played an enormously important role during the war. And once again it must be said that the Children's Home was a jewel in the town. There was never a social institution established in the town that did such wonderful work.

The Folk–Kitchen was located on Brisk Street next to the church. Here they cooked midday meals and distributed them to the poorer members of the Jewish community. The Kitchen benefited from the support of the German authorities, thanks to the assistance of the Field–Rabbi (non–orthodox) at the time, Dr. Tentser. The Kitchen was managed by representatives of every existing party in the town.

Hebrew: Program of support for the Folk–Kitchen for Passover
Yiddish: Passover aid campaign for the Folk–Kitchen (1918)
In the middle of the star: Support your poor brothers
Top point: Flour for Passover
Bottom point: Matzah baking
Out of the star – top: Campaign to provide aid for Passover 1918
Out of the star –bottom: By the Jewish Folk–Kitchen Biale

    The Kitchen was not just an institution where they distributed hundreds of midday meals daily but also a place where many of the youth gathered to enjoy cultural activities. Reading and discussion groups took place there. A dramatic circle was also organised there, that presented performances for the benefit of the Folk–Kitchen. The selling of flowers was also organised, as well as the sale of money–orders for the benefit of the Kitchen.

[Page 136]

Many times it seemed that the German occupation would never end but after three years of keeping the Biale community in restrictive circumstances, the mighty German war–machine collapsed and it was evident that the end of German rule was near. Who would be the next ruler was not yet clear. One felt, however, that the approach of a public–spring, a period of freedom for every citizen, that would not differentiate between nationality or religion, was imminent.

The first sign that the Germans were leaving the town, was the sale of the contents of their stores to the civilian population. The period of transition between the time that the Germans left the town and the arrival of a new power, lasted a few months. At the time when the German administration ceased to function, a few people from the Jewish underworld used the opportunity to rob Jews. These members of the underworld would dress themselves in German clothing and in the evenings they would attack Jewish houses and steal money and jewellery.

The Jewish community organised a militia, that obtained a few revolvers from the German authorities. The militia would wander the streets at night, to guard the Jewish houses from attack. On one of these evenings, they came across two underworld figures from the gang and began to persecute them. After a short chase, both were shot by the militia in a courtyard on Yatke Street.

On a November day in 1918, the last German soldier left Biale and a Polish military mounted unit entered the town.

3. Under the Polish Government

Already the first days of the new reign were signed with Jewish blood. Polish soldiers went into the home of Moshe Richter in the Volye looking for arms and during the inspection they beat the Richters murderously and a few days later, he died. Very often the soldiers would grab Jews for various work, during which the Jews endured all sorts of torture. Gradually the situation began to normalise. Proper officials took lodgings in the town, and the population, including the Jews, began to rebuild everything that was disturbed and interrupted during the war.

The Jewish population was terribly impoverished and exhausted. Here the American "Joint" came to their aid, and sent large quantities of food and clothing to Biale. A committee of representatives of all parties was established and engaged in distributing items to the needy people. A kitchen for children was organised where lunches were sent home for the poor residents.

Allowing the existence of political parties made it possible for Jewish parties in Biale to implement their activities amongst the masses. On their agenda were various parties like: "Bund" and "Poalei Tzion" [workers for Zion] and now an additional party "Agudah" [Association], the party of the orthodox Jews, that although it only recently took its first steps on the political arena, already had behind it the largest section of the older generation. In that time there was also a cluster of nationalists.

The main competition took place between the "Bund" and the Zionists. The "Bund", whose followers were mostly workers, excelled particularly in stirring up fervour and very often would break into Zionist meetings and try to disrupt them. At times, this led to violent scuffles.

In 1918 the Zionists in Biale took action to send delegates to Warsaw for the co–ordinating–conference of their national council.

The elections to the constitution–committee stirred up Jewish spirit in the town. This event brought prominent party–leaders to participate in the mass–gathering. In Biale voting circles, the Zionists scored a victory by electing as a deputy fellow–townsman Advocate Polinari Maximillian Hartglas.

In 1919, for the first time, voting took place in the town for election to the town council, in which the Jewish population also participated. In these elections the "Bund" scored a victory and from the 15 elected Jewish councillors, six were on the "Bund's" list.

After the world war, when life had just begun to return to normal, it was interrupted because of the war between Poland and Soviet Russia. As long as the war–operations were taking place on Russian soil, or far east of Biale, there were fairly weak repercussions in the town; but with the breakdown of the Polish offensive and the retreat of the Polish army, the town began to tremble for fear of war.

[Page 137]

The military forces that were sent to the front lines and passed through the town made their presence strongly felt by the Jewish community with their hooliganism. The soldiers of General Haller's army ("hallertshikkes") and from the Poizner side ("Poznantshikkes") were excessive in their murderous beating of Jews, cutting beards and robbing shops and houses. The Jewish community lived in fear and there was no one to intervene. The whole Jewish community was regarded as Bolsheviks and in any case, they were allowed to treat them as their hearts desired– .

In the summer of 1920 the fighting front came closer to Biale. The Polish defence lines were constantly breaking down. A few months before the Polish army left the town, a grabbing of Jews began. They were sent east to dig trenches. For this work they grabbed Jews exclusively; Christians did not participate at all in the digging of trenches.

Close to the Polish army's evacuation of the town, prominent Bundists were arrested and they were sent away to the Dombye internment Camp.

At the beginning of August 1920 the town was occupied by the Red Army. Before the new regime managed to take its first step, it had to leave again in a hurry because the Bolshevik offensive failed at the Vistula. The Poles began to persecute the retreating Red Army, at a rapid pace.

Panic broke out in the town with the news that the Bolsheviks were leaving town. This frame of mind was not due to sympathy with the new regime, that barely lasted eight days, but simply out of fear for the approaching Polish army. With the Bolshevik regime in the town, Jews and Christians worked together, although the Christians occupied more leading roles, and the Jews – more secondary positions. Yet the Poles saw this Jewish collaboration as a hostile act towards Poland whereas they saw the collaboration of the Christians as their own understanding of doing good for the Fatherland.

A number of Jewish men ran eastwards together with the Red Army for fear of revenge on the Jewish community, by the Poles. But as the retreat of the Russian Army was sudden and turned into a panic–run, the civilian population who ran with them were an encumbrance, so the army compelled them not to allow the civilians to run with them. Most of the Biale runners remained stuck on the way, and after a few weeks almost all of them dragged themselves back to Biale. A few managed to reach Russia itself (amongst them was Shayme Sheinberg, who, with time, became an eminent military personality).

As much as the retreat of the Polish army during the breakdown of the Polish offensive in Russia was marked with Jewish blood, suffering and pain, the advance now meant more brutality for the Jewish population. The Polish army murdered and beat Jews under the pretext that they were Bolsheviks. Robberies were a normal phenomenon and the people from the villages would come into the town every day with sacks, in order to take home the spoils that were stolen from Jews with the help of the soldiers.

We will present here a translation of the interpretation of our fellow–townsman, Advocate A.M. Hartglas, a parliamentary representative, that he took to the Polish government in those days. The document gives a detailed picture of our town in those days in 1920.

"Even before the invasion, people, both Jews and Christians, were taken into forced labour. The latter however, were freed immediately. The Jews were beaten over their heads with rifle butts and they were robbed of their money. This was done mostly by the Poznantshikkes [people from Poznan]. One could only walk about until 10 in the evening but people worked until later than that. Before escorting a Jew to his home they extorted 100 – 500 marks per head. Accusations and intervention by local leaders did not help, because the officer in charge of the mobile–unit who was responsible for this work, was not interested. Violence and more severe robberies did not take place; only the Poznantshikkes were plundering. On the last day, the Poznantshikkes shot Jews in the streets, broke into Jewish homes and stole and in doing so, they wounded a Jewish woman. Before leaving the town the Polish military, on the grounds of a judicial order, shot four spies, amongst them – a Jew. A few days before the Bolsheviks came in, a slaughter took place beyond Grabanov (a village near Biale – M.Y. Feigenbaum). During this slaughter, Biale Jews earned praise from the local headquarters for their diligence in providing help for the wounded and cooked food for the fighting soldiers.

[Page 138]

The Bolsheviks that had entered greeted a member of the citizen militia, a Pole (who fled together with the Bolsheviks). In the beginning the Jewish population kept a distance. They drew nearer only after the meeting at the market place. The Bolsheviks were respectably restrained and they committed only one robbery in the house of Mrs. Hartglas. The reason for this was that they found implements belonging to her son, a soldier in the Polish army. The local Christian Communists remained in order. The Jewish Communists who betrayed the opponents of the Bolshevism were worse. In the concerts that were organised by the Bolsheviks, the number of Jewish youth participating outweighed the number of other participants (Biale Jews made up 75% of the population).

The "Revkom" (revolutionary committee – M.Y.Feigenbaum) consisted of a soldier – a Russian, Yulyev, a Pole and a Jew (both – local). Candidates for Revkom membership were Jews. At the head of the division there were also non–Communists from among the residents of the town. The Agricultural division was taken over by a local Pole, Provisions — a Christian, a Communist (who ran away with the Bolsheviks), Education — a Christian, a Communist (fled), Health – a local Jew. The militia consisted mainly of the unemployed, and was made up mostly of Jews. The head of the militia was a non–Communist. Mainly Christians took up official placements in Communist positions, who were not necessarily Communists. Jews were mostly in the police force and secretaries in offices. They were not Communists in the main but were afraid of the consequences – so they fled (with the Bolsheviks – M.Y.Feigenbaum).

The Zionist, Rubinshtein, did not care about the repeated threats and refused to accept a position with the Bolsheviks, not even as an overseer of the Jewish school system.

When the Polish soldiers re–entered, they immediately shot two Jews who happened to be passing by in the suburb of Volye and robbed them. Later, without any motive, they arrested Fisher the Zionist, and the councillor and warden Lebenberg, and one, a contractor, (of whom they first enquired if he was a Jew) and then stood them up against the wall with the intention of shooting them. Thanks to the fact that a few local Christians intervened on their behalf – they were freed.

The local residents were not happy with the fisherman Akiva (Kivve) Kamyen, who at the command of the magistrate, guarded the ponds of Chrabye Vielopolski and did not allow them to catch fish there. They pointed him out to the soldiers who wanted to shoot Kamyen. The intervention of the Christian community saved him. Six more Jews were murdered that were encountered behind the town. The Bolsheviks took Eliezer Wasserman to work with his horse–and–cart. On his return, with a Polish identity document, the soldiers stopped him on the road between Yaneve and Biale, confiscated his horse–and–cart, removed his clothes, tore the identity card and forced him into a pit, intending to shoot him. One soldier, however, took pity on him and they let him go. Six viorst from Biale he met other soldiers who beat him mercilessly, forced him into the river and ordered him to lie on the river bed. An officer ran up, reprimanded the soldiers and rescued him.

The robberies lasted almost without interruption and on a grand scale, although without excessive cruelty. Jews locked their stores. The robberies appeared to be normal acts of vandalism. Like: the items and books that were stolen from Rozenshine were piled up in a heap and set alight. The local Christian community and those from surrounding areas spoke to the soldiers, the thieves, and suddenly appeared with sacks in order to take the spoils. A few Jews on military duty and deserters fled Biale with the Bolsheviks. The town administration decided on a vote of confidence applicable to all those who worked with the Bolsheviks. They recognised that this was unavoidable, in order not to give the Bolsheviks the opportunity to introduce their decrees exclusively, and broaden their power. Until now, there have been no records of persecutions against those who worked with the Bolshevik forces who were almost exclusively, pure Poles. The boycott–agitation continued on its way. The citizens took a kind of decision, that was being considered by the magistrate, that refused to pay salaries to Jewish officials, and would not share with them the flour that was left by the Bolsheviks and that was divided amongst all the officials.

Only Jews were grabbed from the streets for labour, regardless of age. Soldiers attacked Jews in the streets and beat them. They also went through the houses confiscating belongings. When they entered they asked who the occupants were: a Jew or a Christian. If a Jew, they confiscated and if a Christian – they left. Mainly those of Yavorske's voluntary cavalry indulged in this activity.

The local management only came into existence in the afternoon of the 26th August. The leader at the time, Porutshnik Zalevski, gave the impression of being a man of good will, decidedly against any kind of cruelty or victimisation of Jews. One could therefore expect an improvement in relationships. I went to him bringing a victim. He immediately took up the matter keenly and warmly.

[Page 139]

He immediately sent out patrols. Regarding forced–labour, he turned to the Polish police with a request that it should communicate with the magistrate about providing him directly with the necessary number of workers. His senior, Captain Stokolski, and others believed that one of the reasons for the victimization was the closing of the stores. I explained that the stores were closed because of the earlier arrests by the Polish soldiers".

A few weeks after the victory of the Polish army at Warsaw, the then head of state, Jozef Pilsudski, travelled through Biale. Information was given that his train carriage would stop at the Biale train station, and that he would receive delegations. He asked the members of the Jewish delegation who presented themselves to him about the fate of the Jewish population during the war. The delegation began to tell him in a very delicate way, about the suffering that the Jewish community had to endure at the hands of the Polish soldiers. Pilsudski interrupted them and said: "my dear sirs, you must be making a mistake and mean the Bolsheviks". Understandably, the delegation had nothing more to say.

After the invasion the Jewish community experienced a very painful Sabbath when all around it was already quiet and order ruled. This was the Sabbath when the court–martial of Zalmenke, a Jew from Konstantin, took place. He was accused of spying for the Bolsheviks. Jews stood around Mevyuse's house, where the court proceedings were held, and waited anxiously for the verdict. In the afternoon the Jew was led out and taken in the direction of the jail, which was also the direction of the cemetery. Nobody knew the verdict and they followed the Jew who was being escorted. When it was apparent that he was not being taken to the jail and was being taken further, it became clear that the Jew was sentenced to death. They took him to the cemetery and there he was shot.

The war was also over and the wounds that were caused by the war started to heal slowly. The economic situation rose again to normal levels, the factories became active and the stores again displayed merchandise as before the war. The intensive building activity that developed in the town created employment for Jewish tradesmen and workers.

Many Biale residents were part of the mass–emigration that began from Poland to America immediately after the war. Information about the good life in America, in contrast to the situation in which Polish Jewry lived at that time, both political and economic, intensified the scale of emigration from Biale to America. Whoever had the possibility to do so – emigrated. Those who emigrated were mainly workers and women with children who were travelling to their husbands and parents, who had emigrated there even before the war.

It was now no longer a disgrace to emigrate to America. With the dollars that people received, there was certainly nothing to be ashamed of; on the contrary, they even brought the recipients some importance in the town.

The emigration drew out considerable productive strength from Biale. Also Warsaw, as the capital, lured and attracted the youth. The war–refugees left the town. As a result, this emigration had a negative effect on many aspects of social life. This was most conspicuous in the "Yavne"–School and in the Children's Home. The "Yavne"–School lost its reputation for excellence and was converted to a school under the name of "Folk school". The Children's home was soon closed.

The Riga peace–treaty between Poland and Russia had already been sealed a long time before, but the incitement against Jews, who were decried as Bolsheviks, still did not stop. The land was flooded daily with a spate of Jew baiting literature from the so–called "Rozvoy". This was an organisation that proposed the familiar Endek economic boycott against Jews [an anti–semitic organisation]. This organisation was also active in Biale. At its head stood Pietshitzki who used to utter inciting speeches against Biale Jews at mass–meetings. Later he was succeeded by the teacher Novotarski. Tensions between the Jewish and Christian communities grew but the Jews did not allow themselves to be provoked and did not give the Christian community an opportunity to unload their wrath.

As careful and guarded as the Jewish community was in this regard, yet an incident did occur whose consequences could have been very tragic for the Jewish community:

[Page 140]

On Lag Ba'omer in 1922, the Jewish youth of Hashomer Hatza–ir, went on their annual march in the forest on the Volye. At the head of the line was the Maccabi orchestra. While they were marching near the Krashevski–Highschool, Christian students threw inkstands from the windows on to the heads of those who were marching. In the evening when the youth marched from the forest back into the town, a few Christian youth on the Volye started fighting with the marching youth. Alongside the marching youth were a few strong young Jewish men who scolded the Christians severely.

Pietshitski, the leader of "Rozvoy", heard about this incident and decided to use this opportunity to get even with the Jews. Rumours began to circulate in the town that there were plans for a pogrom for the Jews. In this connection "Rozvoy" announced that a mass–gathering would take place on one of the approaching Sundays.

A delegation from the Jewish community went to the Governor of the province, Rudnitzki, and informed him about the rumours, requesting that he take proper preventative measures. His answer avoided the issue. A day later the community received a letter from the Governor, in which he informed them that due to the aggressive behaviour of the Jewish youth, he could not take responsibility for the consequences of the incident on the Volye. The Zionist Societies immediately informed the National Council in Warsaw. A few days later the Governor turned to the community and asked them to return his letter to him. The community fulfilled his request.

One Sunday a mass–gathering took place, called by the "Rozvoy" at which Pietshitzki, who has already been mentioned, delivered an anti–semitic speech. After the gathering, a line formed that reached the building of the Governor. There a few resolutions were read out, and the mass quietly dispersed.

The tension and the irritation, however, continued for days. Ambushes of Jews took place during which the authorities, and the police in particular, behaved in a completely passive way. The police avoided intervening even when cases of ambushing Jews occurred in front of their eyes, like, for example, during the ambush of Matityahu Adlershtein. The events of these days resounded in the presentation that the Jewish deputation delivered to the parliament.

In general, the relationship between the Jewish and Christian communities was peaceful and there were no clashes unless they were fired up from above. There were, however, single cases when Christian youths attacked Jews and beat them. Such incidents increased in the years leading up to the Second World War.

When we talk about relationships between the Jewish and Christian populations, one must note that in this domain great changes took place in comparison to the period before the First World War. Jews used to participate in events that were arranged by Christians like: theatre performances, concerts, balls, dance evenings, lectures etc. where they enjoyed themselves undisturbed. Christians again used to come and enjoy themselves at Jewish balls and dance evenings. The fact that Jewish children were studying in government schools also brought them closer. Jewish students used to visit their Christian friends and vice versa.

In the town's volunteer fire service Jews and Christians worked together in harmony for many years. In "Podlaska Life" of 5. 1. 1934, number 1/177, we read that the regime decorated these Jewish firemen for excellence and long service: Lieutenant Ya'akov Hershberg – 35 years of service; Avrom Orlansky and Antshul Beckerman – 25 years of service; Avrom Brovarek, Ya'akov Goldreich, Yosef Rozenberg and Berel Hershberg — 10 years of service. We can see from this list that the participation of the Jews in the fire service was very significant and would certainly have been impossible if the relationships between Jews and Christians had been strained.

In the league of air–defence, a Jewish division was created, led by Michash Hoffer. Thanks to his achievements in this field, Michash Hoffer was honoured by the government and awarded a "Cross for distinguished service".

It was entirely unnecessary to have a pogrom to shake up Jewish life, because the extermination–policy in the economic domain regarding Polish Jewry also reached Biale, and the consequences of this policy began to have a catastrophic effect on the Biale Jewish community. This happened after a relatively short time. The Jewish community in Biale that was never noted for a large number of wealthy residents and most people belonged to the middle or working classes, managed to tear itself away from the voluntary ghetto in which it found itself until the First World War.

[Page 141]

The Jewish way of life was completely changed in all respects. The reign of the religious fanatics disappeared, although their numbers in the town were quite marked. The excommunication of the Biale Zionists, proclaimed by the Biale Rabbi, serves to reveal the extent of the influence of these religious fanatics on Jewish life in the town. A chassid [a follower of a Jewish religious movement] handed the Rabbi part of a journal "El Al", a publication of Hashomer Hatza–ir, in which the chassid discovered a "terrible heresy", a poem by D. Shimonowicz–Shimoni. The Rabbi did not think for long and on a certain day, sent Yoel, the beadle of the synagogue, to knock on the doors of the Jewish houses with a hammer and call the people to the synagogue. To a synagogue packed with religious Jews and ordinary curious people, they turned on the lights and after a short sermon from the Rabbi, in which he banned the Biale Zionists, the beadle, at the Rabbi's command, blew the shofar and with that the banning ceremony ended.

Whoever was familiar with the former Biale can imagine what such a banning act by the Biale Rabbi, Reb Shmuel Leib, of holy memory, would mean in the period before the First World War. Now, however, the banning ceremony resounded quite weakly with the community.

The Jewish parties carried out their activities legally and each, in its own way, stimulated those in its circle of influence. Each party established a library and there was an enormous number of readers in the town who enjoyed the libraries. Dramatic circles existed in the town that often gave quite successful performances. The numbers of informed youth grew, that actively participated in all political fields and pursued education and knowledge.

The standard of living rose. Alcove–living disappeared and almost every family had its separate dwelling. In order to marry a child, one had to first prepare a decent dwelling and proper furniture, not to mention a decent dowry. The cloth and calico clothing and the Hambursk boots disappeared completely. They were replaced with elegant suits and dresses and the income of the people improved no end. In most houses meat and pastry made from white flour was prepared daily. Going to the home of a rich man with a little pot to ask for gravy for a sick person also stopped. The Jewish worker and tradesman ceased to labour from sunrise to sunset.

It was, therefore, really very painful to see how the extermination–policy of the Polish government against the Jewish population forced a continuous lowering of living standards. The economic noose became tighter around the Jewish throat. The first signs of this campaign against the Jews, was the Grabski-policy that began to empty the Jewish houses of their belongings.

Many Biale residents were carried away with the stream of emigration that increased then in Poland, and again mainly the youth. This time the doors to the United States were already closed to immigrants and the emigration went to the countries of South America, France, Belgium, Canada, Mexico and Cuba. A large percentage of Biale emigrants went to the Land of Israel.

Besides the emigration overseas, there was a flow of people from Biale to Warsaw and other big cities where it was easier to find work. Those who were active in all the parties also left and the result was a decline in the social life of the town.

After the Pilsudski–upheaval, in May 1926, there was a little relief in the economic situation of the Jewish population, but this was only a pause to catch one's breath. The general economic crisis of 1930 that affected Poland did not exclude Biale. A couple of large local wood merchants went bankrupt and dragged many families with them into abysmal poverty and brought about the liquidation of as much as two credit–institutions in the town.

The Polish Fascist government called "Senatzia" imposed a repression policy against Jews that ensured that the Jewish population would not recover from this economic crisis. Together with all Polish Jewry, Biale Jewry was also submerged in an economic abyss, that almost paralysed Jewish social life in the town. The Jewish population embraced apathy and resignation.

The Jewish shopkeepers lost their Christian customers, the Jewish tradesmen did not receive work from the Christians, and they were not able to make a living from the Jews. In order to hasten the pauperisation process of the Jewish masses, the tax office added high taxes to Jewish enterprises and in this way, one enterprise after another was systematically liquidated.

In these years people would remember with longing the tax burdens that the Jews had to bear during the Czarist regime. They would recall that the extent of the taxes in those times was worth the value of a tallit or a pair of candlesticks that the sequestrator Kshimovski would confiscate in the case of not paying the taxes. Now this seemed quite comical. Now, when the Polish tax officials would take entire households, the Jew would still remain in debt to the tax office.

[Page 142]

The Jewish youth found themselves in a hopeless situation: the working youth did not have stable employment, and if they did work, their earnings were minimal. The youth who were studying were not allowed into the High schools. So the town actually had an army of "street–surveyors" as the unemployed youth were then called.

In this pathetic economic situation, the Jewish community was not in a position to maintain its institutions on its own. A few social institutions were active in the town that, in a very limited way, helped the poorer classes in the community.

The Jewish hospital, the pride of the Jewish community, was more closed than open because there were no means to maintain it. When they received a few hundred dollars from their fellow townsmen in America, they opened the hospital and when the overseas support was exhausted, the hospital was closed.

Many families became "clients" of the "Food Kitchens" where every Friday evening challot that had been collected from the community were distributed and many Jewish children benefited from the help from the society "Toz" [Towarzystwo Ochrony Zdrowia (Society for Safeguarding the Health of the *Jewish Population; TOZ*)].

Some of the Jewish youth, embittered by their circumstances, found their way to the Communist movement.

In his article about the Biale circle, the author B. Gurni (former vice Governor in Biale) says that Jews made up 39.34% of the general number of members of the Communist party in the circle. It is apparent that the author does not take the slightest trouble to analyse the reason for this fact. For him it is sufficient that he can brand the Jews as an incubator for Communists. Because of the lack of proper material we will not contest the number that the writer provides, we merely want to state that the economic termination–policy and the anti–Semitic course of Polish rule were the main causes for the large number of communistically disposed Jews.

From the Communist side, they conducted propaganda that presented a Soviet–federation as a paradise for the Jewish population, that knows no boundaries, where people live free and with equal rights like all other Russian citizens.

Regarding the relationship of the Magistrate to the Jewish population, we will cite a few facts.

The town authorities of Biale, where the Jews made up nearly 40% of the population in 1938, knew only one thing: Jews had to fill the town's treasury, but they should not receive any compensation from the town's budget.

The contribution of the Jewish population was much larger than the contribution of the remaining 60% of the Christian population. In addition, the Jewish population who were mostly shopkeepers and tradesmen also paid, besides the direct taxes to the town authorities, indirect taxes to the state treasury. This was in the form of supplements in favour of the town authorities when purchasing trade and work patents. When it came to employing Jews in council positions, the town authorities granted permission to employ two Jewish officials (one of whom was later removed) and two to three tax collectors but only after long battles with the Jewish council members.

Of the general expenses sum of 270,000 zlottes from the preliminary budget of the town council for the year 1933/4, only 10,550 zlottes were allocated for Jewish purposes; that means 3.9% of the general expenditure (6500 zlottes for the Aged Home; 100 zlottes for the "Tarbut" library; 100 zlottes for the "Cultural" library; 500 zlottes for the Benevolent Society; 300 zlottes for "Toz"; 50 zlottes for Yivo; 1000 zlottes to cover expenses for the sick in the Jewish hospital). And even this minimal amount was not paid out easily by the town authorities. Each time there were difficulties in extracting one of the sums from the council treasury on the account of these subsidies.

While mentioning the magistrate, we will name the Jewish council members.

The Jewish representation in the first elected town council consisted of the following council members: Moshe Rubinshtein and Moshe Kavve (Zionists); Gedalyahu Braverman, Moshe Rodzinik, Nachum Vorek, M. Hochman, Chaim Brodatsh and Geltman (Bund); Yonah Shteinman and Yosef Zinger (Po'alei Tzion); Yisroel Bialer, Moshe Chaim Vizenfeld, Zushe Rozen and Moshe Meilech Zilberberg ("Agudah"); Moshe Lebnberg (non–party member).

Even though the Jews were a majority in the town council, they did not manage to elect even a deputy mayor and had to be satisfied with two Jewish aldermen. This probably happened because of the attitude of the Bund council members, who refused to co–operate with the other Jewish council members. It is, however, a question whether the authorities would have confirmed the election of a Jewish deputy–mayor.

[Page 143]

In the elections for the second town council in 1923, 13 Jewish council members were elected:

Ya'akov Aharon Rozenboim, Yoel Zilberberg and Yisroel Cohen (Zionists); Baruch Vinograd and Menashe Tzeshinsky (Handworkers' Union); Eliezer Tselnikker and Moshe Kramarzsh (Tenants' Union); Isaac Sheinberg, Yisroel Bialer, Zushe Rozen, Dovid Viseman, Chaim Levi Rubinshtein and Yitzchak Levi ("Agudah").

In the second town elections too, which also had a greater number of Jews, no Jew was chosen as deputy mayor and the Jewish representation to the office of alderman was assigned to the council member Yisroel Cohen. Today it is difficult to say whether the Jewish representatives tried to appoint a Jewish candidate for election as deputy mayor or whether they abandoned this idea, knowing in advance that the government would not confirm the election of a Jewish deputy mayor. Also during the term of office of this council, as in the first council, the Jewish representatives were not able to reach any positive outcomes, except for the insignificant sums that they received as subsidies for a few Jewish institutions in the town.

In the third council that was elected in 1927, the number of Jewish representatives was reduced to seven councillors. The government bodies already tried to change the voting statutes, so that the council would no longer have a Jewish majority. Aiding the decrease of the number of Jewish representatives was the division of the Jewish streets.

Members of the town council that were elected in 1927 [Hebrew]
The members of the town council that were elected in 1927 [Yiddish]

Seated from left: first –– Mayor Zakshevski
Standing: second –– Avrom Stricher, fourth – Yisroel Goldshtein, sixth – Boruch Vinograd
Eighth – Volvish Veitzman, after him – Chaim Levi Rubinshtein, Dovid Veisman
Second from right: Emil Vineberger

At that time the following were elected: Yisroel Goldshtein (Zionists); Boruch Vinograd and Avrom Stricher (Handworkers' Union); Dovid Veisman and Volf Veitzman (Small–traders' Union); Chaim Levi Rubinshtein ("Agudah"); Yitzchak Pizshitz (Merchants' Union).

In this town council there was one more Jewish councillor, named Eppelbaum, who did not represent Jewish interests, because he was elected from the Communist list. Understandably, he did not have anything in common with the other Jewish council members. After a short time he emigrated overseas and a Christian took his place on the town council.

Due to the Christian majority on the town council, this time the Jews were also grudgingly granted the position of an alderman that was filled by Emil Vineberger (originally from Galicia).

In 1934 elections took place for the fourth town council. Again the Jewish representation was reduced. This was caused by the various new changes to the voting statutes, like attaching village regions to the town, that formerly belonged to the village electorate and also granting voting rights to professional military personnel in the town.

This time five Jewish representatives were elected: Boruch Vinograd and Avrom Stricher (Handworkers' Union); Yitzchok Levi and Dovid Viseman (Small–traders' Union); Chaim Levi Rubinshtein (Gerrer Chassidim).

It is worth mentioning that the Jewish parties that participated in the elections did not achieve one mandate. Almost every elected Jewish councillor represented the interests of the Jewish social organisations in the town. This demonstrates that the Jewish community saw themselves compelled foremost to defend its economic needs.

[Page 144]

In 1938 the last town council elections took place before the Second World War. The Jewish community showed complete indifference to these elections. The Hand workers' Union and the Small–traders' Union presented a joint list of candidates of whom only three councillors were elected:

Avrom Stricher, Moshe Rodzinek and Advocate L. Goldfarb.

The decline in numbers of the Jewish representation from the first elected town council until the last amounts to a full 80%, at a time when the decline of the Jewish population compared to the Christian population in the same period amounted to only 16%. We see clearly how far the government bodies went in their efforts to reduce the Jewish representation in the town council, at a time when the community was large in number yet her influence over the management of the town's interests was minimal.

They not only wanted to remove whatever Jewish influence there was in the town's economy but also endeavoured, in the area of representation in the town, to remove even the least Jewish participation.

The Community

The first elected community authorities (council and management) in Biale, took place in 1924. The Jewish population voted publicly for its representatives in the community. In these elections, and also in later elections in the town, the political parties and the economic organisations took part. The workers' parties never participated in the elections of the community.

Unfortunately we do not possess the proper archival material to cast light upon this chapter of the Biale community. We will therefore endeavour to create a picture of its activities, according to details that remained in our memories based on clarification from the former community secretary, Baruch Vinograd (in Israel), and articles gathered from that time that appeared in the town's press.

The law regarding the communities, that was issued by the Polish government, stipulated that the activities of the community should not extend beyond the framework of a religious institution. With proper harmonious co–operation amongst the wardens of the synagogues, the community could still manage to accomplish something substantial in many areas of Jewish life.

Amongst the Biale community authorities in positions of power, the relationship between the representatives of the religious and the other authorities was always equal. The wardens of the religious wings used to try to ensure that in the preliminary budget, the needs of the religious should be satisfied first. To assist them they had the community law and it was not necessary to enter into any conflict. These wardens were not interested in large municipal taxes, and did not want their voters to bear any resentment because of high municipal tax payments. The income from the slaughter of animals and whatever was received from municipal taxes was sufficient to cover the expenses for the needs of the religious sector.

The main sources of income for the community were from municipal taxes and the slaughtering of animals but in both cases the income was less than it actually should have been. There were wardens who took the trouble to see that their relatives, acquaintances and clients should not, God forbid, "be wronged" by the municipal assessments. So actually the rich paid insignificant sums, and even this they did grudgingly.

We present here a list of municipal tax payers, as we found in the "Biale Weekly News" number 29, of 23. 7. 1937:

Number of Municipal tax–payers	Sum from the annual municipal tax – zlottes
159	5
130	10
41	15
62	20
28	25
30	30
2	35
20	40
28	50
12	60
25	75
13	100
10	125
11	150
1	175
1	200
1	225
3	250
4	300
2	350
1	600
Total 584	18465

[Page 145]

From the above list of municipal tax–payers, it must be stressed that it does not include all those who should have paid the tax. It is difficult to imagine that of a population of more than 7000 people, there should not be more than 584 tax–payers, that amounts to not more than 8.3% of the general number of the Jewish population. If we accept that on average there were 5 persons per family, it means that there were approximately 1400 families in the town, and of this number, more than 60% did not pay tax. One can assume that the community never had a precise register of the Jewish population.

We see also that starting from 100 zlottes a year and higher, the number of tax–payers is an insignificant minimum. Even in difficult economic circumstances in the town, a much larger number of Jews could be found who were able to pay a higher tax than 100 zlottes. This justifies our assertions that the rich got off with paying insignificant sums in favour of the community.

The management chairmen, Binyamin Klieger and Pinchas Nortman, waged a difficult battle to introduce a proper tax register for the community and for implementing a true budget that would satisfy other areas of Jewish life and not just the needs of the religious. They did not, however, manage to win a majority vote for their proposals.

For a long time the Zionist and hand–workers' factions waged a bitter battle in the community to take over control of the slaughtering of animals. The slaughterers did not want to release such a lucrative undertaking from their hands and the wardens of the "Agudah" came to their aid. And when slaughter finally came under the auspices of the community, the slaughterers waged an endless sabotage.

This is what appeared in the town's press:

"The slaughterers slaughtered without a note of consent from the community. The community did not want to provide these notes because they did not want to add to the income of the slaughterers. The Rabbi agreed to a decision by the community council and management committee to suspend the slaughterer Y. from his activities for 2 months without pay. In protest the slaughterers organised a strike one day, but after a warning from the Rabbi, they discontinued the strike." ("Podlassier Life", number 6 of 31. 12. 1926).

"Next, the slaughterer F. was fined 100 zlottes for slaughtering fowls without tabs from the community" (Podlassier Life", number 29/145 of 27. 7. 1934).

These punishments, however, did not help much because the slaughterers maintained that slaughtering was their private enterprise, and that no one has the right to interfere in their matters.

In 1932 a slaughterer received a weekly salary from the community of 75 zlottes. In addition they received free meat for a whole week. When one takes into consideration that a qualified worker earned 30 zlottes a week in those days, one can comprehend to what extent the slaughterers were "wronged" by the community.

The community economy was managed negligently and the community was immersed in debt. We read in "Podlassier Life", number 19/51 of 23. 9. 1932, that the inventory of the community was auctioned for an amount of 70 zlottes for a debt of 1200 zlottes, that the community owed to a government institution for insurance for employees ("Zupo").

We will present here a few figures from the community budgets, that we found in the town's press.

In 1927 the Rabbi receives a salary of 600 zlottes a month, and 500 zlottes a year for his rent ("Podlassier Life", number 23, of 16.9. 1927).

The preliminary budget of 1933 amounted to 75,000 zlottes. The income was estimated from the following sources: for uncollected municipal taxes for 1932 – 8500 zlottes, from the cemetery – 3500 zlottes, from the community houses – 7000 zlottes, for taxes for 1933 – 16,000 zlottes and from slaughter – 40,000 zlottes.

Among the expenditure entries, there appear: For the hospital – 10,000 zlottes, for the Benevolent Society funds – 600 zlottes, for "Toz" – 500 zlottes, for the library of "Tarbut" and the "Culture League" – 200 zlottes, for the Talmud Torah – 5500 zlottes, for the Jewish National Fund and Keren Ha'yesod – 200 zlottes (Podlassier Life", number 5/70 of 3. 2.1933).

The above–mentioned expenses amounted to 17000 zlottes. What kind of expenses took precedence over the remaining sum that amounted to a whole 58,000 zlottes? The greatest part of this sum was swallowed up to maintain ecclesiastical positions and an insignificant amount was used to pay the salaries of the office staff, that was very small: it consisted of: Boruch Vinograd – secretary, Shlomo Hochberg and Yechiel Hayblum – officials.

From the budget figures presented we see, however, that the community assigned 0.27% for cultural purposes; for social purposes – 14.80% but for ecclesiastical positions and for the Talmud Torah, that were of a very low level, added to this the small expense required to maintain the community office, all amounted to 84.66% of the preliminary budget.

Regarding this, it must be noted that the preliminary expenses for the ecclesiastical positions were always paid out according to the preliminary budget but in contrast, the subsidiaries were almost never paid according to the budget stipulations – they were always paid less. The best proof of this is the miserable circumstances of the Jewish hospital, that was more often closed than in use, because it never received the amount allotted in the preliminary budget.

[Page 146]

Just these few figures that appear in the community budget for 1933 present a picture of the activities of the community. It is therefore no wonder that the community did not have any influence and authority, even in matters that were within its jurisdiction. In these circumstances, in 1927, the butchers, in complete agreement with one another, arbitrarily raised the price of kosher meat: 3 zlottes for a kg. veal and 3.50 zlottes for a kg. beef. Only with the intervention of the government were the prices of kosher meat set at: 1.80 zlottes for a kg. veal and 2.40 zlottes for a kg. beef (Podlassier Life", number 10 of 11.3. 1927).

In the last years before the Second World War, the community became a battle ground due to the employment of a town Rabbi in place of Rabbi ShmuelmLeib, of holy descent, who passed away. For years the town was reluctant to take a new Rabbi and his role as teacher was filled by Moshe Utshtein. With time the teacher fell into disfavour with the "Agudah" and it began to put strong pressure on the community regarding the employment of a new Rabbi. The Zionistic wardens continually dragged their heels about employing a new Rabbi, but the religious wing took to the matter energetically. Various rabbinic candidates presented themselves. A Rabbi from Yavorshzne, Rabbi Tzvi Hirshhorn was elected.

Many positive measures were accomplished by the community authorities during their activities.

In the town there were communal buildings that appeared in the official books as having private owners. There were also so–called "legacies". The income from these assets was designated for specific social purposes.

The transfer of the buildings and "legacies" mentioned in the name of the community was no easy matter. It was a difficult legal procedure involving great expense and constant vigilance of the issues, in order to lead them to a conclusion.

These were the assets that were legally transferred into the power of the community:

The Jewish hospital, study houses and synagogues (also the Volye synagogue), Talmud Torah, receiving guests, the ritual bath–house, Tille's house on the market place where the finance bank was situated, the house of the "Garden of Eden" (a nickname) at number 6 Briske Street (where the community was located), three shops in the market place, three shops at number 3 Briske Street and one shop on Yatke Street.

The income from the cemetery was taken away from the Chevrah Kaddishah. Clearly, this was not accepted lightly, because previously the cemetery was the property of the Chevrah Kaddishah.

The Jewish hospital had existed as a separate institution that received a subsidy from the community. Thanks to the efforts of the chairman of the management committee, Binyamin Klieger, and the community secretary Baruch Vinograd, the hospital was changed to a community institution. The hospital budget was included in the preliminary budget of the community. The greatest concern for the community authorities was to ensure, as far as possible, the continued existence of the hospital.

The community carried out capital renovations to the synagogue and the study house. To paint the synagogue and the study house, artistic painters were invited from the town and from other areas. The community made a great effort to bring order to the arrangements for receiving communal guests and to the synagogue courtyard itself [where guests were usually housed]. The premises that were set aside for this hospitality were occupied by the poor who were not locals, as well as by poor people who were sick and had nowhere to go. The sanitary conditions in the house were shocking. After extensive efforts and great expense, the house again became a place for hospitality. The synagogue courtyard was neglected and unclean. Bringing order, and permitting the authorities to maintain hygiene conditions there, took a lot of energy and was very expensive. These achievements and improvements robbed the community authorities of time to attend to other issues. Every change brought about battles, struggles and protracted negotiations with opposing sides, that were actually not interested in any reforms in those areas that they represented.

After the liquidation of "Achi–ezer" the medical appliances were transferred to the community office. Until the last day of community activity, these appliances were being lent to the Jewish population. The community used to distribute permits to poor pregnant women. On the grounds of these permits, the woman was accepted, without payment, to the gynaecological section of the Jewish hospital.

The community office would write requests for assistance for the poor in the community, without payment, to all offices. There they would also distribute various permits.

[Page 147]

Of the notices in "Podlassier Life" that we managed to obtain, we see that in the years 1926 to 1933, these were the following management and council chairmen in the community: Ya'akov Aharon Rozenbaum, Binyamin Klieger, Pinchas Nortman, Binyamin Cohen, Arke (Aharon) Viseman, Yitzchak Levy, Moshe Kavve, Shamai Kalichshtein.

We come across the names of the following wardens:

Motl Aydelsberg, Zishhe Rozen, Leibl Goldshtein, Yisroel Cohen, Eliezer Tselnikker, Moshe Kramarzsh, Avrom Stricher, Fyvl Sitner, Tzvi Halperin, Natan Rammes, Yitzchak Berman, Velvl Isenshtat, Moshe Meilech Zilberberg, Isaac Shineberg, Chanina Kashemacher, Yitzchak Petterburg, Mordechai Pyekarsky, Chaim Levi Rubinshtein, Mordechai Yosef Goldshtein, Yoel Shtromvasser, Shual Batshko, Alter Suknov, Iddel Aydelshtein, Avigdor Fyerman, Eliezer Eppelbaum, Yitzchak Cohen, Shimon Lichtenshtein and Yehoshua Aydelshtein.

At the end of this chapter, a tragic event that shook the town must be mentioned. It will be ingrained in the memory of the Jewish population for a long time. We refer here to the fire of the printing office in the courtyard of Reb Aharon Landau.

"One evening on the 4th September 1927, a fire broke out on Narotovitshe Street number 5 (previously Kshivve Street), in the courtyard of Reb Aharon Landau. There in the wooden printing office 5 people were burnt to death: 1. Yitzchak Rubinshtein (a scribe, aged 60); 2. Esther, his wife (aged 58); 3. Yisroel, their son (aged 21); 4. Yocheved, their granddaughter (aged 3), and 5. Yitzchak Rubinshtein (aged 46), from Lubartov, a proof reader in a printing firm, who happened to be sleeping over at the home of the scribe. He left behind in his home a wife and three children. Three Torah scrolls that were in the scribe's possession were also burnt. The next day, on the day of the funeral, the Rabbi declared a day of fasting and asked that the shops be closed until after the funeral. After the funeral, hundreds of people went to the prayer houses to say psalms. It was assumed that the fire was the result of arson and that the victims were killed and robbed by murderers and then set alight. One can also assume that the victims were asleep and were asphyxiated by the fumes". (Podlassier Life, number 22, of 9. 9. 1927).

Many years later, a Jewish water–carrier lay seriously ill in a Christian hospital, and before he died he admitted participating in the robbery of the scribe and in setting the printing office alight.

We will present here a few figures that refer to the numbers of the Jewish population in Biale, from the beginning of the 19th century until 1939.

Year	Jews	Percentage of the whole population
1827	1,091	54.8
1841	2,220	61.8
1857	2,564	66.1
1897	6,382	55.2
1921	6,874	52.9
1931	6,923	39.5
1939	7,493	36.9

The numbers presented indicate that from 1857 to 1897 the Jewish population increased by 148.9%. How can this growth be explained? – it can be assumed that the figures of the previous years were not exact and in 1897, during the great census ordered by the Russian regime, the registration included, more or less, the entire population. That the figures of the previous count were not correct, can also be seen by the numbers of the Christian population, that according to these numbers grew in this period, from 1857 to 1897 as much as 400% (!). One must also take into consideration, that even in the great census of 1897, not all Jews registered, because they were afraid of the decrees – .

From the above figures it can be seen that from 1921 to 1931 the natural growth of the Jewish population concealed the drain that occurred due to emigration. In the last eight years, from 1931 to 1939, the increase in the Jewish population amounted to 570 people that occurred because of the cessation of emigration. The figures also show us that until 1921 the Jewish population formed the majority in the town. The reasons for the large increase in the numbers of the Christian population in contrast to the Jewish population are, that large branches of industry existed in the town at that time, that brought employment to many workers and only of Christian descent.

Workers were brought from all over Poland to work in the aeroplane factory. Besides this, as we mentioned earlier, for election purposes, purely Christian populations, that were previously attached to village communities, were now attached to the town.

[Page 148]

In such a situation as we described earlier, Biale Jewry entered the fateful year 1939. Even in these fateful months before the collapse of the Polish state, the pressure of extermination of the Jewish population was unrelenting and it continued until the last breath drawn by the Polish state.

For 21 years Biale Jews lived under renewed Polish rule that arose, as from the dead, after a 150–year enslavement. With the rise of the Polish state, the Jews of Biale, together with the entire Jewish population of Poland, dreamed the beautiful dream of equal rights, that seemed, in the national spring after the First World War, as self–evident. Disappointment, however, came quickly and they were convinced that the oppressor of the past very soon forgot the recent past and quickly became the oppressor again. The Jewish battle for equal rights in the last years of Polish existence changed into a despondent struggle for naked existence.

The war, therefore, found the Biale Jewish population in a state of despair, dominated by apathy and without prospects. This situation was the reason that, of the entire Jewish population that sat close to the new border between Germany and Russia, only an insignificant number crossed over into Russia. The majority remained sitting and waiting for the arrival of the murdering hordes. Everywhere one could hear one response: — why should we run? What will Hitler do to us? How can our situation become worse? – .

Sources:

1. "Podlassier Life" independent communal weekly, Biale. A number of examples from the years 1926/7 and 1932/4.
2. Testimonies by Alter Vineberg, Asher Hoffer, Moshe Ravon – Tel–Aviv, Gedalyahu Braverman – Petach–Tikvah, Baruch Vinograd – Ramat–Gan, Ya'akov Aronovicz – Argentina, Rabbi Shmuel Ya'akov Rubinshtein – Paris.
3. Janush Urbach: "The participation of the Jews in the Polish war of Independence", 1938.
4. B. Gorny: "A monograph of the province of Bialsk".
5. Bogdan Varshatinski: "The Jewish population of Poland in the 19th and 20th century". Warsaw 1930. Chapter: Jews in cities.
6. National club of the Jewish members of the Lower House in the Polish parliament, at the temporary Jewish advisory bureau: "The involvement of the Jews in the Bolshevik invasion". A Collection of Documents, number 1, Warsaw 1921.

[Page 149]

The Economic Life

A. Trade until World War 1

by M. R.

Translated by Libby Raichman

Until the First World War, open trade, i.e. trade in shops, was concentrated at the market place, as the square with the market orchard in the middle was called, or Volnoshtshi Place – after that time, it included parts of Warsaw, Brisker, Yannever and Yaske streets, that bordered on the market place. Here one could find the more representative businesses, organized, so–called "metropolitan" and also smaller shops.

Of the larger businesses, the following should be noted:

- In the line of manufacturing – Blimmele Mintz (Motl Mintz's wife), Chanele Miriam Fradls (the wife of Reb Yossele Alter, the Gerrer Rabbi's brother), Reb Aharon Landau, Feige Frimmes (Hellershtein ?)
- In the branch of haberdashery – "Varshavsky Department Store" belonging to Biederman, Chavah daughter of Dina (Lieberman), Yossel Gittelman (son of Channe Dovid Wolfs), Dovid Varm, Yakov Shlayme Zeidman.
- In the branch of metal – Meir Orlansky, Boruch Isenberg (son of Moshe Yossel).
- Utensils and glassware – Lidzbarsky (son of Feigele daughter of Rafael), Yakov Rozentsweig (son of Yankel, the son of Asher).
- Wine business – Leibe Bornshtein (Mednik), Chaim Pesach Farbiyak, Yisroel Meir Cohen.
- Food and Grocery – Fishl Finkelshtein.
- Restaurants and Pubs – Reuven Feldman, Moshe Adlershtein, Tzemach Tuchmintz.

Until approximately 1908, there was fairly small trade at the open market from booths, from street stalls or from the usual boxes, where vegetables, fruit, fish, soda–water etc. were sold. Only around 1908 – 1910 did the Russian administration liquidate the market in the middle of the town and moved it to the very end of Brisker Street, opposite the old cemetery. The place received the name "New Market". The garden in the middle of the old market place was significantly enlarged.

In the beginning, a very small number of the small traders moved to the New–Market. Most of them moved to the courtyard of Chaim Levi Rubinshtein, that was a thoroughfare to three streets. For the first time in Biale, fire–protected grain storehouses were built in this courtyard, with ceilings of brick and metal, and metal doors. Later, various wholesale and retail businesses opened in these same granaries. In 1912, a Jewish family from Kyeltz established an egg export business, that used to buy, pack and export eggs to Germany.

The greater volume of trade in produce and wood etc. that was mainly tied to export was conducted from the homes of the big merchants, like Shualke Cohen and others like him. There was already one room in the dwelling, that was set up as a "writing–room" that more or less resembled an office, where clients were received. These merchants already had a "person", i.e. a clerk, that did the bookkeeping, the correspondence etc.

Wholesale trade was carried out mainly in the food line. The biggest wholesaler of food and groceries was Motl Mintz. He conducted his trading from the granaries and from his own house on Yannever Street. Pelte (Paltiel) Oppenheim had his wholesale business on Brisker Street. There were also wholesalers that confined themselves to specific articles only, like: Berele Kozzes, Zissele Rivkah daughter of Akivah – herring and salt; Yehoshua Pyess, Nachum Liebman (Montsharzsh) – flour; Chaim Hofman (Naftsharzsh) – oil/petrol.

On the Sabbath or a Jewish festival, trade came to a complete standstill. It was as if the Jewish divine presence had spread its wings over the streets. All the businesses were closed and locked. The couple of Christian pork shops, pharmacies, Klimetzke's grocery and bookshop, looked as if they were abandoned. You would now meet the Jews who could be seen in the shops or workshops six days a week, going to pray or returning from praying, with prayer shawls in their hands; or Chassidim, who do not carry anything on the Sabbath in the streets – wearing their prayer shawls under their coats. Only in 1911 –1912, one Jewish business whose clients consisted mainly of officials and officers in the town opened at first half a door, and later the whole door, on a Sabbath morning.

[Page 150]

In contrast, on a Sunday, one could sense the revival of trade. In the morning hours the noblemen would arrive in the town from the surrounding palaces. Their covered wagons would concentrate on the north side of the market, from the council building to the Paviat (a district in Poland). They would visit the Jewish merchants who would take their produce from them, lend them money to reap their harvest and carry out other similar transactions with them.

On a Sunday, farmers from the surrounding villages would arrive with farm wagons and gather in the town. At first, the wagons would remain at the market place. Later, when the market was moved to the New–market, the wagons were left in the courtyard around the market. These farmers supported the small traders. On such a Sunday in the town, the farmer would buy everything that he needed for the whole week and would also sell his products.

This trade, big and small, would almost wind down before noon. After a visit to the Catholic church and after ending their prayers there, they would return to their places in the afternoon: the noblemen to their palaces and the farmers to their villages.

Such a Sunday was also the main day of trade for the restaurants and taverns. During the time that the nobleman was busy with his Jewish merchant, with whom he conducted his business, and had somewhere to go and enjoy the few hours, the farmers – who came in their masses, mostly not connected to any particular stall, would go from shop to shop, to find out where they could buy something for one groshen cheaper – this was evident from the restaurants and taverns. There they could enjoy their few free hours and also have a drink. One would actually meet drunken famers in the late afternoons.

During the week, Jewish small trade was done mostly amongst themselves. Every shopkeeper had his own clients. The larger businesses lived mostly from the custom of the officers, from the troops who were stationed in the town, and from the Russian officials.

B. Forerunner Of The Banks

Even before the first banks were founded in the town like: the "Savings Bank", the "Vzayemri Credit", and later also the "Bank Dlaya Handlv e Pshemislav", that was a branch of this bank in Shedletz it already engaged in well–established banking activity. Although this activity was conducted in quite a primitive way, it discharged the tasks of the branch in the economic life of the town in those days. The very big merchants had direct ties with banks or banking houses (Dom Bankovi) in Warsaw. The smaller merchants and the middle class, however, had to approach a middleman to fulfil their most minimal banking needs.

In the area of money transactions, the office of Yechezkel (Haskel) Erlich was active. The office was not an official banking house, with official permission from the government, but quite a homely business, in his house on Brisker Street. This office was connected to the "Banking–House Soloveitchik-Morgenshtern in Warsaw, and I think also in Brisk. Merchants who had to send money to Warsaw or Brisk for merchandise that they had bought there would purchase a draft from Yechezkel Erlich, for his correspondents in the two towns.

The drafts would be written in Russian, because the official bank–houses kept their books in this language. Yechezkel Erlich was not proficient in the Russian language so a Russian–speaking employee would manage the paper–work. Yosef Nachum Shteitelman, a Chassidic Jew, worked from early in the morning into the night, and even on Saturday night after Havdalah, for a reward of 3 ruble a week.

A second source of money transfer was the shipping agents (commissioners), who, besides the purchase of merchandise ordered, would also accept cash money in Biale and transfer it to the appropriate addressees in Warsaw.

Besides the money transfers, the merchants also needed credit. In this area, the middle–men came to their aid, like: Velvele Itshesand Yehuda Yakov, who were mobile banks. The two men acted as intermediaries between merchants, who needed credit, between those who possessed a few hundred rubles, or even greater sums, and kept it, as it was then called, "on percentage" i.e. "on interest". The money was sourced mainly from young couples, who boarded with their parents, from maid–servants, who gathered coin upon coin for a dowry, and from those who managed to save something from their work etc.

[Page 151]

Bigger merchants would take this kind of money on fixed terms. The accepted interest was between 10 and 12 percent annually. The smaller shopkeeper would have to pay 18 percent. The interest was paid weekly. Velvel, Itshes, and Yehuda Yakov would gather the interest from the borrowers every weekend and deliver it to the lenders. In this way the lenders saw their normal weekly income, every week before their eyes.

Jewish Income

by M. Y. Feigenbaum

Translated by Libby Raichman

A. Commerce

Before the First World War, trade in Biale lay exclusively in Jewish hands, as in many other towns in Congress–Poland. It was not at all necessary for Jews to compete with someone who had the same branch of income, because he was entirely free and not restricted. The Christian population avoided being traders, as they regarded it as not very honourable work. In Biale, before the First World War, the number of Christian shops could actually be counted on one's fingers. In 1910 or 1912, the first Polish Consumer–Co–operative "Spollem" opened – this was an expression of open and organized boycott of Jewish trade.

The Christian population did not willingly go to Christian shops, because between the Christian merchant and Christian client there was an abyss; in the Christian shops, the purchaser had to remove his hat, not come near to any article, but allow himself to be served by the staff, take what he is given, and pay whatever price was required, without bargaining. The Christian customer could not bear the tension created by the Christian merchant, who again could not understand the psychology of the purchaser, with whom one had to bargain and beat down the price. The merchant could not suddenly load the wagon with too much merchandise and then remove it again – the Christian customer looked with suspicion at the reality of the situation.

In Jewish stores, the Christian felt free, could choose the articles, test them, bargain and beat the price down and borrow for the purchase, and generally have a chat with the Jewish merchant, who was not aloof. The Jewish merchants understood the habits of their Christian clients well and knew how to approach them. The Jewish shopkeepers were also the buyers of the products that the farmers brought into the town, therefore the farmer felt more attached to the Jewish shopkeeper than to the Christian. The officials and the military personnel in the town were the clients of the Jewish merchants and there they enjoyed good customer service and credit.

Jews took to trading, because as a means of earning an income, it was relatively not difficult. Jews had no access to government and communal work places. One had to learn for many years to do a trade, and in addition, for Jews, trades in those years had very little status. A shop, however, could be opened very quickly, because for that, no qualifications were required, and not even a great outlay of capital. When a child married, the couple would use the dowry that they received to open a shop. As the number of shops increased, so did the competition between the Jewish shopkeepers.

Trade was concentrated mainly in the market place and in Ch. L. Rubinshtein's courtyard, that was bordered by Brisker, Grabanover and Yaske Streets. Single shops could be found on almost every other street and there were also shops in people's houses. In the last years before the Second World War, a great percentage of Jewish traders moved into booths and stalls in the "New–Market".

A large proportion of the shops were small in size, arranged and managed in a very primitive way. Many shops did not even have a glass door, and in the winter, in the days of the greatest frost, people would stand in open shops and warm their frozen hands at a fire–pot. The shops would remain open until late into the night and each shopkeeper would look to see if another had closed his shop. There were, however, also shops that were well appointed and were managed in great style. In Biale many women were involved in trade, making it possible for their men to study Torah.

[Page 152]

Merchandise was brought in from Warsaw and Brisk in wagons, before World War I, and by cars, after the war.

In the town there were also Jews who were involved in big business. They used to buy forests from the noblemen, cut down the trees, some of which were left in their raw state and some were sent to the sawmills to be modified. and exported abroad.

During the Russian rule, the merchants would have to buy a trade–patent and pay a very small tax.

The First World War ruined normal trade. Some of the merchants were impoverished and left the area of trade altogether. Their place was taken by yesterday's poor, who were successful in just this abnormal time.

With the rise of the Polish state in 1918, trade resumed on its normal track, except for Jewish traders; for them, a new chapter began, a chapter full of suffering, that was intended to lead to the decline of Jewish trade.

The fight against Jewish trade ceased to be contained by the written and spoken word, and was replaced by actions that became much stronger for the Jewish traders. The Jewish traders felt as if the extermination–noose that was cast around their necks, was becoming more and more restrictive.

Firstly, excessively high taxes were imposed on Jewish shopkeepers, that they were not in a position to pay. They were only allowed 1 year during which they were unable to pay the taxes, and then the backlog of taxes grew at such a pace that they could not extricate themselves. The tax office did not keep quiet, removed the merchandise from the stores, and the shopkeeper remained sitting in an empty store.

The observance of Sunday as a day of rest was forced on the Jewish population by the Polish government. This resulted in loss of income and brought hardship to the Jewish shopkeeper, who could not afford to rest, 2 days a week. So, they used to sell from the back door, and whoever did not have such a door would stand outside and cautiously admit the purchaser into the locked store. In this way, shopkeepers used to stand on guard outside their shops all Sunday, even in winter in the greatest frost. The police, however, used to persecute the Jewish shopkeepers severely, and put together official reports to their detriment, that carried heavy monetary fines.

In Biale, the downfall of the Jewish merchants was conspicuous, and was caused in the first place by the tax office. Prominent merchants liquidated their shops and opened booths at the new market; some did not even manage to open such a booth and stood there with small tables; still others became travelers to the fairs.

The reciprocal competition was an added cause of the impoverishment of Jewish traders. In this struggle, they forgot to include the taxes in their price calculations, and were later really not in a financial position to pay these taxes. The following example can serve to illustrate the calculation of prices of the Jewish shopkeepers: there were certain articles for which the shopkeepers could receive a bonus after one year, up to a specific percentage, that depended on the volume of trade that he did with this particular article. Taking this bonus into consideration, the Biale merchants would sell the bonus article at a lower price, that they themselves would pay. In the town they used to say, that the merchants also calculated into their prices their walk to the train station (the train station was situated 1½ kilometers behind the town, and the merchants who needed to travel to buy merchandise, begrudged a ride to the station in a horse–drawn cab).

As if the screws of the taxes that pressured the Jewish merchants were not difficult enough, the authorities began to bring Christians from the western areas into Biale, and opened businesses for them. These newly elevated Christian merchants were issued with government credits, that the Jewish merchants never had. All the orders placed by the aircraft factory, by the government and communal officials, as well as by the military, were granted to the Christian merchants.

The aircraft factory on the Volye, that was originally in private hands, was built with nothing less than Jewish money. The Jews were the providers of material and Jewish tradesmen helped with their hands to build the factory. Very often, Jewish merchants and tradesmen would receive promissory notes instead of money, for quite large sums, that were not paid, and it was permissible to protest. If these promissory notes were in Christian hands, who knows if they would have been able to complete the building of this factory, at all. The Christians would have immediately declared that the venture was bankrupt. The Jewish merchants and tradesmen, however, had the patience to carry themselves around for months with protested red promissory notes (red promissory notes were made out only for sums of 1000 zlottes) and allowed themselves to be cheated by the promises that they received from the builders of the factory. They promised them that they would be eternally remembered and thanked for the huge credit that they provided while the factory was being built. All the promises were later forgotten. All these people who helped to erect this enormous factory were later not permitted to cross over its threshold, even when their tenders were much cheaper than those of the Christians.

[Page 153]

The courts of the landowners in the surrounding areas, who had for generations been buyers from the Jewish merchants, and from whom they enjoyed considerable credit, now deserted their Jewish merchants, who had thick books that recorded the credit given to them. They took their orders to the Christian merchants.

The imported Christian traders from western Poland later thanked the Polish population, in particular the Polish intellectuals in the town, that brought them to take over the trade from Jewish hands. In the Hitler period these Christian merchants became the so–called "folk–Germans", who loyally served the Nazis. They helped to destroy a large number of the Polish city intellectuals.

In this period, there were a few Jewish businesses that could be called well–established, where the anti–Semitic attacks had not yet reached the source. Of these once great produce merchants, no trace remained, and the current produce merchants were called sack–Jews, because their trade consisted of buying a sack of produce, and no more.

A few Jewish families still clung to the once rich branch of trade in timber. The economic crisis of 1930 caused the bankruptcy of a few timber merchants in the town, and the results of these bankruptcies were felt for many years.

The decline of Jewish trade in Biale also characterized its organizational framework. In Biale, in the first years after the rise of Poland, a merchant association existed, that used to take up various issues raised by its members. With the increased rate of restriction against Jewish trade, the merchant association ceased to exist, and in its place came the small business association, to which almost all local merchants belonged. This coherence of almost all traders to the small business association was a clear indication that there were no longer any substantially large merchants in the town.

What the Polish regime, with its extermination policy against Jewish trade, did not manage to do, the Germans did, immediately after their occupation of Biale in 1939. A few weeks after occupying the town with the aid of the brown–shirt murderers, Jewish trade ceased to exist altogether.

At the end of this article, we will calculate the branches of trade in which the local Jews were represented.

- Food, fruit and candy, vegetables, grocery, dairy, pubs, cafes, tearooms, butchery, fish, produce, purveying, wine, poultry.
There were shops that sold only wholesale: salt, kerosene, sugar, flour, groats, herring, rice, yeast, beer.
- Manufacture, butter, haberdashery, footwear, confectionary, leather and shoe–making accessories, clothes, elastic, glassware and kitchen utensils, metal and building materials, agricultural machinery, and tools, coals, building timber, firewood, paint, bicycles, old–iron, writing materials and books, combatant materials, furniture, jewelry, hotels.

As far as possible, we will make the effort to recall the largest shops and enterprises that existed at the outbreak of the second World War.

- In the food and grocery line – Yakov Kornblum, Tzivia Bachrach (from Brisk– the main wholesaler;
Chaya Zelda Tzukerman, Mordechai Yosef Goldshtein. Moshe Shor.
- Fruit, candies and cafes – Berl Sandlarzsh, Yitzchak Cohen, Chaim Mordechai Rozenberg.
- Vegetables – Abush Rozenblum.
- Dairy–Blume Goldshtein.
- Taverns–the Adlershtein family, Shimon Lichtenshtein, Moshe Lichtenshtein, Chaya Sapir, Velvl Malina, Yitzchak Berman.
- Wine – Natan Bornshtein.
- Wholesalers: salt and sugar – the partners Dovid Nortman and Feldman; herring and rice – Eliezer Tzelnikker; yeast – the Reich family and Motl Shteingart; beer – Yitzchak Berman, Moshe Lichtenshtein, Yisroel Yitzchak Sapir; flour and groats – Netta Altbier; kerosene and all kinds of kerosene products – "petroleum" that belonged to Isaac (Izshe) Sheinberg and to the brothers Leibl and Shmuel Krizelman.
- Manufacture and butter – Yehoshua Gliksberg, Berish Fishman, Yerachmiel Lichtenboim.
- Haberdashery and footwear – Shmuel Zusman, Yakov Shlomo Zeidman, Yosef Gittelman, Dovid Kligberg, Hershl Cohen, Soreh Leah Tornheim, Leibush Richter.
- Confectionery – Mendl Tokarsky, Mordechai Piekarsky.

- Leather and shoemaking accessories – Yakir Cohen-Tzedek, Yitzchak Grobman, Motl Eidlsberg.
- Kitchen utensils and glassware – Y. Vinegarten (Feigele Rafael's daughter), Moshe Lidzbarsky and Tzirl Rozentzveig (Yankel Asher's daughter).

[Page 154]

- Iron, building material, agricultural machinery, coal – Avraham Orlansky, Meir Orlansky, Avraham Kalichshtein, Shimon Lichtenshtein.
- Building timber – the partners: the Lustigman family and Velvl Aideltuch, the partners: the brothers David and Froyem Viseman with Hershberg (David Kligberg's son–in–law), the partners: Moshe Radzinek and Shmuel Orlansky, the partners: Moshe Kuropatve and Zechariah Eppelboim.
- Firewood – Moshe Rodzinek, Avraham Yitzchak Koralik, Yosef Zshelaza.
- Furniture – Moshe Yitzchak Biederman, Pintshe Aidelman.
- Bicycles – Yitzchak Agress, Yakov Dogodny.
- Jewellery – Avraham Goldshmidt, Chaim Mordechai Goldshmidt.
- Writing material and books – Pinchas Nortman, the heirs of Yoske Vinograd, Vurman (Yoske Vinograd's son–in–law), Nochum Tenenboim.
- Combat material – Michash Hoffer, Berl Goldberg.

A few other occupations need to be mentioned here, that were allied and connected to trade. We mean agents (purchasing agents), car–owners and suppliers ("with government contracts").

The agents in Biale would travel to Warsaw on Sundays with pouches filled with orders from the merchants. On Fridays they would return home, bringing the main orders with them. During the week they would hand over the goods that were ordered to their families at home, and their families would deliver them to the merchants. The Biale agents were very familiar with Warsaw, they knew every little corner there and did not need any addresses of the merchants, from whom they needed to purchase the goods ordered. They, the agents, mostly paid lower prices than the merchants themselves. The agents worked very hard and they were genuinely responsible people who could be relied upon.

In the difficult years for Jewish trade in Biale, at a time when many Christian traders emerged, the Jewish agents in Biale remained without clients. There was no Christian who could or wanted to compete with agents, and even the anti–Semitic Christian merchants had to approach the Jewish agents.

As agents, the following families were active: Pretter, Sheinberg, Rieback (Yakov and his son Aharon), Hayblum, Novomiast, Kamlet, etc.

Local Jews were also pioneers in the organization of inter–town automobile–communication. Jewish-owned trucks travelled from Biale to Warsaw and Brisk from where they brought various merchandise. The pioneers were the agents consisting mainly of the following families: Sheinberg, Rieback and Kamlet.

Jewish "contractors" (suppliers) were active in the town. Until the First World War Shmuel Pizshitz, Shimon Krideshtein and Chaim Levi Rubinshtein were well–known. They would supply the military and the government with various items, and also take on major works with the government.

In the 1880s, Shimon Krideshtein erected his military barracks on Yannever street that stretched until the ends of Garntzarske and Sitnitzke streets.

Ten years later, after Shmuel Pizshitz erected his barracks on Artileriske street, the military left the barracks of Shimon Kriedshtein and moved into the barracks of Sh. Pizshitz. Because of this, there was an ongoing battle in the town between Krideshtein and Pizshitz.

Later Shmuel Pizshitz built wooden barracks on the Brisk highway and in 1901 he built barracks of bricks alongside them.

After the rise of Poland, Wolf Weitzman and Shmelke Shvartz were active suppliers to the military in the town. With the dismissal of the "Ovshem–politic" in the area of economics, they too were distanced from this source of income.

Unfortunately, we have no statistical material about Jewish trade in Biale. The former town–elder in Biale, B.Gurny, in his monograph of the Biale Circle, provides figures for the whole district. What is apparent to us, however, is that they could also be reliable numbers for the town of Biale. This is what he writes: "In 1938, 80% (1640 licenses) for trade in the district, lay in Jewish hands. The Jews were represented mostly in the trades of: haberdashery (84%), leather (78%), food (75%)".

In 1939, almost the same number of Jews lived in the Biale district as in the town of Biale itself, close to 7500 souls. If we should accept that both in the Biale district and in the town of Biale there were the same number of people in trade, then it means that in Biale 820 families were involved in trade.

B. Trades

[Page 155]

It can be assumed that in those years, 70–80 years ago, Biale was no exception to other towns, where a trade was not considered to be an overly honourable occupation and was not much of an attribute for a family. In those years, the merchant took pride of place in Biale Jewish life. Most of the merchants were Chassidim and they prayed in the small Chassidic–prayer houses using the rite of prayer that was inspired by Sephardic liturgy. The tradesmen were concentrated in the synagogue and the study houses and prayed in the Ashkenazi style of liturgy. Even before the 1st World War, there was a positive change in the attitude towards a trade, as a profession.

Biale did not distinguish itself in conducting any form of mass–production, which was the case in neighbouring Mezritsh, with the pig–hair line of business. There were hundreds of workshops in the town and most of them were located in the homes of the tradesmen themselves. It is understandable that the housewife would involve young apprentices in doing the housework, and in their first years they would also at times assist the tradesmen with his work.

Work would begin in the very early hours of the morning – in the summer, from sunrise to sunset, and in winter, work would begin when it was still dark – by the light of an oil–lamp, and they would work until 8 or 9 at night – again by an oil–lamp. There were occasions in workshops where articles had to be completed for transport, every week on a Friday, they also worked through the night on a Thursday. Most craftsmen stood in the workshops and worked together with their workers.

On Fridays the workers were paid their salary. The apprentices were not paid, except on the festivals — when they received a few groshen (small coins) for a haircut.

The work was hard because no mechanical power was used, and work was done in a very primitive manner.

Under the influence of the organized workers' agency, the difficult work conditions changed even before the 1st World war. The workers began to push their employers for various changes and in the first place, they demanded a shorter number of working hours. The expectation of improved social conditions never came into consideration. In the later years, under Polish rule, some workers were insured in a health insurance fund and their employers had to pay a certain fee. In almost all work–places in this period, the 8–hour work day was already observed.

In the Russian period, the Jewish tradesman did not know about taxes at all, but in the Polish period (1918–1939), he became a debtor of the Polish treasury. The Jewish tradesmen were encumbered with such high taxes, that most were not in a position to pay. So, the tax officials actually emptied their homes of every piece of furniture. That was the time, when the idea of a cupboard, built into the wall, was developed so that the tax–officials would not be able to remove their possessions. Many tailors would obtain a receipt from their clients, confirming that the material belonged to them, to avoid a requisition from the tax–officials.

Another law was added regarding Sunday as a day of rest that made it possible for every policeman to harass the Jewish tradesmen. Although the overwhelming majority of the Jewish workshops were situated in the courtyards and not in front, on the streets, the policemen would come and issues warrants for desecrating the Sunday.

The three statistical tables presented here belong to the year 1921, developed under the direction of the engineer Heller, Warsaw 1923, on the basis of a poll about Jewish industrial enterprise in Poland.

What is relevant to Biale are the tables concerning mainly the artisan–workshops, because, besides Ra'abbe's factory, two sawmills and two mills and the vinery, there was at that time in Biale no other Jewish industrial enterprise.

It can be assumed that the figures in the tables are not comprehensive. We see from them that in 1921 there were 402 Jewish work enterprises (of them 26 – not active), with a sum of 861 workers, of whom 758 were Jews.

Table 1

Enterprises	In %	Employed salaried workers	Totaled in %
Stone, clay, glass*	1.1	9.2	19.9
Metal	5	4.1	2.1
Machinery business	1.9	1.3	0.3
Wood	2.1	3.7	6.5
Leather	2.4	2.8	2.8
Textile	1.1	0.9	1.
Clothing	49.5	43.8	42.5
Paper	2.7	1.5	0.5
Maintenance	18.1	18.6	10.1
Chemistry	2.7	3.	3.1
Construction	9.8	6.7	6.7
Graphic industry	1.6	2.3	2.3
Cleaning	2.1	2.1	2.1

*In production occupations "lime pits" – 2 enterprises with 77 salaried–workers, of whom 2 were Jews.

[Page 156]

Table 2

Local Industry	No of active and non-active	Active		Non-Active	Total employed	Owners		Family Member		Salaried Workers						Non-Jews			
		With salaried workers	Without Salaried workers							Jews									
						Number	%	Number	%	Together	%	Men	Women	Children	Together	%	Men	Women
Stone, earth etc Ind.	4	2	2	—	79	2	2.5	—	—	2	2.5	2	—	—	75	95	75	—
Metal Ind.	19	4	14	1	35	21	60	6	17.1	8	22.9	4	—	4	—	—	—	—
Machine and Technical Ind.	7	1	6	—	11	7	63.6	3	27.3	1	9.1	—	—	1	—	—	—	—
Wood Ind.	8	3	4	1	32	7	21.9	—	—	13	40.6	12	—	1	12	37.5	12	151;
Leather skins & similar Ind.	9	4	5	—	24	12	50	1	4.2	11	45.8	9	—	2	—	—	—	—
Textile Ind.	4	1	2	1	8	2	25	2	25	4	50	1	—	3	—	—	—	—
Clothing and fur Ind.	186	88	92	6	377	183	48.5	30	8	163	43.2	77	30	56	1	0.3	—	1
Paper Ind.	10	2	7	1	13	7	53.8	4	30.8	2	15.4	1	1	—	—	—	—	—
Nutrition & enjoyment facilities	68	12	51	5	160	61	38.1	60	37.5	32	20	26	6	—	7	4.4	7	—
Chemical Ind.	10	2	5	3	26	7	26.9	7	26.9	6	23.1	6	—	—	6	23.1	6	—
Building Ind.	37	7	22	8	58	28	48.3	4	6.9	25	43.1	25	—	—	1	1.7	1	—
Graphics Ind.	6	2	4	—	20	7	35	4	20	8	40	4	—	4	1	5	—	1
Cleaning Ind.	8	5	3	—	18	8	44.4	2	11.1	8	44.4	6	—	2	—	—	—	—

1. Enterprises With salaried–workers Without salaried–workers Not active Total			133 217 26 376
2. Employed persons proprietors family members		Number 352 123	in % 40.9 14.3
Jews Men Women Children	173 37 73	283	32.9
Men Women	101 2 total	103 861	11.9 100.

In the later years, before the 2nd World War, Biale possessed the following Jewish tradesmen:

Carpenters, bricklayers, painters, cabinetmakers, blacksmiths, locksmiths, metal workers, turners, electrical technicians, radio technicians, shingle makers, sawmill workers.

Tailors, seamstresses, shoemakers, hat makers, milliners, furriers, *Kushmers*, cutters and stitchers of shoe leather, knitwear producers, makers of wadding, wool combers, knitters, lace makers, embroiderers, corset makers, sock makers.

Watchmakers, goldsmiths, printers, book binders, photographers, grease makers.

Bakers, butchers, vintners, paraffin makers, gruel/porridge makers, gardeners, confectioners, fleecers, fishermen, pitch makers.

barbers, wig makers.

Despite the sweeping policy of the Polish regime to transfer trade and work to the local Poles, there were, until the 2nd World War, trades in Biale that lay entirely, 100%, in Jewish hands, like: hat making, glass making, metal work, wood–lathing, printing, book binding, etc. All attempts to introduce Christian tradesmen in these areas, remained unsuccessful. Even in the aircraft factory, where later, they did not allow any Jewish tradesmen, they were forced to employ the Jewish glazier, Feigenboim, and the Jewish metal worker, Yisroel Felman.

[Page 157]

The aforementioned once vice–governor of Biale, B. Gurny, in his monograph of the Biale Circle, states that Jews in the Biale Circle controlled 56.5% of the entire handwork in the Circle. According to him, until 1939, 1286 handworkers' cards were issued to the Jewish tradesmen. If we should also accept, as we did with trade, that the Jews in the Circle, whose numbers were the same as the number of Jews in Biale, were represented percentage wise to the same degree as the Biale Jews, that would mean that Biale officially possessed close to 643 Jewish tradesmen. We say official, because in fact, there were many Jewish tradesmen who worked without hand–workers' cards, particularly in the province.

In the monograph mentioned here, it states that the Jews in the Circle were educated in: tailoring 80%, painting 90%, hat–making 100%, shoe–making 78%, hairdressing and barber 75%, metal–work !00%.

The participation of the Jews in the Circle, in the free professions, is classified at 25%.

Jews in the town were active in the following free professions: doctors (1 – 3), dentists (1 – 2), advocates (1 – 4), midwives, dental technicians, book–keepers, clerks, forestry experts and business employees.

[Page 157]

Trade
[of the 1880s until 1939]

by Gedalyahu Braverman, Petach Tikvah

Translated by Libby Raichman

Regardless of the fact that Biale was always considered a religious town, and was famous for its great scholars, already in the 1880s, trade was widespread among the Jewish population of Biale, even though trade was not regarded with much esteem.

The main source of income of the Jewish tradesmen in Biale came from the Christian population in the town and the surrounding areas. Biale, as a Circle–town, was home to many officials and military personnel. However hostile the officials and Russian officers were to the Jews, they had to approach the Jewish tradesmen in many instances where there were no Christian tradesmen at all. And if there were any, they were unable to compete with Jewish tradesmen in the superior quality of their work. The Christian shoe–makers were unable to copy a pair of officer's varnished boots that Srulke (Yisroel) Kotshemayinik produced. Who did not talk about Hershl Brisker? People had to wait in a queue to buy a pair of boots or a pair of shoes from him. Aside from the fact that his work was first–class, the materials he used were of the best quality.

True, there were also Jewish shoe–makers who were not as skilled, but these served the farming population who were more willing to allow themselves to be served by the Jewish tradesmen than the Christian.

It is worthwhile telling about a Biale shoe–maker of that time, who conducted his work in a strange way. That was the shoe–maker Sender Motye (he had a son who was a teacher and had his own house at the corner of Grabanover and Proste street). This Sender Motye never measured a client's foot and in particular, that of a woman. He had a little box of sand and he would tell his customers to place their foot in it. Then he would measure the impression that formed in the sand. It is understandable that Sender Motye's clients were recruited only from the Jewish population.

The same occurred with the Jewish tailors, with whom the Christian tradesmen could not compete. The few Jewish military tailors were frequently inundated with work. The clients of the good Jewish tailors were noblemen and officials, as well as wealthy Jews. The clients of the mediocre Jewish tailors were from the Jewish middle–income group, the Jewish workers, and the local town–dwellers.

The Jewish building–trades, like: cabinet making, carpentry and painting, were certainly dependent on the Christian population for work. The cabinet makers and many building carpenters could be found in the villages for almost the whole season, where they would erect houses for the farmers and in the courtyards of the noblemen.

The situation of the bricklayers was different. They were dependent almost entirely on the Jews in the town.

The situation of the painters was better. They did not have to wait for the eve of Passover when Jewish people white washed their houses but received work from the Christian population and from the local officials.

[Page 158]

In the winter, the economic situation for some tradesmen was a difficult one. The building industry ceased, the tradesmen did not have work and they could not exist for long on the money they had saved. They therefore began to look for other work in the winter. Many went away to chop ice on the river, others were employed to put ice in the ice–houses and many would go around the courtyards of the houses chopping wood.

At the beginning of this century, there was a great revival in the building industry. This happened when the administrator of the Biale court, Dikler, built the barracks on the Warsaw highway. For this work, a few hundred tradesmen from Biale and the surrounds were employed.

In the later years when menial work ceased to be a stigma for a family, and the youth who were now grown up, hastily turned to learn a trade, every trade acquired new tradesmen. It is understandable that Biale was not able to absorb so many tradesmen, so many of them left to work in larger towns, returning home for Sukkot and Pesach. This was, more or less, the means of solving the problem of an excess of tradesmen in the town.

With the industrialization of the country, shoe factories came into existence which was a blow to the shoe–makers' trade. The Biale shop–keepers began to bring in beautiful shoes, and in this way took the young customer away from the shoe tradesman. The shoemakers called meetings, threatened the shopkeepers with torment, but after all the fuss, they realized that one cannot go against the times, and that the shopkeeper could not be forced to give up his source of income.

Amongst the cutters and stitchers of shoe leather, there were two rational master craftsmen, Idl Brisker (Hershl Brisker's son) and Froyem the Ginger, who came up with the idea of creating a Workmen's Association of all the Biale cutters and stitchers, to avoid competition. When the shoe–makers came to know about the impending union, that would, in their opinion, adversely affect their pockets, they began to agitate and tried to prevent the association from being established, but all they managed to attract was one cutter and stitcher, Velvl Kiegls.

In 1906, the union of cutters and stitchers came about. A unit was rented from Reuven Kozzes (Shulman) on Grabanover street and there they all worked together. In the town it was called: "The Cutters and Stitchers Union". The following tradesmen worked there: Idl Zeidman (Brisker), Froyem the Ginger, Henech Ostatni Grosh, his son and Avraham Froyems. As workers the following were employed: G. Braverman, Mordechai Yosef (Brayndel Gricheles's grandson) and Yoel Ketzeles. The Union, however, did not last more than a year and fell apart. There were many reasons for dissolving the Union, but the main reason was that one employee wanted to deceive the other and watched to see that only the other employee would do the work.

During the 1st World War, when Biale found itself under German occupation, the situation of the Jewish tradesmen was pitiful. There were no raw materials with which to work, and the population could not afford to acquire anything. Most of the Jewish tradesmen became day–workers for the German government.

After the 1st World War, it took a while before the economic situation in the land stabilized. Great changes were brought into the lifestyle of the population that affected the circumstances of the Jewish tradesmen in the town.

A revival came about in the line of furniture carpentry. Before the 1st World War this was an almost unfamiliar skill in the town. Who was interested in what kind of bed they slept in, and how many generations had already slept in that bed? Who was concerned with what kind of wardrobe stood in the house? After the war life took a great step forward. For a young couple, after their wedding, the issue of furniture became a problem. Furniture factories began to open in the town, and many building carpenters took to this work. With time, there was a noticeable influx of adult youth to this profession.

The building industry in the town came to a halt; Jews no longer built. Jewish bricklayers were assigned to Christian employers, and the latter rather took Christian bricklayers, who regarded themselves as no worse tradesmen than the Jews. So, some of the Jewish bricklayers actually left for foreign lands, and there were no followers amongst the younger generation to this profession.

The cabinet–makers' trade became unstable for the Jews and began to decline. If a Christian built a house, because of anti–Semitism, he gave the work to a Christian.

[Page 159]

The production of machine–made shoes in Biale began even before the 1st World War, when the brothers Hoffer and their brother–in–law Binyamin Klieger established a factory for machine–made shoes, where tens of workers were employed. After the war the work in this factory was not recommenced. Many workers who had previously worked in the aforementioned factory opened factories in partnership and produced machine–made shoes. In the town, before the outbreak of the 2nd World War, there were 5 partner–factories and production was almost stable. The products were sent to Brisk and a part was taken by Biale shopkeepers.

These partnered–factories provided a livelihood for almost all the leather workers in the town and some of the leather shopkeepers.

Generally, the economic situation of the Jewish tradesmen in Biale, in the last years before the 2nd World War, was a difficult one. A revival was noticeable only in the partner–factories of machine–made shoes, and by the furniture–makers and the tailors.

Despite the restrictive policy of the government towards the Jewish population, even relentless anti–Semites were forced to approach some of the Biale Jewish population, if they wanted to have a good article. Even the German murderers could not stop marveling at the work that the Jewish tradesmen produced in Biale.

Factories

by M. Y. Feigenboim

Translated by Libby Raichman

Under the name "factories", we mean enterprises that worked with machines, even primitive machines, that employed a greater number of workers, or those firms that were never classified as workshops.

Already in 1873, in the Volye, there was a small active factory producing wooden nails. The factory belonged to the Ra'abbes until the outbreak of the 2nd World War, when it was appropriated by the Germans. After the war, the factory was nationalized by the Polish government.

The founder of the factory was the German Tyber. In 1873 he built up the factory on a very small scale, as a workshop for producing wooden nails for shoes.

Hersh Ber Ra'abbe, a pious Warsaw Jew, who was a small salesman of Tyber's nails, was, after a while, brought in as a partner in the factory. Their firm was called "Tyber and Ra'abbe". After a few years the partnership was dissolved and Ra'abbe remained the only proprietor of the factory. The name of the factory changed to "Ch. B. Ra'abbe". Ra'abbe enlarged the factory and they began to produce shoe–trees for shoes. Later Ra'abbe established a sawmill.

In 1915, when the German army marched eastwards, the factory was evacuated and moved to Russia. The machines were transported, and a large number of employees travelled with them to Russia where the factory was set up in the town of Nyerecht.

After the 1st World War, when the Ra'abbes returned from Russia, the factory was re–established and began to operate on a very large scale. Besides the wooden nails, they began to produce new items, like: knives, wooden heels, wooden trowels for medicinal purposes etc. The world–famous firm "Bata" were buyers of the Ra'abbes' products.

Ra'abbe's factory was one of the largest of its kind in the Russian empire. Its products reached as far as Manchuria, Middle–Asia and the Caucasus. In 1915, before moving the factory to Russia, 400 workers were employed there, amongst them approximately 100 Jewish female workers. The administrative personnel were entirely Jewish. The factory's doctor was Dr. Gershon Zita, the only Jewish doctor in the town.

After the death of Hersh Ber Ra'abbe, his heirs continued to run the factory. The four sons were: Me'oritzi, Bernard, Vintsenti and Yakov (all lived in Warsaw).

Me'oritsi still strove to observe certain Jewish traditions in his house, but some of his children gave up their Judaism. Bernard became entirely assimilated and after all his children converted, he and his wife followed them. (It is worthwhile mentioning that at the elections to the first Russian parliament, Bernard made the effort and managed to be sent as a representative of the Jewish community in Biale, as a delegate to the election–assembly that appointed a candidate as representative to the Russian parliament). Vintsenti was a social–democrat and an active party–member. He materially supported popular socialistic activities. Yakov went to Paris, without participating directly in the running of the factory managed by the younger generation of the Ra'abe family. Finkelhoiz was the director of the factory until the 2nd World War.

[Page 160]

(This was according to information transmitted in writing by the engineer Moshe Kerner who was a senator in the Polish senate. He was the director of Ra'abe's factory in Biale from 1909 until 1915.)

Various factories existed in the town until the 1st World War. Some of these were liquidated due to the events of the war and were not re-established. We will, as far as possible, list them here.

A Jewish owned sawmill already existed on the Volye in 1866. It belonged to a lady named Bayltshe. The work was done by Jewish workmen.

Another Jewish owned sawmill, also on the Volye, belonged to the estate (more details in the section dealing with the premises of A. Vineberg of blessed memory).

In 1866, on the Volye there was a small factory producing grease for wagons, sulphur on a stick and sticks for penholders. This small factory belonged to Noah and Leibush Friedman. All the machines were built by the owners themselves and were operated by a person turning a wheel. Later the machines were operated and driven with the help of a transmission belt. Most of the workers were Jews.

A shoe factory existed in the town that belonged to the Hoffer brothers (sons of Py-e), and Benjamin Klieger. The factory employed more than 40 workers, shoemakers and cutters. The products were also sent deep into Russia.

Famous in the town and the surrounding area was the factory of Motl Mintz that produced paper for rolling cigarettes. A large number of Jewish workers worked there, mainly women.

For many years there was a water-mill on the river, belonging to the court, that was almost always leased to Jews. Some time before the 1st World War, the mill burnt down and was never rebuilt.

The factory of Zushe Goldreich, that produced slabs for sidewalks (situated in the courtyard that later belonged to Alter Suknov and Volf Mallina) was liquidated in approximately 1912.

The brick-yards in the villages of Seltz and Tzitzibor belonged to the Biale Jews, Chaim Levi Rubinshtein and Yitzchak Goldshtein (Yitzchakl the son of Channe Toibes). The brick-yard in Seltz was renowned in the entire area for the quality of its products.

Of the 2 sawmills that existed until the 2nd World War, one belonged to Yitzchak Pizshitz and partners. This sawmill was burnt down by the German air force during military operations.

The second sawmill belonged to Herzl Tsharni and partners. In this sawmill there was also a steam mill.

Aside from the large steam mill of Ratayevitsh, all the other steam mills in the town belonged to Jews.

The mill on the Yanever highway was the property of Moshe Shneiman and partners. The mill on Artilerisker street belonged to the Krizelmans and Pinchas Nartman. The owners of the mill in Viness were the Urbach and Vizenfeld families. The Finkelshtein brothers ran a mill on the *glinkes* that was erected on the site of the former windmill, that belonged to their father. On Garntsarsker street there was a large paper mill belonging to Leibl Blankleider, and on Yaske street – the small paper mill belonging to Leibl Mindal.

In all these Jewish owned mills, a visible number of Jewish workers were employed doing various tasks.

The Winery (the name Winery, which means a wine house, probably stems from the fact that wine was once produced or sold in that place), produced beer, and in 1908 it was rebuilt by Berish Urbach, on the site of the wooden winery that had burned down in 1904.

All the machines there were powered by a transmitter that was driven by a belt to which a horse was harnessed.

During the 1st World War the winery was requisitioned by the Germans, and on that site, they installed factories that were entirely mechanized, producing: beer, lemonade and artificial ice. In the courtyard of the winery, an electricity producing plant was installed, but only the Germans themselves benefitted from the electric lights.

After the war, the owners of the winery sold the machines of the lemonade and ice factories and remained with the modernized beer factory. The production of beer continued there.

A few score Jewish workers and many families earned a living thanks to the factory. With time, however, the owners of the winery liquidated the beer factory, and erected a steam mill there.

[Page 161]

Leibe Bornshtein, whose house was next to the winery, was called Leibe Mednik in the town because of the mead and wine factory that he had in his house. The mead produced in this factory was particularly renowned and was in demand throughout Poland.

The heirs and workers of the wine-cellars of Leibe Mednik

Leibe Mednik, and later his heirs, employed a number of Jewish workers who were very well treated there.

At the beginning of the Volye, immediately after the river, was a tannery that was bought after the 1st World War by the young family man, Friedberg (from Brisk). The tannery was active until the 2nd World War. The main product consisted of Russian cowhide for the harness makers.

A few Jewish workers worked in the tannery.

Next to the tannery was a small soap factory belonging to the lady Sarah Gelle Golfedder. The production was performed entirely by the family.

A second soap factory, on a larger scale, was situated alongside the so-called Kazioner bath, and belonged to the Oppenheim family. Here too, the factory was run entirely by the family members. The factory of the Oppenheim family was liquidated after the 2nd World War.

Of the five soda-water and lemonade factories in the town, four were owned by Jews.

The Jewish soda-water and lemonade factories belonged to: the Cohen family (Kahan – the son of Shaya Bertshes), the Zinger family (Berele Zinger), Yakov Flichtgreich and Moshe Fretter and Listgarten.

The small number of workers that were employed in these factories were all Jewish.

B. Printing Shops

The first printing shop in the town was established in approximately 1900/1 by a Jew from Minsk, Dvorzshetz, who came from a family that was engaged in printing. It can be assumed that Dvorzshetz's leaving Minsk, the great Russian town and settling in such a provincial town like Biale, was not dictated by economic motives, but was caused by the percentage-norms for Jewish children in the Russian school system. Dvorzshetz's children were indeed immediately sent to the Biale High school.

The above mentioned Dvorzshetz established a large printing shop in the house of Yitzchak Goldshtein (Yitzchakl Channe Toibes) on Yanever street. The printing shop would do printing work only in the Russian language and did not possess Yiddish font. It appears that there was no need for printing work in Yiddish in the town at that time.

During the 1st World War, before the Russian army left the town, Dvorzshetz moved his printing shop to Minsk.

The second printing works in the town was established in approximately 1902 by Yakov Zelig Lubeltshik. Yakov Zelig was by profession a painter but displayed great talent in various areas. Even before he established the printing shop, he turned to making stamps (seals).

The printing shop was run by Yakov Zelig and his two sons, Matityahu and Avraham. After the war Avraham remained the proprietor of the printing shop.

[Page 162]

The printing shop had a large printing machine (100 x 70 centimeters) and a few small printing machines, a machine for cutting paper, and a large assortment of font in various languages. All the machines were operated by human hands or feet.

Polish books, brochures, newspapers and various other printing work were printed in the printing shops, for officials, and for producing posters. There the Jewish newspaper "Podlasier Life" was typeset and printed under the editorship of M. M. Gellenberg.

For many years the printing works was situated on Brisker Street, in the house of Leib Mandelbaum. In the last years before the 2nd World War the printing works moved into the home of Avraham Lubeltshik that he built for himself on Reformatzker street.

The third printing works in the town was established by Moshe Frishtik on Yanever street. The printing shop was a small one and the printing machine was quite a primitive one and required great physical strength. Despite this, however, a few newspapers were printed there during its existence.

The first Jewish newspapers in Biale were printed in Frishtik's printing shop: "Biale Echo", "Biale Voice", published by the local Zionist organization under the editorship of Moshe Rubinshtein.

In 1927 Moshe Frishtik moved his printing works to Warsaw.

The fourth printing works, under the name "Express", was established in 1931 on Pilsodski street by Yisroel Hochman and Dovid Tzeshinski. After a few years the partnership was dissolved and Yisroel Hochman remained the proprietor of the printing works.

The printing works had a printing machine measuring 35 x 50 centimetres, and a small pedal machine. Both were operated by foot. In the last years before the war, they had a paper-cutting machine.

In this very printing shop, the following newspapers were published: "Podlassier Life", under the editorship of Chaim Rozmarin; "Biale Weekly", under the editorship of Chaim Miyodek, and "Podlassier Voice", published by the League for the Working Land of Israel.

The main work generated from this printing works was for officials and private enterprises.

Stamps (seals) would also be produced in all these printing workshops.

It is worth mentioning that due to the efforts of "Rozvye" in Biale a Polish printing works was established in the town in the 1920s. Despite the backing that it received from all sides, it did not last long. The owners went bankrupt and the printing shop was liquidated.

During the 2nd World War both Jewish printing works were confiscated by the Germans and handed over to the German named Vanzshura.

(some of the details were submitted by Yitzchak Shein)

The Biale Estate

by Alter Vineberg – Tel Aviv

Translated by Libby Raichman

There were two estates in Biale: one was related to the Biale Rabbi Yitzchak Yakov Rabinovicz, who, due to his broad and rich bearing, was known throughout Poland. The second estate had no connection to Rabbis, but in a certain period played an important role in the economic life of Biale Jews. I mean, the so-called Radzshivil estate.

In my childhood I heard many legends about the estate. Later, when I was already an adult, I worked there and had the opportunity to move around freely and to verify the authenticity of those legends.

The estate was situated on the Mezritsh highway, immediately after exiting the town, and shared a border with the High School. Entering the estate, on the right side, one could see a building with a tall tower in a neglected condition. On the other levels, there were holes where there were once windows. The front wall, until the first level, was built with longish four-cornered stones, with a high round gate. The arch around the gate was paved with artistically chiseled stones. On each side of the gate were various stone figures, like: guns, cannons on two wheels that the military used to drag, swords etc. The gate was no longer there, and the entrance was boarded up. On the other side of the building, opposite the gate, parallel to the highway, was a mountain that stretched the length of the estate. At the foot of the mountain stretched a little stream. In the summer, the stream was covered with small green leaves. Jewish and Christian women would go there with sieves and buckets and pull out the leaves with which they would feed small ducks. Beautiful dense Ash trees grew between the highway and the small stream.

[Page 163]

The mountain was called Val (a cylinder), because, it was told, the space in the mountain had been filled in. People used to say that under the mountain was a cellar that stretched from the building with the tower, until the village of Slavatshinek. According to the legend, on a few occasions people went into the cellar with lights and torches, in order to see what was there, and how far the cellar stretched, but no one returned. People also used to say that there in the estate, lay a frame of a whale bone, a piece of which was a cure for a fever. If there happened to be an opportunity to enter freely into the estate, people would go and cut off pieces of the frame of the whale bone.

What circulated was, that the entire town of Biale and the area of the Biale embankment (that the Jews used to call Nabialke) until the village of Stirentz, and even further, belonged to a member of the Radzshivil family. Who and what this Radzshivil was, nobody knew. Some said, that he was a nobleman, others again – that he was an emperor, that the whole terrain belonged to him and that all the inhabitants in that area were his subjects. He lived on the estate, that, in time of war, was also his fortress.

If one observed the estate carefully, one could actually assert that this was a fortress. The tower with the holes on the higher levels were definitely meant for shooting the enemy, in the event that it would be necessary.

The schools in Biale and Yaneve were, as was said, built by Radzshivil. Why also the Yaneve school, nobody knew. The fact is, that both schools were similar.

At the end of the last century, one could not freely enter the estate, because it held the prison for the entire circle. On the second floor of the tower building, there was a prison for women, and the windows there were barred. The court-house was situated deeper into the estate and the court-chairman lived there.

The jail was located in four long single-storied buildings, built in a very old style: very thick walls, and vaulted ceilings of solidly baked bricks. To knock out a brick was much more difficult than making a hole in a concrete wall today. On every window there were thick iron bars. When I used to work there, it happened from time to time that I had to break into walls and I saw that the bars were not installed when the prison itself was but were already reinforced when the building was erected.

Nevertheless, it happened that despite the thick walls and the vaulted ceilings, a group of prisoners escaped from there. If I am not mistaken, they were all Jews, and amongst the escapees, were also Biale residents. They made a hole in the ceiling, went into the attic, and from there they managed to escape. This happened at night and in the morning the authorities turned the town upside down. It was told at that time, that the hole in the ceiling was scraped out with knives, a task that naturally must have taken months, and that there were small boats waiting for them at the river. Most of the escapees later went to England. Why the group of escapees consisted only of Jews, and why they were in prison, is a whole other chapter. All the escapees were arrested without a trial, and with them in their cell were others who had already had court sentences. The latter did not escape, and as much as they were tortured, they did not reveal a single detail and claimed that they were asleep and therefore, saw and heard nothing.

In the 1890s , a new prison was built in Biale on Proster street. Then the estate became free for all the residents of the town to walk through. Jews also began to go to the orchard there on the sabbath for pleasure but sometime later, Jews were not permitted to enter.

For some time, this estate was called Finekl's manor, although it was never his[1]. Finekl was the manager there for many years, so people assumed that he was the owner. Everyone who had any contact with this Christian was quite well enriched. There was no shortage of ways to do deals because tens of thousands of acres of land and forests belonged to the estate, that stretched from Bialke on the Brisk highway, to both Slavatshinkes, villages on the Warsaw highway, as well as the villages Prosheki and Stirnetz. In Bialke and in both these two villages called Slavatshinke, there were Jewish tenant farmers, who were the purchasers of the milk.

[Page 164]

The estate also had many houses in the town and on the Volye. The building in the town, that was once occupied by the officials of the district, was the property of the estate, and stretched from the market place, through Yanever street into Patshtover street. Later Shmuel Pizshitz bought the house. It was told that he bought it for 10 thousand rubles, to be paid over 10 years, and that Pizshitz had an annual income from that house that was much more than a thousand ruble. That building housed the district with all its departments, the military and the police. On one floor was the apartment of the Circle-chief. Later, when all these officials moved into Mevyuse's property, they converted the building into shops.

The estate, that was also called the "treasury", once owned a sawmill on the Volye (on the other side of the railway station), that cut the trees from its own forests. The sawmill was definitely the first sawmill – I think that for many years it was the only sawmill in the town.

The estate also owned the watermills in Biale and in the village of Prosheki. I still remember the small mill in Biale, that burnt down together with the bridge over the river. Later, a large 3-storied mill was erected, that stood for many years and also burnt down.

The first lessee of the mill was Moshe Bergshtein, who had a brick building close to the river, and he later owned the first 3-storied house in Biale that Berel Vineberg erected on Reformatzker street and was passed over to Bergshtein in settlement of a debt.

The second lessee of the mill was Dovid Reb Isaacs or Reb Dovid Shachor, a noted Chassid in the town. He held the lease of the mill until it burned down.

Among the Christian workers in the mill, there were also two Jews, Avigdor Moshe Guttenberg and Shimon Maratshnik.

At the end of the last century the estate was sold to a new owner, a Pole. What was said was that the reason for the sale was due to the fact that the Russian government issued a decree that foreign nationals could not possess any immovable property. Because this owner of the estate was a Pole, a national, he had to sell the estate. A new manager came in Finekl's place, also a Pole, and he began to bring in new orders.

The new landowner, however, did not keep the estate long in his possession. In approximately 1900 it was sold to a Jewish girl named Helena Adolpuvna Kogan, a Russian citizen, born in Odessa and living in France. She had a very big business and enterprises with many branches in the Russian towns. The main director of her business was an uncle of hers. After the estate became the possession of this girl, the manager appointed to the Biale estate was a Jew from Odessa – Dikler. A new chapter in the history of the estate began. It became a Jewish estate. The Biale Jews could move around freely in the orchard of the estate and go for walks there whenever they wished. The estate received a new name – Dikler's estate.

Dikler knew how to live in style and was not Russianized like the other Russian Jews who were ashamed to speak Yiddish. In Dikler's home, understandably, they spoke Russian, but in the office, in the street and generally with Jews who used to come to him about various matters, he spoke in a beautiful Ukrainian Yiddish. Later, when I met his father, I saw that this Dikler was raised in a respectable middle-class Jewish home. It was said that Dikler received a large salary, truly like a governor. Under his direction, his office changed from a Polish one and became a Jewish one, where poor Jews sat as clerks, who were not ashamed of their Yiddish.

The contractors, workers, and merchants remained the same. The mill in Prosheki was leased and taken over by two Shedletz Jews who were later called Idl and Asher Proshekier. These two Jews remained at the mill until it burnt down.

Dikler first turned to bringing order to the buildings in the castle. Walls were broken to insert ventilation in order to dry the dampness, bars were removed, and beautiful high windows were installed, the stone floors were lifted and were replaced with wooden boards, new levels were erected - all of great size. Trees and grass were planted at the entrance to the estate, which changed its appearance completely.

The office was installed in the first building at the entrance to the estate. On the second floor of the tower building lived the chief officials and their families, Ruzshinski and Hertzke Vinograd (Yoske, Vinograd's father), who worked on the estate as a woodsman and regarded himself as a great tradesman in this field. He was a fine Jew, religious, but not a fanatic.

[Page 165]

The landowner's sawmill on the Volye was dismantled and on its site a brick sawmill was erected, large and modern. Two Jews who were specialists in the wood industry were brought to manage this facility.

One of the two specialists was a Warsaw Jew, a Gerre Chassid – Segal, who was a very distinguished figure in the town. On the festivals he would go from the Volye to pray in the Gerre prayer house. The second was a young man from M'lav, a religious and intelligent person. On the sabbath preceding the new month, he would go and pray in the synagogue on the Volye. This young man was not embarrassed to put on his hat and do the afternoon prayers in the office. On the festival of Sukkot, he had to have an etrog (citron) in his home.

A Jewish guard named Shpak lived on the premises. He had a very good job there. Hershl Shykes was the regular wagon driver there. He would distribute the wooden boards at the site and deliver material to the train. He was a respectable Jew who lived on the Volye.

Later, Segal's place was taken by Zingerman from Odessa. He was a devoted Jew but a liberated one. Even in those days he would ride through the town to Bialke and back on the Sabbath. In his home, however, he kept a kosher kitchen.

The sawmill grew to such an extent that it became an international firm. Merchants came to Biale from the whole of Poland, and merchants from Germany spent the winter months in the town and transported wood to Germany.

Dikler did not rest and constantly initiated new enterprises. In November 1901 he began to build barracks on the Warsaw highway, for the *Kaluzshesk* regiment, apartments for the officers, a Russian church, and everything that the regiment needed. This was an enormous undertaking that was actually completed in an unbelievably short time. Many workers worked on the site, Jews and Christians. The work could have quickly come to an end, but fortunately Dikler had the sawmill at his disposal, with all its facilities. The machines produced and supplied wood and the tradesmen only needed to complete the task. Today machine work is quite a simple matter, but then, 50 years ago, when even in Warsaw there were no woodworking machines, and everything was made by hand, this was a huge achievement for Biale.

Which Biale resident of the older generation does not remember the building of the barracks? Every courtyard was, after all, full of firewood and off-cuts from construction. The highway was full of women and children who used to carry away heavy sacks containing wood shavings and blocks of wood.

Of all the work in the vicinity of the barracks, 90% was carried out by Jews. Despite Dikler's efforts to bring in Christian tradesmen, because he was already short of Jewish workers, and he wanted to complete the work as soon as possible, nothing came of it – the Christians could not maintain the work-tempo of the Jewish workers. He even brought Russians from deep within Russia, but in the time that they managed to erect one house, the Jews had already completed five houses. Therefore, when the Russians completed one building, Dikler sent them home.

A Christian carpenter, Vintzenti from Grabanov, was also employed there. He was a good tradesman, but he was also slow compared to the Jewish tradesmen. But as this Vintzenti was on good terms with my father-in-law, Gershon Brodatsh, who worked there, my father-in-law retained him. My father-in-law did this with a purpose: As they also had to build a Russian church there, and he, as a religious Jew, did not want to put a hand to such a building, he actually allocated this work to Vintzenti the Christian, and was happy that he managed to extricate himself from church-work.

The roofs were made of shingles and for this work, all the shingle makers and shingle fitters in Biale and from the surrounding villages were employed. They worked frantically and therefore over-exerted themselves.

The carpenters who worked in partnership were Avraham Gril (Braverman) and Velvl Malina. It is worth relating here the tragic incident that happened by their undertaking the carpentry work.

Avraham Gril and Malina used to work at the estate and were therefore candidates to receive this work at the barracks. Godl Binyes (Milboim) also wanted the same work. Godl had the keys of the synagogue, where he was the treasurer, and he kept the prayer shawl of Advocate Kalman Hartglas under his supervision. When Hartglas marked the anniversary of a death, he would come to the synagogue to pray and say the traditional prayer for the dead and Godl used to hover around him. Later, when Hartglas's children were nationally elected, everything there changed, and Hartglas would come to the synagogue on every festival and sometimes on the sabbath. Godl also worked in Hartglas's house. Now Advocate Hartglas appealed for Godl to receive the work at the barracks. When Godl went to Dikler, Avraham Gril and Malina came out of their workshop and, using a piece of wood from a window frame (part of a window), hit Godl over the head.

[Page 166]

They broke his skull. A doctor was brought from Warsaw, who operated on him. His condition was critical, and only thanks to the efforts of Advocate Hartglas, who regularly brought doctors from Warsaw, Godl was saved from death. The court sentenced Gril and Malina to 1½ years in prison and to pay Godl a significant sum of money; they were escorted to the prison. Later they appealed and were freed. The matter however, cost them a lot of money.

Nearly 90% of the brickwork was done by me. The remaining 10% was done by the Christian, Kaminski. I also built 7 brick wells there. The barracks were built in a very modern way, for those times.

The painting work was done in partnership by Hershl Lentshner and Abele Maller. They worked there with many workers.

While the barracks were being built there was a day-guard, a Jew by the name of Moshe. They made a large barracks with tables and benches for him. And this Jew organized a restaurant there and earned a good income from the workers.

Dikler appointed a manager in the warehouse in Slavatshinek. He was a simple village Jew whom they began to call Moshe from Slavatshinek. This Jew made a living there from selling milk products and there were proprietors in the town who went there to sample these things. The Christian manager did not disturb the Jew from acquiring this income and even used to help him to earn his living.

Dikler also conceived a plan to build a distillery and set about accomplishing the task. Two weeks before the Jewish New Year in 1904, the building of the distillery commenced on a site near the sawmill. The distillery was large and very successful. The alcohol produced there acquired a good name.

As regards the distillery, I would like to note an episode that is engraved in my memory.

I began to build the distillery before the New Year and had to complete it in a very short time because of the winter. As it was the time of the festivals, I had to negotiate with the other bricklayers, that they should work on the intermediate days of the festival of Sukkot. In those days people did not work on those intermediate days. The shops were open, the wagon drivers travelled with their wagons, but the poor worker was not allowed to work. I began to attempt to persuade the workers, promising a higher salary, but only a few agreed to work.

At the time when the distillery became active, they began to make fish ponds to breed fish. For this purpose, Dikler brought an engineer, a tradesman in this area. This was also a very serious undertaking. For many Jews, the whole idea of breeding fish seemed strange; they knew that there are fish in the river, but no one breeds them. . . . . .

Before leaving Biale, Dikler still allowed the tower of the castle to be renovated. The roof was removed, and a new roof was made with a beautiful tall dome. The work was done by my father-in-law. Shlaymele Stolyer's son, Menachem Leib Hochberg, made the dome. Menachem Leib regarded himself as one of the best and most talented master carpenters in the entire vicinity. He could understand a plan and could draw up plans himself.

Once, being in the office, I heard that the "girl" bought another property that was truly a Garden-of- Eden, in which she herself planned to settle. There was a palace in the grounds, and a river flowed through the estate. There was also an orchard and a hot-house with the most expensive fruit, that grew there summer and winter.

Some time later, I once came into the office and noticed a depressed atmosphere. One clerk mentioned to me: - you know Mr. Vineberg, we have to make a reception for the landlady. To my question, regarding what he meant by that, he told me, that the "girl" is coming from her recently purchased estate near Warsaw with her Christian husband, the distiller of that place.

That was certainly a tragic event for the office. All the years since the office existed, the "girl" had not once been in Biale, and suddenly she is coming with a gentile husband. It was said that the "girl" settled in the manor that she had bought and married her distiller. After she converted, one could sense that the Jewish office was coming to an end.

Preparations for the reception were made. At the entrance to the estate, a triumph gate was erected, with various adornments as they used to do for the emperor or other great personalities. There was great excitement in the town. People were running to see the gate and all the preparations.

[Page 167]

That day, when the "girl" came to Biale, everyone, Jewish and Christian, ran to look at her. The Jewish population went with curiosity and pain to see the hunchback, as she was called in the town, who, being so rich, fell in love with a gentile and in this way, delivered such enormous wealth into gentile hands. The Christian population was also curious to see the "girl" and were overjoyed with the capture of a Jewish soul.

I was not there but after a couple of days I went to the office, to see what kind of atmosphere there was after the visit of the "girl". I found the staff depressed.

I do not remember how long the Jewish office continued to exist. Details of the liquidation of Jewishness in the office have also been erased from my memory. I only remember that a Christian manager arrived with a truly gentile appearance. We, the Jewish tradesmen, went to him about employment and he promised that all those who worked in the estate would remain working there. There I met the wife of Moshe from Slavatshinek, who told me that that they had already been retrenched from their work.

Jewish tradesmen no longer worked there; only, I think, Ruven Kozzes (Shulman), and that was due to the protection of the noblemen of the Biale region, for whom he used to work.

All the Jewish clerks and the couple of Russians left Biale, and only one remained, a certain Azrilian, a Jew from Odessa, who became a supplier of meat to the military in the town.

Now, as I write these lines, when since those times, 50 years have already flowed away, I still see the estate office before my eyes, as if it had been only yesterday. I see the Jewish office with Dikler at its head, with his bearing and understanding of people and the Jews in particular. I see before my eyes, Dikler's entrance into the office, with the Yiddish or Russian 'good morning'. I remember his arrival at the barracks while they were being built, his enquiries about everything, his attention to everything, his occasional scolding, and his remarks and his jokes in a tasteful Yiddish.

I recall now, that weeks would pass, and one would not see a gentile in the office, only Jews and Jews. An office that engaged with the world was entirely Jewish: Jewish merchants, Jewish tradesmen of all professions, and Jewish day and night guards. A significant number of Jewish families in the town had a comfortable income from this estate, that was an important factor in the economic life of Biale Jews.

Even for work like sanitation – cleaning toilets, that the gentiles had already surely done, came a Jew like Mendele Sitniker (Freedman) and said that he wanted to take that job. They helped him obtain the necessary tools and Mendele Sitniker was employed in this capacity and earned well.

I want to add here another line about the warm attitude of the office towards Jews.

One winter, the office began to distribute wood to the poor. Hundreds of banknotes were distributed (notes that authorized the holder to remove the quantity of wood specified in the note, from the forest).

In Biale, it was a well-known matter, that if things were distributed late, as for example, 'wheat money' for Passover (for the poor), then "nice" young boys would receive it. These people were not satisfied with one single distribution but took whatever they could; they did, because everyone was afraid of them. The wood was distributed to Jews and Christians, but the quiet needy Jew did not receive anything. Firstly, he was embarrassed, and secondly, when he did conceal his shame, these "nice" youths did not allow him to receive anything.

It appears that Dikler was informed about all of this and he asked me to take the hundred banknotes and distribute them; if the hundred was too little, more would be added. I took up his proposition. It is possible that a few years earlier, I would not have taken up Dikler's request because I would have been afraid of the "nice" Biale youth, but this happened in the times of the Bundist activity in Biale when he had already somewhat silenced the gang.

I turned to the trustees of the small Chassidic prayer houses about giving me a list of those who needed wood and each trustee received the required number of banknotes, that he distributed among his people. I distributed the banknotes to the tradesmen and others in need, myself, or through intermediaries. For a few years I distributed the wood, and every winter, no less than 150 banknotes. If I was short of a few more than 150, I would go to the office and would receive them there.

I cannot say if the Biale Jews knew how to appreciate the attitude of the office towards them. It could be, that if Dikler had been a Chassid, and went to pray on the sabbath, they would have valued the benevolence of the office more.

[Page 168]

And this office, that became more and more Jewish, suddenly slipped out of Jewish hands and became absolutely Christian. A colossal Jewish fortune was transferred from Jewish possession into Christian hands. Biale Jews felt the change in their economic situation because they lost a very influential source of income.

Footnote:

    1.   Advocate Apolinari Hartglas writes about it, in his unpublished memoirs:
"At the time of my birth (1883), the castle belonged to the assets of the German Chancellor, Duke Hohenlohe, to whom it was transferred as

an inheritance from the Duchess Radzshivil. Together with him, it was managed by an administrator of German extraction, who assumed a more Polish name, Finekl" – editor.

The Professional [Workers'] Movement

by Yisroel Hochman

Translated by Gloria Berkenstat Freund

In the 1890s, when all of Russia began a great evolution in communal life and new branches of production resulted in even more wage workers, a series of factory enterprises with several hundreds of workers arose in Biala. But, just as everywhere else, a labor system existed then in which the work was done in inhuman conditions, with unlimited hours of work, completely unprotected, dependent on the benevolence of those who provided the jobs.

The first forms of professional work began to arise in Biala in such difficult conditions. The worker, who had been accustomed to looking at the person who provided the work as someone upon whom his life was completely dependent, began to change his opinion little by little.

The rise of various groups of artisans and wage workers, the organizing of *minyonim* [prayer groups of 10 men needed for organized prayer – *minyon* is the singular form of the word] and *shtiblekh* [one room houses of study often organized by the members of the same trade] was the first primitive form of organization, the first actual organization of the workers and artisans. Thus, the tailors in Biala created a prayer group named *Khevre Bokherim* [group of young men]. Its task was to separate the artisans and wage workers from the middle-class Jews. Therefore, the *Khevre Bokherim* took on additional tasks such as: spreading education among the members and *daveners* [those who prayed], teaching them to write, a little bit of *Khumash* [Torah] and *Tanakh* [Torah, Prophets and Writings], as well as self-help activities for the sick. This first primitive form of professional organization lasted as long as the Biala worker did not have any contact with the larger cities and wider world.

Reverberations from the activities of the socialistic parties in Russia reached Biala and the first traces of the workers' movement arose. The young, who were enthusiastic about the revolution, devoted all their fervor to the professional organizing of the workers. Among the intelligentsia, Yewel Tiamkin, Czarni Lewin, Dovid Kruses, Yakov Sztajnman and others excelled with all of their strength and helped not only with organizing, but all led systematic educational and explanatory work among the workers.

An economic revival in the various branches could be observed, which drew in more and more workers. The professional and political work became more varied. The factories of Motl Minc and Raabe, which employed several hundreds of male and female workers, occupied the most esteemed place. All of the other branches also were revived, such as the tailors who were employed, thanks to the demand for ready-made women's and men's clothing. A factory for ready-made shoes opened then at which several dozen workers were employed. These groups introduced greater strength for the political and professional workers' movement.

The workers who joined the political parties demanded something tangible and intensive underground work began. The Bund Party committee in Biala created an "exchange" where workers from the various branches would meet with their representatives and tell them about the conditions at their workplaces.

The most important activists at organizing the working class were: with the tailors: Elya Szimszeles, Khona Niskeles, Nakhum Worek; with the carpenters: Shmai Fridman, Elya Bubkes. The other trades were under the leadership of a group of other activists. The brothers Borukh and Yeshayahu Wajnberg played an admirable role in the political and professional movement. Borukh was a true people's tribune; his speeches were like an intoxicating drink for the masses.

Strikes broke out in 1904-1905 to which all of the workers were drawn. The strikes were partially political, but in greater part economic. They were carried out on a large scale and made an impression.

[Page 169]

Emigration abroad of the Biala workers began after the failure of the revolution of 1905. A breakdown began of the organizations that had been created with so much effort. It continued in this way until the outbreak of the First World War, with no change in the situation.

The first years of the First World War passed under the general signs of a real depression until the evacuation of the Russians. The situation completely changed after the arrival of the German military. Illegal work was no longer necessary to lead a professional organization. However, the hardship was that there was no work. The work that existed was for the military regime where no professional union could have any influence. The majority of the workers were jobless and suffered from hunger; this itself created discouragement. At the end of the German occupation, a tailors' union was created at the existing cultural society, which however did no tangible work. This union, in which the active leaders were Meyram Fridman, Moshe Brawerman and Nakhum Worek, lasted until the German occupiers left Biala.

The date when the first legal professional union in Biala was created is recorded in 1918. The German military regime was crushed and forced to leave Poland. The Polish Republic arose, which gave the workers the opportunity for normal, legal professional activity. Thanks to this, a group of professional organizations was created which had at its disposal an entire house on Grabanower Street, where a workers' canteen was also created. The political party, the Bund, was then located in the same house.

During the first year of Poland's independence, the professional unions of the Jewish workers developed very well. Thanks to the legal opportunities, systematic cultural, professional and political activity was carried out among them. The masses were activated; the young people were drawn into the professional movement. Separate youth sections were created at various trades. Active workers then were: Mordekhai Hochman, Shmai Fridman, Nakhum Worek, Moshe Rodzinek and Gliksberg.

The strong and well-disciplined professional unions carried on their work with full intensity; all actions to better the conditions of the organized workers had the appropriate success and were carried out without any opposition. However, these magnificent organizations did not have a long existence. A large fire which broke out in the unions' building, erased everything. Not even one bench was saved.

From then on the unions moved from one place to another. A short while later they succeeded in renting a small apartment on the second floor in a small alley, where the tailors' union was established with its 200 members, and the leaders were: Leyzer Shneur, Ita Ejzenberg and Gliksberg. The shoemakers' union also was located there and had good leadership, among whom Shmuelka Goldberg and Chaim Eizenberg stood out. All of the other trades such as the carpenters and locksmiths were organized under the name Construction Union.

The well-known year of 1920 drew near. Repressions spread among the professional unions during the time of the Polish-Bolshevik War. Their activists were exiled to camps; the organizations were closed. This was a deathblow for the organizations. The professional activity ceased for a long time.

After the Polish-Bolshevik War, when it finally became peaceful, the former activists did not return to their organizations. The only communal strength came from the young people, who began to re-erect the destroyed unions. The tailors' union arose again illegally. Not having any refuge, it wandered from one house to another. This lasted for three-quarters of a year until the first money fund was created and the union received a small apartment on Grabanower Street, on the second floor, and it was legalized. Little by little other unions arrived; the shoemakers', metal workers' and carpenter organizations were revived. The unions carried out intensive activity, thanks to the active leaders: B. Solman, Sh. Winderbaum, W. Szuster, Semiaticki, Goldhamer and others. The economic actions that were carried out in their time were met with success. However, alas, the economic situation then for Jewish workers in Biala was unfortunate.

[Page 170]

The Jewish workers were scattered in many small workshops and even with the best will they could not improve their situation. In addition, the currency of that time was the mark with its running inflation. The worker, despite the successful actions, could not make enough money for his daily needs. This situation brought new emigration during 1921-1922 and hundreds of workers emigrated to France, Argentina and other nations. The new storm of emigration drained the masses of active strength from among the young people as well as the older ones. A split in the Bund took place in 1922. This created a dispute on party terrain and the professional organizations were weakened as a result and finally fell into ruin.

Only the carpenters' union remained of the professional organizations, which, thanks to a good set of circumstances and great demand for the work [of carpenters], held together well and carried on good professional and communal work until 1927. The leadership lay in the hands of responsible and devoted people, such as: Elya Hofman, Mikhal Krawiec, Zilia Gutenberg, Charasz and Wirnik. All of the workers in the other branches envied the carpenters for their good and steady income. It is no wonder that the actions undertaken by the carpenters' union at that time succeeded.

In 1927 a decline in the carpentry trade began. The stabilization and the normal life brought with it a standstill in the work. The older workers became *meisters* [foremen or their own bosses] and left the union. Only the young remained who could not cope. The political parties lost their influence; the union remained unsupervised; control over its activity as well as over the inflowing money was weakened and the organization of the carpentry workers began to crumble. In addition, this situation led to the only existing union being thrown out of its apartment and its wandering began anew.

Thanks to the efforts of Yakov Szwarcberg and Zelig Libman, an apartment was again rented, into which moved the professional union of the carpentry branch as well as the library of the professional union. A half-year later, financial difficulties led to neglecting the payment of rent; the owner was not paid for a long time, until one evening he decided to throw the entire [library] inventory out into the street. The books roamed around, a little time with one person, another time with another. The legal professional unions of the Jewish workers in Biala ceased to exist from that moment on.

(*Podlasier Lebn* [*Podlasier Life*], number 19, 19th May 1934)

The Artisans' Union

by B. Winograd, Ramat-Gan

Translated by Gloria Berkenstat Freund

The union was founded in 1921. The organizers were: Avraham Lubelczik, Manashe Ceszinski, Borukh Winograd, Yoal Sztromwaser and Tsala Birnbaum. The reason for founding the Artisans' Union was to organize the large number of artisans (about 500) in a uniform economic organization in order to raise their level of achievement.

The artisans were a significant percentage of the Biala Jewish population. Until the rise of the Artisans' Union, their only form of organization was *minyonim* [prayer groups] such as the "Zaposner" house of prayer, which consisted mainly of artisan worshippers, the *Khevra Bokhorim* [Society of Young Men] of tailors and shoemakers, which was located at the *Hakhones-Orkhim* [place for hospitality on the Sabbath and on holidays for poor travelers], and later just in the attic of the synagogue, and from that comes the nickname, "the *minyon* from Golembik." The majority of artisans were concentrated in the large house of prayer.

The cultural level and their conditions were humble – backwards. The competition and hatred among them was very great and the want and poverty ever greater, but some of them could read and write.

The institutions mentioned carried out a registration of all the Biala Jewish artisans according to the particular trades. A managing committee, auditing commission and organizational court was chosen at a general meeting. The statute of the union was received from the Warsaw Central Artisans' Union and the Biala Artisans' Union was legalized with the government as a division of the Warsaw Central.

The managing committee instantly began intensive activity. Gatherings of the artisans were called for each trade and a particular section was chosen from each trade that was occupied with organizational questions connected to the given trade. There was a reading room active every night in the premises of the union and the skilled artisans would read the daily Yiddish newspapers for their comrades, as well as various brochures of literary, hygiene-medical and professional content.

[Page 171]

Over time, Avraham Lubelczik, Avraham Stricher, Menasha Ceszinski, Tsale Birnbaum, Yehosha Eidlsztajn, Khanina Kaszemacher, Moshe Kava, Welwl Eizensztat, Leizer Eplbaum, Yitzhak Peterburg, Nakhum Warek, Yoal Sztromwaser and others were members of the managing committee of the union.

The chairmen of the union over the course of various terms of office were: Avraham Lubelczik, Moshe Kava, Avraham Stricher, Nakhum Warek and Khanina Kaszemacher.

Borukh Winograd was active as the secretary from the rise of the union in 1921 until 1925, and Ayzk Szajn from 1925 until his departure for *Eretz Yisroel*. The last secretary of the union was Noakh Kramarsz.

In the course of its existence the Artisans' Union took an active part in the political and communal life of the city.

The artisans elected an appropriate number of councilmen from their list at the elections to the city council. In 1923 Menasha Ceszinski and Borukh Winograd were elected; Borukh Winograd and Avraham Stricher [were elected] at the elections in the years 1927 and 1934.

The artisans also took an active part in the leadership of the *kehile* [organized Jewish community]. During the elections to the first *kehile* council, four artisans won election out of 15 councilmen: Avraham Stricher, Welwl Eizensztat, Yehoshua Eidlsztajn and Leizer Eplbaum. Khanina Kaszemacher, Yoal Sztromwaser and Yitzhak Peterburg, artisans, were then elected to the *kehile* managing committee.

There were no institutions in the city in which representatives of the Artisans' Union did not take part.

The first premises of the union were located at Brisker Street in Moshe Lebenberg's house. Their second location was at Janower Street in Yitzhak Goldsztajn's house. The last premises of the union were located at Janower Street in the house of the tinsmith, Moshe Elya.

The Artisans' Union carried out energetic action in providing artisans' cards for the comrades, without which, according to the law, it was illegal to have a workshop. Later, there came the action of arranging for master-diplomas for Jewish artisans. It was not an easy thing for a Jewish artisan to receive such a diploma because he needed to take an exam, during which, in addition to showing his mastery of his trade, he also had to show mastery of the Polish language, and Jewish artisans in Biala were very weak in this area. However, it was important that the Jewish artisan receive this diploma because an artisan without a diploma did not have the right to employ apprentices. Thanks to the good relationship that existed between the leaders of the Jewish Artisans' Union and the leaders of the Christian guild organizations, the exams were limited only to questions in the area of the trade and the Jewish artisans successfully passed the exams.

A *gmiles khesed* [interest-free loan] fund existed at the Artisans' Union, which would divide loans among the members without interest, to be paid in installments.

During the course of its existence, the Artisans' Union carried out several events that had great success, such as an artistic evening at *Beis-Am* [assembly hall] that was carried out by the union members, a lecture by Deputy Noakh Prilicki and others.

In 1939 the Artisans' Union suffered the fate of other Jewish communal institutions in the city, which ceased to exist immediately after the German Army marched in.

The Retailers' Union

by Shmuel Kahan, Paris

Translated by Gloria Berkenstat Freund

When the merchants' union in the city ceased to be active because of the anti–Semitic economic policies of the government, which led to the fact that the majority of the large merchants became retailers, the idea developed to create a retailers' union in Biala. The union was founded in 1924. The organizers were Shmuel Kahan, Moshe Rodzinek, Dovid Wajcman, Volvish Wajcman, Dovid Kantor, Yosha Bachrach and Yakov Tokarski.

The main task of the union was to defend the interests of the retailers at the tax office so that they would not be worn down because of the too high tax evaluations. Very often, when the intervention by the union at the municipal tax office did not have an appropriate success, a delegation was sent to Lublin to the local *izba skarbowa* [tax office] in order to intervene, and many times the delegation met with success. It also was important to be represented in the city council and at the *kehile* [organized Jewish community] because matters that were important to the retailers often were on the agenda.

[Page 172]

Volvish Wajcman and Dovid Wajcmen were elected to the city council on the part of the retailers and Shaul Batszka and Yoel Sztromwaser to the *kehile*.

The union tried to have the appropriate representatives at the municipal cooperative bank in order to be of assistance to the comrades in receiving credit there.

The activity of the union constantly expanded and new departments were organized, such as an honorary court to solve various conflicts among comrades in order to avoid turning to a court. An information office for the credit possibilities for the clients was opened. Medical help for the comrades at discount prices was organized.

A *gmiles–khesed kasa* [interest–free loan fund] was created at the Retailers' Union, which carried on vigorous and fruitful activity, helping the members with loans. The fund had a large role in the communal life of the retailers in the city, benefitting from everyone's trust.

The union was in constant contact with the central office in Warsaw, which would carry out interventions with the higher officials at the request of the Biala union and also provided legal help in needed cases.

The union worked with the artisans' union in the city in certain actions.

The budget of the union would be covered by dues from the comrades and by subsidies that the union would receive from the central office in Warsaw.

In 1927 the organization of the union consisted of the following comrades:

Managing committee: Shmuel Kahan (chairman), Moshe Rodzinek, Moshe Feldman, Dovid Wajcman, Yoel Sztromwaser, Yosha Bachrach and Yakov Tokarski.

Inspection commission: Volvish Wajcman, Yitzhak Agres and Ahron Ribak.

Honorary court: Yakov Sztajnman, Volvish Wajcman, Moshe Feldman, Dovid Wajcman, Moshe Rodzinek, Yakov Tokarski and Hershl Kahan.

The union was located for a time in Yoska Winograd's house and, later, at Yatka [butcher] Street at Ides (Yehudis) Henya Resze's [house].

The union continued its activities, helping the shopkeepers in their daily struggle for survival until the dark day of the Germans' arrival in Biala and the entire Jewish communal life ceased to exist.

Credit Cooperation

by A. Wajs

Translated by Gloria Berkenstat Freund

a. Until the First World War

In 1908 the first credit cooperative arose in Biala under the name "Loan and Savings Fund." Later the fund joined the loan and savings fund of *I.K.O.* [Jewish Colonization Organization]. (The founders were: Chaim Levi Rubinsztajn, Yehezkiel Erlich, Kalman Szajnberg and Dovid'tshe Cahan. They would serve daily without any financial reward – ed.)

The Jewish artisans and retailers lived under difficult conditions during that time and the rise of the loan fund was welcomed with great joy. Only a few people, including Zogar, one of the founders of the cooperative, then understood what cooperation was. But, everyone understood that such an institution where the Jewish artisans or the retailers would receive a loan of several hundred rubles was an important accomplishment and therefore everyone enthusiastically devoted themselves to the work.

The Biala loan and savings fund developed quickly and became very popular with the Biala Jewish population, so that after a year of its existence the fund's members numbered 500 with a share capital of 7,000 rubles and 30,000 rubles in deposits, giving out loans of 38,000 rubles.

The number of members constantly grew, so that the volume of business could not satisfy the demands of all of the members and they had to draw more outside capital. And the late community worker, managing committee member of the fund, Dovid'tshe Cahan, may he rest in peace, in addition to his own deposit of several thousand rubles, agitated among the group that they should bring the *groshns* that they had saved to the fund, emphasizing the safety of the institution.

[Page 173]

After two years of its existence, the fund developed with such speed that there constantly was an excess of money. The amount of the loans was tripled from 100 to 300 rubles for a member and in many cases the members benefited from double loans, that is, up to 600 rubles.

The fund satisfied the needs of the poor population, but it did not satisfy the needs of the middle class and of the larger merchants. According to a law of that time, the fund did not have the right to carry on exchange–operations, such as collections and other bank operations. At the initiative of a group of people, with the Messrs Eidl Szwarc and Adolf Boldman at the head, it was decided to create a Society of Mutual Credit in Biala for this purpose.

When one remembers the lack of rights and arbitrariness that reigned in Tsarist times, perhaps it can be understood what effort and obstinacy must have been connected to receiving permission from the Finance Ministry in Petersburg to found such an institution, particularly when all of the signers of the charter were Jewish, and evaluating the earnings of the above–mentioned, they did not stop working for half a year until the charter was finally approved. Naturally, in addition, they made use of the full recommendation by influential Jewish community workers in Petersburg.

During the second half of 1911, the charter was approved by the then Finance Minister [Vladimir] Kokovtsov with the provision that at the opening, the cooperative would number not less than 100 members with a minimum capital of 10,000 rubles.

The information was received with such enthusiasm by the Biala merchant–class that the capital was subscribed with a great surplus at the first founding meeting. Then a managing committee was elected with Eidl Szwarc as chairman and a council with Alter Eidlsztajn as chairman.

The activity of the institution began on the 1st of November 1911. The well–appointed office in a European manner and the hiring of Ayzyk Szwarc as an actual director with a full general staff and co–workers made the institution very popular in the first months of its existence. Almost every day there were new members and trustees of the richest men in the city and the surrounding area. The institution developed at a fast tempo and surpassed all expectations.

After a year of its existence, the Society joined the Petersburger Central Bank of Mutual Credit as a member and over the course of a year it received rediscount credit of 50,000 rubles and was accredited in the same way by various societies and banks in the country and abroad.

The institution developed daily. The deposits grew and it became one of the most esteemed credit institutions in Congress Poland.

On the 1st of August 1914 the institution numbered over 250 members with its own capital of 42,00 rubles, deposits over 150,000 rubles, discount notes up to 300,000 rubles with almost unlimited rediscount credit in various private and share–banks, in the Central Bank in Petersburg and in *Bank Towarzystwo Spoldzielczych* [Bank of Cooperative Societies] in Warsaw. This provided the possibility of expanding the activity of the institution and raised the credit to 5,000 rubles for a member.

There was great trust in the bank so that Jewish and non–Jewish institutions placed their capital in *Wzajemni Kredit* [Mutual Credit] (the official name of the institution).

The activity of the institution proceeded at a calm and exemplary tempo until 1914.

The activity of the Biala cooperative institutions was restricted and paralyzed from the outbreak of the war until 1915. Every day the monetary means flowed out. The Cooperative Bank was evacuated to Minsk in July 1915.

Thus the First World War destroyed two beautiful, exemplary Jewish cooperative institutions in Biala.

(*Podlasker Lebn* [*Poldlasker Life*] 83/18, of 12th May 1935. A. Wajs is probably Ayzyk Szwarc – M. Y. F–M).

[Page 174]

Credit Cooperation

by M. Y. Feigenbaum

Translated by Gloria Berkenstat Freund

a. In Liberated Poland

1. Cooperative Bank

The "credit–cooperative" was founded after the First World War, which actually was the continuation of the "loan and saving" [fund]. Later (1927), the name was changed to the Security Cooperative Bank [*Spoldzielczy Bank Udzialowy* in Polish].

The tasks of the cooperative were: distributing cheap credit to its members, permitting the members to buy goods on credit through the intervention of the cooperative, taking in deposits and savings, accepting collection notes, etc.

The members of the cooperative consisted of artisans and retailers.

At the founding of the cooperative, its activities were carried out in Chaim Lev Rubinsztajn's house. Later, in Jungerman–Fridberg's house (previously Hartglas). In 1929 the bank moved into a large and beautiful building in the center of Wolnoszczi Square, in the community house belonging to Tila Berlin (over Ostrowska's apothecary).

In 1926 the bank passed through a dark crisis that threatened the cooperative with liquidation. At the general meeting of the members in August 1926 new members were elected to the managing committee, which consisted of the dentist, Yoal Zilberberg, Pinkhas Nartman and Yitzhak Arges. Benyamin Kliger stood at the head. The new institutions energetically began the work of assuring the health of the bank. A number of members simply invested large sums of money and thus guaranteed normal activity. Due to the then favorable economic conditions, the institution succeeded, in general, in emerging from the difficult situation in which it had been.

The population again had trust in the bank and again began to bring in deposits and savings. The Inspectors' Union of the Jewish Credit Cooperatives in Warsaw giving its judgment that the activity of the bank had been normalized greatly helped it to receive credit from the Cooperative Central Bank and from the Joint [Distribution Committee] in Warsaw.

The bank never had a director and all of the members' matters and interests were handled by the personnel, according to the decisions and instructions from the managing committee, which would come together for a meeting twice a week. In addition to this, the managing committee members would come to the bank every day, which gave the personnel the opportunity to ask them for advice about various matters.

There was always the feeling of a shortage in the volume of business and therefore they could not always satisfy the requests of the members. In the last years before the start of the Second World War, a member could make use of up to 2,000 *zl.* credit. Loans of up to 300 *zl.* were given in the form of discount notes. When the managing institutions noticed a rise in the profit, they immediately lowered the interest.

The bank leadership maintained a very secure credit policy and always tried to have their members benefit from credit and not permit individuals to have privileges to the detriment of other members. The credit policy led to the bank being able to cope with all economic crises and to continue to exist during the time when all other Jewish banks in the city were liquidated.

The bank was for the common people in the fullest sense of the word. The bookkeeping actually was in Polish, but the everyday language was Yiddish. The bank tried, as far as possible, to help its members. There was no pomposity there; a folksy joke, a witticism, a story could be heard there. A list of immigrants to *Eretz–Yisroel* and city nicknames was kept there. The bank was known in the city as Zionist although the bank authorities represented Bundists and *Agudahnikes* [Orthodox non–Zionist organization], who worked harmoniously together on behalf of the institutions and its members.

The bank ceased to exist with the outbreak of the Second World War. The portfolios of promissory notes and securities were hidden and it is difficult to say what their fate was.

In the course of the existence of the bank, its personnel consisted of: Yakov Ahron Rozenbaum, Moshe Morgensztern, Itka Rubinsztajn, Moshe Orlanski, Motl Wiznfeld, Moshe Yosef Fajgnbaum, Yehudis Warm, Yehosha Fajgbaum, Sura Miendziczecki, Yeshayahu Stolowi, Meir Korman and Menakhem Hajblum.

Active in the administrative bank authority during the last years before the war were: Benyamin Kliger, Yitzhak Agres, Dr. Yoal Zilberberg, Pinkhas Nortman, Moshe Rodzinek, Shmuel Orlanski, Yosef Fridberg, Yakov Kornblum, Asher Fajgnbaum (carpenter), Yehosha Eidlsztajn, Yitzhak Hochberg, Yitzhak Grobman, Yakir Kohan-Tzedek and others.

[Page 175]

Board and Personnel of the Cooperative Bank

Sitting, from the left: Shmuel Orlanski, Yitzhak Grobman, Asher Fajgnbaum, Benyamin Kliger, Pinkhus Nartman, Yithak Hochberg;
Standing: Yitzhak Arges, Yosef Fridberg, Yeshayahu Stolowi, Moshe Rodzenek, Sura Miendziczecki, Motl Wiznfeld, Moshe Orlanski, Yakov Kornblum, Yehosha Eidlsztajn, Dentist Yoal Zilberberg (missing from the personnel - Yakov Ahron Rozenbaum)

Balance on the 31st of December 1936 Biala Cooperative Bank

Active

Treasury	8,698 *zl*
Banks	2,045 *zl*
Securities	1,087 *zl*
Loans	29,132 *zl*
Discounts	62,061 *zl*
Advances on collections	5,538 *zl*
Inventory	1,600 *zl*
Other accounts	971 *zl*
	111,132 *zl*

Passive

Securities	19,152 *zl*
Reserve Fund	5,207 *zl*
Special Fund	521 *zl*
Deposits	56,831 *zl*
On–going Loans	530 *zl*
Debts	22,300 *zl*
Other invoices	5,475 *zl*
Profits in reporting year	1,116 *zl*
	111,132 *zl*

(The balance is taken from the Cooperative Movement, number 10, Warsaw, 10/10/1937.)

In the monograph by B. Gurny, which was published just before the [Second World] war, the number of members of the bank is given as 314 and the bond capital is given as the sum of 20,601 *zlotes*.

2. Merchants' Bank

The Merchants' Bank in Biala was founded on the 5th of January 1925. It was located for a time on the first floor of Mendl Wajman's house at Pilsudski Street. Later it moved to the ground floor of the same house and was organized in an ample form.

The large merchants and even the landowners from throughout the county were involved with the bank. The bank developed at a fast tempo, so that in the course of two years of activity, the bank's own capital reached a sum of more than 15,000 *zlotes*, which at that time was a very astounding sum.

The bank took care of all kinds of bank transactions and made use of its very good reputation in the banking world, benefiting from high credit at various financial institutions. After a short time of activity, the bank was taken in as a member of the Inspectors' Union of the Jewish Cooperative.

However, the credit policies of the institution were not very cautious. Credit operations with individuals were permitted for very large sums. During the economic crisis in the year 1930 several large wood merchants in Biala, with whom the bank was involved, went bankrupt and also dragged the Merchants' Bank into the abyss with them.

In March 1933 a general meeting of the bank members took place to stabilize the position of the bank. It was decided at the meeting to add a surcharge to every security of 25 *zlotes*. Elected to the council at the meeting were: Dr. A. Gelbard, M. Orlanski, Sh. Grodner and A. Lustigman. However, all attempts to again strengthen the position of the bank were unsuccessful. The truth is that Biala did not have any great merchants that were in a position to help rehabilitate the institution and in 1934 the bank completely ceased to exist.

Fishl Finklsztajn was the director of the bank. Working as officers were: Ayzyk Szwarc, Shlomo Hirszson, Pesl Sirkus, Ruczka Dzenczol, Yakov Liberman, Noakh Kramarcz, Garber and Elihu Libman.

[Page 176]. **Balance Report of the Biala Merchants' Bank on the 31ˢᵗ of December 1926**

Active

Cash	4,247.70 *zl*
Discount	69,602.42 *zl*
Interest	2,578.61 *zl*
Moveable assets	2,299.64 *zl*
Collection documents in the portfolio	61,047.51 *zl*
Collection documents with correspondence	8,836.30 *zl*
Correspondents	2,849.18 *zl*
Property payments and bank instruments	3,701.16 *zl*
Bonds	145.- *zl*
Advance on collections	8,264.80 *zl*
Action by the bank for the cooperatives	179.- *zl*
Interest for year 1927	110.37 *zl*
Debts	11,823.62 *zl*
	175,685.31 *zl*

Passive

Interest	17,960.91 *zl*
Securities fund	10,900.- *zl*
Reserve fund	1,270.13 *zl*
Special fund	3,008.- *zl*
Deposits and savings	30,988.35 *zl*
Running accounts	18,174.87 *zl*
Rediscounts	14,367.75 *zl*

Various collections	69,883.81 *zl*
Transitional sums	616.56 *zl*
Receivable accounts	7,868.15 *zl*
Interest for 1927	72.64 *zl*
	175,685.31 *zl*

(The balance was taken from the *Podlasier Lebn* [*Podlasier Life*], number 6, of the 11th of February 1927).

3. Cooperative People's Bank

The bank was founded by the Radziner Hasidim in 1927. At first it was located in a room in the house of a leather merchant, Motl Eidlsberg.

Yehezkiel Erlich was the leader of the bank and the personnel consisted of religious young people such as Elihu Erlich, Shepsl Rozen, Hinekh Szajnberg, Dovid Pocztaruk. The only non–religious one there was the bookkeeper, Wajsman from Radzyn.

In order to receive deposits, which were not abundant among the Jewish population in the city, the bank began to pay higher interest. It should be understood that whoever chased after this interest and did not consider where he was entrusting his money brought his money to this bank. The two remaining banks in the city, which did not want to enter competition with the People's Bank, felt the results of this tactic. (*Podlasier Lebn*, number 19, of the 19th of August 1927)

The bank would carry out risky transactions with "our people" and in chasing after profits they completely forgot to insure the credit given.

The bank did record success at the beginning and moved into the large and beautiful premises of the former *Bank dla Handlu i Przemysłu* [Bank for Trade and Industry] in Chaim Joska Kasztenbaum's house. It belonged to the *Agudah* [Orthodox organization] Inspectors' Union.

In 1931, with the first sign of a tightening economic crisis, the bank collapsed and ceased to exist.

The consequences of the collapse were very serious because the bank owed a large amount of money to small depositors who had taken advantage of the directors of the bank and their assistants. No efforts were made to collect the debts at least to partially cover the debts for which the bank was responsible.

The decline of the bank created anger among a number of Radziner Hasidim who even left the Radziner Hasidim *shtibl* [one–room synagogue].

The bank was never officially liquidated and the holders of debt received none of their savings.

The members of the managing committee were: Yehezkiel Erlich, Motl Eidlsberg, Mordekhai Yosef Goldsztajn, Nukhem Tenenbaum, Avraham Goldszmidt, Moshe Yitzhak Biderman, Shimeon Lichtensztajn and so on. The council consisted of Yitzhak Berman, Shmai Kalichsztajn, Moshe Betsalel Laszczewski, Kalman Szajnberg and so on; in the Inspection Commission: Ayzyk Szajnberg, Leibl Wajntraub, Tzvi Halpern and so on.

4. Cooperative Discount Fund

After the liquidation of the Merchants' Bank, the former officials of this bank, Ayzyk Szwarc and Shlomo Hirshzon, founded this fund that was located at Wolnoszczi Square, in Yisroel Khahan's house.

Despite all efforts, the fund did not develop and was liquated after a short time. It should be recorded that the fund had no influence in the economic life of the Biala Jews.

[Page 177]

5. Cooperative Trade Bank

The founder of this bank was Ayzyk Szajnberg. It was located in the courtyard at Meir Orlanski's and did not play any role in economic life. Its main activity consisted of collecting promissory notes. No loans were given there.

They did not belong to any inspection union and were by controlled by state reviews.

The bank personnel consisted of Shepsl Rozen and Hinekh Szajnberg. The bank ceased to exist with the outbreak of the war.

————————

Workers' Consumer Cooperative, *Einikeit*

by W. Szuster, New York

Translated by Gloria Berkenstat Freund

The rise of the Polish independent nation did not bring with it any easing in the area of economics for the population. The economy, which was greatly harmed during the [First] World War, had still not returned to normal and a new war had already flared up, the Polish-Bolshevik [War]. Workers and the masses were then not in a position to buy the most important major products.

Therefore, the Bund in Biala decided to found a consumer cooperative, where each worker and the general masses could get money to purchase products for low prices and be safeguarded against speculation. The Bundist party and the professional unions called a meeting of their comrades and proposed to them the plan for creating the cooperative.

The plan foresaw that each worker and the general masses in the city could become members of the cooperative on the condition that he bought a share. He was entitled to buy at the cooperative with the payment for the share, but only for his own family. The project was affirmed and the cooperative, *Einikeit* [Unity], arose. The cooperative numbered 255 members (*Lebns Fragn* [Questions of Life] 1919, Bundist newspaper in Warsaw, correspondence from Biala).

The cooperative committee consisted of the comrades Avraham Adller, Nakhum Warek, Moshe Rodzinek, Khanina Kuperszmid and Shmaye Fridman. The sellers at the cooperative were Khone Frajnd, Chaim Wajsgloz and Velvl Kohan. Mainly the most important articles sold, such as kasha [buckwheat groats], flour, rice, oil, salt, herring, soap and so on, would be bought at the state provisions office.

The cooperative had its selling place at the house of Dovidl the stonecutter at Grabanower Street. Later it was located at Mezritcher Street at the house of Yankele the painter.

The cooperative closed when the Bolsheviks drew near to Biala in 1920 and all active Bund comrades were arrested. With the entry into Biala of the Bolsheviks, several Bund comrades, who had been hiding and avoiding arrest by the Polish regime, gathered and they decided to distribute all of the products among the cooperative members. Later, the committee liquidated the cooperative.

(Written based on the material that was found in the Kursky Archives, New York, as well as from the book by Sh. Herc, *Di Geshikhte fun a Yugnt* [*The History of a Young Man*]).

[Page 178]

Cooperative Mechanical Bakery

by M. Y. F–M

Translated by Gloria Berkenstat Freund

The frequent persecutions on the part of the regime against the Jewish population in the area of sanitation created the idea among the Jewish bakers of founding a joint mechanical bakery.

Such a bakery was founded in 1930 as a cooperative, which was joined by all of the Jewish bakers in the city. They rented several large rooms for this purpose in Wajne's and there organized a mechanical bakery according to all of the newest technical standards.

The cooperative was accepted as a member of the Jewish Central Inspectors' Union [of the Jewish Credit Cooperative] in Warsaw, which made it possible for it to obtain certain credits.

The cooperative was dissolved after a very short existence and each bakery returned to being a private bakery. Later, the bakers still strongly lamented the unsuccessful attempt that had cost each of them dearly.

It is hard now to know the reasons for the liquidation of the cooperative.

The Interest-Free Loan Fund at the Small Businessmen's Union

Translated by Gloria Berkenstat Freund

The *gemiles-khesed kasa* [interest-free loan fund] at the Small Businessmen's Union was founded in 1926. The initiators of founding the fund were: Shmuel Kahan, Moshe Rodzinek, M.A. Miszkin, Yosha Bachrach, Dovid Wajsman, Mendl Wajsman, Yoal Sztromwaser and Yakov Tokarski. An inducement to found the *gemiles-khesed kasa* was provided by the news that the Joint [Distribution Committee] in Warsaw was distributing subsidies to such funds.

However, two conditions were placed by the Joint Central in Warsaw: 1) firstly, a fund with the appropriate capital needed to be created on the spot and then the Joint would add its proportional subsidy to the collected capital and 2) the fund had to be a joint fund both for the small businessmen and the artisans.

The initiators contributed to a money collection in the city and in a short time there was success in collecting the appropriate sum. The Joint, for its part, added a subsidy in the amount of 10,000 *zlotes* and the fund began to function.

However, as the leadership of the Artisans' Union had not agreed to the joint fund with the Small Businessmen's Union, the small businessmen founded their own fund and the subsidy that had been received from the Joint was divided between both funds in equal parts. So that the Joint in Warsaw would not know that two separate funds were in existence, every month a joint report was sent to Warsaw. At the first inspection by the Joint on the spot [in Biala], the existence of the two separate funds was uncovered. Later, the two funds received separate subsidies directly from the Joint.

The Small Businessmen's Union's *gemiles-khesed kasa* would distribute loans from 100 to 300 *zlotes* to its members and the loans would be paid back in small installments. They did not charge any interest but everyone who received a loan had to pay several *zlotes* in membership dues.

The Small Businessmen's Union would carry out various events and campaigns that made possible the increase in the capital of the fund and thus received even larger subsides from the Joint.

The *gemiles-khesed kasa* existed until the outbreak of the war and helped a great number of Biala small businessmen. The society, whose number [of members] reached approximately 400, acted with great sympathy toward their fund, paying their loans on time. An insignificant percentage of loans were not paid back. However, the fund never pressed charges in court against a member, because such a step was not permitted by the Joint.

According to *Podlasier Lebn* [*Podlaska Life*] number 28/144 of the 20th of July 1934, elected to the managing committee of the fund were Yitzhak Berman, Tzvi Halpern, Moshe Feldman, Leibl Lipiec, Leibl Blanklajder, Yakov Rozencwajg, Yitzhak Khahan, Avraham Srebrnik and Yakov Tokarski.

Yisroel Liverant, Ruchl Listgartn, Berl Czelazo and Yakov Niewidze worked there as employees during the course of the fund's existence.

Balance Sheet on the 1st of November 1926
of the Interest-Free Loan Fund

Active

Treasury	75.10 *zlotes*
Loans given	8,088.50 *zlotes*
Running accounts in the bank	567.– *zlotes*
Administrative costs	816.07 *zlotes*
	_____
	9,545.67 *zlotes*

Passive

Rescue committee (Joint)	4,475 *zlotes*
Own debts (deposits)	2,410 *zlotes*
Various income	871.17 *zlotes*
Shares of 378 members	1,790.50 *zlotes*
	_____
	9,545.67

(The balance sheet was taken from the *Podlasier Lebn*,
number 1, of the 26th of November 1926)

Received from Shmuel Kahan (Paris)
and Ruchl Listgartn (Kibbutz Ramat David)

[Page 179]

Parties

The Zionist Organization

by M. Bruchl Tel Aviv

Translated by Libby Raichman

It is not known if, in the period of "Chibat Tzion" [Love of Zion], before the advent of political Zionism, there were traces of the movement in Biale. Rather it must be assumed that there were not.

The outcome of the first Zionist Congress in 1897 also resonated in Biale. It is true that, at that time, there was no specific group of people who came into contact with one another regarding the new word "Jewish State" that was thrown about in the Jewish street but certain individuals in the nearby and distant towns reflected on this and even contacted those who proposed this new movement.

Chassidic houses were known to receive a hectographically printed familiar circular by Dr. Cohen-Bernshtein from Kishinev: the weekly (or monthly) journal "The Jew" was published in Krakow. In houses like these, there were also the first small signs — a blue Star of David with the word "Zion" in the middle.

With the emergence of the Chassidic rabbis against Zionism, these first Chassidic sympathizers distanced themselves from Zionism. There were, however, individuals who chose rather to leave the Chassidic study houses. One of these Chassidim was Hertzl Halbershtat, Moshe Cohen's son–in–law, the brother–in–law of the later famous surgeon Dr. D. Cohen of Warsaw.

The first organization of the Zionist group in Biale was established in 1901 by Apolinari Hartglas who was then a very young student at the Warsaw university:
" … at that time, at the beginning of my first summer vacation, between my first and second courses, I took to spreading the word of Zionism in Biale, with all my zeal. I found a few young people from among the Chassidic youth in Biale that I influenced in favour of Zionism. I spent my own money and brought many brochures in Yiddish and Polish from the publishing house "Achiesof" in Warsaw. I organized the first group that gathered together, held discussions and sang Zionist songs. Biale, one of the cradles of the worst, darkest periods of Chassidic aloofness, became one of the fortresses of Zionism in the Polish province".

In an article "Times are Changing" that appeared in "Podlassier Life" number 62 of 11.2.1927, Hartglas describes how difficult it was for him to organize the first Zionist group in Biale, because of his lack of knowledge of Yiddish and he therefore sought the assistance of the Hebrew teacher Sholem Ratshin.

This organized beginning, it appears, was the foundation stone for the Zionist structure that was built later, with longer and shorter breaks but without cessation, until it became this fortress of which Advocate A. Hartglas speaks.

This is what Asher Hoffer, one of the first Zionists in the town, reports about the early days of Zionism in Biale: I cannot recall the year when we, a group of Biale youth, began our activity for the Zionist ideal.

Eliezer Baynish Goldfarb came from Mezritsh to speak about Zionism in the synagogue. The synagogue was packed. People came from all levels of society: Chassidim, opponents of Chassidism, merchants and tradesmen. Even Reb Itshe Meir Cohen and Reb Chaim Levi Rubinshtein of the great Gerer Chassidim came to hear him.

Goldfarb's address in the synagogue made a strong impression on the audience and we, the Zionist youth group in the town, wanted to take this opportunity to recruit more members to our circle.

[Page 180]

Unfortunately, we did not have a great response, due to orders from the Rabbis not to associate with the Zionists. Then the Chassidim began to persecute the Zionists. The Zionists ignored this and a Zionist organization was established in Biale. The founders were: a man named Kamenne from Shedletz, who was an agent for Singer Sewing machines, Chaim Tvarkovsky, who was a military tailor and Sholem Ratshin, a Hebrew teacher from Slutzk, son–in–law of a Biale resident. Meetings were held in quarters that were hired from Shimon Krideshtein. Sympathizers came from Chassidic circles, religious students and tradesmen. If one wanted to enter these premises, one had to creep in unnoticed, literally like a thief, so as not to encounter the persecutors of the Zionists".

In "Podlassier Life" number 7 of 18.2. 1927, Avrom Urmacher added a few details of that first period.

One Passover between 1903 and 1906, a meeting of Zionists took place over a glass of liquor, in the home of A. Urmacher. Amongst others, the following participated: The student A. Hartglas, Reb Gavriel the scribe, Reb Dovid Moshe son of Yossel, Moshe Yaver, Sholem Ratshin, Asher Hoffer, Binyomin Klieger, Avrom Lubeltshik. Hinech Cohen, Avrom Gelblum the teacher from Bork, a few elected Zionists students from the Biale Gimnazye and perhaps 50 religious students who used to come and study in the "religious students' society".

Avrom Podlishevsky came from Warsaw to Biale to arouse interest in the KKL [Keren Kayemet L'yisrael – Jewish National Fund]. He lectured behind closed doors in the home of the Bielsk tailor Chaim Tvarkovsky, to a very limited audience.

In the years 1903 – 1906, our own synagogue was established in the premises of Shimon Krideshtein. Besides praying there on Sabbaths and festivals, people used to gather there in the evenings for various lectures.

Yehoshuah Fisher, one of the oldest Biale Zionists, who had a temperamental and aggressive nature, and who stood at the head of the Zionist activities until the First World War, relates the following:
"Approximately in the year 1903, I turned to the Odessa–Palestine committee in Odessa with a suggestion that I be elected as their representative in Biale. I have been sympathetic to Zionist ideals for a long time but due to my father's antagonism, I was not able to participate actively in the Zionist movement. Now that this antagonism has ceased, I have begun to be active. My proposition was accepted by the Odessa committee. I recruited a substantial number of members who paid an annual fee of around 3, 6, 10, 15 and 25 ruble to the Odessa committee.

Our group numbered approximately 30 members. Of those who were active, I remember: Asher Hoffer, Moshe Kavve, Ya'akov Shteinman, Binyomin Klieger, Moshe Rubinshtein and Moshe Braverman. We used to meet in my home and have discussions on Zionist themes. I managed initially to involve religious students in our ranks. We used to receive a variety of Zionist brochures from the Odessa committee as well as material for implementing fund–raising activities for the Odessa–Palestine committee. The collection of money was carried out on the eve of Yom Kippur in the synagogue, study houses, Chassidic prayer houses and at the cemetery. We would put out plates and the names of the donors who had donated more than 20 kopeks, on a list. The first year we raised 6 ruble and in 1913 – 100 ruble.

At these collections, there was no shortage of incidents, mainly by the influential Chassidim. One Yom Kippur eve, in the Gerer house of prayer, Motl Mintz threw the plate off the table. After that incident I confronted Motl Mintz and warned him that he should not dare to do such a thing again because in retaliation, I would be compelled to react sharply against him, that would bring him no glory. Motl Mintz remembered my warning well.

From time to time we would organize talks by lecturers that we invited from Warsaw. The income was designated for the Odessa– Palestine committee.

It is worth mentioning that sometime after I began the Zionist activity in Biale, I became aware that years earlier there was an active Zionist group that was led by Asher Hoffer, Moshe Kavve and Binyomon Klieger but due to the Tsarist government ban on Zionist activity, the group ceased to exist".

Approximately in 1910/11, the small group of Zionists was strengthened by fresh young blood. A number of the youth joined this group and devoted themselves to the cause with fresh zeal. Contact was arranged with the Zionist movement and the Zionist centres. They subscribed to the Zionist periodic press and read their publications ("Ha'tzefirah", "Razsvet" – in Russian and "Di Velt" – in German and also the Zionist "Kopek Library" that was published in Odessa.

The traditional collections for the Odessa–Palestine committee continued every year on the eve of Yom Kippur in the synagogue and in the prayer houses. Besides that, the practical work, under the guidance of Yehoshua Fisher, consisted of stretching the shekel and in collecting for the Jewish National Fund. These collections took place secretly because such activity was banned by the Tsarist government. The money was sent in the post to Cologne (Germany) where the headquarters of the Keren Kayemet [Jewish National Fund] were housed.

[Page 181]

A fund–raising campaign was also implemented through the "Anglo–Palestine Bank" (now the Bank Leumi of Israel). The value of each share was £1 sterling or 10 Russian ruble. A lottery ticket cost 15 kopeks. One can assume that 60 – 65 people participated. The lottery was won by Pinye Riebak from the village of Ragizshnitze (he later became the son–in–law of Rabbi Shlaymele Goldberg of Kazion).

At first the group assembled in private houses — in the homes of Yehoshua Fisher, Yisroel Firkelshtein (Ritker) or Asher Hoffer. At these meetings, besides dealing with organizational matters, debates would take place about Zionism, that was a common dream and the reality of a small group of inspired people, a dream that warmed everyone's hearts.

The size of the groups attending the gatherings increased steadily, and the private homes became too small for the meetings. They began to think about having their own regular meeting place where members would be able to meet every day and spend time together. It would not be incorrect to say that it was felt that there was a need for such a place, where people would be able to unload the social energy that accumulated and grew with each session, and with each meeting of the members.

It was impossible to create a regular meeting place in the normal way during Tsarist rule, under the watchful eye of the Russian police. The idea was therefore born, to establish a benevolent society under the name of "Achiezer" [My brother's help] that would offer medical assistance to the sick who were in need, lend various medical instruments etc. A society of this nature existed in Shedletz and by following that example and its status, the society was legalized in Biale.

This society "Achiezer" and its important work is a chapter of its own. Here we are interested in the Zionist activity that was conducted in secret between the walls of "Achiezer".

As mentioned, the initiative for establishing the "Achiezer" came from the Zionist group but the actual purpose was hidden immediately, from the first moment. Connections were made with communal leaders and personalities in the town who were drawn in, to work together in the institution. Idl Shvartz was the head of the "Achiezer"–council and the managing committee consisted of Moshe Kavve and others. The youth took responsibility for all the internal work, administration, duties, distribution of medical instruments etc. In this way a venue was created where people could gather every evening, play chess, talk, support one another and most important, be together. The "Achiezer" gradually became almost like a club for the youth, and the community leaders who headed the institution were aware, and consented, because they saw that the only possibility of conducting the fruitful work of the institution was with the involvement of the youth, as only they could accomplish the task with such devotion.

The "Achiezer" had its first premises in the home of the Viness family and later in larger premises in the home of Dovidtshe, the son of Pessel. Here they would gather in secret on Friday nights so that the members and the management of the council would not know. Readings from Zionist literature took place and also meetings with Zionist emissaries from other towns.

In this way, Zionist activity continued for a few years and became more intensive. Contact was established with the centre in Warsaw, although in a round–about way. We learned of the Zionist address in Warsaw via Berlin and Peterburg. The Zionist group in Biale sent a delegate, a certain Dr. Monosovicz, to the 11th Zionist Congress, on a recommendation from Warsaw. He was supposed to come to Biale after the congress to give a report but this did not happen.

Over time, the group came out into the open and organized lectures in the hall that was then currently used, belonging to Yoske Kashtnboim. One of the lectures was given by Rabbi Yitzchak Nissenboim from Warsaw and a second by Dr. Shmuel Isenshtat who spoke about the Hebrew University in Jerusalem.

Already then in 1912 or 1913 the first film from the Land of Israel was shown in the cinema hall. It showed the "Herzlia" High School and the first houses in Herzl Street in Tel–Aviv. If my memory does not fail me, it also portrayed the Passover festivities in Rechovot, that took place at that time during the intermediate weekdays of the festival.

The contact with the Zionist organization in Warsaw was maintained through the press and by articles in the special section for the province in "Ha'tzefirah", where also Biale and her society were mentioned.

[Page 182]

And here is one such article, in which there is a report of Rabbi Yitzchak Nissenboim's visit to Biale.

"In the town of Biale, in the district of Shedletza public lecture was arranged about the Land of Israel and her Hebrew colony. This lecture drew a large audience and amongst those gathered were also Chassidim from the various "Shtiblech" (small prayer houses) for whom matters regarding the land of their forefathers were close to their hearts and they were very keen to know what was happening there. And in Biale there are Chassidim from various streams of Chassidism and they all lived in harmony but when it became known in the "Shtibl" of the Partshuv Chassidim that their counterparts also came to hear this "heretical" lecture, the stability of their movement was fractured and it seemed as if the walls were about to fall into ruin. That day was as difficult for them as the day of the sin of the golden calf … and on the first Sabbath after the lecture, when they took out the Torah scrolls to read, an announcement was made by the warden of the synagogue, that everyone who attended the "Zionist" lecture, dare not, from now on, come to the "Shtibl"…

There was a distinguished teacher among the Partshuv Chassidim in Biale who was greatly respected and had delved deeply into "Sefer Ha'yetzirah". He could literally "create a duck from the dust of the earth" [do the impossible] … and it came to pass that when this punishment by the Partshuv opponents of Zionism reached his ears and spread through the walls of his "shtibl", he feared greatly lest the deadly poison impact upon this holy corner and he hastened to invite the transgressors and described to them the magnitude of their sin, because in the future, the land of Israel will be a home for the Jewish people… God forbid that one should think such foul thoughts, that this is the view of the heretics, the "Zionists", perish the thought. In reality, "in every place that we live, that is where the land of Israel is, that is the opinion of the believers" …

And if this foul thought is central to your beliefs, continued the teacher, then "you will have to fast several times until your wayward thoughts are crushed, then the good God will forgive you". ("From the Cycle of Life" – Ha'tsefirah tractate 174 of 15. 8. 1913).

Finally, the Zionist activity that was conducted between the walls of the "Achiezer" could no longer remain secret and caused anger amongst the leading authorities who were particularly angry because all this Zionist activity carried on for years under their noses and they knew nothing about it. It was real due to a fear that the institution that had developed so successfully would be broken up. Even a Jew like Moshe Kavve, who was quite distant from these groups, in this instance sided with Idl Shvartz who felt most cheated, being the head of the council. There was also a fear that Dr. G. Zita, who was assimilated, would leave "Achiezer". The youth had made up their minds to carry on the work of the institute even if the leadership decided to leave the "Achiezer". The crisis passed without any further agitation.

In the summer of 1914, on Tishah B'Av, the first world war broke out and immediately a black cloud was cast over Jewish life. Biale saw the refugee camps that were filled with the inhabitants of entire Jewish villages of Galicia and Congress–Poland who fled their homes as the front line of fighting approached them. All Jewish social movements in all of Russia ceased their activities for a while and concentrated their efforts on the aid–committee in Peterburg and its divisions, in order to provide for the needs of the refugees. The Zionist movement in Biale held its breath for a while.

In the summer of 1915, with the advance of the German army eastwards, part of the Jewish population of Biale began to leave. Fear reigned amongst them that the battles around the Brisk fortress would last a lot longer and that the closest towns would suffer most. Many went to Russia — to places they were sure that the war would not reach. A small part, mainly the young members of families that remained in the town, went to Shedletz to avoid being drafted into the Russian army.

After the German occupation of Biale in 1915, the Zionists that remained in the town became active again. They thought just then, that having a European government instead of the Tsarist government, would enable them to continue their social life, with more success.

The first Zionist discussions took place between Moshe Rubinshtein and Yehoshua Fisher. They thought about what kind of practical Zionist activity they could initiate, that would draw larger groups of youth into the Zionist movement. The first idea was to organize Hebrew courses for adults. The Hebrew teacher Ya'akov Shteinman was brought into the discussions. After considering one project after another and one program after another, they came upon the idea of establishing a Hebrew school with a children's home near the school, for the children of families whose men were drafted into the Russian army, or had gone to America.

In the middle of the winter of 1915/6, an intensive organizing campaign began, in order to prepare, announce and open the "Yavne" school at Passover in 1916. This was the first real step towards renewed Zionist activity during the German occupation. Details about the school itself and its activities will be dealt with separately in this book.

Right from the beginning, the school demonstrated its strong influence, beyond the bounds of its actual activity and direct purpose. Male and female students of the school aged 12 and 13 used to come home with happy little faces and in good spirits, with songs on their lips and with stories from Jewish history and legends that stirred their fantasies. Grown–up sisters and brothers, who were older than school age, would envy their younger brothers and sisters who were fortunate to still be of school age.

[Page 183]

Reb Chaim Levi Rubinshtein's wooden house on Kshiver street, where the "Yavne" school was situated, became like a flame that attracts all those who yearn for light. At the time of the lectures in the school, small boys used to wander behind the windows or stand a few steps back and listen, to catch something from its original source, straight from the teacher's mouth. Hebrew songs that were sung in the school were immediately heard everywhere.

The school had just opened a few weeks earlier when the first Lag Ba'omer approached and the children were taken on an outing into the forest. The male and female students, dressed in festive clothes, marched in orderly rows, singing Hebrew songs, through the streets of the town. This first public march of the Hebrew school in the town understandably drew with it other young people who participated in the new celebration of this Jewish festival, that until now, had not been commemorated.

All this created a Zionist spirit in the town. The active Zionists were striving to increase and expand their numbers, after this first splendid success.

The Zionist circle grew with members from the so-called "refugees" who slowly settled in Biale. Of those who joined, some were active workers and others, just members. At that time Moshe Barlas, who came from Brisk with his entire family, became an active worker.

In the summer of 1916, further steps were taken to embrace the youth and bring them under the influence of the Zionists. Reading sessions were organized every Saturday afternoon in the big hall in the shul premises. These gatherings were not only accessible to acknowledged Zionists but even to the opponents of Zionism like, for example, active Bundists who had good relationships with the Zionist leadership. Pulye (Raphael) Lederman was even given the opportunity to lecture from a Bundist point of view, and Vaksin (a refugee from Brisk who represented an assimilated leaning, also had the opportunity to participate in the conversations and discussions.

This circle grew, the lectures were well attended and after a short time, a significant Zionist group crystallized. On the one hand, the attendance at the gatherings once a week on the Sabbath diminished (it was not possible to use the synagogue premises during the week) but on the other hand, there were constant additional overflowing discussions with opponents, where the same arguments and counter–arguments were repeated again and again. It was therefore decided to establish a Zionist "Bet–Am" at a different location that would be a gathering place for the Zionist youth, and also for sympathizers. According to the decision "Bet–Am" would have to be led by a specially elected committee, under the leadership of the chairman of the Zionist committee.

The first location of "Bet–Am" was in the house of Meyer Korman in Grabanove Street, in the corner of that narrow street. The premises consisted of two attic rooms and a front room.

"Bet–Am" was opened in the winter of 1916/7 with a solemn opening night. The festivity could be felt not only by the inner spirit but also externally, by the clothes; the crowd wore their Sabbath clothes, were dressed up and excited. From the first moment, Moshe Rubinshtein stood at the head of "Bet– Am", one would say "ex officio", as chairman of the Zionist committee. The other committee–members were elected and amongst them were: Chaim Barlas, Mendel Kavve, Yonah Shteinman etc.

The organizational tasks that were initiated were divided into separate branches. Various subcommittees were elected for each separate area of work. In this way many more members were involved in the activities. Each subcommittee had tasks to perform and at the same time had to present a report to the governing committee. In this way they were able to participate in the meetings. Cultural activities took place often and consisted of readings of literary works and articles on current public affairs. A dramatic group was organized, under the leadership of Moshe Piekarsky, and a choir, under the direction of Shimon Blankleider (the thin one). Later "Maccabi" was established, as well as its wind–orchestra.

One room was designated for the activities of these subcommittees and every day this room was at the disposal of another subcommittee, except when general gatherings and events took place and the entire venue was occupied.

Every Saturday afternoon, the Hebrew circle would gather and each time another member would read the current public affairs in Hebrew and other works in Hebrew. Among the active workers in the Zionist organization were two German Jews who were in the German army: Fritz Kornberg (an architect) and Dr. Shvabe, the chairman of the student rowing club, "Ivriyah", in Berlin who worked in Biale in Police administration. Their collaboration was very important but understandably, they were limited by the bounds of feasibility.

[Page 184]

There was a buffet in the front room of "Bet Am" that was run by the Vineshtein sisters (Dudl Brukirer's daughters). Shayne, a younger sister of theirs (now living in New York) attended the "Yavne" school and brought them into the Zionist circle.

The work was satisfying. The youth came from all levels, even from amongst those who were apparently far removed from Zionism. Firstly, as already mentioned, the school students inspired their older brothers and sisters, and secondly, the "Bet Am" was the only place in the town where the youth could gather and enjoy themselves freely. From the first moment the "Bet Am" was set up on the basis of freedom of religion that even brought them into conflict with the earlier religious Zionists, part of whom actually left and founded the "Mizrachi".

In the summer of 1917, after a period of intensive work, the first general gathering of the "Bet Am" took place that was supposed to be the first meeting of a large and strong group of organised members. Both rooms, that were not particularly large, were packed. After hearing the report of the chairman about the activities of the group, since the opening of "Bet Am", the debates began. And here a strong opposition manifested itself, not against the nature of the activities but against the principle that one person should not be the chairman of both the Zionist committee and "Bet Am" at the same time.

The opposition was led internally by the committee members Chaim Barlas and Mendel Kavve. The opposition influenced almost the whole gathering. M. Rubinshtein, with the support only of Dr. Shvabe, a person with strong organizational skills and pragmatism, defended the idea of one person as chairman, with the argument that this was the only guarantee that the "Bet Am" would remain Zionistic and not become a discussion club as it did in the period of the Sabbath gatherings.

This meeting lasted three evenings. Finally, it was decided that as an alternative to the issue of the chairman, the Zionist committee would also be the committee of "Bet Am". From that time on, "Bet Am" formally became a Zionist organization, as a club and also as a venue for all Zionist activities.

In 1917, with the growth of the Zionist organization in German occupied territory, the central Zionist organization in Warsaw decided to implement a Zionist referendum in all the towns and villages, together with fund–raising for the Jews of Jaffa and Tel Aviv who were driven from their homes by the Turkish government. The primary purpose of the referendum was meant to be a political demonstration for the Land of Israel when in the prevailing atmosphere there was the belief that the current war was a freedom–war for oppressed peoples.

The content of the declaration read:
"In recognition of the enormous merit of providing assistance to our brothers, the pioneers in the land of Israel, we, the Jews of Poland, express a strong desire that will not be broken. The great upheaval in the world that is likely to bring freedom and liberty to all the oppressed nations will also realize the historic Jewish ideal to create a secure homeland in justice for the Jewish people, in its historic homeland, in the Land of Israel".

The signatures appeared under the text together with the addresses of the signatories.

The arm of the "Federation of the Orthodox" known as the "The Jewish word", waged a battle against this referendum and called on all the religious Jews not to sign their names.

The Zionist organization in Biale played a very active role. Members went out in pairs and visited every Jewish home, telling the residents about the Land of Israel and the hope that was being pinned on a favourable solution for our needs, when after the war, nations would sit around the peace table. Tens of sheets of paper were filled in, with hundreds of signatures. Biale participation was also evident among the 200 Polish towns and villages with their 250 thousand signatures.

The various work–committees of the organization expanded and required more place and time. The premises, that were an advantage in the beginning and made it possible to unload Zionist zeal, could no longer satisfy the appetite that came with the eating. Each group (dramatic section, choir, Maccabi orchestra etc.) needed more days, more rooms, larger premises.

The search began for a second suitable place. In the winter of 1917/8 "Bet Am" moved into the house of Moshe Lebnberg on Brisk street, for a short while. It was at this time that the first public clash took place between the Zionist group and the Biale Rabbi.

[Page 185]

In January 1918, news came of the death of the Zionist leader Dr. Yechiel Tshlenov. The committee decided to arrange a public commemoration in the large synagogue. Previously too, Zionist events that were organized in closed locations ("Bet Am", "Yavne" School) were visited by guests who stood outside of the ranks of the Zionist group; this time however, it meant an invitation to the whole community, to come and pay respects to the memory of the Zionist leader. This commemoration was duly announced. On the appointed day, the Biale Rabbi sent for the warden of the synagogue, Gadl the son of Binye, and not only forbad him to open the synagogue but also asked him to bring the keys of the synagogue and removed them from his possession.

The whole afternoon there were stirrings and turbulence. People who wanted to avoid a clash turned to the Rabbi and tried to influence him to allow the commemoration to be held in the synagogue, but without success.

Evening began to fall and people came at the appointed time and began to gather in the synagogue courtyard, but were unable to enter the synagogue. In a matter of half an hour, the entire synagogue courtyard was black with people. This response from the community to this Zionist event was a success.

The stubbornness of the Rabbi threw the Zionist youth into a separate comic–battle, and the members of Maccabi who were assigned to maintain order at the commemoration stood prepared to open the synagogue by force, which was not an easy matter; the synagogue was locked with double doors and heavy locks. It was difficult to decide whether to open the doors by force, as long as they thought that there was a chance that the Rabbi would relent. They also did not want to create the slightest sign of desecrating the synagogue by breaking down the doors.

When, however, it became clear that there was no other choice, an order was given to find a way of opening the synagogue from the inside, and as far as possible, not to break the doors. Three Maccabi members, under the leadership of Asher Feigenboim (Moshe Glezer's son), went into the women's synagogue on the third floor, tore a bar from the window and through this opening, Feigenboim let himself down into the men's synagogue. In a matter of half an hour, the synagogue doors were pried open from the inside. The synagogue was filled immediately and hundreds remained standing outside.

Members spoke about the deceased and even chanted the prayer "El malei rachamim". This prayer should have been intoned by the town's cantor, who did not attend as he was forbidden to do so by the Rabbi. Instead it was done by one of the members (Pintshe Liebman).

This incident, the public struggle with the opponent, and with the Rabbi to add, gave the Zionist leaders in the town the courage to shed their constraints and come out into the open. It was the forerunner of other social struggles and clashes that were waiting in the near future.

After a short time "Bet Am" moved into the house of Kalman Sheinberg on Sadaver street. Here in fact, was the actual, true "Bet Am", the place that attracted the town's youth. The accommodation consisted of five rooms, of which two were combined. By removing the wall that divided the two rooms, one large hall was created for meetings and for gymnastic practice for Maccabi.

The work was divided anew into various subcommittees. Every branch was assigned its time and place appropriately, according to the new circumstances. Every two weeks, public meetings of the so–called "Mo'atzah" (Board) would take place, that consisted of the members of the various subcommittees. Permanent readings were introduced: literary, articles on current affairs from the press, literary laws etc. In one word, a renewed impetus began in Zionist life.

At that time, the Youth of Zion group began to form in the town and later, during Polish rule, the Hashomer Ha'tzair, that began as a scout organization. They all found their place in "Bet Am".

It was in 1918 that in the air one could feel the approach of the end of the war. All around things became a little freer. The borders of the so–called "stockade" that had been locked in the whole time for the military as a fenced off territory, without a connection to the outside world, was slowly torn down. Without knowing how and from what direction, the people received greetings and news from outside. With the advance of the German army deep into Russia, the Jewish military personnel in Biale, who were active in the Zionist movement in the town, left. In a roundabout way, they created some sort of contact between the Zionist group in Biale and the action–committee in Berlin.

[Page 186]

There was almost no connection with Warsaw. For the third Zionist land–conference exit permits could not be obtained from the German "stockade authorities". Gradually, however, it became easier to make contacts and news began to arrive from different sources. In Russia, members were found who had left as the front lines of the war drew nearer. From them we began to receive literature, newspapers, and circulars from Zionist centres and from the "Cultural" organizations in Russia, that gave an idea of the scope of Zionist activity in Russia. Also, the aforementioned Fritz Kornberg in Kharkov was in contact and sent publications of the Zionist youth movement in the Ukraine, where he was also active.

Later it was easier to make contact with Warsaw. One could already send a letter, and a travel permit was easier to obtain. At that time, the news of the "Balfour Declaration" reached us, news that the Germans hoped would not reach the Jewish population.

In short, they emerged from their restricted circumstances to follow a broader path. They foresaw intensive political and social activity, to the same degree as they felt the slow dying of the German war tempo and its approaching end.

At the end of the summer of 1918, the first returnees began to arrive from Russia. On the one hand, there were the ex–leftists with the message of the Bolshevik revolution and its ideals, and on the other hand the Chassidic middle–class element, who, until the outbreak of war, could only be Chassidim of the prayer houses. A few of these returning Chassidim then founded the "Agudat Yisrael".

These elements began to take their place in society. The Zionists, who were until then predominant, had to agree to an inter–party collaboration (in the American aid–committee, where all parties were represented under the chairmanship of Moshe Rubinshtein) and sometimes had to do battle with opposing parties.

In the autumn of 1918, the Zionist movement in Poland was strengthened by the full–blooded power of Yitzchak Greenboim, who returned from Russia at that time. The first task in organizing Jewish life in Poland was Greenboim's project of calling together a general Jewish national convention, at which a national council would be elected, that would stand at the head of Polish Jewry and manage its interests. This idea met with opposition from the "Agudah", the "Bund", the members of the folk party and also Zionist–socialist parties. The Zionist leadership decided in the meantime to call together a pre–conference to this national convention in December 1918. This pre–conference was attended by Zionists as well as those who did not affiliate with the parties.

In Biale, the elections to this pre–conference became the first contest of the Zionist group with other parties in the political battle. The main opposition in this area came from the followers of the "Agudah". They undermined public meetings in the synagogue. They did everything they could to obstruct the idea of a general national Jewish council, that would not be built on Torah and commandments. At one of these gatherings, Itshe Meir Cohen spoke from the side of the "Agudah". Before the war, he was removed from worldly matters but after returning from Russia he felt that he was capable of appearing at a public gathering. His most important argument was that the Zionists do not wear tzitzit [fringed garment].

On an appointed winter's day, the elections for the pre–conference took place in the synagogue. Moshe Rubinshtein and Chaim Barlas were elected.

At this conference, the Biale representatives made their first acquaintance with Zionist customs, and immediately, at this first introduction, occupied a meaningful place in the Zionist movement in Poland.

In January 1919, elections to the constitution parliament of the renewed Poland brought pogroms against Jews in Lemberg, Kieltz and other places; attacks on Jews by the "Halerchiks" and "Poznanchiks" [anti–semitic groups], by cutting beards and other similar "heroic deeds", took place also in Biale.

At this time, the Zionist organization in Biale began to prepare for the election battle. Four constituents were attached to the Biale elections: Biale, Radzin, Vladove and Yaneve. From time to time, conventions were called of all the towns and villages in the four districts. These conventions were held in "Bet Am". An episode that is worth mentioning concerns a Pole from the Mezritsh area who came to the convention and presented himself with an unusual request. He was a liberal Pole who did not agree with the anti–Semitic incitement and wanted to receive a Jewish mandate to the Polish parliament. This election convention, after hearing the speeches of the members Ch. Barlas and M. Rubinshtein, accepted the Zionist election platform and created in Biale a central election bureau, that would manage the election activities in the entire electoral district.

[Page 187]

All the Zionist youth threw themselves into the election campaign with great enthusiasm. Local members worked intensively and made contact with all the towns and villages in the four districts – through frequent circulars, letters and personal visits. Financial support for election expenses was not required from the central organization in Warsaw. Immediately after submitting the list of candidates (on which the following names appeared: advocate Apolinari Hartglas, advocate Alexander Hertz Alshvanger and the engineer Moshe Kerner) that received the number 5, a number–sale was organized in the entire election circle on the same day, that carried the number 5, in order to cover the election expenses. In the two months of the election campaign, the "Bet Am" became the frenzied headquarters.

With the approaching election day, a series of election meetings began, our own and of the opposition. The atmosphere became increasingly heated. Since the elections in the whole of Poland at that time were already over, electioneering by all parties was now free. (Biale was only freed later from German occupation, therefore the elections here, took place later.) The speakers and instructors were therefore able to put all their efforts into this one Biale election circle. The elections took place on a Sunday. On the weekend before the Sunday, a few young Zionist speakers from Warsaw voted: Dr. Esther Mangel, Yitzchak Itkin, Mordechai Yaffe, and Ya'akov Fiantnitsky who spoke at various gatherings. On Friday evening a meeting of the Folk party was held, at which Noach Prilutsky spoke. He was opposed by Dr. Esther Mangel from the Zionist side.

After the meeting, by the way, after close examination, it was decided to assemble the next day, on the Saturday night, at the same place (in the cinema hall of Chaim Kashtenboim), where there would be a meeting of the national register, at which Yitzchak Greenboim would speak.

The next evening Yitzchak Greenboim arrived in Biale. The hall was packed and the audience waited impatiently for the meeting to begin. One could feel the fire in the air. The opposition mobilized all their energies to disturb the meeting and in addition to them, the "Bund" were preparing to cause havoc and prevent Greenboim from speaking. Greenboim stood on the podium, encircled by a strong group of members, but it was impossible to start speaking. A strong Bundist group stood at the ramp in front of the podium and poured out a deluge of screams and heckling that had no connection to the actual problems of the elections. Finally, Greenboim managed to overcome the tumult of the wild screaming. His impromptu speech hardly touched on the elections of the following day, but was a cutting analysis of the Jewish problem regarding the Bolshevik revolution in Russia. With baited breath, the whole hall listened to the speaker. The group of Bundists at the ramp became more infuriated by Greenboim's analysis, and in their rage, they screamed that somewhere in a village, Zionists betrayed their Bundist members. Greenboim promised to investigate the matter. A Bundist then shouted "provocateur!" Greenboim immediately retorted: "For this one pays with blood!" A fight broke out and the meeting could not be brought to a close and one felt that to continue was not possible. After a reception for deputy Greenboim, the members escorted him to the station.

Early on Sunday, all the members went to their assigned positions and performed their tasks with devotion. And now came the days of waiting for the results of the long exhausting preparations. These were days that, on the one hand, were days of release from tension, after weeks of stressful work almost without respite and, on the other hand, a restless, passive waiting for the result. Zionist members hung around impatiently in the corridors of the circle court that served the central election commission. They already knew 10 hours earlier, from their representative in the commission, before the central election commission officially declared the result of the elections, that their work was not in vain. They also knew that their beloved advocate A. Hartglas would increase and strengthen the power of the national group's deputation in the Polish parliament.

The elections to parliament were the first political activity in the renewed Poland, in the general political arena. At the same time, the local government was formed, that included a magistrate, who began to control the activities of the parties and the social organizations and immediately banned the activities of the Zionist organization.

[Page 188]

People, however, did not lose their cool. It was evident from the first contacts with the new government that the line of approach, of asking for legalization, was long and uncertain so they chose a shorter path. There was a decree from the head of state who automatically legalized all the unions that had existed legally during the German occupation and this saved the situation. In truth, even from this point of view, everything was not strictly kosher, yet in this way it was much easier to procure a permit. This dispute with the new Polish government was reported in an article in the Zionist daily newspaper "The Jewish People".

In August 1919, the fourth Zionist land–convention in Poland took place, to which Biale sent two delegates: Moshe Rubinshtein and Ya'akov Aharon Rozenboim. At this convention, the independent organization "Zionist–youth" distinguished itself. Already then, a split began in the lines of the Zionist organization, between democrats and those on the right, that later led to the split between "Al Hamishmar" [On Guard] and "Et Livnot" [Time to Build]. Biale then sided with the democratic group.

In the same year, 1919, there were also elections to the Biale town council, during which all Jewish parties nominated separate lists of candidates. From the Zionist list, Moshe Rubinshtein and Moshe Kavve were elected.

In the town council, all the Jewish councilors, besides the Bundists, built a Jewish faction under the chairmanship of Moshe Rubinshtein, and voted as one. Once, when on the day's agenda there was a Jewish issue for which there was no hope of avoiding a vote against Jewish interests, the Jewish faction disrupted this sitting by leaving the hall. In this way, they upset the legal quorum required for the vote.

There were never any clashes with the Bundist councilors.

From 30th December 1919 until 1st January 1920 there was a convention in Warsaw of Jewish councilors in Poland, in which Biale also participated. The aim of the convention was to unify Jewish activity on the town councils.

In 1920, Biale's participation in central Zionist activity in Poland intensified. As a result, local Zionist activity was diminished, because active members went to work in the central Zionist institutions in Warsaw.

After Purim in 1920, a convention took place in Shedletz, of the Zionist institutions in the Shedletz area. The lecturers at this convention were from Warsaw, one from Shedletz and one from Biale. The lecture of the Biale member was about social work. The social work in Poland at that time, after the first world war, consisted of the aid–committees of "Joint". Almost in the whole of Poland, this work lay mainly in the hands of the assimilated circles or in the hands of the orthodox. In Biale this work was managed by a broad social committee, under Zionist leadership, in which all the parties, from left to right, were represented. The work was conducted in a constructive way which was remarkable at that time. Therefore, the lecture at the aforementioned Shedletz convention was given to a Biale representative. They wanted to know how it worked.

In 1920 there was a crisis in the Polish–Russian war. The fighting front moved ever closer. Life became increasingly difficult; people did not leave their homes because they were grabbed for work. The civil government left the town and they remained under military rule. In the most difficult days, a Polish–Jewish civilian militia unit was established, in which our members participated, in order to keep an eye on everything that could be done for the Jews in the town because the militia had the right to move around freely in the town, even in the hours when it was forbidden to the civilian population. Finally, the town was occupied by the Red Army. The civilian militia ceased to exist.

The Russian military government immediately organized the "Revkom" (Revolutionary Committee) and gradually set up the division of the civil administration. In organizing this administration, the Russians did not necessarily seek a communistic group of fellow–workers but at first employed everyone who volunteered to co–operate. Later the government challenged every person capable of doing administrative tasks to work together.

At that time, there were vigorous debates in the Zionist group, about whether to co–operate or not. Sessions were held regarding the acceptance of official decisions about this matter. A consensus had to be reached, for in the event of a negative decision reaching the government, it would immediately result in a trial by the revolutionary tribunal and an instant death sentence for sabotage. The debate was therefore held in secret and there was an unspoken exchange of opinion without any decisions. Each person therefore made their own decision and no one prevented another from acting according to his own understanding.

[Page 189]

Once a question was raised in a session. It was a Sabbath, 6 days after the Russian military government settled in Biale. Early on that Sabbath day, one of the leading members was invited to a meeting of the division of culture and school matters, that took place in the building of the high school. The member was required to assume the position of inspector of Jewish school matters in the Biale and Yaneve districts. The discussion lasted approximately an hour. The member tried to extricate himself from this appointment, saying that he was a Zionist and that he could only build an educational program that would include Hebrew and Tanach (Bible). The answer was that there would be no interference in the educational program. His reluctance did not help at all as a mandate was written for the member mentioned, on the spot, and he was appointed early the next morning, in order to give him time to find appropriate premises for his office.

That Sabbath afternoon, a session of a small group of members was called, that took the form of a visit to a sick female member, around her bed. During the discourse, the question was mentioned very sharply for the first time. Most were in favour of the position being accepted because of the importance of Jewish schools remaining in Zionist hands. The minority, and amongst them the member selected to hold this office, were of the opinion that they should wait for the outcome of the battle in Warsaw. In the event of Warsaw falling, then they would be able to come into contact with the Zionist central committee.

The next day, Sunday, the appointed member did not go and look for premises for an office. In the evening, placards with notices were posted in the town by the Russian government notifying that in cases of sabotage people would be brought before a revolutionary tribunal within 24 hours. Because of this, it was decided that the appointed member should take over his position on Monday. Suddenly on Monday, however, there was a change in the military situation, and the same evening, the Russian army evacuated Biale.

The retreat of the Russian army, that happened so suddenly, brought a situation where members who worked in Russian administration had to leave Biale, for fear of revenge by the returning Polish government. These members fled eastwards. Some of them stopped on the way, in places where they were not known and later returned. Others fled to Russia.

The reorganization of Zionist activity in the town was difficult after the Bolshevik invasion that caused part of the active members to relocate. The political atmosphere and Polish–Jewish relationships were strained, and did not make the implementation of social practises easy.

After the confirmation of the "Balfour Declaration", an emigration of Polish Jews to the Land of Israel began. The emigration policy of the Zionist organization favoured the emigration of tradesmen. At that time the Zionist organization in Biale established a joiners' workshop that was located in the courtyard of the Freedmans (called: Garden of Eden), in Narutovicz street. There, in the workshop, a number of members acquired a trade and prepared for their emigration to the Land of Israel. The workshop was run by Asherl Feigenboim (Moshe Glezer's son).

In approximately 1920, individuals began to prepare for their emigration to the Land of Israel.

The first person to leave Biale and go on Hachsharah [preparatory agricultural training for prospective immigrants to Palestine] to the pioneering farm Grochov, near Warsaw, was Itte Urmacher. Later, she was actually among the first emigrants to the Land of Israel. Others of the youth that emigrated were Zelig Rozenfeld and Pearl Vizenfeld. Of the older people – Shlaymele Viseberg (hatmaker), Yeshayahu Agress, Alter Vineberg, Sholem Rogalsky, Noach Man etc.

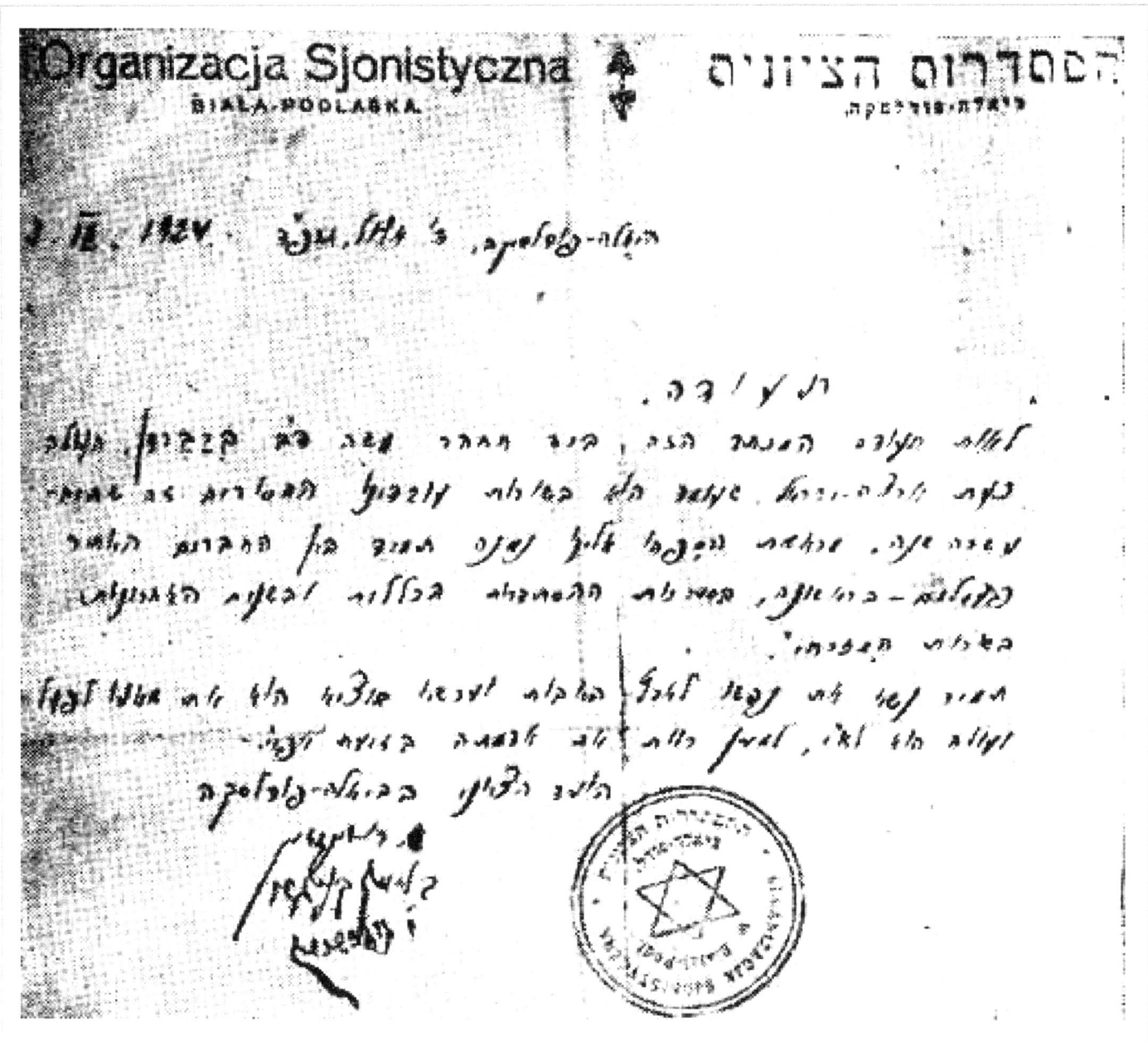

Certificate from the Zionist organization in Biale, for Moshe Braverman on his emigration to the Land of Israel in 1924

[Page 190]

At the end of summer 1922, the end of the term of office of the Polish Constitutional parliament approached. Jews too, had to begin preparing for the election of the new parliament.

In Biale, a circle conference was called for the first time in Poland, for representatives from the entire election circle (4 districts), at which the deputies Yitzchak Greenboim, Apolinari Hartglas and Heshl Farbshtein had to present reports of their activities in the Constitutional parliament. The conference took place on a Sunday. In the morning, there was a public meeting in the hall of Chaim Yaske Kashtenboim. After the meeting the deputies received delegations from various societies and institutions. In the afternoon, a large Zionist meeting was held in the synagogue. The streets on the way to the synagogue were packed and Biale had never seen such congestion in the synagogue and in the synagogue courtyard. In the evening the conference of the representatives of the election circle was held in Kayovske's hall. At this conference, a decision was taken regarding the list of candidates to the second parliament, from the Biale election circle. Afterwards, similar conferences were called in other election circles, based on Biale's example.

In 1923 the great dispute in Polish Zionism began and brought about a split between two groupings: "Al Hamishmar" and "Et Livnot". The "Al Hamishmar" group was in the minority in Biale. Biale sent delegates from the "Et Livnot" group to the 6th Zionist land–conference. The leading members in Biale who belonged to "Al Hamishmar" and who always represented Biale at the land–conferences were elected to this conference in other locations.

The reactionaries that grouped themselves around the Rabbi could not digest the growth of Zionist life and activity in the town and brought out their old weapon from its hiding place, the "ban". The reason for the ban was a fragment from a poem by the poet Dovid Shimonovicz, that was printed on the title page of a periodic publication by Hashomer Ha'tzair, under the name "El Al". This edition, with "appropriate" commentaries, was brought to the Rabbi by a Chassid from Radzin.

The ban that was imposed on the Zionists was announced with all its harshness in the synagogue, by the Rabbi himself, beside kindled lights, accompanied by the blowing of the shofar and vehement curses. These curses from the Biale Rabbi and the calling of the ban made a deep impression on the superstitious masses.

This needed a prompt and not belated answer, that would undo and completely destroy this foolish fear. And the answer came immediately. The next day, it already became known that the Zionists were taking up the battle and would wage it freely and publicly, against the Rabbi and all his accomplices.

From this ban, the first newspaper in Biale was born, named "Biale Echo". In the newspaper, the ban was put to shame. The scene of the ban in the synagogue was presented in the form of a play that made the audience roll with laughter, yet this was necessary.

The Zionist organization in the town was preparing for the community elections and in order to establish an election fund, it organized various events. Amongst these, it was decided to bring Cantor Gershon Sirotta and his daughter to perform in a concert. When everything had already been organized and the posters announcing Sirotta's appearance were already visible in the town, the Zionist organization received a telegram from Cantor Sirotta, saying that unfortunately he was unable to come, because there was an intervention in the name of the Biale Rabbi that he should abandon the idea of visiting Biale. The Biale Zionists did not keep quiet, and after much trouble, they persuaded Sirotta to come to Biale.

A Purim ball was organised at a public venue during Purim in 1924. A special script was written for the ball, a satire about the ban, that began with the words: "I was sent to you by the Rabbi" (a parody based on Bialik "The last word"). The program for the ball was advertised publicly on posters and marked the reading of this satire. This enraged the followers of the Rabbi. They tried with every possible means to effect the removal of the satire from the program, but the Zionists did not yield to their demands and the satire was recited at the ball.

With this bold battle, the Zionist organization in Biale caused havoc in their attempts to modernize the Middle Ages.

After the ban, the Zionist opponents in the town put pressure on Kalman Sheinberg to remove the "Bet–Am" from his house. Of course, Kalman Sheinberg took all steps to get rid of the Zionist organization that was, unfortunately for him, successful. The Zionist organization had to leave the superb, large premises and move to the house of Mendl Goldfarb on Mezritsh street. In their new premises, there was also the contemporary, now wealthy, "Tarbut" library, and various lectures were arranged there.

[Page 191]

The completion of the dissertation by M. Bruchl

With the departure of Moshe Rubinshtein from Biale, first to Warsaw and later to the Land of Israel, the activities of the general Zionists in Biale were weakened. Also the splitting of the Zionist organization worldwide, understandably, echoed in Biale. The further downfall of the organization of the general Zionists in Biale was therefore a natural phenomenon.

Until the beginning of the 1920s, Biale possessed one Zionist organization, where all those disposed to Zionism in the town were grouped together. The "Mizrachi", however, existed as a separate party, and aside from cultural activities, co–operated with the Zionist organization in all matters. The Hashomer Ha'tzair was then purely a scout group, under the authority of the Zionist organization, during all necessary party activities. In this period, various Zionist groups began to rise in Biale — according to the pattern set by other towns in Poland, that were directly in line with the central organization in Warsaw. Not only did they not co–operate with the earlier Zionist organization in the town, but often went against her. Of course, the newly formed groups drew a number of members from the former Zionist organization to them and almost severed the flow of youthful power in its ranks.

In this period Hashomer Hatzair changed from a scout group and became an independent youth organization with its own political orientation. The Revisionist party came into existence and waged a bitter battle with the local Zionist organization. The "Hechalutz" movement came into existence and was very active, drawing the working youth into their ranks. "Hechalutz" sent its members on Hachsharah (agricultural training farms that prepared prospective emigrants to Palestine) and tried to encourage them to emigrate to the Land of Israel. In the 1930s, the right wing "Po'alei Tzion" established a branch. In Biale there was also an active division of "The league for a working Land of Israel".

Of course, these differentiations within the Zionist camp strongly affected the former unity of the Zionist organization in the town, that had now become a division of the general Zionist organization in Warsaw, and in which there again existed the factions "A" and "B". The members of the older generation remained in this organization, without the youth. The difficult social situation had its effect, throwing the members into complete apathy.

A group of general Zionists on the occasion of the Aliyah of Asher Hoffer to the Land of Israel

Standing from right: Yisroel Goldshtein, Shmuel Zusman, Zelig Yakobovsky, Shmuel Orlansky, Yostina Zeidman, Ya'akov Kornblum, Dovid Kantor, Dovid Nortman, Boruch Tselnikker
Sitting: Moshe Morgenshtern, Ya'akov Shteinman, Asher Hoffer, Binyomin Klieger, Ya'kov Aharon Rozenboim, Yitzchak Agress
Third row: Shmuel Viezenfeld, Hershl Orlansky and Chaim Miyodek

At the head of the Zionist organization in Biale after the departure of Moshe Rubinshtein, were: Yisroel Goldshtein, M.Mishkin, Binyomin Klieger, Asher Hoffer, Ya'akov Aharon Rozenboim etc.

For many years Chaim Miyodek was the secretary, who excelled in his intensive work. In the last years the Zionist organization was located in Tshasnem street, in the house of the butcher Moshe Goldshtein.

[Page 192]

It needs to be mentioned that despite the splintering of the Zionist organization into different groups – a situation that prevailed in Biale in the last few years before the war – all the Zionist groups were united in their activity for the "Keren Kayemet L'yisrael" (The Jewish National Fund").

From "Podlassier Life" number 29/9 of 26.7.1933, it can be seen that during the elections to the 18th Zionist Congress, that took place in the town on 23rd July 1933, 968 votes were cast out of 1027 members with voting rights.

List number 1. ("Al Hamishmar") — 59 votes; List number 2. ("Et Livnot") — 5 votes; List number 3. ("Mizrachi") – 132 votes; List number 4. 0 votes; List number 5. Bloc for a Working Israel" – 514 votes; List number 6. Revisionists – 251 votes; List number 7. — 7 votes.

M. Y. Feigenboim

[Page 192]

Hashomer Hatza'ir

Translated by Ofra Anson

Edited by Yocheved Klausner

Hashomer Hatza'ir was one of the first youth movements in Biala. We say one of the first, because *Pirchei Zion* [Flowers of Zion][1] was really the first. Yet, when *Hashomer Hatza'ir* was later established, almost all members of *Pirchei Zion* joined *Hashomer Hatza'ir*.

Before we turn to write about *Hashomer Hatza'ir*, something should be said about its forerunner, *Pirchei Zion*.

In 1918, there were already quite a few young people who had graduated from the *Yavneh* School. They were good friends, and felt they needed a place to meet and pursue their cultural life. The group used to meet in the evenings and holidays in the *Yavneh* School, have lectures on literature and host debates. The name *Pirchei Zion* was taken from a Warsaw newspaper, and later the group joined *Pirchei Zion* in Warsaw.

The founders of this group were: Eliezer Eideltuch,[2] Zelig Rosenfeld, Mirtshe Blankleider, Hantshe Zineman, Solomon Zarok, Arie Lamas, and Sara Kramarzs. The members elected a committee, chaired by Zelig Rosenfeld, and Eliezer Eideltuch as secretary. *Pirchei Zion* had 60–70 members, who paid monthly membership fees.

The leaders of Pirchei Zion

From right, sitting: Sara Kramatzs, Eliezer Eideltuch, Arie Lamas;
Standing: Mirtche Blankleider, Zelig Rosenfeld, Shlomo Zarok and Hentche Zinamon

As the name of the group indicates, it was a nationalist organization, its political orientation having been shaped while they studied in the *Yavneh* School. This youth movement drew the attention of the leaders of the local Zionist organization, Moshe Rubinstein and Haim Barlas, who supported *Pirchei Zion* and helped with the work involved in running the group.

The group received from the headquarters in Warsaw a variety of materials, which guided its activity. As time passed, they built a library which included both Hebrew and Yiddish books.

As mentioned above, upon the entrance of *Hashomer Hatza'ir* to Biala, *Pirchei Zion* ceased to exist, almost all of its members joining the new youth movement. The library also became the property of *Hashomer Hatza'ir*.

In 1919 a young man from Warsaw, Solomon Yankaviak, came to Biala with the Polish army. He was a member of *Hashomer Hatza'ir* and it was his initiative to bring the organization to Biala. Among the founders were: Abush Liberman, Zelig Rosenfeld, Eliezer Eideltuch, Tova Rubinstein,[3] Hanna Zineman, Arie Lamas, and Sara Kramarzs.

Hashomer Hatza'ir was similar to the scouts' youth movement, encouraging both national orientation and the love of the Land of Israel. At first it recruited about 70 youngsters; later on the number increased to 100. Most members were former students, men and women, of the *Yavneh* School. All paid monthly membership fees.

[Page 193]

The youngsters of *Hashomer Hatza'ir* were divided into groups; each group had its own leader. The groups met several times a week for small–talk and physical exercises. On Saturdays all members would meet, to hear a talk given by the chair–person Abush Liberman, to learn Hebrew songs, and to have a good time. Often, the chair of the Zionist movement, Moshe Rubinstein,[4] came to these Saturday meetings to talk about Zionist matters and biblical themes.

To avoid interference with its activity, *Hashomer Hatza'ir* became a section within the *Tarbut* [culture] society, which was legally registered with the Polish authorities.

At first, the relationship between *Hashomer Hatza'ir* and the Scouts' organization in the city was quite good. The Scouts even used to invite *Hashomer Hatza'ir* to take part in public drilling exercises at Polish formal events. Later, however, the behavior of the Polish Scouts group changed: they could not accept the fact that Jewish youngsters carried the International Scouts' standard. *Hashomer* suffered a lot of bullying from the Polish Scouts, who were assisted in this by the whole kingdom. *Hashomer Hatza'ir* recruited many of the high–school students, but the school objected to their participation. They thus had to hide their activity from the public, not always successfully, as the meeting place was situated in a Christian neighborhood. After the fall of Joseph Trumpeldor in the battle of Tel–Hai, the *Hashomer Hatza'ir* of Biala took on his name.

One of the main concerns of *Hashomer Hatza'ir* was cultural activity, which gave its members the opportunity to learn and develop. Evening courses were initiated, where members could broaden their education in subjects such as Hebrew, Polish, mathematics, science, geography, etc. There were classes for the history and geography of Eretz Israel, as well as Hebrew literature. Later, when the courses stopped, high–school students used to teach their peers who were eager to study. The library developed, thanks to the intensive work of the librarian, Haim Rosmarin. Often, a newsletter was hung on its wall, and every two months a newspaper, named *Mehayeinu* [from our life] was published. It included a variety of articles and poetry in Yiddish, Hebrew, and Polish. The following members were involved in the newspaper work: Joshua Hafer, Rose Yakobovsky, and Leibel Finkelstein. They were responsible for both its content and graphical lay–out.

The "Reuven Group of Hashomer Haza'ir

Standing from right: Selig Rosenfeld, Arie Lamas, Butche Finkelstein, Eliezer Eideltuch, Josef Nochevitz;
second row: Yankavyak (Warsaw), Gershon Rosmarin, Moshe Rubinstein (both from the leading committee),
Appelboim (Warsaw), Abush Liberman (the leader of the group);
third row: Sara Kramarzs, Toibale Rubinstein, Hantshe Zinaman, Pearl Weisenfeld, and Gitl Weissglass.

[Page 194]

Lag–Baomer excursion of Hashomer Hatza'ir
(before departure from the public school courtyard)

The activities of *Hashomer Hatza'ir* were held in different localities. In the beginning, the elementary school on Gravanover Street was used; after this building burned down the new location of the school was used, in the rabbi's place on Mezritch Street. During the summer members used to gather in the rabbi's back yard, in the open air. During the winter *Hashomer Hatza'ir* went to *Beit Ha'am* [the peoples' house] for physical exercises, using Maccabi's sport facilities.

Hashomer Hatza'ir was under the influence of the Zionist party in the city, which, in turn, used to rely upon its members for different party–related tasks. They were sent to collect money for *Keren Kayemet* [Jewish National Fund], hang wall posters, distribute the Shekel stamps, etc.

Often, *Hashomer Hatza'ir* performed theater shows in *Beit Ha'am*, with great success. Every *Lag Ba'Omer* [35 days after Passover] *Hashomer Hatza'ir* used to organize field–trips to the meadows around the city and these practically became an annual nationalist demonstration. Members would gather in the early morning in the courtyard of the rabbi's house, all dressed in *Hashomer Hatza'ir* khaki uniform, and be organized in military–like groups. After hearing a short talk from the president of the Zionist movement, and headed by the *Maccabi* orchestra, they marched through the city to the fields. At night, all the Jewish community waited for them on the street to greet them as they returned to the city. The impression of this event was felt for weeks after it took place.

With the Bolshevik invasion in 1920 the activity of *Hashomer Hatza'ir* stopped. The archive of the organization was hidden in Reuven Feldman's attic. The Red Army stayed in town for a few weeks, and after it left normal activity began again.

We should note that the religious community did not approve of *Hashomer Hatza'ir*. Yet they did not have the power or the means to stop their children from going to a youth organization. They had an opportunity to pursue their objection to *Hashomer Hatza'ir* during the 1920s. One of the Radzin Hasidim whose daughter went to *Hashomer Hatza'ir* sent the rabbi a question written in the Torah script, and showed him a song by David Shimonovitz, starting with "*Al Tishma*" [do not listen, or do not hear]. He presented this as proof that *Hashomer Hatza'ir* encouraged Jewish children to convert, heaven forbid. It came after several incidents of disputes, and the rabbi of Biala did not think long before excommunicating *Hashomer Hatza'ir* and the whole Zionist movement. This was an excommunication with the full ceremony, including calling the people to the synagogue, lighting candles, and having his helper blow the Shofar.

The excommunication did not do a lot of harm. True, in the beginning the number of members dropped, but this was largely due to migration from the city of people looking for a purpose in life and who were no longer satisfied with *Hashomer Hatza'ir* activities.

[Page 195]

In the early 1920s the romantic–scouts period of *Hashomer Hatza'ir* was over, as most of its members graduated from school.

The economic crisis among Jews had deepened, and the youth had to turn to vocational training. Those still in school had to decide whether to continue their studies beyond elementary school or to look for an occupation. Some could not make a decision; quite a few went to do physical work. The situation brought about organizational change in *Hashomer Hatza'ir*, its second period. The majority of its members were now working people, and even those still in school were psychologically ready to learn a trade. Willingly or unwillingly, contrary to the wishes of the older members, there was a barrier between them and the new ones. The working youth were the main force behind the separation. Some of them were organized in trade unions, and were influenced by its ideology. At the same time there was a crisis among the school youth, which had an opposite effect.

The local leadership tried different ways to bring the two parts to work in harmony. It organized joint courses: Nathan Zigelnik and Lea Orlanski made a great effort for this purpose, they worked hard to make it work, but life took its course. Their activity did not yield the expected results. Work–related issues became the main topic in the discussions in *Hashomer Hatza'ir* and the questions raised were of a practical, realistic, nature. Yet, this development was not unique to Biala; it happened in all cities and towns.

During this time *Hashomer Hatza'ir* started to establish Kibbutzim in Israel. The leaders in the headquarters of *Hashomer Hatza'ir* coined the notion of *hagshama atzmit* [self–realization, self fulfilment]. The poem of Davis Shim'onovitz "*Al tishma beni musar av*" [son, do not follow in your father's footsteps] became a slogan calling every young person to stop studying, to leave their parents' home, go on *Hachshara* [training], and get ready to immigrate for the hard labor awaiting in Eretz Israel. This call, however, was too harsh for the students in Biala, and only a few of them took it on.

A group of Hashomer Haza'ir

The new course taken: The central leadership strengthened the working youth of *Hashomer Hatza'ir* in Biala. It helped them to take over the local leadership, and to dismiss those who were not interested in *hagshama atzmit* and had no wish to make Aliya.

[Page 196]

The local leadership of the young workers started its work in a difficult time. The active members went on *Hachshara*, and with a limited working force, collaboration between right (the Revisionists, General Zionists [liberals], and *HaMizrachi* [religious]) and left (the Bund and Communists) had to be established in order to find a new way to crystalize a socialist orientation. The central leadership sent help, first Moshe Platnikov, then Yitzhak Lehrer, and after his Aliya to Eretz Israel – Moshe Smolyar. They wanted to preserve the two main achievements of *Hashomer Hatza'ir*, the support for *Keren Kayemet* and the *Tarbut* library.

This is when the third period of *Hashomer Hatza'ir*'s existence started, a period of search for a political way. Members who could not or did not wish to identify with the political orientation left *Hashomer Hatza'ir*. Some members joined the Left *Poalei Zion*, others joined the communists, other left political activity altogether. Some started a new youth organization – *Magshimim* [the fulfillers].

Except for *Hashomer Hatza'ir*, no other youth movement devoted to working in Eretz Israel operated in Biala. Thus, only *Hashomer Hatza'ir* could take on the initiative of establishing *Hechalutz* [the pioneer]. The local leadership decided to start a *Hechalutz* group, an organization which would attract young persons who sympathized with the Zionist cause but were too old to join *Hashomer Hatza'ir* and found no interest in other organizations.

Hechalutz developed and sent many members on "hachshara", arranged work for other members, made Aliya and live in Israel to this day.

Hashomer Hatza'ir also organized a workers' league for Eretz Israel, which attracted those who were sympathetic to the idea. All members of *Hechalutz* automatically belonged to that league. This is how the workers' wing of the Zionist movement came to be in our city.

Hashomer Hatza'ir was also involved in the establishment of the *Poalei Zion* party, though it had a right wing orientation, and in the *Ha'oved* branch of this party.

A group of Hashomer Hatza'ir

Almost all political organizations and activities went through *Hashomer Hatza'ir*, who constantly looked for collaboration in order to strengthen the socialist–Zionist influence in the city.

As active members went on *hagshama* [made Aliya], those who stayed took their place and fulfilled the necessary tasks.

[Page 197]

Hechalutz group and several Hashomer Hatza'ir members

Standing from right: Hanna Grinberg, Sara Gittelman, Rivka Feigenboim, Itke Plat, Haim Liverant, Leibel Feigenboim, Bloome Rosenbloom, Fania Tzelinker, Asher Grinblatt, Rachel Listgarten, Mulie Urmacher; sitting: Jacob Gelburd, Feige Tzukerman, Jacob Gliksberg, Bloome Edelstein, Itzhak Lehrer, Lea Shneiman; sitting in front: Aron Miadek, Jeshayahu Stallavi, Shalom Knijshnik, Hershel Eidelman.

The third period lasted until the Second World War, when many members fled to Russia.

A group of members of the "League for Labor Eretz Israel"

Standing from right: Solomon Hochberg, Yurberg, Rivka Grodner, two whose names are unknown, Shalom Knijshnik, Abraham Nochevitz, Lea Nochevitz, Aranski (a Hebrew teacher);
sitting: Josef Grinstein, Ytzhak (Aizik) Shien, a Shaliach [messenger, delegate], Eliezer Eideltuch, Hershel Nochevitz, Maskal

Of those who stayed through the Hitler hell, almost nobody survived. Yet even in the most difficult days under the German regime, the activity of *Hashomer Hatza'ir* continued, both by members from Biala and those who were deported by the Germans from other places.

The brave death of Godya Steinman was strong evidence of the loyalty to *Hashomer Hatza'ir* values. Godya Steinman was an illegal representative of the central leadership. She worked with the underground movement, jointly with other members. Godya was cruelly interrogated in the Gestapo jail of Biala, in an effort to make her provide details regarding the activity and the people participating in that activity. Yet she withstood all the tortures and did not divulge any information.

This Information was provided by E. Eideltuch,[5] Y. Ofer, and A. Greenblat

Translator's Footnotes:

1. a. Translations of some of the Hebrew terms are given in square brackets in the text.
   b. Some of my family members are mentioned in the article; see reference numbers in the text and below.
2. Eliezer Eideltuch was my father.
3. My cousin
4. My uncle
5. My father

[Page 198]

The Revisionist Organization

by Jacob Bernstein: Tel Aviv

Translated by Ofra Anson

Edited by Yocheved Klausner

It is difficult to write about the period that the revisionist organization operated in Biala after such a long time. Without any documents or written sources, I will do the best I can and remember.

At the end of 1926, a group of young people from the General Zionists' Party were caught up by the ideas and slogans propagandized by the Zionist Activists headed by Ze'ev Jabotinsky. We youngsters demanded an immediate change in the tactics of the Zionist organization. This demand brought about constant conflict with the local Zionist committee, of course. As a result, five of us were charged and appeared before the Party Court. The trial lasted a few weeks, and was a stormy event. As far as I remember the chair of the court was Binyamin Kliger, and Jacob Aron Rosenboim and Asher Hoffer were members of the court; Israel Goldstein was the prosecutor, and we were our own defenders. Our verdict was to avoid any Zionist activity in Biala for six months. The accused were Leibel Bialer, Moshe Leibson, Haim Miodek, and Jacob Bernstein. We appealed to the party court of the central Zionist committee in Warsaw, which cancelled the verdict and granted us full rehabilitation.

Despite the rehabilitation, our dissatisfaction kept increasing, until we started the first revisionist group in Biala in the beginning of 1927.

A Revisionist group

From the right by the flag: Henia Tzeplinski, Rachel Rosenbloom; standing: Tepermana, Sara Shwartzberg, Franie Argess, Rivka Teitelboim, Slove Hershberg, Haia Weissmann, name unknown, Ita Gefen, Rivka Belmann, Leibel Bialer, Rachel Weissmann, Josef Salmanovitch, Tchipe Jak, Simha Grinberg; sitting: Eliyahu Lerner, Jacov Goldfarb, Golde Davidson, Kreidstein, Jacob Cohen, Israel Loevenberg, Hana Shneimann, Fishel Loevenberg, Srebernik; kneeling: Maya Kramarsash, Haia Urmacher, Tzirl Sheinboim; in front: Sara Rubinstein, Feige Weinstein

The members of the first committee of the revisionist organization were: Jacob Cohen, Isaak Goldberg, Abraham Rotenberg, Leib Bialer, Moshe Leibson, and myself.

Two to three years later, Revisionism was already deeply rooted in Biala. People from all social standing joined the organization. *Beitar* [revisionist youth movement] and *Hatzohar Alliance* [revisionist Zionist organization] were the most popular. Each revisionist event and each activity became a big happening in Biala and attracted a lot of attention and recognition. On Passover 1932 a Bazaar for the Jewish National Fund was organized in the movie theater *Mirazsh*. All Zionist youth movements took part in this activity, competing with one another. Beitar had a corner in the bazaar and excelled in the way it was laid out.

[Page 199]

The cultural and sporting activities of *Beitar* consisted of courses in Hebrew, Yiddish literature, singing and sport. Most popular were lectures and talks delivered by persons from the central committee. These always attracted many people. It is worth noting that among the visitors were Aba Achimeir, Dr. Wolfgang von Wiesel, Aron Propes, and Menachem Begin. Every year *Beitar* organized summer camps for the young members and sent the older ones to trade study and military training.

The *Beitar* convention which took place in Biala in 1934 made a strong impression. We celebrated the seventh anniversary of *Hatzohar* and five years of *Beitar*, with the participation of Menachem Begin. During the assembly Biala's Beitar received a standard.

Among the big events organized by the revisionist party in the city was a petition to evacuate the Jewish population from Poland. Despite the objection of the left–wing party, the majority of Biala Jews signed the petition.

I would like to mention some members of the revisionist party who were active during this period.

Baruch (Boleck) Hoffer was an example of a devoted member. He was an officer in the Polish army and used his expertise to give *Beitar* members military training. He was the founder of the revisionist organization The Soldiers' Alliance, and led it for several years.

Leib Bialer was the secretary of the party for five–six years. He initiated some of the most important activities in the city.

Samuel Glucksberg and Sender Glucksberg, who later became the commanders of *Beitar*, promoted the spread of nationalist ideas among Biala youth with enthusiasm and devotion.

The following were active in *Beitar* and in *Hatzohar* during different periods: Joel Shapiro, Samuel Swartz, Ita Gefen, Eli Goldstein, Haim Silberberg, Sara Swartzberg, Heinech Bialer, Shalom Feigenboim, and Blooma Kalichstein. All were killed during the German occupation.

The *Mizrachi*

by Moshe Bravermann, Avraham Brandweinman, and Yehuda Beitl

Translated by Ofra Anson

Edited by Yocheved Klausner

The *Mizrachi* organization in Biala started in 1916. No need was felt for it before that. The religious persons who sympathized with the Zionist idea were integrated into the general Zionist movement in the city. The first dispute between the orthodox and the free Zionists occurred in *Beit Ha'am* [the house of the people] which was located in Meir Korman's home, with the first signs of desecration of the Sabbath. Joshua Fisher, Joshua Baruch Rabinowitz, Moshe Bravermann and some others, seeing that their protests did not help, left the Zionist organization of the city and established the *Mizrachi*.

As the Zionist organization lost the apartment of Meir Korman, it was rented by Asher Blumenkrantz, who gave most of its space to the *Mizrachi*. A year later, when this place grew too small for the party, it moved to a three–room apartment in Motl Mintz's house, on Yanever Street.

Members of the committee were: Moshe Bravermann – chair, Joshua Fisher, Moshe Frishtick, Isaak Hochberg, Berl Zshelazo, Moshe Bankhalter and others.

A permanent contact between the local party and the *Mizrachi* center in Warsaw was established, who sent directions regarding the daily running and the activities to be held. Most of the work concerned recruiting the youngsters into the party's lines and attracting the adult population, who were not interested in Zionism, to the Zionist idea. The general Zionist activity, such as the National Fund, Keren Hayesod, elections to the Sejm and the municipality were performed together with the Zionist organization.

Members often gathered in the party's office, where they held cultural activities such as Hebrew evening classes taught by the teacher Jacob Steinman, talking and discussing Zionist issues and *Eretz Israel* matters. For the people in the city, hearing Hebrew singing from people that were truly devoted orthodox Jews was a novel experience.

The visit of the Member of the Sejm Heshl Farbstein, the chairman of the *Mizrachi* federation in Poland, aroused a lot of excitement. It was in 1922, the eve of the elections to the first *Sejm*. Two other representatives came to the *Mizrachi* conference in Biala, Isaak

Grinboim and Apolinari Hartglass. The visits of Zionist leaders were festive days for Biala's Jewish population. Farbstein's appearance in the Beit–Midrash left a strong impression on the religious audience and increased the flow of new members.

[Page 200]

*A group of members of the Mizrachi on the occasion of the Aliya
of Yehoshua Fisher and Moshe Braverman in 1924*

*Standing from the right: name unknown, Gedaliahu Kramarejsh, Moshe Levi, Berish Liebman, Rotenberg, Jacob Nirenberg
sitting: Itzhak Hochberg, Asher Hoffer, Moshe Braverman, Joshua Fisher, Moshe Frishtik, Abraham Brandweinmann;
in front: Motl Hoffer, Moshe Bankhalter, Jacob Kramarjsh, David Orbach, Samuel Koltan, Menachem Goldsac, Motl Hochberg*

In the context of Heshl Farbstein's visit in Biala, a characteristic episode comes to my mind. The representatives stayed at Isaak Pizshitz's place. It was during the nine days before 9th of Av, and Farbstein avoided meat dishes. Grinboim and Hartglass followed him. Therefore they called Yakir Cohen–Tzedek's son, who was just about to finish a *Masechet* [Tractate], and they joined him in his study. When they were done they had the customary *Seudat Mitzvah* [ceremonial meal]. In *Seudat Mitzvah* they could eat meat.

After Joshua Fisher and Moshe Bravermann left for Israel, the activity of the organization declined. After a while the activity resumed, led by Israel Finkelstein, Moshe Levi, Jacob David Rubinstein, Leibel Migdal, Berl Zshelazo, Avraham Brandweinmann and others. New members were recruited and a general assembly was called by the committee of the party. The party was located in Berl Zshelazo's apartment, on Yanever Street. The first activity to be organized was Hebrew evening classes. From time to time Avraham

Zhito from Lakov, a well–known activist in the *Mizrachi* Party, came to Biala. He used to lecture with a lot of enthusiasm about *Mizrachi*'s goals and affairs.

In 1925 the committee brought from Warsaw Samuel Landau z"l, one of the *Mizrachi* leaders. *Agudat Yisrael* [an orthodox party] tried to interrupt his speech in *Bet Hamidrash*, but failed. Samuel Landau's manners strongly impressed the people who came to hear him. In a meeting between Samuel Landau and the local committee it was decided to establish a farm where the local *Mizrachi* members could train for the kind of work awaiting them in *Eretz Yisrael*. Samuel Landau with some local members went to Isaak Pizshitz, who owned a piece of land in Valla, a neighborhood outside Biala, next to his sawmill. Isaak Pizshitz agreed and, with the financial support of the *Mizrachi* center in Warsaw, a farm was founded.

Some 50 members stayed permanently on the farm, and learned agriculture in order to become agronomists. Cultural activity was also an important part of the farm's life. On Saturdays, people from the city used to go out to the farm, to take a look at the fields cultivated by young religious men and women. After a year of training on the farm many youngsters made Aliya to *Eretz Yisrael*. The farm contributed to the recognition of the *Mizrachi* in the city.

[Page 201]

When the airplane factory was built in the neighborhood, the farm was disassembled, because the land was sold to a non–Jew.

The visit of the preacher Rabbi Isaak Dines, who came to Biala for the National Fund, was used by the *Mizrachi* for its activity. His appearance in *Bet Hamidrash* left a strong impression on the large audience. Parties were held in the apartments of Israel Finkelstein and Moshe Isaak Biderman, and Rabbi Dines sang songs of Zion beautifully.

In 1927, there were about 70 members in the party. A Talmud class was operating, led by the *Melamed* Benjamin Hersh Eidelman, who also learned with the *Beit Hamidrash* attenders. Yet after a short while he stopped coming. We believed that the *Agudat Yisrael* rabbi convinced him to leave the *Mizrachi*. Some members went to the rabbi and argued that they wanted to study the Torah, but it did not help. His argument was that if we want to learn *Torah* we should come to *Beit Hamidrash*. Yet the *Mizrachi* members would not compromise and Berl Zshelazo taught the class.

Agudat Yisrael constantly fought against the activity of the *Mizrachi* in Biala, and the rabbi supported that struggle. Despite that, the number of *Mizrachi* members increased to 80 in 1927/8. That year the committee members were: Israel Finkelstein, Berl Zshelazo, Avraham Brandweinmann, Leibel Migdal and Jacob Weissmann.

In 1928 the lawyer Simha Bunimb**Error! Bookmark not defined.** Feldman, a *Mizrachi* activist and former Member of Parliament, settled in Biala. Dr. Feldman enjoyed much sympathy from the local Jewish population, thanks to his simple ways. His presence in the city strengthened the Zionist movement; some people became devoted advocates for its promotion. Thanks to the energetic behavior of Dr. Feldman, many people became involved in the successful communal activity on behalf of the settlements in *Eretz Yisrael* after the bloody clashes of 1929.

Dr. Feldman was especially respected by the people for his religious devotion. Biala had never seen a lawyer who prayed with the public in *Beit Hamidrash* day in and day out, walking with the *Tallit* under his arm in the streets. He would not appear in court on Saturdays. Even the *Hasidim* used to say that he is "a righteous man".

Those days Yehuda Beitel, a member of the central committee of the *Mizrachi* youth in Poland, settled in Biala. Thanks to him *Mizrachi* youth organizations, *Hashomer Hadati* for religious boys and *Bruria* for religious girls, were established in the city. The evening Hebrew classes resumed.

In 1931 the *Mizrachi* youth and the *Mizrachi* pioneers' organization held a regional conference in Biala. The president of these organizations in Poland, Rabbi Elimelech Neufeld, came from Warsaw. That year three other members of the central committee in Warsaw paid a visit to Biala's branch: Levi Youngster, Moshe Krone, and Josef Zimberknop. These visits revived the spirit of the *Mizrachi* members in Biala.

In 1932 a delegate from the religious workers of Eretz Yisrael visited Biala: Nathan Gardy from kibbutz Rodges. He took part in fund raising for the religious workers in Israel, *Keren Tora ve'Avoda* [the Fund for Torah and work]. A special talk was organized for the religious women in the city. After his speech the leader of the women in the *Aguda* synagogue, *Beit–Yaakov*, came to the presidential table and committed the synagogue to raise a monthly contribution for the fund. This commitment was an important step, which gave moral and material support to the joint activity in the city.

The *Mizrachi* in Biala strongly encouraged its members to make Aliya, taking every opportunity to do so. Thus, members went to Israel as rabbis.

Those days the members of the committee were: Avraham Brandweinmann, Yehuda Beitl, Leibel Migdal, Gedalyahu Cohen, Jacob Weissmann, Jacob Gefen, Shalom Kreiselman, Rachel Lustigman and others.

Mizrachi operated in the city until 1938, when Poland was conquered by the German Hordes, and the terrible sentence on the Jewish people in Poland was signed.

[Page 202]

Poalei Zion Left

by Avraham Lavi (Lemberger) Haifa

Translated by Ofra Anson

Edited by Yocheved Klausner

August 1917. In the middle of the First World War, a group of young people gathered on a Saturday afternoon in a small attic on Miedzyrzec Street and laid the cornerstone for *Poalei Zion* Left in the city. Their names – the teacher Yona Steinman, the brothers Avraham and Moshe Solski, Zisl Greenberg, Israel Yitzhak Sapir, Josef Singer, Menachem Finkelstein and others. The meeting was illegal, and the activity was delayed until the German army evacuated Biala in the winter of 1918.

After the war *Poalei Zion* in Biala started different activities, gaining support from different parts of the population. In some respects, this was due to the influence of Yona Steinman, popular in all circles, who led the new party and displayed the theoretical background for its program. The party worked from a small place in the house of Shmerele Hochman (Shmerele the baker) on Grabanover Street.

For legal reasons, the work was under the umbrella of the library, which was registered in the Polish government as a branch of "The association for evening education for workers in Warsaw".

Poalei Zion was started not only because of traditional Jewish reasons, but also for reasons of socialist ideology. Many members already felt the yoke of work on their backs. True, some members came from petit bourgeois homes, but they were on their way to becoming workers. They could not join the Bund because they were devoted to Zionism; and they did not find their place in the Zionist organization in the city because of its bourgeois reputation, so they looked for the golden middle way which would meet both needs.

The proportion of the elderly among the members was small in comparison to the other parties which operated in the city. But the number of young members organized in the "Youth" movement constantly grew and most of the party's work was devoted to them. The small location of the party was always busy and bubbling with life.

The small, modest party soon gained support among a large portion of the Jewish people, and two of its members, Yona Steinman and Josef Singer, were elected to the Municipal Council.

The leadership of the party consisted of distinguished people, who were among the founders of the party: Yona Steinman, Zissel Grinberg, Avraham Solski, Josef Singer, and Menachem Finkelstein. Later – Avraham Solski, Sheine Weinstein, Sara Weissman, Avraham Lemberger, Nachum Heibloom, Moshe Friedman, and Avraham Semiatitzki.

The party had a big library, which was enriched from time to time with new, high quality books. After a year, when the party felt the signs of hardship, the library remained the only activity and became the center where members could get together.

Similar to other parties in the city, *Poalei Zion* experienced a dramatic crisis, its income declined, including the contribution of the father–organization for local activity and new books.

During its existence, the party experienced many difficulties and crises. Nonetheless, it succeeded in avoiding inner conflicts. When the dispute between "right" and "left" took place in the party in Poland, in Biala all members joined the "left", thus avoiding struggle and splitting. Since that time the party was called *Poalei Zion Left*.

When it was operating, the party used to invite party leaders from other places to clarify the essence of *Poalei Zion* and its calling. Among others, Isaac Shipper, the well–known and well respected historian came before the election to the *Sejm* (before the split between "right" and "left"). His visit remained etched in the audience's memory for a long time. After the split, Jacob Zerubbabel, Moshe Erem, and Shimon Ibshitzer (member of the Brisk City Council) came for a visit.

From the small location on Grabanover Street the party moved to Miedzyrzec Street, with the library. During the move, however, Avraham Solski, who faithfully worked for the library, felt sick, and it was moved to his house so that he could continue to take care of this cultural treasure in his free time, as he always did with endless devotion.

[Page 203]

A flower sale by the Left wing of Poalei Zion

Standing from the left: Levinstein, Abraham Semyatitzki, Lea Feigenboim, Haim Kave, Singer, Adlerstein, Moshe Feigenboim;
second row sitting from the right: name unknown, Hershel Felsenstein, Josef Singer, Abraham Solski, Menachem Finkelstein, Fradel Feingenboim, Mindel Woletzki;
third row, sitting from right: Sara Warshawski, Dostche Appleboim, Kamien, Cohen, Eliyahu Knizhnik, Semiatitzki,

B. Srebernik, B. Levin;
in front: Haim Rubinstein, Hana Rosmarin, Sara Bednarosh, Haim Eidelmann

With time, many of the members passed away, but three founders who out–lived their friends could still be seen taking a walk on the *Brieten Trotuar* [the wide sidewalk]: Avraham Solski, Josef Singer, and Menachem Finkelstein. With the death of Avraham Solski, not only the two remaining friends but the whole party felt orphaned.

In 1930–1933 the party started to renew its lines. New members filled the abandoned locality. Yet there was something missing: the idealism and romanticism of the first years; the cultural events; even the party's propaganda was weak. Only one thing was common to all: the will to get to the top of the list to go to Eretz Israel and leave the suffocating atmosphere of the diaspora as quickly as possible.

In a short while many of the alia–candidates of Poalei Zion in Biala, including the writer of this chapter, met in the streets of Jerusalem, Tel–Aviv, and Haifa. They fulfilled the role of the party and became true *Poalim* [workers] in Zion.

During the 1930s, when *Poalei Zion* ceased to exist in Biala, the archive was sent to the center of the party in Warsaw.

* * *

In the 1930s the party became *Poalei Zion Right*. Its chairman was Aizik Shein (until he made Aliya). Together with *Hashomer Hatza'ir* and *Hechalutz* they became affiliated with the "League for the Workers in *Eretz Yisrael*" which was very active at the time.

(M. I. P…m)

[Page 204]

The National Funds
(Keren Kayemet le'Israel and Keren Hayesod)

Translated by Ofra Anson (Ideltuch)

Edited by Yocheved Klausner

Working for the national funds was always an important part of the activity of all Zionist parties. The activities of the Zionist parties in the town were often accompanied by drama, competition and struggles; yet all these stopped when it came to collecting money for the Jewish National Fund and Keren Hayesod (the United Israel Appeal). For this, special committees were established, made up of members of the different Zionist groups.

Money for the Jewish National Fund was raised on set days during the year: Tamuz 20th (the anniversary of Herzl's death), 15th of Shevat (by selling bags of fruit from Eretz Israel), Hanukah, Purim, and Lag Ba'omer. On top of these special days, Jewish National Fund boxes were distributed to households and were emptied from time to time; money was collected from vows, Yizkor, and collecting plates in synagogues for Kol Nidrei; greeting cards and calendars were sold too. Jewish National Fund tokens were also sold at every family celebration.

At the beginning, Jewish National Fund work was organized by a committee from "Beit Ha'am headed by an authorized signatory. Later, the committee comprised representatives of all Zionist organizations, who chose the authorized signatory. The authorized signatories were (at different times): Moshe Morgenstern, Yitzhak Hochberg, Abraham Brandweinman, Jacob Aron Rosenboim, and Aron Ribak.

A few details are worth noting. In 1920, during the Polish–Bolshevik war, Binyamin Kliger had to leave Biala and flee east. He had some money belonging to the Jewish National Fund, which he had no chance to give to the committee. During all the time he was away this money was hidden, sewn into his clothes. When he returned to Biala he returned the full sum.

In 1922, when Yitzhak Hochberg served as the authorized signatory, a movie showing life in Eretz Israel was brought to Biala. The film played during a full week in H. Y. Kastenboim's movie theater and was seen by all the Jewish population. For some of them it felt like a holiday, others carried the impression of the pictures from Eretz Israel for a long time. The income generated was quite high.

Another source of income was jewelry donated to the Jewish National Fund. A list of such donations was published in the "Jewish Folk", Warsaw, number 94, 5.12.1918:

"From Biala 304. Feige Urmacher – a silver chain; 305. Rivka Fischer – a golden watch; 306. Rachel Rubinstein — a golden ring; Rachel Weitzmann – a golden ring".

Flower sale on behalf of the Jewish National Fund (Keren Kayemet Le'Israel)

Standing from right, first row: Hershel Heibloom, Hershel Cohen, name unknown, Motel Tietelboim, Joshua Piva;
Second row: name unknown (first name Roske), Judith Hopfer, Rachel Mann, her cousin Mann, Breindel Rosental, Sheinberg, Mindel Shlivke, Hana Goldapple, Joel Srebarnick;
Sitting: Moshe Preter, Binyamin Eisenstat, Rachel Listgarten, Yeshayahu Stalavi, Roise Rubinstein, Hana Shneimann;
In front: name unknown, Solomon Hochberg, Haya Sara Zubermann, name unknown, Rachel Holzheker

Income Report, Jewish National Fund, Biala Podlaska, 1933

Activity	Hachalutz	Hashomer Hatzair	General Zionists	Poalei Zion	Visa	Mizrachi Youth	Mizrachi	Beithar	The Worker
Boxes	266.09	65.89		22.75	17.33	31.24		12.5	
Greeting cards and calendars	5.95	17.15						0.8	
Bowls	4.48					2.25			
Vows and Yizkor	30.68		3.51						
Hanuka	24.05	4.9							
Shvat 15th	10.3	6.25				13.67			
Purim	3.9	9		5.15					
Lag Ba'Omer		11							
Tamuz 20th	4.05	4		9.7					6.8
Usishkin Village	303.24	106.38	200.12	27.49	28.34		35	1.5	
Flower days	110.57	106.63	2.27	7.37	8.37		68	1.72	
Family celebrations	22.85	10.57						3	
Notes and telegrams	19.5			4.5		4.75			
Foresting Eretz Israel		13.7							
Rain Donation	12.5	16.44							
Pocket boxes		17.59							
Special activity	1.5								
Left from 1932									

Secretary and treasurer: Yeshayahu Stolovi
Authorized signatory: Y. A. Rosenboim

Minutes of the Audit committee

We have checked the books of the Jewish National Fund in Biala Podlaska, the income receipts
and all documents related to the bookkeeping, and found that all has been done in good order.

The audit committee: M. Morgenstern, Rachel Listgarten, Y. Weismann.

Biala Podlaska, 5th of Heshvan, 1933.

("Podlaska's Life", number 40, 19.10. 1934)

The financial report of 1934 presented above shows that despite the diversity of Zionist groups operating in Biala before WWII, all were united in working for the Jewish National Fund.

During the week of Passover 1932, the Jewish National Fund held a bazaar in H.Y. Kastenboim's hall, and brought a festive feeling to the Jewish population. It left a very good impression.

* * *

Following the setting up of the United Israel Appeal (Keren Hayesod) at the Zionist international conference in London in 1920, Zionist activity in Biala resumed and the town started collecting money for a settlement fund, which was called "Keren Hageula" [Redemption Fund, O.A.]. The major operation on behalf of the United Israel Appeal started in 1922. Rabbi Yitzhak Dines and Shapiro came to Biala from the center in Warsaw. Their presence in the town stirred the people, and a large sum of money was promised, of which some was given in cash, and some in periodical payments. These commitments were based on future income, and were far greater than the assets the Zionist already had. Contributions to the United Israel Appeal became an annual event, together with the annual collection of funds for Zionist organizations. Binyamin Kliger chaired the United Israel Appeal committee, which included delegates from the different Zionist groups.

[Page 206]

The "Bund"

Gedaliahu Braverman (Petah Tikva [Israel])

Translated by Ofra Anson (Ideltuch)

Edited by Yocheved Klausner

a. From the start to 1918

Different stories have been told about the establishment of the Bund in Biala, some of which have become real legends. This is not surprising. In almost a hundred years, Jewish life in Biala had not changed. The dominant slogan was to go "baderech hayeshara" [in the righteous path]. To respect the rich man, who held the power to help others earn a few pennies; and of course, the religious officials, whom everyone was obliged to honor as they were Those who taught you to be a Jew. And what about the authorities? One would not dare to express a thought or a word of complaint.

When I was a young boy, I used to hear stories about the Bund, passed on by word of mouth. Like everywhere else, the women were first to get news of this wonder, and the first to spread the word. A woman in Biala, who happened to hear a noise or a rumor about this "nuisance", could not rest in peace until she had whispered it in her neighbor's ear, adding, "let's keep it a secret".

Each one passed the story on to the others, asking them to keep it secret. Slowly these secrets became stories, fantasies, and legends.

One of the many legends was that a group was established, who, heaven forbid, does not like the Emperor, and wish to choose another one instead. For that purpose, these people go out into the woods, where no one else goes, and there they choose their Emperor. He sits on a high place, and all those present swear their loyalty to him by raising two fingers of their right hand. Even the name of the chosen Emperor was spread around, Naske Hudesls, second only to king Matias (Matityahu). It was also known that the Emperor was chosen for a set number of months; after that, a new one was chosen.

I cannot say who first brought this "Treif" [abominable] idea to Biala, and took the risk of involving others, because I have heard so many different versions of this story. Some thought it was Baruch Srule (Israel) Mulyers (Weinberg), who came back from London at the time, where he adopted the idea of a free life. Others thought that workers from Biala, who were employed in Warsaw, became involved with the Bund there and were sent back with a mission to organize a group in Biala. What is undisputed is that the Bund pioneers in Biala were apprentice carpenters, led by Baruch Weinberg (who himself was a carpenter when he was young).

The first political process

It seems that the rumors and the legends which spread in town with regard to the Bundists in Biala reached the head of the police. At the end of 1900 several young carpenters were arrested, among them: Baruch Weinberg, Elye (Eliyahu) Bobkes (Hofman), Avraham Solomon Mendix and others. Shortly afterwards, their trial started in the headquarters of the prison on Proster Street. The arrest, and then the trial, shook Jewish Biala like a storm. The Jewish community became fearful, because who knows what kind of problems and troubles the Bundists might bring upon them.

On the day of the trial, a group of Jews gathered in front of the prison. Some were relatives of the defendants; others were news seekers. The trial was a strange event in town: Jewish youth in trouble with the government? Never heard of such a thing! Shloimale Goldberg and Yosel Wetshik were present at the trial. They told the people that the defendants stood proudly in front of the judges; they fired their defense lawyers and presented their ideology themselves.

[Page 207]

Baruch Weinberg gave a three–hour speech, explaining to the judges the difference between Russia and West European countries, where the people are sovereign, and enjoy full political freedom; only Russia was left behind, and the people, who have no rights, are now struggling to achieve their aspirations. Baruch spoke with such glowing enthusiasm that the judges were shaken. They could not understand from where this Jew took the courage to stand there and express such complaints and claims against the beloved Russian Czar. They were sentenced to exile in Siberia with hard labor, and soon after the trial, they were indeed sent to Siberia. A few years later, the Czar pardoned all political prisoners, and they returned to Biala. However, Avraham Shloimale Mendix had a nervous breakdown, and his father sent him to an asylum in Nizshne from which he never returned.

The Bund Goes Out in the Open

At the beginning of 1901, the Bund stopped hiding, with the slogans: "Out into the streets"; "Bring the tidings of freedom to the poor and downtrodden masses"; "Plow the abandoned field and see the new fruit".

A committee was set up, with a mission to approach every young worker, men and women, to talk with them, and explain to each of them what they needed to know and understand. The meeting place was in an orchard, named "Birzshe" and to avoid the attention of the police, they used to say that they were going on a field trip. They decided to meet three times a week. They split up into groups, by occupations, each with its own meeting point in the park. Representatives from the party brought propaganda, calling on the workers to wake up and get ready for the new times.

Among the shoemakers, the leaders were: Haim Fishtshatzer (a shoemaker) and Hersh Ber Aronovitch (a saddler). Among the carpenters: Shame Friedman, Elye Shimshele and Itzale Stolier. Among the painters, who were quite a large group – Itzale Maler and Leizer Maler. Among the young women – Chinke Brachies and Sheindle Grinberg.

Although the movement recruited many youngsters, and everybody knew who the party representatives were, the committee continued to behave like an underground organization, for security reasons. The meeting place and time of the committee were kept secret. Party representatives reported their activity to the committee, including names of devoted and trustworthy followers; the latter were then promoted to a higher rank named "political members". As such, they were allowed to accompany central–party members and sometimes meet with the committee. Initially, the committee consisted of the founding members, those who organized the party. When the party grew, committee members were elected.

A hidden activist and the beginning of the political movement

At that time, the Tyomkin family lived on Proster Street. They were famous in town, though they were not involved with the religious community in Biala. Their son, Haim (Yevel), studied at Petersburg University. During his visits to Biala he had direct contact with the Bund committee, and took part in their meetings and get–togethers.

When I was honored with the rank of "political member", my contact member once ordered me to come to a certain street at a given time the next morning. When I arrived, my contact told me to go to Braganaver Street, from where a second party member led me to Pesachl Mantcher's home, to a small chamber, half dark, lit only by an oil lamp standing in one corner; the flame spread a faint light on the people present, who were waiting in silence for the others. Soon, Elye Shimeles came in with the student Haim Tyomkin. The student climbed on a chair and started lecturing, explaining to us the idea of "social democracy".

[Page 208]

In 1904 I met Tyomkin again, at a party meeting. By then the party had many members, and used to hold general meetings in a field. On sunny Saturdays, many came out to Lamas field to hear Tyomkin speak. These meetings have remained etched deep in my memory. In the middle of one talk, when all the people were totally involved in the speech, suddenly we heard a scream: "Oy". We stood where we were, as if electrified, and the speaker stopped his words. Above our heads a red flag was flapping. When the speech was over, somebody from behind declared "It's a hard world we live in!" [Lit. "The night is dark!"]

The reforms introduced by the Bund

The Bund did not limit itself to propaganda and preaching about the wrongs of the present life. It also took action to improve working conditions, which were miserable, both economically and spiritually. The workers were strongly dependent on their employers; wages were extremely low and the working day often lasted from dawn to dusk. The Bund took upon itself to improve working conditions, and started negotiating with the employers. They established a strike committee, which started to teach the employers what exploitation and honesty meant. The first group to go on strike were the tailors, who were eager to improve their conditions, and included many long–serving workers. In order not to make too many waves in town, they started with modest demands: a 10–hour working day and a less derogatory attitude, particularly for the young apprentices.

As much as these demands look modest in today's terms, at the time they were revolutionary in Jewish economic life. The employers just could not grasp the idea that workers could have a say with regard to their working hours. How is it possible – they argued – to work only 10 or 12 hours a day before the holiday when they have to deliver the work to the customer? The demand that an apprentice–boy is not a servant was beyond their understanding. Although the employers were confused, they understood that the demands came from a social movement. In the end, they understood that they had to give ground, and after they gave in to the tailors, employers in other trades had to follow.

In one place, it was extremely difficult to improve working conditions: Motel Mintz's cigarette factory. Motel Mintz was a *Hassid* who owned a house on Yanever Street. Apart from the cigarette factory, he also owned a cloth shop in the market. He was an assertive person, who believed that nobody had the right to interfere with his business. When it was explained to him that new times had come, times when a young working woman also wants to be a human being and have a few hours for herself, he roared: "not in my business"; and added "they can stop working altogether and be completely free" – and refused to talk anymore. The girls left work and showed him that they could survive weeks and months without a job. At the end, when they realized that he was not going to listen, the town declared a boycott on his merchandize and his shop, and he had to give in.

The movement enters the orthodox schools and the Hassidic world

In those days, most parents wanted their children to grow to be distinguished students, good Jews, but not a crafts–person or a worker. What, a tailor? A shoemaker? These entailed no prestige for the family, and were doomed to a hard, and poor, future. A scholar, on the other hand, had a different path, lined with privileges and a comfortable life paid for by his rich father–in–law. For that reason, a large proportion of the young Jewish men avoided vocational training and turned to study the Torah in the *Beit Midrash* or Yeshiva.

The Bund members did not connect with the youth, whom they wanted to go into vocational training instead of living like parasites. They wanted them to learn about the wide world by reading Russian literature (secular Yiddish literature was still in its infancy). Under the influence of the Bund, David Kroses (Goldfarb), Joel Itzel, and Hanina'le Kling and others left their studies and joined the Bund.

The student members of the movement helped those who had left the *Yeshiva* and turned to general studies. David Kooses was one of them. He came from an extremely orthodox family and his father studied *Mishnayot* in the *Beit Midrash* between *Minha* and *Ma'ariv* [the two evening prayers]. David Kroses now studied secular books with the same devotion with which he had previously studied the *Torah*. He studied Russian so well that he later became a teacher of the language.

[Page 209]

Beside the workers, youngsters from rich homes also joined the movement, such as Motl Minz, whom I mentioned earlier. In the movement, members developed a sense of solidarity, togetherness, and freedom, values for which one should be ready to sacrifice one's own life. The heroic behavior of Hirsh Lekert in Vilna was used as an example.

A short while after the Bund started its activity in Biala, traditional life started to change. Workers worked for a set number of hours a day, and after work they washed themselves, changed clothes, and went out to the "birzshe" to meet with other members, and enjoy political and cultural activities.

The older generation, which was deeply rooted in the traditional religious life, did not want their children to go astray. They warned the boys to keep away from the Bund, but were stricter with the girls. Parents were afraid that their daughters would meet, heaven forbid, a man. We have to understand that beside the Bund other radical changes were also taking place, against the old generation's will. They were angry with the girls, cursing the rebellious ones who wanted to leave the traditional life, but to no avail.

The Bund did not campaign against religion as such. However, when people started reading popular scientific and philosophical literature that explained to them many natural processes, their point of view changed, and it affected their religious beliefs. Many of them became anti–religious.

The assemblies of the Bund

As the party grew, it began to hold general assemblies; in summer – in a field or a grove; in winter – either in the *Beit Midrash* or in a *Hassidic* synagogue. These assemblies became an important part of the town's life, and had a festive and cultural nature. Problems, and the danger of falling into the hands of the Czar's soldiers, were forgotten. When the meeting was held in a field far from the town people really let go.

On New Year's Eve of 1903, it was agreed to meet outside the town, after dinner. At the set hour, masses of people gathered in the forest. Baruch Weinberg gave a speech. He spoke about life outside the country, the living conditions of laborers, and promised that the social–democratic parties, together with the Bund, would fight for the same conditions in Russia. When night fell and it became dark, they could not see each other, and only the excited words cut through the silence, promising to fight the darkness. When the assembly was over, some Bund members formed a gate through which all the participants passed. It was thus possible to count them – 400 men. On their way home, they were singing revolutionary songs.

The gatherings in *Beit Hamidrash* were organized in such a way that if the police approached, an agreed signal was given, and *Beit Hamidrash* was evacuated by jumping out of the windows. By the time the police arrived, nobody was to be found. Sometimes the people who came to *Beit Hamidraash* to pray did not like the "bond" using the place, and mimicked a false alarm so that the Bund members would flee.

In summer, getting together was not a problem; the forest, grove, and orchard could be used as meeting places. In winter, however, meeting places became a serious problem. They looked for a store where they could meet. In the courtyard of Hershl Lentchner's house on Grabanaver Street, a certain Shmuel had a sweet shop. They used to go in, stand by the shining shelves and discuss important issues, sometimes even quietly singing revolutionary songs. The store was so crowded that it was difficult to move. The shopkeeper then moved his business to a larger store, and more people could take part in the meetings.

[Page 210]

The community cares for the poor

In those days, if a poor person fell ill, there was no one to care for them, and provide medical care. People with contagious diseases stayed at home and were not isolated. No effort was made to build a Jewish hospital for the poor.

One time, a young working orphan boy fell sick (he had no mother and his father had been taken to the army). He worked for Gershon Shuster, who himself was a very poor craftsman. He was lying in the workshop without any medical care, and when the Bund found out about him, it was too late. When the Bund activists Elie Shimsheles and Itzale Stalier went one evening to the workshop to look for the sick boy, he was already dying. He asked them for help, but died within few hours. The next day, the Bund organized the workers, and turned the funeral into a demonstration against the leaders of the community. By the open grave, Elie Shimsheles described in tears the visit they had paid to the deceased the night before, and how the boy had cried for help.

The Bund took upon itself to ensure medical care for the poor. They searched for ways to collect money to build a Jewish hospital. The opportunity soon came. When one of the rich men of the community died, a delegation went to the deceased's family, asking for a sum of money, and the funeral was held up until the family donated the money. The family wanted to avoid the Bund's intervention, so they turned to Baruch Weinberg and argued that it was a community affair, and the Bund should not interfere; they also understood the need for a Jewish hospital, but this had nothing to do with the Bund.

What Baruch answered them is not clear. According to one rumor, he said that donation is philanthropic in nature, and the Bund, indeed, should not interfere. Nevertheless, since it was a serious matter, the sum requested was raised and the funeral went ahead.

Political strikes

The Bund tried to organize strikes. However, in a small town it was not easy. We shall describe one such strike here.

After the tragic incident of the priest Gapon in St. Petersburg, the Bund stopped the protest strikes. In Biala, the Bund explained the incident in St. Petersburg to the public, and decided to hold a general strike that would include all employees, of industrial, service and sales workers.

A workers' strike was quite feasible, as the employers did not stand in the way. Closing stores, however, was a difficult matter. Closing shops used to be a punishment measure taken by the city's authorities to express dissatisfaction with the population. The Czar's police warned against the strike, and Jewish shopkeepers found it difficult to follow the Bund's request.

The night before the strike, Bund members went to the bakers and told them not to bake for the next day; they went to the butcheries and groceries and asked them not to open their shops the next day. That evening the Czar's police started to have a feeling that something was happening. In those days, the streets were lit by petrol–lamps, which were lit every evening and hung on a high post. That night all lamps were broken by heavy stones, and the town was dark.

When the police found out that a strike was planned for the next day, they raided the houses of Bund activists and arrested a few of them, such as Elie Shimsheles, Shama Friedman, and Shiye Binyamin Leibeles (Joshua Mandelboim). Yet this did not stop the strike.

[Page 211]

The next day, a frozen winter day, the workers stayed at home; some groceries were open, some were closed. The police went to each shopkeeper who did not open his store, and brought him from his home to the store; yet as soon as the police left, Bund activists told him to close. If he refused, they closed the doors from the outside. When they could not do that, they threw stones into the shop. The police were after the Bund activists throughout the day, but could not stop them; they considered calling in the army to help. The police did manage to catch about ten men, who were imprisoned for a few months. Some were sent out to other regions after they were released. Among them was Feivel Mitten, nicknamed "Jabe". [Frog]

"The Fighting Unit" of the Bund

Officially, the Bund was against terror, but there was a group of armed activists who were ready to take any action, and to use physical force if necessary. This armed group called itself "The Fighting Unit", and included members of the movement with a very high level of commitment. People who wanted to join this group were examined carefully before they were admitted. The first question they were asked was whether or not they were ready to sacrifice their life if needed. If the candidate answered "yes" with no hesitation, he was recruited; but if he thought for a second, he was rejected.

The armed group included 30 healthy young men. I remember a few of them, for example: Anchel Katzap (Bekerman); Moshe Ishtsher, Haim Fishtshatzer; Nachke Feldman; Shiya Benyamin Leibekes; the white Meir, and Haninale Kling. If I am not mistaken, Yesha'ayahu Weinberg also belonged to this group. The armaments came from the center. They used to practice the equipment outside the town, overseen by Leiser Molyer who came from Lodz and was experienced in training such groups.

Informers

Informers troubled the Bund in Biala. They did not come from inside the Bund, but from the general public, and for several reasons: for easy money, which the police were ready to pay informers, and as a revenge on those who led Jewish children astray. There were frequent arrests, and the prison in Biala often hosted members of the Bund.

The armed group of the Bund decided to find the informers and punish them. Three of the informers were indeed discovered. One of the informers, a craftsman, became so frightened that he left Biala with his family. The second one, a merchant, was shot and wounded in his store. The third was an embittered person, who was not afraid of anyone, and always carried a gun. He went to Warsaw by train quite often, in the Czar's service, riding first class. He used to hide, avoiding contact with strangers and thus suspicious people. But to no avail: one summer evening he was caught and punished as he deserved.

The way in which the death sentence was executed is interesting. From the train station the informer used to travel into town by carriage, with a covered roof so that he could not be seen. On the evening of the operation, an elegantly dressed lady approached him, and asked him in Russian to allow her to travel with him in the same carriage. When the carriage reached the bridge over the river, the lady pulled out a gun, shot him a few times, and disappeared. It was not generally known that the lady was actually a disguised member of "The Fighting Unit" of the Bund of Biala.

Open demonstrations

At the end of 1905, the Czar's government published a manifesto about the constitution and general elections to the parliament (*Duma*). The Bund in Biala called a general assembly to explain to the population the real meaning of the freedom the Czar was giving his subjects. The meeting took place in the synagogue, which was filled with people from all walks of life. The speaker came from the center, and his words enchanted the audience. After the meeting, "The Fighting Unit" formed a ring, in which most of those present were caught, and led them through the town for a demonstration, shouting slogans against the Czar.

[Page 212]

The police were at that time in Pijshits's house in the market, at the end of Yanover Street. The chief of the police was Kareniov, who was known for his liberal attitudes. When the demonstration left the synagogue and started marching towards the police station, and the policemen heard the noise and the anti–Czar shouts, Kareniov left his room and prevented his men from confronting the crowd.

The demonstration went smoothly through the town up to the prison on Proster Street, where some Bund members were imprisoned. In front of the prison, they demanded the release of the prisoners and sang revolutionary songs.

Fighting with the underworld

Before the Bund started to operate in Biala, the Jewish community had been terrorized by criminals. Thieves, delinquent youth, hooligans, and parasites bullied the Jews and blackmailed them in different ways. On Purim and Simchat Tora they used to get drunk, go into the synagogues and attack whoever came near them. Sometimes people had to hide behind closed doors for fear of them; nobody stood up to them.

The Bund tried to work with these outlaws, to change them to normative workers. Yet they succeeded with only a few; most remained untouched by these efforts. At the beginning these negative elements were upset by the new power which had arrived on the Jewish streets. It disturbed their freedom to do as they liked. They tried to behave provocatively during the meetings organized by the Bund; pull faces, talk and shout during speeches. Yet they were not met with fear, nor with submission, and were asked to leave. They tolerated this attitude for the time being, but prepared for a future confrontation.

The Bund in Biala had a strong belligerent spirit; some members were strong and heavily built. For example: Antshe Katsap (Backerman); Chonke Niskeles (the painter); the white Meir, Avraham Kamelmaker and others, who always carried guns. This group did not fear the criminals at all. One day it was discovered that criminals were preparing to pick a fight the next day. That day Chone Niskeles met one of the criminals; he blocked his way and said: you want to fight? What are you waiting for? and pulled out his Browning revolver. The criminal fled without a word.

Self defense

During the pogroms in Russia, when the Czar's forces wanted to suppress the revolutionary spirit by setting the Russian population against the Jews and organized a pogrom, the Bund organized Jewish self–defense. They called the Jewish people to prepare for a possible attack. They organized an armed camp, recruiting people from the general, non–Bundist population. They had different means of defense: spears, stakes, revolvers, weights and stones, and pieces of iron.

Biala's Jews did not fear the civilian population, which generally was not interested in politics, and had negative feelings towards the Russian regime. Rather, they were afraid of the Russian soldiers stationed in the town. There were eight artillery units in different army camps located around Biala, close to the highways to Warsaw and to Brisk.

On Sundays, when the soldiers were allowed to go into town, they used to get drunk and attack the Jews they happened to meet. They would make a disturbance, accompanied by Russian expressions such as: "jidi masheniki" (Jewish liar) and "rasresiat vas nada" (you should be cut to pieces). There was fear of a serious attack on the Jews which would result in loss of life.

One Sunday about 1903, news arrived that the soldiers planned to attack the Jews and their houses that evening. The self–defense group took their arms and stood in groups next to the Jewish homes. Indeed, in the evening drunk soldiers came shouting "davai Jidi!" [give us Jews], intending to storm Jewish houses. The waiting self–defense men resisted, prevented them from robbing, attacked them using their armaments, and the soldiers withdrew. It should be said the soldiers were unarmed; had they been armed, who knows what the results of their attack would have been.

[Page 213]

The next day the self–defense members were in a very high mood. Each group shared their previous night's experience with the others. Some of them had been attacked themselves. The soldiers never came back.

The crisis

In an effort to repress the revolutionary movement, the Czar decided to establish an organization of peoples' representatives, and on the other hand kept looking for ways to destroy the revolutionary elements. The ruler wanted to subdue the revolutionary enthusiasm and encourage despair about possible change. The change in mood was felt in Biala too. Guides from the center stopped coming, and the work of the Bund almost ceased. The more energetic members turned to cultural and social activities, but these, of course, were on a smaller scale than activities led by a party.

As long as the party was there, with a united ideology, people were more willing to put their own interests aside. However, when the party stopped its activities, the members started to look around, to seek out their own goals. One result of this process was emigration from Biala. Among those who left were: Leiser Maler, Elye Shimsheles and his fiancée; Avraham Kamelmaker with his sister; David Kroses (who went to Paris and returned after a short while); Hane Niskeles, the white Meir and others.

The young heirs of the Bund in Biala started to take over the party and continue its work. When Haninale Kling (one of the Bund activists in Biala) started to get ready to leave, he told me, Elyahu Reiseles (Klatch); Moshe Benyamin Tsharni, and two others that he would hand over to us the armaments collected by the armed Bund group, "The Fighting Unit".

It was about 1908. At the set hour, we were led by Haninale Kling to "Zapye" forest. He pointed at a high tree with a bent, broken looking treetop, and said that the armaments were hidden under that tree.

When we arrived at the tree, he touched the ground with a piece of metal he had on him, and found the place after some time. We dug with some tools we had with us, until we found an iron box. We took it out, and only after a long time managed to open it because it was rusty. We were shocked when we opened the box: all the arms were lying in water. We counted more than thirty revolvers, some of them rusted beyond use. Parts of them were made of nickel and were still a little shiny. Knives and bullets were also rusted. We spilled out the water and started to clean the arms with our handkerchiefs. We were so busy that we did not notice the time. When it got dark, we put oil on everything, and stuffed it back in the box. Haninale left with tears in his eyes.

What happened to the box later – I do not know. Some trees were uprooted by Christians to develop a business. I went there a few times and found our tree in the middle of a flowering garden. During the First World War, the Germans occupied Biala and cut down all the forests, including our marker tree.

The Bund stops its activity

The bourgeoisie were overjoyed at the decline of the Bund. They were quite annoyed by the constant demands of their workers, the strikes, and the demand to close stores and groceries. It was said that in the Gur *Shtiebl* [Hassidic synagogue] the fall of the Bund and the defeat of the strikers was celebrated on *Simchat Tora*, and that a special song was sang:

"Yente the beauty
A telegram arrived;
All strikes are finished,
No more threats
Be happy on *Simchat Tora*."

[Page 214]

They maintained and developed the library. They used to go out to the forest on Saturdays where they held discussions on different problems. They were sure that the crisis was a short–term one. In 1910 they decided to celebrate May Day. The event was organized in the same way as it had been in previous years. Each member of the group, that is, Elyahu Klatch, Moshe Benyamin Tsharni, Moshe Finkelstien, Joel Fingerhut and I were responsible for encouraging workshop workers and readers from the library to be out on the street on the evening of the First of May.

It was decided to hold the assembly on Yanover Avenue, to go down to the field, to a secluded corner next to the Jewish cemetery. That evening two of the organizers went down to the corner to wait for the people, while the other organizers went out to send the people to the meeting place. Only two or three people were on the streets so it would not look suspicious. At the meeting, Elyahu Klatch explained the meaning of May Day, and reviewed the political situation. After that, participants went home.

The first attempt to found a professional organization

In 1909, Nehemiah Hoffer set up a workshop for mechanical shoe making in Biala. After some time he recruited his two brothers, Asher and Mathithyahu, and his brother–in–law, Benyamin Kliger, as partners. The workshop developed into a factory which employed some forty workers. The work methods followed those of modern industry, with travelers (Mathithyahu Hoffer), who went to the distant towns to set up production. In this factory there developed the first professional organization in Biala. They conducted their activities under quite primitive conditions, without a secretary and without a location. They used to meet on the street to discuss their affairs. They even called a strike on behalf of the workers.

During the First World War

During the German occupation, the Bund could not be active in any way. They thus turned to social work. They helped set up a public kitchen, as well as organizing literature and drama groups. New members joined the Bund: Mordechai Hachman, a refugee from Brisk Miriam, who was born in Biala but lived in Vilna and came to stay with her mother; an old–time Bund activist, Chone Freind, returned to Biala; Shimshon Blankleider (the fat); Avraham Striecher, Ester Eidelman and others.

At the end of the war, when news about the revolution in Russia arrived, the revolutionary spirit in Biala also revived. Bundists felt that the time for intensive activity had come, on a large scale if possible. Bund members who had stepped aside after the 1905 revolution failed became active again: Shama Friedman; Bahum Vorek; Eliahu Hofman, Hersh Ber Aaronivitz and others.

With the establishment of Poland, a new chapter opened in the history of the Bund in Biala.

[Page 215]

b. Between the World Wars

by V. Schuster

Translated by Libby Raichman

In Biale, in the years 1917 – 1919, there was an intensive process of awakening, and the organization of the workers. A youth–organization was established as well as professional trade unions like: needle–workers' union, metal–union, wood–union, bakers' union etc. A cultural club was founded, as well as a library and a dramatic circle. The best journals, books and newspapers in Yiddish were acquired and read in a reading–hall facility. All these institutions were absorbed into the large Bundist club in Grabanover Street, named after Bronislav Grosser, in the home of Motl of the winery. A consumer–co–operative was also established to enable the members to purchase food items at normal prices.

Through these professional unions, the "Bund" influenced the working masses, both politically and economically, and strengthened their socialistic awareness. These professional unions were led by the most capable Bundists: Shimon Blankleider – secretary of the central professional union; Moshe Rodzinek – secretary of the tailoring–section and Shmuelke Goldberg – secretary of the leather–branch.

The organization of the young workers by the "Bund" was not an easy matter because one needs to consider the circumstances in which they lived at that time. As they were spiritually miserable and economically poor, it was necessary to awaken in them the feeling of a new world and to teach them the path to freedom. To teach these youth, the Bund appointed one of their most talented members, Tanna Fryned, an intelligent person who was very knowledgeable. He would deliver lectures to the youth, gave them the appropriate books to read and led social clubs. Their thoughts and passions brought the young Jewish workers out into a social environment that lifted their spirits above their grey everyday life and gave them the hope of a more beautiful tomorrow. Thanks to this cultural activity, workers and leaders of the Biale "Bund" later emerged.

The "Bund" was already organized, and having an influence on the professional unions, stepped into the electoral–action to the first town council for the first time. It called together meetings in the synagogues and in the halls that local members frequented. Members also came from Warsaw such as Hershel Himmelfarb, Yakov Patt and others. They strove to persuade the population that the "Bund" was not just a class party, but also a defender of national Jewish interests. As a result of the propaganda that the "Bund" promoted, it managed to influence the appointment of 6 council members: Moshe Rodzinek, Shimon Blankleider, Nochum Vorek, Chaim Brodatsh, Gedalyahu Braverman and Mordechai Hochman.

In 1920, when the Polish military began their retreat from Kiev, a wave of arrests and persecutions on a large scale began, against the leaders of the Jewish working class. In the midst of this, the Grosser club with all the institutions was burnt down and everything was lost in the fire. Some time later, the whole Bundist committee was arrested and its members were deported to the Dombiye camp. Among those deported were: Shimon Blankleider, Nochum Vorek, Moshe Rodzinek, Tanna Fryned, Fyvel Gold, Zissel Izenberg, Eliyahu Goldman and others.

In the first months of 1921, after the war between Poland and Russia had ended, intensive construction work by the "Bund" in Biale began again. Members returned from the army, from the prisons, and from the camps where they were interned. Many of the members who returned were no longer in a fit state to throw themselves back into political activity, because some of them were sick, or physically broken, and others began to prepare themselves to leave Poland. It therefore became the lot of the younger Bundists to proceed with the work. The young Bundists threw themselves into socialistic enlightenment activity with a new enthusiasm. A new committee of the following members was elected: Chaim Visegloz, Velvl Shuster, Eliezer Shnur and Berel Solman. Together with the fresh committee, older members became active again and guided the youth on how to proceed with Bundist activity. In addition, members of the older generation distinguished themselves; in particular: Tanna Fryned, Shimon Blankleider and Fyvel Gold.

At the outset, they undertook to rebuild the professional unions. The first, the needle–workers' union, was organized in the home of Shragge the shoemaker, on Proster Street. The management consisted of these members: Velvl Shuster – chairman, and Berel Solman – secretary and treasurer. The union also became a place of cultural activity. Discussion evenings and various lectures were arranged there. Later the professional unions for leather, wood and metal were organized. All the unions were led by Bundists. At the head of the leather union was the member Yechezkel Vloss. The metal union was led by the member Fyvel Gold and the wood union by the member Velvl Charash.

[Page 216]

The "Bund" brought the best lecturers from Warsaw to lecture to the Jewish population on topical political problems. The town had the opportunity to hear the voice of the "Bund" again.

The Jewish working youth with their strong drive for education, their yearning for joy and their desire to uplift themselves, sought to satisfy, to a great extent, the ideals of their own organization. For the "Bund–youth", whose organisation was both an instrument of struggle and an educational institution, stood the difficult question of training the necessary core group of speakers and leaders for the organization. The core–group had to come from amongst the youth themselves; there could not be any talk of bringing unfamiliar teachers or those who stood outside of this camp. It had to be one of their own, kneaded from the same dough. From everywhere, individual youth came forward who had acquired a certain amount of knowledge, and also possessed the ability to impart their knowledge to others. However, it was necessary to give the younger lecturers and the culturally active speakers a program and a method, in order for them to personally clarify the role that they were taking upon themselves. For this purpose, young Bundists would travel to Mezritsh, where the regional centre of the "Bund" was located, and there they would receive instructions in how to perform their tasks.

The institution "Culture–League" was created in Biale with the aim of centralizing all the work of the "Bund". The "Bund" in Biale always aspired to uplift the worker spiritually and morally. They managed to achieve this by systematic club–activities, through courses, camps, gatherings, public readings, concerts, presentations and by various other means.

As has already been mentioned, the library that was established in 1917 was entirely destroyed in the fire at the house of Motl of the winery. At the professional unions, a library was again erected, that was later taken over the Communists. The "Culture League" therefore decided to turn to the Bundists in America, requesting that they assist in establishing a library. Thanks to the determined efforts of the member Fyvel Gold, it did not take long before 10 large crates arrived containing Yiddish books. Every month the "Culture–League" would receive the latest literary publications, and in that way the library became the second home for a large section of the young workers.

The committee of the Youth Bund "Tzukunft" (future)

From right: Volf Shuster, Devorah Shuster, Klieger, Vechterman, Zinger, Leah Goldshtein and Berel Bekkerman

The "Bund" as a political party was not satisfied with only cultural activities. At a meeting of the "Bund" committee, it was decided to organize the porters, the coach drivers, bakers and meat workers. It was also decided to turn to the headquarters in Warsaw about sending a suitable person who would be capable of managing these unions. The appeal was accepted in Warsaw and a member, Leibl Kersh, was sent as an instructor. He was truly suited to the position, both as a speaker and in his management skills. He took to organizing the unions, enthusiastically.

Separate unions were organized with one central office. The porters voted in an election and selected Avigdor Richter as leader, and in addition, the "Bund" member, Yitzchak Vechterman. The secretary was L. Kersh, the official from Warsaw. At the head of the management of the meat union stood Shlayme Stop's son, Yakov Tsharny; chairman of the management of the bakers' union was Kolker.

In 1933, it was decided to turn to the PPS (Polish Socialist Party) about organizing a joint 1st May demonstration. Conferences were held with the Polish Party leadership and it was decided to celebrate the workers' holiday jointly. That year, the 1st May demonstration was an impressive event. The professional unions of the porters, bakers, meat–workers and tailors marched with their banners bearing inscriptions, with slogans against Fascism, against anti–Semitism and for workers' rights. The porters rode in front on horses and the demonstration made a strong impression on the townsfolk. After the demonstration, a meeting attended by a large crowd was held in the hall of the cinema "Mirage", where Jewish and Polish speakers appeared and from both sides the struggle for the worker and the peasant–government was stressed.

[Page 217]

A flower sale on behalf of the "Culture League" 1927

Front from right: Feige Smolarzsh, Chaim Zinger, Tsirl Mayerzon, Moshe Shneiderman, Shayndl Zusman, Shualke Yurberg, Esther Shneiderman, Mannes Rodzinek
Sitting in the middle: Fyvel Virnik, Shlayme Kupershmidt, Shmuel Chaim Vinderboim, Elye Hofman, Chanah Bravarek, Gedalyahu Braverman, Avrom (surname unknown), Moshe Finkelshtein, Wolf Shuster, Shmuelke Goldberg
Standing: Gittel Aronovitsh, name unknown, Moshe Koralik, Menuchah Koralik, Hershl Eppelboim, Devorah Belman, Yitzchak Brodatsh, Leah Izen
4th row: Mintshe Aydelman, name unknown, Feige Potshtaruk, Avrom Koralik, name unknown

In 1938 Biale became a centre of anti–Semitic unrest. The anti–Semitism was already emerging in an organized boycott of Jewish trade and Jews being beaten in the town; a fear came over the people.

The "Bund" decided to turn to the PPS (Polish Socialist Party) for help in combatting the organized boycott. The PPS then proposed its plan to fight against the boycott. Their plan was, that when the anti–Semites stood with placards at the Jewish shops and would not allow Christian customers to enter, then the "Bund" would create a money–fund and the PPS would use these funds to provide suitable people who would be prepared to repel anti–Semitic attacks. The "bund" however, did not have any money and therefore decided to organize a collective–action amongst the Jewish population. They went out to the Jewish merchants in the town and presented the proposition of the PPS. The merchants agreed to the proposition and raised a suitable sum for this purpose. It is understandable that the issue was complicated enough and not easy to accomplish. A few meetings were held with the leaders of the PPS and it resulted in the forging of a group of Jewish and Polish workers whose task it was to form a resistance to the anti–Semitic hooligans. The PPS hired mostly unemployed people for this group. The first fight with the anti–Semitic picketers broke out at the shop of Glikke Mendiks (Lichtenboim – manufacturing store) and the hooligans were driven away. The Jewish population breathed more freely. In organising this action, the following members of the "Bund" were active: Yitzchak Vechterman, Avrom Koralik, Fyvel Virnik, Gedalyahu Braverman and Moshe Shneiderman.

In this way, the Bundist activity continued in Biale until 1939, when the town fell under the rule of German tyranny, during which, after a few years of difficult struggle, no sign of the Jewish population remained in the town.

V. Shuster (New York)

Additional Details:

We will add details here that have a connection to the activities of the "Bund" in Biale, according to articles that we extracted from a number of copies of "Podlassier Life", and from the Frans Kursky archive in New York.

In 1905, on a winter's evening, a discussion took place in the synagogue between the Bundist, Boruch Vineberg and the anarchist Aydl the laundress's son. The "Bund's" "*bo'yuvkes*" (guards) stood around the synagogue, let everyone in, but allowed no one to leave (Podlassier Life", number 31 of 10.8.1934).

A revolutionary military organization was established, with which Boruch Vineberg and Velvel Tyomkin were associated. Through a member of this military organization they managed to buy a whole sack of revolvers for 12 or 16 rubles ("Podlassier Life" number 33 of 24.8.1934).

Members of the "Bund" stole crates of revolvers from the stables in Kshiver Street, that belonged to the policeman, Mossik. The revolvers were confiscated from Chaim Zeidman (Chaim Zeidman had a permit to sell guns) – the editor "Podlassier Life", number 34, 31.8.1934.

[Page 218]

On the night of Simchat Torah, the mayor, the policeman Romanovsky, was found drunk on a pile of mud in the middle of the market place, without his sword. This was done because of his persecution of the Bundists. After a promise that he would no longer meddle in the affairs of the "Bund", they returned his sword to him. ("Podlassier Life", number 36, of 18.9.1934).

At the time of the proclamation of the constitution in Russia, the Biale "Bund" issued a written proclamation.

After the failure of the December uprising in 1905, the Russian High Official, Kedrov, called the "official state Rabbi", a certain Shlaymele, and warned him that if the "Bund" in Biale did not stop their activities, there would be a pogrom in Biale. The "official state Rabbi" contacted Boruch Vineberg and asked him to see that the activities of the "Bund" did not bring about a pogrom in the town. Boruch Vineberg answered that the "Bund" was not afraid of a pogrom.

While serving in the military in 1905, the Bundist "*Samo'obrona*" came to blows with a band of Christian conscripts. Because of this incident, military service in Biale went through a calmer period than usual. ("Podlassier Life", 5.10.1934).

Correspondence from Biale (Sedletz region)

"We began to prepare here for the 1st May, much earlier. A few meetings were held with attendances of 40 to 80 people – current events in Russia and the 1st May were discussed.

The entire population of the town said that the "strikers" were preparing for the 1st May.

At last the 15th April arrived (the old style), where 350 notifications from headquarters were distributed in Polish and Yiddish. The notifications were very well distributed.

On the morning of the sabbath, the 16th April, the police arrested 2 people who were interrogated and were then allowed to go free. In the town there was a mood of unrest. On Sunday 17th April, before nightfall, a few groups of people went around and ordered the workers not to go to work the next day.

The police were also restless. They ran around like poisoned mice, but without consequences. The police came to a few people at night — but also without consequence – nobody was at home. They therefore prepared 4 brigades of soldiers for Monday 1st May.

It was nice to see how all the workers walked around in the streets, in their sabbath clothing; everyone felt free and holy. It made a great impression on the workers that the Christians united with them, by going around to the workshops and removing those who were working.

The general strike was magnificent, but they could not demonstrate in the streets because the soldiers were spread throughout the town. It was enough that Biale had displayed such great courage that the town had never seen – a general strike. They were unable to demonstrate, but from deep in our hearts, the cry rings out: Down with autocracy! The 1st May lives! Freedom in Russia lives!

On the sabbath, the night of the 16th April, the PPS distributed pamphlets but not with much success, because before anyone had time to read a pamphlet, the police had already collected them".

("The Bund", mouthpiece of the general Jewish Labour Bund in Lithuania, Poland and Russia. May 1905, number 7, in its 2nd year).

"The Biale government commissioner distinguished himself with his own laws: public readings, meetings, dramatic presentations, were according to his laws, not allowed in "jargon". In refusing, he often explains: "in Palestine you can perform in jargon". Recently we wanted to present "The Broken Hearts". This time the High commissioner gave in to a "compromise". He announced that he would only allow the presentation, on 2 conditions: 1) that the booklet should be translated into Polish and 2) allow Russian censorship of the booklet. We complied, and he allowed it. However, on Saturday, when we came for the written permission, he changed his mind, said that he did not handle the matter correctly, and banned the presentation. No complaints and no pleading helped – the presentation did not take place. In addition, we suffered a great financial loss."

(Life's issues" number 324, Tuesday 22nd July 1919).

Biale –Shedletz

Political members 50 – town councillors 6; Preferential votes 772.

Cultural facilities

Workers' Club, named after Br. Grosser – Prosta Street 32, members: 260

Co–operative movement

Labour Co–operative "Unity".
"Workers' Calendar" 1920, according to the Jewish calendar 5680 – 5681, published by "Life's Issues", Warsaw).

(From the Bund archive of the Jewish Labour movement, named after Frans Kursky, New York; rewritten by co–writers from the archive, H. Kempinski, submitted by V. Shuster, New York).

[Page 219]

The Rise of "Agudat Yisrael"[1]

by Moshe Braverman, Tel Aviv

Translated by Libby Raichman

At the end of the German occupation, those Biale residents who went to Russia during the war began to return. Among them was Yeshayahu Veitzman (Volvish Veitzman's older brother), who was called in the town Yeshayahu Shlaymeles**Error! Bookmark not defined.**. Yeshayahu Veitzman was a distinguished Gerer Chassid and, thanks to him, the "Agudah" was established in Biale.

I would like to relate a few details of the rise of the party in Biale, as it is engraved in my memory.

One evening Yeshayahu Veitzman and Yechezkel Erlich met in the local "Achiezer" (the "Achiezer" served as a neutral place for all parties). Amongst various other topics, Yeshayahu then raised the question about establishing an "Agudah" party in Biale. Yeshayahu Shlaymeles began to provoke Yechezkel Erlich about the matter and then the following conversation took place:

Yeshayahu: "Haskel, an "Agudah" needs to be established in Biale".

Yechezkal: "What do you mean by an "Agudah"? What do you mean, establishing?"

Yeshayahu: "Renting a unit with a few rooms where our kind of people can meet and experience life, because we see how all the sinners lead their Jewish life and they can be seen everywhere. We Chassidic Jews also need to organize ourselves and become a power".

Yechezkel: "You say, rent a couple of rooms, meet each other, when?"

Yeshayahu: "Between the afternoon prayers and the evening prayers. A committee of 10 – 15 people will be chosen, and they will carry out the work. The committee will meet from time to time and every question that is on the agenda will be dealt with. It is understandable that a chairman and a secretary will be chosen, who will lead the session, and each question that is dealt with will have the opinion of every person. The opinion that receives the most votes will be accepted and implemented".

Here Yechezkel was already becoming impatient and began to give Yeshayahu a piece of his mind. "Shaya, have you gone mad, God forbid, or did you become a skeptic there in Russia?" What has become of you? Why have you come with such heretical notions, with new ideas to introduce into Biale? Do you not remember how we conducted ourselves in the town before the war, when there were issues about a ritual slaughterer, a cantor, the ritual bath or similar town matters? We used to call a meeting in the Rabbi's house, we would call Reb Nachan, Moshe the big one, Moshe the small one, Dovid Reb Isaacs and a few other community leaders. Each one gave his opinion. We argued, discussed, but in the end, we took the advice of Reb Noach or Moshe the big one".

While in Russia, Yeshayahu became very skilled in such matters. He had a sharp mind and was very determined and was unmoved by Yechezkal Erlich's surprised response.

The Gerer Chassidim were on Yeshayahu's side and the matter became a serious one. Yeshayahu's plans began to become a reality. In the town at that time there were other powerful individuals like: Noach Gurfinkel from Lomaz, a talented speaker, Natan Rammes, Nachum Tennenboim and others, who were not as interested in an "Agudah–Party", as in hindering the activities of the Zionists and "Mizrachi", who then had control of Jewish life in the town. These individuals began to help Yeshayahu to accomplish his plan.

Although I too was a member of "Mizrachi", yet I was present at the gathering to establish the "Agudah", that took place in the home of Itshe Meir Zishes. At this gathering a management committee was selected and at the end, they drank a toast. In this way the "Agudah" in Biale emerged. I think that the committee consisted of: Zusha Rozen, Nachum Tennenboim, Meir Yud and others.

* * *

Our fellow–townsman David Patshtaruk relates the following about the "Agudah":

In the latter years, before the 2nd World War, the committee of the "Agudah" consisted of the following persons: Meir Yud, Chaim Levi Rubinshtein, Motl Aydelsberg, Isaac Sheinberg and Aharon Viseman.

The "Agudah" also had a youth organization "Youth for peace and belief in Israel" and later "Workers for "Agudat Yisrael". During its existence, the following served on the committee of "Workers for Agudat Yisrael": Shlayme Asher Utshtein, Asher Goldzak, Avigdor Rubinshtein, Dovid Patshtaruk, Eliyahu Erlich, Henach Shteingart, Reuven Zilberberg, Eliyahu Henech – righteous–priest, Tzvi Rozenboim, Yosef Barnboim, Yakov Utshten, Shmuel Frankreich and others.

The members would get together every evening and study a page of Gemara with additions (critical commentaries on the Talmud).

Thanks to the "Agudah", a one–grade Bet–Yakov–School for girls was established.

Translator's footnote:

1.   Orthodox religious movement

[Page 220]

The Communist Movement

by Gottl Biederman

Translated by Libby Raichman

After the Russian revolution in 1917, when power came into the hands of the labour party "Bolsheviks" (Communists), a Communist party also emerged in Poland that organized branches in the province.

The echo of the Russian revolution was at first revived in the Bundist workers' ranks, and it came about in such a way.

At the end of the 1st World War, when Biale was still under German occupation, the news about the Russian revolution reached Biale, and evoked in every worker that was versed in socialistic ideals a joy and deep respect. In their hearts lay a striving and a desire to unite with the activists in Russia.

The events in Russia were expressed at the meetings of the Biale Bundist organization. Friction arose within the party and, as a result of this, a splinter group from within the Bund itself was created, that was called "Kombund". A short time later, the group split from the "Bund" and began to exist as an independent political group of that time, under the name "Royte" [Reds].

The rise of the "Royte" began in Biale in the 1920s. The greater part of the "Bund" members in Biale, mainly the youth, joined the "Royte". The older and more prudent members remained in the "Bund". The "Royte" began to pursue intensive activities in the economic, cultural and political realms.

Despite the fact that the "Royte" was an illegal organization, whose followers were severely persecuted by the regime, it did not deter the youth from joining its ranks. In these ranks one not only met youth from impoverished backgrounds who were always concentrated in radical left parties, but also youth from the middle classes, from wealthy homes and some from the student body.

The Communists controlled the professional unions and the large Bundist library that was located there. The older active Bundists were not able to do anything, because most of them were tradesmen and therefore could not join the professional unions.

The "Royte" carried out a few successful economic strikes in the Jewish workshops, and as a result their importance grew in the town.

In the premises of the professional union, discussions were organized on various themes, and active Bundists were invited. At that time in Biale, there was a movement that organized dramatic circles. In this area, the Communists refused to be excluded, and organized their own dramatic circle under the direction of G. Braverman. This cultural activity was conducted under the shield of the professional unions that were, at that time, legalized by the regime.

In an altogether different chapter, the political activity of the "Royte" is presented. These activities would put the whole local government on alert, from time to time. Their propaganda and manifesto always had the aim of demonstrating affiliation to Soviet power in Russia, and their intention to spread this power over all other countries. This, understandably, brought out Polish people of power from the woodwork.

Sometimes at night, the "Royte" would stick slogans on all the fences in the town, that related to Soviet power in Russia. An altogether separate aspect of their activity was suspending red flags with matching slogans that they would throw over the highest telephone wires.

Sometimes the "Royte" would reveal their activity in a very risky way. On the days of the festivals, they would throw their pamphlets displaying the marching military, from behind fences or from the corridors of houses.

The police turned all their efforts to catch those who were distributing the pamphlets but for a long time they did not manage to do so. One youth who was engaged in this activity excelled at playing tricks right under the noses of the police and then disappearing. The police eventually discovered the identity of the trickster who distributed the pamphlets and arrested him. During the investigation, the police tortured the youth so terribly that he broke down and joined the police force as a colleague. He left Biale. It appears that the police transferred him to another location.

[Page 221]

Some time later, after the arrest of the youth, the leaders of the communist group in Biale were arrested. It is not known whether this happened as a result of the provocation by the arrested youth or by another person. The trial of those arrested took place in Biale and they were sentenced to many years in prison. When they were freed from prison, after serving their sentences, they were very weak and one of them was taken to a hospital in Warsaw, where he died. Another victim was the youth, Moshe Rykler. While in the Biale prison, he became so ill that the authorities freed him before he served his full term. The state of his health, however, was already so critical that every attempt to save him was unsuccessful, and in a short time he died.

The Jewish communist group kept in contact with the Christian communists in the surrounding villages, and it can be assumed that also, in Biale itself, Jewish communists were in contact with Christians that were communists.

During the elections to the town council in 1927, the communist group managed to put forward their own list of candidates, from which only one councillor was elected, a Jew. During their election meetings Christians also participated.

As already mentioned, the professional unions were legalized and had the right to organize meetings on the 1st May. The authorities knew well, that at the head of the unions stood a communist committee, but as long as the unions benefited from the legality, they were not prohibited from arranging such meetings. At one of these 1st May meetings, the authorities took revenge on the participants. It happened in this way: the meeting took place at the New Market and police with secret agents encircled the crowd. When the meeting ended, and the masses marched to the premises of the professional unions, in order to resolve matters, the police threw themselves at the marching crowd and beat them brutally with their rifle–butts.

Finally, the authorities locked the premises of the professional unions and their activities were declared illegal.

When an organization was established in Poland to gather funds for Jewish colonization in Biro–Bidjan, that needed to develop a Jewish republic, the communists in Biale organized one division of this organisation. Through them, a "Mofer" group was created in the town that was a branch of the central organization, whose aim was to collect money to help political prisoners. The Biale "Mofer" group used to come to weddings and social events to collect money for this purpose, and they would issue official receipts on writing pads that they received from their headquarters.

The decline in communist activity in the Jewish street in Biale began in the 1930s. A few of the active members were dissatisfied and withdrew from their activities. Other activists went abroad and to Warsaw. The decline was also caused by the closing of the professional unions and the arrest of the leading members. It can, however, be assumed that the situation was also the result of the general circumstances in the Polish communist party, that was "kominteren" ("commented on"/viewed) with suspicion and as a result, the activities of the whole party were brought to a halt.

In the time mentioned, the Biale communists were almost not involved in any activity. They managed, however, to gain access to various institutions and societies, so that they could, at every opportunity, express their political position. In this way they crept into the Bundist "Culture–League" and, I believe, also into other Biale organizations.

This passive activity of the Jewish communists endured until the outbreak of the 2nd World War. During the occupation of the town by the Soviet army in 1939, the Jewish working class did not play a dynamic role, as they did in 1920, during the Bolshevik invasion of Poland. With the retreat of the Red army from Biale, a small part of the Jewish communists went toc; a much larger part remained under German occupation.

Additional Details:

We will add here details about the communist activity in the town that we discovered in a few copies of "Podlassier Life".

On Wednesday the 5th October 1932, an important political trial took place in the local district court. On the bench where the accused sat were 7 young men and 2 young girls aged 17 to 21.

They were accused of the following:

On the 26th June there was a funeral of a young deceased worker.* At the funeral, the accused organized a communist demonstration at the cemetery. Without their hats, they sang songs and afterwards they formed a line and demonstrated in Sadover Street, shouting anti–government slogans at the same time.

[Page 222]

Four of them were sentenced to 2 years in prison and the loss of their civil rights for 5 years; three were sentenced to 1 year in prison, taking into consideration the time that they were in prison before the trial; two were allowed to go free.

("Podlassier Life" number 21, of the 7th October 1932)

On Tuesday evening, the 13th June 1933, unknown persons hung 2 red flags on the telephone and electricity wires; one flag on Yanover Street and one on Grabanover Street. Simchah Platt of Biale, who was accused of hanging the flags, was sentenced by the local district court to 4 years' imprisonment, on the 20th September 1933.

("Podlassier Life" number 23 and 38, of 16th June and 29th September 1933).

On Tuesday 2nd October, an important political trial began in the local district court.

On the bench where the accused sat were 29 people – 17 Jews and 12 Christians.

The charges laid against them were, that in the region of Biale, from 1930, they carried on illegal communistic activity, whose aim was to bring change to the ruling order with force, and that they demonstrated by using propaganda, hanging banners etc.

After a 2–day court adjournment, the following judgement was handed down:

---

* This means Moshe Rykler – M.Y. Feigenboim

1 (a Jew) was sentenced to 5 years in prison; 2 (Jews) – to 4 years; 1 (a Christian) to 3 years; 4 (2 Jews and 2 Christians) – to 2 years; 6 (2 Jews and 4 Christians) to 1 year; 2 (Christians) – to 6 months in prison; the remaining were freed. All those convicted were regarded as *preventz* arrests.

("Podlassier Life" number 38, of 5th October 1934)

An Anarchistic Group in Biale

by Gedalyahu Braverman

Translated by Libby Raichman

The widow, Aydl the laundress, was known in Biale. When her oldest son Moshe was twelve years old, she entrusted him to her relative, the shoemaker Shimon Karshnboim (Krempl), with the view to him teaching Moshe his trade of shoemaking. At that time, a man named Leibl worked for Shimon who originated from Lomaz and had previously worked for a few years in Cherson (Russia). At work Leibl would constantly talk about the beautiful life in Cherson, that shoemakers earn a lot of money there, that in the town there is a circus with many animals and a Russian theatre. Every Sunday the workers go to the circus and to the theatre. Watermelons lie around in the streets.

Moshe listened attentively to the stories that made a deep impression on him. Moshe was influenced by Leibl and wanted him to go with him to Cherson, and both of them set off. For a long time, not a word was heard from Moshe.

My parents were neighbours of Aydl the laundress, and I would hear how Aydl was heartbroken that her Moshe had left home years earlier and that she did not know what had happened to him, and she would shed tears of longing for her child.

In 1903, the door of my house opened, and an adolescent young man entered, with a small parcel under his arm. He limped a little on one leg. I recognized him immediately, that this was Moshe, the son of Aydl. the laundress.

A few days later, when he had already happily reconnected with his family, he came to me and had a conversation with me. He told me that he had just returned from Odessa, where he worked and was active in anarchistic circles. He had already been in prison there, from where he had just escaped and where he was wounded in his leg. He said that he wanted to establish an anarchistic group in Biale.

Moshe began to meet with people with whom he was acquainted and managed to influence a few of the youth with his ideas and an anarchistic group emerged in the town. Aydl's son Moshe began to attend Bundist gatherings and there he propagated anarchism.

Some time later, Moshe went to Argentina, but the anarchistic group in Biale continued its activity.

After Moshe, the son of Aydl departed for Argentina, an official came to Biale to lead the anarchistic group. If I am not mistaken, they called him Sashke. He was a young and handsome youth and did not give the impression of being a worker, but rather a student.

My brother was also active in this group. Using a hectograph (copying machine), he helped to copy various appeals and policy statements that the group released from time to time.

[Page 223]

The group attempted to draw into their net the Christian workers at Ra'abe's factory, who were under the influence of the PPS (Polish Socialist Party). On a certain day, I think, that both a Jewish and a Christian festival coincided, Sashke and I (Sashke was a frequent visitor in our house), went together to a gathering of Christian workers that took place in the home of a friend of theirs, who lived in the courtyard of Reb Aharon Landau.

In my conversations with Sashke, he would tell me that the anarchists were using terror tactics to acquire money for their movement. They would send demands to the rich and to wealthy firms, demanding specific sums, and if they did not receive the sums required, they would attack them with weapons, and even with bombs, and used violence to pressurize them into giving them the money.

Rumours actually began to circulate in the town about attacks that took place on the Lomaz Highway that has forests stretching on both sides. People used to say that armed young men, in need of money, came out of the forests and when people refused to give them money, they threatened to shoot them to death.

Once, a wagon–driver from Lomaz was attacked on the Lomaz Highway and when he refused to stop, they shot his horse dead.

At that time there was a strike at Motl Mintz's cigarette factory. Motl Mintz was a stubborn Jew and could not under any circumstances grow accustomed to the idea that these were different times, and that his attitude to the worker had to be more tolerant. This time the workers handed over the strike to the anarchists. One evening they treated Motl Mintz's factory to a small bomb, that tore away an entire wall. Only now, Motl Mintz understood with whom he was dealing.

Once, Purim time, at dusk on the sabbath, when the crowd went for a walk on the "broad sidewalk", a terrible explosion suddenly resounded over the town. Within a few minutes, the street was emptied. The crowd dispersed in shock and returned home. When the tumult was over, it was discovered that a bomb had exploded in Yoske Kashtenboim's courtyard. The explosion was so strong that all the window panes in that area fell out.

At the time of the activity of the anarchistic group in Biale, there were incidents where their members were arrested, but the arrest of a member of theirs, Binyamin Prikashtshik (a nickname), ended most tragically.

Binyamin was the son of a poor shoemaker who lived on the Volye, named Berel, whose nickname was Bonde. The young man had worked for many years as an employee in the factory of Motl Mintz, and there he earned the nickname Prikashtshik (a clerk).

Due to the fact that an informer had denounced him, Binyamin was arrested and transferred to the Warsaw Citadel, where he died in 1907.

Additional details:

The leadership of the Biale anarchists were: Masha Rubinshtein (Aryeh Mabatshnik's daughter), Froyem Fridman (Shmuel Shammai Zimmel's son), Leib Rubinshtein (nickname "Lopetik" – a shovel), Moshele Chaikels. The latter two were arrested in Biale and sent to a penal colony.

The bomb in Chaim Yoske Kashtenboim's house was the result of a conflict between Chaim Yoske and a shopkeeper, whom he wanted to evict from a shop in his house. The anarchists came to Chaim Yoske to say that he should not evict him from the shop, but instead of negotiating with them, Chaim Yoske called the police. The anarchists fled and then came the bomb.

Yonah Shteinman (New York)

[Page 224]

The Cultural Life

General Overview

by M. Y. Feigenboim

Translated by Libby Raichman

We had noticed earlier, that until the beginning of this century, almost no sign of cultural activity was evident in our town. The Enlightenment movement that blossomed in Brisk barely 40 kilometers from Biale, did not even find the slightest resonance in town. The Rabbinic order and the Chassidic movement that were strongly rooted in the town determined the essential tone of Jewish life, that was based on strong religious traditions. Every deviation from accepted lifestyles was truly considered as heresy and in the struggle against it, every method was kosher.

Yet, notwithstanding the rigid religious regime, there were a few attempts at enlightenment in those days.

Until the First World War

In 1884, there was turmoil in the town concerning Christian images that might be discovered in the house of prayer. What it amounted to was a matter regarding a small Hebrew arithmetic book, "Tsofnat Pa'anach" (meaning "revealer of secrets"), that was found in the possession of one of the religious young men who studied in the House of Prayer. In the conventional signs in this book, real Christian images were seen…

In the years 1890 to 1893, a group of young people organized a library. At a gathering in the Lamoz forest, they collected amongst themselves 10 to 15 Ruble. With this money they bought Yiddish books from Warsaw – novels by Solomon Rabinovich (Shm"R), Bloshtein and others. Each member paid 3 – 5 koppikes a week, and after a while, when they had collected about 30 Ruble, they bought Hebrew books from Warsaw. The librarian was Avrom Urmacher. The Biale Rabbi came to know about the secret library and managed to remove the Hebrew books that he burned at his home. The Yiddish books were divided amongst the members, and in this way avoided the same fate.

At the end of the 19th century, a group of Zionists established a "Young Men's Society" with the aim of studying Chumash (Pentateuch), Rashi, Shulchan Aruch, and also secretly promoting Zionistic ideas. The group would gather in the private school of A. Urmacher. Young tradesmen who were religiously inclined belonged to this "Young Men's Society".

After the discovery of the previously mentioned secret library, the group moved out of Urmacher's school on the orders of the Rabbi, and moved into a unit on Proste Street, but the Zionists continued to be in contact with them. On Purim, when the young men of the group were reading the Megillah, the two Zionists, Asher Hoffer and Mendl Pizshitz, brought to the attention of the congregation that it was not appropriate in a holy place, to bang with sticks and bars at the mention of Haman's name. And they actually did not bang. This incident was referred to the Rabbi, and he ordered the young men not to have any dealings with the "Young Men's Society".

In the years 1890 to 1893 in Biale there also existed a secret circle of young men that studied Hebrew and Russian. This group also arranged to receive books from Mezritsh. In the publication "Podlassier Life" number 19, of 19th May 1934, it says: "the book "Ahavat Tzion" (Lovers of Zion) by Avraham Mapu, that played a pioneering role in the Enlightenment movement in Russia, was lost on its way from Mezritsh to Biale. The book is passed from hand to hand and is read in secret places. Finally, one young man was "caught" in the act, with the forbidden book in his hand.

The "catcher", a zealous Chassid, became so excited with his discovery that he ran out into the street with the book and began to rant wildly: "Help! It's burning!" "The Jewish faith is in danger and the fire must be extinguished!".

[Page 225]

In that period, one must include the activity of a society named "Anti–fanaticism". From the name itself, it is already clear what the aim of this society was. All we know about the activity of this society is that it published 3 editions of a newspaper named "Anti–fanaticism", written by hand.

Time, however, does what it wants. Even in the darkness of the Biale "ghetto", signs of the rise of culture in Jewish life began to penetrate. The religious circle continued their stubborn resistance, but the assailants became stronger and stronger.

Without doubt, the high school students who came from Russia to study in the Biale government high school (gymnasium), played a great part in the rise of culture amongst the Jewish population in Biale. They made contact with the Jewish youth and influenced them to engage in worldly education. The Biale fanatics were powerless against these students because they could not throw the parents out of the Chassidic small prayer houses. The Biale religious Jews regarded the students at the high school as "half Jews".

The decline of the Biale rabbinate after the death of Reb Yitzchak Rabinovicz was an important reason for the weakening of the authority of the religious circle in the town.

The first school in the town was founded by Avrom Urmacher in the previous century. The school was situated in Yatke Street. Later, other schools were established by: Yakov Shteinman, Gedaliah Kravyetz, (who was called the Mezritsh teacher), Michael Fireman, Volf Nuchovitsh, Avrom Yakov Krideshtein and Avrom Kramarzsh.

When we mention here the word 'schools', it should not be understood in the literal sense of the word. These were not schools at all, even for those times. All these schools were arranged in a very primitive way, were situated in only one room already equipped with school furniture, and mostly in the home of the teacher. Not one of the listed teachers had any teaching qualifications and they were all self–taught. The schools used to have approximately 30 students, girls and boys, who came separately and studied separately. They studied a little Yiddish, Russian and arithmetic. Yakov Shteinman was the only teacher who also taught Hebrew and Bible. His school bore the popular name at that time, "Modernised Religious School".

As mentioned, the girls and boys studied separately, because no teacher would then have risked teaching boys and girls together. The boys were recruited from traditional religious schools, who were already studying with Gemarra teachers and whose parents wanted them to be able to write. These boys only came to the so–called school for a short time, an hour or two, when they were free from their religious schools. Their instruction was unusual, and the teacher used to sit and wait for his students. The reward was also minimal.

The teachers who established schools also gave lectures in the wealthier homes. At the same time, they had a number of rivals in the town. These were the so–called "writers", who used to come to people's houses and teach the residents to write a letter in Yiddish with a gentile address. Some teachers from religious schools also took eagerly to this work and taught people to write letters using a handbook of sample letters.

Of the teachers who gave lectures in people's homes, one named Sholem Ratshin, the son–in–law of a Biale resident, was particularly outstanding. This Sholem Ratshin, who was an active Zionist, was already giving lectures in Hebrew.

In the religious schools of the Gemarra teachers, teachers used to come in and teach the students to write. Some teachers were Christian and amongst them was the teacher Baranovsky, who was particularly well–known.

Before the First World war, a few Biale Jewish children were studying in the local high school, and in the so–called Government boarding school for girls.

At that time, Dr. G. Zita and his wife Bieyelinke, a dentist, and Advocate Kalman Hartglas organized evening courses for the Biale Jewish youth where, among other subjects, they also learned the Polish language.

The attempt to establish libraries was partially successful, but Yiddish literature was then still too poor, and books in other languages were read very little by the Jewish youth.

A group of young people organized a secret library in the home of the teacher Yakov Shteinman. Over time a space was also created there for readings by the Jewish high school students who studied in the local gymnasium.

A second illegal library was established by the "Bund", that also had revolutionary literature.

Before the outbreak of the First World War, private libraries existed at the shops that sold textbooks such as: Avrom Urmacher, and Munish Zaltzman. For a certain fee, one could borrow books to read.

[Page 226]

The first distributors of newspapers in the town were Binyamin Kavve and his wife Chavah. They used to receive the newspaper "Frined" ("Friends") from Petersburg and "Hatzfirah" (one of the first Hebrew newspapers) from Warsaw and distributed these newspapers to their subscribers. Later, they were already operating from the street, next to Chaim Yaske Kashtenvoim's house, and sold items from the Warsaw Yiddish press like: "Hinte" ("Today"), "Moment", and various Jewish periodicals and newspapers in other languages.

We also know about the theatre activity of the Biale youth, in the time preceding the First World War. Amongst others, a performance of Y. Gordon's "Hashe the Orphan" was presented that made a lasting impression on the visitors. It is interesting to note, that the religious circle did not react to this.

From time to time, wandering Jewish troupes would find their way into Biale and give performances in Chaim Yoske's hall. We also know about an impressive Sholem Aleichem evening that took place in Biale, whose proceeds were intended to buy up Sholem Aleichem's work from the publishers. Such a campaign was organized throughout Poland at that time and it appears that our town also contributed its share to this undertaking. Noach Prilutzky came from Warsaw for this evening.

The "Bund" and the Zionists used to organize public readings on literary and cultural themes, and also distribute various brochures amongst the population.

During the First World War

The flare-up in the cultural realm, however, came during the years of the First World War, under the German occupation. Precisely then, when the Biale population was suffering from hunger, need and cold, precisely in those war–time years, the Biale youth craved education and knowledge, with the intensity of those who thirst for water.

In the first place, the Zionist group advanced in their daring feat to organize a Hebrew school. It founded the Hebrew school "Yavne", that had numerous male and female students between its walls. For the first time in the history of Jewish Biale, the town had a school of which it could truly be proud.

The dramatic group that participated in the Sholem Aleichem evening, with the participation of Noach Prilutzky (Warsaw)

Sitting from right: Yoel Itzl Shneider, Shayne Perl Aidelshtein, Yakov Aharon Rozenboim, Dasye Felznshtein Standing: Name unknown, Itshe Sherman (Itshe Genzeles), Chaye Rozenboim and Fyvel (surname unknown)

[Page 227]

During the war years, a girls' school started, run by Perl Shuvak (Moshe Tocker's daughter), and Perl Fishman (Shlayme Fishman's daughter). This school that was housed in the home of Rottenberg, on Reformatzke Street, had a high level of education. There, the language of instruction was Polish. In the first years after the First World War, the school was closed.

The activities of the Parties brought fruitful results. The Zionist Party founded the "Bet–Am", in premises that housed a library, a reading hall, a dramatic circle and Maccabi with its orchestra. From time to time, various productions took place in "Bet–Am" such as: theatre productions, concerts, touring events by Maccabi, and a variety of lectures.

The "Bund" legalized its small library with the occupying regime and established a drama circle. In 1915, a few members of the "Bund" founded a literary–dramatic society. The military non–orthodox Rabbi at that time, Dr. Tenser, also helped with the legalization of this society with the German regime, and thanks to his efforts, the society received a 2–storey locale on Garntsarske Street, as well as a piano and furniture.

This society was of a non–political nature and was occupied solely with cultural activities. The musician Shimon Blanklider (the fat one) organized a choir, and a dramatic circle emerged under the direction of Gedalyahu Braverman. Various lectures and artistic evenings would often take place in the premises of the society.

With time, a buffet was organized in these premises, where the visitors could purchase sugared tea with bread, for low prices. In those bitter war years, when hunger was a frequent visitor in Jewish homes, the possibility of receiving a glass of sweet tea and bread at a minimal price was a great achievement.

The society was managed by a committee consisting of: Fulle (Refael) Lederman, Gedalyahu Braverman, Mordechai Hochman, Shimon Blanklider (the fat one), Moshe Rodzinek, Tzalke Voksin (a refugee from Brisk and others

Quite often, performances of the dramatic circles and the mandolin orchestra took place in the town, in the hall of Chaim Yoske Kashtenboim, and Kyavske, and in the seminar where the Germans procured a small theatre hall.

The Jewish Social circle received great support for their cultural activities from the Jewish military personnel in the German army.

At the end of the war, the party "Po'alei Tzion" (Workers for Zion) emerged and there too, a library was established.

In this way, during the entire period of occupation in the town, a vibrant cultural activity existed, in the most difficult economic circumstances.

In the Renewed Poland

With the rise of the Polish regime in 1918, changes came about in the cultural life of the town.

Firstly, the town lost its "Yavne" school and was never again privileged to have a Jewish school.

It is difficult to find someone from Biale who would be able to clarify how and why, suddenly, overnight, the "Yavne" school was converted to a "Folk–School". Although the teachers were then still the same, yet, the standard of education dropped. Hebrew continued to be the language of instruction, but some subjects were already being taught in Polish. The school continued to remain under the influence of the Zionist organization but constantly struggled for its survival, until 1923, when it closed completely.

At the time when the "Yavneh" school was suddenly converted to a "Folk–School", a private school arose in the town, under the direction of Nachman Shivak, that advanced successfully. The school, however, could not withstand the competition from the free state Folk–Schools, and after a few years, it closed.

After the liquidation of these schools, attempts were made to establish new schools, but these remained unsuccessful. Attempts to create a school were made both by the Zionists and by those in the Yiddish circles, who were advocates for the Yiddish language. Even "Tarbut" schools were active – and the "Jewish Schools Organization", but these were only intermediary and after a short time, ceased to exist.

At that time, Jewish children filled the state schools. The two state high schools in the town were no longer boycotted by the Jews, as they once were in Tsarist times; however now, on the contrary, the administrators of the high schools restricted access to Jews, citing a shortage of places.

In the premises of the liquidated Folk–School, a state school was established for Jewish girls, who were freed from studying on the Sabbath; but with time the school ceased to exist, and the Jewish girls of this school were transferred to another school where they had to attend the school on the Sabbath, just as the rest of the Jewish children did in all the state schools. In the beginning the frequenting of the schools on the Sabbath by the Jewish children evoked a reaction from the religious parents, but later, in hindsight, no protest was noticeable, even in very religious circles.

[Page 228]

A few years before the outbreak of the Second World War, the Agudah Circle founded a "Bet Yakov" school whose activity continued until the war. The school was housed in a room in Tille's home, at the market–place.

It should be mentioned that the teacher Luba Vinetroib-Tuchshneiderran a pre–school, almost without interruption, that was even active during the Second World War.

From time to time, a private school run by Volf Nuchovicz, was active.

A flower sale on behalf of the Jewish School Organisation Division, in Biale. 25. 4. 1927

In the first years after the rise of the Polish state, the sisters Varshavsky, teachers from Warsaw, were involved particularly with preparing male and female students in the town for the examinations in the two state high schools.

In the town a few years before the war there was a man named Aronsky from Volin who was active as a Hebrew teacher and successful in his work.

Students of the Hebrew evening school under the leadership of M. M. Gelenberg

[Page 229]

Evening courses were frequently organized where, for a minimal payment, young people learned Hebrew. The first courses that offered other subjects besides Hebrew were organized by Hashomer Ha'tza'ir. Later Hashomer Ha'tza'ir established evening classes for Hebrew only, that was taught in the Folk School by the teacher M. M. Gelenberg. When the courses organized by Hashomer Ha'tza'ir ceased to exist, the teacher Gelenberg suggested offering the courses himself, at first in the home of Golda Vineberg (Alter Vineberg's wife) and later in the house of the Friedmans, on Kshivver Street. Gelenberg managed to attract several learners in the town. Hebrew courses were later managed by Moshe Smoliar and the aforementioned teacher, Aronsky.

M. M. Gelenberg was one of the initiators and founders of the Esperanto courses in the town, that were implemented by A. Urmacher.

When the war broke out in 1939, there were 2 libraries in the town: one at the "Tarbut" organization and one at the "Culture League". Both were completely destroyed during the Nazi rule.

The dramatic circles displayed an intensive activity, often performing the works of Y. Gordon, Peretz Hirshbine, Sholem Aleichem, Mendele Mocher Sforim and others. The dramatic circle that grouped around "Bet Am" was directed by Motl (Mordechai) Pyekarsky. The other dramatic circles were mostly led by the director Gedalyahu Braverman.

Thanks to M. M. Gelenberg's initiative, a dramatic circle was formed, named Y. L. Peretz, that presented Molier's "The Miser" on stage, under the direction of Berel Manperl from Mezritsh.

From time to time artistic troupes from Warsaw and individual artists would visit the town, and appear on stage with their own programs, such as poetic recitalists, singers and humourists.

The Blanklider musical family, with their artistic activity, enriched Jewish cultural life in Biale and earned well. They brought a musical atmosphere to every cultural presentation, wherever it was necessary. A part of this family was involved as organizers and conductors of orchestras and choirs, and Shimon Blanklider excelled particularly (he was called "the thin one", to differentiate between the second Shimon who was fat). This Shimon Blanklider displayed great organizational talent and, as such, he was the founder and director of the Maccabi orchestra. He organized many choirs and mandolin orchestras in the town, with which he would often give concerts. If a gymnastic teacher was needed at the "Yavne" school, Shimon Blanklider was called, and he was trusted with the position in which he excelled greatly. The Blankliders also gave private music lessons. It is worth noting that in those times, when antisemitism was at its worst, the Christian community had to approach the Blankliders if they wanted to enjoy good music.

Almost until 1930, Maccabi was very active in the realm of sport, and also possessed a fine wind–orchestra. The general apathy and resignation that descended upon the Jewish population of Biale also brought about the downfall of Maccabi. The "Bund" also had a sport club for a certain time, called "Morgenshtern" (Morning Star).

At the beginning of the 1920s, attempts were made to release a weekly newspaper, but they were not successful. Only a few numbers of the "Biale Echo" were published that were distributed by the Zionist organization in Biale. This was a strong militant newspaper against the Biale clergy, with the Rabbi at its head. In the same year, a literary edition was also published under the editorship of the teacher M. Gelenberg.

In 1926, the weekly newspaper "Podlassier Life" began to be published. It was edited by M.M. Gelenberg, thanks to whose efforts the newspaper developed and was published for a few years.

From 1932, the following weekly newspapers were published with breaks: "Podlassier Life", an independent social weekly; "Biale Weekly", a national social weekly for Biale and the surrounding areas; "Podlassier Voice", an independent social periodical. From a number of copies that we managed to receive, it is evident that in the year 1938, the "Biale Weekly" was still being published in the town under the editorship of Chaim M'yodek.

Gelenberg was also the founder of a literary circle that used to organize literary judgements and brought noted lecturers from Warsaw, almost every sabbath.

The Jewish Citizen Club ("Club Avivatelsky"), that could be found in the home of the dentist Yoel Zilberberg, would arrange lectures/readings, mostly in the Polish language.

[Page 230]

When war broke out, there were three Jewish newspaper kiosks: Chavah Kavve (at the end of Volnoshtshi Place, at the entrance to Yaneve Street); Chaim Kavve (in Volnoshtshi Place, near Chaim Yoske's house) and Ahron Riebak (the end of Volnoshtshi Place at the porter's intersection).

At the end of this overview, the Biale teachers and so–called "writers" should be mentioned, who made the effort to bring knowledge and culture to the Jewish population in the last 70 – 80 years of Jewish life in Biale. The list is almost comprehensive.

Asher Avrom Kodnyers
Yishayahu Eliezer (Shya Leizer, not Muzshinek, the writer of petitions).
Meir Dovid Goldberg (writer from Brisk)
Sholem Ratshin.
Nechama Shriber (a nickname).
Dos Cozzakl (a nickname).
Avrom Yakov Krideshtein.
Elchanan (sent out from Kovno– Lithuania).
Avrom Urmacher.
Yakov Shteinman.
Michael Fireman (North America).
Gedalyahu Kravyetz
Volf Nuchovitsh.
Moshe Kramarzsh.
Yonah Shteinman (North America).

Shlomo Izenberg.
Matityahu Kligsberg (Israel).
Avrom Gvirtzman.
Chaim Barlas (Israel).
Yitzchak Leib Mizel.
Rozshe Varshavsky-Lebenberg
Chayah Shein.
Kanalboim (student from Warsaw).
Nachman Shivak.
Tuvia Binshtok (North America)
Rafael Myerzon (Belgium).
Luba Vinetroib-Tuchshnider.
Mordechai Goldberg.
Feldman (daughter of the upholsterer).
Shimon Blanklider (the thin one).
Yishayahu Idl Lemberger.
Menachem M. Gelenberg.
Yakov Nordman (Israel).
Yitzchak Lerer (Israel).
Moshe Smoliar (Israel).
Aronsky.
Renya Goldshtein-Suknov (Australia).
Golinsky.

Sources:

1. "Podlassier Life", independent social weekly newspaper, Biale (copies from the years 1926/7 and 1932/4).
2. Evidence taken from: Alter Vineberg, Asher Hoffer, Moshe Rubinshtein and Gedalyahu Braverman.

The "Yavne" School

by M. Raboun/Tel Aviv

Translated by Marc Zell

The first modern, national Hebrew school in Biala known as the "Yavne" Hebrew School was established around Passover time in 1916 during the German occupation in the First World War.

The organizers and founders of the school were Moshe Rubenstein, Yehoshua Fisher and Yaakov Steinman. The physician, Dr. A. Meller from Altona outside of Hamburg (Germany), assisted in realizing the idea for the school. He was a Zionist who found himself at that time in Biala as a German military doctor.

The founders of the school had thought for years about establishing a Hebrew–language school in the town. But the idea could not be realized because the Czarist authorities refused to grant permission to open such a school. Besides, the organizers were doubtful whether the school would have any pupils, because they did not believe that the religious groups in town would tolerate the existence of a modern school.

During the early days of the German occupation these same persons wanted to commence public Zionist activity in town by organizing evening classes in Hebrew. As they first set about realizing their plan they changed direction and decided instead to create a modern, nationalistic, co–educational Hebrew–language school.

[Page 231]

Governing Board of the Yavneh School

From right: Yakov Steinman, Yehoshua Fisher, Hanna Miriam Mintz, Moshe Rubenstein and Yonah Steinman

In order to ensure that they would have enough students, just before the school was to open, the organizers were inspired to create a children's home to prepare the vanguard class of pupils for the school.

The requisite permission to open the school was obtained from the German occupation authorities by Mrs. Hanna Miriam Mintz with the help of the Military Rabbi Dr. Tenzer.

The school was located in an annex off the courtyard of Chaim Levy Rubenstein's house and later at the end of its existence in the home of Motel from Weiness [?] on Grabanower Street.

At first only two classes were opened but shortly afterwards there were four classes in operation.

The board of trustees for the school consisted of: Mrs. Hanna Miriam Mintz, Moshe Rubenstein, Yehoshua Fisher, Yaakov Steinman and Yonah Steinman.

The faculty comprised: Yaakov Steinman, Yonah Steinman, Shlomo Eisenberg, Shimon Blankleider, Yeshayahu Idel Lemberger, Abraham Gewirtzman (a refugee from Brest–Litovsk), Chaim Barlas (refugee from Brest–Litovsk), Yitzhak Leib Meisel (refugee from Pinsk), Matityahu Kligsberg. Later the following teachers joined: Michael Feierman, Wolf Nuchowicz, Gedalyahu Krawiec, Moshe Kramarz, the Warszawski sisters (from Warsaw) and the female college student Kanalbojm (from Warsaw).

The following subjects were taught in the school: languages Hebrew (language of instruction), German and Polish; arithmetic, history, Bible, geography and natural science, singing, drawing, handcrafts and physical education. After the lectures they would learn Chumash [five books of Moses] with Rashi. At the beginning of the school's operation Talmud was also studied. Early in the school day before classes began they would hold public prayers and after the school day – mincha. Characteristically, the girl pupils who were exempt from prayers did not want to be excluded from the class and used to spend the whole time praying, not out of piety, but more because they did not want to be seen to agree to and recognize that there were any differences between them and the boys.

The school was not part of any school district and operated independently. The curriculum was developed at the school itself using its own staff.

Textbooks, school supplies and books for the school library were brought in from Warsaw. Later on books were ordered from Germany.

Studies were conducted at a very high level and were quite intensive. The pupils made good progress in their studies, especially in Hebrew. The pupils were well developed in social skills. The Rabbi Dr. Sh. Pozanski wanted to accept several of the Yavneh pupils into his teachers' seminar in Warsaw even without examination (as related by Chaim Rozmarin). Those pupils who had decided to continue their education in the municipal public high school (gymnasium) had no difficulty passing the entrance examinations. They proved to be more advanced in general studies than their Christian classmates.

Governing body and Teachers of the Yavneh School

From right: Abraham Gewirtzman, Yakov Steinman, Yeshaya Idel Lemberger, Moshe Rubenstein, Shlomo Eisenberg, Hanna Miriam Mintz, Yehoshua Fisher, Yonah Steinman, and Shimon Blankleider

At the founding of the school there were approximately 100 pupils within its walls, which later grew to about 200 pupils. Sadly, due to the lack of space, more pupils could not be accepted.

Most of the students paid tuition and only a small percentage was exempt from paying.

[Page 232]

Pupils and Teachers of the Yavneh School

The school's budget was covered principally by tuition. There was also income from different events such as artists' night, flower sales. Wood for heating the school in wintertime was usually obtained from the German Civil Administration. When the Polish state was established, they used to get a subsidy from the Joint.

In its early days the school did not have paid administrative personnel, except for the custodian, Yosef, a refugee from Brest–Litovsk.

The town's Jewish community had a positive and respectful relationship with the school. Even in the religious community there was no tension or persecution. The school had among its students a significant number from religious homes.

The school used to put on traditional Hanukkah and Purim events, various types of other events, Lag B'Omer and Tu B'Av outings, etc. These events used to take place far from away from the school area and were transformed into grandiose productions of the Zionist movement for the national idea. These events used make a strong impression on the population for a long time.

The annual memorial for the Zionist leader, Dr. T. Herzl, was a major new development in town. The event took place in the Yavneh School.

Pupils and Teachers of the Public School ("Volkschul")

[Page 233]

This memorial with its ceremonial presentation was particularly etched in the pupils' memories. A giant portrait of Herzl (painted by the artist Yeshaya Idel Lemberger) in a black frame was hung on the wall illuminated by two kindled candles. The evening used to begin with the prayer "El Maleh Rachamim" chanted by Pintche Liebman accompanied by the school choir. This was followed by lectures on the life and work of the founder of the Zionist Organization. Many members and supporters of the town's Zionist Organization also used to attend the memorial evening.

Relations between teachers and pupils were very warm and full of respect from the pupils towards their educators. Near the end of its existence a female teacher, a college student and a Bundist from Warsaw arrived at the school. She tried to influence some of the students in the upper class against Bible studies. Following an intimate discussion by the principal with the students, the lady was completely discharged.

When the Polish State was established, there was confusion among some of the teachers, the level of learning had fallen, aggravating the financial situation of the school. It is impossible for me to remember the circumstances under which the name "Yavneh" for the school disappeared and it started to be called the "Volkschul" [LMZ: "Public School"].

Nachman Sziwak's Private Elementary School

Translated by Libby Raichman

The school was founded in 1919 by Nachman Sziwak, who came from a village near Mezritch. At first the school was located in the home of Yeshayahu Reizwasser, the tailor, on the first floor on Prosta Street. There was only a single class in which some 10 pupils between the ages of 10 to 14 learned. The educational level of the pupils was not the same for all. Nachman Sziwak was the sole teacher and used to study the following subjects with the pupils: Hebrew, Yiddish, Polish, and arithmetic. There were no school facilities to speak of.

Sometime later the school was transferred to the home of Alte Cohen on Prosta Street. There three classes were set up.

The following teachers were active in the school: Nachman Sziwak (Polish and arithmetic); Tuvia Binstock (Hebrew); Falic Meyerson (Yiddish and geography); Mordechai Goldberg (Bible); Lyube Weintraub (Polish and arithmetic in the lower grades).

The school was privately owned and was maintained by student tuition (about 100 students) and was well liked in the town.

The school was shut down after several years of operation, because the students went to study at the mandatory government–run school.

Pupils and Teachers of Nachman Sziwak's Private School

The Teachers sitting from right: Tuvia Binstock, Nachman Sziwak, Lyube Weintraub-Tuchshneider, Falic Meyerson and Mordechai Goldberg

[Page 234]

Evening Courses to learn Polish

by Gedalyahu Braverman

Translated by Libby Raichman

It was in the years 1905/6 when, under pressure from the revolutionary movement, the Tsarist regime softened its treatment towards the Polish population a little and ceased to persecute the people for learning the Polish language.

As is known, in revolutionary circles at that time, a slogan was served to the intelligentsia of all nations that inhabited Russian territory, that they should go out to the people, engage with their problems and initiate the provision of elementary education.

The strata of Jewish intelligentsia that Biala possessed at that time consisted of a small number of assimilated Jews. They decided to take up the call and established evening courses for the Jewish youth. The assimilated, however, remained true to the cause and instead of conducting the courses in the Yiddish language, the language of the masses, they taught the Jewish youth Polish. The initiators and founders of these courses were: Dr. Gershon Zitta and his wife Byelinke, a dentist, Advocate Hartglas (the father), the manufacturer Ra'abe etc.

Most of the students consisted of Bundist youth who endeavored to convert the purpose of the courses to a meeting place where they could continue to spin the thread of Bundist activity that was interrupted by the failure of the revolution. The Bundist students enrolled to learn with the teacher Goldman, an employee at Ra'abe's factory, and an active Bundist leader.

At Goldman's lectures they were involved in political conversations and discussions. For appearance's sake, their books lay open, in case of a visit by the organisers of the courses.

The young, lovely Miss Yanka Hartglas was also a teacher of the courses (daughter of Advocate Kalman Hartglas and sister of the former representative to the Polish parliament, Advocate Apolinari Hartglas). For them, this was perhaps their first contact with the local Jewish population.

Engraved in my memory is a very good impression of her attitude towards the working youth. She never gave her students the feeling that with her education she was superior to them. She was vivacious and cheerful; by her crossing the threshold of learning, the experience became a lively and joyful one.

She approached the courses in a very serious manner, and she very much wanted us to enjoy the classes as much as possible. If she was at times unable to attend a lecture, she would inform us in advance, and would send her younger brother as a substitute. Miss Hartglas would have conversations with us about natural science and tried very hard to influence us to further our education.

The courses continued for two years.

An Attempt at Culture

by M. Rabon

Translated by Libby Raichman

It must have been in the years 1908 – 1910 that a group of so–called 'children from established homes', got together and founded a small culture group. These young boys already knew a little Russian and secular studies, that they learned from private teachers, from students at high school and from the Russian high school In the town.

Their meeting place was in the home of the Hebrew teacher Ya'akov Shteinman, who lived in the annex of the house of Binyamin Leibele Mandelboim on Brisk Street. There they rented half a room that was separated by a screen, behind which was a small library, mainly with Russian books. The members would meet in this room almost every evening.

The library housed about 200 books – some of these were given by the members and some comprised supplements to the Russian newspaper "Ruskaya Slava" in Moscow, to which the group subscribed. The members paid a monthly contribution.

Their activities had to be conducted in secret, to avoid the eyes of the Russian police and also to avoid the neighbours, from whom the parents could find out about their meetings. For this reason, they worked out various routines to which the members had to adhere when going to their meeting place, as well as internal rules. They met only at night so that they could come unnoticed.

[Page 235]

The group consisted of quite a small number of members. Most of the boys were between 16 and 18 years of age and also a few girls from Chassidic homes. Among others, the following were members of the group: Leibl Goldshtein, Yisroel Cohen, Dovid Lustigman, Channah Feige Mintz, Berel Ernkrantz, Manye Kashtenboim, Moshe Rubinshtein and Hinde Shachor.

The situation was more dangerous for the girls than for the boys, because imagine what would have awaited them at home if their parents found out about their meeting with boys, and also with high school students, who were certainly gentiles.

After a short time, a few Jewish high school students were drawn into the group who used to read classic Russian works aloud. Every evening one of the high school students would read the work of a specific Russian writer. Among these students, there was one named Kattelyansky,[1] a year 8 student who had a particular leaning towards humorous writers. He would lecture twice a week; one evening he would read the works of the Russian writer Gogal, and in the second – the work of Sholem Aleichem. Some of the other high school readers were: Issak Tiyamkin, Yuzshek Hartglas and Kantarovicz.

Footnote:

1. He was a medical doctor in New York. He later gave up his medical practice and became a singer of Jewish folk music, of which he published a collection.

The "Tarbut" Library

by M.Y. Feigenboim

Translated by Libby Raichman

The "Tarbut" library was one of the finest Zionist cultural institutions in the town. Despite all the discord that existed in the Zionist camp, in this institution the gatherings were harmonious and collaborative.

To understand the origins of this library, one must return to those years when all the Zionist activity in the town was concentrated in "Bet–Am". Already then, when "Bet–Am" was situated in Sadover Street, the library possessed a significant number of books and began to distribute them for reading. Reizl Belman and Isaac Shein were the librarians. The Zionist movement "Hashomer Hatza'ir" also had a library, an initiative of Chaim Rozmarin, that was established with a small number of books from the earlier youth organization "Parchei–Tzion".

The library grew in size, and besides Yiddish books, it also possessed books in Hebrew and Polish. After removing the Zionist organization from its location on Sadovver Street, and the Hashomer Hatza'ir from the building of the former Folk–School on Mezritsh Street, the two libraries encountered difficulties in their activities.

Flower sellers for the benefit of the "Tarbut" library

In the first row, standing from right: Yurberg (sister of Tsirrel), Mordechai Lashtshevski, Tsirrel Yurberg, Shor, Asher Rozentzveig, Maya Batshko, Esther Zinger, Sholem Gliksberg, Chaye Rozentzveig
In the 2ⁿᵈ row seated from right: Chaim Rozmarin, Rayzl Belman, Chayele Fishman, Yosef Feldrib, Yisroel Goldshtein, Yitzchak (Isaac) Shein, Yonah Shein, Toybele Rubinshtein, Yocheved Biederman
In the 3ʳᵈ row seated from right: Avraham Zinger, Tsharni (Hershel Shachor's daughter), Meilech Rozmarin, Blumme Zilberzon, Beile Milboim, Leibl Bialar, Moshe Orlanski
In front: Kanakshrein, Yerucham Lipyetz, Dintshe Cohen

[Page 236]

Then the idea arose of merging the two libraries, an idea that was actually accomplished. The library that was called the "Tarbut Library" was run by representatives of the General Zionists and Hashomer Hatza'ir.

Thanks to the determined efforts of the chairman of the "Tarbut" organization, Yaakov Aharon Rozenboim, they managed to find premises in the communal house of Tille Berlin on Valnoshtshi Square. Now the activities of the institution actually proceeded normally and very intensively.

For some time, the library was managed by Yosef Feldrib who, with his devotion and his energetic activity, increased the number of books considerably.

Aside from the fee charged to the readers and various undertakings, other sources of income were: theatre presentations, lectures, flower selling and subsidies from the community and from the town council.

When the libraries were combined, it was decided that it would house books in three languages. It continued in this way until the end. In order to differentiate between the different language books, the Yiddish books were bound in green covers, the Hebrew books in blue, and the Polish books in black.

The librarians who were active there were, among others: Mulye Urbacher, Yehoshua Kligger, Itke Rubinshtein, Asher Rozentzveig, Asher Greenblat and Sheindl Grodner.

In 1933 there were 2385 books in the library. Of them: 1170 were Yiddish books, 405 Hebrew books and 810 Polish books. The number of readers amounted to 200 (according to "Podlassier Life" number 18, of the 12th May 1933).

During the war, when the premises of the Library initially housed refugees, the "Tarbut" chairman, Yaakov Aharon Rozenboim, moved the books to the premises of the Judenrat on Brisk Street, and he took care of them so that the book–treasure would not be pillaged.

After the liberation of Biala from German occupation in 1944, the few Jews who remained alive returned to the town and found no trace of the "Tarbut" library. The Christian merchants would wrap their merchandise in pages of the Exodus from Yiddish religious books and other books that had been in the library.

The Bundist Library

by Gedalyahu Braverman

Translated by Libby Raichman

The "Bund" had a tradition of organizing gatherings on the fast day of Tishah B'Av [9th Av], when people did not work. At one of these gatherings in 1905, Eliyahu Shimshelles (Yustman) proposed the establishment of a library. His proposal came primarily to maintain the existence of the Bundist movement in the town, as there was then a crisis due to the decline of the revolutionary movement in Russia.

From the fees of the members and from the money that was collected, a few books were purchased, written by the following authors – Mendele Mocher Sforim, Sholem Aleichem, Y. L. Peretz and Sholem Ash.

The books were legal but utilizing the books to establish a legal public library was prohibited in Tsarist Russia; so the books were exchanged among the readers in an illegal manner.

A while later, when various active members dispersed, the books were moved to Eliyahu Klotz and to me. We became the actual managers of the wandering library. To this work we attracted the following members: Shimon Blankleider, Moshe Binyomin Tsharni, Yoel Fingerhut, Betzalel Birnboim and others.

As its first task, the group set out to increase the number of books. In order to procure proper funding, we relied upon their original existence.

At that time, a cinema already existed in Biala, in the home of Chaim Kashtenboim, that was called "Illuzion". From time to time we would rent the premises from the proprietor of the cinema for an evening and then went out into the town selling tickets for the cinema show. This brought us certain profits and afforded us the possibility of buying new books. We would also organize lotteries for the purpose of buying books and utilize the festival of Purim, when donations were distributed, and our members would go around in disguise, collecting for the illegal library.

When we already had a larger number of books, we found an old Jewish lady who agreed, for a certain fee, to keep the books at her place, on condition that only the books would be kept there and that no one should come there, except for the members that she knew. It was further suggested that we carry the books under our clothes and in this way we exchanged the books among the readers.

In the last years before the First World War, when the political activities of the "Bund" almost ceased, a group gathered around the library, among them even those who had no connection to the managing group of the party, such as Yonah Shteinman, Refael Lederman and others. They saw the library as a cultural accomplishment.

[Page 237]

As the circle around the library grew, they managed to acquire a room in the home of a widow on Kshivver Street. The library began to be active according to our wishes. But it did not last long. Suddenly, the widow explained that a policeman had asked her about something that had a connection to our library. The books were removed from there and distributed among various members.

In this way, more or less, the work of the library continued until the First World War.

During the First World War the library was situated in the house of Mrs. Rivkah Eidelman on Proste Street and operated legally. The development of the library, however, was restrained because Biala was in a war region, cut off from Warsaw, and there was no possibility of our buying new books.

With the rise of the Polish regime in 1918, when the American Aid Society sent our members certain sums of money as an aid activity for Passover, part of this money was used to buy new books for the library.

The number of readers reached a few hundred and from time to time gatherings of the readers were organized, during which certain newly published books would be introduced, and readers were involved in taking care of the books.

When the "Bund" moved into the house of Motl of the winery, on Grabanovve Street, their library was also moved across. Unfortunately, it did not exist for very long. On a frosty winter's night, a fire broke out in the house and everything was lost in the fire.

A short time later, the professional unions began to gather the books belonging to the Bundist library that were spread among its readers. The library at the union was constantly being enlarged thanks to the income that flowed in from theatre performances and flower selling.

When the professional unions were taken over by the communists, the library also came under their authority.

At that time, the "Culture League" decided to establish the Bundist library again. An appeal was made to a friend, Fyvl Gold, in America, who was in constant contact with the Culture League, and who became active in America gathering books for the newly established Bundist library. Thanks to him, hundreds of books arrived in Biala from America.

Until then, the "Culture League" was located in a loft on Proste Street; then it was moved to Yanevve Street, to the home of Moshe Elye (Eliyahu) the metal–worker, where the new library was organized.

The library had approximately 300 readers. It possessed more than 1000 books and the monthly fee was 30 groshen (according to "Podlassier Life" number 7, of 16th February 1934). The member Moshe Shneiderman ran the library for a long time, and his place was later taken by the member Koralik.

During Nazi rule in Poland, Eliyahu Hoffman packed the books and stored them in the attic of his house. After the expulsion of the Jews from the town, the Christian population pillaged the books and destroyed them.

The Library of the Left Leaning Po'alei Tzion

by A. Labi

Translated by Libby Raichman

In approximately 1917, through the initiative of Yonah Shteinman and A. Solski, this library was established that was not political, even though it was under the management of the left leaning Po'alei Tzion. In the beginning the library was located in the premises of the "Youth" (a youth organization of Po'alei Tzion), in the house of Shmerl Hochman, on Grabanovve Street. Later the books were moved to A. Solski on the Brisk Highway.

The library had 400 Yiddish books, with about 150 readers borrowing them. The library was managed by Shayne Vineshtein, A. Solski and Menachem Finkelshtein. It was possible for the readers to exchange the books twice a week. The income from established flower selling and theatre performances meant that it was always possible to purchase new books.

During the Bolshevik invasion, in 1920, the work of the library was disrupted.

After the war, the library was re–established. It was located in the house of A. Solski, and for a certain time on Mezritsh Street in the house of the Tzinammons. The library was called "The Library at the Society of Evening Courses for Workers".

[Page 238]

In 1927, the number of books reached 1200 (according to "Podlassier Life" number 23 of 1927). The library possessed the latest publications of Yiddish literature. A. Solski, who managed the library, devoted his heart and soul to it. After his death, the library was liquidated, and the books were sent to the headquarters of Po'alei Tzion in Warsaw.

Maccabi

by Nachman Vineberg

Translated by Libby Raichman

Maccabi was established in Biala in 1916. These members of the Zionist organization – Moshe Rubinshtein and Mendel Kavve, called a gathering of a group of young people, explained the significance of Maccabi, and proposed the creation of such a sporting organization.

The following members formed the inaugural group: Avraham Lebenberg, Butshe Finkelshtein, Abush Lieberman, Bunim Rubinshtein, Yaakov Zeidman and the writer of these lines. We tackled the task of organizing this movement and managed to attract many young people to our ranks, both from among the students and from among the working youth. Yaakov Shteinman was a very enthusiastic member who brought members from the working youth; these were young people who could use a saw, a hammer etc. and on whom one could count, should there be a need to 'harden one's fists'.

Later a committee was elected that consisted of these members: Bunim Rubinshtein, Zalman Gottlieb, Fallik Mayerzon, Yaakov Zeidman and Goldshtein (Shepsel Goldshtein's son).

We began with physical exercises in Chaim Levi Rubinshtein's courtyard where the "Yavneh" school was then situated. The courtyard was not sufficiently suitable for exercising and we moved to the *blonye* and to the Yanevve highway.

We used to do gymnastics with various equipment, and swimming, boating etc. Our first instructor was a Christian man from the Volye (I cannot remember his name). When we set up our orchestra, he was also our bandleader. Afterwards, Shimon Blankleider (the thin one), became our instructor and bandleader.

After a time, the "Bet–Am" opened on Sadovve Street. Many older inactive members helped us with funding and in this way we could allow ourselves to purchase exercise equipment, establish a string–orchestra, a wind–orchestra, and engage a bandleader. Thanks to these older members we made contact with Jewish and non–Jewish soldiers in the German army and before the soldiers left the town, we were able to buy various orchestral instruments for a small sum.

The Maccabi Committee

From right: Yaakov Zeidman, Zalman Gottlieb, Bunim Rubinshtein, Fallik Mayerzon and Goldshtein

[Page 239]

The Maccabi Committee

When the Germans left Biala, there was chaos, shooting and plundering. A civilian militia was then created, in which the Maccabi members played a large part.

The Polish military units marched into Biala in 1918, and at the request of the Zionist organization, the Maccabi orchestra welcomed them; and though they were thanked very politely, yet, a day later, they were falsely accused of being fired at, from a window of a Jewish dwelling at the market place.

Sometime later, a Jewish soldier named Yankovicz arrived in Biala from Maccabi in Warsaw, who was trained in physical fitness. He taught us gymnastics on a variety of equipment – using the rings, the horse, the ladders etc. It did not take long before we excelled in all the disciplines. One Saturday, we organized a gymnastics evening at "Bet–Am". The audience were so inspired by our performance that they embraced and kissed many of us. For many weeks, people in the town spoke about our performance.

The Maccabi orchestra was at that time the only orchestra in the town and it would participate in all the events that were organized by the Zionist organization. It would also play during the intervals at theatre performances, at dance evenings and during Lag Ba'omer excursions.

The Maccabi orchestra in the forest on Lag Ba'omer

[Page 240]

We had very successful musical evenings and we even had invitations from Mezritsh to go there with our orchestra. The Christian population would also invite our orchestra to their events.

The following members played in the orchestra: Abush Lieberman, Asherl Feigenboim. Moshe Rabinovicz. Friedman (from Gan-Eden), Yitzchak Myoddek, Ruzal, Zshamme (his nickname), Leibl Lebenberg, Dovid Lieberman, Berish Rubinshtein, Froike Friedman, Eliezer Aydltuch, Leibl Hoffer, Nachman Vineberg, Aryeh Lomaz, and others.

The Maccabi members actively assisted the Zionist organization with its propaganda activity. They participated keenly during the first parliamentary elections and in many other Zionist political events.

Until my departure from Biala in 1920/21, Maccabi had approximately 30 active participants and many other members that used to support us financially. Its budget was covered by members' fees, from various contributions that we received, and from the income from the sport evenings and the orchestra.

The Maccabi soccer team

First row, standing from right: Berish Rubinshtein, Sanne Karshenboim, Moshe Rozenfeld, Yerucham Lipyetz,
Hinech Lebenberg, Mulye Urmacher, Asher Feigenboim
2ⁿᵈ row: Dovid Lemberger, Berel Feigenboim, Chaim Heshl Mallina
3ʳᵈ row: Asher Rozentzveig, Avraham Blushtein and Sholem Gliksberg

Additional details:[1]

In the 1920s, there was a managing committee at the head of Maccabi consisting of Dr. Yoel Zilberberg, Dr. Antony Gelbard, Berish Rubinshtein and Asherl Feigenboim.

A Maccabi football team was organized in which the following participated: Asher Rozentzveig, Yerucham Lipyetz, Hinech Lebenberg, Sanne Karshenboim, Moshe Rozenfeld, Dovid Lemberger, Mulye Urbacher, Sholem Gliksberg, Avraham Blushtein, Berel Feigenboim, Chaim Heshl Mallina, Yitzchak Rozenboim, Mendl Bendarzsh and others.

The number of members far exceeded 100. The sport sections were managed by the instructors Hoffer and Berish Rubinshtein. Countless tours and excursions were conducted.

The Maccabi organisation was attached to the Maccabi headquarters in Warsaw from whence instructors would come and conduct various courses in Biala. The Maccabi orchestra grew and perfected its musical standards.

Maccabi on the occasion of the emigration of its members Berish Rubinshtein and David Lemberger to the Land of Israel

[Page 241]

During its existence, the orchestra was directed by: Shimon Blankleider (the thin one), a Christian who was a worker at Ra'abe's factory, and Shentz and Gongalinski from the military orchestra that was stationed in the town.

The on–going emigration of the Biala youth, the burden of living prudently, and the difficult economic situation that cast an apathy on the Jewish population, were the cause of the decline of Maccabi in Biala. The orchestral instruments that were at first stored, in the hope of better times, were later sold. The archive was transferred to the authority of the Zionist organization, and one of the finest youth organisations for physical culture in the town ceased to exist.

Later, attempts were made to revive Maccabi, but they were not successful.

Footnote:

1. The additional details were provided by Eliezer Aydeltuch and Dov Rubinshtein.

The Press

by Chaim Rozmarin

Translated by Libby Raichman

Few people of the Biala Jewish population know that 40 years ago Biala already had its own newspaper. Of course, when we say "own newspaper" one needs to take into consideration the circumstances in which those people lived, who were bold enough to publish a newspaper.

The newspaper that we are talking about was published in 1894 and bore the name "Anti–Fanaticism". They had to dedicate their struggle against the fanaticism of that time, that imposed a heavy burden on those who searched for a path to free thinking.

The editor of the newspaper was the Hebrew teacher Sholem Ratshin and his fellow–journalists: Moshe Kavve, Avraham Urmacher, and Zaltzman from Shedletz.

The newspaper was written by hand, by Hinech Vinograd, and was published in three copies: one for Biala, one for Shedletz and one for Yanevve. The enlightened members of the community would carry the written "forbidden" item under their coats and when they had an opportunity they would sit in the small prayer house with the Talmud and read the newspaper.

The newspaper was, in total, published only three times, with a format of 12 pages. The outcome of the task that it was meant to fulfil on the Jewish street was not fulfilled because it almost did not reach its audience. Besides that, the difficult circumstances of publishing a newspaper like this, at that time, resulted in the interruption of the publication of further editions.

No one remained with copies of that newspaper. The only item that we received was a poem that was printed in the first edition of "Anti–Fanaticism", written by Moshe Kavve.

The poem called "Israeli", from which I tremble in part, characterizes the reasoning of the enlightened people of the past.

1.
A wanderer I was
And now I am still
Whoever read my story
Knows how great is my strength

2.
Many rivers of blood
Were bled from me
Yet I know full well
How great is my strength.

3.
How much hardship I have had
In the course of my life
Yet it did not harm me
Because the name "Jew" is my duty.

4.
Bathing in my blood
Is the smallest of matters
Because my name Jew
They cannot change.

From the time since the "Anti–Fanaticism" was published, many years passed and Biala did not dream of having its own newspaper. Only in 1924, the first printed newspaper was published, called "Biala Echo" under the editorship of Moshe Rubinshtein. Four issues of this newspaper were published and one issue of "Biala Shtimme" [Biala Voice]. The newspapers were dedicated to the struggle with the "Agudah" [the religious party] during the community elections at that time.

In the same year, a literary publication of 12 pages appeared, called "Unzer Vort" [Our Word] under the editorship of Menachem Gellenberg. For Biala, the publication of this type of newspaper was something new.

[Page 242]

Gellenberg made the greatest effort to convert the newspaper to a weekly publication. I am reminded of a curiosity that shows how little we then believed in the success of the initiative. The meeting that was supposed to take place about the release of the newspaper was arranged in the Jewish community hall. A large number of people were invited to attend.

That evening, when we had to go to the hall for the meeting, I came to Gellenberg so that we could go together. As we approached the door of the hall, Gellenberg prodded me to enter first, and I prodded him to go before me. We were not sure if anyone had responded to the invitation and we were embarrassed for ourselves.

The event, however, exceeded our expectations. People did respond, an editorial board was created, and there was an undertaking to release a weekly newspaper called "Podlassier Lebn" [Podlassier Life].

The first issue was published 26th November 1926. Gellenberg was the literary editor of "Podlassier Lebn" and Fishl Finkelshtein was the editor responsible for distribution. Other active writers were: Isaac Shvartz and Yaakov Goldshtein. "Podlassier Lebn" was warmly received by the Biala Jewish community.

It seemed that with this beginning "Podlassier Lebn" would be published regularly, without interruption, but the illness of the editor Gellenberg resulted in temporary suspensions. In 1927, after publishing 32 issues, "Podlassier Lebn" ceased to be published.

In 1932, a newspaper was published in Biala called "Biala Vochenblat" [Biala Weekly], issued by the Zionist organization in Biala under the editorship of Shmuel Vizzenfeld.

This newspaper had a Polish side that was rare in all of Poland, because among the hundreds of provincial newspapers that were published in Poland, there was no newspaper like this one. After 18 weeks, the newspaper ceased to be published.

On 20th May 1932, the first issue of the renewed "Podlassier Life" was published under my editorship. The newspaper received considerable approval and support among the readers in Biala, and abroad. The newspaper was backed by various activities, thanks to which we actually managed to publish regularly, and under very difficult conditions we reached our jubilee issue, that involved great expense and effort – an outcome that no other newspaper in the province achieved.

("Podlassier Life" number 19, 19th May 1934)

The Biala weekly newspapers

Additional details:

The newspaper "Biala Echo" and "Biala Voice" (together they published 5 issues) were distributed by the Zionist organization in Biala, which resulted in an excommunication served on the Zionists.

The "Biala Weekly" was again renewed in January 1936 under the editorship of Chaim Myoddek. From a number of copies that we have in our possession, it is evident that the newspaper was still published in 1938.

The "Biala Weekly", that was originally published under the editorship of Shmuel Vizzenfeld and later under the editorship of Chaim Myoddek, had contributing writers: Yaakov Goldshtein, Yostina Zeidman, Yaakov Aharon Rozenboim, Moshe Urlansky and others.

In 1938, a few issues of a weekly newspaper called "Podlassier Shtimme" [Podlassier Voice] were published, an independent societal periodical. This periodical was published through the "League for a working Land of Israel".

In "Podlassier Life", under the editorship of M. Gellenberg, we meet writers who contributed to the weekly newspaper: Yaakov Goldshtein, Avraham Urmacher, Yaakov Cohen, Avraham Lubeltshik, Isaac Shvartz, Yitzchak Perlov (from Brisk) Isaac Beckerman (Paris) and others.

In the renewed "Podlassier Life", under the editorship of Chaim Rozmarin, the contributing writers were: Leibl Finkelshtein, Menachem Finkelshtein, Avraham Lemberger, Yisroel Hochman, Moshe Y. Feigenboim, Boruch Vineberg (London), Aharon Beckerman (Paris).

[Page 243]

The "Biala Echo" and "Biala Voice" were printed in the printing works of Moshe Frishtik. The "Podlassier Life", under the editorship of M. Gellenberg, was printed in the printing works of Avraham Lubeltshik and the other weekly newspapers in Yisroel Hochman's printing works "Express".

"Podlassier Life", under the editorship of M. Gellenberg, would be published with 6 or 8 pages. The other weekly newspapers were published with 4 pages and a few hundred copies of all were printed.

The price of a copy was: the weekly newspaper under the editorship of M. Gellenberg, 20 groshen, later – 25 groshen, and the other newspapers – 10 groshen.

M.Y. Feigenboim

Dramatic Circles

by Gedalyahu Braverman

Translated by Libby Raichman

After 1905, with the decline of the revolutionary movement, some of the youth devoted themselves to other cultural work, and also to the theatre.

A dramatic group was also created in Biala that consisted of workers and the educated members of the community, such as: Eliyahi Shimshelles and his girlfriend, Itzele Stolyer, Hershl Izzes (Liebman), Itshe Maller, a young lady from Viness (a gymnast – I cannot recall her name), Chaye Sorre Goldfarb and others.

The group was preparing to act Yaakov Gordin's "Chashe the Orphan". Their rehearsals for the play lasted a few months. How did they know how to act and to portray the essence of the characters? At that time, groups like these existed in many towns and after completing their performances in their own town, they would go on tour in the neighbouring areas. Before beginning their rehearsals of "Chashe the Orphan", the Biala group attended a few performances of the troupes that came to Biala; they specially travelled to Mezritsh, to see how this play was presented there.

Young boys and girls were going to take part in a theatre performance, and it is difficult to describe today what kind of impression this news made in the town. On the one hand, there was complete contempt from the older generation; on the other hand, there was admiration on the part of the youth and also envy from some young people, towards those who had the honour of stepping out on to the stage.

The performance of "Chashe the Orphan" by the Biala circle was a great success. Understandably, everything bore the stamp of simplicity. The group did not manage to present more than this one performance.

At the beginning of the German occupation, during the First World War, I got together with Shimon Blankleider (the thin one), to discuss preparing a theatre evening. Shimon accepted my proposal and we began to prepare for this evening. I arranged the literary aspect, a one–act play and readings, and Blankleider attended to the music – a performance by a mandolin orchestra. The income from the performance was donated for the benefit of the Folk–kitchen.

A while later, we organized an artistic evening again. With the same group that performed at the previous evening, we presented "The Eternal Song" by M. Arnshtein, and "Mazel Tov" by Sholem Aleichem. Shimon Blankleider performed again with his mandolin orchestra.

When the literary–dramatic society was established at the Folk–kitchen, in which Fulye Lederman and I participated, we decided to present on stage Yaakov Gordon's "The Slaughter", which at that time was a stage hit.

We organized a dramatic circle that consisted of Esther Aidelman, Fulye Lederman, the writer of these lines and his wife, Mishe Vineshtok (a refugee from Brisk) and others. The presentation met with very great success and brought in a significant sum of money for the Folk–kitchen.

This group implemented a few other successful evenings in theatre halls at which the following were performed: "Es Brent" by Y. L. Peretz, "Mentshen" by Sholem Aleichem and others. Besides this, we organized evenings in the premises of the literary–dramatic organization.

After the rise of Poland, I founded a dramatic circle in the premises of the "Culture League" of the "Bund". I appealed to the members Eliyahu Geltman and Yechiel Tzelnikker to assist with the management of this circle.

We did not have any theatre training, but because we had a love and respect for the theatre, our productions were at a high level. Most of the plays that we produced were plays that we had seen presented by touring theatre troupes from Warsaw. Among others we performed L. Kobrin's "Dorfs–Yung" [Village –Youth]. We presented the play in the way we had seen it performed by a Warsaw troupe in Biala, under the direction of the noted artist Yaakov Viselitz.

[Page 244]

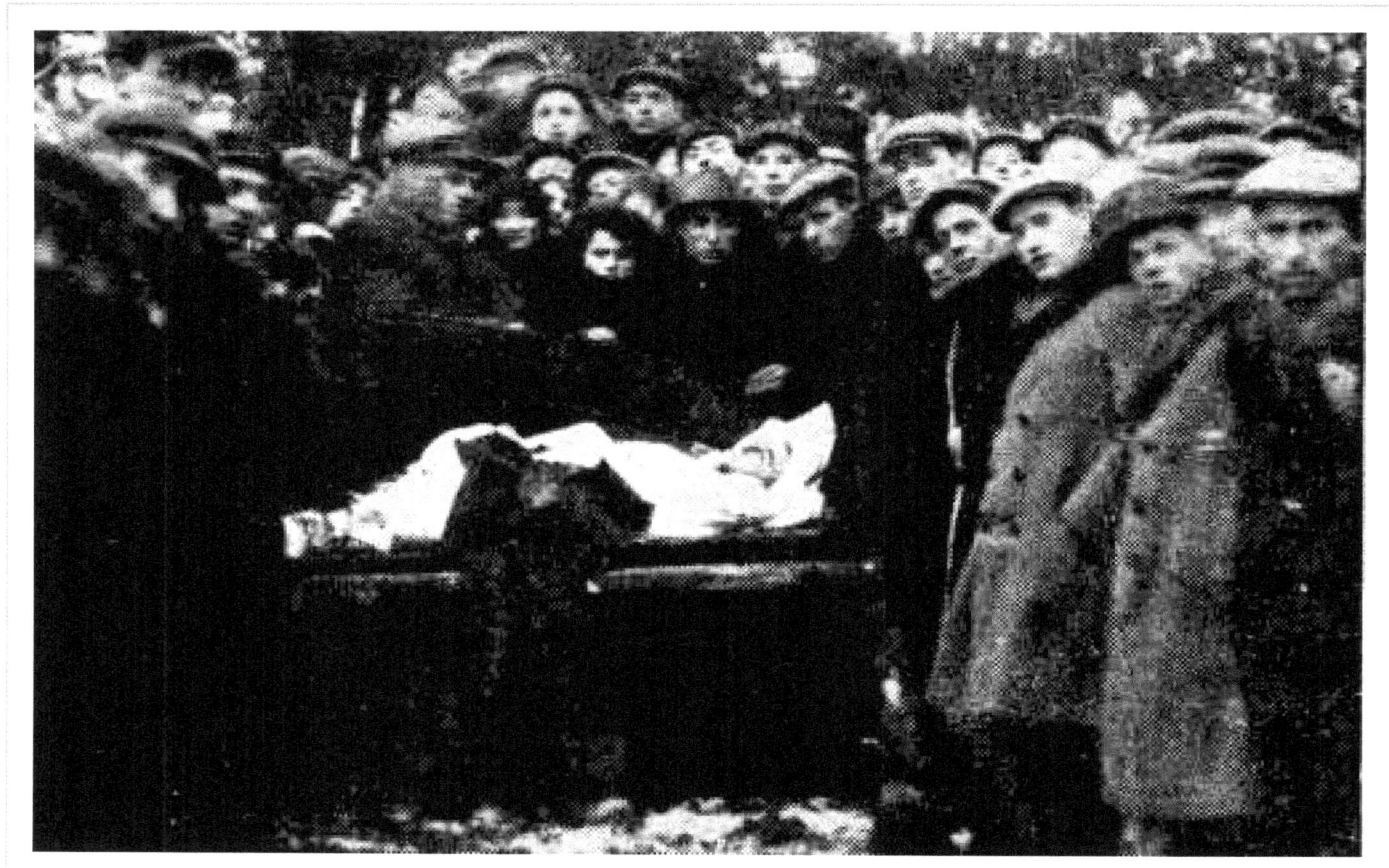

The funeral of Aronovicz

I would like to relate here two events that occurred during my activities with the dramatic circle in the town that are distinctly engraved in my memory.

In 1927, I brought into the dramatic circle of Hashomer Ha'tza'ir the play "On the Edge of the Vistula" by F. Bimka. This play depicted the Jewish–Polish relationships of that time. The group consisted of people of very great talent such as: Michtshe Lieberman, Sarah Biederman, Sarah Rubinshtein, Leibl Finkelshtein, Chaim Liebman, Shmuel Vizzenfeld, Chaim Rozmarin and others.

When we commenced our work, we did not consider that we might have interference from the government in presenting this play because the play appeared in a legally printed book.

After working for some time, when we were already preparing to stage the play, and even the props were completed (painted by Yaakov Bornshtein), we travelled to Warsaw, to acquire the permit and a copy of the censor. Only then we discovered that the government would not allow us to present this play. The incident caused us great upset. I particularly regretted that I did not manage to put this talented group on stage.

The second incident was the tragic death of the young fellow actor Yehuda Leib Aronovicz.

That was in 1925. At the Bundist dramatic circle, I introduced Yaakov Gordon's "God, man and the Devil". The role of Mottele's father was assigned to the new actor, Yehuda Leib Aronovicz. On a wintry Saturday evening, this play was staged in Kayovsky's hall. I also took part in this play. Suddenly I noticed that Aronovicz sat down abruptly on the chair and did not utter one word. I went down from the stage and gave instructions to lower the curtain. There was a stampede in the hall, and everyone ran to the stage feeling that a calamity had occurred. We notified the audience that an actor had fainted during the play.

The dramatic group with the stage manager Gedalyahu Braverman

Standing from right: Yaakov Shvartzberg, Shmuel Litman, Liebe Shvartzberg, Chaim Liebman, Yaakov Frinde, Moshe Shniderman
Sitting: Gedalyahu Braverman, Avraham Varshavsky, Yosef Mapier, Dovid Zegman, Miriam Frinde, Yehudit Zegman

[Page 245]

Aronovicz was taken immediately to the medical practitioner, Krochmalsky. He gave him an injection, thinking that this would pass, but Aronovicz remained unconscious. The performance was not completed and, in a depressed mood, the audience left the hall.

We took Aronovicz home and did not leave his bedside. Seeing that his condition did not improve, we consulted a team of doctors who established that a vein had burst in Aronovicz' head. Aronovicz died during this consultation. This tragic incident had a depressing effect on the town. Some of the religious people saw this as a punishment from God.

It is clear that after such an incident, for a certain time, a silence descended upon the activity of the dramatic circles in the town.

The second winter after the tragic incident, the dramatic circle of the "Bund" resumed intensive activities. Besides theatre performances, we organized readings about theatre problems. The lecturers were Dr. Michael Vichert and Alter Katzyuzne from Warsaw.

In the 1930s, the professional union organized a dramatic circle and invited me to be its director. It was energetic work. We performed "Yo'el" by Peretz Fishbine; "Tuvia the Milkman" by Sholem Aleichem; "For our Faith" by Sholem Ash, and others.

Finally, the participants in the dramatic circles with whom I worked in the town, in the course of almost 20 years, need to be mentioned here – understandably, as much as my memory is able to recall all the names.

Devorele Toibe, the inn keeper's daughter (maiden name Rozenboim – died in Paris), Yechiel Tzelnikker, Avraham Stricher, Esther Aydelman-Stricher, Refael (Fulye) Lederman, Chaim Zinger, Perl Kashemacher, Shifrah Braverman, Moshe Magid, Chaim Rubinshtein, Shimon Blankleider (the thin one), Shmuel Myendzizshetzky, Moshe Feldman, Shmuel Vizzenfeld, Sarah Biederman, Chaim Rozmarin, Yehudit ZegmaniError! Bookmark not defined., (all perished), Yeshayahu Iddel Lemberger (went to Russia in 1920), Motl (a tailor who worked for Eliyahu Klotz), Solman (son of the Warsaw medical practitioner), Miriam Frinde, Velvl Charash (both arrived from Argentina and left for Birre–Bidjan), Eliyahu Geltman (left for Cuba in 1927), Malye Vineshtein (America), Avraham Varshavsky, Sarah Rubinshtein, Yaakov Bornshtein, Chaim Liebman, Beile Bargman (all in Israel), Masha Solsky (Belgium), Shayne Hendl Grinshtein, Sorrele Viseman–Friedman (America), Chayah Semyatitzky, Dovid Zegman, Michtshe Lieberman (all in Paris), Leibl Finkelshtein (Australia), Sarah Bednarzsh (Canada).

The Dramatic Circle of "Bet–Am"

by M. Y. Feigenboim

Translated by Libby Raichman

Motl (Mordechai) Pyekarsky (son–in–law of the tailor Mendl Nuchovicz), came to Biala before the First World War. He directed this dramatic circle and would very often arrange artistic performances in Hebrew with the students in the "Yavneh" school. There he presented D. Pinsky's "The Eternal Jew".

Pyekarsky always set as his goal productions from a classical repertoire, and his theatre presentations were always of a high standard. It was not known how Pyekarsky came to be in theatre, but in the town people used to say that he was once an artist in a wandering theatre troupe. Whoever was present at his rehearsals with the dramatic circle saw that Pyekarsky was not an amateur in this field, and that he was truly skilled in the art of theatre.

The first dramatic circle of the Zionist organization that Pyekarsky organized consisted, amongst others, of: Feige Itte Urmacher, the Vineshtein sisters (the daughters of Dudl Brukierer), Shayndl Grinberg, Itta Lashtshevsky, Yaakov Aharon Rozenboim, Yohah Shteinman, Shlayme Izenberg, Pintshe Liebman, Abush Lieberman, Shimin Blankleider (the thin one), Yeshayahu Iddel Lemberger, Shmuel Myendzizshetzky, and Yaakov Zeidman.

Motl Pyekarsky presented classical works such as: "Widely Scattered and Dispersed" by Sholem Aleichem, "With the Stream" by Sholem Ash, "The Villain" by Peretz Hirshbine, etc.

His crowning presentation on the Biala stage, that was also his last production, was "Uriel Akosto" by Gutshkov. This was a magnificent challenge for a provincial theatre group. For many months Pyekarsky worked on this project with his group, most of whom were members of Hashomer Ha'tza'ir.

[Page 246]

The props and the make–up were specially brought from Warsaw, loaned by the troupe of the Warsaw Central Theatre. The artist Shlosberg arrived with the props and she had no words to describe her enthusiasm for the performance that took place in the evening of one of the intermediary days of Passover.

The following took part in this splendid presentation: Liebe Urmacher, Channah Tzinnamon, Abush Lieberman, Butshe Finkelshtein, Pintshe Liebman, Yisroel Goldshtein, Eliezer Aydeltuch, Dovid Lemberger, Chaim Rozmarin, Arye Lomaz etc.

The artistic decorations were completed by Dovid Lemberger and Leibl Finkelshtein.

The Dramatic Circle at "Bet–Am"

Standing from right: Yosef Festman (from Brisk) Feige Itte Urmacher, Shmuel Myendzizshetzky, name unknown, Shayndl Grinberg, Yaakov Aharon Roznboim, Malkah Blankleider, Yaakov Zeidman.

Sitting: Itta Lashtshevsky, Malye Vineshtein, Yonah Shteinman, the director – Motl Pyekarsky, name unknown, Shimon Blankleider
In front: Yeshayahu Iddl Lemberger, Butshe Finkelshtein, Shlayme Izenberg

The Dramatic circle at "Bet–Am" that presented "Uriel Akosta"
under the direction of Motl Pyekarsky

Standing from right: Eliezer Aydeltuch, Bernard Lieberman, Chaim Mordechai Goldshmidt, Pintshe Liebman,
Birnboim, Yosef Yehoshua Visebrot, Yitzchak Shein, Moshe Orlansky, Sanne Karshenboim
Sitting: Butshe Finkelshtein, Liebe Urmacher, Abush Lieberman, Motl Pyekarsky, Yisroel Goldshtein, Arye Lomaz
In front: Chaim Rozmarin, Dovid Lemberger, Chantshe Tzinnamon

Purim Plays at the end of the 19th Century

by Gedalyahu Braverman

Translated by Libby Raichman

At the end of the 19th century in Biala, there was a group that used to gather on the Sabbath and on the festivals, in a house, where in a friendly manner they enjoyed themselves with a prepared alcoholic beverage, mostly a small cask of beer. On these occasions, they would delight in a little of the cantorial tunes for the High Holy days, a folk song, and even snatch a little dance.

The group consisted of the little Kiegls (Streamwater), the four brothers (the sons of Meir Kiegl – a shoemaker on Yanneve Street): Velvl, Yosef, Isser and Moshe; Moshe Koshkes (a goldsmith, a metal worker); Avraham Gril (Braverman, a carpenter); Mendl (a baker); Mendl Roizes (a painter); etc. From time to time, this group presented the theatre performance "Joseph and the Brothers".

The shows were of course, connected to Purim, when people would dress up in disguise. This was very popular among the Jewish population at that time.

The performance of "Joseph and the brothers" was divided into two parts. The first was called "The Sale of Joseph" that depicted the manner in which Joseph was sold to the Ishmaelites, and the second part, "The Glory of Joseph", showed Joseph as second in command to the king in Egypt. These two parts were not performed in one evening, because it would have taken too much time and, besides that, the actors would not have had the opportunity to change their clothing so quickly and each part required another costume; so one Purim they performed the first part and the next Purim, the second.

The way they prepared for the show was very different from the current manner when the actor receives his printed or written script. The entire content of this presentation was memorized by a few actors who would sing the content in the form of a song. The rest of the actors learned their lines in this way.

The rehearsals would only take place in the winter evenings, because after a long day's work in the summer, they would rather go for a walk than engage in theatre performances.

Initially, the performances were organized in the following way: the group would notify Shmuel Pizshitz, the town's wealthy man, that on Purim they would afford him the honour of presenting "The Sale of Joseph" at his house. The group did not expect a fee and were satisfied with the honour that the wealthy man granted them. On Shushan Purim [the day following the festival of Purim], Pizshitz invited guests to a meal and the group would perform for them, in one of the large lounges in his house on Brisk Street.

The actors came dressed up and ready to present their show. Mendl Becker performed the role of the old father Jacob. He used a women's wig on his face, in place of a beard. Mendl Roizes played Reuven [the eldest brother] and he too had a wig as a beard, but a smaller one. The other brothers put soot on their faces that suggested that they were beginning to grow beards … Their costumes were more or less appropriate for the roles of the players. A gravestone fashioned like a board symbolized mother Rachel's tomb, at which Joseph lingered and sang a lamentation when the Ishmaelites were taking him to Egypt.

The last time, the group did not perform at the home of the wealthy Pizshitz, rather the performance was presented in one of the large rooms of the Talmud Torah and the entrance fee was a couple of koppeks.

Additional details:

According to Alter Vineberg, he only recalled Purim Plays in the years 1881/2. The group that performed consisted of: Itzele Horb Mendl Roizes, Avraham Gril, Hershl Gril etc. Alter Vineberg also remembers that the group managed to stage performances in a few different places on the same evening, for example: at the Moscow Rabbi [in Biala], (Rabbi Chaim Berlin, Tille's second husband), in Viness and at Shmuel Pizshitz.

[Page 248]

The Religious Life

General Overview

by M. Y. Feigenbaum

Translated by Ofra Anson

In many aspects, our town lagged behind other towns in Poland. Yet, religious life was more developed than in other places. I do not mean the way religious life was organized, nor how people practiced; these followed the pattern set in earlier times.

Biala was known as a Hassidic town and was even documented as such in world Jewish literature, for example by Y. L. Peretz in his story "Between two Mountains". Biala was the home of Rabbi Berish Landoy and his son, Rabbi Aharon. Rabbi Berish had a reputation as a great scholar, and many Hassidim came to him from all over Poland. The last story published by Opatoshu, "The Silent man from Wurk", was written about Rabbi Berish Landoy. The court of Rabbi Yitzhak Jacob Rabinowitz, well known around Poland, was in Biala, and his Hassidim were called "the Bialer Hassidim". Several communities of Bialer Hassidim can be found today in Israel. Their Rabbi is the grandson of Rabbi Yitzhak Jacob. Naturally, the rabbinic courts were very influential in the community and in the religious life in town.

There were also *Mithnagdim* in Biala, but there was no hostility between the two groups.

By the turn of the 20th century, there were no more Hassidic courts in Biala and religious life was mainly influenced by the town's Rabbi, Shmuel Leib Zak. Although most of the time he sat in his room with his books, and hardly mingled with the members of the community, his word was a command for the religiously observant.

Generation after generation, people were trained to adopt a strictly religious way of life. Men knew that their spare time should be devoted to prayers and learning. Praying and studying lasted from the cradle to the grave. Lullabies included messages of the importance of Torah studies. When a boy was a little older, he went to the *Heder*, where he learned the whole day and in winter even in the evenings. When he graduated from the *Heder*, he continued studying either in a Hassidic learning institution or in a Yeshiva. Only those who could not learn went to work. Parents would do everything they could to motivate their sons to study. The parents' dream was that their son would grow up to be a scholar. At the same time, those who started working were not cut off from religious life. They kept praying three times a day, and on Saturday they learned *Chumash* (Pentateuch) and read psalms like everybody else. I do not mean to say that there were no ignorant men in Biala, but everyone knew how to use the prayer book. Even those who could not read Hebrew were no strangers to it.

When the young men who were studying got married, they were often supported by their parents-in-law and continued their studies. The young men who started a business often let their wives run the store while they themselves went to study. Those who had to make a living themselves went to study a page of Talmud in the evenings. Indeed, Biala was known to be a town where many people studied.

Jewish women also were educated to keep to the tradition of a strictly religious way of life. The Rebetzin [Rabbi's wife, O.A.] taught the girls to pray, and the mothers did the rest of the training.

[Page 249]

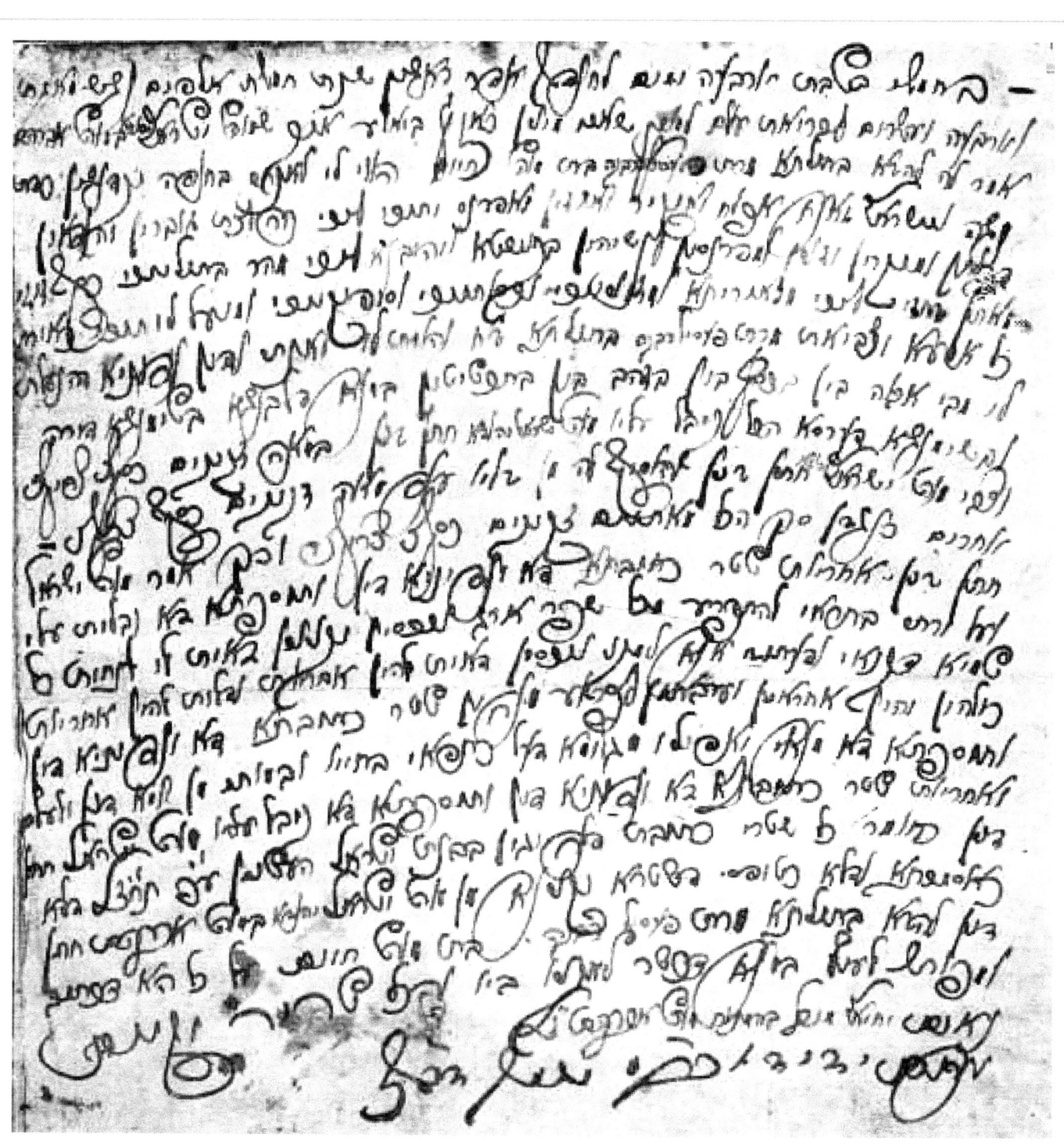

Marriage contract (Ketuba) written in Biala in 1864

Among the women, the proportion who were illiterate and who could not pray was higher than among the men, particularly among the poor. The morning after the wedding, the bride's head was shaved and she wore a coif, and later – a wig.

At the turn of the century, and particularly during WWI, radical changes took place and religious life became looser.

Before Saturday or a holiday, one could see and feel which tradition was the dominant one. The local governors could have their way during the week, but Saturdays and holidays belonged to the Jews.

On Saturdays and holidays the Jews were not in exile in a Christian society, but the other way around. All the shops and workshops were closed, and a sacred atmosphere rested upon the town. Even in the remote villages, the Christians knew not to enter them on a Jewish holiday.

Until WWII, Jews determined the town's life on Saturdays and Holidays, despite the changes in religious life. Time, of course, brought about change, and some of the restrictions were somewhat released. The spirit of revolution in the Czar's regime affected life in town. WWI brought its own changes and the aspiration for freedom and equality also affected religious life. The streets on Saturday did not look like Shabbat at the turn of the century anymore. Shops were closed, except for two pharmacies, a colonial shop, and two other businesses (the pharmacies and the colonial shop had been open since before WWI).

[Page 250]

Orthodox teacher Feiga Shnur and her girl students

Still, on Saturday one would not see a Jewish person with a cigarette on the street. Behind closed doors, there were people who broke the rules. The only visible change on Saturdays was that young men and women walked on the streets together.

Yet, when the High Holidays approached, the fear of doomsday brought back the old religious life. For the whole month before the New Year, early each morning, men went to the synagogue to hear the Shofar and read psalms. Traditional tunes and prayers could be heard from workshops, and people went to visit their ancestors' graves.

When WWII broke out, the yard of the synagogue included the synagogue and two places of learning, a learning place in Vollia, about 10 Hassidic prayer houses, and another few *Minyans* of Hassidim and Mithnagdim. The Talmud Torah on Proster Street was also active until the war.

There was a Yeshiva, established after WWI, which stayed until the last days of WWII. Mordechai Shimonowitz was the first headmaster, Rabbi Israel and the manager David replaced him. It was founded by Jews from East Poland and most of the students came to Biala from other parts of Poland.

Dr. Dov Yarden, a former student in this Yeshiva, wrote:

"I was about 11 years old when an emissary from Novardok Yeshiva, located in Biala Podlaska, came to our town, Motal (near Pinsk, birth place of Haim Weizmann). He gave a speech in the synagogue, encouraging the audience to send their children to the Yeshiva in Biala. My parents and the Kolodney family accepted the offer.

My father came with me [to Biala, O.A.]. He presented me to the head of the Yeshiva, Rabbi Mordechai, a pleasant, handsome, man. My father praised me, and mentioned I knew the sacred language. Rabbi Mordechai said that it is not the language that should be sacred, it is the heart. The main difference between Novardok and other Yeshivas was the moral teaching. Most of the day was devoted to studying the *Talmud*, like in other places. Rabbi Mordechai and his assistants taught us, and we memorized the lesson either by ourselves or with a friend. Yet, some hours a day were assigned to moral studies. We used different books, such as *"Chovot HaLevavot"* ["Duties of the Hearts", O.A.], written by Bahya Ben Yosef Ibn Pakuda (skipping the first, "philosophical", "gate" [section, "sha'ar" in Hebrew. O.A.] because of unexplained fear); *"Sha'arei Teshuva"* by Yonah Gerondi; "The Prince and the Monk" by Ibn Chesdaii; *"Mesillat Yesharim"* ("Path of the Upright", O.A.) by Rabbi Moshe Haim Luzzatto, and others. We dwelled particularly on the essays of Rabbi Yosef Yoizel Hurwitz, the founder of the Yeshiva *"Madregath HaAdam"* ["Stature of Man", O.A.], based on conversations he held over the years. We used to read the books for about half an hour, and then went out to discuss what we had read. Each older student took one or two young students with him and, with one on his left and one on his right, walked up and down the study house and discussed a moral idea. We used to call these conversations "Burse". On the origin of this name there was a story that Rabbi Yoizel (or "the elder", as we used to call him out of respect), while visiting the study house and seeing the enthusiastic moral discussions between the students, said amazed: "This is like in a real burse!"

Apart from studying in the educational institutions, men went into the Hassidim prayer houses to study Torah. The teacher, Benjamin Hersh Eidelman, used to study in *Beith Hamidrash*, each evening and Saturdays, with those who were interested.

There was a *Tehilim* Group in town, who regularly came to the praying house to read psalms. There was a group of Shabbat keepers, who went around the town Fridays before candle lighting to remind the traders to close their shops. On Saturdays, they used to patrol the streets to check if smoke came out of any chimney, and if they detected some, they entered the house and asked them to turn the fire off.

[Page 251]

Occasionally they went to the train station to make sure that Jews did not ride the train on Saturdays.

The *Mikve* [ritual bath, O.A.] was in a sealed building on Bud Alley. The building was renovated during WWI. The wooden walls were replaced by metal ones, and showers were installed. After the war, it was used mainly by the orthodox.

The following persons were active in the religious life of Biala:

Rabbis:

Rabbi Nahum Wolf Bornstein (the father of the well-known Rabbi Avreimale from Sochachow). He lived in the market, in the house of Israel Wichnem (later rented by Motl, the leather trader). The Rabbi had a Yeshiva in his home.

Rabbi Shmuel Leib Zak became the town's rabbi after him. He came from Szczebrzeszyn. He lived on Brisker Street, in the house of Motye Shuster. He died in Otwock, in the winter of 1932, and was buried in Biala.

The last Rabbi was Zvi Hirshorn. His previous position was in Yavoshna. He lived in the Market, in the house of Motl the leather trader.

Rabbinical Judges:

Before WWI: Rabbi Leib Zak (he specialized in writing contracts according to Jewish law. People invited him for their more important contracts, personal matters or property selling. His contracts were accepted by the official notary); Rabbi Yakir, Rabbi Yitzhak Kalman; Rabbi Menke (the son of the Rabbi from Tykocyin, he had the reputation of a great scholar). After the war, Rabbi Moshe Otchen (the son in law of Rabbi S. L. Zak).

The Rabbis and the judges were paid from the earnings of the slaughterhouse and by the community. Later, after Polish independence, they were paid by the community (which now had responsibility for the slaughterhouse).

Slaughterers:

Gershon Mendel, Shimon, Haim (all before WWI); Salman's Mendele (he was a great scholar and published a book by the name of "Memories of Menahem"); Meir Yod; Shmuel Rubinstein; Jacob Polonjetzky and Keibele Winetraub (from Markuszow, the son in law of Mendele the slaughterer).

Cows were slaughtered in the slaughterhouse; fowls were slaughtered at the slaughterer's home and later in the prayer house yard.

Supervisors:

Gitl Bashe's Baruch; Moshe Hofer; Zelig Hersh (before WWI) and Meir Aranowitz (nicknamed Pishke [box, O.A.]).

Purgers:

Elijahu Mordechai and Gdljahu Leib (both before WWI); Davidche Grinstein (from the Kitties); and Shlomo Eliezer Frankreich (Shlomo Lazar).

* * *

Let us list as many scholars and teachers as possible that worked in Biala during the last 70-80 years of Jewish life. The great scholars were, among others: Berish Landoy, Rabbi Nahum Wolf Bornstein, Noah Shahor, Itche Moses, Moshe Latzes (called "Big Moshe"), Leibish, Siskind, Haim Asher, Aharon Lipke, Menke, Itchke's Heinch (a young man, son of the teacher Itchke Patel), Aharale Judah Jacobs, Moshe Yaff, Wevel Goldfarb, Meirl Kalishiner, Gavriel Sofer, the brother in law of Shalom Vinograd (his name was forgotten, he later became an atheist and died young), Komlet (the husband of Ita Gampl), Baruch Eisenberg, Small Moshe, Rabbi Shmuel Leib Zak, Yehezkel Erlich, Shimon Kreidstein, Joel Meir Hilbloom, Benjamin Hersh Eidelman, Benjamin Gewirzman (Sotche's), Mendele Shohat, Baruch Shalom Kreidstein, the son of Mendel Rososher (a youngster), the brother of Moshe Kaveh, Israel (son of Hershel Yanover, died young).

Teachers:

Moshe Kalman
Avreimale Kodiner
Eizeek
Feivale Lubliner
Jacob Nathan
Israel Yitzhak Heigenbaum
Shmuel Hersh Appleboim (father of Nera the teacher)
Mendel Appleboim
Leibish Katz (a nickname)
Leibele Rososher
Arieh's Leibish Jacob
Tzalke

Welel Lutwak
Moshe David (son of the teacher Tzalke)
Welvel Idl Athe laundryman
Shia's (Yeshajahu) Sender
Aharon Lipe
Kive (Akivah)
Tuviah
Yehuda Leib Ashberg
Elijahu David
Shepsel's Elijahu
Wowele's Elijahu
Eliezer Leib
Shmuel Yankl Rubinstein (father of the teacher Menahem Rubinstein, and grandfather of Rabbi Shmuel Rubinstein, Paris)
Itzl (Yitzhak) Nahum
David Walf
Peie's Hersh Haim Moshe
Artchele's Hershl
Shlomo Kreidstien
Nahum Petke (teacher of very young children)
Tuvia Glikeles
Motl Domatchewer
Avraham Avele
Avreimale Janover (teacher of very young children)
Jonah Krokewer
Nuske (the son in law of Welwel Lutwak)
The teacher from Badker
Pesah Rishon [Pesah the first, O.A.] (teacher of very young children)
Pesah Sheni [Pesah the second, O.A.] (teacher of young small children)
The teacher from Radzyn
Hershl Shtrikenmacher (teacher of very young children)
Tuviah the Ginger
Moshe Haim Kligsberg
Binem (Bunim) Rososher (also produced wine for *Kiddush*)
David Leibele (son in law of Shalom the butcher)
Yizthak Moshe Bobkes [a type of cake, O.A.] (nickname, his wife made the cakes)
Leibele Ketche (nickname)
Avraham Yitzhak (son of Hain Hushler)
Moshe Itzikl (his mother was the sister of Shmuel Moshe the butcher)
Avraham Simha
Mendele
Itchke Potls (nickname)
Moshe Srul (Israel) Potls (nickname)
Haim Asher
Shakele Feigenboim (teachers for girls)
Hersh Ham' Sender Matias
Baruch Shalom Kreidstein
Yankl (Jacob) Brahie (Brahyahu – a *Talmud Torah* teacher)
Haim David Appleboim (a *Talmud Torah* teacher)
Nahum Eidelman (a *Talmud Torah* teacher)
Neta Appleboim (nicknamed Shteker)
Berele Appleboim (Neta's brother – teacher of very young children)
Joel Meir Heicloom
Feivele (teacher of very young children)
Menahem Rubinstein (the father of Kihele's husband)
Benjamin Hersh Eidelman (the son in law of Welvele the butcher)
Moshe (Israel Yitzhak's) Feigenbaum
Yitzhak Orkelesh (a *Talmud Torah* teacher)
Haim Gitl Milboim

Hershele Bankhalter (son in law of Simhale Sofer)
Hershele (teacher of very young children)
Elijahu Davidl Gutman (teacher of very young children)
Fleck (nickname – a teacher of very young children)
Shmuel Gliksberg
Haim Israel Finklstein
Moshe Michl (teacher of very young children in *Talmud Torah*)
Mendl Rososher
Aharon Hil (Yehiel) Weinberg
Welvel Yustman (Rososher)
Shlomo Haim Shwartzbard (a *Talmud Torah* teacher)
Ben-Zion.

[Page 253]

Until the First World War, the so-called "Kazyonne" Rabbis were also active in Biale. The classification "Kazyonne Rabbi" speaks for itself; these were Rabbis for the authorities, and not for the Jewish population. These Rabbis received their salaries from the community and an additional income for keeping the registry of Jewish births.

Of these Kazyonne Rabbis, the people of the town would remember one called Yosef Dryzin.[1] In approximately 1889, he came from Russia, having been appointed by the Governor. He was a liberal person and was driven out of the town by the community.

A Biale resident, Shlaymele Goldberg, became the Kazyonne Rabbi after him. He had once worked for the public registrar and later passed examinations to become a Kazyonne Rabbi. Shlaymele died even before the First World War and there were no Kazyonne Rabbis in the town after him. Under Polish rule, the Rabbi Moshe Utshtein, a judge of rabbinic law, would receive the oath of the Jewish soldiers in the town's regiments and was the guardian of the Jewish soldiers in the town.

This is how religious life continued in the town, almost without disruption under all the political regimes. With the occupation of Biale by the Germans in 1939, this life ceased to pulsate. Pious Jews were forced to shave their beards, wear peak caps, and because of forced labour, even had to desecrate the Sabbath. The prayer houses were filled with newly arrived refugees and people no longer prayed there.

Footnote:

1.   Dreizyn Josef (1843-1894), Yiddish lexicographer and storyteller, born in Minsk. For a while, he was a rabbi, known as a scholar. In 1891 he and his family converted to Christianity and he became a missionary. In 1887, he published a Russian-Yiddish dictionary, which was widely circulated. He also wrote "The Joker", "A Wife of Two Living Men", and more, based on folk stories (Encyclopedia Judaica).

The *Talmud Torah*

Translated by Phillip A. Applebaum

Before a *Talmud Torah* was built in the city, poor Jewish children whose parents could not afford Jewish education did not remain without Torah learning. There were the so-called *Talmud Torah* teachers who, in their own houses, taught the poor children without a fee and the community rewarded them for it.

Around 1894, the community purchased the house near the prison on Prosta Street and there organized the *Talmud Torah*. The Jewish poorhouse was also there.

Around the First World War, the officers of the *Talmud Torah* instituted wide-ranging reforms. This probably was done under the influence of the Yavne School.

The poorhouse was removed and a major renovation was undertaken. Modern school benches were installed in some of the rooms, and also a detention room was set up ... A school office functioned under the management of Moshe Braverman and for the first time in the history of the *Talmud Torah* there was registry of students. The most important of all the reforms was the instituting of secular studies several times a week for several hours. The teachers were Volf Nuchowicz, Michael Fejerman, Gedalia Krawiec and Moshe Kramarz.

During the period of Polish sovereignty the condition of the *Talmud Torah* worsened in all respects and again, neglect was the order of the day. The Jewish ritual slaughter of chickens took place in the school yard in full view of the children.

The *Talmud Torah*'s budget was mostly covered by a subsidy from the Jewish community and the remainder from a minimal tuition.

The *Talmud Torah* Committee, at various times, consisted of Moshe Laces ("Big Moshe"), Leibish Sourimfer, Moshe Uczen, Binyamin Cohen, Meir Jud, Yisrael Eliyahu Szapiro, Moshe Melech Silberberg, Yerachmiel Lichtenbojm. Some of the committee members came on Shabbat in the summer to hear the students recite their lessons.

Administrators of the *Talmud Torah* in the decades before the Holocaust were Selig Frajnd, Moshe Melech Silberberg and David Silberberg. The administrators also sold *shechita* coupons.

The teachers were Chayim David Epelbaum, Yankel Brachja, Yitzhak Urtszeles, Menachem Rubinsztejn, Velvil Rososzer, Shmuel Kligsberg, Binyamin Hersh Edelman, Nachum Edelman, Moshe Michl, Chayim Yisrael Finskesztejn and others.

Information received from Moshe Braverman, Asher Hoffer and Alter Weinberg.

Additional Details:

232 students study in the *Talmud Torah*. The Christian teacher, Zelichowski, instructs the students the Polish language. A Talmud-Torah teacher earns 30 zlotys a month in salary (Podlashier Leybn, number 4 of 28 January 1927).

Administrator of the *Talmud Torah* was Moshe Melech Zilberberg. And the teachers that worked there: Chayim Szwarcbord, Chayim Yisrael Finkelsztajn, Chayim David Epelbaum, Binyamin Ze'ev Ajdelman (Podlashier Laybn, number 18 of 12 August 1927).

Despite the fact that most recently the *Talmud Torah* teachers are paid 10-15 zlotys a week, they declared a strike on 15 January 1933 (Podlashier Laybn, number 3/68 of 20 January 1933).

The preliminary community budget provided a subsidy for the *Talmud Torah* at the level of 5,500 zlotys (Podlashier Laybn, number 5/70, of 3 February 1933).

[Page 254]

Houses of Prayer

by M. Y. Feignbaum

Translated by Ofra Anson

The Synagogue

Even the oldest people in Biala did not know in detail how the synagogue came to be built. According to the accepted story, Prince Radziwill built it. It seems plausible that he helped with building materials, or even with money. The older people only remembered that, before their time, it was painted by the Christian artist–painter Tzishewski. Why was the work, in a holy Jewish place, entrusted to the hands of a Christian, when Jewish builders were available? Is it possible that the Jewish builders were not qualified enough?

At the end of the 19th century, the synagogue underwent a major renovation, which cost few hundred rubles. During the renovation, the plaster was repaired, and a new coat of paint applied.

The entrance was to a corridor that was a little lower than the street. Steps led from the corridor to the synagogue, which was about a meter and a half lower. The corridor included a Holy Ark, Elijah's chair and a bowl of water to wash the hands.

The Synagogue and the Beit Hamidrash

A closed cellar with names was on the left side of the synagogue. The Permanent Candle was on the west wall of the synagogue, next to the entrance. The Holy Ark stood next to the eastern wall, which was quite simple, with no special decorations. A few steps led to the Holy Ark, and the lectern stood right next to it. The stage was in the middle, surrounded by metal bars and wood. The access to the stage was from the south to the north. High windows were located on the walls, except for the western one. Looking at the windows, one could see how thick the walls were, more than half a meter. The walls were covered with wood up to the height of two meters. Around the walls were benches and stand and next to these stood benches and tables.

The women's section was on three sides of the synagogue: south, north, and west. On the southern and the northern sides there were two attached wings on the ground floor.

The entrance for men and women was from the front, on the west side. Women could watch the service through a thick window with bars.

Over the synagogue, there was an attic, with a round opening on the western side. A stone–paved pavement led to the building, with two large stones on its side, where brides and grooms used to stand during the marriage ceremony (*Huppa*).

Until the end of WWI, oil lamps and candles in a big copper chandelier hung from the ceiling and smaller candleholders on the walls behind the benches lit the synagogue. After the war, electricity was introduced.

The synagogue had a hand–written book of prayers (*Siddur*) made of parchment, size A4, which had been mended in a few places. It had several beautiful *Parochet*, artistically made. The most beautiful one, artistically sewn and carefully finished, was saved for the high holidays. It was decorated with two verses, embroidered with silver yarn: "*Tikuu Behodesh Shofar*" (blow the Shofar, O.A.) and "*Ki Bayom Haze*" (on this day, O.A.). During the Ten Days of Penitence, the *Parochet* with "Remember us for Life" was used, and on regular Saturdays the one with "And Israel will keep the Shabbat" embroidered on it was hung.

During the thirties, an old book was discovered, with a note–book of the "Eternal Candle" society, which operated in Biala in the past.

[Page 255]

A few years before WWII, the synagogue was renovated again. This time the builder was an acquaintance from Miedzyrec, the synagogue builder, Hersh Liber Podolak.

There were three *Minians* in the synagogue: the early *Minian*, the cantor's *Minian*, and Moshe Kaveh's *Minian*.

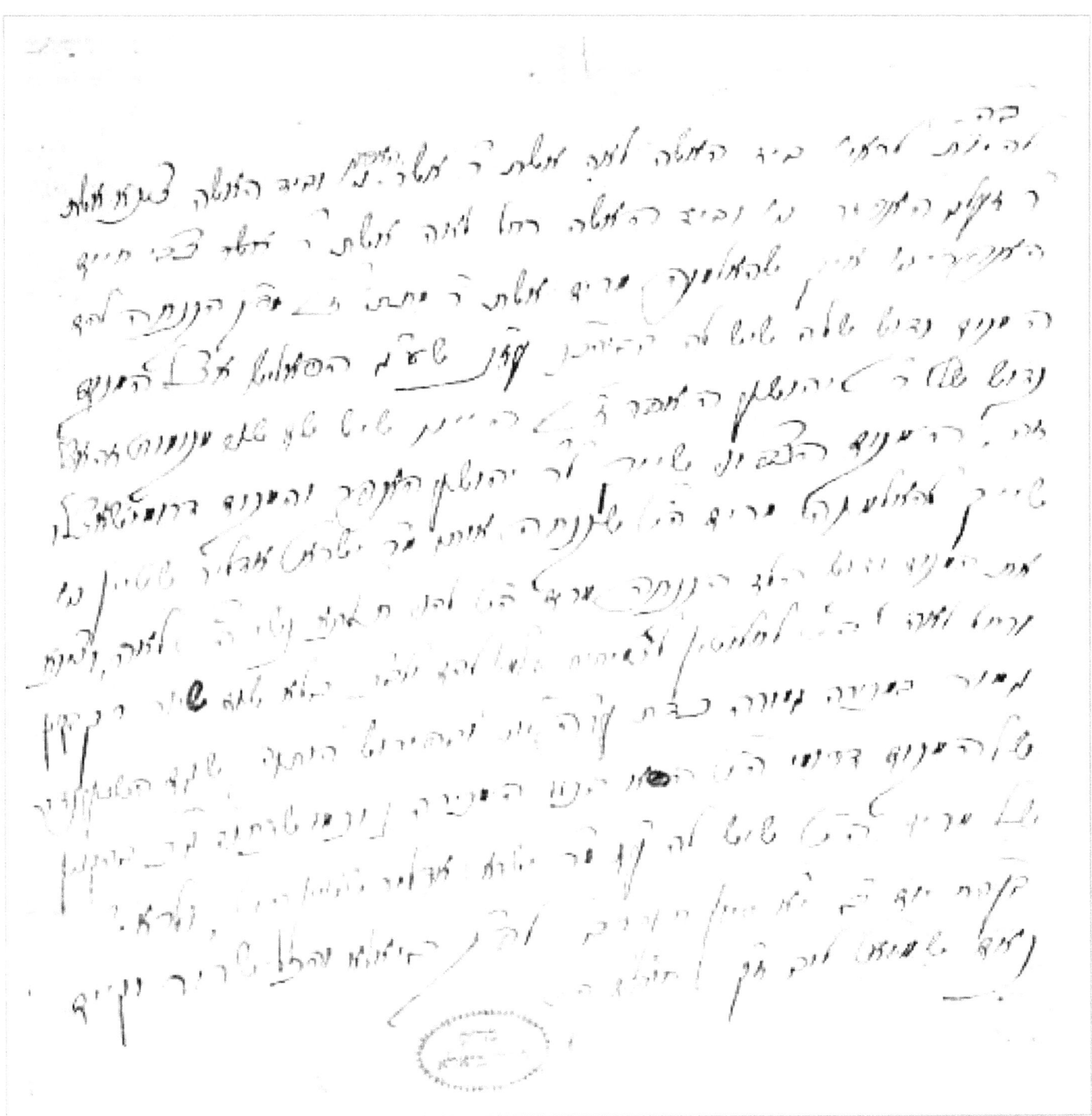

Contract of purchase of a place in the synagogue, written by Rabbi S. L. Zack

The janitors (*Gabaim*) of the Synagogue were: Moshe Feikes, Godel Binik (Milboim), and Yosel Wetchik.

The cantors were: Mechl from Russia, Joshua'le, and Moshe Yehuda Hacohen from Lithuania, who served for about 15 years, until WWII. He was known to be extremely orthodox, and devotedly supported the Novgorod Yeshiva in Biala.

Among the others who conducted the prayers were: Shimale Kreidstein and Benyamin Kliger.

The Germans destroyed the synagogue.

Further Details:

It would appear that this was not the first synagogue in Biala. People used to call another place "the old synagogue yard". It was the place where the houses of Moshe Haim and Treinele and Godel Binik Hthe carpenter were on Proster Street, and up to the houses of Hiench and Alther Kawal (Jarnitzki), with an entrance on Grabnover Street.

The first *Minian* was called "the waking up *Minian*". It was the *Minian* of porters and wagon owners, who used to get up very early for work, and got up early even on Saturdays. Sholkele Feingenboim, the lame girls' teacher, led the prayer for this *Minian*. The Gabai was Avigdor Reicher (nicknamed Tato).

The second *Minian* was the cantor's *Minian*. The important people prayed in this *Minian*, for example: the lawyer Heartglass, Idl Schwartz, Israel Cohen, etc.

[Page 256]

Moshe Kaveh's *Minian* was the third. The people who prayed in this *Minian* were mainly artisans, some Hasidim who used to pray in the Sephardic style. The prayer leaders were, until WWI, Mendele Melamed, later the writer Yeshayahu Eliezer (Shaii Laizer).

Before the Shtibels [literally, a small home; it means a small praying place, O.A.] for the Gere and the Radzyn Hasidim were built, they prayed in the women's section on the left hand side of the synagogue. When the Hasidim left, the *Minian* named the "Tailors' *Minian*" came onto the first floor. The shingle makers also prayed with them. The outstanding members of this *Minian* were Rabi Yosl Koliatsh (second name), and Rabi David Baruch the requests writer. The reader was Rabbi Gabriel Rosenstein.

In the women's section, on the second floor, prayed the "shoemakers' *Minian*". This *Minian* was respected because they had a good prayer leader, Yoel Kigl (Shtromvaser), on one hand, and a good choir on the other. Their reader was Ben–Zion the teacher.

P. Gold (New York)

The Beith Hamidrash

The Beith Hamidrash was built in 1892/3 in the same place where the old, small, Beith Hamidrash had been. This was about to collapse and had to be demolished. The initiators of the building were Motl Shenker and Izik Shahor (the father of Tile Berlin). The money was collected from donations by the residents.

The builder was Israel Weinberg, and the furniture made by Shmuel Shmai Simels (Friedman).

The building was made of bricks, and the roof made of tin.

The women's section was on the western side, and it had two entrances on the side. The window from the women's section into the Beith Hamidrash had thick bars.

Two large doors, on the southern and the northern sides, led to halls, and from there, a few steps led to the Beith Hamidrash itself. The bowl for hand washing was located by the southern entrance, on a high brick stove. By the entrance from the southern side stood a bookcase. The Ark stood in the middle of the inner eastern wall, a few steps higher than floor level. The lectern was on its right side. Left to the ark was the Rabbi's place. The stage was in the middle, and it could be reached from both north and south. Four wooden poles were located next to the stage, up to the ceiling. There were three big windows that let a lot of light come in.

The Beith Hamidrash was full of tables and benches. On one table by the western wall book–sellers, not necessarily from Biala, used to sell books and other items for religious purposes. Beith Hamidrash could hold some 500 people. Electricity was installed in 1918. Oil lamps were in use before that.

Major renovations took place a few years before WWII. The tin stoves were replaced by white stoves. A fresh coat of paint was put on the ceiling and the walls by local experts: Abraham Lemberger, Haiim Yosef Knuzcnik, and the Rosenker brothers.

Many *minyanim* prayed in Beith Hamidrash fron early in the morning. All day long one could see people studying the *Gemara*. In the evening there were more people studying, among them: Goldfarb (Velvele?) and the teacher Benyamin Hersh Eidlman.

Friday night *Psalms* were read in public. During the last period, the tailors Pesach Saks (nickname) and Sheime Bekerman (from Sanies) were the readers.

Among the leaders of the prayers were: Rabi Manes, Eizshe Libman, Soshe Rosen, Joel Greendlass, and Haiim Shye (Yeshaayhu).

The *minyan* the rabbi prayed with The Gere Hassid Zalmn Zak led the prayer.

The *Gabayim* of Beith Hamidrash were Moshe Tuvya Stolier, Itzke Koval, Yosef Nathanson, Michael Eizenstat, Zile (Uziel) Stolier (Feigenboim).

Janitors: Shalom, Yankel, Avraham Thevel, , Avreimale, Noah, Joel Greendlass, and Haiim Shye (Yeshaayhu).

After WWI, the yeshiva operated in the women's section.

[Page 257]

During the Nazi occupation, Beith Hamidrash was converted to host refugees. They burned every item made of wood during the freezing weather. Even the wooden floor was used. Like the synagogue, Beith Hamidrash was taken over by the Germans during the war.

Further Details:

The first *minyan* was the *Mitnagdim* [the Orthodox Jews that opposed the *Hassidic* movement, O.A.]. These were mainly artisans, who also did odd building jobs for Beith Hamidrash.

On the eastern side sat: Velvele Waserman, the architect and the chief planner of Beith Hamidrash; Shlomele Stolier and his son, Menachem Leibele, sat next to him; the brothers Shaulke and Itschke Eidelman (Kavales); and Moshe Toker, The Gampel family also sat at the eastern wall, because Leibish Gamplel was Gabai and administrator of Beith Hamidrash when it was built, and worked for Moshe Batchke, who donated handsomely to the building.

The second *Minian* was the *Hassidic* one. The best known of them was Rabbi Zalman, the son of the former Rabbi, a brother of Avreimale Sochatzover, and Rabbi Heikel Lichtzier. The *Hassidim* named the *Toiter* [the dead, O.A.], from Broslov.

P. Gold (New York)

The Additional Beith Hamidrash

At the northern side of the Synagogue's courtyard stood the "Additional" Beith Hamidrash. It was built by a few Jews from the Russian army to commemorate their survival in the Russian–Japanese war.

It was built after the Russian–Japanese war. The initiators were Shmerl Pep (nickname) and Heinch Koval (Yarnitzki). The money was raised from the reserved Russian army stationed in Biala. The workers came from the reserved army, and Alther Weinberg supervised the work.

Human skulls were discovered while digging the foundations for the Beith Hamidrash.

The entrance was on the southern side, and led straight to the Beith Hamidrash. The floor was a bit lower than the door step. Indoors, on the western side, was another door, which led to a small room.

By the eastern wall stood a wooden Holy Ark and a lectern. In the middle of the large room stood a table to read the *Torah*. Tables and benches stood around the walls.

Over the Holy Ark was the permanent light with the inscription: "Donated by Meir, son of Rabi Yehuda Leib Goldhamer" (the eldest son of Leibele Shemes, on behalf of Feivel Gold, North America).

The women's section was built over the Beith Hamidrash. It looked like "r", and was closed, with wooden bars of 1.5 meters high. The steps to the women's section were on the western side of Beith Hamidrash. Next to the entrance of the women's section was a little apartment.

Most of the years, the *Gabai* was Jacob Velvel Hershberg, the blacksmith.

A *Heder* operated there during the last years before WWII.

This Beith Hamidrash also hosted refugees during the war, and here too all the wooden pieces were burnt.

The Germans destroyed the Additional Beith Hamidrash too, and thus no sign of Jewish life remained in the synagogue's courtyard.

The Beith Hamidrash of Volia

Some say that Jews settled in Volia before they settled in the town. To find its Beith Hamidrash one had to walk out of the town, cross the river to its left bank, away from the path, almost out at the green. It was built like a Hasidic Shtible: without a stage in the middle and without a built Holy Ark. Four wooden stands were in the middle, and it had a women's section.

It was a low building. It stood on wet ground, and its foundations had to be changed from time to time.

Two *minyanim* prayed there. In the first prayed the *Motnagdim*, and then the Hasidim (*Alerlii Hadasim*)

[Page 258]

Prayer Houses of Chassidim and the opponents of Chassidism[1]

by Fyvl Gold, New York

Translated by Libby Raichman

The Kotzk Prayer House

The Kotzk Chassidim were the first Chassidim in Biale, so their prayer house in the street of the bathhouse was the oldest. It is my opinion that it already existed in the first half of the previous century.

The Kotzk Chassidic Rabbinic court was the closest to Biale. The most important and first travellers of Biale were: Reb Herzl Cohen (Reb Shualke and Reb Yisroel Meir's father), Reb Izik Shocher Tsharny as well as my great-grandfather Reb Yakov Eliezer Pishtshatzer.

The Chassidic prayer house was a traditional large synagogue, with four pillars in the centre, the holy ark in the east, and the lectern for reading from the Torah in the middle. There was a room on the right that was filled with religious books.

The Kotzk Chassidim had split a few times. The last split occurred between the Sokolov and Pillev Chassidim and the prayer house remained in the hands of the Sokolov Chassidim.

The most eminent Chassidim there were: Reb Boruch Sender and his son Reb Dovid (Kligberg), Reb Shmuelke Pizshitz, the tar makers, the scholars: Hersh Chaim Melamed (of the Pyes, great-grandfather of Elye (short for Eliyahu) Marks (New York), the teacher Binyomin Hersh, Reb Yakov Goldhammer (my father's brother, who was called Yankel of the bubkelach, Shayne Chaye's; the teacher Reb Dovid Leibele (son-in-law of Sholem Katzeff).

The Ger House of Prayer

This prayer house, situated in Potshtovve Street, was enclosed by a high fence. It had a large courtyard with tall trees. One would walk up a few steps and enter the foyer. On the right side of the foyer was the entrance to the prayer house, and on the left side - the residence of the beadle. The prayer house was large and bright. At the eastern wall was an entrance to a smaller room, where shelves of religious books were housed.

At the eastern wall, on the left of the holy ark, sat those of very distinguished descent: Reb Yisroel Meir (a younger brother of Reb Shualke, and son-in-law of the first Rabbi of Gur, Reb Itshe Meir, the exalted Torah reader in the prayer house; Reb Yossl Yunever (the father of Dina Yunever), who in his later years left for the Land of Israel; Reb Leibl Dine (of holy memory). Reb Leizer (Eliezer Mintz (of the "Varshavsky Magazine"), and Leibele Dovid, son of Reb Isaac.

Besides those mentioned above, there were other members of distinguished families who prayed there: Reb Eliyahu Mintz, Reb Bunim Leibele, the sons of Reb Shmelke (Shmelke) and Yakov Kahan's grandfather, a son-in-law of Reb Isaac Shocher. In Biale, if one wanted to reprimand someone, they would ask: "what are you, a Reb Shmelke?"), Reb Dovid Tzvi (the grandfather of the Orlanskes) etc.

At the table between the southern and western side stood Reb Shualke (Reb Hertzl's oldest son, regarded as the wealthiest Jew in Biale), who conducted himself in an unassuming way and sat together with the common people. Yirmiyahu Bedner (also Bedder) and his family also sat at this table.

The Prayer House of the Gur Chassidim (winter 1944/5)

[Page 259]

On the Sabbath, prayer services were held three times. The first was called "Reb Yossele's prayers". Reb Yossele was the brother of "words of truth", and brother-in-law of Reb Noach Shocher. He stood in a place of honour, at the large printed prayer "Hodo". Next to him: Reb Mendl Buchner (Reb Chaim's youngest son-in-law), the family of Reb Moshe and Zishe Cohen, Reb Yechiel Hersh and other "P'nay" [leading citizens]. Reb Yossele, who wore a tallit with the largest display of silver embroidery at the collar, was a quiet and unassuming man. His strength was manifest on Simchat Torah, when he was given the honour of reciting the "Atah Har'aytah", and an additional soul entered into this quiet Yossele as he delivered the prayer with confidence, pride and contentment. The last two verses poured out with immense rapture (his wife Chanele would gather round, flat stones the whole year, to make her utensils kosher on the eve of Passover. She would ask my mother that when she baked matzah at our place, she should ask those who rolled out the dough, to have pity on her and say, "for the sake of good matzot").

The second service was called Moshe Latze's, or Moshe the big one. Reb Moshe, the big one, was Reb Noach Shocher's oldest son-in-law, and was regarded as one of the great scholars in the town. He was the main ambassador of the Rabbi of Gur in their rabbinical court in Biale.

The leaders of these prayers were: Reb Yosef Lubliener (the only one who studied the Jerusalem Talmud) and Reb Leibele Shocher. The Torah reader was Reb Zalman, of holy memory.

The third prayer service was called Reb Meirl Kalushiener's. This prayer service was conducted from 2pm to 3pm. The main objective for these worshippers was study.

Reb Meirl Kalushinner was regarded as a great and astute scholar (his first wife was the daughter of Reb Yisroel Meir).

The leaders of these prayers were: Reb Hershl Urtsheles and Reb Motl Mintz, and the Torah reader – Reb Meir Korman.

Aliyot to the reading of the Torah were sold, with exception for a few congregants of distinguished descent, as well as for a bridegroom, for the father of the bridegroom or for a Bar Mitzvah. The prices of these call-ups would rise on the Sabbath, before the new moon, at the beginning of a new month, even more on the festivals, and mainly on the High Holy Days. The person who paid the highest price (minimum 25 Rubel) would bring in the prayer "Atah Har'aytah" (Motl Mintz), and Yisroel Cohen bought "Chatan Brayshit". There was also an annual fee, the highest being 12 Rubel and the minimum one Rubel. The fee was collected by snatching the worshippers' tallitim on the Sabbath and then requiring the person to pay their fee for the return of their tallit.

The youth sat and studied in the Ger house of prayer, as well as in all the other Chassidic houses of prayer. The two eminent Talmudic Chassidim were: Reb Yosef Refael (Reb Yisroel Meir's oldest son-in-law – the first trustee of the synagogue, from the earliest times, that I can remember; three of his four sons were Rabbis in the small towns), and Reb Shimon Ahreles (a brother-in-law of Reb Leibl Dine, the father of Aharon and Yakov Gelblum) would often walk over to the young students and help them.

The Radzin Prayer house

As is known, the Radzin Chassidim wore a blue thread in the tassels of their prayer shawl and undergarment; due to this, there was a major dispute between them and other Chassidim and they were severely harassed; they were not allowed to approach the synagogue lectern, and not allowed to be called up to the Torah. They were, therefore, very stubborn. (In Biale, a stubborn person would be asked: - who are you? A grandchild of Reb Shabtai? – meaning Reb Shabtai Finkelshtein).

Reb Shabtai Finkelshtein was a son-in-law of the famous Shocher family who initiated the construction of the Radzin prayer house in Biale, a sufficiently large prayer house in Vansk Street, that was built of brick.

Those who assisted him, both with money and with professional knowledge, were: the Goldreich family, Reb Chaim Pesachof the wine store, and Reb Tzemach Shenker (Tuchmintz). These were Chassidim truly, to the core.

In later years, the main person of distinguished descent was Reb Yechezkel Erlich, one of the scholars in the town. The following were also regarded as distinguished: Reb Kalman Sheinberg (of Reb Shabtai's and Reb Urele's family) and Reb Zishe Goldreich.

Eminent worshippers were, among others: Reb Arye Tabatshnik, a handsome Jew and a passionate leader in prayer, Reb YehudaYakov and the "targovnik" (a nickname – father of Yoel Itzl Schneider, New York).

The Partzev Prayer House

After much wandering, over various premises, the Partzev Chassidim chose a place for prayer, in a unit in the house of the brothers Itshke and Shualke Eidelshtein (Kovalle's), that was located close to the Rodzin prayer house, and the prayer house of the opponents of Chassidism.

The eminent Chassidim who belonged there were Reb Leibe Bornshtein and his son-in-law Reb Chaim Rammes. Their prayer leaders were: Reb Natan Rammes (son of Reb Chaim), and the teacher Reb Aharon Yechiel Vineberg.

The Lomaz Prayer House

[Page 250]
The Lomaz Chassidim did not have their own house of prayer. Before the Viness fire, their prayer house was situated on Proste Street, at the corner of Kshivve Street, opposite Reb Aharon Landau's courtyard. After the fire they were at first in the premises of Berel Kozzes (a Lomaz Chassid), later in occasional premises only for the Sabbath and the festivals. Their last place of prayer was in the premises of the well-known honey-cake baker, Alte Treinele, in Proste Street.

Of the older eminent Lomaz Chassidim there were: Reb Velvl Lutvak (husband of Treinele well-known for her hospitality and father of the sisters: Shifrah and Alte), the scholars Reb Paltiel Oppenheim (son of Yeshayahu of Zeif – who had a wholesale food store) and the teacher Reb Menachem Rubinshtein (the husband of Alte Treinele and father of Rabbi Shmuel Yakov Rubinshtein in Paris, the author of the book "Sh'ayrit Menachem" that was published in three volumes, in Paris in 5714 [corresponding to 1953].

The Lomaz prayer house produced three distinctive characters: Reb Boruch Yakov Brodatsh (Gershon Chaim Kubele's son, brother of Chaim Brodatsh – New York, a local quick Torah reader, who managed, on a Shabbat, to read the weekly Torah portion at a few different prayer houses in the town; Yosef Marchbein (of the Patotz's – nickname), founder and leader of the Socialist- Revolutionaries in Biale; and Chaninalle Kling, one of the leaders of the "Bund" in Biale, during its period of glory.

Pillev Prayer House

The Pillev (Pullavi) Chassidim had their prayer house in the home of Moshe Tuvia on Proste Street. Before the Second World War, they had to leave the prayer house, and on the Sabbath and festivals they prayed in the Talmud Torah.

Mezritsh Prayer House

The Mezritsh Chassidim also wandered around from one location to another, until they settled in the house of Moshe Yitzchak Stollier at 29 Proste Street.

The eminent Chassidim there were: Reb Berish Urbach (of Viness) and the cantor Izshe Liebman.

The Aleksander Prayer House

This prayer house was situated in the courtyard of Reb Aharon Landau and later in the house of Meir Korman.

Aside from Reb Aharon Landau, the most eminent worshippers were: Reb Volvish Goldshtein (son-in-law of Sh. Pizshitz), the Gampel family, the Rabbi, Reb Moshe Utshen, Reb Chaim Lieberman (of the Kozzes – a nickname), and Reb Aharon Zilberberg (Shkop – nickname).

The Lublin House of Prayer

Their place of worship was situated in the premises of Fyvele Melamed on Grabanov Street, but only until the First World War.

The Damatshev House of Prayer

They had their prayer house in the courtyard of Chaim Yaske Kashtenboim. People knew little about it, but it did exist before the First World War.

Shedletz House of Prayer

A prayer house like this was created a few years before the Second World War, and was situated in Viness. Their prayer leader was Yechiel Urbach (a son of Berish)

The House of Prayer of the Opponents of Chassidism

This prayer house was situated on Vansk Street and was built as a synagogue, with a large reading desk in front of the lectern for reading the Torah, and a smaller one in front of the holy ark. They also had a women's section.

The builders of this non-Chassidic house of prayer were stubborn scholars and religious artisans, adversaries of Chassidism. The entire fit-out and accessories in the women's section were given by the renowned lady, Feige Frimmes (she had a house and a factory on Varshevve Street).

Eminent worshippers who belonged to that house of prayer were: Reb Menkin Dine, Reb Nachman Rozenkrantz, the brothers Yehoshua and Eliezer Hoffer (of the Pyess) and their brother-in-law Reb Moshe (grandfather of Gittel Rozenblatt, New York).

When Reb Yehoshua died, it was told that in his will, he bequeathed to the prayer house religious books to the value of 300 Rubel and also a sum of money (he made a good living, but was not a wealthy man. Typically, the children of the above mentioned distinguished persons, Reb Moshe, Reb Yehoshua and Reb Eliezer Pyess, were Chassidim).

The Tarshish House of Prayer

This was a typical Chassidic house of prayer and their worshippers were not the followers of any particular Rabbi.

They were mostly young people of Chassidic families, who were frowned upon in the Chassidic prayer houses, because they wore pressed collars with neckties, short forelocks, polished boots and clothes that were of good quality. In jest they were called "Jonah the prophet's Chassidim" because the prayer houses spat them out (threw them out).

[Page 261]

The founders of this prayer house were Asher Hoffer (of the Pyess), Moshe Lebenberg, Yoske (Yosef) Vinograd, Asher Feigenboim and others.

The prayer house was situated at Asher Feigenboim's (carpenter) on Brisk Street. Later, until the First World War – in the house of Leibe Mendik. In the first years of the First World War – in the house of Asher Hoffer on Yatke Street. Later, until the Second World war – back to Asher Feigenboim. The leaders in prayer there were: Asher Hoffer (also the Torah reader), Binyomin Klieger, Moshe Lebenberg, Yakov Goldshtein, Leibele Krideshtein, Yossele Glezer (called a Rodzinner), Moshe Biebergal, and Shpiegel (from Lodz, son-in-law of Hersh Yakov Zshelazni).

The Society of Talmudic Students

There was a saying in Biale: "A Talmudic student says the blessing for wine over wood shavings". For a young man it was impossible to secure a call up to the Torah. He had to wait until he was married. So, a group of young men got together and created their own prayer group. That happened at the end of the 19th century. The young worshippers later married but their prayer group was still called the Society of Talmudic Students.

The society reached a high level when their leader was Reb Moshe Mordechai, a man who was renowned in his time (called the Kesselerke's son-in-law – later went to live in Tsfat in the Land of Israel). He would study with the worshippers on the sabbath during the day, and in the evening, they arranged a third meal at the end of the Sabbath, with Sabbath hymns. After the departure of Reb Moshe Mordechai, a young man, whose name I do not remember, studied with the group. (He was the brother-in-law of the painter Chaim Yehoshua Blushtein).

Their place of worship was in the house of the brothers Moshe and Meir Zuberman. Later, in places where they received hospitality. Finally, in the women's synagogue, to the left, on the second floor.

They had two fine prayer leaders: Hersh Bernshtein (a tailor, who immigrated to Canada) and Yossele Platt (a shoemaker of Lashitz).

Original footnote:

1.   This information refers mainly to the period until the First World War.

Cantors

by Feivel Gold, New York

Translated by Ofra Anson

Biala, the town we loved and that we all miss, does not exist anymore, not even the sign of a grave.

Let us remember the cantors we all knew, loved, heard, and enjoyed. They did not use any technology or tricks when they prayed. They knew very well who they represented and to whom the prayer should be directed.

The old cantor

I never knew his name. He was very old, may have reached hundred years, and was a cantor in Biala for more than 60 years. He prayed solely, without any help, even on Saturdays, and because he held the position – no other cantor could be hired. Hearing the high tones on Saturday prayers, I knew he had a rich baritone voice when he was young.

Shimale Kreidstien

The most handsome person in the big synagogue. He was a cantor who served mornings and evenings and blew the Shofar. An old person with a small beard, gray hair and a beautiful young tenor voice. He was dressed like a *Hasid* rabbi. In his time, he was the only cantor who I heard singing the confession on Yom Kippur in the old, traditional, tune. Yosel Wetchik and Althar Cheshler were his assistants.

Aaron Yehiel Melamed

Aaron Yehiel Melamed was called Beile Hishe's husband. He was born in Parczew, and served as a cantor during the High Holidays as long as the old cantor held his position. Before holding the service in Biala, he used to pray in the small settlements around Biala. He had a nice tenor voice, and used to cry a lot while praying. He reached high tones when he sang the prayer for the 10 persons assassinated by the Romans and considered to be Jewish martyrs. He cried so hard, as if he himself was going through the tortures.

Joshua'le – the new cantor

In his youth, he studied in *Beith Hamidrash* with the rabbi of Biala. He was a gentle young man, a scholar, and sang beautifully. He became a cantor following the advice of the Rabbi, though he had lung disease. The orthodox Jews of Biala believed that the Rabbi helped him reach high tenor tones. Before he became a cantor in Biala, he worked in a few other towns. In Biala, people took pride in having such a handsome and talented cantor.

[Page 262]

He organized a good, large choir. Biala was enchanted by his soloists, such as: alto – Yosele Solovei (Yosl Zied), Yankl Motl Kaves; Tenor – David Sara Rivkes (Hochberg); Bass– Shmuel Moshe Antsheliches. For me, his best composition was for "*lo amut ki ehyeh*" in the "*Halel*". Second best was "*venathna tokef*". In general, what he said or sang, alone or with the choir, was full of sweet feelings. On Saturdays, in "*av harachamim*", when he got to "*Kama yomru hagoiim...*", he sang it loud and with such pathos, we were sure it went straight to heaven.

Manes

Manes was the cantor of the big *Beith Hamidrash*. He was a Hasid of the old Rabbi of Lublin, the prophet. He was an old person, short, with a nice white beard, and a good bass voice. His Priestly Blessing (*birkat hacohanim*) was particularly original and beautiful. His assistants were Noah Shames and Pinie Beker (the father of Kotchemeinik).

Eyzshe Liebman

He was born in Lomza, and people called him "the husband of Sara Hanna Miriam's daughter". Sara'le was the one who made the living. She had a big family, and ran a food store in the shop of Moshe'le, the son of Yankel. Eyzshe used to sit in the Rabbi's *Beith Hamidrash* and study. He came into the store to wish it success.

When the cantor of *Shaharit* in *Beith Hamidrash* suddenly died, the Rabbi was asked to find a replacement. Thus, Eyzshe Liebman became the cantor after Manes died. He was the first cantor I heard praying "*Ani ha'ani mima'as*" in the traditional tune, and with a choir – his own children. He sang nicely, though there were people who complained that his voice was not clear enough. He used to pray with devotion and strength. His first-of-the-month blessings, *Hallel* and *Avinu Malkenu* were particularly beautiful and original.

Feigale's Meir

Kotsk Hasidim loved *Tikkun*. Naturally, when you start a little *Tikkun*, dancing and singing are involved. Indeed, the Kotsk Hasidim had a reputation as the best music players.

Feigale's Meir (the writer's cousin), the son of Haim Ortcheles, was the best cantor the Kotsk Hasidim ever had. Rabi Haim Ortcheles died very young in Biala, when his eldest son, Meir, was not even 13 years old. Yet, Meir had already learned his father's sweet singing, and the Kotsk Hasidim in Biala liked him a lot. After the death of the Kotsk Hasidim's Rabbi, he joined the Pilever Hasidim (led by the Kotsk Rabbi's younger son). Sokolover Hasidim, whose rabbi was the Kotsk Rabbi's eldest son, were quite sorry he did not join them.

When the *Shaharit* cantor of *Beith Hamidrash* suddenly died, the Rabbi sent for Meir. Meir argued that his voice was not strong enough for *Beith Hamidrash* and that he was already committed for the *Musaf* in the Pelevers' praying place, but the Rabbi convinced him. He worked hard to learn the Ashkenazi prayers for New Year's Eve, and he prayed with the well known Kotsk devotion and sighs.

He is the only cantor of Biala that has a grave, because he died in Israel.

Hershale the Rabbi's son

Hershale, the youngest son of Biala's Rabbi, sometimes served as a cantor. He had a high, young, tenor voice. The Hasidim in Biala used to compare him with Mendel Buchner. He played the violin, and prayed the *Musaf* with a large choir. His *Kol Nidrei* was a big success, and people came to hear him from far away. He had a very nice melody for "*Yishtabach*", and the Hasidim in Biala adopted it. He had a very popular melody for "*ve'ak kulam*", which became a folk song – "Yente Geneshe received a telegram saying that all strikers were killed".

He was a rabbi in Siedlce, and died very young. His son became the rabbi of Biala in Tel-Aviv, Israel.

Mendel Azarekaver

He was a Hasid of Biala's Rabbi, and used to spend all the holydays with the Rabbi. He held the position of cantor in the morning prayers. Before the prayer he used to go to the Rabbi's *Mikve*, and his ginger beard became like a shining piece of red wood. He used to say "*Hamelech*" by the stage, and run with the same breath to the column, while the Hasidim moved to free his way. He prayed with such devotion, as if he meant to pull the heaven down to earth or the earth up to heaven.

[Page 263]

Moshe of Peia

Peia's Moshe was the cantor for the morning prayers in the *Mitnagdim*'s praying house, together with Rabbi Mneke. He used to sing the first "The King" with such a force, that his voice became hoarse.

I do not know why, but the devil got hold on him, the eldest and distinguished member of a well-known family, and one of the handsome persons in the *Mitnagdim*'s praying house. Each year he lost his voice during the high holidays, until he was in his 90s.

Menke the (*daian*) judge

Being a judge in Biala, where there were hundreds of certified Rabbis, was not a mean achievement. Rabbi Menke was the most handsome Jew in in the *Mitnagdim*'s praying house, and led the *Musaf*. He had a very nice baritone voice. He prayed with all his heart and pain. His assistants were: Haim Naftcharz (Hoffman), Arie's Baruch Jacob, and a son of Yosel Miner. His *Hakafot* in *Simhat Tora* were well known.

Itzke Moses

Itzke Moses was married to the granddaughter of the Kock Rabbi. He was raised in the Warka Rabbi's yard, a decedent of a well-known *Hasidic* family. Yet, even without all that heritage, he was suited to be the *Musaf* cantor in the Gere praying room, where the aristocracy of Biala prayed. He was over 70 when I met him. He was one of the Geres' great scholars, with an aristocratic-patriarchal grace.

His sweet, deep, baritone came into full expression when he prayed "*Ithgadal*" during *slihot*, or "*Barechu*" on New Year. I remember he used to pray in tunes that were also popular among the Kock Hassidim. He had a choir of six singers, three of whom – Leibish Commissioner (Heibloom), his brother Simha Heibloom, and Itzhak Lipes – were cantors themselves in the Gere praying room; the first in Biala, the second in Losice, and the third in Miedzyrzec. The other three singers were: Hershele David son of Iizik, Yoske Yehiel Hersh, and Moshe Yenterl (who died in Israel).

Mendel Buchner

Mendel Buchner was married to Yocheved, the daughter of Rabbi Noah Musinke. It means that big Moshe, small Moshe, and the Gere's rabbi (who recently passed away in Jerusalem) were his in-laws. He had a nice voice, good diction; he was clear and composed nice tunes. He was much respected in the Gere's praying place. He led the morning prayers on Saturdays and holidays, and took on leading the evening prayers after Itzke Moses left Biala. He had no help, and figured out how to present the most difficult prayers clearly.

His tune to "*kachomer beyad hayotzer*" (like putty in His hand) was based on a folk song "Everyone knows that there is no school on Sunday". This tune was arranged by Joseph Rumshinsky and sang by Molly Picon in the play "Yankele".

Leibish Ortcheleres

Leib Commissioner (Ortchelers) resembled Mendel Buchner. He liked the stage, and prayed with Hassidic ecstasy. After Mendel Buchner took on the leading of the evening prayers, Leib became a candidate for leading the morning prayers. Yet, his business, which involved long hours of daily train riding, was an obstacle. He used to go to Warsaw to buy merchandize and distribute it, so leading the morning prayers was physically impossible. After WWI, when his children had already left home, telephone connections and automobile transportation allowed him to quit traveling, and he became the morning cantor of the Grere praying place.

Whenever I think about my relative Leibish Ortchelers, I remember the way he used to sing *El Adon* on Saturday.

[Page 264]

The Rebbe's Court

by Asher Hoffer, Tel Aviv

Translated by Gloria Berkenstat Freund

When one said the Rebbe's Court in Biala, everyone knew that one meant the residence of the Biala Rebbe, Reb Yitzhak Yakov Rabinowicz.

The Biala Rebbe was descended from the *Yid Hakadosh* [the Holy Jew] – Yakov Yitzhak Rabinowicz of Peshischa [Przysucha], but he inherited the position of Hasidic rebbe from his father-in-law, Reb Yehosha, may his memory be blessed, of Lentchna [Łęczna], who did not leave any sons. Reb Yehosha was the Ostrower (Lublin region) Rebbe and his Hasidim were called the Ostrower Hasidim.

I cannot remember in which year Yitzhak Yakov Rabinowicz came to Biala and founded his court. I assume that the reason for moving the court from Ostrower to Biala was that Biala had a train station and Ostrower did not and the Rebbe did not want his Hasidim to come by horse and wagon.

The Rebbe established his court at the end of Mezricher Street, where he had an apartment, a house of prayer and a *mikvah* [ritual bath] built for him. The land and the buildings were the possessions of the Rebbe.

The Hasidim, who paid monthly money, supported the Rebbe's court. There were very rich Hasidim who let it cost them a great deal of money to support the court. They would pay a *pidyon* [redemption – a sum of money] when taking a *kvitl* [piece of paper with a petitionary prayer] to the Rebbe.

Several young men from the city and married young men who *zenen gezesn oyf kest* [sat on *kest* – young men who studied while their fathers-in-law paid their expenses] studied at the Rebbe's house of prayer. Young men from other cities, who would *ezen teg* [eat daily meals] at the homes of the city's middle class and also sleep in those houses, also studied there.

Hasidim from Warsaw, Siedlice, Lublin, Brisk, Mezrich, Łuków and other cities came to the Rebbe.

Life at the [Rebbe's] court was led in a rich manner. Life flowed quietly and monotonously during the weekdays. There was a commotion on the eve of holidays and on the holidays. The highpoint of the revival and tumult at the court was on the holiday, when Hasidim arrived from all corners of the country.

On a regular *Shabbos*, two or three *minyonim* [plural of *minyon* – 10 men required for prayer] of Hasidim would come to the Rebbe from the surrounding *shtetlekh* and then a bit of excitement was noticeable in the court. Reb Mendl Mezricher would come every *Shabbos* from Mezrich. Reb Mendl played host for his [the Rebbe's] sermon, which the Rebbe recited at his table and which he wrote out at the end of *Shabbos*. After the Rebbe's death, these were published in books (*Divre Binah* [*Words of Understanding*] and *Yishre Lev* [*The Upright of Heart*], revised by the Rebbe's son, Reb Avraham, the Lubliner Rebbe).

I saw before my eyes how the court appeared on the eve of holidays, on the holidays and during the Days of Awe.

On *Shabbos*, the young men, the so-called *kest-eidemlekh* [sons-in-law who were being financially supported while they studied], and the older Hasidim would arrive for the first *slikhos* [penitential prayers recited in the days before Rosh Hashanah and Yom Kippur]. The older Hasidim, who could not remain for Rosh Hashanah, would go home immediately in the morning, on Sunday. However, the young men remained until after Yom Kippur. A pot of pearl buckwheat would be cooked for these young men every day. The cooks, Yakov Slawatiszer and, later, Shimshon Parcewer, would be employed doing this. The young men would pay three *groshn* for a bowl of cooked food. The Biala young men brought bread from home and ate with those from outside Biala at the house of prayer.

On Rosh Hashanah, approximately 800 Hasidim would arrive. The house of prayer was packed and many Hasidim prayed in the courtyard. Immediately after Rosh Hashanah many Hasidim went home and others came for Yom Kippur, but not in such a large number.

Of the prayer leaders with the Rebbe on the Days of Awe, I remember: Moshe Orczechower, as a *baal Shakharis* [leader of the morning prayers]; Monish Morgnsztern of Brisk, Najtl, rabbi of Neishtot, Benyamin Gampl of Warsaw, Uzial Wajnberg of Biala and the Rebbe's younger son, Hershele, later the Siedlicer Rebbe, would lead the *Musaf* [additional prayers]. Hershele prayed with the choirboys.

The Hasidim who had arrived for the Days of Awe would stay at the inns of Hersh Yakob Czelazni at Garncarsker Street and with Moshe, the Rebbe's *Shamas* [rabbi's assistant].

It became quiet at the [Rebbe's] court after the Days of Awe and as lonesome as the autumn days that stretched out through them.

Thirty or 40 Hasidim came from away for *Sukkous* [Feast of Tabernacles], the majority young men who would need to appear for the draft and came to ask the Rebbe to pray for them so that they would be saved from gentile hands.

During Chanukah, the *kest-eidems* would come for the entire eight days and older Hasidim for the Chanukah *Shabbos*.

During the Chanukah evenings, the young men at the house of prayer would plays cards without pictures of people, instead of [the regular] cards. Cards were not supposed to be kept in the house of prayer because they had pictures of people on them. The cards without pictures were numbered from 15 to 20. 15 instead of a nine card, 16 [a 10 card], 17 a jack, 18 a queen, 19 a king and 20 an ace. For each number there were up to four playing cards without pictures and each card was marked in the middle with a number from one to four. One meant red, two – green, three – diamonds and four – clubs. Alter Cukerman, who we called Chaim Josl's Alter, was the one who drew the marks on the cards.

[Page 265]

Purim passed very cheerfully at the court. True, there were no arrivals of Hasidim but the Rebbe's house of prayer would be filled by the city's Hasidim and other members of the middle class, who would come to the Rebbe to tax themselves and see how the Rebbe *pravet tish* [lead a communal meal at which a rebbe's followers are present].

Ayzshe Libman would lead the entire *Purim-shpil* [Purim play] at the rabbi's house. He would impersonate the rabbi with a large hump, paste on a large flax beard and long *peyes* [side curls]. He would get on the table and recite witticisms; the audience would hold their sides in laughter. The impersonated rabbi had a Purim wife and the role would be carried out by Chaim Moshe's [son], Shmuel (Shmuel Kligsberg, a *melamed* [religious teacher]). The role of the Purim servant would be played by Yosef Meir, whom the Purim rabbi would call Yospe Mirl; he was called *Tsigarele* [cigarette] in the city. The Purim play would last until late at night. [People in] all kinds of disguises would come from the city and the Rebbe would give them all money. Mikhalkele Droszkarcz would come on a wooden horse, as well as young men from the *shtibl* disguised as officers.

It also was joyful in the *khederim* [religious primary schools] with the *rebitizin* [wife of the rabbi or teacher]. The women of the city would come together there. We, the young men who were studying at the Rebbe's house of study, would sneak into the *rebitizin's kheder* to see the performance of *The Selling of Joseph*, which a group from the city would come to perform. The *rebitizin* would treat the *Purim-shpilers* [actors] and also give them a fine coin.

Immediately after Purim, they began in the courtyard to prepare for Passover. They would bring the hand grinder from the attic and begin to grind the *shmurah* [grain grown under religious supervision] that hung the entire winter from the house of prayer ceiling. The *shmurah* wheat would be sent every summer from Łosice by Reb Yehuda Bekerman from his own fields (he was the owner of a courtyard near Łosice). Every *erev Pesakh* [the eve before Passover], Reb Bekerman would send a horse-drawn carriage to the Rebbe and the Rebbe would send six *shmurah* matzos that had been baked in the Rebbe's house of prayer.

We young men would turn the handmill and beautiful flour would emerge. For this work, we would receive whiskey at night from the Rebbe. We would work like this for two to three days, grinding the wheat and, meanwhile, be spared from learning which, for us young men, was also a great prize…

As we already had the flour, we needed to bake the matzos. This work also was carried out by the young men and the *kest-eidems* who studied at the house of prayer. The kneader was Itsl Cukerman; we called him Itsele Minister. Another one was a flour strewer, a third a water pourer. The Rebbe would mostly do the cutting with a wooden knife and we young men would roll the matzos with glass rolling pins. There was a large baking oven in the antechamber of the house of prayer and there we would bake the matzos. The baker shoveler was Alter Note, the bagel baker (the husband of Rayzele, the maker of little cakes). Every evening, the Rebbe would distribute whiskey to the helpers.

Erev Pesakh, we would again bake *shmurah* matzos and we young men would be the bakers and, therefore, we would receive one *shmurah* matzo.

On Passover, several Hasidim who did not have wives or children and had to submit to the draft would come to the Rebbe. The young people would need to bring permission from their wives that they agreed that their husbands could leave their homes for Passover. The guests would be at the Rebbe's court for the entire eight days of Passover.

On *Shavous* [spring holiday celebrating the receiving of the Torah], there would again be a large number of Hasidim, who would come to receive the Torah at the Rebbe's [house].

Summertime, the Rebbe and the *rebitzin* would travel to various cure spots and often even abroad.

Thus, life in the Rebbe's court flowed the entire yearly cycle, year in and year out.

The entire Jewish population of the city acted with great reverence for the Rebbe [including] *Misnagdim* [opponents of Hasidus] and Hasidim from other rebbes. The government also had respect for the Rebbe.

The Rebbe died in Warsaw in 5665 (1904) and was buried at the Warsaw Cemetery.

Shortly after the Rebbe's death, the Rebbe's courtyard was burned and, in general, a rabbinical court ceased to exist in Biala.

[Page 266]

Rabbis and Rebbes in Biala
(Material about religious leaders in Biala)

Meir Edelbaum, New York

Translated by Gloria Berkenstat Freund

Edited by Libby Raichman

A. Rabbis

The first Biala rabbi who we find in the historical material was, it appears, one of the great ancestors of the well-known rabbis. The name of this rabbi is "Yosef Hurvitz, who settled in the holy community of Biali, he is the very honored master and teacher of Mordechai Segal, may his righteous memory be blessed".

This is how he signed the approbation that he gave that appears on the well-known book of sermons, *Words of the Covenant* of Avraham Zvi, son of the rabbi and kabbalist... Meir. The approbation is dated the 2nd of Cheshvan [5th of October] 5489 (1728).

Not only was the Horowicz family of great lineage, but the Biala Rabbi himself cites in his approbation the endorsement of the well-known Brisker Rabbi, Yisroel Iserl whom he called "in-law." To be an in-law of the greatest rabbis of his time demanded a great deal of self-worth. This shows that the Biala Rabbi was a well-known rabbinical personality, which was very natural for Biala, which at that time was considered among the most respected *kehilus* [organized Jewish communities] in Poland.

In any case, the interval of time between him and his successor, Reb Euzer, a son of the famous Rabbi, Reb Abishl Frankfurter, was probably not a very long time. In 5514 [1754], when Avraham Abish, the Mezritcher Rabbi (successor of his father, Reb Tzvi-Hirsh), was welcomed as a rabbi in Lithuania, his son Reb Euzer, was then welcomed in his place as the rabbi in Biala. It is therefore assumed that Reb Euzer was the rabbi in Biala after Reb Yosef, although we cannot say for sure if there was not someone else as rabbi in Biala between him and Reb Yosef.

After Reb Euzer, and perhaps much earlier than even Reb Euzer, the Rabbi was a certain Reb Yehuda Idl. We learn about Reb Yehuda Idl from his grandson, Reb Yehuda Leib, Rabbi in Zager, son of the well-known *Gaon* [genius], Reb Shimkha Tiktiner. The above-mentioned Reb Yehuda Leib wrote in his introduction to his book, *Shalmei Simkha* [*Complete Joy*], Vilna 5566 [1806]: Yehudah Leib descendant of the Gaon ….. Reb Simchah of blessed memory … and so I am the son of Rivkah, the daughter of the great luminary, Mr. Yehudah Iddel of Kotzk, and of Biali, and of Mezritsh, of the family of the Korahites". This Reb Yehuda Leib died in the year 5596 [1836], two years after Reb Euzer probably became the rabbi in Mezeritch. He was either the rabbi in Biala before Reb Euzer or after him.

After Reb Euzer or after Reb Yehuda Idl, the rabbi was one of those rabbis who led the bitter quarrels against the well-known Rabbi, Reb Yonoson Eibeschitz. His name was Reb Yitzkak. He was a son of the very well-known Rabbi, Reb Meir Asch (Eisenstadt based on the name of the city in Mer, where he was the rabbi [Kismarton], later known as Eisenstadt]), the author of the well-known book of responsa, *Panim Me'irot* [*Illuminated Face*].

This Reb Yitzhak previously was the rabbi in Nesvizh [Niasviž], as was well known the second place of residence of the princely Radziwill family, and possibly, that Reb Yitzhak was a member of the entourage of the princely court (by the way, Reb Yitzhak was an in-law of the Liser Rabbi, Reb Mordekhai, the oldest brother of Reb Abushl Frankfurter; both, as is well known, born in Mezritch). He was connected by marriage to Reb Yakov Emdin, with whom Reb Yonoson [Jonathan] Eibeschitz was engaged in many controversies.

When Reb Yakov Emdin began a fight against Reb Yonoson Eibeschitz, whom he suspected of being a follower of Shabatai Tzvi, the entire rabbinic world, with few exceptions, stood in flames in this quarrel. Reb Yitzhak, the Biala Rabbi, with his father-in-law, Reb Borukh Marc (who previously lived in Biala and later in Konstantyn), who was probably in addition a scholar as well as a rich man, threw himself into the struggle and did everything in his power to persecute and degrade Reb Yoncson Eibeschitz. Reb Yitzhak even went on a long trip through the cities in Volyn and Galicia to recruit rabbis against the followers of Shabatai Tzvi and Jakob Frank, including Reb Yonosn Eibeschitz and tried to convince the Council of the Four Lands, which held a meeting in the *shtetele* [small town] of Konstantyn to excommunicate Reb Yonoson Eibeschitz.

It is worth adding that Reb Yonoson Eibeschitz and the Biala Rabbi, Reb Yitzhak, had known each other since their early youth. Reb Yonoson became an orphan at an early age and Reb Yitzhak's father took Reb Yonoson, who had the mind of a prodigy, and studied Torah with him (had something happened between the two friends in their youth that influenced their later quarrels?).

We will provide two letters whose author was none other than the Biala Rabbi, Reb Yitzhak, and which meant a great deal in his time. Although these two letters were mainly dedicated to the matter of Jakob Frank, Reb Yitzhak did not forget to attack Reb Yonoson Eibeschitz in them.

The first letter is taken from the instruction book, Amsterdamin 1759, the year of acquisition.

5520 [1760]. This book is a collection of letters from a number of prominent men in Poland from the Great Council of the Four Lands in connection with the sad events that occurred in Podolia two years earlier – here they are talking about Jakob Frank and his followers, who later converted [to Christianity].

[Page 267]

This letter is provided with the heading: The letter of the honorable president of the Rabbinic court of Biala, says that Yehonatan will die like a villain on 27th Elul, for "he had power over the angel and prevailed" - Hosea 12:4.

It is not clear who made use of this sharp and ugly pompous curse, which is a paraphrase of the words, "Should Abner have died the death of a knave?" in the well-known elegy by King David over the death of Abner, the commander of the Army of Israel, who was murdered by David's army commander, Joab, when he defected to David after the death of Saul. David then felt strongly affected by Joab's traitorous act and he called out in resentment: Should Abner have died the death of a knave?

The author of the heading of the letter curses Reb Yonoson Eibeschitz and says: "Should Yonoson have died the death of a knave?" – that he should die like a vile person. Then this author found an appropriate expression in the telling of the story from the Torah about the struggle between Jacob and the angel, "Jacob wrestled with an angel." The [numerical equivalent of the] letters of the word *veyosher* [*vov, yud, shim, resh*] are equal to the number of the year 5515 [1755], when the letter was written: Jacob is the name of the one who liked to argue with Reb Yonoson; *malekh* [angel] alludes to Reb Yonoson in the sense of the *Midrash* [commentaries], that the angel with whom Jacob wrestled was the guardian angel of Esau. While in Reb Yitzhak's letter the date cannot be found, there is an opportunity to suspect that Reb Yitzhak wrote the transcription. It makes no sense that Reb Jakub Edmen, the author of the book, should write about himself, "Jacob wrestled [*veyosher*] with an angel, and prevailed…"

"he had power over the angel"

And here is the content of the letter:

He who revives life, will give him a blessing, and give him life, to my master the rabbi, the famous Gaon, beloved teacher, the Rabbi Ya'akov, may his light shine.

After enquiring about your well-being, all this is about those who believe in Shabtai Tzvi, may his name be erased, and delivered to a reporter from the Rabbi, the Gaon, our teacher the Rabbi Reb Meir, president of the Rabbinical court of the holy community of Horodenka, that was written to the holy community of Brod. It was copied from the evidence that was written in the body of the letter of the Rabbi, the Gaon, the president of the Rabbinical court of Satnov, may God protect and preserve him, who publicly revealed the shame of the followers of Shabtai Tzvi. And for a married woman of the followers of Shabtai Tzvi, it will be regarded as a mitzvah to commit adultery and desecrate the Shabbat and the text of their prayer, and the celebration of their festivals.[1] And there were among them, those who were taken in iron chains to the master, the Bishop.[2] And God will save our brothers of flesh and blood from the contaminated thoughts of these arrogant people. And also, the wording of the great excommunication that was imposed in the holy community of Lvov, and the holy community of Lutzk, and the holy community of Brod, and the holy community of Dubno, and all the chronicles explained in the Book of Kolboh [book of Halachah, first printed in Naples in 1490]. Anyone who marries, or enters into business transactions or eats of the food of any man or woman of the wicked that are mentioned above, they will be excommunicated like them. And also, any two people who know that someone belongs to these wicked ones, they are compelled to testify in the Rabbinical court and publicize the matter. The ban will also fall on everyone who will study this heretic literature, the books of the Rabbi Natan[3], a prophet of the Shabtai Tzvi movement, and Nechemiah Chia Chivan[4], and the meaning of their amulets, and their flawed books, *v'avo el ha'ayin*. And everyone who is in possession of the contaminated books mentioned above, or the style of their new amulets, may we never hear or see their likeness, the ban will fall on him too, if he does not burn them, or references to them. The ban mentioned above will also fall on everyone who discovers golden coins. They will be excommunicated and excluded from all the sanctity of Israel. Also, the copying of the prayers that are prayed to his daughter [Chavah Frank, daughter of Ya'akov Frank] may her name and her memory be erased.[5] And today, they will be counted, and their ban will be completed in all the borders of Israel before Kol Nidrei. The Rabbi the Gaon, the teacher Chaim Katz, president of the Rabbinic council of the holy community of Lvov[6], stood among a few of the people of the sect of Shabtai Tzvi, may the name of the wicked rot, before the bishop and his ministers, and God gave Chaim Katz graciousness, and the officials gave him permission to excommunicate the followers of Shabtai Tzvi and take them to prison. And now that the punishment has commenced, he will be satisfied. At the end of all this, all the Jewish people realized that the essence of his words were truth and righteousness, and that "Jacob will rejoice and Israel will be glad" [Psalm 14:7, Psalm 14:7], in our righteous savior and in the building of the heroic city of Jerusalem; and that the wicked will be cut off and that no trace of them will remain, may their names be erased. And these will understand the curse and they will be caught on the side of the ban; in the holy community of Lantzkron[7], the holy community of Busk, the holy community of Aziran, the holy community of Apatshene, the holy community of Kribtshin. Their Rabbi, out of madness, made himself into a prophet, and some repulsiveness that would prevent any entry into Gan Eden[8]. I will see to sending merchants to Danzig or to Frankfort Oder [today, a town in Germany on the Polish border] with foreign currency, for expenses.

And a time will come when man will have peace, the people of Israel will be quiet and at rest, as a green olive tree. [Jeremiah 30:10, Jeremiah 46:27]. Avraham, the community leader of the holy committee, of the holy community of Lublin, and his son the Rabbi[9], are regretful of the past issues, and say: what should we say, and what shall we speak, that the devil tempted us and there were some personal and financial links in some respects.

All the early writings falsely accused and defamed him. But today it is clear, that he Yonatan, the eldest son of the devil, perverted the people of Israel. The holy committee hurried to impose a ban on his books and his amulets. I was in the holy community of Konstantin for two weeks with our in-laws, our teacher, the Rabbi Baruch, may God preserve him. There was a great commotion caused by the confusion that was provoked in the holy community of Yampoli [Podolye][10]that was ensnared in a bad trap with a perplexity of false charges in Pablimash (?) and all the dignitaries were taken in metal chains, may God have mercy upon them, to which all the people of Israel responded, and said, that because of this sin, the blood of Israel was shed in that region. Because of that uproar, I was forced to wait until it was announced in the synagogue, and the Rabbi, our teacher, Pinchas[11], promised that his regret and the announcement of the ban would be published in the holy community of Zalkva. So, his respected mind will be at rest, and the letter would be delayed until the new moon [Rosh Chodesh] of Cheshvan, [the 8th month in the Jewish calendar] in 1747 here in Bialah. And I have come to repeat for the last time, to write an answer that is focused simply on Warsaw and specifically on these two great men – the Rabbi who is our teacher, the Rabbi Avraham Katz from Zamut and the Rabbi, our teacher Baruch, may God preserve him.

And with this I will leave in peace, with thanks to our Rabbis. May God grant that they will be raised up higher and higher, and 'the righteous will flourish like the palm tree' [Ps 92:13]. Likewise, I pay my respects to you, the holy Yitzchak, of the Burial Society, as in the case of Bialah.

[Page 268]

A second letter about the same matter, which is also of historical value, dated 14th Kislev *b'shir"h* (1837) *lp"k* here in Bialah, via Danzig.

After greeting him, I wrote to his highness about the Rabbi, his excellence, the teacher, the Rabbi Itzik, of the holy community of Levertov and also about the Rabbi, the luminary of the exile, the Rabbi Avraham Gutman, may God preserve him, the President of the Rabbinical court of the holy community of Dribnin, with a bundle of manuscripts from his honour, the Rabbi, the Gaon, our teacher, the Rabbi Avraham. And I did not know if the writings would reach his honest hand, and I came to repeat for the third time, and to inform of the words that were said in truth, a conciseness, according to the brevity of the speaker; that the voice will be loudly heard because of the enormity of the desecration of the name of God, what had happened in the holy community Lvov where one of the believers in Shabtai Tzvi, the name of the wicked will rot, came on the day that he publicly desecrated the Sabbath, and allowed smoke to rise to the height of his nose, in anger [2 Samuel 22:9], who dared to communicate with God and defied the honour of the Rabbi, the Gaon, our teacher Chaim Katz, in the presence of the Bishop; and God was with him, and for this he was condemned to death. In this way, all the evil people of the land will disappear. I was also in the holy community of Konstantin, with the distinguished Rabbi, our teacher Baruch, mentioned above, together with the community leader of the "Four Lands", that is, Reb Avraham of Lublin, and behold he regrets the past, with total remorse, firm, and abiding. He asked us, to request his pardon, of His Highness, to ask for forgiveness for what he said, for he is not the master in this matter, that all the manuscripts of Reb Yehonatan are written in one style, that falsely accuse with lies; and now I will speak the truth to Jacob [Micha 7:20]. In the end, we will see that the essence of his words is true, that this man was caught and excommunicated in the gathering of the wicked, the people of the holy communities of Lantzkron, Aziran, Kaposshetz, Kribshtin. And I sent evidence of the ban to those who studied the books and manuscripts of that heretic, Reb Yehonatan, and those who write the incantations according to their style. And with this, I will go out safe and sound with thanks to the Rabbi, bringing peace to the holy, learned Yitzchak, and putting his mind at rest, as in the case of Biale.

These two letters, among many others, are important documents. In them, we have a report of one of the rabbinical eyewitnesses and chief fighters in the war that Jewry led against Jakob Frank and his followers.

From the letter we see that the matter of excommunicating everyone who was suspected of having Sabbatai Tzvi tendencies was not so simple. It simply could not be assumed that entire Jewish communities such as Łyskornia, Busko, Ozeran [Ozeryany, Ukraine], Kopyczynce and Krivtchin would have declared themselves as followers of Jakob Frank and that at the congress of the leaders of the Council of the Four Nations they would be excommunicated. Perhaps he means the avowed and hidden followers of Sabbatai Tzvi and the Frankists. We must accept with caution Reb Yitzhak's words about the excommunication of everyone who studied the books, manuscripts such as Reb Yonoson's "who study the books, the manuscripts of Reb Yehonatan and those who write the incantations according to his style".

There cannot be any talk here about an excommunication that the Council of the Four Lands placed on Reb Yonoson Eibeschitz. The Council of the Four Lands did not take any clear position in the quarrel. Certainly, Reb Yonoson Eibeschitz found the strongest following in Poland. Even the Vilna *Gaon* [the Vilna Sage, Rabbi Eliyahu *ben* Shlomo Zalman], then not as well-known and influential as he was later, took the Rebbe, Reb Yonoson, as Polish Jewry later called him, under his protection. Therefore, it is assumed that Reb Yitzhak was describing only the rabbis who were Reb Yonoson's opponents, that they excommunicated him. On the other hand, Reb Yonoson's followers excommunicated their opponents.

In his second letter, Reb Yitzhak again mentioned the quarrel with the Frankists, in which the well-known Lemberger Rabbi, Reb Chaim Kac-Rapoport, an in-law of Reb Yitzhak Bialer, played a main role.

It is also interesting to mention that the Bialer Rabbi said, incidentally, that because of postage, which it was difficult for him to spend, he would send Reb Yitzhak Edmen the letter through the people who were traveling to Danzig and Frankfurt on the River Oder. Therefore, it appears that Biala Jews traveled to fairs in Frankfurt and traded with Danzig.

Reb Yitzhak died in the year 5535 [1775].

After the death of the Rabbi Reb Yitzhak, his place was taken by his brother, the Rabbi Reb Sabbatai, who died in 5550 [1790].

The Rabbi Reb Yosef probably followed him. We know very little about him. According to the well-known researcher about rabbinical lineage, Reb Yosef Lewensztajn, the rabbi in Serock, his [Reb Yosef's] father was supposed to have been the author of a book on Torah named *Kokhavi Yakov* [*Star of Jacob*]. While such a book is not mentioned in the lists of published books, it is assumed that what is being discussed is a manuscript. He died in the month of Elul 5563 [approximately September 1803].

We do not know who the rabbi was after him. We know of a Biala Rabbi, Reb Avraham Abele, who died in 5593 [1833] at the young age of 32. This Avraham Abele came from Warsaw. His father is recorded as "The great, sharp-witted, famous, master, our teacher, Rabbi Chaim of Warsaw, may his light shine".

[Page 269]

This Rabbi, Reb Chaim may his light shine, was none other than the well-known Warsaw Rabbi, Reb Chaim Davidzon, ancestor of the famous Warsaw Davidzon family. When the son died, the father was still alive, which can be seen by the words, *Nero Yair* – May his light shine. We know this from the eulogy that the famous preacher and popularizer of the Dubner *Magid* [preacher], Reb Dov Berish Flam of Mezritch Poldaska, gave about him and after the publication of his book *Avel Yakhid* [*Individual Mourner*], which contains a series of eulogies and was published in Warsaw in the same year, 5593.

That Biala was thought of as a great and illustrious rabbinate is seen in that this Reb Avraham Abele whom Reb Berish Flam eulogized and called "the Rabbi, the great luminary, the astute, venerated, and perfect". He must truly have been a great prodigy, occupying such a position as a young man. He was then in total 32 years old when he died. That he was a man with great knowledge of Jewish law can also be seen in his response that he exchanged with the prominent rabbis of his time, such as the famous Warsaw Rabbi, Reb Shlomo Zalman Poizner. In an answer to the Biala Rabbi in his book "Chemdat Shlomo", a section of the "Yoreh De'ah", part 28, he writes to him: "To my friend, the great luminary, of honoured name and glory, he is Avraham Abele, the President of the Religious court of the holy community of Biali, in Lithuania. May his light shine."

The renowned *Gaon* [genius] Reb Meir Rottenberg, the author of the book of responsa, our teacher, our Rabbi Reb Meir, earlier the Rabbi in Wlodowa near Biala and then in Zamocz, asks a question of the young Biala Rabbi, "the Great Luminary" taken from the section "Choshen Mishpat" [4th part of the Shulchan Aruch]," from Yoreh De'ah [section of the book of Haturim and the Shulchan Aruch].

His successor possibly was Reb Moshe Mikhl whose father, Reb Fishel Strzyzover, was widely known as a great kabbalist and author of the famous book of kabbalah, *Olam Hafukh* [*Upside Down World*].

About Moshe Mikhl, who died in the year 5596 [1836] in Biala, we know that he was one of the great students of the Kotzker [Rebbe] and close friend of the *Khidushei haRim*[a], Reb Yitzhak Meir Alter the heir of Reb Mendele Kotzker and founder of the Gerer [Hasidic] dynasty. A story was told about him that once while traveling with the *Khidushei haRim* to Kotzk, they traveled past a *shtetl*, and no one invited them in. The *shtetl* was punished because of the great dizziness [he suffered] because of the insult to the Torah [in the person of] the *Khidushei haRim*. A fire broke out as soon as they left there. It is plausible that Reb Moshe Mikhl was the first Hasidic rabbi in Biala.

The successor of Reb Moshe Mikhl was another Kotzker Hasid and the Kotzker's in-law, Reb Nakhum Zev Borenstein, previously the rabbi in the small *shtetele* [town] Olkusz. Reb Nakhum died in 5648 [1888]. He was considered among the Torah giants in Kotzk and his book *Agudas Eizov* [*Bundle of Hyssop*] on Jewish law is a scholarly book. He led a *yeshiva* [religious secondary school] in Biala and he established a generation of scholars and Hasidim. All sorts of miracles and wonders were told about him. One is connected to the birth of his well-known son, Reb Avrahamele**Error! Bookmark not defined.**, the Sochoczewer Rebbi and the author of the famous scholarly books, *Avnei Nezer* [*Stones of the Crown*] and *Eglei Tal* [*Drops of Dew* – book on the 39 labors prohibited on the Sabbath], which made him famous as a genius of his generation even in Lithuania. It is told that once on Purim, Reb Nakhum was engrossed in learning when the entire Jewish world was enjoying the joys of Purim, and that the world could only have existed in the merit of Torah and would not have had any existence that Purim if Reb Nakhum Zev had not illuminated all seven heavens and heavenly palaces with his nightly study of Torah. Because of this, he was given a son who illuminated all the world with his knowledge and *tzedakah* [charity] and the great Kotzker *tzadek* [righteous man], Reb Mendele, chose him as the husband for his daughter, Tzina. And although the Kotzker

[Rebbe] would chase away all of the Hasidim and spent his time locked away from them, and even from his great students, he made an exception for his young son-in-law and guided him in study and observed him all of the time.

After Reb Nakhum Shmuel Leib Zack was the rabbi. Reb Shmuel Leib was a very old man when he died during the winter of 5692 (1932). In Biala and in the area, he was considered a great *tzadek* and we would go to be blessed by him. He was a student of the famous *gaon* [sage], Reb Yosef Shaul Natanzon, rabbi in Lemberg and of the author of the *Khidushei haRim*, the first Gerer Rebbe. Reb Shmuel Leib *hot gegesn kest* [financial support while a young groom studies religious texts] with the famous *tzadek*, Reb Yehosha (Shiele) Ostrower, because Reb Shmuel Leib was a son-in-law of the Ostrower's brother-in-law, Reb MosheYehuda Lieb, who was a son-in-law of the Lentshner *Tzadek*, Reb Shlomo Leib.

Reb Shmuel Leib Zack was lenient in his interpretation of the laws of fasting, and on *Tisha B'Av* [fast commemorating the destruction of the Temples in Jerusalem], 1904, during the great fire in Biala, he announced that they should not fast more than half a day. It should be understood that not everyone wanted to make use of the rabbinical permission, but even those who favored a rigorous interpretation of the laws among the Hasidic Jews did not dare to criticize the Biala Rabbi's permission out of great respect [for him].

Additional Facts:

It is clear that Reb Yosef Hurwicz was not the first rabbi in Biala. However, attempts to learn the name of the previous rabbi were not successful.

Biala belonged to the old Jewish communities in Poland. The city was established by the end of the 15th century and Jews were already settled in the area, mainly in Brisk-Dalita [Brest-Litovsk].

[Page 270]

It is therefore assumed that after the rise of Biala Jews settled there.

So, it can be seen from the acts of the Brisker municipal court that by the end of the 16th century Jews were found in Biala. As is described in the court proceedings, the relationship between the princely Radziwill family of Biala and the Chodkiewicz family was strained. In 1589, Chodkiewicz's militia men attacked the *arendar* [leaseholder] of Radziwill's court, Yisroel *ben* (son of) Eliezer, beat him, placed him in chains and threatened to burn him alive. The same fate awaited the Jew, Marek Yakovich (Mordekhai *ben* [son of] Yitzhak?], Eliezer *ben* Yeshayahu and Joseph's wife – all subjects of Radziwill. However, it was fortunate for them because they were saved at the last moment by one of Radziwill's militiamen.

In his treatise, *Yidn in Biala* [*Jews in Biala*], Dr. M. Hendl writes that in 1621, the Jewish community in Biala was already well-established. Therefore, it cannot be considered a community without a rabbi.

According to various sources we see that the names of rabbis are mentioned who sat on the rabbinical seat in Biala even before Reb Yosef Hurwicz, such as:

Reb Ahron Shmuel (*Maharshak* [abbreviation for *Morenu haRav* – our teacher, our rabbi – *Shmuel Kaidanover*]): rabbi and author, 1614 in Vilna, 1676 (1679) Krakow. Rabbi in Biala (near Brisk) in Nikolsburg, in Glogau, in Fürth, in Frankfurt on Main and in Krakow. One of the great rabbis of his generation. During the days of the Ukrainian [Chelmnitski] pogroms, 5408-5408 [1648-1649], he escaped from Biala to Vilna and Lublin. He was wounded; his two daughters were murdered and several of his treatises, his manuscripts, *Birkat ha-Zebah* and *Tiferet Shmuel* (novel interpretations of the Talmud), *Birkat Shmuel* [sermons], *Emunat Shmuel* (*General Encyclopedia*, Masada Publishing House, Tel Aviv, volume 6, page 302/3) were lost.

It is assumed that Reb Ahron Shmuel (*Maharshak*) was the rabbi in Biala for a very short time. Incidentally, here we have a confirmation that the tragic events of 1648-1649 reached Biala.

Reb Eliyahu *ben* Shmuel, in his book of responsa, *Yad Eliyahu*, that was published in Amsterdam in the year 5472 – 1712, in question 17 says: A matter that came before me when I was in the holy community of Biali, in the year 1691, concerning the selling of leavened food on the eve of Passover.

(A question concerning the sale of *khometz* [foods containing leavening] on the eve of Passover that he was asked when he was the rabbi in Biala in 5451 – 1691). The rabbi carried on a correspondence with the Brisker Rabbi, Reb Yisroel, about this question.

Reb Eliyahu *ben* Shmuel died in 5495 – 1735.

The mentioned rabbi was probably born in Lublin. In around 5442 – 1682 he settled in Brisk and there studied with the *Mofet haDor haMaor haGadol* [the greatest of his generation, the great light] Mendel Katz, may his light shine. Reb Eliyahu was the rabbi in several large Jewish communities in Poland and Lithuania, as well in Eibeschitz [Ivancice] (now Czechoslavakia [Czech Republic]). From his book, *Yad Eliyahu*, which is the only one that remained of his many innovations and writings, we see the Torah war that was carried out between him and the Brisker Rabbi, Reb Yisroel, the Hamburger Rabbi, Reb Moshe *bar* Mordekhai Ziskind, the Bamberger Rabbi, Reb Mendl Rotschild, and so on.

Reb Tzvi Hirsh *kharef* [sharp student], a son of the Lemberger chief rabbi, Reb Naftali Hirtz Ashkenazi. It can be seen from his book, *Kos Yeshuos* [*Cup of Salvation*], that he was the rabbi in Biala. He died in 5508 – 1748. It is difficult to say if he was the rabbi in Biala before Reb Yosef Hurwicz or after him.

Here we will add still more names of Biala rabbis who were not mentioned in the treatise by Meir Edlbaum.

It is assumed that after Reb Yitzhak, the Bialer rabbinate was inherited by his brother, Yehuda (a son-in-law of Reb Naftali Hirtz *bar* Khenokh, the Zulkewer Rabbi – book *Anaf Etz Avot* [ancestral family trees] of Shmuel Khenokh Kahane, Krakow 5664 [1903]; also Dr. M. Hendl *Yidn in Biala* [*Jews in Biala*] – about the Jewish community and outside world) and not his brother Shabtai, who was the Bialer rabbi in later years.

It appears that the position in the chapter, "B. Biala *Kehile*" in the treatise of Dr M. Hendl's *Yidn in Biala*, about the nomination of Reb Yosia *ben* Yakov in 1765 as the Biala Rabbi, has a connection to Reb Yosef, *baal Kokhavi Yakov* [author of *Star of Jacob*]. It can be assumed that the rabbi, who the duke had dismissed, was the previously mentioned Reb Yehuda.

Reb Yosef *ben baal Kokhavi Yakov* died in 5663 – 1803. However, it is probable that he was not the rabbi in Biala until the end of his life because Reb Shabtai, the brother of the mentioned rabbis, Reb Yitzhak and Reb Yehuda, who also was the Bialer Rabbi, died in 1790 [5550] (previously, he was the rabbi in Szereszow).

Reb Menakhem Nakhum Ginzburg was probably the rabbi in Biala after Reb Shabtai. We see this in the book, *Penei Levi* [*Faces of Levi* – treatise about ritual circumcision], published by the mentioned rabbi's grandson, Reb Naftali-Yosef *haLevi* Fraind (Piotrkow 5664 [1904], rabbi in Rózan (Lomza region). The author writes in this book: "The Gaon, Reb Menachem Nachum, the President of the Religious Court in the great Biale, wrote booklets in his handwriting about the debate, and it appears that he composed all about ("*Ba'al Ha'Trumah*").

Reb Menakhem Nakhum belonged to the famous family of Baron Ginzburg, Petersburg. His father, Reb Kalman *gaon* and Hasid, was the Siemiatyczer Rabbi and died in 5543 –1783. Reb Menakhem Nakhum had two sons: Reb Moshe, Rabbi in Siemiatycze and in Kolna, and Reb Asher, Rabbi in Kraœnik.

[Page 271]

In the book *Penei Levi* it is said about Menakhem Nakhum's son, Reb Moshe:

Reb Moshe of Kolno, mentioned above, the son-in-law of the wealthy, exalted Reb Mordechai Blumkes of Biala (and he is the father-in-law of the rich, the grand and the eminent Reb Hirtzel Ha'Cohen, Reb Aharon Sheinberg, and Reb Izik Shachor). The son-in-law of the Gaon *mufh"d,* Reb Tzvi Hirsh Furlicker (Friluker) of Brisk.

The author of the book, *Daat Moshe* [*Law of Moses*] (Warsaw) 5671 [1911], Moshe *ben* Tzvi Hirsh, belonged to this rabbinical family. For some reason, his name was Rozenbaum. He died in Biala in 5750 – 1890.

The last Biala rabbi was Reb Tzvi Hirshhorn, previously the rabbi in Jaworzno. He was welcomed as a rabbi six years after the death of Reb Shmuel Leib, a holy person. After the arrival of the Gestapo in Biala in 1939, Tzvi Hirshhorn illegally crossed the German-

Russian border near Semiatycze and went to his parents in Lemberg. The *rebbitizen* [rabbi's wife] remained in Biala with her sister and they were deported to Mezritch, from which they were sent to the Treblinka death camp.

M.Y. Fajgnbaum

B. Hasidic Biala

The victorious march of Hasidism did not bypass Biala. It is assumed that the zealous rabbis from this place such as the Biala Rabbi, Reb Yitzhak (later the combatant of the followers of Shabtai Tzvi and followers of Reb Yonoson Eibeschitz), looked with suspicion at each new religious phenomenon in Jewry, particularly in their communities and, of course, were afraid of the new sects – the Hasidim – but they were unable to prevent the victory march of Hasidism. Biala, like all other *shtetlekh* in the area, became almost exclusively Hasidic. The only two cities in the area that were able to preserve their old path were Brisk and Mezritch.

It is difficult to establish when the first Hasidic sprouting actually appeared in Biala and who was the first leader of the Hasidic movement. It is believed that the first Hasidic rabbi in Biala was the Kotzker Hasid, Reb Moshe Mikhl. There is no proof that the previous rabbi, Reb Avraham Abele was a Hasid. We have not found any proof for this in the Hasidic books. The fact that from Reb Moshe Mikhl on, the rabbis in Biala were only Hasidim, is enough proof that long before this, Biala had a large Hasidic population that could impose a Hasidic rabbi on the *kehile* [organized Jewish community].

It is also assumed that Biala was a fortress of Kotzker Hasidim. This is shown by the fact that the first two Hasidic rabbis from Biala, the above-mentioned Reb Moshe Mikhl and his successor, Reb Nakhum Zeev Bornsztajn, were Kotzker Hasidim. There were other Hasidim there at that time: Wurker, Lentshner [Łêczna] or Ostrower, as they called themselves after the death of Lentshner [rebbe], when his son and successor settled in Ostrowa, etc. The Ostrower were, it appears, the second in number. After the split of Reb Mordekhai Josef Eibeschitz from the Kotzker court, new Hasidim came to there who later were known as Ridziner Hasidim. The Kotzker themselves later were divided between the Gererand Kotzker. This happened when Reb Mendele Kotzker died and Reb Itshe Meir Alter the *Baal Khiddushei haRim* [author of commentary on Torah] began to control the position of Hasidic rabbi. The majority followed the *Baal Khiddushei haRim* and the other remained with Reb Dovid, who controlled the position of Hasidic rabbi in Kotzk after the death of his father.

Although Biala was more geographically Lithuania than Poland, based on the character of its Jews, it was more of a Polish-Jewish *shtetl* in the sense that it was almost exclusively Hasidic. The third Rabbi, Reb Shmuel Leib Zak, was a Hasidic rabbi. One can assume that his selection occurred not only because of his Hasidus and piety – there were many such Hasidic rabbis who also were considered to be righteous Jews – but more likely because of his support from the Gerer and Ostrower. [Hasidim].

As already mentioned, Reb Shmuel Leib was a student of and even an intimate of Reb Itshe Meir's heir, Reb Arya Leib, known by the name of his treatise on the Torah and *gemore* [commentaries], *Sefat Emet* [*The Language of Truth*]. His second pedigree was kinship with Lentshne; he was the husband of Reb Shlomo Leib Lentshner ß's granddaughter and thus a cousin of Reb Yankele Bialer, the successor of Reb Shiele Ostrower. Both Hasidic camps had enough strength to conquer the other Hasidic groups and elect a rabbi from among their own, which as a result, gave prestige to their Hasidim.

As it appears, there were respected Hasidim, rich men, scholars and influential people in Biala. From a letter that the *Baal Khiddushei haRim* [Yitzhak Meir Rotenberg-Alter wrote to his followers in neighboring Metzritch, when a quarrel between the *misnagdim* [opponents of the Hasidim] and the Hasidim blazed there, it can be seen that the Biala Hasidim became involved and tried to influence the Mezritcher to stop the quarrels. Biala also was well-known for the Hasidic marriage matches it made between people with good lineage. Reb Itshe Meir's ([known as] *Khiddushei HaRim*) grandsons or sons-in-law were born in Biala. Reb Mordekhai Alter, the last of the old Gerer dynasty in Poland, who died in Jerusalem, was a son-in-law of the well-known Biala scholar and Gerer Hasid, Reb Noakh Shur. Reb Avrahamele Chechanower, one of the best-known experts on Jewish law at his time, who began to lead the rabbinate after the Kotzker also was related to Biala by marriage. Two of his famous sons, Reb Berish, who became famous later as the Biala Rebbe, and Reb Yankele, Nashelsker Rebbe, were sons-in-law of the same father-in-law.

[Page 272]

As we are speaking of aristocratic matches, we must also remember another important match, although in the *misnagid* sector. The Moscow Rabbi, Reb Chaim Berlin, the son of Reb Naftali Zwi Yehuda Berlin – *haNetziv* [acroynym of his name] – Volozhiner, married into the famous Biala family Shur, taking as his wife, Tila, the daughter of Reb Yitzhak Ayzyk Shur. The Rabbi Reb Chaim Berlin was then already famous because of the great rabbinical positions that he had already occupied. He lived in Biala and was not engaged in rabbinical matters. Apparently, being a rich son-in-law, he became connected with well-known booksellers and collected a rich rabbinical library. During the years when he, so to say, sat quietly in Biala and devoted himself to Torah, he was called to take over the leadership of the well-known Volozhiner *Yeshiva* [religious secondary school], which had experienced its great crisis. He did not remain in Woloczin for long and he settled in Jerusalem, where he was soon recognized as one of the personalities there.

As has already been mentioned, Biala was Hasidic through and through. More than that, in the history of Hasidus, Biala also created a concept. We do not mean to say that Biala created something on-the-spot like Przysucha or Kotsk. Biala Hasidus did not create its own doctrines. Yet the name Biala served to underline a center that drew thousands of Jews from Poland to warm themselves in the Hasidic fire that the rebbes who settled there ignited.

The first rebbe who settled in Biala or, more correctly said, the Biala resident who became a rebbe and led a rabbinate there, was Reb Berish Landau.

Reb Berish, born in about 5580 [1820], was the second son of the Chechanower [Ciechanów] *Gaon* [genius] and Rabbi, Reb Avraham Landau. It appears that Reb Berish was the only one among Reb Avraham Chechanower's five sons (all became Hasidic rebbes], who in his youth was not engaged with Hasidus and did not visit any rebbes. Although, like his father, Hasidus was also not unfamiliar to him (Reb Avraham was in his youth with the rebbes, Reb Bunem and Reb Fishele Strikewer, but he did not engage in Hasidus and did not even pray in the customary Sfard [Sephardic] manner), he was only engaged in studying Torah.

Reb Berish's father-in-law, the rich man and Hasid, Reb Itshe Meir, who had a tavern in Biala, gave his son-in-law *kest* [financial support while a young groom studies religious texts]; he did not even think of becoming a rabbi as his father had. He became involved in commerce and opened a whiskey distillery with a partner, and he toiled thus until he emerged penniless from his factory and remained a poor man. Then, his industrious and capable wife, Rukhla, the *rebbitzen* [rabbi's wife], took over the worry about earning a living and opened a tavern and he sat busy with study and prayer. However, he decided to spend several hours a day at the tavern, not, God forbid, to help his wife, but to watch over the simple Jews with whom he would spend time to assure that, God forbid, they would not drink or eat without reciting a blessing.

How did he become a Hasid? Once he was invited by his friend, Reb Feivele Dancig, Gritser Rabbi, to a *bris* [ritual circumcision]. Reb Feivele was much older than him and, in addition, he was one of the Hasidim of the Prophet of Lublin, Reb Yakov Yitzhak. After this, he and other bright young men left Przysucha for the *Yid Hakadosh* [the Holy Jew – Yakov Yitzhak]. After the Jew's death, he [Reb Berish] became a Hasid of Reb Bunem Peshischa [a Yiddish spelling of Przysucha]. Then [he became a Hasid] of Reb Bunem's son, Reb Avraham Moshe and when the latter died, he became Reb Yitzhak Vurker's Hasid. Reb Feivele knew Reb Berish well and knew of his vanity about his learning and about his virtues. Consequently, it was important for him to reach out to Reb Berish both about Hasidus and his rebbe, Reb Yitzhak Vurker. Whereas his Rebbe was supposed to be his *sandek* [man who holds the male child during a *bris* – ritual circumcision], he told him of the Chechanower Rebbe's son, who it was worthwhile to befriend. It seems that Reb Yitzhak Vurker made a great impression on Reb Berish, and he became one of his greatest Hasidim. Incidentally, he was the only Vurker Hasid in his family, while his brothers traveled to [were followers of] Reb Mendele Kotsker.

In Vurka, he mainly was a friend of Reb Yitzhak's second son, Reb Menakhem Mendl and, when Reb Yitzhak died, he became the right hand of [the new Rebbe] Reb Mendele Vurker.

As is known, Reb Mendele Vurker was a frightfully quiet man; even his teachings of *Torah* would consist of short sentences, and his Hasidim, even his greatest Hasidim, in the main did not understand the teaching of the Rebbe. They all would come to Reb Berish to have him explain the Rebbe's teachings. Reb Mendele himself would often use affectionate language: the *Bialer ganof* [Biala thief] knows. When Reb Mendele died in the year 5628 [1868], the Vurker Hasidim made Reb Berish their rebbe and leader.

[Page 273]

He remained in Biala and led in the Vurker way of Reb Mendele until 5636 [1876], when he died. He had a great name and a large number of well-known Hasidim, who themselves were worthy of being rebbes, were his students. The most famous of them were Reb Yehiel Dancig, a son of Reb Feivele Gricer and founder of the well-known rabbinical dynasty in Aleksander near Lodz, Reb Yankl Nadriziner who was Reb Mendele's son-in-law and then himself became a rebbe, the future Skerniewicer Rebbe and Reb Mendele's son, Reb Shimeon and other prominent men.

After Reb Berish's death, the Hasidim took Reb Berish's student, Reb Yehiel of Aleksander (near Lodz) as their Rebbe. Reb Berish's son would travel to [the Rebbe in] Aleksander. After the death of Reb Yehiel his son Reb Yisroel Yitzhak, who was called *Yismakh Yisrael* [*Israel Will Rejoice*] from the name of the book of which he was the author, became the Rebbe.

When the *baal* [author of] *Yismakh Yisrael* died, a number of Hasidim took as their Rebbe Reb Ahron Landau, Reb Berish's son. A second son of Reb Berish's, Reb Elimelekh Menakhem Mendl, later became the Strikower Rebbe.

Reb Ahron Landau became the Rebbe in 5670 [1910]. The celebration among his followers of his agreement to become the rebbe of the Biala court was immeasurable. Masses of Hasidim began to arrive in Biala and they would dance with ecstasy along the entire road from the train to the city. However, his rabbinical position did not last a long time. The same year, around Passover time, he became ill and he died on the second day of *Shavous* [7th day of Sivan 5670/14th of June 1910] in Warsaw. At his funeral, which took place in Warsaw, a gathering of 50,000 Jews took place.

After his death, his son, Reb Menakhem Mendl, took his place. After two years of being the Rebbe in Biala, he moved to Warsaw. There, he continued as the Bialer Rebbe, to whom Hasidim from many Polish cities were drawn. He sat for fifty years and wrote Torah treatises and writings on Hasidus. Until now, only the book, *Shemesh u'Magen* [*Sun and Shield*], has been published, in Israel by his son, Reb Yehiel Landau.

Reb Menakhem Mendl died in Brooklyn [New York] in 5698 [1938].

A second chapter in the history of Biala Hasidus was written by a second famous Rebbe, Reb Yitzhak Yakov Rabinowicz. He came from a great Hasidic ancestry, being a great grandson, a direct male descendent of the *Yid Hakadosh*, whose name he carried.

Hasidim say: his father, Reb Nusan Dovid, the Szidlowcer Rebbe and successor of the Rebbe, Reb Yerakhmiel the Jew's son, said that when his wife bore him a son, he should be shown the child at once. The reason for this was his fervid desire to name one of his children with the name of his great grandfather, the *Yid Hakadosh*, namely, Yitzhak Yakov. Every time his wife bore him a son, Reb Nusan Dovid looked at the child and said, "Not him." And it is worthwhile to know, that all of the sons of Nusan Dovid became famous Hasidic Rebbes. When the later Biala Rebbe was born and his father looked at the small face of the just-circumcised child, Reb Nusan Dovid's face brightened; "I mean him," he called out enthusiastically and naming the child, he announced the name with great joy: *Veyikarei Shemo b'Yisrael* [From the Book of Ruth, words recited at a *bris* – ritual circumcision] – "May his name be called in Israel, Yitzhak Yakov."

Hasidim further say: Reb Nusan Dovid would take the child with him to the rebbes to whom he would travel, particularly, to the sage of his generation, Reb Yehezkiel Kuzmirer, who was the greatest student of the *Yid Hakadosh*, and to the great *tzadek* and *gaon*, Reb Chaim Tsanser. The Hasidim said that when the small Yitzhak Yakov was seven years old, his father was with the Kuzmirer *Tzadek* and when the *Tzadek* looked at the small boy, he was very impressed with him and said: "A great Polish Rebbe." The Reb Chaim Tsanser's Hasidim similarly gave the young child great praise and called him Rebbe.

While still a child, he became the groom of the only child of Reb Shiele Ostrower, with whom he studied a great deal. After the death of his father-in-law in 5633 [1873], he was crowned as a rebbe with the agreement of the great righteous men, particularly from the great *tzadek*, Reb Yitzhak Schizczer. He became famous as a great rebbe. His wisdom and his regal conduct enraptured Hasidim. They saw in him the heir of the rebbes from Peshischa and Lentshen and, after a number of years in Ostrowa, he settled in Biala where he generously steered his Hasidim. Thousands of Jews were drawn to Biala from all over Poland.

Reb Yankele Bialer became ill in the month of Adar 5665 [1905] and died in Warsaw while there for treatment. He was buried at the Warsaw cemetery near his father-in-law, Reb Shiele Ostrower. Although the latter had left a will that no one should be buried for four ells [about 15 feet or more than four and half meters] from him, after a special judgment of the great rabbis, the Bialer Rebbe was buried near him. The judgment was inscribed on the headstone.

[Page 274]

Reb Yankele Bialer left four sons who were rebbes and two sons-in-law who also were rebbes. The oldest son, Reb Nusan Dovid, settled in Partchev [Parczew] and became famous as the Partchever Rebbe. The second son became his successor in Biala, but later, Rebbe, Reb Meir Shlomo Yehuda, the Biala Rebbe – *Mishlei* [acronym created by using the first Hebrew letters of his name; *Mishlei* is also the Hebrew name of the Book of Proverbs] became the rebbe in Mezeritch, near Biala, and became known as the Mezeritcher Rebbe. The third son, Reb Avrahamele, became rebbe in Lublin (author of *Yeshuos Avraham* [*Salvation of Abraham*], a book about

Genesis, part one, published by his son Ahron Nusan Dovid Rabinowicz, Lublin, 1934). The youngest son, Reb Hershele, became well-known as the Shedlitzer [Siedlce] Rebbe, but he died a year before his father's death.

The oldest daughter, Matele, who was a great *tzadekus* [righteous woman], was the wife of the Radzyminer Rebbe, Reb Mendl. When she died, only those who had been to the *mikvah* [ritual bath] that day were permitted to approach the *mitah* [board on which a body is borne for burial]. The second daughter, Chanale, was the wife of the Skierniewicer Rebbe, Reb Yosele (rabbi in B'nei Brak, Israel), son of Reb Shimeon Skierniewicer.

Reb Yankele Bialer is the author of the Hasidic books: *Divrei Binah* [*Words of Wisdom*] on the entire Torah and *Ishrey Lev* [*Honesty of Purpose*] on *Shabbosim* [Sabbaths] and the holidays.

Thus, Biala recorded an important chapter of great rabbinical and Hasidic personalities, who had an effect there and from there to illuminate the heavens of the Jewish people. Alas, this was in the past. The cruel enemy, the Germans and their partners, may their names be erased, destroyed the Jewish people in Poland and everywhere they [the Germans] had control and, together with them, the holy community of Biala Podlaska, referred to in old documents as *Biala d'Lita* [Biala of Lithuania] and *Biala Gadol* [Biala the Great].

Translator's footnote:

a.   *Khidushei haRim* – Yitzhak Meir Alter was known as the *Khidushei haRim*. It is customary for a Torah scholar to be known by the name of his most famous book. *Khidushei* is Hebrew for innovations; *haRim* is the acronym for *haReb* – the Reb – Yitzhak Meir.

Original footnotes:

1.   This focus in Reb Yitzhak's letter relates to the incident in the *shtetl* Lanckorn.[7] While there, a market took place. Frank was caught with 20 of his students who had gathered in secret at the house of one of their members in a dance around a half-naked woman and kissed her.

2.   Meant the Bishop Mikołaj Dembowski of Kamieniec-Podolski.

3.   Natan of Gaza, the prophet of the Sabbatai Tzvi movement.

4.   Nehemiah Hiyya Hayyun – of the Sabbatai Tzvi movement, author of the book, *Mehemnuta deKola* [*Faith of All*], which justified the actions of the futile men believing in Sabbatai Tzvi.

5.   Chava Frank, the daughter of Jacob Frank. She also was thought of as a godly symbol by the Frankists.

6.   This position in Reb Yitzhak's letter is not clear. The date of his letter, 5517, coincides with the year 1757, when an argument took place between the rabbis and Frankists before Bishop Dembowski. The second, similar argument took place in Lemberg two years later. It is possible that the position relates to the beginning of the era of the fight with the Frankists.

7.   He means Łyskornia not Lanckorn.

8.   He means the Busker Rabbi, Nakhman *ben* [son of] Shmuel *haLevi*, who became a Frankist.

9.   This *Parnes-haKodesh* [monthly leader] and his son at first stood on the side of Reb Yonoson Eiberschits. The son, who was a rabbi in Lublin, even dared to excommunicate Reb Yakov Edmen. This evoked rage on the part of Reb Yakov Edmen's followers, and they ousted him from the position. The family had other losses and even cases of death. Under the pressure of the blow that the family received, Reb Avraham, as well as his son, expressed their regret.

10.   Meant the blood-libel against the Jews in Yampole [Podolia].

11.   Son of the chairman of the Lublin Jewish community.

[Page 274]

A Portrait of Rabbi ShmuelAryeh Leib a Holy Person, of Blessed Memory, the Rabbi of Biale[a]

by Shmuel T. Halevi Rubinshtein, the Rabbi in Givatayim

Translated by Libby Raichman

"The Biale Rabbi", that is how he was called by all those of his generation in the country of Poland, who remembered his name with awe and admiration. They all understood the devotion of this genius and mystic, the righteous prodigy, the Rabbi Shmuel Leib, the holy person, who served in our community for 42 years, from 5651 [corresponding to 1881] until 3rd of Tevet 5692 [corresponding to 1922].

He was not a speaker, and not a man of words. I do not recall him ever going up to the bimah[1] to preach or deliver a religious sermon in any one of the synagogues of our town. I hardly ever saw him disseminate knowledge; nevertheless, his influence was recognized in the town. They all knew that he was a genius and master of the Torah, one of the few remnants of the generation, and considered him a miracle worker, a wonder Rabbi, and that every blessing that he uttered would be a sign of good things to come. And they would come to him from all parts of the country to seek salvation and compassion because they knew that he pronounced the spirit of God. They feared his stringency and tried not to disobey him in any matter to do with Judaism and the needs of the religion, because those who refused knew that the matter was in his soul, and for that reason, all his words were like burning coals.

His holiness was spread over his face and his white beard and it all emitted awe and fear. That great fear and the penetrating look in his eyes made people afraid to approach him and only chosen individuals of those who came to his house would debate with him and with others who were interested, and turned to him for his help and advice. There was always a barrier, a wall of iron between him and the community. Very little is known to us about his life, but even the few details in our possession provide perfect evidence about the greatness of his scholarship and the originality of his personality.

He was born to his father Reb Chaim Yisrael in the town of Hurodna in Lithuania, in 5607 [corresponding to 1847]. His father was a learned man, and later a preacher in a few congregations and finally, in the town of Terespol that was close to Brisk-D'Lita. There his young son Shmuel Leib sat and diligently studied Torah, until he became renowned as "the prodigy of Terespol".

From there, he dispatched responsa[2] correspondence to the great Rabbis of his generation and used to exchange letters with the Gaon[3] Rabbi Yosef Shaul Natanzon, the Rabbi of Lvov, whose great treatise "Sho–el Umeishiv" [Question and Answer] elicited many scholarly questions from Rabbi Shmuel Leib of Terespol. The Rabbi of Lvov believed, according to the letters, that the inquirer was certainly the Rabbi of Terespol, a young man who signed: Shmuel Leib, the holy person of Terespol; in fact, he was then only a boy of 13. It is told that when his father, the preacher, would go from town to town to speak, he once took his young son Shmuel Leib with him, and reached Lvov. There they went to the house of the Rabbi, Reb Yosef Shaul, to introduce themselves and become acquainted. When they entered, the Rabbi asked: from where are you? From Terespol, the father answered. The Rabbi asked, and how is your Rabbi, Reb Shmuel Leib, who it seems, is a great and sharp–witted scholar. Here the boy intervened and remarked: Reb Shmuel Leib is not such a great scholar. The Rabbi immediately slapped him on his cheek and reprimanded him, scolding him for daring to offend a Rabbi and a scholar. The father could no longer restrain himself, turned to the Rabbi and said: Take it easy Rabbi, my small son is none other than the Rabbi Shmuel Leib with whom you have been corresponding on new interpretations of the Law. The face of Rabbi Yosef Shaul lit up at the sight of the "young but clever" and said: I have never seen something like this, in all my life.

The youth spent a few months within the walls of the Rabbi of Lvov and from there he returned to Poland via the town of Radom. There he was seen by Reb Yoav Yehoshua, the author of "Chelkat Yoav" [The Portion of Yoav], who was the Rabbi in Kintzk, who kept him in his house for a few weeks and where together they were immersed in the laws of Torah. The Chassidim of Gur in Radom heard from the Rabbi Reb Yoav Yehoshua that this boy was an amazing expert and extremely sharp and they began to tell the youth about the greatness of their Rabbi, Rabbi Yitzchak Meir of Gur, author of the "Chidushei HaRabbi Yitzchak Meir" [New interpretations by the Rabbi Yitzchak Meir], and they tried with all their might to persuade him to travel to Gur to receive Torah from him. He took these words to heart and travelled to his home to request permission from his father, who was opposed to Chassidism, to allow him to go to the Rabbi in Gur; and it was like manna from heaven, when his father the Lithuanian responded to his son's request and took him to the Rabbi in Gur.

[Page 275]

When Reb Chaim Yisrael went inside to the holy man, he said to the Rabbi of Gur: "I have brought my son, the youth, to learn Torah from his honour, his holiness, but it is not financially possible to keep him here at my expense. The "Chidush HaRabbi Yitzchak Meir" answered him: "When I take him into my hands, he will not be short of anything". (This was seen in "Ramzei D'Chachmata" of the Rabbi, may the memory of this righteous man be blessed, at the end of the book on the life of the author, may the memory of this righteous man be blessed, that was published by his son Reb Dov Berish, may the Lord avenge his blood).

In 5620 [corresponding to 1859], the youth of Terespol was accepted as a student to the master, Rabbi Yitzchak Meir of Gur and endeared himself to him. There he studied together as a team with his grandson, the young man Reb Yehuda Ari Leib author of "The Language of Truth", may the memory of this righteous man be blessed.

Every day, he would go to the holy man within, to receive regular lessons from the Rabbi. In this way he continued with his studies until he entered into the covenant of marriage with the daughter of Rabbi Moshe Yehuda Leib (who was interred in Jerusalem), the son–in–law of the famous Chassidic Rabbi, Reb Shlomo Leib of Lantznah, a contemporary of the Chassidic Rabbi Simcha Bunim of Pshischah. When Reb Shmuel Leib became engaged to the granddaughter of the Chassidic Rabbi of Lantznah, the righteous man was no longer alive (he died in 5603) [corresponding to 1843], but his son, the righteous Reb Yehoshua of Ostrov, author of "The History of Man", succeeded his father and promised to support the young couple after their marriage so that that they should live in Ostrov in the shadow of their righteous uncle. It is told about an intelligent letter that the youth Reb Shmuel Leib prepared for the uncle of his fiancée, the righteous man of Ostrov, in which he asks him to send him the cost of his maintenance during the time that he lived in Gur as a boy, and a student of our master, our teacher, our Rebbe of Gur. He explained his request as follows: In the Jerusalem Talmud, in the 3rd section, in chapter 1, it says: He who eats of the food of his friend, should be ashamed to face him and turn his face to another side, and the prophet says: (Isaiah 30:20) "but your eyes will see your teachers" – Is it not, that a student must look at the face of his teacher, and how can I look at his face, when I am eating his bread and am strengthened by his purse?"

He too, his uncle from Ostrov knowing the answer of Abraham our forefather to his guests (Sutah 10:2), "after they ate and drank and were ready to leave, he said to them: because you have eaten of mine, it is as if you have eaten of the God of the universe, give thanks and blessing to He who spoke, and the world came to be". From this, it is understood – that you are not eating the bread of your Rabbi, but you and I, and your Rabbi, the Admor[4] – our master, our teacher, our Rebbe of Gur, we are all eating of the food of the God of the universe".

When the young man married his wife, Yehudit Sheindl he lived in the shadow of the righteous man of Ostrov and ate at his table together with his cousin, our beloved Rabbi, Reb Yitzchak Ya'akov Rabinovitsh, who later became known as the Admor of Biale, and was called Reb Yankele of Biale. A great friendship began between these two cousins.

In Ostrov the young married man Reb Shmuel Leib continued to devote himself to Torah and engage in piety, within the framework of his uncle, and even after his marriage he continued to travel to the Rabbi of Gur and received lessons from him until the latter died in 5626 [corresponding to 1866].

In 5639 [corresponding to 1879], he was accepted as a Rabbi in the small town of Vludavka and from there he rose to the throne of the rabbinate in 5642 [corresponding to 1882], in the town of Shabarshin in the district of Lublin. With the influence of his cousin Reb Yankele of Biale, he travelled to the Admor, the great preacher, Reb Avraham of Trisk. Many great masters, teachers and Rabbis of the generation travelled there, and the Rabbi of Shabarshin was regarded among them as a great expert in both the Talmuds [the Jerusalem and Babylonian Talmuds].

It is told that the preacher of Trisk spoke words of Torah at his table and recalled a saying from the Gemarra. After the blessings after food were recited, those who sat at his table asked each other whether they knew the source of the Talmudic saying that the preacher had quoted from the Gemarra. Among them were the great scholars of the generation and they did not know where to find the saying.

The preacher entered the room and asked them for the source of the saying in the Gemarra. So, the preacher said: go to the synagogue and ask the Rabbi from Shabarshin and he will show you the saying because he is an expert in the Gemarra and there is no one like him. The Rabbi of Shabarshin immediately showed them the saying, to the great amazement of the scholars who questioned him.

It was known that the Rabbi of Shabarshin was appointed by the preacher of Trisk to test his grandchildren during their lessons. One day when the Rabbi Reb Moshe Mordechai of Lublin, the Admor of Trisk, came to Biale to discuss rules of Jewish law, he visited the Rabbi and reminded him that he was tested by him in Trisk when he, the preacher, was on the threshold of his later years, may the memory of this righteous man be blessed. That was in the winter of 5690 [corresponding to 1930].

In the year 5648 [corresponding to 1888], the Rabbi of Biale died – the Gaon Reb Z'ev Nachum Burnshtein, the father of the Rabbi Reb Avraham of Sucht'chuv. Reb Z'ev Burnshtein was famous as a genius and a great Chassid, one of the most important Chassidim of Kotzk, and the father–in–law of the old Rabbi of Kotzk. The Biale community was proud of him. With his passing, it was difficult for our community to choose a Rabbi who was capable of filling the place in Torah and piety. For three years the community remained without a Rabbi, until esteemed members turned to Rabbi Shmuel Leib, a scion of saints [holy person], the Rabbi of Shabarshin, to appoint him as the Rabbi of the town. It is quite probable that the Chassid, the Admor, Reb Ya'akov of Biale, who was, as mentioned, the cousin of Reb Shmuel Leib tried silently to have him appointed as the Rabbi of Biale because they had recognized influence in the town, and apparently the Chassidim of Gur in Biale, who had the most say in these matters, did not oppose this appointment either, because they knew of the genius of this Rabbi, that he was the student of the "Chidushei HaRabbi Yitzchak Meir"[5]. The Admor, the author of "The Language of Truth", readily agreed to this appointment, because he remembered him from their youth when they studied together as a team. And indeed, in 5651 [corresponding to 1891], the Rabbi appeared at the gates of Biale and everyone in the town came out to meet him because his knowledge of Torah and his reverence went before him, as one of the great men in the land.

In particular, the most prominent scholars in the town amused themselves with him. Rabbi Noach Shachor (father–in–law of the Admor of Gur, blessed be the memory of the righteous), whose friends admired him greatly for his knowledge of Torah and his righteousness, encouraged him to act stringently in his jurisdiction, without hypocrisy and discrimination.

It is no wonder then, that in every butcher shop, the laws of *Kashrut* were meticulously observed, for the butcher knew that if the Rabbi were to perceive that there was failure in the observance of the laws, he would be condemned and lose his source of income. So, when a plaintiff appeared before him in dread and fear, his judgement was received as if it was a punishment of fire, for which there was not a hair's breadth opportunity for appeal.

Once, he was told that on the Sabbath, in one of the barbershops, people were being shaved behind closed doors. The Rabbi went to the place of the incident with his supporters, to fulfil his duty, burst inside and caught the shavers red–handed. Those being shaved fled immediately with soap suds on their faces, and the Rabbi slapped the face of the barber, reprimanded him severely, and the barber did not dare to desecrate the Sabbath in this shameless way again.

Even the head of the synagogue and the large prayer house would not introduce a single custom that the Rabbi had not agreed to, and everything was suspended pending the approval of the Rabbi. I remember that when we established the large prayer house in our town a "Magen David was painted above the door at the entrance to the building, that then symbolized the revival of Zionism.

[Page 276]

The Rabbi immediately sent word via the beadle to remove the symbol and scrape it off, for it is forbidden to introduce a new passion into the old prayer house. Understandably, on that day, the Zionist symbol was removed from the wall of the prayer house despite the thoughts of the local Zionists.

However, in spite of his decisiveness and insistence, he was kind–hearted, good–natured, pitied the poor and helped everyone who was downhearted and weak. His home was open to the poor, and his daughter, the righteous Rochele, would cook lunch in his house every day, and on his orders would distribute the food to the poor in the town, and to every beggar.

The Rabbi was particularly famous for the simple and easy way that he taught about fasting on the four public fast days. Since the First World War and after, Reb Yoel, the beadle, would make the following announcement in the synagogue on the fast of the 17th Tammuz and on the fast of Tish'ah B'Av: "on the orders of the Rabbi, people who are frail must not fast at all. Those for whom it is difficult to fast should eat at 1pm in the afternoon, and then complete the fast in the evening". For this, he was unique in his generation, and renowned throughout the State of Poland, as a Rabbi who permits eating on the days of the fast (understandably, except for Yom Kippur).

It was said that he had a source for this view, in the words of the Rabbi Yom Tov ben Avraham, in the tractate of Shabbat, in which he says that he who eats well every day, he is able to fast for a complete day and will not endanger his life, but for he who eats food sparingly to stay alive, it is dangerous to fast, lest he die, and according to the language of the Gemarra: "For him, it would be his day to die". In the light of these words by Rabbi Yom Tov ben Avraham, the Rabbi used to say that during the days of the war, people suffered the shame of hunger, and had very little food, therefore there is reason to exempt those from fasting who are frail, and to bring a little relief to those who find it difficult to fast.

It is interesting that the Rabbi, Reb Meir Yechiel HaLevi from Ostrovtzah, may the memory of the righteous be blessed, who was known as one who was well informed about fasting and was strict in his observance of the fasts, once met a Jew, a resident of Biale, and asked him to sit alongside him and inform him of the exact language utilized by the Rabbi of Biale on matters of fasting. He wanted to know this because it was told that the Rabbi of Biale permitted eating on the days of the fasts, as if he was negating the decree of "the four public fasts"[6] – seeing that he listened well to the language of the announcement, the Rabbi said to the resident of Biale: I am comforted, I am comforted, for I have a basis for easing the restrictions in this way.

The Rabbi was generally very lenient on questions regarding "what is forbidden and what is permitted", because he had broad shoulders in these matters. With his expertise as an arbiter and his professional orientation about the quality of the question, he was able to solve difficult questions that many others struggled to solve. In our town there was a scholar who sat all day in the Chassidic prayer house, diligently studying Torah (out of respect, I will not mention his name). He reviewed the *Shulchan Aruch*[7] all his days, particularly "*Yoreh De'ah*"[8]. Once a lady came to him to ask whether a chicken was kosher, fit to eat. The learned man looked into the matter and pronounced the chicken unfit for eating. The lady remained silent and approached the Rabbi to confirm the judgement. She then returned and complained to the scholar. Why did you say that the chicken was not kosher, and the Rabbi said that it was! The learned man then took the "*Yoreh De'ah*" under his arm and went to the Rabbi to argue with him about the matter, for in his opinion, the chicken was certainly not kosher. When the learned man began to speak, the Rabbi approached his bookshelf, and took out the book of responsa "*Chacham Tzvi*" and showed him that in that book it is explicit to permit, and forbidden to waste, the money of the Jewish people – and the Rabbi continued to reprimand him, saying that if you are not expert in the later Deciders[9], you are forbidden to teach.

Also, in matters relating to what is permitted for women who have been abandoned by their husbands, he was known as a great expert, and great Rabbis sought his opinion in discussions. The Gaon, Rabbi Chaim Solovitchik, the Rabbi of Brisk that was close to Biale, asked the Rabbi many times to consider a judgement of an abandoned wife who had come to him, and to express his opinion as an arbiter, and he always agreed with his judgement. The Rabbi of Brisk used to say: after the directive of the Biale Rabbi, there was nothing more to think about.

My teacher, the Gaon, Rabbi Moshe Shapira, may the memory of this righteous man be blessed, was the Rabbi of Lublin. A dispute erupted between him and Rabbi Ya'akov Me'ir Biederman, the brother–in–law of the Admor of Gur, may the memory of the righteous be blessed, regarding the provision of charity boxes in aid of the Yeshivah for the Wise of Lublin. Rabbi Ya'akov Me'ir, as head of "The Treasury of Rabbi Me'ir, the miracle worker", opposed this, saying that this was overstepping the boundary, and undermined the distribution of the Lublin charity boxes. So Rabbi Shapira turned to all the Rabbis of the communities in Poland, and set before them a booklet in the *halachah*, indicating that there was no prohibition of any kind, and asking for their agreement in writing, with their signature, regarding this matter.

When the rabbi had gathered 300 signatures about his booklet, he came before the Rabbi of Gur to show him the opinions of the great Rabbis, to allow the matter to proceed. The Rabbi paged through the signatures and did not react at all. When he reached the signature of the Rabbi of Biale, he ceased paging through any further and called his brother–in–law Rabbi Ya'akov Me'ir and showed him the signature of the Rabbi and passed judgement: there is no longer a need to focus on the booklet; after the judgement of the Rabbi of Biale, there is nothing to answer.

As far as he pledged his soul to assist those who were unfortunate, one can learn from "what is permitted to an abandoned wife", that he allowed an abandoned wife to marry after many great Jewish scholars did not find a way to allow her to marry. And he, with his expertise, made every effort to reveal what was concealed in the law, to free her from the bonds of an abandoned wife, and this was the case. A woman suffered greatly from her free–thinking husband until he finally changed his religion but did not want to give her a *get*. One day he drowned in the sea and his body was not found. When the woman came to the Rabbinic court requesting that they allow her to marry as a widow, the wise men of the generation did not want to allow it, as there was no witness to the fact that he died in the sea, only that he drowned – perhaps he came out of the water, that he is alive, and we do not know. According to the law that is explained in the *Shulchan Aruch*, *Even HaEzer*, paragraph 17, section 32: "He was seen falling into the sea, even if he drowned in the ocean, there are no witnesses to the fact that he died, perhaps he went out from another place", because the law says: if the water does not have an end, the wife is forbidden". The woman was persistent and knocked on the portals of the Rabbinic court but there was no one to entertain her plea, until the Rabbi of Biale was asked to consider a judgement and he judged that she be permitted to marry according to the book "*HaKannah*", attached to the books of *Kabbalah*[10], that says, "water that has no end" – it is possible that the drowned man was saved and went out at another place, and we did not see – all this applies to a person who believes in the Holy One, blessed be he, who has no end or boundaries – it is possible that he was saved, but he who does not believe in God's help, and does not believe in water that has no end – he has no hope and certainly drowned and died. And the Rabbi continued to pass judgement: perhaps he was afraid and repented when he was in the water, also here, one should not fear that perhaps he was saved and is still alive because it has already been said (*Avodah Zarah* 17:1) "anyone who spreads heresy – dies". Therefore, this woman is allowed to marry anyway, because her husband is certainly already dead. And when Rabbi Me'ir Shapira, may the memory of the righteous be blessed, told about the permission given, he said, the reasoning for this, is surely very "strange" but he certainly utilized only one section of the basic laws, whereas the Rabbi of Biale gave permission based on other laws.

In addition to his righteousness and his piety, it is also worth pointing out his wisdom, his original thought, and his quick grasp that always enabled him to approach matters directly and in a clear manner.

[Page 277]

The Rabbi Reb Menachem Rubinshtein of Biale (the father of Rabbi Shmuel Rubinshtein, the Rabbi of the Paris community) once went to the Rabbi Reb Shmuel Arye Leib to ask him for a letter of recommendation and intercession to one of the leaders of the town. The Rabbi wrote the letter and when he reached the signature, he concluded: "his dear friend" etc. While doing this, he spilled drops of ink on the word "his friend". The Rabbi searched for a pocket–knife to remove the drops of ink on the word. Rabbi Menachem was very sorry that the Rabbi was going to so much trouble for him, and remarked; Rabbi, there is no need to delete so much. The Rabbi answered: You have forgotten Rashi's explanation about what is written in the Torah (Genesis 33:4) "And Esau ran to meet him" and he kissed him" – Rashi says: "the dotting above the word[11] indicates that he did not kiss him with all his heart". Now go and see, if spots of ink remain on the word "his friend", the leader of the community might think that I am not "a friend" with all my heart. It is therefore necessary to remove the spots properly.

One of the residents of our town told me that he once came to the Rabbi to ask his advice about what action to take in his business, as he was anticipating a great loss and he himself did not know what measures to take to prevent the loss. The Rabbi hesitated and said: who am I – am I a trader that I can advise you on matters of trade? The man was not discouraged, and the Rabbi turned to him and asked: Do you lay Tefillin every day? Yes, said the man. And do you say the evening prayers every evening? Here the man hesitated and said: when I have time, I pray. The eyes of the Rabbi lit up immediately and he said: if you would say the evening prayers, and you said the prayer "*Hashkivaynu*"[12], in which it says: "provide us with good counsel of your own", then you will be provided with good counsel. Now you ask me for good advice. Promise me that you will say the evening prayers every evening, and God will provide you with good advice of his own.

In my childhood, I heard from my elders that the Rabbi was very famous in his youth as a Gaon, as a scholar and a great innovator, but in the midst of his best years, he devoted himself to the law of hidden wisdom, that is, the law of *Kabbalah*[13] and began to engage in 'practical Kabbalah'[14] until it affected his health significantly and caused a fatal interruption to the course of his studies and his scholarly progress in areas of the law, and in the law that is revealed.

Indeed, I still remember him when he was closeted in his house, occupied with his books, and on very rare occasions we would see him appear in the street or in the synagogue. It was not at all easy to be received by him in his house because he was always engaged in scholarship in his sanctum, studying the books of *Kabbalah*. His son–in–law, Rabbi Moshe Utchn, served as the Rabbi in our town and directed all the communal affairs of the Rabbinate – only in urgent matters, his son–in–law tried to take people into his room and disturb him from his studies.

However, this was only what appeared to be, for the Rabbi was actually engaged in writing responsa,[15] matters of the law that touched on practice, such as writing legal documents of divorce, religious sanctioning of ritual baths etc. for various communities, both near and far. In particular, he criticized ritual slaughterers and examiners and rebuked the butchers who did not practice according to the accepted custom. He also regulated the laws of *Kashrut*[16] so that not a single hair's breadth would be altered from what was the custom in the holy communities, in ancient times.

We have already said that he was by nature inclined to lighten his directive and take pity on the finances of the people. I remember, that on the morning of the eve of the Day of Atonement, he would stand next to the door of his room while a long queue of women formed before him, with questions about the ritual lawfulness of the slaughtered chickens that were used as atonement on Yom Kippur, the Day of Atonement. Each person held a chicken and showed him the fowl to be examined. He looked at the mark (on the chicken) in question, nodded 'right', 'right', in his particular Lithuanian pronunciation. It is interesting that in his holy presence, the women who were asking about their chickens did not forget to ask the Rabbi to bless them for a good year, and a command for salvation. The Rabbi blessed them and urged them to return home quickly, for there was much work waiting for them in their homes, for the forthcoming great day.

Despite all his greatness in Torah scholarship and knowing his personal value, he humbled himself before the righteous of his generation. When Rabbi Mendele Landau, the Admor, of Strikov, came to our town to honour his father the righteous Rabbi, Rabbi Berish of Biale, on the day of the anniversary of his father's death that fell on 25th Sivan, he would go to the grave of his father, with a group of Chassidim. At the graveside he would receive notes on pieces of paper, and his grandson, the young man Reb Shlomo Asher, would come, and in the name of his grandfather, he would ask them to commemorate his name.

In addition, it was his custom to send a note to the Admor of Gur, for the Rabbi of Gur valued him and held him in great esteem.

In his last years he was very ill with bladder problems and suffered terrible pain, yet his face lit up with a supreme light, as if his pains brightened his soul and shone from his holy face.

When he lay sick in Warsaw, the great pious Rabbis visited him, and he would apologize to them, that he had a dilemma with the blessing in "*asher yatzar*"[17] since no urine flows from him, only through a tube. And he whispered to my teacher and my Rabbi, Rabbi Meir Shapira, that he suffered greatly from the power of the blessing, that is not in his hands to decide, more than from the intense pain of his affliction itself. When my teacher returned and related this to his students, he stressed with great admiration how touching the piety of the Gaon, the righteous man, was.

In 5691 [corresponding to 1931], on the festival of Tu Bi'shvat[18], the completion of the first circulation of the "Daf Ha'yomi" of the Talmud occurred, and the Rabbi of Lublin announced an appeal to raise money – an amount of 27 zlotte and 2 groschen[19] per page of the Babylonian Talmud (containing 2,702 pages). And the Rabbi of Biale then lay in the clinic of Dr. Frishman in Warsaw. When he heard about the large festive meals that were being organized on the day of the completion of the Talmud, he sent the above–mentioned amount to the house of the Chassidim of Gur, at 19, Nalboki Street, and asked them to send him 'shirayim'[20] from the festive meal that, as far as he knew, was a great event. The fact that a large community of Torah scholars completed the Talmud at one and the same time made a huge impression on donors in Warsaw, and many followed his example and donated, like him.

In the last weeks of his life, he was very ill, and he was taken to Utbutzk near Warsaw, and his daughter pleaded with him to return home, and he answered her that his time had not yet come and that there was still time for him to travel. He intimated that at the end of the days of the festival of Channukah, he would return home. And indeed, at the end of the holy Sabbath, on the eve of the 3rd of the month of Tevet, 5691 [corresponding to 1932], his soul departed in purity after the blessing of the Havdallah[21] ceremony. He was 85 years old. The leaders of our town tried to bring him from Utbutzk, to be buried in our town. People came from all the surrounding areas to honour the spiritual shepherd, who sustained the people of Israel in holy communities, over a period of more than 35 years. Students from the Yeshivah of Nuvharduk, from Mezritsh nearby, walked a distance of 25 kilometers to attend his funeral. All the Rabbis in the vicinity came to eulogize the deceased. In particular, Rabbi Meir Shapira came from Lublin, the capital town of the district, and stood on the verandah of the house of Rabbi Yitzchak Radzinner (Berman) in Brisk Street and delivered a eulogy in a wailing voice, a bitter cry, and below stood the entire community, in their tens of thousands, at the Gate of Cheshbon, with their heads bowed towards the coffin of their righteous and holy Rabbi.

[Page 278]

Rabbi Shapira read this verse (1 Samuel 3:3): "And before the lamp went out Samuel lay down in the temple of God". And he said, I am witness to the great Rabbi of Biale, whom I saw a few times before his passing and his face hovered in loftier worlds and in the palaces of heaven. His body suffered much pain, but his spirit and all his efforts were directed towards worlds of holiness, worlds that do not belong or have a connection to our low and dark world, and the lamp of God – the light and soul of this righteous Gaon – has not gone out yet. It will still shine, it will lie down and hover high above, not here, but in the palace of God, in heaven, the place of the holy angels, and the Tana'im[22] and Amora'im[23], masters of the Torah.

And here the eulogizer turned to the coffin and announced: Great Rabbi of Biale! You were so concerned for the people of your town, to make things easier for them on the days of the fasts, knowing the frailty of their bodies, and the fragility of their health. May you know that today there are many homes among the Jewish people where many fast days are observed, not because they are obliged to fast, but because they do not have food. They suffer the shame of hunger due to the terrible affliction that reigns in your town and in the surrounding towns. Therefore, go and advocate before the Throne of God, that the time has come to bring salvation to the Jewish people, so that they should not have to suffer hunger and poverty anymore.

Jews of Biale, be aware, that in this coffin that you are accompanying now, does not lie a withered body of a righteous and holy person, for here rest the holy Scrolls of the Law, with letters that are shining and burning with fire, a pillar of scholarship who served you in holiness for more than 40 years. You are escorting a Rabbi, a spiritual shepherd, of whom there is none like him in this entire generation. Those who had gathered, cried bitterly. The journey of the funeral lasted from the morning of the 3rd day, the 5th Tevet to the afternoon under a shower of snow. At the cemetery, the Admor, Rabbi Moshe Baruch Morgenshtern, the great Rabbi of Vludava, eulogized and the whole community filled a big sack of notes that were lowered into the grave alongside the body. His son–in–law, the Rabbi, the teacher of righteousness, Rabbi Moshe, said some words of his eulogy as the coffin was lowered into the grave and then stopped, overcome by much wailing. He could not complete his eulogy because of his great sorrow and mourning. In silent mourning the community returned to town and mourned: A Rabbi like this will not arise again in our generation.

The Rabbi left behind a son, an eminent Torah scholar, the Chassid, Rabbi Dov Berish may the Lord avenge his blood, and two sons–in–law: the teacher of righteousness, the Rabbi Moshe Utchan, a chassid from Strikov, and Rabbi Chaim Yechiel Tzitrinboim, his daughter, the righteous Rochele, may the Lord avenge her blood, grandchildren and great–grandchildren, his granddaughter Mrs. Esther Yehudit Oleh who lives in Bnei Brak, in Israel, his grandson Mr. Ya'akov Utchan in America, his great grandson Avraham Mordechai Hershberg, a Rabbi in Chicago, whose grandfather the Rabbi, may the memory of the righteous be blessed, still managed to ask Rabbi Shapira to accept him into the Yeshivah of the Wise in Lublin because he is a talented young man and was orphaned by the death of his father. And indeed, after the death of his grandfather, the youth came to the yeshivah. There he was persistent and very diligent in his studies and was the author of the book "Machshavat Ha'kodesh"[24], about the succession of holy ones. And today he is considered one of the most distinguished Rabbis in America[b]; but more than all of this, the Rabbi left behind a "good name", that only few in a generation succeed in attaining. Among the great Rabbis of Biale, his name will shine eternally.

*A certificate issued for a letter purchased and written in a Torah Scroll,
inserted in memory of the Biale Rabbi Shmuel Leib, a scion of saints, of
blessed memory*

[Page 279]

An Addition to the Article about the Rabbi Shmuel Aryeh Leib, a scion of saints

The Biale Rabbi felt that in Jewish law, in matters between an artisan and a businessman, the evidence of the artisan was more reliable. A workman also benefited from a lawsuit judged by the Rabbi, as he was more trusted than his master.

A typical lawsuit before a rabbinic tribunal came before the Biale Rabbi: the distinguished Chassid Yechiel Hersha grain merchant of Gur, became destitute and did not have the money to trade. Moshe Lederman, a respected Chassid of Gur, collected 100 Ruble among the Chassidim and gave it to Yechiel Hersh, without telling him, that it was meant as support. Some time later, Yechiel Hersh wanted to return the 100 Rubel, but Moshe Lederman claimed that he did not recall having lent him money. The matter reached a lawsuit before the Biale Rabbi. The verdict was that the person who was loaned the money was believed more than the lender. The 100 Ruble was donated to the Talmud Torah[25].

When I was called up for military service during the war, my father took me to the Rabbi to ask him for a blessing. The Rabbi gave me his hand and said: "may you survive in peace".

A couple of weeks after my returning home from captivity, when I worked for Gadl Shlosser, Mendl Mulyer came in and asked me to repair a lock for the Rabbi. I went home to put on a *tallit katan*[26]. (Biale residents will recall that the rabbi had a weakness of inspecting the *tzitzit*[27]) and I went to repair the lock. The Rabbi was asleep while I was working. A couple of hours later, Mulyer came to call me again, to go to the Rabbi.

When I came to the Rabbi, I asked him if he had something else to repair. No, was his answer. He only wanted to pay me for my work.

Rabbi, you need not have called me specially for this. I would have come when I was passing by.

– Payment for work done during the day may not be withheld after sunset.
– Tell me, who are you, young man? – the Rabbi asked.
– Fyvl, the son of Leibele Meir Fishtshatzer – was my answer.
– Where were you during the war?
– In captivity.
– Did you at least come home with all your limbs?
– Yes. Thanks to you, your blessing Rabbi, that you gave me on the day before I had to present myself for military service.
– Long life to you.
– Shrage Fyvl, are you a locksmith?
– Yes.
– Are you a good locksmith?
– Pertaining to your question, I have been an artisan for two years already.
– Can you make a key for a lock?
– Yes. That is my trade. I can also make a lock.
– I do not need a lock. I need a good tradesman to make a key for a good lock.
– I have not had a lock for which I could not make a key.
– Shrage Fyvl, I need a good locksmith who will be able to adjust a key for the gates of mercy.
– Rabbi, for that, you are a better mechanic than I am.
– No, every observant Jew can be the mechanic, he just needs to be worthy of it.

Fyvl Gold (New York)

Original footnotes:

    a.   This article about the Rabbi, Reb Shmuel Aryeh Leib the second last Rabbi in Biale for over 40 years (1891 –1932), is presented here in the Hebrew original, as the author sent it.

    b.   The head of the Yeshiva, Rabbi Yehuda Aryeh Frommer, gives his lesson. He is the heir of the Rabbi and Senator, Rabbi Meir Shapira, who died young. He repeats his lesson for us, on the same evening at the concluding meal when a young lad – almost a boy, repeats the entire lesson by heart, swaying his long blonde sidelocks at the same time.

Who would have expected that this young boy would become the current Rabbi Reb Mordechai Hershberg, of Chicago, whom I have heard speaking at the American embassy in Venezuela, as well as in Colombia, to a selected audience where he spoke about the greatness of America and its Jews, and about his friend, the Vice President, Dick Nixon?

(Dr. Shashkes – "About the remaining Jews in Lublin" – an article that appeared in "Latest News", number 1552, of 5. 2. 60, where among other articles, there is one about the festivities on the completion of the Talmud that took place in 1938 in the "Yeshivah of the Wise of Lublin").

Translator's footnotes:

1. A bimah is a podium.
2. Responsa – letters of questions and answers.
3. Gaon – a genius. A Rabbinic title given to a scholar of great stature.
4. Admo"r – acronym for the Hebrew words *adonaynu, moraynu v'rabaynu* – our master, our teacher, our Rabbi. A title given to a Chasssidic Rabbi.
5. Chidushei HaRabbi Yitzchak Meir – The interpretations of the Rabbi Yitzchak Meir.
6. "the four public fasts" are: Fast of Gedalyah, Fast of Esther, Fast of the 17th Tammuz, Tish'ah B'Av.
7. Shulchan Aruch – Code containing a detailed body of Jewish Laws, published 1550–1559.
8. Yoreh De'ah – This is a section in the Shulchan Aruch, a compilation of halachah by Rabbi Jacob ben Asher.
9. Deciders – Arbiters. Rabbinic authorities on halachic questions.
10. Kabbalah – Jewish Mysticism.
11. The word is "Va'y'shakayhu" meaning – and he kissed him. In the Torah text, there is a dot above each letter of this Hebrew word. The Rabbis inserted these dots because they doubted whether the kiss of Esau was genuine.
12. Hashkivaynu – the first word of a prayer in the Ma'ariv (evening service) that begins "grant that we lie down in peace, Lord our God".
13. Kabbalah – Jewish Mysticism.
14. Practical Kabbalah – concerned with incantations and miracles.
15. Responsa – questions and answers on religious law.
16. Kashrut – ritual lawfulness.
17. Asher Yatzar – a blessing said before the morning service, blessing God, who heals all flesh.
18. Tu Bi'Shvat – a festival occurring in the month of Shvat, that celebrates the new year of the trees.
19. Zlotte and groschen are Polish currency. A groschen is a small coin.
20. Shirayim – remnants of food that a Chassidic Rabbi has blessed and tasted that the faithful share and consider a blessing.
21. Havdallah – the candle lighting ceremony at the end of the Sabbath that separates the Sabbath from the weekdays.
22. Tana'im – teachers, authorities quoted in the Mishnah.
23. Amora'im – interpreters, sages who interpreted the words of the Tana'im.
24. Machshvat Ha'kodesh – The Concept of Holiness.
25. Talmud Torah – tuition free elementary school maintained by the community.
26. Tallit katan – a four–cornered fringed garment worn under a shirt by observant Jews.
27. Tzitzit – the four tassels on the tallit katan.

The Rabbi Reb Tzvi Hirshhorn[a]
(The last of the Biale Rabbis)

Y. N.

Translated by Libby Raichman

Rabbi Tzvi Hirshhorn was born in 1900, in the small village of Komyonka-Strumyaluba that was close to Lvov and was called Kominke in Yiddish. His father Reb Shmuel was a merchant who traded on a small scale and struggled to make a living. When the First World war broke out, Rabbi Tzvi's parents fled to Lvov, the capital of eastern Galicia. In those days of scarcity, their financial situation eroded completely, and they suffered poverty and destitution. As the family had been uprooted from its place and did not take root in a new place, by the end of the war, the family were in very poor financial circumstances.

Tzvi was of Bar Mitzvah age when his parents moved to Lvov, and already then, his remarkable talents stood out – his diligence, his character as a boy of vision, his refinement, and his aspirations. His parents deprived themselves of food so that they could provide their only son (they also had a daughter) with a suitable Torah education with the best teachers, and he succeeded in his studies. In Lvov he entered the yeshivah "Embracing Torah Scholars", under the influence of the heads of the yeshivah, Rabbi Berel Karnil and Rabbi Aharon Linvand.

However, the religious beliefs of Tzvi Hirshhorn, who was called Hirsh Kaminer (named after his town), were not in accordance with the ways of Belz Chassidism. Regarding his views and mindset, he belonged to a group of observant youth. He finally found his place in the "Youth of Agudat Yisael"[1] and in the small synagogue of Ziditchuv, in Lvov, that served as a kind of base for "young people". From here, Tzvi Hirshhorn expanded his horizons.

[Page 280]

The finest Charedi youth gathered in the small study house in Zidichuv, led by Rabbi Gershon the young cripple, Moni Pulturok, Lippa Gershon and others. Most of them were from Chassidic families of Hushyatin, Churtkuv, Buyan and Kupitchnitz.

Tzvi Hirshhorn who studied diligently with this group, had acquired a little secular enlightenment in his home. Over time, he organized groups of young people in the small prayer houses as the "The Youth of *Agudat Yisrael*", where he was one of the leaders. As he was active in *Agudat Yisrael* and connected to Rabbi Meir Shapira of Lublin, and the Rabbi of Churtkov, Rabbi Yisrael Friedman was one of the leaders of the association, he was accepted among the pious of Churtkov. Hirshhorn travelled to Churtkov every time the Rabbi who lived in Boino, visited there. These journeys made a deep impression on him, and he found that the Rabbi, according to the Chassidic expression, "uplifted his soul" and influenced him greatly. And the unmarried man came to Zlutchov in the summer of 5684, [corresponding to 1924], to the completion of a tractate, that turned into a conference of the youth of *Agudat Yisrael*, and he became one of the most internationally powerful youth of the *Agudah* movement in Poland.

He married the daughter of Rabbi Nachum Pluhar, a Hoshyatin Chassid from Krakow, that was closer to the centre in Warsaw, than Lvov. From that time on, he visited Warsaw more often and participated in meetings and in the sessions of the youth of Agudat Yisrael.

However, he suddenly fell silent. He was not seen at any of the party meetings and did not take part in any of its activities. He was then in Kubrin and studied Torah from the Rabbi of the town, Rabbi Pesach Pruskin, one of the great Torah scholars in Lithuania. He advanced in his studies and was ordained as a Rabbi, by the Rabbi of Kubrin and other great Torah scholars.

In 5692 [corresponding to 1930], he was chosen as the Rabbi in Yabuzsnu, in the district of Krakov. He returned to his work with the "Youth of *Agudat Yisrael*" and took part in national committees and his speeches were the main event at these meetings. He published articles in the newspapers of the association: "Dos Yiddishe Togblat"[2], "Ortodoksishe Yugnt Bletter"[3], "Darkeinu"[4], and others. They excelled in their polished style and their beautiful, rich language. Everything that emanated from his pen was steeped in his personality, yet his power as a speaker was even greater.

In 1932, he was elected chairman of "Youth *Agudat Yisrael*" in Poland and since then he stood at the head of the organization and directed its course. Together with the Rabbi Moshe Ephraim Moshkovitz of Ostrik, and Yerucham Berliner of Lodz, and others, he worked to instill Torah into the ranks of the youth of the *Agudah*. His aim was to establish the study of Torah into the lessons in the small *yeshivot*[5]. The main activity of the Youth *Agudat Yisrael* organization, was to push the activities of the party to the next level, to a place that it deserved, as a means to an end.

At the large last gathering before the Holocaust, in 5697 [corresponding to 1937] in Ma'arinber, Hirshhorn appeared on behalf of "Youth *Agudat Yisrael*", requesting more intensive activity for the organization. This was, incidentally, his first appearance at an international gathering of *Agudat Yisrael*, and his talent was fully revealed. There he inspired many great people, while still a young man, at the beginning of his path in life, and in the midst of his diligence for personal advance.

As a result of a controversy in his community due to rivalry, Hirshhorn decided to leave Yavuszna because his refined personality was disgusted with the dissension, and even more, by the means used by its disputers. In 5698 [corresponding to 1938], he was chosen as Rabbi in Biale–Podlaska, a town filled with scholars, Chassidim, and famous Rabbis who studied there. But, immediately after moving over to his new community, the Second World War broke out.

He fled to safety from the Germans, may their name be erased, to Lvov, his previous place of residence. He lived there during the days of the Soviet conquest and after that, during the days of the German conquest.

The bitterness of the Holocaust affected him. He saw the loss of his birthplace the destruction of tens of thousands of Jews in the town, together with the Jewish community of Lvov. He was saved from the first deportations in the summer as his friends and admirers hid him for a certain time, until he too was killed in May 1943, at the age of 42, together with the magnificent Jewish community of Lvov.

According to the book "These are a memorial", second volume, New York. The institute for Research into Orthodox Jewry.

Original footnote:

    a.   This article about Rabbi Reb Tzvi Hirschhorn, the last Rabbi of Biale (1938-1939), is published in Hebrew according to its source, as we found it.

Translator's footnotes:

1.   Agudat Yisrael – literally, the "Society of Israel". Agudat Yisrael was a religious party in Israel.
2.   "Dos Yiddishe Togblat" – The Yiddish Daily.
3.   "Ortodoksishe Yugnt Bletter" – Orthodox Youth newspaper.
4.   "Darkeinu" – Our Path.
5.   Yeshivot (singular yeshivah) – Talmudic colleges.

Rebbe Berish Landau

Translated by Gloria Berkenstat Freund

The first Biala Rebbe was the Rabbi and *Gaon* [genius] and holy Rabbi Berish Landau, a son of the *gaon* and holy Rabbi Avrahaml, the Ciechanower Rabbi, to whom all *gaonim* of the generation related with great reverence. Rebbe Berish was born in approximately 5580 [1820].

While still young, Berish left for the Vurker [Warka, Poland] Hasidim. The Vurker Rebbe, Reb Yitzhak, took Reb Berish under his wing and loved him very much.

The Vurker Hasid, Reb Itshele Tenenbaum, said: When Reb Berish was still in Warka, people spoke ill of him to his father, that he, Berish, neglected his studies and spent time at friendly, festive meals, as were then undertaken by the Vurker Hasidim. Once when all of Reb Avrahaml Ciechanower's sons were gathered on a *Shabbos* [Sabbath] in order to welcome their father, the *tzadek* [righteous man], he called every one of his sons to his room and talked with them. He did not call Berish. Berish walked around the front room apprehensively. When his mother saw her son was worried, she could not control herself; she went in the room of the Ciechanower *tzadek* and she insistently questioned him for so long until he finally called in Berish. He talked with him for two hours and when he came out, the Ciechanower *gaon* said to those in attendance: I gave my son the name Ber; he is truly a bear, someone who likes sweets, may blessing fall on his head.

[Page 281]

Reb Berish would recite words of Torah at a prepared table even during the week and the Hasidim would provide wine, like on a *Shabbos* or holiday. Once he came to Ciechanow to visit his father and Hasidim came with him. He felt himself there in Ciechanow as if he were at home: at a prepared table he recited Torah for the Hasidim. The Ciechanower followers of his father looked askance and went to his father to complain about Reb Berish. When Avrahaml Ciechanower heard this, he answered them: – I beg you, go to my son's meal and offer him a bottle of wine in my name.

Reb Berish was the rebbe in Biala for about eight years. The rebbe's court was located on Krzywa Street.[a] [He] died n 5636, on the 22nd of Tamuz [14th of July 1876]. However, he left five sons: Reb Ahron, Reb Simkha-Bunim, Reb Itshke from Mlawa, Reb Elimelekh Mendl from Wolya and Reb Yekutiel from Wengrod. They were worthy of becoming rabbis, but they did not want to take on the burdens of a rebbe. They agreed that the *tzadek* [righteous man], Reb Yehiel from Aleksander who was one of Reb Berish's esteemed students, should become the successor to Reb Berish.

Thousands of his Hasidim, followers and great people of the time came to Reb Berish's funeral.

A joyful celebration took place on Reb Berish's *yahrzeit* [anniversary of a death]. His brothers, sons, grandsons, Hasidim and followers would gather in Biala in the house of my grandfather, Reb Ahron Landau, to take part in the joyful celebration. The figures, who are well engraved in my memory, were: my grandfather's brothers – Reb Itshke from Mlawa, Reb Yekutiel from Wengrod, Reb Mendl Elimelekh Menakhem from Wolya (later the Strikower Rebbe); my grandfather's sons – Reb Vovtshe, my father and Reb Yisroel from Lodz; the grandsons – Reb Mendl Szedlecer, Reb Yakov Yitzhak, Kinewer Rabbi and Reb Berish from Piotrkow; the elders of the generation – Reb Yisroel from Linik, Reb Dovid Sanaker, Reb Hirsh Leib Minsker, Reb Moshe Chelemer from Warsaw, Reb Borukh Mordekhai Sokol from Brisk, Reb Lipe Lukower, Reb Yisroel Yitzhak from Lukower, Reb Yisroel Dovid from Lodz and Reb Nota Kaminski; the *Anshei Biala* [people of Biala] – *Moyre-Hoyroe* [rabbi competent to decide questions of religious law] Reb Moshe Utszen, Reb Yehezkiel Erlich, Reb Moshe *der groyser* [the large one], Reb Moshe *der kleyner* [the small one], Reb Ahron Slawatitszer, Reb Ahron Zilberberg, Reb Leibl Mednik, Reb Ruwin and Reb Yakov Szulman, Reb Chaim Liberman and Reb Yisroel Hofer.

Reb Nota, Reb Ahron Landau's father-in-law, would come to Biala every year to the joyful celebration. Once he did not have the money for expenses; he sold his cow and came. When he came the next year, he said that he never had such a blessed and prosperous year as the past year.

The joyful celebration began at night. Everyone would gather in the private house of prayer that was built in 5628 [1867] before the time of Rebbe Reb Berish (on Krzywa Street). The young men of the house of prayer would adorn the house of prayer with varied colored lanterns in which candles burned. The beautiful light spilled out of the 16 house of prayer windows and lit the entire area. After *Maariv* [evening prayers], they went together for an evening meal at my grandfather's house. Early in the morning, after *Shakharis* [morning prayers], they left the house of prayer for the cemetery to Reb Berish's *ohel* [monument over the grave of a prominent person]. Space in the *ohel* was scarce and a number of Hasidim and followers had to wait outside. The *ohel* was flooded with *kvitlekh* [notes to a Hasidic rebbe requesting a blessing]. After reciting Psalms and *Kaddish* [memorial prayer], they returned home and the *sudes mitsvah* [banquet held for a religious event] began.

(Taken from the preface to the book about his father, Reb Menakhem Mendl Landau, *Shemesh u'Magen* [*Sun and Shield*], written by Reb Yehiel Landau, a grandson of Reb Ahron Landau.)

In the book "Tif'eret Yisrael"[1], Freeman, we read something about Reb Berish:

"The moderate Admor[2] from Varke, once visited the Admor of Kotzk, escorted by his student, the Admor of Biale. On the morning of the holy Sabbath, the Admor from Biale was invited to the Rabbi of Kotzk to drink coffee together with him, and the great scholars of Kotzk who spent time with their Rabbi at this hour. It was the custom of the Rabbi of Kotzk to debate matters of Halachah[3] at gatherings such as these, and mostly, regarding the Rambam[4]. And the Rabbi of Kotzk reviewed the well–known argument of *Mishneh Lamelech* (chapter 17, of the Halachah regarding the Rambam laws of the Sabbath). Why do we need a verse from the Torah "you shall bring", to give special permission to allow salting meat on the Sabbath, when salting meat is not usually forbidden on the Sabbath? Those present provided an answer.

And you, young man, what is your view about this? – the Rabbi of Kotzk turned and asked the Admor of Biale. According to my understanding, it is not that difficult – he answered, – because the sacrifices of the sabbath were "burnt offerings" and the head was not flayed or cut, so it was salted with its skin, and salting hide is usually forbidden.

You see – the Rabbi of Kotzk turned to those around him – this is how you learn. (This means erudite)".

On the death of Reb Berish, on 6th Tammuz 5636, corresponding to 16. 6. 1876, the following article was published in edition number 24, of the "Tzefirah"[5].

"In Mezritch (close to Biale), the past Sabbath, the 27th Sivan, was a dark, gloomy, overcast day for the Biale community that is near to us, for death was plucked from it, when the Rabbi, the *Gaon*[6], the righteous famous Rabbi, The Rabbi, Dov Berish Landau died, may the righteous memory of this man be blessed. He was the son of the Rabbi, the *Gaon* etc., The Rabbi, Avraham Landau, may the memory of this righteous man be blessed, of Tshechanova. In every town, in every place that this bad news reached, crowds of Chasidim gathered, and they came to the town of Biale the next day, to pay their last respects to their Rabbi; on that day he was brought to the cemetery with great honour. The most important of the Chasidim carried him on their shoulders. *VaYerav b'vat Biale*[7] – he increased in the daughter of Biale, pain and wailing. God will reward you who mourn him, with comfort, and be gracious to his ashes.

Orginal footnote:

a.   At the left entrance in Reb Berish's courtyard on Krzywa Street was located his *yeshiva* [religious secondary school], (F. Gold, New York)

Translator's footnotes:

1.   "Tif'eret Yisrael" (Hebrew) – The glory of Israel.
2.   Admo"r – acronym for the Hebrew words *adonaynu moraynu v'rabaynu* – our master, our teacher, our Rabbi. A title given to a Chassidic Rabbi.
3.   Halachah – legal aspects of Jewish traditional literature.
4.   Ramba'm – acronym for Rabbi Moshe ben Maimon – Maimonides.
5.   Ha'Tzefirah – one of the first Hebrew newspapers of the 20th century.
6.   Gaon – a genius. A rabbinic title given to a scholar of great stature.
7.   The original text of this quotation is a verse from Lamentations 2:5 and reads: *and he increased in the daughter of Judah.* The author has replaced the word "Judah" with the word "Biale" so that it applies to the people of Biale in particular. Expl: Rabbi Yitzchok Javen, Fr.

[Page 282]

Rebbe Ahron Landau

Translated by Gloria Berkenstat Freund

I spent approximately two years in the house of my grandfather, Reb Ahron Landau, before he became a rebbe. Here, I will describe several episodes that remain in my memory.

The image of my grandfather, who evoked reverence, stands before me even now. Mainly, I remember the time from *erev-Shabbos* [Sabbath eve] to *motse-Shabbos* [the close of the Sabbath] in his house. *Shabbos* to him was literally uniting with a *yeseyre neshome* [an additional soul]. His face shone like a godly angel, particularly when saying *Sholem Aleikhem* [peace upon you, said when greeting someone] and at *kiddish* [sanctification of the wine]. I am unable to describe the beauty and splendor of him sitting at the *Shabbos* table, his pleasant attitude while eating and drinking. His face smiled to everyone sitting around; he would speak with everyone, and always found pleasant words for everyone. His conversations always were interwoven with words of Torah. Following the blessing after eating, all of the children stood around him and he would distribute pumpkin seeds and sometimes nuts, as he sat and amused himself with us.

He rose in the morning and then as he went through the *Shabbos* day, he studied the Torah portion for the week, the *Midrash* [commentary] and the *Zohar* [Kabbalah]. While he prayed, he truly inspired everyone who stood in his presence.

The concluding evening meal *motse-Shabbos* was a time for oneself. My grandfather recited words of Torah and there was singing. The meal would last until the middle of the night.

My grandfather was called Reb Ahron Landau in the city without any nickname, as was customary in the Polish cities. Outside of Biala, he was known as Reb Ahrom Bialer.

He possessed a stately appearance. His weighed his words. He spoke gently, pleasantly and modestly to everyone, small and large. He had a *gmiles-khesed* [interest-free loan] fund, was involved with *Hakhnoses Kale* Society [society to help poor young brides] and was a hospitable man who had no equal. There was not a week that he did not have a poor guest with him in his house. He tended to make the bed himself for the guest. He was a member of the *Khevra Kadishe* [burial society] and would accompany the deceased [to their burial].

Both the most-esteemed in the city to the water carrier would come to seek advice from him. His modesty and love of his fellow Jews was apparent in all his ways and deeds.

He was a manufacturer-merchant. Reb Leibish Sauerimper, with the help of my grandmother, ran the business on Brisker Street honestly, trustworthily. My grandfather himself would make the purchases in Warsaw and Lodz. He would go to Warsaw on business matters. The news that Reb Ahron Bialer was coming quickly spread and people would gather from all strata to consult with him. One came for advice in business, another in family matters, a third to ask about his well-being and there were those who came because of curiosity. The door to our house, where he stayed, did not close for a second. People came and went to have had the merit of spending several minutes in the presence of Reb Ahron.

After the death of the Rebbe, the *Yismakh Yisroel* [he rejoiced in Israel], a great number of the Aleksander Hasidim, many followers of my grandfather and also those who had for a long time not had any connection to the Rebbe, crowned my grandfather, against his will, as their teacher and rebbe. The group of his Hasidim and followers grew from day to day. Every Tuesday a train left Warsaw for Biala with cars fully packed with my grandfather's Hasidim; they would sing the entire way. Various legends circulated during the short time of his rabbinate that were full of praise for him.

I heard from my uncle, Reb Vovtshe that my grandfather, Reb Ahron, during the time of his illness, when he lay in Otwock, said to his relatives:

– I assure you that I will get well, but provided that I am left to rest because I am not in a condition to carry such a burden.
His illness lasted seven weeks; he died on the second day of *Shavous* [holiday commemorating the receiving of Torah] 5670 [1910].

His death had a terrible impact in all circles [of Jewish society]. The then Warsaw Yiddish press wrote:

"The second day of *Shavous* 5670, the Rebbe, Reb Ahron Landau of Biala died. Warsaw had not seen such a large funeral in a long time. More than 50,000 men took part. Among them were the rabbis and rebbes from: Skierniewice, Amszinow [Mszczonów], Radzymin, Novominsk, Otwock, Sokołów, Ciechanow, Wengrod, Tomaszow, Kraznik and so on, as well as the entire Warsaw rabbinate."

(Taken from the preface to the book about his father, Reb Menakhem Mendl Landau, *Shemesh u'Magen* [Sun and Shield], written by Reb Yehiel Landau, a grandson of Reb Ahron Landau.)

[Page 283]

Our master and Teacher
Rabbi Yitzchak Ya'acov Rabinowicz

Translated by Libby Raichman

He was born on the 14th Tevet 1847, the third son of the Admo"r[1] Rabbi Natan David of Shidlovetza, the grandson of the "The Holy Jew" from Pashischa, after whom he is named.

Chassidim say that the Adm"r of Shidlovetza during a Brit Milah, would look into the faces of the sons that had been born to him, to see if he should name them after his grandfather *"Ha'Yehudi"* [The exemplary Jew]. It was only after the birth of his third son, the Admo"r of Biala, that he found the child worthy of being called by this name.

While still in his childhood, he was recognized for his strength in Torah, and the sages, the Admor'rim of that generation, Rabbi Yechezkiel of Kozmir, Rabbi Chaim of Tzanz, and others, respected him greatly and said of him, that his future would be to enlighten the people of Israel with the light of Torah.

The righteous Rabbi Yehoshua'le of Ostrov, the author of *"Toldot Adam"* [The History of Man], the son of the righteous Rabbi Shlomo Leib of Lantzna, took him at a young age as a husband for his daughter. His father-in-law was also his Rabbi and leader in holiness, and the Admo"r of Biala, always saw himself as the faithful student of his father-in-law. His book "Yashrei Lev" was named after his father-in-law.

After the death of the Admo"r, Rabbi Yehoshua'le of Ostrov in 1872, his son-in-law, the young married man Rabbi Yitzchak Ya'akcov, had not yet reached the age of 30, yet the Chassidim of his father-in-law, chose him as their Rabbi and their leader. Rabbi Yitzchak Ya'acov refused to accept this great honor, until Rabbi Ya'acov Aryeh of Radzimin, of the elders of the great Amori"m of that generation, wrote to him saying that it was his duty to accept the leadership, because that is the Divine will. Only then, the Rabbi Yitzchak Ya'acov responded to their insistence and became their Rabbi and their leader.

While he was leader and Rabbi of thousands of Chassidim, it was his custom to travel to an elder of the most righteous of the generation, the holy preacher of Trisk who loved him very much. When the preacher was asked by his sons, why he favors the righteous man of Biala, more than all the righteous of the generation, he answered them: "they come to test me, and he comes to listen to me".

The righteous Rabbis of the generation, the holy Rabbi Reb Yechiel of Alexander, the holy Rabbi Reb Ya'acov of Purisov, and others, admired him. The holy Gaon Reb Yechiel Meir of Gostinin, one of the great scholars of the Admo"r of Kotzk, despite his old age, visited him a few times and said: "If I had the strength, I would travel to this righteous man regularly". Also the holy Rabbi Reb Yisrael of Pilov, the grandson of the Admo"r of Kotzk admired him, and said of him: "a sage who is superior to a prophet".

His manner of worshipping God was inspired by an internal fire that warmed all those who approached him and visited him frequently. This was his weekly routine, and how much more so, on the Sabbath[2]. According to the stories of the Chassidic elders, his face was aglow on the Sabbath, with such intensity that it was difficult to countenance.

In the words of his son, the holy Rabbi Reb Avraham Yehoshua Heshel of Lublin, in the introduction to the book "Yishrei Lev", says, that his father's special feelings that he heard from him personally, regarding the holiness of the Sabbath, came to him, because he was born on the 11th of Tevet, the day that was recognized as the day that the famous epistle of the Sabbath, "The Epistle of Shabbat" was sent to the Rabbi Avraham Ibn Ezra, and therefore, and as a result, he was honored with the celebration of the Sabbath. And he concludes, that from his father's words, he learned that the roots of his soul are hewn from the holiness of the Sabbath. And also in his testament, he feels that his words of Torah that are specific to the Sabbath, will be printed for the first time "because of this I am sure, that the Lord will advocate honestly for me".

The words of Torah of the Admo"r of Biala, are in part, gathered and printed in his book containing six sections, called "Words of Wisdom", about the Torah and the festivals and matters dealing with the Sabbath "Yishrei Lev" [Honesty of Purpose].

His wonderful books that are absolute treasures of original ideas, and explanations of the sayings of the great Chassidim, from whose wells he drank, and from whose teachings he gleaned, and shared with others, in clearly articulated language, appropriate for every soul; and at times, he blends a deep theme into a few lines, in a poetic phrase, so that it will be understood by everyone. The basics of Chassidism are explained by him in a new light, and in his words, he presents the essence of Chassidism based on a solid foundation, such as the explanations of matters regarding travel for Chassidim, or the issues of setting the table, "leftovers", and similar matters. Everything receives his full and proper explanation.

He was a fierce opponent of the "Enlightenment", and at every opportunity, he appealed to his Chassidim to distance themselves from it. He struggled against heresy, without compromise, and some of the realities can be observed in the words that are written in his book "Yishrei Lev"; that "the war of Gog and Magog[3], is the heresy of God's providence, may he be blessed. That is the way of bringing, heaven forbid, the people of Israel to heresy by their learning the external wisdom of the heretics. In truth, every Jewish person therefore, needs to seek to be rescued from the snare, and as we see from the legacy of the Messiah, this spiritual impurity becomes stronger, and precious souls are ensnared by the study of external wisdom". In his explanation of the song "Bnei Hechal", he writes, that Rabbi Yitzchak Luria of blessed memory, amended the words, Bnei Hechal, saying, that at a third Sabbath meal nowadays, the essence of dining is meant to save us from Gog and Magog, that is the heresy in the customs of the Jewish people. And among our sages of blessed memory, and in this song, we say "they are cast out, they may not enter, these[4] insolent dogs" for they are the heretics and the infidels.

The righteous man of Biala became seriously ill at middle age and suffered greatly. With true devotion he went about his life, as usual, and continued to read Torah for many hours despite his severe suffering. He died in 1905, at only 58 years of age.

He left behind his four sons who continued the holy dynasty: Rabbi Natan David of Partzeva, Rabbi Meir Shlomo Yehuda Leib of Mezritsh, Rabbi Avraham Yehoshua Heshel of Lublin, and Rabbi Yerachmiel Tzvi of Shedllitz, and his two sons-in-law, Rabbi Aharon Menachem Mendl of Radzimin, and Rabbi Tzvi Kalish of Skarnovitz, who, at the end of his days, was the President of the Rabbinical court of Bnei-Brak.

When the heresy arose among the Jews of Europe, the evil axe was also raised on the house of Biala, many were killed in the terrible Holocaust. At the mercy of the Lord, his grandson, the holy Rabbi Yechiel Yehoshua, who led the Admori"m of Biala, survived, the son of his son, Rabbi Yerachmiel Tzvi. He continued the golden dynasty of the *"Yehudi"* [The Jew], the holy Rabbi Shlomo Leib of Lantzna, in the holy city of Jerusalem.

Translator's footnotes:

    1.   Admo"r – stands for Adonaynu Moraynu and Rabaynu meaning, our Master, our Teacher and our Rabbi. It is the title of a Chassidic Rabbi.
    2.   A joyous Chassidic gathering to celebrate the Shabbat.
    3.   Armageddon
    4.   Aramaic quote. "these" refer to forces of evil that are likened to insolent dogs.

[Page 284]

The *Khevra Kadishe*

Received from Alter Wajnberg and Asher Hofer

Translated by Gloria Berkenstat Freund

It is appropriate that the *Khevra Kadishe* [burial society] was founded right at the beginning of the Jewish community in Biala. From the treatise *Yidn in Biale* [*Jews in Biala*], by Dr. Hendl, we know the facts about the activity of such a society a hundred years ago. Here we will add several facts about the *Khevre Kadishe* for the last 70-80 years, with many facts, it should be understood, that we succeeded in receiving.

Alas, the activity of the society in the social area during the last tens of years of its existence was very backward compared to the activity of the society in the earlier generations. The least that the society did was distribute *talisim* [prayer shawls] to grooms for their weddings and it provided shrouds for the poor deceased.

The society had a *pinkas* [chronicle of the society], but no one had a reason to look into it. After long efforts, the historian Dr. M. Hendl barely prevailed in receiving permission to look at it.

Khol HaMoed Pesakh [during the intervening days of Passover], the *gabbaim* [sextons] of the society for the coming year were elected.

The *Khevra Kadishe* would gather for *kiddush* [blessing over the wine] and banquets: each *Rosh Khodesh* [celebration of the new month], the last day of Passover, *Simkhas-Torah* [holiday celebrating the completion of the yearly reading of the Torah and the start of the new yearly cycle of readings] and *Lag b'Omer* [holiday traditionally celebrating the end of a 2nd century plague]. However, the main banquet would be celebrated on the 5th of Kislev. On this day, the members would fast the entire day and assemble at night to recite penitential prayers for a pardon of their sins if they had not conducted themselves in keeping with Jewish law during a burial and perhaps, God forbid, given offense to the remains. A true banquet would take place after the penitential prayers. The active members would mainly take part in this banquet.

. We will record the names of the *gabbaim* and members of the society during the last 70-80 years. Understand that the list is not complete.

Gabbaim: Moshe Tuvya Stolier, Moshe Bergsztajn, Yehoshua Hofer (Faya's [son]), Reb. Ahron Landau, Chaim Pesakh Farbiak, Tzemekh Tuchminc, Chaim Levi Rubinsztajn, Yisroel Openhajm (Itshke Shaya's [son]), Yoel Itsl Lerner (the Zeszencz[1]) and so on.

Members: Yisroel Wichnas, Reb. Menke, Moshe Hofer (Faya's [son]), Velvl Czito (called Velvl Doctor). Meir Korman, Zelig Hofer (Faya's [son]), Dovid Hofer (Faya's [son]), Yerakhmiel the *soyfer* [scribe], Yerakhmiel *der kleiner* [the small one], Yisroel (bricklayer) Wajnberg, Velvl Mas, Matisyahu Moshe Batszko, Borukh Dovid the *shneider* [tailor], Berl Batszko, Borukh Dovid the *shneider*, Berl Batszko, Uziel Fajnbaum, (Zisl the *stolier* [carpenter]), Moshe Malekh Zilberberg, Mendl Tokarski, Yoal Sztromwaser, Khanina Kaszemacker, Moshe Ahron Perl, Dovidl Geltman, Moshe Mordekhai Geltman, Yakov *Shoykhet* [ritual slaughterer], Idele Eidlsztajn,

Dovtshe (Dovid) Kitie (nickname), Mendl Kitie (nickname), Dovid Potsztaruk, Yoel Gringlas (*shamas* [synagogue caretaker] at the house of prayer), Eliezer Libman, Chaim Libman, Chaim Yeshayahu the *shamas*, Kalman Rozenbaum, Yeheil Rozenbaum, Dovid Parcewer, Yehoshua Rubinsztajn, Shlomo Yosef Cukerman, Yoel Meir Hajblum (*melamed* [religious teacher]), Shlomo Chaim the *melamed*, Borukh Yankl Brodacz, Moshe Potsztoruk, Yerukhem Lajzerzon, Dovtshe Pesl's [son], Boez Lustigman, Yaker Kohan-Tzadek, Tsalke Openhajm (Itshke Shaya's [son]), Hershl Szajnberg, Motl Minc and so on.

————————

Translator's footnote:

1.   It is uncertain if Zeszencz is a nickname, a toponymic name, an occupational name or something else.

The Cemeteries

Translated by Gloria Berkenstat Freund

The cemeteries, which were located at the Brisker highway, were probably not the first in the city. As was the custom in the city, on *Tisha B'av* [ninth of Av, commemorating the destruction of the 1st and 2nd Temples in Jerusalem] important Jews would visit the graves of their parents in the *Zofie Wald* [Sophie's Woods], although in our time there was no evidence that there were graves there.

At first, the cemetery at the Brisker highway extended over to the new market, but at the building of the Warsaw-Moscow highway, which ran through the new market and would cut the cemetery into two parts, they exhumed the bones of the corpses and brought them to the right side of the cemetery. The cemetery was fenced in with a brick wall in which was a stone with a Hebrew inscription that *kohanim* [members of the priestly class] should walk a distance of four cubits [about 6 feet or 1.8 meters] from the fence. During the First World War, the Germans dismantled the brick wall.

More than 60 years ago, headstones could still be found there on which could be seen dates from 130-140 years earlier. Finding eternal rest at this cemetery was the sister of *Shakh* [Shabbatai HaKohen], who escaped from Chmielnicki's troops during the years 1647-1648 with her brother and, on their way, they also stopped in Biala. (See: *Yidn in Biale* [*Jews in Biala*], chapter 6, "The Organized Jewish Community and the External World."

[Page 285]

After the brick wall was removed, they surrounded the cemetery with a wooden fence. The Christian population, however, would systematically disturb the fence around the cemetery and would drive their cattle and pigs there to graze. All interventions by the organized Jewish community had no success. During the last years before the Second World War there was no longer any sign of the former cemetery.

The cemetery also suffered the same fate as the previous one on the Brisker highway. During the Second World War, it was destroyed by the Germans and later it was plowed and seeded.

After the Nazi occupation, the survivors exhumed the bones of the Jews who had been shot, who were buried in various places in the city, and they buried them in a common grave at the destroyed cemetery. A memorial was erected on the common grave, which was dynamited by the Christians.

Received from Asher Hofer, Alter Wajnberg and according to the facts from the written testimony of Gedalyhu Braverman.

[Page 286]

<u>Hassidic Biala in Literature</u>

Between Two Mountains[1]

by Y. L. Peretz

Translated by Ofra Anson

You must have heard about the Rabbi from Brisk and the Rabbi from Biala. Only a few people, however, know that the tsaddik from Biala, Rabbi Noah'ke, used to be a devoted student of the Rabbi from Brisk. He studied with him for quite a few years, then he disappeared for several years. After this self–imposed exile, he reappeared in Biala.

He left for the following reason: they studied the *Torah*, but he felt that it was a dry *Torah* … They studied, for example, the questions women bring to the rabbis, such as separation of meat and milk, financial laws … Very well! Reuven or Shimon come to settle a dispute according to the religious law, or a servant or a woman come to ask a question – then the learning comes alive, it is related to the lives of people and there is a government in the world. Otherwise, Noah felt that the *Torah*, that is, the body of the *Torah*, what is seen from the outside, the shell, the coating, is dry. He felt that it was not the *Torah* of life! – The *Torah* has to live. They did not learn *Kabala* in Brisk. The Rabbi from Brisk was a fanatic "avenger and guard" against it. If anyone touched the Zohar or the Pardes, he used to curse and excommunicate him. Once, he caught somebody with a Kabala book, and he ordered his students to shave off the man's beard like a non–Jew. And what do you think? This poor man lost his mind and became depressed. Moreover, nobody could help him! One does not play around with the Rabbi from Brisk! On the other hand, how could one get away from the Brisk Yeshiva?

He thought about this for a long time.

One night he had a dream. In his dream, the Rabbi from Brisk came to him and said: Get up Noah, I will take you to the lower Garden of Eden[2]. He took him by the hand and led him. They entered a large palace. It had no doors or windows apart from the door through which they entered. Yet, it was full of light. Noah thought that the source of light was the shiny crystal walls.

They went on and on but he could see no end to the palace.

– Hold on to my coat, – said the Rabbi from Brisk – the palace has countless halls, and if you leave me, you will get lost forever…

Noah held on to the Rabbi, and they went on and on. The halls were empty of chairs or any other furniture.

– Nobody sits here – explained the Rabbi from Brisk – you just keep walking and walking. He followed him. Each hall was larger and lighter than the previous one, and the walls shining with different colors. Yet they did not meet anybody on their way.

Noah got tired. He was covered with sweat, with cold sweat. He was cold and his eyes were hurting from the permanent shiny light…

Suddenly he felt lonesome. He missed people, he longed for friends, for human beings. But they were all alone in that palace.

– Do not long for anybody – said the Rabbi from Brisk– this palace is just for you and me… One day you too will become the Rabbi from Brisk!

Noah panicked; he held on to a wall in order not to fall. The wall burnt his hand, not with fire, but with ice.

– Rabbi – he screamed – the walls are made of ice, not of crystal! Just ice!

The Rabbi from Brisk did not answer.

Rabbi Noah shouted again:

[Page 287]

– Rabbi, take me out of here! I do not want to be alone with you here! I want to be with my people!

After he said that, the Rabbi from Brisk disappeared, and he was alone in the palace.

He did not know the way in or out. The walls imposed cold fear on him. His longing for people, his need to see a human face, be it a shoemaker or a tailor, grew stronger and stronger. He started to cry bitterly.

"God almighty" – he begged – "take me out of here. I would rather be in hell with other people than be here all alone!"

That moment, a simple Jew arrived, with a red cart–driver belt at his waist and a long whip in his hand. He did not say a word, but took Noah by his sleeve, led him out of the palace, and disappeared. What a dream!

He woke up early in the morning, almost with the first light, and the first thing he wanted to do was to run to the *Beth Midrash* and solve the dream with his fellow students who spent their night there. Passing through the market, he saw an old carriage, ready to go, a driver standing by its side, a large red belt at his waist, a long whip in his hand, resembling the man who led him out of the palace in his dream.

He was sure it was not a coincidence. He thus approached the driver and asked:

– Where are you going?

– Not your way! – answered the driver quite rudely.

– If you are going – he begged – may I join you?

The driver thought for a while, and then answered:

– Can't you walk? A young man like you cannot walk? Go, on your way!

– And where should I go?

– Your eyes will lead you – answered the driver and turned his back on him – not my business.

Rabbi Noah understood, and went into exile. Some years later, he was found in Biala (I am not telling you how he got there, although the story would leave you speechless). I myself arrived in Biala about a year later. Rabbi Yehiel invited me to be a teacher in his home.

I was not sure I wanted to take on this job. You should know that Rabbi Yehiel was extremely rich, unbelievably rich. Each of his daughters had a dowry of a thousand gold coins and his children married into the most distinguished rabbinical families. Indeed, his youngest daughter–in–law was the daughter of the Rabbi from Brisk. You see, if the Rabbi and the other in–laws were *Mithnagdim* [to the Hassidic movement, O.A.], then Rabbi Yehiel must be one too. I, on the other hand, am a Hassid of the Rabbi from Biala… How can I integrate into such home?

On the other hand, I was attracted to Biala. If I take the job, I will be close to my Rabbi, live in the same town, which is not to be sneezed at! I considered all possibilities, and decided to go.

Rabbi Yehiel himself, I found, was a simple man. I bet his heart was with the Hassidim. He was not a scholar, and when the Rabbi from Brisk was discussing a religious matter, he looked at him as a rooster looks at people. He did not mind that I was a Hassid of the Rabbi from Biala, though he himself was a *Mithnaged*. When I told the family something I had heard from my Rabbi, he supposedly yawned, but I could see that his ears opened. His son, the son–in–law of the Rabbi from Brisk, on the other hand, wrinkled his forehead, looked at me with a mixture of anger and humor, but never argued with me. In general, he did not speak much.

One day, it was time for Rabbi Yehiel's daughter in law, the daughter of the Rabbi from Brisk to have a child. All women are at risk when giving birth, but she was in greater risk than most. Her father, you remember, had ordered the beard of a student who held a book he did not approve of to be shaved. The *tsaddikim* punished him – he had no male descendants: his two sons died within 5–6 years and his three daughters had only girls. Moreover, his daughters had difficult deliveries, and almost died at each birth. Everybody knew that this was the result of the curse of the *tsaddikim*. He himself, however, with his bright eyes, failed to see it. Alternatively, it was possible that he refused to see it. He continued to hold on to his objections – with excommunications and violence.

I was very sorry for his daughter, Gitl. First, she was a human being. Second, she was a kosher Jewish soul. She was the purest person in the world.

She made sure that all poor brides would have a proper wedding, such a delicate creature! Yet, she was going to die because of her father's intolerance! I started using all I had to convince the family to send to the Rabbi from Biala some redemption or at least a pleading note.

[Page 288]

With whom should I talk?

I tried to talk with the son in law of the Rabbi from Brisk. I knew he loved his wife dearly; they did not hide their feelings. One could see their love in their movements and their facial expressions. Yet, he was the son in law of the Rabbi from Brisk! He spat, kept walking, and left me standing with my mouth open.

I went to Rabbi Yehiel himself, but he said: she is the daughter of the Rabbi from Brisk. I cannot do anything against his will, even if my life depended on it. I tried with his wife – a decent woman, but very simple – who answered me: if my husband orders me, I will send the Rabbi from Biala my best festive coif and expensive earrings. Without my husband's agreement – I send nothing. Not a penny.

– And a note? What harm could a small letter cause?

– Nothing behind my husband's back! – Tell me yourself how should a good wife behave, and leave me alone. She walked away, hiding her tears. Her mother's heart already sensed the risk…

I ran myself to the Rabbi from Biala as I heard the first scream.

– What can I do? – Asked my Rabbi – I will pray for her!

– Rabbi, give me something for the poor woman. A note, a coin, a small cameo, whatever…

– Heaven forbid, said the Rabbi, it can make things worse. All these work only for those who believe in them. These people have no faith…

What could I do? It was the first day of Succoth, she was having a difficult delivery, and I could help her. I decided to stay with the Rabbi from Biala and every now and then, I looked at him, begging, hoping he would change his mind.

The severity of the situation was clear, three days in labor! They did what they could: women cried in the synagogue, graves were measured in the cemetery, thousands of candles were lit in the synagogue and the Beith Midrashim, charity was donated… All cupboards in Rabbi Yehiel's home were open to the public, a mountain of coins was put on the table for the poor to come and take what they wanted and however much they wanted.

My heart broke.

– Rabbi, I said, it is written: "Charity protects from death".

He answered: The Rabbi from Brisk may come.

That moment Rabbi Yehiel came in! He ignored the Rabbi, grabbed me by the collar, and said:

– A carriage is waiting outside, go and bring the Rabbi from Brisk… He should see with his own eyes what is going on….

I could see that Yehiel understood the situation. He looked so bad, the dead looked better than him…

I drove and thought to myself that if the Rabbi from Brisk came, something should come out of it. We should try to make some sort of peace, not between the Rabbi from Biala and the Rabbi from Brisk, they had no dispute, but between both sides, the Hassidim and the Mithnogdim… When he comes, he will see with his own eyes…

Yet, heaven was against me. As I left Biala a terrible storm started. The sky darkened, a horrible wind blew, and it seemed to come from all directions at the same time. This is when Christians cross themselves and say that it is going to be a difficult ride. The driver showed me the sky with his whip… The wind grew stronger and tore the clouds as if they were made of paper, the clouds were blown one after the other and some became like towers of ice in a river. I felt three and four floors of clouds over my head. At the beginning, I was not even worried. I am not afraid of getting wet, and thunderstorms do not disturb me. The driver begged me to go back to Biala, but I was determined to get the Rabbi from Brisk.

I knew I was taking a risk, but I heard cries of a woman giving birth in the wind, I heard the knuckles of the Rabbi's son in law cracking in the falling rain; I saw Rabbi Yehiel's face getting darker, his burning eyes losing their vitality. Go, go, I said, and we kept going.

[Page 289]

It was pouring. We were hit by the rain from above and the horses' shoes splashed us from underneath. The road was covered in rainwater, we were almost swimming. We lost our way, but held on.

I arrived with the Rabbi from Brisk on the day of *Hosanna Raba*. The truth is that the storm stopped as he got into the cart. The clouds broke off, and the sun came through the dark sky. We entered Biala dry and calm. Even the driver said in his own language – a Rabbi is a Rabbi.

We went in. The women fell on him like locusts, crying bitterly. I could not hear the woman in labor from the other room, either because of the noise made by the crying women, or because she was too weak to groan. Rabbi Yehiel did not even see us, he stood with his forehead in the window's glass. He must have had a headache.

The Rabbi's son in law too did not turn to greet us. He faced the wall, and I could see he was trembling and his head hitting the wall.

I could not stand it. I felt the sorrow and the fear surrounding me, getting closer and closer. I was getting cold, body and soul.

The Rabbi from Brisk was a strong, tall man. He was charismatic, full of authority, like a king. He had a long white beard, divided in two, one end tucked in his belt, the other rested on it.

His thick, white eyebrows covered half of his face. When he raised his eyebrows and one could see his eyes, the women almost fainted. He shouted like a lion: enough women.

Then, in a soft voice, he asked:

– Where is my daughter?

He went in, and I stayed, thinking to myself: he is so different from the Rabbi from Biala! He raises fear with his eyes, eyebrows, and his voice. The Rabbi of Biala, on the other hand, looks at you with warm, good eyes, in such a calm way, straight to the heart; his look is soft, and his voice is extremely sweet, it wraps the heart, lightly and calmly caresses it… He does not raise fear but induces love. One's heart goes after him, and the soul wants to merge with his… Like a summer bird flying to heaven… and here – horror and fear! He went into the room to his daughter who was in labor!

I feared for her. I ran to the Rabbi from Biala. He greeted me immediately at his door with a smile.

– Did you see the honor of the Torah? – He asked – the pure honor of the Torah.

I calmed myself down, seeing his good smile.

* * *

Indeed, everything went fine. A baby boy was born on *Shmini Atzereth*. On *Simhath Torah* the Rabbi from Brisk discussed *Torah* issues at the dinner table. The truth was that I wanted it differently, I wanted a happy, lively celebration like the one they have with the Rabbi from Biala. I was afraid to say anything, because I was the tenth in the Minyan, and we were going to do the blessings.

What can I tell you? If the Torah is an ocean, the Rabbi from Brisk is the whale in that sea. With one movement, he swims through ten *Masachoth*. With another he swims through *Shas* and *Poskim*. He splashes, boils, raises waves – as if he was the sea itself. My head was spinning, but I was still not satisfied. I felt that I did not experience the real joy of the holiday. I was daydreaming, but the noise at the table brought me back. I saw that everybody was sweating, but I was cold as ice. I knew that at the Rabbi from Biala's was warmth, there was light, they discuss a different Torah… Each word is uttered with love and devotion… Angels fly in the house, their white, large wings are heard and felt. I wished I was there, but could not leave.

Suddenly, the Rabbi from Brisk asked:

– What kind of rabbi do you have here?

– One by the name of Noah – someone answered.

[Page 290]

"One by the name of Noah"! My heart broke. Flattery! Flattery!

– Does he have super–natural power? – He kept asking.

– Few, we are not interested… The women tell us sometimes…

– He takes money for that…

Why did they tell the truth? That he took little money but handed out a lot of charity.

The Rabbi from Brisk thought for a while and asked:

– Can he study?

– They say that he is a very prominent scholar.

– Where is he from?

Nobody knew, and I had to answer. A small conversation started between him and me.

– Noah, did he live in Brisk in the past? He asked me.

– If the Rabbi was in Brisk? I think he was.

– Ah, you are one of his Hassidim! I felt he looked at me as if I was a spider.

He turned around to face the others, and said:

– I once had a student named Noah…He was quite smart, but the other side appealed to him. I warned him once, twice, and I wanted to warn him the third time, but he disappeared. Could this be the same Noah?

– Who knows?

He started to describe him: thin, short, black beard, black curled sideburns, and soft, thoughtful, vice.

– It is very possible that this is the same Noah. Said the people.

We started with the blessings. When we had finished, the unbelievable happened. The Rabbi from Brisk got up, called me to a corner, and whispered, Take me to your Rabbi, my former student. Make sure nobody knows!

I did as he wished. In the middle of the way, however, I startled:

– Rabbi, what is the purpose of your visit? I asked.

He answered simply:

– During the blessing, I was thinking that actually I judged him without hearing his side… I want to see with my own eyes. May be – he added – with God's help, I will rescue one of my former students.

– You know – he added jokingly – if your Rabbi is the same Noah that studied with me, he can be one of the biggest scholars, even become the Rabbi from Brisk one day!

I was afraid.

* * *

And the two mountains met. I wonder how I survived it.

On *Simhath Torah*, the Rabbi from Biala used to send his Hassidim to take a walk in town. He himself sat on his porch, to watch them and enjoy.

Biala was not as big as it is now. It was a small town. The houses were small and low, except for the synagogue and the learning house of the Rabbi. From his porch, however, the Rabbi could see the whole town lying beneath him, with the mountains in the east and the river on the west…

He sat and looked, and saw a few Hassidim walking quietly. He started to sing a tune, they heard him, and went on their way singing. Groups were passing by; they went out of town, all singing. Singing with devotion, a real *Simhath Torah*… The Rabbi himself did not leave the porch.

Suddenly, the Rabbi heard different footsteps. He got up, and saw the Rabbi from Brisk.

– Welcome Rabbi! – He said modestly with his sweet voice.

– Thank you Noah! – answered the Rabbi from Brisk.

– Come in Rabbi, have a seat!

The Rabbi from Brisk sat, and the Rabbi from Biala stood in front of him.

– Tell me Noah! – Said the Rabbi from Brisk lifting his eyebrows – why did you run away from my Yeshiva? What did you miss there?

– I was missing some air to breathe, Rabbi – Noah answered. I felt I was suffocating. I could not catch my breath.

– How come? What are you telling me Noah?

– It was not me, my soul needed more air, more space – explained Noah softly.

– Why, Noah?

– Your Torah, Rabbi, is pure law! It has no mercy in it! No grace! Moreover, it has no joy, not enough free space… It is made of iron and copper, it has iron laws… It is elaborated, deep, but only for a talented minority!…

[Page 291]

The Rabbi from Brisk said nothing, and the Rabbi from Biala continued: Tell me, what do you have to offer to the people who cannot study? For the lumberjack, for the butcher, for the worker, for the simple people? Especially, what do you have for those who have sinned? For the non–scholars?

The Rabbi from Brisk kept quiet, as if he did not understand anything that had been said. The Rabbi from Biala went on with his sweet voice:

– Excuse me Rabbi, but I have to tell you the truth… Your Torah was hard, hard and dry, because you are the body of the Torah, not its soul.

– The soul? – asked the Rabbi from Brisk, scratching his forehead.

– Of course! Your Torah, Rabbi, is only for the scholarly minority. Yet, the Torah should be for everybody! The *Shechina* should rest on us all!

– And your Torah, Noah?

– Do you want to see, Rabbi?

– To see? Torah?

– Come, Rabbi, I will show you. I will show you the joy, the joy that shines from every Jew.

The Rabbi from Brisk did not move.

– Please Rabbi, come with me. It is not far.

He took him by the sleeve, and I followed them quietly.

– You can follow us – He told me – You, too, will see today. The Rabbi from Brisk and yourself will see a real *Simhath Torah*.

I saw the same *Simhath Torah* I saw the previous years, but I saw it in a different way. Through a veil.

A large, wide sky – almost to infinity, and blue, so blue it was a pleasure to the eyes. In the sky, the light was white, nearly silver, clouds flew across, and one could see how they danced with the people, in honor of the *Torah*. The town underneath put on a green dress, a dark, lively green, and it seemed that the greenery was dancing, hugging, and kissing.

Groups of Hassidim walked around in the green. Their coats, those made of silk and those made of cotton, shone like mirrors. The hems of the festive clothes brushed against the dancing green, making a joyful holiday. All the Hassidim looked up to the Rabbi's porch with thirsty eyes, absorbing inspiration from the Rabbi's shining face, and sang higher and higher, brighter and brighter, sacred tunes…

Each group sang its own tune. In the open air, however, the tunes mixed, and the Rabbi on his porch heard one, rich melody. The sky sang, the wheels sang, the earth sang. The entire world sang.

God almighty, I thought, this is so sweet, I am going to melt.

Suddenly, the Rabbi from Brisk said sharply – It is time to pray *Minhah*! – And everything disappeared.

Silence. I felt I fell from heaven, and I saw what I have seen every year. A simple sky above, simple grass underneath. Hassidim walked around in poor, torn clothes that have seen better days… The tunes were broken, unrelated pieces… I looked at my Rabbi – and his face was dark.

* * *

They parted, remaining opponents as before. The Rabbi from Brisk went home, and did not change his attitude.

Yet, the meeting had some effect after all. The Rabbi from Brisk stopped chasing after the Rabbi from Biala.

Translator's footnotes:

1. The two mountains are the Rabbi from Brisk and the Rabbi from Biala. O.A.
2. According to Jewish tradition, there are two gardens of Eden: a lower and a higher. The lower is an earthly paradise with luxurious vegetation, to be enjoyed by the spirits of those who followed all the religious laws; the higher, the celestial, is where the immortal souls of the righteous who learned *Torah* rest. O.A.

[Page 292]

The Silent Man From Wurk

by Y. Opatoshu New York

Translated by Ofra Anson

This is the last story Opatoshu (Yosef Opatovski) published in "The Daily Morning Journal" a few days before he died.

The Jews of Wurk could not remember such a cold month of Shvat as there was in 1859. It was so cold that the water in the houses froze. On Shvat 15, when they went to pray in the synagogue, frozen birds were glued to the fences.

Late in the afternoon, a *Minyan Hassidim* went to the prayer house of Mendele, the Rabbi from Wurk. Some sat there and learned, others stood and exchanged stories about the former Rabbi from Wurk, the late Rabbi Yitzhak. The young janitor prepared the Rabbi's table, which was covered with a white table cloth. He put on the table dates, carobs, figs, and wine.

By the wide opening under the tiled roof, stood an old, gray Aba, who had also served the former Rabbi of Wurk. Although he hardly knew the prayers, he learned the janitor's work from Rabbi Yitzhak. Rabbi Mendele from Kock once asked Rabbi Yitzhak: "Why did you take on such an ignorant janitor?" Rabbi Yitzhak from Wurk answered: "If I had taken on a scholar, he would have become ignorant over time. So it is better to take an ignorant person who will at least learn scholarly expressions".

Old Aba brought in some wood, to warm the prayer house for Shvat 15 dinner. He said in a hearty voice:

"– – – Do not pray, do not study, but do not upset God".

Here and there, a Hassid who was in the middle of learning, or a Hassid who was praying, caught the tune and joined in quietly:

– "Do not upset the Father in heaven".

Just then, a carriage stopped at the Rabbi's yard, and Rabbi Berish from Biala stepped out. Berish was a great scholar, and one of the most important Wurk Hassidim. Berish himself already had a few Hassidim. He belonged to both the Wurker and the Kock Hassidim. Because of the frost, he entered the *Beith Hamidrsh* half dead. Old Aba greeted him with a bottle of spirits:

– It is like a fire outside, right?

– Really dangerous, – said Berish and cleaned drops of ice from his beard and sideburns. He took a second glass of spirit and said to Aba: – Tell the Rabbi that I need to see him right away.

The Hassidim, who considered Berish some sort of a Rabbi, surrounded him and, with a lot of respect, asked him what was the matter.

– We need to pray for Rabbi Medele from Kock who is lying on his death–bed.

– Wai, wai – – –

The janitor returned, taking small quick steps, and called Berish to the Rabbi.

Berish went to the sink and washed his hands for a long time. He put the towel old Aba gave him across his eyes.

"The Wurker's courtyard is like home, it smells like mother and father, like old cherry wine. Kock, on the other hand, is always in a rush, restless, fearful.

Rabbi Berish traveled between the two courtyards. How could he bring some Kock to Wurk? Rabbi Yitzhak from Wurk had two sons. The first, Jacob David was a big scholar, and devoted a lot of his time to study. The younger, Menachem Mendel, did not study, he liked horses, he got friendly with cart drivers, and the Hassidim of Wurk did not approve of his behavior. Rabbi Yitzhak, however, liked him. After Mendele got married, he surrounded himself with the smartest and finest young men. a sort of a "guard" that he headed.

With this "guard, he walked in the fields and the forest, ate all his meals, and kept all their activity a secret. The people used to murmur, "What are they doing there? What are their big secrets?" Even Berish from Biala, who at that point was already very close to Rabbi Yitzhak from Wurk, could not stop whispering: "Why doesn't Mendel study? Why does he waste his days and nights?"

Came *Shavuot*. After the festive meal, the Hassidim came to *Beith Hamidrsh* for *Tikkun Hatzot* ("Midnight Rectification", O.A.) and when they started to study, it was almost dawn. Berish from Biala saw Mendele and his gang entering the market and followed them. They went into a wine cellar, and he went after them. They put on their *Tallit*, prayed the Morning Prayers and sat down to drink some wine. Berish saw all this from his hiding place.

[Page 293]

After they had each had two glasses of wine, Mendel said to his "guard":

– Do you know what a Jew should do? A Jew has to do three things: Scream silently, dance in a standing position, and when he begs on his knees, do it proudly. When he had finished, all his gang bowed their heads, put them on the table and cried. Rabbi Berish from Biala was sure that these smart youngsters filled their glasses with their tears.

This is what young Mendel brought from Kock to Wurk.

That *Shavuot*, Rabbi Berish from Biala became a Hassid of Mendel, and remained his Hassid until Mendel passed away.

When Rabbi Berish came to the chamber of the Rabbi from Wurk, the Rabbi came forward to greet him. The Rabbi was forty years old; Berish was seventy–three. The Rabbi had dark eyes, a black beard and sideburns and pale skin. He looked like his own father, whom the children used to call "Black Yitzhak". Rabbi Berish from Biala had blue eyes, a light blond beard and sideburns, and transparent skin. The room seemed to light up when he came in.

They greeted each other, and looked in each other's eyes, which were full of tears as if both understood simultaneously that the days of the Rabbi from Kock were numbered. The Rabbi's eyes asked:

– Rabbi Itche Meir is in Kock?

– It has been two weeks now.

The Rabbi closed his eyes.

– When did it happen? Yesterday? The day before? He did not want to become a Rabbi after his father's death. People think he is a Tsaddik, one who fears God and never talks. The Rabbi frowned and said:

– Did you come to tell me that the Hassidim want to make you their new Rabbi? Remember, we are accountable for every Hassid that comes to us; also remember that when a Tsaddik carries out God's will, people's hearts are attracted to him.

The Rabbi held the hand of Berish from Biala in his, and kept silent.

And Berish from Biala? He was in Kock. A week after *Shavuot* Rabbi Mendel from Wurk gave a speech. The Rabbi from Kock asked him:

– Are you coming from Wurk? Was there an audience?

– About three thousand Hassidim.

– Did Mendel from Wurk greet each one of them personally?

– He did, each one.

Well, this is the best sign that this silent man must be a Rabbi. Only a Rabbi can shake hands with three thousand people and not become a leper…

The Rabbi from Wurk left Berish's hand, and lifted his two hands:

– Do you hear me, Berish? Let us scream silently.

They sat together in silence, knowing that they serve God with their thoughts and that a Hassid should behave exceptionally: If the law says you must never hurt your friend, the exception is that you must never hurt yourself.

They sat without talking. They prayed Mincho, they prayed Ma'ariv, they bemoaned the death of the Rabbi of Kock, but did not utter a word. Then Rabbi Mendel from Wurk raised a question: "What is One?" Berish did not answer immediately, and the Rabbi closed his eyes and said: "One is the one and only!" and he was silent again, such silence that one could hear and touch it. They sat like that for hours and hours. Suddenly, the two Tsaddikim stopped the silence together, as if they had coordinated it ahead of time, and said:

– We need to study a lesson for Shvat 15. We must have a lesson, according to what Rabbi Mendele from Kock used to say: "He who learns Torah will be rewarded in this world and in the other world".

Berish went to the door. He became angry with the group of Hassidim who stood there doing nothing. The Hassidim received Berish with open hands and enlarged eyes:

Reb Berish, we were waiting for you, and did not hear anything.

– It is impossible! – Berish lifted his hand – We had a meal, he taught me a very difficult lesson, and he did not leave me until I answered all his questions. Did you not hear any of that? Actually, you are right; the whole conversation between us was only in our thoughts…

The Hassidim sat around the table, and Berish from Biala started the lesson of Shvat 15.

[Page 294]

Poland

by Y. Y. Trunk

Translated by Ofra Anson

Chapter 35

The kingdom of Biala. Rabbinic Marquise. All are crown princesses. The dynasty of Biala holds the golden key to prosperity. Silk and velvet.

I have already written about the love story, a Romeo and Juliet kind of love story, between two rich families in Lodz. The current love story, between two rabbinic courts, took place in 1905–6. It pictures the atmosphere of that time.

The rabbinic court in Biala did not have many Hassidim. Yet, its genealogy, "*yihuss*", was one of the best in Poland. Their blood relations could be found in almost all the important rabbinical dynasties in Poland and in Wolin. If I were to count the ancestors of the court of Biala, I would have to write the full history of the Hassidic movement. It is enough to note that the Biala court stemmed from "The Holy Jew from Peshischa a very important *yihuss* for Hassidim, and this is only the beginning. Hassidim from Wolin will tell you about their rabbinic dynasty, and how it is blood–related to the Biala court.

Although Biala did not have many Hassidim, it was managed like an empire. The life style was aristocratic, like the courts of Radzyn and Sadagora. The Hassidim used to say that, for the needs of the Rabbi's court, God puts in a hundred Zloty bill each time a purse opened. This must have been true; money came in buckets from the Hassidim. Biala had its share of poor people, and there were quite a few beggars, supported by the Biala court. The rich did not want to live in Biala, where lazy beggars were always dependent on the Rabbi to provide them with food.

The Rebbetzn, the first lady of the Biala court, the grandmother of the hero of our story, was treated in Poland as a Marquise. It would take an hour to describe her *yihuss*. Moreover, she was beautiful, the only refined daughter in a court of the important rabbinic dynasty of Wolin. She was of a good disposition, but held that she has the right to her own place in the world. She was not the only one to think that. Since she was a baby, the people around her had kept pointing this out. The Hassidim, men and women, talked about the *yihuss* of her ancestors. She understood very well that either because of her rabbinic blood, or because of her beauty (an orthodox woman may also look at the mirror), she needed to go to Warsaw to have her dresses sewn. Moreover, she needed to hire the same seamstresses as the most rich and ancient Polish aristocracy. Biala's Hassidim understood that this is how it should be, and that their Rebbetzn deserves it by God's will. They opened their wallets and spread the court with gold. She was known to be one of the prettiest and most elegant women in Poland, not only among the Jews, but among the Polish aristocracy as well.

As I have already said, the court in Biala conducted an aristocratic life style. Nevertheless, although there was a son in the court, he was not the only crown prince; all the sons in the court were crown princes. Each of them had a group of people around him, who looked at "their" crown prince as the one who would inherit the court when the Rabbi reached 120 years. Meanwhile, they kept their wallets open, to have first access to the abundance that would flow when "their" crown prince became the Rabbi. Naturally, there were also beggars who prepared themselves for an idle life by the new Rabbi's table. Each son in the Biala court felt and behaved like the future Rabbi, each daughter in law felt and behaved like a Rebbetzn.

[Page 295]

The Rabbi, the crown princes, and the Hassidim were sure that the Biala court would stand solid until the Messiah came. Even when the Messiah's *shofar* would be heard, and all would have to leave Poland and move to Jerusalem, the Biala court would not cease to exist. Meanwhile, the princes who would run the Biala court in the future had to prepare themselves. They began their training in the cradle. When they went to the *Heder* some of them had a private server that would not move from their side. Nothing but silk and velvet was good enough for the gentle body of a grandson of the Biala court.

Chapter 36

Biala's elderly look at the baby in the cradle. A bride is brought from Sochatchov. The bride is a member of Poalei Zion (a Socialist–Zionist movement, O.A.). The Russian Czar gains priority over nice dresses. Is this wedding possible?

Joshua'le – the hero of our story – was one of the princes in the Biala court. He was the eldest son of the Biala Rabbi's first–born son. This meant that he was the first in line to the crown. Since he was born, the Hassidim sought after him. They struggled to peep in the pram to see him and could not wait for him to grow up. They started calling his name and his mother's name asking for prosperity. As I have already said, the Biala Hassidim were sure that God put the golden key to prosperity in the hands of the Biala dynasty.

When Joshua'le started walking, he was dressed only in silk and velvet. He carried a golden *yarmulke* on his little head as if it was a crown. He had a special caretaker who did not leave him for a moment, followed his step, searched his mouth, and served him. Naturally, the caretaker was handsomely paid.

He grew up to be a fine young man, and reached the age of marriage. He was thin and gentle, pale, with two beautiful innocent eyes. His long, curled sideburns and his silk and velvet clothes made him look like a real rabbinic prince. His pale, gentle face was covered with the respect of generations of important Rabbis. The Hassidim were sure that the Biala dynasty was about to begin a new stage.

The search for a bride began, and matchmakers brought a bride from the Sotchachov court. It was agreed that Biala had enough rabbinic *yihuss*, and the blood of a genius in the Torah should be added to the family.

Rabbi Avreimale from Sotchachov was still alive then. At that time, Sotchachov was the Torah center, not only in Poland but also all over the world.

The bride was the granddaughter of Rabbi Avreimale, daughter of Rabbi Shmuel, the famous, only son of Rabbi Avreimale. Shmuel sometimes replaced Rabbi Avreimale. I have already written a lot about him in the first chapters of this book. In Sotchachov, outstanding scholarship was not sufficiently appreciated. Money did not flow into the court as in other Hassidic courts. When the Rabbi's wife, the Rebbetzn Tzine, a daughter of the Rabbi from Kock, heard that in Biala the Rebbetzns are dressed like Polish nobility, she did not want even to consider a possible match.

She was a descendant of The Holy Jew from Peshischa who was admired in the Kock court. They also admired Rabbi Avreimale, his daughter the Rebbetzn Tzine, and, needless to say, the Rabbi's son Shmuel. Thus, marriage with a granddaughter of the Holy Jew from Peshischa was so important that they were willing to disregard the fact that the Sochachow court did not like the way they read the *Gomorra* in Kock.

All this happened around 1905, the time of the great revolution. A revolution in Jewish life also took place in those years. Everything changed. *Yihuss*, rabbinic courts, did not matter as much anymore. The workers' movement penetrated to the court of Rabbi Avreimale. Dobrish, Shmuel's daughter, who was supposed to be the bride of the delicate grandson of the Biala court, inherited the extremist tendencies of the Kock court and of her grandmother Tzine. She was strongly influenced by Poalei Zion.

[Page 296]

Because of her strong character, she could not compromise. She brought her socialist ideas home, to Rabbi Shmuel's doorstep. The Sochachow court was known for its scholarly merits and Rabbi Avreimale as an expert in the laws of the Sabbath. His book, *Eglei Tal* (drops of dew, O.A.), which discussed the 39 tasks forbidden on Saturday, was a masterpiece. His granddaughter, however, was an atheist. She challenged her family, for example, by writing at home on Saturday.

We do not know how Dobrish came under the influence of Poalei Zion. We do know, however, that Poland was shocked to see how deeply atheism had penetrated into the Jewish community. They had to make sure that Dobrish would not make any scandal. Her father, Rabbi Shmuel, was a strong man who did not let any question go unresolved. Now he had to hide what was going on in court, the great Torah center. The other rabbinic courts seemed to have avoided the revolution.

The common attitude in the Sochachow court was that when Dobrish got married she would have other things to worry about than fighting with Poalei Zion against the Russian Czar and against the old Jewish life. The beautiful clothes would overcome politics.

Dobrish was my age. Matchmakers suggested her as a possible bride for me, among other brides who lived all over Poland. My grandfather Baruch liked the idea of intermarriage with the Sochachow court. He thought that a rich family does not need the prestige of other rich families, but the respect of the Torah. His only daughter married into the family of Joshua'le Kotner. For his only grandson he wanted a bride from the court of Rabbi Avreimale of Sotchachov.

Rabbi Shmuel knew that choosing a groom for Dobrish without asking her opinion was a waste of time. He asked her if she would marry me. She answered with Kock wit:

– Thank you, but I do not need a son of a rich family.

It was clear that there was no point in asking her again. Meanwhile, different people told Rabbi Shmuel that Dobrish was attending illegal gatherings of Poalei Zion in Sotchachov. He decided to go along with the groom from the Biala court, without discussing it with Dobrish. He was sure that once she was married and moved from Sotchachov to Biala, the crazy socialist ideas would evaporate.

Now, all the fancy dresses of the women in the Biala court became an asset, rather than a disadvantage. Rabbi Shmuel thought that the beautiful clothes would take Dobrish's mind off Poalei Zion and the Russian Czar.

The Biala court had no idea what a terrible bride was coming from Sotchachov. The matchmakers knew how to hide and keep secrets, and the distance between Sotchachov and Biala prevented gossip-mongers from spreading the word.

Nobody asked Dobrish, and the *Thnoim* (the marriage contract, O.A.) were signed. The Biala court showed its aristocratic affluence. The Rebbetzn Tzine, the daughter of the Rabbi from Kock, had one look at the silk and velvet dresses of the women of the Biala court, their pearls and diamonds, turned her back and murmured sharp words of disapproval. Under normal circumstances, she would have stated her opinion loud and clear. Yet, she had to pay her respect to the descendants of the Holy Jew, and not spoil Dobrish's wedding.

The groom, Jushua'le, was more quiet and gentle than his relatives. With his long sideburns, his silk and velvet clothes, he really looked like a prince. Rabbi Avreimale himself, though he was more interested in the scholarly prestige of the Baila court, looked at him and told Rabbi Shmuel:

– He looks like a grandson of the Holy Jew.

Dobrish looked at the event as a comedy. She laughed with her friends from Poalei Zion and said: Let them play! I am not going to marry such a bourgeois rabbinic bloodsucker anyway.

[Page 297]

Chapter 37

Only God knows one's heart. The Bund secret. Those who seek, find. Poland is shocked and the Sotchachov court sends back the marriage contract. Dobrish's letter to the groom. The dialectic of the revolution discontinues.

Only God knows what is in one's heart. Nobody can see the worm which lives inside the most beautiful apple. A period of unrest came along. When legends take the front of the stage – the logic of all traditions is quiet.

Who could imagine that pale Joshua'le, the prince dressed in silk and velvet, who had his own servant and all the Hassidim wanted to work for him, would join the "Bund" in Biala? Who could believe that when he asked his servant to leave him alone and close the door, when the Hassidim were sure that he was studying the mystic writings, he was actually reading the books of Karl Marx?

In court he behaved in the usual rabbinic way. He kept his long sideburns, the clothes, the servant and the Hassidim followed him, a great show. At the same time, he belonged to the "Bund".

The reason was the following:

A Russian troop was stationed in Biala. The soldiers were mainly Cossacks and Circassians. The "Bund" was active among them, trying to make them join the revolution, and had managed to organize several revolutionary cells. This activity was extremely dangerous.

They figured that the rabbinic court was the best and safest hiding place for their written materials. Moreover, they had their own man in the Biala court, Joshua'le. They ordered him, therefore, not to change his rabbinic behavior.

Joshua'le obeyed the party's orders, and never came to their meetings. Only three or four members knew that he belonged to the organization. It did not cross the minds of the gendarme and the secret services that the center of Biala's revolutionary militant organization was in the rabbinic court.

Everything went well for quite a while.

However, there was one provocateur, who looked and searched until he found a lead. He showed the Russian gendarme where to look for the propaganda center of the revolutionary militant organization. The gendarme could not believe his eyes and said to the provocateur:

– You must be crazy! Alternatively, the "Bund" wants you in jail.

The provocateur insisted he was right, and the gendarme had no choice but to enter the rabbinic court and search for the terrible enemy of the Czar.

They gently knocked on the rabbinic closed doors.

All the Rebbetzns and the servants grew pale, and could not understand what the matter was. They spoke calmly and politely to assure the gendarme that there must have been some misunderstanding. Some of their rivals probably dropped a word in Petersburg to get them into trouble, and the government issued an order to search the rabbinic court. The truth would come out soon, and the mistake or the lies would be revealed.

The Rebbetzns indeed calmed themselves down. They did not inform the Rabbi, who was praying in his special room, because they did not want to disturb him.

The gendarmes started the search, and they knew how to do it. They went to Joshua's chamber, and soon found what they were looking for.

The gendarmes themselves could not believe their eyes when they found the stamps of the revolutionary military organization and a package of propaganda pamphlets to be distributed among the Cossack and Circassian soldiers.

[Page 298]

One cannot imagine what happened in the Biala court. The Rabbi had to be disturbed in the middle of praying, to be told the horrible news.

The shaken gendarmes remained polite to the flabbergasted Rebbetzns. They were also polite to Joshua'le, but took him with them. The case was so important that they were afraid to hold him in the Biala prison and transferred him to Warsaw under heavy guard.

* * *

The news fell on the Hassidim of Poland like thunder on a clear day. If revolutionary activity had been found in the Biala court, this must be the end of the world. The Jewish way of life was under attack; nobody could trust his own children anymore.

In Sochachow they thought: not only did Dobrish's engagement to Joshua'le not make her leave Poalei Zion, but also the grandson of the Holy Jew himself was involved in revolutionary activity. Rumor was that the young, pale, well–dressed man with long sideburns would be sent to Siberia for the rest of his life. They did not think of respect or prestige, and immediately sent the marriage contract back to Biala. The engagement was over!

The Biala Hassidim knew that they had to open their wallets wide to pay for the Mitzvah of prisoners' redemption; they also knew that they would be re-embraced from heaven. They had to act quickly, and not to save a thousand or even ten thousand. God and the Holy Fathers would multiply each sum spent ten or hundred times. Indeed, money started pouring in. They started with the Biala gendarmerie, bribing left, right and center. In no time, the Biala gendarmerie obeyed the Biala Hassidim. They destroyed the documents that could be used against Joshua'le. The agents who searched his chamber swore by the name of all the saints that they had not found anything and it was all a big mistake. Then they went to Warsaw, and the delegate of the Czar could not resist the bribery.

Sure enough, Dobrish heard about Joshua'le's heroic revolutionary activity.

The engagement was over. Dobrish sat down to write a letter to her former groom, the pale orthodox man, whom she would rather die than marry. Actually, she wrote, our parents arranged our engagement without asking us, and broke the engagement without asking us. This does not matter now. If you want me, I am willing to marry you.

Joshua'le, who heard about her revolutionary activity, answered: Yes, I would like to.

They met in Warsaw a few times. Although she was from Poalei Zion and he was from the "Bund" (both socialists, but the Bund was not Zionist; O.A.), they fell for each other.

In both rabbinic courts, that of Biala and that of Sochachow, matchmakers continued to bring possible matches. This time, Dobrish used the sharp tongue she had inherited from her grandmother Tzina, and told her father, Shmuel:

– I give you three weeks to revive the engagement with the Biala court, or I will live with him without getting married.

Rabbi Shmuel was shattered. He knew his daughter, and knew that she was sincere.

[Page 299]

Careful, diplomatic negotiations started between Biala and Sochachow. The marriage contract was restored, but the wedding was modest and quiet, in Warsaw, not as originally planned in Biala. Bells did not ring; only close relatives knew the exact date. Under other circumstances, this wedding would have been a major event in the Hassidic world.

*

Joshua Rabinowitz (the name of the Holy Jew from Peshischa) lived first in Lodz, and later in Warsaw. We were good friends. He used to come with Dobrish to my place, and I used to visit him with my wife Hanna.

Joshua was an example of a person who managed to combine "Bundist" thought with deep Jewish socialism. There was no contradiction between the tradition represented by the Holy Jew and the "Bund". Both stem from the same Jewish historical thought: the dialectic of the revolution and beyond.

Joshua remained an orthodox Marxist. He saw in me a metaphysicist and idealist. We had many arguments, but we both were good "Bundists".

He was in the Warsaw Ghetto during WWII, in the "Bund" underground organization, until the Germans sent him to his death. Dobrish had been shot by the Germans while walking on the street with her youngest daughter, whom she named Tzina after her grandmother. The Germans used to shoot the child in front of the parent, and then shoot the adult. One can imagine that Dobrish was happy to leave this world.

Biala's "Yard"[1]

by A. Litwin

Translated by Ofra Anson

None of the Hassidic courts in Poland was as glorious and magnificent as the Biala Court. Neither the Gere nor the Turzysk courts succeeded in setting up a "table"[2] like the Biala court had. Biala's Rabbi, Yitzhak Jacob, had a top rabbinic *yihuss*. He was the grandson of the Holy Jew from Peshischa, and a great–grandson of the best disciples of the Baal Shem Tov.

His nickname was "the cripple". Naturally, only the "Mithnogdim" dared to call him by that name, not the Hassidim, although it was true. He had a limp.

He was very talented, and very smart. He knew how to handle his Hassidim, men and women worshiped him. A poor woman, who always paid redemption for her only son (that is, she donated to the court for the safety of her son, O.A.), used to complain only of one thing: why was she not born a man? If she was a man, she could have stood close to the Rabbi.

I would like to present some more evidence of the uniqueness of the Biala Rabbi. Usually, only a few Hassidim lived with their Rabbi in the same town. Living in the same location meant that they knew the Rabbi and his family inside out, and lost respect for him. The opposite happened in Biala. The most important and the most devoted Hassidim lived in Biala.

This was possible only because the Rabbi knew how to run a "kingdom". During the High Holidays, he assured that his Hassidim would be in awe. Dressed in white, surrounded by seven Shofar, he alone read the whole book during the service. By the table, discussing the Torah, he did not speak clearly, and the warden explained to the others what their Rabbi meant. No rabbi could so artistically make believe he had risen to heaven for a long time, and had suddenly remembered to come back to earth as the Rabbi of Biala.

Like many other rabbis, the Rabbi of Biala was too proud to go around asking for donations and redemption fees. The funds came of their own accord. Each Hassid, even the poorest one, was committed to a weekly donation. Rich Hassidim donated a lot of gold. Each note for a woman cost a Ruble. In his closet, the Rabbi held the most expensive wine, worth thousands of Rubles. Table manners were meticulous and meals were like a royal ceremony.

[Page 300]

Except for cameos, the Rabbi used to give *Seguloth* (merits, O.A.) for the sick, which actually were instructions in hygiene. Young people who were close to the court told me that the old Rabbi used to read "*Hatzfira*" (a Hebrew newspaper, not accepted by the orthodox. O.A.) in the toilet. Moreover, in his chamber he had a collection of books of general knowledge. These books were packed away secretly after his death, five years ago, and taken by people who had an interest in general education. Nobody in the court knew about these "unclean" books.

The Rebbetzn, the wife of the Rabbi of Biala, was a special woman. She used to be very pretty and had the reputation of being an elegant woman. While the Rabbi enjoyed the admiration of the wives of the Hassidim, the Rebbetzn was the goddess of the Hassidim themselves.

She had the intellectual and spiritual abilities to run the court like a marquise, to ensure an aristocratic atmosphere, including glamorous companions. She made the court into a palace. She had her own secretary, a handsome and healthy warden (both male, O.A.), who followed her everywhere. She used to go for walks with the warden, leaning on his shoulder.

She used to dress according to the latest fashion of Paris and Berlin, She ordered her dresses abroad, in the leading fashion shops. The price of a dress was 800–1000 Rubles, 100 Rubles for an umbrella. Diamonds were studded in her garters. When one of her daughters got married, she ordered a dress embroidered with gold for herself, as beautiful as the wedding dress of the bride.

I would like to bring two indications of the admiration of the Rebbetzn by the Hassidim. Once, she went to a store in Vienna, to buy some cosmetics. Next to her stood a rich woman, probably a German marquise. The marquise argued that the price they were asking was too high, and left. The Rebbetzn paid the full price for the cosmetics fancied by the German marquise. Later the marquise came back to the store to buy what she had chosen before she left, yet it was too late. She got very angry and asked: – Who was the milliner who bought it? When she learned that it was just a Rabbi's wife, she almost lost her mind. The German newspapers published the story, but the Rebbetzn won...

One dark night, the Rebbetzn lost a hairpin. It was, of course, diamond studded. When the Hassidim heard about it, they came to search for it, and did not leave until it was found.

The Biala Court was a real palace. It had a large garden; a carriage and horses always stood at the ready. Each child had his or her own house, servants, and a group of Hassidim as companions.

The Rabbi and the Rebbetzn had four sons and two daughters. One daughter is the Rebbetzn of Radzymin (Radzymin, Gere, Biala, and Turzysk were the most important rabbinic courts in Poland and Wolin). One daughter fell in love with a simple young man from town. The relationship was stopped as soon as it was discovered. Their youngest son, Hershele, was very talented. He was a singer and played the violin, a painter, and, on top of everything, very good looking. In the evenings, he used to hide his sideburns under his hat, sneak out, and go out with young women from the town.

The old Rabbi of Biala died just before the first Russian revolution. Hershele became the Rabbi but actually the old marquise, the old Rebbetzn, ran the court. Nevertheless, it did not last long. Six months after he became a Rabbi he died in Siedlce.

A war of inheritance started between the other brothers, as often happened in many other courts. The result was the end of the Biala kingdom. The glamorous court with the Jewish marquises and princesses ceased to be forever. Small kingdoms were set up, though, in Miedzyrzec, Siedlce and other places. None of them, however, had the prestige and admiration enjoyed by the Biala Court. The Biala Court is lost, the ways leading to it are blocked and only a small number of the former thousands of Hassidim and pilgrims have remained loyal to the dynasty. Many others joined other courts. The old Rebbetzn, the Jewish marquise, went to live with her daughter in Lublin, unhappy in her later years. Yet, there were enough loyal Hassidim to provide her with a good pension, and she kept up her high standard of living until she passed away.

("Yiddishe souls", Volume 6, published by "Folk Building", New York, 1917)

Translator's footnotes:

1. "Yard" is equal to the "court" as used by Y. Y. Trunk in the chapters from Poland. (O.A.)
2. "Table" "tish" in Yiddish, is an event in court, when a table is laid for the Rabbi and his Hassidim. (O.A.)

[Page 301]

Social Institutions

The Hospital

by M.Y. F–M

Translated by Gloria Berkenstat Freund

It can be seen from the treatise in this book by the historian, Dr. M. Hendl, that the Biala Jewish population already possessed its own hospital in 1742. Consequently it is notable that at the beginning of the 20th century Jewish Biala did not have such an institution. The reason can be seen to be that, in case of an illness, well–to–do Jews could obtain treatment without a hospital, particularly at that time when the word "hospital" in general was intimidating to the psychology of the Jews. Only the poor strata was directed to hospital treatment which, despite their complete superstitious fear of a hospital, was the only recourse they had when one of them became ill. It appears that for the poor class, the city *gabbaim* [sextons] of the 18th century were more concerned than in the later years and who knows if Biala, in general, would have obtained such an important social–medical institution if not for the accident of death of a rich woman in the city which we already have mentioned in the treatise, "Jewish Biala in the Past Generations."

Jewish Hospital Building

The building of the hospital, according to the building plan of the Biala architect, Wolodka, began in 1909. The masons were the municipal artisans, Alter Wajnberg and Hershl Nowomiast.

Yudl Szwarc, Dr. Gustaw Zita, Moshe Kawa, Yitzhak Piczic, Wolf Goldsztajn, Moshe Lebnberg, Kalman Szajnberg, Zalman Zak, the lawyer Kalman Hartglas and Chaim Yoska Kasztenbaum were members of the hospital building committee. The driving force of the committee was Yudl Szwarc.

The construction ended in 1911 and a solemn ceremonial opening took place the same year, to which the governor of Siedlce came.

The erection of the hospital cost approximately 20,000 rubles, which was received from Shmuel Piczic after the death of his wife, Ita Brukha – 6,000 rubles; 4,500 rubles, the inheritance from Shmuel from Venice after the death of his father; Hersh Ber Raaba; and the so–called "girl" from the courtyard, Helene Kagan, donated 2,000 rubles. The rest was collected among the population.

Yudl Szwarc, Yitzhak Piczic, Dr. Zita and the *dozores* [members of the communal council] were hospital trustees until the First World War.

Dr. Zita led the hospital, which had 10 beds at the start of its activity. Of the personnel who were active there, I remember the nurse Ayzyk Finklsztajn, the guard Alter Czeszler and the cook Dwoyra Finklsztajn.

The hospital was supported by a hospital tax, by payments by the sick and from donations that would be collected among the population.

During the First World War, the hospital was requisitioned by the German occupying regime for military purposes.

[Page 302]

Flower sale in aid of the Jewish Hospital

After the First World War the hospital income came from the following sources: subsidy from the *kehile* [organized Jewish community], grants from the city hall, payments by the sick and support from the *landsleit* [people from the same town] abroad, mainly in North America.

The hospital also had income from Tila's house at the market and from several shops in Yatka Street, which the woman mentioned [Tila] transferred to the hospital.

Active in the hospital in the era between the two world wars were the following doctors and other co–workers: Dr. Joakhim Zater, Dr. Antoni Gelbard, Dr. Sz Tenenbaum (Siedlce), Dr. Butshe Finklsztajn (from Biala), Dr. Pinkhas Erdman (Bialystok) and Dr. Goldenberg. Nurses: Wolf Szor, Dovid Przewuzman, Musawicz (the youngest son of the Kobriner *feldsher* [barber–surgeon]). Nurses [female]: Miss D. Biderman (Ahrela Slowaticzer's daughter) and Chava Rogalski. Midwives: Chava Manhajmer–Szor, Sonya Wajnsztajn-Kelmanzon and Sura Kramarcz.

Flower sale in aid of the Jewish Hospital

[Page 303]

הילפס-אקציע לטובת דעם יודישען שפיטאל אין ביאלע-פאדל.

אויפרוף

צו אלע ביאלער לאנדסלייט אין ניו-יארק:

די שענסטע און וויכטיגנסטע יודישע אינסטיטוציע אין אייער אלטער היים, **דער יודישער שפיטאל אין ביאלע**, געפינט זיך אין זעהר א קריטישער פינאנציעלער לאגע און ראנגעלט זיך שווער פאר זיין עקזיסטענץ.

דער אלגעמיינער קריזיס, וועלכער האט זעהר שטארק געטראפען אונזער שטאדט און שטארק פערארימט דעם גרעסטען טייל פון אונזער בעפעלקערונג האט קאטאסטראפאל געווירקט אויך אויף די הכנסות פון יודישען שפיטאל. מיליב דער אלגעמיינער קריטישער לאגע האט מעהר קיינער גיסט די מעגליכקייט זיך פריהאם צו קריהרען און יעדער טראכטער מיט געקומען אין שפיטאל ווי צו בעקומם די נעהטיריגע מעדיצינישע היליף.

דער ברייטער קרייזם און ארבעטשלאזיקייט אין ביאלע האט געדרונגען ערציי, אז דער יודישער שפיטאל איז שטענדיג אינגערשאלט מיט זייער ערנקע קראנקע.

אריב פיר וועלן אין דער נאהטענטער צייט ניסא צוהאלפסן קיין פינאנציעלע היליף רעכען, די וועגאר, או דער יודישער שפיטאל זאל צטשלאסען ווערען. מרבר טם אזי זאל מפיקלענעכדע חיצדוום דאם מינגעלטן קראננען. וועלבעס מאר אבער אין קיין סאל ניטט דערלאוען ווערען, בעוונדערטס אין אוג קריטישען מאמענט.

די עקזיסטענץ פון יודישען שפיטאל איז א לעבנסנ-נויטווענדיגהיים פאר דער גאנצער ביאלער בעפעלקערונג.

מיר אפעלירען דעריבער צו אייך ביאלער לאנדסלייט אין פריינט פון יודישען שפיטאל: —

העלפט אונז מיט אלע מעגליכקייטען וויטער אויפצוהאלטען די עקזיסטענץ פון יודישען שפיטאל, וועלכער איז ווירקליך דער שענסטער און ברייטיגסטער יודישער אנשטאלט אין ביאלע.

פארזיצענדער: (—) ב. קליגער.
הידענטער: (—) ד"ר נעלבאום.
קאסיר: (—) ב. זידינאָגראד.
היטעם, טיוורער: (—) ז. ראזען.
סקרעצער: (—) ז. ליידעראנט.

שפיטאל קאמיטעט

ביאלע-פאדל. דעם 15טען סעפטעמבער 1931.

Appeal from the Hospital Committee to the Biala landsleit [people from the same town] in New York [requesting financial assistance]

The *feldsher* [barber–surgeon] at the hospital during the last days of the Second World War was Berish Wajsman (from Lomaz [Łomazy]).

The two Jewish hospital doctors up to the Second World War

From the left: Dr. Erdman, Borukh Winograd (kehile [community] secretary), Dr. Goldenberg, Zalman Liverant (hospital secretary)

Administrators of the hospital after the First World War were Benyamin Kliger, and after him, Zalman Liverant, who held this office until the day that he was shot by the Germans.

Hospital Committee [in Biala] in 1935

Sitting from the right: Benyamin Kliger, Moshe Hava, Dr. A. Gelbard;
Standing: Zalman Liverant, Khanine Kaszemacher and Borukh Winograd

The hospital was closed often during this era and this was during the long months without monetary means because the *kehile* never paid the designated subsidies on time and also never in the amount that they had designated.

In 1939, during the Second World War, the Red Army requisitioned the hospital and during their evacuation from the city they took parts of the hospital equipment, such as medical apparatus and instruments, with them.

During the German occupation in the Second World War, the hospital was always filled with the sick. Dr. Gelbfisz, who had been specially brought from the Warsaw ghetto, led the hospital. Dr. Hochman (a refugee from Germany), Dr. Rubensztajn (came from Warsaw) and the *feldsher* Berish Wajsman worked with him.

Additional Facts:

According to what Yakov Goldsztajn [wrote] in *Bialer Vokhnblat* [*Biala Weekly Newspaper*], number 10 of the 6th of March 1936, the inspiration for building the Jewish Hospital in the city was the Biala Rabbi Yitzhak–Yakov Rabinowicz. He spoke about this with Yudl Szwarc several times.

In the same issue of the *Bialer Vokhnblat*, Yakov Goldsztajn says that a certain Mrs. Minc had left a bequest for the building of a Jewish hospital in Biala. The bequest, lying in a bank over the course of 100 years, had grown to 500 rubles.

[Page 304]

Reb Moshe Kohan left several thousand rubles in his will for the building of a Jewish hospital in Biala (P. Gold, New York).

In 1932 a clinic was opened at the hospital for the poor population (*Podlasker Lebn*, number 15/19 of the 23rd of September 1932).

In the preliminary budget of the *kehile* [organized Jewish community] for the year 1933, the subsidy for the hospital was anticipated to be a sum of 19,000 *zlotes* (*Podlasker Lebn*, number 5/70 of the 3rd of February 1933).

The subsidy of the Jewish hospital in the preliminary budget of the city hall was anticipated in the amount of 3,000 *zlotes* (*Podlasker Lebn*, number 4/69 of the 27th of January 1933).

The payments by the sick, who were treated in the hospital in the years 1930/1, added up to seven to eight thousand *zlotes* a year. (*Podlasker Lebn*, number 42/107 of the 27th of October 1933).

A subsidy for the hospital in the amount of 12,000 *zlotes* was anticipated in the *kehile* preliminary budget in 1934 (*Podlasker Lebn*, number 5/121 of the 2nd of February 1934).

The hospital budget in the year 1934 was established as 20,000 *zlotes*. Eight thousand *zlotes* was expected from the sick, subsidies and donations. The *kehile* was supposed to cover the remaining 12,000 *zlotes* (*Podlasker Lebn*, number 1/117 of the 5th of January 1934).

In the Health Service for the Welfare of the Population

Received from Alter Wajnberg and Asher Hoper

Translated by Gloria Berkenstat Freund

Let the names be remembered here of those who over the course of the last 70-80 years of Jewish life in Biala carried medical help to the Jewish population.

Doctors:

Until the First World War: Dr. Brudniak, Dr. Davidzon (from Lithuania; a former *yeshiva* [religious secondary school] student. Coming from a patient, he fell on the stairs and died), Dr. Gustav Zito (from Warsaw; came to Biala from Łomazy). Between both wars [the First and Second World Wars]: Dr. Yaakhim Zatler, Dr. Przigoda (from Warsaw; was in Biala for a time as a military doctor in the Polish Army in 1920), Dr. Antoni Gelbard (from Warsaw), Dr. Shlomo Tenenbaum (from Siedlice), Dr. Butshe Finkelsztajn (fellow townsman; later active as a doctor in Byten), Dr. Pinkhas Erdman (from Bialystok), Dr. Goldenberg, Dr. Sznajer (eye specialist; brought by the health insurance fund). During the Second World War: Dr. Bergman (probably from Katowice), Dr. Hochman (refugee from Germany), Dr. Rubinsztajn and Dr. Gelbfisz (from Warsaw).

Dentists:

Until the First World War: Bruk (Motl Minc's son-in-law) and Bielinke. Zilberberg (from Brisk, from the First World War until the expulsion in September 1942). In various eras between the two World Wars: L. Winikamien, Mrs. Gelbard, Celniker (from Siedlice), and Mrs. Labendrzowa (from Radzyn – until the expulsion in September 1942).

Royfeim:

Actually these were *feldshers* [unlicensed medical practitioners], but they were called by the name *royfe* [a doctor, usually without medical training] in the city and we will not change this folksy name.

Velvl Zito (called Velve Doctor, died in 1897 on the day of the *bris* [ritual circumcision] of his great-grandson, Velvl Eidltuch, who was given the name after his great grandfather), wrote prescriptions, which would be accepted by the apothecary. The Jew was an active member of the *Khevra-Kadishe* [burial society] his entire life. Chaim *Royfe* (father-in-law of the barber Rozmarin). Both were active until the First World War. During the First World War, Yosef Itshe Asz was occupied with healing the sick.

Feldshers:

Until the First World War: Meir Mikhl Laufman and Fridlender (called *Warszawer* [Warsaw] *Feldsher*). Chaim Musawicz (called Kobriner [from Kobrin– from before the First World War until the expulsion in June 1942), Solman (called *Warszawer Feldsher* – came from Warsaw during the First World War and returned in the 1920s), Berish Wajsman (from Łomazy – arrived several years before the Second World War – until the expulsion in September 1941).

Midwives:

Until the First World War: Ides Royzner and Ruchl Salamon (received eternal exile for political activity in Penza– Russia). Between both wars: Chawa Manhajmer-Szor, Sonya Wajnsztajn-Kelmanzon and Sura Kramarcz.

[Page 305]

Achiezer

by Moshe Braverman - Tel Aviv

Translated by Gloria Berkenstat Freund

During *Khol haMoed* [intervening days of] Passover 1911, 10 to 15 people from the Zionist organization came to together to consult about creating a location in which Zionist activities could be carried out. According to the then conditions it still was possible to carry out such political and communal activity under the shield of a philanthropic society for which one could receive legalization from the Russian regime. Therefore, at that deliberation, it was decided to found such an institution in the city under the name *Achiezer* [a welfare organization], which would distribute medical help to the poor population and, simultaneously, make use of their premises for Zionist activity.

According to the laws such an institution had to have a minimum of 10 members with an assessment of three rubles from each [member]. Obviously, as there were 10 members, the request for legalization was accepted by the *gubernia* [province].

Permission from the *gubernia* arrived before *Shavous* [the holiday commemorating the giving of the Torah to the Jewish people] and immediately after *Shavous* the founding management committee was called together. The creation of such a modern institution for the poor sick evoked great interest among the Jewish population and several hundred people came to the gathering and enrolled as members, with a minimum payment of one ruble a year. There also were those who committed themselves to paying 10 rubles a year and even more. The managing committee obviously was led in line with the strength of the Zionist organization. According to the agenda, it was necessary to elect a temporary managing committee, council and audit committee. However, in order for it to be possible for the institution to lead the Zionist work, provisions were made that more Zionists would be chosen for the organizational leadership of *Achiezer*. However, in order to mask such a step, the managing committee also elected several who were not so well known in the city for their Zionist activity. Moshe Kawe, Moshe Rubensztajn, Yakov Finkelsztajn and Avraham Finkelsztajn were elected then to the first managing committee.

At first, *Achiezer* was located in Viness. Later, a place with four rooms was rented in Dovtshe Pesl's [house]. The first room served as a waiting room; the second for the managing committee and the secretary who would welcome the people; the third room served as a reception room for the sick who were examined there by the doctors; the medication, medical instruments and tools for the sick were found in the fourth room.

They contacted all of the doctors in the city, Jewish and Christian, who agreed to distribute medical help to the poor without any payment. Dr. Gustav Zito would come twice a week, Monday and Thursday, from four to six o'clock in the afternoon and every time he would take eight to 10 sick people. Dr. Szilingowski, Dr. Florinski and Dr. Wajczechowski would take three or four sick people every day at their homes, based on a note that each sick person received from *Achiezer*.

The distribution of medicines for the poor population was arranged in the following manner: *Achiezer* maintained contact for a time with the apothecary Ernkranc and later with the apothecary Ostrowski. Those interested would turn to the apothecary with a prescription from the doctor, on which had been recorded a price, not knowing for whom the medicine was designated. *Achiezer* placed a stamp on the prescription and signed it. The sick people paid *Achiezer* 50 percent of the price and received the prescription from the apothecary without cost. The very poor would receive a signed prescription without cost. At the end of every month the apothecary would send all of the prescriptions with the invoices [to *Achiezer*]. Five hundred to 1,000 prescriptions would be collected over the course of a month at a cost of several hundred rubles. *Achiezer* would receive a discount of 40 to 50 percent from the apothecary. The full price was paid for imported medicines. *Achiezer*, wanting to make sure of the accuracy of the price for the prescriptions, would often send the prescriptions with their prices to the Brisk *Bikor-Khoylem* [society to help the sick poor] Hospital, where a large apothecary with a Jewish pharmacist would verify the prices. For every *kopeke* recorded as more expensive than the official price, the apothecary had to pay a fine of 10 rubles.

Food provisions such as milk, egg, butter, meat and other articles of food for the sick poor were also distributed according to a certificate from a doctor. *Achiezer* notes for all of the products were willingly accepted in every shop. Each milk seller and merchant who received such a note would receive payment according to street prices. The sick were not forced to take the products from a designated place; they had a free choice to take them wherever it was convenient for them.

[Page 306]

The arrangements for receiving such food coupons were: a relative or an acquaintance of the sick person would give a doctor's certificate to *Achiezer* for the necessary products for the sick poor as was designated for as long as such provisions were needed. Meetings of the managing committee would take place several times a week at which the requests for product distribution would be considered and arranged.

The activity of *Achiezer* expanded considerably. One of the most important medical aids was to send members to sit at each sick person's bed every night.

Achiezer numbered from 1,500 to 2,000 members, with membership dues that reached several thousand rubles a year.

Tools and various medical instruments that were needed by the sick, such as water bottles, bladders for ice, inhalation tools, thermometers, supports, rubber pillows and so on, were given for a time. Such tools were given not only to poor patients but also to others, even the rich strata, because such tools were also unavailable in the rich houses. *Achiezer* helped all classes of the population in this manner.

The budget for *Achiezer* was completely and exclusively used for medical help. *Achiezer* had no other expenses, except for rent. Everyone who helped *Achiezer* in its activity did so without any payment.

The institution was very well received in the city, even among the Christian population. There was a case when the then district official, Tufikin, and the mayor, Sologub, came on a visit to *Achiezer* and saw, according to the book of minutes, how the managing committee designated the food distribution for each patient (the books were written in the Russian language). They could not keep from expressing their happiness with the arrangements. Yet they found one transgression. A Hebrew stamp, *Achiezer*, was on the table. This was forbidden according to the laws of that time. Moshe Kawe immediately on the spot took a small knife out of his pocket and cut the stamp in front of them and they were satisfied.

Achiezer founded a matzo bakery for Passover for the poor population in Biala, whereas in other *shtetlekh* [towns] in Poland, private matzo bakeries existed several weeks before Passover, which would hire girls and women from the poor population for the work. They would be paid from three to four *gildn* daily. The work was not easy, both rolling and kneading. The tempo of the work had to be very fast and, in addition, they stood on their feet from six in the morning to late in the evening hours in the most difficult working conditions. They would use from 15 to 19 *pood* (a *pood* is about 16 kilograms [about 36 pounds]) of flour a day, and with only 15-20 female workers. In addition the heat of the baking ovens had an effect on the workers, so that after several days of such intense work their hands and feet would be swollen. The price of the baked matzo varied. In the morning hours when the strength [of the workers] was fresh, they baked the matzos for the rich classes who would pay a higher price than for [the matzo] that was baked later in the day or at night when the male and female helpers were already completely exhausted. It should be understood that the matzos from the evening hours were not as beautiful or as thin as in the morning hours.

At the initiative of *Achiezer*, a mixed committee of women and men was created who set as their task to bake matzo for the poor population. Taking part in the committee were Rywka Fiszer, Chana Miriam Minc, the writer of these lines and so on. We rented a certain place where not just 20 helpers could be located, but from 40 to 50, and these volunteers were from the more well-to-do population. Women from all strata were invited to work as volunteers. Everyone had to work only a few hours a day when it was convenient for them. Every few hours the work force changed. They came dressed in the prettiest and best clothing, fresh and cheerful, every woman and man in his place, without any coercion or pressure from anyone, and they worked. There was no question of early or late, of the "first" or the "second" oven. It was considered an honor to contribute a few hours a day to the charitable matzo bakery for the poor population. It was one of the most beautiful communal events in Biala. Instead of the poor working as usual for the rich, here the rich worked for the poor. The most difficult and the most responsible work at the baking oven was carried out by Ayzyk Finkelsztajn without any payment.

In addition to baking matzo for the poor population without any payment, they also distributed flour to bake matzo and other holiday food products to the poor.

[Page 307]

Thus, this charitable work extended for several years. The outbreak of the First World War in 1914 brought a pause [in the work of *Achiezer*]. The income of *Achiezer* shrank and, not having the necessary medical help on the part of doctors, who were either mobilized or evacuated to deep Russia, *Achiezer* closed. The premises were requisitioned; the remaining items were moved to a room in Yisroel Finkelsztajn's [house].

At the beginning of 1915, when the writer of these lines was freed from the military, he and Moshe Kawe began to revive the activities of *Achiezer*. In one room we carried out the work on a much smaller scale, which continued until the Germans occupied the city.

During the German occupation, *Achiezer* was led by new strength such as Leibish Sauerimper, Yizroel Finkelsztajn, Chaim Rames, Moshe Melekh Ziberberg, Yisroel Elihu Szapira, Yoal Szapira. The Biala rabbi's son, Dovid Zak, stood at the head.

They rented new premises at Grabanower Street at the corner of Prosta Street in the house of the shoemaker Shraga.

Achiezer succeeded in drawing German military doctors, such as Dr. Al Meler (a Jew) and Dr. Barteles (a Christian), who would distribute medical help to the Jewish population, visiting the Jewish sick in their houses. They would also come several times a week to the premises of *Achiezer* and there accept patients. Other German military doctors would accept Jewish patients who would be sent to their homes. This was all done without payment. Naturally, this activity was not consistent because of the conditions of war. The military doctors would not remain on the spot for long.

At the beginning of 1916 the *kehile* house at Brisker Street 6 was successfully taken over and *Achiezer* was set up there. The premises were beautiful and appropriate.

Dr. Barteles put us in contact with the German headquarters where, thanks to his efforts, we received permission to open a Jewish apothecary, despite the fact that Major Funk, an outspoken enemy of the Jews, was then the head of the command. However, for certain reasons, the apothecary was not erected.

Dr. Barteles later put us in contact with the German civilian managing committee in the city, which was led by the chief, Paputin. Thanks to him, Biala families were successful in contacting their relatives in America, from whom they had not received any news since the Germans entered Biala. An exchange of letters began in the German language, which was written at the *Achiezer* premises. The civilian managing committee would send the letters to America and other countries. There was also success in arranging the departure from Biala of two groups of women to their husbands and parents to their children in America. Among others then, Beiba Beker went to his son, Abela Maler's daughter-in-law to her husband, Velvele, and others.

An entirely different chapter during the time of the German occupation in Biala was providing the Jewish population with matzos for Passover. During the German occupation, baked goods made from flour from the flour mill were forbidden for the civilian population. The Jewish population received permission for a greater quantity of flour for matzos before Passover. A committee was founded at *Achiezer* with the following composition: Moshe Lebenberg, Fishl Finkelsztajn, Yisroel Elihu Szapira, Hershl Shachor, Moshe Braverman (secretary) and so on, who were involved with distributing the flour. The flour was distributed to the Jewish population based on [ration] cards and every family was taxed by the committee with a certain payment for *maot-khitim* [assistance to the poor for

Passover] for the poor part of the population. A lot of money flowed in, which made possible the distribution of not only matzos for Passover, but also potatoes, meat, wine and so on.

The matzo distribution and the *maot-khitim* distribution lasted for the entire time of the [First World] war.

The activity of *Achiezer* continued for a time after the rise of the Polish state, but the beautiful institution ceased to exist after several years. The newly arisen Jewish *kehile* moved into the *Achiezer* premises and the place was too crowded for the two institutions. After the end of the war, many active communal workers left Biala and, as it lacked a group of communal workers who would devotedly dedicate themselves to the institution, *Achiezer* failed. The medical instruments remained in the premises of the *kehile*, which would lend them to the population against a pledge, but there was no one interested in administering this and the instruments actually were pillaged.

[Page 308]

The Children's Home

Submitted by Chana Rywka Rapaport–Rubinsztajn

Translated by Gloria Berkenstat Freund

The children's home in the city was founded in 1916 during the German occupation in the First World War. At the time of the *Yavne* [religious Zionist] School, this was a further link in the glorious chain of activity by the Zionist organization in Biala.

We know the main reason the Zionist elements in the city were moved to make an effort to erect a magnificent institution in the city from their study about the *Yavne* school system. However, in addition to that reason, there was also the necessity to found such an institution for other reasons, such as the then great need that existed in the families where the men were in America or mobilized in the Russian Army. These families truly remained without a means of living and the children were found in a neglected state. It was necessary to tear these children from this desolation, and this blessed Zionist institution from the Zionist circles that, in fact, had in mind another purpose, also showed that they not only cared about the soul of the child, but also for its body. Biala, before as well as later, never possessed such an exemplary social institution.

The children's home was located in a three–room apartment in Moshe Lebenberg's house on Brisker Street.

The institution was led by a women's committee, which consisted of the women Chana Miriam Minc, Rywka Fiszer, Chana Rywka Rubinsztajn, Rayzl Zinger (these women were the initiators and founders of this institution), Sura Barlas (refugee from Brisk), Glika Lichtenbaum, Ita Laszczewski, Waksin (refugee from Brisk) and the sisters Helman, Caruk, Morgensztern. Chana Miriam Minc was the chairwoman of the committee, the vice–chairwoman was Rywka Rubinsztajn, and Sura Barlas was the secretary.

Committee of the Children's Home
The Leadership of the Children's Home

Sitting from the left: Rywka Fiszer, Chana Miriam Minc, Chana Rywka Rubinsztajn, Rayzl Zinger;
Standing: Yona Sztajnman, Yehosha Fiszer, Moshe Rubinsztajn and Yakov Sztajnman

The committee set as its task taking the children from desolate and poor families, as well as orphans. They fed, clothed, provided education and even took care of them in the after–school hours.

Children's Home – The Children with the Women's Committee

The Women's Committee from the right: Miriam Helman, Waksin (Brisk), Liba Helman, Chana Rywka Rubinsztajn, name unknown, Chana Miriam Minc, Rywka Fiszer, Glika Lichtenbaum, Sura Barlas, Caruk, Morgensztern, Rayzl Zinger, Ita Laszczewski.

[Page 309]

There were 60 children in the institution; more could not be taken in because of budget difficulties.

The women who took an active part in the activities of the children's home righteously and capably carried on their work without any reward. Only the women who ran the kitchen were paid.

The woman on duty would come at eight o'clock in the morning and give the cooks instructions on what and how to prepare food for the children. Miss Richter ran the kitchen.

All of the children at the children's home were students in the local *Yavne* School. After finishing the instruction at the school, they would march to the children's home, standing in rows, where they would eat lunch. After eating, the students would begin to do their homework under the supervision of the women on duty. After finishing their homework, the small children would amuse themselves and the older children would be engaged in various conversations. The women on duty would wash the children, clean and wash their heads. After eating the evening meal, the children would go home to their families. There were cases in which arrangements were made for the orphans to go to families to sleep.

The children of the children's home were dressed in special uniforms that the women's committee had arranged to be made for them out of cloth they received from the government.

The children's home was closed on Shabbos [Sabbath] and holidays. The children would be given food products to take home for holidays.

Every Passover, a traditional *Seder* [Passover ritual meal] would be arranged on the second *Seder* night at the children's home for the children. The *Seder* would be led by the teacher, Yakov Sztajnman. No outside guests were allowed to attend the *Seder*. The expenses connected with preparing the *Seder* would be covered by the Women's Committee from their own pockets.

At the beginning, the budget of the institution was covered by the Women's Committee itself, which collected a certain assessment among its own members and also would receive some support from sympathizers. Later on, the civilian managing committee covered a large part of the expenses and also gave food products. Twice a month, movie tickets for the movie presentations were given to the Women's Committee by the civilian managing committee, which would sell the tickets among the Jewish population and thus receive a source of money. Once a month they carried out a flower sale and from time to time the Zionist dramatic circle at the community center arranged a presentation for the benefit of the children's home. From this income the Women's Committee was able to pay tuition money for the children to the *Yavne* School.

Links with the civilian managing committee succeeded thanks to the sister of Field Marshal Pan [Mister] Lizingen, who was active in Biala as a nurse. This nurse would come over to the laundry that was run by Mrs. Chana Miriam Minc and a close acquaintance developed between the two.

The military field rabbi, Dr. Tencer, also supported the children's home and, in addition, tried to reduce the influence of the Zionist circles, under whose influence the institution was founded.

With the rise of the Polish state, the Women's Committee began to come up against budget difficulties because they did not receive any subsidies or support from the regime. Therefore, they would lead the children to the so–called children's kitchen after the lessons. In this kitchen, which was supported thanks to products received from America, the children would eat lunch and afterward they would march to the children's home. There they would do their homework and spend the time until night when they would go home.

The children's home was liquidated in 1919. The reasons were, firstly, budget difficulties and, secondly, many children emigrated to America with their families as soon as the gates to America opened after the First World War.

Throughout the entire era of the existence of the children's home, there was no particular incident recorded nor any unpleasant cases with the children. There were never any disputes among the children themselves or between the children and the Women's Committee. The children did not lag behind the other children in their studies and a number of them even excelled in learning.

The relationship between the children and the Women's Committee was sincere and warm. The children were strongly bound to the women of the committee, who made such a maternal effort with the children. Years later this connection strongly came to expression in many cases.

[Page 310]

TOZ

by Baruch Vinograd

Translated by Gloria Berkenstat Freund

The founding of the *TOZ* [*Towarzystwo Ochrony Zdrowia Ludności żydowskiej* – Society to Protect the Health of the Jews] Society in Biala, whose task was to protect the health of the Jewish population, is dated as the year 1925. The director of the Jewish hospital, Dr. A. Gelbard and the *kehile* [organized Jewish community] secretary, B. Winograd from Biala, were invited to the county conference of the *TOZ*, which took place that year in Lublin. During the conference in Lublin the Biala representatives were asked to found a division of the *TOZ* in Biala.

The initiators, Dr. A. Gelbard and B. Winograd, spoke about the important task of *TOZ* and justified the need to create a division of *TOZ* at the founding meeting at the *kehile* premises, which was called then, with the participation of all strata of the Jewish population in the city. The assembled showed great understanding of the matter and everyone present declared themselves members on the spot.

Elected to the managing committee were Dr. A. Gelbard – chairman, Mrs. Baltsha Piczic – vice chairwoman, A. Robak – treasurer, Borukh Winograd – secretary, managing committee members Mrs. Bayla Wiznfeld, Mrs. Manya Yungerman, Mrs. Hela Orlanski, Mrs. Lyuba Szwarc, Mrs. Fanya Fridberg, Dr. Butsha and Mikhasz Hoper.

The managing committee worked out a preliminary budget and energetically went to work. The income consisted of subsidies from the *kehile* and city hall, member dues, public collections and entertainments, but mainly from the subsidy by the *TOZ* central committee in Warsaw.

The actual activity of the *TOZ* began in 1926 and continued until the outbreak of the war in 1939.

Each year of its existence, the *TOZ* would arrange summer camps for poor, weak children during the two to three summer months. The *TOZ* rented the large area in the rabbi's courtyard at Mezriczher Street for this purpose. Appropriate buildings were erected there with tables and chairs for 100–120 children as well as a kitchen and other sanitary conveniences. The entire area was fenced in and completely planned. Clean sand was brought in for a certain area for sunbaths for the children. A large number of trees were planted so the children would have somewhere to hide from the sun. Every session, which numbered 100–120 children, lasted only one month. The children would receive good nutrition four times a day. Almost all of the children would significantly increase in their weight, tan in the sun and be refreshed. The payment was minimal and 50–60 percent of the children were taken without any payment. The summer camps were active from eight in the morning until four in the afternoon. Over the course of a summer, 250–300 children would make use of the camps. The children would be under appropriate pedagogical and medical supervision during their entire time there.

According to the allocation of the *TOZ* central, every summer a certain number of sick children would be sent out of Biala to Czechoczinek, Otwock and so on.

The TOZ Summer Camp in Biala

A free clinic for all school children, for the students of the *Talmud Torah* [free religious school for poor children], *khederim* [religious primary schools] and the *yeshiva* [religious secondary school] was opened by the *TOZ* at the Jewish hospital. Free medications were given out there. Thanks to the frequent medical examinations for the children and the visits of a doctor and a hygienist to the *Talmud Torah*, *yeshiva* and *khederim*, the main illnesses were eliminated and cured, particularly mange (parasitic skin disease). In necessary cases the sick children were sent to the x–ray station at the Warsaw *TOZ* central at the expense of the Biala *TOZ*. During the winter months many hundreds of children were irradiated with sun lamps at the clinic at no expense.

According to an agreement with the *TOZ* managing committee, the dentist, Yoal Zilberberg, accepted all of the children who were under the supervision of the *TOZ* and gave them dental help, such as healing and removing sick teeth as well as filling teeth completely without cost. The *TOZ* would provide the dental medications.

[Page 311]

One of the main tasks of *TOZ* was to prevent illnesses. This was successful to a great extent, thanks to frequent visits to the *Talmud–Torah*, *yeshiva* and *khederim*, giving hygienic instruction and directions. Over the course of the winter months, rolls and a glass of milk, without any payment, were distributed to many children every day. Large quantities of cod liver oil for all of the children in the city, without exception, were also distributed during the winter months. All poor children would have their hair cut systematically and they received baths without cost in the military bath establishment paid for by *TOZ*.

Every month *TOZ* would distribute pieces of soap in significant quantity to the poor Jewish population to wash clothes. Public lectures on popular hygiene themes would be organized. Medical journals, such as *Folksgezunt* [*People's Health*] and so on, were distributed, as well as leaflets with hygiene instructions and information.

The *TOZ* was very popular and beloved among the Jewish population in the city. The income undertakings of the *TOZ* always had the best results. The Purim balls, especially, were popular, from which each year the income would be designated exclusively for the summer camps. This mass participation of the most widespread strata of the Jewish population in the *TOZ* enterprises and the sympathy and interest shown served as a stimulus for the *TOZ* managing committee to continue the responsible and important work on behalf on the Biala Jewish population.

The *TOZ* office was located in the Jewish hospital. The administrative expenses of *TOZ*, in general, were minimal, about 10 percent of the general budget, and this gave the managing committee the ability to use all of the income only for constructive medical and professional purposes. It is worthwhile to mention that Dr. A. Gelbard, during the entire course of his activity as chairman of the *TOZ* managing committee from 1925 to 1937, that is until his move to Warsaw, carried out all of the medical exams of the children, gave lectures on hygiene and medical themes entirely without any material compensation. In addition, he always showed an understanding and warm relationship to the *TOZ* activity. A new managing committee would be elected at the annual general meeting. Of the members of the managing committee [those] particularly active there [who] excelled were: the vice chairwoman Boltsha Piczic, Mrs. Fanya Fridberg and Mikhash Hofer. In the course of the existence of the *TOZ*, the women, Luyba Wajntraub–Tuchsznajder, Bela Jakubowicz, Toybele Rubinsztajn and so on worked with the pedagogic and educational personnel of the summer camp. The teacher of singing and sport was the talented member of *Shomir HaTzair* [Young Guard – Socialist–Zionists], Shloymke (Shloma) Hochberg, who showed great dedication and love for the children, teaching them gymnastics exercises and songs in Hebrew, Yiddish and Polish every day.

At the end of each season at the summer camps, with the participation of the children and their parents, representatives of the state, *kehile* and other communal institutions and invited guests, the children would appear with songs, recitations and sports exercises, which were arranged each time in a very joyful manner.

It is also worth remembering Dovid Przewuzman, the medic and hygienist at the *TOZ*, who showed great devotion and zeal with minimal reward. The main cook at the *TOZ* summer camp in Biala over the course of its activity was Sura Breyna Liberman, who was a [capable person] and was never late in preparing the tasty and nutritious food for the children.

The *TOZ* was also popular among the Christian population in the city. So the subsidies of the *TOZ*, although very modest, were always supported by the Christian councilmen of all political views at the city hall. It was characteristic, too, that even the anti–Semitic *Podliaszak* (an *Endeke* [anti–Semitic Polish National Party] weekly in Biala) at that time (published in 1936) dedicated a special article on its first page to the *TOZ*, praising its important activity, and particularly the summer camps; emphasizing that the *TOZ* drew support from all parts of the Biala population.

The activity of the *TOZ* lasted until the outbreak of the Second World War. Along with the entire Jewish population that was annihilated by the German beasts, the hundreds of Jewish children who the *TOZ* cared for with so much love and devotion also perished.

The archive of the *TOZ*, along with the medical instruments, remained at the Jewish hospital.

Alas, of all of those who worked with the *TOZ*, only two people survived: *TOZ* secretary Borukh Vinograd (Israel) and Mikhash Hoper (Brazil).

[Page 312]

Activities Report of the *TOZ* Society

From the 1st of August 1927 to the 31st of March 1933.

1. School infirmary	– 6,338 free visits.
2. School infirmary	2,325 prescriptions.
3. Bathed at the expense of *TOZ*	10, 492 children.
4. Free baths for the jobless	1,380.
5. Haircuts at the expense of *TOZ*	6,185.

6. Washing 7,097 pieces of underwear for poor children

7. 1,067 children who on average gained 1.30 kilograms in weight benefitted from the summer camps.

8. 59 children sent to summer camps: Otwock, Domaczewo, Czechoczinek, Druskenik.

9. 73 children healed of ringworm.

10. 285 children free irradiation with quartz lamps.

11. Distribution of cod liver oil to 327 children.

12. Distribution of more than 10,000 brochures about hygiene, leaflets, calendars, periodicals and so on.

13. More than 2,000 young people did gymnastic exercises at the *TOZ* sports ground.

Income	*Zlotes*
1. Subsidy from the *TOZ* central	15,788.–
2. Subsidy from the city hall	5,483.08
2. (there are two number 2s) Subsidy from Seimek	1,000.–
3. Subsidy from the Jewish community	1,380.–
5. (there is no number 4) Subsidy from the sick fund	1,895.–
6. From members' dues	3,124.55
7. Grant for undertakings and donations	7,588.62
8. Grant for payments for the summer camps	8,077.90
9. Subsidy for school hygiene	861.15
10. Grant for sun lamp	324.–
11. Grant of various income and loans	220.08
Total	45,742,38

Expenses	*Zlotes*
For summer camps	25,266.09
2. For school hygiene	7,576.80
3. School clinic	3,090.99
4. Sun lamp	689.88
5. Milk, medicine and cod liver oil	1,289.02

6. Hygienic information	1,160.02
7. Physical education	589.87
8. Administrative and office expenses	5,093.79
9. Members' dues on hand	553.14
10. Various payments	383.55
Balance on 1st of April 1933	49.23
Total	45,742.38

Report About the Summer Camps from the *TOZ* Society for 1933

Income

Payments from children	169.– *zl.*
From the sick fund	105.– *zl.*
Collected by the aid circle in *Podlaskier Lebn*	662.– *zl.*
From other collections	110.50 *zl.*
Subsidy from the *TOZ* central	400.– *zl.*
Total	1,446,50 *zl.*

Expenses

Food for the children	1,009.47 *zl.*
For the location	125.– *zl.*
Remodeling and administrative payments	101.25 *zl.*
Management personnel	61.– *zl.*
Pedagogic personnel	115.– *zl.*
Various expenditures	51.95 *zl.*
Total	1,463,27 *zl.*

The average growth of the children reached 1.10 kilos [2.4 pounds].

Eighty–nine children were accepted completely without cost and the remaining children for a minimal payment, beginning with one *zlote* monthly.

Chairman: Dr. A. Gelbard
Secretary: B. Winograd
Auditing commission: A. Szwarc, M. Yungerman, A. Lubelczik

(*Podlaskier Lebn* number 19/84, of the 19th of May 1933 and number 44 of the 10th of November 1933.)

[Page 313]

The *Moyshev–Skeynim*
[The Old Age Home]

by M. Y. F – M

Translated by Gloria Berkenstat Freund

A painful problem in the city was the poor and lonely old people. There was no one to be involved with them or to care for them. One could meet old people, the majority of whom were sick, lying around homeless at the entrance to the house of prayer, in the women's gallery and at the *hakhnoses orkhim* [inn for poor Sabbath and holiday guests].

Various plans were proposed in the columns of the newspaper *Podlaskier Lebn* [*Podlaskier Life*] published in the 1920s and, among others, the idea of erecting a building for a *moyshev–skeynim* [old age home]. The editorial board of *Podlaskier Lebn* took upon itself the accomplishment of this plan. But, like many plans in our city that were outlined but whose feasibility was not analyzed, this plan did not have a solid base under it. Instead of turning to the population to create the means to care for the old people, they turned to the population with an appeal to construct a building for an old age home. It was clear that such a plan did not have the least prospect of success.

Not having any other material, the notes from a number of issues of *Podlaskier Lebn* and *Biala Vokhnblat* [*Biala Weekly Newspaper*], which are in our possession, give us a picture of the interest [in an old age home] that existed in the city until the outbreak of the Second World War.

On Sunday, the 12th of December 1926 in the city hall room, a meeting took place that was supposed to consider the question of constructing a Jewish old age home. The assembled declared on the spot [they would contribute] 6,000 *zlotes* to be paid out over the course of two years. Those artisans in attendance declared a payment in kind, that is, to provide support with the necessary work until the old age home was built. A committee was elected of nine people: Eidl Szwarc, Yitzhak Piczic, Yisroel Kohan, Fishel Finkelstajn, Dr. Antoni Gelbard, Pinkhas Nortman, Moshe Kava, Yitzhak Arges and Yakov Herszberg. Chosen for the audit commission were: Yisroel Goldsztajn, Ayzyk Szajnberg and Dovid Wajsman. The committee had to start carrying out the construction plan immediately. (*Podlaskier Lebn*, number 4, of the 26th of December 1926).

In the preliminary budget of the city hall for the year 1927/8, a subsidy in the amount of 1,000 *zlotes* was designated for the old age home. (*Podlaskier Lebn*, number 13, of the 27th of April 1927).

The old age home received one *zlote* daily from the city hall for each person. The city hall subsidy anticipated that there would be 20 old people and more than 30 people were supported by the subsidy (*Podlaskier Lebn*, number 28, of the 25th of November 1932).

The old age home was under the managing committee of the Jewish councilmen's club. The subsidy for the old age home was recorded in the preliminary budget for the year 1933/1934 with a sum of 6,500 *zlotes* (*Podlaskier Lebn*, number 4, of the 27th of January 1933).

After the eviction of the old age home they succeeded in receiving a new premises at Leib Akerman's at Sadowa Street (*Podlaskier Lebn*, number 28, of the 20th of July 1934).

On Tuesday, the 13th of July 1937, in the evening, a meeting took place in the premises of the *kehile* of people interested in an old age home with the purpose of reorganizing the two existing committees, that is the "men's" and "women's" committees and to transform them into a permanent committee.

A report about the financial condition of the old age home was given at the meeting.

A closing report was given for the period from the 1st of April 1936 to the 1st of April 1937. The balance appears as follows:

Income	Zlotes
Balance on the 1st of May 1936	28.58
Subsidy from city hall	3,222.49
For distributed lunches	642.64
Subsidy from the kehile	183.90
Donations	45.68
Rent for part of the space	50.–
For unpaid debts	328.63
Total	4,501,92

Expenses	Zlotes
Food for the old men and women	3,241.13
Salary for the administrator	650.–
Janitor	60.–
Heating and lighting	155.14
Cleaning and laundry	125.75
Water	60.–
Clothing and mending	96.79
Various small expenses	98.96
Balance on the 1st of April 1937	4.15
Total	4,501.92

[Page 314]

A report was also presented from the "club" action, whose income reached nearly 500 *zlotes* (along with the items and products).

The Moyshev–Skeynim with the committee members

Sitting from the right: Chaim Miodek, Moshe Lebnberg, Vice Mayor Y. Abramowicz, Shmay Kalichsztajn and Avraham Lebnberg. (Near him, the managing committee member Sh. Gornsztajn)

Those gathered decided to attempt to create a society named *Moyshev–Skeynim* in Biala (in agreement with the certified statute from the government), whose members would be the legal owner of the institution. For this purpose it was decided to dissolve both existing committees and to create one joint committee that would carry out a canvassing action in the shortest time possible for the members of the society in Biala.

The Messers Shmay Kalichsztajn, Meir Orlanski, Yitzhak Berman, Itsl Lewi, Borukh Winograd, Chaim Miodek, Moshe Lebenberg, Moshe Rodzinek, and Khanina Kaszemacher joined the new committee.

L. Szwar, Kladnyev, Minc, Wajnztok, Kelmanzon, Sznajdmil were members of the women's committee (*Bialer Vokhnblat*, number 28, of the 16th of July 1937).

We see how in 1934 there was not even a start of the great plan of 1926 about erecting a building for the old age home. In general, the question of building was not even on the agenda, only simply collecting the minimal means to be able to feed the old people who came to the institution, which was called the old age home.

Thus, the lonely and sick old people in the city struggled for their existence, and Jewish society did not appear to help them. During the German occupation, during the Second World War, the situation of the old people was tragic because then society in general was entirely helpless and dejected.

Women's Aid Committee

Translated by Gloria Berkenstat Freund

During the 1920s there was a Women's Aid Committee in the city whose task it was to support impoverished and lonely sick people. The source of income for this committee was member dues, various events and incidental collections.

The committee numbered 250 members and at its head stood the women Baltsha Piczic – chairwoman, Rywka Nowominski – secretary, Yokheved Biderman – treasurer.

Report from the 16th of December 1925 to the 1st of January 1927

Income	Zlotes
Remaining in fund to the 16th	70.74
Taken in from the hospital committee of the community	25.–
From family entertainments (weddings, engagements)	133.57
Flower day, the 7th of April 1926	222.12
Performances (Warsaw Troupe of H. Balbirski)	221.36
From various voluntary contributions	59.51
From weekly dues from the members	1,343.10
From the *Gemiles–Khesed*	20.83
	2,096.23

Expenses	Zlotes
Products 3 to 4 for 40 people – 430 kilos (*challahs*, breads and various dry foods)	1,049.85
Sugar for 40 people, 360 kilos	401.70
Wood	30.–
Potatoes	23.90

Prescriptions for 40 people	113.78
Support in cash for 94 people	234.80
300 quarts milk, 12 people	139.25
Various publications (receipts, printing, stamps, pouches, pins and so on)	102.95
	2,096.23

[Page 315]

A *gmiles–khesed kase* [interest–free loan fund] existed at the committee, which distributed small interest–free loans to the street and market sellers to be paid back weekly. In order to permit the existence of the fund, the women's committee instituted separate voluntary monthly dues from their members.

The leaders of the *gmiles–khesed kase* were the women: Baltsha Piczic – chairwoman, F. Lubelczik – secretary and R. Laszczewski – treasurer.

It is difficult to say if the committee existed until the outbreak of the Second World War or if it ceased to exist earlier (the reports were taken from *Podlaskier Lebn*, number 7, of the 18th of February 1927 and from number 1/2 of the 7th of January 1927).

Report of the *Gmiles–Khesed Kase*

Volume of business from the 1st of June 1926 to the 1st of January 1927

	Income	Expenses
Fund	2,226.65	2,285.17
124 loans given to 57 people	1,732.–	2.211.–
Printing expense, receipts		15.65
Monthly fees and so on	553.15	
	4,511.82	4,511.82

Balance on the 1st of January 1927

	Passive	Active
Treasury	58.52	
Loans given (39)	479.–	
Printing expenses	15.65	
Monthly payments		553.17
	553.17	553.17

Other Voluntary Institutions in the City

by M. Y. F – M

Translated by Gloria Berkenstat Freund

Beis Lekhem

In about 1885 such an institution [*Beis Lekhem* – bread for the needy] was already active in the city, whose task was to go to the Jewish houses and collect *challahs* [Sabbath bread] and bread on Fridays. The collected *challahs* and breads would be distributed among respectable needy people who were ashamed to go to houses and ask for bread as the bolder poor people would do.

Members of this institution would come, disguised, to weddings where they would entertain the crowd and collect money for the *Beis Lekhem*.

The driving force of *Beis-Lekhem* was Yakov Yitzhak, the carpenter, and he had Moshe Dovid, the ropemaker (Szajnbaum), to help him.

During the First World War the *Beis-Lekhem* ceased its activities.

The institution became active again in the 1930s. The difficult economic situation for the Jewish population called it back to life.

Not having any information about the activity of the *Beis-Lekhem* during the era mentioned, we will provide the facts that we have found in a number of issues of *Podlaskier Lebn*.

The flower sale for *Beis-Lekhem* that took place at the beginning of 1933 brought in 85.47 *zlotes* (*Podlaskier Lebn*, number 75/10, of the 10th of March 1933).

Because of an incident between those receiving matzo and the *Beis-Lekhem* committee, the institution ceased to collect and distribute bread (*Podlaskier Lebn*, number 29/94 of the 28th of July 1933).

Flower sale in aid of Beis-Lekhem

Sitting from the right: Avigdor Richter, the Radziner tailor (nickname), Avik Rozenblum, Krugman, Mrs. Laszczewski, Mrs. Sztajngart
Right, standing: Pinkhus Garnsztajn. (The names of the remaining are unknown.)

[Page 316]

Each week the *Beis Lekhem* was forced to buy 15 to 20 kilograms of bread to add to the bread collected from the population (*Podlaskier Lebn*, number 33/98 of the 25th of August 1933).

In 1933 the *Beis Lekhem* committee consisted of Shimkha Barlas, Zalman Zak, Abush Rozenblum and H. Y. Krugman (*Podlaskier Lebn*, number 45/110 of the 17th of November 1933).

Hakhnoses Orkhim

Until 1907, the *Hakhnoses Orkhim* [society to provide beds for guests for *Shabbos* or holidays] was located in two rented rooms in Shlomole Krajdsztajn's house on Janower Street.

In 1907 a building was erected in the synagogue courtyard for the *Hakhnoses Orkhim*. The initiator for this was Yosl Wetshik (Gotgrid). The money was collected in the city. The construction was carried out by the bricklayer, Alter Wajnberg.

Emissaries from *yeshivus* [religious secondary schools] and poor people who would come to the city to collect contributions would spend the night at the *Hakhnoses Orkhim*.

There was an apartment in the house for the overseer of the *Hakhnoses Orkhim* and for the apartment, which he received without cost, he had to clean the *Hakhnoses Orkhim*.

After the First World War, the apartments were taken by Biala residents and the *Hakhnoses Orkhim* no longer fulfilled the task for which it had been created.

Linas HaTzedak

None of the remaining Bialer remembers its rise. The task of this society [for visiting the sick] was to send two people every night to every sick person in the city to spend time with him and thus help those living with him who would be busy with the sick one all day. The members of the society would pay a *kopike* weekly on behalf of the institution. On the last day of Passover they would come together to drink wine.

Velvl Mas, the bookseller, led the society at the end of the last century (19th century).

After the First World War, we no longer heard about the existence of this institution.

Ezras Kholim

From the *Podlaskier Lebn* [we learn] that during the 1930s a society named *Ezras Kholim* [aid for the sick] existed in the city.

The members of the *Ezras Kholim* would pay weekly dues in the amount of 10 *groshn*. The sick poor would receive medical help, such as medical exams from doctors, prescriptions and milk from the *Ezras Kholim* without cost.

On the 18th of August 1933, the society arranged a concert by Cantor Moshe Kusewicki of Warsaw and thus received significant income. In the summer of 1934 an aid group for *Ezras Kholim* was inaugurated in *Podlaskier Lebn* (*Podlaskier Lebn*, number 42/10, of the 22nd of July 1932 and number 99/24 of the 1st of September 1933).

[Page 317]

Personalities, Figures, and Types

Translated by Ofra Anson

Edited by Yocheved Klausne

Political activists

Apollinaire Maximilian Heartglass

by Itzhak Greenboim

He was the youngest of us, our real "last born". He joined "Kadima" (Forward), a group established in Warsaw University, during the early twentieth century. He came from Biala after graduating the local High–School with distinction. His father was a lawyer, and, as far as I know, it was the only Jewish home speaking Polish only.

This was all we knew about his background. We were not interested in our members' past, willingly adopting any person expressing devotion to Zionism. We were holding hands for over fifty years, and I still cannot understand how Heartglass, a high school student from Biala who had no Jewish education, came to be aware of, and love, the Jewish people, the nationalists, and the Zionists. I did not ask him, and he did not tell me; we had no time for such intimate relationships, being busy and continuously struggling, since the first day we met in the law faculty in Warsaw and in "Kadima".

Young Heartglass was very capable, sharp minded, quick to perceive and analyze. He was broad minded. He used to write papers and scholarly research, satirical poems and prose; he drew smart, witty, cartoons, and understood art and the history of it. He planned to move to Munich, to study in its well–known academy of art, and become a painter. This was his childhood dream. During meetings he was always drawing and scribbling while listening to the discussion, sometimes coming up with portraits of the participants. Yet he gave up this childhood dream, and went along the path paved by his parents: after graduation and army duty he went back home to work with his father's law firm. He worked with dedication, learning to enjoy the profession. Yet as long as he did not have a family of his own, he looked into other possibilities, such as journalism and Zionist activism. During these periods, he used to leave his parents' home, devoting himself to his new work. If one could make a living from journalism in those days, it is very possible that he would have become a publicist. He completely neglected painting: he probably did not believe in his talent, and did not want to become an artisan painter.

Writing came easily to him. Polish was his first language. He and Kirshrot were our only members who had mastered the language like a Polish person. We used to tease him that even his slips of the tongue were of a Polish, rather than a Jewish, nature. We used to say that Jewish sayings and idioms emerged from his sub–conscious in a Polish form, though the Polish found it rather irritating and incomprehensible. He did not learn Hebrew as a child, but only when he started thinking that he would have to emigrate to Eretz Israel. Growing up in a Yiddish speaking town, he understood the language, but could not speak it. I once asked him to write his articles in Yiddish himself, and not rely on me to translate. When he showed me his paper, I could not believe how one could express his ideas in a language one only heard and absorbed unconsciously. Yet, he could not speak Yiddish. Even those who demanded that he speak Yiddish during meetings begged him to spare them, and return to Polish.

His articles and speeches never needed editing. His ideas were clear and written without any corrections. His stenographs were printed as is, each idea came out clearly from his mouth or pen without any need for rephrasing. During meetings and conferences, he used to formulate the decisions and the declarations while listening to the speakers.

[Page 318]

Not only was he quick to comprehend, but he could perceive the essence of another person's ideas.

He was an honest and truthful person, with a sense of dignity. He was not a quarrelsome person, but fought fiercely for his ideas and principles. He would not compromise on those; but on small, marginal matters he was ready to compromise in order to avoid anger and upsetting others. Personally, he did not believe that things would turn out all right. In his later years he was disappointed and pessimistic, regarding his own fate and that of the Jewish people and Zionism.

*

How did Heartglass become a Zionist? Now, that he is no longer with us, the only answer I can come up with is his sense of dignity, the dignity of a person who stands upright. Submission and humiliation caused him pain and anger. In a *Hasidic* language, I would say that he felt sorry for the Divine Spirit that wallowed in the dirt of the diaspora. When he demanded that we pursue an extreme action, when he rejected any compromise, he used to argue that our offended personal and national dignity required taking a strong position.

I still remember the conversation we had on our way to the Sejm, during the long negotiations we had with the early Polish governments after Poland's independence. I did not believe that we could convince the government to accept even a few of our basic demands, but we did not want to be blamed for stopping the negotiation. Heartglass, however, argued that long discussions that brought us nowhere were humiliating, and allowed the Polish government to present itself as liberal, ready to come to terms with the Jews. He convinced me to stop the negotiations, and so we did. He was right: no negative consequences were apparent, and we gained more respect.

Kirshrot became a Zionist because he felt attached to Judaism, and believed that assimilation was immoral. He was third generation to an assimilated family. Similarly, Goldsmith (Janusz Korczak) found his way to his people following his frustration from the big lie of his assimilated environment. But Heartglass came because of his offended human dignity – not necessarily in Poland, but in the diaspora in general, and the lack of a homeland, unlike any other people. It was a "gentile" kind of Zionism, but it withstood all the difficulties and illusions, unlike many others who had been deeply rooted in Judaism. Over the past fifty years we have experienced difficulties that shook the foundations of our lives; there have been disappointments and temptations. Some were not strong enough and left us. Yet, Heartglass remained loyal to his people and to Zionism, despite his bitter disappointment from what was happening in our country.

Was it the effect of the Polish concept of "honor"? Possibly yes. Yet for the Polish, "honor" lost its true meaning and became false, masking degradation and cheating. For Heartglass it was a pure, sacred feeling, rooted in the poor condition of the Jewish people living in the diaspora. Zionism based on such a foundation is long lasting and withstands all temptations and obstacles.

*

For fifty years we went hand by hand; since we started our Zionist activity, as university students, until today, after the establishment of the State of Israel. We fought together for Zionism and for Polish Jewry. Together we won a few struggles, and were defeated many times; yet it was always for the Polish Jews and the Zionist movement in Poland and worldwide. There are people, close friends as well as others, who thought they could tear us apart, to set one of us against the other; sometimes they thought they succeeded. They could not imagine that we were completely coordinated, even when Heartglass was appointed to chair the Jewish representatives in the Polish parliament. Even when I decided to leave Poland, when I felt that many Jews were tired of fighting and needed a rest, I knew that Heartglass would stand strong, keeping up our people's struggle for its rights and freedom, and first and foremost – for its dignity and soul.

And he did. He kept up Zionist activity during the terrible period of Poland's decline and the adjustment of the Zionist majority to this decline to the degree of accepting the right for parliamentary representation from a hostile national democratic government, which felt it was time to fulfill its dream and get rid of the Jews from Poland. Together with others who kept up the tradition of struggle, Heartglass kept fighting until Poland collapsed and the murderers invaded Poland.

Heartglass could not believe that a war was going to take place, and that the German nation would lose its humanity under Hitler. He thought that if all the Allies, including Russia, had joined forces from the beginning, Poland would not have been conquered and the Jews would have escaped the Holocaust. All his life he believed there is no penance for that sin. His own world and life were ruined with the demolishing of Poland's Jews.

The Nazis went after him, and almost captured him. Nevertheless, he succeeded in fleeing and joining his daughter in Israel. He never forgave himself for leaving the Polish Jews in such a desperate time, though he knew that the choice was flight or death.

[Page 319]

He could not find his place in Israel. His heart remained in Poland with his brothers and their troubles. He deceived himself that the news of terror, humiliation, and then the extermination, were just exaggeration. His rich experience from the National Council he had chaired taught him that the rumors about the troubles of the Jews were often exaggerated. He learned to feel the truth. This time, however, he refused to know, like a man who sees his loved ones struggle with death and would not admit that they are going to die. He worked in the Rescue Committee, editing bulletins, and saw all the news coming from Poland – but he refused to believe. Once, he told me that he had heard that Jewish children were concentrated in a camp close to Lodz, waiting for extermination. When he learned that the children were killed, he tried to commit suicide. Yet, he took the wrong dose and survived.

He forced me to agree to return to work for the management of the Jewish Agency, which I left because of a severe disagreement, and he would not take his own life. We both kept our word.

*

The Poland born leaders of the settlers in Israel before independence knew about Heartglass; others did not. When he came to Israel, he did not get the working and activity positions he should have received. Naturally, I did all I could to get him a job. Yet he sat at meetings and said nothing. His Hebrew was not good enough, and he lacked the character to push himself through locked doors. He was not capable of promoting himself and demand compensation for his past work. He did not knock on doors, and did not search for intimacy with influential persons. He felt that he would lose face if he demanded recognition for his past activity. Thus, his talent and knowledge of law and politics were not used. When I spoke on his behalf, people did not believe me, but I knew that knowledge and experience earned in Poland or in Czarist Russia were not considered relevant. These people never realized that in the future they would largely follow in the steps taken by Poland before WWII, thinking that they follow Britain and the USA.

When I became Minister of Interior Affairs, I appointed Heartglass to be the director–general, and we renewed the collaboration we started at the Jewish National Council and its representatives in the Polish parliament. Heartglass resumed writing letters, preparing law proposals, and being involved in all the office affairs next to me. These were his happiest days in Israel, and possibly in all his life. I have a sense that he was a bit angry with me that I did not keep my ministerial position, and easily gave it up.

He had no choice but to stay in the ministry after I left. I was appointed to the inquiry committee of the Jewish Agency, and he wanted to move with me and practice law. Yet there was no room for him in my new office. Shapira, who took the ministry after me, recognized Heartglass's ability, but was committed to appoint the head of his party as Director General. He kept Heartglass as a consultant and used to discuss serious matters with him. Things got worse for him after Shapira left the ministry. By then he already suffered from a serious heart disease. He tried to disregard it, and continue to fulfill his duty. I often asked him to take it easy – but he would not listen.

*

Such were the life and the death of Maximilian Heartglass, who chaired the Zionist Federation in Poland just before WWII; who was the director of the National Committee for Jewish affairs; the head of the parliamentary delegation of the Jews in Poland for quite a while during the first Sejm; a Director General of the Ministry of Interior and, later, a consultant. This was how his outstanding talent and rich experience were used in Israel, the country he dreamt of, and to which he devoted his strength and capabilities all his life.

("Al Hamishmar" No. 2950, 29.3.1953)

[Page 320]

1. Apollinaire Heartglass

by M. Y. Feigenboim

Apollinaire Heartglass was born in Biala on April 7th, 1883. His father, Kalman Heartglass, was a lawyer who came to Biala from Warsaw. Apollinaire, like his siblings, was raised in an assimilated Polish home. It was largely his mother who sought to isolate herself and her children from Jewish society. His father, on the other hand, was drawn to the synagogue, spoke fluent Yiddish, and for a while even served as a supervisor in the Jewish community.

Heartglass studied in the Russian high school, and had nothing to do with Judaism. In his article "Times are changing" ("Life in Podlaska", no. 6, February 11th, 1927) he wrote that Jewish children, who thought that he was not Jewish, beat him and injured his head.

In a letter he sent me, he wrote, among other things: "Our home was completely assimilated; my father was the only one with some Jewish, Zionist, inclination. Life at home was Polish. As for myself – I considered converting to Catholicism upon finishing high school. Yiddish was not spoken at home; I learned Yiddish later in life, so I would be able to address Jews in my articles. We did not associate with Jews; all my friends were Christian workers from Biala. We had no Jewish life, except for the Jewish holidays. Later, other Jewish students joined my high school, but they were Russian speaking Litvaks. They treated me like a stranger, though, in general, we were on good terms. The Jewish population was also a stranger to me. We had no relatives in Biala; my mother had an old aunt, Sara Zaltzman, who died when I was young. I remember that, once in a while, I used to enter her shop, located at the end of Lubelske Street and Kishive Street. Suddenly, when I was about 17 years old, with no apparent reason, I realized I was Jewish. I left all my Polish friends, and I declared that from now on I would not be able to be part of their social circles. They accepted my declaration with understanding, telling me I was right. We remained friendly until I fled Warsaw in December 1939. A few of them visited me in Israel after 1946, and we are still in correspondence."

Apollinaire Heartglass graduated from high school with distinction, and went to Warsaw University to study law. There he met Jewish students who were committed nationalists, and it seems that under their influence he became a Zionist.

Heartglass was sentenced to a month in jail for demonstrating against Warsaw's theater when they produced the anti–Semitic play "Rosmaitashtshi". There he met Baruch Weinberg, who had been brought from Biala to the Warsaw jail because of revolutionary activity. Baruch Weinberg wrote about Heartglass: "Years later, when I returned from Siberia for the first time, I was a very good friend of Apollinaire Heartglass. He was a very good person, not a snob, he was modest and honest. When I first met him in jail in Warsaw, where he was held in custody for a month's "administrative period" for taking part in a students' demonstration, he did me a great favor in smuggling out a lot of my writings when he was released, and generously distributed them" ("Life in Podlaska", No. 31/63, December 16th, 1932).

Every time Apollinaire Heartglass came home from Warsaw he used to meet with the Zionists in Biala, take part in their activities and help them organize themselves.

[Page 321]

His mother's efforts to assimilate her children completely into the Polish society were of no avail. It appears that the echo of the uprising of the Jewish street penetrated the Heartglasses' house, the voice of Jewish national and socialist struggles affected the children, who realized they were Jewish and joined their people. Heartglass's brothers and sisters volunteered to give lectures to the town youth and participate in folk–culture activities, gaining even the trust of the Jewish workers.

Apart from Apollinaire, his younger brother Josef was also an active Zionist. After he earned a law and mathematics degree from Warsaw University, in 1913, he went to Kiev, where he was active as a law consultant.

At the time of the Petliura rule in Ukraine, Josef was an active member in the "Self–Defense" [Selbstschutz]. In 1919, while he was with some acquaintances, anti–Jewish demonstrations began in the street. His friends did not allow him to leave the house but, as a member of the Selbstschutz he refused, and he fell in the fight against the Petliura rioters.

After he got his law diploma, Apollinaire Heartglass settled in Siedlce, where he became very active in its social life. At the end of the German occupation in Siedlce during WWI, he was tried by a military court for defending a Polish person who had been attacked by a German. It was a miracle that he survived. In the first election for the Siedlce municipality, he was elected as a member of the municipal Council as a representative of the Jewish Zionists. His brave speeches in the Municipal Council drew a lot of attention.

At that time Heartglass was already very well known. In 1906 he participated in the Russian Zionist congress in Helsinki (Finland), and in 1907 in the congress in Prague.

Heartglass's greatest breakthrough was his election as representative in the Sejm. His knowledge of law and the Polish language made him one of the bravest fighters for the rights of the Jews in Poland. In 1926, after the "Ogoda" agreement (between the Polish government and the Jewish representatives Dr. Joshua (Abraham Osjasz [1]) Thon and Dr. Leon Reich, by which the Jews agreed to support the government in return for more rights for the Jewish people [2]) collapsed, Heartglass became an excellent representative of Jewish affairs in the Sejm.

Each year Heartglass came to the cemetery in his hometown, Biala, to pay his respects to his late father. It was also an opportunity to report to the local community a summary of the Jewish delegates' activity in the Sejm. Not only the Jews came to listen to his reports, but also Christians, even those of higher ranks. The latter could never have enough of his fluent, elegant Polish, despite having to hear his harsh criticism of the way the Polish government treated its Jewish population.

Though he was almost completely absorbed into Polish politics, he found time for Zionist activity. Thus, he went to the Zionist Congresses of 1921, 1923, and 1929. Up to WWII he chaired the Zionist organization in Poland. In 1939 he was the Polish Zionist delegate at the "Round Table" conference in London.

Along with his political activity and practicing law, he was also involved in writing, in Polish, Russian, and Yiddish. He started his journalistic career in 1906, in the Polish newspaper "*Glass Szidovski*" ("The Jewish Voice"). He wrote in Professor Martin Buber's newspaper "*Der Jude*" (in German "the Jew"); in Zionist publications such as "*Chodesh*" ("Month", 1921), "From the Bygone Days" – about the Polish–Bolshevik war. He himself edited the Polish publications "*Tigadnik Szidovski*" ("The Jewish Periodical") and "*Zshisitzie Szidovskie*" ("Jewish life"). In the last years before WWII he worked steadily on the Polish journal "*Apinie*" ("Opinion" O.A.). His first article was translated to Yiddish and published in "*Siedlce Laibn*" in 1912 ("Life in Siedlce", O.A.). In 1918/19 he worked on the Zionistic daily "*Dos Yiddishe Folk*" ("The Jewish People", O.A.). This newspaper closed in 1920, and Heartglass moved to write for "*Heynt*" ("Today", O.A.) published in Warsaw. He taught himself to write in Yiddish, and discussed Jewish politics in Poland and Zionistic matters in general. From his pen came pamphlets and books such as: "Territory and People" (Russian, 1906); "The Basic Ground for the Land–Politics of the Zionists in Poland" (Polish, 1918); his speeches from 1919–1922; "The Jewish National Council in Poland" (Warsaw, 1923). In 1944, the Jewish Agency published his Polish pamphlet "Know the Country" in Israel, for Polish people who came to Eretz Israel during the war.

His years in Israel are another chapter. When he heard the sad new about the tragedy of Polish Judaism, he could not find peace. Like another Polish Jew in London, A. Siglboim, Heartglass could not forgive himself for leaving the Polish Jews in their most difficult time, in their greatest need. He survived by accident, only to keep agonizing over the terrible news.

[Page 322]

Heartglass did have good days in Eretz Israel, for example at the establishment of the Jewish State, though these were rather short. The severe disease which had no doubt been the result of his suicide attempt had already taken its toll, ruining any possible joy in his life.

On March 23rd 1953 we lost our important townsman, a real representative of Polish Judaism. He is buried in the old Tel–Aviv cemetery on Trumpeldor Street.

Translator's Footnotes:

1. https://www.google.co.il/search?q=%D7%99%D7%94%D7%95%D7%A9%D7%A2+%D7%98%D7%94%D7%95%D7%9F&oq=hvuaug+yvi&aqs=chrome.1.69i57j0l5.11881j0j8&sourceid=chrome&ie=UTF-8, 20.9.2018
2. https://he.wikipedia.org/wiki/%D7%9C%D7%99%D7%90%D7%95%D7%9F_%D7%A4%D7%99%D7%99%D7%9A ×ᵃ
20/9/201

---

2. Moshe Rubinstein

The name Moshe Rubinstein (my maternal uncle, O.A.) is associated with the most beautiful period in the Jewish life of Biala in the last generation. It may rightly be argued that he was the main personality who shaped this period. I am talking about the years of WWI and the first years of the Polish regime. It is no exaggeration to say that, in those years, Moshe Rubinstein was regarded as a prominent activist who enjoyed recognition in the Zionist circles and was respected by his opponents. He made an enormous contribution to the Zionist movement in our town and, indirectly, he also contributed a great deal to other parties (i.e. not socialist. O.A.) who, although opposing the Zionist struggle, under the leadership of Moshe Rubinstein had to rise to a much higher level, and learned a lot from his political strategies. He was the first social activist in Biala, who taught his fellow activists how to behave in a parliamentary way in meetings and assemblies.

Moshe Rubinstein was an active Zionist since before WWI. Yet, then, the conditions did not allow him to let out the burning energy accumulated in him.

The German occupation in Biala during WWI brought with it the opportunity to develop Jewish community life, and Moshe Rubinstein assumed these activities with all his talent and commitment. Thanks to him, various institutions were established, activities that the people never dared dream of, and he became the pride of the Jews in Biala.

Moshe Rubinstein was the initiator and the founder of the fully Hebrew school, *Yavneh*, which he directed. And when arguments broke out, and he left the running of the school, it rapidly went downhill, the level of studies dropped, and it closed down. Around the *Yavneh* School, Moshe Rubinstein organized flourishing Zionist activities. In after-school hours the building became a Zionist *Beit Am* ("People's House", a cultural center, O.A.). Who does not remember the beautiful Children's house of WWI? It was also Moshe Rubinstein's initiative.

All his time and energy he invested in organizing the Zionists in Biala, and with great success. Because of him, Biala, a provincial town, became known as one of the most active in Poland. Who does not remember the lively activities that took place in *Beit Ha'am* in Biala? No other party in Biala was as active as the Zionist party. If Biala had *Maccabi*, so loved by the Jewish citizens, it is also because of Moshe Rubinstein, who inspired the creation of the national sport organization. He helped *Maccabi* to develop, accompanying its activity with his alert eyes.

[Page 323]

When the first youth movement, Hashomer Hatza'ir, was established in Biala, Moshe Rubinstein helped with the organization and took an active part in shaping its national character. Many activities took place during this period, both political and cultural. It is unbelievable how Moshe Rubinstein, this Zionist activist, mobilized the great majority of Biala's youth to take part in these activities.

Moshe Rubinstein also tried to legalize at least part of the Zionist institutions and initiations. Through these efforts, he earned recognition and respect among the Christians as well as among the Jews. At one point, the local council and the leaders of the Jewish community considered having a Jewish deputy–mayor. The Polish political party agreed to support it under the condition that Moshe Rubinstein would be the candidate. However, he was already getting ready to emigrate to Israel.

It was not easy for Moshe Rubinstein to organize all the Zionist organizations in town under one roof. Except for motivation and organizing ability, of which he was not short, it was also necessary to conduct a bitter campaign with the other Jewish parties in Biala. Here too he excelled, unwilling to compromise any of his Zionist principles. The struggle with the *Aguda* (ultra–orthodox party) was another chapter in the life and activity of Moshe Rubinstein. Since Rabbi Shmuel Leib Zak was associated with *Aguda*, it was actually a struggle against the chief Rabbi of Biala. Moshe Rubinstein threw himself enthusiastically into this struggle, and thanks to his activity, the influence of the orthodox declined. In those days, having an open dispute with the town's rabbi was not easy, and demanded a lot of courage.

When the town's rabbi ordered the closing of the synagogue to prevent the Zionists from holding a memorial meeting for the late Zionist leader, Dr. Yehiel Tchlenow, Moshe Rubinstein decided to open the door from the inside, and the *Maccabi* youth carried it out. One has to be familiar with that "arena" to be able to appreciate such action. When the rabbi of Biala supported "*Aguda*" in the elections, Moshe Rubinstein stood against him with no fear whatsoever. He led the campaign by calling for assemblies, and especially by publishing in the free–distributed newspaper *Bialer Echo* ("The Echo of Biala", O.A.). Having a printed newspaper for the first time in town was by itself an outstanding achievement of this brave Zionist leader.

The rabbi of Biala decided to forbid the famous cantor, Gershon Sirota, from giving a concert on behalf of the Zionist organization, but his efforts were to no avail. At first Gershon Sirota complied with the rabbi's letter. Moshe Rubinstein, however, knew who had more influence on Sirota than the rabbi, and sent this person to change his mind. Gershon Sirota came to Biala, and with his great artistic talent increased the Zionists' elections fund nicely.

Moshe Rubinstein had an open campaign against the opponents of Zionism; all his opponents respected him for his honest and noble behavior. When the help–committee was set up in Biala, with resources that came from the Central Committee of the JOINT in Warsaw, it was clear to all that Moshe Rubinstein should be its chair.

During the invasion period of 1920, Moshe Rubinstein collected evidence of the anti–Jewish events and secretly sent it to the Jewish delegates in the Sejm in Warsaw. When the Bolsheviks occupied the town and started to set up their administration, they turned to Moshe Rubinstein to take responsibility for the Jewish children to attend school. He took his time, until the Bolsheviks were suddenly evacuated. The central Zionist committee in Warsaw learned to appreciate the Zionist organization in Biala, and in many important activities relied on the local activists.

At the beginning of 1921, Moshe Rubinstein was invited to work in the central Zionist committee, and moved to Warsaw. There he worked closely with Izsak Grinboim, and they have been friends to this day. With his move to Warsaw the Zionist activity in Biala naturally declined. In 1923, with the rise of the dispute around the question of enlarging the Jewish Agency, he took the radical position and joined *Al Hamishmar*. When the right–wing group, *Et Livnot* ("Time to Build", O.A.) became the majority, he left his work in the Zionist central committee along with other members of *Al Hamishmar*.

[Page 324]

Moshe Rubinstein lived up to his principles. He practiced himself what he preached to others. In 1925, he left Poland for Eretz Israel. In Eretz Israel he did not look for clerical work, he did not go around telling others what he did in Poland, nor did he ask to be compensated for his Zionist activity. He took hard, physical work, which he had never done before. In 1926–1928, he worked on "*Zionist Leaves*" which was distributed in Warsaw with the *Al Hamishmar* newspaper, and wrote a column by the name of "Letters from Eretz Israel".

In the years to come he became active in the American Zionist society, never pushing himself to a higher position. When he met with people from Biala, his old hometown, he surely remembered the lively period his life, of which he had all the reasons to be proud.

[Translator's note: Moshe Rubinstein was my mother's eldest brother. We adored him, and considered him the head of our extended family. He had four daughters, nine grandchildren, and after he left us a number of great–grandchildren were born.]

3. Joshua Fisher

Joshua Fisher was not born in Biala; he came from Minsk–Mazowiecki. He came to Biala after he got married. In his youth he was strongly built, always walked quickly, his eyes looking around, and had a handsome face.

He opened a tavern, and immediately showed every one that he was not afraid of the strong lads or the informers. First, because he had an iron fist; secondly, he could speak Polish better than all the informers could.

Joshua Fisher, however, was not a typical tavern–owner, as we knew them in Biala. He was a learned man, who used to read a lot. One could find at his place the Hebrew newspaper *Hatzfira*, and on Saturdays one would find him reading the Bible or Ahad Ha'am's book, *Al Parahsat Drachim* (At the Crossroads, O.A.).

He belonged to the Radzyn Hassidim, but, at the same time, was an enthusiastic *Hovev Zion* (Lover of Zion, O.A.). He was not an active Zionist because of his father's objection. Yet, the minute his father dropped his objection, Joshua Fisher took on Zionist work with all his heart. He started a branch of the Odessa Palestine Committee and kept connections with Odessa. He started to recruit supporters to the Zionist idea from the orthodox community. He held meetings of *Hovevei Zion* in his home, where youngsters used to sneak in so that nobody would recognize them.

Joshua Fisher was the first in Biala to send out young men with bowls to collect money for Eretz Israel in religious learning places, synagogues, and cemeteries on Yom Kippur eve. When a Hassid from Gur tried to throw the bowl to the ground, he received such an earful from Joshua Fisher, that he never again came close to a bowl.

In those days, a very famous feldsher (equivalent to an assistant–physician in the USA, O.A.) lived in Biala, Meir Michel Laufman. He was known for his large medical practice, and his success in healing the sick. Yet he was a very difficult man, nobody would go against him. Joshua Fisher, however, did stand up to him. When a few members of Joshua Fisher's wife's family fell sick, and wanted to call on Meir Michel for help, Joshua Fisher called in physicians and other feldshers.

In his tavern, he used to bring together activists for the illegal Polish Socialist Party (PPS), and quite a few campaigns were instigated there. Since the activists were not very literate, Joshua Fisher was their secretary and reported their activities to the center in Siedlce. They used to talk with him and consult him. His collaboration with them enabled him to prevent a pogrom in Biala, after there was one in Siedlce. Thanks to his intervention among the PPS activists, the Jews in Biala escaped bloodshed. His underground name in the PPS was "Grubi".

The PPS activists liked and completely trusted this Jew with his little Jewish hat, and they came to him for help in the most difficult moments. One such episode is worth telling.

[Page 325]

The Christian workers of one factory decided to strike, although the PPS was against it. A leader from Siedlce was sent to the workers' meeting, to convince them that the strike was not necessary. The local PPS activists were surprised that he could not convince the workers, who were determined to achieve their goal. They called in Joshua Fisher in a hurry, who spoke to the workers, explained to them why the strike would not lead anywhere, and convinced them with his burning words.

During WWI Joshua Fisher did not own a tavern any more, but dealt with gas–lamps and with distributing gas.

During the war, he built the Yavneh School, and his wife, Rivka, was one of the founders of the children's home.

Joshua Fisher was one of the founders of Beit Ha'am, but did not stay there for long. He left it and the Zionist organization because they did not keep Shabbat. Nevertheless, he did not sit idle. At that time *Hamizrahi* started operating in town, and religious youngsters joined it.

Joshua Fisher was among the few who were not afraid to stand up to strong people. He got annoyed with the Radzyn synagogue and left to pray in Tarshish; there he had an argument with one of the rich persons and moved to the Bet–Hamidrash [House of Torah study].

After Polish independence, Joshua Fisher was involved in the elections to the first Sejm and Senate. In the elections of the Jewish community, he again came into conflict with the Zionist organization, as he demanded harsher struggle against "*Aguda.*

With the Bolshevik invasion in 1920, and the withdrawal of the Russian army, Polish soldiers took Joshua Fisher from his home with the intention of executing him. By chance, the court attendant, Stanislaw, saw it from far away and came running to save Joshua Fisher from certain death.

A little later, when life started to go back to normal, Joshua Fisher and some friends of his conducted a large colonial business. One morning they closed everything and Joshua Fisher with his partner, Moshe Braverman, went to Eretz Israel.

When they arrived, he was worried about Braverman, and what he would do in Eretz Israel. For himself he did not worry as much. After a while, Braverman found a job in a bank, while Joshua Fisher suffered, working in different hard, physical jobs.

Nevertheless, as he once told me, he had always been drawn to agriculture, and this is what he wanted to do in Eretz Israel. A few years later, he had an opportunity to fulfil his dream. A group of religious persons went to start a new settlement, known today as *Kfar Ata*, where the successful textile factory Ata was located.

The difficulties that Joshua Fisher encountered in *Kfar Ata*, and the things he did there, are an important chapter of this settlement. Here I want to write only about one dramatic moment.

The Arab neighbors gave *Kfar Ata* a lot of trouble. Among them was one shepherd who stood out in his anti–Jewish actions, and was considered by his partners a big hero. One evening, Joshua Fisher and another man went to their fields; suddenly, the shepherd hero and another Arab were right in front of them, taking their sheep to pasture in the Jewish cultivated fields. Joshua Fisher ordered them to leave immediately, but they started a fight. Joshua Fisher turned to the hero, severely beat him, and took his shepherd's stick. The other Jew struggled with the second Arab. Once Joshua Fisher finished with the hero, he turned to help his mate, leaving in the field two badly wounded Arabs.

The blows the hero suffered made quite an impression, and after that the Arab neighbors let the Jewish settlers alone. The beaten hero came back to ask for the stick Joshua Fisher had taken from him, a stick that looked like a baton. Joshua Fisher did not want to part with the baton he won, and the hero left in disgrace.

Joshua Fisher was among those who appeared before the British investigation committee in Eretz Israel after the riots of 1929. There he heard so many lies, and he took it so hard, that it broke his spirit. He was sick for a long time.

The hard life Joshua Fisher had was shared by his devoted wife, Rivka Fisher, who was a social activist in Biala.

[Page 326]

During the regime of the Russian Czar, her home in Biala was a meeting place for Zionists, and a number of Zionist institutions were founded there.

When the Keren Hage'ulah Fund was established, she donated almost all her jewelry to the fund.

Adjusting to Eretz Israel, and the hard physical labor she had never done before, did not come easy to Rivka Fisher. Yet, she accepted every hardship with love, and never complained. Taking part in building the country filled her with joy.

If you come to *Kfar Ata* and ask about Mr. Fisher, even the youngest child will immediately show you the house of the most important man, the first mayor of *Kfar Ata*.

Joshua and Rivka Fisher grew old in sickness and misery. In their later years they ran the charity fund for the needy in *Kfar Ata*.

Moshe Smolyor

by Jacob Aaron Rosenboim

Jacob Aaron Rosenboim was a devoted, valuable member of the community. For him, public activity was not a means for his own benefit. He was a man of European manners who was at home in the Russian language and literature. He contributed original ideas and new meanings to each conversation. We had the feeling that he carried us with him to the well of wisdom from which he drew for many years. He belonged to the generation of the *Maskilim* (a Jewish social movement that sought to combine one's general education with Jewish religious way of life), for whom the struggle between Jewishness and being a *Mentch* (human being, O.A.) had not been reconciled. He did not neglect the *Talith*, but he did not stick to tradition. I always felt that he had succeeded in finding the main road. Being a Jew and being a *Mentch* were very clearly expressed by him. With his gentle soul, his pure conduct, his attraction to people and social life, he was a complete *Mentch*, in a way that only those who were deeply rooted in the Jewish tradition and, at the same time, drank from European culture could be.

Tolstoy and Gorky, the distinguished Russian writers, were his favorites. Yet a conversation could not end without his mentioning Mendele Mocher Sforim and Shalom Aleikhem. As an educated person, at the beginning of the 20th century, his knowledge was broad and sound. He could cite chapters written by Gogol, Dostoyevsky, Bialik, Tchernichovsky, and others. He did a lot for the people in town. He handled the loan–bank; he was a chair of the Zionist Organization; he always represented the Zionist party in the community; he was the head of the community council; he was the representative of the Zionists in the municipal council; ran the "*Tarbuth*" society, was active in several other organizations and institutions and participated in the weekly newspapers that appeared in town. He was well known and respected in Jewish circles.

Jacob Aaron was a devoted Zionist. He came to the Zionist movement with the *Maskilim* generation. The truth is that he did not wait for the revolution to bring relief, so he did not become a Zionist because he was desperate. He always saw Zionism as a means to heal the Jewish people and gather it in Eretz Israel.

WWI, the death of millions, the destruction of towns, and later the pogroms in Ukraine and Poland, strengthened his Zionist commitment, to which he devoted a large part of his life.

He was a Zionist activist, not expecting any personal reward. He was active with the National Funds – the Jewish National Fund and the United Israel Appeal. He wished to establish a Hebrew *Tarbut* school in Biala. He planned it for a long time, but was not able to bring it to fruition. He loved the Hebrew language, and saw it as an important element of Zionist education.

He brought his daughters and son to follow him to Zionism. He made sure that his children, too, would absorb the best of both Jewish culture and the world's treasures. He sent them to study at the Polish High School, but made sure they also had a Jewish education.

In 1939, when the German-Polish war was over, the Jews in Biala started to flee to Brest, then in Russia. I heard a rumor that Jacob Aaron Rosenboim was among the refugees.

[Page 327]

I made every effort to find him and to invite him to stay with me, but I did not find him. I later heard that he returned to Biala to be with his wife and son.

After the war, I learned that during the Nazi occupation Jacob Aaron Rosenboim was active in the Jewish community, bravely representing the interests of the Jews during this tragic period. In this cruel time, he risked his life with false Nazi documents, hoping that one day he would see the light again. With others, he was sent to the Majdanek concentration camp in the last transport.

Baruch Weinberg

Baruch Weinberg was very well known in his hometown, Biala Podlaska. He was known for his honesty and sense of justice; he could not stand any injustice. He hated exploitation, and employers feared him. When people wanted to mock someone for their revolutionary talk, they used to say: "Ah, he is growing to be a Baruch"…

Baruch was the founder of the *Bund* in Biala, and he gave it all his heart. He was a carpenter, but he organized strikes not only in his workshop, but also in other occupations as well. He had good rhetoric ability, and was popular as a revolution advocate. He was blessed with natural intelligence, which he cultivated by reading both Jewish and general literature; he developed like a real propaganda person, armed with a broad knowledge of socialism, working conditions and rights. He became so famous that the police kept their eyes on him; he was arrested and twice sent to Siberia. From Siberia, he managed to escape to London.

After a while he gave up carpentry and studied printing. He used each free moment to develop social activities. He became Morris Meyer's partner in the Yiddish newspaper, *Di Zeit* (The Time, O.A.), and published a weekly under the name *Der Friend* himself. When he opened his own printing shop, he became the publisher of Dr. M. Zalkind's Yiddish translation of the Talmud (only tractate *Berakhot appeared in print*), investing in it a lot of love and quite a big sum of money.

Being ideologically a left wing socialist and an activist, Baruch Weinberg was the president of the "Workers' Circle" in London. Yet, his love for Jewish culture and the Yiddish language were so great that he compromised his party's ideology and accepted any Jewish cultural activist with open arms.

In 1937, he went to America to visit his brother Joshua, and the immigrants from Biala organized a warm welcome for him. From all across the county people came to see the famous "Baruch", whom everybody kept talking about.

He passed away on July 14th, 1941, in London.

(From "*Theater Notebooks*", New York, 1943).

[Translator's note: Baruch Weinberg was my father's uncle].

Yeshayahu Weinberg

He was born in Biala on June 15th, 1888. He was drawn to revolutionary activity when he was still a schoolchild, and went through all the phases of that vigorous period: secret meetings, jail, demonstrations, Cossack pogroms, etc. At the same time, he swallowed literature, both Jewish and general, like a hungry person, and became an autodidact. In December 1905, he moved to London. He became an active member of a theatre club, searched for the finest concerts and best English theater performances, studied art and became a walking encyclopedia of art. He became the secretary of the "Amalgamated Society of Tailors and Seamstresses." He founded the *Hazamir* (Nightingale, O.A.) Association, and was one of the founders of the "Workers' Circle". Later he started writing in *Di Zeit*, under the pseudonym *Molomut*, about theater and music. In 1915/16, he became very active in the "Russian Immigrants' Committee" and was one of the founders of the *Temple Theatre*.

[Page 328]

In 1920, Weinberg came to America, and a bit later, he became the local editor of *Forwards* in Detroit, where he started his journalism and social activities. He wrote under the pseudonyms "*Brandweiss*", "*Winogorski*", "*Meloman*", "*X*", "*Riverson*". The crowning glory of his work was his book in Yiddish, "*The Jewish Institutions and Schools in Detroit*", which received very good reviews from all Yiddish critics.

For several decades, first in London and then in Detroit, he threw himself wholeheartedly into Jewish cultural work, helped all cultural institutions with counsel and activity, and donated funds from his own pocket to meet their needs. Weinberg cultivated Yiddish theater in particular, not only by writing reviews, but also by advocating for the importance of maintaining the Yiddish language. His home was open to all theater lovers.

In his last years, Joshua Weinberg was very sick. Yet, like a committed soldier, he did not step down from his duties. On April 15th 1943, his weak heart stopped beating.

(From "*Theater Notebooks*", New York, 1943).

---

1. Elie Shimsheles (Elijahu Yustman)

by Gdaliahu Braverman

If you came to Biala at the beginning of the *Bund's* activity, and asked the workers who brought about the greatest achievements for their organization, you were sure to hear the name of Elie Shimsheles.

Elie Shimsheles was born in an extremely poor home. His father was a baker. The boy had a strong will to study, and envied the children whose parents sent them to teachers, where they would learn to write Yiddish and Russian as well as math, and bring home copybooks full of round, written letters. Elie's father did not have money for tuition fees; he did not have money even for copybooks. He promised little Elie that, as soon as he (Elie) started working, from his first salary, he would start learning. So, when Elie became 12 years old, he was sent to a carpenter to learn the profession, hoping that he would soon start earning.

It is easy to say "he would soon earn money"; to make money he had first to learn the skills, and at that time, this did not happen quickly. The new apprentice spent the first few years as a servant, serving the master and the other workers, not to mention the master's wife. The apprentice–in–training was sent to bring food from the house to the workshop, or shopping, rather than learning the profession. When he was asked to do something close to carpentry, it was usually to sharpen the tools. This is how days and months passed by. When Elie got enough courage to ask the workers for a piece of wood to try sawing or polishing, they used to mock him: — look at this tot, he is in a hurry – and ask him with an evil smile: — aren't you ready to be a master yet?…

For three years, Elie learned almost nothing. When the *Bund* started operating in Biala at the turn of the century (20th, O.A.), one of its first activities was to change the conditions of the apprentice children.

Elijahu Bobkes (Hoffman) and Baruch Weinberg came to work with the same master, Shmile Shome Simels (Samuel [Friedman] Shamai Simels). They taught Elie and, in a short while, he became a carpenter.

During work, Elie found out that Elijahu Bobkes and Baruch had some secrets, whispering and transferring small packages they hid in the tall boxes. When Elie became more friendly with the two new workers, he asked them about the packages. This is how Elie Shimsheles learned about the revolutionary group.

When Elie, who had a soft heart and mourned the deep poverty of his parents and people like them, heard that there are people that are ready to fight for others, he felt that his wishes had come true and that he must join the fight with all his might.

In 1903, when the *Bund* grew and became a large organization, Elie Shimsheles was already an important activist in town.

[Page 329]

People respected him, and he was accepted by all because of his simple way of behavior and original thought. He did not use high language and complicated sentences, drawn from written materials — as was the fashion those days — in order to demonstrate intelligence. On the other hand, he took it upon himself to deal with matters that others did not want to do. If there was a dispute between an employer and his employees, Elie went to talk with the stubborn employer, and this was often enough to soften the latter's heart and to give in to his workers' demands.

Elie started reading and studied the problems that concerned either him or the working force. In the *Bund*, he ran a group of the more knowledgeable members.

With time, Elie became the central nerve of the *Bund* in the town, member of the most secret *Bund* committee, which was at the top of the party.

Elie had a natural rhetorical talent, something quite rare in those days. He had a lot of success with any audience. If a poor speaker was sent to Biala from the region, and Elie saw that the audiences were falling asleep, he would come forward and the participants would wake up. He knew how to approach people and to speak to their hearts and feelings.

David Kruses, who was in Paris and had the opportunity to hear some good speakers, wrote that if Elie was in Paris and went into politics, he would have been one of the more popular speakers.

More than half a century has passed, and I still feel Elie's warm and lovely approach to all around him. His consistent readiness to be involved in action gave us the feeling that we stood in front of a prophet who could see the future.

Later, after the failure of the revolution, the *Bund's* activity in Biala died away, the beautiful dream dissipated, and hearts were filled with deep despair. Elie decided to start a theater club in town. With this step, he meant to fight the apathy of the workers and cultivate their interest in cultural activities.

During the first period of his *Bundist* activity, Elie thought about starting a library. His initiative brought about the beginning of an illegal library in town. I myself was among the founders of this library and those who ran it until it was destroyed by the German vandals. I regularly saw, with my own eyes, its first creator, Elie Shimsheles.

About 1907, Elie and his girlfriend, Dovale the joker's daughter, left Poland. For a long time we did not hear from him. I could not believe that such a devoted activist for the workers would step aside and give up his work for workers' rights. It hurt me greatly when after a while I learned that Elie was in America, running a grocery store, and struggling to make ends meet.

2. David Kruses (Goldfarb)

The son of orthodox parents, a student in a *Hasidic* religious school, he was attracted to the revolutionary movement, which penetrated into religious institutions, too. He replaced the religious books with general ones, and committed himself to revolutionary activity.

At that time, David Kruses was the representative of the *Bund* in Biala. He frequently appeared in assemblies, where he defended the attitudes of the *Bund*, and was well accepted by the public.

There were times when the progressive intelligentsia in town considered him as trouble. Thirsty for knowledge, he turned to the Jewish high school, and learned a lot from it. He initiated an intelligentsia–club, where high school students met with advanced laborers. The club used to get together in the apartment of Jacob Steinman, the teacher, where they used to talk about current political issues and read about different cultural characters.

David Kruses was drawn to the big world. The small town really suffocated him, especially after the *Bund's* activity ceased because of the failure of the revolution.

[Page 330]

He decided to go to Paris, the cultural center in the eyes of many young people.

He left for Paris in about 1909. He sent letters back to Biala, reporting his impression from the large sphinx, Paris.

Soon after he arrived in Paris, David the simple boy, who felt for social problems and had the workers' needs in front of him, saw the poor state of the French workers. In his letters he told us that the working class was excluded from the Parisian paradise and enjoyed very little luxury.

David was soon disenchanted by the glowing beauty of Paris, and within two years returned to Biala. Some misunderstanding at the border led to his arrest for a few months.

He came out of jail depressed and bitter. From time to time, he took a group of *Bundists* out to the field for a lecture. Yet he did not talk about politics, but about everyday problems.

After he returned from Paris, David became depressed, not interested in earning a living. He gave the impression that he was desperate on one hand and looking for something that would take him out of his mundane, daily life on the other.

During WWI, when the front got closer to Biala, there was serious talk about evacuation to Russia, to avoid the war. David was among those who left for Russia.

After the war was over, and the revolution in Russia calmed down, there was still no sign of David in Biala. During the 1930s, Elijahu Reiseles (Klatz) suddenly received a letter from him. He wrote that he lived in Latvia, had married, taught in a high school, and asked about some of his friends.

There was no news from him after this letter. We have no knowledge of what happened to him during WWII.

---

1. Elie Bobkes (Elijahu Hoffman)

by P. Gold

Elie Hoffman was a carpenter, and one of the founders of the *Bund* in Biala. He was tall, his head leaning forward a bit, buried between his shoulders, his blond hair hidden, always holding a pipe – with tobacco when he could afford it, or empty when he had no money.

He was arrested with other *Bund* members by the Czarist regime and sent to Arkhangelsk (Russia). He came back ill with tuberculosis. He stayed in Biala for a short time and went to America. He arrived in America during the economic crisis, and had a very difficult time, but never lost his smile. When he was asked how he was doing or what he was doing, he used to answer: "It is cold on Broom Street". Immigrants from Biala to New York used this phrase for many years.

Elie came back to Biala and married the daughter of Avreimale, the music player. Jews say that musicians have beautiful daughters; this was definitely true for Elie's wife. Together they worked, fell sick, but brought up a family.

The 22nd anniversary of the *Bund* was celebrated in Gedaljahu Braverman's home. Elie, the oldest and the first *Bundist* in town, was asked to say a few words. Instead of a speech, he sang the *Bund* oath.

The second time I met him in his own home. I then understood why he was usually absent from the *Bund* meetings. It was Passover eve of 1920, the Workers' Help Committee decided to give him a donation for the holiday, and it sent me with the money. The mother of his children lay in bed, smiling, but terminally ill and in great pain. Elie himself had to work, to take care of the children and his bed–ridden wife. Seeing that, I understood why he could not be active. How he kept his smile is still beyond me.

In 1921 the *Bund* split. In a meeting in Abraham Adler's house to discuss the issue, Elie took the stage and shouted: — Friends! This is an attack on our own mother!

[Page 331]

Those who created the split were always against the *Bund*, and even the other part will not let us be for long. We have always been an independent party, and we will continue to exist as such; we swear to remain completely faithful to the *Bund*.

From time to time, my friends in Biala wrote that Elie had another hemorrhage. In one letter they told me that after one such episode, when he recovered somewhat, he said to the friends around him: — there are 40 Zlotys in the pillow case, belonging to the *Cultural League*; take it because my wife (the second one) might find it and spend it all.

In his letters, he never mentioned his condition. They were always full of his humor, although "it was cold on Broom Street"…

2. Tankhum Freind

by P. Gold

Tana, as people used to call him, was the son of Seilig, a supervisor in a *Talmud Tora* (religious school).

I first met him in the *Heder* of rabbi Motel Domatchewer, and later we studied together with the best teacher of the higher *Talmud Tora*, Drogetchin. After school, I became an artisan, and Tana went to Lithuania to study in a *Yeshiva*. A few years later he went to Lodz and became a clerk for a young family from the *Hasidic* intelligentsia. The wife suggested that he should teach her children, who went to the local High–School, the Bible and other Jewish topics, and, in return, she offered to teach him Russian and Polish.

In Lodz Tana met with workers, and with the popular *Bund* activist, Ephraim Lazar Zalmanovitch, who had a lot of influence on him.

After WWI, I met Tana in the administration building of the literature and theater society, and in a *Bund* committee.

He was considered part of the *Bund*'s intelligentsia. He was not a speaker, but a conversation person. The organization gave him responsibility for the youth: it set up the "future" organization, to get the young together and to send them lecturers. He himself had a group that met every Saturday in Elie Bobke's home.

In the Krakow *Bund* meeting, Tana and Baruch Stechanovski (now the chairperson of the *Bund* in Belgium) represented Biala. They were both, then, from the more leftist group of the *Bund*. When the consumers' cooperative *Einikeit* (Unity, O.A.) was formed in Biala, Tana became a clerk there.

In July 1920, Tana was arrested with other *Bund* members from Biala. They were sent to several jails and camps and then they were sent to the well–known concentration camp, Dombie.

After the Soviet–Polish war the JDC started to reconstruct Brisk Cooperatives were developed, and Ort (Organization for Vocational Craftsmanship, O.A.) opened vocational training schools. As the *Bund* had a say in the cooperatives, Tana came to Brisk to work with the administration. Later he became a teacher in a Cyszo school (the central association of Jewish schools in the Republic of Poland, O.A.).

While he was a teacher in Pinsk, he became involved in the local municipality and worked as a clerk. I was told that the students loved him; they trusted him and saw him as an older brother and friend.

Occasionally I saw his name in the folk–newspaper of the *Bund*, but not as a speaker. Later Tana taught in Piotrkow and Chenstochow. During Hitler's time, he worked in a factory and, in the evenings, he ran a Jewish school in the ghetto. He was active in the *Bund's* underground, and served as a courier. He escaped Aktzias, but not death. He disappeared just before the Germans' defeat.

[Page 332]

3. Hirsh Richter (Lazar the Carpenter)

He was born in Biala–Podlaska, but at a very young age he moved to Warsaw and grew up in a very poor Jewish neighborhood, in Stawki Street. He was still a boy when he heard about the *Bund*, but its stubborn campaign against Zionism kept him away. He came closer to the radical Zionist circle "*Hatkhija*" (The Revival, O.A.), when Izsak Tabenkin, Izsak Grinboim, and Josef Shprintzak were among its leaders. Later he belonged to the group of *Poalei Zion* (Zion's Workers, O.A.) that joined the Zionist proletariat, to which he stayed loyal for almost forty years, until his death. He won his social position thanks to his thoroughness, restraint, his spirit and self–sacrifice. He never went to school, but he had a deep internal intelligence and natural ability to solve the most difficult daily problems. When he entered *Poalei Zion*, they were busy mainly with discussing theoretical problems, and he was one of the people that preferred practical work to professional and theoretical arguments; under this slogan, he organized the "workers' opposition" in the party. Being involved with the public, he knew what was going on in each workshop and factory, and had a great influence, especially among his fellow woodworkers, although most of them belonged to the *Bund*. He was popular among the Jewish workers and the poor, both in Warsaw and in the provinces – they called him Lazar the Carpenter. His decisiveness often brought about a strong clash between him and the leaders of the party, when he blamed them for deviation from the party's main ideology. The Czar's police often arrested him because of his party activity; sometimes he was badly beaten during his arrest. In 1909 he was recruited to the Russian army for three years, but, when he was released, he immediately resumed his political activity.

In 1914 someone informed on him, and he was arrested and sent to a period of forced labor in the Urals. He stayed there with two central *Bund* members, W. Medem and W. Alter, who tried to talk him out of Zionism, but to no avail. He was freed after the revolution of 1917 and became one of the Communist leaders of the *Poalei Zion* party in Russia. In 1920, the Central Committee of the party decided to annex "*Poalei Zion left*"; he bitterly fought for each ideological principle. He promoted the daily support of the workers in Eretz Israel, and the idea of integrating into the world Zionist organization. In 1924, he fulfilled his long–lasting wish and moved to Eretz Israel. The Jewish workers remembered him well, especially in Tel–Aviv, where he stayed during 1924–1927. However, the party center in Warsaw called him back to Poland.

When the war began, he left Warsaw but returned immediately to continue his four–decade activity. Indeed, he was present in all areas of the underground activities. His nature did not allow him to be passive, and he demanded armed resistance. The Nazis sent him to Lublin concentration camp, where he suffered until he died at the age of 58.

(Melech Neishtadt: "The Destruction and the Uprising of Warsaw Jewry".

[Page 333]

Rabbi David Pizich

by Elijahu Mazor Tel–Aviv
(Former President of Warsaw Community)

When I commemorate the sacred Jews, rabbis, *Hasidism*, believers, activists and good doers with whom I was in Warsaw, a city with the biggest Jewish community in Europe, who were killed during the terrible holocaust, I turn to the mission with great respect, with deep sorrow and pain. There is no comfort.

This time I will commemorate a Jewish activist, a member of the community committee in Warsaw, a scholar, *Hasid* and a modest man, Rabbi David Pizich from Mlawa and Biala–Podlaska. Rabbi David Pizich was elected to the community committee as a representative of *Agudat Israel* (Orthodox Party, O.A.), chosen by the Rabbi of the Sokolow Hassidim.

I was at the time the president of the community committee, and I was very familiar with his rich activity in the social committee and the rabbinical committee. Rabbi David who was a wealthy merchant, always found the time for public affairs, with special attention to the poor and needy. He used to donate money and food for holidays, making sure not to offend or shame anybody.

During WWII, he kept up his good work, despite the constant danger of death. He sacrificed himself to help his miserable brothers. Once, the Gestapo ordered the community committee to come to an emergency meeting on Saturday. Four members were arrested, including Rabbi David Pizich. It took effort and tricks to release him. He stayed in the Warsaw Ghetto almost to the end, and was among the last to leave it. He died in Poniatow with the other pure, sacred victims.

His sons, who live in Israel, brought his ashes from Poniatow and buried them in the old cemetery on Trumpeldor Street, Tel–Aviv. They erected a stone in his memory and in the memory of his family members killed during the holocaust.

(This article was published in Hebrew, as the author submitted it.)

[Page 334]

Religious Persons and Figures

Rabbi Dovid'l Karliner

by Dr. Shmuel Elyashiv

Translated by Ofra Anson

Edited by Yocheved Klausner

1

Rabbi David Freidman (Dovid'l Karliner) was born in Biala in 1827. At the age of six he was recognized as a genius, and attracted the attention and sympathy of the most respected scholars of his time – Rabbi Shlomo Eiger, Rabbi Leib Katzenelenbogen, Rabbi Tevele Minsker, and others. Leading scholars found a special pleasure in being entertained by the young genius, asking him about difficult problems and hearing him analyzing the *Talmud*.

We know one interesting fact about Rabbi Dovid'l Karliner's childhood. Rabbi David Tevel (Tevele from Minsk), came to Brisk when Dovid'l, who was growing up in Brisk, was nine years old. Rabbi David Tevel, known as the genius from Minsk, was to become the Rabbi of Brisk. Some scholars and leaders of the community objected to his appointment, and in order to thwart it, pushed little Dovid'l to the stage after Rabbi Tevel's talk. The young boy enthusiastically took to arguing with the great sage, tearing to pieces his hard–to–understand talk. The Rabbi from Minsk went back home with nothing, yet from that day on he dearly loved the young boy and never stopped watching over him.

The greatest Jewish personality of that time, who showed the most sincere interest in the young star, started to worry that the boy's talent might be spoiled because people treated his childish wisdom too lightly, and played with it too much. The genius from Brisk Rabbi Leib Katzenelenbogen, who supervised little Dovid'l, stated that the child should be taken away from Brisk to a quiet small town, where he could study and develop with no interruptions, as soon as possible. Dovid'l was taken to his elder brother in Kamieniec, where he studied the *Talmud* in a peaceful environment. His greatness increased daily, and people all over Poland and Russia talked about him constantly, telling of the wonders of his sharp mind and deep thoughts.

2

Rabbi Shmariahu Luria, one of the monumental Jewish figures at the turn of the 20th century and one of the wealthiest, took an interest in the young genius. He brought the boy to his rich and peaceful home, dressed him in the finest array and tried his best to make him "*Maor Hagola*" [lit. the light of the Diaspora], by providing him with the best conditions for studying, under the supervision of Shmariahu Luria's father in law and the learned, wealthy Rabbi Salman Rivlin from Shklob (whom Maze described in his memories as "the Jewish Taras Bulba").

Rabbi David Freidman acquired his knowledge by learning from the original texts, largely ignoring interpretations and commentaries transmitted over the generations. Freed from daily worries, enveloped in the feeling that he could search for knowledge independently, he took to work on his classic book, his life's work, "*Piskei Halachot*" (Halachic Rulings, O.A.), which put aside the interpretive literature and struggled directly with Maimonides with the fresh approach of a learned person who goes his own way. The complete book had not been published when the current article was written, but the first manuscript has already brought its author a respected place in the rabbinical literature.

Later, Shmariahu Luria married his daughter to the young genius, and his second daughter married the well–known writer and Israeli pioneer, Yechiel Pines. The two brothers in law were good friends throughout their life, influencing and enriching each other's thinking. They stuck together during the excommunication that the Jerusalem rabbis declared on Pines, while Rabbi David Freidman published his manifest "*Emek Beracha*" (The Valley of Blessing, O.A.) where he severely criticized the "black rabbis" and their right to excommunicate a person (they sent out black dogs in Jerusalem with notes with the name of those excommunicated tied to them).

[Page 335]

After Shmariahu Luria's death, Rabbi David Freidman received a rabbinical position in the small town of Karlin, a suburb of Pinsk. In this quiet town, he could continue his work, and he stayed there all his life. From all corners of the world, people who studied the *Tora*, and saw him as the greatest authority of his generation, came to his small house. Among the ordinary people, he was known as

"Rabbi Dovid'l Karliner". He was called Rabbi Dovid'l because of his miniature figure, and because of his love and attraction to every Jew who came to him for advice or consolation. The biggest communities, such as Minsk and Vilnius, did all they could to bring him to be their rabbi. They had not had a Rabbi with a reputation of the genius Karliner for many years. In 1881, he finally received a formal appointment, and with great effort he agreed to leave the quiet atmosphere of the small town. Yet the big fire of Minsk broke out, and he stayed in his tranquil Karlin.

3

He was not the kind of scholar who neither knows nor cares about the wide world, one who sits in his own room learning and praying for 18 hours a day, day in and day out. He was involved with the *Hovevei Zion* movement (Lovers of Zion, O.A.), which had just started its activity. He wrote enthusiastically about the new movement in the newspaper "*Halevanon*" (in 1875), supporting it with his rabbinical authority. He had an extensive correspondence with Hirsh Kalischer, the first spokesperson of *Hibat Zion* (grandfather of Rabbi Hayut), with Elijahu Griditzer and others. He went to the Katowice Conference (1884, O.A.), where he shared the presidency with L. Pinsker. He was vivid and active, he inspired thoughts and made proposals which have not lost their relevance even today; he brought his knowledge and his fresh, learned thoughts to the young movement, which had just started to search for its form of activity. For example, he already spoke about colonizing Transjordan. He talked about an idea that only later came into being with the foundation of the Jewish colonial bank: to establish a folk–bank, a bank that would depend for a large part of its activity on small shareholders. Yet they found out that this was not possible because of the Russian law.

He was always interested in the building of *Eretz Israel*. At that time, young Pinsker was a high–school boy, and Haim Weizman was involved with the local *Hovevei Zion*, and the house of the Karliner Rabbi was the center of these noisy youngsters. Unfortunately, as time went by, the people around the Karliner rabbi started to provide him with bad and false information about the development of the movement, which estranged him from it. Yet, he did not mind the changes in *Hibat Zion*, he remained with the principles of the Katowice Conference, for which he had left his study and his books in order to enable the Jewish people to return to their homeland.

4

Beyond the scholar, the *Talmud* authority, and the Lover of Zion, Friedman-Karliner was an interesting person. From the outside, he was a small person, a childish figure; one would wonder how he stood on his legs. With this physiology, he conducted a unique life style, working 18–19 hours a day, without sleep and with little food. He was the first to wake up in the morning, right after the cockcrow, in summer and in winter; he opened the shutters, started the fire, and sat down to work, a routine he kept up for decades, throughout his long creative life. What for? To keep up his spirits! He was a heavy smoker, always holding a cigarette in his mouth; completely separated from the materialistic world, deep in thought for hours, enveloped in his cigarette smoke.

It is a wonder how a person who led such a hard life lived to the age of 87 and did not change, keeping a sharp, fresh mind until the end. All knew his beautiful, special face.

[Page 336]

His image was used to decorate children's books and the cover pages of albums, and many people saw it a hundred times without knowing who he was. This is how they built the image of *Maor Hagola*, a photograph made by an artist, the brother of his daughter in law. It was taken from the street, through an open window, while he was sitting, deep in thought, eyes wide open, but seeing nothing of the world.

5

The hardships during the war put out the quiet fire which burnt in the big soul, dwelling in a weak, almost ghostly body. With the confusion caused by the unbelievable catastrophe, people used to come to see him as if he was a saint. People stood by his door for hours, to hear the quiet, slow words of his prayers, which, in his late life, he used to say repeatedly, in a low voice, word after word, constantly holding the book of prayers in his hand. The sound of his prayers brought comfort to the listeners. From the far end of Russia, thousands of poor soldiers wrote to him asking for a blessing before they went to the front. Whoever had some trouble travelled to Karlin, seeking the blessing of the man considered sacred. He did not like it. It often unnerved him. His modest, *mithnaged* (the opponents to the *Hasidic* movement, O.A.) nature did not allow him to be admired like a *Hasidic* rabbi. Yet, he felt the pain of the people calling on him, never said a harsh word, and gave everyone his sincere, quiet blessing.

(A chapter from the book written by Dr. Shmuel Elyashiv, the former Israeli ambassador to Russia, the grandson of Rabbi Dovid'l Karliner — his son's son.

Taken from "The Jewish Newspaper of Africa", July 6th, 1956.)

Bialer Yichus (pedigree, O.A.)

by Pavel Gold

Translated by Ofra Anson

Edited by Yocheved Klausner

At the turn of the last century, there was a well–known Jewish banker from Siedlice, "Temerl the richest person in Poland. Temerl was an energetic and very orthodox woman, but God punished her – she had no son to say "*Kadish*" after her, just daughters. She decided to buy herself sons, the best scholars. The first son–in–law was the greatest Polish genius, Itche Meir, known later as the first Rabbi of Gur. Temerl's second daughter married the already well–known Rabbi from Kotsk (she was his second wife). From Biala, Temerl choose two sons–in–law – Rabbi Herzl Cohen and Rabbi Itzik Tcherno (black).

1. "The *Hoseh*" (The Prophet)

During the life of the two great scholars, Rabbi Herzl Cohen and Rabbi Itzik Shahor (black), Rabbi Herzl, known as the prophet, was the better off, both in Tora and in wealth. Why was he called the prophet? There are two suggestions: first, because he used to visit the *Hoseh* from Lublin; the second and more accepted reason was that a well–known Polish Jew, whom Rabbi Herzl used to visit, became very ill. Rabbi Herzl and a group of students were studying Mishnah. Suddenly Rabbi Herzl stood up, closed his book, banged the table and said: "I will get my carriage ready, I am going to a funeral". Later it turned out that the sick person had passed away exactly at that moment.

After both Rabbi Herzl and Rabbi Izik had passed away, more of the wealth stayed with the first family, while scholarship remained more in the second. Both families were of the highest social status in Biala. With their family relationships they enjoyed the highest social position in Poland.

[Page 337]

2. Rabbi Noah (The Giant of Biala)

When I met Rabbi Noah, he was more than 60 years old: a small person, with a short, white beard, stuttering a little. On the rare occasions he was in the street, he was running from his home on Janover Street to the Gur synagogue on Potchtava Street, or back. Except for New Year and the Day of Atonement, he prayed alone. To the Gur synagogue he came every few weeks, either to read the Tora or for a Yahrzeit. He constantly studied the Tora in his own home, with several chosen students who were attracted by his knowledge. He did not get involved in the daily affairs of the community, but when an extraordinary issue arose, he was one of "the seven elders" called to a meeting with the Rabbi to find a solution.

In the *Hasidic* world, his influence went beyond Biala to Poland at large. When Rabbi Mendele of Kotsk died, Rabbi Noah was a young man and said: I am going to Gur – and took with him a large group of students, not just from Biala, but from all over Poland. After the funeral of "*Sfat Emeth*" (Language of Truth, a book by Rabbi Yehuda Arie Leib Alter, the Gerer Rebbe, O.A.), he approached the Rebbe's son (who was also Rabbi Noah's son in law), who inherited the position, and said: congratulations Rabbi.

About Rabbi Noah's sharp mind, his fellow Hassids used to say – do not talk about it, the devil should not hear … The first night of New Year, and after the Day of Atonement, he used to stand up in the synagogue, in a place that made him visible to all. He reached out his hand and, with a smile, answered everyone that said to him, "Happy New Year", or "May you be signed and sealed in the book of life", with "To you too".

When Rabbi Noah died, during the Ten Days of Repentance of 1909, all businesses and workshops in Biala closed. Hundreds of rabbis came to the funeral, which was the largest seen in Biala.

Some anecdotes were told about Rabbi Noah, which shed light on the way people saw this uncrowned Rebbe. A Jewish wood cutter sawed some wood for him. When he was done and had to be paid, Rabbi Noah was busy with teaching. The wood cutter was impatient, and when he heard that the Hassidim did not listen but talked to each other, he said: hear Noah, I am worse off than you, because I came to you to cut wood…

Salman, whose nickname was "the presser", was a supervisor in a yeshiva for young children and known for his mischief. He once came out to the street with a long pipe. The youngsters laughed and called out: Salmanke, where did you get this pipe? He answered: – – I forcefully took it from the yard of a small, dirty shoemaker. They all shouted at once: Oh, Salmanke, you are in trouble! You will not live through the year. It is Rabbi Noah's pipe. Salman quickly returned the pipe.

One Friday night, the silver candlesticks were stolen from Rabbi Noah's home. On Monday morning, the candlesticks were laid by his door step. Rabbi Noah's home caught fire several times, but the fire immediately went out. Soon after his death, the house burnt down completely. Orthodox people took it as a sign that God's spirit lived in the house in which Rabbi Noah studied. He was a small person in body, but a giant in the Tora.

3. Rabbi Moshe Cohen

Rabbi Moshe Cohen was a rich dealer in wooden boards. He lived like the aristocracy, in a big beautiful house (on the corner of Grutke Lane and Kotchteln; it burnt down about 1911), with a closed porch, and windows made of glass. During *Succoth* the porch served as a *Sukkah*. Rabbi Moshe Cohen was the head of the community, and showed a sincere concern for the town. He initiated important institutions such as *Linat Tsedek* (helping the sick, especially staying with them at night), *Lehem Oni* (food donations), etc. When somebody complained about the amount of tax demanded, Rabbi Moshe Cohen used to free him from paying, but did not invite him to meetings anymore, and forbade him from being called to read the Tora.

[Page 338]

He was a well established Gur Hassid. His sons and his son in law, Herzl Halbershtat, were the only ones in the Gur synagogue who were allowed to wear pressed collars and carry little bottles of spirit, while others were not. Even his youngest son (who later became a famous surgeon in Warsaw), went to the Biala's High School after his uncle's death, and used to come to the synagogue from time to time with cut *payot*, and nobody said anything.

He was not the richest person in town, but in his will he left a few thousand Rubles for building a Jewish hospital in Biala.

4. Rabbi Moshe Moses (The Great)

Many years ago there was a food store on Mezhyrichi Street (Rabbins Street), run by a respected woman by the name of Lhotse Moses. She had a son, known in Biala for his learning. Rabbi Noah took him as his first son–in–law. He was called Moshe Lhotse's or Moshe The Great. The nickname "The Great" he earned rightly by both his learning and his size.

Tall and wide, a big head, with a long, thick, brown beard and *payot*, never touched by scissors, he had a light, clear face, with two big, blue eyes, which got lost in his big thick eyebrows. Till this day I am convinced that he who never saw Moshe's face, never saw a true Rabbinic face in real life or in a picture.

Moshe the Great used to learn in his own home, with a limited number of other men – the men who were afflicted by the craze of studying during lunch time, which, for them, was a sign of advanced learning. In the Gur synagogue he enjoyed a lot of respect. People waited for him to start the prayers even when Noah was still alive. On Simchat Tora and Purim the celebrations were sponsored by him. In Biala he was considered the ambassador of the Gur court (his youngest brother in law was the Ger Rabbi) and the business ambassador of the famous Gur lottery, of which he was the chief agent.

5. Rabbi Moshe Shahor (the Little)

Little Moshe was the son of Rabbi Noah and the son–in–law of Shaulke Cohen. Like his older brother–in–law, he was considered a great scholar, with a sharp mind and thorough knowledge. In Biala he was known for his orthodoxy and never looked at women, which brought about funny situations.

He used all his stubbornness when he was praying in front of the people. From "Shma Israel" to "God Is True" he used to read sweating, with all his might, so as not to miss or misread a word. If, towards the end, he suddenly made a mistake – he would start again from the very beginning. He always preferred to pray reading the book, even though in praying from the book one cannot go as deep into praying as doing it by heart.

After using the toilet, he would take a handful of water and pour it down his trousers, in winter as in summer.

For Passover he always got new clothes, to avoid the slightest possibility of leavened food being left over. He lived on Potchtava Street, in Rabbi Shaulke's house, close to the Ger synagogue. When he went to the synagogue during Passover, he went with his hands tucked into his sleeves, and waited until someone opened the door for him, so as not to touch the door handle.

He was a stranger to the daily, materialistic world. He spent his life praying and learning, considering himself to be one of the greatest scholars in town.

[Page 339]

6. Rabbi Shimele Kreidshtein (the "Skoreyi")

Rabbi Shimale Kredshtein was the most interesting person in the big synagogue. A great scholar, from a respected background, smart, he could lead the prayers well and blow the *shofar*. Once he was rich, as he owned army camps, and was a committed *Mitnaged* (against the *Hasidic* movement, O.A.). He was the only one in the synagogue not dressed as a *Hasid* but in the Rabbinic fashion: a satin gown, wide coronet *Tallit*, wide silk *gartl* (a belt which separates the impure lower part of the body from the spiritual upper part, O.A.), *Streimel*, and open shoes with white socks.

All his life, Rabbi Shimale Kredshtein led the morning prayers during the high holidays, and the regular prayers during the year. When the old cantor did not let a young cantor take his place (he had a permanent position), Rabbi Shimale Kredshtein led the prayers during Saturdays and holidays too, with the help of Alter Cheshler and Yosel Wetshek.

He was called "Skoreyi" – "express" because he was very quick, in walking, praying, and reading. It was difficult to follow him, particularly the simple people who prayed with him in the same synagogue. When one made a comment about it, he would answer with a smile: who told you to play around instead of learning when you were a child?

He was smart, but stubborn, and this was his dispute with Shmelke (Shmuel) Pizshitz, forgetting that although both of them were smart and stubborn, Shmelke Pizshitz was much wealthier than he was.

Rabbi Shimale was a brave man. When a Russian officer wanted to joke with him and cut one of his *Peot*, he ripped off the officer's shoulder strap.

He was called to the Czar's court once, and when he realized that the judge was drunk, he advised him to go home to sleep and delay the trial for another time.

Rabbi Velvel Moses

Translated by Ofra Anson

Edited by Yocheved Klausner

Rabbi Velvel Moses was born in Biala in 1862. His father, Idel, was a scholar and a well–known *Hasid*. He died quite young, only 36 years old. His grandfather, Alexander Siskind Moses from Biala, belonged to the Przysucha and Kotsk *Hasidic* group. He donated a lot to the needy and to various institutions. He supported the Polish revolution of 1863. Velvel Moses's mother, Letse Leah, was the daughter of Rabbi Yehuda Leib Heinsdorf from Warsaw.

Velvel studied the Tora in different *Heders*, but especially from Rabbi Zeev Nahum (the father of Rabbi Avreimele, the genius from the Przysucha court, the author of *Egley Tal* [drops of dew, O.A.]) and at a rather young age got his Rabbinical certification from the great Rabbi Chaim Soloveitchik from Brisk.

In 1878 he married Rivka, the daughter of Rabbi Reuven Israel Halevy Frankel, from the old Kotsk Hasidim, who had a farm and was known for his philanthropic work and rich library. Her mother, Golda, was the daughter of Rabbi Yehuda Leib Kushmirak, a very rich man, who, in his old age, visited *Eretz Israel* under the influence of Moshe Montefiore and Rabbi Dr. Nathan Adler from London. During his visit, he gave a large sum of money to buy the land around Jericho; when this plan did not materialize, the money was used to buy apartments for Jews in the old city of Jerusalem.

For many years, Velvel lived in "*Kest*" with his parents–in–law (a period immediately after the marriage, when the father–in–law is obliged to feed the new couple, so that the man can devote himself to learning. O.A.), he was a Gur Hasid, assembled a group of young men around him, and studied Mishnah, *Talmud*, and Kabala in his own, private Yeshiva. He authored many new interpretations in his special method of study. A small portion of it was burnt in Kalisz during the German occupation and WWI.

When the "*Kest*" was over, he became a merchant, first in Rasashitz and then in Turek. He kept learning alone and teaching others. In 1896 his wife died in Turek. A year later, he married his niece, Hana Miriam, the daughter of Rabbi Josef Mendel Herman. Some years later, he went to Kalisz, where he was involved in commerce and industry. In 1905, he was nominated as the head of the court of the Jewish community in Kalisz. He held this position for 29 years, while he also worked to teach Tora to the people.

In 1927 he visited *Eretz Israel* (some members of his family had already immigrated there), and ten years later he settled there with all his family. He did not want to go into the Rabbinate. His home became a center for Torah lovers.

[Page 340]

We should note that a man who for many years was a merchant and industrialist succeeded in convincing other merchants to start and study Tora.

Rabbi Velvel Moses died in Tel–Aviv on 1.2.1949.

(Encyclopedia of the Founders and the Builders of Israel – David Tidhar, Tel–Aviv, 1949 [Hebrew]).

The Rabbi Shmuel Tanhum Levi Rubinstein

Translated by Ofra Anson

Edited by Yocheved Klausner

He was born in Biala Podlaska in 1915. His father, Rabbi Jacob David was a Hasid and a scholar. At the age of 5, he knew the book of Isaiah by heart, and has been called the genius from Biala. In 1924–5 he studied in the *Talmud–Tora* in Bialystok.

Until the age of 15, he studied in the "*Metivta*" in Warsaw, where he had a difficult time. When his teacher, the genius, Rabbi Yehuda Meir Shapiro, opened the Yeshiva of Lublin's Scholars, Shmuel started to learn there seriously and without worries. Most of his knowledge he gained from this teacher. He immigrated to *Eretz Israel* in 1935, after the genius from Lublin died. It was a hard landing. He lived in poverty. He taught *Talmud* in different high schools in Tel Aviv, and taught Torah in the private synagogue of Jacob Gesundheit on Ben–Yehuda Street, in Tel Aviv.

When Rabbi Yechiel Rabinovitz from Tel Aviv began to publish "*Maimonides La'am*" (Maimonides for the people, O.A.), with a new interpretation that ordinary people would be able to read easily, someone suggested to him the name of Rabbi Shmuel Tanhum Rubinstein as an interpreter. "This is the man!" – said the genius Rabbi Avigdor Amiel (Tel Aviv's chief Rabbi), when Rabbi Yechiel Rabinovitz came to ask his advice. Rabbi Amiel knew Rabbi Shmuel Tanhum from the days when he established "the assembly of authors" to produce the "collected method". During this work, he became familiar with Rubinstein's thorough knowledge and his popular, simple approach to complicated matters. Then Rabbi Rubinstein began to write his interpretation of Maimonides.

When he completed the interpretation of the first part of Maimonides' "*Yad Hazaka*" (literally – Strong Hand, yet the name comes from the fact that it comprises 14 books, Yad (14) in Hebrew. O.A.), that is, "the Book of Knowledge", he brought the draft to the old genius Rabbi Iser Zalman Meltzer, one of the greatest interpreters of Maimonides, and asked for his approval. When Rabbi Meltzer saw the draft was vowelized, he asked, almost angrily: "Does his honor think that children will learn Maimonides, that he published it vowelized?" Yet, he agreed to speak to the young man and inquire into his knowledge. He asked him questions, went deeper and deeper into the *Talmud* and its meaning. Later they spoke about Maimonides and his interpreters, and when Rabbi Meltzer saw that Rabbi Rubinstein was familiar with all the aspects of Maimonides, he took the draft again and started reading it seriously.

He studied the manuscript for a long time, and then he took his pen and willingly wrote: "I hereby acknowledge the initiative of Yechiel Rabinovitz to publish the books of Maimonides, vowelized, so that children and adult merchants will find it easy to study. Also, the knowledgeable Rabbi Shmuel Tanhum Levi Rubinstein has done well in adding a necessary, short interpretation, with sources and proofs, which will help readers. I am sure the readers will enjoy his comments, which have been composed with a lot of talent". He finished by recommending all those who are interested in studies to "take this blessing into their home".

Rubinstein continued to work on Maimonides' writings, even after he became the chief rabbi of Givatayim.

After the death of Rabbi Yechiel Rabinovitz, Mosad Harav Kook took the initiative to continue the publication of the new edition of Maimonides. This institution had already published other books from "*Yad Hazaka*" with Rubinstein's interpretation. To date, the following books have been published: "The Book of Knowledge", "Love (of God)", "Women" (for which Rubinstein was awarded with "Rabbi Kook Award" from the Tel–Aviv municipality in 1958), and "Separation". "Civil Laws" was the last book of this edition of "*Yad Hazaka*".

Apart from the books mentioned above, Rabbi Rubinstein published articles about the Torah in the monthly magazine "Sinai", and papers of criticism and biographies in periodicals and newspapers.

For a few years, he taught *Talmud* in the "course for high Judaic Studies" for teachers in Tel–Aviv, under the leadership of Dr. David Levin. Nowadays he lectures in conferences on Oral Torah, organized by the "Rabbi Kook Institution" in Jerusalem.

Rabbi Shmuel Tanhum Levi Rubinstein is a popular rabbi, giving talks and lessons to the public in his region and beyond it. He is one of the few rabbis in Israel that is involved with the youth in his city, and once a month he prays in the youth Minyan established in Givatayim, mainly at his initiative, and talks with them afterwards.

(Cited from an article in "Ayin Beayin" ["Eye to Eye"], No. 51, December 19th, 1958.
This article was originally published in Hebrew.)

————

[Page 341]

Rabbi Shmuel Jacob Rubinstein

by Shmuel Tanhum HaLevi Rubinstein, Givatyim's Rabbi

Translated by Ofra Anson

Edited by Yocheved Klausner

Rabbi Shmuel Jacob Rubinstein was born approximately in 1887. His father, Rabbi Jermya Menahem, was a Hasid of Lomazy, a disciple of Biala's Rabbi, the genius Rabbi Ze'ev Nahum Bornstein, the author of *"Agudath Ezov"* (a bundle of hyssop, O.A.), the father of Rabbi Avraham from Sochaczew, the author of *"Avnei Nezer"* (the Jewels in the Crown, O.A.).

Rabbi Shmuel Jacob was considered one of the best scholars in Biala. When he was young, he studied under the genius Hasid Rabbi Noah Shahor from Biala, the father in law of the Rebbe Rabbi Avraham Mordhai from Ger, who died in Jerusalem in 1948.

With his father, Rabbi Shmuel went to the Rebbe Rabbi Zvi from Lomazy, the grandson of Rabbi Menahem Mendl from Kotsk. He stayed there to study for 26 years, a good scholar, sharp, and talented.

After the death of Rabbi Zvi from Lomazy, Rabbi Shmuel, together with his father, became the Hasidim of his son, Rabbi Avraham Pinhas Morgenstern from Siedlce. He remained faithful to him all his life. Others followed him and went to see the new Rebbe.

In 1931 (?) he went to Paris to visit his brother who settled there. He received a position in the *"Ateret Cohanim"* synagogue, also known as *"Passage Kushner* 148. In 1948 he received a position as a Rabbi in *"Agudat Hakehilot"* (the communities' association, O.A.) in Paris, on Pove Street 10, replacing the late genius Rabbi Joel Leib Halevi Herzog (the father of the late genius Rabbi Yitzhak Halevi Herzog, the chief rabbi of Israel).

Rabbi Shmuel Jacob Rubinstein was not only a scholar, but also a prominent speaker and preacher, who attracted many Parisians who came to benefit from his knowledge and wisdom. He composed a book, *"Sheerit Menahem"* (Remnants of Comfort, O.A.), three volumes of interpretation based on the great *Hasidic* commentators, ordered according to the weekly portion of the Torah read in the synagogue.

In 1960 he published his second book, *"Shemen LaNer"* (Oil for the Candle, O.A.), two volumes of articles about Jewish laws and legends, updated to the current era. This book too, shows a rich mind and a thorough knowledge of Jewish literature.

In the summer of 1948 Rabbi Rubinstein visited Israel. He gave lectures in different places, and enchanted the public with his knowledge, sharp mind, and wisdom.

Rabbi Rubinstein would love to settle in Israel and end his life there in study and work, but he finds it difficult to leave his community in Paris, in which he has invested so much, before he finds an appropriate replacement.

(The article about Rabbi Shmuel Jacob Rubinstein was published in Hebrew, as sent by the author.)

[Page 342]

Portraits

by M. Y. Feigenboin

Translated by Ofra Anson

1. Jacob Steinman

Jacob Steinmann was born to a poor family, and from early childhood had great passion for studying. Indeed, he left home and went to study in a Lithuanian *yeshiva*, something that was quite rare among Biala's youth in those days. He was away from home for many years, and when he came back he was a grown man, yet he was neither a scholar nor a rabbi, which brought a lot of grief to his parents.

He came back with a thorough knowledge of the Bible, the Talmud, and the Hebrew language. Like other *yeshiva* students, beside his Jewish studies, he learned to read Russian, which was not completely a foreign language for him. He also learned, and excelled in, mathematics. The Russian revolution in those years also influenced him.

Equipped with his wide knowledge of Judaism, new information on current affairs and Russian, he entered teaching, starting by giving lectures in private homes. At the same time, he taught the Bible to a group of young men, and some youngsters whom he guided in acquiring knowledge.

Yet, Steinmann's real passion was to open a modern *Heder*. During that time in Biala, there were several "schools", where the young boys of the *Heder* learned little reading and writing in Russian and some mathematics for one hour a day. The rest of their time they spent in the traditional *Heder*. Steinmann, however, wanted to set up a *Heder* where the young Jewish children would get all their education, both Jewish and general, in one place, with a unified pedagogical approach and supervision. *Heders* like this had been opened in a number of towns and were called *Heder Metukan* (revised *Heder*).

To open such a *Heder*, one needed permission from the Russian administration. The Rabbi, who did not want to allow such a "heretic" institution, gave permission to inform on Steinmann to the Russian police, and the permission was denied.

Steinmann was not frightened, and with the help of a group of parents, who were religious but not fanatic, and wanted a better education for their children, worked with all their resources to open a *Heder Metukan*. After several delays, the necessary permission was given to Jacob Steinmann's younger brother, Jonah Steinmann, and the new *Heder* opened.

The Bible and Hebrew were taught at a very high level in this *Heder*. It became the foundation of Hebrew education in Biala.

Characteristically, after the Rabbi gave permission to prosecute Jacob Steinmann and to inform on him to the Russian police, Rabbi Aaron Landau invited him to come and teach his daughter at home.

After Jacob Steinmann's marriage, his apartment became a meeting place for the youth, who did not realize how isolated they were.

The greatest time of his life was during WWI, when he, together with other Zionists, established the Hebrew school, "Yavneh". It was clear to everybody that the pedagogical leadership of the school should be entrusted to Jacob Steinmann. This was the happiest period in his life, which overall, was not very easy.

If a generation of young people who knew Hebrew and learned to love the language grew up in Biala, it was definitely the work of Jacob Steinmann. Even now, when any of his students, who have spread all over the world, some of them cut off from the language for years, hear the word "Yavneh", they will cite a Hebrew song learned from Jacob Steinmann.

[Page 343]

It should be remembered that one of the problems which the "Yavneh" school had to deal with was the parents of children of the same class. Some of them had never been to school, and came from homes with a variety of educational approaches. Teaching and running the school were not an easy task for Steinmann, especially as he wanted the school to be of a high level and run in good order.

No other teacher could attract the students the way he did. The discipline that students demonstrated during his lectures was the result of the respect, love, and fear they felt for him. When he pointed a finger at a standing student and ordered him to sit, everybody knew that this student had already been sentenced.

When Steinmann left the public school, he left teaching altogether. His wife opened a haberdasher, and he helped her to earn a living. He was active in the Zionist organization, taking part in reading evenings.

During Grabski's time (Poland's prime minister in 1920 and in 1923-25, O.A.), who limited Jewish life, this affected Jacob Steinmann too. At that time, his wife fell ill and died.

Her death devastated him. He was left with four children. With all the hardships he encountered, he gave his children a good education. They went to the public high school, where they were among the best students. They were also among the few children who had a Hebrew education at home.

The tragic death of his beloved younger daughter Godhe, who was active in the underground anti-Nazi organization and was caught and tortured, broke Steinmann completely. He spent his life in his room, stunned. He did not sit for long, as in Succoth 1942 he was transferred, together with almost all the Jewish population of Biala to Mezhyrichi, from where he was sent to the death camp of Treblinka.

(Moshe Rubinstein provided some of the details.)

2. Menachem Mendel Gelenberg

Gelenberg was not "a Bialer, he came from Terespol, near Brest. The years he spent in Biala, however, left a distinctive mark on its cultural life.

Before he came to Biala, people did learn some Hebrew, but with him around, learning Hebrew became a mass phenomenon. Each evening the large hall in the public school was packed with people. Although Gelenberg was not a qualified teacher, he had the ability to excite both students and their parents to learn the language.

He was a thin man of average height, a pale face that showed his poor health, and shining eyes. You could see him always walking quickly, deep in thought, with a book under his arm. He never parted from a book and sometimes he was so deep in reading that he forgot to eat.

Because of his stormy temperament, evening courses in Hebrew were not enough for him. He looked for additional activity, and, as it happened, he found it in Yiddish and not in Hebrew. This brought about conflicts with the Zionist organization. As a result, the Zionist organization denied responsibility and support for the evening courses of *Hashomer Hazair*. Gelenberg continued with the courses single-handed, without support.

The years Gelenberg stayed in Biala were a time of cultural activity, which enriched the life of the Jewish society.

[Page 344]

He was the initiator and executor of the publication *"Undzer Wort"* [Our Word, O.A.]. He aspired to make it a weekly journal, and accomplished it with the establishment of *"Podlasier Laben"* [Life in Podlaska, O.A.], which he edited. He was constantly watching out for creative activity. The weekly journal was of high quality and his article in memory of I. L. Peretz (11 years after his death), was read in the literary circles in Warsaw, who wondered about the talent brought up in the periphery.

He made a lot of effort to found a Jewish school in Biala. He had no success, mainly because he could not compete with the government's public schools, preferred by parents interested in general education. Moreover, during the period of economic hardship parents could not afford to pay the tuition fees of a private Jewish school.

Gelenberg was the first to introduce the work of I. L. Peretz to Biala. He directed the theatre group to perform Molière's show "The Miser", translated by Peretz. The performance was a success.

He spent all the money he made on books, as he liked to read. In his home you could find the whole series of *HaTkupha* [The Period, a journal for literature and philosophical thought, O.A.], in an impressive binding. Yet, he sold the series when *Habima* [the theatre, O.A.] came to Warsaw and he needed money to go to Warsaw to see the show.

Gelenberg brought the love of literature to Biala. He organized various literary activities and discussion evenings. Every Saturday he organized an open reading event, to which he invited a speaker from Warsaw. Thus, from the stage of Biala you could hear literature experts, philologists, and artists.

Despite his extensive activities, Gelenberg became bored with provincial life and went to Warsaw. In Warsaw, his talent was soon recognized and he was invited to edit the "*Kleiner Volkszeitung*" [Small Folk Newspaper, O.A.]. Anybody who knows what it means to entrust the editing of such a serious children's newspaper to the hands of a young, provincial man, will appreciate Gelenberg's intellectual level and his writing talent.

Gelenberg did not edit the children's newspaper for long. The active Jewish life in the capital drew him into the Communist organization. Understandably, not much is known about his activity there, but as a result, he was released from editing the newspaper.

Despite the secrecy of his communist activity, once I did find an item in a Warsaw newspaper:

In 1930 the Chief of staff Pilsudski went for a vacation to the Isle of Madeira. For his birthday, on 29 March, people organized to send him a greeting card by post. Gelenberg undertook the mission, and sent the card, but instead of congratulations, he sent allegations and kept a copy for himself. The police searched his room and found the copy. In those pre-war years, such a deed would have one sent for many years to jail and, indeed, Gelenberg did not escape such a sentence.
Gelenberg disappeared during WWII, and has not been heard of since.

Some details:

Gelenberg published articles in "*Volks Zeitung*" published in Warsaw [People's Newspaper, O. A.], "*Literaturbühne*" [Literature Stage, O. A.], and "*Front*". Parts of his works were published in "*Literarische Blätter*" from Warsaw [Literary Pages, O. A.], "*Jiddish auf der Warschauer Gassen*" [Yiddish on the Street of Warsaw, O. A.], an important work on Yiddish life (1930). He also published in the Warsaw journal "*Foroint*" (June 9th, 1930) [Forward, O. A.] "*Problemen und Thematik*" [Problems and Issues, O. A.]. He also translated a play in three acts by R. K. Sherif, "*The end of Wondering*", three-act play, Warsaw, 1930, 130-7 and wrote poetry in a fine style. He was lost during WWII.
(Source: the Lexicon of New Yiddish Literature, volume 2, 207/8 – sent by Jacob Cohen, New York).

[Page 345]

3. Moshe Kave

I knew Moshe Kave since my early childhood. I remember him with a long, wide, white beard, because of which he was sometimes called "the grandfather". A large, wide person, with a majestic appearance. He looked more like a rabbi than like a bookbinder. Always dressed in long clothes, with a small hat on a big, silver head and with a steady little smile on his clever face.

Rumor was that Moshe Kave became an *apikoros* when he was young. He worked at a bookbindery in Klimetzki's crystal shop, where he used to sit and work with a bare head. In those days, putting on a paper collar or wearing shoes instead of boots, was perceived as getting into bad company. Moshe Kave's behavior was terribly delinquent. They said that he returned to the right way after the sudden death of his older brother, who was a great learner.

I knew Moshe Kave as an orthodox Jew, who read a chapter of Leviticus, for example, to refresh himself on Saturday afternoon, when he got up. He was observant, but not fanatic, and tolerant of other people.

Moshe Kave had a weakness for the printed word. It was not common in those days that a simple worker would be literate, or interested in Yiddish newspapers and books. It is possible that this weakness was a result of his vocation. He was one of the first readers of a Yiddish newspaper in Biala. He was also subscribed to the "*Freund*" [Friend, O.A.], sent to him from Petersburg. It was well known that he was up-to-date in world news; he even knew that over the sea was a state named America. There is no king there, but some sort of a governor named president, and that even a shoemaker can one day become the president.

He was so eager to read that he used to cut out the chapters of serial stories and bind them together in the bookbindery where he worked. Over time, he collected quite a few books, and opened a small library.

Moshe Kave was a clever, outgoing person, and a good artisan. He was also a courageous man; he went against rabbis and rich, powerful people, and called the ordinary people to revolt against them more than once.

He was the only artisan whom the powerful people in Biala called upon to take part in different activities in order to gain public trust and participation. He was on the committee that planned the Jewish hospital, and the committee for distributing financial assistance before Passover.

Moshe Kave also liked to write. He wrote in the first newspaper printed in Biala, "*Antifanatism*", and in Gelenberg's "*Podlasier Leben*" [life in Podlaska, O.A.].

Moshe Kave was one of the organizers of the craftsmen in Biala, and was their president for many years. He was active in the community as their representative. He was also one of the first Zionists in town, and represented the organization in the municipal elections during the beginning of free Poland.

The Christians also had a lot of respect for him. He used to work for different property owners in the neighborhood, for clerks, and for organizations.

Moshe Kave was blessed with good common sense and wisdom. Once I asked, during a conversation, "why did you not send your son to study? You were always aware that children should develop, and I believe that you could afford it."

He answered me, "yes, I understood this, but I did not send them to study because there should not be too much distance between parents and children, because they may become strangers. Do you see this person?" he asked, pointing at his neighbor, a Jewish craftsman, "he scarified himself to let his son study, and you should see how this son treats his father now, he is ashamed of him. What would happen if my son Antshel was a doctor? He would have lived in Warsaw, and if I wanted to visit him I would have to ring the doorbell first; the domestic help would go to inform him that some Jew wants to see him, and I would have to wait for an answer, whether or not I can come in. On the other hand, if my Antshel becomes a merchant and lives in Warsaw, and I come to Warsaw, I can go into his home as if it was mine. We would embrace each other and kiss. My Antshel will send *his* children to study and there will not be as large a gap between him and his children as there would be between my children and me if I let them study."

[Page 346]

The name of Moshe Kave was commemorated in the town during his lifetime, with the establishment of a *Minian* after his name. As far as I know, he was the only one in town to gain such respect especially during his life. Similarly, people always called him by his full name, Moshe Kave, unlike other craftsmen, who were usually called according to their vocation: Alther the plasterer, Nachman the bookbinder.

For a long time, Moshe Kave's *Minian* prayed only on Saturday mornings. On Friday nights and the high holy days he used to pray in Tarshish, where I had the pleasure of hearing him talking and discussing politics. I remember that after WWI he once said, "Ah, what an important process is taking place in the world, it is possible that more important events will happen in the future, and I would love to live and see them."

Moshe Kave waited for the important events to happen, but, unfortunately, they were extremely tragic. The Nazi occupation came. A Hitler follower cut his beautiful, majestic beard, which survived 1920 when Polish soldiers cut Jews' beards, on the first day of the occupation.

With the loss of his beard, he lost his charm, and aged all of a sudden until it was difficult to remember the ever-young spirit and vital Moshe Kave. He hid his face in a kerchief. Instead of the Jewish small, woolen hat, he wore working clothes and complained about the hardship of the times, something he never did before.

He was alone at home, while his daughter, who used to live with him, went to Russia with her husband and children. Moshe Kave, loved by all, stayed alone in the Jewish quarter until June 10th, 1942, when he voluntarily joined the transport to the death camp, Sobibor.

4. Idel Schwartz

Idel Schwartz was not born in Biala. He came to Biala as the son in law of Rabbi Yehezkel Shahor, and later of Rabbi Shmuel Pizshitz. He was knowledgeable in both Jewish and world literature. He had a nice library, including some rare books.

Idel Schwartz was one of the few people in Biala who travelled beyond the boundaries of the town, and even beyond the Polish border. He visited Western Europe, and knew well the big Russian cities, which he often visited for business. Wherever he went, he looked for libraries with interesting books.

Each time he visited Warsaw, he went to the library of the Jewish Institute and read for hours. About one of these visits he once wrote in "*Podlasier Leben*" [Life in Podlaska, O.A.]; you could read between the lines that a well-read person wrote it.

Idel Schwartz was very active on the Jewish hospital board. He was also one of the initiators of an old-age home and other social services.

He was an aristocrat and learned man, but at the same time, a person of the people. He liked to talk to ordinary people, to tell them stories and jokes. He used to pray in the synagogue of ordinary people.

He had a well developed sense of justice. During the dispute between Shimele (Shimon) Kreidstein and Idel's father in law, Shmuel Pizshitz, Idel supported Shimele more than once. When Shimele was arrested during this dispute, it was Idel who collected the money to bail him out.

Idel Schwartz was observant, but a tolerant person, who hated the militant clergy. During the 1930s, the clergy in Biala became aggressive. He used to publish short articles in *Talmudic* Hebrew in the "*Bialer Wochenblatt*" [Biala's weekly, O.A.], arguing that aggressiveness is against the Jewish way of life. Only a few people knew that it was Idel Schwartz who wrote these articles.

All his life Idel Schwartz was one of the biggest and more established merchants in town. He dealt mainly in forests [timber, O.A.], which brought him into contact with the property owners in the area.

[Page 347]

Often, such property owners would mock a Jewish merchant or show him their supremacy, but they treated Idel Schwartz correctly.

He went bankrupt during the economic crisis of the 1930s. He became poor, but remained the same proud aristocrat he had always been, dressed in a black jacket and a black brimmed hat.

He saw the Germans occupying Biala for the second time, but he did not share the tragic end of the Jewish life in Biala: he passed away in the summer of 1941.

5. Alter Zukerman - (The Edison of Biala)

An average person, with a short, trimmed beard, dressed in a typical Jewish outfit: a long coat and a little hat. A pair of dreaming eyes, always deep in thought. He was a craftsman, but knowledgeable, who came to the workshop from learning, a rare phenomenon those days, as work was not appreciated.

For many years Alter studied Tora in the Rabbi of Biala's place, then he married and studied at his father in law's expense. During his studies, he always worked a bit with metal. When the time came to look for a livelihood, that is, at the end of the time his father in law had promised to support him, he opened a locksmith's workshop, though it was only a hobby.

Alter had an artistic sense, and he could literally revive dead metal. Behind the artistic hands was a genius brain, which did not rest for a minute, always thinking about inventions and innovations. Some of these I will describe as best I can, either from my own memory, or from what I heard at home as a young child.

Once, the iron safe of Rabbi Shaul'ke Cohen, one of the rich people of the town, was shut tight and none of the professionals could open it. After all had failed, he decided to call in Alter, who had just finished his studies and become a locksmith. Nobody believed he could do it, and Rabbi Shaul'ke sat calmly at his desk, leaving Alter to work on the safe, which had quite a few Imperials (Russian gold coins) inside it. Next to Alter stood a blacksmith, whose wife worked in Rabbi Shaul'ke's house. It did not take long before the heavy iron door gave in, and screeched open. Alter went to Rabbi Shaul'ke's office to tell him he was done. The blacksmith remained by the open safe, and helped himself to few Imperials. He later became a partner in a power plant, while Alter was just paid for his time.

Soon Alter's reputation as an expert in opening stubborn safe doors spread. Another artisan would have probably used it to charge high prices, but Alter had no drive to become rich; he did it for the art in it. This proved to be the right way.

He was often called in to open boxes in the country. In such cases, he would charge 10 rubles if he finished the work before midnight, and 25 rubles if he worked beyond midnight. Sometimes he worked for hours, and the case opened just few minutes before midnight and he got the 10 rubles. Another person would have fiddled around a little longer to make 25 rubles. Alter, however, never did, despite the urgent advice of his friends.

For a while, the post used to wash stamps and reuse them. Alter looked for ways to stop this fraud. He developed a device that made holes in the glued stamps, with no damage to the envelope of the stamp. Someone in the town sent it to Petersburg in order to register it as a patent. The machine did not reach Petersburg, and the person who was supposed to send it argued that it got lost on the way.

[Page 348]

Years later, a letter came from abroad with the holes invented by Alter.

For a long time Alter worked on a lock that only one key would open, so that even a good duplicate of that key would be useless. When the lock was finished, he gave it to a friend of his, a well-known merchant, to hang on the door of his store and said, If a thief breaks into your store, you should know that I am the thief. People said that thieves did try to break in, using all their knowledge and technology, but to no avail.

Alter was an excellent metal-engraver. Merchants used to order hooks with special signs from him to mark the logs in the forest. For the soap factory, he made a stamp with a fish, the factory symbol. The fish on the soap looked alive, so detailed were the fish scales. Years later, when the stamp broke and Alter had already died, it was taken to Warsaw to be fixed. The people in Warsaw were amazed at the talent of the artisan who made it, and could not find anybody capable of such artistic work.

During WWI, the Germans recognized his talent and helped him build a large workshop with all the machinery. Surprisingly, this scholar knew each machine, and how to operate it, although he had never seen it before. You can imagine what a good professional he was, if the particular, pedantic Germans appreciated his work. He was the only Jew allowed by the Germans to walk outdoors during the night.

Alter also did repairs, and started to study telephones a long time before the first telephone was installed in Biala. I often heard from my mother that Alter and my grandfather, who also had a weakness for technology, used to stretch a cable to the neighbor's house, and sent her home to hold a little box tied to the cable next to her ear. Alter and my grandfather would speak, and she could hear their voices in the box.

When the Germans left in 1918, they left electricity lines and turbines. No one knew how to use electric light, and the houses had no installations for electricity. Mysteriously, Alter knew about electricity and how to use it. In a short time, he taught his fellow-craftsmen, and together they started to prepare the houses in Biala for using electricity. They also electrified the synagogue.

Thanks to Alter Biala's homes were lit, but Alter himself started to deteriorate. He was always physically weak; he fell ill, and could not be cured. The brilliant brain of old Alter stopped, along with his warm heart.

6. Hershel Zak - (The Mathematician)

A *Hasid*, with a wild-grown, black beard, two long hands, which were always in the way like two sticks. Hershel Zak used to mix with "the high windows" [important decision makers, O.A.], though he did not master the Russian language very well. He used to bribe people left and right. He was a contractor, and took building jobs. In his work, he used his knowledge of mathematics, which was much appreciated by the Christians and brought him a lot of work.

He never went to school, and his knowledge of mathematics was probably a result of natural talent.

Students from the Biala gymnasium often visited Hershel Zak, who was able to solve problems they couldn't. Within a few minutes he had it clearly written out for them.

When they built the military hospital, it was trusted to the hands of Hershel Zak. The military doctor responsible for the hospital's construction, a general, heard about Hershel Zak's mathematical ability and decided to put the legend to the test.

[Page 349]

The general gave Hershel a very difficult problem to solve. It did not take long before he had it solved, even without paper and pencil, leaving the general open-mouthed. The general then said that Hershel must have a strong visual memory.

When Hershel Zak gave the general a problem, he thought and calculated, but even using paper and pencil, and failed.

Hershel used to multiply large numbers by large numbers in one row very quickly. He calculated the sum of the largest columns of numbers with one hand on the sheet of paper while grumbling under his nose.

Before WWI, several cement producers became partners. They invited Hershel Zak from Biala to Warsaw to put all the accounts in order, which he did during a few evenings. He earned a nice sum of money for that work. Rumor was that anyone else would have needed many weeks to do the accounting.

This is what our Moshe Kerner, who was a senator in the Polish senate and a former director of a big factory in Biala, said:

"I remember a man, who was always thinking, walking like his head was in the clouds. His name was Hershel Zak, a Ger Hasid.

He came to my factory once, for some business. He sat in my office and explained to me what he wanted. He had a very special intonation. I felt the urge to examine whether or not what was said about his mathematical ability was true. He asked me to give him a problem. I remembered a problem I struggled with in my first year as a student. An exercise that even students of the polytechnic did not know how to approach.

Hershel got up from his chair, went to the corner of the room, turned to the wall, and covered his face with his hands. After several minutes, he returned to his chair and gave me the right answer. I was astonished.

I met him in Warsaw a few years after WWI. He was quite poor."

7. Haim Mustovitch - (The Kobryner)

His name was Haim Mustovitch. Yet, you could walk around the whole town looking for him under this name, and no one would know whom you were talking about. However, if you asked for Kobryner, everyone, young and old, would lead you straight to the feldsher (paramedic) called "Kobryner".

As his nickname shows, he came from Kobryn. Although he lived most of his life in Biala, his dialect remained Lithuanian.

An average size man, with constant infection, leaking eyes, a bunch of hair on his chin, dressed in European clothes even though it was considered to be an *apikorosim*'s outfit; yet he was forgiven. On Saturdays and holidays he came to pray dressed in a frock coat, with top hat, wrapped in a large *tallit*, praying with the ordinary people.

He did not receive medical training in any high school. Indeed, rumor has it that he never went to any school at all. He learned medicine in a Russian hospital where he worked as an orderly, and from his rich practice.

There was no home in Biala, rich or poor, where the "Kobryner was not the home-doctor. During WWI, there was a typhoid epidemic in Biala and the "Kobryner" went from home to home to heal the sick.

[Page 350]

Rabbi Haim was a man of the people. He was committed to his work and he did not let others wait for his help; he made home visits even in the middle of the night. When he entered a home to treat a sick person, he somehow brought with him an immediate sense of relief. After examining the patient, he used to say, in his Lithuanian accent, "sha, have no fear, he is not dying yet. Give him some chicken soup, milk, and compote".

Sometimes he would stay by the sick person for a while, describing cases he had treated.

Once a little non-Jewish girl with a very swollen head was brought to him. The physicians did not know what was wrong with the child. The "Kobryner" examined her, and he diagnosed that the girl had put a pea into her nose. He took the pea out. The swelling started to go down and within a short time it was completely gone.

The "Kobryner was called to a girl who suffered from a long-standing disease. All the doctors had given up on her life. Her family members were crying, asking him to have mercy on her and save the young life. He examined her and said that only warm liquefied lard would save her. After few weeks she started to recover and was completely healed. The other doctors could not believe the miracle. Later on this girl went to America.

The "Kobryner had a very big practice, treating Jews and Christians. The farmers from the surrounding villages used to bring their sick family members, using wagons during the summer and on sleds in the winter, to "Professor Kobrinski", as they used to call him. He worked hard, but he was never nervous, and always welcomed everybody with a smile, ready to help. It was not necessary to make an appointment or take a number in his clinic. When he was at home, he was always ready to go on a home visit. Even on Saturday during the meal, between eating the fish and eating the onions, he sometimes treated a patient.

He was very popular and well respected, but he never exploited this. He never bargained, putting whatever wax was given to him in his wallet.

He was never full of himself, and never played the role of a doctor who had come to examine the patient and write a prescription. When necessary, he made the patient's bed by himself, or put a compress on him/her or whatever needed.

On Saturdays, one could find him in the company of artisans, talking politics with them. He always said, with regard to the declarations of the Polish government on the rights of the Jews, "what is the good of a written constitution, if it is not applied in real life?" He used to take walks with people and explain to them how the human body works.

He had a good sense of humor, and liked to tell jokes and anecdotes, which later were told in the town. His wife, who was quite a nervous woman, woke him at night once, and complained, "Oh, Haim, I am not feeling well. He answered, "Sleep, Rachel, sleep, who does feel good and happy these days?"

Writing prescriptions was a difficult task for him, as he never even went to elementary school. The local pharmacy, however, learned to understand his handwriting. The Kobryner however, was not a great believer in medications. Rather, he preferred to use his common sense to develop appropriate cures.

If a doctor visited a patient, the family would often call the "Kobryner later and ask his opinion on the medication the doctor had prescribed. The "Kobryner" was not insulted in these cases. Rich households often called in several doctors to treat their sick, hiding the prescriptions in order to have a few independent opinions. Then they called the "Kobryner", showed him the prescriptions, asked for his advice, and followed his decision.

The doctors in town were too full of themselves to talk with the members of the household, but the "Kobryner always explained the disease in his original way. He used to move his finger on the table, showing the human organism, and pointing at where the problem was. People said that one could see the disease on the palm of his hand!

Naturally, the "Kobryner was like a thorn in the eye for the other doctors. They started to look for ways to get rid of him. One day they started to trouble him, demanding that he take examinations and provide diplomas.

[Page 351]

In the end, he had to take the exam, which he failed. And how could he pass it? It was in Polish, a language he did not understand properly! The authorities asked him sophisticated theoretical questions instead of giving him a patient to treat. As a result of this failure, he had to stop practicing.

The "Kobryner started to have a difficult time. How could the "Kobryner" stop treating patients? Even if he agreed to it, the public could not let him stop. People did not care whether he had a diploma or not. The "Kobryner" continued to be the doctor of the community. The pharmacies learned to hide his prescriptions from the authorities. The other doctors, however, did not let go, which brought the "Kobryner" to court more than once. He was punished, but kept going from house to house to treat the sick.

This lasted until the Germans came in. On June 11th 1942, the "Kobryner was sent, with the other Jews, to the death camp at Sobibor.

8. Benjamin Konolstein

He was a giant, tall, wide, strong hands, big head, and two small eyes. In my father's workshop, someone measured his back; its width was 80cm. Summer and winter, he was dressed in a long frock and black boots. During the summer, he wore a small Jewish hat, in the winter an old cap.

Benjamin was born to a family of builders. All were heavily built, and like them, he became a builder too. There was a story about his father, Idl Tzines, that a log fell on his head at work once. He got angry and shouted to the other builders, "Hey there, why do you throw tooth-picks at me?" Once, after having a heavy lunch, Idl Tzines went to work on the scaffolding with a loaf of bread under his arm, and by the time he reached the top, the bread was all gone.

For years, Benjamin worked in Lodz and in Warsaw at a furniture workshop, and excelled in this too. Yet, his specialty was in smoothing the wood. With his sharp hammer, he made the wood so smooth, as if it was done with paper. Like many others in those days, he never attended school. Nevertheless, he could build according to a plan. When someone needed to build something, they would turn to Benjamin. When an improvisation was necessary, Benjamin could invent something.

Once he saw how porters struggled to get an iron box up some stairs. He commented that it would have been easier to take it in through the window. Indeed, when the bank had to move its big safe, the work was trusted to Benjamin's hands and the job was done without the noisy porters.

In the army camp on Artillery Street stood an old metal stable, tilted and almost falling over. The army officers asked the property owners to fix it or to build a new stable. The owners consulted Benjamin. He came with several other workers, and for a number of days they worked at the stable, laid cylinders, tied ropes, and cut pegs. When everything was ready, he sent the workers home. The next morning the stable stood upright. The columns in the corners and in the middle of the wooden walls had been straightened, and the stable stood as new, ready to be used. Other builders came around to try to understand how Benjamin managed to straighten such a ruin, but they could not find out.

Every time he finished a job, he was cheated, and he very often worked almost for free.

Sometimes he worked in the countryside, going out on Sunday early morning and coming back Friday evening.

[Page 352]

There were times when he worked with his brother, Gdalyahu, for the local Lord, Mevis. Other Jews also used to work there. They used to take with them food for the whole week, and live there. For all the other workers, their provisions lasted to Friday, but Benjamin and his brother declared on Wednesday that Friday had already arrived. They had sharp knives, and when they sliced bread, each slice was no less than 5-6 cm.

Benjamin had the hands of an artist. He could do whatever he saw. I remember that, when I was a child, he once told us how he tried to make a violin. He worked on it for a while and then, when it was almost finished, his children started jumping around and screaming, "Oh, a violin! Oh, a violin!" The noise upset Benjamin, and he gave a shout, "What? A violin?" He banged the unfinished violin on the table and broke it.

Before soles for boots were produced in Biala, Benjamin supplied soles to the shoemakers. His endless curiosity led him to take a new boot and examine it to learn how it was made.

No matter how busy and troubled by work he was, he always found the time to make his own wine for Passover. Sure, if one makes wine, one needs different tools. Benjamin made his own tub and wooden barrels. He used to go to others that made their own wine and give them a taste. He told my mother how he squeezed the raisins, demonstrated the action with his strong hands, and said with teeth grinding, "I grated the raisins like a rooster…"

Benjamin liked to talk to other craftsmen about their work and what they did. He could not stand sloppy performance at work. When asked by a fellow craftsman to show him how to make steps, which were not easily done by Biala's artisans, and only a few were ready to take on such a job, Benjamin always did. He used to remove the tiles from the floor to the workshop, lie on the floor with the ends of his garment widely spread like two bats, mark the steps, calculate and explain how it should be done.

Although Benjamin looked like a strict person, he was soft hearted and loving, with the soul of an artist which had never been realized.

He died after a short illness at the beginning of the Nazi occupation, and thus was spared the tortures of the Holocaust.

9. Jacob Virnik

Born in 1889 in Vola. As a young man, he became a carpenter, and a member of the "Bund". In 1906, he left Biala and settled in Warsaw, when he worked as a carpenter.

During WWI, he was recruited to the Russian army. He was decorated for his heroic performance in the battle by the river Bzure.

After the war, he stopped building houses and started to manage houses.

During the Bolshevik occupation, in 1920, he fought in the Polish army. There too, he acted heroically by the Vistula River, and won the highest decoration of the Polish army.

After that war, he resumed his building operation and managing houses. He became a partner to some important Polish people.

During WWII, after the German occupation of Warsaw and the exile to the ghetto, he was the head of a quarter, and did his best to ease the life of the people. On August 22nd 1942, he was sent to Treblinka. Somehow, he managed to go to the work camp and not the extermination camp. Thanks to his talent, which was obvious in each job allocated to him, the Germans respected him, and let him be the last candidate to go to the gas chambers.

[Page 353]

When they started to enlarge the gas chambers in the death camp, Jacob Virnik was assigned to this job. Because he was involved in different kinds of work, he could freely move between the camps, and frequently visited the death camp. No other person saw so many horrors as he did, and stayed alive.

The revolutionary spirit of his youth, which attracted him to the "Bund" in Biala, and was depressed later in Warsaw, woke up again in Treblinka. He was the living spirit among the Jews in the Treblinka work camp. He encouraged them to fight, and was one of the organizers of the uprising which broke out in August 1943.

During the uprising, he managed to run away and, after a few days of wandering, arrived in Warsaw, where he knew Christian members of the underground, who helped him to hide as a Christian. His appearance also helped him do so.

His fighting spirit did not let him remain idle even in the worst of times. He often looked for hiding Jews, and brought them money, which he got from the underground movement. As for himself, he was a clerk in the Warsaw municipality.

At the end of 1943, he wrote a brochure about Treblinka, which the underground distributed all over the world, and made a big impression. His brochure was the first to let the world know what really went on in Treblinka, about the huge death camp the German monsters had built in the wilds of Treblinka. It was translated into many languages.

Virnik participated in the uprising against the Germans in Warsaw in 1944. Later he continued to fight in Pruszkow, where he was freed by the Soviet army during the winter offensive action.

After the war, Jacob Virnik settled in Wroclaw, where he became a building inspector.

He went to London to visit his relatives, and spent some time in Sweden. In 1949, he made Alia to Israel.

Here I am, sitting with Jacob Virnik, who, with his big, thick mustache, looks more like a Polish farmer than a Jew, and he tells me episodes from his eventful life. He ensures me that he has a great passion to achieve one other thing in his life. He, who was one of the builders of the huge death-machine in Treblinka, who stood by the door of hell, wanted to build a model of the death chambers of Treblinka, the grave of so many Polish Jews.

And he realized his dream. A model of Treblinka was presented to the museum of Kibbutz Lohamei HaGeta'ot, which Jacob Virnik planned and built [as of 2010, the museums exhibits a revised model. O.A.].

10. Hershel Nuchovitz

He taught himself furniture carpentry from a very young age. During WWI he worked in a German carpentry in Vola. It appears that he worked with an excellent German carpenter, and learned the vocation thoroughly.

Hershel Nuchovitz was blessed with a lot of patience, and liked to be fully involved in his work. A lovely young man, who never got angry, and always had a cigarette in his mouth, even if it was not lit.

When *Purim* masked balls became fashionable in Biala, Hershel decided to have an original mask that would leave its impression in town. All winter he worked on it in the evening, keeping it secret; even those close to him and members of the household knew nothing about it. When his mother brought his dinner to his room, he never let her in, but stretched his hand through a crack in the door and took the food. When *Purim* came, Hershel and his brother went to the ball as Moses and Aaron, dressed in costumes made of different materials and fabrics. Indeed, he won the first prize.

For the next ball, Hershel made the costume of a goose. Again, he worked all the evenings of the winter, gluing feather to feather.

[Page 354]

We used to say that Hershel liked to get himself sucked into his work. Actually, he had an ambition to work out things that were outside his vocation. He wished to invent something in his life. I would like to write something related to this wish.

It was after General Nobile crashed in his failed attempt to reach the North Pole by airplane. Hershel read a lot about this expedition, and became interested in airplane building. Sometime later, he showed me many calculations, and explained to me that he had found a way to prevent airplanes from crashing in case they fall on the ground. I looked at his calculations, but did not understand much. I asked him if he learned physics, and he replied that he read a lot on airplane building. He asked me to write up his invention in Polish.

Hershel did not speak to me about it anymore. I heard that he went with Isaak Pizshitz to an engineer of the airplane factory in town. The engineer looked at the calculations, and said that Hershel might have an original idea there, but each detail had to be further developed.

Hershel took to the work. Meanwhile, however, Hitler came with his airplanes. Hershel went to east Poland, but could not escape the Germans.

From the beginning of the century, Jewish children in Biala did not go to public schools. The Heartglass family was the only one to send its children to the state's high-school at the end of the 19th century. This family was a newcomer to Biala, and was an assimilated family. At the turn of the 20th century, things changed and even children from Hassidic families started to attend public schools. Still, very few went and acquired high education. The Nazis, of course, put an end to all this.

In the next sections, I will tell about some of the people who graduated from higher education.

11. Dr. David Cohen

He was born in Biala in 1889. His father, Moses Cohen, was a devoted Ger Hassid. When his father died, David was a young boy, and left in the custody of his brother-in-law, Herzl Halberstadt. In those years, Halberstadt was already a Zionist, and wore "German" clothes. Because of these sins, he had been exiled from the Ger synagogue. Herzl Halberstadt busied himself with his young brother-in-law David, and sent him to the state high school of Biala.

A few years later, the family moved to Warsaw, leaving David behind to finish the sixth year of the gymnasium. During his studies, he was caught up by revolutionary ideas, which were common among Jewish youth as well as among Christian youth.

David finished his studies in Warsaw, and went on to medical school. During WWI, Warsaw University was evacuated to Rostov (Russia). David went with the university to Russia, where he finished medical school. After the war, he returned to Warsaw, took some additional courses, got his diploma, and started practicing.

His desire was to specialize in surgery. He wished to become an assistant to the well-known surgeon, Professor Dr. Radlinski, who practiced in the university hospital "Swienti Duch". This hospital was beyond reach of most students in Poland before WWI. Jewish students, who were subject to the *numerus clausus*, did not even dare to dream about specializing there.

[Page 355]

David Cohen had an extraordinary talent for surgery, and became Professor Radlinski's first assistant, which carried quite a high prestige in the Polish medical milieu.

In Warsaw, David married his school mate, Dr. F. Sirkin (from the famous Sirkin family), who was a Zionist activist.

David Cohen himself was a well-known Cosmo-political person, totally assimilated, with no understanding whatsoever of the Jewish problems. All the efforts of his wife and her friends to involve him in their Zionist enthusiasm were in vain. He had his own craze, medicine, to the study of which he devoted himself with all his might. Beyond his activity in the operating theatre, he was also involved in research, and he published in professional journals. Beside medicine, he also loved music.

When he took on a social activity, it also had to do with medicine. He sponsored an institute for the mentally ill, and was active in the association for medical help.

Despite assimilation and Cosmo political attitudes, David had a soft spot for his hometown, Biala. It was very difficult to visit him in the hospital "Swienti Duch", and the Polish priesthood had a strong influence on the hospital's religious approach. Nevertheless, Hershel Zak, the Ger Hassid from Biala, was a regular guest of David Cohen. Hershel Zak came to the hospital quite often, with his long coat (*Capota*), his boots, and his long, wild, knotted beard, talking to Dr. Cohen loudly in Yiddish in front of the Christian doctors. He used to bring stew (*cholent*) to the Jewish patients, some of whom came specially from Biala to be operated on by Dr. Cohen. Zak's word always helped, because Dr. Cohen respected him, remembering him as a neighbor from his childhood in Biala.

About 1934/5, Dr. David Cohen was nominated as the head surgeon in the Jewish hospital in Warsaw. The hospital had no shortage of candidates for that position, but Dr. Cohen was elected unanimously. One had to be highly qualified to be able to get such a high position in such a large hospital, where physicians such as Dr. Nathanson, Dr. Platau, Dr. A. Soloveichick, Dr. G. Levin, and Dr. Lubelski were practicing.

On top of his work in the hospital, Dr. Cohen had a private surgery clinic in Warsaw, which was well known in Warsaw and in the whole province.

Dr. Cohen continued his medical practice and scientific activity until WWII broke out. At the end of August 1939 he was mobilized to the Polish army. He stayed with his unit in Rovno until they merged with the Soviet-Russian army.

He was afraid to return to Warsaw, which was already under German occupation. He stayed in Rovno, and threw himself completely into medical work. Soon he became famous as the "great surgeon from Warsaw". The German blitz offensive of Russia caught him in Rovno. Yet, even under the German occupation, he continued his medical activity. The story goes, that the Germans took him from the operating table to his death.

His wife and daughter managed to escape the Nazis and emigrate to Israel via Italy. Dr. F. Sirkin-Cohen continued to practice medicine in Israel. Their daughter finished high school in Israel, graduated the Technion in Haifa, and works in architecture.

Dr. D. Cohen is still remembered as a distinguished surgeon. His name is carried with respect and gratitude. Some of his students are working in Israel in respected medical positions. When his assistants come across a difficult and complicated operation, they say to themselves, "Our Dr. Cohen did it 20 years ago, when medicine was not as developed as it is today."

Written according to the information provided by: His spouse Dr. F. Sirkin-Cohen Moshe Ravon, Yitzhak Shein.

[Page 356]

12. Dr. Butche Finkelstein

Born to Fishel and Tzipora, he was one of the few youngsters who attended the state gymnasium before WWI. The war interrupted his education, and after the war he was the first Jew to graduate from the state high school. He then went on to medical school at Vilnius University, where he earned his diploma.

He was a very nice young man, modest, with a good sense of humor and he loved socializing.

We knew several young men in Biala that, after finishing the gymnasium, became very snobbish, pretended not to know Yiddish, and never spoke it for fear that it would spoil their Polish accent. Butche Finkelstein was far from such a snob. He was an active member of *Hashomer Hatsair*, and was a group leader until he went to study out of town. He was friendly with everybody, and used to think of ways to develop a conversation on different subjects. He was also a teacher in the evening classes of *Hashomer Hatsair,* much liked by his students. He also improvised a lot on the melodies sung in *Hashomer*.

Despite all his activity in *Hashomer Hatsair*, he was one of the best students in his class, and still found time to be active in *Maccabi*, and to participate regularly in the dramatic club in "*Beit Haam*", where he appeared on stage more than once. He did not worry about his Polish accent, and always spoke Yiddish; lively, vivacious Yiddish with a lot of humor.

When asked, "Butche, what will you do after graduation?" he used to answer, with his special humor, "I will return to Biala and set up a business with the undertakers…"

He did, indeed, return to Biala and started practicing medicine. When he had time, he returned to social activities, this time working with the group that tried to revive *Maccabi*.

From Biala he moved to Biten (Wolyn). There, he continued to work in his profession, and built a family. As in his home-town, he became involved in social activities, and was much loved and appreciated by the community.

When WWII broke out, he was recruited into the Polish army. He fell into the hands of the Germans, and has not been heard of since.

13. Dr. Nathan Tsigelnick

His father was very religious, a *Melamed* [a teacher of young children, O.A.] somewhere in East Poland. His mother was from Biala, from the Rosentswiges, who made up her mind to ensure her son's and daughter's future at all costs.

At first, she was not pleased with her son's performance in school. His poor achievements in the preparatory course led to his being expelled from the gymnasium. Yet, this expulsion shook young Nathan, and ignited in him a strong ambition.

He sat down to study, as if he was glued to the chair. A year later, he retook the exams, and was accepted to the second year of the gymnasium. It did not take long for him to become one of the best students in his class. He studied day and night, but still found time for *Hashomer Hatsair*.

In the upper classes, when a special event devoted to the sea took place, Nathan was nominated to prepare a lecture about the sea. The Polish teacher approached him after his speech, and said, "Very good, very good, but it lacked some warmth" (meaning it was not patriotic enough).

After finishing high school, Tsigelnick chose medicine for a profession. He went to study in Vilnius, where he got his medical diploma. He must have excelled at the university, because he received many letters of recommendation from his professors, including one from Professor Rosee (Professor Rosee researched the brain of the late Marshall Pilsudski).

[Page 357]

These letters helped him to get a position in the Jewish hospital in Warsaw, a hospital to which many young Jewish doctors applied, but only a few were accepted.

The German occupation caught him in Warsaw, where he continued to work in the Jewish hospital. In Warsaw's Ghetto he worked in a responsible position in the Ghetto's Jewish hospital. He got married in the Ghetto, hoping to see better days. The German killers, however, got him, and the shine of a bright star on the medical horizon was turned off.

14. Shimon Goldsmith

He was the son of Abraham Goldsmith. He was a short man, somewhat fat, with a round face and a pair of smiling eyes. From the *Heder* [religious school, mainly for young children. O.A.] of Aaron Yehiel he went to the gymnasium, and soon developed as an outstanding student. He was one of the few Jewish students in Biala's high school that took the matriculation exams at such a young age. He did the exams very well, but failed in the end, because he spelt Pilsudski's name with a "z" instead of an "s".

That summer, his sorrow doubled with the death of his mother. Her death caused him a lot of grief. A year later, he took the exams again, and won his matriculation degree with no difficulty.

He could not enter a Polish university, and went to study in Bologna, Italy. During his studies, he took to writing in the Polish language. A serious publishing house in Warsaw published his book about Pirandello and his father. The book had very good reviews in the Polish press.

He was about to finish medical school in 1939, when the war broke out, and he was located by the Polish representative in Italy and returned home. He brought with him many manuscripts, but he never published any of them because of the war.

At first, Shimon was in Russia but quite soon he returned to Biala and went to Warsaw. There were rumors that he was on the German side of Warsaw. In the chaos of those days, he disappeared.

[Page 358]

Social Workers, Writers and Personalities

Ya'akov Kahan

by Yosef Zide, Los Angeles

Translated by Libby Raichman

About 6 years ago our fellow-townsman Ya'akov Kahan appeared at a meeting of the Biale Aid-Organisation in Los Angeles. His arrival invoked in me a feeling of great satisfaction, because he came at a time when our small group needed a person with understanding and intelligence, who would be able to assist in instilling more life into our fine group of ex-Biale residents.

We, as well as other former Biale residents, knew Ya'akov from our hometown and it occurred to us that he, Ya'akov would be the ideal person to carry on the work of the Biale fellow-townsfolk in California.

As Ya'akov had not been in Los Angeles very long, he felt a little strange, and incidentally, he was not in the best of health. Yet, he agreed to become the chairman of the organization.

For many years now, his conscience troubled him. There was so much work to be done in Jewish life, so many needs to provide for, amongst the Jews who remained alive after the greatest destruction. His activities were not only centered on local Jewish life, but also on the Jewish land of Israel - the country that became the hope of all the homeless, persecuted, and unfortunate Jews, and the country that brought honour, courage and hope to all the Jews in the entire world.

If his life had flowed normally, without the disruptions and struggles that he had to endure, Ya'akov Kahan, with his broad understanding and earnest approach to people, problems, and situations, would have occupied an important position as a social worker in local Jewish life much earlier.

But there were many setbacks in Ya'akov's path in life, starting from his childhood.

At 2½ years of age, he was an orphan. His father died and left a wife and 5 children, of whom Ya'akov was the youngest. His extensive, aristocratic, wealthy Chassidic family - (his mother was descended from the distinguished Shachor family, a niece of the great scholar Reb Nachum Shachor) – the latter provided the widow with financial assistance and assumed the role of a father, in raising the orphans.

In his childhood, Ya'akov already felt the taste of oppression, the feeling of protest and rebellion against his guardians and advisors, and those who passed their opinion, enclosed his life, and led him to accept his fate. These feelings of protest and resignation that he gathered, influenced his life to a large extent.

Even in his later years, life did not bring him much luck or joy. Illness and family problems restrained him, weakened his energies, and prevented him from taking a more active part in the activities that were so dear to him. He believed, however, that the time would come when circumstances would change, and he never gave up the idea that he would be able to fulfil his duty and his wishes for the important goals that he set for himself.

When Ya'akov settled in Los Angeles with his wife Ray, his health improved and his life normalized and it was in the Biale Aid-Organisation that he began his first period of social activity. In the realm of aid-work, with the co-operation of assistants, he proved to be a true master. He served as a fine example for other larger fellow-townsfolk organisations here in the town.

At the same time, he quietly and modestly began his work in his beloved organization, "Jewish National Labour Union", where he had been a member many years earlier. He devoted a lot of time, health, and energy to carrying out the responsible work that was entrusted to him.

It is therefore no wonder that Ya'akov earned much praise and recognition from his friends, his acquaintances and everyone who worked with him. And justifiably, the leader of the organisation, when introducing Ya'akov as the chairman of the organisation-enterprise, said: I present to you here the chairman of the evening, our member Ya'akov Kahan himself, of the "Jewish National Labour Union".

This is our Ya'akov, the pride of all the people of Biale.

[Page 359]

Aharon Beckerman

by Y. Papiernikov

Translated by Libby Raichman

He was born in Biale-Podlaska in 1897. In the years 1914 – 1918 he was dragged into forced labour in Frankfurt-on-Main (Germany). In 1918, he was drafted into the Polish army and taken into captivity to Petluria. In 1922, he returned from military service and lived in Warsaw until 1926. From 1926 he lived in Paris. He was an associate contributor to the Argentinian "Press", "New Press" (Paris), "Paris Journal" and many other publications. He published books about Dostoyevsky, Anatol Frans, B. Glozman and P. Bimka. His manuscripts included monographs about Lenin, Anri Barbis, Zola, and other autobiographies, a diary of the time of the 2nd World War, and others. He was deported on 6th March 1943.

("A Yizkor Book to the memory of the 14 Jewish Writers who were killed", Paris, 1946)

Aharon Beckerman was a fellow-worker and regular contributor to "Podlassier Life" (M.Y. Feigenbaum).

There are people who win trust with the power of great simplicity and warm popularity, draw people close to them, and make them feel comfortable from the time they first meet.

This was the kind of person that the literary critic and essayist Aharon Beckerman was.

I met him in Warsaw, in 1921/2 on Dzsikke Street, in the small bookshop of Goldfarb Publishing House. When he heard my name from Goldfarb, he turned to face me as if to an old acquaintance that he did not recognize – and with surprise asked: This is you, Papiernikov? Why are you quiet about it? Here is a 'sholem aleichem'! and – Beckerman stretched out a short, coarse hand, that suited his middle-sized frame. He had a full round face and a pair of light, good-natured eyes.

When we left Goldfarb together, I could not keep up with Beckerman, not in his walk and not in his speech. He spoke about Weissberg, who was then the frequent hero of the day, among the Jewish writers' family in Poland. Beckerman believed, like me, that Weissberg's war against the incompetent, self-crowned in the world of literature – was correct, but clumsy, and to demonstrate his solidarity, he promised Weissberg that he would work with him on his literary publications.

I never met Beckerman in Weissberg's home. He also almost never appeared at the literary society at 13 Tolmatzke Street. After a few chance meetings with him in Warsaw, I met him again at the first Jewish Cultural Congress in Paris, after a break of fifteen or sixteen years. I met with him at cultural conferences, literary social events and at gatherings of the Paris left-writers' group. Just as the first time we met in Warsaw – I also saw him in Paris again, lively, creative, full of literary plans and – with concerns about providing for his wife and children, to whom he was very devoted.

It was in 1937. Besides being a writer and a publisher, he was by trade a handbag-maker, in French a "Marokanner", a worker who ate, as one says: the bread of his sweat, who led an unassuming, quiet, pure family-life, that was cruelly cut short – with the Nazi invasion into France.

After Beckerman's death, besides the published monographs about Dostoyevsky, Anatol Frans and Boruch Glozman – there remained many unpublished writings, and amongst them – a handwritten extract from his diary, where he wrote about the first day of the Nazi occupation of France. He died in Auschwitz.

(Y. Papiernikov "Latest News", Tel-Aviv of 5th April 1957).

1. Yossel Birshtein

by Ya'akov Kahan/Yosef Zide, Los Angeles

Translated by Libby Raichman

Born in 1920 in Biale-Podlaska, 1936 in Melbourne, since 1950 in the State of Israel on kibbutz Gevat.

Tallish and longish-faced is he – Yossel Birshtein. He looks at you a little strangely, he looks at you and observes you. Therefore, he can be silent for long periods and hear, not just hear, but listen. Despite all these intellectual characteristics of his nature – he has very strong hands. Not any hands – but strong hands. Perhaps this is all because I know Birshtein as a kibbutznik – and many kibbutzniks are actually like that. That he is black-haired with deep brown eyes, is not necessary to add.

They were born in the same year, came to Australia in almost the same year – Yosel Birshtein and Yossel Bergner, the painter, my son.

[Page 360]

Both served in the Australian army during the war and settled in Israel at almost the same time. Our friendship, our acquaintance, and our attachment, came about not only for literary reasons, but also for personal and familial reasons.

Yossel Birshtein began writing songs; good songs, and even released a collection of songs. But for so long, he saw himself as inept – as a poet, until he decided, that he was in truth more prosaic than poet. And he descended from the winged poetic Pegasus and settled himself firmly on a simple labouring work-horse. He writes prose, good prose, more under the influence of American-English than ordinary European modern prose, like Yiddish and Hebrew. And in that case, the Yiddish influences are those of Bergelson, rather than anyone else. He took up the challenge of writing a kibbutz novel. And the kibbutz-novel is – in the broad sense of the word – not merely an Israeli novel, but a universal search for the integration of man and machine, town and village, one and many, Jew and non-Jew. Here recently, we heard Birshtein reading a chapter of the novel for members of the kibbutz – one could see how the people on the kibbutz exchanged glances and smiled at each other: finally, someone is writing from the depths of our souls . . . . but before he undertook this theme, the methodical Birshtein first tested his strength with good prose, short stories with Israeli landscapes and ordinary characters.

He is a family man, he has two children and an attractive wife, Margaret, who comes from German speaking Jews and only learned Yiddish from Yossel, and learned to understand modern literature well.

On the kibbutz, it is like this: to get in is not easy, the kibbutz community has to accept you. You have to work hard. There are no exceptions. Therefore, however, it is easy to leave. Overnight. Pack up the packages and away. And, as it is written in the Pentateuch: he came in by himself, he went out by himself. And no matter how much one yearns for more freedom to move around – one thinks it over three times. Yossel has been on the kibbutz for seven years already – when these words are being written. He is a shepherd of sheep. In prose, it sounds like a song, but in truth it is hard labour. The sun burns as if hell were not below, but above . . . . And the sheep want you, not only to be their friend, but that you should be a kind of very clever sheep, that walks on two feet . . . . I saw Yossel at work, he actually looked like the pictures of Jacob serving Laban to be able to marry Rachel, but the sweat poured like beans from his longish face, and the weariness was manifest from every organ in his body. Later in the evening, I saw him on the slippery floor of the milking stable, three-quarters naked, moving himself around on a small stool from one sheep to another, and the sheep – as it is when milking these animals – with their bottoms towards the face of the talented young prose writer, one who is an expert and reflects on the complicated souls of men and women, with reserved expressions on their faces . . . . Certainly, it is foolish and trite to say: but this is the way, the path of suffering of highly valued writing. This is the way of the sacrifice. If Birshtein reads these words – he will smile, but this is the truth.

2. Yitzchak Perlov

He was born in 1911 in Biale-Podlaska, in Poland, spent his youth in Brisk, later Warsaw. During the 2nd World War in Russia, later in Poland, then Germany and since 1947 in the Land of Israel. He lives in Tel-Aviv.

One fine day, Yitzchak Perlov, who came from a lovely town, not far from Warsaw, arrived at the premises of the Warsaw literary society at 13 Tolmatzke Street. He was very young, very tall, and very thin and had a lost smile. And although we were all, at that time, not old – we all said: well, we all have talent to write poems – some more than others and some less, but we are envious of you, Perlov, we envy your youth and youthful faith. Because we had by then already experienced the great literary storms, and the years after the storms always bring a little skepticism. But the whole world of faith existed in Yitzchak Perlov. If we were unable to open the gates of sustenance for him – as he did not think much about earning a living, he continued to suffer hunger. And when a possibility arose, he remained sitting in a corner of the literary society premises, overnight.

And here a relevant story should be mentioned. The extent of overnight stays in the premises of the society had begun to reach epidemic proportions. The police, who always kept an eye on the premises, began to suspect that there was a political motive behind it and issued a warning. And I, as secretary of the association, received sharp instructions that the overnight stays had to stop. So, I quietly told all the potential night lodgers that: no more!

[Page 361]

And the same to Perlov, but just then it happened to be a cold night. I went home and I left the premises empty. But my conscience was tormented. At about 3am, I telephoned the premises. Perlov answered . . . . he heard my voice and became disturbed. He was . . . . caught out. But when I heard his voice – I was happy, a sign that on that cold night he did not sleep in the streets. That moment of joy has remained with me as a ray of light throughout my life.

Very soon Perlov, the lyric poet, became the writer of lyrics for the singer, Lola Folman. It soon proved to be, that this was not only a literary-artistic match, beginning forty days before the commencement of her singing career and his, the writer of the words. This was a match proclaimed in heaven and also simply, a personal match; and they were "as one flesh" according to the verse in the book of Genesis (2:24). And they went on a concert tour throughout Poland, the slender poet, and the little singer. The lines of hunger disappeared from his face but not the dimples and the charming smile.

And years passed. The Perlovs wandered and endured the years of the third destruction in the remote regions of Russia. They bore a beautiful little boy whom they named Ben-Ami; they were in the camps in Germany and then wandered with the legendary ship "Exodus" to the Land of Israel and returned to Germany . . . . and now it is 1950 and I visit them at the sea-shore in Jaffa, in a small house in "Dzshebelya". Lola sings and Perlov is now writing fewer songs and more novels, autobiographical descriptions, and he is already popular in a few parts of the world. They are readily printing his works in America, in the "Forverts", and his books are often published. His work is presented to the public at evenings attended by large audiences.

And now it is 1954 – 1956 -- from Dzshebelya they moved to an apartment in the middle of Tel-Aviv – north. And we are both members of the committee of the Yiddish Writers' Association in Tel-Aviv. Lola sings and Yitzchak writes. He is a novelist, according to his profession. That dream of making a living has been realized, and they are not short of anything.

And he is, as always, most respectful. And here a story needs to be told. The writers' association receives Chaim Lieberman, the eternal opponent of Sholem Asch. But Perlov, after all, has admiration for both of them, and now he has a chance to speak. He holds a glass of Carmel wine in his hand and praises the grand guest and ends by saying: From you – our guest – I have learned a lot, but I have also learned from Sholem and therefore, to life (Chaim), and to peace (Sholem) – to Chaim Lieberman and Sholem Asch! A wonderful poetic pun. May it be ascribed to Perlov.

("My Lexicon", Montreal 1958)

Published works by Yitzchak Perlov: "Prunza Verde" (songs and poems), Warsaw, 1934: "Untergang" ("Decline") (songs and poems), Warsaw, 1934; "Estrade-Lieder" (three booklets) Warsaw; "Unzer Likoy Chamah" ("Our Solar Eclipse") (songs and poems), Munich, 1947; "Exodus 1947" (poems and songs), Munich, 1948; "Our Rainbow" (ballads and songs), Munich, 1948; "The People of the Exodus" (novel), Buenos Aires, 1949. Published also in English: "The people of the Exodus", Tel-Aviv, 1960; "Der Tsurik-gekummener" ("The returnee") (a novel in 2 volumes), Buenos Aires, 1952; "In Eigenem Land" ("In Our Own Land") (short stories), Buenos Aires, 1952; "Matilda Lebt" ("Matilda is Alive") (short stories), Buenos Aires, 1954; "Ahava V'nedudim" ("Love and Wandering") (stories), Tel-Aviv, 1954; "Dzshebelya" (novel), Buenos Aires, 1955; "Flora Ingber" (novel), Buenos Aires, 1959; "Myne Zibn Gute Yor" ("My Seven Good Years") (novel), Tel-Aviv, 1960.

Translations: "Dr Zhivago" by Boris Pasternak (2nd edition), Tel-Aviv, 1959.

Articles published in periodicals - in Brisk-D'lita: "Yung Peozye" "Young Poetry", "Yoni Polessye; in Warsaw:

"Shtivel Oifn Bruk" ("Boots on The Pavement"); "Zalbe-acht" ("Eight of us"); "Varshever Bletter" ("Warsaw News").

Contributor and associate in: "Podlassier Leben", Biale-Podlaska; in Warsaw – "Literarishe Bletter" ("Literary Papers"); "Unzer Hoffenung" ("Our Hope"); "Velt Shpiegel" ("World Mirror"); "Hynt" ("Today"); "Moment"; "Folks-Tseitung" ("Folk Newspaper"); "Radio" (all until the 2nd World War). In New York – "Forverts"; "Die Tzukumft" ("The Future"); "Oifkum" ("Rebirth"). In Tel-Aviv – "Letste Nyes" ("Latest News"); "Illustrierte Velt" ("Illustrated World").

Plays that were performed (in 3 acts) on the stage in Poland, in 1939: "Tsvishen Goldene Zangen" ("Between Golden Ears of Corn"); "Abi Men Zet Zich" ("As Long as One Sees Each Other"); "Men Fort Oif Gappe" ("One travels on Contraband").

Hundreds of songs, monologues, and sketches – sung, recited, and performed by the most popular stage artists.

Ya'akov Cohen

Translated by Libby Raichman

Born in Biale in 1900 to his parents Aharon and Alte. He studied in the "chedorim" – the traditional religious classes, and in the small Chassidic house of prayer; secular studies – with private teachers. During the 1st World War, he became an active member of "Mizrachi" and was socially active. He continued his studies and excelled in universal knowledge. He was familiar with Hebrew, Yiddish and world literature. During the Polish-Bolshevik war, he was mobilized and served for three years.

He returned from military service in 1922, and returned to his national and social work. He left "Mizrachi" and joined the General Zionists.

[Page 362]

He established the Revisionist and Betar organisations in Biale, and was their chairman. He participated in the Revisionist assemblies and was elected to an all-Polish council, and later secretary of the council.

He was one of the co-founders of the Biale newspaper "Podlassier Life". He published songs in "Time" and "Rebirth" (Volin) and theoretical articles in a series of Revisionist publications.

He married in 1929 and settled in Bialystok. There too, he was the chairperson of the Revisionist organization and the leader of the Galil (northern Israel) unit of Betar. With the split in the Revisionist organization he crossed to the "Jewish State", becoming the chairperson of their Bialistok organization. He founded the "Covenant of the Soldier" in Bialistok and was their chairman.

He was active in the small-business union and was the chairman of the Colonial-Food-Branch. He established the loan facility in the union and initiated the creation of the Small- Business Co-operative. He was the secretary of the Jewish Combatant Organisation, was active in the Boycott committee against Hitler's Germany, and participated in cultural campaigns.

During the 2nd World War, he participated in campaigns to assist refugees who were arriving in Bialistok.

During Soviet rule, he worked as a manager in a warehouse, was arrested and sat in jail for 3 months. He was then exiled to Russia, to a camp in the remote north. After the amnesty for Polish citizens, he was liberated from the camp and settled in Dzshambul, where he tried to organize Zionist activity.

In 1948, he returned to Bialystok. There he became the leader of the Culture and Propaganda Bureau of the provincial government, chairman of "Unity", of "Co-ordinating Committee of all Zionist Parties" of the provincial committee, and representative of the Jewish National Fund. He administered the campaign to assist those who were fighting in the land of Israel and mobilized fighters for the Israeli army. He was involved with the school (being a teacher there for some time too), with the library and with the dramatic circle. He was a correspondent for the radio and for the Yiddish Press-Agency and wrote in "The New Life".

In the same year, he travelled to Paris. There he was elected as a council member of the Organisation of General Zionists, and member of the management committee of the Biale society in France. He visited the French provinces and Belgium and gave lectures there. At the same time, he contributed to the local Jewish Press.

In 1954, he emigrated to North America, where he was a contributor to the "The Lexicon for the New Yiddish Literature".

He published the following books: "Three Years in the Polish Military", Bialystok, 1930; "In and Around Zionism" (essays and dissertations), Bialystok, 1932; "From One's Own Garden" (aphorisms and songs), Paris, 1949; "On The Paths of Jewish Existence (essays), Paris, 1950; "Labyrinths of the Mind" (aphorisms and proverbs), Paris, 1951; "Folk-spirit and Land" (essays), Paris, 1952; "To A New Life" (short stories), Paris, 1953; "Living and Thinking" (essays), New York, 1959.

He contributed to the following newspapers and journals: "Rebirth", "Time" (Volin); "Podlassier Life" (Biale); "Island" (from Bagish); in Bialystok: "The New Life"; Our Lives"; "Good Morning"; "The Voice"; in Warsaw: "Truth"; "Opinion"; "Mosti"; in Paris: "Our Word"; "Zionist Voice"; "The Way" (Mizrachi); "The Way" (Progressive); "Our Voice"; "The Voice", Bergen-Belsen; in America: "The Future"; "American"; "The Bialystok Voice"; "The New-York Weekly"; "Anew"; "Yom-tov-gazette" (South Africa); "The Zionist Voice" (Mexico) etc.

Ya'akov Falatitzky

Translated by Libby Raichman

Born in Lodz in 1912, and arrived in Biale aged 3. He studied in a cheder (religious elementary school) and later in the Yiddish Folk-school and the general Polish school, in preparation for the high school examinations. Already in his youth he displayed an inclination to write.

At the beginning of 1928, Falatitzky wandered over to his father (Gedalyahu Stollier) in Argentina. In Buenos Aires, he was active in the local Hashomer Ha'tzair and led a group in the town. During the day, he worked with his father as a carpenter, and he studied at night. He completed elementary school, went through the high school course with private tuition but did not complete it. He studied in a school of Journalism and became interested in the arts, like theater and painting, and heard about lectures at the university on these subjects.

He began to contribute to the newspaper "Morning-Newspaper" with humorous children's stories and general reporting, until the newspaper ceased publication in 1940.

[Page 363]

In 1938, Falatitzsky organized the youth organization "Dror", and became the editor of the youth journal "Youth-Vanguard" (Yiddish and Spanish). At the same time, he contributed to "Yivo" and one of his works about the youth was published in the third volume of Yivo writings (Zionist Youth Organisations in Buenos Aires).

In 1939, he was invited to Montevideo (Uruguay) as manager of the Jewish National Fund. There he established "Dror" and became its first chairman. There he published a monthly journal (16 issues), "Montevideo Voice", and contributed to the local "Folk-newspaper".

After he returned from Argentina, he took over the position of editor of the Histadrut-Newspaper, "Our Time". He later became the secretary of the office of the Jewish Agency in Latin America. He was also the secretary of the first Israeli Consulate in Buenos Aires. He wrote in various periodicals in South America – in Yiddish and Spanish.

In recent years, Falatitzky returned to active party-activity in the Poalei-Tzion Organisation, where he was a regular member of the central committee for many years. In 1951, he was elected as a delegate to the Zionist Congress in Jerusalem.

After returning from the congress, he again took over editing the party-newspaper, "New Times" (formerly "Our Time"). He was also invited to edit the periodical writings of the Latin-American Bureau of the Histadrut "Anales del Trabassa de Yisrael", in Spanish.

Falatitzky was a member of the management of the literary-union and general secretary of the Yiddish Cultural Congress. He was a regular contributor to the journal "Wood Industrial", where he published humorous stories under the pseudonym "Fala", that had a wide readership. Now he is preparing to publish a collection of the humorous stories that were printed.

Yosef Zide

Translated by Libby Raichman

Yosef Zide was born in Biale in 1899. His father, Moshe Mordechai Petelnik (a nickname meaning "maker of button-holes"), was a beadle, an assistant to the Biale Rabbi. His mother, Esther Dzshadeliches (a nickname meaning "a beggar"), was a seamstress. Between the two of them, they barely made a living.

As a young boy, Yossele was a singer with the Biale cantor Yehoshuale. He was musically gifted, and his warm, sweet alto-voice enchanted the listeners. On the festivals, the synagogue was packed with people who came to hear the cantor and marvel at Yossele's singing.

After going through the religious elementary schools with various teachers, and studying in the Chassidic study-houses, Yosef left Biale in 1919. After a year of wandering in different countries, amongst them 6 months in a camp in Holland, he arrived in New York in 1920.

In the first years, like most of our fellow-countrymen in New York, he worked in a factory making women's hats. He worked very hard and hardly made a living. In 1922, he married a Biale girl, Rikl Valetzky (the daughter of Shmuel Moshe the butcher).

In 1928, he stopped working in the factory and settled on a farm not far from New York. He and his wife both worked very hard, but they loved their work. They lived on the farm until 1945. During that time, two children were born to them – a son and a daughter. The children received a modern Jewish education.

Yosef Zide was active in the Biale association for immigrants from his town, organized the farmers, and founded a branch of the Jewish-National-Workers'-Union.

In 1945, he became a resident of Los Angeles. He also bought a farm here and worked hard to make a living. In Los Angeles, he was one of the founders of the Biale Aid-Organisation, and was secretary for many years. He was active in the Yiddish Culture-Club, was a devoted worker in the only Yiddish Middle-School, and was always surrounded by a group of intelligent, cultured folk-people.

Already in his childhood, Yosef Zide had absorbed an exceptional love for Yiddish music and for everything Yiddish for the common people. He loved the Yiddish language, Yiddish culture, was interested in Yiddish education and assisted in spreading these ideals. He was a serious reader of Yiddish literature. He was, in the true sense of the word, a Yiddish folk-intellectual.

Yosef was the type of Jew who, with his idealism and perseverance, wanted to transplant and maintain the spiritual treasures that we brought from the old country, a task that was very difficult and brought many disappointments.

[Page 364]

He was a product of a period of our Jewish life in Poland that built up movements, social and political, and brought forth personalities that nourished Jewish spiritual life in the whole world. These personalities emerged from the Jewish folk-masses, that struggled and fought for a better and brighter tomorrow.

By nature, Yosef Zide was a warm, sincere person with feelings for the Yiddish speaking common people. His greatest pleasure was to be able to help a friend. He lived the life of an honest, idealistic, hard-working, cultured person.

In the last few years, his economic situation improved significantly. He gave up the farm and was preparing to visit the State of Israel that year. His cruel death on 28th June 1959 put an end to his plans.

Great was the loss and sorrow for his wife Regina, who worked together with him through the years. She was a staunch and devoted life-companion, and with exceptional loyalty, she eased his suffering in the last months of his life. Great is also the loss and sadness for his children, family, and friends. The loss is also great for our Biale Aid-Society, that has lost one of its loyal and devoted workers, whose memory we will always carry in our hearts.

Advocate Avraham Yitzchak Gottlieb

by Zalman Gottlieb, Buenos Aires

Translated by Libby Raichman

He was born in Shedletz in 1843. At age 16, he married Pearl Rozenberg, aged 15. It appears that after the wedding they settled in Biale, because all their children were born in Biale.

Avraham Yitzchak came from a fanatically religious home. His parents would not allow him to study at school but, as he possessed exceptional talents, he studied privately and later passed his examinations. He mastered the following languages thoroughly: Hebrew, Polish, Russian, German, French, and English.

His passion for learning was so strong, that even though he was married, he went abroad to perfect the languages, leaving behind his wife and children, without even having the possibility of assuring them of some kind of maintenance. During his stay abroad, he visited Germany, France, England, and North America. After he returned from abroad, he became an advocate. He never took on a case of a Jew against another Jew, and it was out of the question that he would consider a case of a Christian against a Jew.

Before a court hearing, Avraham Yitzchak would appear in special clothes, according to the ordinance of the czarist regime, at that time. On Friday at noon, he would remove his Gentile vestments (that is what he called them), put on his Jewish clothes, and began to prepare to welcome the Sabbath. It is understandable that after noon on a Friday he would no longer receive any clients.

As a religious Jew and a Gerrer Chassid, he was one of the first to arrive in the Gerrer small Chassidic house of prayer on a Friday evening. On the Sabbath and festivals, he would sit engrossed in Jewish books.

In 1915, during the 1st World War, when the Germans occupied Biale, he was appointed as a civil judge. In 1916, he became ill and died.

(Reported by his grandson Zalman Gottlieb – Buenos Aires)

Fyvel Friedman

by F. Gold

Translated by Libby Raichman

He was one of the first Bundists in Biale (an older brother of Miriam, a noted Bundist in Biale). Because of the persecutions by the Tsarist government, he left Biale, with the idea of emigrating to America. However, due to lack of money, he remained stuck in Denmark.

He became a painter in Copenhagen and an active member of the local Danish Social-Democratic party. In time, he became the largest painting contractor. When the Social-Democrats were managing the administration of the town in Copenhagen, he became the painter of all the town's houses, and later the government buildings, and the royal homes and castles.

He generously supported all the Bundist institutions in Poland, particularly the "Central Yiddish School Organisation" and the "Folk-Newspaper".

Characteristically, the "Morning-Freedom" in North America, in one of its assaults on the "Bund" in Poland, mentioned Fyvel Friedman, the "Bundist-Capitalist and frequent visitor to the Danish royal court".

After the 2nd World War, we did not manage to find any information about his fate.

[Page 365]

Bernard Lieberman

by Arthur Lederman

Translated by Libby Raichman

A son of Chavah Dinnes. Tall, slim, and charming. He studied at the Biale High School, interrupted his studies, and went to Warsaw, where he learned the trade of a dental technician.

In the 1920s Bernard Lieberman went to Paris and it was told that he suffered great distress there. Then suddenly the news reached Biale that Lieberman had become very wealthy in Paris. He took his whole family over to France and settled them there.

Former Biale residents living in France used to write home about Lieberman's wealth. He bought the most beautiful palaces and parlours, and the most expensive furniture and carpets. In his palaces, his guests would be served by servants and valets, dressed in tailcoats, and wearing white gloves. He used the best textile-brands, had his own theatre box at the opera, bought tens of houses in the capitals of Europe and villas at the sea front (in Warsaw, he bought the large house at 17, Foksal street).

Bernard was not satisfied just to be a millionaire as his bubbly temperament demanded creative activities. He became the president of many industrial and finance ventures. For his merit as a philanthropist, he was crowned by the French government with the title: "Officer of the Legion of Honour".

Without considering his career as a millionaire, Bernard Lieberman remained an ordinary folk-person. In the circles of Parisian high society that he frequented, he did not conceal his Jewishness, and often emphasized his Jewish persona; a Yiddish folksong or a good Yiddish joke always found a good listener. He gladly mentioned his childhood, when life was difficult for him. Bernard Lieberman responded positively to all who turned to him for help, and those who learned about him from his birth-town, Biale.

When the Germans occupied Paris, during the 2nd World War, they shot Bernard Lieberman.

(Adapted from an article by Arthur Lederman I "Podlassier Life", number 50 of 22.12. 1933).

Dr. Yehuda Leib Davidson

by Yosef Babitsh Prozshani

Translated by Libby Raichman

We suffered a great loss in these days. From the town of Biale, in the region of Shedletz the sad news was received that on the Sabbath, the 24th day of Tishrei that passed, the noted Hebrew writer, Dr. Yehuda Leib Davidson, died suddenly of heart failure, aged 56. Here I would like to mark his presence, and relate a little of his obituary that appeared after his death in "HaZman".

The deceased was one of those outstanding people of the elite, of whom there are so few amongst us now. He excelled as a man who, to a great extent, embodied both general enlightenment and the Hebrew language. He read and learned much of our Hebrew literature, the old and the new, and also wrote Hebrew in a beautiful style, polished and precise. The deceased was a very enthusiastic Jew, warm-hearted, with a strong emotional attachment to his people and his traditions; these attributes were revealed, not by his various theories, but from the depths of his heart and his soul. He was nationalistic and Zionistic, in the full sense of these words. Central to his ideals was the revival of our nation in the land of his ancestors, and the development and building of spiritual and historical beliefs. These were his wishes in his short life, and to these ideals, he also dedicated his literary talents.

Dr. Yehuda Leib Davidson was born in 5617 (corresponding to 1857), in the small town of Kapolya, in the province of Minsk, from which there emanated wise men and famous writers, born to honourable parents, from distinguished families amongst the people of

Israel. His father, Reb Aharon, was a great expert in Torah, as well as an enlightened man and an interpreter of the Hebrew language. He was given the title of an enlightened teacher, one of a kind, at that time, who knew the grammar and the Bible with interpretations from "Ha'Biur" ("The Explanation" - Moses Mendelssohn's translation of the Pentateuch into German) – something that caused resentment amongst all the scholars in Kapolyah. Influenced by this enlightened teacher and master of the Bible, the boy became a teacher who was master of the Gemarah, and succeeded greatly in his studies and very soon became known in the town as a "genius". When he turned 12 years of age, he left the town of his birth and travelled to the Yeshivah in Mir. He studied in this Yeshiva for 2 years and then his uncle, the Rabbi, the Gaon, Rabbi Yitzchak Yechiel Davidson, may his memory be blessed, the head of the Rabbinical court in the town of Karelitz, brought him to study Torah with him. This Rabbi, who was an expert in the world as it exists, and removed from fanaticism, found personal fulfillment in the poetic phrases and the poems of the young man and encouraged him to continue to improve his knowledge of the Hebrew language.

After the death of his uncle, the young man came to the city of Minsk, where he had wealthy relatives, and he entered the Yeshivah Gedolah there. At the age of 19, while living in this city, the desire arose in him to learn the Russian language, that was foreign to him. There he found a Hebrew teacher who began to teach him the Russian language for one hour a day, free of charge. He also acquired a little knowledge in accounting and the German language, but he did not abandon his study of the Talmud, and the Hebrew language and its literature. But when this learning became known to his relatives, they were angry with him and drove him out of their house, in a manner that left him without food and a place to live, in that big city. But, with the help of the teacher that is mentioned here, in this bad time, he succeeded in obtaining a few lessons teaching Hebrew language and Talmud and in this way, he managed to exist on a meagre diet.

[Page 366]

At that time, Davidson wrote an important article called, "Taking Preventative Steps Against Adversity", that was printed in a series of 4 parts in the newspaper "The Voice", of Rakdinson. This article stated the necessity to establish a high school for Jewish knowledge in Russia, according to the example of the study houses in Berlin and Breslau. It attracted the attention of the readers and writers, and amongst them also the deceased M.L. Lillinblum, who extolled his virtues. After this article, he wrote a few others about working the land and the development of industry amongst the Jews of Russia.

In 1882, the young Davidson came to Warsaw; there he applied to the editor of "HaTsfirah" (Chaim Zelig Slonimsky), to see if he could help him a little. Slonimsky received him warmly but could not assure him of anything. With great effort, he managed to secure a few lessons, that earned him 10 rubles a month. Then he rented a small room in an attic below the roof, and began to prepare himself with great diligence for the high school curriculum. Over a period of two and a half years, he managed to acquire all the information and knowledge that was required for the high school, to enable him to receive a matriculation certificate. This matter was, at that time, miraculous, in the eyes of the teachers in the high school. His achievement was announced in the Polish newspapers, "Koriyor Varshavsky and "Koriyor Porangi". That year he entered the faculty of medicine at the university.

During his time at the university, he earned a living from different sources: a little from teaching, a little from an allowance from the university, and a little from various literary works. Regarding the latter, it would not be superfluous to relate this fact now: he placed an advertisement in the weekly Hebrew-Polish newspaper, "Izrailitta", that a student of the university who knows Hebrew literature, seeks work as a teacher. The noted Polish writer Klimins Yonusha answered the advertisement and suggested that Davidson teach him to read books in the Jewish language, so that he would be able to read for himself what was written in these books, and for these lessons, he would pay him one ruble per hour. Davidson accepted his offer and began to teach him to read Jewish literature. After two weeks passed, Klimins realised that the exercise was futile, that he was wasting his time and his money because it was too difficult for him, and that he would never achieve his goals. Klimins ceased to learn, and instead suggested that Davidson should translate for him a few of the works of the exceptional writers in Jewish literature into a free translation of the Russian language, and that he personally would translate the Russian translation into Polish. For this purpose, Davidson chose the works of Abramovicz, "The mare" and "The Travels of Benjamin the Third", and translated them into Russian, and Klimins Yonusha translated them into Polish. The translations of these books sold in the thousands, which did not please the anti-semites in Warsaw, and they abused and cursed Yonusha because he did this.

In 1890, he graduated from the university and was awarded a degree as a doctor in the field of medicine. After he completed his university studies, he secured a position as a doctor in the small town of Kletsk in the region of Minsk. In 1898, after living there for 7 years, he moved to the town of Prozshani in the Grodno region. Then he married the daughter of the noted Zionist, Mr. Eliezer HaCohen Kaplan from Skapin. After 2 years, they moved again to the town of Biale, where his life was cut short while he was still in the prime of life.

Dr. Yehuda Leib Davidson wrote articles of great value regarding world Jewry, in "HaMelitz", "HaTsefirah", "Pardes", "HaEshkol", "HaShaluach" and others. Besides these, he left hand-written documents; among them were books deserving of being published. The deceased left behind him a young wife, and an only son aged 13.

The people of the town of Biale recognized the worth of the deceased and gave him a proper final honour. They eulogized him in accordance with Jewish law, and gave him a special burial place. May he rest in peace.

("HaZman", Vilna 1912, number 225. The article mentioned above also appeared in 1912, in "HaTsefirah" number 221, with minor changes).

Fritz Kornberg

by Moshe Ravon

Translated by Libby Raichman

Sunday 15th Av 1916 was an ordinary summer's day that, incidentally, did not have any special significance for the Jewish population. For the "Yavneh" school, however, it was one of those age-old celebrations that was renewed, not of a specifically religious character, but almost as a school holiday. This holiday was celebrated for a whole day, with a school excursion to the forests around the town. The children marched happily in rows, starting with the little 6 to 7-year-old children from the preparatory classes, up to the older 14 to 15-year-old students. A joy spread over all the little faces, and from their mouths flowed the songs that they managed to learn in the few months of the school's existence. This school holiday could also be felt in the town, because a large part of the adolescent youth joined the walk with the students of "Yavneh".

After spending a summer day like this one in the forest, playing various games and engaged in other activities, they returned from the forest, via the Volye, into the town. On the return march of the school, a German soldier was walking from the town to his residence on the Volye. He came across the procession of children, led by their teachers, singing songs in a foreign language. Despite all his efforts, he could not understand a single word – so this soldier approached a teacher who was leading his class and asked: "who are these children and in what language are they singing? The answer: "Jewish children and Hebrew songs". This answer was a startling revelation for the soldier. It was as if he was wrenched from existing reality and entered into a dream-world. He turned around, and instead of going home on the Volye, he walked in his dream into the town.

[Page 367]

The children arrived back at school and were sent home. This German soldier could not rest. Questions and more questions. Some of them were very naïve, and unintentionally, made us smile. It felt though, that here stands someone close, in whom a spark had become ignited.

After talking for an hour, it transpired that the soldier was a Jew from Berlin, named Fritz Kornberg, an architect and painter. He knew so little about being Jewish that a Biale Gentile could serve him as a Rabbi . . . All his Jewish baggage consisted of perusing articles by Martin Buber.

Kornberg served as a driver in the German army and stood alone on the Volye. He fulfilled his military duties during the week and was free on a Sunday.

On the first Sunday, after the first meeting, Kornberg appeared at the school. He began to take more of an interest in the details of the learning program, the teachers, organization etc. And soon he suggested working together, understandably in secret, because the military authorities must not know that he maintained close contact with the civilian population. In the school's learning program, two hours were set aside each week for every class to have drawing lessons. The teacher was Yeshayahu Idl Lemberger. According to Kornberg's suggestion, he would take over a part of this education on a Sunday. In his lectures Lemberger would be present, to provide the necessary pedagogic theory, that he did not have. The rest of the days, Lemberger would continue the lectures on his own.

In this way Kornberg entered our circle and worked together with everyone. In "Yavneh" school, he participated in all pedagogic and other consultations and meetings, and in the same way, also in all other areas of Zionist activity in the town.

However, he not only contributed, he also gathered all the information that was necessary for him to become more Jewish. Firstly, he started learning Hebrew. His teacher was Ya'akov Shteinman. One must confess that this was very, very difficult for him. There were many Hebrew sounds that he could not memorize, under any circumstances. Until the end, he used to pronounce a "yud" as a "zsh". For example, he would say "zsheled" instead of "yeled"; a typical indication that he was a foreigner. In the beginning, before he began to learn Hebrew, he tested every written letter separately to see how many hand movements were needed for each letter, compared to the same letter in Latin script. This demonstrated to him the practicality of writing the script from "right" to "left" . . .

Kornberg began to visit Zionist homes and in this way, he penetrated a Jewish environment, and saw Jewish daily life from both a national and religious perspective. He became a family friend in these houses, at family celebrations, and other occasions. He sat down amongst everyone, and with his eyes, mouth, and ears, he absorbed every phenomenon and every custom. He asked about everything and requested explanations; so much so that – how was it not possible to recognise Kornberg as one of us?

He took an interest in the economic life of the Jews. Unfortunately, during the First World War, the economic situation was in ruins and unstable, so that it was difficult for him to learn about it. The existence of Jewish tradesmen was a great revelation for him. In the beginning, when he was told about it, he simply did not want to believe it. In his free time, he would be accompanied and shown live people in the workshops, Jews with beards, with various work-tools in their hands. He was beside himself, and could not believe what he saw. His sketch pad, from which he was never parted, was filled with drawings of different types of people in workshops with work-tools in their hands.

As mentioned, Kornberg used to participate in all Zionist activities. It is superfluous to work out how, and when, just as it is improper for us to speak about ourselves.

It would not be unreasonable to tell a little episode, that reflects a character trait of Kornberg.

It was a Channukah evening at the end of 1916, in the "Yavneh" school. This evening was not only a celebration for the students but also for the parents, friends, and mainly for all the Zionists in the town. As a special guest, Dr. Shvabbe, a German military man, a Zionist, also from Berlin who served in the German police administration, was also invited. The acquaintance with Dr. Shvabbe came about when arranging a Zionist matter with the police. Since then contact with him was maintained, but in a more cautious way than with Kornberg.

Dr. Shvabbe and Kornberg were two different characters. The former: head, organizational talent, Zionist experience from his activities amongst the Zionist academic youth in Berlin. The latter: heart and soul, and in the realm of Zionist activity, he began to take his first steps with us.

[Page 368]

At the Channukah evening, I found the opportunity to formerly introduce the two Berlin Jews, and left them to talk to each other. But the discussion did not last long. After a short time, Kornberg was standing next to me. I felt that a cordial relationship was not established. What happened? -- Dr. Shvabbe asked Kornberg: "are you an academic?" – "No, architect" -- was the answer.

If I am not mistaken, Kornberg was in Biale until around 1917. With the advance of the German army into Russia, Kornberg's automobile-division went to Kharkov. There Kornberg immediately found his way to the "Zionist Youth" and assisted them greatly in connecting with groups abroad.

When I came to Israel, at the end of 1925, I got to know that Kornberg was in Jerusalem. As an architect, he was supervisor of the construction of the university buildings on Mount Scopus. Understandably, I immediately visited him in his house, in the suburb of "Talpiyot" (Jerusalem). The house was built according to Kornberg's special, artistic style. In the house, on the walls, amongst other drawings, I found a part of Biale, and also a few drawings of female students of "Yavneh" school (Mirtshe Blankleider with a violin, Itke Rubinshtein and others).

In the events of 1929, the house, that was the last in the suburb, was burnt down by Arab aggressors. With that, all the memoirs of Biale that Kornberg had, in the form of artistic drawings, were burnt too. It took a few years before Kornberg managed to renovate and bring his house to life again. Unfortunately, he was not destined to remain there for long. When he was working around the house, in the garden that he tended with so much love, he died of a heart attack.

[Page 369]

Women Characters

Translated by Ofra Anson

Edited by Libby Raichman

In presenting a few portraits of women in the years before the genocide, particularly from the earlier period, this is not to say that this exhausts everything that can certainly be said about Biale women who were active in the political and social life in the town. If we relate here information about Gadye Shteinman and Chavale Rodzinnek, we are mentioning only two young heroic women, but there was no shortage of women of the younger generation in the town, who languished in jail for years for their political convictions; women who left their warm homes, went off as pioneers to the Land of Israel, and lived a difficult and heroic life to build the country. There were, of course, a significant number of women in the town that were active in providing social support for the needy classes.

We have only limited information on this topic; unfortunately, we did not manage to obtain sufficient material to increase the number of women's profiles.

Tille Berlin

by Yitzchak Shein, Tel Aviv

Translated by Ofra Anson

Edited by Libby Raichman

In the most beautiful part of the town, in the middle of the market, on the wide sidewalk, stood a big house. The courtyard was built up on all sides, with a thoroughfare into Zakashtshelne Street, across the road from the Catholic church. The entrance from the market side, was through a wide, carved gate, with a wooden floor. The walls were paneled with wood.

Ostrovsky's pharmacy was on the ground floor, and his apartment on the first floor had 6 –7 rooms and a balcony opposite the market orchard.

In the town the house was called the 'communal house'. Not many knew how the name originated, or that the house once belonged to Tille Berlin.

Tille was the daughter of Reb Yitzchak Isaac Shocher, a wealthy landowner. She was married to Shmuel Falik (I do not remember his surname), a big, wealthy timber merchant who traded with Germany. One spring, when he dispatched a huge transport of timber on the Vistula River to Danzig, a catastrophe occurred. The stormy waves of the river tore the wooden rafts apart and the entire timber transport went into the sea and tens of boatmen drowned.

Besides the loss of money, he still had a lawsuit against him, and he had to pay large sums to compensate the families of the boatmen. He became an impoverished man. The disastrous situation affected him so severely that after a short time he died of a heart attack.

Tille, the surviving childless widow, did not panic and took over her husband's business. She set herself the goal of paying all the debts that she inherited. She began to buy timber herself, transporting it again by water.

At that time, in the 1880s, nearly all the forests around Biale and also the Biale estate belonged to Duke Hohenlohe. When the Russians issued a decree forbidding foreign citizens from owning large estates, the Duke began to liquidate and sell off his fortune.

Tille was one of the largest buyers of the Duke's forests, and the transactions amounted to hundreds of thousands of Rubles. The Duke himself was a frequent visitor in Tille's house. It is understandable that from such huge transactions she became very wealthy. She truly lived a royal life, with her own coaches and coachmen, yet, she kept a kosher home and wore a wig.

A few years later, she married a second time, to the Rabbi, the Gaon (genius), Reb Chaim Berlin, the eldest son of Reb Naftali Tzvi Yehuda [his initials] (NTZY"B), head of the Yeshiva of Volozshin.

Reb Chaim Berlin was formerly a Rabbi in Moscow (before Rabbi MZA"H). After his marriage to Tille, he left the rabbinate and settled in Biale in a magnificent aristocratic home, and studied Torah day and night. (Many years ago, when I met Rabbi Meir Berlin (Bar–Ilan), I spoke to him about the family relationship — I thought that he was Reb Chaim's nephew – and he said to me: "we are closer than you thought – because he is my brother". In answer to my question about the age difference, he replied: "Chaimke was born when my father was 19, and I was born 40 years later, to his second wife").

[Page 370]

One Saturday afternoon, in 1892 or 1893, when Tille went for a walk with her two nieces Henye and Rochel (my mother), Tille felt unwell and died of a heart attack at the age of 50.

After "shivah" [7 days of mourning], her husband, Reb Chaim Berlin, opened the metal cash box in the presence of the heirs and counted 560 thousand Ruble in cash, besides expensive jewellery and valuable items. In those times, that was a colossal fortune. As mentioned, Tille was childless, and there and then her sisters and brothers divided her fortune amongst them, each one of them receiving their share of more than 60,000 Ruble in cash.

They also found items that people had pledged in exchange for loans for large sums, given by Tille. Every item was noted and to whom it belonged, and the heirs returned these to the owners without requesting repayment.

After receiving his inheritance, Reb Chaim left for the land of Israel, where he died in Jerusalem in Tishrei 5673 [corresponding to 1913] at a very old age.

The heirs gave away various buildings that had belonged to Tille, for benevolent purposes. The house on Potshtovve Street – for the Gerer house of prayer; shops on Yatke Street – for communal use, and the famous house at the market – for the Bikkur Cholim society that tended to the sick. The rules indicated that the income from the houses would be managed by the members of the family. This money was used to support the poor with prescriptions for medications that the pharmacist Ostrovsky used to distribute with a 50% discount. It was also used to send poor sick people to hospitals and spas. With the emergence of an elected Jewish community organization during Polish rule, everything came under its authority. During the 1930s the community provided premises in the house and at the market for the "Tarbut Library", the "Bet Ya'akov" School and the artisan organization.

I would like to add a few details about the family from which Tille Berlin is descended, a family that played an outstanding role in Jewish life in Biale.

The head of this dynasty was Reb Noach Shocher. Hs family were originally from Nis'vyezsh and Vilna. His son, Reb Yitzchak Isaac Shocher, had 9 children:

1. Reb Noach Shocher – the father–in–law of the Gerer Chassidic Rabbi, author of "Sfat Emet" ("Words of Truth") and father–in–law of the Gerer Rabbi, Avraham Mordechai Alter, who died in Jerusalem on the eve of Shavuot 5708 (1948).
2. Reb David Shocher – my grandfather.
3. Reb Saime Shocher – lived in Lublin
4. Reb Yechezkel Shocher – father–in–law of Idl Shvartz (of the same family but from a different branch).
5. Tille Berlin.
6. Maite Rozenkrantz, wife of Nachman Rozenkrantz, an antagonist [orthodox Jew opposed to Hassidism] in this family. (Their house on Yanneve Street had a common border with the Jewish hospital).
7. Zissl Mintz – mother of Motl Mintz.
8. Chanele Alter–the wife of Yossele Alter, a brother of "Sfat Emet".
9. Chayele Rubinlicht – the grandmother of Shmuel and Yakov Kahan.

The family had a fund that held a very large sum of money that was established by the Nyes'vi'ezsh and Vilna Shochers. The interest from this fund was given as support for needy relatives, between 50 and 300 Ruble, distributed through a lottery. On the recommendation of two family members the needy relative was included in the lottery. The winner of the lottery had to wait 3 years to be able to participate in the lottery again. A significant sum of money from Tille's inheritance was given to this fund.

by B. Wineberg, London

Translated by Ofra Anson

Edited by Libby Raichman

1. Rivkah Akivaches

In Yatke Street, almost at the intersection of Briske Street, was a large courtyard, on which open wagons and covered wagons always stood, that had come from the surrounding small towns and villages. This was a large gateway courtyard that was always noisy and bustling with Jews and non–Jews who came to Biale to trade or to take care of other matters.

On the outskirts of the courtyard stood a large house, that was very long and had steps leading up, to enter. The house was an inn, where the "guests" would warm themselves in the winter and drink a glass of tea, and in the summer, they would take off their heavy clothes.

The courtyard was known by the name "Rivka Akivaches's courtyard", the name of the woman who managed the business. Rivkah Akivaches was an exceptionally beautiful woman. She was tall, slender and gracious in her movements and although she was dressed as was customary at that time, a turban on her head, and cheap non–matching dresses and blouses, her gracious and charming beauty was apparent. She was a very clever woman and even Chassidim came to take advice from her.

[Page 371]

I did not know who her husband was. Since I can remember, from my earliest childhood, she had no husband, but she had daughters who were pretty and aristocratic in all their ways. Their beauty was a refined one, a heavenly one – if one can express oneself like that – and their attitude to people was most decent and courteous. Besides managing the inn, Rivkah Akivaches was engaged in making acid. The acid that she produced was not only for domestic use but also for "export" to the surrounding towns, hamlets and villages. She would also travel to Danzig and bring herring from there. She had a good income, and the children, her daughters, received a good upbringing for that time. People even mumbled that she was spoiling the girls, by allowing them to learn to read and write.

What seems to me today is that there was a secret mystery surrounding Rivkah Akivaches's house. As much as was possible in those times, she separated herself from everyone and came into little contact with the town, even though so many people came into her house. Her seclusion was not due to arrogance, from looking down on others. No, it was more a restraint, a kind of withdrawal from the general public.

I remember that every Yom Kippur eve, my father, may he rest in peace, would go to Rivkah Akivaches's house and bring a large wax candle from there that he put into a small box with sand, together with other candles that burnt from before "Kol Nidrei" [opening prayer for Yom Kippur] until after "Ne'ilah" [closing prayer]. These wax candles were designated for souls of someone in Rivkah Akivaches's family. For whom? Only Rivkah and my father knew that.

I met Rivkah Akivaches's daughter in London and I remembered these trivialities of that remarkable, almost biblical figure, Rivkah Akivaches. That was a woman who grew in my eyes like a giant, a mysterious giant, that overcomes a cruel life with firm resolute steps, for a specific purpose, with a specific goal, without taking into account what the world around says or thinks about him. This was a rare woman, a rare person, of rare character, who, I am sure, was not forgotten by those who knew her, and can still remember her.

May this portrait be a replica of the wax candles that my father, may he rest in peace, placed for her in the house of prayer. May it be a memorial candle to the great soul of this remarkable woman, Rivkah Akivaches, who was distant, and carried her pain deeply buried within her, without looking for sympathy from the masses, who were often cynical about her.

2. Pesl the "Deaf"

Pesl the "Deaf" was a woman of average height, with a very beautiful face. That was all, I think, one could say about a woman of those times, who was not permitted to show her own hair or her whole ear, and was not allowed to wear a corset … and as Pesl the "Deaf" was an observant, kosher Jewish daughter, she wore a wig and did not wear a corset, yet she appeared gracious and full of charm.

If she was really deaf, I do not know; who her husband was, I do not know either. I only know one thing: whoever spoke of Pesl the "Deaf"**Error! Bookmark not defined.**, mentioned her name with respect and with reverence. In the town, her name was a symbol of goodness, beauty and perfection.

Pesl the "Deaf" was a woman of immense, almost insatiable energy, a woman with great business instincts and talent, which at that time was a rarity, even among the men of Biale. In addition, she was very charitable, and had a broad and open hand for anyone who needed help.

At the corner of the market place (today Volnoshtshy Place) and the street that leads to the Mezritsh Highway, stood the large shop that Pesl the "Deaf" ran, with a large stock and a variety of merchandise, intended particularly for people who could afford to spend money – a shop that could be compared to the big shops in Warsaw at that time.

I do not remember a Biale Jew ever going into the shop of Pesl the "Deaf" to buy something. No, this was a shop specifically for the noblemen, Polish counts and local counts who lived on their estates around Biale. These noblemen would descend a few times a week, with their carriages that were drawn by four horses, harnessed in "tandem" in the summer, and sleighs with "Troikas" in the winter.

[Page 372]

At Pesl the "Deaf" you could procure all sorts of wines, liqueur and brandy (at that time there was still no monopoly on liquor), all spices, and in addition a variety of toys, and even cradles for children. The shop was always packed with merchandise and also with customers.

Already then, there were many military personnel in Biale. There were old barracks, new ones were built, and the town was always full of officers, colonels, and even generals. It is therefore understandable that the shop of Pesl the "Deaf" also had many buyers from among the military personnel, and even they treated her with the greatest respect. With her aristocratic bearing, she also earned the greatest respect and the deepest regard from the Polish noblemen in the vicinity, who always liked to joke – often cruel jokes – about women, mainly about Jewish women.

Pesl ran her shop in a purely businesslike manner: "I have the merchandise that you need – buy, pay and enjoy". It was not the humble spirit that we still see today in the Jewish businesses in many European towns. She was a proud merchant, an honest merchant, who sold merchandise but not her soul.

3. Esther the "Lizard"

A small shriveled little woman, with a cap on her shaved little head, in which two lively eyes were set, that looked angrily at people and at the world; a small pointed nose, that hung over a small mouth, that talked constantly, mumbled constantly, cursed or blessed.

There was an enormous metal shop on the side of the market whose wall stretched from Briske to Grabanovve Street. The shop was very long and at the other end it had a door that led out onto a large courtyard with warehouses that were always filled with various metal products. One always saw buyers in the shop, both gentiles and Jews. On a Sunday, it was impossible to pass by on the sidewalk alongside the shop, because hundreds of gentiles were pushing to get into the shop to buy something: a file, a ploughshare, a pound of nails, a mechanical transmitter….

The owner of the shop was Esther the "Lizard". She was not only the owner, but she ran the shop and was also the manager of this large business.

She was a physically weak woman, religious, and more than that, an extreme fanatic in all her prejudices. To this day, it is the greatest wonder to me, how she, with her lack of strength, could manage such a large business. It seems, however, that often a strong spirit, striving to achieve something, has the power to fill the weakest body.

Esther the "Lizard" had this striving. Her ideal was the family, and this gave her the strength to overcome her physical weakness.

Her husband, Moshe Yosl, was the opposite of his wife; a handsome Jew, with a fine pointed beard that was not too large, and a smiling face, who constantly sat at home and studied. They had a large family and a high standard of living, that in those times had high expenses. And Esther the "Lizard" had the task of providing the means for these expenses. The whole family, married sons and their children, had all their needs satisfied by the income from the shop that was run by this weak little woman, who possessed such boundless strength and energy.

Every 15th of Shvat [Tu Bishvat], Esther would distribute presents to her customers — "bags", paper bags with a variety of fruit. I remember that my father, may he rest in peace, being one of her customers, would come home every "15th" with such a bag, filled with good things. She was very charitable and gave generously to charity. There was talk in the town that she supported a few needy families. People knew about her secret donations and for that she was respected and valued, yet she was still regarded as an unpleasant person.

After her death, her children took to running the business, but it no longer functioned as it had before. With each passing day, it deteriorated, and the huge, famous metal shop became a small shop that did not provide sufficient income for those who worked there. It lacked the knowledge, the work and the spirit of the small emaciated little woman, that supported such a large family, and also fed many people outside of her family.

(The characters described by Boruch Wineberg were extracted from a number of editions of "Podlassier Life" in 1933).

[Page 373]

Godya Shteinman

by Dina Arbitman, Kibbutz Ein Hashofet

Translated by Ofra Anson

Edited by Libby Raichman

Her name was Golda – we called her Godya, as this name suited her. She had golden hair, blue eyes, a friendly laugh and a constant smile. Her great charm and her good nature brought her many friends amongst the children and also amongst the adults.

Our dear mother died when Godya was six years old. Godya was a baby who did not manage to be nourished by the love of her mother, who excelled in her wisdom and kindness. We were afraid that the sadness that prevailed in our home after the tragedy would break Godya 's spirit, so we decided to send her to relatives in the neighbouring town of Mezritsh. Godya started going to the "Tarbut" school and, although she did not know the Hebrew language, she soon caught up with the other children and was much loved by the teachers. The headmaster of the school asked her father to allow her to remain for at least one more year because, he said: "she is an example to all the children in her class".

Godya returned home and began to study at the primary school. After a few weeks she was placed in a higher class. At home, she gladdened our hearts. She did not let her father wallow in sorrow, and she was a ray of light for us all. My father, of blessed memory, my sister Reizele, my brother Shmuel, of blessed memory, were primarily concerned for her.

After Reizele left for America and Shmuel, of blessed memory, went to Warsaw to study, the two of us remained at home with our father. I saw myself not only as an older sister to Godya, but also as a mother. I felt an enormous responsibility for her destiny, I wanted to give her the mother's love that she lost at such a young age. Despite her deprived childhood, she was happy and mischievous and, thanks to her great talent, she also excelled in her studies. She stood out in primary school and later in High School. The Holocaust put an end to her studies.

Our home was a house of Hashomer Ha'tzair. Many friends found it a place of stimulus and calm. Lunches and dinners often became symposiums on literature, Bible etc. My father was like an older friend to us and guided us even in discussions in our group. He helped us to acquire knowledge in Hebrew and to read the newspapers that the movement published in Poland and in Israel. My father instilled in us a love of Israel, the pioneering movement and the Jewish people, both the good and the difficulties. Godya was a committed student and quickly understood what her role was in the Polish High School, where anti–Semitism permeated the entire environment. She proudly defended her people and did not hide her Jewish identity. At the age of 12, she joined Hashomer Ha'tzair. She was the first to participate in song and dance, and also the first to take on tasks that required effort. Her thirst for knowledge intensified her desire to read and to delve into social and sociological topics.

Once, a member of the central leadership of Hashomer Hatzair happened to come to Biale and was present at a discussion in Godya's group; when he listened to her eloquence and her serious train of thought, he requested from the movement that she be sent to a seminar. He remarked: "look after Godya, in the future she will fill a very important role in the movement", but that was not to be her fate.

Godya was modest, forthright, helped her friends who had difficulties with their studies, and also found time to be active in the movement.

When I was about to emigrate to Israel and Godya was then just 16, she was made a member of the leadership of the movement. I made Aliyah on Rosh Hashanah 1938, and Godya was about to finish High school. Because she was so young, she took special examinations and received her matriculation certificate with distinction. All my hopes and all my efforts were to bring the two of them, my father and Godya, to Israel, to my kibbutz. I made many plans for Godya's future in Israel, but the cruel war broke out and ruined all my plans. Godya remained there to fulfil her role in the movement and also to support my aging father.

Recently I found out that people advised Godya to escape and that they were prepared to help her, but she refused. Without considering the many dangers, she devoted herself to working in the underground, and was even appointed to be a member of the central leadership of the movement.

The Nazis transferred her and her father from the apartment in the main street to a tiny room in the ghetto. The room was used for important meetings and decision making, and fateful decisions were often made there. Many young people found support and refuge there. Even in 1939, during the war, I received letters from them.

Godya was continually active in the ghetto and received instructions from the central leadership in Warsaw. The end came when a train worker was caught with a letter containing instructions, addressed to her.

I did not manage to gather full details about her last moments, but I know only this: Godya, my wonderful, dear sister, still in the prime of her life, died a hero's death. Despite the cruelest torture in the Gestapo prison, and despite their promises of freedom – she remained loyal to her character until the last moment and did not reveal even one name to the enemy. Through punishment and torture, until the last moment, she gave her young soul with courage, holiness and purity.

* The article about Godya Shteinman is presented in the original Hebrew, as submitted by the writer.

Chavale Rodzinek

by M. Y. Feigenboim

Translated by Ofra Anson

Edited by Libby Raichman

She was a tall and slim girl with a pair of dreamy eyes; the daughter of Moshe Rodzinek, well–known in the town for his communal activities. The war of 1939 caught her on the threshold of her dreams:

She had completed her studies at the High School and wanted to study medicine. All the sorrow of the premature severance of her youth spilt out on her face. The most difficult experience for her was to see her father taken together with the members of the Judenrat, the Jewish Council, to Majdanek, but at the same time, this was the spur for her to actively fight against the Germans.

Chavale wrote a valuable page in the history of the struggle and fight with the German beast.

[Page 374]

Her name is mentioned in the publication of the Jewish History Institute in Warsaw. We will note here just a few episodes from Chavale's experiences in this dark period. At the time of the deportation from Biale during Succot 1942, when she and her mother were taken to Mezritsh, she decided that on no account would she allow herself to be locked up in the ghetto. She arranged with her mother that she, Chavale, would leave for Warsaw and that her mother would then follow. Chavale jumped down from the truck that was travelling in the direction of Mezritsh, was shot and lightly wounded in the foot and flung herself back on to the truck. On their approach to the Voronyetz forests where the trucks stopped, together with her mother she ran from the vehicle. After wandering in the Biale vicinity for a few weeks, her mother went to the Mezritsh ghetto and Chavale – to Warsaw.

By chance, in Warsaw she turned to a Christian man who worked at the Jewish Aid Council, who had been condemned to death by the Germans in Lodz, but managed to escape from the clutches of the Nazis. The Christian was the first person to report to London the information about the extermination camps in Poland. Chavale trusted this man with the truth, that she was Jewish, and expressed her preparedness to participate in actions against the Germans. He brought Chavale into the ranks of the underground movement as a liaison officer and distributor of illegal literature. A few days after her arrival in Warsaw, she received Aryan documents, and was provided with an apartment where illegal leaflets were printed and Aryan documents were produced. As a liaison officer, Chavale would often travel to Pyeterkov, Skarzshisk, Kyeltz, Radom and others. She used to manage to get into the ghettos and camps, where she distributed money, documents and illegal literature. She would bring Jews to Warsaw and put them in contact with appropriate persons. On one of these visits to Pyeterkov with a few other liaison officers, they were discovered by the Gestapo and, while escaping, the Gestapo opened fire and only Chavale and one other liaison officer survived.

During another visit in Lodz, together with the Christian man who brought her into the underground movement, she was detained by a member of the Gestapo. It was clear that the man, for whom there was already a warrant, would not come out alive. Chavale, however, managed to influence the Gestapo member with the promise that she would meet him the next day.

Once, just before the Warsaw uprising, Chavale and a girlfriend overheard German officials' telephone conversations, with the aid of a special device. When the colleague who was supposed to join them at a specific time did not arrive, they destroyed the device. They had barely managed to do this when the Gestapo arrived at their dwelling and took them to their headquarters in Warsaw. There they were undressed and, although nothing was found on them, and they did not confess to anything, they were flogged until their bodies were completely black and blue. They had already lost all hope of getting out of there, but with that, the murderers told them to go. They did not want to go home in such a state during the day, so they went into a church and stayed there until the night.

In Warsaw, Chavale had contact with more than a hundred Jews who were on the Aryan side and whom she used to provide with money and documents. From time to time, she also met with a few Biale residents who were on the Aryan side in Warsaw. In Autumn 1944, when the Warsaw uprising broke out, Chavale could be found among the ranks of the fighters against the Germans. She worked as a nurse, carrying aid to the wounded rebels. She was caught by the Germans, and together with other Warsaw residents, was chased ahead of the German tanks that were attacking a barricade of the rebels. There she was wounded in her right breast and in one leg.

With the collapse of the uprising, Chavale was taken to Germany. She worked there in a hospital for foreigners, as a nurse and an interpreter. She stole medications from the hospital and brought them into the camp where she found herself, in order to alleviate the suffering of the sick. With the approach of the front lines to the camp, the Germans decided to transfer the camp inmates to west Germany. Before their departure, camp inmates were confined to a shed. Chavale managed to persuade a German doctor to open the door of the shed for a few minutes and, together with others, she escaped to a village.

After the end of the war, Chavale went to Belgium and from there, back to Poland.

[Page 375]

Types

Moshe Tuvia the carpenter

by Boruch Vineberg

Translated by Libby Raichman

I remember Moshe Tuvia from the time when I was still a small boy, even before the great fire in the shul courtyard, in which half the town went up in smoke. That was approximately 45 or 46 years ago (written in 1933 — i.e. 1888/9.).

He was a man of medium height, with a beautiful, white, long beard (that I was sure he combed, if not every day, then at least every week), with large lovely eyes that were covered by the long hair of his brows. He spoke softly and in a gentle manner and always had a loving smile on his lips.

Moshe Tuvia the carpenter was a pious Jew who was also able to teach a chapter of Mishnah. I think that he used to teach the congregants in the synagogue a few times a week.

With his natural instinct for social work, for helping his fellow–man, for providing for the needs of his townsfolk, Moshe Tuvia was always occupied with communal matters.

A "poorhouse" existed in the town, a wooden ruin in the grounds of the cemetery. The grave–digger lived in one half and in the second half – with the broken roof, window panes knocked out, wet and sloping walls, without a floor – was the place where a few neglected, sick, and crazy people lay about in darkness and in filth, like the worms.

In those times, the feeling of responsibility to provide for the sick and the unfortunate was not developed at all. The most that was done for the unfortunate was to give them a piece of bread… In the winter, they would wander over to the women's synagogue, naked, dirty and neglected.

Moshe Tuvia the carpenter supported this poorhouse with all his strength. He sacrificed himself for these sick and lost souls. He went to the poorhouse that was, by the way, quite a distance from the town, a few times a week, and there he would comfort and help those who could still understand when they were spoken to, and often also took food to sustain the hungry.

I do not recall any of the "rich" communal leaders ever taking an interest in these victims, at that time. It was only Moshe Tuvia the carpenter, with his natural feeling of assisting, of supporting and providing for those who were not able to take care of themselves, who always did his duty towards his unfortunate fellow–men.

Biale, like other towns and villages, had a book of records in which all the important events in communal life were recorded – events in religious life (there was no other life in the town then), or an occurrence against religious life, were all written down. This book of records was entrusted to Moshe Tuvia the carpenter.

Even as a boy, I held Moshe Tuvia the carpenter in high esteem and respected him for his self–sacrifice for the unfortunate, unlucky people of Biale. To this day, his memory is precious to me.

Shmerele Becker (Hochman)

by Gedalyahu Braverman

Translated by Libby Raichman

At the end of the 19th century, Biale was a fortress of strictly religious Judaism. The slightest deviation from established practices was immediately deemed to be heresy, and in the struggle with heresy, all means of punishment were kosher.

Not everyone followed the rules. There were individuals in the town who had the courage to peep into the big, wide world. Shmerele Becker could be found amongst these individuals.

Shmerele was an ordinary folk–person with a small shop on Grabanovve street, where he sold herring, a few portions of lime with which the women would whiten their chimneys in honour of the Sabbath and festivals, a container of kerosene, a few tallow candles, and other small items. This is how he made a living.

One could always find Hebrew books on Shmerele's table, with which he was regularly occupied. Shmerele not only absorbed the new words for himself, and the new thoughts of the enlightenment literature, but he was also bold enough to share these new ideas with those whom he met.

The most effective means of keeping the masses strictly observant was the promise of hell or paradise after death. And who would want to exchange momentary pleasure for eternal life?

Shmerele had a particular leaning, to dispel the idea of the other world with the Leviathan and the legendary bull [these were promised to the righteous, to sustain them in the world to come]. He allowed himself to joke about this to the women who used to buy from him. He had a special quality of speaking in a gentle tone with a smile on his face, that would not offend the listener, even when they heard such heretical thoughts.

Slowly Shmerele's heretical thoughts began to spread and the devout residents in the town actually began to suspect him of heresy, recognizing in him Jeroboam, the son of Nevat [an expression applied to one who sins, and causes others to sin too], who wants to lead Jews astray from the righteous path. At that time the "Bund" was already active in Biale. From the beginning, the Bundists began to draw the masses away from the influence of those in ecclesiastical positions, so that they would be able to accept the new doctrines of socialism. They used Shmerele's arguments which were of significant help to them in their endeavors.

Shmerele never attached himself to any party on the Jewish street. He never told his children to which party they should belong. They were free to act according to their own understanding. He only made the effort to see that his children possessed as much knowledge as possible.

Aside from his age, Shmerele was also a spiritually broken man in the last years before the Second World War. The world changed, way past all his pessimistic ideas.

In a discussion with me, in the last summer before the war, he said to me: — you, Braverman, know how distant I was from being influenced by the triumphs over the old world, because I never felt in them any perfect victory. But the level that the world has reached is remote from the power of my imagination.

Shmerele, Shmerele, even the actual truth has greatly surpassed your power to grasp the great destruction whose approach you foresaw.

[Page 376]

Leibe Mednik
(Reb Yehuda Leib Bornshtein)

by Ya'akov ben Yechezkel Tel Aviv

Translated by Libby Raichman

Reb Yehuda Leib Bornshtein was born in the year 5691 (1831), in Mezritsh, to parents of moderate means. While still a young man, he came to Biale and opened a small factory making wine and mead (that is why he was called Mednik). He also produced wax candles, that were at that time a modern item. He inherited the profession from his father Moshe, of blessed memory.

Reb Leib's house was always open to anyone in need. It was of no concern to him that he was not regarded as one of the rich men in the town, but he secretly supported many families. Respectable, lonely people ate at his table for many years and he took care of all their needs.

It often happened that people came to Reb Leib in the middle of the night, asking for help with a sick person, or a shy Jew knocking on his door on a freezing night asking for wood to warm his house. They knew that they would find Reb Leib sitting over a book late at night. He never resented that they came to him so late. God forbid. On the contrary, he was particularly considerate of them. Reb Leib understood that the Jew who came was not only suffering from the cold but also from hunger, and he gave him everything, every food item in his house.

His hospitality extended beyond the borders of Biale. A preacher, an emissary from a yeshivah, a book seller or just an ordinary person, all knew his address.

In his house, there was a particularly large room for visitors where beds were arranged. It happened very often that one of his children or a grandchild would wake at night and notice that his pillow or bed–covering was missing. Reb Leib removed the item for his visitors. It was his custom to prepare the bed personally for an important guest. When his children, at times, interrupted him and said: — Dad, it is not appropriate for your esteem, to serve others, — he used to answer: I know well, what I must do. You should think that I am preparing the bed for myself … It happened that some guests felt so at home that they stayed for weeks and months.

On the Sabbath and on the festivals, he would send a messenger or a grandchild to the prayer houses and small Chassidic synagogues to see if there were Jews there who had nowhere to eat. When Reb Leib returned from praying with his guests, there was a commotion and frantic running in his house. His wife and his daughters felt helpless, as they had not prepared enough food for so many people.

Hush, hush children – Reb Leib would say to calm the members of his household – you will find a solution, by giving each one a smaller portion of food. Above all, there is enough wine and challah, so Jews will not go hungry.

[Page 377]

On more than one occasion Reb Leib embarrassed his family by his conduct. They felt that their father overstepped the boundaries of what was feasible. He gave interest-free loans to people and never saw them again. He had the generosity of spirit to take a garment that the tailor had just delivered and give it to an impoverished Jew.

His children reported their concerns to the Rabbi, Reb Shmuel Leib of holy ancestry, who was the only one who could influence Reb Leib. The Rabbi managed to stop him from these practices but after a short time he continued in the same way as he had done before.

Reb Leib died at a very old age, in 5683 (1923). When he was sick, he did not forget his friends and the poor. He kept asking whether they were well cared for.

He had the privilege of dying calmly, in the presence of all his children and good friends. He said farewell to them all, leaving a will, in which he said that his children should continue his tradition of charity and hospitality.

If, in the world, there are 36 righteous men, then Reb Leib Mednik must be counted amongst them.

A former student of the Biale Yeshivah, Dr. Dov Yarden (now in Jerusalem), writes about Reb Leibe Mednik:

"Reb Leib Mednik, my night innkeeper, was one of the most prominent benefactors of the town. Like many of the townsfolk, he too was a "chassid", a righteous person. He had a big wine business and from this he acquired the name "Mednik", that is to say: he produces or sells mead (wine made from honey). He excelled in many ways. His relationship with the yeshivah students who stayed at his house was like a father to his sons. At night, he would get up to see if the yeshivah boys were properly covered, and if he saw that a blanket had fallen to the floor, he would pick it up silently and cover the sleeping guests.

Aside from having a place to sleep at night, I was also included at his table on the Sabbaths. The Sabbath table in his house was set mostly for members of the community: sons and daughters, grandsons and grand–daughters and other relatives, and in addition to them "guests" who were invited for the Sabbath. They would recline around the tables that were set with everything good, as the elderly master of the house, Reb Leib, an imposing patriarchal figure, sat resplendent at the head, and ruled over the whole house".

Abik Ogrodnik (Abush Rozenblum)

by Berel Fakman Montreal

Translated by Libby Raichman

A Jew, a strong man, with majestic confident footsteps on Biale's cobbled streets. It was difficult to recognize the diaspora Jew in him. He was rooted in the earth, body and soul and his face glowed from his abundant success.

His gardens lay beyond the town and from the time he sowed the earth he waited impatiently and anxiously, looking out for the first sprouting of a blade of grass, or a leaf. Every spring, he experienced anew the miracle of God's creation.

As a wealthy land–owner, he was conspicuous amongst those around him, with his joyful confidence and blessed down–to–earth manner. In contrast, there were small busy merchants who wandered around the market place amongst the farmers' wagons in order to buy a sack of grain, a basket of eggs etc. He did not look upon these merchants with disrespect – on the contrary, he took pity on these people who waved wands, were hungry and lacked income.

When he used to walk through the streets and stole a glance into the pitiful little Jewish shops, he understood that such a trader, together with his whole family, must go hungry.

When Grabski's government reached the Jewish shops, and made more demands to choke the Jewish shopkeeper, then Abik made it his goal to alleviate their plight as far as possible and he began to distribute small loans.

At the beginning of the 1930s, when a large part of the population had become greatly impoverished and really hungered, Abik renewed the institution "Bet Lechem" [house of bread]. In the beginning, care was taken to ensure that the poor person would not know from whence the help came. Later he organized for every needy person to buy a ticket for 10 groshen every week and for that he would receive a specific quantity of bread and food for the Sabbath. In this way, the poor man felt a certain softening in his distress, as he had "paid".

It is remarkable that this hardened and toil weary Jew, at the same time, had such feeling for the suffering of others, particularly for the sick. He felt that it was his sacred duty to visit them and give them some pleasure. In his same simple way, he organized a society "Bikkur Cholim" [visiting the sick] into which he put his heart and soul, in his desire to bring comfort to those who met with this fate. To assist him, he chose women that were most suited to this task.

When he bought the large building on the corner of Brisk and Market streets that housed 24 shops, there were only a few who paid rent. When he accepted a promissory note from one of these shop–keepers, he knew that it was not worth anything, because in any case, they would not be able to pay. From where and with what could they pay? Particularly as they were not afraid that Abik would evict them from their shops.

This Jew also had a feeling for education. He truly swelled with pride when he saw his youngest son Chaim in uniform, coming home from Gimnazye [High School] with his bag of books under his arm.

[PS. An "ogrod" is a "kitchen–garden" – where vegetables are grown. He was a grower of these items, hence the nickname.]

[Page 378]

2. Mordchele Vinetroib

I became acquainted with Mordchele in the 1920s, in the rooms of a professional society, on the third floor, on the corner of Prost and Grabanovve street.

One would hear various stories about this society and my curiosity prompted me to go up there and see with my own eyes what happens there.

Here indeed, under a bent ceiling, at a table, Mordchele sat dozing in a very faded military great–coat, with a disheveled head of hair, that moved up and down, fearing that he would fall asleep. Through his half–closed eyes, he saw a young boy in a small coat that he had outgrown, and a little Jewish hat, glancing at the large picture of Karl Marx.

— Whom are you looking for, little friend? – I heard a sleepy voice say and he stretched out his hand and asked: — how old are you, little friend? Certainly, a victim of capitalism and clericalism?

I asked him to speak in language that I could understand because his words were unclear to me.

His sleepy face became heated and his gentle eyes began to spurt fire. He started to search for suitable words, in order to explain what he meant. I stood confused. His sudden motive to rob me of my spiritual treasure, with promises of equality and freedom in the future, stabbed at my heart.

— Sit, little friend – he brought me the broken chair on which he had been sitting.

— Yes, young friend, you will grow to be a great crusader for the holy cause; I can see that you want to know everything.

Since then I saw Mordchele quite often.

Mordchele lived at the Volye with his poor mother but he seldom went home, because he could not help his mother and he could not eat there.

That was the time when the leftist workers' movement ruled the minds of a large section of the youth, and all the remaining movements were given titles by the workers' movement such as: "small–minded citizens", "dark elements", "chauvinists" and "social – fascists".

Mordchele was the one that a part of the naïve and innocent youth looked up to. For them, he was the messenger for the crusade in search of a beautiful and just life.

Surrounded by the youth, he was beloved and respected. He had the run of the house in many well–to–do houses and felt very much at home there. Even the religious Jews were not afraid of him, because in their eyes he was idle and unworldly. Women used to slip him a spoon so that he could join them when they ate. They did not have to ask him too many times; mine, yours, what difference does it make. That the revolution would come, whatever the day, of that he was sure.

He had no skill in any trade. He had no time and no head for such prosaic matters.

When his followers learned that Mordchele was giving a lecture, in the local hall or in a private house, the venue was packed. It was truly difficult to breathe there but who expected the flaming, fiery words to fall from his mouth, about the rotten capitalistic order. He ignited a fire in the hearts of the youth with his deep faith in the fact that very soon, the exploiting world would collapse. His logical arguments had such an effect on the listeners that they felt happy to give up their own lives for this sacred purpose. Even though he was never short of fiery material against the clerical–capitalistic order, yet he would allude to authorities such as: Comrade Lenin, Marx, Engels and Lasalle.

Once, as he emerged radiant from such a meeting, he met Hinech Goldfeld, who asked: — Mordchele, when are you going to buy yourself a new pair of pants? He did not think too long and answered: — one hour after the revolution.

One morning, when I went down to the courtyard (of Itshe Koval), I saw Mordchele in an unappetizing, ragged suit of clothing, with a yellow liquid dripping out of his pocket. When I drew his attention to his pocket, he quickly answered that this was his breakfast that a female friend had placed there.

He opened the parcel and called out: — look what a bourgeoisie breakfast. I am not accustomed to anything else, only rolls with butter and underdone eggs. Who has food in mind when the closing accord of the conference, from which I have just returned, is screaming in my ears: Strengthen! Hurry! You understand what that means …

He told me that when he came to me the previous evening, it was already dark in the house. So, he lay down there on the table (a table from Yitzchak Pretter's bakery), and it seems that he fell into a deep sleep and did not even feel that it rained a little.

[Page 379]

In later years, when I once walked in the streets of Warsaw, I heard behind me, a popular revolutionary song being sung in a familiar steamy, low tone. I turned around and saw that the tune came out of a metal tub that someone was carrying on his head.

— give me a whistle! – I heard Mordchele's voice say.

He became a metal–worker. He arrived as an apprentice to a master who provided him with food and a place to sleep.

The last time I saw him was at the beginning of October 1939. Half of Warsaw lay in ruins and the German mobs went wild in the Warsaw streets. It was teeming with people, everyone was searching for a relative, an acquaintance, from whom to take advice: To stay – or to flee. Here I met Mordchele, neglected, but smiling. His entire possessions a straw mattress in his boss's cellar, but he did not take it to heart.

When I asked when he would go west, Mordchele began to complain about all those cowards who were fleeing the liberated country. – who will be here in the fateful moment? – he actually said, angrily.

The end: he entered into the count of the destroyed 6 million.

Friend Mordechai Vinetroib was the grandson of Leibele Rososher, the greatest teacher of Gemara in the Talmud Torah. Mordechai's mother was widowed young, and she and the children moved in with her father, who lived in the Talmud Torah.

Mordechai was versed in Jewish learning, he was renowned for being like a walking dictionary. He used to frequent the home of Yisroel Shualke where he ate twice a day, and it was there that he found Dr. Piness's foreign dictionary that he learned almost by heart. He read extensively in Yiddish about Jewish and world literature. He inherited a double dose of his grandfather's idleness. When the American parcels began to arrive after the First World War, he was often given fresh clothes, but these did not last and, before long, he was again wearing ragged clothes. Gedalyahu Braverman wanted to teach him to sew gaiters and Avrom Nuchovicz wanted to teach him carpentry but nothing came of either profession.

That friend Mordechai needed the social revolution, is clear for all to see …

Mordechai was amongst the most intelligent and learned in the Communist movement in Biale. In a few letters to me, he tried to lead me on the "right path". When he saw from my answers that I was, poor thing, a "lost cause", he used to say, in conversations with acquaintances, "Fyvel is a counter–revolutionary, on whom I have pity" … .

F. Gold

Boruch Sholem the Teacher (Krideshtein)

by F. Gold

Translated by Libby Raichman

1. Boruch Sholem the Teacher (Krideshtein)

He was the son of Shlaymele (Shimmele's brother) Krideshtein. He was also called Boruch Sholem the Kositinerin. His father was a Gerrer Chassid and he himself, a Biale Chassid. He was amongst the most observant in the town and a mystic. He had the desire, through Kabbalism, to create a living creature. Truly, not as large as the Golem of Maharal – [Rabbi Yehuda Low of Prague, 16th century – legend ascribes to him the creation of a Golem, a clay figure that came to life]. Yet, as he said, he could do that but not at the level of the Gaon of Prague. He therefore decided to create a small duck from clay and blow into it the spirit of life…

He prepared himself for this by studying the entire night, fasting and running to the Mikveh a few times during the day. Biale was in confusion. A fear fell over the town; what will happen if he succeeds and the duck will, God forbid, rebel in him? And what will be if he does not succeed? Until the Biale Rabbi called him and, on a handshake, forbade him to be involved in such matters.

2. Motl Domatshever

In the beginning, Reb Motl was the "third hand "of the most highly regarded teachers. Later the "second hand". He had approximately 30 students, ranging from 10 to 13 years. He was originally from Domatsheve and served in the Tsarist army for 8 years. He was the teacher of Shmuelke Pizshitz's children, even after they were married.

He was a tall Jew with a small grey beard, cleanly and well–dressed. He used to walk in the middle of the street and not on the sidewalk, with a red cane in his hand. Because of the tall hat that he wore, the students called him "vertiche".

He liked a child to shout out "the Rabbi is coming" when he entered the school room and everyone should be seated at 3 tables that were arranged in the shape of a "U". But the students would call out the "vertiche" is coming and he would take a deep sniff of snuff and ask: "who said "vertiche", may all evil befall you?" He struck the one whom he suspected, mainly on the head, dragging his hair with his hat.

[Page 380]

He used to teach the lesson while walking around the room between the tables, with his stick on his shoulder, like a soldier with his rifle. For this reason, the students also called him "Cossack". He began each lesson with the words: "it is certainly quite (clear), that whoever does not pay attention to learning, will soon get cholera" (will amount to nothing). Making trouble for a student was a trivial matter for him.

He was regarded as an angry teacher and a beater but one had to see the tenderness that he showed to a student who wanted to learn, but did not have the ability, to see him fuss over a student that accidentally hurt himself, or was stung, did not feel well, or who entered the room in winter, frozen. He would tear his handkerchief to tie a student's wound – an act he did with great pity and love, even for a bad student.

He spoke and wrote Russian and Polish well, and of course, Hebrew and Yiddish. He was one of the best and most beautiful swimmers in Biale. He was famous for freestyle (crawl) swimming and water–treading, in the town.

At the age of 78, he drowned in the Mikveh (apparently from a heart–attack).

3. Shualke Cohen

Everyone in Biale knew Reb Shualke, the son of Reb Herzl or at least had heard of him. Aside from being one of the finest Jews in the town, and of prestigious descent, he was also among the wealthiest Jews in Biale but, as it appears, very unworldly. Reb Shual could really not understand how it was possible that a poor man did not even possess at least 300 ruble. … Being an old–fashioned banker (lender), mainly for the aristocrats, brokers would keep his company and assist with his businesses. Two brokers in particular were spoken of, who became wealthy by hiding their cigarettes in Reb Shualke's safe, in order to rein in the evil inclination to smoke …

Notwithstanding his wealth and prestige, Reb Shual was a very modest man. In the Gerrer house of prayer, he did not occupy a seat of honor but sat at a table in the middle with poor people; opposite Mendele Sitnikker who delivered clay, the convert, and at the other end of the table, Irme (Yirmiyahu) Beder. He had a small crown on the collar of his prayer shawl, the smallest lulav on Sukkot and he was the last person to follow the cantor in the procession on Hoshanah Rabbah.

An example of the simple manner in which he conducted himself will be understood by his fellow–townsfolk who have Chassidic roots. When these small prayer houses were short of money for their expenses, then on the Sabbath after prayers congregants would grab the prayer shawls from the Chassidim. Early on Sundays, they would have to buy back the prayer shawls to be able to begin praying. In this way, the prayer houses received money. Once on a Sabbath, people were standing at the door of the Gerrer prayer house and young Chassidim were removing the prayer shawls from the congregants. The Chassidim let Reb Shualke pass through. Hearing a noise behind him, he turned around and when he saw what was taking place, he took off his overcoat, and from under his overcoat, his prayer shawl (Gerrer Chassidim do not carry anything on the Sabbath and wear their prayer shawls on them, under their overcoats), and he himself threw his prayer shawl in, amongst the others.

4. Yossel Vetshik (Gotfried)

He was strongly built, with a big red beard, a red face, and a red neck. With his deep voice he was, one might say, the reserve leader in prayer and the official reciter of psalms in the synagogue, particularly every morning during the month of Elul. Being the beadle for the Chevra Kaddishah [Burial Society], he would walk at the front of every funeral procession with his alms box, shaking it and calling: "charity will save from death".

In his youth, he was a tailor who did alterations and no–one in Biale knew exactly how he became an important person in the magistrate's office, under Russian rule and later under Polish rule, without being able to read or write (besides praying), but he would mechanically sign, Yossel Gotfried. With his finger, he would flip the pages of the books that contained the registry of births, until he found what he was looking for. Finding documents where he was mostly witness at the birth gave him his income. He lived into his nineties. He was the best purchaser of a good bottle of brandy and a roasted goose.

5. Pesach SkosError! Bookmark not defined.

If there is any truth in the legend that a ladies' tailor told the Vilna Gaon, that it is easy for him to be a righteous man, sitting in his prayer house of books, then that story is made to measure for Pesach Skos. To say that he was a "religious person" or an "honest Jew" is not saying enough.

He was a ladies' tailor but Pesach Skos was the most acknowledged reader of the morning prayers. His rendering of the psalms, standing on the side at the pulpit, was legendary (hence the nickname "Skos") [a legend]. For his recitation, verse by verse, with the resounding answer from his workman Shayme, the son of Sonia (Bekkerman), he was renowned in Biale.

[Page 381]

Because of the First World War, he lost his income. He died a tsaddik [a righteous man] from hunger, around 1922.

6. Moshe Bass

No longer did anyone in Biale count the years of his life. He was the bass player in the Biale band and the founding father of almost the entire band–family in Biale.

At weddings, he would sit, sleeping, and strumming on the bass. When the band was already playing the mitzvah dance for the bride and groom, he would still be playing the accompaniment for the seating of the bride. The band wanted to pay him his share so that he would no longer play, but there were two obstacles attached:

1. without playing, he did not want to take a share,
2. the enquiries about him from the in–laws, who wanted the remedy for living a long life.

Moshe Bass had claim to the first Minchah [afternoon prayer], before the Sabbath in the large synagogue. He was old, blind, and weak, but as long as the soul had not left his half–blind eyes, he maintained his right.

And although he was called Moshe Bass, he sang his "you are one" with a squeaky little voice.

7. Alter Nemirover

This Jew of medium height, with a bent shoulder and colorless beard, was the shadow (good) of the Biale Rabbi, Reb Yankele. His ardent devotion to the Rabbi was inconceivable for the ordinary person. No decisions could be taken in the courtyard without Reb Alter Nemirover first having the agreement of the Rabbi.

When the Biale courtyard was once on fire, he cried out: — help Jews, it's burning! help Jews! I am running to the Rabbi! – he ran out from the Rabbi with another cry: — water! water! nothing can help, only water! – a short while later, Reb Alter was seen running with the ladder to the orchard. As a non–Jew was already walking on the Rabbi's steps, the non–Jew also used this ladder. He ran with the ladder to dip it in the Mikveh (ritual bath), so that the Rabbi would be able to go out from his room and put out the fire. His two popular phrases in broken Polish originate from that fire in Biale: "the whole town is burning" and "send the non–Jew".

8. Yitzchak Urtsheles

Almost everyone in Biale knew Reb Yitzchak Urtsheles, the teacher. He was a gemorra teacher in the Talmud Torah. His students would sing and pray loudly in the morning. They sang certain sections of the Pentateuch and Song of Songs, and in particular, his rendering of the weekly section of the Pentateuch remained in the memories of his students.

Reb Yitzchak Urtsheles's ways were not unusual but in the following three events, he was definitely the only one in Biale.

After he boarded with my great–grandfather Reb Urtshe Katzev for three years, he took his dowry of 500 gulden and went out to trade. Just as "a cow represents half an income", he rather purchased an ox …

He was born in Rososh. On an anniversary of a death, he once went to Rososh to visit his father's grave. On the way, he stopped to recite the afternoon service, and became so confused that he returned to Biale. Something was unfamiliar to him – he did not see Lamoz on the way, and Rososh, against the evil eye, had grown and spread so much, with a train, a river, bridges, large houses, long wide streets …. Well, let it be so, a religious Jew should not think about such things. He said the evening prayers, said the mourner's prayer, ate his evening meal and sat down to study the whole night. In the morning – he prayed, said the mourner's prayer again and went to visit his father's grave. When he could not find his father's gravestone, he realized that he was in Biale and not in Rososh.

When he came to Biale to board, he took it upon himself to do a good deed, to provide the Chassidim in the Kotzk synagogue with a fresh drink of water with their third meal, and also finger–bowl water before saying grace. Even in the worst weather, he did not falter, even though he was close to 60 years of age. In his old age, the younger Chassidim wanted to take over from him but he did not allow them to do so and would give this interpretation: — you must understand me, as long as a person lives, he sins. In the next world, when the bad angel will say: another barrel of tar, the good angel will shout: a ladle of water; so, the more water I carry, the better.

9. Meir Tallitmacher

Meir Tallit–macher was a Jew from Kotzk. He was a Cabbalist and well versed in the holy books. Those who lived in the mud huts said that he was one of the 36 righteous people in the world. His custom of performing the midnight service was so stirring that it moved stones.

[Page 382]

About his tallit–making, it was said that when a tallit was ordered for a bridegroom, the tallit was only ready when the bridegroom was about to attend his children's marriage ceremonies… He made two or three tallit katan [four–cornered undergarment worn by orthodox Jewish men] per week (if he had orders). He made a living, as they say in America, from fast days. On official fast days, all the Biale Jews fasted, but Reb Meir used to fast four or five days a week. He died on a Sabbath, a day when a religious Jew may not fast.

10. Idl Tzinnes (Kanalshtein)

Idl Tzinnes was a strong man. He was a carpenter. When he was over 60, he could still easily carry an iron ball, a task with which four young carpenters struggled. He was known, not for his strength but for his eating. Two examples will be illustrated here.

In his old age, when he and his wife were suffering from a cold, the uncouth assistant surgeon (Papinsky) wrote a prescription for him. On the way into town to get the prescription, he bought two home–made breads. On the way home, he tasted the prescription. Not bad, a little sweet, the bread is tastier. Before he reached home, there was no sign of the bread or the prescription.

At the wedding of his grandson, he discovered that there was rice in the world and that it was not bad. So he told his wife to cook a bowl of food for him, from two pounds of rice and ten pounds of potato.

11. Chaim Chaveles

At first glance you would have said that he is a strong man. Tall, chubby and good–natured. He was a driver of a horse–drawn cab. He could throw two pood (40 Russian pounds each) weights two stories high and catch them again by the handle.

In the town, people told of a bet that he took, carrying an iron ball weighing close to 20 pood, from the corner of Yaneve street to the monastery (a distance of approximately ¾ of a viorst) [former Russian measure of distance, equal to .66 of a mile]. That time he won 25 ruble and those who scoffed used to say – and more …

12. Moshe Bukkes (Puterman)

Moshe Bukkes was a men's tailor. Besides tailoring he had other sources of income. He was happy when he was asked to make a long satin coat worn by religious men. Firstly, it was for a fine Jew, and secondly, it did not have to fit very well – the wearer of the coat did not have to dance with Graf Pototzki's daughter…. What was important was, that it had to be wide enough. He also paid particular attention to width and size when sewing pants and loose robes for Jewish children; never mind, they will grow into it …

He earned a second income at Sukkot time. He used to provide Jews with a cheap means of blessing the Etrog. For half a day, each of his sons ran around to residents of the town with a separate lulav and Etrog, to enable them to say the blessing.

Half the day, Moshe Bukkes would stand near Pizshitz's house in the market place and tell stories and jokes, while waiting for the task that was most dear to him, to be a second witness to Yossel Vetshik on marriage and birth documents, or God forbid, on a document concerning a death. Here Moshe Bukkes would demonstrate his competence: it was no small matter to sign "Moshko Puterman" in Russian. He marked on the paper signs resembling small eggs, grinding holes, corns on feet, fishing rods, details above and below, shafts for a wagon, half and whole wheels, complications. Every mark had to be put in the right place and there was not much space on the paper. A difficult task, but a fine and honorable occupation… particularly as he was paid for that, a sixer, a tenner and sometimes a drink of brandy too.

Moshe Bukkes would have been wealthy if not for his wife and children. As soon as his wife opened her mouth: "Give me a gulden!", all the children with one voice, as in a choir, answered: "I am hungry!" and as luck would have it, his second wife would also ask for a gulden, but the choir was no longer there; on the contrary, the choir would often give him a gulden ….

13. Yos Drozshkarzsh (Gerrman)

Everyone in Biale knew Yos the cab driver [driver of the droshky] (Yossel Broder). There was another cabdriver in Biale who was well–known, Saske with the horse, save him please. But it was Saske's horse that was famous and not he, himself. For example, the horse would go no further than the first bridge over the Voliye. If one wanted to catch the Brisk train at 9 in the evening, one had to leave with Saske for the Warsaw train around 11 in the morning….

Yos was ashamed that he was an ignorant person. To be fair to Yos, there were people in the town who were more ignorant, but Yos had a few admirable qualities that earned him his reputation: honesty, simplicity, goodness, his ability to engage in conversation and to pray aloud.

[Page 383]

Yos Drozshkarzsh had the privilege of being the only cab driver whom the Biale Rabbi would often hire to take a ride, and to make a distinction, also the authorities used his services. But unfortunately, poor thing, he had no luck with his horses. Before the First World War, he downgraded from his original two horses to a pushcart. For many years, he saved money to buy a young horse, but he had no luck, because whatever he managed to save, his money kept losing its value during the war and in the post–war period. So, is it any wonder that on Rosh Hashanah (Jewish New Year) when "v'chol ma'minim she hi" was recited, he shouted ma–ma–sha? He was so heavy hearted that he shouted, Mama. When he once earned a little extra, he said to his fellow–men who always endured the sins of the rich: — may we all possess, what I have earned.

Once, in a discussion with his brother, he said to him: — you are a good friend to me, that I know, but me to you, I do not know (he meant the opposite). When he was called to the Torah, he wanted to follow the portion in the Torah but because of the oven–fork and the shovel (style of the writing), he could not overtake the reader, so he shouted – whoa! halt! …

His "fair" complaints to the authorities: Why, in Biale, does the snow not remain still, it's melting affects riding with a sleigh. Why do they make a Sabbath in the middle days of a festival, it affects one's income? He himself saw that boys from Mezritsh came from Mezritsh on the Sabbath. That means that in Mezritsh it was not the Sabbath and in Biale it was …. Why do they allow the ginger–haired book–seller to sell books in the synagogue; he bought a kalboinik (siddur that has all the prayers for the whole year) and found no instructions in it on how to repair a step….

As he was exchanging good wishes with another person, he expressed the wish that they should not need to receive assistance from one another — Yos said that he hoped that he would not live to approach the other and that the other should not live to approach him….

———————

In the town, they would tell whole mountains of stories about Yos. We will jot down a few of them here.

One Simchat Torah [festival of the rejoicing of the Law], Yos was given the honour of carrying a Torah during the procession around the synagogue but the Torah was damaged as it did not have an etz chaim [one of the wooden rollers on which the Torah is rolled]. Yos was angry and said: — I do not want a lame Torah.

One Sabbath Yos was given an honour of being called to the Torah and it just happened to be the portion of "the rebuke". When Yos came down from the bimah [the raised section where the Torah is read], somebody informed him that the section of the Torah with which he was honored was full of curses. Yos waved with his hand and called out: — I immediately saw that the letters were crazy.

During the High Holy Days, those who listened to Yos's praying scoffed at him, and later had much to tell about his Hebrew. In the prayer "V'chol ma'a'minim she hi" were the words:

"ha'bochen u'bodek ginzay nistarot" meaning: who tries and searches for the most hidden secrets, that Yos expressed as: "a boche a budke, genzene strawnes" meaning: a crier, a booth, a goose's trout;

"V'chol ma'a'minim she hu bochen klayot" meaning: and all that believe that He searches the innermost parts, he read as: "uv'chol mamasha bochtes kluven", meaning: and all mother's examined vice; "hakatzar b'za'am ma'arich af" meaning: he is slow to anger and long–suffering, he read as: "a kirtze bezem mach op", meaning: make up a short broom.

Once Yos came to the Rabbi and asked the Rabbi to inform him of the date when he had yahrtzeit [anniversary of a death] for his father. The Rabbi then began to enquire of Yos and question him, hoping that perhaps, he would after all, get a word out of him, that would have some connection to the date of his father's death. After the Rabbi had already labored extensively in a long careful investigation, Yos called out: — Rabbi, I know nothing. I know only one thing. When the bells in the Cloister began to peal on Christmas eve, my father's pious soul went out through forbidden t …

(M. Y. Feigenboim)

[Page 384]

Folklore

Biale possessed a rich treasure of folklore, in which legends, stories, customs, characteristics, words, jokes etc. are all intertwined. If it were possible to restore the folklore–treasures of our town, then one would have a picture of Jewish life in Biale in those days, when almost every Jewish family was called by a nickname and not by their family names.

Unfortunately, we managed to gather only a fraction of this treasure. But even this small portion adds a special colour to the period of the last Jewish generations in Biale.

We managed to add clarifications regarding the nicknames because, firstly, today one cannot clarify the source of each nickname, and secondly, even the nicknames that allow themselves to be explained needed to be a separate task, whose scope could not be compressed into the framework of this book.

Words, Aphorisms, and Jokes
by Biale's Sharp Minds and Fun Lovers

by M. Y. Feigenboim

Translated by Libby Raichman

This is what they used to say about Shualke Cohen who was one of the two richest men in the town:

A friend of his from another town turned to him for a small loan. At the end of his letter, the friend added: — "God willing, I will pay". Shualke answered in writing: — You did indeed present me with a good guarantee, and it is truly good with "God willing" but what if, God forbid, God is not willing?

*

Chaim Peisach, the warden of the Chevra Kaddisha [burial society], while lying on his death–bed, called to Yechezkel Erlich who came to visit the sick: Haskel, you now have a good opportunity to send greetings with me, to your father …

*

Motl Mintz used to ask: — Why does the cantor wait before beginning the rendering of the Shmoneh Esray aloud, and when he comes to "Adonai eloheichem emet", he does not even turn around, and continues to pray?

This was Motl's answer: — if the cantor would have to wait until the Rabbi says "emet", he would wait in vain.

*

A Chassidic Jew who liked to play cards died in Biale. At his funeral, women followed the procession, crying, and asked – oy, good angels should come out to meet you. – A friend of the deceased, also a card player, said to the acquaintances: — I think that aces are better…

*

A Biale teacher used to pass judgement over his wife every day and to add, shouted – you have enough for yesterday, — then his wife would ask of him: give me for today too, so that once and for all, the debt will be cleared.

*

In Biale and the vicinity there was a very well–known jester, Vigderl (Avigdor) Blankleider. Once, when he happened to have two weddings at the same time, there was a substitute for Avigdor at one of the weddings. As the substitute began to seat the bride, he spoke and spoke, but not even a tear appeared in the bride's eyes. He became so angry, that he shouted: — Nasty woman! Why are you not crying? …

*

The Chevrah Kaddisha person, Meir Korman, used to say: — you can put the deceased into my bed and I will sleep soundly with him.

*

Shlaymele ` [Watchmaker] (Lederman), who behaved in the town as if he were a heretic, gave his children a religious education. So his son Fulye (Rafael) once asked him: — father, you do not observe all these things, so why do you send me to study them? To that Shlaymele answered: Fulye my child,

[Page 385]

you should know everything, but may your mouth become crooked if you should ever use it…

*

Shmerl Hochman was also renowned in the town as a free person, and yet he would go and pray every Sabbath morning. When people used to ask him: Reb Shmerl, how come you are in the synagogue? – his answer was: one must leave the house and allow one's wife to sweep, so that you will not become entangled between the bristles of the broom….

*

Motl, the son of Peshke (Rozmarin), was known for his jokes.

During the ten days of repentance, a Chassid who was known for his frequent bankruptcies stood in the Radzin prayer house, and recited "Avinu Malkeinu" – "our father, our king". Behind him stood Motl, and when the Chassid said, with great devotion, "Avinu Malkeinu m'chok et kol shitrei chovoteinu" – "Our father, our king, erase all record of our debt", Motl called out – and what will happen to the huge debts? …

*

Yitzchak Pizshits had a dog named Karol, and Pinchas Nartman had a dog named Balak. Once Motl came into the bank to request a loan. When the official asked him: — and who are the guarantors? – Motl did not have to think long and said: Karol Pizshits and Balak Nartman….

*

In his later years, it became very difficult for Motl to walk. Once, when he met the well–known dance teacher in the town, Motl turned to him and said: — you teach everyone to dance; teach me at least, to walk …

*

There is bread, there are potatoes, dance Yosef Itshe!

(A few words from Yosef Itshe Ash, during the German occupation in the First World War).

*

Yehoshua Mirtenboim used to say: — fasting, I do not even fast on Yom Kippur, but I do smoke a cigarette.

*

Two Biale brothers, both porters, when they argued amongst themselves, one would honour the other with the curse: may a spirit enter into your half father ….

Surnames according to towns of origin

by M. Y. Feigenboim

Translated by Libby Raichman

Hershl Lentshner, Shedletzer Bekker, Shimon Likkever (Lukov), Ahrele Slavatisher, the Ostrover, Moshe Lomazer, the Warsaw Feldsher, the Kobrinerin, Ahrke Komaruvker, Ahrke Pishtshatser, Iddele Proshekier (Proshuki), Yossel Terebiller, Mendele Sitnikker, the Zshelechoverin, Tzivia the Briskerin, Dovid Rososher, Meir Tsitsivorer, Moshe Vitorozsher, Simcha Loshitzer, Meir Nossever, the Stirnetserin,, Moshe Voliyer, Yehoshua Ossover, Dovid Koloder, Ahrele Sitshinner, Yossele Vohinner, Yossele Yanever, Chaim Svurer (Svori), Ya'akov Partsever, Itzele Rabinover (Grabanuv), Chavah Dibever, Yisroel Ritker, Yitzchak Radzinner, Yehoshua Ulinker, Mendel Ozerkover, Motl Domatshever, Fyvele Lublinner, Leibele Markushover, Pinchas Kodnier, Chaim Hushliever, Moshe Hishtsher, Shlayml Konstantiner, Bodker Melamed, Bielsker Shnider, Moshe from Slavatshinek, Shmuel Vlodaver, Binyomin Kozevilke (Koza–Vulka), Ahrele Kitelner, Dovid Sosnovitzer, Hershl Vishnitzer, Yonah Krakever, the Lyutbak.

Surnames according to Grandmothers and Grandfathers

Yankel – Beila Frimme Gittels, Yossel – Chanah Dovid Volfs, Yossel – Chavah Bashe Shmerkes, Yossel – Asher Shia (Yehoshua) Payes, Chaim – Sorrele Chanah Miriams, Yehudit–Shmilke (Shmuel) Mirreles, Gedalyah – Hershl Binyomin Moshe Tsives (Tsivia), Yehoshua – Yitzchak Yisroel Elyes (Eliyahu).

Surnames according to occupations

Work

Alter Mulyer – bricklayer, Alter Shlosser – locksmith, Asher Stolyer – joiner, Menashe Maller – painter, Moshe Glezer – glazier, Leibke Shindlmacher – maker of roof shingles, Moshe Blecher – metal worker, Dudl Brukirer – paver, Binyomin Koval – blacksmith, Moshe Tokker – turner, Binyomin Tshesler – carpenter, Leibishke Shnider – tailor, Shmuel Shuster – shoemaker, Irma (Yirmiyahu) Kessler – boiler maker, Nachman Inebinder – bookbinder, Velvl Rimmer – harness maker, Velvl Mozshonzshnik – greased carts , Zavele Sherer – barber, Dudl Farber – dyer, Chanah Leah the Licht tzierin – candlemaker, Ya'akov Shimon Bashleger – iron bender, Yehuda Leib Smoliarnik – pitch burner, Asher Kashemacher – maker of groats/gruel, Piniele Bagel–Bekker – bagel baker, Raizele of the thin Pletzelach – cakemaker, Altele of the kichelach – kichel maker, Mottele Kicher– of the kitchen, Dudl Sarver – waiter, Avigdor Badchan – jester, Avrom Goldshmidt – goldsmith (also his surname), Temele the Vattemacherin – maker of wadding, Yossel Milner – miller , Mendel Bendelmacher – maker of ribbon and lace, Elye – wine, Irme (Yirmiyahu) Bedder – bathkeeper, Shlayme Matzevah–Kritzer – inscriber of gravestones, Dovid Bekker – baker, Izesheliche of the Bilkes (Bulkes) – white loaves/cakes, Moshe Zaygermacher – watchmaker, Asher Tzukernik – confectioner, Berish of Vines– winemaker, Leibe Mednik – maker of med (mead), Moshe Dovid Shtrikken macher – rope maker, Feige the Kniterin – maker of candle wicks, Froyem Shtepper – quilter, Shye (Yishayahu) of soap, Zishe of sawdust, Kivele Fisher – fisherman, the Mangelnitshke (Mangel), Rochl Leah the Parrikn–macherin – wig maker, Tzalke of the wooden boards – (used to transport the boards from the sawmill), Yontl Drozshkarzsh – (cabdriver), Dovid Leib Fessel–Firrer (Assenzatziye) – barrel carrier, Shye Leizer (Yeshayahu Eliezer Proshenye–Shriber– (writer of petitions), Nachman Shriber – (teacher of writing), Chaim "Roffe" – (doctor), Meir Michl the Feldsher – (doctor's assistant), Rochl Leah the Banke–Shtelerin – (applied the cupping glasses to those with a fever).

[Page 386]

Trade

Nachum Montsher – flour dealer, Motele Tabatshnik – tobacconist, Chanah Rochl – of the yeast, Chaim Naftsher – petroleum, Itshe Meir of the tea house, Gittel the Koylerke – coal, Gittele of milk, Yitzchakl of the feathers, Chaya Tzviah of soda–water, Moshe Izik of old furniture, Toibele the inn–keeper, Mendele Tandeter – dealer in 2nd–hand clothes, Kreindele of the children's shoes, Chavele of the pages (newspapers), Shimon the Milchiker – milkman, Leibe of the cellar – (vegetables), Moshe Betsalel the store–keeper of iron, Hinech Shmatnik – dealer in rags, Duvtshe Fisher – fisherman.

Ecclesiastic

Chaim Shochet – slaughterer, Idl. Sofer– scribe, Shlayme Lozer (Eliezer– one who removes forbidden veins from meat, Hershele Melamed – teacher, Pesach Tehillim–zoger – reciter of psalms, Feige the Tikkerin – bathkeeper, Yankele (Ya'akov) Shamash – beadle, Avremele Mocher–sforimnik – bookseller, Velvele Bagreber – grave digger.

Mocking Surnames and Nicknames

by M. Y. Feigenboim

Translated by Libby Raichman

Ox, astatni–grosh, ucha, amp, oppalala, adzshumes, ayber, onpoyer, imre, onufre.

Lady's boot, bull, bear, noseless, bezrutshke, Bolshoi, Bolshevik, bolomotsh, bubkes, wretched boy, bartek, big bad boy, carob, bow down, botshkele, lead bird, bembekyeche, broom, arsonist, blister, misfortune, blind, buffalo, chubby.

Little goose, noise of a cricket, fat, a crude Jew, big, getsh, gorontse, golden calf, paradise, gold tooth, non–Jew, ginger, triangular piece of cheese.

Thin, pest, awkward.

Hen, hunch, tall, little hand, tea cake, wood, chandelier.

Vetshik, white carrot, wolf–man, vertiche.

Frog, forger, nag, policeman, zshentsh, zlatte–rontshke, zatshes, soldier, zshadeliche, zshazshele, zshamme.

Chaitshik.

Tshumberl, deaf one, deaf, Turk, devil, dead purse, dozen, tatu, smear, tsherske, small bag, tryne, clash, scratch oneself, tuchmanke, dancer, lively one, wicked person, heavy shoe, trotske, ruminant, trumpet, forelock, dance, snuff sniffer.

Lizard, boy, blood of a beast, box.

Loose shirts, hooligan.

Mild/soft, load, doll, shovel, liorke, lilkele, liovke, laymerl.

Mirshke, metsh, peculiar, poppy cake, mostiever–kamf, mischievous, Mikado, my step – your step, minister, angel.

Nose, small nose, niyeboyis, successor to the crown, 90s, smell.

Nightingale, suche–duppe, legend, stimske, stop, stach, quiet, sheaf, savitske, saske, sik–sak, s'knepl, suchenoz, spudnitse.

Amalek, small ox.

A mark, scab, pollepon, animal forequarter, rabid, pep, dirt, pototz, preles, prondik, potelyuk, polker, provetz, prisoner, piyus, pantile, mouth, parsnip, pentemelache, pocket handkerchief, pindzsheriche, ferkop, ponk, pidiak, petke, a pole, parshke, pritzl, sporty, button hole, pip, break, pekl–mekl, button– holer, gratitude.

Tsuker–bob, toy/plaything, cigar.

Small island, cheat, kitten, gruel, small duck, kozshol, kremenoz, short, dwarfs, hernia, butt of a gun, squint, ketshe, kuliatsh, Cossack, katsap – nickname of a great Russian, kigelichesforem, kigl, white loaf, taffeta, klet, konye–po–itsh, cat, kotshemoinik, kopyan, krempl, pickpocket, kytush, koshetz, kunepye, kulevenever, kakashte, kaponde, heads, intestines, wood–pile, log, galosh, krakus, kakkerulik, kayito, katik, small tub, kitayetz, cold–udder, head, excrement, bone, scratch, kupke, small bones, emperor, complainer, drags his feet, cold–doshe, log/block.

Rust, rondel, scab, rusty.

Black, black one, dirty, one who messes, disturb, agreeable, currant cake, shalonik, stabber, shkop, broken earthenware pot, jumper, shma–kolineche, shataneche, wading, sponger, interferer, fashionable, non–Jewish boy, convert, proud, dawdler, roan horse, shmoch.

––––––––––

[Page 387]

Customs and Charms

by M. Y. Feigenboim

Translated by Libby Raichman

It can be assumed that the following customs and characteristics were not specific to Biale, and that they were known and accepted in other towns and villages in Poland as well; but as they were accepted in Biale, we feel that it is appropriate to record them.

Moshe Ahrele used to walk through the town every Friday at 12 during the day calling: — leaders, into the bath–house!

On Friday evenings, the beadle of the synagogue would walk through the town calling: — into the synagogue!

Every Friday evening the assistant at the cheder (religious school) would take his students into the synagogue to hear Kiddush (Friday evening prayer for wine). When the cantor recited the Kiddush, the children would respond aloud "amen" and receive a sip of wine from the traditional Kiddush cup.

When a male child was born, the assistant to the teacher of the youngest children, who already had a claim to the family of the newborn child and hoped to have him as a student, took the small children of the beginners' class every evening to the woman who had just given birth, and read the prayer Kriat Shma [prayer said before going to bed at night] with the children, at her bedside. After the reading of this prayer, the children were given sweets and candy. This continued for a whole seven days, until the watch–night (the night before the circumcision). As the watch–night was regarded as dangerous, because of demons that lie in wait for the child, the beadle of the synagogue would bring the Mohel's [circumcisor's] knife and place it at the head of the bed, under the birth mother.

At slichot time, in the days preceding the High Holy days, the beadle of the synagogue would wake the community with three knocks on their shutters. If, however, there was a death in the community, he would only knock twice.

In the Hebrew month of Elul, the last month of the year, the students who studied the Pentateuch began to recite about ten chapters of psalms in the synagogue every day. The leader in prayer was Yossl Vetshik. He would say a verse and the children would repeat it.

Due to a case of Blood–Libel that was supposed to have taken place in Biale (see a separate chapter), it became customary in many homes before Passover to heat the oven after cleaning the house.

Because of an event that was tied, apparently, to the pouring of water on the clothes of a dead person (more about this later), in many houses it was accepted not to go out alone at night to pour out this unclean water. When the water was disposed of, they would call out three times: — beware, beware, beware. Although later it was apparent that the whole matter of pouring water on the clothes of the dead was implemented by a baker's lad, still the custom remained.

After the "Sabbath call–up" (the Sabbath before the wedding, when the bridegroom was called to the reading of the Torah), the bride and groom did not go out alone at night, only with an escort.

On the day of the wedding, the bride was not permitted to go out into the street alone. It was accepted that on the day of the wedding, the bride should carry a small knife.

These customs no longer exist, and had already diminished even before the First World War. Some practices remained but instead of calling out "to the bathhouse" or "to the synagogue", the beadle would walk around the town before candle–lighting and would knock with a hammer on the doors of the shops, or on the shutters, announcing how many minutes still remained before candle–lighting. In recent years, this task was performed by the beadle Azriel.

During thunder and lightning, the women would engage in this practice: they would put a quart of water on the window sill and a broom in the kitchen. If a non–Jew was in their house at the time, they tried to prevent him from leaving ….

———————

Clothes and Fashions of 80 years ago

by M. Y. Feigenboim

Translated by Libby Raichman

Men: Loose shirts, trousers, and waist–coats – all made of cloth, boots, small hats, the so–called "Jewish hats", half silk scarves instead of cravats. Trousers were tucked into boots.

Women: Long dresses of various materials, home–knitted socks, lace–up shoes (later buttoned), long hair plaited. Immediately after the wedding heads were shaved, and a cap or a turban was worn. In those days, if someone dared to wear a sheitl (wig), the religious people would pull it off.

[Page 388]

Tales and Legends

"Stoyontse" The "Upright" Burial

Translated by Libby Raichman

The members of the Chevra–Kadisha used whatever means possible to extract as much money as they could from bereaved families. We could tell a lot about these tricks but here we will relate just one incident.

On a frosty Sabbath day, Pessel Cohen died. On that Sabbath evening, when the shops were opened, Pessel's son Duvtshe (Dovid), went into the store of Chaim Pesach, who was at that time the trustee of the Chevra–kaddisha. Duvtshe began to cry to him about the death of his mother, and started to tell what a precious mother and modest woman she was.

Chaim Pesach, who was an ardent Radzin Chassid, and long–standing trustee of the Chevra–kaddisha, stood calmly, warmed his hands at the fire–pot and added to the praises of the son for the deceased mother.

When Duvtshe began to talk about practical matters, that means, when was the Chevra intending to arrange the funeral, Chaim Pesach placed himself before Duvtshe and glared at him and asked: — and have you taken care of the Chevra? – Duvtshe stood there, stunned, and called out: — Chaim Pesach, my mother bought a cemetery plot while she was still alive.

Chaim Pesach did not flinch, but calmly explained to Duvtshe the matter of the plot that his mother had bought.

— Listen here, Duvtshe – he began – it is indeed true, that your mother, may she have a bright future in Gan Eden (the Garden of Eden – paradise), bought a cemetery plot, but one is permitted to tell the truth, even about a deceased. You know, however, Duvtshe, may it remain just between us, that your mother was stingy, so she paid us for a small plot and we can bury her in that plot, but only "stoyontse" (standing/upright). If you wish, and are agreeable to burying your mother "stoyontse", so be it. However, if you wish us to bury your mother lying down, you must pay an additional amount towards the cemetery plot that your mother bought.

Duvtshe remained standing, dumbfounded. He did not expect a story like this at all. He began to put in a word to Chaim Pesach about justice and righteousness, but it did not help at all. Chaim had one answer: — what do you want, Duvtshe? What your mother, of blessed memory, bought, we are giving back to her. If you agree to bury your mother in a standing position, then go in health and peace and tomorrow everything will be done in the best possible way.

And when Duvtshe saw that Chaim Pesach was not at all impressed by his moral talk of justice and righteousness, so he began to ask Chaim Pesach: — what is the cost? – and now Chaim Pesach drummed up a sum that left Duvtshe in shock. His mother, he was thinking, left a small inheritance, but what kind of in–laws are these Chevra–kaddisha people? But allowing his mother to be buried in a standing position did not appeal to Duvtshe. So he had no choice other than to pay the necessary sum of money so that his mother could be buried in a Jewish cemetery, like all Jews.

(This article was published in Podlassier Life – but it was not possible to get a copy)

Without Success

Translated by Libby Raichman

Shayme Shnider (Bekkerman) became very friendly with the members of the tailors' society. They were a group of professional tailors who sewed shrouds for the dead, in the home of the deceased. But all Shayme's requests to be taken into their society brought no result.

It happened in the town, that the wealthy Chaim Yoske Kashtenboim died. The tailors' society demanded a high price for sewing the shrouds, to which the family did not want to consent. So they started to look for a way out. A few brothers from the so–called "Tsherske" family undertook to sew the shroud but they were looking for some sort of tailor that would at least cut the linen, so they turned to Shayme Shnider. The people of the tailors' society heard about this and let Shayme know that if he did not get involved they would admit him to the society. So Shayme remained sitting at home, and the "Tsherske" brothers managed somehow to find a solution without him. (The tailors' society then spread a rumour that the "Tsherskes" sewed Chaim Yoske's riding breeches [trousers].)

After this Shayme began to demand more boldly from the tailors that they should allow him into the society, as they promised, but again without any progress. Sometime later, Shayme told acquaintances that the reason that the tailors would not take him into their society was his own fault. And this is how it happened.

When he, Shayme, nagged the tailors even more strongly to take him into their society, one evening in the synagogue Nechemyele Yossl Vetshikkes (Gottfried), called him into a corner and said to him: — Listen, Shayme, do want to come into our society? – of course I do – Shayme answered.

[Page 389]

Hearing his answer, Nechemyele pulled out a large glass from his pocket and asked Shayme: — Shayme, you see this glass? Tell me, can you undertake to drink such a full glass of 59 in one gulp? When Shayme saw the glass, and heard 59, he became confused, and with downcast eyes said: — I do not know if I can do it. – If so – said Nechemyele – you are not fit to be in our society. — And Shayme was again excluded from the tailors' society.

(Heard from Ya'akov Aron Rozenboim – **M.Y. Feigenboim**)

The Dead Man

by M.Y. Feigenboim

Translated by Libby Raichman

This incident happened many years ago, before the First World War. At that time Biale did not yet have electric lights to light up the streets at night. The couple of gas lamps at the corners of a few streets hardly helped to expel the darkness that fell on the town at nightfall. Most streets and lanes were not paved and in the middle of the autumn rains people waded through the mud, up to their knees. It is understandable that in these autumn nights no one was seen walking in the streets and lanes. People sat in their homes and, as most of the Jewish population were far from a Torah or a book in those days, they occupied themselves by telling various stories and happenings about ghosts, spirits, demons, not good ones, and about the dead that come to the synagogue every night to pray. For these tales, there was no shortage of witnesses who confirmed that they themselves managed to be present at these bizarre events ….

On one autumn Sabbath night, a woman went out with her slop–pail on to the threshold of her house, and threw out the dirty water. At that moment, a white figure floated by. From shock the woman dropped the slop–pail from her hands, went back into the house and began to faint.

The people in the house tried to cheer up the woman, wanting to find out what happened, but the woman did not wake up. With that, a lamenting cry was heard from outside, and one could distinctly hear the words of the crier: water was poured on my clothes, how will I now reach the grave….

For the household, it became clear what happened here and a terrible fear fell upon them. The woman did not stop fainting and lay almost unconscious. The lamenting cry outside did not stop and one could constantly hear, quite clearly: — water was poured on my clothes, how will I now reach the grave? … The neighbours also heard the wailing outside and they too fell into shock. Through the walls, they communicated what happened here, and for each one it was clear that a neighbour poured water on a corpse that was surely going to pray in the synagogue….

The shock was so great, that those on the top floor were even afraid to go close to a window to peep outside. The neighbors began to deliberate about what to do. Some suggested that a few men should go outside and ask for forgiveness from the corpse. But there were no volunteers among the men who were prepared to take such a step. Even the bold Shmuel Shuster, who had completed his service in the Russian army, sat at his shoemaker's bench, truly paralyzed.

The corpse did not go away and his lamenting cry carried in the stillness of the night and increased the fear of the residents of the house. As there were no daring men to go out to the front of the house and ask forgiveness from the corpse, they began to recite psalms everywhere. This was no simple reciting of the psalms but a heart–wrenching cry from people who know and understand how great is their sin. The corpse continued to lament for a time and then it became quiet outside. The people in the house, however, did not calm down and, with full confidence, awaited the severe punishment that would befall them.

It is understandable that in that house no one shut an eye that night, even when it later became quiet outside. They recited the psalms with crying and pleading voices the entire night.

As soon as the day began to dawn and there was some movement in the little street, the residents of the house peeped outside and saw nothing unusual. The men went to the Rabbi and told him what had happened at the end of the Sabbath next to their house. The Rabbi ordered that a minyan of men [a quorum of 10 men required for communal prayer] should go to the cemetery, pray, and ask forgiveness of the dead. Time passed quickly and the people of that house could still not forget that terrible night. If something bad happened to a family in that house, they were convinced that this was punishment for that night.

Since then it became a custom in Biale that when pouring out dirty water at night they would go in pairs, and they would also call out 3 times: beware, beware, beware.

[Page 390]

Years later, one evening Shmuel Shuster sat in the synagogue before the Sabbath amongst a group of Jews and told them heroic stories from the time when he was a soldier in the Russian army. Just then the baker's boy, Shaloime, who was nearby, called out: — Reb Shmuel, if you are really such a hero as you say, why were you afraid to go out of the house that Sabbath evening, when they poured water on the corpse? That was me, Shaloime, I was the corpse, walking then in my white work–clothes to the bakery.

(published by me in the "Biale Weekly" under the pseudonym "Bialski" and not having a copy, I have written it anew – M. Y. Feigenboim)

[Page 390]

The Muddy Neighbourhood

by F. Gold

Translated by Libby Raichman

Everyone in Biale knew where the earthen huts were located. Officially the street was called the French Street, because that area belonged to a Frenchman and was not town land. Jews could not buy plots of land there (according to the old Russian laws). As a result, the Frenchman leased pieces of land for 99 years. About 40 to 50 families lived there.

The Biale "skyscrapers" were in the earthen huts, in Japanese style – deep, because they were built into the ground, and from this the name earthen huts is derived.

Most of the mud was in the earthen huts. This happened for two reasons:

1.   when the Russian engineers built the tarred highway to Brisk, they forgot to construct a canal through the tarred road, to carry the rain water to the river.
2.   because the wagon–drivers and cab–drivers lived there and the street led to the large nobleman's court. When the wagons drove up in the water, they would make the mud wider and deeper.

In Biale they used to joke that the area belongs to a Frenchman because, when Napoleon fled Russia, he arrived in Biale at the earthen huts in the spring, when the mud was in full swing. The French were then unable to leave and the Russians could not enter. And so this remained French territory.

Stories

by M.Y. Feigenboim

Translated by Libby Raichman

The Biale Rabbi, Rabbi Shmuel Leib, of blessed memory, was completely removed from the external world. Once a lady came to him with a question concerning religious law – while she was cooking meat in her kitchen, she went outside for a while, leaving no one in the house. When she returned, she found a Christian man in her kitchen.

The Rabbi, not knowing what a Christian was, asked the lady: — where was this Christian, in the pot or on top of the pot?

*

The Biale Rabbi, Rabbi Shmuel Leib, of blessed memory, was informed that Avrom Urmacher the photographer worked on the Sabbath. The Rabbi did not have to think long, and sent for Urmacher.

When Urmacher came to him, the Rabbi began to reason with him, not to work on the Sabbath.

— but Rabbi – Urmacher defended himself – I don't work, I just give a squeeze.

— only a squeeze? — the Rabbi snapped – so you can take a gentile woman and she can give the squeeze….

*

Chaim Pesach (the trustee of the Chevra Kaddisha) had a shop that sold drinks and dairy products and employed a few girls. Chaim Pesach's wife, wanting to ensure that the girls did not eat the milk products, thought of an "original" idea. As soon as the girls arrived at work in the morning, she treated them to meat grits….

*

Mendl Goldfarb (also known as Mendl Spokoyinne) was known in the town as a big joker and jester.

Mendl lived in Shedletz for a few years. One winter's day he came to Biale and, on meeting Ya'akov Velvel, one of the firefighters, proposed this business deal:

Seeing that the winter in Shedletz is a mild one, that there is no ice and no hope of there being ice, and seeing that Biale has quite a severe winter, he suggested the following plan to Ya'akov Velvel – that he should engage a non–Jew from amongst the firefighters, and fill train wagons with water that Mendl would provide at the Biale train station. By the time the wagons reach Shedletz, they will be full of ice (Shedletz is a few train stations away from Biale). In addition, Mendl described what a good business this could be.

Ya'akov Velvel grabbed at the proposition and, as a pledge, invited Mendl to have a drink with him. They got drunk, parted amiably and Ya'akov Velvel remained standing and waiting for Mendel's arrival with the wagons ….

*

[Page 391]

Mendl Spokoyinne once went to a restaurant late at night with an American visitor and wanted something to eat. The restaurateur suggested only a small roasted goose. Mendl turned to the American and told him that all there was to eat was a roasted crow. The American pulled a face and answered that he did not eat crows. Mendl, however, agreed to eat the roasted "crow" and the restaurateur brought the "crow" to the table. Mendl calmly ate the "crow", the American looked at him with pity and – paid.

*

Once Mendl went to the barber and saw a religious young man, a very idle person, sitting in the chair. Mendl glanced at him and called out: — you, shlimazl (person with bad luck), do you also need to have a haircut with an uncovered head? – the young man became confused and embarrassed and began to ask – Reb Mendl, how is it possible to have a haircut any other way? How is it possible any other way? – Reb Mendl repeated the question and said – when one side of your head is being cut, you can hold your hat or your yarmulke (skull cap) on the other side, and with that Mendl demonstrated for the young man how to cover half his head with his hat. The young man remained sitting as if he had been struck, and quietly defended himself, promising that in the future he would do that.

*

Once an antique dealer came to Biale and met Motl the son of Peshke (Rozmarin). They spoke and Motl promised the Jew that tomorrow morning early he would show him a rare antique. On that account, the antique dealer gave Motl a proper shnaps (brandy).

Chaim Pesach's wife had a habit of walking around in her house in the morning in her panties. It was there that Motl took the antique dealer the next morning, and showed him the antique....

*

In Biale one often heard the expression "a dish of groats with a yarmulke". Where did this come from?

On the first night of Slichot (days preceding the High Holy Days when penitential prayers are recited) they would cook groats in the Chassidic prayer houses. After the penitential prayers, after midnight, the Chassidim would seat themselves at the tables and have the meal. Usually they would cook such a dish in large pots at the home of one of the Chassidim and, in addition, there was also a chassid who knew about such things.

It happened once that a chassid who was overseeing the pots of groats did not notice at all that his yarmulke had slipped off his head and fallen into the pot of groats. When they began to spoon out the groats from the pot with a large wooden ladle, in the Chassidic prayer house, the person serving felt that the ladle had become very heavy. He thought that he was scooping up a large piece of meat. But when he turned the ladle over into the plate, he saw a cooked, fatty yarmulke....

(This was heard being told in the "Tarshish Shtiebel")

*

The town's wealthy man, Shmuel Pizshitz (a Kotsk Chassid), was travelling home on a Friday, on a rainy autumn day, from his saw-mill on the Volye. As he sat in his closed coach, he noticed the village man Mendl Rososher, also a Biale Kotske Chassid, walking on the tarred road in the rain.

Pizshitz instructed the driver to stop the coach, and when Mendl came closer, Pizshitz called: — Mendl come in; and then added: "there are those who achieve their goals in one hour".

What? So cheaply you, Shmilke (Shmuelke), want to buy a place in the world to come? Mendl asked, and remained standing.

So, what do you want, Mendl? Shmuel Pizshitz asked.

It costs a gold coin – was Mendl's answer.

Pizshitz resented such cheek and told the coach driver to drive on. He travelled a little further; it was raining harder and Pizshitz, it seems, felt bad about leaving a Jew in the street in such weather, and one of his own chassidim too. So he asked the driver to stop. When Mendl again came closer to the coach, and Pizshitz called: — Mendl, you will receive a gold coin, and come in.

Mendl came closer to the coach and said: — have you got the gold coin? When he received an affirmative answer, he called out: — then pay! When he received the gold coin Mendl entered the coach.

(Heard from a grandson, Koppel Pizshitz, son of Dovid Pizshitz, former Warsaw synagogue warden)

[Page 392]

In the town they used to narrate the following legends

by F. Gold and Gedalyahu Braverman

Translated by Libby Raichman

That Napoleon visited the Biale synagogue during his march to Russia.

*

That in the Biale cemetery there were the graves of a daughter of the Prague Maharal and of a son or son–in–law of Hagaon Harav Yom–tov Lipmann (17th century commentator on the Mishnah).

*

That when the Jews of Biale had to carry a few dead persons from the tarred highway, they found two corpses in the cemetery that had already been dead a couple of hundred years, not touched and still in their shrouds, as if they had just been buried.

*

That the Biale Rabbi, Yitzchak Ya'akov Rabinovicz, conducted a lawsuit in his synagogue between a living and a deceased miller.

*

That at night, dead people called a Jew to the Torah who was passing through Biale, near the synagogue. He went to the Rabbi, who told him to go to the synagogue, and gave him his prayer shawl and his walking stick (as a child they showed me the person who was called up, but he was not allowed to be questioned).

*

That a dead mother took a son of hers who had fallen asleep between the afternoon and evening prayers out of the synagogue through the railings, before the dead come and pray in the synagogue.

*

Reb Berish Landois's wife used to sell wine for Kiddush. Once, when she did not have money to buy fresh wine, she asked her husband, Reb Berish, if it was possible that there was no money. He answered: — you will have wine. – From that little bit of wine that was at the bottom of the large bottle. For years she sold all sorts of wine, and the bottle was full. With the money that she gathered from selling wine, the courtyard on Kshiver Street was purchased, that was later known as "Reb Aharon Landois Courtyard".

*

I happened to hear the following legend, that had a connection to the old cemetery on the Brisk highway.

Many years ago, the person in charge of Biale was an enemy of the Jews. One fine day he decided to erect a cloister in no other place than alongside the Jewish cemetery.

He began to build the cloister, but every time they finished building a wall, it would sink into the earth, and the building of the cloister never ended.

The Jews, seeing that they would not be able to prevail upon the evil man to stop building the cloister, decided not to continue to bury the dead there, and they established a new cemetery, at the end of the present day's Proster Street. Only when the Jews ceased using the earlier cemetery did the enemy of the Jews manage to complete the building of the cloister.

The "Hero" from Biale

by A. Litvin

Translated by Libby Raichman

The Biale Jews remember well the name of the person they called "Samson the mighty". The name was faithfully handed down from grandfathers to grandsons, from father to son, for generations, and served as a topic of synagogue conversations in the long winter evenings.

His name was Shimshon–Leib– this wonderful man, who was a water carrier or a tailor. He could only live under the marvellous Radzshivils, those noblemen who at the very end of summer made "montshkes" (paths for sledges, from sugar–flour) and their coach was harnessed by bears.

And it happened that the nobleman Radzshivil came through the town in the middle of Tammuz on a "montshke". As if in a real shevat–frost, his sledge rode on a sugar–sledge path, carried by a trio of eagles–horses.

Shimon Leib approached slowly from the side, caught the side of the sledge with his hand, and the three eagles from the Radzshivils' best horse–stable suddenly stiffened, as if rooted to the earth.

The sledge–path was good: for many weeks, the farm–hands toiled; the sledge was even better and lighter, but swifter than the sledge were the eagle–horses, but it did not help: Shimon Leib put three fingers into the sledge and the three eagle–horses came to a standstill.

Radzshivil turned around and saw something that his forefathers would not have believed; a slovenly Jew with a torn peak cap took the liberty of making fun of Radzshivil.

[Page 393]

But instead of being angry, the nobleman came down from the sledge, and slapped the Jew on his shoulder: you are a bold man, Shimonke! I like people like that! You are strong, Shimonke! But I will show you someone stronger than you: a Russian soldier, a Katsap (nickname of a great Russian soldier), actually from Moscow. If you bring him down – you will receive 5 gold coins.

A week later they brought Shimon Leib to Radzshivil's court. One of the most splendid forms of entertainment for the Polish nobility at that time was supposed to take place there: a battle between two opponents, a boxing match between two mighty men – between the thin "zshidek" (Jew), Shimonke, and the fat, red katsap of Moscow.

The katsap immediately approached Shimon Leib and, without preamble, and without questions or complaints, pushed his five fat, red fingers into Shimon's face.

Shimon's whole head was turned to the side.

Without saying a word, Shimon Leib took a step firmly and confidently towards the katsap, grabbed him by the head, lifted him up high and dropped him to the ground. There was no longer any katsap…. scattered bones lay on the ground.

No harm was done to Shimon. This was a boxing match…

One can easily imagine that "Shimonke" was a treasure for these insane noblemen like Radzshivil. Sitting in company somewhere in Paris, amongst other such crazy noblemen like him, he had something to boast about. Nobody had in their court such a remarkable "Shimonke" like him.

And "Shimonke" actually felt like the darling son, somewhat specially privileged by the nobleman. He was allowed such "tricks" – that if it were anyone else, and not "Shimonke", it would have cost him his head.

Once the nobleman Radzshivil, in his usual manner, travelled over the sledge–path in his sledge, pulled by bears. "Shimonke" was there, not at the back of the carriage but in the front. He ran ahead and teased the bears.

The bears began to yield. The nobleman could go no further. He told the coachman to use all his strength to stop. He crawled out alone from the sledge and said to his Jew:

"Listen Shimonke, do you think that it's a great feat to tease bears, when they are harnessed? Now, prove yourself – I will unharness the bears and then tease them".

This was not said in jest; this was an order.

"Shimonke" had to position himself as before, opposite the bears; the bears were unharnessed and one hastily set upon Shimon Leib. Other Jews stood at a distance: some on fences, some on roofs, hardly alive from fear and horror. One blink and ….

"Shimonke" was already riding on the bear. With both hands, he bent the bear's head to the side. Then, with the right hand, he delivered a blow to the head and jumped off.

The bear gave a jump, wounded. He could no longer bite: his whole lower jaw with his teeth and tongue were lying on the ground….

It is not known what role Shimon played in the town itself, amongst Jews. But all the gentiles were terrified of the burly hero. In all the surrounding villages, the toughest gentile youths fled when they saw "Shimonke", even from a distance.

But in one village apparently, the gentile youths did not know "Shimonke". When he once passed through their village, the gentile youths ran after him and cursed him: Jew, Jew….

"Shimonke" continued calmly on his way but, when he was sick of the youths' abuse, he turned around, took one of their hats, and approached the nearest house. With one hand, he lifted the house from its foundations and with the other hand he put the hat underneath – and continued on his way as if nothing had happened.

They say that the hat is still lying under the house to this day. But since then, in that village, they also knew who "Shimonke" was….

("Jewish souls", volume 1)

––––––––––

In the series "Legends and Tales of the former Biale" that I published in the Biale weekly under the pseudonym "Bialski", amongst others, I also published the legend "The Wedding steps at the Synagogue". There it is told about a Biale hero with the name of Shmuel Zbitkever. One can assume that this legend actually has a connection to the mighty Shimon Leib. It is possible that over the generations, the real name was forgotten and it is difficult to establish which of the two of us, A. Litvin or the writer of these lines, has provided the correct name. It is worthwhile noting that the name Zvitkever has a connection to the wealthy Warsaw family that is mentioned in the history of Warsaw in the 18th century.

We will briefly relate the legend about "The Wedding steps at the Synagogue".

[Page 394]

One day, when Radzshivil was travelling behind the town, his coach stopped before a barricade of two gigantic round wagon steps and could not go any further. These two steps were placed on the highway by the wealthy Zbitkever.

Radzshivil ordered that all travelling farmers be stopped and challenged them to remove the steps from the highway. The farmers made an enormous effort but were unable to move the steps from their place.

Just then, Shmuel Zbitkever, who set up these steps, appeared and began to move them in the direction of the town. Radzshivil stood and marvelled at the strength of the Jew.

Shmuel Zbitkever moved the steps to the synagogue and fitted them close to the entrance of the synagogue. On these two steps, they would place the canopy for every wedding. Even if the wedding was arranged to take place at the distant Volye, they would bring the bride and groom for the ceremony in front of the synagogue on these two gigantic steps. Even in winter, in the most severe frost and deep snow, the weddings would take place on these two steps in front of the synagogue. During the First World War this custom ceased.

M. Y. Feigenboim

A Blood Libel
[a case of Blood Libel]
A False accusation of Ritual murder

by M.Y. Feigenboim

Translated by Libby Raichman

As soon as the Jewish festival of Passover drew near, there were notices in the press of blood–libel against Jews in various lands and towns. It would therefore be interesting to report on a case of blood–libel that actually occurred in our town many years ago, that ended quite tragically, although the event is perhaps unknown.

I have not managed to establish the exact date of this occurrence. It appears that it took place under the rule of the former Poland.

And this is the story. The eve of Pesach amongst the Jews was in full swing. Suddenly, like a thunder on a bright day, the rumor spread on the Jewish street that in the synagogue courtyard, in an oven of an abandoned house, a body of a child was found.

The Jewish population immediately understood what this meant and what it smelt of. But before they could react, the police were already going around looking for the lost child, and they actually found it in an oven in the synagogue courtyard.

It is understandable that they did not take too long to look for a party guilty of the murder. It was clear to the police that a dead child in the synagogue courtyard, on the eve of Passover, meant that the Jews murdered for ritual reasons.

Suspicion fell on the cantor, still a young man, much loved by the congregation, whom they arrested.

Terror enveloped the Jewish community. The impending festival was forgotten and there was a fear of the approaching market–day, when many Christians arrive in the town, so they locked themselves into their homes and waited for the unknown terrible end.

They did not have to wait long for the judgement. Already three days after the occurrence, the cantor was sentenced to death by chopping off his head.

The suffering of the Jewish community was terrible, knowing that a young man was paying with his life for a death he did not cause.

In those moments of immense despair in the Jewish community, an old Jewish resident presented himself to the police, an elderly man named Uziel, who took upon himself the guilt, in order to save the young cantor from death.

The cantor was allowed to go free, and having the "right" criminal in their hands, they treated him cruelly. This Jew, Uziel, endured the most severe torture in the short time that remained of his life, but he did not for one minute show any sign of despair and dejection.

On the fourth day after the occurrence, they beheaded Uziel in the synagogue courtyard.

Legend has it, that it was decreed that if the Jew Uziel was sentenced to death, then, however far his head would fall after they beheaded him, that place would never be built on. And therefore, a piece of land on the eastern side of the synagogue was never built on. It was also decreed that his family should not live within 10 cubits around the area where his head fell after being beheaded.

The hero of the Biale blood–libel was buried in the old cemetery (near the Brisk highway). Many people still remember how, on the anniversary of his death, a woman from his family (his wife was a relative of Motl Rozmarin's family) would take herself off, with a little pot of paint, to refresh his gravestone, of which there is no memory today.

Since then, there is a custom that dates back to that time, that after preparing for Passover evening in the home, one heats the oven.

(Revised anew according to my article in "Podlassier Life" number 14/79, of the 10th April 1933.
From the series "Legends and Tales of the Former Biale" that I published under the pseudonym "Bialski". – **M. Y. Feigenboim.**)

Additional details:

In the first edition of the publication "The Jews in Poland", published by the committee for the publication of "The Jews in Poland", New York, 1946, the historian Dr. Rafael Mahler, in his treatise "Jews in Former Poland", page 277, amongst others, writes about the bloody theme of blood–libel: "… in the year 1710, a Jew from Biale paid with his head for a similar "discovery".

In his treatise, Dr. Hendl also mentioned in the book the case of blood–libel in Biale in 1710, that ended with a death sentence for a Biale Jew.

In A. Litvin's book, "Jewish Souls", it is told about "the holy one in Biale and his last will". In this chapter, A. Litvin tells about cases of blood–libel in various towns in Poland and Lithuania, and about those holy ones who died because of the blood–libels. Amongst other cases, he writes: "Biale has forgotten the name of this holy person", who gave up his life for his people. I do not know if the memorial prayer is said for him in the synagogue but the legend remained alive amongst the people.

After the beheading of the holy one – so the legend goes – the head spun around on the spot where the bloody sentence was carried out and called out: many, many generations should be aware of this place and no one should build a house where innocent Jewish blood was spilt.

For hundreds of years Biale observed this testament. No one dared to desecrate the remembrance of this holy person. This gloomy place is a monument for him, who sacrificed himself for the entire community.

Fyvl Gold (New York) writes: "the body of the holy person was stolen during the night and buried in the cemetery. Overnight, grass covered his grave and it was not possible to locate the site of the grave."

Hinde Muzshinek, the wife of Yeshayahu Eliezer (Shai Lazer, the writer), told me that when her eldest daughter, Golda, married and was supposed to take a dwelling in the house of Binyomin Leibele (Mandelboim), in the synagogue courtyard, Hinde's father, Reb Moshe Chayes, did not allow it, saying that they are still obliged to observe the message of the holy one, who was a relative of theirs, not to live in that place.

[Page 399]

Destruction and Annihilation

by M.Y. Fajgenbaum

Translated by Gloria Berkenstat Freund

The war that broke out between Poland and Germany on the 1st of September 1939 bloodily burst into Biala on the first day. The first bombs from the German airplanes fell on Wolya [a suburb of Biala] on Friday morning; they were targeted at the airplane factory there. Simultaneously, bombs also fell on civilian houses, and among them, a Jewish house in which the entire family of the cabinetmaker Avraham Tajtlbaum perished.

The population witnessed the disorganization and chaos that ruled in all areas on the first day of the war. The airplane factory was almost undefended and no Polish airplanes were seen that would disrupt the German air assaults. However, it was hoped that this was only the beginning and that a radical change would come quickly.

There was no sign of the Polish government, which had trumpeted for the war by bragging that they were "united, strong and ready." The chaos and disorganization increased from day to day. The German bombers flew freely across the Biala sky and sowed devastation. The population lay in the fields throughout the day and, when the German bombers ceased their work at night, began moving and first of all buried the victims of the day.

The airplane factory already lay in ruins for a long time; there were almost no more Polish military in the city. However, the German bombers did not stop their rampage. Among the destroyed houses were: the magnificent house of Hartglas (burned and later taken over by the Germans), the *Folks-shul* [public school] at Grabanower Street (Motl Weine's house), Shimeon Lichtensztajn's house at Brisker Street, Papinska's house at Janower Street and so on.

Erev [eve of] Rosh Hashanah, several German tanks entered the city and, while shooting, went through Brisker Street in the direction of the Brisker highway. A Polish officer and a small group of soldiers opened fire on the tanks at the new market. As a result of the fight the majority of stalls at the new market were burned.

The Polish Republic ceased to exist after two weeks of war. The idea of life under German rule threw the Jews into a desperate mood. Meanwhile, Biala was not occupied and remained "no-man's land."

On one desperate day, hope suddenly began to glimmer for the Biala Jews that the Russian Army was marching west because, in accord with the German-Russian Pact, the Russian Army would occupy the Polish area to the Wisła [Vistula]. That is, Biala would belong to Russia.

The news actually was confirmed. The Russian Army occupied Biala on the 26th of September 1939, moving further west.

The holiday of *Sukkous* [Feast of Tabernacles] was celebrated by the Biala Jews with mixed feelings. They were happy that they had not fallen into the hands of the Germans, but they were haunted by an unease about the future.

The Soviet regime did not rush to bring order to the city. A certain restraint on their part was noticed; they left the initiative in the hands of the population. Various committees arose in which Christians were exclusively represented. Meanwhile, Jews avoided any cooperation with the new regime, remembering well the bitter experience of 1920.

The shops were closed more than they were open. The lack of raw materials was felt immediately and an exchange of goods among the population began. Long lines of buyers filled the open shops and bought everything they saw.

The Biala Jews were not destined to celebrate the holiday. At the end of September, the radio news reported that the boundary between Germany and Russia would be the Bug River and not the Wisła. The news spread in the city lightning fast and threw terror into the Jewish population.

[Page 400]

Although the Russian military personnel denied the news about withdrawing in conversations with the population, we began to notice signs of their withdrawal to the east: they began to remove from the city everything that was valuable in their eyes and load it on trucks. During this activity, they did not even treat with respect the Jewish hospital, from which they removed valuable medicine, equipment and instruments.

For the Jewish population, the question actually became whether to leave the city and go to the other side of the Bug [River]. This was possible because the Russian regime did not disrupt the exodus to the former Polish eastern areas. However, the Biala Jews had had bitter ordeals in this area during the First World War and in the year 1920. Then, during the era of transition, the Jewish population suffered with fear, but those who left suffered greatly in unfamiliar areas. Understand that no one then, even in their fantasy, imagined the terrible end that Germany would bring to the Jewish population. They anticipated a difficult life, but when had the Polish Jew had an easy life?

They knew that life under the Soviet regime was not easy. Everyone lived with the hope that the war would not last long; it would end with Germany's defeat and they would find themselves in a freer and more open world. However, those who went to Russia would first of all be transformed into a large group of refugees that was immediately exposed to suffering. The strongest were afraid of the idea of being hermetically sealed within the borders of Soviet Russia which they could not leave after the war. However, those who decided to leave the city had one answer: "We do not want to be with the Germans and, particularly, not with the Hitler Germans." It is estimated that 500-600 Jews left, the majority men who left their families in the city because it was assumed that the German persecutions would mainly be turned against the men.

Jews from all strata left for Russia. The majority of them had never had any connection with communism. A number of Jews remained in the city who qualified as sympathizers of the Soviet regime.

We cannot have any complaints against the Biala Jews as to why they did not leave their birth city for Soviet Russia, because if Jewish leaders of the largest Jewish world organizations did not know of Hitler's plans of annihilation in regard to the Jews, how should shtetl Jews have known?

The End of 1939

On the 10th of October 1939, the Russian Army left the city and the German Army arrived in its place; this threw great fear on the Jews so that many who could not decide to leave the city earlier now did so.

Several hours after their arrival, the Germans took Jewish hostages (using a list provided to them by the mayor). Christians wearing white armbands appeared in the street and their first task was to grab Jews for work. The Germans had no lack of work and the Poles again zealously provided more Jews, even more than had been requested.

The German regime immediately ordered the opening of the shops and endeavored to have the city return to its normal appearance, which actually happened over the course of several days. A curfew was brought in that lasted until the Germans left the city. The Jewish population had less free time to move in the streets than the Christian population.

Abschrift

Verordnung

Im Auftrage der Deutschen Militär Behörde ordne ich an, dass alle Juden, die innerhalb der Stadt Biala-Podlaska wohnhaft sind, binnen 12 Stunden vom Datum der Bekanntmachung bei der Stadtverwaltung (Eingang von der Poststr.) ihre genaue Wohnungsanschriften anzugeben haben.

Die Nichtanmeldung der Wohnung während der oben angegebenen Frist verursacht die Aberkennung sämtlicher Rechte, die den Bürgern der Stadt Biala zustehen.

Männer und Frauen im Alter von 16. bis zum 50. Lebensjahre verpflichtet die Anmeldung persönlich vorzunehmen

Biala-Podlaska, am 17.X.1939

gez. Bürgermeister

Ing. A. Walawski

Za zgodnosc odpisu

Przewodniczący
Miejskiej Rady Narodowej
w Białej-Podlaskiej

Order for the Biala Jews to report their addresses to the city hall

Meanwhile, the managing committee of the city was in the hands of the military regime and it appeared that they still did not have any anti-Jewish instructions.

[Page 401]

So, the regime gave Jews permission for trips to Warsaw and Lodz, for which Jews left and began to bring back various goods. The trade blossomed. Freed from the heavy chains of the Polish finance regime, the Jews breathed more freely, forgetting where they were. However, the bustle of trade lasted a very short time because in November 1939 the well-known Gestapo entered Biala and a long-lasting era on a road of suffering and terrifying death began for the Jews.

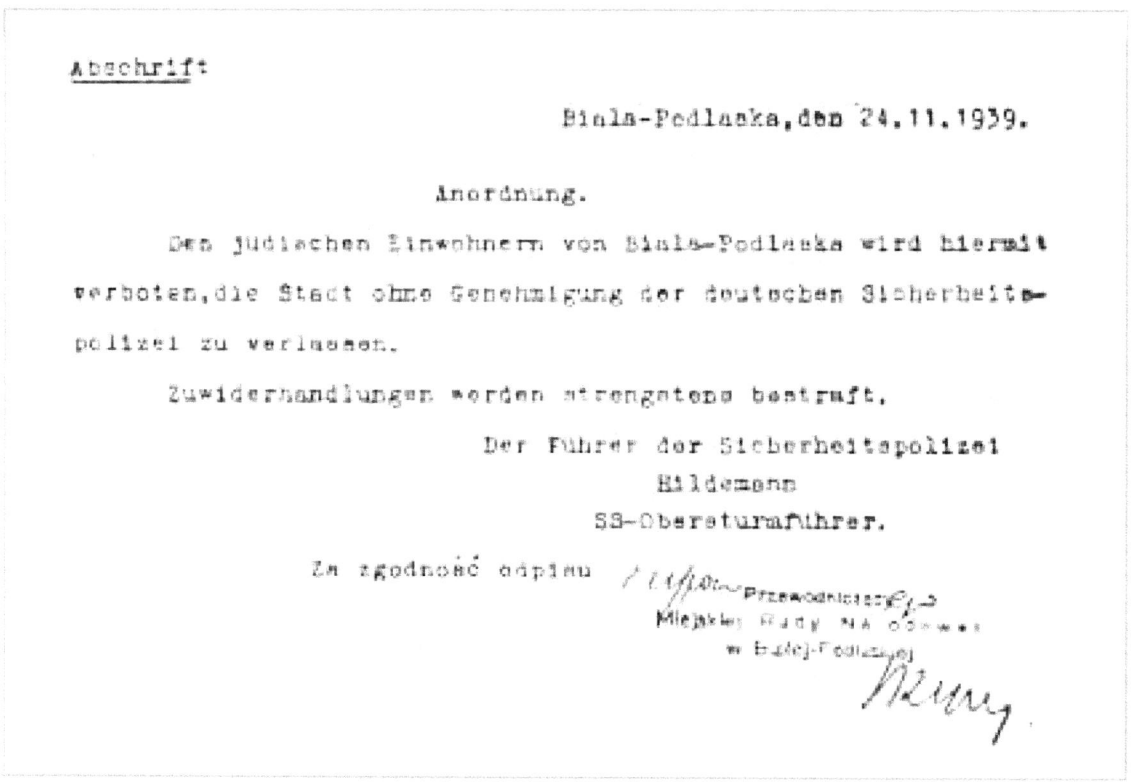

Prohibition against leaving the city

The Gestapo was quartered in the chateau of the Raabes' factory on the Wolya. Its first contact with the Jewish population was the demand for a monetary payment of several tens of thousands of *zlotes*. In order to force the payment to be paid quickly, the Gestapo arrested a number of Jews and threw them in prison where they were continually tortured. The Jews were freed from prison after the payment of the appropriate sum.

The appearance of the members of the Gestapo in the street brought panic to the Jews and they would run from the street. The printing press owner, Avraham Lubelczik, hearing that the Gestapo was coming to him, had a heart attack and fell on the spot.

The Gestapo found the *shamas* [synagogue caretaker], Yoal Gringlos, who stood forlorn in his *talis* [prayer shawl] and *tefilin* [phylacteries] in the house of prayer. They led him out to the street, and brought several Jews with a ladder, on which the *shamas* had to sit in his *talis* and *tefilin*. The Jews placed the ladder with the *shamas* on their shoulders and had to go through the streets of the city.

The arrival of the Gestapo caused several dozen Jews to run from the city. This time, however, it was difficult to smuggle oneself across the border because it was already well guarded. Among those escaping was the Biala Rabbi, Rebbe Zvi Hirszhorn.

Every Jew who encountered the brown [shirt] murderers on the road would be murderously beaten. They robbed the goods from the Jewish shops, even taking the money from the cash drawer.

The economic life of the Jews was paralyzed. The Germans actively undertook the liquidation of Jewish positions. The large Jewish businesses were requisitioned; the goods were taken out to trucks and the owners were thrown in prison, demanding high payments from them. The workshops and the tools were taken away from the Jewish artisans.

A number of Jewish merchants, wanting to save their existence, gave their businesses to Christian acquaintances, assuring themselves with various agreements. A very small number of these Christians kept the agreement, but the larger number of them immediately tried to get rid of the Jews. Understand that this was not difficult to accomplish because the Jew was already without rights and helpless.

In November 1939, the Gestapo Commissar, Hildeman,[a] ordered that every Jew, starting at age six, from the 1st of December 1939 must wear a yellow *Mogen-Dovid* [Shield of David– Jewish Star] of 15 centimeters [almost six inches] on the left side of their chest. The sign of disrepute was later traded for a white armband with a blue *Mogen-Dovid* that had to be worn on the right arm. Jews were forbidden to leave the city without the permission of the German regime.

One day, all of the former members of the last-elected *kehile* authority [organized Jewish community] were called to the Gestapo. The former *dozores* [members of the Jewish community council] were ordered to immediately organize a *Judenrat* [Jewish council].

[Page 402]

Other members who previously did not belong to the *kehile* were attracted to the *Judenrat*. The *Judenrat* officiated at the premises of the *kehile* at Brisker Street.

Then the Germans had an address to which to turn with all of their demands. The *Judenrat* would constantly receive orders for various goods, which reached high sums of money that had to be covered by the Jewish population. Orders for hundreds of Jewish workers would be sent to the *Judenrat*, and understand that the workers were not paid for their work, but very often they would be beaten while working. The *Judenrat* had to organize a labor office so that it was able to provide the demanded number of workers every day. The *Judenrat* had to pay a number of the workers for their work because they simply did not have the means to live.

The occupying regime quickly assumed the entire state apparatus and the former Polish officials helped them a great deal. These officials let out on the Jews their entire rage at Poland's defeat. Where they had the opportunity, they let the Jews feel it.

The tax office quickly became active again and it began to demand all of the ordered taxes from the Jews. The officials Gerech and Kunicki particularly excelled at this. If a Jew did not pay the tax debt quickly, he was thrown in prison and tortured there.

The Pole Bielecki, who went around every day requisitioning Jewish residences for the Christians whose previous apartments were suddenly too crowded, dealt with the establishment of the housing office. Christians heartily helped the Germans in clearing out the furniture from the Jewish houses; Cibulski, the prison guard, particularly distinguished himself in this.

Every Pole who held the office, who had a connection to Jews and where the representative of the *Judenrat* took care of various matters, asked for gifts from the Jews just like the Germans. Their requests had to be met. In this area, it was particularly good to fill [the requests of] the mayor Antoni Walawski, his aide, Szczepan Szczepanski and the above-mentioned official from the housing office, Bielecki.

In the ranks of these Christians were found the early initiators and inspirations for imprisoning the Jews in a ghetto and this was a smaller one.

Jews from Suwałki and Serock were brought to Biala at the end of 1939. These Jews were gathered in the middle of the markets in their cities and as they stood, they were taken out of their cities in the Lublin *Województwo* [administrative district]. The Jews were not permitted to take anything with them and from the market they were driven into the train wagons. We learned from the Jews what kind of inhuman torturing they had already gone through during the few months of German rule.

Two thousand refugees were brought to Biala, of which the Jewish population took a large number into their residences; a very large number were quartered in the synagogue, houses of prayer and Hasidic *shtiblekh* [one room synagogues]; and a number of refugees left for Warsaw and other cities.

The Year 1940

At the beginning of 1940, Jewish prisoners of war from the former Polish Army who were from the former Polish eastern districts were brought to Biala.

The road that led the prisoners of war to Biala was marked with a bloody harvest [of bodies] and with the graves of their comrades. The imprisoned were brought from Germany to Lublin and from there, on a frosty day, they began to drive them on foot to Biala. On the road, the German escorts made the ranks of the prisoners more sparse by firing on them with automatic weapons. The prisoners of war were interned in Poczice's barracks on the Brisker highway.

In these barracks, the Stormists [*Sturmabteilung* – Stormtroopers] began to build a camp with the help of the Jewish workers whom the *Judenrat* would provide every day. The mayor, Walawski, decided to inform the Jews that this camp was being built for the Biala Jews, where they would be driven at the beginning of April. Such news, understand, brought despair and dismay among the Jews.

The prison was full of Jews, who were truly harassed. Who was not in prison then? One as a payment, another for taxes; merchants for not being willing to say where they had ostensibly hidden their goods; artisans for not being willing to show their hiding places for goods that they had ostensibly made. In connection with uncovering hidden goods, they brought the Biala merchants Yosef Gitlman, Fishl Wlos and Moshe Yitzhak Biderman from Lublin to the jail.

[Page 403]

Jews began to work sometimes at forced labor and received a salary of two *zlotes* a day, which was not enough on which to live.

Oprowizatsia-kartn [ration cards] were implemented, from which the Jewish population would receive almost nothing. A portion of the population found a solution; they traded illegally, looking for income wherever they could. Although it was forbidden for Jews to travel on the trains, Jews would take the risk of a trip on the train to Warsaw. They would dress like Christians and bring goods from Warsaw.

Several shops were open during the day, but since they did not receive anything officially, what were they permitted to sell? However, the trusted customer could receive everything.

Edicts were constantly harming the Jews. The last Jewish economic positions were liquidated by the Germans. Even the small Jewish shops were closed and the goods were taken from them. Several Jewish shops remained on Grabanower Street, where the owners were changed each time by the regime. The smallest shop had a sign with a large *Mogen Dovid* that was bought at the administrative district for a large payment.

At the entrance to Grabanower Street from the market and from Prosta Street, two large linen banners were hung with the inscription: "Plague – Danger! Entry is forbidden for Aryans." Jews were forbidden to set foot on the Wolnoszczni Square (market).

With the Jews forbidden to appear at Wolnoszczni Square, it became difficult to approach the post office. In addition, the Jews had, in general, no desire to stand in a line at the post office and be exposed to various harassments. Therefore, the *Judenrat* made great efforts to be allowed to organize a post office division. The efforts succeeded and a post office division arose at the *Judenrat* where there was also a telephone. Every day two *Judenrat* members would go to the German post office and there take care of the postal matters for the Jewish population.

On the eve of the Days of Awe, the Wolya Jews were ordered to enter the city and Wolya was cleared of Jews.

Jews were forbidden to use their balconies. If the balconies were made of metal, they [the balconies] were taken, along with all of the metal that the Jews had and given to the regime (Poles had to provide only three kilos [6.6 pounds] of metal).

*Prosta Street. A sign on Hershl Sznajman's house with the
inscription: "Jewish quarter"
[Photographed winter 1944/45]*

The situation in the synagogue and in the houses of prayer to which the homeless Jews had been brought was sad. They lived in terrible conditions. They particularly strongly felt the cold winter. Every crumb of wood in houses of prayer disappeared. The refugees tore out the floors, took down the double windows; the fences in the Jewish quarter disappeared and even the trees at the cemetery; everything was devoured in the fires at which the refugees tried to warm their limbs.

We were very satisfied that the cold winter day quickly left and the long night ended.

[Page 404]

We would board ourselves up in the houses, where we told the news of the day and waited for the defeat of the Germans.

Although the border between Germany and Russia was heavily guarded, several Bialers succeeded in smuggling themselves across to the Russian side. We learned from them that a large number of Biala refugees wanted to return home because the life of a refugee became tiresome, particularly as they heard there [in Russia] that the Jews on the German side were living and it was not bad economically.

In May 1940, a train arrived in Biala with those repatriated from the Russian side and among them were many Biala Jews. Those returning were truly surprised by the good behavior toward them on the part of the Germans.

In the course of the decisive battles in western Europe, the Germans did not forget the Jews and they were reminded that Germany was victorious.

On a beautiful morning, the Biala *Judenrat* was called to the Gestapo. There the Jewish councilmen were arranged in a row and the Gestapo man Kot read the news from a German newspaper that a Weizmann Legion to fight against Germany had been created in Eretz Yisroel. Therefore, a Jewish land would be created there with the English king at the head. After reading the notice, Gestapo members with sticks entered the room and severely beat the Jewish councilmen.

In March 1940, the Jews were ordered to register for forced labor. Many of the Jews tried to obtain certificates from doctors to say that they were not capable of working and placed the certificates with the *Judenrat*.

In June 1940, the sad chapter of forced labor began for the Jews. Jews from Mezritch [Międzyrzec] were brought to Biala and, later, also from other cities. The camp at Piczic's, at the barracks was full of Jewish workers. The Jews were employed with repair work and lived in the camp in the most terrible conditions. The Biala Jews were spared. A very small number of them worked at the repair work in the city itself. Every day, after the work, they would return home. The majority of the Biala population had made provisions for workplaces that were recognized as forced labor by the regime.

Notice forbidding the use of balconies

[Page 405]

The repair work was carried out under the leadership of the German engineer, Grinenfeld, who had his headquarters [in Biala]. The work suppliers and guards for the workers were Stormists, with their aides – the *volks-Deutschen* [ethnic Germans].

Jews did not intend to suffer in the camps and began to look for ways to find their way out of them. They did not have to look for long because every German had already found a Jewish go-between who was occupied with freeing Jews from the camps and a trade of slaves from the camp began. Understand that not everyone was able to pay such a ransom price, so the poor remained in the camps until deep autumn.

On one hand, the Stormists freed Jews from the camps for a fat reward, but on the other hand, wanting to erase the traces of this commerce, they tried to maintain a strong regimen, both at work and in the camps. One day, the Stormists' guard went to the meadow and, for no reason, shot several Jewish workers from Mezritch.

On a July morning in 1940, the Jewish population was surprised by an extensive search for the men. From all sides [of the city], Jewish men were led in the direction of the barracks at Artilerisker Street. It gave the impression that they planned to take away all of the Jewish men from the city. The women experienced hours of shock and could not even move because it was still early and because the curfew forbid going out in the street.

When all of the men were assembled at the large pit at the 9th Pulk [regiment], the Germans went to work: carrying out a selection among those assembled. They examined every work card and decided: home or remain on the spot. The majority were freed and those held were led away to a train and from there in an unknown direction.

On the same night, similar searches were carried out in most of the cities in Lublin administrative district, so it was quickly learned that those held had been taken to Belzec for forced labor.

The Biala *Judenrat* spared no effort to extract the Bialers from Belzec. However, this succeeded only after a certain time. Among the Jewish victims who fell there during the work was the Biala young man, Motl Hafer.

Autumn time 1940, the *Judenrat* was freed of the burden of providing workers because a labor office was created that was occupied with this matter.

Order to deliver up all Metals

[Page 406]

Abschrift

Aufruf.

Auf Befehl des Obergruppenführers der SS-u-Polizei-
führers beim Stabe des Generalgouverneurs für die besetzten
polnischen Gebiete vom 20.Januar 1940, haben sich sämtliche
Juden - auch getaufte - der Zwangsarbeit zu unterziehen.

Zur Eintragung haben sich alle Männer vom 16.bis zum
vollendeten 25.Lebensjahr

sofort

im Lokal Jüdische Gemeinde Pierackiego 8 zu melden.

Sämtliche männlichen Juden vom 12.bis 15.Lebensjahr
und vom 25.bis 60.Lebensjahr haben sich sofort im Lokal
Pierackiego 8 zu melden.

Alle Erfassungspflichtigen haben ihren Personal-
ausweis,Handwerker ein Verzeichnis der in ihrem Besitz
befindlichen Handwerkszeuge,mitzubringen.Fabrikbesitzer
müssen die genaue Grösse der Fabrik angeben.

Nichtmeldung zur Registrierung wird mit 10 Jahren
Zuchthaus bestraft.

Biala Podl.,den 1.März 1940.

Bürgermeister

(-)A.Walawski

Ing.A.Walawski

Za zgodność odpisu

Przewodniczący
Miejskiej Rady Na.odowej
w Bialej-Podlaskiej

Announcement to register for compulsory work

Working as officials at the labor office were the Jews Emil Wajnberger, Tuchsznajder, Edek Slobodzki (from Warsaw), Doba Krajzlman, Lewi (a son of Yitzhak Lewi), Chrielewski, Cymerman (from Sulwalk) and a young woman from Serock. Although the officials were sent by the *Judenrat*, from whom they would receive their salary, the *Judenrat* had a very weak influence on them. The official, Slobodzki, particularly made use of his office, and extracted a great deal of money from the Jews.

The *volks-Deutsch*, Leman, a former worker at the municipal airplane factory, ran the labor office, which was designed only for Jews. Jews would say of him that he was a fair "gentile." His "goodness" consisted in taking money from the Jews and this already was a good trait. He did not turn over any Jewish workers who had transgressed to the Gestapo or to the Nazi *sondergericht* [special court]; only he alone would teach a lesson on the spot. He often battered Jewish workers until they were bloody. Jews accepted this as love, rather than falling into the paws of the Gestapo. Very often, Leman beat Jews without any reason, but Jews explained it as being a result of his nervousness and with wanting to show that the labor office was a true Nazi office.

There was an instance when several young Jewish men were transferred to the Gestapo for not reporting for work punctually and the *sondergericht* sentenced them to a year in prison. Among those sentenced was the young man, Ziglman, from Garncarsker Street.

Later, the labor office did not have to strain to force the Jewish workers to work. Rather the opposite; the Jews themselves demanded employment from the labor office because they needed to have a few *zlotes* that could be earned while working. They also did not want to appear jobless to the Germans. In particular, after all of the hard labor conditions, the situation became more favorable than in a labor camp. After an entire day of work and after all of the blows received at work, in the evening they came home and had a warm environment.

At the time, they began to pay the Jewish workers for their work. A worker would earn about 3-4 *zlotes* a day. The Jewish workers would do piece-work in the carpentry factory and earn approximately 10 *zlotes* a day. The Christian workers who also worked there could not produce such earnings. Every night the Jewish carpenters would bring sacks of wood from the work and sell it in the Jewish quarter. The price of bread, in comparison to other articles, was still cheaper (from 75 *groshn* to one *zlote* a kilogram).

The Jews were mainly employed by the military and by German firms that carried out various work for the military. Among those firms were: Benz, Maier, Zager-Werner, Stuag and Zid.

The firms Benz, Maier and Zager-Werner carried out their work at the airfield. The remuneration from the firms was little, but the workers would receive plentiful blows. The Benz firm particularly excelled in the area of beating Jews. The leader of the labor office, Leman, would send Jews to the firm who had sinned.

At the Zid firm, the Jews were employed in erecting barracks for the security police at the Janower highway. The reward here also was weak and there was no lack of blows.

[Page 407]

The Jews were employed repairing the highways by the Stuag firm. The work was difficult and terrible. The workers would pave the highway with heated tar, which would emit gases that would burn their faces. For this work, the Jewish workers were not given any means of protection and a very large percentage of them would be brought to the Jewish hospital in serious condition.

Jews also worked in the large enterprises that belonged to the *volks-Deutschen* and to the Poles, such as: in the sawmill and the carpentry shop of Zawidzki that was located in Hercl Czarne's sawmill and the Raabes' factory; in the carpentry shop of Hauschild, that was located in Piczic's sawmill.

Summer 1940, when they began to take Jews for forced labor and send them to labor camps, a group of Biala Jews wanting to assure themselves of a workplace to avoid forced labor erected a brush factory at Garncarsker Street under the leadership of the Mezritch tradesman, Munye Sucharczik. At the beginning, the *Judenrat* led the factory, but it was soon taken over by the German, Wanczura, a brother-in-law of the vice district administrator, Fritsh.

This German, Wanczura, also took over the soap factory of Sura Gele Goldfeder at the Wolya and turned it into a large enterprise. The professional leadership was found in the hands of the Jewish refugee, Bibrowski, and his helper was Volvish (Volf) Wajcman. This enterprise was not really for the Germans; he requisitioned both Jewish printers, Lubelczik's and Hochman's, and erected a large printing plant at Pulsudski Street.

The Biala Jews had "equal rights" in the area of work and even received "state posts." Thus the Jews worked in the administrative district and other German offices, such as: messengers, mechanics, drivers. Who even speaks of military workplaces? There, they literally could not go without Jews.

Despite the fact that the labor office provided Jewish workers for all German workplaces, they would still grab Jews for work from the street. There were Germans who could not give up the pleasure of walking through the streets and chasing after Jews. These Germans, in general, did not need to have Jews to work, only to bully them.

The Year 1941

At the beginning of 1941, the Germans arranged an expulsion rehearsal in the city. On a winter morning, the gendarmerie and the security police went through the city, grabbed a few old Jewish people, women and men, and took them to the village of Opole, near Rososz. Several days later, all of those taken out came back. It was difficult to understand what the Germans intended with this.

War illness – typhus – spread widely in the Jewish quarter. It reigned in the Jewish houses where there was overcrowding and where they lived under difficult hygienic conditions. The courtyards also were polluted because their sanitary facilities were not suitable for such a large number of residents. The sanitation division at the *Judenrat* could not catch up with the cleaning.

The Biala *Judenrat* also had the Jewish hospital, which was over-crowded, under its control. At the beginning of the German occupation, in general, there were no Jewish doctors in the city and the Jewish sick were forbidden to see Christian doctors.

Summer 1940, Jewish doctors came to Biala: Dr. Bergman (is supposed to have come from Katowice), Dr. Hochman (a refugee from Germany, came from Warsaw) and Dr. Rubinsztajn (came from Warsaw). In 1941, the Warsaw surgeon, Dr. Gelbfisz, came to Biala. The *feldshers* [traditional barber-surgeons], Chaim Musawicz (the Kabriner) and Berish Wajsman (from Łomazy), were active.

A help-committee existed at the *Judenrat* under the name Jewish Social Self-help that would also receive subsidies from the Jewish regional help-committee in Lublin. At the head of the committee was Moshe Rodzinek. The committee endeavored to ease the need of the poor by distributing lunches and distributing medical help without cost. However, the financial means of the committee were too small to be able to ease the need on the Jewish streets. The committee was located at Grabanower Street in the house of Yakov Kornblum. The committee kitchen was active in the former bakery of Yitzhak Fogel on Prosta Street.

In spring 1941, the Germans began to rush to build military objects in Biala and its surroundings and mainly air bases. Jews were employed in all of the works and this time their conditions became more favorable in the work camps than a year earlier. It was clear to the population that Germans were preparing for a jump to the east.

[Page 408]

In the middle of the preparation for the war, a number of edicts against the Jews again were issued, of which we will here enumerate only a few of them.

Jews were forbidden to leave their residences. Christians were forbidden to permit Jews to enter their houses and, in general, have any contact with Jews. This was motivated by the fact that Jews were covered with lice and typhus would be spread through them.

Jews were forbidden to travel in coaches and by horse and wagons.

All Jewish immovable estates were confiscated and the Jews had to give the rent money to the guardianship that was organized for this purpose. Even the owners of the houses were obliged to pay rent for their apartments. The guardianship collected the rent regularly and the Jews had to remodel the apartments at their own expense and clean the streets and courtyards.

The confiscation law was also valid for the houses of prayer and the synagogue. As the homeless were living in the latter, the *Judenrat* had to pay rent for them. The *Judenrat* dared to subtract from the rent the expenses that were connected with cleaning the toilets near the synagogue. For such daring, the *Judenrat* representative, Yakov Ahron Rozenbaum, received a slap from a German comptroller, who had come specially from Lublin about this matter. However, the *Judenrat* was stubborn and again subtracted the expenses.

Among the fresh anti-Jewish edicts was an order to pay the Jewish workers 20 percent less than the Christian ones. The earnings of the Jewish workers decreased and the scarcity grew. A kilogram of bread now cost six *zlotes* and in time the price reached eight *zlotes*.

After Passover, the city was flooded by the German military, which kept on storming to the east. We saw that the last preparations for a new bloody struggle were ending. It was clear that it was the threshold of the war between Germany and Russia. This feeling of war evoked a hope from the city Jews that the war between Germany and Russia would speed up Hitler's end, although they trembled at the prospect of the fresh, bloody turmoil. Meanwhile, the prices on all goods rose sharply. The price of bread in those days reached 12 *zlotes* a kilogram.

Shabbos night, the 21st of June 1941, in the middle of the night, the German Army crossed the Russian border and began to push east. The hope of the Jews quickly faded away and the fear of the next day increased.

During the first weeks of the war between Germany and Russia, Russian prisoners of war would constantly be brought to Biala. The prisoners would ask for a piece of bread or matches when they were led through the streets. However, no one filled their requests because the Jews paid very dearly for a piece of bread.

Announcement about petechial typhus illnesses that mainly spread among Jews

[Page 409]

Moshe Ganski and Akiva Jurberg, arrested for offering a piece of bread to the imprisoned, were transported to the Auschwitz camp, where they perished. The Polish Biernacka was arrested for the same sin, but they succeeded in extracting her from the Nazi talons.

The Russian war prisoners were treated terribly in German captivity. However, cruelty was the fate of the Jewish-Russian war prisoners. The German rulers made the greatest effort to find Jews among the prisoners and to annihilate them.

Once, when Biala Jews were working at repairing the Brisker highway, a freight train passed by with Russian war prisoners. Seeing the workers, they began to shout. Suddenly, one began to shout in Yiddish: "Comrades! We are being taken to be shot!" The Jewish workers recognized one of those shouting, the son of the shoemaker, Goldberg, from Janower Street.

In autumn, the so-called Jewish *Ordnungsdienst* [ghetto police], who were provided with complete clothing and a hat on the pattern of the Warsaw ghetto, was organized by the *Judenrat* at the order of the administrative district. The task of the Jewish police consisted of keeping order in the Jewish quarter (mainly expressed by not permitting walking on Grabanower Street, which was the central street in the quarter); providing to the labor office Jews who were in no hurry to go to work; and watching over the sanitary conditions in the quarter. Later, when a "prison" was created at the *Judenrat* to hold arrested recalcitrant tax payers, the *Ordnungsdienst* was busy with arresting the accused and with guarding the "prison" so that the Jews would not "run away."

Yakov Goldsztajn (commandant), Hinekh Bialer, Asher Rozencwajg, Motl Finklsztajn, Moshe Preter, Chaim Fridman, Fishl Lebnberg, Yakov Tokarski, Lajbzon and Chonen (a saddlemaker from the Wolya) belonged to the *oranungsdient*. The secretary was M. Hercman (former bookkeeper at the Raabes' factory). After the commandant, Goldsztajn, was shot in the summer of 1942, the refugee from Sulwalk, Cymerman, was designated in his place.

In autumn, at the order of the regime, the office of the *Judenrat* was moved from Brisker Street to Yakov Kornblum's house on Grabanower Street. This was done with the intention of ousting the few Jews who lived outside the designated boundaries of the Jewish district.

On a November day, Thursday, the security police went to the Warszaw highway between Biala and Mezritch and shot every Jew they met. Among the murdered was the flour merchant, Berl Czelaza, of Grabanower Street. It seems this was because of the order that forbad Jews to leave the area in which they lived.

And how could the Jews remain sitting at home and watch how families were dying of hunger? They actually ignored the dangers and started on their way, where a bullet often reached them and they never came home. Jewish houses drowned in the sadness and tears.

Confiscation of immovable property

[Page 410]

Christmas Eve, the representatives from the *Judenrat* were called to the district headquarters, where they were given an order to collect all of the furs from the Jewish population. The *Judenrat* reported this order to the Jewish population and the office of the *Judenrat* was transformed into a fur camp. Not all of the Jews hurried to give their furs to the Germans and they burned or destroyed them in another way, although they were threatened with death.

A few days after the passage of the period to turn over the furs, the security police set out on a search of Jews. Men and women were stopped and they were taken to the security police. It was learned from the first freed Jews that the search by the security police was for Jewish furs. The search gave rise to a Jewish victim: the security police found a fur under a coat of a Jew, probably someone abnormal, and he was shot.

Abschrift
_____

Der Kreishauptmann   Biala Podlaska,den 1.9.1941
Straßenverkehrsamt

           Anordnung.

Betr. Regelung des Droschkenfuhrwesens.

Zur Regelung des Droschkenfuhrwesens erlasse ich nachstehende
Anordnung:

1) Alle in den öffentlichen Verkehr zu stellenden Droschken
    sind dem Straßenverkehrsamt zur Prüfung und Zulassung vor-
    zuführen. Ein Rechtsanspruch auf Zulassung besteht nicht.

2) Für jede zugelassene Droschke wird eine Zulassungsbeschei-
    nigung ausgestellt,welche der Fahrer stets bei sich zu
    führen und auf Verlangen dem Beamten des Verkehrsdienstes
    vorzuzeigen hat

3) Es werden zwei Standplätze für Droschken im Stadtgebiet
    Biala Podlaska bestimmt:
         a) Standplatz am Stadtplatz,gegenüber der Polizeiwache;
         b) Standplatz am Bahnhof,gegenüber dem Bahnhofgebäude.

    Andere Plätze dürfen nicht als Standplätze benutzt werden.
    Die polnische Polizei bestimmt die jeweils erforderliche
    Anzahl der Droschken für den Fahrdienst am Bahnhofplatz
    und für den Dienst in den Nachtstunden.

4) Die Fahrpreise regeln sich nach den Tarifsätzen der von mir
    festgesetzten Droschken-Tarifordnung.

5) Jede Droschke ist durch Aufmalen der zugeteilten Nummer mit
    weißer Farbe an der äußeren Rückseite kenntlich zu machen.

6) Die Beförderung von Juden ist verboten.

7) Der Genuß alkoholischer Getränke während der Fahrdienstzeit
    ist untersagt.

8) Jugendliche unter 16 Jahren dürfen mit dem Führen von
    Droschken nicht beauftragt werden.

9) Unbegründete Ablehnung von Fahrten, insbesondere Deutschen
    gegenüber, ist unstatthaft.

10) Zuwiderhandlungen gegen diese Anordnungen werden mit Geld-
     strafe bis zu 1.000 Zl. oder mit Gefängnis bis zu 3 Monaten
     bestraft. Gleichzeitig kann die Einziehung der Droschke ver-
     fügt werden.

11) Diese Anordnung tritt mit dem Tage der Bekanntgabe in Kraft.

                         Der Kreishauptmann
                         gez.Kühl.

     Za zgodność odpisu

Przewodniczący
Miejskiej Rady Na.odowej
w Bialej-Podlaskiej

Prohibition on the use of horse drawn coaches

Rumors reached Biala that the Jews in the occupied eastern area of the former Poland were being tortured and annihilated by the Nazis. And that among the victims were Biala Jews who had escaped from their homes in 1939 and considered themselves saved from the Nazi talons. We learned from Mrs. Sura Khohan (née Preter), who returned from Slonim, about the frightening slaughter of the Jewish population that the Germans had carried out there. Among the murdered in the slaughter were several Bialers who had gone there in 1939, such as Moshe Orlanski and his wife and child, Sura Khohan's husband and so on.

The city was full of German officials and they were all busy with the Jews. Woe to the Jew in whom these officials interested themselves.

A division of the *S.D.* [*Sicherheitsdienst*] (Security Service) was located on Pilsudski Street (Mezritcher), which the S.S. people, German and Glet, led. In addition to the gifts that the division would demand from the *Judenrat*, it also demanded reports from the *Judenrat* about what the Jewish population thought and said. The *Judenrat* did not hurry to provide such reports. Once, when the S.S. men were insistent in this matter, it was written in short that the Jewish population was full of concern about the oncoming winter, how to obtain potatoes, firewood and other needed things. The S.S. men, hearing such a report, entered a wild rage and began shouting: the Russians have taken back Minsk, Vilna and Riga; are the Jews talking about this? The members of the *Judenrat* were escorted out of the office with blows.

A *volks-Deutsch* named Apel was located at the Biala gendarmerie. This gendarme was surely a wagon driver for a Jew because he spoke Yiddish well, constantly adding small bits of wagon-driver curses. The Jews gave him the nickname, Yankl *Morde* [chin or snout]. This gendarme would apply pressure on the Jews and there was not a day on which he would not catch a Jew in a sin and batter him. If he found a piece of meat in a Jew's house, he would carry on a real pogrom in the room. He broke everything with an axe and threw it out through the window and then beat those in the house. When the Jewish shoemaker, Borukh Frajner, who was friendly with him, asked him: "Apel, what do you want from us?" He would answer: "May you know of cholera! With all of your bag and baggage, there is no end to you!"

[Page 411]

The Polish police *przodownik* [leader] Drwencki (came from Pomer), was active at the gendarmerie and he was a privileged person there because he spoke German. This Drwencki had his methods of blackmailing the Jews who he knew were involved in commerce. He was a constant visitor of the Jews, but it was difficult to satisfy his appetite by giving him the most beautiful and best. After everything, he would turn the Jew into the gendarmerie.

The Biala security police, who were housed at Grabanower Street, literally in the heart of the Jewish quarter, rampaged. Among them, those who stood out with their special cruelty were: one Peterson (nicknamed "blond murderer" by the Jews) and another, with a fat head, whom the Jews would call *Psil* [idol, graven image]. The security police had a forge at the new market and woe to a Jew who these two security policemen would take to the forge, ostensibly to work. Such a person would remember his visit there for long weeks. When the two security policemen were noticed from afar, the street would empty of people.

The Biala security policemen would attack Jewish houses at night and rape the women there. After doing this disgraceful act, they would loot the residences.

A special militia was active at the administrative district, which consisted of *volks-Deustchn* and was called the *Sonderdienst* [special services]. Their leader for a time was one Grzimek, who caused great problems for the Jews. The *Sonderdienst* would come to the Jewish quarter to grab Jews for work and, in addition, they heavily beat them.

The agents of the Biala Criminal Police also exerted influence over the Jews. They knew which Jews were employed in trading and smuggling and they constantly blackmailed them, extracting giant sums and items of worth from them. The agents Constanti Baldiga, Wolanski and Golenbiowski excelled here. In addition to being a blackmailer, Baldiga was also a murderer. In the winter of 1941-42, he shot the first two Jews in the city, the carpenter, Wajsberg (the son of the carpenter, Khanan) and a young man from the former Polish eastern sector.

The Polish police also constantly reminded the Jews of their existence. Here, too, the Jews stood with their pockets [wallets] and paid so that the Polish policeman would overlook [things] and stop bothering them. What Jews then were [considered] legal in regard to German law? What did a Jew still possess in his house after everything had been confiscated? And a Polish policeman knew very well where to look…

The officials at the Biala administrative district would constantly demand presents from the *Judenrat*, which reached great sums. Their conduct in relation to the *Judenrat* was cynical. They constantly assured them that no more edicts would come, but actually they themselves created and issued anti-Jewish orders. The *Judenrat* knew well the worth of their assurances.

Of all of the exterminators, the "most tolerable" for the individual Jew was the Gestapo. It did not grab Jews for work; it did not come into the Jewish quarter to beat Jews. It was in contact with the *Judenrat*, sending orders there for giant sums, extorting the last *groshn* from the *Judenrat*, which was constantly a debtor. Several Jewish artisans were swamped with work for the Gestapo. In time, the Gestapo arranged a tailoring workshop [in its facilities], where the brothers Nakhman and Yoal Zuberman, Meir Rajc and Ahron Wolkowicki customarily worked. The constant shoemakers for the Gestapo were Borukh Frajner and Nekhmia Dorfman. The materials were provided by the *Judenrat*.

These artisans from time to time would get a hint of news from the hangmen about Jews and confide it to a few chosen people in the quarter. They would know who had been brought to the Gestapo prison at the Raabes' factory or who had been taken out to be shot in the Grabarker and Wulker forests.

One of the first Jewish arrestees at the Gestapo prison was the Biala resident, the apothecary, Michasz Hofer. The Gestapo probably did not know itself why they were holding him, but it did not want to free him. Hofer would be in the city the entire day, but he had to return to the prison to sleep. The members of the Gestapo extorted valuable items from Hofer and after many months they freed him from prison.

The Year 1942

Dejected, resigned and full of apathy, the Jewish population strode into the new year of 1942, which was the last year for them in their city of birth. The suffering before death was even more difficult and the rope around the neck was drawn even tighter.

On a winter night the *Judenrat* was informed that two young, Jewish men had been thrown into the cellar where they had worked by the security police. One of them was the son of Khanan Rajch. It was already known that there was the smell of death [associated with this]. The young people were supposed to have sawed a board there in order to take the wood home. This was noticed by a security policeman who threw them in the cellar. The *Judenrat* began its efforts to extract the two young men. The security police demanded a sum of 10,000 *zlotes* that even at that time was a very serious sum. Yet, the sum was collected and was given to the security police. However, only one young man was freed because in between Rajch had already been shot.

[Page 412]

Every day, Christians would come and tell of the murdered Jews who lay outside the city. They had been shot by the Germans who saw them there. The record of the carrying out these executions comes from the gendarme, Leon Busch, a *volks-Deutsch* from the Poznan region.

Thus, the gendarme Busch shot two others at the Wolya, near the church, including Liptshe (Adlersztajn), the son of the [female] butcher. A few weeks later, the wife of Pinyele, the bagel baker from Mezritch Street, perished from one of his [Busch's] bullets at Szidorska Street.

During the first week after Passover, tens of Jews were arrested, mainly those who were once punished for violating the Nazi laws. After spending the night at the Polish police post, the Gestapo took them away on the Janower highway in the morning and shot them there, near the Jewish cemetery. Among those shot were the butcher, Yudl Jurberg and Adlersztajn (his wife Tsvya), as well as the Sulwalker homeless one, Bernsztajn (a brother of the photographer, Osif Bernsztajn), and so on.

On a June evening, the Polish police carried out arrests among the Jewish population. That night, the arrestees were imprisoned in the Polish police post and, in the morning, they took them out to Wulker forest and shot them there. Among those shot this time were: Chaim Fridman (nickname *Beznozek* [without legs]), Nakhum Tenenbaum's son-in-law, and Yakov Goldsztajn, commandant of the Jewish *Ordnungsdienst*, who was arrested the day before by the gendarmerie.

The young Moshe Lichtenbaum (Leibe Mednik's grandson] was among the arrested Jews at the Polish police post. He was arrested during the day because of a sharp answer he gave to a Christian who had insulted him. His parents, seeing the evening arrest, immediately understood that fresh executions were being prepared. They began to make efforts to save their child. It is easy to imagine the mood of the parents who had to return home at seven o'clock (the curfew time for the Jews) without their son. They went outside in the morning and learned that the Jews arrested the day before had actually been shot. However, their son remained at the Polish police post. They began to shake with joy. Moshe Lichtenbaum had been arrested by the ruddy security policeman, Peterson, who was known by the Jewish policeman, Moshe Preser. He asked the murderer for hours to free Lichtenbaum, but he could not prevail on him. This Peterson, however, it appears, wanted the young man to go through a struggle with death and ordered the Polish police to come to take the Jews to the Gestapo, imprisoning Lichtenbaum in a separate cell. Thus, the young man and the Jews who had been shot went through their last suffering before their death, [Lichtenbaum] not suspecting that he would be saved. This Lichtenbaum said that it was clear to everyone that they were going to their death and they spent their last hours reciting the *vide* [confession of one's sins].

At the same time, a group of Janower Jews were shot in Wulker forest and among them the Biala resident, Leibl Rodzinek, who had made efforts to free the Janower Jews. Rodzinek was also supposed to be helped by the Christian woman, Konopka, but instead of helping him, she handed him into the hands of the Gestapo.

There was a series of shootings. However, German cynicism went so far that they did not stop the court hearings against the murdered Jews. Thus, for example, there was a court hearing for leaving his place of residence for the Biala resident, Noakh Wajnsztajn (from the village of Proszeki), that took place in Lublin. At that time, he had been transferred from the Biala prison to Lublin. His two daughters did not rest and did everything to save their father. They engaged the well-known lawyer, Hafmakl-Ostrowski who had access to the German courts and, therefore, they were asked to pay really legendary sums. The Jew was not present at the court hearing. With joy, his daughters heard the verdict freeing him and they waited impatiently every moment to see their father. However, there was nothing for them to await. As the lawyer told them, their father had been sent away to the east…

In the middle of the hardships, the *Judenrat* received an order from the administrative district official, Lipkow, to put together a list of candidates who wanted to travel to Eretz-Yisroel or America. The *Judenrat* did not issue placards about this announcement, but individuals learned of this and thought: be listed or not be listed. In the circles of the *Judenrat* this was treated with mistrust for the entire matter. They simply said: the Germans would not become involved with a Jewish exodus during the full fervor of the war. In general, the Jews did not strongly like to appear with their names on the lists that were being provided to the Germans. And as long as the administrative district no longer applied pressure for the list, the *Judenrat* forgot about it.

[Page 413]

The majority of the population lived from their work. A number of Jewish artisans still carried on with their workshops. On the other hand, the official merchants remained an insignificant percent of the employed. Twenty or 30 small shops were found in the Jewish quarter, mainly on Grabanower Street.

Naturally, smuggling occurred on a large scale in the Jewish quarter to obtain even more food. Jewish artisans would work for Germans and for the Christian population and from them they would receive various products. The Jewish workers would also bring various goods from their workplaces.

The main article smuggled was flour. This article would be obtained in the Jewish quarter, along with the flour that was designated on the bread ration card. Nearby, various groups were also dragged along. The agents of the criminal police knew about the smuggling and were well paid for this and, consequently, made sure that the business would not be harmed. Understand that these costs made the price of bread and cereals more expensive.

Potatoes, which were a very important food, were provided by the *Judenrat*, which would receive the potatoes from the Polish *rolnik* [farmer] according to the instructions of the regime, but here, too, they had to give gifts.

The butchers would smuggle in meat. However, smuggling was very risky and they did not have the help of the agents of the criminal police, but the opposite; the agents would beat them fearlessly. Very often, the butchers would cut [the meat] very badly. However, it is clear that meat was very expensive and only a small part of the population could permit themselves the luxury.

The Jewish intelligentsia, besides doctors, lived in very difficult conditions because they lost their economic base. The change in status that befell them was not easy, in particular because the adjustment took place under German blows. They sold everything in their houses that they had acquired over the course of years of work. Particularly difficult was the situation for the members of the intelligentsia who were refugees, for whom their surroundings were completely unfamiliar. They did not even have any contact with those who had influence at the labor office who would have made it possible for them to receive the appropriate workplaces.

The Filipówer Rabbi, who had been brought with the Sulwalker Jews, was living in Biala. After the death of Rabbi Moshe Utszen (who died of typhus in the winter of 1940/1), all of those who had need of a rabbi turned to this rabbi. The Filipówer Rabbi had the reputation of a scholar and also was well versed in worldly knowledge. Taking into consideration that there was no house of prayer in the entire quarter, not one *kloyz* [small synagogue], not any religious institution, it was understandable that the rabbi's influence on the life of the quarter was minimal.

During the Days of Awe, there were places where large *minyonim* [prayer groups of at least 10 men] prayed. There were also small *minyonim* in private apartments that prayed three times a day the entire year.

There was no cultural activity in the Jewish quarter. Everyone was busy with themselves and with coping with their daily hardships.

The large *Tarbus* [secular Zionist] library was moved from Wolnoszczi Square to the premises of the *kehile* at Brisker Street. Yakov Ahron Rozenbaum, the chairman of the Zionist organization, carefully protected the treasure. At first, the Bundist library was moved to the apartment of Elihu Hofman (*Bubkes)* [nickname meaning nonsense]. He took great care of the books, but because of the constantly growing overcrowding in his apartment, he had to take the books out to the stall. Only Mrs. Liuba Tuchsznajder's Froebel school [kindergarten] at Grabanower Street existed in the quarter. The school ostensibly had the permission of the Polish school supervisor.

Many young people studied with perseverance at home and prepared to take exams as soon as the German chains were thrown off.

Although it was forbidden for Jews to buy newspapers, they would receive Polish and German newspapers in the quarter. The radio news, which the Germans would broadcast through a megaphone at the market orchard, would be gathered by children and delivered by them in the quarter.

Illegal publications came into Jewish hands very often, but it was difficult to see an organized hand in this. A Jew simply received a page from a Christian acquaintance and would bring it to [other] Jews.

News Gatherers

[Page 414]

The short, frosty winter days would pass. At night, we sat imprisoned in the houses and considered Hitler's defeat. The Germans installed a radio location in the Biala city garden that would give political news several times a day. One was drawn to the radio loudspeakers, but Jews were afraid to risk it because if they were caught listening to the radio their lives were insecure.

As the passion to hear the news of Hitler's defeat was great, they had an ingenious idea: they would send small children to the loudspeaker to grab the ether-waves and they would delight the Jews with a little news.

Children stood outside in the frost; their small noses and eyes dripped, but the childish minds strained to take in even more news. When the radio broadcast ended and the children returned to the Jewish quarter, the adults were waiting and overwhelmed them with a flood of questions. However, the children did not want to answer because each of them had a circle of news-takers and they did not want to tell [the news] to strangers.

We will describe one such group here. Among other news gatherers was a small boy, Nota Osnhclc, who specialized in catching the radio news near the radio loudspeakers in the market orchard. [He was] a child of about 11 or 12. Before the war he went to a Polish public school and to a *kheder* [religious primary school]. He was an emaciated child, really skin and bones, with a pair of glowing eyes and a sharp, very sharp, little mind.

Several times every day, this child would leave the Jewish quarter discreetly for the radio megaphone. Badly dressed, there he would jump from one foot to the other in the cold and take in every reverberation from the wide world.

So this young boy would give an overview of all of the news he had heard that day on the radio to his group every evening and take part in the political conversations. They would sit and gape, hearing the child relating the war communications. [He] never ate his fill; his small voice vibrated weakly, but he enumerated all of the places of the battlefields clearly and exactly, even from the Far East, with the ringing names so strange to our ears. The child's mastery of politics was astonishing.

In the circle for which the child Nota was the news bringer, people who had no idea about politics would come at night. However, they marveled at the young boy who breathed hard, had no strength to speak and yet "operated" the fighting ships, all kinds of airplanes and other heavy weapons.

When they would call for Nota from his home, it took a long time until the child could tear himself away from the political debates. And Nota's mother would complain: So, Nota, what will be? I do not know how we will get wood or something else for the house and you are busy with politics? And when the child would leave, people would often call to him: so, in fact, is there such a child among the Christians! Who has such a child who can be so clear about all of today's political problems as this child?

The circle to which the child, Nota, would provide the radio news, also had two other news gatherers and very talented politicians.

[One of them was] Chaim Zilberberg, the youngest son of the dentist, Yoal Zilberberg. A young man of 20, he had been sickly from birth and was a constant client of doctors. He graduated from *gymnazie* [secondary school], where he was one of the best students, just before the war. Chaim Zilberberg was freed from forced labor as someone who was sick. He would diligently study the German press the entire day and would find what was unsaid between the lines, from which he would construct his political theses. His room was filled with maps, on which he would follow the war operations. His mother would often make scenes about the maps, afraid that during a search there could be a bad outcome with such material; how does a Jew come to have maps?

The other one was Moshe Lichtenbaum, Leibl Mednik's grandson, a young man of 18. He studied in *kheder* [religious primary school] and studied worldly subjects privately. Before the war, he was harnessed in the business of his parents. He was also dedicated to politics with his entire being and was clear about every battlefield. His work was dependent on the German press, which he received through various ruses and shared with the young Zilberberg.

Moshe also was freed from forced labor because he had a problem with a foot from childhood on. However, he gave up his privilege and settled into his work as a carpenter in the workshop of the *volks-Deutsch* Kraskowski. Entering a workshop had cost him several hundred *zlotes* and he did this with a purpose. There was a radio in the house of the *volks-Deutsch* and Moshe was a strong enthusiast for hearing a little radio from abroad; as a result, it was the right decision for him to go for instruction as a carpenter. He became friendly with the *volks-Deutsch*, who was an old communist, and [Moshe] very often spent time with him in his house. There he would manipulate the radio and receive a great amount of news from London.

[Page 415]

This young man also remained in contact with comrades who worked for prominent men as house workers and in whom the brown [shirt] tyrants had trust, leaving them the keys to their residences when spending time in Germany on furlough. Moshe was the first to make use of these places to listen to the radio from abroad. He would spend entire nights there, and what could be a better place for hearing the radio from abroad than in a Nazi's house? Moshe was really "stuffed" with news from abroad. When Jews would take him into a small group, he spoke for a long time before they let him leave.

Moshe did not want to leave the radio news to the young boy, Nuta. Mainly, he did not have the patience to wait until Nuta would give the report. He himself ran to the radio loudspeaker in the municipal garden. He was successful at the beginning, but later he had his bones severely broken for wanting to listen to the radio. When it was very difficult for a Jew to approach the radio loudspeaker, Moshe could be found standing at the gate of Yisroel Shualke's courtyard and one would see how he strained his ears to catch something from the loudspeaker. In the middle of the busiest work in the workshop, he would disappear when it came time for the news from the radio.

The First Expulsion

Shabbos, the 6th of June 1942 (21st of Sivan 5702), a rumor spread in the city that all Biala Jews had to leave the city. We later learned that the county district had informed the *Judenrat* that on Wednesday, the 10th of June, all of the Jews who were not employed by the labor office had to appear at the train to leave. The order concerned all of the Jews in the county. All of the provincial cities would become free of Jews and all of the working Jews from the entire county would be located in Biala.

Yakov Ahron Rozenbaum, the representative of the *Judenrat*, dared to ask the consultant, Lipowski: Where are you sending the people? The official answered: To the west. The representative of the *Judenrat* again remarked that he knew that the Jews from the west were being sent to the east, so why had the Biala Jews become so displeasing that they were being sent to the west? The official remained embarrassed for a while, but he regained his composure and said: "You see in what conditions the people are living in the synagogue and in the remaining prayer houses." To this Y. A. Rozenbaum responded: "Yes, true, we would not be against bettering the situation of the people, but we know that, in general, this is not in the interest of the government, so why does it bother you that the people will die here?"

A group of Jewish carpenters who worked in the carpentry shop of the volks-Deutsch, Kraskowski, which was located in the Gerer Hasidic shtibl [one room prayer house]

From the right: Wowtshe Rozenbaum (Lodz), Asher Fajenbaum, Moshe Fajenbaum, Shimshon Justman, Yosef Ejdlman, Shlomo Cyker, Itshe Kanier (Serock), Yakov Brodacz, Chaim Zavl Milbaum, Zilie (Euzial) Fajenbaum, Berl Sznajderman, Moshe Lichtenbaum, Benedict Kraskowski;
From the front, sitting: Frei (Grodna), Yehosha Fajenbaum;
From the back, standing: Szulman (eastern section), Zile (Euzial) Gutenberg

The official had no right to a place in the discussion. Not having more to say, he answered: "You, Rozenbaum, see everything in black; therefore, with that attitude any collaboration with you will not be possible."

The *Judenrat* began an energetic action to repeal the edict and boarded up all thresholds [houses]. At the Gestapo, they asked why they had not been entrusted with such "a piece of work."

The *Judenrat* succeeded in learning that the edict had come from Lublin, but it did not provide any number of how many should be deported. The administrative district was interested that in the deportation numbers should be more specific.

After all efforts by the *Judenrat*, it became clear who could remain and who must leave. All of those who had work cards as well as merchants and artisans who were employed by the administrative district had the right to remain, along with their wives and children up to the age of 14. These women and children needed to receive separately stamped receipts from the labor office and from the captain to legitimize themselves for the regime. Every emigrant had the right to take up to 10 kilograms of hand luggage. For not conforming to this order there was the threat of death.

[Page 416]

The regime, for its part, informed the *Judenrat* that the entire action had to be led by the *Judenrat* and the Jewish *Ordnungsdienst* [ghetto police]. If they could not control the situation, the regime would be forced to engage with it, and that could lead to unwanted consequences.

On Tuesday, the *Judenrat*, through notices in the street, informed the Jewish population of everything and designated an assembly point at the synagogue courtyard.

On *Shabbos*, as soon as it was clear that one could escape from the expulsion with a work card, a large part of the population began to make an effort to obtain such a card. Many succeeded by making high payments to receive a card for living.

Young men, who had gone around with young women for years and did not intend to get married during the time of war, quickly got married in order to save their brides [girlfriends] from expulsion and thus legalized their brides as their wives. Fictitious marriages also took place in order to save Jewish women.

There were those who could not legally save themselves; they decided on the spot not to appear and to hide during the time of the *aktsia* [deportation]. Many ran away illegally in time to the closest villages, to Christian acquaintances and to neighboring Mezritch. Those who decided to leave began to prepare for the road and to prepare packs.

In the provincial *shtetlekh* [towns] of the county, the Jews ran to the forests. In general, they did not intend to appear for the migration.

Tuesday afternoon, the taxation office in Biala also showed what it was capable of doing. Almost all of the officials, accompanied by policemen, started going through the Jewish quarter demanding of the Jews the required and also even more unevaluated taxes for 1942. They demanded extremely high sums that had to be paid immediately because, if not, they threatened arrest and appearing the next day for the deportation transports.

The same day, Yakov Malina went to the administrative district to take care of some matter. At night, we learned that Malina was taken away outside the city in an auto and shot by the agent, Baldiga.

Tragic moments took place in families; parents could not cope with their children nor children with their parents. No one had the strength to say to the other – remain. Because death called out from every order.

On Wednesday, the 10th of June, 700 souls in their holiday clothes with packs of various sizes assembled at the synagogue courtyard. People streamed there from all directions. The Jewish *Ordnungsdienst*, which had been enlarged to 50 people specially for this purpose, went from house to house and reminded people about the obligation to appear at the synagogue courtyard. Those who belonged to the lucky ones and remained in the city moved freely in the Jewish quarter, where no controls were enforced.

The representatives of the regime arrived at the synagogue courtyard and watched the scene. They sent home some of the crippled, sick and nursing women. They ordered that the sick, those not capable of being transported, should remain at home. Understand that this strengthened even more the impression that the people were only being evacuated to another city. Many who had decided not to appear now took their packs and came to the synagogue courtyard.

At around two o'clock in the afternoon, when the synagogue courtyard was full of Jews, the group along with Jewish *Ordnungsdienst*, accompanied by several gendarmes, was led to the train where it was turned over to the *Sonderdienst* [special services] of the administrative district. A number of weak Jews were brought to the train by auto.

It is difficult to list all of the Bialers who marched in the procession to the train. Several faces have remained etched in my memory: Moshe Kawa, known and beloved by everyone, went, resigned and prematurely old. Near him walked the good-natured teacher, Yoal Meir Hajblom. Among the lines could be noticed the merchant Yosef Gilman and his family, Pintshe Eidlman and his wife and small son, Hercl Czarni and his wife.

The Jews had to wait at the train station until morning because it seems the deportation had been carried out early and no wagons had been prepared for the people. The *Judenrat* brought bread and coffee to the train several times.

Early Thursday, a freight train arrived and by around 11 o'clock in the morning, the people were already in the closed wagons. The train moved from the spot in the company of a Stormist and several Ukrainians guards, in the direction of Łuków.

[Page 417]

The *Judenrat*, at any cost, wanted to learn to where the people had been sent. They learned from the Łuków *Judenrat* that the train left in the direction of Lublin; from the Lublin *Judenrat* – in Majdan Tatarski – came the news that the people had gone in the direction of Chelm. And Chelm reported that the train had passed through the city on Friday evening in the direction of Wlodawa. The last news came from Wlodawa, from which they reported that they knew nothing and that they should not be asked such questions again.

At Wlodawa, the thread was torn. And because such an answer was given from there, it was surmised that in Wlodawa they did know what had happened to the people.

The administrative district also learned about the constant rumors that there was news from the people who had been sent away. It, therefore, tried to tap the pulse of the *Judenrat*, but the *Judenrat* answered: "We called the people to report for emigration and where you sent them, you know and not us."

Actually, the *Judenrat* learned where the people were being sent. It came to light that the last train station of their wandering was Sobibor, 37 kilometers from Chelm, in the direction of Wlodawa. Before the war, Sobibor was well-known as a small train station between forests in the Wlodawa area, from which wood would be transported.

Later, we heard that many Jews had been brought to Sobibor and they were left sealed for several days in freight cars without food and without a drop of water on a hot summer day on a side train line in a forest. Afterwards, the bodies were thrown out of the train cars and burned there.

Weeks passed and the thinking about the uprooted victims did not cease. It was natural that the German regime became the inheritor of the few possessions that the victims had left in their apartments. The apartments that had been left were thoroughly cleaned.

The month of July passed relatively calmly and the month of August arrived, which was so rich in bloody events.

On Monday, the 3rd of August, in the afternoon, Ahron Brodacz was arrested at the district administration. At the same time, the *Sonderdienst* began to search for Menakhem Finkelsztajn. Not being able to find him, it arrested the *Judenrat* chairman, Yitzhak Piczic, as a hostage, threatening to shoot him if Finkelsztajn did not appear. After a short time, Menakhem Finkelsztajn appeared at the district administration and Yitzhak Piczic was freed. The news about the arrest of the two Jews made a strong impression in the city because they knew that both had been visitors at the district administration and had "support" in the person of the officials, Engineer Debus and Naulinger. Relatives and friends warned them of the consequence of maintaining contact with the Nazis, with whom they would from time to time have success in obtaining a favor for a Jew for a good reward.

Right after the arrest of Ahron Brodacz, a search was carried out in his residence by the *Sonderdienst*. Consequently, his sister and his wife, Chaya Fajbenbaum, and her two sisters were held.

For an entire afternoon, the families of the arrestees made every possible effort to learn something, but without success. No one knew what to say, but everyone was calmed, believing that this was a misunderstanding that would quickly be clarified. Thus the day passed without any success until the curfew arrived for Jews, seven o'clock at night, and the families of the arrestees had to return home with mixed feelings of fear and hope.

The end was a tragic one. That same night, all of those held, the women and the men, were shot. They said in the city that this was the German officials wanting to erase the traces of their contact with these Jews and that the official, Naulinger of Passau (Germany), had a hand in the murders.

In the middle of the night, on Monday into Tuesday of the 4th of August, we suddenly heard heavy military steps in the streets of the Jewish quarter. As soon as the sun began to come up, we heard the wild Gebril, *Mener raus* [men, out]! The entire Jewish quarter was surrounded by gendarmes, security police, Polish police, Gestapo and Goering's troops – the pilots, all armed with machine guns and grenades. Grabanower Street was full of men, who were chased to the corner of the street (in the direction of the new market). Those who were late were accompanied on their way with blows from rifle butts. After a time, the Germans began to check the work cards. The checking lasted several hours and all the men were freed.

However, these almost "innocent" checks that morning cost the Jewish population 19 victims. Among them were: Zalman Liverant, Yukl Listgartn, Fridman (from eastern Kresy ["Eastern Borderlands" of Poland], a former war prisoner), and so on. Many of those who returned alive had been severely beaten and bloodied during the check.

[Page 418]

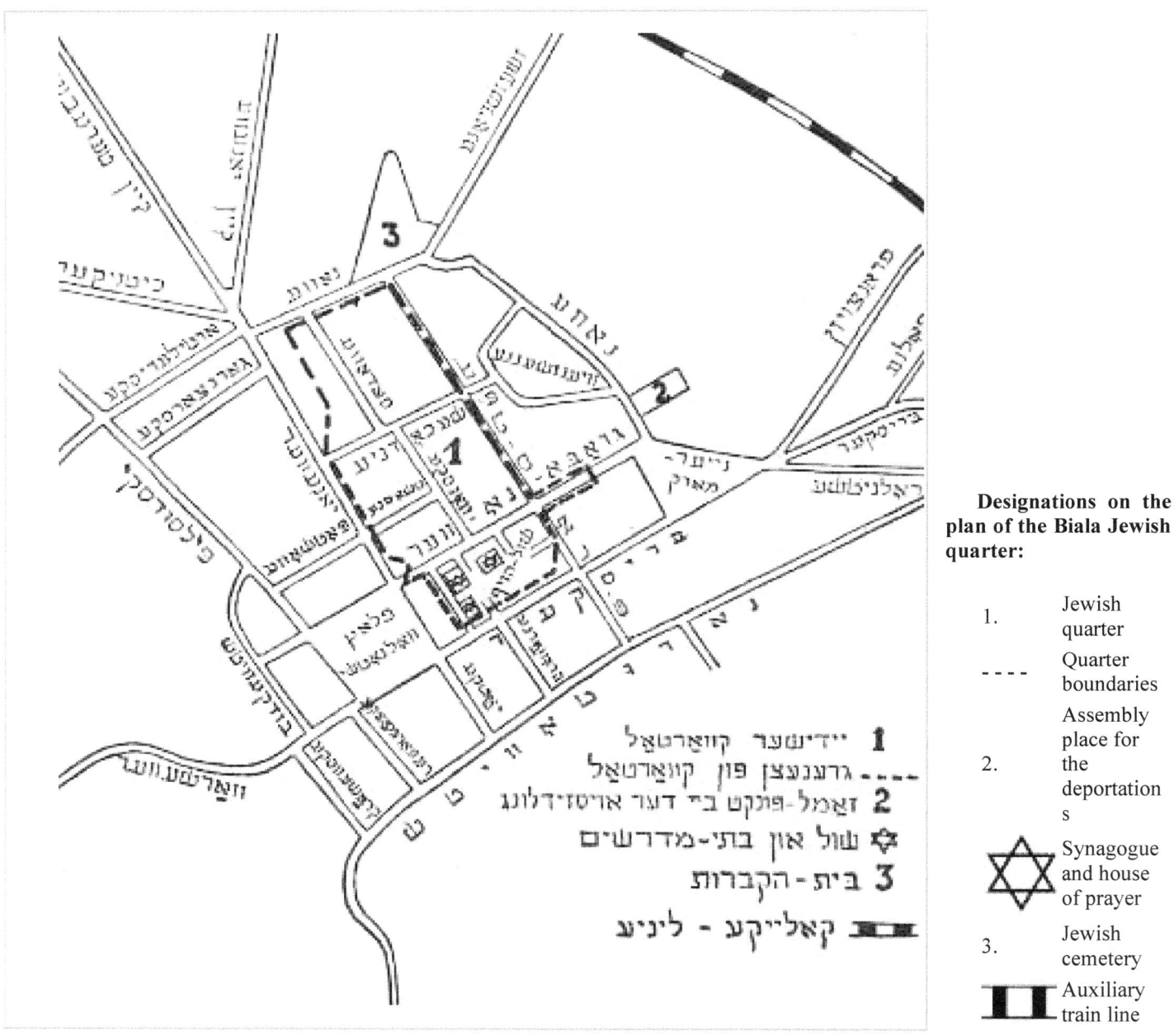

Plan of the Biala Jewish quarter during the Nazi regime

Designations on the plan of the Biala Jewish quarter:

1. Jewish quarter

---- Quarter boundaries

2. Assembly place for the deportations

✡ Synagogue and house of prayer

3. Jewish cemetery

Auxiliary train line

Faisker,[b] the Gestapo man, led this *aktsia* and the *volks-Deutsch*, gendarme Leon Busch, excelled particularly bloodily.

On the part of the accused, witnesses such as the shoemaker, W. Ivanicki, former Biala vice-mayor, appeared. After he gave his testimony, Faisker stood up and gave the following statement: "I expected that Jews would appear here against me. I can also understand the appearances of Poles as witnesses against me. But how does Ivanicki come here? This Ivanicki, who was a Gestapo confidant who denounced tens of Poles to the Gestapo and brought about their death – how dare he appear in court against me?"

Ivanicki was arrested on the spot. The court sentenced him to 10 years in prison, to losing his rights as a citizen for 15 years and the confiscation of his possessions on behalf of the state treasury (provided by Yehosha Wajsman – Israel.)

The events in the city began to unwind with particular speed.

On Friday, the 7th of August, the *Judenrat* announced that, according to the order of the regime, all Jews had until six o'clock in the evening to move to the smaller quarter, according to how it had earlier been planned.

The Jewish quarter that was located between the streets, Grabanower and the synagogue courtyard alleys (except for several houses bordering on the new market), Janower (only on the right side), Prosta (from the court on) and Cmentarne, would now be enclosed like a four-cornered box between the streets (without the synagogue alleys – from Wolnoszczi Square to Prosta), Prosta, only on the left side (from Grabanower to Przechodnia), Janower, the right side until Przechodnia and Przechodnia only the right side.

There really was the threat of suffocating in such a narrow cage. Although the quarter was not closed, people already lived in stalls, so that it was an instrument of torture deciding where to go.

The *Judenrat* still tried to intervene with the *S.D.* representative, Glet, who had promised to try to have the order revoked, and it was actually soon withdrawn.

In a conversation between the *S.D.* [*Sicherheitsdienst* – Security Service] man and the *Judenrat* representative, Y. A. Rozenbaum, the former blurted out that the order would certainly be revoked because other mass means were being planned against the Jews. However, what kind of mass means these were, they could not learn from him, but time lifted the veil of this mystery.

On Monday, the 10th of August, a rumor spread in the city that freight cars were standing at the train station in which 400 men would be taken from Biala to Lublin. This information was confirmed because all of the German offices were telephoned from the train station and they were asked about the Jews who were supposed to leave. Everywhere they answered that they did not know anything.

Wednesday, in the morning of the 12th of August, a search was carried out for the Jewish men by an unfamiliar security policeman with the help of the Ukrainian militia. The detained Jews were taken to an assembly place on the Wolya. Among those held were many workers from the *Wehrmacht* [German armed forces] and from the German workplaces, which made efforts to free them. The *S.D.* representative, Wida, announced the search to the *Judenrat* who left for the assembly point at the Wolya and freed all of the Jews.

[Page 419]

Abschrift

Anordnung.

Auf Grund der Verordnung über Aufenthaltbeschränkungen im
Generalgouvernement vom 13 September 1940(VBlGG I S.288)und der
dazu ergangenen Ergänzungen ordne ich mit sofortiger Wirkung an:

Die in der Stadt Biala-Podlaska aufenthaltberechtigten Juden
dürfen:

1.den ihnen als Wohnbezirk zugewiesenen Stadtteil nicht ver-
lassen.

2.von der Grabanowskastr.und Prostastr.nur die innerhalb des
jüdischen Wohnbezirkes liegenden Strassenseite,sowie von der
Janowskastr.nur den dem jüdischen Wohnbezirk angrenzenden Fussteig
(vom Stadtplatz aus rechter Fussteig der Janowskastr.)betreten.

3.die Janowskastr.selbst un die dem jüdischen Wohnbezirk nach
aussen angrenzenden sonstigen Strassen und Platze nicht betreten.

4.den Weg zu u.von der jüdischen Bade-u.Entlausungsanstalt nur
in geschlossenen Abteilungen unter Führung des jüdischen Ordnungs-
dienstes durch die Prostastr.u.Narutowiczastr.benutzen.

Ausgenommen von dem Verbot ist die Benutzung der öffentlichen
Strassen durch Juden,die zur Arbeit eingesetzt sind und sich auf
dem Wege zu oder von der Arbeitsstelle befinden.Diese Juden haben
ihre Arbeitskarte vom Arbeitsamt oder eine Ausnahme-Genehmigung mit
Lichtbild von der Kreishauptmannschaft,Abteilung Passstelle,als Ausweis bei sich zu führen.

Für die in den übrigen Gemeinden des Kreises Biala-Podlaska
aufenthaltsberechtigten Juden gilt vorstehende Anordnung sinngemäss.

In der Stadt und sämtlichen Gemeinden des Kreises Biala-Podlaska
ist Ariern,die nicht im behördlichen oder polizeilichen Auftrag
handeln,der Zutritt zu jüdischen Wohnbezirken und Einzelwohnungen,
sowie jeder Verkehr mit Juden,verboten.

Zuwiderhandlungen gegen diese Anordnung werden nach den beste-
henden Bestimmungen bestraft.

Biala-Podlaska,den 10.August 1942.

Der Kreishauptmann

gez. Kühl

Za zgodnosc odpisu
Przewodniczący
Miejskiej Rady Na ...
w Białej-Podlaskiej

Restriction on movement for Biala Jews

It did not take long and there again was panic in the city because the search for men was resumed. An order came simultaneously from the district administration that the *Judenrat*, the aid committee and [those in] the disinfection colony should appear immediately at the square of the district administration.

To those assembled at the square of the district administration, the official, Lipkow, asked the assembled women of the aid committee and of the disinfection colony to go home, and he disappeared. A vehicle with unfamiliar security police and a few Ukrainians arrived at the square. The Jews were loaded into the vehicle and they were taken to the train.

Despair reigned in the city because it was clear that with the removal of the *Judenrat* the city had been abandoned and the end of the tragedy was approaching. We were sure that a search would soon be made for men because many were still missing from the number that had been caught during the morning search. It really did not take long before a new search began.

The catching of 400 Jews was not easy because the majority of the Jewish workers were already at the workplaces. Therefore, the search persisted an entire day. And when the nightmarish day turned to night, a dead Jew with a smashed head lay in the gutter at Narutowicz Street and in a small room lay a woman who had been shot, Mrs. Brukha Adlersztajn (Moshe'e the saloonkeeper's daughter-in-law), who would not let herself be raped by a Ukrainian who took part in the deportation.

It became clear that in the morning the *S.D.* man again succeeded in freeing a Jew because the unfamiliar leader of the deportation was not on the spot. However, as soon as he arrived at the assembly place and saw that Jews were being freed, he ordered that they be held. He left for the German offices and, it appears, it was his right to carry out the search and he encountered no more interference, but on the contrary, strong cooperation.

Around nine o'clock at night, the freight train left in the direction of Lublin, taking approximately 400 Jews in the sealed cars, among them the majority of the *Judenrat* and of the aid committee.

Here began all the while, it seems, the exertions of other mass means regarding Jews by the above mentioned *S.D.* man, Glet. Firstly, they eliminated the *Judenrat*, from which they had received so many gifts, but at the same time, the *Judenrat* had been too active and too often asked for the annulling of various edicts. In the process, they [the *Judenrat*] pulled along the members of the aid committee and of other institutions, helping the foreign security police fill the contingent of Jews who had been seized who he [Glet] had to bring somewhere else.

In August, Godya Sztajnman (the youngest daughter of the well-known Hebrew teacher, Yakov Sztajnman), the member of *HaShomer HaTzair* [the Young Guard – Labor Zionists], was arrested. It was said that this talented girl had taken part in illegal activities, that emissaries from the movement would meet in her residence. She fell into the hands of the Gestapo because of the arrest of a Polish train official who had been arrested on the train with illegal literature and given Godya's name and address. Godya Sztajnman spent a very short time in the cellar of the Gestapo prison. It turns out that the experienced murderers were convinced that they would get nothing from the physically weak young woman, despite the tortures she endured there. We learned of the severe torture that Godya endured from the Jewish tailors who worked there, and from them we learned that Godya Sztajnman had been taken from there in a car in an unknown direction and shot.

[Page 420]

At the same time, Glika Lichtbaum (Leibe Mednik's daughter) was arrested and she was shot by Agent Baldiga, which supposedly happened because Glika had demanded [the payment of a debt] from a *volks-Deutsch*.

The German extermination machine then was already in full operation and during the first phase of the annihilation of the Jews, it tried to concentrate the Jews in order for it to be easier to be able to exterminate them.

The military regime told the Jewish workers that whoever wanted to work for them must be restricted to the barracks; that is, to sleep in the barracks under German supervision. The military regime also began to give food to its Jewish workers. The Jews did not want to lose their workplaces and therefore were forced to be restricted to the barracks. Every night one could see this scene: the workers came home from work for a short time and immediately were assembled at the synagogue courtyard and, standing in military order, they were marched away to the barracks. Whoever had a desire to spend the night at home received the administration of 40 blows over his body in the morning. They were only freed from work in the camp on Sunday so they could see their families.

Meanwhile, one of the 400 Jews who had been sent away in the direction of Lublin, the former war prisoner, Grosman, came running back. A fresh picture of the tragedy unfolded from his words.

We learned that the 400 men had been taken to the camp at Majdanek, several kilometers outside Lublin. There they changed into camp clothing. However, an order soon came to return the clothing. Officials from the train authority came and chose around 350 men for work in building a new train line in Golomb, between Demblin and Pulow, Lublin *woyewodztwa* [administrative division]. Fifty men remained in the Majdanek camp, the majority older people and among them Y.A. Rozenbaum, Yitzhak Piczic, Moshe Rodzinek, Moshe Chaim Wizenfeld, Yisroel Bialer, Shmuel Krajzlman, Yakov Shlomo Zajdman, Yakov Velvl Herszberg, Berl Goldberg (pharmacist), Khanan Wajsberg, and so on.

The work in Golomb took place in unbearable conditions. Heavy labor, little and bad food. One was shot for the slightest weakness. Perishing there among others were Fishl Kantor, Eliezer Lerner and Blumenkranc (Yukl Listgartn's son-in-law).

Just before Rosh Hashanah, almost all of the Biala Jews returned from Golomb.

The wives of the members of the *Judenrat* who had been sent away began to make efforts to bring back their husbands. In the German offices they were promised that their requests would be filled, but they did not keep their promise. Meanwhile, Eliezer Celniker was designated as the new chairman of the *Judenrat*, who with several remaining members of the *Judenrat*, tried to begin some kind of activity.

On *Shabbos*, the 19th of September, it was ordered that *Judenrat*s of Biala, Janowa and Konstantyn should report to the *S.D.* representatives.

During the day of *Shabbos*, they already knew the results of the visit: it was ordered that several kilograms of gold be collected from the Jewish population and be delivered to the *S.D.* The order was motivated by the idea that the *S.D.* would defend the Biala Jews to the higher powers. The Janower and Konstantyner *Judenrat*s were told that by Friday, the 25th of September, all of the Jews must move to Biala from their towns.

Around Tuesday, the 22nd of September, the *S.D.* man, Glet, sent for the wives of the two *Judenrat* members, Piczic and Rozenbaum, who had ceaselessly tried to make him bring back their husbands from Maidanek.

[Page 421]

When the two women came to Glet, the *S.D.* man, they found the *Judenrat* chairman, Eliezer Celniker, there. Glet asked the women in his [Celinker's] presence how much their husbands meant to them because there was an opportunity to free them. The women answered that their husbands were dear to them, but, alas, they did not have any large sums of money. The women tried to speak about bringing back all of the Biala Jews, but from the start the *S.D.* man did not want to hear about it. Finally, after long pleas from the women, Glet agreed to try to free all of the Jews. Therefore, the women were obligated to provide him with 45,000 *zlotes*. He emphasized that the money needed to be given to him very quickly because he would probably be going to Lublin either Saturday or Sunday to take the gold assembled by the *Judenrat* and while there he would make efforts to free the men. He observed that everything must be very secret; if not, the women would be responsible for their lives.

Around Wednesday, the first arrivals of the Janower and Konstantyner Jews appeared. Small wagons of Jewish families followed. Only a small group of Jews remained in Janowa, as workers in the *Wigoda* [horse farm] there.

The arriving 3,000 Jews were partly quartered with their friends and acquaintances. Everyone who did not have a place to go remained on the street with their bag and baggage.

On Wednesday night the refined murderer, Glet, visited the quarter. He promised to give apartments to the immigrants. Meanwhile, he asked Yitzhak Preter, the baker, to distribute bread among the refugees, promising to give him back flour on Monday.

The *Judenrat* had already given the assembled gold. Whether the provided quantity, about two kilograms [almost four and a half pounds], satisfied the *S.D.* members or not was difficult to learn.

Around seven in the evening, the women came to the office of the *S.D.* and delivered the 45,000 *zlotes*. Glet again told the women that around *Shabbos* or Sunday he would be in Lublin and he believed that he would be successful in freeing the men. As it was already seven o'clock, he gave the women a certificate that they had permission to be in the street at the later hour.

That there was going to be an expulsion was clear to everyone. All Jewish settlements in the entire Lublin *woyewodztwa* [administrative district] were included in the expulsion designation. However, the Biala Jews did not expect that their total annihilation was approaching.

Rumors spread from the administrative district that they did not mean the Biala Jews. Only those Jews arriving from the small *shtetlekh* [towns] were designated for deportation. Therefore, the majority of Biala Jews thought that in general a deportation was being prepared for migrants, among whom there would naturally be transported many Biala Jews. However, there was a solution to this; this had been learned from the first Biala deportation and from the large deportation in Mezritch – hide. Therefore, the building of hiding places was in full fervor. No money was spared in this purpose and a hiding place was created in every house.

The Jews arriving from the *shtetlekh* who were capable of work besieged the labor office and demanded that they be given workplaces because this was a way of rescue during the first Biala expulsion. Now, they spared no money to obtain a work card.

Friday, erev *Sukkous* [the eve of the Feast of Tabernacles], there was busy and exasperated movement in the quarter. They sensed the closeness of the danger. The news that various officials had taken even half-completed work from the artisans increased the panic.

The *Judenrat*s from Janowa and Konstantyn gathered gold from their *landsleit* [townsmen] the entire day, which was given to the *S.D.*

During the day, the workers from many workplaces came to take their things because they were assigned to the barracks. They spoke about the seven camps that would be in the city: 1. at the Stuag firm; 2. at the Zid firm; 3. at the *Ostbahn*; 4. at the water management inspection (the only place where women would also be); 5. at the air field; 6. in the military bakery, and 7. the largest camp would be at the *Wehrmacht*, when they would also eat and sleep as workers of a private firm which had the right to employ Jews.

The Jews were divided into three categories: one – those quartered [in the ghetto/camp]; the second – those who had prepared hiding places; among them a small percentage with Christians (among those who had prepared to hide were also men who, although in barracks, did not want to leave their closest ones); the third category consisted of every Jew who did not have a place to hide, or did not want to hide and was ready for everything.

[Page 422]

The Second and Last Expulsion

On *Shabbos*, the first day of *Sukkous* [Feast of Tabernacles] (26th of September 1942), at around 5 o'clock in the morning, rifle fire was heard in the Jewish neighborhood and it was clear that the bloody events had begun.

A. At the Assembly Square and in the Ghetto

As it appeared, the expulsion *aktsia* began before five o'clock in the morning. When we heard the noise of the rifles, many Jewish lives had been cut short.

Taking part in the action were: Gestapo, security police, the gendarmerie, Polish police and soldiers from the *Luftwaffe* [German armed forces] who had surrounded the quarter around 10 o'clock at night.

As soon as it began to turn blue [sunrise] outside, the ousting of people from their residences began, and they were driven to the square, to the "pig market," where they were told to sit on the ground.

Doors were broken open in houses where the door was not answered quickly enough. The Germans entered the houses like rampaging animals and beat the people. Whichever one of them had the desire to do so fired his rifle and victims fell. The sick who lay in bed and could not go to the assembly spot were shot in their beds.

Glet, the *S.D.* man, ordered the Jewish *Ordnungsdienst* [Jewish ghetto police], Hinekh Bialer, to enter the residence of Chaim Gotlen in the courtyard at Prosta Street to see if Jews were present there. Bialer entered the residence and found Jews, whom he told to hide. He reported to the *S.D.* man that there were no Jews present. However, Glet did not believe him and entered the residence and found several Jews who had not yet hidden and he immediately went outside and shot Bialer on the spot.

The Jews in the street who had gone to the assembly spot were beaten and many of them were shot.

The three Grodner sisters and a young brother arrived at the street and hurried to the assembly spot. Before them appeared the security policeman, Peterson, and when he saw the youngest sister, an amazingly beautiful child, he called out: It is a shame that such a child should go to Mezritch; it is better that she remain. A shot was heard; the child faltered and fell on the cobblestones with a shattered head. The sisters and the young brother were chased to the assembly spot.

At the assembly spot, the Jews sat dejected and full of fear. Every second, the Germans chose a Jew, took him to the side and shot him. A long mass grave was created near the house of the Christian, Szidlawski.

Jewish blood flowed in the residences, in the streets and at the assembly point. Everywhere the eyes reached, one saw Jewish corpses.

Peterson, the security policeman, Busch the gendarme, and the commandant of the Polish police, Kuchczewski, rampaged the most cruelly.

The pig market – assembly point during the expulsion
Photographed Winter 1944-45

[Page 423]

Many hiding places were immediately uncovered by the hangmen. The people were led out to the assembly place under a hail of blows and many fell dead on the spot.

When there were enough Jews at the assembly place, they began to choose people who were capable of work for the camp at the airfield and for Malaszewicz's former Polish airport near Terespol.

They brought Zushe Goldberg, the Serocker young man (a friend of the above mentioned Godya Sztajnman), who had worked at the security police the entire time, where they had the best opinion of him. A few security police with Peterson at the head were angry with him because he had not permitted them to rob the storehouses where he worked. The suffering that the young man went through, before he parted with the world, is truly indescribable. He was severely beaten with crowbars; afterward, they poked out his eyes, laid him on a concrete well and again murderously, ceaselessly beat, tortured and humiliated him.

The young man acted heroically. He did not ask for mercy, but flung his brave words in the faces of his torturers: "You are heroes" – he said – "compared to the unprotected Jews. However, the world and also the Jews will see what kind of heroes you will be when you lose the war." This caused a terrible rage among the torturers. The young man breathed out his soul with immense suffering.

It was demanded of the people who sat at the assembly point that they surrender their money and jewelry, threatening them with death for not handing it over. As they had surmised that they would be transported to the death camp, Treblinka, no one had taken anything with them. They then regretted this because they loaded the Jews into wagons and sent them to Mezritch.

The older people and children were loaded into wagons and it was arranged to transport the young people on foot to Mezritch. Because of the large number of wagons that remained unfilled, the young people were also loaded into the wagons.

Wagons stretched out, stuffed with Jews, dejected, full of fear, at first not knowing where they were being taken. At the end of the Biala county, where the Woroniecer forest is located, many of the Jews were taken out of the wagons, led into the forest and shot there.

The corpses in the streets and in the residences, from which they were slid out of the windows, were taken to the cemetery by the Christian workers from the city hall. After several days of lying there, the corpses were buried by the Christian workers.

The Gestapo entered the Jewish hospital where there were 15 sick and two nurses who did not want to leave the sick, and ordered the nurses to feed the sick…

The Christians made use of the darkness of the night and began to rampage in the Jewish houses. They dragged out whatever they could. They even took the clothing off the corpses that lay in the streets.

Abschrift

Stadtverwaltung   Biala Podlaska,den 28 September 1942
in Biala Podlaska

Bekanntmachung

Auf Grund der Anordnung des Herrn Kreishauptmanns vom 24.d.Mts.gebe ich hiermit zur Kenntnis der Bevölkerung,dass das Betreten des ehem.Judenviertels ohne besonderen Ausweis unbedingt verboten ist.
Plünderungen von Häusern,Geschäften usw.werden mit dem Tode bestraft.

Der Bürgermeister
(-)Ing.A.Walawski

Za zgodność odpisu

Przewodniczący
Miejskiej Rady Narodowej
w Bialej-Podlaskiej

Prohibition for non-Jews to enter the former Jewish quarter

[Page 424]

On Sunday, the second day of *Sukkous*, all of the Reich's Germans and *volks-Deutschn*, who had come en masse in holiday clothes, were invited to the Jewish quarter. They wandered through the quarter, looking for hiding Jews. They had already looted the Jewish houses for the most beautiful and the best things.

However, the Germans ascertained that a large percentage of Jews had not appeared at the assembly place. They brought bloodhounds to find the Jews in their hiding places. A fresh day arose of bloody work for the murderers. The scenes of the first day were repeated; everywhere lay Jewish victims and blood flowed in rivers.

The district headquarters took Jewish workers from the camps, who began to carry out the possessions from the abandoned houses and brought them to the synagogue and the house of prayer.

<u>Odpis</u>

Zarząd Miejski w Białej-Podlaskiej
    Zakład Oczyszczania Miasta

                        Zarząd Miejski
                        w Białej-Podlaskiej
                        29.WRZ.1942
                        L.dz.3942/42

        Meldunek

        Do
            Pana Burmistrza
                    m.Białej-Podlaskiej

        Na zarządzenie p.Burmistrza z dnia 26.IX rb.
Nr.dz.3996/42,donoszę że żaden z robotników Z.O.M.
nie jest z pochodzenia żydem,jak również na terenie
zabudowań Z.O.M.żaden z żydów nie ma żadnego schro-
nienia.-

        Jednocześnie nadmieniam,że wydałem polecenie
robotnikowi Z.O.M.Janowi Grabowskiemu zamieszkałemu
w budynku Z.O.M. by bezwzględnie żadnemu żydowi nie
pozwolił na zatrzymanie się w Z.O.M.,w wypadku gdyby
miały miejsce takie wypadki - żydów skierowywał
wprost do najbliższego posterunku żandarmerji, a nie
wypuszczał ich swobodnie.-

                        Kier.Z.O.M.(-)W.Iwanicki

Biała-Podlaska dnia 29.IX.1942 r.

                    Za zgodność odpisu

                    Przewodniczący
                Miejskiej Rady Narodowej
                    w Białej-Podlaskiej

*Order of the Mayor, A. Walawksi and his assistant, W. Iwanicki,
after the expulsion, about holding the Jews and giving them to the gendarmerie*

Where the Jewish workers entered a residence, they immediately called out: "Men, come out!" And the men who heard their call joined the work group and at night they went with them to the camps. Wherever a Jewish worker had the opportunity, he reported that Biala was *Juden-rein* [empty of Jews] and that they must leave for Mezritch at night.

The Gestapo came to the Jewish hospital for a second time and, going from bed to bed, they shot all of the sick. The two nurses also shared the same fate as the sick.

A hiding place was also discovered in the hospital and the Jews there were shot on the spot. Among those shot was the *Judenrat* chairman, Eliezer Celniker.

The Jews who were gathered at the assembly point on the second day of the expulsion were also sent away to Mezritch.

The roads that led to Mezritch were full of Jewish victims. Anyone who desired to stop the wandering Jews did so and gave them into German hands. Thus at the well, the Grobman sisters were stopped and the *Sonderdienst* [special services] shot them there on the spot.

From Thursday on, the fourth day of the expulsion, they stopped shooting Jews. The Gestapo took over the management of the former Jewish quarter. Announcements appeared in the streets that the Jews could freely walk to Mezritch until Tuesday the 1st of October 1942. Every Jew who was found in Biala county after this period would be shot.

And actually, during those days, no Jews were shot. Both those who freely appeared and those who crawled out of hiding places were sent to Mezritch.

The Gestapo chose a group of 50 men from the people, who, since Tuesday, had appeared on their own for the expulsion, to clean the houses in the Jewish quarter. Among them were the two women, Matl Cyker (Froim Cyker's wife) and Masha Gelburd (a daughter of Yosele Wohiner), [and] the men Yitzhak Eksztajn (barber), Yitzhak Chonen and his son Gedalihu, Khanina Kaszemacher, Noakh Rodzinek, Antshl Bekerman, the Bekerman brother (the sons of Yosef Sanie), Shmuel Liberman (tricot-knit weaver from Siedlce), Yitzhak Grobman, Borukh Fajgnbaum, Polosecki (a carpenter from Łomazy), Dovidl Geltman, Shlomo Cyker (Matl Cyker's son), Shimshon Justman, Shlomo Sztajngart (Motl Arya's son), and so on.

[Page 425]

The workers were quartered in the barracks that were located at Shabati Finkelsztajn's spot (the barracks were erected there at the beginning of 1942 and until the expulsion Jews, who were constantly removed from the streets that were located outside the outlined Jewish quarter, lived there). At night they would let the workers into the barracks, bar the doors and windows with boards, and the municipal firemen guarded them until the morning, when they would be let out to work.

The first employment for the workers was to go around and board up all of the Jewish houses. Then they began to go from house to house and clean everything. They took the things to specially arranged warehouses, and the more valuable things were later transported to Germany.

A large part of their work during the first weeks of the expulsion consisted of burying victims right there on the square.

As soon as Tuesday passed, the shooting of every Jew encountered began again. This time only by the Gestapo, which turned the square in the Jewish quarter into a cemetery.

Actually, there was no difference between the cemetery at the square in the Jewish quarter and the official cemetery, because German vandalism also reached there; all of the headstones and brick walls around graves were hacked to bits and used for various purposes.

The 50 Jewish workers at the Gestapo were witnesses to enough awful scenes. Jews were brought every day to the barracks, for whom they had to prepare mass graves. At night, the victims, in only their underwear, were led to the pits in pairs and shot. The remaining victims who were waiting for their turn would hear the shooting and see what soon awaited them through the cracks in the barracks walls.

When the shooting stopped, the Jewish workers ran with shovels to cover the mass grave.

They brought the *Judenrat* member Dovid Kantor and his daughter, Sura, to the square. He asked the Gestapo man, who had received more than one gift from Kantor's hand at the time, to let them live because they were young and could still work. Several revolver shots were heard and two lives were extinguished.

Mrs. Szayndl Kornblum, who had been brought there with her husband, Yakov, proposed giving away all of their possessions if they would give them their lives, but the Gestapo man laughed cynically and fired his automatic weapon.

Mrs. Etl Richter asked a Jewish worker that they not tell her son, who was in one of the Biala camps, about her tragic end. That same evening, she was led out of the barracks, just in her shirt, and shot.

More than one worker witnessed the shooting of his own wife, his children and those closest to him, who were discovered in hiding places. He looked terrified and was silent. And thus the victims also were silent because the least hint that a close person was being shot could bring death.

The ghetto square (Shabse's Garden) in the middle of the barracks where the Jews were pushed after they were thrown out of their residences. After the expulsion, they installed the Gestapo workers there. Here, various detained Jews were imprisoned after the expulsion until they were shot at night there on the square.
On the right – Khanina Kaszemacher's house, where the Gestapo workers were later held; to the left: Motl Minc's house.

[Page 426]

And thus, in front of the worker, Khanina Kaszemacher, they shot his wife, Perl. The worker, Shmuel Liberman, filled in the grave of the squirming body of his son. Noakh Rodzinek watched as they shot his brother, Avraham.

There was a case when the co-worker at the *Judenrat*, Idl Cymbolist, and his pregnant wife, Nekhama (Moshe Szenker's daughter), were brought to be shot. After long efforts by the workers, they succeeded in persuading the Gestapo man that Cymbolist be taken to work. However, in the middle of the work, another Gestapo man noticed him and drove him back into the barracks of the Jews being held to be shot. When the workers asked the Gestapo man for mercy, that Cymbolist should be taken to work, he told them that he could not help because the Jew was brought here with his wife; if he wanted to continue working, what would they do with his wife? They could not and they were not permitted in such a case to separate a man and wife. They actually were not separated, but hurled together into a grave.

There also were cases when Jewish girls were stopped and forced to dance naked in front of the prepared graves, at which time they were then shot.

The entire space there with all of its neighboring courtyards was transformed into a Jewish cemetery

B. In Hiding Places and other Means of Rescue

The hiding places were made at various places, after contemplating the matter for the entire night. Thus in cellars they installed brick walls that divided the cellars in two. One part continued to be as it was, but the second part was entered through a raised board in the house floor. Small rooms in residences were hidden with boards and a secret entrance was made in the wall that was hidden with a bed or with a cupboard. Various plank beds were created in attics and in stalls.

There was great crowding in almost all of the hiding places because people who had not been counted [in the planning for the hiding places] had to be allowed into them at the last minute. In the hiding places that were located in the attics, the people actually lay naked because of the great heat. The worst hardship was with small children who cried constantly and could easily betray the hiding places. There were cases in which such children were simply suffocated.

The Jewish workers at the Gestapo in the quarter later found dead children in the attics and the cellars, in cells and in stalls. There was a hiding place where the woman, Rywka Berzowski (her girlhood name, daughter of Shepsele the carpenter), had labor pains and because of her screams, she suffered the same fate of the previously mentioned children; she was choked (in Chaim the baker's house at Prosta Street).

Food and water were prepared for a short time in the hiding places, but for how long could one lie like this? In general, the Polish firemen who worked so zealously in uncovering Jewish hiding places helped the Germans. They even tore off the roofs in some houses where they had a suspicion that a hiding place was located.

In many hiding places, they lay for long days and did not know what was happening outside. And if one risked going out to learn something, he usually did not return; he was detained and shot.

There were places where people lay for months. In an attic hiding place at Chaim the baker's house people lay until the middle of January 1943 – more than three and a half months. When the Jewish workers in the quarter noticed them, the people were in a terrible condition. This was a good hiding place, arranged with bedding so it was not very cold and there was enough food for the entire time. They were able to use an oven with *cholent* [Sabbath stew] that was in the house since before *Sukkous* [Feast of Tabernacles]. They had a hardship with water. When they noticed from inside the hiding place that quarter workers were carrying water, they began calling to them to give them water. At night, the workers provided them with enough water and food. When they were asked why they did not go to Mezritch, they answered that they wanted to wait here until the new year; perhaps a change would come in the situation of the Jews.

Unable to wait for the change, several weeks later they left their hiding place. One by one they left for Mezritch. However, only one arrived there – the young man Ekerman (Shayma, the tailor's son-in-law). The remaining people, it appears, met death on the road.

[Page 427]

In another hiding place (in the attic in Moshe Yitzhak Biderman's house, Janower Street), they found several dead Jews in March 1943. It was difficult to determine the cause of their death.

The Jews who had hidden with Christians also could not stay there for long. The Christians were afraid to keep them because they were threatened with death. One by one, over the course of weeks, the Jews were drawn to Mezritch. Jews hidden in the villages were almost all detained and shot.

A negligible percentage of the Biala Jews tried to save themselves by obtaining Christian passports, the so-called *kennkartes* [identity documents], but here, too, they met with great difficulties. Extraordinary sums had to be paid for the *kennkartes*, and everywhere one turned, they were blackmailed by the Christians, who took the last *groshns* and, in the end, they [the Jews] returned to the ghetto.

After the war, among those from Biala who had obtained *kennkartes* and were accepted as Aryans and survived were: Gutsha Goldfeld, Mikhasz Hofer and his wife and daughter, Manya Warm and her brother Leibl, Emil Wajnberger, Berl Sandlarsz and his wife and daughter Hela, Krusa Rozensztajn and her daughters Ida and Chana, Chaim Fridman, lawyer Leon Goldfarb, Bronya Fuks and so on.

Young women made attempts to be sent to work in Germany as Christians, but they did not succeed. Women who traveled on the trains [hoping] to be caught for work in Germany did not achieve their goal, not having any documents with them to show from where they originated. Instead of their dream to become slave-workers in Germany, they found their death. As it was described, Doba Altbir (Nuta Altbir's daughter), was found among the victims.

Some went to the forests with the hope of joining the Russian prisoners of war who had escaped from the German prison camp, like the family of Eplbaum, the butcher, at Janower Street. Here, too, the end was tragic. The prisoners of war, who did not carry out any partisan actions against the Germans, took everything from the Jews, left them naked and barefoot and drove them away.

Individuals created hiding places in the forests; every night they went to a nearby peasant house and bought something to eat. However, here too, in the forests, they were persecuted by death. The Jews were either murdered by the Christians or by the Germans. Such a case took place in a bunker in Holier Forest where, in the summer of 1943, the Sznajderman brothers (Ruchl Leah's sons, Brisker Street 4), Khanan Tenenbaum (Dovid the baker's son), Hinekh Chohen (Yitzhak Chohen's son) and a young man from Mezritch were shot by gendarmes. A Christian from the village of Selc had reported to the gendarmerie about their bunker.

After the liberation of Biala by the Russian Army in July 1944, coming back from hiding places were: Berish Urbach, Rywka Bachrach, Faywl Buchhalter, Shmuel Gwazda and his wife, Ruzshka Drenczol, Sura Wiznfeld, Ester Wajnsztajn, Avraham Nuchowicz and his sister Rywka, Nekhemia Pocztaruk, Moshe Yosef Fajgenbaum, Chaya Feldman and her two sons, Yitzhak and Shmuel, Yitzhak Fridman, Noakh Rodzinek, Gedalihu Ridlewicz, Moshe Sztajnberg and his sisters Elka and Elda Szliterman.

C. In the Camps

We previously mentioned the belief that there were supposed to be seven camps in the city. During the expulsion, this belief was shown to be correct. The majority who belonged to the camps or to the private firms that were recognized by the regime were located in the camps at the beginning of the expulsion and were not handed over to the deportation action. During the first days of the expulsion, a certain number of Jews entered the camps. A number of them succeeded in remaining there; others were given to the Gestapo and were shot.

The majority of the Jews were concentrated at the *Wehrmacht* that was located on the Warsaw highway, near the barracks of the former 34th regiment.[c] The *stabszahlmeister* [paymaster] was Zeeman and the *oberstabszahlmeister* [chief purser] was Shilf. They designated as an *uber-Jude* [chief-Jew], the Jew, Sokolowski.

There were workshops in the camps for carpenters, locksmiths, shoemakers and tailors at which a number of Jewish workers were employed.

Every morning a military guard took several hundred Jews from the camp to the *Vineta* camp that was a division of the camp of the 34th regiment. There, the Jews would work at various heavy labor. And for it they would receive food. At night the German soldiers brought them back to the central camp. Jewish workers who had earlier worked in private firms that were recognized as important by the regime would also be taken to work and brought back at night by the Jewish *Ordnungsdienst* [ghetto police], a few of whom were located in the camp. The midday food would be taken to them at their workplace.

[Page 428]

German soldiers would come into the camp every morning and take groups of Jews to work at the military units. The remaining Jews in the camp worked at various hard labor.

On Sunday, the second day of the expulsion, the camp had a Jewish funeral. The young man, Chaim Hofer, had hung himself after hearing that his wife and child had been deported.

On the days of the deportation, when over the course of several days the remaining Jews in Biala were permitted to freely walk to Mezritch, small Jewish boys near the camp of the *Wehrmacht* [German armed services] at the Warsaw highway would sneak around. At night, they would crawl through the barbed wire fences around the camp, sneak into their fathers to spend the night there and, in the morning, disappear from there.

At the camp on the air field, where the firms Maier, Benz and Zagar-Werner were active, the Jews worked at building and sewer system work. A large number of workers were employed with loading wagons with wooden beams for coal pits. The regimen there was bearable at the beginning, but later, it became a terrible place for Jews. Day after day, weakened Jews were bound with wire, thrown in a wagon and taken to the Gestapo in the ghetto where they were shot.

In the camp, the saddle-maker, Yitzhak Winderbaum, slit his throat with a razor and suffered in pain for hours until a German bullet made an end of his life.

In the camp of the water administration, the men were employed at reclamation work and the women and children at field and garden work. The German engineer, Grinenfeld, who extorted all of their expensive possessions from the Jews, was the leader of the camp. The regimen there was bearable. The camp was located near the river.

The Jews worked at various jobs in the German bakery. Hanak, the German, ran the camp. He also stole a great deal of Jewish possessions from his Jewish workers. The small number of Jewish workers lived there relatively well. The camp was located at the mechanized bakery at the Wolya.

In the camp of the firm Stuag that was located in Holier Forest, the Jews were employed at highway work. Civilian Germans and Poles governed them. The treatment there was bearable.

At the camp of the German firm, Zid, which worked for the security police and was under its supervision at the Janower highway, the Jews worked at building the barracks for the security police there on the highway and at sewer system labor. Life there was unbearable. The German foreman, Bitner, particularly distinguished himself with his wildness.

The camp of the *Ostbahn* was found at the railway, where the Jews worked at unloading and loading freight cars as well as at cleaning the train lines. The regimen was lenient.

In almost all of the camps they tried to employ the artisans at their trades to have even more use of the Jews who were held in the camps.

The work for the Jews in all of the camps was not particularly difficult, but the inhuman conditions, the belittling of them, the mockery of them, had a much worse effect than the heaviest physical labor. The food was meager; with the money they had brought with them, everyone bought food that was smuggled into the camps by various means. The sanitary and hygienic conditions were miserable. All remuneration for work for the Jewish workers ended at the moment they crossed the threshold of the camp.

On the first day of the expulsion, many Jews left the camps for Mezritch, where they had their families. They would also try to go to the Jewish quarter accompanied by a soldier, who would, in various ways, receive remuneration for going to the Jewish quarter, which was intended, first of all, to take the men from the hiding places and bring them to the camps. They would also remove money and clothing from the houses. Later, it was almost impossible to go to the Jewish quarter. The soldiers received an order not to go to the Jewish quarter and the camp Jews were forbidden under the threat of death to leave the camp. Despite this, at night Jews risked going into their houses in the Jewish quarter which was constantly guarded by Polish firemen who had many Jewish victims on their conscience, such as Ayzik Orlinski (the son of Avraham), Moshe'le Lajbzon's son, Sura Tsirl, the grandchild of the [female] baker (Suszczik).

[Page 429]

Shimeon Lichtensztajn and a grandson, who left the camp at the air field and wanted to join a group of Jewish workers in the *Wygoda* in Janowa, were stopped and shot on the Janower highway.

During the first week of the expulsion, attempts were made with the *stabszahlmeister* [paymaster] at the camp of the 34th regiment to arrange a bathhouse for the Jews and carry out disinfections. They also tried to have medications brought from the Jewish hospital and from the aid committee. They promised to do everything. At the end of the week, they felt that a different wind was blowing and nothing would come from all of the promises. They saw that the Jews here were held as slaves and, later, it would be even worse.

On Wednesday, the 30th of September, the women and children from the camp at the water administration were taken to Mezritch by vehicle. The women staged a revolt and wanted to leave the vehicles. It resulted in shooting, during which the sister-in-law of Yitzhak Lewi (from Janowa) and the woman Rywka Nowomiski (M.Y. Biderman's daughter) were wounded.

The first week passed and Sunday arrived when they were free from work in the camp of the 34th regiment. The group stood in circles and talked. In one place they were occupied with politics; the "politicians" believed in a quick end to Germany. In a second place, they calculated the fallen victims in the course of the week and many of the living were counted among the dead.

The greater number of workers thought about the situation. During the recent days, the supervision of the camp regime was demanding. The question arose as to whether the Jews would be kept here. One noticed that a large quantity of potatoes had been brought there and this was considered evidence that the Jews would remain…

Jews had good noses and detected that the quiet was before a storm; that something bad was being prepared.

On Tuesday, the 6th of October [1942] (25 Tishrei 5703), at around half past one in the afternoon, Aba Wajsman (the son of Berish the *feldsher* [traditional barber-surgeon]) came into the carpentry workshop and said that there was some news. His father had just returned from the *Vineta* camp where a gathering of all of the workers was arranged at one o'clock. And further: all of the men from the water workshop had been taken away to the train. Probably because the Gestapo members from Lublin had come, supposedly to confer with the local Gestapo. He had just left the workshop and ran to the worker Khanan Cukerman, who had begun to hit his head with his fists and shouted: "Already, now we are lost! The Gestapo has come for us!"

And immediately after him, the Jewish *ordnungsdient* Lajbzon entered and called the group of tradesmen to the camp. The camp already was guarded by the Gestapo, armed with machine guns. The carpenters began to leave the workshop, but then the *stabszahlmeister* came and told them to go back. When everyone was back at the workshop, the director of the workshop (the Pole, Karpinski) closed the door with a padlock.

It did not take long and the Jews were led out of the camp. Where and for what? This, no one knew.

At night, the *stabszahlmeister* entered the carpentry workshop; he told them to stop their work and declared: You are the only 17 Jews who remain in Biala; for how long I do not know; in any case, try to work diligently and do not go outside the camp.

– Of the thousands of concentrated Jews, only 17 remained in the city?

When the 17 tradesmen went to the camp after this, they found it locked. According to the instructions from the regime, they were quartered in a small barracks outside the camp. Absorbed in sad thoughts, they noticed the arrival of a small group of workers. It appeared that a group of 16 workers who had worked in the Holier Forest had also been left. The freshly arrived said that all of the workers from Stuag had also been taken away.

Twilight arrived. The 33 workers sat in the barracks in the dark and a disturbing stillness reigned. Suddenly, a shout was heard: "*Alle Juden raus!*" [All Jews out]. Yes, the Jews thought; they have not forgotten us; they have come to send us away, too. The Jews went outside and saw in front of them an officer and a soldier who told them to stand in two lines. They counted the Jews and they were sure that the order was coming: march! However, they only told a few to go with them, to take bread, marmalade and kerosene for the lanterns. Bringing the bread, marmalade and kerosene, the soldier warned that there should be a proper division and a list should be made of the people. Dovid Gelosn was chosen as the group leader.

[Page 430]

At dawn, the workers in the barracks began to get dressed. The young Pinkhas Grodner, who had been taken away with all of the other workers, sneaked in. From him we learned this: the Jews from the camp of the 34th regiment had been taken away to the train where there already were assembled the workers from the *Vineta* camp and the water management camp. They were told to sit down in the garden at the train station and were forbidden to talk to each other. Later, they also brought the workers from Stuag, from the German bakery and from all the other workplaces at which the people at the camp of the 34th regiment had worked. The Jews were not brought from the firm Zid, the air field or from the ghetto.

Stilhammer, the commander of the Gestapo, gave a speech to the assembled Jews and said that they were being taken to another temporary workplace. "You, men capable of work, nothing threatens you, do not be afraid, nothing will happen to you." He ended his speech with these words. Stilhammer demanded order and discipline.

A large number received his words as true. Those who did not believe him also could not help themselves. One worker, Volvish Wajcman, who did want to help himself and ran, was shot while running by the Gestapo man, Szimanski.[d]

The Jews sat in the garden until the evening. A freight train arrived and when they began to load the wagons, they learned where they would be sent. Although there were enough wagons, they only opened a few. The group was driven into the wagons and, at the same time, murderously beaten with rubber batons. The crowding in the closed wagons was frightening. They understood that the people were not being sent to work and that there was another deception here by the sadists. They began to shout from the wagons – it would be better if you shot us before we suffocate in such crowding! – Shooting is too easy a death for you – was the answer from Szimanski of the Gestapo. The train moved in the direction of Mezritch.

In Biala, they had heard a great deal about how, during the first deportation in Mezritch, Mezritchers had jumped out of the train cars and so the Bialers began to do the same thing. When a door was opened, they would jump. If a door could not be torn open, they jumped out of the small window of the moving train.

However, only a small percentage jumped, knowing that there was nowhere to go; the majority were resigned and let themselves be led to the slaughter. As soon as they nailed the doors of the wagons shut, the dentist Yoal Zilberberg and his son Chaim poisoned themselves.

Pinkhas Grodner did not know where they had taken the people because, as soon as the train began to move, he jumped out and was slightly hurt.

At lunchtime, the *stabszahlmeister* came, opened the camp and told everyone to take their things. He simultaneously said that each worker was permitted to have only two pairs of underwear and one suit. The tradesmen could have two pairs of pants. A heavy penalty was threatened for not complying with the order. The Jews were ordered to immediately give away all of their documents, photographs, money, watches and jewelry because whoever later had something found on them would be turned over to the Gestapo.

During the next days, all of the things [belonging to] the workers who had been taken away were taken out of the barracks into the ghetto, in the possession of the Gestapo.

During the ensuing days, from great distances, the train-jumpers appeared at the camp of the 34th regiment. Among them: the lawyer Leon Goldfarb, Eyzshe Rubinsztajn, the gaiter quilter, Yakov Fridman, Shepsl Lajbzon, Moshe Szajnberg and Zilberzon. From them we learned that the train stopped in Mezritch and they chased Jews from Mezritch into the empty train wagons. We understood that the people were sent to Treblinka.

Now it became clear what was intended in the barracks for the men capable of work in the camps. The "heroes" from the Gestapo did not want several thousand work-capable men and strong men to be assembled at the assembly point who would see the bloody orgies with their closest ones. Who knew what the Jews would do; perhaps, one would suddenly rise up and then another and react to the bloody deeds and Nazi heads could fall as a result. However, when the powerful men were behind the wire fences, then they [the Gestapo] could do whatever their hearts desired to their unprotected wives and children.

A number of those who had jumped from the wagons decided to come to Biala at night and learn if there were still Jews in the camps. Others went to the forest where their end was tragic.

[Page 431]

The leaders of the camp of the 34th regiment and at *Vineta* tolerated the coming of fresh Jews to the camp. What did it bother them that Jews would work as slaves? It was assumed that the Biala Gestapo also knew of the influx of the Jews into the camps and did not react. For them, perhaps it was better that their victims were concentrated back in the camps and thus it would be easier to annihilate them at the appropriate hour.

At the end of October 1942, the number of Jews in the camp at the 34th regiment was 106 men and in *Vineta* 47 men. Among the latter were three disguised women: Golda Szapiro (Avraham Goldberg's daughter), Manya Kowarski (Leibl Goldberg's daughter) and Sura'le Gliksberg (Nakhman Gliksberg's young daughter).

The remaining tradesmen in the camp of the 34th regiment received another barracks under their authority. The food was not the worst; however, there was very little. The 30 dekagrams [.6 pounds] of bread did not still the hunger. However, everyone found a solution. They still had a few *zlotes* and the Christians who worked in the camp would bring the Jews enough bread, despite the ban by the leader of the workshops, the evil man, Karpinski. If they received too little bread, they had ersatz spreads, such as: marmalade, ersatz honey, ersatz cheese of which they received enough. Lunch, which consisted of potato soup with a small amount of fat, would not have been bad if the Christian [female] cooks had wanted to make the effort to prepare them so that we could eat it. After giving out the lunch, some cooked food remained in the pot and the hungry workers would ask for a little more. The Christians would rather spill out the food in the garbage pails. Twice a day, in the morning and in the evening, they would receive coffee that needed to be sweetened, but instead of being in the kettle, the sugar wandered home to the [female] cooks. There were several attempts made by the Jews to run the kitchens themselves, but they did not succeed.

A tragic case took place in the *Vineta* camp. Shmelke Szwarc, a worker there, left for the city with a German and in his stall at Sodower Street dug out a sack of valuable things. This was noticed by a Christian woman (a wife of a prison guard) and she reported this to the Gestapo. Several members of the Gestapo came to the camp and asked that Szwarc be brought to them. Feeling that something was not good, Szwarc gave the sack to a young man. The sack was later taken from the young man by Pinkhas Grodner. Szwarc received heavy blows and he confessed. The Gestapo members stopped the young man and, as soon as he received the first blows, he immediately pointed to Grodner, that he had taken Szwarc's sack. Szwarc was taken to the prison at Prosta Street and the Gestapo took Grodner with them to their headquarters at Raabe's sawmill.

As soon as Grodner arrived at the courtyard, he exited the horse-drawn carriage and disappeared. A search was ordered and he was found hiding among stacks of wood. When he was taken to the Gestapo prison, there at the courtyard, he again began to escape. He reached the fence and began crawling over it. Several bullets threw him off the fence, dead, and he was buried there, near the fence.

Shmelke Szwarc had been brought by auto on an end-of-November night to the ghetto square along with other victims and shot near the Razdiner Hasidic *shtibl* [one-room synagogue].

Sad news would arrive at the camp of the 34th regiment. At the time when here in the camp only a few blows were received for the greatest "sins," in the Zid camp they would be shot for the smallest sin. The sick, who were tolerated in this camp [34th regiment], were shot there in the Zid camp. Thus they shot the worker, Yona Morgnsztern (son of Moshe), because he became sick. The situation in the camps at the air field and in Malaszewicz (near Terespol), where many Biala Jews were located, was very bitter. These camps simply partnered with the Gestapo: every day they would provide a number of Jews, both healthy and sick, to be shot.

Thus passed days and weeks. The workers at the camp of the 34th regiment were not badly treated. However, no one could forget his suffering. Everyone was dejected and a sadness pressed on the heart. From time to time, an evening of singing Yiddish folk songs took place there. However, the Yiddish songs could not cheer them up, but the opposite; they would make them even sadder.

The pious ones would gather for the *Minkhah* [afternoon] and *Maariv* [evening prayers] as a group. They had a very good *baal tefilah* [reader of the prayers]; this was Avraham Gringlos (the son of the *shamas* [sexton] Yoal), who, during the time of war, returned to Biala from Łodz.

At the end of October, a group of young people left the camp for the forest under the leadership of Zilie Gutenberg. The group succeeded in obtaining a few guns and ammunition from the storehouse at the camp, as well as clothing. The Biala district captain [Herbert] Kuhl is supposed to have been shot by the group on the Mezritch highway.

[Page 432]

In the Summer of 1943, Zilie Gutenberg lay wounded in a village; what happened to him is not known. The same summer, the young man, Lustigman, who also belonged to the group that had left the camp, went through the Mezritch forest with a weapon in his hand.

At the beginning of November 1942, the Jews from the camps at the firm Zid and at the *Ostbahn* were transferred to the camp of the 34th regiment. With the 47 Jews at *Vineta*, the number of Jews reached 400. The transfer of the people was motivated by the order that, from the 1st of November, Jews could only be held at the camp at the *Wehrmacht* and only behind wire fencing. As the mentioned two camps did not have any connection to the *Wehrmacht*, the Jews were taken to the *Wehrmacht* camp at the Warsaw highway.

Among the freshly arrived people at the camp, the workers from the firm Zid were mostly neglected, terribly clothed and greatly starved. There were also those sick with typhus among them. A part of the blame for the conditions was due, as the people said, to their group leader, a former war prisoner from the eastern borderlands.

Everyone lived in friendly relationships in the camp of the 34th regiment. The group leader did not do anything on his own and would turn to consult the tradesmen. He did not have the benefit of any privileges. People would often leave the camp for Mezritch to see their families. The people had to report [that they were leaving] so that no food would be taken for them; otherwise at a check this could have a fatal ending. Everyone who had left would be reported that he had not come back at night from the work. However, after a few days, the person would return from Mezritch and he would register in another name so that he would not be turned over to the Gestapo. There were cases where people made such trips several times and they were constantly registered with a new name. However, no one demanded payment from such a person. Consequently, the stories by Jews from the firm Zid about their group leader sounded strange. They said that when it was noticed that someone was wearing a nice garment or an item that pleased him [the group leader], he asked for it. He also was supposed to have plotted in the kitchens so that the nourishment became worse.

The previous camp was reopened because of the arrival of the men. Before this, another barbed wire fence was put around the camp and rings of barbed wire were thrown between both fences. The gate of the camp would be closed at seven o'clock in the evening and opened at five thirty in the morning. The German guard would walk around the entire night in the square outside the camp, coming every time to see if the wire fences had been torn. Two Jewish guards, who had to prevent escapes from the camp, would walk around near the wire inside the camp itself.

Again, several hundred Jews left every morning to work in the camp *Vineta* and would return in the evening. The tradesmen worked in the workshops. The remaining Jews were employed at various kinds of hard labor and there were also those who worked in the warehouses.

There was no problem in the camp with sickness until the arrival of the fresh people. Now, in the two barracks where the people from the Zid were located, lay a very large percentage of the sick. There was no doctor in the camp and they were afraid to demand one. The experience in other camps showed what the visit of a doctor brought. If the doctor determined that someone in the camp was sick with typhus, the sick person would be shot and the camp would be locked for a certain time. Here, we acquired various medicines and several "old time physicians" such as Chaim Rozmarin (dental technician) and Leibl Lebnberg (electrical technician) would go around to the sick…

We constantly argued with the regime that these were influenza illnesses and that an influenza epidemic was now present in the city; it would last a few days and the sick would return to health and begin to work.

Meanwhile, there were also some cases of death. The dead were buried at the Jewish cemetery. Among the dead were the Bialers: Moshe Kornblum (Yakov Kornblum's son) and Spiwak (the furrier's/hatmaker's[1] son from Grabanower Street 2).

The typhus epidemic began to enter the remaining barracks and also did not skip the *Vineta* camp. They began to think about isolating them in a separate barracks. However, they were afraid to do this because isolating them in a separate barracks would catch the eyes of the Germans and could give rise to them being handed over to the Gestapo. However, when there were 60-some sick, the healthy began to demand that they be isolated because it could not be permitted that everyone would become sick.

[Page 433]

On Sunday, the 13th of December 1942, willingly, unwillingly, all of the sick were isolated in a separate barracks. Matisyahu Czelazni, Elihu Zinger and Grubman, who had been through the typhus, were busy with the sick.

At the beginning of December 1942, the *stabszahlmeister*, the leader of the camp of the 34th regiment, asked the group leader to inform the workers that he had received permission to further help the Jews. As long as he was here, nothing bad would happen. He would try to improve the food and escaping from the camp made no sense because almost all escapees were caught and shot.

When the group leader told this to the camp Jews, many on the spot immediately responded: it was significant news because when the German murderers began to assure and calm, the opposite happened. Others were inclined to believe the news.

On *Shabbos*, the 12th of December, the *stabszahlmeister* [paymaster] left on furlough and the *oberzahlmeister* [chief purser] represented him.

On Sunday night, when the camp gate was closed, the Jewish guards who stood inside the camp let it be known that the *oberzahlmeister* [chief purser] Shilf and the *zahlmeister* [purser] Behme had entered the camp.

Both began to carry out an inspection of the barracks. The *oberzahlmeister* Shilf was very drunk. It seems that he had come to train his dog on Jewish bodies. He placed his cane on every Jew he encountered; the dog immediately was up on the Jew, tearing the last bit of clothing and also tearing a piece of flesh. After reveling with the dog and satisfying himself with blood, the drunk left the camp. The incident evoked a very oppressed mood because until then we had not seen such a thing in the camp.

On Tuesday, the 15th of December, the group leader from the *Vineta* camp was called to clarify a matter of evidence. When he arrived at *Vineta*, the workers there asked him if he knew where the 40 workers with shovels were being taken. They had also been given bread because they would work there at night. The group leader answered that he knew nothing about it

When the group leader sat there with several Jews of his acquaintance and ate lunch, he asked the local group leader, Kaze, about the story of the 40 workers, but he also said that he knew nothing about it. Meanwhile, the leader of the *Vineta* camp, a military official, the so-called Balman from Hamburg who played a two-faced role in relation to the Jews, came in. He took the most expensive gifts from the Jews, promised to save them, but during the deportation action from the camp on the 6th of October, he himself gave the Jews into the hands of the Gestapo so that they would not hide. The tailor, Yosef Tiszl, had sewn many diamonds in his [Balman's] suits and the shoemaker, Borukh Frajner, had hidden enough gold rubles in the heels of his boots so he could take them home with him during his furlough trips. Balman carried on a conversation with a sick young man with whom it appeared he had been a very good friend and whose father was in the camp of the 34th regiment. This conversation lasted a long time. Meanwhile, a rumor spread in the *Vineta* camp that the 40 workers who had been taken away had been shot. The group leader had suspected that the conversation between Balman and the Jewish young man had a connection with the case of the 40 workers because he had seen that the young man had gotten up from his bed and had gotten dressed. However, the young man assured them that he knew nothing.

In the evening, when the workers returned from the *Vineta* camp, we learned that 38 of the 40 men had been shot. Among them, Hershl Wajsman (Dovid Wajsman's son) and Rozenberg (Nakhumale Sender's son-in-law) succeeded in escaping on the way.

The escapees were so confused that it was difficult to learn anything from them. However, more or less, we understood the following: military guards had taken them from the camp. A Gestapo man on a bicycle arrived on the road and showed where the men should be taken. The two young men realized that the gesture from the Gestapo man was a bad sign and they began running and near the Graborker Forest they ran into the woods. They were shot at, but they entered the forest and hid. In a short time they heard heavy shooting and shouting.

A fresh sadness poured out over the camp. Fathers cried over the death of their children and children cried over the death of their fathers. Before the camp gates were closed, the leader of the group went up to the *oberzahlmeister* [chief purser] and reported to him that 40 workers had not returned from their work at *Vineta* and that they were not at *Vineta*. What could this mean? The *oberzahlmeister* with his retinue around him remained somewhat puzzled and he asked the group leader if he knew where the men were. The answer was that he had no idea. After thinking for several seconds, the *oberzahlmeiter* said: "They probably are located at the camp at the airfield. Tomorrow I will phone there early." His answer confirmed the sad truth.

[Page 434]

Wednesday was a normal workday; everyone in the camp was at work. The workers who also would work in the *Vineta* camp were taken to the camp by the German soldiers at the Wolya early in the morning.

In the afternoon, the paymaster, Behme, came to the camp. He went through the camp with a group leader who gave him a report about everyone. The paymaster was satisfied that the number of sick had begun to decrease. The group leader asked him about the 40 workers. The paymaster was unruffled by the question and answered that they were working at the air field and that they would return home in the coming week.

In the evening, the workers from the camp *Vineta* returned and they said that the Jewish camp leaders were not there. They were supposed to go to the Christian, Smietanka, who lived near the camp. Among those who had left the camp was also that young man with whom Balman had spoken last night for a long time and who had a father in the camp of the 34th regiment. Would a son not want to save his father? Would he not have told his father to escape from the camp? However, the father remained in the camp as if nothing had happened…

It was a serious matter that everyone would leave the camp at the same time; particularly as there was a large number of sick in the camp and there was nowhere else to go but the Mezritch ghetto. Yet, if the camp [inhabitants] had had the information that the young people did in the *Vineta* camp, of what danger threatened them, everyone would have decided to leave the camp on that winter night. However, they speculated on the attitude of that worker at *Vineta* regarding his father, and alas, cruelly disappointed themselves. On that cruel day, family bonds were loosened; they first tried to save their own souls, not thinking of their closest and dearest ones.

This worker from *Vineta* woke up and began walking away to Mezritch, leaving his father at the camp of the 34th regiment.

After the news about the escape of the Jewish camp leaders in *Vineta*, the mood on the Warsaw highway became tense. Groups were created that began to prepare to escape. Many did not want to hear of it because they felt "firmly established" here – and where would they now go during the winter?

On Thursday, the 17th of December 1942 (9th of Tevet 5703), around 4:30 at night, the Jewish guards at the camp let it be known that the camp was being surrounded. They noticed that outside, in front of the camp gate, two trucks were waiting and the camp square was illuminated by spotlights. Fully armed military guards walked around the barbed wire fences.

The camp Jews thought: Yes, the tragic finale was coming.

In the barracks, the workers stood angry and resigned. It was clear to them that they were going to do the same thing to them here that had been done on Tuesday to the other 38 workers at the *Vineta* camp. They spoke among themselves about acting in a dignified manner during their last hours because the several hundred workers would not be any exception among all the Jews. While it was clear to everyone that the march to death would begin soon, several workers began to prepare packs for the trip, which evoked sarcastic laughter from the others.

An opinion was heard about throwing themselves at the murderers. Some demonstrated that such an action could be organized in advance, particularly because the barracks were isolated, but such a thing had to take place spontaneously.

The Gestapo commissar, Shtilhamer, and two members of the Gestapo, Faisker and Derm, entered the barracks. The commissar called to the workers and ordered the men in the barracks to line up in rows of five and then to translate for the workers what he, Shtilhamer, would say. The commissar began by saying that, since cases of escape were happening in the camp, he believed that the regimen here was too easy. Consequently, the men would be transferred to another camp. Nothing would happen to the workers, but he demanded that there be order during the march. Whoever escaped would be shot and, as a penalty, another 20 men would be shot. He pointed to his wolfhound which he held near him, meaning that the dog also would have something to say and would not let anyone escape.

In the barracks we heard vehicles driving into the camp and driving back out. It was clear that the sick had been taken out. Later, it could be seen that in the trucks that were in front of the camp gates were the Jewish workers from the camp, *Vineta*.

The dark night still reigned. Those already sentenced to death stood in the barracks and waited to be led to their execution.

[Page 435]

Several shots were heard in the nighttime quiet. Later, it was learned that several workers who had approached the barbed wire fence had been shot. In one barracks, they found the worker, Moshe Lajbzon (Yehiel Prondik's son), ripping out the floor, under which one could hide, and he was shot at the camp square. They also shot a worker at the toilet pit where he had tried to hide.

An invasion of the barracks took place on the last morning before the death sentence. The doors opened and the Jews were ordered to go out to the camp square. There, seven men were placed in a row and warned not to escape.

The *zahlmeister* [paymaster], Behme, worked with all of his power to show that he, too, did not trail behind in the "sacred" work of annihilating Jews. He brought the worker, Pinkus Czarni (Shlomo Stop's son), who had hidden in a garbage container, and placed him in the hands of the Gestapo commissar. The commissar led the worker among the barracks and ordered him to stretch out on the ground. However, Pinkus Czarni did not want to carry out the order. The commissar pushed him to the front, aimed a revolver shot at his neck and the Jew fell on the ground, dead.

"You see," the commissar mentioned, "I not only speak, but I also do." He ordered the counting of 20 men and that they be shot, but in the middle of counting, he called out: "As an exception, I spare you now the shooting of 20 men as a punishment."

They counted the columns and it appeared that 231 men were ready for the slaughter. They told the group to hold hands. It was forbidden to look to the side or behind or to speak among ourselves.

With heads down, the condemned began the march to the execution spot accompanied by five members of the Gestapo and 10 soldiers. Leaving the camp gate, on the left near the storehouses, they saw a corpse. Near the German house block, they saw two Christians with two wagons filled with shovels, clear as to their purpose.

The column left on the Warsaw highway and began to walk in the direction of Mezritch. Although it was already the second half of December, the day was not cold, but a dampness hung in the air. The walking Jews turned from the highway to the small Slawaczinska alley that was full of deep mud and made the walk difficult. Suddenly, they were told to sing. The melody of a sad Polish cavalry song was heard and the procession marched further in the mud.

When they ordered us to stop singing, the chords of the death-spreading machine guns carried to those marching. We guessed that this ended with the men who had been taken away by trucks. Among those who perished there were those from Biala: Yakov Wajsman (Arka Wajsman's son) and Manya Kowarski (Leibl Goldberg's daughter). Also, the coach driver Botshkele (nickname), the quilter Yakov Fridman and his young son, Surale Gliksberg, Elihu Zinger, Matisyahu Czelazni, Grubman and so on.

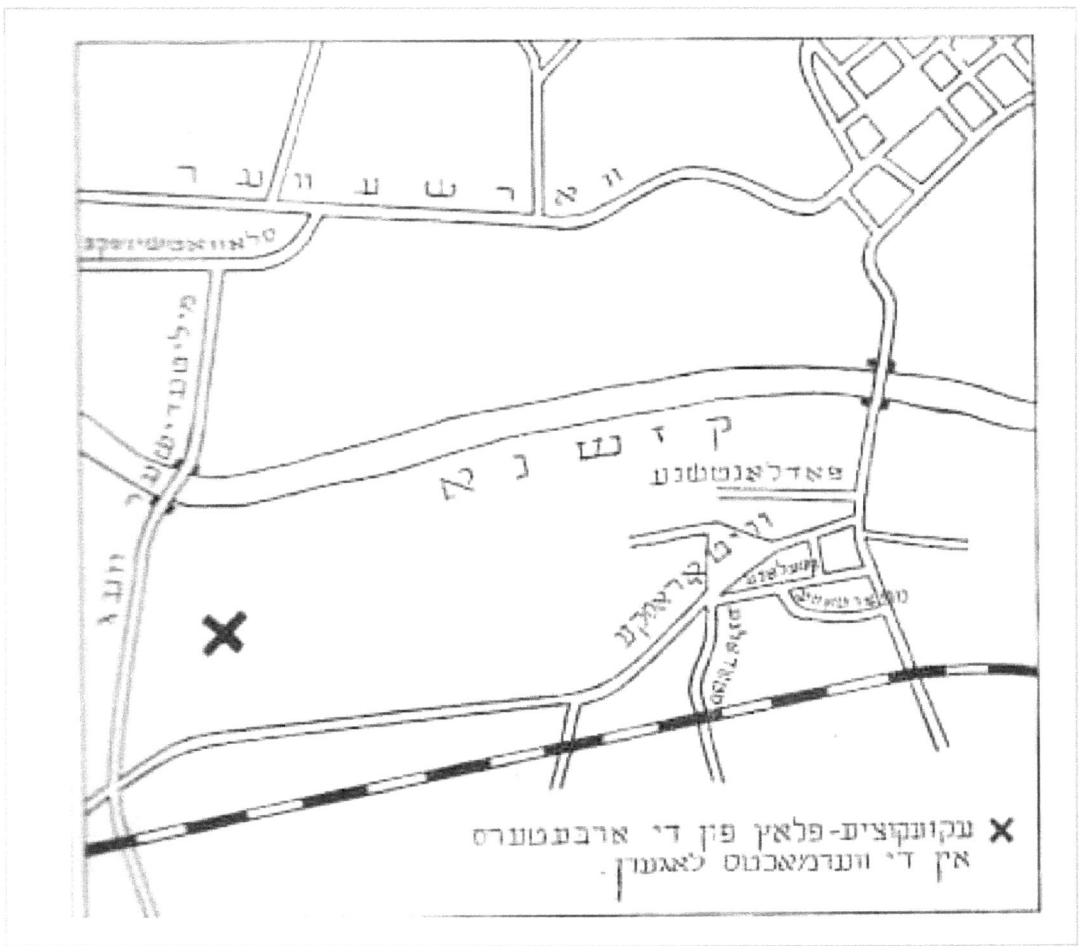

Sketch of the execution place where the Jewish workers from the Wehrmacht camp were brought to be shot on the 17th of December 1942

[Page 436]

The death sentence was delayed. The Jews had seen their grave. A long and deep grave in the meadow that was called Kolichawa. On both sides of the grave lay the dug-up earth, the later covering for the grave.

As soon as they detained the Mezritch Jews, the worker Yisroel Rodzinek tore himself away from the row and began to escape to the right. Soon, there was shooting at him from all sides, but he ran further. The dog did not want to obey his orders and did not want to move from the spot.

This scene took a second and Senior, the worker, a former prisoner of war, gave the order: "Run!" With wilds shouts of "hoorah!" the group ran in all directions. The machine guns and the rifles opened a deafening barrage and shot a hail of bullets at the escapees.

Almost all of the escapees from the execution field went to the Mezritch ghetto; among them was the hero, the first escapee, Yisroel Rodzinek. Among those from Biala arriving at the Mezritch ghetto were the wounded: Yehoshale Wajsman, Yerakhmiel Lichtenbaum and Asher Fajgenbaum (carpenter).

Later, we learned that a number of the escapees from the execution field left in another direction and that, on the road, many of them perished, such as: Yitzhak Kaufman (grain merchant, Yanower Street), Alter Plat (tailor), Yakov Rozenker (painter), Chaim Shimeon Rozenblat (watchmaker), Avraham Gringlas (Yoal, the son of the *shamas* [synagogue caretaker]), Blumenkranc (Yeshayahu Blumenkranc's son) and so on.

After shooting the workers from the camp of the 34th regiment and *Vineta*, the workers at the Gestapo in the Biala Jewish quarter prepared themselves for the same end, because the group leaders, Yitzhak Ekstajn, Shlomo Sztajngart, Shimeon Justman and the Sznajderman brothers, had escaped from there.

At dawn, they assembled all of the ghetto workers at the courtyard of the Gestapo, near Raabe's factory. They brought out a badly beaten Eksztajn and the Gestapo commissar demanded of the Jewish workers that they kill Eksztajn. The commissar, Shtilhamer, called out – If you are afraid of the Jewish neighborhood, we will kill him. Several members of the Gestapo smashed their victim with crowbars. Eksztajn was buried near the fence at Raabe's factory.

The Jewish workers worked at the camp at the airfield until November 1943, and then, according to the Christians, they were shot. There was a group of Janowa Jews there who worked at the Janowa *Wygoda* [horse farm] and later they were brought to the camp at the Biala airfield.

Destruction of the synagogue

[Page 437]

In a testimony at the Katowicer division of the Central Jewish Historical Commission in Poland (number 290), Jerzy Rozenbaum of Warsaw, who was in the Poniatow (Lublin region), said that in October 1943, 10,000 (ten thousand) people were sent from the camp to the Biala Podlaska airfield.

Biala Christians would speak about the Hungarian Jews who were supposedly brought to the airfield. It seemed to be in connection with the people from the Poniatow camp. However, the number of 10,000 seemed exaggerated.

Supposedly, the news from the Christians about the shooting of Jews in November 1943 at the air field was correct because on the 3rd of November 1943 a so-called *sonderbehandlung* [special treatment] took place in the Lublin region, during which a large number of Jews in the camps were shot and the remaining were taken out to Majdanek.

A group of Jewish workers at the Gestapo, after cleaning up the former Jewish quarter, were employed removing every sign of *Yidishkeit* [Jewish way of life] in Biala that supported the vestige of Jews in Biala. They demolished the synagogue and the houses of prayer.

In May 1943, another 17 Jews from the Mezritch ghetto joined the group.

This group remained in the city until April 1944. With the approach of the Russian Army, the last handful of Jews were taken from Biala to Lublin. A small number of the group survived.

The *Judenrat*

We have previously mentioned that one day (in November 1939), the Biala Gestapo summoned the *dozores* [members of the synagogue council] of the previous *kehile* [organized Jewish community] and ordered them to organize a *Judenrat* [Jewish council].

A number of former *dozores* entered the created *Judenrat* and people from all strata of the Jewish population were admitted with them. Its composition was the following: Yakov Ahron Rozenbaum, Yitzhak Kantor, Avraham Stricher, Yitzhak Lewi, Moshe Chaim Wajznfeld, Yisroel Bialer, Dovid Wajsman, Shmuel Krajzlman, Menakham Finklsztajn, Yehosha Goldrajch, Khanina Kaszemacher, Yehosha Eidlsztajn, Yehosha Rubinsztajn, Berl Goldberg and so on.

The *Judenrat* benefited from the complete sympathy on the part of the Jewish population and no bitterness reigned in the city in relation to it. Even the refugees who were brought to Biala by the Nazis did not reproach the *Judenrat*. As far as was possible, the *Judenrat* was tolerant to the homeless brought here, particularly the fact that a large percentage of homeless Jews were employed in its office, headed by the secretary, Rubinsztajn. Many homeless were sent to the labor office as administrative officials and to other German workplaces.

Everyone in the city knew that the members of the *Judenrat* had gone to great lengths in their offices to help but, in addition, there were demands from the Gestapo and it was clear under what difficult conditions the *Judenrat* carried out its work and how risky it was to have contact with the prominent Nazis. And if one of the rich Jews in the city expressed his dissatisfaction because higher taxes were demanded of him, the *Judenrat* let him know that it was ready to accept him as a member of the *Judenrat*. It should be understood that the "wronged" Jew immediately excused himself and apologized because there were no volunteers for *Judenrat* membership in the city.

In the winter of 1941, the *Judenrat* recruited several fresh members and among them was Chaim Rozmarin. Because the latter did not have any desire to be considered by the [German] regime as a member of the *Judenrat*, he ransomed himself for a considerably large payment to the treasury of the *Judenrat*. Yoal Zilberberg, the dentist, also was a large payer so that he would not have to be a member of the *Judenrat*.

There were cases where Jews (among them Avraham Jamnik, son-in-law of Yehosha Gliksberg) brought valuable jewelry to the *Judenrat*; perhaps, thanks to this, he said they could ease the conditions of the Jewish population. The *Judenrat* categorically refused to take the jewelry and answered: If it becomes necessary, we will use this idea with an appeal to the population.

We need particularly to record the courageous and devoted activity of the Biala *Judenrat*, which literally sacrificed itself on behalf of the Jewish population. Its members were the first to bear all the suffering and torture, of which the Jewish population did not even have any idea.

The *Judenrat* constantly stood on watch to have revoked the edicts that fell without end, and once they succeeded.

The daring conduct of the *Judenrat* in relation to the Nazi rulers was shown in the conversation of the *Judenrat* representative, Yakov Ahron Rozenbaum, with the official, Lipkow, which is described in the chapter "The First Expulsion."

[Page 438]

During the first deportation from Biala to the death camp in Sobibor, the *Judenrat* members gave strong hints to the Jewish population not to hurry to the place of assembly, although they could pay for this with their lives. The hints were to remember that the first deportation in Biala (they did not yet know then about the death camps. And they were sure that they were being deported to another city) had not torn out from the city all of those who, according to the order, needed to leave Biala.

The *Judenrat* knew how to make use of the antagonism among the German rulers. The Gestapo often annulled an edict that came from the administrative district. Thus, the *Judenrat* was in a quandary that the Gestapo did not have any idea about the first deportation edict. The Gestapo took umbrage then that the information reached it from the *Judenrat*. Perhaps this was a sign of the passive attitude of the Gestapo during the days of the deportation and why the action took place bloodlessly.

The proud and vigilant attitude of the Biala *Judenrat* certainly gave rise to its members being the first victims in the city. A month before Biala became *Judenrein* [emptied of Jews], the members of the *Judenrat* were taken from the city and tortured in Majdanek.

The Bialers in Mezritch Ghetto

The Biala Jews who were taken to the Mezritch ghetto during the second and last expulsion (from the 26th of September to the 1st of October 1942) really could not find a place to stay. There was barely room in the crowded ghetto for the Mezritcher and here they had brought thousands of Jews from Biala and the Biala *poviat* [district]. In such cases it was clear to the ghetto where they were taking newly arrived Jews, that they were thinking of a fresh expulsion. And, as in every ghetto, they went around with the illusion that this did not mean the local Jews, only those who had been brought in. In any case, they did not want to mix with those freshly arrived in the same situation.

However, the Mezritch *Judenrat* did not have any choice and it distributed the few houses for the Biala Jews. Also here, in the Mezritch ghetto, Biala Jews made efforts to be given work, to lengthen their lives. Perhaps, some convinced themselves that they would save themselves from death. A number of Bialers succeeded through various recommendations to be given workplaces.

The Biala *S.D.* [security service] man, Glet, came to Mezritch for the deportation and asked where the women, Baltshe Poczic and Chaya Rozenbaum, were, from whom he had swindled 45,000 *zlotes* with the promise that he would bring back the Biala Jews from Majdanek. It was said later that during the deportation all of the Jewish women who had worked in the field at Potocki's farm, "Halas," where the women B. Poczic and Ch. Rozenbaum,also worked, were taken from the field in the middle of their work and taken to train cars at the Mezritch train station. Thus the *S.D.* man Glet was sure that he was rid of the two women.

During the deportation, the Biala refugee in the Mezritch ghetto, Dovid Wajsman (who. came to Biala from Warsaw), a brother of the feldsher [traditional barber surgeon] Berish Wajsman, refused to leave his house and in no case wanted to obey the order of the Nazis to go outside. He was shot in the house. Characteristically, as the Jew would constantly argue in Biala: They will not take me to Treblinka. Why is death on the spot bad, but one must go to Treblinka [to die]?

Before the deportation, the number of Bialers in the Mezritch ghetto shrank sharply. Bialers were transported in each deportation from the Mezritch ghetto and their number constantly decreased. These Biala women died in their hiding places during the deportations: Khema Kalichsztajn and Lidzbarski (the wife of Moshe Lidzbarski). Between one deportation and the next, the Bialers carried on the same life as the Mezritch Jews. A life of fear, crowding and filth (typhus raged in the crowded and dirty houses and a number of Bialers died of the illness), a life always in a struggle with death, a life full of sadness and longing for those closest to them who had perished and with hope of Hitler's defeat.

[Page 439]

Biala Jews would risk walking to Biala to remove something of value from a hiding place there. Many never returned from such a walk from Mezritch. Moshe Yitzhak Biderman, his grandson (Rywke Rubensztajn's son), Yehosha Englender, Polya Ribak, Ayzsha Rubinsztajn and others left for Biala and they were never again seen in the ghetto.

After the fourth deportation to the Mezritch ghetto, in November 1942, the number of remaining Biala [Jews] was very small. Several Biala Jews were involved in trade in the ghetto; others would go to work outside the ghetto and try to smuggle something in to earn a living. There were Biala Jews who still had money that they had succeeded in bringing with them during the expulsion from Biala. There also were Biala Jews who would still come to the social division at the Mezritch *Judenrat* for help.

Bialers would meet in the crowded ghetto and, like those from Mezritch, they carried on no activity. Each one lived for himself.

On the long list of Jewish victims in the Mezritch ghetto (those who fell between one expulsion and another, or during the expulsions), the participation of the Bialers was very dignified. We will here record the names that remain in our memory.

The banished Biala Jews still had not become acquainted with the labyrinth of the Mezritch ghetto and the heavy sword of the second deportation had already descended on Mezritch. On the same day, the 6th of October 1942, when the men were led out of the Biala camps, the train which they had been on was held at the Mezritch train station and the empty freight cars were filled with Jews. The first victims here were the Jews from Biala and its county. The Mezritcher had already prepared hiding places and good working places and, therefore, a small percentage of them left in the deportation.

Shot for risking leaving the ghetto to earn some support for the soul were: Itka Plat, Miriam Listgartn and her daughter, Leah Knicznik, Mrs. Fridman (her husband, a tailor from Grabanower Street, came from Lomaz.

In the orgy of blood organized in the Mezritch ghetto by the Biala Gestapo on New Year's Eve of 1942/3, the majority of victims were Biala women and children. Shot with dum-dum bullets that night were: Zisl Rozmarin (née Sirkus), Sluwa Khohan, Mrs. Szajnberg (née Wiernicki), Mrs. Rozen (née Rozenbaum) and the two children of the painter Chaim Yosef Knicznik.

During the search for the escapee from the police, Yisroel Layzer Joczimowski, former commandant of the Mezritch Jewish *Ordnungsdienst*, Avraham Ezra Handlman and Bluma Preter were shot.

Biala victims, mainly from discovered hiding places, fell during the deportation from Mezritch in the ghetto itself in May 1943.

Killed in a hiding place into which the gendarme, Franz Bauer, threw a grenade, were Monya Lustigman (son of Iser), his wife (née Jurberg), the Fraus sister and brother and Monya's two sisters.

The people were led out into the street from a hiding place in the house of Lempert, the butcher, stood at the wall and were shot. Among them were the Bialers: Moshe Fajgenman (Zilie the carpenter's son) and his wife Blume (née Gerszkop), his small son and his wife's sister; Toybele Lustigman (née Rubinsztajn) and her small son. In another place in the ghetto were shot: Meir Orlanski and his wife and the baker, Yitzhak Fogel.

Yosef Elbaum (the son-in-law of Yakov the *shoykhet* [ritual slaughterer]) was murdered in the Mezritch Forest by Poles. His young daughter then succeeded in returning to the Mezritch ghetto with a gunshot wound through her small hand.

Biala youth also tried to escape to the Mezritch Forest from the Mezritch ghetto to free themselves from the Nazi talons, but these attempts were not successful.

In a group that left for the forest were the Bialers Faywl Buchhalter, Moshe Sztajnberg and his sister, Elka, Shepsl Lajbzon, Nakhke Gerszkop and Dovid Rozenberg. The group was able to obtain several revolvers. At a meeting in the forest with Russian prisoners of war who had escaped from the German camps, the Russians with weapons in their hands surrounded the Jewish group, disarmed and robbed them. The Jews returned to the ghetto.

In a second group that left for the forest were the Biala girls Sura Wizenfeld and Bas (from the butchers). During a heavy German search of the Mezritch Forest, the group succeeded in leaving the forest and it returned to the ghetto.

In July 1943, the Mezritch ghetto was completely liquidated and the last few Biala Jews there disappeared together with the handful of Mezritch Jews.

After the liberation of Mezritch by the Russian Army, it appeared that this group of Biala young people was the only one that had had a hiding place in the very center of the city of Mezritch and it (the group) succeeded in remaining alive. This was the Sztajnberg sisters and brother, Buchhalter, the Wizenfeld girls and Bachrach.

* * *

At the end of this bloody chronicle, we provide two reactions from the Nazi camps that had a connection to Biala, as well as two lists of the immovable Jewish possessions in Biala.

In the official government newspaper of the General-Government, *Krakower Zeitung* [*Krakow Newspaper*] of the 17th of October 1942, it is said that, according to the pact between the Biala and Radziner *Kreishauptmannschaften* [administrative districts], all of the Biala Jews were transferred to Mezritch [Międzyrzec]. That after the removal of the Jews from the city, everything became half as expensive. The Christian artisans, who had previously been pushed out by the Jews, now took to the work with zeal.

[Page 440]

Understand that it appeared that the moving of the Jews was not mentioned.

Actually, nothing could be obtained in the city. The Christians themselves would say that the Jews must have taken everything with them… One Christian was afraid to trade with another because the majority of goods were illegal. When the Jews had left, trade had died out.

How much the Christian artisanship "revived" can be seen from the fact that when those in power in Biala needed to have a good piece of work, they came to the Mezritch ghetto to the few remaining Jewish artisans. The Christian artisans in Biala were without work because they did not have the material on which to work that would previously have been provided to them by the Jews.

As is known, after the war, 21 prominent Nazis with [Hermann] Goering at the head, were tried in Nuremberg (Germany) by the International Military Tribunal.

In the stenographic report of the trial is found the witness testimony of Dr. Fritshe, former chief editor of the German news agency (*D.N.B. – Deutsches Nachrichtenbüro*) and head of the news division of German radio. This statement speaks of, among other things, Biala county (volume 17, page 177) because:

Dr. Fritz, the lawyer for Dr. Fritsche, during his examination of his client, asked him questions about the fate of the deported German Jews. To the question from his lawyer about whether he, Dr. Fritsche, had taken an interest in the treatment of the German Jews who were sent as Jewish refugees to eastern Europe, came the answer from Dr. Fritsche: Certainly. For example, I learned various things from a former co-worker who was sent to the General Government and he occupied an administrative post in the Biala Podlaska region. He told me that the area under his control was a Jewish area. He would often describe the appearance of the deported Jews and their housing. He had also reminded me about difficulties, about the employment of Jews as workers and about their work at plantations. His entire description gave evidence of his humane viewpoint. He told me that Jews were better treated by him than in the Third Reich.

Correspondence concerning Jewish immovable property in Biala

To the questions from his lawyer asking what the name of the person was, came Dr. Fritsche's answer: *Oberregierungsrat* [senior government counsel] Hubert Kihl.

In connection with this statement, it is worthwhile to comment that in Biala county, in general, there were no deported German Jews.

The above-mentioned Hubert Kihl was the Biala *Kreishauptmann* [district captain] who was shot on the Mezritch highway (probably by a group of Jews who left the camp of the 34th regiment under the leadership of Zilia Gutenberg).

The appropriation of Jewish immovable property was announced in the report of the 15th of January 1942 by the Biala district captain.

[Page 441]

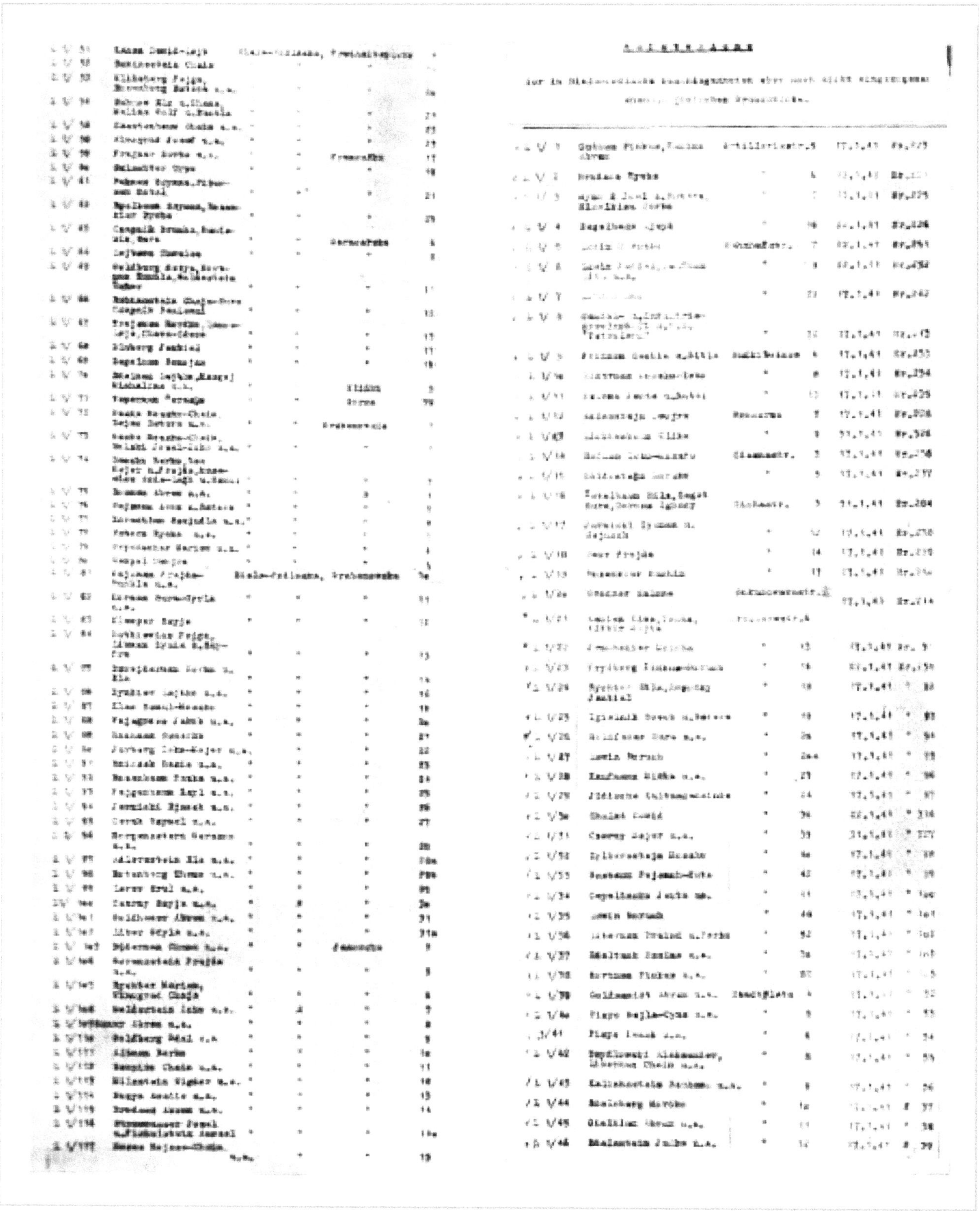

German list of some Jewish immovable property in Biala (annex to letter)

[Page 442]

From the documents that we received from the Jewish Historical Institute in Warsaw it can be seen that, in September 1943, when the German front in Russia had already collapsed, the African Corps of Marshal [Erwin] Rommel was smashed and the Allied armies were standing on Italian territory, the Germans all sat and made lists of Jewish houses whose owners had been murdered.

First of all, this document interested us because we could learn the extent of Jewish immovable possessions that remained in Biala.

From a letter of the 22nd of September 1943, of which we provide a photo here, it can be seen that it speaks of 317 Jewish immovable possessions in Biala, in the month of August 1943. It is difficult to say if this number encompasses all Jewish houses and sites in Biala. From the list that we are publishing here, as it was assembled by the Germans, we see that it contains only 194 entries and an entire series of streets are missing. A number of names are garbled and erroneous. The houses of Ahrele Slawaticzer and of the Rodzineks on Grabanower Street are missing. The houses at Wolnoszczi Square are missing where the shops of Khana Ruchl Reich, Sura Gele Goldfeder, Winograd, Sopir, Yontl Lipiec, Mendl Tokarski and Sura Leah Tornhajm were located. In addition to these, the houses of Avraham Orlandski, Shmuel Fiszman and Tila Berlin on Wonoszczi Square are missing.

Characteristically, rumors went around during the Nazi times about Shmuel Fiszman's house that the Germans sold to the German firm Golinker from Bremen.

Ref	Name	Place	No.
L 1/118	Listiguen Usser u.a.	Biala-Podlaska, Janowska	16
L 1/119	Wiernicki Szyja-Dawid u.a.	" " "	17
L 1/120	Szajnberg Rotera u.a.	" " "	21
L 1/121	Sussezyk Fejga	" " "	23
L 1/122	Wajgaus Gotlib	" " "	26
L 1/123	Jüdische Religions-gemeinde	" " "	29
L 1/124	Kosakowski Kazimiera u.a.	" " "	30
L 1/125	Kajzman Dawid	" " "	32
L 1/126	Bajsrstein Chana u.a.	" " "	34
L 1/127	Knisuła Feja	" " Jatkowa	2
L 1/128	Frydman Dawid u.a.	" " "	3
L 1/129	Schulman Lejzor	" " "	4
L 1/130	Kligur Blumen u.a.	" " "	5
L 1/131	Erlenstor Dwojra u.a.	" " "	6
L 1/132	Kliger Blumen u.a.	" " "	7
L 1/133	Schnew Nie-Mordka	" " "	9
L 1/134	Jabrokowski Szmuel	" " "	10
L 1/135	Rubinsztein Gral u.a.	" " "	11
L 1/136	Korbaum Rindla	" " "	11a
L 1/137	Shelbovie Bereszko u.a.	" " "	14
L 1/138	Kurowik Estera u.a.	" " "	16
L 1/139	Tusklewi Idas	" " "	18
L 1/140	Charni Lejb	" " Koszarowa	45
L 1/141	Felman Lejbko u.Rajchla	" " "	63
L 1/142	Zylberg ug Gitla	" " Kretha	3
L 1/143	Jüdische Kulturgemeinde	" " Losizena	1
L 1/144	Nalewik u.Tajtel u.a.	" " "	2
L 1/145	Jüdische Kulturgemeinde	" " "	3
L 1/146	Szteanberg Berusch	" " "	4
L 1/147	Szcejnman Marjem Gela	" " "	6
L 1/148	Szygiel Wojra	" " Marktplatz	1
L 1/149	Kryger Lajzus	" " "	3
L 1/150	Celkowski Blai under u.a.	" " "	5/6
L 1/151	Bodanki Szamul u.Feajcha Fejga	" " "	11
L 1/152	Oterhede Lejka u.a.	" " Strzeszkiess	9
L 1/153	Eisenman Sube	" " "	19b
L 1/154	Jougleraza Malka u.a.	" " "	16
L 1/155	Wahlmanberla Chaim	" " "	2a
L 1/156	Finkiel Estera u.a.	" " "	22
L 1/157	Schuchmacher Mordko-Jossl u.a.	Biala-Podlaska, Brzotowicza	24
L 1/158	Wajnsztein Szymon u. Grynberg Macia	" " "	26
L 1/159	Wilf Gitla u.a.	" " "	28
L 1/160	Sa Aron u.a.	" " "	32
L 1/161	Uhwat Gwaiej	" " "	33
L 1/162	Gutman Froim	" " "	34
L 1/163	Rogalska Dwojra u.a.	" " "	40
L 1/164	Gutman Jurko u.a.	" " "	41
L 1/165	Uzerna Rajchla u.Koffer Riwa-Rachela	" " "	42
L 1/166	Walecki Chuna-Lejzor u.a.	" " "	47
L 1/167	Kligier Cypa u.a.	" " "	50
L 1/168	Edelman Junkiel u.Lenachem	" " "	52
L 1/169	Chrosnicki Losako	" " Sofn	20
L 1/170	Josar Lejbko u.a.	" " "	24
L 1/171	Kozniunszouk Paulina, Chrosurzycki Szmul-Mordko u.a.	" " "	26
L 1/172	Wajntaum Cypa u.Dwojra	" " Podlasna	16
L 1/173	Obriant Berko u.Perla, Luxsam Ita-Feja	" " Prosta	3
L 1/174	Strycher Aron u.Nachla	" " "	4
L 1/175	Auerbach Salmon u.a., Sussner Szmul-Zelik u.a.	" " "	6
L 1/176	Wielnicki Dumerko u.a.	" " "	8
L 1/177	Jarberg Junkiel u.Siernik Blima	" " "	10
L 1/178	Lichtensstein Szymon u.a.	" " "	11
L 1/179	Kahan Alte	" " "	11
L 1/180	Szcejman Herszko u.a.	" " "	1
L 1/181	Kokowsko Moszko u.Lebenglik Junkiel	" " "	1
L 1/182	Dzieciol Szmul u.a.	" " "	
L 1/183	Fruchtenberg Wigdor-Lejb, Lustiguam Dawid-Szragie u.Chanaleja	" " "	
L 1/184	Wydra Szul-Josek u.a.	" " "	
L 1/185	Pacztaruk Lejzor u.a.	" " "	
L 1/186	Kahan Lejbo	" " "	
L 1/187	Rossenberg Chaim-Mordka u.a.	" " "	
L 1/188	Lustiguam Lejzor-Fejszeli, Szuster Rajzla u.a.	" " "	
L 1/189	Korman Boru-Cyrla u.a.	" " "	
L 1/190	Suchowies Boech u.Chana-Pesja u.a.	" " "	

L 1/193	Zwra Moszko, Szulman Ita-Laja, Bronowicz Junta	Biala-Podlaska,	Prosta		51
L 1/194	Jassler Nachman u. Feperztok Szlona	"	"	"	32
L 1/195	Milbauer Icko, Trej-tman Chaim-Chajkiel, Tokarska Gitla u.a.	"	"	"	33
L 1/196	Lemberglar Dawid u.a.	"	"	"	34
L 1/197	Terebies Utla, Kuzmiecka Dalcza, Apelbaum Szmul u. Zacharia	"	"	"	35
L 1/198	Rubinsztain Jankiel-lozk, Kulawy Szaja-Rejk, Krawczik Jentel u.a.	"	"	"	36
L 1/199	Rubinsztein Icko, Kahn Motel, Rozanbaum Aron, Goldstain Jankiel, Flan-helm Bluma	"	"	"	37
L 1/200	Szapira Srul-Icko	"	"	"	38
L 1/137	Glikzberg Herszko u.a.	Biala-Podl. Jatkowastr. 12		17.1.41 Nr.133	
L 1/135	Cukierman Izyl u.a.	Biala-Podl. Naruntowiczsstr. 15		17.1.41 Nr.171	
L 1/241	Judische Kultusgemeinde	Biala-Podl. Rozmiinastr. 2		17.1.41 " 244	
L 1/242	Weinstein Szewa u.a.	"	9	31.1.41 " 291	

German list of some of the Biala Jewish immovable property (insert to a letter)

[Page 443]

Because of the discovery of the German list of Jewish immovable possessions and in order to complete it, we provide here a list of the Jewish immovable possessions that we created from memory and which do not appear in the German list. This last list contains 98 entries and it is also not complete.

1. Inheritor Rozenszwajg	1 Brisker Street
2. Abik Rozenblum	2 Brisker Street
3. Stores of the *kehile* [organized Jewish community]	3 Brisker Street
4. Yitzhak Berman	4 Brisker Street
5. Mordekhai Yosef Goldsztajn	5 Brisker Street
6. *Kehile* house	6 Brisker Street
7. Moshe Zajgermacher and Gerszkop	7 Brisker Street
8. Benyomin Leib Mandlbaum	8 Brisker Street

9. Inheritor Gerszkop	9 Brisker Street
10. Inheritor Rozenbaum	10 Brisker Street
11. Nakhum Libman	11 Brisker Street
12. Berl Sandlarcz and Yitzhak Fogel	12 Brisker Street
13. Leibe Bornsztajn	13 Brisker Street
14. Zavl Najsztajn	14 Brisker Street
15. The Wajnes	15 Brisker Street
16. Shimeon Lichtnsztajn	16 Brisker Street
17. Inheritor Piczic	17 Brisker Street
18. Lewin (Koczemainik)	19 Brisker Street
19. Benyamin Natanzon and Yosef Feldman	Brisker Street
20. Piczic's barracks	Brisker Street
21. Radziner *shtibl* [one-room synagogue]	Wonska Street
22. Shmuel Kligsberg	Wonska Street
23. Space of Elihu Piwo	Wonska Street
24. The Eidlsztajn brothers (blacksmiths)	Wonska Street
25. *Misnagdim shtibl* [one-room synagogue of the followers of the Enlightenment]	Wonska Street
26. Ponczik	Wonska Street
27. Grodner – Grobman	Wonska Street
28. Wajnberg (inheritor of Avraham Mendl)	Wonska Street
29. Ajzenberg Shmerl	Wonska Street
30. Space of Shabati	Wonska Street
31. Yosef Yuwale (wagon driver)	Wienczenne Street
32. Fayge Firme's [daughter]	Warszawer Street
33. Ajzenberg	Witoroska Street
34. Yehoshua Kop [head] (nickname)	Witoroska Street
35. Avraham Tajtlbaum	Witoroska Street
36. Yitzhak Droczkorcz	Witoroska Street
37. Moshe Hajblum	Witoroska Street
38. Inheritor of Chaim Beker-Murowiec	Prosta Street
39. Moshe Kuropotwe	Prosta Street
40. Yeshayhu Rajzwaser	Prosta Street

41. *Talmud Torah* [religious school for poor children]	Prosta Street
42. Moshe Glezer [glazier] – Fajgnbaum	Prosta Street
43. Shmuel Fajgnbaum	Prosta Street
44. Shmerl Pep (nickname)	Prosta Street
45. Moshe Szajman	Prosta Street
46. Getsl (*dorf-geyer* [men who bought and sold goods in villages])	Prosta Street
47. House in which Avigdor Richter lived	Prosta Street
48. House in which Shmuel Ruvin Wajsbrot lived	Prosta Street
49. Shimkha Rozenfeld	Prosta Street
50. Liba Zusman	Pocztowa Street
51. Inheritor Eidltuch	Pocztowa Street
52. Ahron Kasztenbaum	Pocztowa Street
53. Gerer *shtibl*	Pocztowa Street
54. Rozenszajn	Pocztowa Street
55. Avraham Goldszmidt and Dovid Kligberg	Pocztowa Street
56. Avigdor Fridman	Pocztowa Street
57. Sura Gliksberg	Pilsudski Street
58. Yosef Bradacz	Pilsudski Street
59. Mendl Goldfarb	Pilsudski Street
60. Moshe Rudl's [son] (nickname)	Pilsudski Street
61. Chaim Mordekhai Goldszmidt and Finkelsztajn	Pilsudski Street
62. Inheritor Rozenberg	Pilsudski Street
63. Yakov Libman	Pilsudski Street
64. Lewi	Pilsudski Street
65. Gerszkop and Pinyele Beker	Pilsudski Street
66. Dovid Leib Grinsztajn	Pilsudski Street
67. Avraham Urmacher (annex)	Pilsudski Street
68. Rubinsztajn (near the pump near Dr. Zita's house)	Pilsudski Street
69. Yitzhak Rozenszajn	Pilsudski Street
70. Piczize's barracks	Pilsudski Street
71. Yehiel (a stablehand – near Moshe Glezer)	Przechodnie Street
72. Shmuel Fiszman (shopkeeper)	Reformacka Street

73. Moshe Lebnberg	Reformacka Street
74. Avraham Lubelczik	Reformacka Street
75. Yisroel Makowski	Reformacka Street
76. Yitzhak Fajgenman	Sadowa Street
77. Zalman Zak	Sadowa Street
78. Eidlman (Moshe Ayzyk's son)	Sadowa Street
79. Khanan Eliezer Nauczni	Sadowa Street
80. Yosef Man (Terebiler)	Sadowa Street
81. Kalman Szejnberg (where the community center was located)	Sadowa Street
82. Eidl Zylbersztajn (Praszekier)	Sadowa Street
83. The location of the oilpresser	Sadowa Street
84. Hershl Szchur	Sadowa Street
85. Mendele Fridman (Sitniker)	Sitnicka Street
86. Yakov Rajz	Sitnicka Street

[Page 444]

89. Idele Cukerman (Łomazyer)	Sitnicka Street
90. Chaya Hofer	Sitnicka Street
91. Inheritor Finkelsztajn	Sitnicka Street
92. Synagogue	Szkolna Street
93. House of prayer	Szkolna Street
94. Zakasner house of prayer	Szkolna Street
95. Shimkha Plat and inheritor Zuberman	Szkolna Street
96. Chaim Musawicz	Szkolna Street
97. The house where the laundry wringer was located	Szkolna Street
98. *Hakhnoses orkhim* [hospitality for poor Sabbath guests]	Szkolna Street

* * *

After the liberation of Biala by the Russian Army, on the 26th of July 1944, about 26 Jews returned to Biala from hiding places in the forests. Among the 26 Jews were those not from Biala who found themselves in Biala during the German occupation.

The Christian population saw the return of the handful of Jewish people with no particular sympathy. On the first day, they did not want to sell anything to the Jews and the Jews were forced to ask the soldiers of the Russian Army for bread.

With the repatriation of the Polish citizens from Russia, a few dozen former Jewish residents returned to Biala. They exhumed the bones of the Jews who had been shot at Shabtai Finklsztajn's place and from other places in the city and they buried them in a communal grave at the former Jewish cemetery. With the help of the Bialers in North America, a memorial was erected at the communal grave. However, the memorial stood for only a short time and it was blown up with dynamite. This tragic record of Jewish death also was erased.

The small group of Biala Jews felt that there was no longer any place for it in its city of birth and it left Biala.

* * *

In the dissertation, *Yidish Biala in di Letste Doyres* [*Jewish Biala during the Last Generations*], and *Khurbn un Farlend* [*Destruction and Annihilation*], we looked at Jewish life in Biala at the end of the 19th century to its tragic end.

We saw a life locked in a voluntary ghetto and the struggle to tear oneself out of the ghetto. We accompanied the sprouting communal life that arose precisely in the years of the First World War. We followed the hopes of a more beautiful tomorrow that was dreamed at the end of the First World War that disappeared and its place was taken by the struggle for daily existence. A struggle that lasted until – until the arrival of the people from the *dichter und denker-land* [the land of the poet and thinker]. And again we, the Biala Jews, were in the ghetto, but this time not voluntarily, but forced with brutal strength and from there, from the ghetto, the road led to a horrible death.

We tore toward the light of Western culture and to civilization. A part of the West came to us and annihilated us.

Sources:

1. M.Y. Fajgenbaum: *Podlisashe in Natsi-klem* [*Podlaska in the Nazi Vise*], Buenos Aires, 1953.
2. M.Y. Fajgenbaum: *Podlisashe in Natsi-klem*, Munich, 1948.
3. *Krakauer Zeitung* [*Krakow Newspaper*], 17 October 1942.
4. *Dokumenty i Materiały Tom I Obozy. Opracował Mgr.* [*Magister* – Polish academic degree equivalent to a master's degree] *N. Blumental. Wydawnictwa Centralnej Żydów Komisji Historycznej przy C.K. Żydów Polskich.* [Documents and Material, Volume 1 Camps. Compiled by Mgr. N. Blumental. The Publishing House of the Central Jewish Historical Commission at the Central Committee of Polish Jews], Lódż, 1946.

(Text below in English as printed)

1. "Trial of The Major War Criminals before The International Military Tribunal in Nuremberg."

Translator's footnote:

1. The Yiddish word *kirzsher* can be translated as both furrier and hatmaker. ***Original footnotes:***

a. Tried in Biala after the war. The court proceedings, which lasted three days, took place in the cinema hall of the firefighters. Hildeman, in his six-hour defense speech, first of all, asked for mercy in order to be able to return to his only daughter in Germany. He argued further that he committed all of the actions according to the orders he received from Lublin. At the end, he explained that as Poland is ruled by one party, everyone who carried out the orders of the party now was under the threat that if the party were removed from power, they would be responsible for their actions.
The court sentenced him to death by hanging and the sentence was carried out in the courtyard of the Biala prison. (Told by **Yehosha Wajsman** – Israel)
b. Tried in Biala after the war and sentenced to 15 years in prison. There were Biala Jews among the accusing witnesses, such as: Yitzhak Fridman, Yehosha Wajsman, Yisroel Bekerman and so on.
c. The camp has been exhaustively described because the author was there from the second expulsion until the end.
d. Shot by someone unknown in Biala, summer 1943.

[Page 445]

<u>Survivors' Tales</u>

The Beginning of the End

by Berish Asenhaltz, Tel Aviv

Translated by Ofra Anson

In the early morning of Friday, September 1st, several explosions were heard in the air, shaking the town and waking its residents. People hurried fearfully to the streets, asking what had happened. We were told to be calm, that what we heard was just an experimental explosion. It did not take long before we learned that the Germans had bombed the airplane factory in Vollye. It was clear that the war had begun.

Biala was bombed every day, especially Vollye, though the airplane factory, built in the First World War, was already in poor condition. The town was helpless: there was no way to resist the German airplanes. The bombing caused casualties and fires. One such fire ruined the house of Heartglass. Passersby were shot from the airplanes with machineguns. The dead and wounded, Jews and Christians, were lying in the streets. Many people left for the East and the roads were full of the wounded who had been shot while leaving.

We celebrated Rosh Hashana under the German bombing. We prayed with extreme devotion. The words "Who will live and who will die" had a very realistic meaning that year.

The bombing stopped after two weeks. The German army camped in Siedlce, the Red Army in Brisk. Biala remained "no man's land". The roads and streets, however, were full of refugees. Yet, instead of fleeing to the East, people started moving to the West. The wounded, with broken and swollen legs, asked for some bread and water. Long queues stood in front of the bakeries, hoping to buy a quarter of a loaf of bread.

The municipality recruited Jews and Christians to form a civil militia to keep order in the town.

Four German tanks arrived from Warsaw Avenue. Seeing the militia, they turned and left in the direction of Brisk Avenue.

A Polish officer, together with the town secretary, Limawski, decided to capture the German tanks. They quickly gathered 200 Polish soldiers from the streets, and sent them in different directions to ambush the tanks. In the evening, when the tanks drove back, they came out, but the Germans opened fire, and left some dead soldiers in the street.

On Tuesday, September 26th, Mayor A. Walawski called a number of citizens for a meeting. The Jewish city secretary came in in the middle of the meeting and brought news that Russian tanks had entered the town. He told the Jews in the meeting: "You should welcome the Russian army" and, with a sarcastic smile, put his coat on and left.

Russian officers spoke to the people of the town. The Jews in Biala felt relieved that the town would not fall into German hands. Shops slowly reopened, and the Russian soldiers bought many things, mainly watches. Jewish Russian soldiers quickly made friends with the local Jews, and Succoth was happily celebrated.

The relief was short lived. By Hoshana Rabbah, the German radio declared that the new border between Germany and Russia would be the river Bug.

[Page 446]

It meant that Biala would be under German control. The news spread quickly, causing despair. The Russian soldiers did not believe the German news, yet it soon proved to be true, and the Russians started to leave Biala. The Russians declared their willingness to help anyone that wished to move to Russian territory, to provide transportation to people and their goods.

What will happen now? The Jews in Biala asked this question. Everyone knew that it was going to be terrible, but not everyone could decide which would be worse: leaving everything, to become homeless and wander like the refugees they saw in town in recent weeks, or to stay put under Hitler's government and see what fate brings.

In the streets, one could see army vehicles driving Jewish families to the station. Nevertheless, only a minority decided to leave. The great majority stayed in their homes.

Thursday, October 10, was a beautiful autumn day. The town, however, was like a ghost town, all doors and gates were closed. The last Russian soldiers had left, and the German army was expected.

A car with a German officer arrived from Warsaw Avenue, accompanied by two armed motorcycles. They arrived at Wolnosci Square, and stopped by the store of Abraham Goldsmith. A few minutes later, a Soviet officer arrived at the same place. After formal greetings, the Soviet officer read the order to hand the town over to the Germans.

The German army entered Biala. Two hours later, German soldiers started to arrest Jews as hostages. Christians with white armbands walked in the streets and kidnapped Jews to work for the Germans, where they were bitterly beaten.

This is how it started.

A. In the Miedzyrzec Ghetto

by R. Bachrach

Translated by Ofra Anson

On Friday evening, the first night of Succoth (September 25, 1942), the secret police, gendarmes, and the Gestapo surrounded the Jewish neighborhood in Biala. Early Saturday morning they started to expel the Jews from their homes and hurried them to the new market, to the gathering point. At the same time, Jews were shot in their homes and on the way to the new market. From the market, most of the Jews were taken to Miedzyrzec Ghetto.

Some fifteen people, including me, my father Joshe Bachrach, my mother Reisel, my brother Yitzhak, my grandmother Rachel and Sara Weisman, hid in a bunker in Arke Weisman's house on Grabanover Street. The bunker had a double wall between a store and a room under the store. The entrance to the bunker was through a small wooden board, which opened under a bed. In the bunker, people stood in line; the children stayed in a hole above the heads of the standing people. We were there for several days. My grandmother Rachel could not stand it and went out. She was immediately sent to Miedzyrzec.

News from outside was heard in the bunker from time to time. We heard that Ivanitzki (the vice–mayor) had joined the Polish police in the search for Jews in hiding. We heard Jews screaming as they were shot in the street. We heard that once, the Christian street–cleaners asked Ivanitzki what to do with a dead horse lying in the street and he answered: put the horse on the pile of dead Jews who were taken to the cemetery.

On the last day of Succoth the Germans discovered our bunker and took us to the secret police station on Grabanover Street, in the building of the elementary school. There they put us on a truck and sent us to the Miedzyrzec Ghetto.

In the Miedzyrzec Ghetto everyone looked for work to make a living. Selig Jacobovitch, Tuchshneider, and my father got a job digging up potatoes. Together with my mother, my little brother, and Zipporah Finkelstein, they went to Wysokie, 8 km from Miedzyrzec. A few days later, on Friday, October 9th, we were sent back to Miedzyrzec. On our way, the Germans shot Zipporah Finkelstein.

[Page 447]

The second Action in the Miedzyrzec Ghetto started on Tuesday, October 6th, 1942. This was the first deportation to Treblinka. My two grandmothers, Rachel Rubinstein and Tzivia Bachrach, were deported that day. From Tuesday to Friday, Jews were collected from their working places, bunkers, and other places and gathered in the school. We also went to the school and, a few hours later, we were marched through the streets to the city square. On both sides, gendarmes, Gestapo, the secret police, and Ukrainian and Polish police officers, who kept shooting, guarded us. The way was paved with dead bodies, and the shooting continued after we reached the square.

In the evening, we were brought to a cargo train, with very small windows with barbed wire. We were rushed into the carriages, women and children separated from the men.

I was in the same wagon with my mother, my brother, and my aunts Hadel Bachrach-Sapir and Sara Bachrach–Finkelstien. Luba Tuchshneider was with us too.

About 10 o'clock, the train started moving. People immediately struggled to get to the windows. The barbed wire had been broken and people started to jump out of the train. I was sleeping, but my mother woke me up and pushed me out of the window. This was before Siedlce. I fell into the ditch by the railway. Soon another person who jumped fell on me, hitting my face with his shoe so hard that I lost a tooth. The train guards kept shooting those who jumped, and my leg was wounded.

Together, a group of "jumpers" started running and looking for a place to hide. We reached a village. Some people went to look for us in order to hand us over to the Germans. Each of us bought his way with what he/she had. We learned to avoid villages from then on.

Meanwhile, the wound in my leg gave me a lot of pain, and I could not go on. I asked the others to leave me alone and save their own lives. They refused and carried me on their back for as long as they could. We found a barn and they left me there.

I think that I was unconscious. I do not know for how long I lay there; perhaps 2–3 days. When I gained consciousness, my leg was bandaged, and a bowl of food stood next to me.

It did not take long before the door opened, and the owner of the barn told me that I could not stay there. He said that he could not throw me out of the barn in the state he found me, but he could not take the risk of his neighbors finding out that he was hiding me. That night he put me on a wagon, covered me with hay, and took me to Miedzyrzec.

The Action was still going on in the Miedzyrzec Ghetto. A relative of mine took me to a bunker located in a leather shop by the river. There my wound was cleansed and I got some food.

When the second Action was over, all the people that were in their workplaces came back to the Ghetto. My father was among them, and when he learned that my mother and my little brother had been sent to Treblinka, he fainted, and his hair became white overnight.

Doctor Koses treated my leg. He took out the bullet and treated the wound until it was healed.

The Ghetto was quiet for about three weeks. Suddenly, one evening, there was panic again. Those who worked outside the Ghetto packed up a few things and left. I joined them. We went to the train station, bought a ticket, and went to Biala.

Next to the train station in Biala was a working camp, where Jews were working. I went in and people who knew me hid me. After a week, the camp was dismantled, and its inhabitants moved to a camp on Warsaw Boulevard.

All that day I was hiding in a concrete canal in a field by the train station. In the evening, I went to the station, to buy a ticket to go back to Miedzyrzec. I saw a few Christians who knew me, and I was afraid that they would identify me as a Jew. So I wandered off at a distance, trying not to be seen. A German soldier approached me and started talking to me. I ignored him as if I did not understand German. He told me not to be afraid of him, that he knew I was Jewish and that I understood German.

[Page 448]

He asked me where I wanted to go and if I had money. I gave him money; he bought me a ticket and took me to the trains to the wagon he was riding.

I came to Miedzyrzec at the end of the third Action, which had started while I was in Biala. The Ghetto was full of Germans. This Action took a long time, because it was difficult to gather enough Jews to fill up the transport. They were concentrated in the school and in the basements of the houses around it, where they had to wait before they were taken to the train.

I went to the German brush factory, where I had an acquaintance. They found me a place to sleep. Next morning they wanted to send me to work in the kitchen, but the Jewish supervisor did not allow it. My acquaintance took me to a bunker, which was inside the camp, where an old man with a long, white beard and a boy about 12 years old were staying. The old man started shouting "take out the female"

(I was 16 at that time). I was so tense at that point, that I told him that I was not leaving, and if I went, he would too. He screamed so loud that the Germans overheard him and took us all out.

We were led to the school. Other Jews, who were working in different places, joined us on the way. When I had a chance, I left the group and hid under a big stone next to a heap of wood next to the road. I lay there until it was dark. At night, I went to the camp. The Jewish supervisor of the headquarters' camp wanted to send me away, but I asked him how much money he wanted; he said "a tenner" (a ten rubles gold coin from the Czar regime). I still had some such coins and I gave him one. He took me to the women's dorm, and in the morning, I went to work in the headquarters (washing floors, shining windows, and such).

On the second day, people started suddenly running to the windows. They said that a convoy of dead Jews was passing by. I was washing a window and looked out. On one of the carriages, I saw the head of my father, dressed in a black coat and bare feet. Something inside me pushed me out of the house. I ran after the convoy, and held my father's foot. I could not utter a word, and for a whole month I did not speak. The undertakers begged me to go away before the Germans shot me, but I did not even understand what they wanted from me. One of the street cleaners grabbed me and forced me back into the building. I worked there for a few days, and rumors started, saying that in the next Action even those who worked in the headquarters and in the factory would be taken. People started to leave their work and look for hiding places. I hid in an attic with some other people between bales of straw. The Germans found us and took us to a large square between the camps. More and more people were brought to this place. On the side of the square stood a wooden building, which used to be the workers' dining and later served as a storage room for the Germans. Inside were long tables and benches. I moved slowly towards that building and hid under a bench. An old German spotted me and aimed his gun at me. As I could not speak, I begged for my life with motions. He felt sorry for me and said that the place I found was not a good one because the light falls on it, and led me to the other side of the room. He covered me with a blanket, and told me not to move, because the place would be searched. Sure enough, some Ukrainians came searching with flash–lights, and by a miracle did not get to my corner. I stayed there for two days.

Two days later, I heard steps. The German who saved me came in, with the Jewish supervisor of the camp near the headquarters. He showed him where I was, told him to give me some food, and left. He told me that the Action was over, that people had started to return to the camp and within a few hours, I would be able to go back too. He did not give me any food but asked if I had money left. I showed him the few "tenner" I had; he took one, and left.

A few hours later, when I heard that people were walking by, I came out and returned to the headquarters. I stayed there for more than two weeks. During this time, the Jewish supervisor took all the money I had, and then told me to leave the camp.

[Page 449]

One Friday night in early December, I was forced to leave the camp and return to the Ghetto.

I arrived at the Ghetto at 6pm, in the midst of shooting started by the SS members, Heine and Dukow, from Radzyn and the gendarme Frantz Bower, whom we named "the beater". The Germans in the Ghetto were extremely cruel and were proud of the number of Jewish victims they had shot. Shlomo'le Shuster (called Shlomo'le Bialer, because his family came from Biala), who worked in the Gendarmerie next to Shotz Square, used to say that each time Frantz Bower returned from the Ghetto he marked a little line above his bed for each Jew he had shot.

I was told that by the wire fence at the end of the Ghetto, in a room that used to serve for praying, I could find people from Biala. I went there and met Golda Kalichstein, Basha Rosen-Kalichstein with her two children and the younger sister of Basha and Golda. They made me a place to sleep on the floor next to them. My relative, Nathan Eidelman, who lived in Miedzyrzec, soon came and took me to him. The next day I became sick, I had a high fever, and Dr. Koses, who had treated my leg, came to care for me again.

A day later there was again a panic in the Ghetto; everyone started running and hiding. The Germans were looking for workers for the brush factory in Travnic, and my relatives packed some things and went to work there. I got up, put some clothes on and went looking for a bunker. No one would let me in because of my fever. I went to the school, where the sick went, and lay on the floor among them. I fell asleep. I do not know how many days I slept. All I remember is that one day an undertaker slapped my leg. I opened my eyes but did not know what was happening to me. One day I woke up and felt new strength in me. I got up, went to the sink to wash myself a little and went outside.

The first person I met was Abraham'ele Nussbaum from Miedzyrzec, who lived with the wife of Shimon Blankleider (the thin), a daughter Bela, a son Josel and his wife. A. Nussbaum took me in with them. Mrs. Blankleider immediately washed me with warm water, fed me, and got me a clean bed to sleep in. I stayed there until the fifth Action.

New Years' Eve 1942–43, SS men came from Biala and started amusing themselves by shooting Jews in the Ghetto. Many Jews from Biala were killed and wounded that day.

There were no Actions during the winter months, but Actions resumed immediately after Passover.

Sunday morning, May 2nd 1943 when it was still dark out, news that the Ghetto was surrounded by Germans passed from house to house. People started running, looking for a hiding place. With the first light, we heard the Germans shouting: "All Jews out".

We went to the attic and hid under the straw. We heard a bang on the door, and the Germans came in and took out whoever they found there. They came up to the attic and took us to the gathering place located in the middle of the market.

They chose the young and healthy men and sent them to Majdanek. Those left in the market had to sit on the earth motionlessly. A young man who sat next to me was shot and wounded when he tried to lift himself a little to stretch a leg. He was bleeding and begged for help, but nobody moved, as we were afraid.

Before noon, we were marched to the train. Dead bodies and small children stayed in the market place when we left.

We were marched to the train in lines. Most people went straight, with no protest. We were tired of life. In the same line with me walked Malka Blankleider, her daughter Bela, and her daughter in law (Josel, her son, was taken with the other group). While we were walking, I asked Bela if she would jump off the train if it was possible and told her how to jump. She said that she would not jump, she had had enough and did not want to live any longer.

We went on the train, not too crowded, about fifteen people in a wagon. In our wagon was an old woman, I do not know from where. She asked who intended to jump and divided her money and jewelry between them. She gave me 300 zlotys, a watch and a necklace, telling me that I would need them.

About a quarter of an hour after we left the station, a woman put her stool under me, Bela Blankleider pushed me to the window, which was quite high, and I jumped off the train. Another three people jumped with me. I hid in a canal by the railway, and the train passed. A broken house was close by and I ran and entered it.

[Page 450]

While I was lying there, I heard steps. A Polish person came in and told me not to fear him. He told me that he saw me jumping off the train and getting into the house, that he was from Miedzyrzec, and there was an empty shed next to him. He invited me to go there at night in the dark, and he would make me a place and bring me food.

I was afraid to be alone, and I asked him to wait and watch me from a short distance until night. He promised to do that. Later, when we got closer to the town, some non–Jewish youngsters spotted me and shouted: "Jewish woman"! I tried to buy my way and gave them all the money I had. At the end, the man chased them away. I entered the house he showed me and hid in a corner in the attic.

The Polish youngsters soon came back, looking for me. They did not find me, and went to seek help from a German who did find me. I told him that I could not walk, because I hurt my leg jumping off the train. He pushed me off the stair I was sitting on and I fell through a broken stair. I could see that the German did not want to be bothered with me. Because I said I could not walk, they brought a cart and set me between them. On the way, he whispered in my ear that he did not set me free only because of the Polish pig.

They brought me to the Polish police, where a woman who worked there was called, and they told her: "Take this shit". She led me to a different room, where she told me to undress completely; she searched me and made me jump to make sure I was not hiding anything. Then she told me to get dressed and took me to a cell in a big barn in the police station yard. I saw there Polish people who had been beaten so hard that they lay there and moaned and could not even turn from side to side. One of the beaten youngsters asked me for the jacket I was wearing because I was going to be shot anyway, and he would pray for the Jews. I told him that I would happily give him cholera. A Jew from Miedzyrzec was also there, and when he saw me, he said: "Tomorrow both of us will lie in a grave". He told me that he was hiding with his sister; she was shot when they were found, and he was taken to the police because he convinced them that he had some gold hidden. His first name was Solomon. I do not remember his last name, but I think that he survived and went to America.

On the wall, we saw lists of Jewish names, probably of Jewish prisoners. Some were written with blood. There were dates next to some of the names. According to Salomon, the majority of these Jews had been shot.

In the evening we heard a key turning in the cell door. We were sure that they had come to take us to be shot. Instinctively, we moved to a corner. The door opened, and food was brought in, declaring: "No food for Jews!" We spent the night there, and each time we heard steps close to the cell, Solomon caught my hand and said: "They are coming to take us".

In the morning, about 7 o'clock, some Polish policemen came, and led us all out to the yard. The weather was nice; armed Polish police officers guarded us. After a while, we were taken back to the cell.

By mid–day I heard a group of Jews marching by, I heard Yiddish, and for no reason I felt happy. I was sure I was going to stay alive. The door opened and about twenty Jews entered, most of them women. Of all of them, I remember the nurse from the Jewish police in the Miedzyrzec Ghetto, whose kindness stood out, trying to help in any possible way.

I learned from them that a second transport had been taken from the Ghetto, and because the Ghetto was meant to be free of Jews, they were taken from the gathering place to clean up the Ghetto, and to take the stuff left behind to the stores. The people of this group sat and mourned their relatives.

About 4pm, the group, Solomon, and I were taken to the yard. They arranged us in rows of two and they led us to the Ghetto. They put us in a house close to the Ghetto's external barbed wire. This house became the shop where the different things that had been left in the Ghetto were sold. We were housed on the second floor; they showed us the beds and sent us to the Ghetto to look for bedding and food. A "Shupa" [horse groom, O.A.] remained downstairs.

The first thing we saw in the Ghetto was the terrible condition of the buildings. Broken doors, smashed windows, feathers from torn pillows and bed covers, scattered dishes, etc.

In the Ghetto we could walk around freely. I went together with another three girls; one of them was Bronya Grossman from Lodz. I went to the bunker where my cousin, Ida Kornbloom, stayed, to try to learn what had happened to her. The bunker was in the attic. I went in and heard some noise. I understood that there were some people up there, who hid when they heard my steps. I called: "Ida!" She recognized my voice and came out. I told her that the Ghetto was, as the Germans say, *Judenrein*, and that she must leave the bunker, which was within the Ghetto. I watched the "Shupa" [groom of horses, O.A.] who stood by the building next to the outer wire fence, and when he left his place, I shouted "Now!" One by one they came out of the house and left the Ghetto.

After that, I went from house to house to look for bedding. In the first house, I saw the headless body of an old woman under the quilt I wanted to take. I got scared, I jumped and screamed and stayed standing almost speechless. Later I saw her head from the corner of my eye. I left this house and entered a second one, from which I took a few things. Suddenly somebody grabbed my ankle from underneath. I screamed, and that person covered my mouth and asked me what was going on. There were some people hidden in a bunker in that house, and when they heard Yiddish, one of them came out. I told him what the situation was.

I went on, to the third house. From there I took a quilt, a cover, and pillows. I also changed my dress, which was torn when I jumped off the train. We also found there a long piece of yarn; we took it, thinking that it could be useful if we had to jump out of a window. We packed the bedding, an alarm clock and a few jars of jam in the bed cover, tied it with the yarn and went back to the shop.

We made our beds and went to sleep. Two people were always on guard, watching out of the windows. The guards changed every two hours. We saw the Germans looking for bunkers and hidden Jews in the Ghetto. Those who they found, they either shot immediately on the street or took them to be shot in the graveyard. In the morning, we found dead bodies in the street.

Our group's duty was to bring from the Ghetto all the things left there into the house, made into a store. The big things were brought in on a cart. I worked sorting out the things in the store. New things we packed separately and brought them to the secret police, to Lieutenant Seifert. Among the things we often found jewelry and gold sewn to clothes.

After few days, the Germans left the Ghetto. Jews who were hiding in bunkers came out and came back to the Ghetto. Some of them got a job in the stores.

The commander of the Jewish police was Lovech, a musician from Bialystok, who was a police officer in his past, and most of his time played for the Germans outside the Ghetto. He started to replace workers with his acquaintances. Later on, they gave him what he deserved. He fired me too, and I went back to the Ghetto.

The Ghetto was not a safe place. At night we used to get out of the Ghetto or and stay in bunkers.

[Page 452]

About 8–9 in the morning, when we heard that it was quiet, we went back to the Ghetto, washed ourselves and, refreshed, we slept through the day. Food came from the farmers to the stores. There was no shortage of food.

As the time passed, groups of people left for the fields around Miedzyrzec. A variety of armaments had been found and taken by these groups. From time to time, they would return to the Ghetto to get food and other things. Jews had to be very careful in the fields. On the one hand, the Polish *Armia Krajowa* [The Peoples' Army, an underground resistance group. O.A.] (a militant Polish reactionary and anti–Semitic group); on the other, groups of Russian war–prisoners who had fled the German prison and took to the fields. They used to assault the Jews, take their armaments and any other thing they had, and chase them away. Their tactic was to show friendliness, to sit with the Jews – and Jews were attracted to them – and then to start shooting and take their belongings.

I joined such a group once, but three days after we took to the field, a group of Russian prisoners approached us, behaved in a friendly way, ate with us, then surrounded us with pointed guns, shot and wounded a young man from Miedzyrzec, took everything we had and sent our men away. They invited the girls to stay with them, but we all ran back to the Ghetto.

I then met my cousin Ida Kornbloom, who told me that she was going to a Christian man, to a bunker, because the rumor was that another Action was about to take place, and that I should also leave the Ghetto. I told her I had nowhere to go. She left with a group of people from Miedzyrzec, and later I heard that she was murdered.

Three–four weeks passed. At the end of May, about 9am, when all came back from their night shelters, the Germans surrounded the Ghetto and the sixth Action began. The people who slept in the store were left alone. The Germans did not look for bunkers, nor did they shoot. The arranged us in lines, and led us to the square downtown, where there was a big shed. There were machine–guns all around. When we were all in the square, those who worked in the store were called to step aside. I went out and joined them. The commander Lovech saw me and told a German that I did not belong to the workers. The German approached me and hit me on the back so badly that I lost my breath, and pushed me back to the other group.

Lieutenant Seifert stood by the entrance to the shed, with other "Shupas" [horse grooms, O.A.]. When I came to the gate, I had the courage to speak to him, to remind him that I used to bring him packages, and that he saw me many times visiting the shoemaker Shlomele Bialer. He pointed to an open car with benches, where 8–10 persons were already sitting. He told me to get into the car. More people who were chosen from the square joined us.

The rest of the people were arranged in rows of three and were led to the shed. There they were undressed; men stayed in their underpants, women in blouses, all barefoot. From there they went in lines to the train station, and to a death–camp.

We, who were in the car, were taken to the Polish police station, to the same cell in which I stayed during the fifth Action. A lot of Jews and some Poles were there. The Kleinboims from Radzyn were there too. I went to sleep, and Mr. Kleinboim, who saw how lightly I was dressed, covered me with his jacket. In the morning, we were taken to the stores to sort out pots and dishes.

B. In a Bunker in the Center of Miedzyrzec

Translated by Ofra Anson

After the sixth Action, 150–200 Jews were left in the Ghetto. Quite a few of them were Jews who had jumped from the train in this Action.

Each one looked for a way to survive, most often in bunkers among non–Jews. From Biala I remember Saratshe Waynesfield, Moshe Steinberg with his sister Elke, Fievel Bookhalter, Avraham Nuchowitz with his sister Rivka, Judith Ploer with her little son, Shmuel Gviyosdo with his wife Elke, Sara Freter and her brother Pinches, Peark Bas, and M. Feigenboim.

[Page 453]

Like the others, I used to wander about during the day, not knowing what to do with myself. In the evening, each one of us went to our hiding place for the night's sleep. I did not have a permanent place.

One man, Potash, I think he was the son–in–law of Grodner Kant, sang very well. A group of people used to get together with him in the evenings. He would sing different songs, and people sang along with him.

One day Potash saw me in the Ghetto, and asked me:

–Are you here?

–How do you know me? I asked.

He told me that he saw me once with my mother and aunts, when my mother wanted to arrange me a job in the Court de l'Or factory. Then, he looked from a distance, but my mother impressed him. He remembered me from then.

He asked me where my mother was, and I told him that she had been taken in the second Action. Then he asked me if I had a bunker somewhere, in case the Ghetto should be emptied completely. When I answered in the negative, he had a suggestion for me: they were three persons; he himself, his wife's cousin (named Alte), and somebody by the name of Makover from Lodz. They had a bunker outside the Ghetto, prepared and used during the first Action by a Jew, and Potash knew about it. He said he would ask Makover, and if he agreed, I would be able to join them. I immediately agreed, of course. We agreed to meet with Makover the next day, and if we got along, we would close the deal.

The next day we met with Makover, who looked like a real Christian. He liked me and agreed to take me as an additional partner to the bunker. He told me that they were preparing provisions for a whole year. They already had sugar, fat, buckwheat, bags of potatoes, oil, oil burners, pots, bowls, buckets, bed covers, pillows, matrasses, and the like. He said that if I could make some money, I should buy more food, and that I should make sure to have all my personal needs (that is, underwear, dresses, etc.). I immediately started to collect things from the deserted houses, sold them to Christians, and made 150 Zlotys. I bought some food, and gave the rest of the money to Makover, because we needed some cash too.

The next day I packed my things, and we agreed to meet in a temporary shelter in an empty house across from the bunker. In this house, we stored all the stuff we had prepared before moving into the permanent bunker. We also slept in this house, and in the morning, we went back to the Ghetto. A few days passed, and Potash told me that as we were still short of money, they had recruited another two people, Fievel Bookhalter from Biala and Leizer (Eliezer) from Serock.

We decided that in a week, when the moon went down late at night, we would move into the bunker and stay there. The bunker was located in the following place. In the market place of Miedzyrzec stood a hotel where SS people stayed. Next to this hotel, joined to it by a thick wall, stood a low, small house. On the market side of this house was a store for iron–made equipment. Under the store, on the side of the butchers' street, were the storage barns for this store. Over the store and its storage barns was an empty apartment, with an entrance from an external staircase. Over that apartment was an attic with a diagonal roof, which hung from the side of the butchers' street on a wooden wall of 70cm height, went up to a small window, and then went down, on the side of the market, to the apartment's ceiling. On the side of the market, where the roof descended, there were holes through which we could see all that was going on in the market, but we were hidden from the outside world.

We could not stand in the bunker; we could only sit or walk bent over. The only place we could stand was by the small window and stick out a head. On the wall of 70cm, on the side of the butchers' street, were cracks through which we could see the staircase leading to the apartment and the yard. One of us always sat there to keep an eye on the entrance. When a suspicious movement was detected, the person gave a sign and we kept quiet. The entrance to the bunker was through a covered opening in the ceiling of the first room.

At night, a guard who walked around the house watched the store and its storage sheds.

[Page 454]

We waited a week as agreed and, about 1am, we started to move to the bunker. We waited until the guard was on the market side of the building, and we ran with our luggage, slippers on our feet or barefoot, and entered the apartment. Most of our belongings were already in the bunker. We waited in the apartment for a while, until the guard finished his tour, and climbed quietly into the bunker.

The internal arrangement in the bunker was as described below. The side of the small wall overlooking the butchers' street had been left free, so we could freely access it. The entrance had also been left free. In the middle, under the small window, stood two oil burners. Next to the built wall, which was attached to the hotel, were the food products and conserved food. The mattresses were moved away a bit from the wall and, a little further on, old straw pillows, under which stood the buckets of water, divided the attic. A stone closed the entrance in the ceiling. Next to the entrance, we prepared a brush and paint. The last one to enter painted the ceiling around the entrance in case it had been scratched accidentally. We did not use a ladder, but we came in and out using a window that was close by and with the help of someone.

We entered the bunker on a Monday in mid–July, 1943. During the day, the tin on the roof got hot, and we were sweating a lot. We looked out from time to time, and we saw a Jew walking through the market. After three days of silence, we decided to go out Friday night, to pass the Shabbat in the Ghetto, and possibly stay for a few more days. We went to sleep dressed in our clothes, and agreed that the first to wake up would wake the others. Fortunately, we slept very well, and when we woke up the moon was high in the sky and we could not go out. We had to delay our plan for the next night.

Saturday morning we heard gunshots from the direction of the Ghetto. We understood what was going on, and stayed in, trembling with fear. About 8pm, we heard steps on the stairs, then in the apartment, and then scratches on the entrance to the bunker. We recognized that these were Jews and opened the door. The same happened on Sunday. In total, four people came to us: Moshe Steinberg from Biala, his sister Elke, Saratshe Waynesfield, and Goldberg from Miedzyrzec. I do not remember who came first. We were now 10 people in the bunker. They told us that some Polish people had shot Germans out of the Ghetto and soon after that the Germans entered the Ghetto. Whoever they found, they shot on the spot, and now the Ghetto was completely empty. Only two Jews were left in the secret police, the shoemakers Shlomo'le Bialer and Siskind Leshtshuk, a Pole who lived close to the Ghetto and was the main dealer in Jewish belongings, organized a group of Polish youngsters who went from house to house looking for bunkers, taking the Jews out to the Germans, who immediately shot them.

That Sunday we saw a "Shupa" standing by the church in the Market, supervising the cart leaving the city. They hid two people, probably Jews, and took them away.

One day a group of young Poles came into the apartment under the bunker, shouting "Jews out!" They searched the apartment and left. I cannot express how we felt.

A week or ten days later, we saw through the crack in the wall how Leshtshuk and his gang went into the house we had stayed in before we moved to the bunker. Soon they went out, and Leshtshuk was in a hurry. We understood that they had found Jews. Not long afterwards, a "Shupa" came in. They found about 10 Jews, and they immediately shot them with a machine gun.

The days passed by. We saw the young Poles roaming about, but they did not return to our house. It is possible that they could not believe that Jews would hide next to a hotel that hosted Germans and above an iron shop.

Meanwhile, each one adjusted to life in the bunker and to the other people. In our small world in the attic, human nature expressed itself, in both positive and negative ways. On one hand, fate had thrown a set of individuals to live together. On the other hand, each individual or each couple lived their own life.

[Page 455]

For eating, the women used to boil potatoes, clean groats, etc. Makover, as the head of the bunker, used to cook and divide the food for the others. Usually we had potatoes and groats. As we got our portion, we swallowed the food quickly; in fact, so quickly it seemed that we could see the bottom of the plate before we started eating. Food was not an issue of dispute in the bunker, and meals passed smoothly.

The men changed the water once a month, late at night when it was dark. The street where our bunker was located went up to the river. Most of the houses were empty; only two Christian families lived on the street, close to the river. The men went quietly and carefully to the river. In one place they spilled the dirty water, and in another filled fresh water to drink and cook.

The summer was very hot. The tin roof over our heads got very hot, and the sweat ran like water. We undressed as much as possible, but to no avail. Through the cracks in the wall, we saw that there was a world out there, where people conducted free lives. Non–Jews were walking freely in the streets. On Sundays, we saw the girls dressed in their best, going to the church near the hotel. It made us jealous and we wondered whether we would ever live to leave the bunker and live a normal life. Sometimes we became desperate, losing all hope, and believed in nothing.

In the evenings, when the outside became quiet, we made sure the bunker was also silent, not to be heard in case someone went by. When the outside was noisy, we let ourselves express our feelings, not necessarily in a nice way. Couples fought, one young man talked to the girlfriend of another, and the two men had a fight. Since there were several couples in our bunker, there were occasions when almost everyone fought with everyone else. Potash then opened the door of the bunker and shouted: "Go down! Why do we need to be discovered and led to extermination? Go of your own free will!"

The man from Miedzyrzec had a Polish acquaintance; we used to send him to buy things we needed with the help of his Polish friend. He was one of the best bunker members, but it seems that he could not overcome his human weakness. He did not contribute all his money to the general pool, but kept some for himself. When he went to shop for the bunker, he used it to buy things for himself and his girlfriend. At night, after we went to sleep, we could hear the sound of unwrapping sweets and the smell of sausage.

Potash used to read quietly to us selections from Shalom Aleichem and Gretz, books that we had in the bunker. Later we brought some more books from the Ghetto. A few times, he read and translated for us something in Hebrew, but I cannot remember what it was. He also quietly sang Yiddish songs for us. I remember one song, about Yom Kippur in the synagogue, when the congregation prayed with respect and devotion.

On the market, the Germans set a loudspeaker, which was used for announcing the news from the front a few times a day. We could clearly hear the news, but we did not believe it. On the other hand, our member from Miedzyrzec, whose Christian friend had a hidden radio, brought us news from an English radio station, and we compared the sources.

Several months passed, and the relationship between the people was tense. In the autumn, Makover, who was afraid that we would be discovered, went to find a new bunker with Christians in a village. As I said, Makover looked like a Christian, and he was best suited for the job. He never came back, and only nine of us were left in the bunker. After a while, our member from Miedzyrzec heard from his acquaintance that somebody had recognized Makover in the street, turned him in, and Makover was shot.

Meanwhile, the sanitary situation in the bunker deteriorated. We almost never washed our bodies. We had lice and fleas, and we took turns in getting rid of these. We had only oil and matches against the pests.

The old wound in my leg opened, infected, and the infection got deeper and deeper, and the leg started to blacken. In addition, a gland became swollen, and wounds appeared on my skull. We decided that when two men went shopping, I would go down with them, buy medications in the pharmacy, and some loaves of bread in the bakery.

[Page 456]

That time of the year, the night fell quite early. It was dark out, but the Christian shops were still open. If I remember correctly, that day was a Catholic holiday, "All Saints". We saw Christians walking with flowers in their hands.

I went into the pharmacy and asked for medications. The pharmacist looked at me and told me to go into an inner room. I did not know what his intentions were, and when I entered the room, I looked for a window to jump from if I had to run away. The pharmacist gave me an injection in the hand, two ointments (Ichthyol and Rivanol), a bottle of oxygen, and cotton wool. I paid him and left. Outside I waited for the two men with whom I came. I went into a bakery and asked for bread. The Christian owner asked how many loaves, and I answered five or six. He looked at me and said he had no bread, and I went out and quickly left. As the winter approached and we had to protect ourselves from the cold, we decided that on a dark night all the men would go to the Ghetto and bring pillowcases, yarns, and a rope. They filled the pillowcases with hay and straw, and brought them in. The women sewed them together and the men laid it under the roof tied to the beams. We also made two walls, four or five meters apart, and put our mattresses between them.

The man from Miedzyrzec remembered that he had seen a small iron stove, and it was brought in. Little by little, we brought from the Ghetto bits of pipe. One dark night we lit a little lamp between the walls we built, and one of the men went out and around the house to make sure the light could not be seen from the outside.

We put the stove in the middle and pulled the pipes to the hotel's wall, where we made a hole. Making the hole in the wall took us almost a full week. We hit the wall, and waited to see if the noise was heard anywhere. When it was ready, we put the pipe through it. Coal we brought from a cow shed we found somewhere and broke its lock.

When the winter came, we realized that the amount of bread was going down; the bunker family was larger than initially planned. One dark night we broke into a bakery our member knew from Miedzyrzec, and took all the bread we found. We broke into bakeries several times, each time a different one.

When the rain came, we wanted to collect the fresh water. We found a place in the diagonal side of the roof where we could bend the tin a little and make a little hole. When it rained, we put our buckets under the hole and collected the water.

One day the men came back carrying sacks with three dead sheep they took from a sheep house. We skinned them, hung the skin and cooked the flesh. This was the beginning. Later we started to go to villages, pretending we were partisans. We made a wooden pistol, painted it black, and took it to with us in case we had to frighten someone.

We prepared food in the following way. In the darkest night of the month, about 11pm, usually when it was snowing so footprints were covered, or when it was frozen and no footprints were left, the men went to the farms. They entered a farmer's house with the "gun" in their hand, closed the people of the house in one room, and took all the food they found. They looked especially for salt, bread and lentils. Once they brought some buckwheat; a few times they brought slaughtered sheep, half a cow, and once they brought pig. They avoided pigs because of the noise they make when slaughtered. Apart from food, they did not take anything. Only once they took boots they needed.

Overall, the winters passed fine. There was no shortage of food, though we strongly felt the shortage of salt. I remember that once we cooked liver without any salt. We did not want to fry anything, to avoid the smell that could reveal our existence. We ate the pieces of liver, but since then I cannot touch liver.

The man from Miedzyrzec once bought from his Christian acquaintance a pistol and bullets. The pistol, however, did not fire the bullets, and all our efforts to make them useful did not succeed.

[Page 457]

Yet our men used it as they used the wooden gun, frightening the farmers, who feared the partisans.

As I described earlier, the space between the walls that we built from straw pillows took up only a small part of the attic. Around it, we always had a guard watching the surroundings through the cracks in the wall. Quite often we saw the Poles who worked in the iron shop lifting their heads and looking in our direction. We were constantly afraid that they had seen us.

I suffered a lot from the wound in my leg, and when I was on guard, outside the small heated place, I had a lot of pain. Potash was the only one who was aware of my suffering, and he quite often replaced me and sent me inside. Secondly, I suffered from the wounds on my head, which developed and covered my entire skull. Since we all had lice, the parasites entered my open wounds, causing me a lot of pain. Some of the people in the bunker took me for a parasite because of that. I got a small ration of oil and water to wash my hair a little and to clean the lice from my wounds. It did relieve my pain considerably.

Quite often there were quarrels in the bunker. When food had been brought in, each one stole something. When the theft was detected, we accused one another of stealing; we quarreled, and offended one another. At the same time, we were friendly; we ate together and told stories and anecdotes.

One day, our guard saw a couple coming our direction. They climbed the steps to the apartment below us. We held our breath, and listened. We heard them talking about what needed to be done in the apartment. We understood that they intended to come and live there. We became depressed, as this would certainly have been our end. We stopped believing in the future, sure that the end was around the corner.

When the couple left, we decided to demolish the apartment. At night, our men climbed down, broke the doors and the windows, took out the floor tiles, and left the apartment in ruins. A few days later, the couple came again and, seeing the apartment's condition, left and never returned.

Another time that we were in danger of being discovered was when we heard a fight and screams from the house of the Christian family who lived on the way to the river. A short, fat man left the house in anger and ran to a house next door to us. As soon as he left the house, we saw smoke and fire coming out of it. The fire got stronger and stronger, and we were afraid that our wooden house was going to catch fire. Firefighters came, many Polish people gathered round, and some of them climbed to the apartment below to get a better view of the fire. We felt that either we would die by the fire or be discovered by the Poles. We were lucky: the fire was put out without damaging our house.

All winter we heard from the German megaphone on the market: "Smolensk", "Smolensk". By the end of the winter we heard "Kovel". We already knew, from the Christian acquaintance of our member from Miedzyrzec, that the Russians controlled Kovel. Hearing that from the Germans, hope entered our hearts, and we started believing again.

Before Passover, the Hungarian army came into Miedzyrzec, with Jewish soldiers who carried guns just like any other soldier. We saw the Hungarian army walking in daylight in the market and the surrounding streets. For a few days we observed the Jewish soldiers, where they went in the mornings, in groups, alone, with no guns. We learned from our informant that by order of the Germans, the Jewish soldiers were concentrated in a separate working group. We decided that two of our men would go down and seek contact with the Jews. One night, two men went to the Jewish working camp, somewhere by the river, and waited until the morning. They made themselves known to a few of the Hungarian Jews. They were surprised by the strange reaction of these Jews. One wanted to kidnap them and give them in. Another chased them away, shouting "Run away!"

[Page 458]

Our men immediately fled, of course. They hid all that day in the burnt house next door, and returned to the bunker in the evening.

Meanwhile, we felt the German movement more and more. Tanks and artillery entered the city from the east. The city filled with the German army. The hotel next to us filled with German high officers. Together with the spring, when the nights became shorter by the day, it became difficult or impossible to conduct our "normal" life. We could no longer go to a village to bring food in one night. We had to hide in a field during the day and come back the next night. Bringing water became difficult, because the Germans were active in the streets all night.

One night, farmers in a field attacked our men, and their pistols were taken. Fortunately, they escaped alive.

We were desperate. We could not come up with anything that would enable us to hold on. We felt that we would not be able to go on for long.

Yet, we found some opening outside. The German army did not stop moving. Tanks, artillery, big wagons with fat horses, and soldiers filled the market place and the streets. We could not believe it, but we sensed that the war would soon be over. We started to feel that we would live to see it end.

A few weeks passed. We thought that we heard the sound of shooting from a distance. We could not be sure, because this sound could very well have been from one of the army camps around the city. Yet we heard the shooting clearer and clearer, until one day we heard artillery exploding quite near. Yet we had to get some bread (we still had some other supplies). One night the men went down, sneaking to a bakery they knew, broke in and stole all the bread they found. We had to make sure we had enough in case the artillery bombing got closer and it would not be possible to go out of the bunker.

The shooting grew louder by the hour. From both the Russian and German sides shells flew over the city, and could be heard day and night. We understood that the bunker, which was attached to the highest building in town, was no longer safe. We decided that each of us would take a loaf of bread and leave it. It was about July 20, 1944. We all left the bunker on a clear day, taking nothing but bread, and went to the Ghetto, to a house close to the riverbank. The house was closed with wooden boards, but we found a small window through which we were able to crawl in.

In our hurry to escape the three–way danger – from the Germans, from the Poles, and from the shells flying over our heads in the bunker – we thought we had found the right place. We soon realized that we were wrong. The house was the last one in the neighborhood, with an open space around it, and close to the river. The Russians were just across from us, and their shells not far from us. Every few minutes we heard a shell launched, and a new hole formed in the empty space next to us.

We understood that we were in great danger. Our Miedzyrzec man said he knew about a house with a solid–built cellar. We waited until it became dark and left this house. One by one, we crawled out and started running, under the shelling and the red sky, to the house recommended by our Miedzyrzec friend. While we were running, we saw a shell entering the house we had just left, destroying a wall. It was a miracle, as if a good angel was guarding us.

We ran bent to the ground, afraid of the shells flying and whistling over our heads. We met some Poles running, who shouted: "There are Jews here too!" Yet, in that situation, they too were running for their lives and left us alone. We immediately turned another way, until we got to our new shelter, which was also close to the river.

[Page 459]

We went in and, in a corner, covered with a lead, we found an opening through which we went down to the cellar. The cellar had a small, high,window, overlooking the river.

The night passed, and another morning came. The artillery bombing strengthened, and got closer. Each time a shell was shot close by, pieces fell from the cellar walls, and we became covered with sand and pieces of bricks. We clearly heard the movement of the German armaments. Was it possible that the Germans were withdrawing? We could not imagine that.

The noise around us declined a bit. We opened the window and peeped outside, and saw metal helmets, masked with green, crossing the river, and we heard calls in Russian. We started to argue – the person from Miedzyrzec said the soldiers were Russian; the rest of us did not believe that the Germans had withdrawn, and said they were from Vlassav.

Not long after, we saw large groups of soldiers speaking in Russian, and among them were women wearing Red Cross uniforms. The person from Miedzyrzec said that we should go out, because if they found us they would throw a grenade into the house and kill us all. He did not wait, and went out, calling: "Welcome, liberating army!" The soldiers approached us, pointing machine guns at us and asked: "Who are you?" We answered "Jews". A Jewish officer immediately came out. I cannot describe our joy. We hugged him and kissed him and all the soldiers.

The Russians took us to the center of the city, and the Germans left. We felt free, though we could not believe that we could walk in the street and not hide. When the Russians reached the market, we suddenly heard shooting from the direction of the church, and we saw Russian soldiers wounded. We were told that a group of German soldiers had remained in the church, and when the Russians got nearer and opened the gate the Germans opened fire.

We heard that Leshtshuk was treating wounded Russian soldiers in a yard not far from the church. We went there, and saw him giving orders and care for the wounded. We started shouting, and told the officer what Leshtshuk had done, how he looked for hiding Jews and handed them in to the German murderers. We all screamed together, until the officer shouted at me (it seems that I was louder than the others): "Who is the commander here, me or you?" He asked that only one of us speak. We told him everything, and Leshtshuk, with an ironic smile, answered: "You are Jews." The officer asked him to come with him, led him to the Ghetto, and we all followed. He took his gun out, shot Leshtshuk once, and gave us the gun so each of us could shoot him too. We undressed him, took off his boots, and left him lying. We felt some revenge, seeing Leshtshuk lying there for eight days, with the hungry dogs and cats nibbling on his body, and his wife pulling her hair out.

The artillery continued to shoot for a few more days. We chose an apartment on the market where a family used to live but had probably run away. We changed our rags and put on what we found. We were sure that no Jews were left except the nine of us. We remembered our family and friends; we longed for them, and felt deep sorrow that they had not survived the two years of the war.

We started to get organized in the apartment we had chosen, and started looking for food. In the apartment, we found a box of different liqueurs and wine. We opened the bottles and got drunk.

The Russian army poured into town and with it more Jewish soldiers. Our apartment became a meeting point for the Jewish soldiers.

After Miedzyrzec was liberated, more Jews came out of their hiding places. Jews that had hidden in the fields and in the wild also came. We heard that the Polish Armia Krajowa (Polish resistance underground) murdered Jews on their way to Miedzyrzec.

[Page 460]

Still, we did not reveal our bunker; we could not believe that we were free. Who knows, we may need to go back there one day…

Yet, we did not go back. I started a new life, wandering around the city, concentration camps, different towns, until I boarded the ship Exodus–Europe 1947, and after five months on board arrived in Israel.

[Page 460]

Leaving Home

by A Bialer

Translated by Ofra Anson

The minute it became clear that the Russians were leaving Biala, a decision had to be taken: To take to wandering or stay home. The town was restless. People were divided into two camps: "runners" and "stayers". It was not an ideological issue. The "runners" were motivated by fear of the Germans; the "stayers" were motivated by the fear of becoming homeless, and the belief that they could hang on until the war was over.

A horse and wagon stood in the yard of Abik Rosenbloom, with the belongings of his son, Yoske. He left the town with his wife and children. The family parted from the travelers. The mother bent towards her daughter Franie, and said: My daughter, take my suitcases, they hold all my property, go with Yoske and save yourself. Franie replied: not without you. All who were present wept.

Only a few of Biala's Jews fled to the other side of the river Bug. The border stayed open for a short time, people and commodities moved back and forth, and people established a new home on the Soviet territory. After a while, the border was closed, and the movement between the sides stopped. The economic behavior started to take shape according to the Soviet policy. Not all, locals as well as refugees, got used to it. Many refugees refused citizenship, being afraid that the Soviets would not let them return home after the war. Yet, there were refugees from Biala who decided to start a new life, and travelled to central Russia. They turned to the right authorities and were sent to Ukraine and Byelorussia. These Jews became Russian citizens, had a place to live and a place of work.

Meanwhile, a German committee was set up in Brisk trying to control the stream of people from Soviet Russia to the German-controlled territories in Poland. The committee sat in the train station in Brisk, and the roads leading to it were full of refugees, the majority of whom were Jews. The sight of long rows in front of the German committee was painful. The committee members did not treat them kindly and their sarcastic remark: "Jews, where are you going? Our Fuhrer does not like you", made no impression on the Jews. The Russians also did not like the rushed return back to Poland. The refugees from Biala used all the connections they could to "win" their return home.

The committee finished its work. Only a few were allowed to go back to Biala. The Germans gave the list of the people who applied to return to Poland to the Soviet regime, who soon used it against them.

Those who did not get permission to return expressed their disappointment. In Minsk, a demonstration was organized with the slogan: "Send us home". The Soviet authorities demanded of the demonstrators to leave the area to a radius of 100 km. Since the refugees did not fill the orders quickly enough, harsh means were taken against them. One night, activists of the Soviet administration visited the houses of the refugees, taking them to a gathering point. By morning, they were on the train, on their way to their assigned destination in the far parts of Russia.

In 1941, when the war between Germany and Russia started, the refugees from Biala were spread over the remote areas of Russia. Many in working camps, a few in Polish areas, and the great majority in Ukraine and Byelorussia where they worked in Kolkhozes, factories, and cooperatives.

[Page 461]

During the terrible war, the Biala refugees in Russia experienced difficult times along with the Soviet population. Jews were recruited to the Russian and the Polish army and fought against the Germans on different fronts. Those who lived in middle Asia worked in different places and some were in trade. Like other refugees, the Jews from Biala had no knowledge of the terrible fate of the Polish Jews.

After the war, Russia let the Polish refugees go back to Poland. At this point, people had already heard about the German murders, but they still hoped that it was not all true. They started their journey home, but the closer they got to the border the less hope they had. Arriving in Terespol, the first border city in Poland, they immediately felt the Polish hate towards the Jews.

In Biala's train station they were "welcomed" with stoning. Most did not get off at "home" and chose to continue the journey. After a while, some returned to Biala to see the destruction, to stroke the stone over the mass grave, and shed tears. The home, of which we dreamt for seven years, was no longer a home, but a graveyard.

Some Memories

Leon Fokman

Translated by Ofra Anson

In October 1939, Biala's Jews became very depressed. They saw the Soviet army withdrawing behind the river Bug, which became the border between Germany and Russia. Some of them, mainly young people, decided to leave the town and cross to the other side of the Bug.

The majority of Biala's refugees concentrated in Brisk where life was hard. As they started to get their life into some routine, the Soviet administration ordered all refugees to move 100km away from the border.

Meanwhile, Russia opened a recruitment office for refugees who were willing to settle in Russia where each person would find work in his occupation. Many refugees, including some from Biala, registered. The first group traveled to Russia via Pinsk and Zhitkovichi. In Zhitkovichi, passengers were divided: half were sent to Mazyr, the other half to Gomel. From there they were distributed between different cities and towns in the far end of Russia.

Quite a few refugees from Biala ended in Gomel, where they established a community. When we arrived, we looked for other people who came from Biala, either in the First World War, or in 1920, when they joined the withdrawing Red Army. Among them were Yeshaya Idl Lemberg, an artist painter (son of Aharale Bekster), and the Oppenheim family (from the soap factory in Volya), who were very happy to meet us, and invited us to their homes.

Each of them wanted to hear news about their relatives and of Biala in general.

Exhumation of the "Kedoshim" who were shot during the Nazi regime in Biala and buried in various places. After the war, they were interred in a communal grave in the destroyed Jewish cemetery

Not all the refugees could adjust to the demands of the new life.

[Page 462]

Some decided to find a way to go to Brisk and from there to return to Biala. Some were caught by the Russians trying to cross the border, and were sent to Siberia to work in the fields. The work in freezing temperature was hard, the nutrition poor and insufficient, and quite a few lost their lives.

Exhumation of the "Kedoshim" who were shot during the Nazi regime in Biala and buried in various places. After the war, they were interred in a communal grave in the destroyed Jewish cemetery

Those who stayed where they were sent could not relax for long. The war between Russia and Germany broke out and families were torn apart again. The men were recruited to the army, the women evacuated to the heart of Russia. Some of the Biala refugees remained in their place, and shared the tragic fate of Jews after the Germans marched in.

I remember the Biala men who went with me to the army, and were killed fighting the Germans.

Jacob Warsawski, a carpenter, lived on Sadower Street (his father was a builder). Left a wife and a daughter.

Tsemah Tuchmintz, a bookbinder. Left a wife and a son.

Simha Liberman (came from the Tshein area). Killed in service in the Polish army, freeing Warsaw.

The three mentioned above were my friends. Yet, many more Jews from Biala fell fighting against the Germans in the Russian and Polish army.

By early 1945, the German animal was already in pieces. People started travelling across Europe. They were drawn back to their land, to their homes. Those from Biala who lived in Russia, sent to populated Russia's remote areas, also shared the hope of returning and uniting with their relatives.

Early 1946. The first transport of Polish Jews from Russia crossed the Polish border, but the local population was hostile. The train bringing the Jews was stoned. The Jews of Biala, who had left their homes in 1939, returned home. their hearts pounding, hoping to reunite with their loved ones; instead they found that almost all the Jews had gone and those who were killed in Biala were buried haphazardly around the town. Their bones were exhumed and buried in a communal grave in the ruined Jewish cemetery and a memorial stone was erected.

Some of those who returned from Russia continued and emigrated to Germany, Lower Silesia, Lodz, and Szczecin.

[Page 463]

The monument at the communal grave

The few who stayed in Biala had set up a committee, which was in touch with the central Jewish committee in Warsaw and with Biala Jews around the world.

The actions of the Polish reactionaries in Biala soon started to shake up the small Jewish community. Soon, two victims were killed. Two young Jewish lives, who had survived Hitler's hell, shot by Poles. A young woman named Staretz (granddaughter of Harash), and a young man called Silberstein from Miedzyrec (the husband of Hanna Charny from Biala). They were shot on the train from Lukow to Miedzyrec.

One summer night in 1946, a loud explosion shook the town. The memorial stone on the communal grave had been destroyed. It was clear that it was impossible to stay in Biala and, one by one, the Jews left for Lower Silesia.

From what I heard, a few dozen decided to settle in Reichenbach. A help committee had been established there by Baruch Vinograd, Sisl Izenberg, Ida Charny, Berish Osenholtz, Hershel Appelboim, Haim Josef Kanizshnik, Leon Pakman, and Hersh Joel Rotenberg.

This committee operated in all of Lower Silesia where people from Biala were settled. The committee was connected to people from Biala throughout the world, and collected donations, money and goods. These were distributed according to family size.

Every year, on the first day of Succoth, the committee organized a memorial service for the Kedoshim from Biala, to which people came from all over Lower Silesia. The people from Biala felt very close to one another. Mutual visits took place, as if all were members of one family.

The people from Biala in Poland and Lower Silesia took great pride in the establishment of the Jewish state. Like the rest of Polish Jewry, people from Biala supported the Jewish settlement in Palestine, and its help committee donated money to the Hagana (the largest organization that fought against the British mandate in Palestine between 1920 and 1948, O.A.). The committee also supported the volunteers from Biala who went to fight in the Independence War.

In 1949/50, when the Polish government allowed Jews to emigrate to Israel, most of the people from Biala took the opportunity and made Alia. Jewish community life in Lower Silesia disappeared. With the emigration wave of 1956/7, the last Jews of Biala in Lower Silesia left for Israel.

The monument destroyed

[Page 464]

In Liberated Biala
(A chapter of memories)[1]

M. Y. Fiegenboim

Translated by Ofra Anson

It is the second day that we[2] are wandering around the bunkers and cannot believe that we are free from life in the bunker. Is it possible that the Nazis' chains, made of the hardest metal, have crumbled? Yet, next to the closed garden, where our bunker was, we saw soldiers from the Red Army, putting up a wire fence.

What do we do with this freedom? Where does one go? How do we start a new life after such bloodshed?

We did not want to leave the bunker without a sign from the owner of the garden. The desire to have a look at the town, to see what was going on, was, however, strong. Thus, like Noah's dove, I went into town to bring news from the new world.

The roads leading to the town were quite empty of people. A strange thought came to my mind: Is it possible that other Jews use different roads to go into town? Could there be many Jews, like me, coming out from their grave–life, and would I be able to meet old friends and relations?

I remained standing at the entrance to the town, by the corner of Grobonower Street, shocked by its emptiness. I started to walk along the street, where the secret police had been located. I went slowly, step by step, like a thief. I was sure I would soon hear the frightening shout: Stop Stay where you are! Yet nobody called, and I went on. It was very early in the morning, and all doors and windows were still shut, though some Christians were standing next to their houses. Wolnoztchi Square was empty. Two Red Army soldiers stood on the roofs of the municipality and the post office building. Flowers were lying next to the post office, probably in memory of the Poles shot by the Nazis. The doors of several stores were broken; clearly, they had been looted.

I arrived at my parents' house on Brisker Street. The thought that I was the only one of my whole family that had come back, shattered every bit of me. A sad hope that another family member might return crossed my mind. The will to live left me at home. Our store was closed, and the gate broken. I saw some Christians, and we started to talk. The circle around us grew bigger. Some of them recognized me and kept asking: Where did you come from? I asked if they had seen any other Jews. One told me that, the day before, he saw a Jewish woman with two sons. They were walking on Lomaser Avenue. Later, I wondered who they might be, but I did not pay attention to all the details, and I could not go to look for them.

I learned that the German people that had lived in my parents' house had left with the German army and that the house was empty. I wanted to climb into the house over the neighbor's fence (Moshe Liebenberg's yard), when a Christian stuck out his head from the window and asked me what I was doing there. I told him I wanted to climb over into my house. He understood that he was looking at a Jew, and started shouting:

Go away! This is not yours! Your good time here is over!

I answered him sharply, but did not climb over to my house. This first encounter was quite discouraging. I realized that, for the moment, the bunker was still the safest place for us. Indeed, I started walking in the direction of the bunker.

We went around the closed garden, enjoying the world in daylight. Each of us took small steps, enveloped in our own thoughts. I am sure that everyone asked himself or herself the same question: why only me?

The camp of the Red Army next to the garden kept growing. From time to time soldiers entered the garden, for no reason, and asked us who we were. We told them our story in broken Russian. Every other word we emphasized that we were Jewish (Ivri).

[Page 465]

They said that we were free to go into town. We were not in a hurry to leave the garden until one day, at noon, soldiers came and asked us to leave. They led us to believe that the front line would soon be in this area. Having no alternative, we left and went into town.

We arrived at the corner of Sadove–Pcehodnie and Wonska. We sat on a bench, and held a conversation with some Christians. We were immediately identified as Jews, and the crowd around us became bigger. People wanted to know where we had been hiding, and we answered: In the forest. We looked around. We saw so many faces, and not one Jew. Here was the garden where the Gestapo soldiers had their blood–orgies with Jewish victims. The whole square had become one big communal grave.

A young woman came, and asked where the Jews were. People pointed at us. She came closer and, with a compassionate voice, said: You must have suffered a lot. I think I saw a tear in her eyes, and she left. Who knows, I thought, if she herself is not Jewish, and who instead of hiding in a bunker, lived among the wolves.

We sat there quite a long time, talking with the Christians. Typically, none of them asked if we were hungry, none offered us a slice of bread.

When the sun started to set in the west, we heard shooting, a sound that grew stronger and stronger. The Germans lined on the other side of the town were shooting, and the Soviet Army shot back.

With my bunker mate Kanyer, I went back to the bunker. We left the town, but when we came to French Street, we saw several Red Army soldiers peacefully eating their dinner. We continued, undisturbed, constantly hearing the whistling of the bullets above our heads. A hundred and fifty meters before the garden, Red Army soldiers shouted to us that we should immediately leave, as this was the new front–line. Declaring that we were Jews did not help, and we had to turn back.

We went toward Lomaser Avenue. Yet, when we put a foot on Kschiwer Street, we felt such lethargy and apathy that we started to walk back, agreeing to stay in our house and, if necessary, to hide in the hiding place there.

We climbed over the fence, and sat on a bench in the midst of the overgrown grass. We sat for a while, listening to the silence of the night. Slowly we moved from the yard into the house, and fell on a mattress. After a year in the bunker, we finally spent the night like humans, in a house. When we woke up, it was already daylight. Fearfully, we peeped out of the window. After a while, we saw the Red Army, and we were relieved.

I started to look around the apartment. The Germans had taken almost everything. What was left was thrown on the floor. The entrance door was a bit broken; it seems that someone came in and made himself at home.

I went out through the gate, and looked at the street. The same houses, the same shops, but the Jews had disappeared.

I reached the synagogue yard. I did not recognize it. The synagogue, Beit Hamidrash, had disappeared, and the other Beit Hamidrash had also disappeared. The Nazis had razed all these buildings to the ground. In the past, white-haired heads filled the synagogue yard. Our children had been slaughtered, and in the synagogue yard and the narrow streets around it, where generations of Jews had experienced joy and sorrow, Christian children were now playing. We heard that the walls of Jewish dwellings had been broken down and tiles taken out in search for hidden treasures.

I went to the place where the Germans had their offices, to look for abandoned documents; alas, in vain. The Christians told me that the Germans took some documents with them and burnt the rest. Similarly, I could not find anything where the Jewish police station was, and it had now become a Polish police station.

[Page 466]

The same day that I stood by our house gate, the Christian neighbor told me that the apartment now belonged to him. I asked him: how come? He said that the previous tenant had sold him the apartment, and I had no more right to it. He started shouting that he would not let anybody take the apartment from him, and that the former tenant left him many things in it. I understood he intended to use the things left for him in order to establish his precedence before the authorities and, for the moment, to prevent me from entering the apartment.

I went straight to the municipality, where I found a few clerks I knew who were idly roaming the rooms. There were also people with a band on their arm, so-called "police" or militiamen. I asked one of these militiamen to accompany me and take all the things out of the apartment. They made it clear that they could not do it themselves. A soviet officer came in, and the clerks told me to talk to him. I told him in Polish what was going on. He understood, and immediately ordered one of the militiamen to go with me.

The Christian, however, also had not sat still. He brought some other Christians who started arguing with me, saying that I should not quarrel with the woman, and give up the apartment. I asked them: Is it right? She has an apartment and I have nowhere to stay. Do you want me to return to the forest? They said they could see my point, but since the previous tenant had given her the apartment, I should let her have it and not fight for it. They saw that they would not convince me and went away.

We started to get hungry. The little food we had was in the bunker. We went from one bakery to the other, and each one told us they had no bread. We did not want to turn to the Christian who hid us, because our close relationship with him could put him at risk. We tried to get some food in different places, with no success. A policeman promised to give us some eggs for Saturday. Yet, when we came to take the eggs, a Christian came in with a murderous look in his eyes and began shouting that we should leave the place. To the person who promised us the eggs he shouted: What? You give them food? Better give them some poison! Shoo them away! An upheaval started, children came running, and the policeman himself asked us to leave his home.

We left, and the children kept running after us, screaming: "Jews!" "Jews!" The children harassed us for quite a while. They called after us "Jews!" when they saw us on the street or on the balcony of our apartment. We thus tried to avoid the streets.

At night, I went to a Christian that used to be our neighbor and asked for food. She gave me bread and marmalade. Her husband brought us some food few times, climbing over the fence and avoiding the gate.

A few days later, we made a deal with a bakery and regularly got bread.

On Saturday morning the Germans resumed artillery shooting in the town. The house of Benjamin Cohen and the house of Benjamin Leib Mandelbaum were hit and damaged.

On Sunday morning we went to the bunker to bring our stuff. In the garden, we saw clear signs of the front line. Many trees were lying broken; bullets had cut the fence on the side of the bunkers in several places. The barn too was in pieces. Our bunker, however, stood undamaged.

Jews that had been hiding in bunkers or in the forest returned to town. Haia Feldman, daughter of Moshe Milner, with her two sons; Avraham Nochovitz, with his sister Rivka; Sara Weisenfeld, Rivka Bachrach (my first cousin, O.A.), Roske Dzebtchol, Shmuel Gwiosdo with his wife Elke, and Mrs. Morgenstern (from Grobonower Street) came first. Emil Weinberg, Berl Sondlarzch with his wife and daughter Hela, Michash Hofner (whose wife and daughter had survived), and the advocate Leon Goldfarb, who had all survived with Aryan papers, came later.

Finding a roof over their head was not an easy task for the survivors.

[Page 467]

We had to negotiate with the Christians delicately, not to fight with them harshly. It usually helped.

Meanwhile, the town had filled up with the Red Army, and military camps were moving towards the west, in the direction of Warsaw.

We longed to see a Jewish face, and we employed different tactics in order to identify Jewish soldiers in the Red Army. When we saw a soldier on the street, we used to loudly ask each other whether or not he was Jewish. Quite often the soldier would say: "True, I am Jewish". If we saw a soldier who looked like a Jew, we used to ask: "*Amcha*?" (from our people, O.A.). In many cases he answered "*Amcha*".

We started to meet with the Jews of the Soviet army. We looked for them, and they looked for us. We learned from them of the Holocaust, how Hitler had spread destruction in the most remote parts of Russia, wherever his army reached. The Jewish soldiers told us that all the way from Russia to Biala they had not met any Jews but us. The Red Army soldiers were much friendlier than they were in 1939. Hitler's cruelty hit all of us. Everyone had something to cry for, survivors grew closer and more open to one another. Russian Jews rediscovered their ethnicity; soldiers were looking for Jews everywhere they went. They heard the tragic story of survivors, and told them their own sad experiences. They used to assure us that we were going towards a better future, that they were going to take revenge on the Fascists. In every conversation, someone would suddenly ask: Why don't we have a country of our own, like other people? We told them about the Zionist movement which strived to build a Jewish state in *Eretz Israel*.

Among the Jewish Red Army soldiers were some writers. They too came closer to us, but kept to the general party line.

I remember an episode that took place in my home. We, a group of Biala Jews, sat with a Jewish officer who visited me quite often. He was a bit drunk, and opened his heart. We finished eating and talked again about the experiences of recent times. He started to cry bitterly, and shouted: The Christians in my town killed my wife and child, robbed me of my home. We Jews are hated all over the world! It took a while for him to calm down.

Many of the Jewish officers wanted to help us in any possible way. I sent my first letter to Israel with their help. One of them told the chief army physician, General Ibragimow, that a young woman had come out of the bunker with a swollen leg. The general was so moved by her story that he arranged for her to be hospitalized for an operation free of charge (the young woman was R. Bachrah, my cousin, who wrote the chapter about Miedzyrec Ghetto; O.A.).

Jews also served in the N.K.W.D. They too looked for contact with us. They wanted to find out who were the Christians who treated us badly, and to take revenge. We told them that if the problem had to do with individuals, it would be worth it.

One day, a Jewish colonel brought me a letter from a Jewish Russian writer, Ilya Ehrenburg. He asked for material on the Nazi era, to help him write the "Black Book" which would describe the cruelty of the Nazis.

It seems that the Russian Jewish soldiers who came to visit me in my apartment and to whom I read parts of my memoirs that I had written in the bunker had told I. Ehrenburg about it.

In my answer, I wrote that I wished that a search committee would be sent to look for the mass–graves in Biala and around it. I never got a reply.

The second Polish government in Lublin sent out a manifesto, showing photographs of the members of the cabinet. It included the photo of Emil Sommerstein, the Jewish representative, with his patriarchal beard. The manifesto promised full equal rights to the remnants of the Polish Jews.

[Page 468]

We believed that the higher authorities would indeed enforce a liberal policy with justice for the remaining Jews. Yet, how were they going to eradicate the widespread hatred towards the Jews? We had already seen that, though the Nazis had been expelled from Poland, Nazism remained deep in the heart of the Christian population.

г. Москва

17 октября 1944 г.

Уважаемый товарищ!

К Вам, как к одному из немногих евреев — [...] Бялой Подляски, спасшихся от немецкой казни, я обращаюсь с [...] просьбой.

По поручению Антифашистского Еврейского Комитета, я, с группой товарищей-писателей, работаю сейчас над созданием "Черной Книги", которая должна будет рассказать миру о зверствах, совершенных немцами над еврейским [народом].

В эту книгу должны войти документы, письма и рассказы очевидцев, свидетельствующие о зверствах немцев [...].

Я Вас прошу помочь мне в создании "Черной Книги" и написать обо всем, что произошло с еврейским населением Вашего города во время немецкой [...], [...] содержать лично Вам и Вашим близким. Пишите подробно, сообщая точно, указывайте даты, фамилии и имена жертв, [...] немецких офицеров, [...] и имена [...].

Если у Вас, или у кого-либо из Ваших знакомых, сохранились немецкие [приказы], распоряжения, объявления, [...] письма погибших евреев, пришлите их мне.

Присылайте для "Черной Книги" все, что Вы найдете нужным полезным. Очень рассчитываю на Вашу помощь.

Письма и материалы шлите мне по адресу: Москва ул. Кропот.
дом N 10, Антифашистский Еврейский Комитет.

Уважающий Вас

/И. Эренбург/.

*Letter from the Jewish–Russian writer **Ilya Ehrenburg** to M. J. Feigenbaum to send documents for a planned "Black Book" on German atrocities*

Walking with a young woman on Wolnoschtzi Square and speaking Yiddish, we heard two Christians that walked by, saying: Here they come again. The other one answered: "Lady, they will all come back, you will see". Yes, we were thinking, we wished his words would become true.

Christians from the town used to visit my home. Often, we discussed matters of the day. They wanted to show that Polish people had helped the Jews during the bad times. I used to push them to the wall with facts, from their general passivity to those who had actively helped our mass killing. Having no reply, they used to tell me that I should not spit in the well I was drinking from.

One rainy, early morning, a group of German prisoners of war marched on Brisker Street. How miserable the former murderers looked now.

[Page 469]

Ripped clothes, bare feet, and untrimmed facial hair, some with no hats on. "Good hearted" Polish people gave them some bread.

A few Jewish young men came from the east, after staying with the partisans in Wolyn. They told us how the Christians partisans had harassed them, including killing some of the Jewish partisans. Hell and death awaited the Jews all over.

The first letters from Biala Jews who had gone to the far end of Russia began to arrive. The post delivered these letters to me. I used to read the letters, which came from Uzbekistan, Georgia, Kazakhstan, and other remote places, and sarcastically smile. They were written in such a peaceful mood! They inquired about everything and everyone, full of joy and hope that we would see each other soon. I read and wondered: Don't people know that their families have been destroyed and their homes ruined? Did news about the brutal German conduct in front of the whole world never reach Russia? Is it possible that none of the people from Biala in Russia had heard about the Jewish bloodshed? Or maybe people there knew everything and believed that it would not happen to them?

What could we answer the letter–writers, who were there in Russia? That they do not have even a remote relative among the few survivors in Biala? How can one deliver news that will cause such a shock?

I waited a while before I composed a standard letter to reply all the letter writers.

My address became the place where people looked for their families. Through correspondence with me, they sometimes found relatives spread out in Russia, relatives they were looking for during the war, e.g., the two brothers Hershberg (sons of Jacob Velvel Kovals), from Wolia.

זכרון קודש

לקהל קדושים הרוגי

ביאלה-פודלאסקה

(ביאלא גדול)

אנשים נשים וטף שנספו על ידי הנאצים
וגרורריהם ימ"ש בשנות הרעות תרצ"ט-תש"ה

הרניבו גוים עמו כי דם עבדיו יקום
וכפר אדמתו עמו

Sunday, October 23, 1960, a memorial board for the Holocaust victims of Biala Podlaska was unveiled in the Chamber of the Holocaust on Mount Zion in Jerusalem. Dozens of people born in Biala Podlaska participated in the event

Footnotes:

1.   This chapter was written in a notebook several months after Biala had been freed (July 26, 1944).
2.   Sara Freter, her brother Pinchas (a refugee from Serock and the writer of this chapter. The four of us hid in two bunkers in a garden on French Street, not far from the cemetery.

[Page 470]

Bialers in the World

In Israel

by M.Y. Feigenboim

Translated by Pamela Russ

From the historical discourse of Dr. M. Hendel, we learn that already in the 16th century Biala Jews had arrived in Israel. Just as from other cities, there were individuals from Biala who also went to the Land of Israel in those years to be able to die in the Holy Land, or to appease the desire of being close to holy places.

The memoirs of Yehoshua Yelin, in the chapter about the growth of the Jewish settlement in Jerusalem in the years 1834–1864, tell of the creation of "*Kolel Warsaw*" [*center for Torah study for married men*] where it was decided that Dovod Yelin would become the head and trustee (he was the father of the abovementioned Yehoshua Yelin), whose partner became the "*HaRav HaGoan* Reb Meir, of blessed memory, of Biala" (one of the *dayanim* [rabbinic court judges] in Jerusalem).

In the period of the "Second Aliyah"[a] Nekhemiah Goldwasser (son of Nissen Goldwasser) came to Israel, and with great difficulty left Israel only to return to Biala before World War One.

Before World War One, you would hear about individual Biala Jews who were living in Israel, such as these two Gerer *chassidim*: Reb Moshe Mordechai (the coppersmith's son–in–law) in Tzfat, and Reb Yosel Junewer (father of Dena Junewer), who left for Israel to die there (P. Gold, New York). Shloimele the hat maker (Weisberg) made great efforts to make *aliyah* to Israel. He had even already sold his huge house on Mezryczer Street and was ready to leave. However, in the middle of all that, the World War broke out and Shloimele had to resign himself from his dream. After the war, Shloimele was one of the first in Biala who left with his entire family to emigrate to the Land of Israel.

At the time of World War One, a Bialer, Melman, a soldier in the Russian army, fell into a Turkish prison and arrived in the Land of Israel where he remained.

After World War I, *aliyah* to Israel began. This took place in small numbers, because first Biala Jews were not great supporters of emigration. Second, the stream of emigration from Biala flowed towards America where the Biala Jews had family and friends whom they could count on for help in setting themselves up in the new land. The small *aliyah* from Biala to Israel had a different character than the earlier *aliyahs*. The new group did not go to the Holy Land to die there or for religious motives, but first and foremost to build a Jewish home, and second, to be rid of the difficult political regime that had installed itself in the liberated Poland.

Among the Bialer who were in the first *aliyah* to Israel after World War I, there were: Avrohom Visenfeld (from Wajnes, Kaspi Zilberger (of the Szkops – served with the Israeli border police), Shloimele Hitelmakher ["*hat maker*"] and his family, Zelig Rozenfeld, Yeshayohu Agres, Sholom Rogolski, Dovid Aranowycz, Alter Wajnberg, the brothers Shlomo and Feivel Avijes (Niskele Muljer's sons), Yitzkhak Zak (Hershel Zak's son), Noakh Mann and Mottel Likhtenberg (Khaya Zelda's son).

In the middle of the 1920s, when the social life among the Jewish population in Poland became much more difficult, a greater *aliyah* to Israel began. During these very years, the following made *aliyah* to Israel from Biala: Yehoshua Rozenboim (Bashe Shmerke's son), Feige Yita Urmakher, Gutman Moshe (Eliyahu Dovidel the *melamed* [teacher]'s son), Yehoshua Shajnboim (Moshe Dovid Shtrikenmakher ["rope maker"]'s son), Yehoshua Ofar, Dovid Lemberger, Moshe Ashberg, Shloime Tzaruk, the brothers Yakov and Shimshon Hajblum, Menkhem Goldzak, Yehishua Fisher, Moshe Braverman, Moseh Bankhalter, Moshe Lewi, Moshe Stolowi, Moshe Rubenstajn, Malke Rames, Malke Migdal, Eliyahu Feldman, Przekupnik, and so on.

[Page 471]

After the unrest in Israel in the year 1929, the youth *aliyah* from Biala increased. They tried to enter the land in any way possible, both legally and illegally, often linked to great dangers.

A small percentage of those Biala residents who could not establish themselves in Israel left and returned to Biala, or emigrated to other countries.

The majority of Bialer settled in Tel Aviv and a small number in *kibbutzim* [collective farms].

The skilled workers among the Bialer worked in their trades, and those who did not have a skill from back home undertook all kinds of work, mainly by moonlighting [bypassing labor laws] in construction work. Of great significance, our compatriot Alter Wajnberg benefitted greatly from this, and he became known in Tel Aviv as one of the best brick masters, and also taught this skill to a group of young *olim* [those who made *aliyah*], and they became known in Tel Aviv as "*Kvutzat Vineberg*" ["Wajnberg's Group"].

The well–known Zionist community activist in Biala, Yehoshua Fisher, was among the founders of Kfar Ata, a settlement in Israel near Haifa, and for many years was the settlement head there.

One of the first residents of Bnei Brak was the Bialer Moshe Gutman. His hut was one of the first houses there that spoke of a new life that would begin in that vast area.

After World War II, when the Biala Jewish settlement was totally erased from the earth's surface, the majority of the small group of surviving Bialer made *aliyah* to Israel. Some of them came as illegal immigrants, still under the British mandate's rule, and the rest arrived as immigrants to the Jewish State.

Today the Biala *landsleit*[1] comprise about 500 families in Israel. Mostly, the Bialer are concentrated in and around Tel Aviv. The rest are spread out across the country, in cities, villages and on *kibbutzim*.

The majority of the Bialer in Israel work in their own workshops, in cooperative endeavors, and as workers in other workshops and factories. A significant number works in the agriculture field – both in private farming and as co–workers in *kibbutzim*. Some work in trading and in other independent professions.

In the organizational domain, the Bialer in Israel did not demonstrate any great initiative and activity. They tried to organize a Bialer association, but without success. In the year 1932, during our compatriot Berish Bernstajn's visit to Israel from America, with his resourcefulness, an initiative–group was established which was meant to lead to the founding of a Bialer association, but nothing came of this.

After receiving the first tragic news about the devastation of our city and place of birth, a Bialer committee was set up in Tel Aviv that undertook a huge collection of clothes from the *landsleit* and sent several large containers with the clothes to Biala (the containers never arrived in Biala and remained somewhere in the middle of the route that went through Persia and Russia). This committee held the first large memorial in Tel Aviv to remember the destroyed Biala Jewish community.

With the arrival of the first *Olim* (new immigrants to Israel) of the Biala survivors of the devastation, the Bialer established a loan fund that helped the newly arrived *Olim* with financial assistance. But after a short time of activity, the committee ceased to exist and the loans were not reimbursed.

In the year 1952, when the Bialer *landsleit* in America expressed their preparedness to perpetuate in Israel the memory of our destroyed home town [place of birth], it was suggested that they establish a *Gemilas Chesed* fund [non–profit assistance to individuals and families] in the name of the Biala community, that would distribute constructive assistance to the new *Olim* with the consent of the Bialer in America. The fund was established under the name "*Kupat Gemilat Chasadim Al Shem Kehilat Biala Podlaska*" [*Gemilat Chasadim* "Bestowing Kindness" Fund in the name of the Biala Podlaska community].

Today, this *Gemilas Chesed* fund is one of the most respected and best organized institutions in this region of the country. It is, as well, an important helping tool for the *landsleit* and a monument for the destroyed Biala Jewish community.

In the eight years of its existence (October 1, 1952 – September 30, 1960), the capital in the fund reached the sum of 28.881 pounds. The capital is used primarily for loans. During this time, 426 loans have been distributed, with a sum of 103.931 pounds, of which 82.230 pounds were reimbursed. At the end of the abovementioned period, the sum of 21.701 pounds came from the borrowers.

The *Gemilas Chesed* fund became the meeting place of the Biala *landsleit* in Israel and takes the position of an association. There is no problem that an association would address that the administration of the fund does not deal with.

[Page 472]

These are some of the issues. Sadly, there are Bialer who are dependent on social assistance that is not under the mandate of the *Gemilas Chesed* fund. But in order not to leave these needy people without any help, a separate social fund was created under the *Gemilas Chesed* fund, which has undertaken to allocate this type of help to the Biala needy. This aide is given in a respectful manner, and sometimes even in significant amounts. This social fund goes under the name *"Keren Asher u'Binyomin le'Ezrah Socialit"* ["A Fund of Asher and Binyomin for Social Assistance"]. This fund perpetuates the memory of two Bialer respected Zionist community activists, Asher Hofer and Binyomin Kilger, of blessed memory, who were among the founders of the *Gemilas Chesed* fund.

The *"Keren Asher u'Binyomin le'Ezrah Socialit"* fund was in existence almost from the same time as the *Gemilas Chesed* fund. During this time, a sum of 16.113 pounds was distributed.

In order to perpetuate the memory of our compatriot Alter Wajnberg, of blessed memory, who was one of the first Bialer in Tel Aviv, whose house was the gathering place for the Bialer in Israel whom Alter would assist with words and action, a stipend–fund was established in his name. Annual stipends are allocated for students of Bialer parents – students who are outstanding in their studies. The monies of these stipends are fully supported by the monies of the *Gemilas Chesed* fund.

This stipend–fund with the name of Alter Wajnberg has existed for six years (October 1, 1954 – September 30, 1960). In this period of time, 22 stipends have been distributed, in the sum of 1.929 pounds. This fund is maintained by the *landsleit* in Los Angeles.

The *Gemilas Chesed* fund administration organizes an annual memorial gathering in memory of the murdered Biala Jews. The gathering is attended by almost all the Bialer compatriots spread across the country.

The executive of the fund are the following: Moshe Reuven – chairman; Yehoshua Kliger and Yakov Gliksberg – vice chairmen; Shimshon Herzberg and Leon Pakman – treasurers; Asher Grinblat – secretary; Yehoshua – bookkeeper; Yehoshua Ofer, Chaim Libman, Chaim Yosef Knizhnik, Roza Liverant, Zalman Dogodni, Bluma Spikhler, Bela Shajnboim, Pnina Goldendrot, Dov Osenholcz, and Shmuel Fishman. Revisions–committee: Aron Mjodek and Gedaliah Kohn.

The destruction of our old home has brought closer together those Bialer *landsleit* in Israel who are at a distance [from one another] – those who are woven into the daily struggle for existence, but with the satisfaction of knowing that they are free citizens in a free State of Israel, which generations have dreamed of and hoped for.

Original footnote:

    a.   The Second Aliyah was an important and highly influential Israeli immigration movement (aliyah) that took place between 1904 and 1914, during which approximately 20,000 Jews, mostly from the Russian Empire, migrated to Ottoman Palestine.

Translator's Footnote:

    1.   *landsleit* – plural of "landsman"

In North America

A. New York

Translated by Pamela Russ

It is assumed that the first Bialer in North America arrived at the end of the nineteenth century when the immigration from Russia to North America (because of the pogroms against the Jews in the year 1881) dragged along with it several Bialer. A small number left because of economic reasons, others to avoid military service in the Russian army. There were also some immigrants who were connected with the so–called *"shaikehs"* [bandits]. In the 1890s, the Bialer Jewish underground, that consisted of fine young men and "strong" ones, greatly bothered the population. The police knew of their activities and would always collect a group of them and send them deep into Russia. These groups were called "*shaikes*" (in his pamphlet "The Bialer Courtyard", A. Wajnberg tells of escaping from the Bialer inmates of the castle prison, and he adds: "Why they were sitting in prison, is a completely different chapter.")

It should therefore be noted that this was connected to the "*shaikes*" and that the fleeing Bialer inmates waited in prison for their deportation to Russia. Many of these "*shaikes*" ran away from their place of deportation, and emigrated to England, and later to America where they became useful workers.

After the revolution was choked off by the Czarist powers from the year 1905, emigration from Biala to America began that was an emigration primarily of workers. The number of Biala emigrants to America, until World War One, is said to be about 400 men.

Just after World War One, when mass emigration to America began, Biala was significantly represented therein.

[Page 473]

At that time, women went to their husbands who were in America even before the war, children went to their parents, parents went to their children, and youths who saw a future for themselves in the United Sates [went as well]. This is how the emigration from Biala to North America went without interruption, until the so–called "quota" was reached in the United States – a quota that practically locked the gates to new emigrants.

The majority of the Biala immigrants remained settled in New York where a large Jewish community already existed. The newly arrived from Biala certainly preferred to stay with Jews rather than going west, where the number of Jews at that time was still small. It was easier to set themselves up among the Jews where you could make use of any of the supports that were available. Clearly, not knowing the language of the land also influenced them to remain among Jews. Every newcomer tried to get work in his own vocation. Those who did not have a skill took all kinds of work. A large number of the unskilled Bialer went into hat production.

Strange, lonely, and sometimes helpless, is how the newcomer felt in the new country. There were also those who couldn't acclimate themselves. They were consumed by a yearning for their home and they returned to Biala. Among others, those who returned until the First World War were: Nakhman Morgenstern (Einbinder – went back to America after the war), Elya Bubkes (Eliyahu Hofman), Khanina Kashemakher, Shmuel Ekstajn, and so on. So, understandably, associations of compatriots were set up, whose goal was to establish a meeting place where you could get together, somewhat appease the mutual yearning for the home that was left behind, and help each other in words and action. Just as with other *landsleit* in America, this is how it went with the Bialer.

Already in the year 1907, the first Bialer Society was established in New York, but because of some of their power hungry members, the society did not have a long life, and it fell apart.

In the year 1910, the Bialer "Branch" of the Workmen's Circle was established, but many Bialer could not find a place for themselves in this organization, and this once again led to the re–establishment of the Bialer Society. Around the founding date of the Society, there were disagreements among the Bialer in America, but the year 1913 is officially recognized as the year of the establishment of the Bialer Society.

In the year 1935, the Bialer Women's Association was established in New York, and in the year 1953, the Bialer-Hlusker Independent Society was established.

Each of the organizations conducts its activities at its own level, but in order to distribute help to those *landsleit* outside of America, the "Bialer Relief Committee"* was established at the outbreak of World War One, that existed only for a few years. During our compatriot Borukh Wajnberg's visit to America from London in the year 1937, under his initiative the "Bialer Central United Relief Committee" was established, and in this relief committee were representatives from all the Bialer organizations.

Understandably, this refers to the organizational form of the Bialer *landsleit* in New York, which are the majority of the Bialer family in America. The Bialer *landsleit* in other American cities also have their associations.

And, of the organizational forms, [this also refers to] the activities of the individual organizations that established our *landsleit* in New York.

The Bialer "Branch" of the Workmen's Circle which was established on January 3, 1910, at that time was marked with the number 402. The founders were: Nakhum Apelboim, Khaim Wajnglas, Avrohom Bukhwald, Avrohom Handwerker, Jack Gold, Albert Liliental, Yakov Rozenboim, Dovid Shumakher, and Izidor . This organization at that time bore an extraordinary proletariat character. Many Bialer *landsleit* who did not sympathize with this "Branch", kept themselves apart from the organization. In the year 1915, a dispute between two members took place in this organization that resulted in a splitting and the founding of a new organization under the name "Bialer Radical Unit ("Branch") 569." With time, however, the misunderstandings were put aside, and on January 1, 1926, the two factions united under the old name and marked itself with a new number, 226. *Landsleit* from Mezrycz and Lomaz also belong to the Bialer Division of the Workmen's Circle.

The principles of the Workmen's Circle are that their members are not permitted to be strike breakers, and during elections, they must vote for the candidate that emphasizes the workers' party.

The members pay a fee, and enjoy various support, such as: medical help, life insurance, sickness support, free burial for the member, his wife, and children (until the age of 18), free access to a large number of hospitals, and when a member is sick, friends are sent to visit him.

[Page 474]

The Bialer Division of the Workmen's Circle in its time helped sustain the "Culture League" in Biala and, by sending a large number of books, enabled the Bund in Biala to re–establish a library. The organization used to support the weekly "*Podlaser Leben*" [Podlasker Life]. It also provided financial support to Biala political prisoners, as long as the "Branch" was convinced that the patron would be honestly helping the political prisoner.

In America, the "Branch" supports all cultural and social institutions, with the first in line, the cultural institutions of the Workmen's Circle. It also helps the Jewish Workers' Committee; the campaigns for: *Histadrut*, Combined Jewish Appeal (*Magbit*), HIAS [Hebrew Immigration Aid Society], YIVO [*Yidisher Vissenshaftlekher Institut* – an organization that preserves, studies, and teaches the cultural history of Jewish life throughout Eastern Europe, today based in New York City], and a number of other local organizations and institutions, let alone for strike activities and other disputes in which the American workers' movement is involved. The active involvement of the "Branch" received recognition for its genuine contribution to the Jewish social life in New York.

The "Branch" is represented in the Bialer Central–United Aid Committee and devotes the greatest energy so that the efforts of the aid committee should be as fruitful as possible.

It is important to mention that when these lines were written, the "Branch" celebrated its 50th anniversary, a period of 50 years of life, creating and inspiring.

The administration of the "Branch" consists of: Khaim Wajnglas – chairman; Yakov Rozenboim – vice–chairman; Sam Zajdman – finance secretary; Khaim Bradacz – protocol secretary; Moris Walecki – treasurer; Av. Stein – hospitals; elected committee – Khaim Bergman, Feivel Gold, Yakov Fast, Viliam Silver, Alter Morgenstern, Ava Sarna.

As already mentioned, not all Bialer were able to belong to the Bialer "Branch", so several Bialer had the idea of founding a Bialer association, creating a place where all Bialer *landsleit*, of all political convictions, could meet and share their pains and joys. The need for these few *landsleit* was to have an association to which all Bialer could belong and feel at home rather than feel restricted.

A "*landsmanschaft*"[1] organization in America is for its members like a community in their birthplace, because in America there were no city communities. The *landsmanschaft* organizations were established not only for the healthy and living, but also for the sick and more – for the deceased. The first concern for this type of organization is – where do you get a piece of land for a cemetery for these members, after 120 years? The other activities of a *landsmanschaft* are designed in accordance with the characteristics of its membership.

Organizing a Bialer association was not such a simple thing to do. It required a lot of time, energy, and strong will.

After the Society which was founded in the year 1907 fell apart, in the year 1908 an effort to revitalize it was made by the *landsleit* Jack Gold and Khaim Wajnglas, but with no success. Only in the year 1913 was the Bialer Society finally successfully organized. The founding meeting took place in the house of Mrs. Gitel Marks-Rozenblat who is noted as the mother of the Bialer in America. The initiators of the founding were: Max Nowim, Khana Kaufman, H. Blumberg, Urcze Czarny, Yankel Rosen, S. Sherman, B. Buchwald,

Khaim Wajnglas, Jack Gold, Rosner, Roza Nowim (the first secretary), Khaim Bernstajn, Louis Gotfried, Dovid Kaufman, B. Blekhman, Charlie Wajnglas, Alex Nowim, and Berl Blumberg.

This is what Yankel Rozen tells of the beginning times of the Society's activities:

"The first meetings took place at Gitel's (Marks) and Meyer Nowim's home. Later we rented places on Clinton and Delancy streets. The membership fee was ten cents a week, later $1.25 for a quarter, and registration fee of twenty–five cents. We were all young then, between 20 and 25 years old, and a small percentage were in the middle years, and there were no elderly at all.

"We used to hold our meetings on the second and fourth of each month. We had large meetings because at that time there was no radio or television yet… I would advertise every meeting, free of charge, in the "*Forwartz*" ["Forward" – Yiddish newspaper] and in the "*Vorheit*" ["Truth" – Yiddish newspaper]. We had small expenses. Rent cost us eight dollars per quarter.

"When I became secretary of the Society we bought the cemetery. It appears that we paid $1,500, paying out the sum monthly. There were not many Bialer at that time, and for a long time the cemetery remained empty. It never occurred to us that we would have to buy a second cemetery…

"In our location on Delancy Street, the president was Lemele (Louis Gotfried). If Lemele did not want to give a *chaver* [friend] the floor, and the other person wanted to speak, Lemele would shout out:

[Page 475]

"Shurrup! This is not Biala!" We were more frightened of his eyes than of his hammer…

More than once there were stormy meetings and the participants became incensed. There was once an incident when a large number of Bialer wanted to invite as a friend a certain Bialer who did not behave properly in Biala, but here in New York he repented, and worked to make a living. But the majority opposed this [membership]. There were also many young Bialer who did not want to belong to the society. But as they got older, they came to us and we accepted them without requiring a large fee from them.

To the most important tasks of the Bialer Association belongs the distribution of mutual relief to the *landsleit*, medical assistance, being involved with sick *landsleit*, and sending visitors while they are ill, and maintaining their own cemetery (a piece of land that was bought from a general cemetery).

The Bialer Association today is one of the most respected organizations on the Jewish street in New York. The society takes part in all activity for benevolent purposes and dispenses sums of money for the Land of the Jews, such as for the campaign of the *Histadrut* and for the Combined Jewish Appeal. It also actively participates in the assemblies of the local organizations and institutions.

The Bialer Association can proudly claim that it brings into the Central United Aid Committee much larger sums of money than the other Bialer organizations because the members of the Association comprise the wealthier Bialer *landsleit* who are able to do this and have the good will to help everyone, particularly our own *landsleit*.

Today's administration of the Society are: Motel Rozenzweig – president; Yerukhem Lipecz – vice president; Hertz Markus – secretary; Khaim Bradacz – protocol secretary; Nathan Silverman – treasurer; Max Nowim – chairman of the cemetery committee; Moris Edelstein – hospitals. Elected committee: Khaim Wajnglas, Yonah Stajnman, Avrohom Lerner, Jack Rozenboim, Khana Kaufman, Jack Gold, and Moris Singer.

The current Bialer Women's Association was founded in the year 1935 by a group of Bialer women who, even though they've been in America for a long time, still felt bound up to their birthplace with all their sentiments. The push to establish one such organization was the calls for help from the old home, in which there was an expression of need from the poor Jewish population, the difficult situation of the Jewish hospital, seniors' home, and so on.

Each request put to the Bialer Society of the Women's Association, is answered with this: Start your work, and we'll be with you.

The beginning was fine, and from then on the Association was active, not only as a Bialer organization, but also as a participant in general Jewish life. The aid from the Association is not limited only to Bialer, but all Jewish institutions that need and call for help find an open door in this Association, and no one leaves without support.

The Association is in close contact with the Bialer "Branch," and holds its meetings in the same location as the "Branch" and also on the same evenings. The women members of the Association feel like one big family and this helps cement the unity and wholeness of the "Bialer Central United Aid Committee" that for so many years has borne the responsibility for aid for our Bialer around the entire world.

The largest part of the money collection of the "Bialer Women's Association" is given over to the aid committee.

Let the names be marked here of those who have worked for 25 years and do everything possible to have their assistance reach more people who are in need: Gitel Stern, Gitel Marks-Rozenblat, Malka Orbant, Esther Gold, Czirele Landau, Brajna Bluberg, Sarah Adler, Rivkah Kaufman, and Khaya Lewin.

The organization of the "Bialer-Hlusker Independent Society" is a brother compatriot organization of a completely different type. Other than the mutual aid that is given here to the members, the Association plays a more political–cultural role in the social Jewish life in America.

The organization was established during the period of McCarthyism, after which, as a consequence, other fraternal organizations died out.

The Bialer Association, as good as other similar organizations in the land, adopted a three-point program: contributions for the wellbeing of the members, for the Jewish nation, and for the country, the United States.

The members of the Association are like one family that rejoices in the festivities and is sad when, God forbid, there is a tragedy. Medical help is also given to the members for a very low fee. Funerals are arranged upon the death of one of its members or a family member, and they also will acquire a grave, if needed.

[Page 476]

The Association also runs cultural activities, organizing lectures and various cultural undertakings during which they familiarize the members with Jewish culture and Yiddish literature, beginning with the classics such as: Mendele, Sholom Aleichem, and Y.L. Peretz, to the end. The spreading of books is encouraged, Yiddish and English books of Yiddish and other authors. The society believes that the future of the Jewish nation lies in planting cultural valuables, in English and Yiddish, into the minds of the Jewish youth. Therefore, greater efforts are placed on cultural activities, such as lectures, concerts, and discussions.

The Association takes part in various activities and discussions that are relevant to, first of all – the Jewish nation, and second – the American people. That is how, for example, the Association, along with other similar societies with which it collaborates, took a position and let its voice be heard against the swastika plague that broke out in Germany in December 1959. All the Jewish organizations were summoned together to cooperate against the re–nazification of West Germany and against the spread of anti–Semitism.

The first "Bialer Aid Committee" was established at the outbreak of World War One, and existed without interruption for several years. The "Bialer Branch" and the "Bialer Society" founded the aid–committee. From time to time, the aid–committee would send significant sums of money to Biala for the benefit of the Jewish hospital and to distribute for the needy people.

With the renewed organization in the year 1937 of the "Bialer Central–United Aid Committee," the systematic aid activities were renewed for our birthplace, Biala. The aid–committee regularly supported the Jewish hospital, soup kitchen, seniors' home, "TAZ" [Jewish Health Organization], and "Culture League." The committee would also provide a few hundred dollars for *maos chitin* [basic food for Passover, i.e., matzo, etc.] for every Passover eve.

After the devastation of World War Two, the "Bialer Central–United Aid Committee" undertook the activities with great zeal, and reached Bialer everywhere, wherever there was a need, and from wherever there was a call for help.

We will cite only a few numbers here of the aid activities that were conducted by the aid–committee in the three years from 1948 until 1951.

Approximately 700 food packages were sent to Israel.

In Paris, a loan–and–save fund was founded for the new immigrants of our *landsleit*, and through ORT [Jewish education and vocational training non–governmental organisation], ten sewing machines were sent there.

To Poland and Germany, medication was sent to the *landsleit* in the camps in Germany, where they had a chance of getting out of there but did not have the necessary monies to do so.

The first support was given to the newly arrived *landsleit* in America.

It collaborated with the campaigns of the *Histadrut* and the Combined Jewish Appeal, and other Jewish aid–organizations.

Altogether, in these three years, about $13,000 was distributed.

The "Bialer Central–United Aid Committee" accepted the proposition of the *landsleit* in Israel to perpetuate the memory of our destroyed birthplace, Biala, by setting up a *gemilas chesed* fund [non–profit loan fund], whose goal is to help, in a constructive manner, the Bialer *landsleit* in Israel, particularly, the new *olim* [emigrés to Israel]. As soon as the fund was set up, the aid–committee sent in a significant sum, and aims that in the future the fund should receive an influx of funds that would enable it to fulfill the needs of the Bialer *landsleit* in Israel.

The monies for the aid projects are raised through various methods, such as help from the *landsleit* and various projects that are organized by the committee.

The aid–committee is in contact with the *landsleit* outside of New York, such as: Chicago, Detroit, Cleveland, Philadelphia, Los Angeles, and even Montreal (Canada).

The Bialer *landsleit* in America have good reason to be proud of their aid activities which they have been carrying on now for almost half a century.

Currently, the administration in New York of the "Bialer Central–United Aid Committee is: chairman – Sam Zajdman; vice–chairmen – Jack Gold, Moris Singer, Elya Marks, Gitel Stern; finance secretary – Avrohom Lerner; protocol secretary – Yonah Stajnman; treasurer – Jack Gold. Administration committee – Motel Rozenzweig, Khaim Bradacz, Sarah Adler, Yakov Rozenboim, Khaim Wajnglas, Philip Gold, Ada Czarny, William Shuster, Moris Walecki, Nakhman Gliksberg.

1960

Compiled with the support of the published works that were printed by the *landsleit* in New York, and added material from Khaim Wajngals, Sam Zajdman, Yankel Rozen, Sarah Adler, and others.

Translator's Footnote:

1. *landsmanschaft* – society, club, or association of Jews who come from the same district, town, city.

[Page 477]

B. Los Angeles

Translated by Pamela Russ

Just as the majority of Jewish immigrants that arrived in North America, the newly arrived Bialer settled in the eastern part of the United States. In the crisis years in America, from 1929, the movement from east to west began. In particular, the migration during the first years of World War Two should be mentioned. With this, the Jewish population did not remain behind. Masses of Jews came to Los Angeles and by now, today, there is a nice Jewish community there that is strong in its cultural activity.

Also, many Bialer migrated to Los Angeles. By chance, I happened to meet Nakhke Feldman who told me how many Bialer are in Los Angeles, and he proposes organizing a Bialer Association.

Once, while sitting at my sister's, Max Burgman and his friend, who was introduced as Yosel Zeid, came to visit. I recognized his voice immediately because Yosele Zeid was a chorister for the cantor in the Bialer synagogue. In my day, he was the beloved child of the cantor and of all Biala. Also during our meeting, we began talking about setting up a *landsmanschaft*. But because of some impediments, and because many Bialer were busy with various other organizations, nothing came of our idea.

The end of World War II came. At the end of 1945, the horrific news came out of Europe. From relatives, we learned that in certain camps in Germany there were Bialer who needed help, and once again we began to talk about a *landsmanschaft*. By chance, *landsman*[1] Aron Gold, of blessed memory, came to visit from New York. He was an idealist who sacrificed himself for people and forgot his own personal issues. He was an activist with organizational skills. It was a great merit for us Bialer to have such people in our lineup. He began to organize the Bialer in Los Angeles.

The first meeting took place in May 1947, in the home of Mashe and Sam Wirshup, where a president, Nakhke Feldman, was elected. As secretary, we elected Ina Wolf; even though she was American born, but as a former secretary in Chicago, she was exemplary in her work. I was elected to manage the relief activities.

We began our work, and first we initiated a correspondence with the Bialer committee in the camp Landsberg (Germany). We found relatives in America of these *landsleit* in Germany and helped them make contact with each other.

Since the number of Bialer in Los Angeles is small, we brought in friends to help with the work, and we called our organization "Bialer and Surrounding Areas Aid Association."

Our first banquet took place in the year 1948, in "Ad Palace Temple." Friends and *landsleit* came. We had financial success and strengthened the existence of our *landsmanschaft*.

We pledged to provide $1,200 for the Israel campaign and in the first three years of our existence we donated close to $1,000 to the money–campaign of the Bialer Central Aid Organization in New York.

After the death of our *landsman* Nakhke Feldman, we elected Max Steinen as president. We continued providing help to our *landsleit* wherever they needed. We sent food and clothing to everyone who came to us, and did not deny anyone our aid.

When Yakov Kahan came to Los Angeles, a new chapter in our activities began. With his organizational skills, and with his Gerer *chassidic* fire, Yakov threw himself into the work and tried to position the Bialer *landsmanschaft* in Los Angeles as among the finest institutions in the city. After the sudden death of Max Stein, Yakov Kahan was elected by us as president of the Bialer *landsmanschaft*.

Yakov Kahan brings a vitality to our meetings that take place once a month. Each time, the meetings take place in the home of a different landsman where we gather at set tables in a homely, friendly environment. A bond develops among the friends, and business deals are even made.

We send money for the loan fund, social fund, and scholarship fund of the *landsleit* in Israel. We send help there to individuals who for various reasons cannot access the social fund.

We are involved as an organization in many projects of local Jewish life, such as in all kinds of campaigns. We are particularly active for the *Histadrut* campaign. We, the small group of Bialer have become a recognized name in Los Angeles.

[Page 478]

In acknowledgement of the great activity of our president Yakov Kahan, in May 1954, we organized an impressive evening in his honor, and published a journal. The evening, crowned as a huge success, caused a great clamor within Jewish Los Angeles. They simply wondered how such a small group as these Bialer could carry out such a substantially rich evening.

Our activities are colorful and filled with spiritual content. We celebrate *yomim tovim* [Jewish holidays], and in particular, it is already a tradition for us to celebrate Chanuka in the Kahan home. A traditional Chanuka lighting ceremony takes place there. In that fashion, we raise a larger sum of money for our activities.

Our Yosel Zeid has a large share in our culture activities. Almost all of the culture programs of our projects are prepared by him.

At all the meetings, Yosel is the writer, reader, and singer.

Mrs. Rae Kahan, the wife of our president, and the finance secretary of our *landsmanschaft*, is very active. She announces our meetings and other festivities.

Sam Wirshup has been treasurer since the founding of the *landsmanschaft* and he is the shipper of packages.

When we glance back on our ten–year–activity, we have to confess that at the very beginning we didn't dream that such a small group of people would be able to conduct such a multi–pronged job. At that time, we didn't dream that we would be able to measure up to the elderly and to many of the other larger *landsmanschaften* in Los Angeles. This multi–branched work is to the credit of the devoted president, all our friends, men and women, who helped us and continue to help in our work.

1958
Dovid Gordon

Translator's Footnote:

1. Landsman – compatriot, native; a fellow Jew who comes from the same district, town, or city, especially in Eastern Europe

---

In Argentina

by Yakov Aranovitch, Buenos Aires

Translated by Pamela Russ

The first Bialer to step on Argentinian soil was Moshe Justman, known in Biala as Moshe Eidel's the washerman ["*der veshin's*"], who used to wash laundry in wealthy homes in town. Moshe, an orphan without a father, became a shoemaker at a very young age, and in the first years of the century he left to go to Russia. He worked there and became politically active. He became caught up in the revolutionary storm that swept across Russia in those years. He supported the anarchistic movement and became a serious activist for this ideal. After a few years in Russia, he returned to Biala where he organized the anarchy group.

As other revolutionary movements, the anarchists were severely harassed by the Czarist powers. Many of them were arrested, others emigrated to other countries, and among those was Moshe Justman.

In the year 1906, Moshe Eidel's came to Buenos Aires. He came along with a cousin of his, a girl from Brisk. Since the girl did not want to remain in Buenos Aires, where there was a lot of prostitution, Moshe took her to her sister in the distant colony of "Klara," in the province of Entre Rios. On account of the difficulty of communication, in those years, Moshe could not return to Buenos Aires right away, so he had to remain behind for a significant amount of time.

In that colony, Moshe did not find any satisfaction and he went to the town of Kopije. There he found himself in a very difficult financial state and so he went to work in a store. After a short time, he left the store and went to a shoe workshop. Because of his skill in this trade, he was hired as the manager of this workshop. In the year 1908, he married a daughter of a colonist and he opened a shoe store in that town. The difficult economic crisis that developed in the colonies had a severe impact on the stores in the nearby towns. Moshe dissolved his store and left for a larger city, where he once again undertook a trade.

Years went by and Moshe lived through good and bad times, as many others in Argentina. In the year 1942, he moved to Buenos Aires and began work as a merchant, sending all kinds of articles to the city provinces. Meanwhile, his sons and daughters grew up, got older, married, built their own homes, and were busy with business. The last few years, Moshe was already a pensioner and received, according to the local laws, a significant monthly fee from the government.

In the year 1910, Moshe brought over his younger brother who married here and settled in a colony near the town of Basil Basa. He is still in this colony today and leads a beautiful Jewish life.

[Page 479]

Among the first Bialer immigrants to Argentina was Khilish Rozenwartzel, son of Berke and Khaya Hodel from Biala. He came to Argentina in the year 1909, leaving behind a wife and two children in Biala. I don't know why he emigrated from Biala, nor do I understand it even a little, because he belonged to the *chassidic* circles, who in those years did not want to emigrate from Biala. Khilish died here. His son Shloime'le, a gaiter stitcher, like many other Bialer, came to Argentina in the 1920s because of the anti–Semitic regime in Poland and because of the terrible social situation of the Jews living there. After he was there for some time, he brought his bride over from Biala, married, and set himself up according to the possibilities of that time.

In the first years after World War One, Khaim Rozenman (surname Krokus) left Biala for Argentina. He died in the 1930s.

A few years after the Bolshevik invasion in Poland, the carpenter Shameh (Shamai) Fridman came to Buenos Aires. He worked in his trade. The times then were very bad and he earned very little. But in a short time, he brought over his wife and children. All of them went through hard times here. The children grew up, started earning a living, and life became a little easier. Later, the children began to trade, and they succeeded in earning some money. Shameh still worked in his trade, but independently on a small scale. The Second World War began. The children had a beautiful workshop of women's clothing and employed a number of workers. Shameh left the workshop and joined the children's business. Things improved, and they didn't live only for themselves, but remembered family and friends.

In the year 1925, Wolfish Shor and his wife, a midwife, came to Buenos Aires. His wife was very successful in her practice here, and Wolfish went into trade. In the year 1947, Mrs. Shor died.

In the years 1925–26, more Bialer came. The majority were not married. Skilled workers got work in their fields, and the unskilled undertook jobs of peddling (driving with pieces of material through the surrounding villages and houses with the materials). They all went through hard times until they were able to succeed in something.

Six of those who came in the years 1925–26 left, going illegally to North America. They left because of the difficult social situation that was going on at that time in Argentina. Four of that group successfully reached New York and their relatives there. Two of this group were detained in Cuba and sent back to Argentina.

One of the two that were sent back later went to Montevideo (Uruguay). This was a certain Beryl Nukhowycz who at that time was a waiter in Akule's [fish] restaurant in Biala. Since he was unskilled, this abovementioned Beryl experienced difficult times in Uruguay. He brought over his wife and children, and with time, things improved for him. The children grew up, studied, and assisted with earning a livelihood. During the later years, thanks to his children, he became wealthy, having set up a large confectionery store. His son married, and together with his wife, emigrated to Israel as *chalutzim* ["pioneers" who settled in Israel and worked in agriculture].

In Montevideo, there are three other Bialer families. One of them is the family of Leibel Feigenboim (a son of Zilya the carpenter).

At the end of 1928, the largest group of Bialer came to Argentina; 15 people, almost all of them unmarried. Again the same thing, everyone is looking for work in his own vocation. The unskilled do whatever there is to do so that, because of the difficult economic situation that there was in the country, they would be able to earn enough to live. Some of the newly arrived could not survive the difficult challenges for existence, and they returned to Biala.

In the year 1929, a group of Bialer went to South America – I was among them – to Argentina. The rest settled in Brazil, where today there are about 15–20 Bialer families.

In the year 1931, the Bialer Moshe Perl and his family came to Buenos Aires from Biala. His brother Yosef was already there. Zalman Gotlieb and his wife (of the Perls) came as well. Moshe Perl brought machines from Warsaw that produce cutlery, but he experienced many years of hardship until his product was acknowledged and accepted. Before he arrived, they used to import these items from other countries.

Before the outbreak of World War II, Nakhman Gliksberg arrived with the very last ship.

Time ran by. Everybody slowly worked their way up. The men brought over their wives and children, and brides, while others married here. Families became bigger and took on citizenship. During the Second World War, the economic situation in the country improved and in general the opportunities developed for the immigrants.

[Page 480]

After World War II, some Bialer came here, such as Itzele Friedman, Tzvi Jawor, and so on, who seemingly established themselves.

In the course of the last 25 years, the number of Bialer in Argentina greatly increased. May they continue to increase. They married off children, who are already building their own families, such that there already exists three generations of Bialer.

According to my calculations, there are about 200 Bialer families in Argentina. The Bialer work in different vocations – in trade and in industry, but everything on a small scale, such as in tailoring, furniture making, knitting, quilt making [stuffing], leather, and metal works. The majority is self–sufficient, and only a small percentage of Bialer work for others. There are Bialer who own beautiful shops in the downtown streets of Buenos Aires. Many have their own homes, which is not an easy thing to achieve here, and almost all of the Bialer make a nice living.

In social life, the Bialer do not have a significant place, with the exception of the two *landsleit*, Zalman Gotlieb and Yakov Palaticki. Individuals support each important institution, but the Bialer are not involved in these respectable institutions, such as community, school, banks, cooperatives, YIVO [Institute for Jewish research], "*Yiddisher Wiessenschaflicher Institut*", and so on.

It is worthwhile to mention a beautiful deed of our compatriot Zalman Gotlieb and his wife. In the year 1955, they celebrated their silver wedding anniversary in a festive manner. The Gotliebs presented an idea to all those invited guests, requesting not to give them any gifts but instead to spend the funds for the building of a Jewish synagogue. Thanks to this request, a significant sum was put together for the abovementioned task.

The Bialer in Argentina accomplished something positive in the philanthropic area.

According to my initiative, several projects were undertaken until World War Two, with great material success, in order to support three widows.

After the terrible devastation of European Jewry during World War Two, a Bialer committee was spontaneously developed, as happened for many other *landsleit* in Argentina, with the goal of helping our surviving Bialer. At the head of the committee, among others, were the author of these lines, Zalman Gotlieb, Shameh Friedman, Yakov Weisglas, Avrohom Dogodni, Nakhman Gliksberg, and Beryl Fishleder. The committee sent a few boxes of good new clothing and shoes to Poland. Soon, $200 was also sent to the Bialer committee in Lower Silesia (Poland).

Many of the second generation, primarily girls, pursued middle–school education, primarily in commercial school. The graduates of this school have jobs in banks, business offices, and so on. A Bialer completed his studies in medicine and is a respected doctor. This is Dr. Yosef Ribak. His mother is the daughter of the Bialer *shochet* [ritual slaughterer] Shmuel Rubenstajn. His father, Leibel Ribak, died several years ago. Dr. Yosef Ribak came here with his mother when he was an eight–year–old child. In Biala, he studied Jewish subjects, but when he came to Argentina he began to study worldly subjects with great eagerness, and successfully completed his studies. Dr. Ribak is a nationalistically inclined Jew and is not embarrassed to use the Yiddish language.

Some of the Bialer youth become distant from Jewish life and we, to our great dismay, mark two incidents of mixed marriages of Bialer youth.

In the year 1948, because of the United Israel Appeal, there was a split in Argentina within the Jewish population. There were two camps: a national one and progressive one that conflicted with each other.

The split, understandably, did not bypass the Bialer *landsleit*. Because of the shared conflict and argumentation there could be nothing substantial created by the Bialer. The only thing that we, a group of nationally disposed Bialer, established through my initiative in the last few years was a publication. The book was by our landsman M.Y. Feigenboim, by the name of "Podlaska in the Nazi Vice."

1956

[Page 481]

In France

Translated by Pamela Russ

The first Bialer Jews came to Paris in the year 1905 after the failure of the revolution in Russia.

The large immigration from Biala to France began in the year 1919. Almost all of the Bialer settled in Paris. The newly arrived Bialer worked as carpenters, bag makers, in tailoring, in upholstery, and a large number were merchants in the market.

In the year 1928, there were about 60 Bialer in Paris, and they organized a union for shared relief. At the head of this union were: honored chairman – Bernard Liberman, chairman – Abish Liberman, secretary – Simon Levin, treasurer – Moshe Rikhter, aid treasurer – Tukhmincz, senator – Max Bluberg, administration member – Fingerhut, review committee – Jack Grodner and Zauerman.

Until the war in the year 1939, the number of union members grew to one hundred. The union conducted cultural and social activities. The loan fund that was established in the union gave tremendous help to the Bialer *landsleit* to settle in France.

Understandably, when the destruction befell the Jews in France during World War II, the Bialer *landsleit* were not left behind. Around 30 Bialer were deported from France by the Germans and did not return after the war. A significant number of the Bialer saved themselves from death during the Nazi occupation by crossing the border into Spain and Switzerland, and also by migrating to the free French zone or to North Africa. There were some Bialer who fell into German imprisonment as French military and survived.

After the war, a number of Bialer came to France. Thanks to the aid from the Bialer *landsleit* in America, many newly arrived people were able to establish themselves successfully in Paris. Many of those freshly arrived in Paris went to other western European countries, and also to Israel.

Today, the Bialer union has about 120 members and is one of the most respected in Paris. This union in Paris has perpetuated the memory of the destroyed Bialer settlement by putting up a monument.

The union frequently holds meetings, and in that way provides an opportunity for the Bialer to get together in a homely setting. There is a loan fund in the union that helps the needy. Every year, a yizkor [memorial] event is organized in memory of the Bialer martyrs. The union tries to make the youth of the Bialer *landsleit* feel connected to the birthplace of their parents.

At the head of the union is the administration, in the following order: president – Shmuel Kahan, vice president – Gedaliah Kromarzh amd A. Tukhmincz, treasurer – Moshe Rikhter, secretary – Yitzkhok Wajngarten, administration members – H. Herczberg, Simon Levin, Reuven Rozenker, Baverman, Jurberg, Dovid Zegman, Gliksberg, and Stulmakher.

(The details were submitted by the Bialer union in Paris in the year 1954.)

In Canada

by Noakh Bresker, Montreal

Translated by Pamela Russ

The Bialer settlement in Canada is, in relative terms, still young, even though it is marking its 200th anniversary of existence. A significant immigration of Jews to Canada first began at the end of the 19th century. After World War I, a mass immigration took place, which increased since the gates to North America were locked before the flood of immigration. In particular, the youth from Poland and Rumania flowed to Canada, since they saw no future for themselves in their countries of birth.

In the year 1920, the first Bialer stepped into Canada. He was Yosel (Yosef) Klempner (Szternfeld), a son of the known Bialer resident, Yermiyahu Kesler. His difficulties and experiences were the same as all the immigrants at that time. In a short time, he brought over his wife Khana Kliger (a daughter of Mendel Bendelmakher [ribbon, string maker]).

The first Bialer did not forget their friends back home. In Montreal, Yosel searched for the family Wiener, an uncle of Khana Bresker. The uncle brought over his niece (Khana, a daughter of Yitzkhok and Gitel Bresker – from the police). Our first Bialer brought over their sisters and brothers.

With the outbreak of World War II, immigration to Canada stopped completely. At the end of the war, we find the following 20 families in Montreal:

[Page 482]

Yosel Klempner (4 people), Yitzkhok Rozen (earlier Rozenker – 6 people), Max Locszewski (brother of Itke Rozen – 5 people), Yedidya Klempner (Yermiyahu's older son – 6), Noakh Bresker (brother of Khana Bresker – 4), Leyale Frishman (daughter of Aron Yekhiel Melamud – 4), Khana Kalina (earlier Bresker – 4), Motel Kliger (son of Mendel Bendelmakher – 2), Beryl Kilger (brother of Motel – 2), Leybel Kliger (brother of Motel – 3), Feyge Shultz (sister of Motel Kliger – 4), Elye (Eliyahu) Baumholcz (2), Zavel Baumholcz (5), Nakhum Goldricz (4), Soroh Turowycz (daughter of Aron Yechiel Melamed – 3), Khaim Mjodek (4), Malke Klempner (sister of Yosel), Frieda Liberman (now in Israel – 2), Avrohom Libman (3), and Khaim Baumholcz (4).

After the war, these Bialer came to Montreal:

Max and Yehudis Greenberg and a daughter (Max, son of Feivel Leshner, and Yehudis – a daughter of Avik Agrodnik – 3), Yakov Goldschmidt (5), Aron Rotenberg (5), Meyer Rzepa and Khayale Pakman (4), Beryl Pakman (2), Hershel Pakman, Yosel and Esther Rikhter (Yosel – Esther Perele's grandson, Esther – daughter of Mikhalkele Drozhkarz – 4), Hershel Gitelman (5), Y. Puterman (Moshe Buke's son), M. Shneiderman, Moshe and Gitel Karalik (2), M. Bukhinyek (4), Reuven Lerner (the tombstone etcher's grandson – 4), Yehoshua Gershkop (4), Hodel Bukhinyek (3), M. Fruchtenberg (now in Winnipeg), Avrohom Salski (now in New York – 2).

According to today's numbers there are 36 families in Montreal with 114 souls, may they increase.

Let us mention here the Bialer who have left us for eternity.

Yosel Rikhter, Soroh Turowycz, Czarne Baumholcz, Meyer Zhefa, Henya Riva Klempner (daughter of Yedidya), Hershel Laskin (10–year–old son of Max Locszewski, and the wife and two young daughters of Khaim Mjodek (Soroh, Khana Eidel, and Yaffa), who tragically died on their trip to Israel (in the El Al airplane that was shot down in Bulgaria in the year 1955).

Their memory is etched respectfully in our hearts.

According to our information, there is an organized body of Bialer only in Montreal because the majority of them are there. There are several Bialer in other cities in the country but we were unable to make contact with them.

The first efforts of organizing a Bialer *landsmanschaft* were made in March 1935, when we received a notice from the Bialer community about help for their institutions. At that time we met at the home of Yosel Klempner and it was unanimously decided to establish an organization of Bialer and the surrounding areas, for those who live in Montreal. An administration was elected: Noakh Bresker – chairman, Yosel Klempner – vice chairman, Motel Kliger – protocol secretary, Shimon Kolina – finance secretary, Yitzkhok Rozen – treasurer, Itke Rozen, Khana Kolina, Khana Klempner, Leyale Frishman, and Faige Schultz.

Several projects were organized and the profits from them, along with personal donations – a larger sum of money – were given over to the Biala institutions: hospital, visiting the sick, library, and sponsorship of political prisoners.

With few disruptions, the Bialer *landsmanschaft* existed the entire time. The work intensified after the war. After we received notices that there were Bialer in Lodz and in the camps in Germany and Italy, we raised a larger sum of money and sent packages of food and clothing. We brought a few families over to Canada. At that time, we worked together with the Bialer in New York, with whom we keep in constant contact. From that time on, the memorial assembly is held every *Isru Chag* of *Sukkos* [the day following the last day of the holiday of Sukkos]. The Bialer in Montreal gather together then and, with great emotion, they honor the memory of the Bialer martyrs who were murdered by the Nazis.

Among the local Bialer, there are no wealthy men. A large portion of them remained as workers in their professions. There are some Bialer businessmen who work with clothing, construction, and the printing industry.

The children mainly work in independent professions, such as: three medical doctors, five engineers (in various areas), one teacher, and so on.

The Bialer here are active socially. You find them in all the organizations and social institutions, such as: Zionist ones (*Poalei Tzion*, Women's Pioneers, associations), leftist workers' organizations (Jewish fraternities), schools, press, and so on.

The differences do not interfere with the unity of working together in the *landsmanschaft* for the benefit of our Bialer. Here, in the *landsmanschaft*, all party differences are forgotten, and we are only Bialer.

Recently, a new administration of the *landsmanschaft* was elected. The chairman's office was given to the first Bialer in Montreal, Yosel Klempner. Also, some newly arrived people were elected onto the administration, such as: Beryl Pakman – vice chairman, and Yehudis Grinberg.

The monthly meetings have a family flavor.

[Page 483]

We celebrate together at our festivities and the same, Heaven forbid, at opposite events. At this time, our activities are concentrated on creating models for helping the Bialer in Israel.

The existence of the *landsmanschaft* gives us a feeling of closeness to our city of birth, and helps us hold onto the memories of a colorful and all–time Jewish life that resounded in the city where we spent the best years of our youth – in the Jewish Biala that was destroyed, and where our dearest ones were gruesomely wiped out.

We will remember them always and memorialize them with great respect.

In Australia

by Hershel Orlanski, Melbourne

Translated by Pamela Russ

In the 1890s, there was already a Bialer Jew [in Australia]. At the same time, a second Bialer Jew settled in neighboring New Zealand. These two Bialer Jews did not come directly from Biala, but from London where they lived. It is understood that these two

Jews were influenced by the immigration of the English to Australia, and they flowed together with the flow of the English immigration to the distant East.

The influx of Bialer to Australia began only a few years after World War One.

The first Bialer Jew who came with this migration to Australia was Faivel Ovjes (son of Niskele Muljer). He came in the year 1924, and lives to this day in Melbourne.

Some years later, the others that came were: Yakov Friedman, may he rest in peace, Khaim Jurberg, may he rest in peace, Shmuel Jurberg, may he rest in peace, Yeshayohu Blankleider, Simkha Eidelman, Khaim Lustigman, Avrohom Semjoticki, Hinde Schneider, Avrohom Perkelwald, Shmaye Friedman, Beryl and Mikhel Feigenboim, Motel Perkelwald, may he rest in peace, Melekh Suknow, Asher Grinblat, Yakov Dogodni (went back to Biala). These mentioned are the Biala pioneers in Australia.

After acclimatising themselves, they began bringing over their families and friends, and as it went, they set themselves up in the land. The majority settled in Melbourne, and only some in Perth.

At the beginning of the 1930s, Australia was in the grip of an economic crisis, and the immigration was completely stopped.

Only around 1936/37 did another migration begin. Thanks to the efforts of relatives and friends who were already residents there, or because of permits (permission for entry) directly from the government, the following Bialer came before World War Two: Khaim Suknow, Herhsel Orlanski, Yakov and Esther Zukerkand, Etel Schneider, may she rest in peace, Yakov and Avrohom Schneider, Rivka Rodziner, Max Wrubel, Miriam, Avrohom, Aron and Khaim Feigenboim, Yosel Birstajn (now in Israel), Raizel Birstajn, Gitel and Yisroel Blankleider, Yitzkhok Friedman, Breindel Fridman, may she rest in peace, Pesakh Semjocki, Yeshayohu Rozenboim, and his daughter Soroh Lieba Soroki, Sheyne Teperman, Avrohom Kohen, the brothers Yisroel and Moshe Dzhenstal, Rokhel Dorfman, Moshe Grinblat, may he rest in peace, the brothers: Binyomin, may he rest in peace, Moshe and Leybel Perkelwald, Avigdor Shnur, Sheindel Feigenboim (now in North America), Leybel Nukhowicz, and so on.

Some of the immigrants of both groups did not come directly from Biala, but from other countries of emigration, such as France, Belgium, and so on.

Some of the Bialer came with families. Others managed to bring over their families before the outbreak of war, but some did not manage that.

After the war, the following came: the Orlonski sisters (two daughters of Avrohom Orlonski), the Lerner brothers, Moshe Piterman, Y. Dorfman, Shmuel Gwiazda and his wife, Rivkah Nukhowycz, Khaim Malina, Moshe Teperman, Mindel Konicki–Feigenboim, Meyer Zinger, Berish Urbakh, Manje and Leybel Wurm, Velvel Wajnberg, Aron Semjoticki, the Rozenshein sisters, Khaim Hofman, Raizel Kornhendler, Pinkhas Wobnik with his wife and children, Lebel Finkelstajn, Ruzhke Dzhenszel, Aron Birman with his wife and son.

The majority of those mentioned came with their families, and just as with the earlier immigrations, the majority of them settled in Melbourne. Almost all of them worked as small merchants and in small industry, and set themselves up quite well.

Shortly after the outbreak of World War II, in the year 1940, a Bialer *landsmanschaft* was set up in Melbourne where they established their mission to organize and prepare aid for the Bialer Jews who were victims of the war, to remain in contact with the *landsleit* in other countries, so that in the moment of need they would be ready with the necessary help. The murderous result of the war put a halt to our plans.

(Some details – from Yosel Birstajn, Kibbutz Givat, Israel)

———————

[Page 484]

Our Compatriot, Yakov Wirnik, a Witness at the Eichmann Trial in Jerusalem
(addendum to the portrait of Yakov Wirnik on page 352)

Translated by Pamela Russ

On June 6, 1961, before a court in Jerusalem, in the trial against the German monster–murderer Adolf Eichmann, described as a witness is Yakov Wirnik, who today is 72 years old and lives in Rishon Letziyon.

Yakov Wirnik was brought to the death camp Treblinka on August 23, 1942, during the expulsion in the Warsaw ghetto. A picture of the model of the camp Treblinka, that was completed by the witness and is in the museum of Kibbutz *Lokhamei HaGeta'ot*, was hung up on the wall of the courtroom. Yakov Wirnik, who was among the builders of Treblinka, indicating the model, explained the goal of each object in the camp. His descriptions greatly disturbed the listeners. He recounted:

As they arrived, the people remained standing between two large barracks. The men remained outside. The women were taken inside a barracks where their hair was shaved off. The people were taken into the gas chambers, the doors were locked, and a motor was left running, as it would fill the chambers with gas. After 40–45 minutes, all the people there had suffocated.

Yakov Wirnik saw, when they opened the doors of the gas chambers, how the bodies of those who were gassed were pressed and stuck together. When the dead were taken out of there, he saw the gas chambers which had rooms the size of seven by seven meters, with somewhat of an inclined floor. When the people inside suffocated and were already dead, they rinsed off the floors with a hose or with buckets of water.

There was a barracks there that was called the "Lazarett." They brought the elderly there, seated them on benches and shot them all from the back.

Until the end of 1942, they would bury the dead in large ditches. But at the beginning of 1943, they ran tests for burning the bodies, but the tests did not work. Then an SS man came forward, with the rank of unit–leader [*Scharführer*], who demonstrated the burning of the bodies spread out on iron rails. This SS man stood close to the fire and shouted: "Flawless! Flawless!" (in the best order).

On August 2, 1943, there was an uprising in the camp. The witness, who was one of the leaders of this uprising, succeeded in escaping from Treblinka.

He returned to Warsaw and found a hiding place with his Christian friend, Stephan Pszibiszewski. Wirnik joined the underground movement and, disguised as an Aryan, he got a job in the Warsaw magistrate. As a night guard against air strikes in Staszic palace in Warsaw, he sat at night and drew the plan of the Treblinka death camp. He also wrote the brochure "A Year in Treblinka," because he assumed that no one would know anything about this camp. The brochure was published in Polish and in English. It was sent to North America and Professor Gorky sent it over to London.

[Page 485]

Index of Names and Places
[Page numbers refer to the bracketed page numbers in the original copy]

Translated by Max Wald

Surname (in capitals) or Place name	Name	Remarks	Page number(s)
א Alef			
FRANKFURTER	R'Abushl	Rabbi	266
MAHLER	Abeleh		166,307
ABRAMOVITS	Y.		314
	Abraham		217
	Reb Abraham son of R'Hisday		250
FROYEMS	Abraham		158
	Reb Abraham son of Reb Chaim		17,106,107
MEDNIKS	Abraham Shlomo		206,207
	Abraham (Lubliner)	Monthly leader of the community	267,268
	Abraham	Trisker Magid [the preacher from Trisk]	275
	Abraham Abeleh	*Melamed* [Torah teacher]	252
	Abraham Yitzhok	*Melamed* [Torah teacher]	252
	Reb Abraham Moshe	The Pshischer Rebbe	272
SIMCHA	Abraham	*Melamed* [Torah teacher]	252
	Abraham Tevel	*Shamash* [synagogue attendant]	256
YANOVER	Abrahamaleh	*Melamed* [Torah teacher]	252

	Abrahamaleh	*Klezmer* [Jewish musician]	330
KODNYER	Abrahamaleh	*Melamed* [Torah teacher]	251
	Abrahamaleh	*Shamash* [synagogue attendant]	256
AGRESS	Yitzhak		154,172,174,175,191 & 313
AGRESS	Yeshayahu		34, 84,130,190 & 470
AGRESS	(Family)		460
AGRESS	Franyeh		198, 460
AGRESS	Wife		460
ADLER	Abraham		177,330
ADLER	Dr. Natan	Rabbi	339
ADLER	Sarah		475, 476
ADLERSTEIN			203
ADLERSTEIN	Blumeh		197
ADLERSTEIN	Bracha		59,419
ADLERSTEIN	Liftsheh		55, 412
ADLERSTEIN	Moshe		34,59,64,130,149, 419 & 426
ADLERSTEIN	Matityahu		41,140
ADLERSTEIN	(Family)		153
ADLERSTEIN		Butcher	55,412
ODESS			78,164,165,180,222
	Aaron	Railway Porter	34,131
VOVELES	Aaron	*Melamed* [Torah teacher]	252
	Reb Aaron Menachem Mendel	Radzimineh Rabbi	274,283
SLAVATISHER	Aaron		75, 281,302, 442
	Reb Aaron Shmuel (MAHARSHAK)		270
JAKOBS	Ahreleh Yehuda		251
AVYESS	Feivel		470,483
AVYESS	Shlomo		470
OTSHEIN	Yakov		219,278

OTSHEIN	Moshe	*Dayan* [Judge in religious court]	45,56,146,251,253,260, 277,278,281,413
OTSHEIN	Shlomo Asher		219,277
	August II		89
	August III		108
	Ostrik		280
	Ofah		469
OPPENHEIM	David		16
AUERBACH	Berish (Australia)		65,427,483
AUERBACH	Berish	from Vainess	160,260
AUERBACH	David		200
AUERBACH	Yanush		46,148
AUERBACH	Yechiel		260
AUERBACH	(Family)		160
	Ortche	Butcher	381
	Uri ben R'Shimon		10,96
ORMACHER	Abraham		34,77,91,130,180,224,225,226, 229,230,241,242,390,443
ORMACHER	Chaya		198
ORMACHER	Liba		246
ORMACHER	Molyeh		197,236,240
ORMACHER	Feiga Iteh		84,189,204,245,246,400
AZOULAY	Abraham		17,106
AZOULAY	Chaim Yosef David	HIDA (the acronym of his name)	10,17,29,96,106,124
	Aziran		267,268
	Azrilyan		167
GINSBERG	Asher Zvi Hirsh	ACHAD HA'AM (his pseudonym)	324
AHIMEIR	Aba		199
OTVOTZK			251,252
IBRAGIMOV		General	467
PROSHIKER	Idel		164
EEDES	Henie Reshes		172
IVANITZKI	W.		49,418,424,446

IZMIR			16
IZHEVITZER	Shimon		202
ITKIN	Yitzhak		82,187
	Itche Meir		272
POTELS	Itchke	*Melamed* [Torah teacher]	251,252
EYBESCHÜTZ			270
EYBESCHÜTZ	Yonatan	Rabbi	17,18,106,107,266,267,268,271
EGER	Shlomo		334
	Eidel	the laundrywoman	217,22,251,478
EDELTUCH	Eliezer		192,193,197,240,241,246
EDELTUCH	Velvel		154,304
EDELTUCH	Yerucham		443
EDELMAN			443
EDELMAN	Benyamin Hersh		201,251,252,253,256,000
EDELMAN	Herschel		197
EDELMAN	Chaim		203
EDELMAN	Yosef		415
EDELMAN	Mintche		217
EDELMAN	Nachum		252,253
EDELMAN	Natan		449
EDELMAN	Pintche		85,154,416
EDELMAN	Rivka		237
EDELMAN	Simcha		483
EDELMAN-STRICHER	Ester		214,343,345
EDELSBERG	Motl		45,72,147,171,174,175,437
EDELSTEIN	Idel		45,147,284
EDELSTEIN	Itchke		256,257,259,378
EDELSTEIN	Alter		173
EDELSTEIN		Brothers, blacksmiths	443
EDELSTEIN	Yehoshua		45,72,147,171,174,175,437
EDELSTEIN	Shaulke		257,259

Surname	Name	Remarks	Page number(s)
EDELSTEIN	Sheyna Perl		226
	Ayzik	*Melamed* [Torah teacher]	251
EISEN	Leah		217
EISENBERG			443
EISENBERG	Ite		169
EISENBERG	Baruch		149,251
EISENBERG	Zisel		215,463
EISENBERG	Chaim		169
EISENBERG	Shlomo		230,231,245,246
EISENBERG	Shmeryl		443
EISENSHTAT			17,20,110
EISENSHTAT	Benyamin		204
EISENSHTAT	Velvel		45,147,171
EISENSHTAT	Michael		256
EISENSHTAT	Dr. Shmuel		79,181
EICHMAN	Adolf		484
EILINITSH			89
	Reb Itzik	Lubartever Rabbi	268
	Itzel (Yitzhak) Nachum	*Melamed* [Torah teacher]	252
	Itzele	nickname: humpback?	247
	Itzele	carpenter	207,210,243
	Itzele	painter	207,243
	Elchanan		230
ALTONA			17,106,230
ALTBIR	Doba		65,427

[Page 486]

Surname (in capitals) or Place name	Name	Remarks	Page number(s)
ALTBIR	Nete		65,153,427
	Alter		453

	Alte from the "Kichelech"	Alte "from the cookies" [sold cookies in the market]	251,252,260
ALTER	Avram Mordechai	The Gerer Rebbe [Rabbi of Gur]	271,337,341,370
ALTER	W.		332
ALTER	Chanaleh Miriam Fradel's	probably Fradel's daughter	149,259,370
ALTER	Yoseleh		149,259,370
	R' Eliyahu Ben Shmuel	Rabbi	270
	Eliyahu David	*Melamed* [Torah teacher]	252
	Eliyahu Mordechai	*Menaker* [Porger, removes veins from the slaughtered animal]	251
	Eliyahu Shepseles	Shepsel's son	252
	Eliezer son of R'Baruch	From Greece	17,106
	Eliezer son of Yeshayahu		270
	Olikeh		89
ELYASHIV	Dr. Shmuel		334,336
ELLIE	Ester Yehudit		278
ALEKSANDER		near Lodz	273,281
	Alkexsander the First		20,111
OLKUSH		the name of a place?	269
OLSHWANGER	Edward, Eliyahu, Hertz		82,187
	Alter	Carpenter	261,301,339
	Alter Neta		265
NEMIROVER	Alter		381
Amsterdam			17,18,19,106,107,108,266,270
AMSHINOV			282
	Anna	princess	9,10,95,97

OSTROV			264,271,273,275
OSTROVSKI		Pharmacist	174,305,369,370
OSTRE (Ostrov?)	PLACE?		14,103
ESSENHOLZ	Beyrish		445,463,472
ESSENHOLZ	Neta		56,414,415
	Esther the "Lizard"		372
	Ester Pereleh		33,129,482
OPATOSHU	Yosef		248,292
OPOTCHNE			105,267
OFOLE			51,407
APPELBOIM	Nachum		473
OPPENHEIM	Itchke		284
OPPENHEIM	Yeshayahu		260
OPPENHEIM	Israel		284
OPPENHEIM	Family		161,461
OPPENHEIM	Paltiel		149,260
OPPENHEIM	Tzalkeh		284
APEL			54,410
	Efraim		19,109
AKULAH			479
AKERMAN	Leibl		313
ARONOVITZ	Gitel		217
ARONOVITZ	David		470
ARONOVITZ	Hersh Ber		207,214
ARONOVITZ	Yehuda Leib		244,245
ARONOVITZ	Yakov		4,6,46,94,148,478
ARONOVITZ	Meir		251
ARONSKI			197,229,230
ARBANT	Malkah		475
ARBITMAN	Dinah		373
OREOL			332
TABATSHNIK	Aryeh		223,259
ARKHANGELSK			330

ORLANSKI	Abraham		41,66,68,75,140,154,429,431,442,483
ORLANSKI	Aizik		66,429
ORLANSKI	Hershel		191,483
ORLANSKI	Leah		195
ORLANSKI	Meir		74,149,154,175,314,400
ORLANSKI	Moshe		53,174,175,235,242,200,000
ORLANSKI	(Sisters)		483
ORLANSKI	Shmuel		154,174,175,191
ORENSZTAIN	M.		243
ASH	Yosef Itsheh		92,304,385
ASH	Sholem		236,245,361
ASHBERG	Yehuda Leib		252
ASHBERG	Moshe		470
Oshvyentshim-Auschwitz			359,409
ASHKENAZI			34,131
ASHKENAZY	Zvi (The Wise)	HCHACHAM ZVI	17,106
KODNYERS	Asher Abraham		230
PROSHEKYER	Asher	Pharmacist?	164

ב Bet

BABITCH	Yosef		365
BODKER (nickname)		*Melamed* [Torah teacher]	77,180,252
BAUER	Franz		74,439,449
BATCHKOH	Berel		284
BATCHKOH	Moye		235
BATCHKOH	Matityahu Moshe		257,284
BATCHKOH	Shaul		45,147,172
	Batchkeleh (Nickname)		71,436
BAKRACH	Yoshe		171,172,178,446
BAKRACH	Yitzhok		446
BAKRACH	Zviya		153,447
BAKRACH	Rivka		65,74,427,439,446 466

BAKRACH	Raizel		446
BAKRACH-SAPIR	Hodel		447
BAKRACH-FINKELSZTEIN	Sarah		447
BALABAN	Prof. Meir		29,124
Bolonia			357
BALBIRSKI			314
BALDIGA	Constanti		54,57,60,411,416,420
BALMAN			69,70,433,434
Bolechov			109
Bamberg			270
BANKHALTER	Hersheleh		252
BAS			74,439,453
BASILBASAH			478
BRARANOVSKI			225
BARVIS	Henri		359
BARGMAN	Beyla		245
BARGMAN	Chaim		474
BARTOSHEVITZ			9,95,96
BARTELESS	Dr.		307
BARLASS	Chaim		80,82,83,92,183,184,186,192,230,231
BARLASS	Simcha		316
BARLASS	Sarah		308
BARENBOIM	Yosef		219
BORENSZTAIN	Avramaleh	Sochatshover Rabbi	251,257,269,275,295,296,339,341
BORENSZTAIN	Beyrish		471
BORENSZTAIN	Chaim		474
BORENSZTAIN	Yakov		198,244,245
BORENSZTAIN	Leybeh Mednik		55,149,161,217,259,261,281,376,412, 414,420,443
BORENSZTAIN	Moshe		376
BORENSZTAIN	Nachum Zev	Rabbi in Byala	251,269,271,275,339,000
BORENSZTAIN	Natan		153

BORKOVSKI			93
	Basheh Shmerkess	She was (probably) Shmerke's wife	470
BUBER	Prof. Martin		321,367
BOIMHALZ	Elyahu		482
BOIMHOLZ	Zavel		482
BOIMHOLZ	Chaim		482
BOIMHOLZ	Tcharne		482
BUCHALTER	Favel		65,74,427,439,453
BUCHVALD	Abraham		473
BUCHVALD	B.		474
BUCHINYIK	Hodel		482
BUCHINYIK	M.		482
BUCHNER	Mendel		259,262,263
	R' Bunim of Pshischa	The Pshischer rebbe	272,275
BUNIM	Leibeleh		258
BOSK			267,268
Buenos Aires			4,6,46,361,362,363,364,478,479,480
BORGMAN	Max		477
BUSH	Leon		55,59,412,418,422
	R' Bachya		250
BIYALI	Pioter Yanovich		89
Bialystok			302,304,340,362,451
BIALER	Heinech		53,61,62,199,409,422
BIALER	Yisrael		42,43,60,72,142,143,420,437
BIALER	Leibl		198,199,235
	Byalke		163,165
BIBERGAL	Moshe		261
BIBROVSKI			51, 407
BIDERMAN		(Warsaw Magazine)	149
BIDERMAN	Gotel		220
BIDERMAN	D.		302

Surname	Name	Remarks	Page number(s)
BIDERMAN	Yocheved		235,314
BIDERMAN	Yakov Maier	Rabbi	276
BIDERMAN	M.Y.		49,65,66,74,154,176,201,403,427,429,439
BIDERMAN	Sarah		244,245
BITNER			66,428
BITEN			304,356
	Beibe	baker	307
BEITEL	Yehuda		201
	Beiltche		160
BIMKO	P.		244,359
	Binem Rushosher (Russian)	*Melamed* [Torah teacher]	252
BINSHTOK	Tuvia		230,233
	Biyelikeh	Dentist	225,234,304

[Page 487]

Surname (in capitals) or Place name	Name	Remarks	Page number(s)
Bielsk-Podlaski			10,29,87,96,124
BYELETZKI			49,402
Byernantzka			53,409
BIRMAN	Aron		483
BIRNBOIM			246
BIRNBOIM	Tzaleh		170,171,236
BIRSZTEIN	Yosel		359,360,483
BIRSZTEIN	Margaret		360
BIRSZTEIN	Raizel		483
BLOCH	Dr.		35,132
BLANKLEIDER	Avigdor		384
BLANKLEIDER	Bella		449
BLANKLEIDER	Gitel		483
BLANKLEIDER	Yosel		449
BLANKLEIDER	Yeshayahu		483

BLANKLEIDER	Israel		483
BLANKLEIDER	Leibl		160,178
BLANKLEIDER	Mirtche		192,368
BLANKLEIDER	Malkah		246,449
BLANKLEIDER	(Family)		229
BLANKLEIDER	Shimon	"the thin one"	80,183,229
BLANKLEIDER	Shimon	"the fat one"	214,215,227,229,236
BLOSZTEIN			224
BLUBERG	Breine		475
BLUBERG	Max		481
BLOOMBERG	Berel		474
BLOOMBERG	H.		474
BLUMENTAL	N.		76,444
BLUMENKRANZ			60,420
BLUMENKRANZ		Yeshayahu's Son	72,436
BLUMENKRANZ	Asher		199
BLUMENKRANZ	Yeshayahu		72,436
BLUSZTEIN	Abraham		240
BLUSZTEIN	Chaim Yehoshua		274,278,471
BLECHMAN	B.		474
Bnei Brak			274,278,471
BENAYAHU	M.		29
PRIKASHTIK	Binyamin		223
	Ben-Zion	*Melamed* [Torah teacher]	252,256
BEGIN	Menachem		199
BEDNARSH	Mendel		240
BEDNARSH	Sarah		203,245
Bohemia			69,70,433,434,435
BAAL MACHSHAVOT		Pseudonym of Dr. Isidor	336

		Israel Elyashiv	
Belsec			50,405
BELMAN	Dvorah		217
BELMAN	Rivka		198
BELMAN	Reizel		235
Bentz			51,66,406,428
BEKERMAN	Aaron		242,359
BEKERMAN	Antchel		41,63,140,211,212,42
BEKERMAN	Berel		216
BEKERMAN		Brothers	63,424
BEKERMAN	Yehuda		265
BEKERMAN	Israel		59,418
BEKERMAN	Sheimeh		65,256,381,388,389
	Ber Bolecover	From Bolechov	29,109,124
BERGELSON			359
BERGMAN	Dr.		52,304,407
Bergen Belsen			362
BERGNER	Yosel		360
BERGSTEIN	Moshe		31,91,126,164.284
	Berdele	Nickname	36,134
Berlin			79,80,81,181,183,185,300,367
BERLIN	Chaim (Rabbi)	Rabbi	247,272,369,370
BERLIN	Tileh		45,75,146,174,236,256,272,369,370,442
BERLIN	Meir (Rabbi)	Rabbi	369
BERLIN	Rabbi Naftali Zvi Yehuda	the NATZIV (acronym of his name)	272,369
BERLINER	Nate Yerucham		280
BERMAN	Yitzhak		45,147,153,176,178,200,000,000
BERNFELD	S.		291,124
BERNSZTEIN			55,412

BERNSZTEIN	Osip		55,412
BEREZOVSKI	Rivka		64,426
BEREZOVSKI	Shepseleh	carpenter	64,426
	Berele Koze	"Berele the goat"	149,260
Brody			18,107,267
BRODATSH	Aaron		58,417
BRODATSH	Baruch Yakov		260,284
BRODATSH	Gershon		165,260
BRODATSH	Chaim		42,142,215,260,474,400,000
BRODATSH	Yosef	miller	263,443
BRODATSH	Yakov		415
BRODATSH	Yitzhak		217
BROVAREK	Abraham		41,140
BROVAREK	Chana		217
BRAVERMAN		in Paris	481
BRAVERMAN	Abraham		165,166,247
BRAVERMAN	Gdaliyahu		42,46,94,142,148,157,158,214,215,217,285 307,328,330,376,379,392
BRAVERMAN	Hershel		247
BRAVERMAN	Moshe	in Israel	78,180,189,199,200,201-,219,253,305,325,470
BRAVERMAN	Moshe	Professor	169
BRAVERMAN	Shifra		243,245
BRANDVEINMAN	Abraham		200,201,204
BRODNIAK	Dr.		304
BROCHEL	M		4,6,77,179
	Baruch Gitel Bashess	*Mashgiach* [*Kashrut* supervisor]	251
	Baruch Ben David	from Greece	17,18,19,106,107,108,266,268
	Baruch David	Tailor	284
	Baruch David Aryeh		263

BROK		Dentist	304
	Breindel Grileches		158
BRILL		Minister	17,18,106,108
BRIN			18,108
Brisk (Lithuania)			9,10,14,15,19,20,30,34,35,36,79,80,92,96,101,102, 103,108,109,110,125,131,132,150,151,159,161,183, 242,243,246,264,269,270,271,274,276,281,304,308, 317,326,331,334,339,343,360,445,460,461,478
	Berechyahu	grave digger (cemetery attendant)	285
Bremen			75,443
Bresslau (Wroclaw)			353,366
BRESKER	Gitel		481
BRESKER	Chana		481
BRESKER	Yitzhok		481
BRESKER	Noach		481

ג Gimel

GOGOL			326
GOLD			Locksmith
GOTTLIEB	Abraham Yitzchak	lawyer	364
GOTTLIEB	Zalman		238,364,480
GOTTFRIED	Yosel		33,129,206,255,261,316,339,380,382,388
GOTTFRIED	Louis		474
GOTTFRIED	Nehemia		388,389
GOLOMB			60,420
GOLD	Aaron		477
GOLD	Ester		475
GOLD	Jack		473,474,475,476
GOLD	Faivel		215,216,237,256,257,279,304,330,336,364,379,383 390,392,395,470,474,476
GOLDAPPEL	Chana		204
GOLDBERG		Shoemaker	53,409

GOLDBERG			454
GOLDBERG	Izak		198
GOLDBERG	Berel		60,72,154,420,437
GOLDBERG	Zusheh		62,423
GOLDBERG	Leibel		68,71,431,435
GOLDBERG	Maier David		230
GOLDBERG	Mordechai		230,233
GOLDBERG	Shloymaleh		78,181,206,218,252
GOLDBERG	Shmuelke		169,215,217
GOLDHAMMER		Professor	169
GOLDHAMMER	Yakov		258
GOLDHAMMER	Laibeleh		257,279
GOLDHAMMER	Maier		257
GOLDWASSER	Nechemya		470
GOLDWASSER	Nisan		470
GOLDZAK	Asher		219
GOLDZAK	Menachem		200,470
GOLDMAN	Adolf		173, 234
GOLDMAN	Eliyahu		215
GOLDENBERG		Dr.	302,303,304
GOLDENRAT	Pnina		472
GOLDFARB			359
GOLDFARB	Beynisch		77,179
GOLDFARB	David Kroses		168,208,213,256,329,000
GOLDFARB	Velvel		251,256
GOLDFARB	Haia Sara		243
GOLDFARB	Yakov		198
GOLDFARB	L.	Lawyer	43,65,67,144,427,430,466
GOLDFARB	Mendel		85,191,390,391,443
GOLDFEDER	Sara Geleh		51,75,161,497,442
GOLDFELD	Gutche		65,427
GOLDFELD	Heinech		378

[Page 488]

Surname (in capitals) or Place name	Name	Remarks	Page number(s)
GOLDRICH	Nachum		482
GOLDREICH	Zusheh		160,259
GOLDREICH	Yehoshua		72,437
GOLDREICH	Yakov		41,140
GOLDREICH	(Family)		259
GOLDSZTEIN			238
GOLDSZTEIN	Eli		199
GOLDSZTEIN	Bloomeh		153
GOLDSZTEIN	Volvish		260
GOLDSZTEIN	Yakov Beile Frime Gitels		242,261
GOLDSZTEIN	Yakov		53,55,409,412
GOLDSZTEIN	Yitzhak		160,161,171
GOLDSZTEIN	Israel		43,86,143,191,198,235,246,313
GOLDSZTEIN	Leah		216
GOLDSZTEIN	Leibl		45,147,235
GOLDSZTEIN	Mordechai Yosef		45,147,153,176,443
GOLDSZTEIN	Moshe		86,192
GOLDSZTEIN	Schepsel		238
GOLDSZTEIN-SIKNOV	Renya		230
GOLDSCHMIDT	Avraham		154,176,443,446
GOLDSCHMIDT	Chaim Mordechai		154,246,443
GOLDSCHMIDT	Yakov		482
GOLDSCHMIDT	Moshe		247
GOLDSCHMIDT	Simon		357
GOLINSKI			230
GOLINKER			75, 443
GOLENBIOVSKI			54,411
GOMEL			460,461

GUMPEL	Binyamin		264
GUMPEL	Leibish		257
GUMPEL	(Family)		257,260
GONGOLINSKI			241
GONSKI	Moshe		53,409
Gasko			446
GAPON		Priest	210
GARBER			176
GORDON			326
GORDON	David		478
GARDIN	Yakov		22,229,243,244
Garvolin			25,118
GORENSZTEIN	Pinchas		315
GORENSZTEIN	S.		314
GORKI			326
Giv'atayim			274,340,341
GABRIEL		*Sofer* [scribe]	77,180,251
Gevat (kibbutz)			360
	Gedaliah Leib	*Menaker* [porger, remover of veins]	251
	Gedalya	from Simyatich	124
GVIAZDA	Elkeh		65,427,453,466,483
GVIAZDA	Shmuel		65,427,453,466,483
GVIRZMAN	Avraham		230,231
GVIRZMAN	Binyamin		251
GUTMAN	Eliyahu David	*Melamed*	252,470
GUTMAN	Binyamin	Rabbi	268
GUTMAN	Moshe		470,471
GUTENBERG	Avigdor Moshe		164
GUTENBERG	Zilyeh		68,75,170,415,431,432,440
Gotchkov			245
GORNY	B.		46,142,148,154,156,175
GURFINKEL	Noach		219

GORKA		Professor	484
Gzhimek			54,411
	Gitli	Daughter of R'Yosef	17,106
GITTELMAN	Hershel		482
GITTELMAN	Yosef		49,58,149,153,403,416
GITTELMAN	Sara		197
GINZBURG	Asher	Rabbi	270
GINZBURG		Baron	270
GINZBURG	Menachem Nachum	Rabbi of Byala	270
GINZBURG	Moshe		270,271
GINZBURG	Kalman		270
GIRONDY	Yonah		250
Gloge			270
GLAZMAN	B.		359
GLIKSBERG		Professor	
GLIKSBERG	Yehoshua		73,153,176,437
GLIKSBERG	Yakov		197,472
GLIKSBERG	Nachman		68,431
GLIKSBERG	Nachman	New York	476
GLIKSBERG	Nachman	Buenos Aires	479,480
GLIKSBERG	Sholem		235,240
GLIKSBERG	Shmuel		199
GLIKSBERG	Sara		443
GLIKSBERG	Saraleh		68,71,431,436
GLET			53,59,60,61,73,410,418,419,420,421,422,438
GEZUNDHEIT	Yakov		340
GELASEN	David		67,430
GELBARD		Dentist	304
GELBARD	Dr. Antony		175,240,302,303,304,000,000,000,000
GELBORD	Yakov		197
GELBORD	Mashe		63,424
GELBLUM	Avraham		77,180
GELBLUM	Aharon		259

GELBLUM	Yakov		259
GELBFISH		Dr.	52,303,304,407
GELTMAN	Elyahu		42,142,243,245
GELTMAN	Dudel		63,284,424
GELTMAN	Moshe Mordechai		284
GELENBERG	Menachem Mendel		162,228,229,230,241,242,243,343,344,345
	Getzl		443
Ger			274,300
GOERING			58,440
GERMAN			53,410
GERECH			49,402
GERSHKOP			443
GERSHKOP	Yehoshua		482
GERSHKOP		Heirs	443
GERSHKOP	Nachkeh		74,439
GEFEN	Ita		198,199
GEFEN	Yakov		201
Grabanov			39,137
GROBMAN	Yitzchak		63,153,174,175,429,443
GROBMAN	(Sisters)		63,424
GRAVSKI			42,141,343,377
Grodno			9,96,366,415
GRODNER	Jaques		481
GRODNER	Pinchas		6,68,430,431
GRODNER	Rivkah		197
GRODNER	(Sisters)		62,422
GRODNER	Sheindel		236
GRODNER	Shlomo		175,443
Grochov			84,189
GROSSMAN			60,420
GROSSMAN	Bronia		451
GROSSER	Branislav		215
GERDI	Natan		201

GROBMAN			69,71,433,436
GRIDIZER	Elyahu		335
GRINBOIM	Yitzchak		82,83,84,186,187,190,199,200,317,3223,332
GRINBLAT	Asher (Israel)		187,236,472
GRINBELT	Asher (Australia)		483
GRINBLAT	Moshe		483
GRINBERG	Zisel		202
GRINBERG	Chana		197
GRINBERG	Yehudit		482
GRINBERG	Max		482
GRINBERG	Faywel		482
GRINBERG	Sheindel		207,245,246
GRINBERG	Simcha		198
GRINGLAS	Avraham		68,72,431,436
GRINGLAS	Joel (Yoel)		48,68,256,276,284,401,431
GRINENFELD		Engineer	50,66,405,428
GRINSZTEIN			92
GRINSZTEIN	Davidtche		251,284
GRINSZTEIN	David Leib		443
GRINSZTEIN	Yosef		197
GRINSZTEIN	Shaineh Hendel		245
GRETZ	H.		29,124,455
	R'Gershon Heinech	The Radziner Rabbi	33,129
GERSZON		Shochet [ritual slaughterer]	251
GERSZON		Shoemaker	210

ד Dalet

	Dobele the *Badchen*'s	son of the *Badhen* [entertainer, comedian]	329
	Dobrish		295,296,298,299
DOGODNY	Avraham		480
DOGODNY	Zalman		472
DOGODNY	Yakov		154,483

DAVIDSOHN	Avraham Abele	The Byala rabbi	268,271
DAVIDSOHN	Aharon		365
DAVIDSOHN	Golda		198
DAVIDSOHN	Chaim	The Warsaw Rabbi	269
DAVIDSOHN	Dr. Yehuda Leib		304,365,366
DAVIDSOHN	Yitzchok Yechiel	Rabbi	365
Domatcheveh			379
Dombye			38,137,215,331
Danzig			19,98,108,109,267,268,369,371
DANZIG	Yechiel	Rabbi of Alexander	273, 281
DANZIG	Israel Yitzhak	Rabbi of Alexander	273
DANZIG	Fayveleh	Gritzer Rabbi	272,273
DOSTOYEVSKI			326,359

[Page 489]

Surname (in capitals) or Place name	Name	Remarks	Page number(s)
Dokodov			11,98
DORFMAN	I.		483
DORFMAN	Nechemya		54,411
DORFMAN	Rachel		483
Dubno			267
	Reb David		250
	Reb David	Rabbi of Kock	271
DAVID		Sanaker	281
DAVID		Partzever	284
DAVID	Baruch		256
DAVID	Wolf	*Melamed*	252,258
DAVID	Moshe	Yosl's (probably Yosl's son)	77,180
	Reb David'l	The Karliner rabbi	334,335,336
Dvorzhets			161
Dukov			449

Jambol			362
DZIENTCHOL	Israel		483
DZIENTCHOL	Moshe		483
DZIENTCHOL	Rozhke		65,176,427,466,483
YONEVER	Dina		258,470
DINES	Yitzhak	Rabbi	201,205
DIKLER			158,164,165,166,167
DEBOS		Engineer	58,417
Detroit			328,476
DEMBOVSKI	Mikolay	Bishop	267
DEMBLIN			60,420
DERM			70,434
DERVENTZKI			54,411
DRIBNIN			268
DREIZEN	Yosef		252

ה Hey

Haag			321
HOHENLOHE		Prince	163,369
HAUSER		Dr.	92
HAUSSCHILD			51,407
HOCHBERG	David		262
HOCHBERG	Yitzchak		174,175,199,200,204
HOCHBERG	Motel		200
HOCHBERG	Menachem Leib		166,257
HOCHBERG	Shlomo		44,145,197,204,311
HOCHBERG	Shloimele	Carpenter	166,257
HOCHBERG	Sara Rebeka		262
HOCHMAN		Dr.	52,303,304,407
HOCHMAN	Israel		51,162,168,243,407
HOCHMAN	Mordechai		42,142,169,214,215,227
HOCHMAN	Shmereleh	Baker	202,237,375,376,385
HALAS			73,438

HALBERSZTAT			19,109
HALBERSZTAT	Herzel		77,179,338,354
HALLER		General	38,82,137
HALPERN	Zvi		45,147,176,178
HOLZHEKER	Rachel		204
Hamburg			17,18,69,106 107,230,433
HANOVER	Natan		19,108
HANAK			66,428
HANDELMAN	Avraham Ezra		74,439
HANTVERKER	Avraham		473
HOFMAN	Eliahu Bobkes		56,168,206,170,214,207,217,328,330,413,331,473
HOFMAN	Chaim		149,263
HOFMAN	Chaim	Australia	483
HOFFMAKEL-OSTROVSKI		Lawyer	55,412
HOFFER	Asher		46,77,78,85,86,94,148,179,180,181,191,198,200,214,224,230,253,261,264,284,285,304,472
HOFFER	Baruch		199
HOFFER	(Brother)	Brothers	158,160
HOFFER	David		284
HOFFER	Zelig		284
HOFFER	Haia		444
HOFFER	Chaim		65,428
HOFFER	Yehudit		204
HOFFER	Yehoshua		149,260,284
HOFFER	Israel		281
HOFFER	Leibel		240
HOFFER	Motl		51,200,405
HOFFER	Michash		41,54,65,140,154,310,311,411,427,466
HOFFER	Moshe		251,284
HOFFER	Matityahu		214
HOFFER	Nechemia		214
Horodna			274

Horodenka			267
HARTGLASS	Apolinary	Lawyer	31,32,47,91,92,126,127,165,166,174,225,234,255,301,320,399
HARTGLASS	Yanku		234
HARTGLASS	Yozhek		235,321
HARTGLASS		wife	39,138
HARTGLASS	Kalman	lawyer	31,32,47,91,92,126,127,165,166,174,225,234,255,301,320,399
LURIA	Rabbi Yitzhak	HA"ARI	29,105,124,283
Horchov			14,103
HEGDEM	Gerszon		280
	Hodes'l Chantche's	Chantche's (Chana's) daughter	34,131
HOROWITZ	Yosef	Byala rabbi	266,269,270
HITLER			46,48,53,56,74,92,148,318,319,409,414,439
HAIBLUM	Hershel		204
HAIBLUM	Yoel Meir		58,251,252,284,416
HAIBLUM	Yechiel		44,145
HAIBLUM	Yakov		470
HAIBLUM	Leibish		154,263
HAIBLUM	Menachem		174
HAIBLUM	Moshe		443
HAIBLUM	Nachum		202
HAIBLUM	Simcha		263
HAIBLUM	Shimshon		470
HEINSDORF	Yehuda Leib		339
HEINE			449
HILDEMAN			48,49,401
HAYLPRIN	Y.		29,124
HIMELFARB	Hershel		215
	R' Heinich Itchkes		251
	Hinich Ostatni Grosh		158
HIRSCH	Leib	From Minsk	281
HIRSHBEIN	Peretz		229,245

HIRSZHORN	Zvi	Byala Rabbi	45,48,146,251,271,279,280,401
HIRSZHORN	Shmuel		279
HIRSHZON	Shlomo		176
HELMAN	Liebe		308
HELMAN	Miriam		308
Helsinki (Helsingfors)			321
HELLER		Engineer	155
	Henyeh		370
HENDEL	Dr. Michael		4,6,7,9,88,95,270,284,285,301,395,470
HERMAN	Yosef Mendel		339
HERZ	S.		177
HERZOG	Yoel Leib Halevi	Rabbi	341
HERZOG	Yitzhak Aizik Halevi	Rabbi	341
HERZBERG	H.		481
HERZBERG	Shimshon		472
HERTZL	Dr. T.		204,232
HERTZMAN	M.		53,409
HERSCH	Chaim Moshe Feyes	*Melamed.* His mother's name was Feya?	252,258
HERSCH	Chaim Sender Motyes	*Melamed*	252
HERSZBERG			154
HERSZBERG	Avraham Mordechai	Chicago Rabbi	278
HERSZBERG	Berel		41,140
HERSZBERG		Brothers	469
HERSZBERG	Yakov Velvel		41,60,140,257,313,390,420,469
HERSZBERG	Slava		198
	Hershel Ortsheles		252,259
(SEIDMAN)	Hershel Brisker	from Brisk	157,158
	Hershel Yanover	From Yanov, *Melamed*	252
	Hershel Lentshner		166
	Hershel Sheykes		165

Hersheleh David R' Aizik's			263
Hersheleh	Melamed		252

ו Vav

WABNIK	Pinchas		483
Volhyn			103
VOITSHECHOVSKI	Dr.	Dr.	305
VOLODKA		Architect	301
VALAVSKI	Antony		49,63,71,93,400,402,404,408,423,424,445
Volozhyn			272
VOLANSKI			54,411
VOLYA			282
VALETSKI	Morris		474,476
VALETSKI	Mindel		203
VALETSKI	Rykel		363
VALETSKI	Shmuel Moshe		363
WOLF	Ina		477
WOLKOVYITZKI	Aharon		54,407
VANZURA			51,162,407
WASSERMAN	Eliezer		39,138
WASSERMAN	Velveleh		257

[Page 490]

Surname (in capitals) or Place name	Name	Remarks	Page number(s)
WAKSEN			308
WAKSEN	Tzelkeh		80,183,227
Voronietz			62
WARM	David		149
WARM	Yehudit		174
WARM	Leibl		65,427,483
WARM	Mania		65,427,483
VOREK	Nachum		42,142,168,169,171,100,000,000

VARSHAVSKI	Abraham	244,245
VARSHAVSKI	Yakov	462
VARSHAVSKI	Leona	228,230,231
VARSHAVSKI	Sarah	203
VARSHAVSKI-LEBENBERG	Rozhe	228,230,231
Warsaw		11-484
VASHUTINSKI	Bohdun	46,94,148
WUHRMAN		154
WURKE		280
WIDE		59,419
WEISENFELD	Abraham	470
WEISENFELD	Beila	310
WEISENFELD	Motel	174,175
WEISENFELD	Moshe Chaim	43,60,72,142,160,420,437
WEISENFELD	Perel	84,189,193
WEISENFELD	Shmuel	191,193,242,244,245
WEISENFELD	Sarah	65,74,427,439,452,454,466
WITGENSTEIN		20,110
VON WEISEL	Dr. Wolfengang	199
WEICHERT	Dr. Michael	245
WEINBERG		443
WEINBERG	Aaron Yechiel	252,259,261,357,482
WEINBERG	Alter	30,46,84,94,126,160,162,166,190,229,230,247,253,257,284,285,301,304,316,470,471,472
WEINBERG	Berl	164
WEINBERG	Baruch	30,126,168,206,207,209,217,218,243,320,327,328,370,372,375,473
WEINBERG	Golda	229
WEINBERG	Velvel	483
WEINBERG	Israel	30,126,206,256,284
WEINBERG	Yeshayahu	30,126,168,211,327,300
WEINBERG	Nachman	238,240
WEINBERG	Uziyel	264

WEINBERGER	Emil		43,51,65,143,406,427,466
WEINGARTEN	Y.		153,481
WEINGLAS	Chaim		473,474,475,476
WEINGLAS	Charlie		474
WEINTRAUB	Leibl		176,251
WEINTRAUB	Mordcheleh		378,379
WEINTRAUB-TUCHSCHNEIDER	Liubeh		56,228,230,23,311,413,447
WEINSZTOK	Misha		243
WEINSZTOK		Wife	314
WEINSZTEIN	Ester		65,427
WEINSZTEIN	Dud'l	Paver	177,184,245
WEINSZTEIN	Noach		55,412
WEINSZTEIN	Malyeh		245,246
WEINSZTEIN	Feige		198
WEINSZTEIN		Sisters	80,184,245
WEINSZTEIN	Sheine		80,184,202,237
WEINSZTEIN-KALMANSON	Sonya		302,304,314
WEISSBERG			54,411
WEISSBERG	Chanan		54,60,411,420
WEISSBERG	Shlomaleh		84,189,470
WEISSBRAT	Yosef Yehoshua		246
WEISSBRAT	Shmuel Reuven		443
WEISSGLAS	Gitel		192,193
WEISSGLAS	Chaim		177,215
WEISSGLAS	Yakov		244
WEISSMAN			176
WEISSMAN	Abeh		66,429
WEISSMAN	Arkeh		45,71,147,219,435,446
WEISSMAN	Berish		52,66,73,303,304,407,429,438
WEISSMAN	David		43,69,72,143,154,171,172,178,313,437
WEISSMAN	David	Warsaw	73,438
WEISSMAN	Hershel		69,433

WEISSMAN	Chaia	198
WEISSMAN	Yehoshua	49,59,71,401,418,436,472
WEISSMAN	Yakov	71,201,205,435
WEISSMAN	Mendel	175,178
WEISSMAN	Froim [Efraim]	154
WEISSMAN	Rachel	198
WEISSMAN	Sarah	446
WAISMAN-FRIDMAN	Saraleh	202,245
WEISSENBERG		359
	"White Underpants" Nickname	36,134
WEIZMAN	Wolf	43,51,67,143,154,171,172,407,430
WEIZMAN	Dr. Chaim	50,250,335,404
WEIZMAN	Yeshayah	219
WEIZMAN	Rachel	204
Vilna		9,23,54,89,96,114,214,266,270,335,356,366,370,410
	The VILNA GAON	268
Vienna		34,131,280,300
Vinograd		75,442
WINOGRAD	Heinich	241
WINOGRAD	Baruch	43,44,45,46,143,144,145,146,148,170,171 303,310,311,312,314,463
WINOGRAD	Yoskeh	154,164,172,261
WINOGRAD	Sholem	92,251
WINDERBOIM	Yitchak	66,428
WINDERBOIM	S.	169
WINDERBOIM	Shmuel Chaim	217
Winnipeg		482
WINIKAMIEN	L.	304
WIENER		481
	Vincenti	165
Vissoka, Lithuania		10,96
Vielopolski		38,138

VIRNIK (WERNIK)	Yakov		352,353,484
VIRNIK (WERNIK)	Faivel		170,217
VIRSHOP (WIRSHOP)	Masha		477
VIRSHOP (WIRSHOP)	Sam		477,478
Vishnitz			31,126
VISHNITZER	Dr. M.		124
Vlodava			10,19,21,58,82,96,108,109,111,112,186,269
Vlodavka			275,417
VLASS	Yechezkel		215
VLASS	Fiszel		49,403
WECHTERMAN	Yitzhak		216,217
	Velvel	son (or husband) of Eidel the laundress	251
	Velvel	*Litwak* (the Lithuanian)	251,252,260
	Velvele	Itches (Itche's son)	150
	Velvele	grave-digger (cemetery attendant)	285
	Velvele	Butcher	252
WENGROVE			10,96,281,282
VRUBEL	Max		483

ז **Zayin**

Zabludov			20,110
ZAGER			266
ZAGER-WERNER	Zager-Werner		51,66,406,428
ZAVIDSKI			51,407
ZATLER	Dr. Yoachim		302,304
ZOLA	E.		359
ZOLEVSKI		Parutchnik [delegate to a commission]	39,138
ZOLESIYEH			92

Surname (in capitals) or Place name	Name	Remarks	Page number(s)
ZALTZMAN			226,241
ZALTZMAN	Sara		320
ZALKIND	Dr. M.		327
Zamosz			268
ZAMIT			268
SOMMERSTEIN	Dr. Emil		467
ZAKSHEVSKI			93,143
ZVITKEVER	Shmuel		393,394
ZUBERMAN	Chaia Sara		204
ZUBERMAN	Joel		54,411
ZUBERMAN		Heirs	444
ZUBERMAN	Maier		261
ZUBERMAN	Moshe		261
ZUBERMAN	Nachman		54,411
ZVIRMAN			481
ZUNDERLAND		Lawyer	34,130
ZUSMAN	Lieba		443

[Page 491]

Surname (in capitals) or Place name	Name	Remarks	Page number(s)
SUSMAN	Sheindel		217
SUSMAN	Shmuel		153,191
SIEGELBAUM	A.		322
SIEGELMAN			51,406
ZITO	Dr. G.		79,159,182,225,234,300,000,000,000
SEID	Ester		363
SEID	Yosef		262,358,363,364,477,478
SEID	Moshe Mordechai		363
SEIDMAN	Idel		158
SEIDMAN	Chaim		218
SEIDMAN	Justina		191,242

SEIDMAN	Yakov		238,245,246
SEIDMAN	Yakov Shlomo		60,149,153,420
SEIDMAN	Sam		474,476
SEIFERT		Lieutenant	452
SILBERBERG	Aaron		260,281
SILBERBERG	David		253
SILBERBERG	Chaim		56,67,199,414,430
SILBERBERG	Joel	Dentist	43,56,67,73,143,174,175,230,240,304,310,414,430,437
SILBERBERG	Moshe Meylech		43,45,142,147,253,284,307
SILBERBERG	Reuven		219
SILBERSON			67,430
SILBERSON-SPICHLER	Blume		235,472
SILBERSTEIN			463
SILBERSTEIN	Idel		443
SINGER		Po'alei Zion Left	203
SINGER		"Bund"	216
SINGER	Abraham		235
SINGER	Elyahu		69,71,433,436
SINGER	Ester		235
SINGER	Chaim		217,245
SINGER	Yosef		42,142,202,203
SINGER	Maier		483
SINGER	(Family)		161
SINGER	Reizel		308
SINGERMAN			165
	Zisele Rivka Akibaches	Akiva's (wife)	149
ZYSKIND		Train Porter	270
ZYSKIND	Reb Zyskind		251
ZYSKIND	Mordechai		270
ZYSKIND	Moshe	Hamburg Rabbi	270
ZYSKIND		Shoemaker-cobbler	454

ZLOTOPOLSKI			321
Zlotshev			280
	Reb Zalman		253
ZALMAN	Bialer	from Byala	16,105
	Zalmankeh		40,139
SEGMAN	David'she		244,245,481
SEGMAN	Yehudit		244,245
ZELIG	Hersch	Mashgiach [supervisor]	251
ZELMANOWICZ	Efraim Leizer		331
ZELMANOWICZ	Yosef		198
ZEEMAN		Stabzeilmaster [Staff number champion?]	65,427
ZAK	Aaron		23,115
ZAK	Dov Berish		275,278
ZAK	David		307
ZAK	Hershel		348,349,355,470
ZAK	Zalman		31,126,256,259,301
ZAK	Chaim Israel		274,275
ZAK	Tchipe		198
ZAK	Yitzchak		470
ZAK	Laibl	Dayan [judge in religious court]	251,258,259
ZAK	Sheindel		275
ZAK	Shmuel Leib	Byala Rabbi	30,33,35,41,45,126,130,131,141,146,248,251,269,271,274, 271,269,251,390,377,323
ZERUBAVEL	Yakov		202
JABOTINSKY	Zev		198
SZAMEH		Nickname	240
Zhulkve			268
SZYTOH	Abraham		200
SZYTOH	Velvel		284,304
Zhitkovice			461
SZELAZOH	Berel		178,199,200,201

SZELAZOH	Berel	Zhelanov Street	53,409
SZELAZOH	Yosef		154
SZELAZNI	Hersh Yakov		261,264
SZELOZNI	Matityahu		69,71,433,436
SZELECHOVSKI			253
SZEPA	Maier		482

ח Chet

NISKELES	Choneh		168,212,213
CHIDUSHEI HARIM		Gerer Rebbe [Rabbi of Gur]	258,269,271,274,275,000
CHAYUT		Rabbi	335
Chaim ORTSHELES			262
R'Chaim ASHER			251,252
Chaim BEKER		Moravietz	64,65,92,426,443
Chaim HOSHLEVER			252
Chaim CHAVALES			382
Chaim Yishayahu			256,284
Chaim PISTSHAZER			207, 211
R' Chaim Zanser			273,283
Chaim		Doctor	304
Chaim Shochet		Slaughterer	251
Chaikel Lichtsyer			257
Haifa			202,203,471
Chanan			53,409

ט Tet

TABENKIN	Yitzchak		332
TOLSTOY			326
TOKARSKI	Yakov		53,171,172,178,409
TOKARSKI	Mendel		75,153,284,442
TARGOVNIK		Nickname	259
TORNHEIM	Sara Leah		75,153,442

THON	Dr. Yehoshua		321
GLIKELES	Tuvia	*Melamed*	252
	Tuvia der Geler	"Tuvia the yellow one", *Melamed*	252
	Tuvia	*Melamed*	252
TVARKOVSKI	Chaim		77,78,180
TUCHMINTZ	A.		481
TUCHMINTZ	Tzemach		149,259,284,462
TUCHSZNAYDER			51,406,446
TOPIKIN		(Governor)	306
TUROVITCH	Sara		482
TUREK			339
TIOMKIN	Isaac		235
TIOMKIN	Yevel		168,207,208,217
TIOMKIN		(Family)	207
TEIBER			159
TEITELBAUM	Abraham		47,399,443
TEITELBAUM	Motel		204
TEITELBAUM	Rivka		198
Tiktin			10,14,96,103
TISHEL	Yosef		69,433
TEVELLE	David	Rabbi	334
TEMEREL			336
TENENBAUM	Itcheleh		280
TENENBAUM	David Beker		65,427
TENENBAUM	Chanan		65,427
TENENBAUM	Nachum		55,154,174,219,412
TENENBAUM	Dr. S.		302,304
TENZER		Rabbi [Rabiner] Dr.	37,135,227,231,309
TEPERMAN			198
TEPERMAN	Moshe		483
TEPERMAN	Sheina		483
Terespol			35,62,68,91,131,274,343,423,431,461

TRAVNIK		449
TROK		89
TRUMPELDOR	Yosef	193
TRUNK	Chana	299
TRUNK	Y. Y.	294
	Trayneleh	255,260
Trisk		275,300
Treblinka		62,67,73,271,343,352,353,423,430,438,447,448,484
Chortkov		280
TCHARNI (CHERNY)		235
TCHARNI	Ortshe	474
TCHARNI	Ortshe Motl	34,131
TCHARNI	Ida	463
TCHARNI	Eida	476
TCHARNI (SHACHOR)	Aizyk	336
TCHARNI	Benyamin	34,131
TCHARNI	Herzl	51,58,160,407,416
TCHARNI	Hershel	34,131
TCHARNI	Haia	475
TCHARNI	Chana	463
TCHARNI	Yakov	34,131,216
TCHARNI	Moshe Benyamin	213,214,236
TCHARNI	Pinchas	70,435
TCHARNI	Shlomo Stop	34,92,131,216,435
TCHIZHEVSKI		254
Chicago		4,7,278,476,477
TCHLENOV	Dr. Yechiel	81,184,323
TCHECHOTSHINEK		310
TCHECHANOV		281,282
TCHECHANOVSKI	Baruch	331
Tchechanovce		10,96

| Czenstochov | 18,19,108,331 |
| TCHERNICHOVSKI | 326 |

[Page 492]

Surname (in capitals) or Place name	Name	Remarks	Page number(s)
י Yod			
YAVOR	Moshe		77,180
YAVOR	Zvi		480
Yavorzhne			45,251,271,280
YAVORSKI			39,138
	Yozef II		9,96,111
YATZHIMOVSKI	Israel Leizer		74,439
YAMNIK	Abraham		73,437
Yampol			268
	Jan Kazimierz	Polish King	9,96
Janow			226,33,39,55,60,61,66,72,82,84,93,120,129,138 163,186,241,420,421,429
YANKOVYEK	Shlomo		192,193,239
	Yankel Brachiya	*Melamed* [Torah teacher]	252,253
	R'Yankel	Nadriziner Rabbi	273
	Yankel	Shamash [synagogue attendant]	256
	Yos	Carriage driver?	382,383
	Yosel Janover	From Janow	258,470
	Yosel KOLYATSH		256
	Yoseleh Glezer	Glazier	261
	Yoseleh VOHINER		424
	R' Yoseleh Zvi	Rabbi in Bnei Brak	274,283
	Yoskeh Yechil Hersh's		263
YATZKOVITCH	Marek		270

YAKOBOVSKI	Bella		311
YAKOBOVSKI	Zelig		191,446
YAKOBOVSKI	Roiza		193
YARNIZKI	Heinich		255,256,257
	R'Yehuda (Biala Rav)	Biala Rabbi	266
	Yehuda Chasid		16,29,105
	Yehuda Yakov		150
	Yehuda Yakov		259
	Yehuda Leib		109
	R'Yehuda Leib	Rabbi	266
	R'Yehoshualeh	Ostrover Rabbi	264,271,273,275,283
	Yehoshua KAPP		443
	Yehoshualeh Chazan	Cantor	255,261,269,363
	R' Yoab Yehoshua	Kinzker Rabbi	274
	Yoel Itzel	Tailor	208,226,259
	Yoel Ketzeles		158
YOD	Maier Shochet	Ritual slaughterer	219,251,253
	R' Yozel	Rabbi	250
Jolyew			39,138
YONASHA	Klemens		366
YUNGERMAN	Maniya		310,312
YUNGERMAN	(Family)	(Family)	161,174
YUNGSTER	Levy		201
	Yonah Krakover (Teacher)	*Melamed* [Torah teacher]	252
YUSTMAN	Eliyahu	(Elie Shimsheles)	168,207,210,213,236,243,328,329,330
YUSTMAN	Velvel		252,253
YUSTMAN	Moshe	son of Eidel the laundress	222,478
YUSTMAN	Shimshon		63,72,415,424,436
	R' Yosi (Yosef ben Yakov)	Biala rabbi	11,98,268,270
	Yosyeh	Tailor	16,104

	Yosef		232
	Yosef Ben R' Peysach Bialer		16,1`7,105,106
	Yosef Katzev	Butcher	27,122
	Yosef Yoelke	Coach owner	443
	Yosef Lubliner		259
RUBINSTEIN	Yosef Maier		265
	R' Yosef Refael		259
JURBERG		*Hashomer-Hatzair*	197
JURBERG			235
JURBERG	Idel		55,412
JURBERG	Chaim		483
JURBERG	Ekivah		53,409
JURBERG		Paris	481
JURBERG	Tzirl		235
JURBERG	Shvalke		217
JURBERG	Shmuel		483
JURBERG-LUSTIGMAN			74,439
KUZMIRER	R'Yechezkel	From Kuzmir	273,283
	Yechiel	Horse Trader	443
	Yechiel Hersh		92,259,279
	R' Yechiel Meir	Gostininer Rabbi	283
		"The Holy Jew"	264,272,273,282,294,299
YELIN	David		470
YELIN	Yehoshua		470
	R' Yakov	Lubliner Rabbi	17,106
	Yakov Eliezer Pishtshatser	From Piitchatz	258
	R' Yakov Arye	Radziminer Rabbi	283
	Yakov ben Yechezkel		377
	Yakov Hersh	Cemetery attendant	285

	R'Yakov Yitzhak	The Choze of Lublin [Seer of Lublin]	272
	R' Yakov Yitzchak	Carpenter	31
	Yakov Natan	*Melamed*	251
	Yakov Slavatitsher (Slavic)		264
	R' Yakov Zvi		283
	Yakov Royzes	Royze's husband or son	247
YA'ARI	A.		29,124
JAFFE	Mordechai		82,187
JAFFE	Moshe		251
Yafo (Jaffa)			184,361
	R' Yitzchak (Baiala Reb)	Byala rabbi	17,18,106,107,108,110,266,267,270,271
	Yitzchak ORTSHELES		252,253,381
	Yitzchak DROSHKARZH		443
	R' Yitzchak	Rabbi of Wurk	272,280
	Yitzchak LIPES		263
	Yitzchak Moshe Bobkes	*Melamed*	252
	R' Yitzchak Kalman	Dayan [judge in religious court]	251,285
	R' Yitzchak'l SCHISHER		273
	R' Yakir	Dayan [judge in religious court]	251
YARDEN	Dr. Dov		250,377
Jerusalem			17,105,106,124,181,203,272,275,283,321,335,339,340, 341,363,368,370,469,470,484
	Yerachmiel Sofer	Scribe	284
	Yerachmiel	Nicknamed "the short one"	284
Yericho [Jericho]			339
	Yirmiyahu	Bathhouse attendant	258,380

	Yeshayahu Eliezer		230
	Yeshayahu David		31,126
	Israel		281
	Yisrael Ben Eliezer		270
	R'Israel		250
	R'Israel (Isser'l)	Rabbi in Brisk	266,270
	Israel David	From Lodz in Brisk	281
	Israel Hersh Yanovers		251
	Israel Vichnes		251,284
	R'Israel		281
	R' Israel	Rabbi in Pilev	283

כ Kaf

KHODKYEVITCH	Family	Family	270
KHARASH			463
KHARASH	Velvel		170,215,245
Charkov			368
COHEN			203
COHEN	Abraham		483
COHEN	Abraham David		23,115
COHEN	Aaron		361
COHEN	Itche Meir		33,77,82,129,179,186,219
COHEN	Alte		361
COHEN	Binyamin		45,147,253,466
COHEN	Gedaliah		63,201,424,472
COHEN	Dr. David		77,179,338,254,355
COHEN	Dudtzser		172
COHEN	David'tche		78,284,305,388
COHEN	David'tche Pesls	Pesl's husband or son	78,284,305,388
COHEN	Dintche		235
COHEN	Heinech		77,180
COHEN	Heinech	Yitzhak Cohen's son	65,427

COHEN	Herzl		258,271,284,336,380
COHEN	Hershel	Binyamin's son	153,172
COHEN	Hershel		53,204,410
COHEN	Velvel		177
COHEN	Zishe		259
COHEN	Chaim		34,131
COHEN	Yakov		198,242,344,361,362
COHEN	Yitzchak		45,63,65,147,153,161,178,424,427
COHEN	Israel		43,45,143,147,176,235,255,259,313,379,415
COHEN	Israel Meir		149,258
COHEN	Moshe		31,126,129,259,304,300,000,000
COHEN	Sluveh		74,439
COHEN	Shoel'ke		149,258,338,347,380,384
COHEN	Shimon Leizer		26,120
COHEN-BERNSTEIN	Dr.	Dr.	77,179
COHEN-PRETER	Sara		53,410,453,464
COHEN-TZEDEK	Eliahu Henich		219
COHEN-TZEDEK	Yakir		153,174,200,284
KAHNA	Shmuel Zeinvil		270
	Chinkeh Brachies		207
CHMIELNITZKI			19,108,284
KHMIELEVSKI			51,406
CASPI-SILBERBERG			470
Chelm			58,90,417
Chentchin	KENTSHIN		21,112
Kerson			222
Kfar Ata			325,326,471
KATZ	Abraham	Zamoter Rabbi	268
KATZ	Mendel		270

[Page 493]

Surname (in capitals) or Place name	Name	Remarks	Page number(s)
KATZ-RAPAPORT	Chaim	Lemberger Rabbi	267

ל **Lamed**

Surname (in capitals) or Place name	Name	Remarks	Page number(s)
LABENZHOVA		Dentist	304
Lodz			48,68,76,280,281,294,331,351,374,401,431,444,451,453,462
LAUFMAN	Meir Michael		304,324
LAZER	(Eliezer)		453
LOMAZ			26,29,33,52,63,74,119,124,129,219,222,262,304,407,424,439
LOMAZ	Aryeh		192,193,240,246
London			205,206,243,322, 327,353, 370,371,374, 415,473,483,484
LANDAU	Avreimaleh	Chechanover Rabbi	272,280,281
LANDAU	Aaron	Biala Rabbi	33,45,138,147,149,223,248,260, 273,281,282,284,285,342,392
LANDAU	Itchke		281
LANDAU	Elimelech Mendel		281
LANDAU	Berish	Biala Rabbi	248,251,272 273,277,280,281,392
LANDAU	Berish		281
LANDAU	Vovtshe		281,282
LANDAU	Yanke'le	Nashelsker Rabbi	272
LANDAU	Yechiel		273,281,282
LANDAU	Yakov Yitzchak	Kinever Rabbi	281
LANDAU	Yekutiel		281
LANDAU	Israel		281
LANDAU	Menachem Mendel	Strikover Rabbi	273,277
LANDAU	Menachem Mendel	Biala Rabbi	273,281,282
LANDAU	Mendel		281
LANDAU	Tzirele		475

LANDAU	Rachale		272
LANDAU	Shmuel		200
LANDAU	Simcha Bonim		281
LANDSBERG			477
LANDSKRON			267,268
Los Angeles			4,7,358,363,472,476,477,478
LASKIN	Hershel		482
LASHTEVSKI-ROSEN	Ita		245,246,308,482
LASHTEVSKI	Max		235,482
LASHTEVSKI	Moshe Bezalel		176
LASHTEVSKI		Wife	315
Loshitz			10,26,96,120,263,265
LAVIE-LEMBERGER	Abraham		202,237,213,256
Lobartov			21,46,111,147,268
Lowitz			451,452
Lublin			11,17,23,29,49,50,52,53, 55,58,59,60, 61,66,72,89,92,98,114, 171,264, 267,268,270,274,275,276, 277,278,280,300,310,340, 370, 401,402,407,408,412,415,417,418, 419,420,421,429,437,467
LUBELTSHIK	Abraham		51,77,161, 170,171,180,242, 305,310,312,401,407,443
LUBELTSHIK	Yakov Zelig		161
LUBELTSHIK	Matityahu		161
LUBELTSHIK	F.		315
LUBELSKI		Dr.	355
LEWIN	Dr. David		340
LUSTIGMAN			68,432
LUSTIGMAN	Isser		74,175,439
LUSTIGMAN	Boaz		284
LUSTIGMAN	David		235
LUSTIGMAN	Chaim		483
LUSTIGMAN	Monyeh		74,439
LUSTIGMAN		Family	154
LUSTIGMAN	Rachel		201

LUZATO	Moshe Chaim		250
Luck			267
Lukow			10,11,58,89,93,96,98,105, 200,264,417
LOURIE	Shmariahu		334,335
LIBMAN	Abraham		482
LIBMAN	Aizhe		256,260,262,265
LIBMAN	Eliyahu		176
LIBMAN	Eliezer		284
LIBMAN	Berish		200
LIBMAN	Hershel		243
LIBMAN	Zelig		170
LIBMAN	Chaim		244,245,472
LIBMAN	Chaim	Nachum's Son	284
LIBMAN	Yankeleh		177,443
LIBMAN	Nachum		149
LIBMAN	Pintshe		81,185,233,245,246,
LIBMAN	Sara		262
LIBERMAN	Abush		192,193,238,240, 245,246,481
LIBERMAN	Bernard		246,365,481
LIBERMAN	David		240
LIBERMAN	Chava Dines		149,365
LIBERMAN	Chaim		260,281
LIBERMAN	Chaim	"Forverts" newspaper	361
LIBERMAN	Yakov		176
LIBERMAN	Michtshe		244,245
LIBERMAN	Freda		482
LIBERMAN	Shmuel		63,64,424,426
LIBERMAN	Simcha		462
LIBERMAN	Sara Breineh		311
LIDZBARSKI	Moshe		73,438
LIDZBARSKI	Feigaleh Rafaels		149
LIDZBARSKI		Wife	73,438

Livorno			17,29,106,124
LIWERANT	Zalman		39,58,138,303,418
LIWERANT	Chaim		197
LIWERANT	Israel		178
LIWERANT	Roza		472
VONLIESINGEN		Field Marshal	309
LITWIN	A.		299,393,395
LITMAN	Shmuel		244
LITMAN SHREIBER		Writer?	230
LEIBZON			53,66,409,429
LEIBZON	Moshe		70,435
LEIBZON	Moshe (Israel)		198
LEIBZON	Mosheleh		66,429
LEIBZON	Shepsel [Shabtay]		67,74,430,439
	R'Leibish		251
LEIBISH	Yakov Aryeh's	*Melamed*	251
LEIBISH KATZ		*Melamed*	251
	Leibel		222
	Leibeleh KETSHEH	*Melamed*	252
	Leibeleh	Russian	251,379
	Leizer	Painter	207,213
LEIZERZON	Yerucham		284
LAJNWAND	Aaron	Rabbi	279
Leipzig			20,110
LICHTENBOIM	Glike		60,217,308,420
LICHTENBOIM	Yerachmiel		71,153,253,436
LICHTENBOIM	Moshe		55,56,412,414,415
LICHTENBOIM	Motel		470
LICHTENBOIM	Shimeon		45.47.66.147.153.154.176.399.429.43
LILIEN			336
LILENBLUM	M.L.		366

LILIENTHAL	Albert		473
LINIK			281
LISTGARTEN			161
LISTGARTEN	Yoikel		58,60,418,420
LISTGARTEN	Miriam		74,439
LISTGARTEN	Rachel		178,197,204,205
	Liseh		266
LIPA	Gershon		280
LIPIEC	Yontel		75,442
LIPIEC	Yerucham		235,240,475
LIPIEC	Leibel		178
LIPIEC	Moshe		263
	Lipeh Lukover	From Lukow	281
LIPKOV			57,59,73,412,415,419,438
LEBENBERG	Abraham		238,313
LEBENBERG	Heinich		2240
LEBENBERG	Israel		198
LEBENBERG	Leibel		69,240,432
LEBENBERG	Moshe		31,39,43,81,126,138,142,171,184,261,301,307,313,443,464
LEBENBERG	Fishel		53,198,409
LEDERMAN	Arthur		365
LEDERMAN	Moshe		279
LEDERMAN	Rafael		80,183,227,237,243,200,000
LEDERMAN	Shlomele		384
LEHRMAN	Yissachar Ber		19,109
LEVY		Yitzhak's son	51,406
LEVY			443
LEVY	Yitzchak		43,45,51,66,72,143,147,314,406,429,437
LEVY	Moshe		200,470
LEVIN	B.		203
LEVIN	Dr. G.		355
LEVIN	Haia		475
LEVIN	(Charny)		168

LEVIN	Israel		91,157,262,443
LEVIN	Shimon		481
LEVINSTEIN			203
LEVENSTEIN	Yosef	Rabbi	268

[Page 494]

Surname (in capitals) or Place name	Name	Remarks	Page number(s)
LEHMAN			51,406
Lemberg-Lwow			14,18,19,82,103,107,109,186,267,268,271,274,279,280
LEMBERGER	David		240,246,470
LEMBERGER	Yeshayahu Idel		230,231,233,245,246,000,000
LEMPERT			74,439
LENTSHNE			264,273
LENIN			359
LERNER	Abraham		475,476
LERNER	Eliyahu		198
LERNER	Eliezer		60,420
LERNER		Brothers	483
LERNER	Yoel Itzel		284
LERNER	Ruven		482
LEHRER	Yitzchak		196, 197,230
LESHTSHUK			454,459
Leczna			33,129

מ Mem

Modena			105
Madera			344
MAHLER	Dr. R.		29,124,395
MAZOR	Eliahu		333
MOZIR			461
MOSES	Idel		339
MOSES	Itzchka		251,263

MOSES	Alexander Ziskind		339
MOSES	Velvel		339,340
MOSES	Hana Miriam		339
MOSES	Latzeh		338
MOSES	Latzeh Leah		339
MOSES	Rivkah		339
MATYS	(Matityahu)		206
	Motyeh	Cobbler	251
	Motel		245
	Motel Domatshever (*Melamed*)	*Melamed*	252,331,379
	Motel	From Venice	47,215,216,231,237,300
	Motel SHENKER	Pub owner	256
	Moteleh		250
Majdan Tatarski			417
Majdanek			60,72,73,373,420,437,438,449
MAHARAM ASH	R' Meir	Rabbi	17,106,110,266
	R' Meir	Horodenka Rabbi	267
	Meir "der weisser"	"The white one'	211,212,213
	Meir the Talit Maker	Talit [prayer-shawl] maker	381,382
	R'Meir	Rabbi from Byala	470
	R' Meir Yechiel	Ostrover Rabbi	276
	Meir Feigeles	Feigele's husband or son	262
	Meir knoch		92
	R' Meir	Rottenburg Rabbi	
	"Mayer"		51,66,406,428
	Meir'l Kalusziner		251,259
MALASHEVICZ			62,68,423,431
MALINA	Chaim Heshel		240,483
MALINA	Yakov		57,416
Malinin-Borenin			342
MOLYER			229

MANN			204
MANN	Yosef		443
MANN	Noach		84,190,470
MANN	Rachel		204
MONOSOVITZ or MANASZON		Dr.	79,181
MANGEL	Dr. Ester		82,187
MANDELBOIM	Benyamin Leib		162,234,395,443,466
MANDELBOIM	Yehoshua Binyamin Leibele's		210,211
MANHEIMER-SHER	Hava		302,304,479
Montevodeo			363,479
MONTEFIORE	Moshe		339
Montreal			476,481,482
R' MANES			256,262
MANPEREL	Berel		229
MASS	Velvel		284,316
MOSIK			217
MOSKAL			197
Moskow			19,89,108,234,336,369
MAPU	Avraham		30,125,224
MAKOVSKI	Israel		443
MAKOVER			453,455
MOROTCHNIK	Shimon		164
MORGENSTERN			308
MORGENSTERN	Abraham Pinchas	Lomaszer Rabbi	341
MORGENSTERN	Alter		474
MORGENSTERN	Hersheleh	Lomaszer Rabbi	341
MORGENSTERN	Yonah		68,431
MORGENSTERN	Munish		264
MORGENSTERN	Moshe		68,174,191,204,205,400
MORGENSTERN	Moshe Baruch	Vlodaver Rabbi	278
MORGENSTERN	Nachman		473

MORGENSTERN		Wife	466
MORD			33, 130,262
Marienbad			280
MARCHBEIN	Yosef		260
Markushov			251
MARKUS	Hertz		475
MARKS	Eliye		258,476
MARX	Karl		297
MARKS-ROZENBLAT	Gitel		260,474,475
MAGID	Moshe		245
MOSHKOVITCH	Moshe Efraim	Rabbi	280
MAHARAL			379,392
MUZYNEK	Golda		395
MUZYNEK	Hinda		395
MUZYNEK	Yeshayahu Eliezer		230,256,395
MUNISH			226
MUSOWITZ			302
MUSOWITZ	Chaim	The "Kabriner"	52,304,349,350,351,400,000
MAZ"E		Moskow rabbi	334,369
MYADEK	Aaron		197,472
MYADEK	Chaim		86,162,191,198,229,200,000,000
MYADEK	Chana Eidel		482
MYADEK	Yafa		482
MYADEK	Yitzchak		240
MYADEK	Sara		482
MIGDAL	Leibl		160,200,201
MIGDAL	Malka		470
MAIZEL	Yitzchak Leib		230,231
MAYER	Morris		327
MAYERSON	Tzirl		217
MAYERSON	Refael		230,233,238
	Michalkeleh Droshkarsch		265,482

MICHELSON	Zvi Yechezkel	Rabbi	29,124
MILBAUM	Beila		235
MILBAUM	Godel		81,165,166,185,255
MILBAUM	Chaim Gatl		61,252,422
MILBAUM	Chaim Zawel		415
Munchen			76,317,361,444
Minsk			19,54,161,173,252,335,365,366,410,460
Minsk-Mazowieck			282,324
MINTZ	Eliyahu		258
MINTZ	Eliezer		258
MINTZ	Blimaleh		149
MINTZ	Zisel		370
MINTZ	Chana Miriam		231,306,308,309
MINTZ	Chana Faiga		235
MINTZ	Motel		78, 149,160,180, 199,208,209, 223,259,284, 304,370,384, 425
MINTZ	Woman		303
MINTZ	Woman		314
MIENDZYRZECKI	Shmuel		245,246,445
MIENDZYRZECKI	Sara		174,175
Miriam			365
MIERTENBAUM	Yehoshua		385
MISHKIN	M.A.		86,178,191
Milave (Mlawa)			165,281,333
MALACH	Chaim		16,105
	R' Menachem Mendel	Wurker Rabbi	272,273
MEDEM	V.		332
MEVIUS			40,91,139,164,342
Miedzyrzec	MEZRITCH		10,19,21,23,26,2228,29,50, 51,53,57, 61,62,63,65,66,78,78,72, 73,74,77,82,88,93,96,109,111, 112,122, 179,216,224,233, 240, 243,255,263, 264,269,271,274, 277,281,300,343,373, 374,376,383, 404,409,421, 422,423,426, 427,428,429,430, 432,434,435,436,438, 439,440,446,447,448,449,450,452,457,459

	Mechel	Cantor	255
Melbourne			359,483
MELMAN			470
MELER	Dr. A.		230,307
MELTZER	Iser Zalman (Rov)	Rabbi	340
	Mendel Ozerkover	From Ozerkov	262
	Mendel	Baker	247
	Mendel	Painter	279
	Mendel	From Miedzyrzec	264
	Mendel Kitiye		284
	Mendel Russusher	The Russian	251, 252
	Mendel Roizes	Roize's husband or son	247

[Page 495]

Surname (in capitals) or Place name	Name	Remarks	Page number(s)
	Mendel Shochet	Ritual slaughterer	251
SHTRITZ	Mendel		33,129
MENDELE	*Mocher Sfraim* [Book salesman]		229,236,326,366,476
	Mendeleh *Melamed*	*Melamed* [teacher]	252,256
	R' Mendeleh	Kotzker Rabbi	269,271,272,336,337
	Mendeleh Shochet (R'Zalmans)	slaughterer	251
	R Menkeh Dayan	Dayan (judge in the religious court	251,260,263,284
	R' Mordechai	Liesser rabbi	266
BLUMKES	Mordechai	Blumke's husband or son	271
	Mordechai Yosef		158
	R' Mordechai Yosef	Izbitzier Rabbi	271
	Miriam		214,364
	Moshe		166

	Moshe Areleh		387
	Moshe Ozsheraver		211
	Moshe Itzikl *Melamed*	*Melamed* (Tora teacher)	252
	Moshe Ishtcher		211
BAS	Moshe		381
	Moshe *der Groyser*	"The Big One"	219,251,263,281,338,
	Moshe *der Kleiner*	"The short one"	219,251,263,281,338
	Moshe David *Melamed*	*Melamed*	251
VISHNITZER	Moshe		31,126
	Moshe Zeigermacher	Watchmaker	443
	Moshe Chaies	Chaia's husband or son	395
	Moshe Toker	The Turner	227,257
	Moshe Tuvia Stolier	The carpenter	260
	Moshe Chelmer	From Chelm	281
	R'Moshe Michel	Biala Rabbi	269,271,285
	Moshe Michel *Melamed*	*Melamed*	252,253
	Moshe	From Smyatitch	16
	R' Moshe Mordechai	Trisker Rabbi	275
	R' Moshe Mordechai		261,470
	Moshe		264
	Moshe Srul Potels	*Melamed*	252
	Moshe	from Slavatchinek	166,167
	Moshe Peyas	Peya's husband or son	260,263
	Moshe Paykes		255
	R' Moshe	Rabbi in Pressburg	19,109
	Moshe Rudels		443
	Moshe Elye	Tinsmith	171,237
	Moshe Kalman	*Melamed*	251
	Mosheleh Chaikels		223

ב Nun

NAUCZENY	Chanan Eliezer		443
NOBILE		General	354
NOVOTARSKI			40,139
NOWOMIAST	Hershel		301,443
NOWOMIAST	Family	Family	154
NOWOMINSKI	Rivkah		66,74,314,429,439
NOWIM	Alex		474
NOWIM	Marks		474,475
NOWIM	Roza		474
NATANSON	Binyamin		443
NATANSON		Dr.	355
NATANSON	Yosef		256
NATANSON	Yosef Shaul	Lemberger Rabbi	269,274
	Noskeh Hodesls	Hodesl's husband or son	206
	NAPOLEON		20,21,25,110,390,392
NORDMAN	Yakov		230
NORTMAN	David		153,191
NORTMAN	Pinchas		44,45,145,147, 154,160,174, 175,313,385
NEULINGER			58,417
NUCHOWICZ	Abraham		65,197,353,379,427,400,000
NUCHOWICZ	Berel		479
NUCHOWICZ	Hershel		197,353,354
NUCHOWICZ	Wolf		225,228,230,231,253
NUCHOWICZ	Yosef		193
NUCHOWICZ	Leibl		483
NUCHOWICZ	Mendel		245
NUCHOWICZ	Rifka		65,427,453,466,483
NUCHOWICZ-FAIGEBAUM	Leah		197,203
NISBAUM	Avremaleh		449
	Noskeh *Melamed*		252

	Nach Shamash		256,262
	Nachum Petke	*Melamed*	252

ס Samech

SENDERS	Nachumaleh		69,433
CHAYUN	Nechemya Chiya		267
SCHREIBER	Nachman		230
	R' Nachman ben Shmuel Halevi	Bosker Rabbi	267
	Neta		281
New-York			4,7,80,177,218, 235,256,257, 259,260,280,292,300,303, 304,330 361,362,363, 470,472,473,476,477,479,482
Nizhne			207
	R' Neitel	Rabbi	264
NEUMARK	Ben-Zion		35,132
NEUFELD	Elimelech	Rabbi	210
NEUSTADT	Melech		332
Nei-Shtetl [New Shtatl)			264
NAYSZTEIN	Hersh Ber		261
NAYSZTEIN	Zavel		443
NISBAUM	Yitzchak	Rabbi	79,181,182
NEWIDZI	Yakov		178
Njeswiezs			9,89,95,266,370
Nierecht			159
	Nikolai II Czar	Czar	33,129
Nikolsburg			270
NIXON	Richard		278
Nirenberg			75,76,440,444
NIRENBERG	Yakov		200
ASHKENAZI	R' Naftali Hirtz	Lemberger Rabbi	19,109,270
	R' Naftali Hirtz	Zlotchever Rabbi	270
NATAN HA'AZATI	Natan Ha'azati		267
Sobibor			58,73,346,351,417,438

Satanov			267
SAURIMPER	Leibish		253,282,307
Sochaczew			295,296, 298,299
Sologov			306
SOLOWEJCZYK	Dr. A.		355
SOLOWEJCZYK	Chaim	Brisker Rabbi	339
SOLOWEJCZYK-MORGENSTERN			150
SALOMON	Rachel		304
SOLMAN		Barber-Surgeon	304
SOLMAN	B.		169,215,245
SOLSKI	Abraham	New-York	482
SOLSKI	Abraham		202,23,237,238
SOLSKI	Masha		245
SOLSKI	Moshe		202
SANDLARZ	Berel		65,153,427,443,466,
SANDLARZ	Heyla		65,427,466
SAPIR	Chaia		75,153,442
SAPIR	Yosef		244
SAPIR	Israel Yitzchak		153,202
SOKAL	Baruch Mordechai		281
Sokolov			26,29,116,119,120, 282
SOKOLOVSKI			65,427
SOROKI	Sara Liba		483
Sarnak			26,120
SARNE	Eva		474
Sashke			222,223
Suwalki			49,51,53,55, 73,402,406,409,437
SORKARTSHIK	Munye		51,407
SOKOLOV	Moshe Baruch	Rabbi	45,147, 160
SOKNOV	Alter		45,147,169
SOKNOV	Chaim		483
SOKNOV	Melech		483

SEDZIK			66,429
STOLOWY	Yeshaiahu		174,175,197,204,205
STOLOWY	Moshe		470
Stanislav			325
STOKOLSKI			90,193
STARETZ			463
Syoag			51,61,66,67,406,407, 421,428,429,430
STEIN	Avraham?		474
Stirnetz			63,163,424
STERN	Gitel		475,476
STRICHER	Abraham		43,45,72,143,144,147, 171,214,245,437
Strikov			277,278
SITNER	Fayvel		45,137
SILVER	William		474
SILVERMAN	Nathan		475
SINGER	Morris		475,476
SIROTA	Gershon		85,190,323
Siroki			33,130
SIRKUS	Pesel		176
SIRKIN-COHEN	Dr. F.		355
SLOBODSKI	Eydek		51,406
Slavatiych			17,106
Slavatchinek			163,166
SLONIMSKI	Chaim Zelig		366
Slutsk			9,14,19, 77,95,96,103,108,109,180
SMOLARZ	Faiga		217
SMOLIAR	Moshe		1,962,292,320,326
Smolensk			457

[Page 496]

Surname (in capitals) or Place name	Name	Remarks	Page number(s)
SEGAL			165

Seltz			65,160,427
Semyatitch			16,105,270,271
SEMIATZKI			203
SEMIATZKI	Abraham		169,202,203,483
SEMIATZKI	Aaron		483
SEMIATZKI	Chaia		245
SEMIATZKI	Pesach		483
SENDER	Motyia		157
SENDER	Sender R'Shayes	Melamed	252
	Senior		71,436
Serock			49,51,62,268, 402,406,415,453
SPIVAK			69,432
SKOLIMOVSKI			445
Skopin			366
Skarzhsik			374
Skiernivitz			282
SZREBERNIK			198
SZREBERNIK	Abraham		178
SZREBERNIK	B.		203
SZREBERNIK	Yoel		204

ע Ayin

EDELBAUM	Meir		4,7,88,266,270
EDELSTEIN	Morris		475
	Uziel		394
	R' Ozer	Rabbi	266
OFER-HAFER	Yehoshua		193,197,470,472
Azza [Gaza]			267
	Azriel	Shamash [synagogue attendant]	387
ETINGER	Henryk	Lawyer	34,130
Eyn Hashofet		Kibbutz	373
ELBOIM	Yosef		74,439

EMDEN	Yakov ben Zvi	YAVETZ	17,18,29,106
EMDEN	Nechama		17,106, 107,108, 124,266,267, 268
AMIEL	Moshe Avigdor	Rabbi	340
ENGLANDER	Yehoshua		74,439
ENGELS			378
APPLEBAUM			143
APPLEBAUM		Warsaw	193
APPLEBAUM		Butcher	65,427
APPLEBAUM	Eliezer		45,147,171
APPLEBAUM	Berele		252
APPLEBAUM	Davidtche		203
APPLEBAUM	Hershel		217,463
APPLEBAUM	Zecharia		154
APPLEBAUM	Chaim David		251,252
APPLEBAUM	Neta		251252
APPLEBAUM	Shmuel Hersh		251
EKERMAN			65,426
EKSTEIN	Yitzchak		63,72,424,436
EKSTEIN	Shmuel		473
ERDMAN	Dr. Pinchas		302,303, 304
ERLICH	Eliyahu		176,219
ERLICH	Yechezkel		150,172, 176,219,251,259,281,384
ERENBURG	Ilya		467,468
ERENKRANZ		Pharmacist	305
ERENKRANZ	Berel		235
EREM	Moshe		202

פ Peh

FOGEL	Yitzchak		52,74,407,439,443
PODOLIAK	Hersh Liber		255
POLDLISHEVSKI	Abraham		77,180
POZNASKI	Dr. S.	Rabbi (Rabiner)	231
PAT	Yakov		215

POTOZSKI			73,438
POTASH			453,455
POTZTARUK	David		176,219,284
POTZARUK	Moshe		284
POTZTARUK	Nechemia		65,427
POTZTARUK	Faiga		217
FAYANS	A.L.		4,6
PAISKER			59,70,418,434
PALATITSKI/FALATYCZKI	Yakov		362,363,480
POLONYETZKI	Yakov	Slaughterer	74,251,284,439
POLOSETZKI			63,424
FOLMAN	Lola		361
PONCZYK			443
PONYATOV			72,333,437
PONYATOVSKI	Stanislaw August	Polish King	110
Pasao			58,417
PEST	Yakov		474
PAPUTIN		Chief	307
PAPIYERNIKOV	I.		359
PAKMAN	Berel		379,482
PAKMAN	Hershel		482
PAKMAN	Chaihale		482
PAKMAN	Leon		461,463,472
FARBIAK	Chaim Pesach		149,259,284,384,388,390, 391
FARBSTEIN	Heshel		84, 190,199,200
Paris			4,7,46, 148,213,242,243, 245,252,260,277,300, 329,330, 341,359, 362,365,476,481
Partzeve			261,273
FUTERMAN	I.		482
FUTERMAN	Moshe Bokes		382,482
Pozen			55,82
POISNER	Shlomo Zalman	Warsaw Rabbi	269
Polav/Pulawi			60,420

SUCHARTZIK	Munia		280
FUNK		Major	91
FUCHS	Bronia		65,427
PIONTNITSKI	Yakov		82,187
Fiorda-Perth			110
PIWO	Eliyahu		443
PIWO	Yehoshua		204
PIZSHITZ	Ite Bracha		301
PIZSHITZ	Boltche		60,73,310,311, 314,315,421,438
PIZSHITZ	David		33,391
PIZSHITZ		Heirs	443
PIZSHITZ	Yitzchak		43,51,58, 72,143,160,200, 301,313,354,385,417,420,437
PIZSHITZ	Mendel		224
PIZSHITZ	KOPEL		391
PIZYK	Shmuel		34,49,50, 60,91,92,130,154, 164,247,258,260,301, 339,346,351,379,382,391,402,404
PITERMAN	Moshe		483
FAIGENBAUM		Glazier	156
FAIGENBAUM	Abraham		483
FAIGENBAUM	Aaron		483
FAIGENBAUM	Asher	Carpenter	71,174,175,261, 415,436
FAIGENBAUM	Asher	Glazier	81,84,185,189, ,240
FAIGENBAUM	Berel	"Maccabi"	240
FAIGENBAUM	Berel	Australia	483
FAIGENBAUM	Baruch		63,424
FAIGENBAUM	Zeliye		74,256,284,415,479
FAIGENBAUM	Chaia		58,417
FAIGENBAUM	Chaim		483
FAIGENBAUM	Yehoshua		174,415
FAIGENBAUM	Yitzchak		443
FAIGENBAUM	Israel Yitzchak		251
FAIGENBAUM	Leibl	Israel	197

FAIGENBAUM	Leibl	Uruguay	479
FAIGENBAUM	M.I.		4----480
FAIGENBAUM	Michael		483
FAIGENBAUM	Miriam		483
FAIGENBAUM	Moshe		74,203,415,439
FAIGENBAUM	Moshe	Glazier	84,185,443
FAIGENBAUM	Moshe	*Melamed*	252
FAIGENBAUM	Fradl		203
FAIGENBAUM	Rivka		197
FAIGENBAUM	Sholkaleh		252,255
FAIGENBAUM	Sheindel		483
FAIGENBAUM	Shalom		199
FAIGENBAUM	Shmuel		443
FAIGENBAUM-GERSZKOP	Bluma		74,439
	Faiga Frimes		149,260,443
	Faivel		226
	Faivel Frog	Nickname	211
	Faivele LUBLINER	*Melamed*	251
	Faivele	*Melamed*	252,260
	Feinkl		163
FIREMAN	Avigdor		45,147
FIREMAN	Michael		225,230,231,253
Philadelphia			476
Philipova			56
PHILIPOVER		Philipover Rabbi	56,413
PILSUDSKI			40,42,139,141,344,357
FINGERHUT			481
FINGERHUT	Yoel		214,236
Pintchev			14,103
	Pinyele	Bagel Baker	55,262,412,443
Pinsk			9,10,19,96, 108,109,250,331,461
PINSKI	D.		245

PINSKER	L.		335
PINES	Dr.	Dr.	379
PINES	Yechiel		334

[Page 497]

Surname (in capitals) or Place name	Name	Remarks	Page number(s)
FINKELHAUS			160
FINKELSTEIN	Abraham		305
FINKELSTEIN	Aizik		301,306
FINKELSTEIN	Dr. Butche		192,193,238,245,246, 302,304,310,356
FINKELSTEIN		Brothers	160
FINKELSTEIN	Devorah		301
FINKELSTEIN	Chaim Israel		252,253
FINKELSTEIN		Heirs	443
FINKELSTEIN	Yakov		305
FINKELSTEIN	Israel Ritker		78,181,200,201, 305,307
FINKELSTEIN	Leibl		193,242,244, 245,483
FINKELSTEIN	Motel		53,409
FINKELSTEIN	Menachem		58,72,202, 203,237,243,417,437
FINKELSTEIN	Moshe		214,217
FINKELSTEIN	Fiszel		149,175,241,307,313
FINKELSTEIN	Tziporah		356,446,447
FINKELSTEIN	Shabtai		64,76,259,425,443,444,465
FINKELSTEIN-CYNAMON			443
Piotrkov			270,281,331,374
PIATSHITZKI			40,41,139,140
PIAKARZKI	Mordechai (Motel)		45,80,147,153,183,229,245,246
PICON	Molly		263
PIRANDELLO			357
Pishatz			25,29,119,124
	R' Fiszel Shtrizhever	From Shtrizhev	269

FISZLEDER	Berel		480
FISZMAN	Berish		153
FISZMAN			227
FISZMAN	Shmuel	Hotel owner?	75,227,442,443
FISZMAN	Shmuel		472
FISZMAN-ORLANSKI	Chaialeh (Hela)		235,310
FISCHMAN-MAIMON	Yehuda Leib Hacohen	Rabbi (Rabiner)	272
FISCHER	Yehoshua		32,39,78,79, 128,129,138,180,181, 182,199,200,230,231, 308,324,325, 326,470,471
FISCHER	Rivkah		204,306, 308,325,326
PLATT	Itke		74,197,439
PLATT	Alter		72,436
PLATT	Yosel		261
PLATT	Simcha		444
PLATAO		Dr.	355
PLOTNIKOV	Moshe		196
FLAM	Dov Berish		269
FLORINSKI		Dr.	305
FLUR	Nachum		280
PLUR	Eliezer		443
PLUR	Yehudit		453
FLICHTENRAJCH	Yakov		161
FLEK		Nickname: *Melamed*	252
	R' Pinchas	Rabbi (Rabiner)	268
	Pinchas Ben Shmuel		10,97
	Pinchas Maier		34,35,131,132
	Pesach Skos		256,380
	Pesach Rishon ["the first"]	*Melamed*	252
	Pesach Sheni ["the second"]	*Melamed*	252
	Pesachl Montsher ["the little one"]		207
	"Pesil" [nickname]		54

Peterburg			9,19,79,96,108, 173,181,207,210, 226,270,297,345,347
PETERBURG	Yankel David		255
PETERBURG	Yitzchak		45,147,171
PETLIURA			359
PETERSON			54,55,62, 411,412,422,423
FELDMAN			153
FELDMAN	Elyahu		470
FELDMAN	Chaia		65,427,466
FELDMAN	Yosef		443
FELDMAN	Yitzchak		65,427
FELDMAN		Schoolteacher	230
FELDMAN	Moshe		172,178,245
FELDMAN	Nachkeh		211,477
FELDMAN	Ruven		149,194
FELDMAN	Shmuel		65,427
FELDMAN	Dr. Simcha Bunim		201
FELDRYB	Yosef		235,236
FELZENSTEIN	Dasia		226
FELZENSTEIN	Hershel		203
FELMAN	Israel		156
Penza			304
PESTMAN	Yosef		246
	Pesl the "deaf one"		371,372
Perth			483
PEREL	Yosef		479
PEREL	Moshe		479
PEREL	Moshe Aaron		284
PERLOV	Ben-Emi		361
PERLOV	Yitzchak		242,360,361
PERKELVALD	Abraham		483
PERKELVALD	Binyamin		483
PERKELVALD	Leibl		483

PERKELVALD	Motel		483
PERKELVALD	Moshe		483
Prague			15,103,379
	Fradl Shemed		91
FROMMER	Yehuda Aryeh		278
FRANCE	Anatol		359
FRANK	Chava		267
FRANK	Yakov		18,19,107,108,266, 267,268
Frankfurt Am Oder			268
Frankfurt Am Main			18,108,270,359
FRANKREICH	Shlomo Eliezer		251
FRANKREICH	Shmuel		219
FROPESS	Aaron		199
Proshuki			55,163,164,412
Pruzhane			10,27,29,96,122,124,365,366
	Froim [Efraim] the Yellow one		158
FRUCHTENBERG	M.		482
PRUSKIN	Pesach	Kovriner Rabbi	280
Prushkov			353
FRIEDBERG	Yosef		174,175
FRIEDBERG	(Family)	Family	161
FRIEDBERG	Sonia		310,311
FRIEDLANDER		Barber-surgeon	304
FRIEDMAN			84,189,229,240
FRIEDMAN	Avigdor		443
FRIEDMAN	Itzele	Buenos Aires	480
FRIEDMAN	Breindel		483
FRIEDMAN	Chaim		53,65,409,427
FRIEDMAN	Chaim (Beznosek)		55,412
FRIEDMAN	Yakov	Australia	483
FRIEDMAN	Yakov		67,71,430,436
FRIEDMAN	Yitzchak		65,418,427

FRIEDMAN	Yitzchak	Australia	483
FRIEDMAN	Israel	Chortkover Rabbi	280
FRIEDMAN	Leibush		160
FRIEDMAN	Mendeleh Sitniker		167,380,443
FRIEDMAN	Miriam		169
FRIEDMAN	Moshe		202
FRIEDMAN	Noach		160
FRIEDMAN	Faivel		364
FRIEDMAN		From the Kresen ?	58,418
FRIEDMAN		Wife	74,439
FRIEDMAN	Froim		223
FRIEDMAN	Froike		240
FRIEDMAN	Shamai		168,169, 177,207,210 ,214,479,483
FRITZ			51,407
FRITCHE		Dr.	75,440
FREIND	Zelig		253,331
FREIND	Yakov		244
FREIND	Miriam		244,245
FREIND	Naftali Yosef Halevi	Ruzhaner Rabbi	270
FREIND	Tana		169,177,214,215
FRAINER	Baruch		54,69,331,410,411, 433
PRILUTSKI	Noach		82,187,226
FRITZ	Dr.	Dr.	75,440
FRISHTIK	Moshe		162,199, 200,243
FRISHMAN	Dr.		277
FRISHMAN	Leahleh	Dr.	482
PRETER	Bluma		74,439
PRETER	Yitzchak		60,421
PRETER	Moshe		53,55,161, 204,409,412
PRETER		Family	154
PRETER	Pinchas		453,464
FREY	Woman		415
FRANKEL	Golda		339

FRANKEL	Ruven Israel Halevi		339
Pressburg			19,109
PERETZ	Y. L.		34,131,229,236,243,248, 286,344,455,476
PSHIVISHEVSKI			484
PSHIGODA		Dr.	304
Pshischa			273,282,294
PRZEWIZMAN	David		302,311
Przsemysl			14,103
PRZEKOVNIK			470
Petach Tikvah			46,148

צ Tzadik

TZADOK			308
	Tzalke	*Melamed*	251
TZADOK	Shlomo		192,470
	R' Zvi Hirsh	Rabbi	266
FRILOKER	R'Zvi Hirsh		271

[Page 498]

Surname (in capitals) or Place name	Name	Remarks	Page number(s)
HALBERSTATER	R' Zvi Hirshele	Byala Rabbi	19,29 ,109,124,271

ק Kof

CUKER	Motel		63,424
CUKER	Froim		63,424
CUKER	Shlomo		63,4`5,424
CUKIERMAN	Alter		264,347,348
CUKIERMAN	Ideleh		444
CUKIERMAN	Itzil		265
CUKIERMAN	Chaia Zelda		153,470
CUKIERMAN	Chanan		66,429
CUKIERMAN	Faiga		197
CUKIERMAN	Slomo Yosef		284

CUKIERKAND	Ester		483
CUKIERKAND	Yakov		483
CYBULSKI			49,402
CYGELNIK	Dr. Natan		195,356,357
"Tzid"			51,61,66,67,68, 69,406,421,428, 430,431,432
CYTRYNBAUM	Chaim Yechiel		278
CYTRYNBAUM	Rachleh		276,277,278
CIMBALIST	Idel		64,426
CIMABLIST	Nechama		64,426
CIMBERKNOP	Yosef		201
ZIMERMAN			51,52,406,409
CHINOVITCH	Moshe		88
CYNAMON			238
CYNAMON	Efraim		26,120
CYNAMON	Chana		192,193,246
	Zineh	Sochashover Rebbetzin)	269,295,296,298
Tzitzibor			160
CELNIKIER	Eliezer		43,45,60,63, 143,147,153, 420,424
CELNIKIER	Baruch		191
CELNIKIER		Dentist	304
CELNIKIER	Yechiel		243,245
CELNIKIER	Franya		197
TZEPELINSKI	Henya		198
TZESHINSKI	David		162
TZESHINSKI	Menashe		43,143,170,171
Tzefat (Safed)			10,96,261,470
KOBRIN			10,96,280,349
KOBRIN	L.		244
KOGAN	Helena Adolfovna		164,301
KOGUT			450
Kodnya			26,119
KAHAN	Yakov		258,358,363,370,477,478

KAHAN	Rey		358,478
KAHAN	Shmuel		171,172, 178,258,370,481
KOWALEVSKI		Engineer	93
KOWARSKI-GOLDBERG	Manya		68,71,431,435
Kovno			230
KAWE	Antshel		345
KAWE	Benyamin		226
KAWE	Chava		226,230
KAWE	Chaim		203,230
KAWE	Yankel		262
KAWE	Motel		262
KAWE	Mendel		80,183,184,238
KAWE	Moshe		42,45,58,78,79, 83,142,147,171,180,181, 182,188,241 251, 255 301,303,305 306,307,313,345, 346,416
KAWEL			457
KAUFMAN	David		474,475
KAUFMAN	Chone		474
KAUFMAN	Rifka		475
KOSAKL		Nickname	230
	Koze (goat)	Nickname	69,433
KOZES	Dr.	Dr.	449
KOT			50,404
Katowitz			52,72,304, 335,407
KOTELANSKI	Chaim		235
Kolodny			250
KOLTON	Shmuel		200
KALICHSZTEJN	Abraham		154,176
KALICHSZTEJN	Blumah		199
KALICHSZTEJN	Golda		449
KALICHSZTEJN	Cheyma		173,438
KALICHSZTEJN	Shamai		45,147,176,314
KALINA	Chana		482

KALINA	Shimon		482
Kalish			339
KALISHER	Hirsh		335
Kolna			270
KOLKER			216
KAMINSKI			166
KAMINSKI	Neta		281
Kamyomka			279
KAMIEN			203
KAMIEN	Akiva		39,138
Kamienets Litovsk			28,122,334
Kamienets Podlaski			18,107,108,267
KAMLET			251
KAMLET	Aita Gumpels		251
KAMLET	Family	Family	154
KAMELMACHER	Abraham		212,213
Kamene			77,180
KANALBOIM			230,231,233
KANALSTEIN			235
KANALSTEIN	Idel Tzines		351,382
KANALSTEIN	Binyamin		351,352
Konopka			55,412
KANTOR	David		64,72,171,191,425,437
KANTOR	Fiszel		60,420
KANTOR	Sara		64,425
KANTOROVITCH			235
KANIER	Itsheh		415,464
KANITZKI-FEIGENBAUM	Mindel		483
Constantin (Wolhyn)			18,107,108,266, 267,268
Constantin			26,40,60,61,93,120,139, 420
Kopotchetz			268
Kapolye			365

Kapizha			478
	Kopel Ben Yitzchak		9,96
Copenhagen			364
KAPLAN	Eliezer Hacohen		366
KATZ	Nete		256
KAZISNE	Alter		245
KATZENELENBOGEN	Leib		334
Kock			10,96,258,266, 269,295
Kokovtzew			173
KAROL XII		Swedish King	89
KORALIK	Abraham		217,237
KORALIK	Abraham Yitzchak		154
KORALIK	Gitel		482
KORALIK	Menucha		217
KORALIK	Moshe		217,482
KORTCHAK	Yanush		318
Karlin			335,336
KORMAN	Meir		80,174,183, 199,259,260,284,384
KORNBLUM	Ida		451,452
KORNBLUM	Yakov		52,53,64,69, 153,174,175, 191,407,409,425,432
KORNBLUM	Moshe		69,432
KORNBLUM	Sheindel		64,425
KORNBERG	Fritz		80,81,183,186,366,367
KORNHENDLER	Raizel		483
KARNIL	Berl	Rabbi	279
KORENYOW		Governor	32,128,130,212
KARPINSKI			67,68,429,431
KARSHENBAUM	Sanyeh		240,246
KARSHENBAUM	Shimon		222
KASHTENBAUM	Aaron		443
KASHTENBAUM	Chaim Yosef		31,79,82,84, 93,126,176,181, 187,190,204, 205,223, 226,227,236,260,301,305,388
KASHTENBAUM	Manya		235

KASHEMACHER	Chanina		45,63,64,72, 174,171,284,303,314,424, 425,426,437,473
KASHEMACHER	Perl		64,245,426
KOIFMAN	Yitzchak		72,436
KOCHAZHEVSKI			64,245,426
KOCHAYEVSKI			93
KONITZKI			49,402
KOSEVITZKI	Moshe		316
KUPERSCHMIDT	Chanina		177
KUPERSCHMIDT	Shlomo		217
Kurow			14,103
KUROPATVA	Moshe		154,443
DE LEOR	Kurt		448,453
KUSHMIRAK	Yehuda Leib		339
KUSZCZYC	Abraham		30,126
Lochamei Haghetaot		Kibbutz	353,484
KIEHEL	Hubert		52,68,75,407,410,419,432,440
	Kieve [Akiva]	Melamed	252
KAIYOVSKI			84,92,190,227,244
Kiev			215,321,460
Kielce			82,186,374
KIRSCHROIT			317,318
Kishinew			77,179
KLADNYEV		Wife	314
KLOTZ	Eliyahu Reisels		213,214,245,330
KLIGBERG	Baruch Senders		258
KLIGBERG	David		153,154,258,443

[Page 499]

Surname (in capitals) or Place name	Name	Remarks	Page number(s)
KLIGSBERG	Sender		199
KLIGSBERG	Moshe Chaim		252

KLIGSBERG	Matityahu		230,231
KLIGSBERG	Shmuel		252,253,265,443
KLIGER			216
KLIGER	Benyamin		44,45,77,78,86, 145,146,147,158,160,174, 175, 180,191,198,204,206,214, 255,261,303,472
KLIGER	Berl		482
KLIGER	Yehoshua		236,472
KLIGER	Leibl		482
KLIGER	Motl		482
KLIGER	Mendel		481,482
KLIGER-KLEMFNER	Chana		481,482
Cleveland			476
KLEINBOIM			452
KLIMETZKI	W.		91,92,93,149,345
KLING	Chaninale		208,211,213,260
KLIF			17,106
KLEMPNER	Henia Riveh		482
KLEMPNER	Yedidiya		482
KLEMPNER	Yermiahu		481
KLEMPNER	Malka		482
KLEMPNER-SZTERNFELD	Yosef		481,482
Kleck			366
KNIZHNIK	Eliyahu		203
KNIZHNIK	Chaim Yosef		74,256,439,463,472
KNIZHNIK	Leah		74,439
KNIZHNIK	Shalom		197
KEDROW		Governor	218
Koeln			78,191
KEMPINSKI	Ch.		218
KERNER	Moshe	Engineer (Senator)	82,160,187,349
KERSH	Leibl		216
KRAVIETS/ KRAWEC	Gedalyahu		225,230,231,253

KRAVIETS/ KRAWEC	Michael		170
Kravtzow			33,130
KROCHMALSKI			245
KRAMARZ	Gdalyahu		20,481
KRAMARZ	Yakov		200
KRAMARZ	Maye		198
KRAMARZ	Moshe		43,45,143, 147,225,230,231,253
KRAMARZ	Noach		171,176
KRAMARZ	Sara		192,193,302,304
KRONE	Moshe		201
KRASKOVSKI	Benedict		56,414,415
Krakow			23,29,76,89,179,270,280
KROSHNIK			98,270,282
KRASHEVSKI			9,93,95
KROGMAN	H. I.		315,316
Krivtchin			267,268
KREIDESZTEIN			198
KREIDESZTEIN	Abraham Yakov		226,230
KREIDESZTEIN	Baruch Shalom		251,252,379
KREIDESZTEIN	Leibaleh		261
KREIDESZTEIN	Shlomo		252,316
KREIDESZTEIN	Shimeon		77,78,154,180,251,255,261,339,346
KRAIZELMAN	Dobe		51,406
KRAIZELMAN	Laibl		153
KRAIZELMAN	Shalom		201
KRAIZELMAN	Shmuel		60,72,153,420,437
KRAIZELMANS		Family	160
KSHIMOVSKY			31,42,127,141

ר   Resh

RAABE			48,51,53,54,68, 72,159,160, 222,234,301,325,352,401,409,411,431,436
RAABE	Bernard		32,127,159
RAABE	Hersh Ber		159

RAABE	Vincenti		159
RAABE	Yakov		159
RAABE	Maurici		159
ROBAK			310
RABINOVITZ	Avraham	Lublin Rabbi	264,274,283
RABINOVITZ	Aaron Natan David		274
RABINOVITZ	Hershele	Szeidlicer Rabbi	262,264,274,283.300
RABINOVITZ	Chanale		274
RABINOVITZ	Yehoshua Baruch		199
RABINOVITZ	Yehoshuele		295,296,297, 298
RABINOVITZ	Yechiel		340
RABINOVITZ	Yitzchak Yakov	Biala Rabbi	162,225, 248,264,271,273, 274,275,283,299,303,3811,392
RABINOVITZ	Motele		274
RABINOVITZ	Meir Shlomo Yehuda	Mezritcher Rabbi	274,283
RABINOVITZ	Moshe		240
RABINOVITZ	Natan David	Szidlevzer Rabbi	273,283
RABINOVITZ	Tzine		299
ROGALSKI	Chava		302
ROGALSKI	Shalom		84,190,470
Rogizhnitze			78,181
ROGINSKI			30,125
Radom			274
RADZIMIN			282
RADZYN			11,14,23,27,29, 82,98,103,122,124,176,177, 178,186,304,449,452
RODZYNEK	Abraham		64,426
RODZYNEK	Havale		369,373,374
RODZYNEK	Israel		71,436
RODZYNEK	Leibl		55,436
RODZYNEK	Manes		217
RODZYNEK	Moshe		42,43,52,60, 142,144,154,169, 171,172,174, 175,215,227,310,314,373,407,420
RODZYNEK	Noach		75,442

RODZYNEKS		Family	75,442
RADZINER		*Melamed*	252
RADZINER	Rifka		483
RADZINER		Nickname: Shneider (tailor)	315
RADZHIVIL			9,10,95,96,109,162, 163,254,266,392,393,394
RADZHIVIL	Dominik		20,89,110
RADZHIVIL	Michael Kazhimierush		89
RADZHIVIL		Family	9,11,12,270
RADZHIVIL	Karol		89
RADZHIVIL (SHERATKA)			89
RADLINSKI		Prof. Dr.	354,355
RAVITCH	Meleh		359
Rovno			355
ROZMARIN	A.D.		304
ROZMARIN	Gershon		193
ROZMARIN	Chaim		69,73,162,231,235,241,242, 244,245,246,432,437
ROZMARIN	Chana		203
ROZMARIN	Motl		385,391,394
ROZMARIN	Melech		235
ROZMARIN-SIRKUS	Zisel		74,439
ROZEN-ROZANKER	Yitzchak		482
ROZENBAUM	Baila		475
ROZENBAUM	Devorale		245
ROZENBAUM	Vovtshe		415
ROZENBAUM	Chaia		60,73,226,421,438
ROZENBAUM	Yehoshua		470
ROZENBAUM	Yechiel		284
ROZENBAUM		Heirs	443
ROZENBAUM	Yakov (Jack)		473,474,475,476,
ROZENBAUM	Yakov Aaron		43,45,53,56,57, 59,60,72,73, 83,86,143,147,174,326,327,389, 408,413,415,418,420,437,438

ROZENBAUM	Yezhy		72,437
ROZENBAUM	Yitzchak		240
ROZENBAUM	Yishayahu		483
ROZENBAUM	Moshe		271
ROZENBAUM	Zvi		219
ROZENBAUM	Kalman		284
ROZENBLATT	Shimon		72,436
ROZENBLUM	Abik Ogrodnik		153,315, 316,377,443,460, 482
ROZENBLUM	Blume		197
ROZENBLUM	Chaim		377
ROZENBLUM	Yoske		460
ROZENBLUM	Rahel		198
ROZENBERG			69,433
ROZENBERG	David		74,439
ROZENBERG	Chaim Mordechai		153
ROZENBERG	Yosef		41,140
ROZENBERG		Heirs	443
ROZENBERG	Perl		364
ROZENWORCEL	Berke		479
ROZENWORCEL	Chaia Hodel		479
ROZENWORCEL	Chilish		479
ROZENWORCEL	Shlomeleh		479
ROZENTHAL	Breindl		204
ROZENMAN	Chaim		479
ROZENFELD	Zelig		84,189,192,193, 470
ROZENFELD	Moshe		240
ROZENFELD	Simcha		443
ROZENCWEIG	Asher		53,235,236, 240,409
ROZENCWEIG	Chaia		235
ROZENCWEIG		Heirs	356,443

[Page 500]

Surname (in capitals) or Place name	Name	Remarks	Page number(s)
ROZENCWEIG	Yakov		149,187
ROZENCWEIG	Motl		475,476
ROZENKER		Brothers	256
ROZENKER	Yakov		72,436
ROZENKER	Ruven		481
ROZENKRANZ	Meite		370
ROZENKRANZ	Nachman		260,370
ROZENSTEIN	Moshe Gabriel		256
ROZENSHEIN	Ida		65,427
ROZENSHEIN	Chana		65,427
ROZENSHEIN	Yitzchak (Itzke)		39,138,443
ROZENSHEIN	Kroseh		65,427
ROZENSHEIN		Sisters	483
ROSE		Professor	356
ROZEN	Zushe		43,45,142, 143,147,219, 256,303
ROZEN	Shepsel		176,177
ROZEN-KALICHSTEIN	Bashia		449
ROZEN-ROZENBAUM			74,439
RATAYEWITZ			160
ROTENBERG			227
ROTENBERG	Abraham		198,200
ROTENBERG	Aaron		482
ROTENBERG	Hersh Yoel		463
ROTSHILD	Mendel	Bamberger Rabbi	270
RATSHIN	Sholem		77,179,180,225, 230,241
ROMANOVSKI			218
ROMMEL		Fieldmarshal	75,442
RAMES	Chaim		259,307

RAMES	Malka		470
RAMES	Natan		45,147,219,259
Rossasz			26,51,119,381,407
Rossoszitz			339
Rostow			354
RASNER			474
Rishon Letzion			484
	Rivka		266
	Rivka Akivaches		370,371
RUBINLICHT	Chaialeh		370
RUBINSZTEIN			443
RUBINSZTEIN	Avigdor		219
RUBINSZTEIN	Itke		174,236,368
RUBINSZTEIN	Eizhshe		67,74,430,439
RUBINSZTEIN	Ester		46,147
RUBINSZTEIN	Bonim		238
RUBINSZTEIN	Berish		240,241,470
RUBINSZTEIN		Dr.	52,303,304,407
RUBINSZTEIN	Chaim		203,245
RUBINSZTEIN	Chaim Levi		31,43,45,77, 79,91,93,126,143,147, 149,151,154,160, 172,174,179,183,219,231,238,284
RUBINSZTEIN	Yhoshua		72,284,437
RUBINSZTEIN	Yocheved		46,147
RUBINSZTEIN	Yakov David		200,340
RUBINSZTEIN	Yitzchak Sofer	Scribe	45,147
RUBINSZTEIN	Yitzchak	Lubartov	46,147
RUBINSZTEIN	Israel		46,147
RUBINSZTEIN	Leib		223
RUBINSZTEIN	Masha		223
RUBINSZTEIN	Menachem		252,253,260,276,341
RUBINSZTEIN		Suwalki	73,437
RUBINSZTEIN	Roizeh		204
RUBINSZTEIN	Rahel		204,446,447

RUBINSZTEIN	Shmuel Shochet	Ritual slaughterer	251,480
RUBINSZTEIN	Shmuel Yankel		252
RUBINSZTEIN	Shmuel Yakov	Paris Rabbi	46,148,252,260,277,300
RUBINSZTEIN	Shmuel Tanchum Halevi	Rabbi in Givatayim	274,340,341
RUBINSZTEIN	Sara		198
RUBINSZTEIN	Sara	Israel	244,245
RUBINSZTEIN-LUSTIGMAN	Toibele		74,192,193,235,311,400
RUBINSZTEIN-RAPAPORT	Chana Rifka		308,309,470
RUBINSZTEIN-RAVON	Moshe		36,39,42,46,78,79, 80,82,83,85,94,134, 138,142,148,162,180,182, 183,184, 186,188,191,192,193, 230,231,234,235,238, 241,305, 308,322,323,324,393,355,366,470,472
Rodges		Kibbutz	201
RODNITZKI		Staroste	140
RVIGA	Abraham		16,29,105,124
RUZAL			270
Rozhan			270
RUZHINSKI			164
ROIZNER	Ides		304
Rome			19,108
ROMSHINSKI	Yosef		263
Rechovot			79,181
SHEIN	Rachel (Shein)		370
RYBAK	Dr. Yosef		480
RYBAK	Yakov		154
RYBAK	Leibl		480
RYBAK	Poliya		74,439
RYBAK	Pinyeh		78,181
RIVLIN	Zalman		334
Riga	RIGA		54,410
RIDLEVITZ	Gedalyahu		65,427
RITB"A			276

RAIS	Yakov		443
RAISWASSER	Yesahiahu		233,443
	Reizele		34,131
	Reizele from the Pletzelach	Reizele "from the little cakes" (she sold little cakes)	265
REICH	Chana Rachel		75,442
REICH	Chanan		54,411,412
REICH	Dr. Leon		321
REICH	Family	Family	153
REICHENBACH			463
REIMONT		St.	90
REITZ	Meir		54,411
REIKLER	Moshe		221
RICHTER	Avigdor		33,129
RICHTER	Avigdor	Porter	216,255,315,443
RICHTER	Ester		482
RICHTER	Hirsh	Carpenter	332
RICHTER	Yosel		482
RICHTER	Leybish		153
RICHTER	Moshe	Paris	481
RICHTER	Moshe Tatu		38,136
RICHTER	Ethel		64,425
RICHTER			309
Ramat Gan			30,46,88,89,148, 399
Reshitza			460

ש **Shin**

Schau			325
	Shloyme	Cemetery attendant	285
SHAPIRA			204
SHAPIRA	Yoel		199,307
SHAPIRA	Israel Elyahu		253,307
SHAPIRA	Meir	Liblin Rabbi	276

SHAPIRA	Moshe	Minister	319
SHAPIRA-ORLANSKI	Golda		68,431
SHOR			235
SHOR	Wolf		302,479
SHOR	Moshe		153
SHOSHKES	Dr. Chaim		278
	R' Shabtai		268,270
	R' Shabtai COHEN	The SHACH	19,109,284,392
	Shabatai Zvi		16,18,105,106, 266,267
SCHWABE		Dr.	80,184,367,368
SCHWACH		S.S. man	50,405
SCHWARTZ	Idel		32,78,79,127,173,181,182,255, 301,303,305,313, 346,347,370
SCHWARTZ	Aizik		173,176,241,242,310,000
SCHWARTZ	Luba		310,314
SCHWARTZ	Shmelke		68,154,199,431
SCHWARTZBARD	Shlomo Chaim		252,253
SCHWARTZBERG	Yakov		170,244
SCHWARTZBERG	Liba		244
SCHWARTZBERG	Sara		198,199
SHUVAK			227
SCHWEITZER	Isidor		473
SHULMAN			415
SHULMAN	Yakov		281
SHULMAN	Ruven Kozes		158,167,281
SHULTZ	Faiga		482
SCHUMACHER	David		473
SCHUSTER	Devorah		216
SCHUSTER	Wolf		169,177,215, 216,217,218,476
SHACHOR	Aizik		258,271
SHACHOR	David R'Aizik's	Son of R'Aizik	31,126,164,219,370
SHACHOR	Hinda		235
SHACHOR	Hershel		235,307,443

Surname (in capitals) or Place name	Name	Remarks	Page number(s)
SHACHOR	Yocheved		263
SHACHOR	Yechezkel		346,370
SHACHOR	Yitzchak Aizik		256,272,369
SHACHOR	Leibele		258,259
SHACHOR	Noach		164,219, 251,259,263,272,275 ,337,338,341,358,370
SHACHOR	Noach	Nyeswetch-Vilna	370
SHACHOR	Sheime		370
SHTOLMACHER			481
STEITELMAN	Yosef Nachum		150
STEIN	Max		477
STEINBERG	Moshe		65,74,427, 439,452,454

[Page 501]

Surname (in capitals) or Place name	Name	Remarks	Page number(s)
STEINBERG	Elke		65,74,427,439, 453,454
STEINGART	Henich		219
STEINGART	Motel		63,153,424
STEINGART		Wife	315
STEINGART	Shlomo		63,72,424,436
STEINMAN	Godya		59,62,197,343,369, 373,419,420,423
STEINMAN	Yonah		42,80,142,183 202,230,231, 237,245,246, 308,342,475,476
STEINMAN	Yakov		59,78,79, 168,172,180,182,191,199, 225,230,231,234,308,309,342, 343,367,419
SZTILHAMER	Raizele		373
SZTILHAMER	Shmuel		373
SZTILHAMER			70,71,72,430,434,436
SZTROMWASER	Isser		247
SZTROMWASER	Velvel		158,247
SZTROMWASER	Yoel		45,147,170,171, 172,178,256,284
SZTROMWASER	Yosef		247
SZTROMWASER	Meir		247

SZTROMWASER	Moshe		247
Sztcheczyn			462
SHTEFANSKI	Stefan		49,402,405
Szidlovski			62,422
SZIEWAK	Nachman		227,230,233
SHEIN	Chaia		230
SHEIN	Yonah		235
SHEIN	Yitzchak (Aizik)		171,197,203,235, 246,355,369
SHEINBAUM	Bella		472
SHEINBAUM	Yehoshua		470
SHEINBAUM	Moshe David	Rope maker	315,470
SHEINBAUM	Tzirl		198
SHEINBERG			204
SHEINBERG			74,439
SHEINBERG	Aaron		271
SHEINBERG	Aizik (Ayshe)		43,45,143,147,153 ,176,177,219,313
SHEINBERG	Henich		176,177
SHEINBERG	Hershel		284
SHEINBERG	Moshe		67,430
SHEINBERG		Family	154
SHEINBERG	Kalman		31,81,85, 126,172,176,185, 190,259,301,370,443
SHEINBERG	Shaime		38,137
SHILINGOVSKI	Dr.	Dr.	305
SHILF		Paymaster	65,69,427,433
SHIMONOVITS	Mordechai		250
Shimanski			67,430
	Shimaleh, Chana Rives		92
SHIPER	Dr. Yitzchak		202
SHLOMOVITZ	Yesko		29,124
Schlossberg			246
SHOLEM ALEICHEM			226,229,236, 243,245,326,455,476
	Shalom	Butcher	252,258

	Shalom	Shamash (synagogue attendant)	256,285
SLIWKA	Mendel		204
SZLITERMAN	Elkeh		65,427
	Shlomo		450,451
	Shlomo Chaim	Melamed	284
	R' Shlomo Leib	Lentzer Rabbi	269,271,275,283
	Slomaleh Shuster	Cobbler	449,452,454
	Shmuel		209
	Shmuel from Venice		301
	Shmuel (Ben Yitzchak)	Son of Yitzhak	10,11,19, 97,98,109
	Shmuel (Ben Meir)	Meir's son	9,96
	Shmuel Moshe Antshelikhes		262
	Shmuel Moshe	Butcher	252
	Shmuel Falik		369
	Shmuel Faibish Ben Natan Fiszel	Nathan Fishel's son	19,109
	Shmuel the shopkeeper		16,104
	R'Shmuel	R' Avrahamale Sochatshever's son	295,296,298
FRIEDMAN	Shmuel Samer Zimels		223,256,328
	Simcha Tiktiner	From Tiktin	266
SCHMIDT			460
	Smileh Pop	Melamed	252
Shmyetanko			70,434
	Shimeon Ahareles	Probably Aharon's son	259
	R'Shimeon	Skiernivitzer Rabbi	273,274
	Shimeon Shochet	Slaughterer	251
SHIMONOVICH-SHIMONI	David		41,85, 141,190,194,195
	R'Shmelke		258
	Szmerel Pep		257,443

SHAMA"R			224
	Shimshon Partsever	From Partzev	264
SZNIR	Avigdor		483
SZNIR	Leizer		169,215
SZNIR	Faiga		249
SZNAIDMIL		Wife	314
SZNAIDER	Dr.	Dr.	304
SZNAIDER	Abraham		483
SZNAIDER	Hinda		483
SZNAIDER	Yakov		483
SZNAIDER	Ethel		483
SZNAIDERMAN	Ester		217
SZNAIDERMAN	Berel		415
SZNAIDERMAN	(Brothers)	Brothers	65,72,427,436
SZNAIDERMAN	M.	Montreal	482
SZNAIDERMAN	Moshe		217,237,244
SZNAIDERMAN	Rachel Leah		65,427
SZNAIMAN	Hershel		403
SZNAIMAN	Chana		198,204
SZNAIMAN	Leah	.	197
SZNAIMAN	Moshe		160,443,466
Szczebrzeszyn			251,275
SHEDLINITZKI		Minister	17,106,107
Seidlice			10,11,16,21, ,23,24,25,29,30, 32,33,77,78,79,83, 90,96,98,105,111, 112,115,116, 118,128,131,180,181,182, 188,241,264,300,301,302 304,317,320, 321,325,364,390,424,445
Szentz			241
SHERIFF	R. K.		344
SHERMAN	Itche		226
SHERMAN	M.		474
Shereshov			270
SPACK			165
SPIEGEL			261

SPRINGER			34,130
SPRINTZAK	Yosef		332
SFAT EMET		Gerer Rabbi (the Rabbi of Gur)	271,275,337,370
	Shraga	Cobbler	215,307
	Sara Tzirl *di bekerin*	"The woman baker"	66,429
TIDHAR	David		340
TOSFOT YOM TOV			392
Tel-Aviv			4,7,79, 95,148,181,184,203, 262,270,32,,332,333,340, 360,361, 369,445,471,472

NAME INDEX

A

Aaronivitz, 257
Abramovicz, 452
Abramovits, 602
Abramowicz, 396
Achimeir, 241
Ackerman, 81
Adelstein, 66
Adler, 416, 425, 591, 592, 603
Adlershtein, 158, 169, 180, 184
Adlerstein, 72, 246
Adlersztajn, 511, 521
Adller, 213
Agers, 39
Agres, 108, 205, 208, 585
Agress, 158, 185, 227, 230, 603
Agrodnik, 598
Aguda, 50, 52
Ahimeir, 604
Ahrele, 478
Aidelman, 185, 300
Aidelshtein, 274
Aideltuch, 185
Aitkin, 105
Ajdelman, 314
Ajzenberg, 552
Akerman, 395, 608
Akivaches, 457, 458
Akulah, 608
Alderstein, 603
Aleichem, 273, 274, 277, 286, 288, 299, 300, 302, 566, 591, 688
Aleikhem, 353, 411
Aleksander, 607
Alexander 1st, 138
Alshvanger, 225
Altbier, 184
Altbir, 82, 531, 606
Alter, 153, 180, 337, 340, 417, 422, 457, 607
Altona, 606
Amiel, 426, 662
Amshinov, 607
Antsheliches, 326
Apel, 510, 608
Apelboim, 589
Appelboim, 233, 575, 608
Apple, 65
Applebaum, 54, 82, 313, 662
Appleboim, 246, 311
Aranovitch, 594
Aranowitz, 311
Aranowycz, 585
Aranski, 239
Arbant, 608
Arbitman, 460, 608
Arges, 207, 209, 395
Argess, 241
Arkhangelsk, 608
Arnshtein, 299
Aronovich, 5
Aronovicz, 121, 178, 301, 302
Aronovitch, 251

Aronovitsh, 261
Aronovitz, 608
Aronowitz, 55
Aronski, 608
Aronsky, 276, 277, 279
Asch, 446
Asenhaltz, 557
Ash, 118, 288, 302, 477, 609
Ashberg, 312, 585, 609
Asher, 185, 311, 312, 345, 349, 636
Ashkenazi, 17, 40, 134, 336, 609, 658
Ashkenazy, 609
Assenzatziye, 478
Asz, 384
Atinger, 39
Auerbach, 604
August Iii, 136, 604
Avijes, 585
Avyess, 603
Aybeshitz, 133, 134, 135
Aydelman, 261
Aydelman-Stricher, 302
Aydelsberg, 177, 265
Aydelshtein, 177
Aydeltuch, 295, 303, 304
Aydltuch, 293
Azarekaver, 327
Azoulai, 123, 133, 152
Azoulay, 604
Azulai, 7, 16, 17, 33, 34

B

Baal Machshavot, 613
Babitch, 609
Bachrach, 95, 184, 204, 205, 214, 531, 544, 558, 579
Bachrach–Finkelstien., 559
Bachrach-Sapir, 559
Bachrah, 579
Backerman, 255
Badchan, 478
Bagreber, 479
Bakrach, 82, 609, 610
Bakrach-Finkelsztein, 610
Bakrach-Sapir, 610
Balaban, 24, 34, 152, 610
Balbirski, 610
Baldiga, 65, 69, 72, 510, 516, 521, 610
Balman, 88, 537, 610
Banke–Shtelerin, 478
Bankhalter, 242, 243, 313, 585, 610
Bar Chaim,, 134
Bar Khenokh,, 336
Bar Meir, 134, 137
Bar Natan Fytl, 136
Bar Shimon, 6, 122
Baranovsky, 272
Barazovski, 81
Barbis, 444
Barenboim, 610
Bargman, 302, 610
Barkovski, 119

Barlas, 105, 117, 221, 222, 224, 232, 279, 280, 387, 389, 400
Barlass, 102, 103, 610
Barnboim, 265
Barteless, 610
Bartoshevicz, 121, 122
Bartoshevitz, 610
Bartoszwycz, 6
Barvis, 610
Bas, 544, 564, 610, 656
Bashleger, 478
Basilbasah, 610
Bass, 471
Batchke, 319
Batchko, 54
Batchkoh, 609
Batshko, 177, 287
Batszka, 205
Batszko, 357
Bauer, 95, 544, 609
Baumholcz, 598
Baverman, 597
Bayltshe, 192
Beayin, 426
Becker, 118, 305, 465
Beckerman, 79, 98, 169, 298, 444
Beckman, 48
Bedder, 321, 478
Beder, 470
Bednarosh, 246
Bednarsh, 613
Bednarzsh, 302
Bedner, 321
Begin, 241, 613
Behme, 88, 89, 536, 537, 538
Beitel, 244, 612
Beitl, 242, 245
Beker, 326, 386, 553, 636
Bekerman, 254, 319, 329, 528, 555, 614
Beker-Murowiec, 552
Bekker, 478
Bekkerman, 260, 471, 483
Bekster, 571
Belman, 261, 286, 287, 614
Belmann, 241
Ben David, 134
Ben Meir, 6, 122
Ben Reb Naftali Hirtz, 136
Ben Shlomo Zalman, 333
Ben Shmuel, 7, 123, 335
Ben Tzvi, 134
Ben Yaakov, 8
Ben Ya'akov, 124
Ben Yechezkel, 465
Ben Yitschak, 20
Ben Yitzchak, 122, 123, 124, 137
Ben Yitzhak, 7
Ben Yitzhak, 6
Benayahu, 613
Bendarzsh, 294
Bendelmacher, 478
Bendelmakher, 598
Berezovski, 615
Bergelson, 614
Bergman, 62, 383, 505, 589, 614
Bergner, 445, 614

Bergshtein, 115, 154, 197
Bergstein, 35, 614
Bergsztajn, 357
Berish, 338, 351, 352, 366, 367
Berkenstat Freund, 201, 203, 204, 206, 207, 213, 214, 328, 330, 351, 353, 356, 357, 377, 383, 384, 387, 390, 395, 397, 399, 492
Berlin, 96, 207, 287, 305, 318, 337, 456, 457, 549, 614
Berliner, 350, 614
Berman, 177, 184, 212, 215, 346, 397, 551, 614
Bernfeld, 614
Bernshtein, 325
Bernstajn, 586, 590
Bernstein, 66, 240
Bernsztajn, 511
Bernsztein, 614, 615
Bertoszwicz, 6
Berzowski, 530
Betsalel, 212, 478
Beznosek, 66
Bialar, 287
Bialer, 16, 17, 50, 64, 73, 76, 93, 133, 171, 240, 241, 242, 333, 337, 339, 340, 353, 354, 507, 522, 524, 542, 560, 563, 565, 570, 611
Biali, 112, 133
Bialik, 108, 411
Bibergal, 611
Bibrovski, 62, 611
Bibrowski, 504
Biderman, 59, 81, 94, 212, 244, 379, 397, 498, 530, 532, 543, 611, 612
Biebergal, 324
Biederman, 83, 180, 185, 265, 287, 301, 302, 344
Bielecki, 497
Bieletzki, 59
Biernacka, 507
Bimka, 301, 444
Bimko, 612
Binies, 103
Binshtok, 279, 612
Binstock, 284
Binyomin, 600
Birman, 600, 612
Birnbaum, 203
Birnboim, 288, 304, 612
Birshtein, 445
Birstajn, 600
Birsztein, 612
Biten, 612
Bitner, 612
Bittner, 83
Biyali, 611
Blankeider, 102
Blanklajder, 215
Blankleider, 192, 221, 231, 232, 257, 258, 280, 281, 288, 290, 295, 299, 302, 303, 454, 476, 560, 561, 600, 612, 613
Blanklider, 275, 278, 279
Blecher, 478
Blechman, 613
Blekhman, 590
Bloch, 41, 160, 612
Bloomberg, 613
Bloshtein, 271
Blosztein, 613
Bluberg, 591, 597, 613
Blumberg, 589
Blumenkranc, 540

Blumenkrantz, 73, 242
Blumenkranz, 90, 613
Blumental, 613
Blumkes, 336, 655
Blushtein, 294, 325
Blusztein, 613
Bobke, 416
Bodker (Nickname), 609
Boimhalz, 611
Boimholz, 611
Boldman, 206
Bolechover, 136
Bolekhiv, 136
Bookhalter, 564
Borenstein, 334
Borensztain, 610
Borgman, 611
Borkovski, 611
Bornshtein, 180, 184, 193, 301, 302, 323, 465
Bornstein, 311, 427
Bornsztajn, 337, 552
Bosch, 71, 76
Bosk, 611
Botshkele, 539
Bower, 560
Brachies, 251
Bradacz, 553, 589, 590, 592
Brandveinman, 615
Brandweinman, 242, 247
Brandweinmann, 243, 244, 245
Brandweiss, 413
Braranovski, 610
Bravarek, 261
Braverman, 50, 55, 100, 121, 171, 178, 189, 190, 198, 218, 228, 243,
    250, 258, 261, 262, 264, 266, 268, 275, 277, 279, 285, 288, 299,
    301, 302, 304, 314, 357, 384, 386, 410, 413, 415, 464, 465, 469,
    488, 585, 615
Bravermann, 242, 243
Brawerman, 202
Bresker, 598, 599, 616
Bril, 134, 136
Brill, 616
Brin, 616
Brisker, 189, 190
Brochel, 615
Brodach, 50, 70, 71
Brodacz, 357, 515, 517
Brodatsh, 171, 198, 258, 261, 323, 615
Brodniak, 615
Brok, 616
Brovarek, 169, 615
Browarok, 48
Bruchl, 217, 229
Brudniak, 383
Bruehl, 19
Bruell, 17
Bruhel, 4, 99, 110
Brukierer, 302
Brukirer, 222, 478
Buber, 407, 453, 611
Bubkes, 201
Buchalter, 82, 611
Buchhalter, 95, 531, 544
Buchinyik, 611
Buchner, 322, 326, 327, 611

Buchvald, 611
Buchwald, 589
Bukhinyek, 598
Bukhwald, 589
Bunim, 611
Burgman, 593
Burnshtein, 342
Busch, 511, 518, 524
Bush, 66, 611
Butchkela, 90
Butsha, 391
Byeletzki, 612
Byernatzka, 64

C

Cahan, 206
Caruk, 387, 389
Caspi-Silberberg, 644
Cava, 70
Celniker, 383, 522, 528
Celnikier, 672
Ceszinski, 203, 204
Chaikels, 269
Chamilevski, 61
Charash, 259, 302
Charasz, 203
Charni, 39, 70, 89
Charny, 575
Chavales, 636
Chaveles, 473
Chayun, 658
Chayut, 636
Chechanower, 337, 338
Chelemer, 352
Chelinov, 103
Cherny, 638
Chesdaii, 310
Cheshinski, 50
Cheshler, 325, 424
Chidushei Harim, 636
Chinovitch, 672
Chivan, 332
Chmielnitzki, 644
Chodkiewicz, 335
Chohen, 531
Chonen, 507, 528
Chossid, 132, 133
Chrielewski, 504
Cibulski, 497
Ciechanower, 351
Cimablist, 672
Cimbalist, 672
Cimberknop, 672
Cohen, 25, 29, 35, 38, 40, 50, 54, 64, 79, 82, 95, 99, 105, 136, 142,
    147, 154, 157, 159, 171, 176, 177, 180, 184, 194, 217, 218, 224,
    241, 245, 246, 248, 284, 286, 287, 298, 314, 318, 320, 322, 422,
    423, 424, 430, 433, 439, 440, 447, 470, 476, 483, 579, 643, 644
Cohen-Bernshtein, 217
Cohen-Bernstein, 99, 644
Cohen-Preter, 644
Cohen-Tzedek, 185, 644
Cohen–Tzedek, 243
Cozzakl, 278
Cuker, 671

Cukerman, 329, 357, 533, 554
Cukierkand, 672
Cukierman, 671
Cybulski, 672
Cygelnik, 672
Cyker, 515, 528
Cymbolist, 529
Cymerman, 504, 507
Cynamon, 672
Cytrynbaum, 672
Czar Nicholai The Second, 38
Czarne, 504, 598
Czarni, 201, 516, 538
Czarny, 589, 592
Czelaza, 507
Czelazni, 329, 536, 539
Czelazo, 215
Czeszler, 378
Czito, 357

D

Dancig, 338
Danzig, 623
Darm, 89
David, 16, 35, 133, 154, 185, 312, 623
Davidsohn, 623
Davidson, 241, 451, 452, 453
Davidzon, 334, 383
Davos, 71
De Leor, 676
Debos, 624
Debus, 517
Dejantshul, 82
Demblin, 624
Dembovski, 624
Dembowski, 340
Derm, 538, 624
Derventzki, 624
Derwantzki, 65
Dibever, 478
Dikler, 190, 197, 198, 199, 200, 624
Dine, 321, 322, 324
Dines, 244, 250, 624
Doctor, 31
Dogodni, 587, 596, 600
Dogodny, 185, 622
Domatchewer, 312, 416
Domatshever, 470, 478, 651
Dorfman, 65, 511, 600, 623
Dostoyevski, 623
Dostoyevsky, 411, 444
Dovid, 357
Dovid Reb Isaacs, 197, 264
Dr. Barteles, 386
Dreizen, 624
Dreizyn, 313
Drenczol, 531
Dribnin, 624
Droczkorcz, 552
Drogetchin, 416
Droshkarzh, 642
Droszkarcz, 329
Drozhkarz, 598
Drozshkarzsh, 473, 478

Drwencki, 510
Dryzin, 313
Dukow, 560
Dvorzshetz, 194
Dzebtchol, 579
Dzenczol, 210
Dzhenstal, 600
Dzhenszel, 600
Dzientchol, 624
Dzshadeliches, 449

E

Eckstein, 79, 91
Edelbaum, 5, 111, 330, 661
Edelman, 314, 605
Edelsberg, 605
Edelstein, 39, 48, 238, 590, 605, 606, 661
Edeltuch, 605
Edlbaum, 336
Edmen, 332, 333, 340
Eedes, 604
Eger, 605
Ehrenburg, 579, 581
Eiberschits, 340
Eibeschitz, 331, 333, 337
Eichman, 606
Eichmann,, 601
Eidel, 598
Eidelman, 70, 238, 244, 257, 289, 310, 311, 312, 319, 560, 600
Eidelmann, 246
Eidelshtein, 323
Eidelstein, 54, 93
Eideltuch, 231, 232, 233, 239
Eidlman, 319, 516, 554
Eidlsberg, 185, 212
Eidlsztajn, 203, 204, 206, 208, 209, 357, 542, 552
Eidltuch, 384, 553
Eiger, 420
Einbinder, 588
Eisen, 606
Eisenberg, 280, 281, 311, 606
Eisenshtat, 606
Eisenstadt, 17, 101, 331
Eisenstaedt, 54
Eisenstat, 248
Eizeek, 311
Eizenberg, 202
Eizenstadt, 20
Eizenstat, 319
Eizensztat, 203, 204
Ejdlman, 515
Ejzenberg, 202
Ekerman, 662
Ekstajn, 540, 588
Ekstein, 662
Eksztajn, 528, 540
Elbaum, 544
Elboim, 95, 661
Elchanan, 278
Elinitsh, 606
Ellie, 607
Elya, 201, 204
Elyashiv, 420, 422, 607
Emden, 17, 18, 34, 152, 662

Emdin, 134, 135, 136, 331
Emperor Jozef Ii, 6
Engels, 468, 662
Englander, 94, 662
Englender, 543
Epelbaum, 314
Eplbaum, 203, 204, 531
Eppelbaum, 172, 177
Eppelboim, 185, 261
Erdman, 379, 381, 383, 662
Erem, 246, 662
Erenburg, 662
Erenkranz, 662
Erlich, 181, 206, 212, 264, 265, 311, 322, 476, 662
Ernkranc, 385
Ernkrantz, 286
Esray, 476
Essenholz, 608
Esther The, 459
Etinger, 661
Ettinger, 158
Eybeschuetz, 17, 18
Eybeschütz, 605

F

Faigenbaum, 664, 665
Faigenbaum-Gerszkop, 665
Faisker, 518, 538
Faitil, 19
Faiyans, 4
Fajbenbaum, 517
Fajenbaum, 515
Fajgenbaum, 492, 531, 540, 555
Fajgenman, 544, 554
Fajgnbaum, 208, 209, 337, 528, 553
Fajnbaum, 357
Fakman, 467
Falatitzky, 448
Falatyczki, 663
Farber, 478
Farbiak, 357, 663
Farbiyak, 180
Farbshtein, 228
Farbstein, 108, 242, 243, 663
Fast, 589
Fayans, 663
Fayvish, 19
Feierman, 280
Feigenbaum, 1, 2, 4, 5, 71, 79, 82, 90, 95, 98, 104, 108, 152, 160,
     166, 167, 182, 207, 307, 312, 444, 581
Feigenboim, 110, 188, 191, 223, 227, 231, 238, 242, 246, 267, 271,
     286, 293, 294, 298, 299, 302, 312, 319, 324, 405, 461, 474, 476,
     478, 479, 480, 481, 484, 485, 486, 491, 492, 564, 585, 595, 597,
     600
Feigenboin, 428
Feignbaum, 112, 314
Feikes, 317
Feingenboim, 246, 318
Fejerman, 314
Feldman, 82, 180, 184, 205, 215, 234, 244, 254, 279, 302, 531, 552,
     579, 585, 593, 668
Feldrib, 287
Feldryb, 668
Feldsher, 384, 478

Felman, 668
Felsenstein, 246
Felzenstein, 668
Felznshtein, 274
Fessel–Firrer, 478
Festman, 303
Fiantnitsky, 225
Fiegenboim, 34, 56, 576
Fijytz, 39
Finekl, 196, 197, 201
Fingerhut, 257, 288, 597, 665
Finkelhaus, 666
Finkelhoiz, 191
Finkelshtein, 180, 192, 219, 261, 290, 297, 298, 301, 302, 303, 304,
     322
Finkelstajn, 395, 600
Finkelstein, 64, 70, 79, 93, 98, 100, 233, 243, 244, 245, 246, 247,
     440, 558, 666
Finkelstein-Cynamon, 666
Finkelstien, 257
Finkelsztajn, 314, 383, 384, 386, 517, 528, 553, 554
Finklstein, 313
Finklsztajn, 210, 378, 379, 507, 542, 555
Finskesztejn, 314
Fireman, 54, 272, 278, 665
Firme, 552
Fischer, 248, 667
Fischman-Maimon, 667
Fisher, 38, 46, 100, 101, 156, 167, 218, 219, 220, 242, 243, 279, 280,
     281, 409, 410, 411, 478, 585, 586
Fishleder, 596
Fishman, 34, 96, 137, 152, 184, 274, 287, 587
Fishtshatzer, 251, 254, 348
Fiszer, 386, 387, 388, 389
Fiszleder, 667
Fiszman, 549, 553, 667
Fiszman-Orlanski, 667
Flam, 334, 667
Flatt, 90
Flex, 667
Flichtenrajch, 667
Flichtgreich, 194
Floken, 35
Florinski, 384, 667
Flur, 667
Fogel, 62, 95, 505, 544, 552, 662
Fokman, 571
Folman, 446, 663
Fradls, 180
Fraind, 336
Frainer, 670
Frajnd, 213, 314
Frajner, 510, 511, 537
France, 669
Frank, 18, 19, 34, 135, 136, 152, 331, 332, 333, 340, 669
Frankel, 425, 670, 671
Frankfurter, 330, 331, 602
Frankreich, 265, 311, 669
Frans, 444
Fraus, 544
Freedman, 200
Freidman, 64, 66, 108, 420
Freind, 257, 416, 670
Freiner, 65, 88
Freter, 564, 583

Fretter, 194
Frey, 670
Fridberg, 208, 209, 391, 392
Fridlender, 384
Fridman, 201, 202, 213, 269, 507, 511, 518, 531, 534, 539, 543, 553, 555, 595, 600
Friedberg, 193, 669
Friedlander, 669
Friedman, 71, 82, 85, 90, 95, 98, 192, 245, 251, 254, 257, 277, 293, 318, 350, 413, 450, 596, 600, 669, 670, 689
Friedman-Karliner, 421
Friloker, 671
Friluker, 336
Frimmes, 180
Frinde, 301, 302
Frishman, 346, 598, 599, 670
Frishtick, 242
Frishtik, 194, 195, 243, 299, 670
Fritche, 670
Fritsche, 545, 546
Fritsh, 504
Fritshe, 545
Fritz, 62, 96, 545, 670
Frommer, 348, 669
Fropess, 669
Froyems, 602
Fruchtenberg, 598, 669
Fryned, 258
Fuchs, 664
Fuks, 531
Funk, 386, 664
Furlicker, 336
Futerman, 663
Fux, 82
Fyerman, 177

G

Gabriel, 619
Gampel, 319, 323
Gampl, 311, 329
Ganski, 507
Gapon, 619
Garber, 619
Gardin, 619
Gardy, 244
Garnsztajn, 400
Gefen, 241, 242, 245, 621
Gelasen, 620
Gelassen, 84
Gelbard, 210, 294, 379, 382, 383, 390, 392, 394, 395, 620
Gelbfish, 621
Gelbfisz, 382, 383, 505
Gelblum, 99, 218, 322, 620, 621
Gelbord, 79, 620
Gelburd, 238, 528
Gelenberg, 277, 278, 279, 429, 430, 431, 621
Gelfish, 62
Gellenberg, 194, 297, 298, 299
Gelosn, 533
Geltman, 50, 79, 171, 300, 302, 357, 528, 621
Genzeles, 274
Gerach, 59
Gerdi, 621
Gerech, 497, 621

German, 64, 510, 621
Gerondi, 310
Gerrman, 473
Gershkop, 95, 598, 621
Gershon, 191
Gerszkop, 544, 551, 552, 553
Gerszon, 622
Gesundheit, 426
Getsl, 553
Gewirtzman, 280, 281
Gewirzman, 311
Gezundheit, 620
Gilman, 516
Ginsberg, 604
Ginzburg, 336, 620
Girondy, 620
Gitelman, 598
Gitli, 17, 133
Gitlman, 59, 498
Gittelman, 180, 184, 238, 620
Gittleman, 70
Glat, 64, 71, 72, 73, 74, 76, 94
Glazman, 620
Glet, 510, 519, 521, 522, 523, 524, 543, 620
Glezer, 324, 478, 553
Glicksberg, 85, 90, 93
Glikeles, 312, 637
Gliksberg, 184, 202, 238, 287, 294, 313, 534, 539, 542, 553, 587, 592, 596, 597, 620
Glozman, 444
Glucksberg, 242
Goering, 517, 545, 621
Gogal, 286
Gogol, 411, 616
Gold, 258, 259, 289, 318, 319, 320, 325, 348, 353, 383, 415, 416, 422, 450, 469, 485, 488, 492, 585, 589, 590, 591, 592, 593, 616
Goldappel, 616
Goldapple, 248
Goldberg, 64, 73, 76, 85, 90, 93, 100, 185, 202, 219, 241, 251, 258, 261, 278, 279, 284, 313, 507, 522, 525, 534, 539, 542, 565, 616, 617
Goldenberg, 379, 381, 383, 617
Goldendrot, 587
Goldenrat, 617
Goldfarb, 50, 62, 82, 85, 99, 109, 173, 217, 229, 241, 252, 299, 311, 319, 414, 444, 486, 531, 534, 553, 579, 617
Goldfeder, 96, 504, 549, 617
Goldfeld, 82, 468, 530, 617
Goldhamer, 202, 320
Goldhammer, 320, 617
Goldman, 258, 285, 617
Goldrajch, 542
Goldreich, 48, 93, 169, 192, 322, 618
Goldrich, 618
Goldricz, 598
Goldsac, 243
Goldschmidt, 598, 618
Goldshmidt, 185, 304, 478
Goldshtein, 172, 177, 184, 192, 194, 230, 231, 260, 286, 287, 290, 291, 297, 298, 303, 304, 323, 324
Goldshtein-Suknov, 279
Goldsmith, 404, 441, 558
Goldstein, 50, 54, 64, 66, 110, 240, 242
Goldszmidt, 212, 553
Goldsztajn, 204, 212, 377, 382, 395, 507, 511, 551

Goldsztein, 618
Goldwasser, 585, 617
Goldzak, 265, 585, 617
Golenbiovski, 618
Golenbiowski, 510
Golencyovski, 65
Golfedder, 194
Golinker, 618
Golinski, 618
Golinsky, 279
Golomb, 616
Gomel, 618
Gongalinski, 295
Gongolinski, 619
Gonski, 63, 619
Gordin, 299
Gordon, 273, 277, 299, 301, 594, 619
Gorensztein, 619
Goring, 71, 96
Gorka, 620
Gorki, 619
Gorky, 411, 601
Gornsztajn, 396
Gorny, 619
Gotfried, 38, 471, 590
Gotgrid, 400
Gotlen, 524
Gotlieb, 596
Gottfried, 157, 484, 616
Gottlieb, 290, 291, 450, 616
Grabanuv, 478
Grabski, 429, 467
Gravski, 621
Greenberg, 245, 598
Greenblat, 239, 288
Greenboim, 224, 225, 228, 403
Greendlass, 319
Greenfield, 60
Greenglass, 57, 86
Gretz, 622
Gretz,, 566
Gricer, 338
Griditzer, 421
Gridizer, 622
Gril, 198
Grinbelt, 622
Grinberg, 238, 241, 245, 251, 302, 303, 599, 622
Grinblat, 587, 600, 622
Grinblatt, 238
Grinboim, 105, 106, 108, 243, 408, 417, 622
Grinenfeld, 83, 501, 532, 622
Gringlas, 90, 357, 540, 622
Gringlos, 496, 535
Grinshtein, 117, 302
Grinstein, 239, 311
Grinsztajn, 553
Grinsztein, 622
Grobman, 79, 90, 185, 208, 209, 528, 552, 621, 622
Grodna, 515
Grodner, 76, 84, 85, 86, 210, 239, 288, 524, 533, 534, 535, 552, 597, 621
Grosh, 190
Grosman, 522
Grosser, 258, 263, 621
Grossman, 73, 562, 621

Grozman, 79
Grubman, 87, 536, 539
Grzimek, 510
Gumpel, 619
Gurfinkel, 264, 619
Gurni, 171
Gurny, 186, 188, 210
Gutenberg, 86, 96, 203, 515, 535, 547, 619
Gutman, 313, 333, 586, 619
Gutshkov, 303
Guttenberg, 197
Gviazda, 619
Gvirtzman, 279
Gvirzman, 619
Gviyosdo, 564
Gwazda, 531
Gwiazda, 82, 600
Gwiosdo, 579
Gzimek, 65

H

Hacohen, 317
Hafer, 233, 502
Hafmakl-Ostrowski, 512
Haiblum, 626
Hajblom, 516
Hajblum, 208, 357, 552, 585
Halas, 624
Halbershtat, 137, 217, 423
Halbershtater, 136
Halbershtatter, 152
Halberstadt, 439
Halberstadter, 19
Halberstat, 99
Halberstater, 671
Halbersztat, 625
Haller, 45, 166, 625
Halperin, 54, 177
Halpern, 212, 215, 625
Hanak, 83, 532, 625
Handel, 4, 5
Handelman, 95, 625
Handlman, 544
Handwerker, 589
Hannover, 19
Hanoch, 38
Hanover, 136, 625
Hantverker, 625
Hartglas, 99, 111, 117, 153, 154, 155, 158, 159, 165, 166, 198, 200, 207, 217, 218, 225, 228, 272, 285, 286, 377, 493
Hartglass, 99, 105, 106, 108. 243, 626
Hartzman, 64
Hasofer, 99
Hauser, 117, 624
Hausschild, 624
Hava, 382
Hayblum, 175, 185
Haylprin, 626
Hayyun, 340
Heartglass, 35, 37, 39, 40, 45, 46, 56, 318, 403, 404, 405, 406, 407, 439, 557
Hegdem, 626
Heibloom, 53, 245, 248, 327
Heiblum, 70

Heicloom, 312
Heigenbaum, 311
Heine, 560, 626
Heinsdorf, 425, 626
Heller, 627
Hellershtein, 180
Helman, 387, 389, 627
Hendel, 111, 585, 627
Hendl, 121, 335, 336, 356, 377, 492
Henech, 265
Hercman, 507
Herczberg, 597
Herman, 627
Hersch, 627
Herschberg, 73
Hersh Ber Ra'abbe, 191
Hershberg, 48, 169, 185, 241, 320, 346, 348, 582
Herszberg, 395, 522, 627
Hertzl, 321, 627
Hertzman, 627
Herz, 627
Herzberg, 587, 627
Herzl, 62, 282
Herzog, 427
Herzog, 627
Hilbloom, 311
Hildeman, 58, 497, 555, 626
Himelfarb, 626
Himmelfarb, 258
Hinech, 157
Hirsch, 626
Hirschhorn, 53, 351
Hirshbein, 626
Hirshbine, 277, 302
Hirshhorn, 57, 176, 336, 349, 350
Hirshorn, 311
Hirshzon, 212, 627
Hirszhorn, 496, 627
Hirszson, 210
Hishtsher, 478
Hitelmakher, 585
Hitler, 626
Hochberg, 53, 175, 199, 208, 209, 239, 242, 243, 247, 248, 326, 392, 624
Hochman, 50, 62, 171, 195, 201, 202, 245, 258, 275, 290, 298, 299, 382, 383, 464, 477, 504, 505, 624
Hofer, 55, 61, 65, 311, 352, 356, 357, 392, 511, 530, 531, 554, 587
Hoffer, 82, 109, 110, 111, 121, 169, 178, 185, 190, 192, 217, 218, 219, 230, 231, 240, 242, 243, 257, 271, 279, 293, 294, 314, 324, 328, 625
Hoffmakel-Ostrovski, 625
Hoffman, 289, 327, 413, 415
Hofmakel–Ostrovski, 66
Hofman, 67, 180, 203, 251, 257, 261, 513, 588, 600, 625
Hofner, 579
Hohenlohe, 200, 456, 624
Holzheker, 248, 625
Hoper, 99, 100, 383, 391, 393
Hopfer, 248
Hopper, 48
Horowicz, 330
Horowitz, 626
Hoshlever, 636
Hudesls, 250
Hurvitz, 330

Hurwicz, 335, 336
Hurwitz, 310
Hushler, 312
Hushliever, 478

I

Ibn Haviv, 147
Ibn Pakuda, 310
Ibragimov, 604
Ibragimow, 579
Ibshitzer, 246
Idelsberg, 54
Inebinder, 478
Isenberg, 180
Isenshtat, 177, 219
Itche Meir, 605
Itkin, 225, 605
Itlbaum, 56
Ivanicki, 518, 519
Ivanitsky, 98
Ivanitzki, 558, 604
Iwanicki, 527
Izen, 261
Izenberg, 258, 279, 302, 303, 575
Izenshtat, 134
Izhevitzer, 605
Izmir, 605

J

Jabotinsky, 240, 635
Jacob, 311
Jacob Aaron, 411
Jacobs, 311
Jaffe, 642
Jak, 241
Jakobs, 603
Jakubowicz, 392
Jamnik, 542
Jarnitzki, 318
Jawor, 596
Joczimowski, 544
Josef The 2nd, 122
Jud, 314
Juljov, 46
Junewer, 585
Jungerman–Fridberg, 207
Jurberg, 507, 511, 544, 597, 600, 641
Jurberg-Lustigman, 641
Justman, 515, 528, 540, 594

K

Kac-Rapoport, 333
Kagan, 378
Kahan, 194, 204, 205, 214, 215, 321, 443, 445, 457, 593, 594, 597, 672, 673
Kahane, 336
Kahna, 644
Kaidanover, 335
Kaiser Joseph Ii, 138
Kaiyovski, 117, 676
Kalichshtein, 176, 185

Kalichstein, 54, 94, 242, 560
Kalichsztajn, 212, 396, 397, 543
Kalichsztejn, 673
Kalina, 673, 674
Kalischer, 421
Kalisher, 674
Kalishiner, 311
Kalman, 311
Kalushiener, 322
Kalushinner, 322
Kamelmacher, 674
Kamelmaker, 255, 256
Kamien, 246, 674
Kaminer, 350
Kaminski, 198, 352, 674
Kamion, 46
Kamlet, 185, 674
Kamyen, 167
Kanakshrein, 287
Kanalboim, 279, 674
Kanalbojm, 280
Kanalshtein), 472
Kanalstein, 674
Kanier, 515, 674
Kanitzki-Feigenbaum, 674
Kanizshnik, 575
Kant, 564
Kantarovicz, 286
Kantor, 73, 80, 93, 204, 230, 522, 529, 542, 674
Kantorovitch, 674
Kanyer, 577
Kaplan, 452, 675
Kapp, 640
Karalik, 598
Kareniov, 255
Karliner, 420, 421, 422
Karnil, 349, 675
Karol Xii, 675
Karpinski, 84, 86, 533, 534, 675
Karshenbaum, 675
Karshenboim, 294, 304
Karshnboim, 268
Kashamacher, 79
Kashemacher, 54, 80, 93, 177, 302, 478, 676
Kashemakher, 588
Kashimovski, 36, 49
Kashtenbaum, 35, 101, 105, 675
Kashtenboim, 108, 225, 228, 269, 275, 286, 288, 324, 483
Kashtenvoim, 273
Kashtnbaum, 154
Kashtnboim, 219
Kastenboim, 247, 250
Kaszemacher, 203, 204, 382, 397, 528, 529, 542
Kaszemacker, 357
Kasztenbaum, 212, 377, 553
Kattelyansky, 286
Katz, 311, 332, 333, 336
Katz, 644, 675
Katzeff, 320
Katzenelenbogen, 420, 675
Katzev, 472
Katz-Rapaport, 645
Katzyuzne, 302
Kaufman, 540, 589, 590, 591, 673
Kava, 203, 204, 395

Kavales, 319
Kavalevski, 119
Kave, 100, 246, 430, 431, 432
Kaveh, 50, 54, 101, 102, 103, 107, 311, 316, 318
Kaves, 326
Kavve, 171, 176, 218, 219, 220, 221, 222, 226, 273, 278, 290, 296
Kawa, 377, 516
Kawal, 318
Kawe, 384, 385, 386, 673
Kawel, 673
Kaze, 537
Kazisne, 675
Kazshimierzsh, 122
Kedrov, 262
Kedrow, 677
Kelmanzon, 397
Kempinski, 263, 677
Kenizshnik, 95
Kerner, 105, 192, 225, 434, 677
Kersh, 260, 677
Kesler, 598
Kesselerke, 324
Kessler, 478
Ketzeles, 190
Khahan, 212, 215
Kharash, 643
Khmielevski, 644
Khodkyevitch, 643
Khohan, 510, 543
Kicher, 478
Kiegls, 190, 304
Kiehel, 676
Kiehl, 86, 96
Kihl, 546, 547
Kilger, 587, 598
King David, 331
King Jan Kazimierz, 6
King Karl The 12th, 112
Kirschroit, 676
Kirshrot, 403, 404
Kitelner, 478
Kladnyev, 397, 676
Klatch, 256, 257
Klatz, 415
Kleinboim, 563, 677
Klempner, 598, 599, 677
Klempner-Szternfeld, 677
Klieger, 174, 176, 190, 192. 218, 230, 231, 260, 324
Klif, 677
Kligberg, 184, 185, 320, 553, 676
Kliger, 52, 54, 99, 110, 207, 208, 209, 240, 247, 250, 257, 317, 381, 382, 587, 598, 599, 677
Kliger-Klemfner, 677
Kligger, 288
Kligsberg, 279, 280, 312, 314, 329, 552, 676, 677
Klimetski, 119
Klimetzki, 117, 430, 677
Kling, 252, 254, 256, 323, 677
Klotz, 288, 302, 676
Knicznik, 543
Knijshnik, 238, 239
Knizhnik, 246, 587, 677
Knuzcnik, 318
Kobrin, 300, 672
Kobriner, 62, 379, 384

Kobrinerin, 478
Kobrinski, 435
Kobryner, 435
Kochayevski, 676
Kochazhevski, 676
Koczemainik, 552
Kodiner, 311
Kodnier, 478
Kodnyer, 603
Kodnyers, 278, 609
Kogan, 197, 672
Kogut, 672
Kohan, 213, 383, 395
Kohan-Tzadek, 357
Kohan–Tzedek, 208
Kohen, 19, 600
Kohn, 587
Koifman, 90, 676
Kokovtsov, 206
Koliatsh, 318
Kolina, 599
Kolker, 260, 674
Koloder, 478
Kolodney, 310
Koltan, 243
Kolton, 673
Komaruvker, 478
Komlet, 311
Konicki–Feigenboim, 600
Konitzki, 676
Konolstein, 436
Konopka, 66, 512
Konstantiner, 478
Kook, 426
Korahites, 331
Koralik, 185, 261, 262, 289, 675
Korczak, 404
Korenblum, 87
Koreniov, 156, 158
Korenyow, 675
Korman, 102, 208, 221, 242, 322, 323, 357, 476, 675
Kornberg, 102, 104, 221, 224, 453, 454, 675
Kornbloom, 62, 64, 562, 563
Kornblum, 80, 184, 208, 209, 230, 505, 507, 529, 536, 675
Kornhendler, 600, 675
Kortchak, 675
Koryanov, 38, 39
Kosakl, 673
Koses, 559, 560
Kosevitzki, 676
Kot, 60, 500, 673
Kotchemeinik, 326
Kotelanski, 673
Kotner, 371
Kotshemayinik, 189
Kotshemoyenik, 115
Kotsker, 338
Kotzker, 334, 337
Koval, 319, 468, 478
Kovalle, 323
Kovarski, 90
Kovno, 673
Kowalevski, 673
Kowarski, 534, 539
Kowarski-Goldberg, 673

Kowarsky, 85
Koza–Vulka, 478
Koze, 88
Kozes, 673
Kozevilke, 478
Kozzes, 180, 190, 200, 323
Kraizelman, 678
Kraizelmans, 678
Krajdsztajn, 400
Krajzlman, 504, 522, 542
Krakever, 478
Krakovski, 68
Kramarcz, 210, 379, 384
Kramarejsh, 243
Kramarjsh, 243
Kramarsash, 241
Kramarsz, 204
Kramarz, 280, 314, 678
Kramarzs, 231, 232, 233
Kramarzsh, 171, 177, 272, 278
Kramatzs, 232
Kramatzsh, 50, 54
Krashevski, 122, 168, 678
Kraskovski, 678
Kraszewski, 6
Kraviets, 677, 678
Kravtsov, 158
Kravyetz, 272, 278
Krawec, 677, 678
Krawiec, 203, 280, 314
Krawotzov, 39
Kredshtein, 424
Kreidesztein, 678
Kreidshtein, 424
Kreidstein, 99, 100, 241, 311, 312, 317, 432
Kreidstien, 312, 325
Kreiselman, 61, 73, 93, 245
Krempl, 268
Krideshtein, 185, 217, 218, 272, 278, 324, 469
Kriedshtein, 185
Kriger, 54, 100
Krizelman, 184
Krizelmans, 192
Kroch, 117
Krochmalski, 678
Krochmalsky, 302
Krogman, 678
Krokewer, 312
Krokus, 595
Kromarzh, 597
Krone, 244, 678
Kroses, 252, 256
Kroshnik, 678
Kruger, 100
Krugman, 400
Kruses, 201, 414
Kshimovski, 155, 170
Kshimovsky, 678
Kubele, 323
Kuchayevski, 119
Kuchczewski, 524
Kuhl, 535
Kukzewski, 76
Kunicki, 497
Kunitzki, 59

Kuperschmidt, 676
Kupershmidt, 261
Kuperszmid, 213
Kuropatva, 676
Kuropatve, 185
Kuropotwe, 552
Kursky, 262, 263
Kusewicki, 401
Kushmirak, 425, 676
Kushtsitz, 153
Kushzutz, 35
Kuszczyc, 676
Kuzmirer, 339, 641
Kyavske, 275
Ky–Yovske, 117

L

Labendrzowa, 383
Labenzhova, 645
Labi, 289
Lajbzon, 507, 533, 534, 538, 544
Lajnwand, 648
Lajzerzon, 357
Lamas, 231, 232, 233
Landau, 39, 54, 158, 177, 180, 244, 268, 323, 338, 339, 345, 351, 352, 353, 354, 357, 428, 591, 645, 646
Landois, 488
Landoy, 307, 311
Landsberg, 646
Landskron, 646
Lasalle, 468
Lashtevski, 646
Lashtevski-Rosen, 646
Lashtshevski, 287
Lashtshevsky, 302, 303
Laskin, 598, 646
Laszczewski, 212, 387, 389, 398, 400
Laufman, 384, 409, 645
Lavi, 245
Lavie-Lemberger, 646
Lazer, 645
Lebeberg, 35
Lebenberg, 64, 154, 167, 204, 290, 293, 294, 324, 386, 387, 397, 629, 649
Lebnberg, 171, 222, 377, 396, 507, 536, 554
Łêczna, 337
Lederman, 102, 221, 275, 289, 299, 300, 302, 347, 451, 476, 649
Lehman, 61, 137, 650
Lehmann, 20
Lehrer, 236, 238, 650
Lehrman, 649
Leib, 466
Leibekes, 254
Leibish, 648
Leibish-Katz, 648
Leibson, 64, 240, 241
Leibzon, 83, 85, 95, 648
Leizerzon, 648
Lekert, 253
Leman, 504
Lemberg, 340, 571
Lemberger, 245, 279, 280, 281, 283, 294, 295, 298, 302, 303, 304, 318, 333, 453, 585, 650
Lempert, 95, 544, 650

Lenin, 444, 468, 650
Lentchner, 253
Lentshne, 337, 650
Lentshner, 198, 335, 337, 478
Lerer, 279
Lerner, 73, 241, 357, 522, 590, 592, 598, 600, 650
Leshner, 598
Leshtshuk, 565, 569, 650
Levenberg, 46, 50, 87, 103
Levenstein, 650
Levi, 50, 61, 173, 243
Levin, 246, 426, 440, 597, 649, 650
Levinstein, 246, 650
Levrant, 71
Levy, 54, 83, 93, 176, 649
Lewensztajn, 334
Lewi, 397, 504, 532, 542, 553, 585
Lewin, 201, 552, 591, 646
Leybzon, 84
Liberman, 210, 232, 233, 352, 392, 528, 529, 573, 597, 598, 647
Libman, 104, 203, 210, 319, 329, 357, 552, 553, 587, 598, 647
Librant, 46
Lichtbaum, 521
Lichtenbaum, 72, 90, 387, 389, 511, 514, 515, 540
Lichtenboim, 184, 261, 648
Lichtenbojm, 66, 68, 314
Lichtenshtein, 177, 184, 185
Lichtenstein, 54, 56, 83
Lichtensztajn, 212, 493, 532
Lichtnsztajn, 552
Licht-Tzierin, 478
Lichtzier, 319
Lidzbarski, 94, 543, 647
Lidzbarsky, 180, 185
Liebenberg, 577
Lieberman, 79, 80, 180, 290, 293, 301, 302, 303, 304, 323, 446, 451
Liebman, 180, 223, 243, 283, 299, 301, 302, 303, 304, 323, 326
Likhtenberg, 585
Likkever, 478
Lilenblum, 648
Lilien, 648
Liliental, 589
Lilienthal, 649
Lillinblum, 452
Limawski, 557
Linik, 649
Linvand, 349
Lipa, 649
Lipe, 312
Lipecz, 590
Lipes, 327
Lipes, 642
Lipiats, 96
Lipiec, 215, 549, 649
Lipke, 311
Lipkov, 69, 72, 93, 649
Lipkow, 512, 521, 542
Lipmann, 488
Lipowski, 514
Lipyetz, 287, 294
Listgarten, 71, 73, 95, 194, 238, 248, 249, 649
Listgartn, 215, 518, 522, 543
Litman, 301, 648
Litman-Shreiber, 648
Litvin, 489, 490, 492

Litwin, 374, 648
Liverant, 215, 238, 381, 382, 518, 587
Liwerant, 648
Locszewski, 598
Loevenberg, 241
Lomaz, 152, 293, 303, 304, 645
Lomazer, 478
Loshitzer, 478
Lourie, 647
Lovech, 563
Lubelczik, 203, 204, 394, 398, 496, 504, 554
Lubelski, 440, 646
Lubeltshik, 194, 218, 298, 299, 646
Lubeltzik, 57, 62, 99
Lubliener, 322
Lubliner, 311, 602
Lublinner, 478
Lukower, 352
Luria, 33, 133, 152, 355, 420, 626
Lustigman, 86, 95, 185, 210, 245, 286, 357, 535, 544, 600, 646
Lutvak, 323
Lutwak, 312
Luzato, 647
Luzzatto, 310

M

Madenick, 72
Magid, 302, 602, 653
Maharal, 653
Maharam Ash, 651
Maharam Esh, 17, 20
Maharshak, 335, 603
Mahler, 24, 151, 152, 492, 602, 650
Maizel, 653
Makover, 564, 565, 566, 652
Makovski, 652
Makowski, 554
Malach, 132, 654
Malashevicz, 651
Maler, 251, 386
Malina, 69, 184, 198, 516, 600, 651
Maller, 198, 299, 478
Mallina, 192, 294
Man, 227
Manaszon, 652
Mandelbaum, 194, 579
Mandelboim, 254, 286, 492, 652
Mandlbaum, 551
Manes, 326
Mangel, 105, 225, 478, 652
Mangelnitshke, 478
Manhajmer-Szor, 384
Manhajmer–Szor, 379
Manheimer-Sher, 652
Mann, 108, 248, 585, 652
Manperel, 652
Manperl, 277
Mantcher, 251
Mapier, 301
Mapu, 153, 271, 652
Maratshnik, 197
Marchbein, 323, 653
Marks, 590, 592, 653
Marks-Rozenblat, 653

Marks–Rozenblat, 589, 591
Markus, 590, 653
Markushover, 478
Marx, 371, 468, 653
Mas, 357, 401
Maskal, 239
Mass, 652
Matys, 651
Matzevah–Kritzer, 478
Mayer, 653
Mayerson, 653
Mayerzon, 261, 290, 291
Maz"E, 653
Mazor, 417, 650
Medem, 417, 654
Mednick, 66, 68
Mednik, 180, 193, 352, 465, 466, 478, 511, 514, 521
Medniks, 602
Meisel, 280
Melamed, 325, 478, 479
Melamud, 598
Meler, 386, 655
Meller, 279
Melman, 655
Melman,, 585
Meloman, 413
Meltzer, 426, 655
Menakhem Nakhum, 336
Mendel, 311
Mendele, 655
Mendelssohn, 452
Mendix, 251
Menke, 311, 357
Meshedlitz, 99
Mesimiatitz, 151
Mevius, 654
Mevyuse, 168, 196
Meyerson, 284
Mezricher, 328
Miadek, 238
Michelson, 654
Michelzen, 34
Miendziczecki, 208, 209
Miendzyrzecki, 654
Miertenbaum, 654
Migdal, 243, 244, 245, 585, 653
Milbaum, 515, 654
Milboim, 198, 287, 312, 317
Milchiker, 478
Milner, 478, 579
Minc, 201, 357, 382, 383, 386, 387, 388, 389, 390, 397, 529
Mindal, 192
Minsker, 352, 420
Mintz, 100, 180, 192, 218, 242, 252, 253, 269, 280, 281, 286, 321, 322, 457, 476, 654
Miodek, 240, 396, 397
Mirtenboim, 477
Mishkin, 110, 231, 654
Miszkin, 214
Miyodek, 195, 230, 231
Mizel, 279
Mjodek, 587, 598
Mocher–Sforimnik, 479
Molier, 277
Molyer, 254, 651

Monosovicz, 219
Monosovitch, 101
Monosovitz, 652
Montefiore, 425, 652
Montsharzsh, 180
Montsher, 478
Mord, 653
Morgenshtern, 230, 278, 346
Morgenstein, 86
Morgenstern, 247, 249, 427, 579, 588, 589, 652, 653
Morgensztern, 208, 387, 389
Morgnsztern, 329, 535
Morotchnik, 652
Moses, 425
Moses, 311, 425
Moses, 650
Moses, 650
Moses, 651
Moses, 651
Moses, 651
Moses, 651
Moses, 651
Moses, 651
Moshe *Ben* Tzvi Hirsh, 336
Moshkovitch, 653
Moshkovitz, 350
Mosik, 652
Moskal, 652
Mossik, 262
Mowiness, 56
Mozir, 650
Mozshonzshnik, 478
Muljer, 585, 600
Mulyer, 153, 348, 478
Munish, 653
Musawicz, 379, 384, 505, 554
Musawutz, 62
Musinke, 327
Musowitz, 653
Mustovitch, 434
Muzshinek, 278, 492
Muzynek, 653
Myadek, 653
Myendzizshetzky, 302, 303
Myerzon, 279
Myoddek, 293, 298
M'yodek, 278
Myudak, 110

N

Nadriziner, 338
Naftsharzsh, 180
Naftsher, 478
Nahum, 312
Najsztajn, 552
Napoleon, 21, 138, 485, 488
Nartman, 192, 207, 209, 477
Natan Ha'azati, 658
Natanson, 657
Natanzon, 335, 341, 552
Nathanson, 319, 440
Nauczeny, 657
Nauczni, 554
Naulinger, 517

Naysztein, 658
Neimark, 41
Neishtadt, 417
Nemirover, 471, 607
Neufeld, 244, 658
Neulinger, 71, 657
Neumark, 658
Neustadt, 658
Newidzi, 658
Niewidze, 215
Nirenberg, 243, 658
Nisbaum, 657, 658
Nisenbaum, 101
Niskeles, 201, 255, 256, 636
Nissenboim, 219
Nixon, 348, 658
Nobile, 438, 657
Nochevitz, 233, 239
Nochovitz, 579
Nochowitz, 82
Nordman, 279, 657
Nortman, 52, 54, 174, 176, 184, 185, 208, 230, 395, 657
Nossever, 478
Novomiast, 185
Novominsky, 83, 94
Novotarski, 47, 168, 657
Nowim, 589, 590, 657
Nowomiast, 377, 657
Nowominski, 397, 657
Nowomiski, 532
Nuchovicz, 276, 302, 469
Nuchovitsh, 272, 278
Nuchovitz, 438
Nuchowicz, 280, 314, 531, 657
Nuchowicz-Faigebaum, 657
Nuchowitz, 564
Nukhowicz, 600
Nukhowycz, 595, 600
Nussbaum, 560

O

Odess, 603
Ofar, 585
Ofer, 239, 587
Ofer-Hafer, 661
Ofole, 608
Ogrodnik, 467
Oleh, 346
Olkush, 607
Olshwanger, 105, 607
Opatoshu, 307, 366, 608
Opatovski, 366
Openhajm, 357
Opotchne, 608
Oppenheim, 16, 180, 194, 323, 571, 604, 608
Orbach, 243
Orbant, 591
Orczechower, 329
Orensztain, 609
Oreol, 608
Orkelesh, 312
Orlandski, 549
Orlanskes, 321

Orlanski, 48, 64, 208, 209, 210, 213, 235, 287, 391, 397, 510, 544, 599, 600, 609
Orlansky, 83, 85, 95, 96, 169, 180, 185, 230, 304
Orlinski, 532
Orlonski, 600
Ormacher, 115, 116, 604
Ortcheleres, 327
Ortcheles, 326
Ortsheles, 636, 642
Osenholcz, 587
Osenholtz, 67, 575
Osnholc, 513
Ossover, 478
Ostre, 608
Ostrov, 608
Ostrover, 478
Ostrovski, 608
Ostrovsky, 456, 457
Ostrower, 335, 337, 339
Ostrowski, 385
Otchen, 311
Otshein, 603, 604
Otvotzk, 604
Ovjes, 600
Ozerkover, 478

P

Paisker, 98, 663
Pakman, 575, 587, 598, 599, 663
Palaticki, 596
Palatitski, 663
Paniatovski, 138
Papiernikov, 444
Papinska, 493
Papinski, 56
Papinsky, 472
Papiyernikov, 663
Paputin, 386, 663
Parcewer, 328, 357
Parrikn–Macherin, 478
Partsever, 478
Pasel, 101
Pasternak, 446
Pat, 662
Patotz, 323
Patshtaruk, 264, 265
Patt, 258
Patterson, 76
Peisker, 71, 89
Perale, 38
Perel, 668
Perele, 157, 598
Peretz, 159, 277, 288, 300, 302, 307, 359, 429, 430, 591, 671
Perez, 40
Perkelvald, 668, 669
Perkelwald, 600
Perl, 596
Perlov, 298, 445, 446, 668
Peshischa, 338
Pesl The, 458, 459
Pesl The, 458
Pest, 663
Pestman, 668
Petach Tikvah, 671

Petelnik, 449
Peterburg, 203, 204, 668
Petersburg, 54
Peterson, 65, 66, 510, 512, 524, 525, 668
Petliura, 668
Petterburg, 177
Philipover, 665
Piakarzki, 666
Piatchiski, 47, 48
Piatshitzki, 666
Picon, 327
Picon, 666
Piczic, 377, 378, 391, 392, 395, 397, 398, 500, 504, 517, 522, 552
Piczize, 553
Piekarski, 54
Piekarsky, 102, 184, 221
Pietshitski, 168
Pietshitzki, 168, 169
Pijshits, 255
Pilsudski, 47, 49, 168, 441, 665
Pines, 420, 666
Piness, 469
Pinsker, 421, 666
Pinski, 665
Pinsky, 302
Piontnitski, 664
Pirandello, 666
Pishtshatser, 478
Pishtshatzer, 320
Pisshitz, 50
Piterman, 600, 664
Pitshazer, 636
Piva, 248
Piwo, 552, 664
Pizich, 70, 73, 74, 93, 94, 417, 418
Pizshits, 477
Pizshitz, 115, 117, 158, 172, 185, 192, 196, 243, 244, 271, 305, 320, 323, 424, 432, 439, 470, 473, 487, 488, 664
Pizyk, 664
Plat, 238, 540, 543, 554
Platao, 667
Platau, 440
Platnikov, 236
Platt, 95, 267, 325, 667
Ploer, 564
Plotnikov, 667
Pluhar, 350
Plur, 667
Poczic, 543
Poczice, 498
Pocztaruk, 212, 531
Podlishevsky, 218
Podolak, 316
Podoliak, 662
Poisner, 663
Poizner, 166, 334
Poldlishevski, 662
Polessye, 446
Polonjetzky, 311
Polonyetzki, 663
Polosecki, 528
Polosetsky, 79
Polosetzki, 663
Ponczik, 552
Ponczyk, 663

Poniatowsky, 20
Ponyatov, 663
Ponyatovski, 663
Potash, 564, 566, 567, 663
Potels, 605
Pototsky, 94
Pototzki, 473
Potozski, 663
Potshtaruk, 261
Potsztaruk, 357
Potsztoruk, 357
Potzaruk, 663
Pozanski, 281
Poznaski, 662
Pratar, 74
Preser, 512
Preter, 64, 66, 95, 248, 507, 510, 522, 544, 670
Pretter, 185, 469
Prikashtik, 613
Prikashtshik, 269
Prilicki, 204
Prilotzki, 105
Prilutski, 670
Prilutsky, 225
Prilutzky, 273, 274
Prince Radzhivil Sherotka, 112
Princess Anna, 6, 7, 123
Pritscha, 96
Propes, 241
Proshekier, 197, 478
Proshekyer, 609
Proshenye–Shriber, 478
Proshiker, 604
Prozshani, 451
Pruskin, 350, 669
Przekovnik, 671
Przekupnik, 585
Przewizman, 671
Przewuzman, 379, 392
Przigoda, 383
Pshigoda, 671
Pshivishevski, 671
Pszibiszewski, 601
Puchtaruk, 82
Pudlishevsky, 100
Pulturok, 350
Punk, 116
Puterman, 473, 598
Pyekarsky, 177, 277, 302, 303, 304
Pyes, 320
Pyess, 324
Pyess,, 180, 324
Pyontnitzki, 105

R

R Avraham, 17
R' Baruch, 17, 18, 19
R' Baruch Yavan, 17
R' David, 17
R' Denan, 19
R' Hayim Malakh, 16
R' Moshe, 16
R' Yehuda Hassid, 16
R' Yitschak, 17, 18, 19

R' Yosef, 16
R. Pinhas, 7
R. Shmuel, 7
Raaba, 37, 86, 91, 378
Ra'abbe, 191
Ra'abbes, 191
Raabe, 57, 62, 64, 65, 155, 201, 535, 540, 678, 679
Ra'abe, 191, 192, 268, 285, 295
Rabbi Aharon Menachem Mencl, 356
Rabbi Avraham, 427
Rabbi Avraham Ibn Ezra, 355
Rabbi Avraham Yehoshua Heshel, 356
Rabbi Avrahaml, 351
Rabbi Avreimale, 311, 370, 371
Rabbi Avreimele, 425
Rabbi Baruch, 332
Rabbi Berish, 307, 345, 366, 367
Rabbi Chaim, 334, 354
Rabbi David Tevel, 420
Rabbi Dov Berish, 346
Rabbi Haim, 435
Rabbi Hayut, 421
Rabbi Herzl, 422
Rabbi Hirsh, 19
Rabbi Israel, 310
Rabbi Itche Meir, 367
Rabbi Itzik, 333
Rabbi Izik, 422
Rabbi Jacob David, 425
Rabbi Jermya Menahem, 427
Rabbi Josef Mendel Herman, 425
Rabbi Joseph, 17
Rabbi Maimon, 20
Rabbi Medele, 367
Rabbi Meir Shlomo Yehuda Leib, 356
Rabbi Meir,, 20
Rabbi Menachem, 344
Rabbi Menahem Mendl, 427
Rabbi Mendel, 368
Rabbi Mendele, 366, 368, 422
Rabbi Menke, 327
Rabbi Mneke, 327
Rabbi Mordechai, 310
Rabbi Moshe, 19, 346
Rabbi Moshe Moses, 423
Rabbi Moshe Yehuda Leib, 341
Rabbi Naftali Hertz, 19
Rabbi Natan, 332
Rabbi Natan David, 354, 356
Rabbi Noah, 360, 422, 423, 424
Rabbi Noah'ke, 359
Rabbi Reb Avrahamyehoshua Heshel, 355
Rabbi Reb Meir, 134, 332, 334
Rabbi Reb Moshe Mordechai, 342
Rabbi Reb Shmuel Arye Leib, 344
Rabbi Reb Ya'acov, 355
Rabbi Reb Yechiel, 355
Rabbi Reb Yisrael, 355
Rabbi Shapira, 344
Rabbi Shaulke, 424
Rabbi Shaul'ke, 433
Rabbi Shlomo Leib, 355, 356
Rabbi Shmuel, 347, 370, 371, 373, 427
Rabbi Shmuel Aryeh Leib, 347
Rabbi Shmuel Leib, 153, 176, 340, 341, 342, 347, 486

Rabbi Shmuelaryeh Leib, 340
Rabbi Simcha Bunim, 341
Rabbi Tsevi Hirsh, 19
Rabbi Tzvi, 349
Rabbi Tzvi Kalish, 356
Rabbi Ya'acov Aryeh, 355
Rabbi Ya'akov, 147, 332
Rabbi Ya'akov Me'ir, 344
Rabbi Yakir, 311
Rabbi Yechezkiel, 354
Rabbi Yechiel Yehoshua, 356
Rabbi Yehiel, 360, 361, 362
Rabbi Yehonatan, 18
Rabbi Yehoshua'le, 355
Rabbi Yehuda, 20, 469
Rabbi Yerachmiel Tzvi, 356
Rabbi Yitschak, 20
Rabbi Yitzchak Meir, 341, 349
Rabbi Yitzchak Ya'akcov, 355
Rabbi Yitzhak, 366
Rabbi Yoizel, 310
Rabbi Yom Tov Ben Avraham, 343
Rabbi Yosi, 8
Rabbi Zalman, 319
Rabbi Zeev Nahum, 425
Rabbi Zvi, 427
Rabbi, Yisroel Iserl, 330
Rabinover, 478
Rabinovich, 271
Rabinovicz, 195, 272, 293, 488
Rabinovitsh, 342
Rabinovitz, 426, 679
Rabinowicz, 328, 339, 340, 354, 382
Rabinowitz, 242, 307, 373
Rabon, 285
Raboun, 279
Radhivil, 680
Radlinski, 439, 680
Radzhivil, 112, 138
Radzimin, 679
Radzinek, 185
Radziner, 680
Radzinner, 346, 478
Radziwill, 5, 6, 7, 20, 21, 314, 331, 335
Radzshivil, 121, 122, 123, 196, 201, 489, 490, 491
Radzshivils, 489
Radzyn, 679
Raimont, 113
Rais, 685
Raiswasser, 685
Raizele, 478
Rajc, 511
Rajch, 511
Rajz, 554
Rajzwaser, 552
Rames, 386, 585, 682, 683
Rammes, 177, 264, 323
Rapaport–Rubinsztajn, 387
Rasner, 683
Ratayewitz, 682
Ratshein, 99
Ratshin, 217, 218, 272, 278, 296, 682
Ratstein, 99
Raviga, 133, 152
Ravitch, 680

Ravon, 55, 178, 440, 453
Reb Aharon, 452
Reb Ahron, 351, 354
Reb Alter, 472
Reb Arya Leib, 337
Reb Asher, 336
Reb Avraham, 328, 333, 338, 340, 342
Reb Avraham Abele, 334, 337
Reb Avraham Moshe, 338
Reb Avrahamele, 339
Reb Avrom, 134
Reb Baruch, 134
Reb Bekerman, 329
Reb Berish, 337, 338, 339, 351, 352, 353, 368
Reb Boruch, 134, 135, 136
Reb Borukh Marc, 331
Reb Bunem, 338
Reb Chaim, 123, 322, 457, 602
Reb Chaim Pesach, 322
Reb Chaim Yisrael, 341
Reb Dov Berish, 341
Reb Dovid, 337
Reb Dovid Tzvi, 321
Reb Elimelekh, 351
Reb Elimelekh Menakhem Mendl, 339
Reb Eliyahu, 336
Reb Eliyahu *Ben* Shmuel, 336
Reb Euzer, 330, 331
Reb Feivele, 338
Reb Fishele Strikewer, 338
Reb Gavriel, 218
Reb Hershele, 340
Reb Herzl, 470
Reb Hirtzel Ha'cohen, 336
Reb Itshe Meir, 321, 337, 338
Reb Itshe Meir Alter, 337
Reb Itshke, 351, 352
Reb Kalman, 336
Reb Leib, 465, 466
Reb Meir, 472, 585
Reb Meir Shlomo Yehuda, 339
Reb Meir Yechiel Halevi, 343
Reb Menachem Nachum, 336
Reb Menakhem Mendl, 338, 339
Reb Menakhem Nakhum, 336
Reb Mendele, 334, 338
Reb Mendl, 340, 487
Reb Mendl Elimelekh Menakhem, 352
Reb Mordekhai, 331
Reb Moshe, 137, 322, 324, 336
Reb Moshe Chayes, 492
Reb Moshe Mikhl, 334, 337
Reb Moshe Mordechai, 325, 585
Reb Mosheyehuda Lieb, 335
Reb Motl, 470
Reb Nachan, 264
Reb Naftali Tzvi Yehuda, 456
Reb Nakhum, 334
Reb Nota, 352
Reb Nusan Dovid, 339
Reb Pinchas, 123
Reb Shabtai, 322, 336
Reb Shimeon, 338
Reb Shimon Ahreles, 322
Reb Shlomo Leib, 335, 341

Reb Shmelke, 321
Reb Shmerl, 477
Reb Shmuel, 123, 124, 137, 349, 485
Reb Shmuel Aryeh Leib, 348
Reb Shmuel Leib, 158, 160, 169, 336, 337, 341, 342, 466
Reb Shual, 470
Reb Shualke, 320, 321, 470, 471
Reb Simchah, 331
Reb Simkha-Bunim, 351
Reb Tzvi, 137
Reb Tzvi Hirsh, 137, 336
Reb Tzvi-Hirsh, 330
Reb Urele, 322
Reb Uri, 123, 151
Reb Vovtshe, 352, 354
Reb Ya'akov, 342
Reb Yakov Szulman, 352
Reb Yakov Yitzhak, 338, 352
Reb Yankele, 337, 342, 471
Reb Yechiel Hersh, 322
Reb Yechiel Meir, 355
Reb Yehezkiel Erlich, 352
Reb Yehiel, 339, 352
Reb Yehonatan, 333
Reb Yehosha, 328
Reb Yehoshua, 324, 342
Reb Yehuda, 136, 137, 138, 336
Reb Yehuda Ari Leib, 341
Reb Yehuda Idl, 331
Reb Yehuda Leib, 136, 331
Reb Yehudayakov, 322
Reb Yekutiel, 352
Reb Yerakhmiel, 339
Reb Yisroel, 336, 352
Reb Yisroel Dovid, 352
Reb Yisroel Meir, 320, 321, 322
Reb Yisroel Yitzhak, 339, 352
Reb Yitzchak, 134, 135, 136
Reb Yitzhak, 331, 332, 333, 334, 336, 337, 338, 340, 351
Reb Yitzhak Meir Alter, 334
Reb Yoav Yehoshua, 341
Reb Yoel, 343
Reb Yonatan, 134
Reb Yonoson, 333
Reb Yosef, 133, 331, 334, 336
Reb Yosef Shaul, 341
Reb Yosele, 340
Reb Yosia *Ben* Yakov, 336
Reb Yossele, 321, 322
Reb Yunever, 321
Reb Zalman, 322
Rebbe Rabbi Avraham Mordhai, 427
Rebbe Rabbi Zvi, 427
Reich, 65, 96, 184, 406, 549, 685
Reichenbach, 685
Reicher, 318
Reikler, 685
Reimont, 685
Reiseles, 415
Reitz, 685
Reizwasser, 283
Resze', 205
Revigo, 16
Ribak, 100, 205, 247, 543, 596
Richter, 38, 44, 80, 157, 165, 184, 260, 389, 400, 417, 529, 553, 685

Ridlevitch, 82
Ridlevitz, 684
Ridlewicz, 531
Rieback, 185
Riebak, 219, 278
Rietz, 65
Rikhter, 597, 598
Rimmer, 478
Rishon, 312
Ritb, 684
Ritker, 219, 478
Riverson, 413
Rivlin, 420, 684
R'manes, 652
Robak, 391, 679
Rodnitzki, 684
Rodsienek, 62
Rodsinek, 50, 66
Rodzenek, 209
Rodzinak, 73, 80, 82
Rodzinek, 90, 173, 185, 202, 204, 205, 208, 213, 214, 258, 261, 275, 397, 461, 505, 512, 522, 528, 529, 531, 540
Rodzineks, 549
Rodziner, 600
Rodzinik, 171
Rodzinnek, 455
Rodzinner, 324
Rodzynek, 679
Rodzyneks, 680
Roffe, 149
Rogalski, 108, 379, 679
Rogalsky, 227
Roginski, 35, 679
Rogolski, 585
Roizner, 684
Romanovski, 682
Romanovsky, 262
Rommel, 96, 549, 682
Romshinski, 684
Rose, 682
Rosee, 441
Rosemarin, 87, 93, 95
Rosen, 50, 54, 95, 319, 589
Rosenbaum, 69, 71, 73, 74, 91, 93, 94, 95
Rosenberg, 48, 88, 95
Rosenblat, 90
Rosenbloom, 238, 241, 570
Rosenboim, 50, 54, 63, 106. 110, 240, 247, 249, 411, 412
Rosenbojm, 67
Rosenfeld, 108, 231, 232, 233
Rosen-Kalichstein, 560
Rosenker, 90, 318
Rosenstein, 46, 82, 318
Rosental, 248
Rosentswige, 441
Rosenzweig, 64
Rosmarin, 233, 246
Rosner, 590
Rososher, 311, 312, 469, 478, 487
Rososzer, 314
Rotenberg, 241, 243, 575, 598, 682
Rotenberg-Alter, 337
Rotschild, 336
Rotshild, 682
Rottenberg, 274, 334

Royzner, 384
Rozen, 171, 177, 212, 213, 264, 543, 590, 592, 598, 599, 680, 682
Rozenbaum, 176, 208, 209, 336, 357, 505, 513, 514, 515, 519, 522, 541, 542, 543, 552, 680, 681
Rozenberg, 169, 184, 450, 537, 544, 553, 681
Rozenblat, 540
Rozenblatt, 324, 681
Rozenblum, 184, 400, 467, 551
Rozenboim, 171, 225, 230, 231, 265, 274, 287, 288, 294, 298, 302, 484, 585, 589, 590, 592, 600
Rozencwajg, 215, 507
Rozencweig, 681, 682
Rozenfeld, 227, 294, 553, 585, 681
Rozenker, 540, 597, 598, 682
Rozenkrantz, 324, 457
Rozenkranz, 682
Rozenman, 595, 681
Rozenn-Kalichstein, 682
Rozen-Rozanker, 680
Rozen-Rozenbaum, 682
Rozenshein, 600, 682
Rozenshine, 167
Rozenstein, 682
Rozenszajn, 553
Rozensztajn, 531
Rozenszwajg, 551
Rozenthal, 681
Rozentsweig, 180
Rozentzveig, 185, 287, 288, 294
Rozenwartzel, 595
Rozenworcel, 681
Rozenzweig, 590, 592
Rozmarin, 195, 281, 286, 287, 296, 298, 301, 302, 303, 304, 384, 477, 487, 492, 536, 542, 543, 680
Rozmarin-Sirkus, 680
Roznboim, 303
Rubenstajn, 585, 596
Rubenstein, 279, 280, 281
Rubensztajn, 382, 384, 543
Rubinlicht, 457, 683
Rubinshtein, 117, 118, 154, 162, 167, 171, 172, 173, 177, 178, 180, 182, 185, 192, 194, 217, 218, 220, 221, 222, 224, 225, 226, 229, 231, 265, 269, 279, 286, 287, 288, 290, 291, 293, 294, 295, 297, 301, 302, 323, 340, 344, 454
Rubinstein, 35, 43, 46, 50, 54, 55, 62, 85, 93, 94, 95, 99, 100, 101, 102, 103, 105, 106, 107, 110, 232, 233, 241, 243, 246, 248, 311, 312, 407, 408, 409, 425, 426, 427, 429, 558, 641
Rubinsztajn, 206, 207, 208, 357, 383, 387, 388, 389, 392, 505, 534, 542, 543, 544, 553
Rubinsztein, 683, 684
Rubinsztein-Lustigman, 684
Rubinsztein-Rapaport, 684
Rubinsztein-Ravon, 684
Rubinsztejn, 314
Rudnitzki, 168
Rudzinak, 79, 90
Rudzinek, 96
Rumshinsky, 327
Ruwin, 352
Ruzal, 684
Ruzhinski, 684
Ruzshinski, 197
Rviga, 684
Rybak, 94, 684
Rykler, 266, 267

Rzepa, 598

S

Sabbatai Tzvi, 333, 340
Salamon, 384
Salmanovitch, 241
Salomon, 659
Salski, 598
Sanaker, 352
Sanders, 88
Sandlarsz, 530
Sandlarz, 659
Sandlarzsh, 184
Sandlerz, 82
Sapir, 96, 184, 245, 659
Sarna, 589
Sarne, 659
Sarver, 478
Sauerimper, 354, 386
Saurimper, 659
Schizczer, 339
Schmidt, 689
Schneider, 322, 600
Schneiderman, 82, 91
Schreiber, 658
Schultz, 82, 599
Schumacher, 686
Schuster, 258, 686
Schwabe, 102, 686
Schwach, 686
Schwartz, 37, 86, 100, 101, 318, 432, 686
Schwartzbard, 686
Schwartzberg, 686
Schweitzer, 589, 686
Sedzik, 660
Segal, 197, 330, 660
Segman, 635
Seid, 633
Seidman, 627, 633, 634
Seifert, 562, 563, 634
Semiaticki, 202
Semiatitzki, 245, 246
Semiatzki, 661
Semjocki, 600
Semjoticki, 600
Semyatitzki, 246
Semyatitzky, 302
Sender, 312, 320, 537, 661
Senders, 658
Sforim, 277, 288, 411
Shabatai Tzvi, 331
Shabati, 552
Shabbetai Zevi, 16, 19
Shabbtai Zevi, 18
Shabtai Tzvi, 132, 133, 134, 135, 136, 332, 333, 337
Shachor, 35, 154, 197, 286, 287, 336, 343, 386, 443, 638, 686, 687
Shahor, 311, 422, 424, 427, 432
Shajnboim, 585, 587
Shama"R, 690
Shamash, 479
Shapira, 85, 344, 345, 346, 348, 350, 405, 685, 686
Shapira-Orlanski, 686
Shapiro, 242, 250, 426
Shashkes, 348

Shedlenicki, 18
Shedlinitzki, 690
Shedlnitzki, 134
Shein, 195, 247, 279, 286, 287, 304, 440, 456, 684, 688
Sheinbaum, 688
Sheinberg, 35, 45, 50, 54, 85, 95, 104, 109, 154, 166, 171, 184, 185,
    223, 229, 248, 265, 322, 336, 688
Sheinboim, 241
Shemietanko, 88
Sheni, 312
Shentz, 295
Sheratka, 680
Sherer, 478
Sheriff, 690
Sherman, 274, 589, 690
Sherotka, 112
Shidlovsky, 76
Shien, 239
Shilf, 88, 531, 536, 688
Shilingovski, 688
Shimoni, 48
Shim'oni, 108
Shimonovich-Shimoni, 689
Shimonovicz, 229
Shimonovits, 688
Shimonovitz, 234
Shim'onovitz, 108, 235
Shimonowicz–Shimoni, 169
Shimonowitz, 310
Shimshon–Leib, 489
Shindlmacher, 478
Shineberg, 177
Shiper, 688
Shipper, 246
Shivak, 275, 279
Shlitterman, 82
Shlivke, 248
Shlomovitz, 688
Shlosberg, 303
Shlosser, 348, 478
Shmad, 115
Shmatnik, 478
Shmuel Leib, 341
Shneider, 274
Shneiderman, 261, 262, 289, 598
Shneiman, 192, 238
Shneimann, 241, 248
Shnider, 478
Shniderman, 301
Shnur, 258, 309, 600
Shocher, 321, 322, 456, 457
Shocher-Tsharny, 320
Shohat, 311
Shor, 184, 287, 595, 686
Shoshkes, 686
Shpak, 197
Shpiegel, 324, 447
Shpringer, 158
Shprintzak, 417
Shriber, 278, 478
Shtefanski, 688
Shteingart, 184, 265
Shteinman, 171, 218, 220, 221, 230, 269, 272, 278, 286, 289, 290,
    302, 303, 454, 455, 460, 461
Shteitelman, 181

Shtepper, 478
Shtilhamer, 84, 538, 540
Shtolmacher, 687
Shtrikenmacher, 312
Shtrikenmakher, 585
Shtrikken Macher, 478
Shtritz, 38, 157, 655
Shtromvaser, 318
Shtromvasser, 177
Shtrumvaser, 54
Shulman, 190, 200, 686
Shultz, 598, 686
Shumakher, 589
Shur, 337
Shuster, 253, 258, 260, 261, 262, 263, 311, 478, 484, 485, 592
Shuvak, 274, 686
Shvabbe, 454
Shvabe, 221, 222
Shvartz, 155, 185, 219, 220, 297, 298, 457
Shvartzberg, 301
Shwaba, 103
Shwach, 61
Shwartzbard, 313
Shwartzberg, 241
Shye, 478
Shykes, 197
Shymanski, 84, 85, 98
Shzapan, 59
Siedlecki, 18
Siegelbaum, 633
Siegelman, 633
Sigelman, 61
Silber, 50
Silberberg, 54, 68, 242, 314, 634
Silberman, 50
Silberson, 634
Silberson-Spichler, 634
Silberstein, 575, 634
Silver, 589, 660
Silverman, 590, 660
Simcha, 602
Singer, 87, 90, 245, 246, 247, 590, 592, 634, 660
Singerman, 634
Sinter, 54
Sircus, 95
Sirkin, 439
Sirkin-Cohen, 440, 660
Sirkus, 210, 543, 660
Siroki, 158
Siroky, 39
Sirota, 108, 408, 660
Sirotta, 229
Siskind, 40, 311
Sitner, 177, 660
Sitniker, 554
Sitnikker, 470, 478
Sitshinner, 478
Skierniewicer, 340
Skolimovski, 661
Skos, 471
Slavatisher, 478, 603
Slavatitshor, 96
Slawaticzer, 549
Slawatiszer, 328
Slawatitszer, 352

Sliwka, 689
Slobodski, 660
Slobodzki, 504
Slobovski, 61
Slonimski, 660
Slonimsky, 452
Slowaticzer', 379
Smolarz, 660
Smolarzsh, 261
Smoliar, 277, 279, 660
Smoliarnik, 478
Smolyar, 236
Smolyor, 411
Sochatzover, 319
Sofer, 311, 313
Sokal, 659
Soknov, 54, 659
Sokol, 352
Sokolov, 659
Sokolovski, 659
Sokolowski, 82, 531
Solman, 202, 258, 302, 384, 659
Sologub, 385
Solovei, 326
Soloveichick, 440
Soloveitchik, 425
Soloveitchik-Morgenshtern, 181
Solovitchik, 344
Solowejczyk, 659
Solowejczyk-Morgenstern, 659
Solski, 245, 246, 247, 289, 290, 659
Solsky, 302
Sommerstein, 580, 633
Sondlarzch, 579
Sopir, 549
Sorkartshik, 659
Soroki, 600, 659
Sosnovitzer, 478
Sourimfer, 314
Spack, 690
Spiegel, 690
Spikhler, 587
Spivak, 661
Spiwak, 536
Spokoyinne, 486
Springer, 39, 691
Sprintzak, 691
Srebarnick, 248
Srebernik, 241, 246
Srebrnik, 215
Stajnman, 590, 592
Stalavi, 248
Stalier, 253
Stallavi, 238
Stanislaw, 410
Staretz, 575, 660
Stechanovski, 416
Steilhamer, 89, 91
Stein, 589, 593, 660, 687
Steinberg, 82, 95, 564, 565, 687
Steinen, 593
Steingart, 79, 91, 687
Steinman, 72, 76, 100, 101, 102, 239, 242, 245, 279, 280, 281, 414, 428, 687
Steinmann, 428, 429

Steitelman, 687
Stern, 591, 592, 660
Stilhammer, 533
Stirnetserin, 478
Stiziniach, 79
Stokolski, 46, 167, 660
Stolier, 251, 319, 357, 656
Stollier, 323, 448
Stolovi, 249
Stolowi, 208, 209, 585
Stolowy, 660
Stolyer, 199, 299, 478
Stoppes, 159
Streicher, 93
Stricher, 50, 54, 172, 173, 177, 203, 204, 302, 542, 605, 660
Striecher, 257
Strzyzover, 334
Stulmakher, 597
Subman, 65
Sucharczik, 504
Suchartzik, 62, 664
Suknov, 177, 192
Suknow, 600
Sulwalker, 511
Sulwalki, 61
Sushchik, 83
Susman, 633
Suszczik, 532
Svori, 478
Svurer, 478
Swartz, 242
Swartzberg, 242
Szajman, 553
Szajnbaum, 399
Szajnberg, 206, 212, 213, 357, 377, 395, 534, 543
Szameh, 635
Szapira, 386
Szapiro, 314, 534
Szchur, 554
Szczepanski, 497
Szedlecer, 352
Szejnberg, 554
Szelazni, 636
Szelazoh, 635, 636
Szelechovski, 636
Szelozni, 636
Szenker, 529
Szepa, 636
Szidlawski, 524
Szidlovski, 688
Szilingowski, 384
Szimanski, 533, 534
Szimszeles, 201
Sziwak, 283, 284
Szliterman, 531, 689
Szlomowicz, 24, 151
Sznaider, 690
Sznaiderman, 690
Sznaidmil, 690
Sznaiman, 690
Sznajderman, 515, 531, 540
Sznajdmil, 397
Sznajer, 383
Sznajman, 499
Sznir, 690

Szor, 379
Szrebernik, 661
Sztajnberg, 531, 544
Sztajngart, 400, 528, 540
Sztajnman, 201, 205, 388, 390, 521, 525
Szternfeld, 598
Sztilhamer, 687
Sztromwaser, 203, 204, 205, 214, 357, 687, 688
Szulman, 515
Szuster,, 202, 213
Szwar, 397
Szwarc, 206, 207, 210, 212, 377, 378, 382, 391, 394, 395, 535
Szwarcberg, 203
Szwarcbord, 314
Szytoh, 635

T

Tabatshnik, 322, 478, 608
Tabenkin, 417, 636
Taentzer, 44
Tajtlbaum, 492, 552
Tallitmacher, 472
Tandeter, 478
Targovnik, 636
Tcharni, 62, 89, 638
Tchechanov, 638
Tchechanovski, 638
Tchernichovski, 639
Tchernichovsky, 411
Tcherno, 422
Tchibulski, 59
Tchizhevski, 638
Tchlenov, 638
Tchlenow, 408
Teantzer, 43
Tehillim–Zoger, 479
Teiber, 637
Teitelbaum, 637
Teitelboim, 241
Temerel, 637
Tencer, 390
Tenenbaum, 82, 212, 351, 379, 383, 511, 531, 637
Tenenboim, 185
Tenenbojm, 66
Tennenboim, 264
Tenser, 275
Tentser, 163
Tenzer, 280, 637
Teperman, 600, 637
Tepermann, 241
Terebiler, 554
Terebiller, 478
Tevelle, 637
Thon, 406, 637
Tiamkin, 201
Tidhar, 425, 691
Tietelboim, 248
Tikkerin, 479
Tiktiner, 331
Tiomkin, 637
Tishel, 637
Tiszl, 537
Tiyamkin, 286
Tocker, 274

Tokarski, 64, 204, 205, 214, 215. 357, 507, 549, 636
Tokarsky, 96, 184
Tokker, 478
Tolstoy, 411, 636
Topikin, 637
Tornhajm, 549
Tornheim, 96, 184, 636
Tosfot, 691
Travnik, 638
Trok, 638
Trumpeldor, 233, 638
Trunk, 369, 375, 638
Tsanser, 339
Tsar Alexander The First, 21
Tsar Nikolai, 157
Tselniker, 73, 79
Tselnikker, 171, 177, 230
Tsharni, 159, 192, 256, 257, 287, 288
Tsharny, 260
Tsherske, 483
Tshesler, 478
Tshlenov, 223
Tsigelnick, 441
Tsinamon, 147
Tsinovicz, 112
Tsitsivorer, 478
Tuchminc, 357
Tuchmintz, 180, 322, 573, 637
Tuchshneider, 61, 67, 558, 559
Tuchsznajder, 504, 513
Tuchsznayder, 637
Tufikin, 385
Tukhmincz, 597
Turek, 637
Turovitch, 637
Turowycz, 598
Tuvia, 464
Tvarkovski, 637
Tvarkovsky, 99, 100, 217, 218
Tyber, 191
Tyomkin, 251, 252, 262
Tzadok, 671
Tzalke, 275, 311
Tzaruk, 585
Tzelinker, 238
Tzelniker, 50, 54
Tzelnikker, 184, 300, 302
Tzepelinski, 672
Tzeplinski, 241
Tzeshinski, 195, 672
Tzeshinsky, 171
Tzimeman, 61, 64
Tzinammons, 290
Tzinnamon, 303, 304
Tzinnes, 472
Tzinomon, 29
Tzishewski, 314
Tzitrinboim, 346
Tzukerman, 184, 238
Tzukernik, 478

U

Uczen, 314
Uhrmacher, 99, 108

Ulinker, 478
Urbach, 55, 82, 178, 192, 323, 324, 531
Urbacher,, 288, 294
Urbakh, 600
Urberg, 63
Urlansky, 298
Urmacher, 39, 115, 116, 158, 218, 227, 238, 241, 248, 271, 272, 277, 278, 294, 296, 298, 302, 303, 304, 486, 553
Urmakher, 585
Urtsheles, 322, 472
Utchan, 346
Utchn, 345
Utshen, 53, 67, 323
Utshtein, 176, 265, 313
Utshten, 265
Utszen, 352, 513

V

Vaksin, 221
Valavski, 628
Valetski, 628
Valetzky, 449
Valovski, 119
Vanzshura, 195
Vanzura, 628
Varm, 180
Varshavski, 629
Varshavsky, 180, 276, 301, 302
Varshavsky-Lebenberg, 279
Vashutinski, 629
Vattemacherin, 478
Vechterman, 260, 262
Veisman, 172
Veitzman, 172, 264
Vetshik, 157
Vichert, 302
Vida, 72
Viezenfeld, 230
Vinderboim, 261
Vineberg, 153, 178, 192, 195, 197, 199, 227, 262, 277, 279, 290, 293, 298, 305, 323, 464
Vineberger, 172
Vinegarten, 185
Vineshtein, 222, 290, 302, 303
Vineshtok, 300
Viness, 192, 219
Vinetroib, 467, 469
Vinetroib-Tuchshneiderran, 276
Vinetroib–Tuchshnider, 279
Vinodrag, 50, 51, 53, 54
Vinograd, 117, 171, 172, 173, 175, 176, 178, 185, 197, 296, 311, 324, 390, 393, 575, 631
Vintzenti, 198
Virnik, 261, 262, 437, 438, 632
Virshop, 632
Viseberg, 227
Visebrot, 304
Visegloz, 258
Viselitz, 300
Viseman, 171, 173, 176, 185, 265
Viseman–Friedman, 302
Visenfeld, 585
Vishnitzer, 152, 154, 478, 632, 656
Vitgenshtein, 138

Vitorozsher, 478
Vizenfeld, 171, 192, 227
Vizzenfeld, 297, 298, 301, 302
Vlass, 632
Vlodaver, 478
Vloss, 259
Vohinner, 478
Voiner, 79
Voitshechovski, 628
Voksin, 275
Volanski, 628
Voliyer, 478
Volodka, 628
Volya, 628
Von Weisel, 629
Von Wiesel, 241
Vonliesinger, 648
Vorek, 171, 257, 258, 628
Votchik, 38
Voveles, 603
Vrubel, 632
Vurker, 338
Vurman, 185

W

Wabnik, 628
Wajcman, 204, 205, 504, 533
Wajczechowski, 384
Wajman, 210
Wajnberg, 201, 329, 356, 357, 377, 383, 400, 552, 585, 586, 587, 588, 600
Wajnberger, 504, 530
Wajne, 214
Wajnes, 552
Wajngarten, 597
Wajnglas, 589, 590, 592
Wajnsztajn, 512, 531
Wajnsztajn-Kelmanzon, 384
Wajnsztajn–Kelmanzon, 379
Wajntraub, 212
Wajntraub–Tuchsznajder, 392
Wajnztok, 397
Wajs, 206, 207
Wajsberg, 510, 522
Wajsbrot, 553
Wajsgloz, 213
Wajsman, 212, 214, 381, 382, 384, 395, 505, 519, 533, 537, 539, 540, 542, 543, 555
Wajznfeld, 542
Waksen, 628
Waksin, 387, 389
Walawksi, 527
Walawski, 497, 498, 557
Wald, 1, 602
Walecki, 589, 592
Walf, 312
Wallawski, 59
Wanczura, 504
Wanzura, 62
Warek, 203, 204, 213
Warm, 82, 208, 530, 628
Warsawski, 573
Warshawski, 246
Warszawski, 280

Waserman, 319
Wasserman, 167, 628
Wassermann, 46
Wasskin, 102
Waynesfield, 564, 565
Wechterman, 632
Weichert, 629
Weinberg, 35, 50, 55, 61, 108, 111, 121, 250, 251, 253, 254, 313, 314, 318, 319, 406, 412, 413, 579, 629
Weinberger, 82, 630
Weingarten, 630
Weinglas, 630
Weinstein, 66, 82, 103, 241, 245
Weinsztein, 630
Weinsztein-Kalmanson, 630
Weinsztok, 630
Weintraub, 284, 630
Weintraub-Tuchschneider, 630
Weintraub-Tuchshneider, 284
Weisberg, 65, 73, 585
Weisenfeld, 50, 233, 579, 629
Weisglas, 596
Weisman, 54, 62, 558
Weismann, 84, 249
Weissberg, 108, 444, 630
Weissbrat, 630
Weissenberg, 631
Weissglas, 630
Weissglass, 233
Weissman, 84, 88, 90, 93, 94, 98, 245, 630, 631
Weissmann, 241, 244, 245
Weitzman, 50, 62, 185
Weitzmann, 248
Weizman, 421, 631
Weizmann, 84, 310, 500
Wengrove, 632
Wernik, 632
Wetchik, 317, 325
Wetshek, 424
Wetshik, 251
Wichnas, 357
Wichnem, 311
Wida, 519
Wide, 629
Wiener, 631
Wiernicki, 543
Wiernitki, 95
Wiesenfeld, 73, 82, 93, 95, 108
Winderbaum, 202, 532
Winderboim, 83, 631
Wineberg, 457, 459
Winetraub, 311
Winikamien, 383, 631
Winogorski, 413
Winograd, 55, 96, 203, 204, 205, 381, 382, 390, 394, 397, 549, 631
Wirnik, 203, 601
Wirshop, 632
Wirshup, 593, 594
Wiseman, 50
Witgenstein, 629
Wittgenstein, 21
Wizenfeld, 522, 544
Wiznfeld, 208, 209, 391, 531
Wlos, 498
Wobnik, 600

Wohiner, 528
Wolanski, 65, 510
Woletzki, 246
Wolf, 593, 628
Wolfs, 180
Wolkovyitzki, 628
Wolkowicki, 511
Wolkowitzki, 65
Wolopolski, 46
Worak, 50
Worek, 201, 202
Wrubel, 600
Wuhrman, 629
Wulos, 59
Wurke, 629
Wurker, 337
Wurm, 600
Wyznicher, 35

Y

Ya'ari, 642
Yaffe, 225
Yakobovski, 640
Yakobovsky, 230, 233
Yamnik, 93, 639
Yanever, 196, 478
Yankaviak, 232
Yankavyak, 233
Yankovicz, 292
Yankovyek, 639
Yanover, 602
Yarden, 310, 466, 642
Yarnitzki, 319
Yarnizki, 640
Yatzhimovski, 639
Yatzkovitch, 639
Yavan, 18
Yaver, 218
Yavez, 17, 19, 20
Yavor, 99, 639
Yavorske, 167
Yavorski, 639
Yazshimovski, 95
Yehiel, 360, 362
Yelin, 585, 641
Yenterl, 327
Yeshaayhu, 319
Yishayahu, 478, 636
Yisroel *Ben* Eliezer, 335
Yitzhak Yakov, 339
Yod, 311, 640
Yonasha, 640
Yonever, 624
Yonusha, 452
Youngster, 244
Yud, 264, 265
Yungerman, 391, 394, 640
Yungster, 640
Yurberg, 66, 95, 239, 261, 287
Yustman, 79, 91, 288, 413, 640
Yuwale, 552

Z

Zack, 317, 335
Zager, 632
Zager-Werner, 632
Zajdman, 522, 589, 592
Zajgermacher, 551
Zak, 25, 35, 39, 40, 48, 53, 307, 311, 319, 337, 377, 386, 400, 408, 434, 439, 554, 585, 635
Zakasner, 554
Zakshevski, 119, 172, 633
Zalevski, 167
Zalkind, 412, 633
Zalman, 635
Zalmanke, 47
Zalmanovitch, 416
Zalmenke, 168
Zaloeski, 46
Zaltzman, 272, 296, 406, 633
Zamit, 633
Zanser, 636
Zarok, 231, 232
Zater, 379
Zatler, 383, 632
Zauerman, 597
Zavidski, 632
Zaygermacher, 478
Zaygerman, 476
Zbitkever, 490, 491
Zeeman, 531, 635
Zegman, 301, 597
Zeid, 593, 594
Zeidman, 73, 180, 184, 230, 262, 290, 291, 298, 302, 303
Zelichowski, 314
Zelig, 635
Zell, 2, 4, 5, 279
Zelmanowicz, 635
Zeman, 82
Zerubavel, 635
Zerubbabel, 246
Zhefa, 598
Zhito, 244
Ziberberg, 386
Zide, 443, 445, 449

Zigelnik, 235
Ziglman, 504
Zilazni, 90
Zilberberg, 85, 93, 171, 177, 207, 208, 209, 265, 278, 294, 314, 323, 352, 357, 383, 392, 514, 534, 542
Zilberger, 585
Zilberzon, 85, 287, 534
Zimbalist, 80
Zimberknop, 244
Zimerman, 672
Zimmel, 269
Zinaman, 233
Zinamon, 232
Zineman, 231, 232
Zinger, 171, 194, 260, 261, 287, 302, 387, 388, 389, 536, 539, 600
Zingerman, 197
Zishes, 264
Ziskind, 159, 336
Zita, 191, 220, 272, 377, 378, 553
Zito, 101, 383, 384, 633
Zitta, 285
Zlotopolski, 635
Zogar, 206
Zola, 444, 632
Zolesiyeh, 632
Zolevski, 632
Zshamme, 293
Zshelaza, 185
Zshelazni, 324
Zshelazo, 242, 243, 244
Zshelechoverin, 478
Zuberman, 325, 511, 554, 633
Zubermann, 248
Zucker, 79
Zuckerman, 84
Zukerkand, 600
Zukerman, 432
Zunderland, 158, 633
Zusman, 184, 230, 261, 553, 633
Zvirman, 633
Zvitkever, 633
Zyskind, 634

www.ingramcontent.com/pod-product-compliance
Lightning Source LLC
Chambersburg PA
CBHW062020090426
42811CB00005B/913